Fodor's 04

AUSTRALIA

Where to Stay and Eat
for All Budgets

Must-See Sights
and Local Secrets

Ratings You Can Trust

Fodor's Travel Publications   New York, Toronto, London, Sydney, Auckland
www.fodors.com

FODOR'S AUSTRALIA 2004

Editors: Melisse Gelula, Holly S. Smith

Editorial Production: Ira-Neil Dittersdorf

Editorial Contributors: Roger Allnutt, Melanie Ball, Daniel Cash, Jad Davenport, Matthew Evans, Michael Gebicki, Caroline Gladstone, Malcolm Harding, Graham Hodgson, Alia Levine, Matthew Liddy, Dominic O'Grady, Liza Power

Maps: David Lindroth Inc., Mapping Specialists, *cartographers;* Rebecca Baer and Robert Blake, *map editors*

Design: Fabrizio La Rocca, *creative director;* Guido Caroti, *art director;* Melanie Marin, *senior picture editor*

Production/Manufacturing: Robert B. Shields

Cover Photo (The Olgas, Uluru National Park): Art Wolfe

ISBN 1–4000–1259–7

ISSN 1095–2675

SPECIAL SALES

Fodor's Travel Publications are available at special discounts for bulk purchases for sales promotions or premiums. Special editions, including personalized covers, excerpts of existing guides, and corporate imprints, can be created in large quantities for special needs. For more information, contact your local bookseller or write to Special Markets, Fodor's Travel Publications, 1745 Broadway, New York, NY 10019. Inquiries from Canada should be directed to your local Canadian bookseller or sent to Random House of Canada, Ltd., Marketing Department, 2775 Matheson Boulevard East, Mississauga, Ontario L4W 4P7. Inquiries from the United Kingdom should be sent to Fodor's Travel Publications, 20 Vauxhall Bridge Road, London SW1V 2SA, England.

AN IMPORTANT TIP & AN INVITATION

Although all prices, opening times, and other details in this book are based on information supplied to us at press time, changes occur all the time in the travel world, and Fodor's cannot accept responsibility for facts that become outdated or for inadvertent errors or omissions. So **always confirm information when it matters,** especially if you're making a detour to visit a specific place. Your experiences—positive and negative—matter to us. If we have missed or misstated something, **please write to us.** We follow up on all suggestions. Contact the Australia editors at editors@fodors.com or c/o Fodor's at 1745 Broadway, New York, New York 10019.

PRINTED IN THE UNITED STATES OF AMERICA

10 9 8 7 6 5 4 3 2 1

CONTENTS

DESTINATION AUSTRALIA

Those who live in Australia call it "Oz." The name fits. This is a land so different from any other that it can sometimes seem as if it were conjured rather than created. It casts its spell through para-doxes: it is a developed nation, poised for the Century of the Pacific Rim, yet it is largely unpopulated, a land of vast frontiers—and with a frontier spirit in its people that was lost in other nations long ago, when life became crowded or comfortable or both. Its cities can be at once sophisticated and unpretentious, as can its people. If you love outdoor recreation, imaginative cuisine, natural beauty seemingly without limit, and the idea of an English-speaking nation actually being exotic, Australia was made (or conjured) for you. Have a fabulous trip!

Karen Cure, Editorial Director

Maps

CloseUps

ON THE ROAD WITH FODOR'S

A trip takes you out of yourself. Concerns of life at home completely disappear, driven away by more immediate thoughts—about, say, what marvels will beguile the next day, or where you'll have dinner. That's where Fodor's comes in. We make sure that you know all your options, so that you don't miss something that's around the next bend just because you didn't know it was there. Mindful that the best memories of your trip might have nothing to do with what you came to Australia to see, we guide you to sights large and small all over the region. You might set out to scuba dive among the dazzling marine life of the Great Barrier Reef, but back at home you find yourself unable to forget the exhilaration of scaling Sydney Harbour Bridge, or the pleasure of wandering through a Barossa Valley vineyard. With Fodor's at your side, serendipitous discoveries are never far away.

Roger Allnutt, a freelance writer based in Canberra, is a member of the Australian Society of Travel Writers. His work is published regularly in newspapers and magazines in Australia, New Zealand, the U.S., and the U.K. In addition to traveling he enjoys food and wine, classical music, and tennis. Roger updated the Canberra and the A.C.T., Tasmania, and Smart Travel Tips chapters.

Melanie Ball began her career in freelance travel writing and photography somewhere between London and Johannesburg on an overland expedition truck in 1986. Her search for all things colorful, edible, unusual, and simply enjoyable has since taken her from Ethiopia to England and around Australia, and descriptions of her adventures appear in Australian newspapers and magazines. Based in Melbourne, Melanie is passionate about Adelaide: "It has the best oval in the country for watching Test Cricket." Melanie updated the South Australian chapter.

A native Melburnian, **Daniel Cash** is the former production editor for *The Age,* the city's only broadsheet newspaper, and is currently working towards completing his MBA. He admits his love of the city stems from its passion for culture—"And the center of culture in Melbourne is obviously the MCG, the home of Australian Rules Football," he jokes. Daniel lends his expertise by finding the best of Melbourne's many sights and outdoor activities.

Although he lives in land-locked Denver, Colorado, **Jad Davenport** has made half a dozen journeys across Australia, including a solo drive across the Outback and dive expeditions in the Great Barrier Reef, the Coral Sea, and the unexplored reefs of the far north. He spent 10 years as a war photographer before becoming a travel writer, and he now takes assignments for such publications as *Travel & Leisure, Northwest Dive News,* and *The Washington Post.* Jad updated the Great Barrier Reef and Darwin, the Top End, and the Kimberley chapters.

Matthew Evans, who updated the Sydney and Melbourne dining sections, was a chef before he crossed over to the "dark side" of the industry as a food writer and restaurant critic. He writes a recipe column each weekend and is currently the chief restaurant reviewer for the *Sydney Morning Herald* and a coeditor of the bestselling restaurant guide *The Sydney Morning Herald Good Food Guide.* Matthew has also written four books on food, and there's little that he wouldn't eat so long as he lives to tell the story later. He dines out on average 500 times a year and is starting to worry that all this consumption could become conspicuous.

British by birth, American by education, and Australian since 1979, **Michael Gebicki** is a freelance travel writer and photographer now based in Sydney. Articles about his global wanderings appear regularly in travel publications in North America, Europe, and Asia. His most recent publication, *Outback in Style,* is a collection of 20 small lodges scattered across the country, from the crocodile-infested coastline of the Kimberley to a trout fishing lodge in the Tasmanian Highlands. He updated the Sydney chapter.

As a journalist who has been writing about travel for the past 14 years, **Caroline Gladstone** has been across Australia, the world, and the high seas. She was cruise editor of the Australian industry magazine *Traveltrade* for many years, during which time she cruised on some 25 ships. Caroline, who updated our Red Centre chapter, is now a freelance travel and feature writer, as well as a newspaper sub-editor. Her articles have appeared in *The Australian* and *The Sunday Telegraph* newspapers, and such magazines as *Vacations & Travel* and *Luxury Travel*.

Malcolm Harding, who updated the New South Wales chapter, is a University of Sydney graduate, a visual artist, and and co-publisher of the *Gay Australia Guide*. He travels frequently throughout Australia, writing for the *Sydney Star Observer* newspaper and other publications. He spends his spare time either bushwalking in the Blue Mountains or shaking his groove thing in Sydney's notorious nightclubs.

A fourth-generation Western Australian, Graham Hodgson has spent most of his life in the state's beautiful South West region. His 35-year career spans stints in newspaper journalism, government and corporate communications, regional tourism planning, and regional economic development. He has written about travel in Australia, New Zealand, Indonesia, Malaysia, Singapore, Zimbabwe, Thailand, France, and Italy for numerous newspapers, magazines, and on-line publications. He lives on a small, five-acre holding (an escape from the 21st century), alternating his work commitments with tending to fruit trees, vegetables, chickens, hens, four pet sheep, and two cats.

A staunch antipodean, Alia Levine moved from New Zealand to her family's native New York in 1997. For the last five years, she has worked in the non-profit human rights sector and as a freelance writer and editor. Alia, who updated the Queensland chapter, spends most of her time planning trips abroad and working out ways to pay for them.

Dominic O'Grady, who updated the New South Wales chapter, holds a Masters degree in Australian literature from the University of Sydney. He is also the founding publisher of Australia's gay and lesbian travel magazine, the *Gay Australia Guide*. He was born with a backpack and a laptop, and has been traveling and writing ever since.

A travel writer for *The Age* newspaper in Melbourne, Australia, Liza Power unwittingly kicked off her travel writing career at the age of 19 when she trotted off to South America for a few weeks and returned Down Under numerous months later with a serious dose of wanderlust. Her travels since have taken her from the Dogon lands of Mali to the steppes of Mongolia, as well as the streets of Bogota, the oases of Libya, the wilds of Patagonia, and the highlands of West Papua. Between her overseas jaunts and weekly adventure travel columns she explores her home state of Victoria—which she believes to be site of some of the world's most beautiful and varied landscapes.

You can rest assured that you're in good hands—and that no property mentioned in the book has paid to be included. Each has been selected strictly on its merits, as the best of its type in its price range.

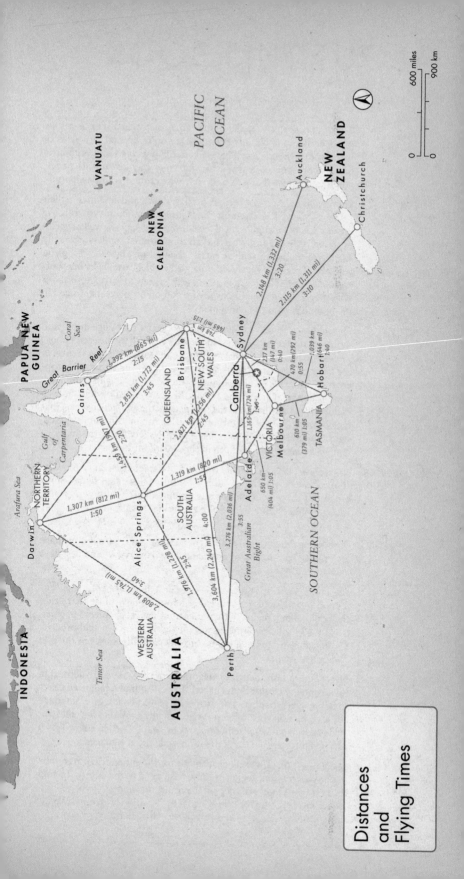

Distances
and
Flying Times

ABOUT THIS BOOK

There's no doubt that the best source for travel advice is a like-minded friend who's just been where you're headed. But with or without that friend, you'll have a better trip with a Fodor's guide in hand. Once you've learned to find your way around its pages, you'll be in great shape to find your way around your destination.

SELECTION
Our goal is to cover the best properties, sights, and activities in their category, as well as the most interesting communities to visit. We make a point of including local food-lovers' hot spots as well as neighborhood options, and we avoid all that's touristy unless it's really worth your time. You can go on the assumption that everything you read about in this book is recommended wholeheartedly by our writers and editors. Flip to **On the Road with Fodor's** to learn more about who they are. It goes without saying that no property mentioned in the book has paid to be included.

RATINGS
Orange stars ★ denote sights and properties that our editors and writers consider the very best in the area covered by the entire book. These, the best of the best, are listed in the **Fodor's Choice** section in the front of the book. Black stars ★ highlight the sights and properties we deem **Highly Recommended**, the don't-miss sights within any region. Fodor's Choice and Highly Recommended options in each region are usually listed on the title page of the chapter covering that region. Use the index to find complete descriptions. In San Francisco, sights pinpointed with numbered map bullets ❶ in the margins tend to be more important than those without bullets.

SPECIAL SPOTS
Pleasures & Pastimes focuses on types of experiences that reveal the spirit of the destination. Watch for **Off the Beaten Path** sights. Some are out of the way, some are quirky, and all are worth your while. If the munchies hit while you're exploring, look for **Need a Break?** suggestions.

TIME IT RIGHT
Wondering when to go? Check **On the Calendar** up front and chapters' **Timing** sections for weather and crowd overviews and best days and times to visit.

SEE IT ALL
Use Fodor's exclusive **Great Itineraries** as a model for your trip. (For a good overview of the entire destination, follow those that begin the book, or mix regional itineraries from several chapters.) In cities, **Good Walks** guide you to important sights in each neighborhood; ▶ indicates the starting points of walks and itineraries in the text and on the map.

BUDGET WELL
Hotel and restaurant price categories from ¢ to $$$$ are defined in the opening pages of each chapter. Expect to find a balanced selection for every budget. For attractions, we always give standard adult admission fees; reductions are usually available for children, students, and senior citizens. Look in **Discounts & Deals** in Smart Travel Tips for information on destination-wide ticket schemes.

BASIC INFO
Smart Travel Tips lists travel essentials for the entire area covered by the book; city- and region-specific basics end each chapter. To find the best way to get around, see the transportation section; see individual modes of travel ("By Car," "By Train") for details. We assume you'll check Web sites or call for particulars.

ON THE MAPS	Maps throughout the book show you what's where and help you find your way around. Black and orange numbered bullets ❶ ❶ in the text correlate to bullets on maps.
BACKGROUND	In general, we give background information within the chapters in the course of explaining sights as well as in CloseUp boxes and in Understanding Australia at the end of the book. To get in the mood, review the suggestions in Books & Movies. The glossary can be invaluable.
FIND IT FAST	Within the book, chapters are arranged in a roughly east–west direction starting with Sydney. Chapters are divided into small regions, within which towns are covered in logical geographical order; attractive routes and interesting places between towns are flagged as En Route. Heads at the top of each page help you find what you need within a chapter.
DON'T FORGET	Restaurants are open for lunch and dinner daily unless we state otherwise; we mention dress only when there's a specific requirement and reservations only when they're essential or not accepted— it's always best to book ahead. Hotels have private baths, phone, TVs, and air-conditioning and operate on the European Plan (a.k.a. EP, meaning without meals). We always list facilities but not whether you'll be charged extra to use them, so when pricing accommodations, find out what's included.

SYMBOLS

Many Listings

- ★ Fodor's Choice
- ★ Highly recommended
- ⊠ Physical address
- ✛ Directions
- ✍ Mailing address
- ☎ Telephone
- 🖷 Fax
- ⊕ On the Web
- ✉ E-mail
- 💳 Admission fee
- ☺ Open/closed times
- ▶ Start of walk/itinerary
- Ⓜ Metro stations
- ▭ Credit cards

Outdoors

- 🏌 Golf
- ⚠ Camping

Hotels & Restaurants

- 🏨 Hotel
- ➳ Number of rooms
- ♨ Facilities
- 🍽 Meal plans
- ✕ Restaurant
- ⟆ Reservations
- 🏛 Dress code
- ↘ Smoking
- ⛉ BYOB
- ✕🏨 Hotel with restaurant that warrants a visit

Other

- ☻ Family-friendly
- 🛈 Contact information
- ⇨ See also
- ⊠ Branch address
- ☞ Take note

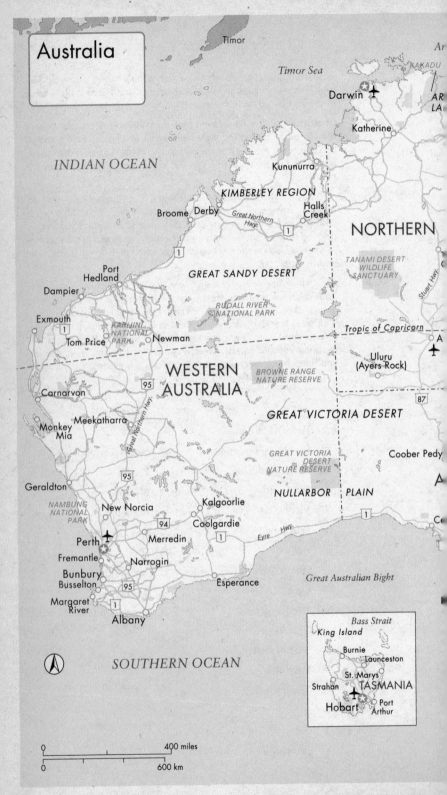

Australia

Timor

Timor Sea

Darwin

Katherine

INDIAN OCEAN

Kununurra

KIMBERLEY REGION

Broome Derby   *Great Northern Hwy.*   Halls Creek

Port Hedland

Dampier

Exmouth

Tom Price   Newman

Carnarvon

Monkey Mia

Meekatharra

Geraldton

NAMBUNG NATIONAL PARK

New Norcia

Perth

Fremantle

Bunbury
Busselton

Margaret River

Albany

SOUTHERN OCEAN

GREAT SANDY DESERT

RUDALL RIVER NATIONAL PARK

KARIJINI NATIONAL PARK

WESTERN AUSTRALIA

BROWNE RANGE NATURE RESERVE

GREAT VICTORIA DESERT NATURE RESERVE

Kalgoorlie

Coolgardie

Merredin

Narrogin

Esperance

NORTHERN

KAKADU

AR LA

TANAMI DESERT WILDLIFE SANCTUARY

Stuart Hwy.

Tropic of Capricorn

Uluru (Ayers Rock)

GREAT VICTORIA DESERT

Coober Pedy

NULLARBOR   PLAIN

Eyre Hwy.

Great Australian Bight

A

Ce

Bass Strait

King Island

Burnie   Launceston

St. Marys

Strahan   TASMANIA

Hobart   Port Arthur

400 miles

600 km

Arafura Sea

PAPUA NEW GUINEA

...DU NATIONAL PARK

ARNHEM LAND

Gulf of Carpentaria

Coral Sea

Weipa

CAPE YORK PENINSULA

Coral Sea Islands

Laura

Cooktown

Port Douglas

Burketown

Mareeba

Cairns

Normanton

Innisfail

GREAT

TERRITORY

Georgetown

Ingham

Townsville

BARRIER

Tennant Creek

QUEENSLAND

Ayr

REEF

Mt. Isa

Cloncurry

66

Hughenden

Mackay

Alice Springs

Longreach

66

Emerald

Rockhampton

Bedourie

Blackwater

GREAT

Birdsville

Windorah

71

Gladstone

Oodnadatta

Charleville

DIVIDING

Lake Eyre

54

Roma

Kingaroy

Nambour

SOUTH

Cunnamulla

71

Dalby

Brisbane

Marree

Toowoomba

RANGE

AUSTRALIA

Lake Torrens

Goondiwindi

Warwick

FLINDERS RANGES NATIONAL PARK

Bourke

Moree

Lismore

Pacific Hwy.

Ceduna

Walgett

Armidale

Grafton

Port Augusta

NEW SOUTH WALES

71

Nyngan

Coffs Harbour

32

Broken Hill

Dubbo

Kempsey

EYRE PENINSULA

Port Pirie

Port Macquarie

Renmark

Orange

GREAT

Port Lincoln

Mildura

Hay

Bathurst Cowra

Newcastle

Adelaide

Young

Sydney

Kangaroo Island

VICTORIA

Murray R.

Albury

Wollongong

Bordertown

Shepparton

Canberra

DIVIDING

Bendigo

Seymour

Cooma

Mt. Gambier

Ballarat

Melbourne

Bega

RANGE

Portland

Colac

Orbost

Warrnambool

Geelong

Sale

Bairnsdale

Wonthaggi

King Island

Bass Strait

Flinders Island

TASMANIA

World Time Zones

Numbers below vertical bands relate each zone to Greenwich Mean Time (0 hrs.).
Local times frequently differ from these general indications,
as indicated by light-face numbers on map.

Algiers **29**	Berlin **34**	Delhi **48**	Jerusalem **42**
Anchorage **3**	Bogotá **19**	Denver **8**	Johannesburg **44**
Athens **41**	Budapest **37**	Dublin **26**	Lima **20**
Auckland **1**	Buenos Aires **24**	Edmonton **7**	Lisbon **28**
Baghdad **46**	Caracas **22**	Hong Kong **56**	London
Bangkok **50**	Chicago **9**	Honolulu **2**	(Greenwich) **27**
Beijing **54**	Copenhagen **33**	Istanbul **40**	Los Angeles **6**
	Dallas **10**	Jakarta **53**	Madrid **38**

Visitors to Australia are inevitably surprised by its vastness. The phrase "tyranny of distance" entered Australian parlance almost at the very beginning of European settlement. Although the country occupies almost the same land mass as the continental United States, its population is only 19½ million, compared with some 285 million in America.

Australia is an ancient land. Originally part of the Gondwanaland supercontinent that included present-day South America, Africa, Antarctica, and New Zealand, the island continent began to migrate to its current position around 100 million years ago. The eastern seaboard is backed by the Great Dividing Range, which parallels the coastline from northern Queensland all the way south into western Victoria. Watered by swift rivers, this littoral region is clothed with rolling pasturelands and lush rain forests. Off the coast of Queensland, the Great Barrier Reef runs from Cape York 2,000 km (1,250 mi) southward. Inland, beyond the Great Dividing Range, semiarid plains cover much of Queensland, New South Wales, Victoria, and South Australia. Deserts cover much of the rest of the country, including most of Western Australia and the Red Centre. Tasmania floats south of the mainland, looking on maps like it's plunging toward the Antarctic.

If you're coming from the northern hemisphere, remember that the compass is turned upside down: The farther north you go *toward* the equator, the hotter it gets. Australia is bisected by the tropic of Capricorn—meaning that overall the continent is rather close to the equator—while the United States and Europe lie well above the tropic of Cancer.

(1) Sydney

The vibrant, cosmopolitan gateway to Australia covers the waterfront with audacious Aussie attitude, sprawl, and pop culture. On the southeast coast of Australia and the state of New South Wales, Sydney is a city surrounded by beaches. And it's a city that whips up some of the most astonishing food on the current world scene, a Eurasian cornucopia overflowing with seafood and exotic flavors. You're bound to spend at least a couple of days here—take hold of them with both hands.

(2) New South Wales

Although Sydney may be the ultimate urban experience south of Hong Kong, southeastern Australia plays virtually all of the continent's rural and coastal variations: historic towns, mountain ranges, seductive sands, subtropical rain forest, and extensive vineyards. All of these variations make for great outdoor activities: hiking, scuba diving, fishing, skiing, trail riding, cave exploring, and rafting.

(3) Canberra & the A.C.T.

The nation's spacious and immaculately landscaped capital city, Canberra sits between Sydney and Melbourne in the Australian Capital Territory (A. C. T.), in the midst of mountain ranges and rivers. Canberra has interesting architecture and museums and is the closest city to some of Australia's greatest national parks.

(4) (5) Melbourne & Victoria

Melbourne, on the southern coast of Australia and the state of Victoria, is the urbane, cultivated sister of brassy Sydney. To the extent that culture is synonymous with sophistication—except when it comes to watching Australian-rules football or the Melbourne Cup horse race—some call it the cultural capital of the continent. Outside of the city you can watch the sundown race of fairy penguins on Phillip Island, marvel at the sculpted South Ocean coastline, sample excellent wines, or explore splendid national parks.

6 Tasmania

From Freycinet Peninsula to the Nut volcanic formation to the wilds of Southwest National Park, Tasmania is a place of intoxicating natural beauty. The island, separated from the southeast coast of Australia by the Bass Strait, is a hiker's dream, rich with wilderness still unexplored. Remnants of the island's volatile days as a penal colony await exploration in numerous small museums and historic sites.

7 8 Queensland & the Great Barrier Reef

A fusion of Florida, Las Vegas, and the Caribbean Islands, Queensland, making up the northeastern portion of Australia, and the Great Barrier Reef draw crowd lovers and escapists alike. Name your outdoor pleasure and you'll probably find it here, whether you wish to explore marine wonders, stroll from cabana to casino, pose in front of the monumental kitsch of the Gold Coast, or cruise rivers and rain forests with crocodiles and other fascinating tropical creatures.

9 Adelaide & South Australia

Come to park-enveloped Adelaide for its biennial Festival of the Arts or simply for a calmer-than-Sydney urban experience. Elsewhere in the state, you can step back in time on Kangaroo Island, explore some of Australia's celebrated wineries and the transplanted German heritage of the Barossa Region, or unwind on a Murray River cruise. South Australia also provides a chance to take in the great variety of Australian wildlife and to trek through Flinders Ranges National Park, one of the best Outback national parks.

10 The Red Centre

The light of the Red Centre—named for the deep color of its desert soils—has a purity and vitality at which photographs only hint. For tens of thousands of years, this vast desert territory has been occupied by Aboriginal people. Uluru, also known as Ayers Rock, is a great symbol in Aboriginal traditions, as are many sacred sites among the Centre's mountain ranges, gorges, dry riverbeds, and spinifex plains. At the center lies Alice Springs, Australia's only desert city.

11 Darwin, the Top End & the Kimberley

From Darwin Harbor to the rocky domes and towers of Purnululu National Park, the Top End and the Kimberley's landforms are stunning and diverse. Besides being breathtakingly beautiful, this area of northern Australia holds many examples of ancient Aboriginal rock art. Darwin and Broome—both far closer to Asia than to any Australian cities—host the most racially diverse populations of the nation.

12 Perth & Western Australia

Those who make it to the "undiscovered country" of Australia's largest state are stunned by its sheer diversity. Relax on beautiful beaches, wonder at coastal formations in Nambung National Park, or swim with dolphins at Monkey Mia or Ningaloo Reef Marine Park. Explore the goldfields east of Perth or the historic towns, wineries, and seaside parks of the Southwest.

GREAT ITINERARIES

Highlights of Australia
16 or 17 days

This tour surveys the misty heights of Tasmania's Cradle Mountain, the steamy wetlands of Kakadu, the central deserts, and the northern rain forests. It finishes in Port Douglas, where you may want to linger if time permits.

SYDNEY
2 or 3 days. Spend a day cruising the harbor and exploring the Rocks. Take an evening stroll past the Opera House to the Royal Botanic Gardens. The next day take a Sydney Explorer bus tour and visit Darling Harbor, followed by dinner at Cockle Bay Wharf or Chinatown. Day Three could be spent in Paddington, with a trip to Bondi Beach. ⇨ *Exploring Sydney and Beaches in Chapter 1.*

BLUE MOUNTAINS
1 day. Stop at Wentworth Falls for a view across the Jamison Valley and the National Pass trail. Pause for refreshments at Leura; then continue along Cliff Drive to Blackheath, with its great hiking and antiques shops. ⇨ *The Blue Mountains in Chapter 2.*

TASMANIA
6 days. Spend the first afternoon strolling Hobart's waterfront. The following day, drive to Port Arthur and explore Australia's convict past. On Day Three, head for Freycinet National Park and hike to Wineglass Bay; then overnight in Launceston. Finish off with two days of hiking in Cradle Mountain–Lake St. Clair National Park before driving back to Hobart for your final night. ⇨ *Hobart, Port Arthur, Freycinet National Park, Launceston, and Central Tasmania National Parks in Chapter 6.*

ULURU
2 days. Fly into Alice Springs to experience Uluru (Ayers Rock), a monolith that resonates with mystical force. Explore its base the first day, spend the night in town, and visit the vast Kata Tjuta (the Olgas) on Day Two. ⇨ *Uluru and Kata Tjuta in Chapter 10.*

KAKADU
2 days. Fly into Darwin and head for Kakadu National Park, with its escarpments, wetlands, and ancient Aboriginal rock art. ⇨ *Kakadu National Park in Chapter 11.*

PORT DOUGLAS
3 days. From Cairns drive north to small, glamorous Port Douglas, where catamarans and sloops cruise to the Great Barrier Reef. Take one day to explore the surrounding rain forest and another for a four-wheel-drive tour to Cape Tribulation. ⇨ *North from Cairns in Chapter 7.*

By Public Transportation
Daily flights depart from Sydney to Hobart (2 hours), from Hobart to Alice Springs via Melbourne (4 hours), from Alice Springs to Darwin (2 hours), and from Darwin to Cairns (3 hours, 45 minutes). From each hub you can rent a car or join a tour to get around.

Darwin · 256 km · Kakadu NP · GULF OF CARPENTARIA · 3 hrs 45 min · 2 hrs · 2 hrs · NORTHERN TERRITORY · Western MacDonnell Ranges · Finke Gorge NP · Alice Springs · Kings Canyon · 450 km · 440 km · Ayers Rock/ Uluru NP/ Olgas/Kata Tjuta Domes · 4 hrs · Flinders Ranges NP · St. Mary's Peak · Wilpena Pound · 2 hrs · Port Augusta · 460 km · Barossa Valley · Adelaide · 70 km

Into the Outback
11 to 14 days

In the raw, brooding Outback, with a little imagination you can go back to a time when the earth was created by the giant ancestral beings from whom the Aboriginal people trace their lineage.

ADELAIDE
2 days. Begin the day with a visit to the Central Market area and a tour of the historic buildings along North Terrace. Stroll through the Botanic Gardens before catching a PopEye launch back to the city center. Later head for the cafés in Rundle Mall. Spend the next day touring the wineries of the Barossa Region. ⇨ *Adelaide and Barossa Region in Chapter 9.*

FLINDERS RANGES NATIONAL PARK
3 days. From Adelaide, drive or join a four-wheel-drive tour via Port Augusta to Flinders Ranges and its towering crimson hills. Take time to ascend St. Mary's Peak at Wilpena Pound, an 80-square-km (31-square-mi) bowl ringed by quartzite hills. ⇨ *The Outback in Chapter 9.*

ALICE SPRINGS
2 days. Spend the afternoon viewing Aboriginal art in the galleries or on an excursion into the West MacDonnell Ranges. The next day head out from Alice Springs on the scenic Mereenie Track, which also links Kings Canyon and Finke Gorge National Park, to visit Uluru (Ayers Rock). ⇨ *Alice Springs and Side Trips from Alice Springs in Chapter 10.*

ULURU
2 to 4 days. Take time to wonder at the magnificent Uluru (Ayers Rock) and then head out to visit Kata Tjuta (the Olgas) and hike through the Valley of the Winds. Spend one or more days on an Aboriginal guided tour learning about indigenous culture and lifestyle. ⇨ *Uluru and Kata Tjuta in Chapter 10.*

KAKADU
2 or 3 days. Kick back and enjoy the warm climate, abundant wildlife, and sandstone caves. When Aborigines camped here aeons ago they daubed the walls with ocher, clay, and charcoal. ⇨ *Kakadu National Park in Chapter 11.*

By Public Transportation
Flights depart daily from Adelaide to Alice Springs (2 hours), Alice Springs to Darwin (2 hours), and Darwin back to Adelaide (4½ hours). Use these cities as bases—either rent a car or take day tours of the sights mentioned.

MAP KEY
Highlights of Australia
Into the Outback

Cape Tribulation
Port Douglas
Cairns

Blue Mountains
Sydney
90 km

VICTORIA
Melbourne
40 min

Launceston
Cradle Mtn-Lake St. Clair NP
Freycinet NP
TASMANIA
Hobart
Port Arthur

Wines & Scenery of the Southeast
10 days

The continent's southeast corner holds serenity, grace, and some wonderful wines along with quiet country towns, Victorian architecture, and a rugged coastline.

RUTHERGLEN
1 day. Rutherglen's vineyards produce Australia's finest fortified wines. A half-day tour introduces you to Tokays, muscats, and ports underpinned with subtle layers of fruit. ⇨ *Murray River Region in Chapter 5.*

BENDIGO
2 days. At the northern extremity of Victoria's goldfields region, Bendigo prospered most from the gold rush of the 1850s and has a rich legacy of Victorian architecture. Ballarat, another gold-rush settlement, hosts reenactments of prosperous days. Between Bendigo and Ballarat lies Maldon, also well preserved. Down the road the Hepburn Springs Spa Centre has flotation tanks, saunas, a relaxation pool, and hot tubs. ⇨ *Gold Country in Chapter 5.*

MELBOURNE
2 days. In Australia's serene and gracious second-largest city spend a day exploring the riverside Southgate complex and the parks and gardens to the east. Then head for the bay-side suburb of St. Kilda for a walk along the Esplanade. Next day tour the Dandenongs, driving through the cool, moist hills of Belgrave and Sherbrooke. ⇨ *Melbourne in Chapter 4.*

GREAT OCEAN ROAD
2 days. Pause at the pretty village of Lorne; then circle rainforested Otway National Park and head for Port Campbell National Park's huge limestone stacks. Overnight in Port Fairy and cross the South Australian border, stopping at Mount Gambier's Blue Lake. Continue to Kingston and drive along the Coorong, a lagoon protected from the ocean by the Younghusband Peninsula dunes and a bird sanctuary. ⇨ *West Coast Region in Chapter 5.*

ADELAIDE
3 days. Devote a day to walking along the North Terrace to the Botanic Gardens and zoo, and another in the Adelaide Hills. The village of Hahndorf, founded by German settlers during the 19th century, is full of stone and timber structures. In the evening visit Warrawong Sanctuary for wildlife-watching. Spend another day seeing the Barossa Region's wineries, fine restaurants, and historic inns. ⇨ *Adelaide, The Adelaide Hills, and The Barossa Region in Chapter 9.*

By Public Transportation
A rental car is the best means of transportation.

Tropical Wonders
13 or 14 days

The east coast's riotous greenery, tropical islands, and year-round warmth, not to mention the spectacular Great Barrier Reef, are difficult to resist.

BRISBANE
1 day. Explore the Queensland capital's city center and the South Bank Parklands. In the evening head for one of the riverside restaurants at Eagle Street Pier. ⇨ *Brisbane in Chapter 7.*

THE SUNSHINE COAST
2 days. Drive an hour north to stylish Noosa Heads, with its balmy climate, scenic beaches, and boutiques, cafés, and restaurants. ⇨ *Sunshine Coast in Chapter 7.*

FRASER ISLAND
2 days. Fly to Hervey Bay and then to Fraser Island to join a four-wheel-drive tour of rocky headlands, the rusting wreck of the *Maheno*, and towering sand dunes. In the interior you'll see paperbark swamps, freshwater lakes, and forests of brush box trees. ⇨ *Fraser Island in Chapter 7.*

HERON ISLAND
2 days. Back at Hervey Bay, fly to Gladstone and then head on to this Great Barrier Reef island, where you can spend your time diving or bird-watching. ⇨ *Mackay–Capricorn Islands in Chapter 8.*

PORT DOUGLAS

3 days. Fly from Gladstone to Cairns, drive to Port Douglas, and spend the first day exploring this relaxed town. Devote another day to hiking the Mossman Gorge trails or cruising the Great Barrier Reef. If the weather sours, head toward Cairns and take the train through the rain forest to Kuranda. Return to Cairns via the Skyrail Rain Forest Cableway. ⇨ *Cairns and North from Cairns in Chapter 7.*

CAPE TRIBULATION

2 days. Keep driving north from Port Douglas to this area of untamed beaches and rain forests. As the spirit moves you, stop for hiking, horseback riding, and beachcombing on half-deserted strands. ⇨ *North from Cairns in Chapter 7.*

COOKTOWN

1 or 2 days. North from Cape Tribulation, the rough Bloomfield Track and numerous river crossings make the four-wheel-drive journey to Cooktown an adventure. Stop along the way at Black Mountain National Park, and the Lion's Den Hotel, a rough pub. ⇨ *North from Cairns in Chapter 7.*

By Public Transportation

Fly from Brisbane to Hervey Bay (one hour), where car ferries chug to Fraser Island from Mary River Heads and Inskip Point. Daily flights connect Hervey Bay with Gladstone (one hour), and it's a two-hour boat trip or 25-minute helicopter ride from there to Heron Island. Daily flights link Gladstone to Cairns (one hour), where you can rent a car to tour Port Douglas and the north. In each region, the best way to get around is to rent a four-wheel-drive vehicle or join a tour.

Map labels

Black Mountain NP
Lion's Den Hotel
Cooktown
Cape Tribulation
Port Douglas
Mossman
Kuranda
Cairns

GREAT BARRIER REEF

Heron Island
Gladstone
Hervey Bay
Fraser Island
Noosa Heads
Brisbane

Sydney

VICTORIA

Adelaide
Barossa Valley
Adelaide Hills
Warrawong Sanctuary
Coorong NP
Hahndorf
Younghusband Peninsula
Kingston
Mt. Gambier
Port Fairy
Port Campbell NP
Bendigo
Maldon
Ballarat
Hepburn Springs
Melbourne
Lorne
Otway NP
The Dandenongs
Rutherglen

TASMANIA

MAP KEY

Tropical Wonders

Wines & Scenery

°C		°F
100		212
40		105
37		98.6
30		90
25		80
20		70
15		60
10		50
5		40
0		32
-5		20
-10		10
-15		0
-20		

Australia is in the Southern Hemisphere, so the seasons are reversed. It's winter Down Under during the American and European summer.

The ideal time to visit the north, particularly the Northern Territory's Kakadu National Park, is early in the dry season (around May). Bird life remains profuse on the drying floodplains, and waterfalls are still spectacular and accessible. The Dry (April–October) is also a good time to visit northern Queensland's beaches and rain forests. You can swim off the coast without fear of dangerous stinging box jellyfish, which infest ocean waters between November and March. In rain forests, heat and humidity are lower than later in the year, and crocodile viewing is at its. prime, as the creatures tend to bask on riverbanks rather than submerge in the colder water.

During school holidays, Australians take to the roads in droves. Accommodations and attractions are crowded and hotel rooms and rental cars are unlikely to be discounted during these periods. The busiest period is mid-December to the end of January, which is the equivalent of the U.S. and British summer break. The dates of other school vacations vary from state to state, but generally fall around Easter, mid-June to July, and late September to mid-October.

Climate

Australia's climate is temperate in southern states, such as Victoria and Tasmania, particularly in coastal areas, and tropical in Australia's far north. The Australian summer north of the tropic of Capricorn is a steam bath. Remember that by comparison no parts of North America or Europe are anywhere near as close to the equator. From the end of October to December (the Australian spring), or from February through April (late summer–autumn), southern regions are generally sunny and warm, with only occasional rain in Sydney, Melbourne, and Adelaide. Perth and the south of Western Australia are at their finest in springtime, when wildflowers blanket the land. Some people would say that spring and fall are the best times to travel to Australia, unless you're dying to get away from a northern winter.

The following are average daily maximum and minimum temperatures for some major Australian cities.

🔲 Forecasts **Weather Channel Connection** ☎ 900/932–8437, 95¢ per minute from a Touch-Tone phone ⊕ www.weather.com.

SYDNEY

Jan.	79F	26C	May	67F	19C	Sept.	67F	17C
	65	18		52	11		52	11
Feb.	79F	26C	June	61F	16C	Oct.	72F	22C
	65	18		49	9		56	13
Mar.	76F	24C	July	61F	16C	Nov.	74F	23C
	63	17		49	9		61	16
Apr.	72F	22C	Aug.	63F	17C	Dec.	77F	25C
	58	14		49	9		63	17

MELBOURNE

Jan.	79F	26C	May	63F	17C	Sept.	63F	17C
	58	14		47	8		47	8
Feb.	79F	26C	June	58F	14C	Oct.	67F	19C
	58	14		45	7		49	9
Mar.	76F	24C	July	56F	13C	Nov.	72F	22C
	56	13		43	6		52	11
Apr.	68F	20C	Aug.	59F	15C	Dec.	76F	24C
	52	11		43	6		54	12

HOBART

	°F	°C			°F	°C			°F	°C
Jan.	72F	22C	May		58F	14C	Sept.		59F	15C
	54	12			45	7			43	6
Feb.	72F	22C	June		54F	12C	Oct.		63F	17C
	54	12			41	5			47	8
Mar.	68F	20C	July		52F	11C	Nov.		67F	19C
	52	11			40	4			49	9
Apr.	63F	17C	Aug.		56F	13C	Dec.		70F	21C
	49	9			41	5			52	11

CAIRNS

	°F	°C			°F	°C			°F	°C
Jan.	90F	32C	May		81F	27C	Sept.		83F	28C
	74	23			67	19			65	18
Feb.	90F	32C	June		79F	26C	Oct.		86F	30C
	74	23			65	18			68	20
Mar.	88F	31C	July		79F	26C	Nov.		88F	31C
	74	23			61	16			70	21
Apr.	85F	29C	Aug.		81F	27C	Dec.		90F	32C
	70	21			63	17			74	23

ALICE SPRINGS

	°F	°C			°F	°C			°F	°C
Jan.	97F	36C	May		74F	23C	Sept.		81F	27C
	70	21			47	8			49	9
Feb.	95F	35C	June		67F	19C	Oct.		88F	31C
	70	21			41	5			58	14
Mar.	90F	32C	July		67F	19C	Nov.		94F	34C
	63	17			40	4			65	18
Apr.	81F	27C	Aug.		74F	23C	Dec.		97F	36C
	54	12			43	6			68	20

DARWIN

	°F	°C			°F	°C			°F	°C
Jan.	90F	32C	May		92F	33C	Sept.		92F	33C
	77	25			74	23			74	23
Feb.	90F	32C	June		88F	31C	Oct.		94F	34C
	77	25			70	21			77	25
Mar.	92F	33C	July		88F	31C	Nov.		94F	34C
	77	25			67	19			79	26
Apr.	92F	33C	Aug.		90F	32C	Dec.		92F	33C
	76	24			70	21			79	26

PERTH

	°F	°C			°F	°C			°F	°C
Jan.	85F	29C	May		69F	20C	Sept.		70F	21C
	63	17			53	12			50	10
Feb.	85F	29C	June		64F	18C	Oct.		76F	24C
	63	17			50	10			53	12
Mar.	81F	27C	July		63F	17C	Nov.		81F	27C
	61	16			48	9			57	14
Apr.	76F	24C	Aug.		67F	19C	Dec.		83F	28C
	57	14			48	9			61	16

CANBERRA

	°F	°C			°F	°C			°F	°C
Jan.	85F	29C	May		61F	16C	Sept.		61F	16C
	58	14			49	4			49	4
Feb.	85F	29C	June		54F	12C	Oct.		68F	20C
	58	14			36	2			45	7
Mar.	77F	25C	July		54F	12C	Nov.		76F	24C
	54	12			32	0			50	10
Apr.	68F	20C	Aug.		58F	14C	Dec.		79F	26C
	45	7			34	1			54	12

ON THE CALENDAR

Annual and biennial events range from international cultural festivals and sporting matches to uniquely Australian celebrations with a distinctly tongue-in-cheek flavor. With the opening of performing arts centers in most capital cities, arts festivals have become major features on the Australian calendar. The dates of some of these festivals may change, so call ahead to check. And remember that the northern winter is Australia's summer.

For more information about those festivals listed below without contact numbers, get in touch with the tourist office of the host city or region. Information about local tourist offices is listed in the A to Z section of each chapter.

WINTER

January	**New Year's Day** is observed as a holiday nationwide.
January	**Sydney Festival**, which begins with harborside fireworks on New Year's Eve, is a monthlong, multicultural celebration with concerts, outdoor movies, circuses, arts workshops, ferryboat races, and fringe theater events.
Jan. 26	**Australia Day** celebrates the founding of the nation.
Feb.–Mar.	**Sydney Gay and Lesbian Mardi Gras** fêtes lesbian and gay life with a month of theater, performances, and art and photography exhibitions, culminating in a spectacular parade.
Feb.–Mar.	**Adelaide Festival of the Arts**, Australia's montlong feast of arts and culture, takes place every even-numbered year.
Feb.–Mar.	**Womadelaide Festival** of world music is staged in Adelaide during odd-numbered years.
Feb.–Mar.	**Melbourne Formula 1 Grand Prix**, held at Albert Park on the outskirts of the city, is Australia's premier motoring event.

SPRING

March	**Canberra Multicultural Festival** is the national capital's major annual event, lasting for 10 days, with a colorful hot-air balloon fiesta, music, concerts, and a street parade.
Second or Third Week in Mar.	**Melbourne Moomba Waterfest** is Melbourne's lighthearted end-of-summer celebration.
Mar.–Apr.	**Easter** holiday is observed Good Friday through Easter Monday.
Mar.–Apr.	**Barossa Vintage Festival**, the best-known wine-region harvest celebration, bears the stamp of the valley's Germanic heritage and highlights the joys of wine, food, music, and culture. The festival takes place around Easter every second (odd-numbered) year, with the next in 2005.
Apr. 25	**Anzac Day** is a solemn holiday honoring fallen members of Australia's armed forces.

SUMMER	
Second Monday in June	Queen's Birthday holiday is observed in every state but Western Australia, which celebrates it in September or October.
July	Camel Cup Races in Alice Springs have to be seen to be believed, as do the carnival's concurrent camel polo matches.
August	Darwin Cup is the premier horse race of northern Australia, bringing a colorful brigade to Darwin from the cattle stations, Aboriginal communities, and islands spread across the breadth of the Top End.
August	Beer Can Regatta in Darwin shows a fine sensitivity to recycling: the sailing craft are constructed from used beer cans!
August	Festival of Darwin celebrates The Dry season.
AUTUMN	
Sept.–Oct.	Warana Festival, usually held over a 10-day period, celebrates Brisbane in spring blossom with arts, entertainment, and a series of gala events, including a festive parade.
Sept.–Oct.	The Birdsville Races bring together station owners and cattle musterers who travel hundreds of miles to the remote town of Birdsville, Queensland, on the edge of the Simpson Desert, for a weekend of horse racing, socializing, and hard drinking.
Sept.–Oct.	Floriade, in Canberra, is a splendid monthlong festival of spring, with special music, dance, and theater performances. The festival's floral show is the largest in Australia.
Sept.–Oct.	Henley-On-Todd Regatta in Alice Springs is a boat race held in a dry riverbed. Crews "wear" the boats, and leg power replaces rowing.
Sept.–Oct.	Fun in the Sun Festival in Cairns highlights the city's tropical setting with a grand parade, entertainment, exhibitions, a yacht race, and a fun run.
November	Melbourne International Festival of the Arts features Australia's top performing artists, along with outstanding international productions, at the Victorian Arts Centre and venues around Melbourne.
First Tuesday of Nov.	Melbourne Cup is one of Australia's most famous sporting events— a horse race that brings the nation to a virtual standstill.
November	Mango Festival in Broome, in Western Australia, is an excuse to throw a rollicking big beach party, with music, a mango cook-off, and even a mango-inspired fashion show.
Dec. 25 and 26	Christmas Day, when almost everything is closed nationwide, and Boxing Day, are observed as holidays in all states, except for South Australia, which does not observe Boxing Day.
December	Sydney to Hobart Yacht Race is one of the world's classic blue-water races. Yachts cross the starting line in Sydney at 1 PM, and the first to finish usually reaches the Tasmanian capital two to three days later. The best vantage points are from the waterline.

PLEASURES & PASTIMES

Beautiful Beaches

Australia is renowned for its beaches. Along its coastline are miles and miles of pristine sand where you can sunbathe in solitary splendor. Sydney has nearly 40 ocean beaches, with such well-known names as Bondi, Manly, Coogee, Bronte, and Maroubra. Queensland's Gold Coast is a 70-km (43-mi) stretch of clean beach washed by warm, moderate surf. This area does not have the box jellyfish that plague the coast farther north (but not the Great Barrier Reef islands) from November through April. Perth's ocean beaches are excellent, too. From South Fremantle on up, there are 19 beaches along the Indian Ocean with wide swathes of sand and good surf.

Bushwalking

With so much bird life, flora, and fauna to admire, hiking—Aussies call it "bushwalking"—is a pleasurable and popular pastime. Every weekend thousands of people head to the tranquillity of national parks in nearby ranges, either individually or with one of the many bushwalking clubs. Get yourself out into one of the country's parks—the Australian bush is a national treasure.

Dining in Oz

Contemporary Australian cuisine emphasizes fresh ingredients, such as seasonal vegetables and fish. Each state has its own specialties, particularly seafood. In the Northern Territory, for instance, grilled barramundi fish is prized as a delicacy. Yabbies (small freshwater lobster) and Moreton Bay bugs (a crayfish-like crustacean), are also highly regarded. "Bush tucker," the food native to Australia, has been rediscovered, and there is scarcely a fashionable city restaurant that does not have some bush food on its menu. Although ingredients such as wattle seed, lemon aspen, emu (a smaller relative of the ostrich), marron (a large freshwater crustacean), and stingray might not all be familiar, they provide an astonishing range of flavors, and chefs with skill and imagination have leapt at the chance to create truly "Australian" dishes. The result is a sort of hybrid of Mediterranean and Asian techniques and spices using these uniquely Australian ingredients—locals call it "Mod Oz," for Modern Australian, and it's quite delicious.

Underwater Australia

With 36,735 km (22,776 mi) of coast bordering two oceans and four seas, Australians spend a good deal of their time in and on the water. Opportunities abound for scuba diving, snorkeling, surfing, waterskiing, and windsurfing. The best known area for scuba diving and snorkeling is the Great Barrier Reef. Prime diving season is September–December and mid-March–May. Western Australia's Ningaloo Marine Park, set in 280 km (174 mi) of Indian Ocean coral reefs off the central coast near Exmouth, is quickly gaining a top-rated reputation among international divers. Unlike the Great Barrier Reef, these reefs lie only a few hundred yards offshore. You can even find good diving close to major cities such as Sydney, Melbourne, and Perth.

Malls & Markets

The best buys in Australia are woolen goods, fashionable leather clothing, sheepskin rugs and car seat covers, arts and crafts, Aboriginal art, and gemstones—particularly opals, diamonds, and pearls. Fine gems can be found in reputable jewelers throughout Australia, but consider going to the source. For opals, look for South Australia's Coober Pedy "milky" stones, and black opals from Lightning Ridge in New South Wales. Western Australia is the place for gold; rare "pink" diamonds, from the Kimberley's Argyle Diamond Mine; and pearls harvested from the waters off Broome in the north. Sapphires and other gemstones are mined in Queensland's ranges. Darwin, Alice Springs, and Kununurra in the Kimberley region are good places to look for Aboriginal art and artifacts, although outstanding examples of Aboriginal art can also be found in the commercial galleries of Sydney, Melbourne, and Perth.

Catch a Wave

Most Australians spend at least part of their youth on surfboards, and the country is well represented in the ranks of world champions. The best surfing beaches are found in New South Wales, Victoria, and Western Australia. Bell's Beach in Victoria and Margaret River in Western Australia are legendary in the surfing world, and several Sydney beaches have surfable waves. For those who prefer warmer waters, Byron Bay in northern New South Wales has been a hangout since the days of the Malibu board. Surf shops are a common sight in most coastal towns in southern states, and boards and wet suits are generally available to rent.

Country Vineyards

The finest Australian wines are among the best in the world, a judgment that international wine shows consistently reinforce. The reds are typically robust, full-blooded wines that dazzle with sunshine and ripe berry flavors. The shirazes and cabernet sauvignons are the foremost Australian varieties, although the pinot noirs can also be exceptional, particularly those from Victoria's Yarra Valley. Among the whites, chardonnay, Riesling, and Semillon are best suited to Australian conditions. The Tokays, muscats, and ports of Rutherglen are exceptional fortified wines: intense, powerful varieties underpinned with subtle layers of fruit that explode in the mouth and only reach their peak after a couple of decades in the cask.

Although vineyards can be found as far north as Central Queensland, all the major wine-growing areas are in the southern half of the continent. Apart from the irrigated vineyards, most lie within 100 km (62 mi) of the coast. You can visit vineyards in several states, including the Hunter Valley, in New South Wales; South Australia's Barossa Region and Clare Valley; and parts of Victoria, Tasmania, and Western Australia.

FODOR'S CHOICE

The sights, restaurants, hotels, and other travel experiences on these pages are our editors' top picks—our Fodor's Choices. They're the best of their type in the area covered by the book—not to be missed and always worth your time. In the destination chapters that follow, you will find all the details.

LODGING

$$$$	**Bedarra Island.** All those world-famous faces jet to this all-inclusive resort, where they can enjoy the ultimate in tropical pampering.
$$$$	**Boroka Downs, Halls Gap, Victoria.** Sumptuous boutique suites with every luxury have up-close views of local wildlife and the Grampians National Park.
$$$$	**Cockatoo Island Resort, Top End.** Tropical foliage surrounds this polished, all-inclusive, luxury island hideaway with a cliff-top infinity-edge pool overlooking the Buccaneer Archipelago.
$$$$	**Convent Pepper Tree, New South Wales.** This luxurious Hunter Valley home is a former convent and surrounded by the vineyards of the Pepper Tree Winery.
$$$$	**Lizard Island Lodge, Great Barrier Reef, Queensland.** This is the reef's most idyllic island retreat—the perfect tropical getaway.
$$$$	**Longitude 131°, Ayers Rock Resort, Red Centre.** You can watch the sun rise and set over Uluru from your bed. The resort is up close to the Rock and very, very comfortable.
$$$$	**Park Hyatt Sydney.** The view of Sydney Harbor from the waterfront rooms doesn't get any better than this.
$$$$	**Silky Oaks Lodge and Restaurant, Mossman, Queensland.** Villas on stilts sit right in the midst of national parkland and overlook verdant rain forest.
$–$$$$	**Kings Canyon Resort, Red Centre.** View amazing landscapes from your whirlpool bath or while sipping champagne on a sunset viewing deck.
$$$	**Adelaide Hills Country Cottages, South Australia.** Nearly 100 acres of rolling countryside surround these charming, secluded cottages.
$$–$$$	**Cape Lodge, Margaret River, Western Australia.** Set amid neat vineyards and overlooking a private lake, this opulent Cape Dutch bed-and-breakfast brings a taste of South Africa to the region.
$$–$$$	**Hatherley House, Launceston, Tasmania.** Set in lush gardens, this exquisite 1830s mansion is now a trend-setting hotel.
$–$$	**Brickendon, Longford, Tasmania.** Children are welcome at this 1824 colonial village and farm, where cottages are surrounded by more than 20 historic buildings.

RESTAURANTS

$$$$	**Rockpool, Sydney.** This seductive chrome-and-glass restaurant fuses Mediterranean, Middle Eastern, Chinese, and Thai flavors.

$$$$	**Sounds of Silence, Ayers Rock Resort.** Dine under a canopy of stars out in the desert as an astronomer explains the Southern night sky.
$$$	**Kuniya, Ayers Rock Resort.** Aboriginal mythology adorns the walls at this Red Centre restaurant, which takes you 'round Australia with dishes from each state.
$$$	**Mead's of Mosman Bay, Perth.** Views of yachts and pelicans plus superb seafood make this Perth restaurant irresistible.
$$$	**Vulcan's, Blackheath, New South Wales.** This modest restaurant turns out amazing slow-roasted dishes, often with Asian or Middle Eastern spices, and luscious checkerboard ice cream.
$$-$$$	**Fee and Me, Launceston, Tasmania.** Tasmania's top dining spot focuses on succulent seafood and dressed-up home-style meals.
$$	**Melbourne Wine Room Restaurant, Melbourne.** Serene, romantic, and modestly glamorous, this is the perfect place to try wines by the glass, paired with stylish Italian cooking.
$-$$	**Hanuman Thai, Alice Springs.** Those who scorn seafood will become converts after sampling the Hanuman oysters (grilled and seasoned with lemongrass and lime) at this new restaurant in Alice.
$-$$	**Hanuman Thai and Nonya Restaurant, Darwin.** Thai-Malaysian flavors have made this dazzling restaurant the city's Asian sensation.

AMAZING WILDLIFE

Cradle Mountain–Lake St. Clair National Park, Tasmania. Keep an eye out for the famous Tasmanian devil and other wildlife as you hike through this alpine park.
Heron Island, Great Barrier Reef, Queensland. The island, a national park and bird sanctuary, is actually part of the reef and is a popular migration and breeding spot for loggerhead turtles and birds.
Kakadu National Park, the Top End. The billabongs (water holes) at Yellow Water, South Alligator River, and Magella Creek attract more than 280 species of birds.
Lady Elliot Island, Great Barrier Reef, Queensland. This 100-acre coral cay is a breeding ground for birds, turtles, tropical fish, and other sea creatures.
Lone Pine Koala Sanctuary, Queensland. Pet the animals at this fauna park outside of Brisbane—and have your picture taken while cuddling a koala.
Monkey Mia, Western Australia. Dolphins show up in Shark Bay anytime to be hand-fed by the rangers, who will share the job with you.
Ningaloo Reef, Western Australia. Giant whale sharks, humpback whales, and turtles abound in the waters off Exmouth Peninsula.
Phillip Island, Victoria. The twilight return of the fairy penguins is a spectacular sight.

Sea Acres Rainforest Centre, New South Wales. An elevated boardwalk takes you above lush coastal rain forest filled with more than 170 plant species, native mammals, and prolific bird life.

Seal Bay Conservation Park, Kangaroo Island, South Australia. Members of Seal Bay's sea lion colony relax on the beach between fishing trips.

Warrawong Sanctuary, Adelaide Hills, South Australia. Rangers lead morning and evening walks through this rain forest, which shelters bandicoots, wallabies, and platypuses.

NATURAL WONDERS

Cape Leeuwin–Naturaliste National Park, Western Australia. Human and animal relics, as well as more than 360 caves, are part of the rugged coastal scenery here.

Freycinet National Park, Tasmania. Gorgeous turquoise bays and soft, sugar-white beaches meet with granite bluffs and thick forests in this park along the island's east coast.

Great Barrier Reef, Queensland. The world's richest marine area supports wondrous undersea life, making for extraordinary diving and snorkeling.

Port Campbell National Park, Victoria. Rugged cliffs and columns of resilient rock stand in the roiling bays that fringe this dramatic section of coastline.

Snowy Mountains, New South Wales. Part of Kosciuszko National Park, this area is Australia's largest alpine region.

Three Sisters, New South Wales. The name of these soaring sandstone pillars in the Blue Mountains comes from an Aboriginal legend of sisters who were saved from a monster by their transformation into stone.

Uluru (Ayers Rock) and Kata Tjuta (the Olgas), the Red Centre. These massive rock formations, which together make up a World Heritage Site, are breathtaking and unforgettable.

THE REAL OZ

El Questro Wilderness Park, Top End. This rugged, million-acre spread offers the chance to jump into life on a working Outback ranch and explore the surrounding terrain.

Harbour Ferry Ride, Sydney. The journey to Manly captures stunning, breezy views of the city.

Lizard Island, Great Barrier Reef, Queensland. The boat crew feed the giant potato cod and the Maori wrasse at Cod Hole, off the outer reef of this island.

Lygon Street, Melbourne. Have coffee at an open-air café here in Carlton, on the bohemian fringe of the inner city.

Mornington Peninsula Wineries, Victoria. Set amid the state's prime vineyards, local wineries produce fine, cool-climate labels to go with the region's exceptional cuisine.

Port Arthur Historic Site, Tasmania. The restored Port Arthur Penal Settlement includes the original church, guardhouse, commandant's residence, prison, hospital, and lunatic asylum.

Salamanca Place, Hobart. One of this city's liveliest gathering spots showcases the island's best crafts and antiques.

Skyrail Rain Forest Cableway, Queensland. The journey takes you 7½ km (5 mi) over rain-forest canopy to the village of Kuranda, near Cairns.

Vineyards of Margaret River, Western Australia. Wine-tasting amid the lush backdrop here makes a memorable experience.

Zig Zag Railway, New South Wales. Riding this vintage steam engine along cliff-side precipices through the Blue Mountains is thrilling.

SMART TRAVEL TIPS

Finding out about your destination before you leave home means you won't squander time organizing everyday minutiae once you've arrived. You'll be more streetwise when you hit the ground as well, better prepared to explore the aspects of Australia that drew you here in the first place. The organizations in this section can provide information to supplement this guide; contact them for up-to-the-minute details, and consult the A to Z sections in each chapter for facts on the various topics as they relate to Australia's many regions. Happy landings!

AIR TRAVEL

The major gateways to Australia include Sydney, Melbourne, Perth, Brisbane, and Cairns. Flights depart from Los Angeles, San Francisco, Honolulu, New York, Toronto, and Vancouver, as well as from London, Frankfurt, and Rome. Depending on your airline and route, you can elect to stop over in Honolulu, Fiji, Tahiti, or Auckland from the United States; Singapore, Hong Kong, Mauritius, Johannesburg, Tokyo, Kuala Lumpur, or Bangkok from Europe. Nonstop service is available to Sydney from Los Angeles.

BOOKING

When you book, **look for nonstop flights, and remember that "direct" flights stop at least once.** Try to avoid connecting flights, which require a change of plane. Two airlines may operate a connecting flight jointly, so ask whether your airline operates every segment of the trip; you may find that the carrier you prefer flies you only part of the way. To find more booking tips and to check prices and make online flight reservations, log on to www.fodors.com.

CARRIERS

When flying internationally, you must usually choose between your domestic carrier, the national flag carrier of the country you are visiting, and a foreign carrier from a third country. National flag carriers have the greatest number of nonstops. Domestic carriers may have better connections to your hometown and serve a greater number of gateway cities. Third-party carriers may have a price advantage.

Qantas—and its subsidiaries, including Eastern Australia, Southern Australia,

Sunstate, and Airlink—is the major domestic carrier. Virgin Australia and Regional Express also provide services. Australian Airlines connects Sydney, Melbourne, and Cairns to Bali, Sabah, and points in northern Asia.

To & From Australia Air Canada ☎ 800/426-7000 in the U.S., 800/665-1177 in Canada, 09/379-3371 in New Zealand. **Air New Zealand** ☎ 800/262-1234 in the U.S., 800/663-5494 in Canada, 0181/741-2299 in the U.K., 13-2476 in Australia, 0800/737-000 in New Zealand. **British Airways** ☎ 800/247-9297 in the U.S. and Canada, 20/8741-2299 in the U.K., 09/356-8690 in New Zealand. **Cathay Pacific** ☎ 800/233-2742 in the U.S., 800/268-6868 in Canada, 0171/747-8888 in the U.K., 09/379-0861 in New Zealand. **Japan Airlines** ☎ 800/525-3663 in the U.S., 800/525-3663 in Canada, 0171/408-1000 in the U.K., 09/379-3202 in New Zealand. **Qantas** ☎ 800/227-4500 in the U.S. and Canada, 0845/774-7767 in the U.K, 0800/808-767 in New Zealand ⊕ www.qantas.com.au. **Singapore Airlines** ☎ 800/742-3333 in the U.S., 800/387-0038 in Canada, 0181/747-0007 in the U.K., 0800/808-909 in New Zealand. **United** ☎ 800/538-2929 in the U.S., 800/241-6522 in Canada, 0845/844-4777 in the U.K., 0800/508-648 in New Zealand.

Within Australia Australian Airlines 1300/799-798 **Regional Express** ☎ 13-1713. **Qantas** ☎ 13-1313. **Virgin Australia** ☎ 13-6789.

CHECK-IN & BOARDING

Always **ask your carrier about its check-in policy.** Plan to arrive at the airport about two hours before your scheduled departure time for domestic flights and 2½ to 3 hours before international flights. You may need to arrive earlier if you're flying from one of the busier airports or during peak air-traffic times. The first to get bumped are passengers who checked in late and those flying on discounted tickets, so **get to the gate and check in as early as possible,** especially during peak periods. Always **bring a government-issued photo I.D. to the airport;** even when it's not required, a passport is best.

Australia's already thorough airport security has been tightened even further in recent months. Be prepared for extensive clothing and carry-on luggage searches. Note that any sharp objects—including knives, scissors, and nail clippers—will be confiscated if found in your hand luggage. To avoid delays at airport-security checkpoints, try not to wear any metal. Jewelry, belt and other buckles, steel-toe shoes,

barrettes, and underwire bras are among the items that can set off detectors.

CUTTING COSTS

The least expensive airfares to Australia are priced for round-trip travel and must usually be purchased in advance. Airlines generally allow you to change your return date for a fee; most low-fare tickets, however, are nonrefundable. Many airlines offer lower fares on-line. It's smart to **call a number of airlines,** and when you are quoted a good price, **book it on the spot**—the same fare may not be available the next day. Also compare quotes from the airlines' Web sites, and the Web sites of discount travel services. Always **check different routings** and look into using alternate airports. Most flights from the United States go over the Pacific, but in some instances it may be cheaper (albeit considerably longer) to fly over the Atlantic and Europe. Also, price off-peak flights, which may be significantly less expensive than others. Travel agents, especially low-fare specialists (⇨ Discounts and Deals), are helpful.

Consolidators are another good source. They buy tickets for scheduled flights at reduced rates from the airlines, then sell them at prices that beat the best fare available directly from the airlines. Sometimes you can even get your money back if you need to return the ticket. Carefully read the fine print detailing penalties for changes and cancellations, purchase the ticket with a credit card, and **confirm your consolidator reservation with the airline.**

When you **fly as a courier,** you trade your checked-luggage space for a ticket deeply subsidized by a courier service. There are restrictions on when you can book and how long you can stay. Some courier companies list with membership organizations, such as the Air Courier Association and the International Association of Air Travel Couriers; these require you to become a member before you can book a flight.

Many airlines, singly or in collaboration, offer discount air passes that allow foreigners to travel economically in a particular country or region. These visitor passes usually must be reserved and purchased before you leave home. Information about passes often can be found on most airlines' international Web pages.

If you'll be flying within Australia (or stopping in Fiji), **book a Qantas OzPass**

from home. This discount air-travel pass is valid for a minimum of two and a maximum of 10 regions of economy-class air travel; the price varies upon the number of regions you select. It's only available outside Australia, and with the purchase of an international Qantas ticket or one of its One World partners (e.g., American).

However, unless you plan to make a number of flights within Australia, and particularly if you're traveling off-season, better deals for most sectors can often be obtained after you arrive in Australia.

🛪 Consolidators **AirlineConsolidator.com** ☎ 888/468-5385 ⊕ www.airlineconsolidator.com; for international tickets. **Best Fares** ☎ 800/576-8255 or 800/576-1600 ⊕ www.bestfares.com; A$59.90 annual membership. **Cheap Tickets** ☎ 800/377-1000 or 888/922-8849 ⊕ www.cheaptickets.com. **Expedia** ☎ 800/397-3342 or 404/728-8787 ⊕ www.expedia.com. **Hotwire** ☎ 866/468-9473 or 920/330-9418 ⊕ www.hotwire.com. **Now Voyager Travel** ✉ 45 W. 21st St., 5th floor, New York, NY 10010 ☎ 212/459-1616 🖷 212/243-2711 ⊕ www.nowvoyagertravel.com. **Onetravel.com** ⊕ www.onetravel.com. **Orbitz** ☎ 888/656-4546 ⊕ www.orbitz.com. **Priceline.com** ⊕ www.priceline.com. **Travelocity** ☎ 888/709-5983, 877/282-2925 in Canada, 0870/876-3876 in the U.K. ⊕ www.travelocity.com.

🛪 Courier Resources **Air Courier Association/Cheaptrips.com** ☎ 800/282-1202 ⊕ www.aircourier.org or www.cheaptrips.com. **International Association of Air Travel Couriers** ☎ 308/632-3273 ⊕ www.courier.org.

🛪 Discount Passes **OzPass**, Qantas, ☎ 800/227-4500, 0845/774-7767 in the U.K., 131-313 in Australia, 0800/808-767 in New Zealand ⊕ www.qantasusa.com. **Pacific Explorer Airpass**, Hideaway Holidays, ☎ 61-2/9743-0253 in Australia 🖷 61-2/9743-3568 in Australia, 530/325-4069 in the U.S. ⊕ www.hideawayholidays.com.au. **Polypass**, Polynesian Airlines, ☎ 800/264-0823 or 808/842-7659, 020/8846-0519 in the U.K., 1300/653737 in Australia, 0800/800-993 in New Zealand ⊕ www.polynesianairlines.co.nz. **Qantas** ☎ 800/227-4500 in the U.S. and Canada, 0845/774-7767 in the U.K., 131-313 in Australia, 0800/808-767 in New Zealand ⊕ www.qantas.com. **SAS Air Passes**, Scandinavian Airlines, ☎ 800/221-2350, 0845/6072-7727 in the U.K., 1300/727707 in Australia ⊕ www.scandinavian.net.

ENJOYING THE FLIGHT

State your seat preference when purchasing your ticket, and then repeat it when you confirm and when you check in. For more legroom, you can request one of the few emergency-aisle seats at check-in, if you are capable of lifting at least 50 pounds—a Federal Aviation Administration requirement of passengers in these seats. Seats behind a bulkhead also offer more legroom, but they don't have underseat storage. Don't sit in the row in front of the emergency aisle or in front of a bulkhead, where seats may not recline.

Ask the airline whether a snack or meal is served on the flight. If you have dietary concerns, **request special meals when booking.** These can be vegetarian, low-cholesterol, or kosher, for example. It's a good idea to pack some healthful snacks and a small (plastic) bottle of water in your carry-on bag. On long flights, try to maintain a normal routine, to help fight jet lag. At night, **get some sleep.** By day, **eat light meals, drink water** (not alcohol), and **move around the cabin** to stretch your legs. For additional jet-lag tips consult *Fodor's FYI: Travel Fit & Healthy* (available at bookstores everywhere).

If sleeping well over a long flight is important to you, Qantas has **first-class and business-class sleeper seats,** which can fully recline. You'll also get in-flight meals prepared by Neil Perry, one of Australia's top chefs, as well as high-quality toiletries and cotton hand towels.

All flights from the United States and Europe to Australia are nonsmoking, as are all flights within Australia.

FLYING TIMES

Flying times are as follows: from New York to Sydney (via Los Angeles), about 21 hours; from Chicago to Sydney (via Los Angeles), about 19 hours; from Los Angeles to Sydney (nonstop), about 14 hours; from Los Angeles to Melbourne (via Auckland), around 16 hours; and from London to Sydney or Melbourne, about 20½ hours via Singapore or Bangkok.

Since flights from the United States to Australia cross the International Date Line, you lose a day on the outward leg of your travels and regain it on the journey home.

HOW TO COMPLAIN

If your baggage goes astray or your flight goes awry, complain right away. Most carriers require that you **file a claim immediately.** The Aviation Consumer Protection Division of the Department of Transportation publishes *Fly-Rights*, which discusses airlines and consumer issues and is available on-line.

Airline Complaints Aviation Consumer Protection Division ✉ U.S. Department of Transportation, C-75, Room 4107, 400 7th St. NW, Washington, DC 20590 ☎ 202/366-2220 ⊕ www.dot.gov/airconsumer. **Federal Aviation Administration Consumer Hotline** ✉ for inquiries: FAA, 800 Independence Ave. SW, Room 810, Washington, DC 20591 ☎ 800/322-7873 ⊕ www.faa.gov.

RECONFIRMING

Check the status of your flight before you leave for the airport. You can do this on your carrier's Web site, by linking to a flight-status checker (many Web booking services offer these), or by calling your carrier or travel agent. Although you aren't required to reconfirm reservations on domestic flights in Australia, it's always smart to do so if it's convenient. You'll be assured of a seat if the flight is overbooked, and you can check on any changes in flight times or planes. Always confirm international flights from Australia at least 72 hours ahead of the scheduled departure time.

AIRPORTS

The major east-coast air gateways are Brisbane International Airport, Cairns Airport, Sydney's Kingsford-Smith Airport, and Melbourne Airport. Perth International Airport is the major international entry point on the west coast, Darwin is the northern gateway, and Alice Springs is the hub of the Red Centre. There are no cost advantages to flying into one city as opposed to another from North America or Europe, although there is certainly a greater choice of flights into Sydney, the major international gateway. Car-rental rates from discount operators are similar in all cities, and rates are much the same from the large agencies such as Avis, Budget, and Hertz. As for convenience, Sydney has more hotels in the vicinity of the airport, as well as a greater choice of accommodations, than any other city. Getting into town is easiest from Sydney, Brisbane, and Cairns airports. Darwin, Alice Springs, and Adelaide airports are all less than 5 km (3 mi) from their respective cities and easily reached by taxi. Melbourne's airport lies farther away from the city, and the highway between is prone to rush-hour delays.

Airport Information Adelaide Airport ✉ 1 James Schofeild Dr. ☎ 08/8308-9211. **Alice Springs Airport** ☎ 08/8951-1211 ⊕ www.ntapl.com.au. **Brisbane International Airport** ☎ 07/3406-3190. **Cairns Airport** ☎ 07/4052-9703. **Darwin International Airport** ☎ 08/8945-5944. **Kingsford-Smith International Airport** ☎ 02/9667-9111. **Melbourne Airport** ☎ 03/9297-1600. **Perth International Airport** ☎ 08/9478-8888.

Airport Transfers Adelaide Airport ☎ 08/8332-0528. **Alice Springs Airport** ✉ Shop 6, Capricornia Centre, Gregory Terr. ☎ 08/8953-0310 or 1800/621188. **Brisbane International Airport** ☎ 03/3860-8600. **Cairns Airport** ☎ 07/4052-9703. **Darwin Airport** ☎ 1800/358945. **Melbourne Airport** ☎ 03/9297-1600. **Perth International Airport** ☎ 08/9478-8888. **Sydney Kingsford-Smith Airport** ☎ 02/9667-9111.

DUTY-FREE SHOPPING

In Australia, there is no limit on what you can purchase, just the limitations imposed by your country of residence.

BIKE TRAVEL

Biking is popular within Australia, where much of the flat terrain is perfect for long-distance cycling, but be aware of the large distances between popular destinations within the country. It's a good idea to select particular areas of interest and enquire about availability and accessibility of bike paths and trails. The Web site of the Bicycle Federation of Australia lists members in each state. The organizations for the region in which you plan to bicycle will be able to provide maps and advice.

Bicycling Information Bicycle Federation of Australia ⊕ www.bfa.asn.au. **Bike Maps Breakaway Bicycle Club** ☎ 1877/829-8899 ⊕ www.breakawaybicycleclub.org.

BIKES IN FLIGHT

Most airlines accommodate bikes as luggage, provided they are dismantled and boxed; check with individual airlines about packing requirements. Some airlines sell bike boxes, which are often free at bike shops, for about A$15 (bike bags can be considerably more expensive). International travelers often can substitute a bike for a piece of checked luggage at no charge; otherwise, the cost is about A$100. U.S. and Canadian airlines charge A$40–A$80 each way.

BOAT & FERRY TRAVEL

Although there are no ferries operating within Queensland, many tour-boat operators make day trips out to the Great Barrier Reef from the mainland. The central points of departure are Townsville, Cairns, and Port Douglas. The *Spirit of Tasmania* ferry service runs between Melbourne and Devonport on Tasmania's north coast. However, this service is mainly used by Australians to transport their vehicles. For visitors it's far more convenient to simply fly and pick up a rental car. You'll need to book or arrive early during the busy school-holiday periods, in particular December–January for Tasmania and July for Queensland. The ferry service that visitors are most likely to use is the Sealink Ferry, which transports passengers and vehicles between the South Australian coastline and Kangaroo Island.

FARES & SCHEDULES

You can pick up ferry and cruise schedules at most state tourism offices, as well as from the individual companies. Tickets can be purchased directly from each travel operator; during high season, check to see if you can book and pay ahead of time. All transport companies accept major credit cards and cash; some take travelers checks.
Boat & Ferry Information Sealink Ferries ☎ 13-1301. *Spirit of Tasmania* ☎ 13-2010.

BUS TRAVEL

Most Australian towns are well served by bus. Route networks of large express companies cover the nation's major highways and link up with regional operators that serve smaller communities. Buses are usually air-conditioned, with toilets and, on some routes, attendants. Drivers run videos from time to time on overhead monitors. One advantage of bus touring is that drivers also act as guides, sharing their considerable knowledge of the countryside and blending illuminating descriptions of the areas you traverse with anecdotes about local characters.

Travel times and approximate one-way costs at press time are: Sydney–Melbourne (15 hours, A$65); Sydney–Adelaide (23 hours, A$127); Sydney–Brisbane (15 hours, A$93); Brisbane–Cairns (30 hours, A$192); Melbourne–Adelaide (10 hours, A$59); Adelaide–Perth (39 hours, A$264); Adelaide–Alice Springs (20 hours, A$177);

Alice Springs–Uluru (Ayers Rock; 6 hours, A$74).
Bus Information Greyhound Pioneer Australia ☎ 13-2030 in Australia ⊕ www.greyhound.com.au. **McCafferty's** ☎ 13-1499 ⊕ www.mccaffertys.com.au.

CLASSES

All bus lines in Australia provide a reasonable standard of comfort. Most have toilets and video systems, and all are required by law to provide seat belts, which passengers are advised to use. Where bus lines offer different fares on the same route, you generally get what you pay for.

CUTTING COSTS

Greyhound and McCafferty's have joined forces to operate a national bus network and offer passes that result in considerable savings, especially when purchased overseas. Most can be bought on arrival in Australia, but at a 10%–15% higher price. If you have YHA membership, VIP or ISIC Backpacker cards, or International Student cards you'll also receive a 10% discount.

Several different passes are available. Distance passes, for example, remain valid for up to a year or until the maximum amount of kilometers has been reached. A 2,000-km (1,240-mi) pass costs A$312; a 10,000-km (6,200-mi) pass costs A$1,195. There are also several regional passes. The one-month Follow the Sun Pass (A$290) is valid along the Sydney to Cairns route; you can also purchase a three-month pass for A$309. Many passes include discounts for accommodations and sightseeing, and are available in the United States and Canada through ATS Tours and in Canada through Goway Travel.
Discount Passes ATS Tours ☎ 800/423-2880 ⊟ 310/643-0032. **Goway Travel** ☎ 800/387-8850.

FARES & SCHEDULES

Details on bus schedules and fares are available from bus companies, tourist information offices, and most travel agents. Tickets can also be purchased from all of these sources. The Greyhound and McCafferty's Web sites provide information on schedules, fares, and passes, and it's also possible to make on-line reservations.

PAYING

You can pay for bus fares with traveler's checks or major credit cards. American

Express and Diners Club are sometimes not accepted by smaller lines.

RESERVATIONS

It's advisable that you **make advance reservations for bus travel.** There are no surcharges for this service. If you book in advance you are guaranteed a seat.

SMOKING

Smoking is not permitted on buses in Australia. The penalty is a fine (and perhaps a sharp crack across the ear from the driver).

BUSINESS HOURS

As a rule, business hours in Australia are weekdays 9–5. This applies to post offices as well. In the Northern Territory, hours are most commonly 8–4:40 for government departments. When a holiday falls on a weekend, businesses are usually closed the following Monday. Note that in tourist areas most shops are open daily except on Good Friday, Easter, Christmas, and New Year's Day.

GAS STATIONS

Around urban areas and major highways, many gas stations stay open 24 hours. In rural areas, however, gas stations are usually open 8–6.

PHARMACIES

Pharmacies are normally open weekdays 9–5:30, Saturday 9–12:30. Most cities have 24-hour pharmacies, usually in the nightlife district. Taxi drivers are the best source of advice for finding after-hours pharmacies.

SHOPS

Shops are normally open weekdays 8:30–5:30, with late closing at 9 PM on either Thursday or Friday. On Saturday shops are open from 8:30 to between noon and 4. Some stores, particularly those in the tourist areas of major cities, may be open a few hours on Sunday. In major cities and tourist areas, shops may have extended weekday hours. Some supermarkets are now open 24 hours.

CAMERAS & PHOTOGRAPHY

The light in Australia is particularly harsh for taking photographs. In the middle of the day especially, contrast is extreme, with washed-out highlights bleached of color and dense shadows that are beyond the contrast range of film. For these reasons, early morning and evening are preferable for taking photographs. For general outdoor photography, a film speed of around 200 ASA is practical. The *Kodak Guide to Shooting Great Travel Pictures* (available at bookstores everywhere) is loaded with tips.

As for protocol, Aborigines might resent a camera being pointed in their direction. However they will seldom refuse a request for a photograph if you have already established friendly contact. If in doubt, ask first. There are no restrictions on photographing government buildings in Australia, although security has been increased. When in doubt, ask at the guards' headquarters.

⬛ Photo Help Kodak Information Center ☎ 800/ 242-2424 ⊕ www.kodak.com.

EQUIPMENT PRECAUTIONS

Don't pack film and equipment in checked luggage, where it is much more susceptible to damage. X-ray machines used to view checked luggage are extremely powerful and therefore are likely to ruin your film. Try to **ask for hand inspection of film,** which becomes clouded after repeated exposure to airport X-ray machines, and **keep videotapes and computer disks away from metal detectors.** Always **keep film, tape, and computer disks out of the sun.** Carry an extra supply of batteries, and **be prepared to turn on your camera, camcorder, or laptop** to prove to airport security personnel that the device is real.

In Australia, your main camera culprits are dust in the Outback, humidity around the northern Barrier Reef, and heat in the Top End. Don't leave your camera or film in a hot car, shade them from the midday sun and sand at the beach or in the desert, and keep them out of the wind and ocean spray when on boats or ferries. Take care to protect your equipment from these environmental factors and you shouldn't have any problems.

FILM & DEVELOPING

Film is widely available throughout Australia. All pharmacies sell film; Kodak and Fuji brands are the most prevalent brands. A 36-exposure roll costs around A$7. In tourist areas, one-hour processing for prints is usually available. Otherwise the standard processing and printing time varies from one to three days.

VIDEOS

Videotapes cost about A$15 and can be found at most places that sell film, but keep in mind that most video cartridges solid in Australia (marked PAL) do not interface with American video players (NTSC).

CAR RENTAL

Rates in Sydney begin at A$50 a day for an economy car with air-conditioning, manual transmission, and 100 free km (62 free mi), although most companies offer rates with unlimited mileage. However, various additional taxes may be levied on the total account, the heftiest being when you pick up a rental car from an airport location. Larger agencies such as Avis, Budget, and Hertz are the most likely to have rental desks located at airport terminals. Rates for car rental from larger operators are similar for all the major cities. However, you can expect to pay more if you rent a vehicle in a remote location. Discount operators offer vehicles at about the same rate in major cities.

Rental agencies generally prohibit you from driving non-four-wheel-drive rental vehicles on unsealed roads. If you do and you have a collision, you may find that insurance will not cover the damage.

Local Agency Britz ☎ 1800/331454, Maui (1300/ 363800).

Major Agencies Alamo ☎ 800/522-9696 ⊕ www.alamo.com. Avis ☎ 800/331-1084, 800/ 879-2847 in Canada, 0870/606-0100 in the U.K., 02/ 9353-9000 in Australia, 09/526-2847 in New Zealand ⊕ www.avis.com. Budget ☎ 800/527-0700, 0870/156-5656 in the U.K. ⊕ www.budget. com. Dollar ☎ 800/800-6000, 0124/622-0111 in the U.K., where it's affiliated with Sixt, 02/9223-1444 in Australia ⊕ www.dollar.com. Hertz ☎ 800/654-3001, 800/263-0600 in Canada, 0870/844-8844 in the U.K., 02/9669-2444 in Australia, 09/256-8690 in New Zealand ⊕ www.hertz.com. National Car Rental ☎ 800/227-7368, 0870/600-6666 in the U.K. ⊕ www.nationalcar.com.

CUTTING COSTS

In Australian cities, most airports and train and bus stations are well supplied with tourism literature and even tourist information offices that will help you track down discount car rentals. In other areas,

check in the Yellow Pages under "Car Rental." The vehicles offered by these discount agencies are usually older than those from the major agencies, generally between two and three years old. Also, there are no provisions for one-way rentals. Vehicles must be returned to the office where they were hired.

If you **join an automobile club** you will often receive substantial discounts on car rentals, both in your home country and when traveling internationally. Another discount strategy is to **book through a travel agent who will shop around.** Steep discounts may also be found if you **look to Internet travel companies.** Major car-rental agencies occasionally offer discounts if you book a vehicle via their Web site.

For a good deal, **book through a travel agent who will shop around.** Do **look into wholesalers,** companies that do not own fleets but rent in bulk from those that do and often offer better rates than traditional car-rental operations. Prices are best during off-peak periods. Rentals booked through wholesalers often must be paid for before you leave home.

Auto Clubs In Australia: **Australian Automobile Association** ☎ 02/6247-7311 ⊕ www.aaa.asn.au. In Canada: **Canadian Automobile Association (CAA)** ☎ 613/247-0117 ⊕ www.caa.ca. In New Zealand: **New Zealand Automobile Association** ☎ 09/377-4660 or 0800/500-444 ⊕ www.aa.co.nz. In the United Kingdom: **Automobile Association (AA)** ☎ 0990/500-600; **Royal Automobile Club (RAC)** ☎ 0990/722-722 for membership, 0345/ 121345 for insurance ⊕ www.rac.co.uk. In the United States: **American Automobile Association** ☎ 800/ 564-6222 ⊕ www.aaa.com.

Wholesalers Auto Europe ☎ 207/842-2000 or 800/223-5555 🖶 207/842-2222 ⊕ www. autoeurope.com. Kemwel ☎ 800/678-0678 🖶 207/ 842-2124 ⊕ www.kemwel.com.

INSURANCE

When driving a rented car you are generally responsible for any damage to or loss of the vehicle. You also may be liable for any property damage or personal injury that you may cause while driving. Before you rent, see what coverage you already have under the terms of your personal auto-insurance policy and credit cards.

Although insurance is included with standard rental vehicles in Australia, you are still responsible for an "excess" fee—a maximum amount that you will have to pay if damage occurs. Fines can be incurred for such accidents as a cracked windshield, which is a common occurrence on Australian roads. The amount of this "excess" is generally around A$2,000, but you can have this figure reduced by paying a daily fee.

REQUIREMENTS & RESTRICTIONS

In Australia you must be 21 to rent a car, and rates may be higher if you're under 25. There is no upper age limit for rental so long as you have a valid driver's license.

SURCHARGES

Before you pick up a car in one city and leave it in another, **ask about drop-off charges or one-way service fees,** which can be substantial. Note, too, that some rental agencies charge extra if you return the car before the time specified in your contract. To avoid a hefty refueling fee, **fill the tank just before you turn in the car,** but be aware that gas stations near the rental outlet may overcharge. It's almost never a deal to buy the tank of gas that's in the car when you rent it; the understanding is that you'll return it empty, but some fuel usually remains.

Rental companies have varying policies and charges for unusual trips, such as lengthy cross-state expeditions around the Top End and Western Australia. Ask about additional mileage, fuel, and insurance charges if you're planning to cover a lot of ground. Also find out if the company charges for each additional driver, and if there's a car seat rental fee if you're traveling with children.

CAR TRAVEL

In Australia your own driver's license is accepted at most rental companies, provided that the information on the license is clear. An International Driver's Permit is required at others (but they will still want to see your own license). The international permit is available from the American or Canadian automobile association, and in the United Kingdom, from the Automobile Association or Royal Automobile Club.

Driving is easy in Australia, once you adjust to traveling on the left. The catchphrase is: **drive left, look right.** "Look right" is the pedestrian's caveat—and a serious one. For Americans, stepping into the street means looking left for oncoming traffic. Do that Down Under and you could get slammed from the right by an oncoming bus.

When you are planning a driving itinerary, it's vital to **bear in mind the huge distances involved.** Brisbane, Queensland's capital, is 1,032 km (640 mi) by road from Sydney, 1,718 km (1,065 mi) from Melbourne, and almost the same distance from Cairns. The journey from Sydney to Alice Springs, the gateway to Uluru (Ayers Rock), is 2½ hours by jet and a grueling 52 hours by road. Between major cities, flying is usually advised.

EMERGENCY SERVICES

If you have an emergency requiring an ambulance, the fire department, or the police, dial ☎ *000.* Many major highways now have telephones for breakdown assistance. Otherwise, flag down and ask a passing motorist to call the nearest motoring service organization for you. Most Australian drivers will be happy to assist, particularly in country areas.

Each state has its own motoring organization that provides assistance for vehicle breakdowns. When you hire a vehicle, you are entitled to assistance from the relevant motoring organization, free of charge. A toll-free, nationwide number is available for roadside assistance.
🚗 **Motoring Organization Hotline** ☎ 13-1111.

GASOLINE

Service stations are generally plentiful, although full service is common only in rural areas. The cost of gasoline ("petrol") varies around the country from about A$1 per liter in Sydney to about A$1.25 per liter in the Outback. American Express, MasterCard, and Visa are accepted at most service stations. Pumps are easy to operate and should be familiar to most drivers from North America and Europe.

ROAD CONDITIONS

Except for some expressways in and around the major cities, most highways are two-lane roads with frequent passing lanes. Main roads are usually paved and well maintained, though traffic lanes are narrower than in the United States. Always **take precautions when you drive through the Outback,** however. Road trains (i.e., truck convoys) can get up to 50 yards long, and passing them at that length becomes a matter of great caution, especially on roads in the bush.

Many Outback roads are unpaved, traffic is very light, and temperatures can be extreme. **Carry plenty of water and always tell someone your itinerary and schedule.** Flash floods from sudden rain showers can occur on low-lying roads. Don't try to outdrive them. **Get to higher ground immediately when it rains.**

ROAD MAPS

Road maps are available at most gas stations, although the choice may be limited. For more detailed maps, look in bookstores in the major cities. If you're planning an extensive road journey, pick up a comprehensive road atlas—such as the annual, widely available *Explore Australia* atlas published by Viking.

RULES OF THE ROAD

Speed limits are 50–60 kilometers per hour (kph) in populated areas, and 100–110 kph on open roads—the equivalent of 31–37 and 62–68 mph, respectively. There are no speed limits on the open road in the Northern Territory. Limits in school areas are usually around 40 kph (25 mph). Surveillance of speeders and "drink-driving" (the legal limit is a tough .05% blood-alcohol level) is thorough, and penalties are high. Seat belts are mandatory nationwide for drivers and all passengers. Children must be restrained in a seat appropriate to their size. These can be hired from car-rental agencies.

Road regulations differ from state to state and even city to city. Traffic circles are widely used at intersections throughout Australia. Cars that have already entered the circle have the right-of-way. At designated intersections in Melbourne's Golden Mile (the central business district), you must get into the left lane to make a right-hand turn. Watch for the sign RIGHT-HAND TURN FROM LEFT LANE ONLY. It's wise to **pick up a copy of the Highway Code** of any state or territory in which you plan to drive from the local automobile association. The Australian Automobile Association has a branch in each state, known as the National Roads and Motorists' Association (NRMA) in New South Wales and Canberra, the Automobile Association in the Northern Territory (AANT), and the Royal Automobile Club (RAC) in all other states. It's affiliated with AAA worldwide

and offers reciprocal services to American, Canadian, and British members, including emergency road service, road maps, and discounts on car rental and accommodations. Reservations must be made through an NRMA or RAC office.

CHILDREN IN AUSTRALIA

Be on the lookout for special children's events at museums, theaters, cinemas, and national parks during school holidays. The "Metro" section of the *Sydney Morning Herald,* published in the Friday edition of the paper, is a good source of information on activities for children. In Melbourne, consult the "EG" section of the *Melbourne Age,* also published on Fridays. Both of these papers are available at most newsstands. Another publication, *Holidays with Kids,* is a good source for vacation ideas.

If you are renting a car, **arrange for a car seat** when you reserve. For general advice about traveling with children, consult *Fodor's FYI: Travel with Your Baby* (available in bookstores everywhere).
Local Information Holidays with Kids Box 206, Thornleigh, NSW 2120 ☎ 02/9980-1284 ✉ info@signaturemedia.com ⊕ www. holidayswithkids.com.au.

FLYING

If your children are two or older, **ask about children's airfares.** As a general rule, infants under two not occupying a seat fly at greatly reduced fares or even for free. But if you want to guarantee a seat for an infant, you have to pay full fare. Consider flying during off-peak days and times; most airlines will grant an infant a seat without a ticket if there are available seats. When booking, **confirm carry-on allowances** if you're traveling with infants. In general, for babies charged 10% to 50% of the adult fare you are allowed one carry-on bag and a collapsible stroller; if the flight is full, the stroller may have to be checked or you may be limited to less.

Experts agree that it's a good idea to use safety seats aloft for children weighing less than 40 pounds. Airlines set their own policies: If you use a safety seat, U.S. carriers usually require that the child be ticketed, even if he or she is young enough to ride free, because the seats must be strapped into regular seats. And even if you pay the full adult fare for the seat, it may be worth it, especially on longer trips.

Do **check your airline's policy about using safety seats during takeoff and landing.** Safety seats are not allowed everywhere in the plane, so get your seat assignments as early as possible.

When reserving, **request children's meals or a freestanding bassinet** (not available at all airlines) if you need them. But note that bulkhead seats, where you must sit to use the bassinet, may lack an overhead bin or storage space on the floor.

FOOD

In Australia, eating out with kids is no problem in family restaurants, which cater to children with high chairs and booster seats. This type of restaurant is usually found in suburbs rather than city centers. Children are also welcomed in casual coffee shops, delis, bistros, and fast-food eateries like Hungry Jack's, Kentucky Fried Chicken, and McDonalds.

LODGING

Most hotels in Australia allow children under a certain age to stay in their parents' room at no extra charge, but others charge for them as extra adults. Be sure to **find out the cutoff age for children's discounts.** Roll-away beds are usually free, and children under 12 sharing a hotel room with adults generally either stay free or receive a discount rate. Note, however, that many bed-and-breakfasts do not allow children.

Home hosting provides an ideal opportunity to stay with a local family, either in town or on a working farm. For information on home and farm stays, home exchange, and apartment rentals, *see* Lodging.

🈂 **Best Choices Brickendon** ✉ Woolmers La., Longford, 7301 ☎ 03/6391-1383 or 03/6391-1251 🖶 03/6391-2073 ⊕ www.brickendon.com.au. **Desert Rose Inn** ✉ 15-17 Railway Terr., Alice Springs, 0870 ☎ 08/8952-1411 or 1800/896116 🖶 08/8952-3232. **El Questro Wilderness Park** 🏕 Banksia St., Kununurra, 6743 ☎ 08/9169-1777 or 08/9161-4318 🖶 08/9169-1383 or 08/9161-4355 ⊕ www.elquestro.com.au. **Esplanade Hotel** ✉ The Esplanade, Albany, 6330 ☎ 08/9842-1711 🖶 08/9841-7527 ⊕ www.albanyesplanade.com.au. **Fremantle Colonial Cottages** ✉ Holdsworth St., Fremantle, 6160 ☎ 08/9430-6568 🖶 08/9430-6405. **Gagudju Crocodile Hotel** ✉ Flinders St., Jabiru, 0886 ☎ 08/8979-2800 or 1800/808123 🖶 08/8979-2707. **Holiday Inn Perth** ✉ 778 Hay St., Perth, 6000 ☎ 08/9261-7200 🖶 08/9261-7277 ⊕ www.

sixcontinentshotels.com. **Hotel Y** ✉ 489 Elizabeth St., Melbourne, 3000 ☎ 03/9329-5188 🖶 03/9329-1469 ✉ melb@ywca.org.au. **Jemby Rinjah Lodge** ✉ 336 Evans Lookout Rd., Blackheath, 2785 ☎ 02/4787-7622 🖶 02/4787-6230. **Lygon Lodge Carlton** ✉ 220 Lygon St., 3053 ☎ 03/9663-6633 🖶 03/9663-7297 ✉ lygonlodgemotel@bigpond.com. **MacDonnell Ranges Holiday Park** ✉ Palm Pl., off Pamn Circuit (Box 9025), Alice Springs, 0871 ☎ 08/8952-6111 or 1800/808373 🖶 08/8952-5236 ⊕ www.macrange.com.au. **Medina Grand Harbourside** ✉ 55 Shelley St., Sydney, 2000 ☎ 02/9249-7000 🖶 02/9249-6900 ⊕ www.medinaapartments.com.au. **Mercure Resort** ✉ Fitzroy St., Leura, 2780 ☎ 02/4784-1331 🖶 02/4784-1813 ⊕ www.mercureresort.com.au. **Monkey Mia Dolphin Resort** 🏕 Box 119, Denham, 6537 ☎ 08/9948-1320 🖶 08/9948-1034 ⊕ www.monkeymia.com.au. **Oakford Gordon Place** ✉ 24 Little Bourke St., Melbourne, 3000 ☎ 03/9663-2888 🖶 03/9639-1537 ⊕ www.oakford.com. **Outback Motor Lodge** ✉ South Terr., Alice Springs, 0870 ☎ 08/8952-3888 or 1800/896133 🖶 08/8953-2166 ⊕ www.outbackmotorlodge.com.au. **Rannoch West Holiday Farm** ✉ South Coast Hwy., Denmark, 6333 ☎ 08/9840-8032. **Ravesi's on Bondi Beach** ✉ Campbell Parade and Hall St., Bondi Beach, 2026 ☎ 02/9365-4422 🖶 02/9365-1481 ⊕ www.ravesis.com.au. **Sullivan's Hotel** ✉ 166 Mounts Bay Rd., Perth, 6000 ☎ 08/9321-8022 🖶 08/9481-6762 ⊕ www.sullivans.com.au. **Woolmers** ✉ Woolmers La., Longford, 7301 ☎ 03/6391-2230 🖶 03/6391-2270 ⊕ www.vision.net.au/~woolmers.

PRECAUTIONS

Prepare children for several environmental and safety precautions. Be especially vigilant at the beach, where strong waves and currents can quickly overpower a child. Children are also likely to ignore the dangers of excessive exposure to sunlight and heat, so **protect children's skin** with a hat and sunblock **stay in cool areas** during the hottest time of the day. Bring plenty of water and sunscreen for the beaches and desert areas—and don't forget mosquito repellent.

SIGHTS & ATTRACTIONS

Places that are especially appealing to children are indicated by a rubber-duckie icon (🦆) in the margin.

SUPPLIES & EQUIPMENT

Department stores and drugstores (called chemists locally) in Australia carry baby products, such as disposable diapers (ask for napkins or nappies), formula, and baby food. Medical supplies like thermometers, cough and cold medicines, lozenges, ice packs, antibiotic ointment, diaper rash cream, bandages, and children's rehydration formula (Pedialyte) are available at local pharmacies, as well as at such major grocery stores as Coles and Woolworth's. Prescriptions can only be filled at pharmacies (also called chemists).

CONSUMER PROTECTION

Whether you're shopping for gifts or purchasing travel services, **pay with a major credit card** whenever possible, so you can cancel payment or get reimbursed if there's a problem (and you can provide documentation). If you're doing business with a particular company for the first time, **contact your local Better Business Bureau and the attorney general's offices** in your state and (for U.S. businesses) the company's home state as well. Have any complaints been filed? Finally, if you're buying a package or tour, always **consider travel insurance** that includes default coverage (⇨ Insurance).

▣ BBBs Council of Better Business Bureaus ✉ 4200 Wilson Blvd., Suite 800, Arlington, VA 22203 ☎ 703/276-0100 🖷 703/525-8277 ⊕ www.bbb.org.

CRUISE TRAVEL

The only major cruise line that calls regularly at Australian ports is P&O, which is known as Princess in other parts of the world. The company's huge *Pacific Sky* sails on 9- to 14-day cruises from Australia to various Pacific islands. Other cruise lines—Cunard and Holland America, for example—sometimes include Australian ports in their round-the-world itineraries. To learn how to plan, choose, and book a cruise-ship voyage, consult *Fodor's FYI: Plan & Enjoy Your Cruise* (available in bookstores everywhere).

▣ Cruise Lines P&O ☎ 800/PRINCESS in the U.S., 800/PRINCESS in Canada, 20/7800-2468 in the U.K., 13-2469 in Australia, 0800/441-766 in New Zealand.

CUSTOMS & DUTIES

When shopping abroad, **keep receipts** for all purchases. Upon reentering the country, **be ready to show customs officials what you've bought.** Pack purchases together in an easily accessible place. If you think a

duty is incorrect, appeal the assessment. If you object to the way your clearance was handled, note the inspector's badge number. In either case, first ask to see a supervisor. If the problem isn't resolved, write to the appropriate authorities, beginning with the port director at your point of entry.

IN AUSTRALIA

Australia has strict laws prohibiting or restricting the import of weapons and firearms. Antidrug laws are strictly enforced, and penalties are severe. All animals are subject to quarantine. Most canned or preserved food may be imported, but fresh fruit, vegetables, and all food served on board aircraft coming from other countries is forbidden. All food, seeds, and wooden artifacts must be declared on your customs statement. Nonresidents over 18 years of age may bring in 250 cigarettes, or 250 grams of cigars or tobacco, and 2 liters of liquor, provided this is carried with you. Other taxable goods to the value of A$400 for adults and A$200 for children may be included in personal baggage duty-free.

▣ Australian Customs Service Regional Director 🖅 Box 8, Sydney, NSW 2001 ☎ 02/9213-2000 or 1300/363263, 1800/020504 quarantine-inquiry line 🖷 02/9213-4043 ⊕ www.customs.gov.au.

IN CANADA

Canadian residents who have been out of Canada for at least seven days may bring in C$750 worth of goods duty-free. If you've been away fewer than seven days but more than 48 hours, the duty-free allowance drops to C$200. If your trip lasts 24 to 48 hours, the allowance is C$50. You may not pool allowances with family members. Goods claimed under the C$750 exemption may follow you by mail; those claimed under the lesser exemptions must accompany you. Alcohol and tobacco products may be included in the seven-day and 48-hour exemptions but not in the 24-hour exemption. If you meet the age requirements of the province or territory through which you reenter Canada, you may bring in, duty-free, 1.5 liters of wine *or* 1.14 liters (40 imperial ounces) of liquor *or* 24 12-ounce cans or bottles of beer or ale. Also, if you meet the local age requirement for tobacco products, you may bring in, duty-free, 200 cigarettes and 50 cigars. Check ahead of time with the Canada Customs and Revenue Agency or the Department of Agriculture for policies regarding meat products, seeds, plants, and fruits.

You may send an unlimited number of gifts (only one gift per recipient, however) worth up to C$60 each duty-free to Canada. Label the package UNSOLICITED GIFT—VALUE UNDER C$60. Alcohol and tobacco are excluded.

⬛ **Canada Customs and Revenue Agency** ✉ 2265 St. Laurent Blvd., Ottawa, Ontario K1G 4K3 ☎ 800/461-9999, 204/983-3500, 506/636-5064 ⊕ www.ccra.gc.ca.

IN NEW ZEALAND

All homeward-bound residents may bring back NZ$700 worth of souvenirs and gifts; passengers may not pool their allowances, and children can claim only the concession on goods intended for their own use. For those 17 or older, the duty-free allowance also includes 4.5 liters of wine or beer; one 1,125-ml bottle of spirits; and either 200 cigarettes, 250 grams of tobacco, 50 cigars, *or* a combination of the three up to 250 grams. Meat products, seeds, plants, and fruits must be declared upon arrival to the Agricultural Services Department.

⬛ **New Zealand Customs** ✉ Head office: The Customhouse, 17–21 Whitmore St., Box 2218, Wellington ☎ 09/300-5399 or 0800/428-786 ⊕ www.customs.govt.nz.

IN THE U.K.

From countries outside the European Union, including Australia, you may bring home, duty-free, 200 cigarettes or 50 cigars; 1 liter of spirits or 2 liters of fortified or sparkling wine or liqueurs; 2 liters of still table wine; 60 ml of perfume; 250 ml of toilet water; plus £145 worth of other goods, including gifts and souvenirs. Prohibited items include meat products, seeds, plants, and fruits.

⬛ **HM Customs and Excise** ✉ Portcullis House, 21 Cowbridge Rd. E, Cardiff CF11 9SS ☎ 0845/010-9000 or 0208/929-0152, 0208/929-6731 or 0208/910-3602 complaints ⊕ www.hmce.gov.uk.

IN THE U.S.

U.S. residents who have been out of the country for at least 48 hours may bring home, for personal use, $800 worth of foreign goods duty-free, as long as they haven't used the $800 allowance or any part of it in the past 30 days. This exemption may include 1 liter of alcohol (for travelers 21 and older), 200 cigarettes, and 100 non-Cuban cigars. Family members from the same household who are traveling together may pool their $800 personal exemptions. For fewer than 48 hours, the duty-free allowance drops to $200, which may include 50 cigarettes, 10 non-Cuban cigars, and 150 ml of alcohol (or 150 ml of perfume containing alcohol). The $200 allowance cannot be combined with other individuals' exemptions, and if you exceed it, the full value of all the goods will be taxed. Antiques, which the U.S. Bureau of Customs and Border Protection defines as objects more than 100 years old, enter duty-free, as do original works of art done entirely by hand, including paintings, drawings, and sculptures. This doesn't apply to folk art or handicrafts, which are in general dutiable.

You may also send packages home duty-free, with a limit of one parcel per addressee per day (except alcohol or tobacco products or perfume worth more than $5). You can mail up to $200 worth of goods for personal use; label the package PERSONAL USE and attach a list of its contents and their retail value. If the package contains your used personal belongings, mark it AMERICAN GOODS RETURNED to avoid paying duties. You may send up to $100 worth of goods as a gift; mark the package UNSOLICITED GIFT. Mailed items do not affect your duty-free allowance on your return.

To avoid paying duty on foreign-made high-ticket items you already own and will take on your trip, register them with Customs before you leave the country. Consider filing a Certificate of Registration for laptops, cameras, watches, and other digital devices identified with serial numbers or other permanent markings; you can keep the certificate for other trips. Otherwise, bring a sales receipt or insurance form to show that you owned the item before you left the United States.

⬛ **U.S. Bureau of Customs and Border Protection** ✉ for inquiries and equipment registration, 1300 Pennsylvania Ave. NW, Washington, DC 20229 ⊕ www.customs.gov ☎ 202/354-1000 ✉ for complaints, Customer Satisfaction Unit, 1300 Pennsylvania Ave. NW, Room 5.5D, Washington, DC 20229.

DISABILITIES & ACCESSIBILITY

Since 1989, legislation has required that all new accommodations in Australia include provisions for travelers with disabilities. Most buildings and streets in the country date from the post-1945 period, and conditions generally for travelers with disabilities are on par with those in North America. The National Information Communication Awareness Network (NICAN) has a free information service about recreation, tourism, sports, and the arts for travelers with disabilities. For example, there are details on special accommodations throughout Australia for people with disabilities. The National Roads and Motorists Association (NRMA) also publishes the *Accommodation Directory,* indicating which properties have independent wheelchair access and which provide wheelchair access with assistance.

🚩 Local Resources **National Information Communication Awareness Network (NICAN)** ✆ Box 407, Curtin, ACT 2607 ☎ 1800/806769 ✎ nican@spirit.com.au ⊕ www.nican.com.au. **National Roads and Motorists Association (NRMA)** ✉ 151 Clarence St., Sydney, NSW 2000 ☎ 13–2132.

LODGING

Despite improvements throughout all lodging classes to accommodate those with disabilities, accessibility often differs from hotel to hotel. Some properties may be accessible for people with mobility problems but not for people with hearing or vision impairments, for example.

If you have mobility problems, ask for the lowest floor on which accessible services are offered. If you have a hearing impairment, check whether the hotel has devices to alert you visually to the ring of the telephone, a knock at the door, and a fire/emergency alarm. Some hotels provide these devices without charge. Discuss your needs with hotel personnel if this equipment isn't available, so that a staff member can personally alert you in the event of an emergency.

If you're bringing a guide dog, get authorization ahead of time and write down the name of the person with whom you spoke.

The major international hotel chains (such as Regent, Sheraton, Inter-Continental, Ramada, Hilton, Holiday Inn, and Hyatt) provide rooms with facilities for people with disabilities at all of their properties. The National Roads and Motorists Association (NRMA), the major motoring organization in New South Wales and the Australian Capital Territory, has an accom-

modation directory with lodging information. Other states have similar automobile associations that publish accommodations listings.

🚩 **National Roads and Motorists Association (NRMA)** ✉ 151 Clarence St., Sydney, NSW 2000 ☎ 13–2132.

RESERVATIONS

When discussing accessibility with an operator or reservations agent, **ask hard questions.** Are there any stairs, inside *or* out? Are there grab bars next to the toilet *and* in the shower/tub? How wide is the doorway to the room? To the bathroom? For the most extensive facilities meeting the latest legal specifications, **opt for newer accommodations.** If you reserve through a toll-free number, consider also calling the hotel's local number to confirm the information from the central reservations office. Get confirmation in writing when you can.

SIGHTS & ATTRACTIONS

Australia's major urban attractions, such as the Sydney Opera House and the Australian Parliament, have special provisions for travelers with disabilities. Many natural attractions are also accessible, including the Blue Mountains and Uluru (Ayers Rock). On the Great Barrier Reef, glass-bottom boat tours are well suited to travelers with disabilities.

TRANSPORTATION

Major airlines are generally accustomed to accommodating passengers with disabilities. They can usually arrange for wheelchairs, seat-belt extensions, quadriplegic harnesses, and padded leg rests.

Only Budget rents out cars fitted with hand controls, but supplies are limited. Hertz will fit handheld controls onto standard cars in some cities. Wheelchair-accessible taxis are also available in all state capitals.

Passengers on mainline trains in Australia can request collapsible wheelchairs to negotiate narrow interior corridors. However, compact toilet areas and platform access problems make long-distance train travel difficult. Both Countrylink, the New South Wales state rail company, and V/Line (Victoria) issue brochures detailing assistance available on metropolitan, country, and interstate trains. Countrylink's (New South Wales) XPLORER and XPT trains have specially designed wheelchair-access toilets, and ramps for boarding and disembarking are provided.

⚡ Complaints Aviation Consumer Protection Division (⇨ Air Travel) for airline-related problems. **Departmental Office of Civil Rights** ✉ for general inquiries, U.S. Department of Transportation, S-30, 400 7th St. SW, Room 10215, Washington, DC 20590 ☎ 202/366-4648 🖶 202/366-9371 🌐 www.dot. gov/ost/docr/index.htm. **Disability Rights Section** ✉ NYAV, U.S. Department of Justice, Civil Rights Division, 950 Pennsylvania Ave. NW, Washington, DC 20530 ☎ ADA information line 202/514-0301, 800/ 514-0301, 202/514-0383 TTY, 800/514-0383 TTY 🌐 www.ada.gov. **U.S. Department of Transportation Hotline** ☎ for disability-related air-travel problems, 800/778-4838 or 800/455-9880 TTY.

TRAVEL AGENCIES

In the United States, the Americans with Disabilities Act requires that travel firms serve the needs of all travelers. Some agencies specialize in working with people with disabilities.

⚡ Travelers with Mobility Problems Access Adventures ✉ 206 Chestnut Ridge Rd., Scottsville, NY 14624 ☎ 585/889-9096 📧 dltravel@prodigy.net, run by a former physical-rehabilitation counselor. **CareVacations** ✉ No. 5, 5110-50 Ave., Leduc, Alberta, Canada, T9E 6V4 ☎ 780/986-6404 or 877/ 478-7827 🖶 780/986-8332 🌐 www.carevacations. com, for group tours and cruise vacations. **Flying Wheels Travel** ✉ 143 W. Bridge St., Box 382, Owatonna, MN 55060 ☎ 507/451-5005 🖶 507/451-1685 🌐 www.flyingwheelstravel.com.

DISCOUNTS & DEALS

Be a smart shopper and **compare all your options** before making decisions. A plane ticket bought with a promotional coupon from travel clubs, coupon books, and direct-mail offers or purchased on the Internet may not be cheaper than the least expensive fare from a discount ticket agency. And always keep in mind that what you get is just as important as what you save.

DISCOUNT RESERVATIONS

To save money, **look into discount reservations services** with Web sites and toll-free numbers, which use their buying power to get a better price on hotels, airline tickets (⇨ Air Travel), even car rentals. When booking a room, always **call the hotel's**

local toll-free number (if one is available) rather than the central reservations number—you'll often get a better price. Always ask about special packages or corporate rates.

When shopping for the best deal on hotels and car rentals, **look for guaranteed exchange rates,** which protect you against a falling dollar. With your rate locked in, you won't pay more, even if the price goes up in the local currency.

⚡ Airline Tickets Air 4 Less ☎ 800/AIR4LESS; low-fare specialist.

⚡ Hotel Rooms Accommodations Express ☎ 800/444-7666 or 800/277-1064 🌐 www. accommodationsexpress.com. **Hotels.com** ☎ 800/ 246-8357 or 214/369-1246 🌐 www.hotels.com. **Steigenberger Reservation Service** ☎ 800/223-5652 🌐 www.srs-worldhotels.com. **Travel Interlink** ☎ 800/888-5898 🌐 www.travelinterlink.com. **Turbotrip.com** ☎ 800/473-7829 🌐 www.turbotrip.com.

PACKAGE DEALS

Don't confuse packages and guided tours. When you buy a package, you travel on your own, just as though you had planned the trip yourself. Fly/drive packages, which combine airfare and car rental, are often a good deal. In cities, ask the local visitor's bureau about hotel packages that include tickets to major museum exhibits or other special events.

EATING & DRINKING

Dining out in Australia was not always a pleasurable experience, as for much of its history Australian cuisine labored under the worst traditions of bland English fare. Happily, post–World War II migration changed that. First European immigrants brought Continental, Slavic, and Mediterranean cooking, then Middle Eastern and Asian immigrants introduced a whole new spicy repertoire. Today every conceivable type of cuisine is available in the capitals, and often in regional towns as well.

Some Australian restaurants serve fixed-price dinners, but the majority are à la carte. It's wise to **make a reservation** and **inquire if the restaurant has a liquor license** or is "BYOB" or "BYO" (Bring Your Own Bottle). Some are both BYOB and licensed to sell beer, wine, and liquor.

Down Under, entrée means appetizer and main courses are American entrées. You'll also encounter the term "silver service," which indicates upscale dining. "Bistro" generally refers to a relatively inexpensive place. French fries are called chips, and if you want ketchup, ask for tomato sauce.

The restaurants we list are the cream of the crop in each price category. Properties indicated by an ✕🍴 are lodging establishments whose restaurant warrants a special trip.

MEALTIMES

Breakfast is usually served 7–10, lunch 11:30–2:30, and dinner service begins around 6:30. In the cities, a variety of dining options are available at all hours. However, the choices are far more restricted in the countryside. Unless otherwise noted, the restaurants listed in this guide are open daily for lunch and dinner.

PAYING

Most major credit cards are accepted throughout Australia, even in small towns, as long as there is a thriving tourist business. However, bring enough cash to cover your expenses in remote areas such as Cape Tribulation, the Red Centre, lonely regions of the Northern Territory, and national parks.

RESERVATIONS & DRESS

Reservations are always a good idea; we mention them only when they're essential or not accepted. Book as far ahead as you can, and reconfirm as soon as you arrive. (Large parties should always call ahead to check the reservations policy.) We mention dress only when men are required to wear a jacket or a jacket and tie.

WINE, BEER & SPIRITS

Australian wine has become something of a phenomenon. Take a walk through the aisles of your local wine shop and you're bound to come across Australian labels such as Rosemount and Lindemans. Australia is the world's 10th-largest wine producer. About two-thirds of all Australia's wine comes from just two areas: the Murrumbidgee Irrigation Area in New South Wales, and the Riverland region of South Australia, where the combination of a warm climate, abundant sunshine, and irrigated vineyards result in massive yields per acre. For more on Australian wine, *see* Pleasures and Pastimes *in* Chapter 1.

There is also a considerable variety of Australian beers, from the well-known Fosters to the products of smaller boutique breweries. International brands are also available. They are customarily drunk well chilled, at which point their true character is muted. Some might say that beer is a way of life in Oz. True or not, pub life is a legitimate subculture worth looking into to get an earful of some local talk, and a mugful of some local grog. Traditional beer is strong and similar to Danish and German beer, although lighter, low-alcohol beer is now readily available. Draft from the tap is the brew of choice, served ice-cold with little head.

Many restaurants and pubs serve liquor. In some states, cafés are also permitted to serve alcohol. Bottle shops, which sell beer, wines, and spirits for consumption off the premises, can be found in most pubs and suburban shopping centers. Cities and wine-growing areas have specialty stores aimed at the wine connoisseur.

In Australia, the legal drinking age is 18. Many bars close around 11 PM; others stay open later on weekends. BYOB (Bring Your Own Beverage) restaurants are growing throughout the country; some have a license to serve alcohol as well. Corkage is usually charged for wines, although the cost varies.

ELECTRICITY

To use electric-powered equipment purchased in the United States or Canada, **bring a converter and adapter.** The electrical current in Australia is 240 volts, 50 cycles alternating current (AC). Wall outlets take slanted three-prong plugs (but not the U.K. three-prong) and plugs with two flat prongs set in a V.

If your appliances are dual-voltage, you'll need only an adapter. Don't use 110-volt outlets marked FOR SHAVERS ONLY for high-wattage appliances such as blow-dryers. Most laptops operate equally well on 110 and 220 volts and so require only an adapter.

EMBASSIES

Embassies and consulates in Australia provide assistance to their nationals in case of lost or stolen passports and documents, major medical problems, and other travel emergencies. U.S. citizens can also obtain tax and voting forms.

🏛 Canada **Canadian High Commission** ✉ Commonwealth Ave., Canberra ☎ 61/6270-4000. **Consulate General** ✉ Level 5, Quay West 111, Harrington St., Sydney ☎ 03/9364-3050. **Honorary Consulate General** ✉ 3rd Floor, 267 St. George's Terr., Perth ☎ 08/9322-7930.

🏛 New Zealand **Consulate General** ✉ Level 10, 55 Hunter St., Sydney ☎ 02/8256-2000. **New Zealand High Commission** ✉ Commonwealth Ave., Canberra ☎ 61/6270-4211.

🏛 United Kingdom **British Consulate General** ✉ Gateway Bldg., 1 Macquarie Pl., Level 16, Sydney Cove ☎ 02/9247-7521. **British High Commission** ✉ Commonwealth Ave. Canberra ☎ 02/6270-6666. **British High Commission, Consular Section** ✉ 39 Brindabella Circuit, Brindabella Business Park, Canberra Airport, Canberra ☎ 1902/941555. **Consulate General** ✉ Level 22, Grenfell Centre, 25 Grenfell St., Adelaide ☎ 08/8212-7280 ✉ Level 26, Waterfront Pl., 1 Eagle St., Brisbane ☎ 07/3236-2575 ✉ 17th Floor, 90 Collins St., Melbourne ☎ 03/9650-3699 ✉ Level 26, Allendale Sq., 77 St. George's Terr., Perth ☎ 08/9221-5400. **Honourary Consul** ✉ Trust Bank Tasmania, 39 Murray St., Hobart ☎ 03/6230-3647.

🏛 United States **U.S. Embassy** ✉ Moonah Pl., Canberra ☎ 02/6214-5600. **Consulate General** ✉ Level 6, 553 St. Kilda Rd., Melbourne ☎ 03/9526-5900 ✉ 16 St. George's Terr., 13th Floor, Perth ☎ 08/9231-9400 ✉ MLC Centre, Level 59, 19-29 Martin Pl., Sydney ☎ 02/9373-9200.

EMERGENCIES

Dial ☎ 000 for fire, police, or ambulance services.

For theft, wallet loss, small road accidents, and minor emergencies, contact the nearest police station. In a medical or dental emergency, your hotel staff will have information on and directions to the nearest hospital or clinic.

It's always wise to **bring your own basic first aid kit.** If you're venturing into remote areas be sure to include a thorough selection of emergency supplies. If you'll be carrying any medications with you, also bring your doctor's contact information and prescription authorizations.

ETIQUETTE & BEHAVIOR

Australians are typically relaxed and informal in their social relationships, and visitors from most other cultures will have little trouble fitting in. Social behavior broadly follows the same patterns as those of North America and the British Isles. Upon introduction, men will shake hands, but this will not usually be repeated on later encounters. A kiss on the cheek is a common greeting and farewell between the sexes, but only once the relationship has moved to a comfortable level of familiarity. Drinking remains an integral part of Australian culture, and drunkenness generally does not incur the same social stigma as in some cultures, provided the behavior remains within reasonable bounds.

GAY & LESBIAN TRAVEL

Politically and socially, Australia is one of the gay-friendliest countries in the world, ranking right up there with the Netherlands, Denmark, and Canada. Gay tourism associations, often associated with a state tourism board, are well established and have plenty to offer lesbian and gay tourists. In 2002, Sydney hosted the Gay Games, drawing millions of athletes and spectators from around the world. Tasmania in particular has recently focused on welcoming gay and lesbian travelers.

Many publications detailing gay and lesbian activities are available. Most major cities—including Sydney, Brisbane, Melbourne, Perth, and Adelaide—publish gay and lesbian newspapers. Sydney's *The Star Observer* has the largest circulation. Local independent travel magazines, like the *Gay Australia Guide* (www.gayaustraliaguide. bigstep.com), also dispense advice. Some newspapers and magazines are also available at lesbian and gay bookstores in North America and the United Kingdom.

🏛 Gay- & Lesbian-Friendly Travel Agencies **Different Roads Travel** ✉ 8383 Wilshire Blvd., Suite 520, Beverly Hills, CA 90211 ☎ 323/651-5557 or 800/429-8747 (Ext. 14 for both) 🖷 323/651-3678 ✍ lgernert@tzell.com. **Kennedy Travel** ✉ 130 W. 42nd St., Suite 401, New York, NY 10036 ☎ 212/840-8659 or 800/237-7433 🖷 212/730-2269 ⊕ www. kennedytravel.com. **Now, Voyager** ✉ 4406 18th St., San Francisco, CA 94114 ☎ 415/626-1169 or 800/255-6951 🖷 415/626-8626 ⊕ www.nowvoyager. com. **Skylink Travel and Tour** ✉ 1455 N. Dutton Ave., Suite A, Santa Rosa, CA 95401 ☎ 707/546-9888 or 800/225-5759 🖷 707/636-0951; serving lesbian travelers.

🏛 Gay & Lesbian Newspapers *Sydney Star Observer* ⊕ www.ssonet.com.au. *Blaze* ⊕ blazemedia.com.au, covers South Australia twice a month. *Brother Sister* ⊕ www.brothersister.com.au, Melbourne's local gay and lesbian newspaper. *Lesbians on the Loose* (LOTL) ⊕ www.lotl.com, Sydney's lesbian monthly magazine. *Q News* ⊕ www.qnews.com.au, covers Brisbane and Queensland twice a month.

🖪 Gay & Lesbian Tourism **Galta** ⊕ www.galta.com.au. **Gay Travel Network** ⊕ www.gaytravelnet.com/aus. **Tasmania** ⊕ www.discovertasmania.com. **Victoria** ⊕ www.visitvictoria.com. **Western Australia** ⊕ www.westernaustralia.com.

HEALTH

Hygiene standards in Australia are high and well monitored, so don't worry about drinking the water or eating fresh produce. The primary health hazard is sunburn or sunstroke. Even if you're not normally bothered by strong sun you should **cover up with a long-sleeve shirt, a hat, and long pants or a beach wrap.** Keep in mind that at higher altitudes you will burn more easily. **Apply sunscreen liberally** before you go out—even for a half hour—and wear a visored cap and sunglasses.

Apply a reliable insect repellent like Aeroguard or Rid to protect yourself from mosquito bites during the summer months (particularly in the north of the continent). Although Australia is free of malaria, several cases of Ross River fever and dengue fever, both mosquito-transmitted viruses, have been reported in recent years. The mosquitoes that transmit these viruses are active in daylight hours.

Dehydration is a serious danger that can be easily avoided, so be sure to **carry water and drink often.** Above all, **limit the amount of time you spend in the sun** for the first few days until you are acclimatized, and **avoid sunbathing in the middle of the day.**

You may take a four weeks' supply of prescribed medication into Australia (more with a doctor's certificate). Medical professionals are highly trained and hospitals are well equipped.

DIVERS' ALERT
Do not fly within 24 hours of scuba diving.

FOOD & DRINK
Australian food, fruit, water, milk and its by-products, and ice pose no threat to health.

MEDICAL PLANS
No one plans to get sick while traveling, but it happens, so **consider signing up with a medical-assistance company.** Members get doctor referrals, emergency evacuation or repatriation, medical hot lines, cash for emergencies, and other assistance.

🖪 Medical-Assistance Companies **International SOS Assistance** ⊕ www.internationalsos.com ✉ 8 Neshaminy Interplex, Suite 207, Trevose, PA 19053 ☎ 215/245-4707 or 800/523-6586 🖷 215/244-9617 ✉ Level 5, Challis House, 4 Martin Pl., Sydney, Australia 2000 ☎ 03/9372-2400 🖷 03/9372-2408 ✉ Landmark House, Hammersmith Bridge Rd., 6th floor, London, England W6 9DP ☎ 20/8762-8008 🖷 20/8748-7744 ✉ 12 Chemin Riantbosson, 1217 Meyrin 1, Geneva, Switzerland ☎ 22/785-6464 🖷 22/785-6424 ✉ 331 N. Bridge Rd., 17-00, Odeon Towers, Singapore 188720 ☎ 6338-7800 🖷 6338-7611.

OVER-THE-COUNTER REMEDIES
Familiar brands of nonprescription medications are available in pharmacies (commonly called chemists).

PESTS & OTHER HAZARDS
No rural scene is complete without bushflies, a major annoyance. These tiny pests, found throughout Australia, are especially attracted to the eyes and mouth, in search of the fluids that are secreted there. Some travelers resort to wearing a net, which can be suspended from a hat with a drawstring device and used to cover the face. These are widely available wherever travelers and flies cross paths.

SHOTS & MEDICATIONS
Unless you're arriving from an area that has been infected with yellow fever, typhoid, or cholera, you do not require any shots before entering Australia.

🖪 Health Warnings **National Centers for Disease Control and Prevention (CDC)** ✉ National Center for Infectious Diseases, Division of Quarantine, Travelers' Health, 1600 Clifton Rd. NE, Atlanta, GA 30333 ☎ 877/394-8747 international travelers' health line, 800/311-3435 other inquiries 🖷 888/232-3299 ⊕ www.cdc.gov/travel.

HOLIDAYS
New Year's Day, January 1; **Australia Day,** January 26; **Good Friday,** April 9, 2004; March 25, 2005. **Easter,** April 11, 2004; March 27, 2005. **Easter Monday,** April 12,

2004; March 28, 2005. **ANZAC Day,** April 25; **Christmas,** December 25; **Boxing Day,** December 26. There are also a small number of extra public holidays specific to each state and territory.

INSURANCE

The most useful travel-insurance plan is a comprehensive policy that includes coverage for trip cancellation and interruption, default, trip delay, and medical expenses (with a waiver for preexisting conditions).

Without insurance you'll lose all or most of your money if you cancel your trip, regardless of the reason. Default insurance covers you if your tour operator, airline, or cruise line goes out of business. Trip-delay covers expenses that arise because of bad weather or mechanical delays. Study the fine print when comparing policies.

If you're traveling internationally, a key component of travel insurance is coverage for medical bills incurred if you get sick on the road. Such expenses aren't generally covered by Medicare or private policies. U.K. residents can buy a travel-insurance policy valid for most vacations taken during the year in which it's purchased (but check preexisting-condition coverage). British citizens need extra medical coverage when traveling abroad. Always **buy travel policies directly from the insurance company**; if you buy them from a cruise line, airline, or tour operator that goes out of business you probably won't be covered for the agency or operator's default, a major risk. Before making any purchase, **review your existing health and homeowner's policies** to find what they cover away from home.

Travel Insurers In the U.S.: **Access America** ✉ 6600 W. Broad St., Richmond, VA 23230 ☎ 800/284-8300 🖷 804/673-1491 or 800/346-9265 ⊕ www.accessamerica.com. **Travel Guard International** ✉ 1145 Clark St., Stevens Point, WI 54481 ☎ 715/345-0505 or 800/826-1300 🖷 800/955-8785 ⊕ www.travelguard.com.

In the U.K.: Association of British Insurers ✉ 51 Gresham St., London EC2V 7HQ ☎ 020/7600-3333 🖷 020/7696-8999 ⊕ www.abi.org.uk. In Canada: **RBC Insurance** ✉ 6880 Financial Dr., Mississauga, Ontario L5N 7Y5 ☎ 800/565-3129 🖷 905/813-4704 ⊕ www.rbcinsurance.com. In Australia: **Insurance Council of Australia** ✉ Insurance Enquiries and Complaints, Level 3, 56 Pitt St., Sydney, NSW 2000 ☎ 1300/363683 or 02/9251-4456

🖷 02/9251-4453 ⊕ www.iecltd.com.au. In New Zealand: **Insurance Council of New Zealand** ✉ Level 7, 111–115 Customhouse Quay, Box 474, Wellington ☎ 04/472-5230 🖷 04/473-3011 ⊕ www.icnz.org.nz.

LODGING

The lodgings we list are the cream of the crop in each price category. We always list the facilities that are available, but we don't specify whether they cost extra. When pricing accommodations, always ask what's included and what costs extra. Properties indicated by an ✕🏠 are lodging establishments whose restaurant warrants a special trip. Except for designated bed-and-breakfasts and farm stays, the majority of prices listed by hotels are for room only, unless we specify that hotels use either the **American Plan** (AP, with three meals included), **Continental Plan** (CP, with a Continental breakfast), **Breakfast Plan** (BP, with a full breakfast), **Modified American Plan** (MAP, with breakfast and dinner), or **all-inclusive** (including all meals and most activities). Surcharges sometimes apply on weekends, long weekends, and during holiday seasons.

APARTMENT & VILLA RENTALS

If you want a home base that's roomy enough for a family and comes with cooking facilities, **consider a furnished rental.** These can save you money, especially if you're traveling with a group. Home-exchange directories sometimes list rentals as well as exchanges.

In most Australian cities you can find fully equipped rentals that include furnishings and kitchens. These can be a great deal, especially for families. Look for the latest listings on the Internet, and check with each state's tourism office for ideas. You can book and pay for an apartment or villa in the same manner you would for a hotel room.

International Agents Hideaways International ✉ 767 Islington St., Portsmouth, NH 03802 ☎ 603/430-4433 or 800/843-4433 🖷 603/430-4444 ⊕ www.hideaways.com, membership $129. **Villas International** ✉ 4340 Redwood Hwy., Suite D309, San Rafael, CA 94903 ☎ 415/499-9490 or 800/221-2260 🖷 415/499-9491 ⊕ www.villasintl.com.

Local Agents Australian Villas 🏠 187 Carlisle St., Balaclava, VIC 3183 ☎ 03/9537-7569.

BED-AND-BREAKFASTS

B&B accommodation has proliferated in Australia—in the cities as well as in country areas. In both, they present an atmospheric, welcoming, and moderately priced alternative to hotel or motel accommodations. Decor and atmosphere vary greatly according to the whim and wealth of the owner. Prices range from about A$70 to about A$200 for two per night. Almost without exception, breakfasts are bountiful, usually consisting of fruit juice, cereal, toast, eggs and bacon, and tea or coffee. Watch out for the word "boutique" in conjunction with a B&B. This implies a higher level of luxury and facilities—but at a higher price.

▶ Reservation Services Bed and Breakfast Australia ⌂ Box 448, Homebush South, NSW 2140 ☎ 02/9763-5833 🖷 02/9763-1677 ⊕ www. bedandbreakfast.com.au.

CAMPING

National Parks throughout Australia have designated campgrounds. Some have hot showers and barbecue areas. A small fee is payable for each night you camp. Even at a remote campsite, a park ranger will usually call in every few days. In less-traveled parts of the Outback, you can camp freely, but remember that you will be on someone's property—despite the likely absence of fences or signs of human habitation. Keep away from livestock. Camp away from water supplies, and don't use soap or detergents that may contaminate drinking water. Leave gates as you find them. Carry your own cooking fuel. Decaying logs are an important source of nutrients for coming generations of plants. **Carry water if you travel into isolated areas,** including national parks. Take a *minimum* of 20 liters per person, which will last a week even in the hottest conditions.

These are the unbreakable rules of Outback travel: If you go off the beaten track, let someone know your route and when you expect to return. If you break down, do not leave your car for any reason. Protect and respect Aboriginal relics, paintings, carvings, and sacred sites, as well as pioneer markers and heritage buildings. Don't sleep under trees because Australia's native trees have a habit of shedding their limbs.

The National Roads and Motorists Association (NRMA) puts out the excellent *Accommodation Directory* (A$7.70

members, A$15 nonmembers) and *Caravan and Camping Directory* (A$5.50 members, A$12 nonmembers). Members of overseas motoring organizations have reciprocal membership rights.

▶ NRMA ✉ 151 Clarence St., Sydney, NSW 2000 ☎ 13-2132.

HOME EXCHANGES

If you would like to exchange your home for someone else's, **join a home-exchange organization,** which will send you its updated listings of available exchanges for a year and will include your own listing in at least one of them. It's up to you to make specific arrangements.

▶ Exchange Clubs HomeLink International ⌂ Box 47747, Tampa, FL 33647 ☎ 813/975-9825 or 800/638-3841 🖷 813/910-8144 ⊕ www.homelink. org; $110 yearly for a listing, on-line access, and catalog; $40 without catalog. **Intervac U.S.** ✉ 30 Corte San Fernando, Tiburon, CA 94920 ☎ 800/ 756-4663 🖷 415/435-7440 ⊕ www.intervacus.com; $105 yearly for a listing, on-line access, and a catalog; $50 without catalog.

HOME & FARM STAYS

Home and farm stays, which are very popular with visitors to Australia, provide not only comfortable accommodations but a chance to get to know the lands and their people. Most operate on a bed-and-breakfast basis, though some also include an evening meal. Farm accommodations vary from modest shearers' cabins to elegant homesteads. You can join in farm activities or explore the countryside. Some hosts run day trips, as well as horseback riding, hiking, and fishing trips. For two people, the cost varies from A$100 to A$250 per night, including all meals and some or all farm activities. Home stays, the urban equivalent of farm stays, are less expensive.

▶ Reservation Services Australian Farm Host and Farm Holidays ☎ 800/551-2012, represented by ATS/Sprint, SO/PAC. **Australian Home Accommodation** ☎ 800/423-2880, represented by ATS/ Sprint. **Bed & Breakfast Australia** ⌂ Box 448, Homebush South, NSW 2140 ☎ 02/9763-5833 🖷 02/9763-1677 ⊕ www.bedandbreakfast.com.au. **Pacific Destination Center** ☎ 800/227-5317. **Royal Automobile Club of Queensland (RACQ) Travel Service** ⌂ Box 537, Fortitude Valley, QLD 4006 ☎ 07/3361-2802 🖷 07/3257-1504.

HOSTELS

No matter what your age, you can **save on lodging costs by staying at hostels.** In some 4,500 locations in more than 70 countries around the world, Hostelling International (HI), the umbrella group for a number of national youth-hostel associations, offers single-sex, dorm-style beds and, at many hostels, rooms for couples and family accommodations. Membership in any HI national hostel association, open to travelers of all ages, allows you to stay in HI-affiliated hostels at member rates; one-year membership is about A$28 for adults (C$35 for a two-year minimum membership in Canada, £13.50 in the U.K., A$52 in Australia, and NZ$40 in New Zealand); hostels charge about A$10–A$30 per night. Members have priority if the hostel is full; they're also eligible for discounts around the world, even on rail and bus travel in some countries.

Australian youth hostels, found throughout the country, are usually comfortable, well-equipped, and family-friendly. Travelers from all walks of life take advantage of these low-cost accommodations, which most often have a selection of dormitory and private rooms around a shared common area, kitchen, and laundry. Note that backpacker hostels, also widely available throughout Australia, aren't YHI members and cater more to late-teen and twentysomething budget travelers. To find these, talk with other travelers, or look for ads on noticeboards at bus and train stations, grocery stores, and cafés.

🛈 Organizations **Hostelling International–USA** ✉ 8401 Colesville Rd., Suite 600, Silver Spring, MD 20910 ☎ 301/495-1240 🖷 301/495-6697 ⊕ www. hiayh.org. **Hostelling International–Canada** ✉ 400–205 Catherine St., Ottawa, Ontario K2P 1C3 ☎ 613/237-7884 or 800/663-5777 🖷 613/237-7868 ⊕ www.hihostels.ca. **YHA England and Wales** ✉ Trevelyan House, Dimple Rd., Matlock, Derbyshire DE4 3YH, U.K. ☎ 0870/870-8808 🖷 0870/770-6127 ⊕ www.yha.org.uk. **YHA Australia** ✉ 422 Kent St., Sydney, NSW 2001 ☎ 02/9261-1111 🖷 02/9261-1969 ⊕ www.yha.com.au. **YHA New Zealand** ✉ Level 3, 193 Cashel St., Box 436, Christchurch ☎ 03/379-9970 or 0800/278-299 🖷 03/365-4476 ⊕ www.yha.org.nz.

HOTELS & MOTELS

All hotels listed have private bath unless otherwise noted. Hotel and motel rooms generally have private bathrooms with a combined shower/tub—called "en suites"—although some bed-and-breakfast hotels and hostels require guests to share bathrooms. Tea- and coffeemakers are a fixture in almost every type of accommodation, refrigerators are found in virtually all motels, and stocked minibars are the norm in deluxe hotels. You can expect a swimming pool, health club, tennis courts, and spas in many resort hotels, some of which also have their own golf courses. Motel chains, such as Flag International, are usually reliable and much less expensive than hotels. You often can check into a motel without booking ahead, but reservations are required for weekends and holidays. Reservations for many Great Barrier Reef and beach resorts can be made in the United States through such groups as Utell International. If you'd like to book a smaller hotel or bed-and-breakfast and you'll be traveling with children, first check that the facilities are appropriate for young ones—and make sure that they'll be welcome to stay.

🛈 Toll-Free Numbers **Best Western** ☎ 800/528-1234 ⊕ www.bestwestern.com. **Choice** ☎ 800/424-6423 ⊕ www.choicehotels.com. **Clarion** ☎ 800/424-6423 ⊕ www.choicehotels.com. **Comfort Inn** ☎ 800/424-6423 ⊕ www.choicehotels.com. **Four Seasons** ☎ 800/332-3442 ⊕ www.fourseasons.com. **Hilton** ☎ 800/445-8667 ⊕ www.hilton.com. **Holiday Inn** ☎ 800/465-4329 ⊕ www.sixcontinentshotels.com. **Hyatt Hotels & Resorts** ☎ 800/233-1234 ⊕ www.hyatt.com. **Inter-Continental** ☎ 800/327-0200 ⊕ www.intercontinental.com. **Marriott** ☎ 800/228-9290 ⊕ www.marriott.com. **Le Meridien** ☎ 800/543-4300 ⊕ www.lemeridien-hotels.com. **Quality Inn** ☎ 800/424-6423 ⊕ www.choicehotels.com. **Radisson** ☎ 800/333-3333 ⊕ www.radisson.com. **Ramada** ☎ 800/228-2828, 800/854-7854 international reservations ⊕ www.ramada.com or www.ramadahotels.com. **Renaissance Hotels & Resorts** ☎ 800/468-3571 ⊕ www.renaissancehotels.com/. **Sheraton** ☎ 800/325-3535 ⊕ www.starwood.com/sheraton. **Westin Hotels & Resorts** ☎ 800/228-3000 ⊕ www.starwood.com/westin.

MAIL & SHIPPING

Mail service in Australia is efficient. Allow a week for letters and postcards to reach the United States and the United Kingdom. Letters to New Zealand generally take four–five days. All mail travels by air.

OVERNIGHT SERVICES

Both DHL and Federal Express operate fast, reliable express courier services from Australia. Rates are around A$76 for a 1-kilogram (2-pound) parcel to the United States and around A$85 to Europe, including door-to-door service. Delivery time between Sydney and New York is approximately three days.

⚡ Major Services DHL Worldwide Express
☎ 13-1406. **Federal Express** ☎ 13-2610.

POSTAL RATES

Postage rates are A 50¢ for domestic letters, A$1.65 per 50-gram (28.35 grams = 1 ounce) airmail letter, and A$1.10 for airmail postcards to North America and the United Kingdom. Overseas fax service costs around A$10 for the first page, plus A$4 for each additional page. There are different rates for posting small amounts of printed matter depending on the destination and the size and weight of the package; the post office will mark the individual rate.

RECEIVING MAIL

You can receive mail care of General Delivery (known as Poste Restante in Australia) at the General Post Office or any branch post office. The service is free and mail is held for one month. It is advisable to **know the correct Australian postal code (zip code) of the area you are visiting.** These are available from the Australian Consulate General. The zip code will allow you to receive mail care of Poste Restante (General Delivery) at the area's General Post Office. You will need identification to pick up mail. Alternatively, American Express offers free mail collection at its main city offices for its cardholders.

SHIPPING PARCELS

Rates for large parcels shipped to other countries from Australia depend on their weight and shape. Some companies provide boxes, and any materials you can fit inside weighing up to 25 kilograms (about 55 pounds) will cost about A$215, excluding any U.S. import charges. You can also consult your airline to find the rates for unaccompanied luggage. Overnight courier services like DHL and Federal Express will deliver packages of any size—for a price.

If you're shipping items in excess of 50 kilograms (110 pounds), it's less expensive to send goods by sea via a shipping agent. Shipping time to the United States and Europe is 10–12 weeks.

MEDIA

The Australian Broadcasting Commission (ABC) operates commercial-free radio and television stations in all states and territories. Commercial radio and television are also available nationwide. Even the smallest country towns have their own newspapers, and these are a good source of local information.

NEWSPAPERS & MAGAZINES

The country's only national paper is *The Australian.* Each major city has its own daily newspaper covering international, national, and local affairs. The *Sydney Morning Herald* is the city's most authoritative source of local and international news. *The Melbourne Age,* its sister publication, is the most respected newspaper in the country. Two tabloids, the *Daily Telegraph* in Sydney and the *Herald Sun* in Melbourne, focus on local affairs. For in-depth analyses of daily financial matters, Australian politics, and the wider world, the *Financial Review* is without parallel. *HQ* magazine is well regarded for its thoughtful, incisive, and often irreverent approach to social issues and the arts. The only Australian magazine that stakes a serious claim as a weekly roundup of national and international affairs along the lines of *Time* or *Newsweek* is *The Bulletin.*

RADIO & TELEVISION

Radio National, the heavyweight of the Australian Broadcasting Commission, is well regarded for its penetrating coverage of local and international affairs, the arts, and lifestyle. ABC local radio is its lighter counterpart. Both broadcast on AM, but the frequencies vary from one state to the next. Triple J-FM is the zany, offbeat sister of these two stations; it's popular with the younger set. ABC Classical FM is an excellent classical music station. Numerous commercial radio stations broadcast from virtually every town across the country.

In addition to commercial-free ABC-TV, Australia has three commercial television broadcasters with national service. Another choice is SBS, which is designed to cater to the needs of Australia's multicultural population, and which broadcasts in several different languages at different times of the day. SBS has an excellent news service weeknights at 6:30 and 9:30, with extensive coverage of overseas events.

Every weeknight, SBS screens foreign-lan-guage movies that are rarely seen on com-mercial television.

MONEY MATTERS

Prices for goods and services can be volatile. Still those cited below may be used as an approximate guide, since varia-tion should rarely exceed 10%. A 10% "Goods and Services Tax" (similar to VAT in other countries) applies to most activi-ties and items, except fresh food.

The Australian dollar's devaluation in re-cent years against many currencies—espe-cially the U.S. dollar and British pound sterling—has made Australia an even more attractive destination for overseas visitors. Although prices appear high at Sydney's five-star hotels, virtually all offer discounts of up to 30% on published rack rates. There are also plenty of cheaper dining and lodging alternatives. Medium-price hotels and hotel-apartments abound in city centers and inner suburbs. For example, double-occupancy rates at the luxury Re-gent of Sydney start at about A$450 a night, whereas the tariff at Victoria Court, a bed-and-breakfast hotel classified as a landmark by the National Trust, is in the region of A$150, including breakfast. Mel-bourne and Sydney tend to be more expen-sive than other cities.

Fares on international flights are usually lower between June and September, and many hotels offer lower tariffs in their off-peak season: April–September in the south, November–March in the Top End. Another way to save money is to buy passes, available for everything from ho-tels and interstate transportation to local bus and train services (⇨ Bus Travel and Train Travel).

The following are sample costs in Aus-tralia at press time: cup of coffee A$2.50–A$4; glass of beer in a bar A$3–A$6; take-out ham sandwich or meat pie A$3.50–A$6; hamburger in a café A$4–A$9; room-service sandwich in a hotel A$12–A$15; a 2-km (1¼-mi) taxi ride A$10.

Prices throughout this guide are given for adults. Substantially reduced fees are al-most always available for children, stu-dents, and senior citizens. For information on taxes, *see* Taxes.

ATMS

ATMs can be found in all parts of Aus-tralia, in small towns as well as in cities. Most suburban shopping centers and malls have at least one nonbank ATM. The most widely accepted cards are Visa, Master-Card, and American Express. Those linked to the Cirrus network are also widely ac-cepted at ATMs. Cards that do not use a four-digit PIN may not be accepted at Aus-tralia's ATMs.

CREDIT CARDS

Credit cards are accepted throughout Aus-tralia by most stores, restaurants, gas sta-tions, and hotels. However, bring enough cash to cover your expenses in remote areas such as Cape Tribulation, the Red Centre, lonely regions of the Northern Territory, and national parks. ATMs are found in every town, and you can with-draw money with a bank or credit card. Visa and MasterCard are the most widely accepted cards. Note that American Ex-press isn't always accepted outside the main cities.

7 Reporting Lost Cards **American Express** ☎ 1300/132639. **Diners Club** ☎ 1300/360060. **Mas-terCard** ☎ 1800/120113. **Visa** ☎ 1800/805341.

CURRENCY

All prices listed in this guide are quoted in Australian dollars. Australia's currency op-erates on a decimal system, with the dollar (A$) as the basic unit and 100 cents (¢) equaling $1. Bills come in $100, $50, $20, $10, and $5 denominations, which are dif-ferentiated by color and size. Coins are minted in $2, $1, 50¢, 20¢, 10¢, and 5¢ denominations.

CURRENCY EXCHANGE

At press time, the exchange rate was about A$1.65 to the U.S. dollar, A$1.14 to the Canadian dollar, A$2.59 to the pound sterling, and A 90¢ to the New Zealand dollar.

For the most favorable rates, **change money through banks.** Although ATM transaction fees may be higher abroad than at home, ATM rates are excellent be-cause they're based on wholesale rates of-fered only by major banks. You won't do as well at exchange booths in airports or rail and bus stations, in hotels, in restau-rants, or in stores. To avoid lines at airport exchange booths, **get a bit of local currency before you leave home.**

F Exchange Services **International Currency Express** ✉ 427 N. Camden Dr., Suite F, Beverly Hills, CA 90210 ☎ 888/278-6628 orders 🖷 310/278-6410 ⊕ www.foreignmoney.com. **Thomas Cook Currency Services** ☎ 800/287-7362 orders and retail locations ⊕ www.us.thomascook.com.

TRAVELER'S CHECKS

Do you need traveler's checks? It depends on where you're headed. If you're going to rural areas and small towns, go with cash; traveler's checks are best used in cities. In Australia, traveler's checks in U.S. or U.K. currencies are easily exchanged at banks, hotels, moneychangers, and Travelex or Thomas Cook offices.

Lost or stolen checks can usually be replaced within 24 hours. To ensure a speedy refund, buy your own traveler's checks—don't let someone else pay for them: irregularities like this can cause delays. The person who bought the checks should make the call to request a refund.

OUTDOORS & SPORTS

BEACHES

Australia is blessed with fine beaches, many of them close to major cities. It is advisable to swim only at designated areas where lifeguards are on duty. Surf is often rough, and many beaches have a treacherous undertow. Volunteer lifesavers monitor almost all metropolitan and town beaches during spring and summer months.

On many Australian beaches, women sunbathe topless; some beaches, like Sydney's Lady Jane and Perth's Swanbourne, are for those who prefer their sunning and swimming au naturel.

BOATING & SAILING

Australians love messing about in boats, as you can plainly see from the number of vessels in Sydney Harbour—one of the finest sailing areas in the world—on a warm Sunday afternoon. The Whitsunday Islands, off Queensland's coast, afford tranquility, warmth, and idyllic anchorages.

F **Australian Yachting Federation** ⊕ 33 Peel St., Kirribilli, NSW 2061 ☎ 02/9922-4333 🖷 02/9923-2883.

CRICKET

Although Australians are often fiercely divided by their allegiance to winter sports, the nation unites in its obsession with the summer sport of cricket. Played between teams of 11 players, this often slow—and incomprehensible to outsiders—game can take place over the course of a day. Test matches (full-scale international games) last for five days. The faster-paced one-day games are gaining popularity. Cricket season runs from October through March.

DIVING

The Great Barrier Reef is one of the world's leading dive destinations, and there are many dive operators all along the coast who can introduce you to its wonders. In Western Australia, Ningaloo Reef is highly rated by scuba divers. Even Sydney has a number of good dive sites, and diving is a popular weekend sport. If you're a novice, consider a resort dive. Once you've passed a brief safety lesson with a dive master in shallow water, you can make a 30-minute dive to a maximum depth of about 10 m (33 ft).

F **Australian Underwater Federation** ✉ 42 Toyer Ave., Sans Souci, NSW 2219 ☎ 02/9529-6496.

FISHING

Records for marlin are frequently broken off the east coast, and the region around Cairns and Lizard Island has won world acclaim for giant black marlin. Fighting fish, including black and blue marlin, mackerel, tuna, barracuda, and sailfish, are found all the way down the east coast. September through November is the best time for catching marlin off Cairns; off Bermagui, the end of November through May.

Barramundi, jack, tarpon, and mackerel attract anglers to the waters of the Northern Territory's Top End, around Darwin and Bathurst Island. Barramundi run from June through November. Rainbow and brown trout thrive in the lake-fed streams of Tasmania, the rivers of the Australian Alps in both Victoria and New South Wales, and in the Onkaparinga River on the outskirts of Adelaide. Fishing seasons vary according to the area but are generally December–May.

GOLF

Australia has more than 1,400 golf courses. Some private clubs extend reciprocal rights to overseas club members on proof of membership; check whether your club maintains reciprocal membership rights with Australian clubs. You can always arrange a round on a municipal course, although you may have to contend with a kangaroo or two watching your form from the rough.

Generally speaking, clubs can be rented, but you'll need your own shoes. In Australia, greens fees at public courses range upward from A$30 for 18 holes.

Classic Australian Golf Tours ☎ 800/426-3610. **ITC Golf Tours** ☎ 800/257-4981. **Swain Australia Tours** ☎ 800/227-9246.

HIKING

Despite the term "national," parks are operated by the individual states in which they are located. For information, contact the National Parks and Wildlife Service in the capital of the state in which you are interested. In Western Australia, contact the Department of Conservation and Land Management. Organized hiking tours can be arranged through the bushwalking clubs listed in the telephone directory of each capital city.

To protect your skin against the sun, **wear a hat and sunglasses and put on sunblock.** Out in the hot Aussie sun, **beware of heatstroke;** symptoms include headache, dizziness, and fatigue, which can turn into convulsions and unconsciousness. Likewise, **avoid dehydration.** Simply **drink every 10–15 minutes,** up to a gallon of water per day in intense summer heat.

Temperatures can vary widely from day to night. Be sure to **bring enough warm clothing** for hiking and camping, along with **wet-weather gear.** Weather in a number of hiking hot spots in Australia can change quickly at almost any time of year. If you are not dressed warmly enough, hypothermia can be a problem. Exposure to the degree that body temperature dips below 35°C (95°F) produces the following symptoms: chills, tiredness, then uncontrollable shivering and irrational behavior, with the victim not always recognizing that he or she is cold. If someone in your party is suffering from any of these symptoms, wrap him or her in blankets and/or a warm sleeping bag immediately and try to keep him or her awake. The fastest way to raise body temperature is through skin-to-skin contact in a sleeping bag. Drinking warm liquids also helps.

Remember to **never drink from streams or lakes,** no matter how clear they may be. Giardia organisms can be a real problem. The easiest way to purify water is to dissolve a water purification tablet in it. Camping equipment stores also carry purification pumps. Boiling water for 15 minutes is always a reliable method, if time- and fuel-consuming. (For information on camping, *see* Lodging.)

SKIING

You can ski in Australia from late June through September. Ski resorts admittedly don't compare too favorably with those in the United States and Europe, mostly due to less significant snowfall and vertical rise, but they retain an appealing bushland character. Cross-country skiing may be more rewarding than downhill because of the vast size of the snowfields and the unusual flora and fauna. The major downhill areas are in the Snowy Mountains region of New South Wales and in Victoria's High Country, though Tasmania also has snowfields. The principal cross-country areas are in Kosciuszko National Park and in Victoria's Alps.

PACKING

The wisest approach to dressing Down Under is to **wear layered outfits.** Frequently, particularly at the change of seasons, weather can turn suddenly. You'll appreciate being able to remove or put on a jacket. A light raincoat and umbrella are worthwhile accessories, but remember that plastic raincoats and nonbreathing polyester are uncomfortable in the tropics. **Don't wear lotions or perfume in the tropics** either, because they attract mosquitoes and other insects. It is also recommended that you carry insect repellent. **Wear a hat with a brim** to provide protection from the strong sunlight.

Dress is fairly casual in most cities, though top resorts and restaurants may require a jacket and tie. In Melbourne and Sydney, the younger set generally wears trendy clothes. Women might want to take along a cocktail dress for evening dining. In autumn, a light sweater or jacket will suffice for evenings in coastal cities, but winter demands a heavier coat—a raincoat with a zip-out wool lining is ideal. **Wear comfortable walking shoes.** You should have a pair of sturdy, good-quality walking boots, as well as a pair of running shoes or the equivalent if you're planning to trek. Rubber-sole sandals or canvas shoes are needed for walking on reef coral.

In your carry-on luggage, **pack an extra pair of eyeglasses or contact lenses and enough of any medication** you take to last a few days longer than the entire trip. You may also ask your doctor to write a spare prescription using the drug's generic name, as brand names may vary from country to country. In luggage to be checked, **never pack prescription drugs, valuables, or undeveloped film.** And don't forget to carry with you the addresses of offices that handle refunds of lost traveler's checks. Check *Fodor's How to Pack* (available at on-line retailers and bookstores everywhere) for more tips.

To avoid having your checked luggage chosen for hand inspection, don't cram bags full. The U.S. Transportation Security Administration suggests packing shoes on top and placing personal items you don't want touched in clear plastic bags.

CHECKING LUGGAGE

You're allowed to carry aboard one bag and one personal article, such as a purse or a laptop computer. Make sure what you carry on fits under your seat or in the overhead bin. Get to the gate early, so you can board as soon as possible, before the overhead bins fill up.

Baggage allowances vary by carrier, destination, and ticket class. On international flights, you're usually allowed to check two bags weighing up to 70 pounds (32 kilograms) each, although a few airlines allow checked bags of up to 88 pounds (40 kilograms) in first class. Some international carriers don't allow more than 66 pounds (30 kilograms) per bag in business class and 44 pounds (20 kilograms) in economy. On domestic flights, the limit may be 50 pounds (23 kilograms) per bag. Most airlines won't accept bags that weigh more than 100 pounds (45 kilograms) on domestic or international flights. Check baggage restrictions with your carrier before you pack.

Airline liability for baggage is limited to $2,500 per person on flights within the United States. On international flights it amounts to $9.07 per pound or $20 per kilogram for checked baggage (roughly $640 per 70-pound bag) and $400 per passenger for unchecked baggage. You can buy additional coverage at check-in for about $10 per $1,000 of coverage, but it often excludes a rather extensive list of items, shown on your airline ticket.

Before departure, **itemize your bags' contents** and their worth, and label the bags with your name, address, and phone number. (If you use your home address, cover it so potential thieves can't see it readily.) Include a label inside each bag and **pack a copy of your itinerary.** At check-in, **make sure each bag is correctly tagged** with the destination airport's three-letter code. Because some checked bags will be opened for hand inspection, the U.S. Transportation Security Administration recommends that you leave luggage unlocked or use the plastic locks offered at check-in. TSA screeners place an inspection notice inside searched bags, which are re-sealed with a special lock.

If your bag has been searched and contents are missing or damaged, file a claim with the TSA Consumer Response Center as soon as possible. If your bags arrive damaged or fail to arrive at all, file a written report with the airline before leaving the airport.

Complaints U.S. Transportation Security Administration Consumer Response Center ☎ 866/289-9673 ⊕ www.tsa.gov.

PASSPORTS & VISAS

When traveling internationally, **carry your passport** even if you don't need one (it's always the best form of I.D.) and **make two photocopies of the data page** (one for someone at home and another for you, carried separately from your passport). If you lose your passport, promptly call the nearest embassy or consulate and the local police.

U.S. passport applications for children under age 14 require consent from both parents or legal guardians; both parents must appear together to sign the application. If only one parent appears, he or she must submit a written statement from the other parent authorizing passport issuance for the child. A parent with sole authority must present evidence of it when applying; acceptable documentation includes the child's certified birth certificate listing only the applying parent, a court order specifically permitting this parent's travel with the child, or a death certificate for the non-applying parent. Application forms and instructions are available on the Web site of the U.S. State Department's Bureau of Consular Affairs (⊕ www.travel.state.gov).

ENTERING AUSTRALIA

You need a valid passport to enter Australia for stays of up to 90 days. In addition, all travelers to Australia, other than Australian and New Zealand citizens, also require a visa or Electronic Travel Authority (ETA). The free ETA, an electronically stored travel permit, replaces the visa label or stamp in a passport, and it enables passengers to be processed more quickly on arrival in Australia. ETAs are available through participating travel agencies and airlines.

To obtain an ETA for Australia, you must: hold a valid passport approved for ETA and travel with that passport; visit Australia for the purpose of tourism, family, or business meetings; stay less than three months; be in good health; and have no criminal convictions. If you're planning on getting a tourist ETA or visa, no work in the country is allowed.

People who don't meet the above requirements should contact the nearest Australian diplomatic office for advice on appropriate types of visas. Fees are applicable for visas. If you travel to Australia on an under-three-month ETA and later decide to extend your visit, then a visa must be applied for at the nearest Australian Immigration regional office (a fee of A$180 is applicable).

If you fly on Qantas you can obtain an Australian visa from the airline. Otherwise application forms are available from one of the offices listed below. Children traveling on a parent's passport do not need a separate application form, but should be included under Item 16 on the parent's form. The completed form and passport must be sent or brought in person to an issuing office, together with a recent passport-type photograph signed on the back (machine photographs are *not* acceptable).

If you plan to stay more than three months you must obtain a visa; contact the Consulate-General for information on the appropriate procedure. A $60 fee is applicable.

For more information on passport and visa requirements, visit the Department of Immigration and Multicultural and Indigenous Affairs Web site (⊕ www.immi.gov.au).

PASSPORT OFFICES

The best time to apply for a passport or to renew is in fall and winter. Before any trip, check your passport's expiration date.

▶ Canadian Citizens **Passport Office** ✉ to mail in applications: 200 Promenade du Portage, Hull, Québec J8X 4B7 ☎ 819/994-3500 or 800/567-6868 ⊕ www.ppt.gc.ca.
▶ New Zealand Citizens **New Zealand Passports Office** ☎ 0800/22-5050 or 04/474-8100 ⊕ www.passports.govt.nz.
▶ U.K. Citizens **U.K. Passport Service** ☎ 0870/521-0410 ⊕ www.passport.gov.uk.
▶ U.S. Citizens **National Passport Information Center** ☎ 900/225-5674 or 900/225-7778 TTY (calls are 55¢ per minute for automated service or $1.50 per minute for operator service), 888/362-8668 or 888/498-3648 TTY (calls are $5.50 each) ⊕ www.travel.state.gov.

REST ROOMS

Australian rest rooms are usually of the highest standards of cleanliness. In major cities, there may be a nominal charge to use them. Railway and bus stations are good places to find public rest rooms. In country towns and at roadside rest areas, rest rooms are usually free. There are fewer facilities in remote areas. Long-distance buses have rest rooms on board.

SAFETY

Given Australia's relaxed ways, it's easy to be seduced into believing that crime is practically nonexistent. In fact, Australia has its share of poverty, drugs, and crime. If you encounter anything it will most likely be theft, and although crime rates are not high by world standards, you need to exercise caution. In major tourist areas such as Sydney's Bondi or Queensland's Gold Coast, the risk increases. When you park your vehicle, hide any valuables. Don't leave anything of value on the beach when you go for a swim. Under no conditions should you hitchhike.

Always be cautious with your money and documents. Be particularly careful when withdrawing money from an ATM, where a number of locals and travelers have been robbed. If you need to withdraw funds, do so during daylight hours, in the company of family or friends, and in a safe location.

WOMEN IN AUSTRALIA

Traveling in Australia is generally safe for women, provided you follow a few common-sense precautions. **Avoid isolated areas** such as empty beaches. At night, avoid quiet streets. You will probably receive attention if you enter pubs or clubs alone. Cafés are a safer bet. Look confident and purposeful.

Don't wear a money belt or a hip pack, both of which peg you as a tourist. If you carry a purse, choose one with a zipper and a thick strap that you can drape across your body; adjust the length so that the purse sits in front of you at or above hip level. Store only enough money in the purse to cover casual spending. Distribute the rest of your cash and any valuables (including credit cards and your passport) between a deep front pocket, an inside jacket or vest pocket, and a hidden money pouch. Do not reach for the money pouch once in public.

SENIOR-CITIZEN TRAVEL

To qualify for age-related discounts, **mention your senior-citizen status up front** when booking hotel reservations (not when checking out) and before you're seated in restaurants (not when paying the bill). Be sure to have identification on hand. When renting a car, ask about promotional car-rental discounts, which can be cheaper than senior-citizen rates.

Unfortunately, however, few of the discounts that Australian senior citizens enjoy within the country are available to visitors, because an Australian "pensioner's card" is usually required as proof of age.
Educational Programs Elderhostel ⌧ 11 Ave. de Lafayette, Boston, MA 02111-1746 ☎ 877/426-8056, 978/323-4141 international callers, 877/426-2167 TTY 🖷 877/426-2166 ⊕ www.elderhostel.org. **Interhostel** ⌧ University of New Hampshire, 6 Garrison Ave., Durham, NH 03824 ☎ 603/862-1147 or 800/733-9753 🖷 603/862-1113 ⊕ www.learn.unh.edu.

SHOPPING

Bargains are not hard to come by in Australia, although as a visitor you might not have the time it takes to look for them. Quality is good and prices are competitive, particularly for such clothing as hand-knitted wool sweaters, wool suits, and designer dresses and sportswear. Bargain hunters can benefit from joining one of the shopping tours in Melbourne and Sydney, which visit one or two factory outlets. Check with your hotel concierge or the state tourist office for information about these tours.

A 10% Goods and Services Tax (GST) is levied on all goods and services, excluding fresh food (but including cooked takeaway restaurant items). The GST is included in the price you pay.

However, you can claim a refund of the GST on goods you take with you as hand luggage when you leave the country. These items must be inspected by customs officials. The refund is paid on goods costing A$300 or more, bought from the same store less than 30 days before your departure. You can buy goods from several stores, provided that each store's tax invoice totals at least A$300. The refund is paid when you leave the country.

KEY DESTINATIONS

Sydney has the best one-stop shopping for such distinctive Australian souvenirs as opals, Aboriginal artworks and artifacts, and bush apparel. City shopping offers competitive pricing, and you can compare products from a number of outlets. Buying from the source may be more rewarding, but it's not really practical in many cases. It would be unlikely, for example, that you would buy opals from the place where they are mined, or an Aboriginal painting direct from the artist. The Rocks and Darling Harbour in Sydney are the best areas to shop for all souvenirs. For Aboriginal artworks, try Alice Springs, Ayers Rock Resort, and Darwin, which have stores that specialize in Aboriginal artworks.

SMART SOUVENIRS

The didgeridoo, a traditional instrument of Northern Territory Aborigines, is a popular Australian souvenir. Unpainted examples start at around A$70, while a more spectacular version will cost from A$200 up. Didgeridoos are widely available from souvenir shops in places such as The Rocks in Sydney. Their biggest drawback is lack of portability. If you don't have the space in your bags, an alternative is a pair of clapping sticks—the percussion section of Aboriginal music—for A$10–A$20. A brightly colored, carved wooden boomerang also makes an excellent souvenir. Tea tree oil, made from the leaves of the coastal mellaleuca tree, is a traditional bushman's salve. It also smells good, and it's usually available from the airport stores that sell "Australiana" products. The cost is around A$7 for a 50-milliliter bottle.

WATCH OUT

Australia has strict laws prohibiting the export of native animals and plants. It's also illegal to take or send items deemed important to Australia's cultural heritage out of the country without a permit.

STUDENTS IN AUSTRALIA

Students and backpackers are entitled to reductions on bus passes available from Greyhound and McCafferty's (⇨ Bus Travel). These 10% discounts are obtained by presenting an International Student Card, YHA cards, and VIP or ISIC Backpacker cards. Some accommodation discounts are also available in conjunction with the pass.

Victoria Street in Sydney's Kings Cross, near the rear entrance to the Kings Cross subway station, is a gathering spot for international backpackers. Here you can sometimes find drivers looking for a rider to share car expenses while exploring the country, or someone heading home who is selling a car. However, several backpackers were murdered in New South Wales in the early 1990s, and backpackers are strongly advised against hitchhiking anywhere in the country. If you are sharing a car and expenses, it would be prudent to let someone know the vehicle's registration number, the people you will be traveling with, and your estimated time of arrival before you depart. Also, as best you can, be sure that your aims and personalities are compatible.

For a guide to backpacker hostels, contact V.I.P. Backpackers Resorts of Australia. This organization sells a V.I.P. Kit, which includes the V.I.P. Backpackers Resorts guide plus a V.I.P. card that entitles you to discounts at all Australian backpacker hostels and on Greyhound Pioneer Aus-

tralia and several other bus lines. The cost of the kit is A$38, including postage.

The NSW Discovery Pass YHA, available to any member of the YHA or its overseas affiliates, allows unlimited economy travel on all Countrylink rail and coach services throughout New South Wales for one month. The pass is available from Countrylink Travel Centres. To save money, **look into deals available through student-oriented travel agencies.** To qualify you'll need a bona fide student I.D. card. Members of international student groups are also eligible.

🖪 I.D.s & Services **STA Travel** ✉ 10 Downing St., New York, NY 10014 ☎ 212/627-3111 or 800/777-0112 🖶 212/627-3387 🌐 www.sta.com. **Travel Cuts** ✉ 187 College St., Toronto, Ontario M5T 1P7, Canada ☎ 416/979-2406, 800/592-2887, 866/246-9762 in Canada 🖶 416/979-8167 🌐 www.travelcuts.com.

TAXES

Everyone leaving Australia pays a departure tax, known as a Passenger Movement Charge, of A$38. This amount is prepaid with your airline ticket. Except for food, all goods and services incur a Goods and Services Tax (GST) of 10%.

TELEPHONES

Australia's telephone system is efficient and reliable. You can make long-distance and international calls from any phone in the country. Australian phone numbers have eight digits.

Hotels impose surcharges that can double or even triple the cost of making calls from your room. Get around this by making calls from a public phone, or by charging to a local account (contact your local telephone service for details). Australia's cellular phones operate on either a GSM (Global System for Mobiles) or CDMA (Code Division Multiple Access) system. All compatible cellular phones will operate in Australia, but check first with your carrier to make sure that your particular phone has been cleared for international access. Some functions—such as message bank callback—will not work outside your home country. Your pager will not work in Australia.

AREA & COUNTRY CODES

The country code for Australia is 61. From the United States, dial 011, then 61, then the local area code. From the United Kingdom, dial 00, then 61. When dialing an Australian number from abroad, drop the initial 0 from the local area code.

Area codes for the major cities are: Sydney and Canberra, 02; Melbourne and Hobart, 03; Brisbane and Cairns, 07; Adelaide, Darwin, and Perth, 08.

DIRECTORY & OPERATOR ASSISTANCE

For local directory assistance, call 1223. For international directory assistance, call 1225. For information on international call costs, call 1800/113011.

INTERNATIONAL CALLS

Calls from Australia to the United States, Canada, and the United Kingdom cost A$1 for the first 10 minutes and then an additional A 30¢–A 50¢ per minute, plus a A 25¢ connection fee. Operator-assisted calls can be made from any phone with IDD (International Direct Dialing) access. Check local phone directories for international operator numbers. For a person-to-person call to the United States, the connection fee is A$3.50, plus A$2.51 per minute. A collect call is known as a "reverse-charge" call.

LOCAL CALLS

A local call costs A 40¢. Australian numbers with a 13 prefix can be dialed countrywide for the cost of a local call. For example, dialing a 13-number for a company in Melbourne when you are in Sydney will be billed as a local call. You can dial 1300 numbers countrywide for the cost of a local call. Toll-free numbers in Australia have an 1800 prefix. Unless otherwise noted, toll-free numbers in this book are accessible only within Australia.

LONG-DISTANCE CALLS

Long-distance calls can be dialed directly using the city code or area code. Rates are divided into two time periods: Day (weekdays 7 AM–7 PM) and Economy (weekdays 7 PM–7 AM and Friday 7 PM–Monday 7 AM). Area codes are listed in the white pages of local telephone directories.

All telephone numbers in Australia have eight digits. Exceptions are toll-free numbers and numbers with the prefix 13. The latter are countrywide and thus carry no area code at all. When you are calling

long-distance numbers within Australia, remember to include the area code, even when you are calling from a number with the same area code. For example, if you are making a call from Sydney to Canberra, you need to include the area code even though both have the same 02 prefix.

LONG-DISTANCE SERVICES

AT&T, MCI, and Sprint access codes make calling long distance relatively convenient, but you may find the local access number blocked in many hotel rooms. First ask the hotel operator to connect you. If the hotel operator balks, ask for an international operator, or dial the international operator yourself. One way to improve your odds of getting connected to your long-distance carrier is to travel with more than one company's calling card (a hotel may block Sprint, for example, but not MCI). If all else fails, call from a pay phone. **⑦ Access Codes AT&T Direct** ☎ 800/435-0812. **MCI WorldCom** ☎ 800/444-4141. **Sprint International Access** ☎ 800/877-4646.

PHONE CARDS

If you plan to make even a small number of phone calls, phone cards are a smart, cost-efficient choice. Phone cards may be purchased from post offices or news agencies. They are available in units of A$5, A$10, A$20, and A$50. Most public phones will accept phone cards.

PUBLIC PHONES

Public phones can be found in shopping areas, on suburban streets, at train stations, and outside rural post offices. Lift the receiver and wait for the dial tone. Insert either a phone card or coins. A local call costs A 40¢. Dial the number.

TIME

Figuring out what time it is Down Under can be dizzying, especially with cross-hemisphere daylight saving time and countries with multiple time zones. Without daylight saving time, Sydney is 14 hours ahead of New York; 15 hours ahead of Chicago and Dallas; 17 hours ahead (or count back seven hours and add a day) from Los Angeles; and 10 hours ahead of London.

From Canada and the States, in order to avoid waking up some Aussie in the middle of the night, **call Australia after 7 PM.** If you're calling Western Australia, call after 9. From the United Kingdom or Europe, it isn't quite as complicated. Call early in the morning or very late at night. When faxing, it's usually not a problem to ring discreet fax numbers at any time of day.

Australia has three major time zones. Eastern Standard Time (EST) applies in Tasmania, Victoria, NSW, and Queensland; Central Standard Time applies in South Australia and the Northern Territory; and Western Standard Time applies in Western Australia. Central Standard Time is ½ hour behind EST, and Western Standard Time is two hours behind EST.

Within the EST zone, each state will sometimes choose a slightly different date on which to commence or end daylight saving from its neighboring state—except for Queensland, where the powerful farm lobby has prevented the state from introducing daylight saving, since it would make the cows wake up an hour earlier. Western Australia and the Northern Territory also decline to recognize daylight saving, which means that at certain times of the year Australia can have as many as six different time zones. Confused? So are most Australians.

TIPPING

Hotels and restaurants do not add service charges, but it is a widely accepted practice to tip a waiter 10%–12% for good service, although many Australians consider it sufficient to leave only A$3 or A$4. It's not necessary to tip a hotel doorman for carrying suitcases into the lobby, but porters could be given A$1 a bag. Room service and housemaids are not tipped except for special service. Taxi drivers do not expect a tip, but you may want to leave any small change. Guides, tour bus drivers, and chauffeurs don't expect tips either, though they are grateful if someone in the group takes up a collection for them. No tipping is necessary in beauty salons or for theater ushers.

TOURS & PACKAGES

Because everything is prearranged on a prepackaged tour or independent vacation, you spend less time planning—and often get it all at a good price.

ADVENTURE TRAVEL

You'll miss an important element of Australia if you don't get away from the cities to explore "the bush" that is so deeply ingrained in the Australian character. Australians pride themselves on their ability to cope in the great outdoors, even if, in many cases, this has never been tested beyond lighting the backyard barbecue. Nevertheless, among the heroes of modern Australia are those men and women who opened this vast, unforgiving land to European settlement—such as Ludwig Leichhardt, who pioneered the 4,800-km (2,976-mi) route between Brisbane and Port Essington (Coburg Peninsula) in 1844, only to vanish without a trace during a transcontinental trek in 1848, or Robert O'Hara Burke, who died in 1861 after completing a south–north transcontinental trip with camels.

Many of the adventure vacations of today were journeys of exploration only a generation ago. Even now, the four-wheel-drive vehicle is a necessity, not a plaything, in the great heart of Australia. Indeed, the country retains a raw element that makes it ideally suited to adventure vacationing. You can still travel for hours or days in many places without seeing another person or any sign of human habitation. From the tropical jungles of the north to the deserts of the Red Centre to the snowfields of New South Wales and Victoria, the landscape is a constant reminder of the continent's age. Without volcanic action or colliding tectonic plates to renew them, the mountains you walk or ride through have been ground down over the eons, and the unique plants and animals you encounter are themselves reason enough to travel to Australia.

With most companies, the adventure guides' knowledge of nature and love of the bush are matched by a level of competence that ensures your safety even in dangerous situations. The safety record of Australian adventure operators is very good. Be aware, however, that most adventure-tour operators require you to sign waiver forms absolving the company of responsibility in the event of an accident or a problem. Australian courts normally uphold such waivers except in cases of significant negligence.

Adventure vacations are commonly split into soft and hard adventures. A hard adventure requires a substantial degree of physical participation: bicycling, bushwalking, skiing, scuba diving, and rafting.

You may not have to be perfectly fit, but in a few cases prior experience is a prerequisite. In soft adventures—camel trekking, four-wheel-drive tours, horseback riding, or sailing—the destination *and* the means of travel combine to make it an adventure.

Australia's vast and varied terrain poses unlimited adventure possibilities for every age and physique. Hard-core outdoor sports enthusiasts can bike, hike, and sail around the country, or raft, ski, and scuba dive infinite points in and around the continent. If you prefer more tame travels, you can simply be an observer as you ride a camel, horse, or four-wheel-drive vehicle through Australia's amazing scenery. And anyone can embark on the ultimate frozen adventure cruise to Antarctica from the Hobart, Tasmania—or at least take the one-day Qantas overflight of Antarctica from Sydney or Melbourne.

Adventure Associates. Box 612, Bondi Junction, NSW 1355 02/9389-7466 02/9369-1853 www.adventureassociates.com. **Adventure Center.** 1311 63rd St., Suite 200, Emeryville, CA 94608 USA 510/654-1879 or 1800/228-8747 510/654-4200 www.adventure-center.com. **Adventure Charters of Kangaroo Island.** Box 169, Kingscote, Kangaroo Island, SA 5223 08/8553-9119 08/8553-9122 www.adventurecharters.com.au. **The Adventure Company.** Box 5740, Cairns, QLD 4870 07/4051-4777 07/4051-4888 www.adventures.com.au. **Australian Wild Escapes.** Box 3116, Asquith, NSW 2077 02/9980-8799 02/9980-9616 www.australianwildescapes.com. **Beyond Tours.** 1 Pony Ridge, Belair, SA 5052 08/8374-3580 08/8374-3091 www4.tpgi.com.au/users/andreacc/beyondtours. **Bicheno Dive Centre.** 2 Scuba Ct., Bicheno, TAS 7215 03/6375-1138 03/6375-1504. **Blue Mountains Adventure Company.** 84a Main St., Katoomba, NSW 2780 02/4782-1271 02/4782-1277 www.bmac.com.au. **Bogong Horseback Adventures.** Box 230, Mt. Beauty, VIC 3699 03/5754-4849 03/5754-4181 www.bogonghorse.com.au. **Boomerang Bicycle Tours.** Box 5054, Kingsdene, NSW 2118 02/9890-1996 02/9630-3436 www.members.ozemail.com.au/~ozbike. **Camels Australia.** PMB 74 Stuarts Well, via Alice Springs, NT 0872 08/8956-0925 08/8956-0909 www.camels-australia.com.au. **Cradle Mountain Huts.** Box 1879, Launceston, TAS 7250 03/6331-2006 03/6331-5525 www.cradlehuts.com.au. **Coral Coast Dive.** Box 35, Exmouth, WA 6707 08/9949-1004 08/9949-1044 www.ningalooreef.com. **Croydon Travel.** 34 Main St., Croydon, VIC 3136 03/9725-8555 03/9723-6700 www.antarcticaflights.com.au. **Discover West Hol-**idays. Box 7355, Perth, WA 6850 1800/999243 08/9486-4133 www.discoverwest.com.au. **Dive Adventures.** 9th level, 32 York St., Sydney, NSW 2000 02/9299-4633 02/9299-4644 www.diveadventures.com. **Ecotrek.** Box 4, Kangarilla, SA 5157 08/8383-7198 08/8383-7377 www.ecotrek.com.au. **Equitrek Australia.** 5 King Rd., Ingleside, NSW 2101 02/9913-9408 02/9970-6303 www.equitrek.com.au. **Exmouth Diving Centre.** Payne St., Exmouth, WA 6707 08/9949-1201 08/9949-1680 www.exmouthdiving.com.au. **Freycinet Experience.** Box 43, Battery Point, TAS 7004 03/6223-7565 03/6224-1315 www.freycinet.com.au. **Frontier Camel Tours.** Box 2836, Alice Springs, NT 0871 08/8953-0444 08/8955-5015 www.cameltours.com.au. **Kangaroo Island Odysseys.** Box 570 Penneshaw, Kangaroo Island, SA 5222 08/8553-1311 08/8553-1294 www.kiodysseys.com.au. **Kimberley Wilderness Adventures.** Box 2046, Broome, WA 6725 08/9192-5741 08/9192-5761 www.kimberleywilderness.com.au. **Mike Ball Dive Adventures.** 143 Lake St., Cairns, QLD 4870 07/4031-5484 in Australia, 1800/952-4319 in U.S. www.mikeball.com. **Morrell Adventure Travel.** 64 Jindabyne Rd., Berridale, NSW 2628 02/6456-3681 www.morrell.com.au. **Paddy Pallin Jindabyne.** Kosciuszko Rd., Jindabyne, NSW 2627 1800/623459 02/6456-2836. **Peregrine Adventures.** 258 Lonsdale St., Melbourne, VIC 3000 03/9663-8611 03/9663-8618 www.peregrine.net.au/antarctica. **Pro Dive Travel.** Suite 34, Level 2, 330 Wattle St., Ultimo, NSW 2007 02/9281-6166 02/9281-0660 www.prodive.com.au. **ProSail.** Box 973, Airlie Beach, QLD 4802 07/4946-5433 07/4948-8609 www.prosail.com.au. **Reynella Kosciuszko Rides.** Bolaro Rd., Adaminaby, NSW 2630 1800/029909 02/6454-2530 www.reynellarides.com.au. **Sail Australia.** Box 417, Cremorne, NSW 2090 1800/606111 02/4322-8199 www.sailaustralia.com.au. **Stoneys High Country.** Box 287, Mansfield, VIC 3722 03/5775-2212 03/5775-2598 www.stoneys.com.au. **Sydney by Sail.** National Maritime Museum, 2 Murray St., Darling Harbour, NSW 2000 02/9280-1110 02/9280-1119 www.sydneybysail.com. **Tasmanian Expeditions.** 110 George St., Launceston, TAS 7250 03/6334-3477 03/6334-3463 www.tas-ex.com/tas-ex/. **Tasmanian Wild River Adventures.** Box 90, Sandy Bay, TAS 7006 0409/977506 03/6278-3070 www.wildrivers.com.au. **Walkabout Gourmet Adventures.** Box 52, Dinner Plain, VIC 3898 03/5159-6556 03/5159-6508 www.walkaboutgourmet.com. **Wilderness Challenge.** Box 254, Cairns, QLD 4870 07/4035-4488 07/4035-4188 www.wilderness-challenge.com.au/page5.html. **Wildwater Adventures.** 754 Pacific Hwy., Boambee South, NSW 2450 02/

6653-3500 🖷 02/6653-3900 🌐 www.
wildwateradventures.com.au. **World Expeditions.**
✉ 71 York St., 5th floor, Sydney, NSW 2000 ☎ 02/
9279-0188 or 1300/720000 🖷 02/9279-0566
🌐 www.worldexpeditions.com.au.

BOOKING WITH AN AGENT

Travel agents are excellent resources. But
it's a good idea to collect brochures from
several agencies, as some agents' suggestions may be influenced by relationships
with tour and package firms that reward
them for volume sales. If you have a special interest, **find an agent with expertise
in that area**; the American Society of
Travel Agents (ASTA; ⇨ Travel Agencies)
has a database of specialists worldwide.

Make sure your travel agent knows the accommodations and other services of the
place being recommended. Ask about the
hotel's location, room size, beds, and
whether it has a pool, room service, or
programs for children, if you care about
these. Has your agent been there in person
or sent others whom you can contact?

Do some homework on your own, too:
local tourism boards can provide information about lesser-known and small-
niche operators, some of which may sell
only direct.

🔁 Tour-Operator Recommendations **American
Society of Travel Agents** (⇨ Travel Agencies). **National Tour Association** (NTA) ✉ 546 E. Main St.,
Lexington, KY 40508 ☎ 859/226-4444 or 800/682-
8886 🖷 859/226-4404 🌐 www.ntaonline.com.
United States Tour Operators Association (USTOA)
✉ 275 Madison Ave., Suite 2014, New York, NY
10016 ☎ 212/599-6599 or 800/468-7862 🖷 212/
599-6744 🌐 www.ustoa.com.

BUYER BEWARE

Each year consumers are stranded or lose
their money when tour operators—even
large ones with excellent reputations—go
out of business. So **check out the operator.**
Ask several travel agents about its reputation, and try to **book with a company that
has a consumer-protection program.**
(Look for information in the company's
brochure.) In the United States, members
of the National Tour Association and the
United States Tour Operators Association
are required to set aside funds to cover
payments and travel arrangements in the
event that the company defaults. It's also a
good idea to choose a company that par-
ticipates in the American Society of Travel

Agents' Tour Operator Program; ASTA
will act as mediator in any disputes between you and your tour operator.

Remember that the more your package or
tour includes, the better you can predict
the ultimate cost of your vacation. Make
sure you know exactly what is covered,
and **beware of hidden costs.** Are taxes,
tips, and transfers included? Entertainment
and excursions? These can add up.

TRAIN TRAVEL

Australia has a network of interstate, country, and urban trains providing first- and
economy-class service. The major interstate
trains are the *Indian-Pacific* from Sydney
to Perth via Adelaide (26 hours Sydney–
Adelaide, 38 hours Adelaide–Perth); the
Ghan from Adelaide via Alice Springs to
Darwin (44½ hours); the *Overland* (night
service) and *Daylink* from Melbourne to
Adelaide (12 hours); and the *XPT* (Express
Passenger Train) from Sydney to Brisbane
(15 hours). Service between Melbourne and
Sydney is on the daytime or overnight *XPT*
(10½ hours). Within Queensland you can
take several interesting train journeys: the
Queenslander and *Sunlander,* which run
along the coast; and the historic *Gulflander*
and *Savannahlander,* which travel through
Outback regions.

Book early whenever possible, especially
for the *Indian-Pacific* and the *Ghan* during
peak times (August–October and Christmas holidays). For more information on
Australia's network of rural and urban
trains, or to make reservations or purchase
discount passes, contact Rail Australia.

CLASSES

Apart from suburban commuter services,
Australia's trains have first and second
classes. Travel in both is comfortable but
far from luxurious. Most people prefer to
travel in their own vehicles. As a result,
Australia's railways have received far less
funding than highways, and the standards
on Australia's train network fall far short
of those found in Europe and the United
States. Except on long-distance trains such
as the *Ghan* or the *Indian-Pacific,* dining
amenities are minimal. Train travel is
moderately priced. However, trains are
used most by the less affluent and senior
citizens, who travel at a considerable discount. First class costs approximately 50%
more than economy.

DISCOUNTS & PASSES

Advance purchase fares, which afford a 10%–40% discount between some major cities, are best bought before departure for Australia, as they tend to be booked up far in advance. It is advisable to **make all rail reservations well in advance,** particularly during peak tourist seasons. Contact your travel agent or the appropriate Rail Australia office.

Rail passes can be purchased in Australia on presentation of your passport. Passes must be presented to the ticket office prior to the commencement of any journey. Rail passes do not include sleeping berths or meals.

The Austrail Flexipass allows a set number of travel days, which don't have to be consecutive, on the national rail network. Because the value of the pass does not ebb away on days when you're not traveling, the Flexipass can be more cost-effective than the Austrail Pass. Four passes are available, from 8 to 29 days. The 8-day pass allows eight days of economy-class travel in a 6-month period and costs A$550. The 29-day pass allows 29 days of travel in the same period and costs A$1,440. The 8-day pass does not allow travel west of Crystal Brook in South Australia, which means that this pass is not valid for service to Perth or to Alice Springs.

The East Coast Discovery Pass allows economy-class travel between any two points from Melbourne to Cairns, with unlimited stops along the way. The pass is valid for six months, and for travel in one direction only. The cost of the pass is A$292.60 from Sydney to Cairns, A$374 from Melbourne to Cairns.

▶ Train Information **Rail Australia** ☎ 13–2147 in Australia, 818/841–1030 ATS Tours in the U.S. and Canada, 800/633–3404 Austravel Inc. in the U.S., 800/387–8850 Goway Travel in Canada, 0171/828–4111 in the U.K.

FARES & SCHEDULES

Rail Australia provides information and booking services for all major train systems across the continent, including the *Ghan,* the *Indian-Pacific,* and the *Overland.*
▶ Train Information **Rail Australia** ✉ Box 445, Marleston Business Centre, Marleston SA 5033 ✉ Box 2430, Hollywood, CA 90078 ☎ 08/8213–4592 ⊕ www.railaustralia.com.au.

PAYING

Train travel can be paid for with American Express, MasterCard, Diners Club, or Visa. Traveler's checks are also accepted.

RESERVATIONS

It's a good idea to **make advance reservations for train journeys.** To get choice seats during high season and holiday periods, you should book (and pay for) your tickets as early as possible.

TRAVEL AGENCIES

A good travel agent puts your needs first. Look for an agency that has been in business at least five years, emphasizes customer service, and has someone on staff who specializes in your destination. In addition, **make sure the agency belongs to a professional trade organization.** The American Society of Travel Agents (ASTA)—the largest and most influential in the field with more than 20,000 members in some 140 countries—maintains and enforces a strict code of ethics and will step in to help mediate any agent-client disputes involving ASTA members if necessary. ASTA (whose motto is "Without a travel agent, you're on your own") also maintains a Web site that includes a directory of agents. (If a travel agency is also acting as your tour operator, *see* Buyer Beware *in* Tours and Packages.)
▶ Local Agent Referrals **American Society of Travel Agents (ASTA)** ✉ 1101 King St., Suite 200, Alexandria, VA 22314 ☎ 703/739–2782 or 800/965–2782 24-hr hot line ⊟ 703/739–3268 ⊕ www.astanet.com. **Association of British Travel Agents** ✉ 68–71 Newman St., London W1T 3AH ☎ 020/7637–2444 ⊟ 020/7637–0713 ⊕ www.abtanet.com. **Association of Canadian Travel Agents** ✉ 130 Albert St., Suite 1705, Ottawa, Ontario K1P 5G4 ☎ 613/237–3657 ⊟ 613/237–7052 ⊕ www.acta.ca. **Australian Federation of Travel Agents** ✉ Level 3, 309 Pitt St., Sydney, NSW 2000 ☎ 02/9264–3299 ⊟ 02/9264–1085 ⊕ www.afta.com.au. **Travel Agents' Association of New Zealand** ✉ Level 5, Tourism and Travel House, 79 Boulcott St., Box 1888, Wellington 6001 ☎ 04/499–0104 ⊟ 04/499–0786 ⊕ www.taanz.org.nz.

VISITOR INFORMATION

Learn more about foreign destinations by checking government-issued travel advisories and country information. For a broader picture, consider information from more than one country.

For general information contact the national and regional tourism offices below and call for the free information-packed booklet "Destination Australia" (in the United States). The Australian Tourist Commission's Aussie Help Line, available from 8 AM to 7 PM Central Standard Time, can answer specific questions about planning your trip. Before you go, contact Friends Overseas—Australia to be put in touch with Australians who share your interests. Membership is A$25.

🖪 Countrywide Information **Australian Tourist Commission** ✉ U.S.: 2049 Century Park E, Los Angeles, CA 90067 ☎ 310/229-4870 🖷 310/552-1215 ✉ U.K.: Gemini House, 10-18 Putney Hill, Putney London, SW15 6AA ☎ 0990/022-000 for information, 0990/561-434 for brochure line 🖷 0181/940-5221 ✉ New Zealand: Level 13, 44-48 Emily Pl., Box 1666, Auckland, 1 ☎ 0800/650303. **"Destination Australia" booklet** ☎ 800/333-0262. **Friends Overseas–Australia** ✉ 68-01 Dartmouth St., Forest Hills, NY 11375 ☎ 718/261-0534.

🖪 Regional Information **Australian Travel Headquarters** ✉ 1600 Dove St., Suite 215, Newport Beach, CA 92660 ☎ 714/852-2270 or 800/546-2155 🖷 714/852-2277 for information on South Australia. **Australia's Northern Territory** ✉ 3601 Aviation Blvd., Suite 2100, Manhattan Beach, CA 90266 ☎ 310/643-2636 🖷 310/643-2637. **Queensland Tourist & Travel Corporation** ✉ 1800 Century Park E, Suite 330, Los Angeles, CA 90067 ☎ 310/788-0997.

🖪 Government Advisories **U.S. Department of State** ✉ Overseas Citizens Services Office, Room 4811, 2201 C St. NW, Washington, DC 20520 ☎ 202/647-5225 interactive hot line or 888/407-4747 ⊕ www.travel.state.gov; enclose a cover letter with your request and a business-size SASE. **Consular Affairs Bureau of Canada** ☎ 800/267-6788 or 613/944-6788 ⊕ www.voyage.gc.ca. **U.K. Foreign and** .

Commonwealth Office ✉ Travel Advice Unit, Consular Division, Old Admiralty Building, London SW1A 2PA ☎ 020/7008-0232 or 020/7008-0233 ⊕ www.fco.gov.uk/travel. **New Zealand Ministry of Foreign Affairs and Trade** ☎ 04/439-8000 ⊕ www.mft.govt.nz.

WEB SITES

Do check out the World Wide Web when planning your trip. You'll find everything from weather forecasts to virtual tours of famous cities. Be sure to **visit Fodors.com** (⊕ www.fodors.com), a complete travel-planning site. You can research prices and book plane tickets, hotel rooms, rental cars, vacation packages, and more. In addition, you can post your pressing questions in the Travel Talk section. Other planning tools include a currency converter and weather reports, and there are loads of links to travel resources.

The Australian Tourist Commission Web site (⊕ www.australia.com) is a good resource for planning your trip to Australia. For more specific information contact the individual states' Web sites: Australian Capital Territory (⊕ www.act.gov.au); New South Wales Government (⊕ www.visitnsw.com.au or www.nsw.gov.au); Northern Territory Government (⊕ www.nt.gov.au); Queensland Government (⊕ www.qld.gov.au or www.queenslandtravel.com.au); South Australia Government (⊕ www.sa.gov.au); Tasmanian Government (⊕ www.tas.gov.au); Victorian Government (⊕ www.vic.gov.au); Western Australia Government (⊕ www.wa.gov.au or www.westernaustralia.net).

SYDNEY

FODOR'S CHOICE

Bondi Beach

Claude's, restaurant in Woollahra

Hemmesphere, cocktail lounge in City Center

Manly Beach

Sydney Harbour Explorer cruise, Circular Quay

Observatory Hotel, The Rocks

Paddington Bazaar, shopping market in Paddington

Park Hyatt Sydney, Circular Quay

Rockpool, restaurant in The Rocks

Sydney Opera House, Circular Quay

Quay, restaurant at Circular Quay

HIGHLY RECOMMENDED

SIGHTS   Chinese Garden of Friendship, Darling Harbour

Royal Botanic Gardens, the Domain

Royal National Park, Sutherland

Taronga Zoo, Mosman

BEACHES   Balmoral

Bronte

Clovelly

Tamarama

So many wonderful hotels, restaurants, nightclubs, and shops can be found in Sydney that there's not enough space to list them all on this page. To see what Fodor's editors and contributors highly recommend, please look for the black stars as you leaf through this chapter.

Updated by
Michael
Gebicki,
Dining by
Matthew Evans

SYDNEY BELONGS TO THE EXCLUSIVE CLUB OF WORLD CITIES that generate sense of excitement from the air. Even at the end of a marathon flight across the Pacific, there's renewed sparkle in the cabin as the plane circles the city, crossing the branching fingers of the harbor, where thousands of yachts are suspended on the dark water and the sails of the Opera House glisten in the distance. Its setting alone, perfected with dazzling beaches and a sunny, Mediterranean climate, guarantees Sydney a place among the most glamorous cities on the planet.

At 4 million people, Sydney is the biggest and most cosmopolitan city in Australia. Take a taxi from Sydney Airport and chances are that the driver won't say "G'day" with the accent you might expect. Like the United States, Australia is a society of immigrants, and Sydney has been their preferred destination. Since the 1950s, the Anglo-Irish immigrants who made up the city's original population have been enriched by successive waves of Italians, Greeks, Turks, Lebanese, Chinese, Vietnamese, Thais, and Indonesians. This intermingling has created a cultural vibrancy and energy—and a culinary repertoire—that was missing only a generation ago.

Sydneysiders, as locals are known, practice a fairly relaxed lifestyle. But it's clear that residents embrace their harbor with passion. Indented with numerous bays and beaches, the Sydney Harbour is Australia's culture and history nexus. Captain Arthur Phillip, the commander of the 11 ships of the First Fleet, wrote in his diary when he first set eyes on this harbor on January 26, 1788: "We had the satisfaction of finding the finest harbor in the world, in which a thousand ships of the line may ride in the most perfect security." It was not an easy beginning, however. Passengers on board Phillip's ships were not the "huddled masses yearning to breathe free" who populated the United States, but the first round of wretched inmates (roughly 800) flushed from overcrowded jails in England and sent halfway around the globe to serve their sentences.

Sydney has long since outgrown the stigma of its convict origins, but the passage of time has not tamed its rebellious spirit. Sydney's panache and appetite for life are unchallenged. A walk among the scantily clad sunbathers at Bondi Beach or through the raucous nightlife districts of Kings Cross and Oxford Street provides ample evidence.

It's good to keep in mind that visiting Sydney is an essential part of an Australian experience, but the city is no more representative of Australia than Los Angeles is of the United States. Sydney has joined the ranks of the great cities whose characters are essentially international. What Sydney offers are style, sophistication, and good, no, great looks—an exhilarating prelude to the continent at its back door.

EXPLORING SYDNEY

Sydney is a giant, stretching nearly 97 km (60 mi) from top to bottom and about 55 km (34 mi) across. The harbor divides the city into northern and a southern halves, with most of the headline attractions on the south shore. You'll likely spend most of your visit on the harbor's south side, within an area bounded by Chinatown in the south, Harbour Bridge in the north, Darling Harbour to the west, and the beaches and coastline to the east. North of Harbour Bridge lie the important commercial center of North Sydney and leafy but bland suburbs. Ocean beaches, Taronga Zoo, and Ku-ring-gai Chase National Park are the most likely reasons you may find to venture north of the harbor.

Within a few hours' drive of Sydney are the Blue Mountains and the Hunter Valley vineyards, areas of spectacular scenic beauty. Although

You really need three days in Sydney to see the essential city center, while six days would allow more time to explore the beaches and inner suburbs. A stay of 10 days would allow trips outside the city and give you time to explore a few of Sydney's lesser-known delights.

If you have 3 days

Start with an afternoon Sydney Harbour Explorer cruise for some of the best views of the city. Follow the cruise with a walking tour of The Rocks, the nation's birthplace, and take a sunset walk up onto the **Sydney Harbour Bridge** 24 for more great views. The following day, take a Sydney Explorer tour, which will still allow you enough time to see the famous **Sydney Opera House** 52 and relax at sunset in the nearby **Royal Botanic Gardens** 53 and **Domain South** 50 and **Domain North** 56 parks. On the third day, explore the city center highlights, with another spectacular panorama from the top of **Sydney Tower** 65. Include a walk around the Macquarie Street area, a living reminder of Sydney's colonial history, and the contrasting experience of futuristic Darling Harbour, with its museums, aquarium, cafés, and lively shopping center.

If you have 6 days

Follow the three-day itinerary above, then visit Kings Cross, Darlinghurst, and Paddington on the fourth day. You could continue to **Bondi** 81, Australia's most famous beach. The next day, catch the ferry to **Manly** 82 to visit its beach and the historic Quarantine Station. From here, take an afternoon bus tour to the northern beaches, or return to the city to shop or visit museums and galleries. Options for the last day include a visit to a wildlife or national park, **Taronga Zoo** 13, or the **Sydney Olympic Park** 87 west of the city.

If you have 10 days

Follow the six-day itinerary above, and then travel outside the city by rental car or with an organized tour. Take day trips to the Blue Mountains, Hunter Valley, **Ku-ring-gai Chase National Park** 83, the Hawkesbury River, or the historic city of Parramatta to Sydney's west. You may also like to explore some lesser-known corners of the city. Travel on the Bondi Explorer bus around the eastern suburbs to **Vaucluse** 6, or the charming harborside village of **Watsons Bay** 7 and its beaches. You could take a boat tour to the historic harbor island of **Fort Denison** 14, play a round of golf or some tennis, or just spend a day shopping or relaxing on the beach.

close enough for a day trip, to get the most out of these places you would do far better to plan an overnight stop.

Numbers in the text correspond to numbers in the margin and on the Sydney Harbour, Sydney, Greater Sydney maps.

When to Visit Sydney

The best times to visit Sydney are during late spring and early fall. The spring months of October and November are pleasantly warm, although the ocean is slightly cool for swimming. The midsummer months of December through February are typically hot and humid, with fierce tropical downpours in January and February. In the early autumn months of March and April, weather is typically stable and comfortable, outdoor city life is still in full swing, and the ocean is at its warmest. Even the coolest winter months of July and August typically stay mild and sunny, with average daily maximum temperatures in the low 60s.

Sydney Harbour

Captain Arthur Phillip, commander of the first European fleet to sail here and the first governor of the colony, called Sydney Harbour "in extent and security, very superior to any other that I have ever seen—containing a considerable number of coves, formed by narrow necks of land, mostly rocks, covered with timber." Two centuries later, few would dispute that the harbor is one of nature's extraordinary creations.

Officially titled Port Jackson, the harbor is in its depths a river valley carved by the Parramatta and Lane Cove rivers and the many creeks that flow in from the north. The rising sea level at the end of the last Ice Age submerged the valley floor, leaving only the walls. In the earliest days of the colony, the military laid claim to much of the harbor's 240 km (149 mi) of shoreline. Few of these military areas were ever fortified or cleared, and as a result, much of the foreshore has survived in its natural splendor. Several pockets of land are now protected within Sydney Harbour National Park. Such areas as North, South, and Middle Heads and the islands that you'll pass on a harbor cruise are still much as they were in Governor Phillip's day.

This tour is based on the route followed by the State Transit Authority ferries on their daily Afternoon Harbour Cruise. The Coffee Cruise run by Captain Cook Cruises follows a similar course. The tour takes in the eastern half of the harbor, from the city to the Heads and Middle Harbour. This is the Sydney at its most glamorous, but the harbor west of the city has its own areas of historic and natural distinction, as well as Homebush Bay, which was the main site for the Olympic Summer Games in 2000. Note that ferries don't actually stop at these locations—this is purely a sightseeing adventure, though you can certainly visit many of these sights by car or public transportation. ⇨ For further details about these trips, *see* Boat Tours *in* Sydney A to Z.

a good cruise

As the vessel leaves the ferry wharves at Circular Quay ▶, the transportation hub just southeast of the Sydney Harbour Bridge, it crosses **Sydney Cove** ❶, where the ships of the First Fleet dropped anchor in January 1788. After rounding Bennelong Point, the site of the Sydney Opera House, the boat turns east and crosses **Farm Cove** ❷, passing the Royal Botanic Gardens. The tall Gothic Revival chimneys just visible above the trees belong to Government House, formerly the official residence of the state governor.

Garden Island ❸, the country's largest naval dockyard, is easily identifiable across Woolloomooloo (say "*wool*-uh-muh-loo") Bay by its squadrons of sleek gray warships. Dominated by several tall apartment blocks, Darling Point, the next headland, marks the beginning of Sydney's desirable eastern suburbs. **Point Piper** ❹, across Double Bay, is famous as the ritziest address in the country. The large expanse of water to the east of Point Piper is **Rose Bay** ❺, bordered by another highly desirable, but somewhat more affordable, harborside suburb.

Beyond Rose Bay, **Vaucluse** ❻ is yet another suburb that conveys social stature. The area is named after Vaucluse House, the sandstone mansion built by 19th-century explorer, publisher, and politician William Wentworth. The house is hidden from view, but you can see the Grecian columns of Strickland House, a former convalescent home. To the east is Shark Bay, part of Nielsen Park and one of the most popular harbor beaches. **Watsons Bay** ❼, a former fishing village, is the easternmost suburb on the harbor's south side. Beyond, the giant sandstone buttress of South Head rises high above the crashing Pacific breakers.

Beaches

The boom of the surf could well be Sydney's summer theme song: forty beaches, including world-famous Bondi, lie within the Sydney metropolitan area. Spoiled by a choice of ocean or sheltered harbor beaches—and with an average water temperature of 20°C (68°F)—many Sydneysiders naturally head for the shore on the weekends.

Food

1

In the culinary new world order, Sydney is one of the glamorous global food centers, ranking right up there with London and New York. Sydney-trained chefs are making their presence felt far and wide, and Australian food magazines are giddy about what's going on at home. "Foodies" vacationing in Sydney are especially in luck—many of Sydney's top sightseeing spots are of equal food interest. The Opera House has the Guillaume at Bennelong, and The Rocks has Quay. Then there are the food burbs of Bondi, Surry Hills, and Darlinghurst, where the smells of good espresso, sizzling grills, and aromatic stir-fry hover in the air.

So what's to eat in Sydney? There's tuna tartare with flying fish roe and wasabi; emu prosciutto; five-spice duck; shiitake-mushroom pie; and sweet turmeric barramundi curry. This is the stuff of Mod-Oz (modern-Australian) cooking, and Sydney is where it flourishes, fueled by local produce and guided by Mediterranean and Asian techniques. Sydney's dining scene is now as sunny and cosmopolitan as the city itself, and there are diverse and exotic culinary adventures to suit every appetite. A meal at Tetsuya's, Claude's, or Rockpool constitutes a crash course in this dazzling culinary language.

Particularly if you come from the Northern Hemisphere, you may find new taste sensations on the seafood menu: rudder fish, barramundi, blue-eye, kingfish, John Dory, ocean perch, and parrot fish; then Yamba prawns, Balmain bugs, sweet Sydney rock oysters, mud crab, spanner crab, yabbies (small freshwater crayfish), and marrons (freshwater lobsters). A visit to the city's fish markets at Pyrmont, just five minutes from the city center, will tell you much about Sydney's diet.

Of course, Sydney food always tastes better when enjoyed outdoors at a sidewalk table, in a sun-drenched courtyard—or best of all, in full view of that glorious harbor.

A Harbor Sail

The often photographed Sydney Harbour offers many boating opportunities; whether aboard a cruiseboat tour or on an active sailing or kayaking trip, being on the water is an essential element of the Sydney experience. *See* the Sydney Harbour section for tours of the harbor by boat.

National Parks & Wildlife

The national parks and numerous nature reserves of Greater Sydney make it easy to experience the sights and sounds of wild Australia or the country's Aboriginal heritage. The lands protected by Sydney Harbour National Park provide a habitat for many native species of plants and animals that are found on no other continent. Ku-ring-gai Chase National Park to the north has engravings and paintings created and left here by the area's original inhabitants, the Guringai Aboriginal people, in a gorgeous park setting. Royal National Park to the south encompasses large tracts of coastline and bushland where you can experience Australia's remarkable flora and fauna in the wild.

Sports

Whether it's watching or playing, Sydneysiders are devoted to sports, and the city's benign climate makes even water sports a year-round possibility. However, cricket—the most popular summer spectator sport—takes place on land. Australia plays both one-day and international test matches against England, the West Indies, Sri Lanka, Pakistan, South Africa, and India at the Sydney Cricket Ground. The biggest winter game is rugby league, but rugby union and Australian-rules football also attract passionate followings.

North Head is the boat's next landmark, followed by the beachside suburb of Manly and the **Quarantine Station** ⑧. Once used to protect Sydney from disease, the station today documents a fascinating chapter in the nation's history. The vessel then enters **Middle Harbour** ⑨—formed by creeks that spring from the forested peaks of Ku-ring-gai Chase National Park—where you'll pass the beach at Clontarf on the right side of the vessel and sail through the Spit Bridge. On the return voyage to the bridge after exploring Middle Harbour, you'll pass by the suburb of **Castlecrag** ⑩, founded by Walter Burley Griffin, the American architect responsible for the design of Canberra.

Just before the vessel returns to the main body of the harbor, look right for the popular beach at Balmoral and **Middle Head** ⑪, part of Sydney Harbour National Park and the site of mid-19th-century cannons and fortifications. During that period, Sydney Harbour was a regular port of call for American whaling ships, whose crews were responsible for the name of nearby **Chowder Bay** ⑫. Sailing deeper into the harbor, the vessel passes **Taronga Zoo** ⑬, where you might spot some of the animals through the foliage.

The vessel now heads back toward the Harbour Bridge, passing the tiny island of **Fort Denison** ⑭, Sydney's most prominent fortification. On the point at **Kirribilli** ⑮, almost opposite the Opera House, you can catch glimpses of two colonial-style houses: the official Sydney residences of the governor-general and prime minister, who are otherwise based in Canberra. From the north side of the harbor, the vessel crosses back to Circular Quay, where the tour ends.

TIMING   This scenic cruise, aboard one of the State Transit Authority ferries, takes 2½ hours and operates year-round. Refreshments are available on the boat's lower deck. For the best views, begin the voyage on the right side.

What to See

⑩ **Castlecrag.** Walter Burley Griffin, an associate of Frank Lloyd Wright, founded this pretty, calm, and prestigious Middle Harbour suburb after he designed the layout for Canberra. In 1924, after working on the national capital and in Melbourne, the American architect moved to Sydney and built a number of houses that are notable for their harmony with the surrounding bushland. About eight of his houses survive, although none are visible from the harbor.

⑫ **Chowder Bay.** In the 19th century the American whalers who anchored here would collect oysters from the rocks and make shellfish soup—which gave the bay its name. Its location is identifiable by a cluster of wooden buildings at water's edge and twin oil-storage tanks.

❷ **Farm Cove.** The original convict-settlers established their first gardens on this bay's shores, now home to the **Royal Botanic Gardens**. The enterprise was not a success: The soil was too sandy for agriculture, and most of the crops fell victim to pests, marauding animals, and hungry convicts. Few of the convicts had any agricultural experience, and for several years the colony hovered on the brink of starvation. The long seawall was constructed from the 1840s onward to enclose the previously swampy foreshore.

14 Fort Denison. For a brief time in the early days of the colony, convicts who committed petty offenses were kept on this harbor island, where they existed on a meager diet that gave the island its early name: Pinchgut. The island was progressively fortified from 1841, when it was also decided to strengthen the existing defenses at Dawes Point Battery, under the Harbour Bridge. Work was abandoned when cash ran out and not completed until 1857, when fears of Russian expansion in the Pacific spurred further fortification. The fort has never fired a shot in anger, although it took a direct hit from the USS *Chicago* when the American cruiser fired on a Japanese submarine that had infiltrated the harbor in 1942. Today, the firing of the fort's cannon signals not an imminent invasion, but merely the hour—one o'clock. The National Parks and Wildlife Service runs 2½-hour tours to Fort Denison. Tours depart from Cadman's Cottage, 110 George Street, The Rocks. ⊠ *Sydney Harbour* ☎ 02/9247–5033 ⊕ *www.npws.nsw.gov.au/parks/metro/harbour/shfortdenison.html* ⊠ *A$22* ☉ *Tours: Mon.–Sat. at 11:30 and 3; Sun. at 11:30 and 2:30.*

3 Garden Island. Although it is still known as an "island," this promontory was connected with the mainland in 1942. During the 1941–45 War of the Pacific, Australia's largest naval base and dockyard was a front-line port for Allied ships. This battle fleet was the target of three Japanese midget submarines that were launched from a mother submarine at sea on the night of May 31, 1942. Two of the three penetrated the antisubmarine net that had been laid across the harbor, and one sank the HMAS *Kuttabul,* a ferry being used as a naval depot ship, with a loss of 21 lives. Despite the ensuing chaos, two of the midget submarines were confirmed sunk.

Part of the naval base is now open to the public. This small park area has superb views of the Opera House and glimpses of the dockyard facilities, including the largest shipyard crane in the Southern Hemisphere. Access to the site is via ferry from Circular Quay.

15 Kirribilli. Residents of this attractive suburb opposite the city and Opera House have million-dollar views. Two of Sydney's most important mansions stand here. The more modest of the two is **Kirribilli House,** which is the official Sydney home of the prime minister and not open to the public. Next door and far more prominent is **Admiralty House** (☎ 02/9955–4095)—the Sydney residence of the governor-general, the Queen's representative in Australia. This impressive residence is occasionally open for inspection.

9 Middle Harbour. Except for the yachts moored in the sandy coves, the upper reaches of Middle Harbour are almost exactly as they were when the first Europeans set eyes on Port Jackson, more than 200 years ago. Tucked away in idyllic bushland are tranquil suburbs just a short drive from the city. Many of the houses in this part of the harbor are set back from the waterline. By the time they were built, planning authorities no longer allowed direct water frontage—in contrast to many of the older suburbs on the south side of the harbor.

11 Middle Head. Despite its benign appearance today, Sydney Harbour once bristled with armaments. In the mid-19th century, faced with ex-

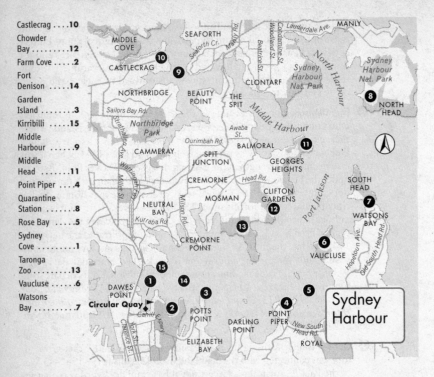

pansionist European powers hungry for new colonies, the authorities erected artillery positions on the headlands to guard harbor approaches. At Middle Head you can still see the rectangular gun emplacements set into the cliff face; however, the guns have never been fired at an enemy.

❹ **Point Piper.** The majestic Gatsby-esque houses in this harborside suburb are a prized address for Sydney's rich and famous. This was once the Sydney home of Tom Cruise and Nicole Kidman, and the record for the suburb's—and Australia's—most expensive house is held by Altona, which fetched A$28.5 million when it sold in 2002.

❽ **Quarantine Station.** From the 1830s onward, ship passengers who arrived with contagious diseases were isolated on this outpost in the shadow of North Head until pronounced free of illness. Among the last to be quartered here, albeit voluntarily, were the victims of Cyclone Tracy, which devastated Darwin in 1974. Ten years later, after its brief use as a staging post for a group of Vietnamese orphans, the Quarantine Station was closed, its grim purpose finally brought to an end by modern medicine. You can take a 90-minute guided tour of the station with a ranger from the National Parks and Wildlife Service, caretakers of the site. Another option is a three-hour evening Ghost Tour—the station reputedly has its fair share of specters. This tour includes supper, and reservations are essential. The basic tour departs from Manly Wharf, while the Ghost Tour departs from the visitor center at the Quarantine Station. Catch a ferry to Manly from Circular Quay and then take a taxi from Manly Wharf, or take bus No. 135, departing the wharf at 1:08 PM. ✉ *North Head, Manly* ☎ *02/9247–5033* ⊕ *www.manlyquarantine.com* ✉ *A$11 basic tour, A$22–A$27.50 Ghost Tour* ☉ *Basic tour Mon., Wed., Fri., and weekends 1:15; Ghost Tour Wed., Fri., and weekends 7:30 PM.*

❺ **Rose Bay.** This large bay was once a base for the Qantas flying boats that provided the only passenger air service between Australia and

America and Europe. The last flying boat departed Rose Bay in the 1960s, but the "airstrip" is still used by float planes on scenic flights connecting Sydney with the Hawkesbury River and the Central Coast.

1 Sydney Cove. Bennelong Point and the Sydney Opera House to the east and Circular Quay West and The Rocks to the west enclose this cove, which was named after Lord Sydney, the British home secretary at the time the colony was founded. The settlement itself was to be known as New Albion, but the name never caught on. Instead the city took its name from this tiny bay.

★ ☾ **13 Taronga Zoo.** In Sydney's zoo, in a natural bush area on the harbor's north shore, lives an extensive array of Australian fauna, including everybody's favorite marsupial, the koala. The zoo has taken great care to create spacious enclosures that simulate natural habitats. The hillside setting is steep in parts, and a complete tour can be tiring, but you can use the map distributed free at the entrance gate to plan a leisurely route. Basic children's strollers are provided free of charge. The easiest way to get here from the city is by ferry. From Taronga Wharf a bus or the cable car will take you up the hill to the main entrance. The ZooPass, a combined ferry-zoo ticket, is available at Circular Quay. ✉ *Bradleys Head Rd., Mosman* ☎ *02/9969–2777* ⊕ *www.zoo.nsw.gov.au* ✇ *A$23* ☉ *Daily 9–5.*

6 Vaucluse. The palatial homes in this glamorous harbor suburb provide a glimpse of Sydney's high society. The small beaches at Nielsen Park and Parsley Bay are safe for swimming, and both are packed with families in summer.

The suburb takes its name from **Vaucluse House**, one of Sydney's most illustrious remaining historic mansions. Most of the Gothic Revival building was constructed in the 1830s for the family of William Charles Wentworth, an explorer and statesman also known as the "Father of the Australian Constitution." The 15-room house is furnished in period style, and its lush gardens, managed by the Historic Houses Trust, are open to the public. The tea rooms, built in the style of an Edwardian conservatory, are a popular spot for lunch and afternoon tea on weekends. The house is one of the stops on the Bondi Explorer bus. ✉ *Wentworth Rd., Vaucluse* ☎ *02/9388–7922* ⊕ *www.hht.nsw.gov.au* ✇ *A$7* ☉ *House, Tues.–Sun. 10–4:30; grounds, daily 10–5.*

7 Watsons Bay. Established as a military base and fishing settlement in the colony's early years, Watsons Bay is a charming suburb that has held on to its village atmosphere, despite the exorbitant prices paid for tiny cottages here. In addition to being a delightful spot on a sunny day, Camp Cove, the bay's main beach, is of some historical importance. It was intended that the convicts who were to be Australia's first settlers would establish a community at Botany Bay, which had been explored by Captain Cook in 1770. However, as Captain Phillip found when he arrived 18 years later, the lack of fresh water at Botany Bay made settlement impossible. After a few days, he set off to explore Port Jackson, which had been named but not visited by Cook. Phillip rounded the Heads and landed on a beach that he named Camp Cove.

In comparison to Watsons Bay's tranquil harborside, the side that faces the ocean is dramatic and tortured, with the raging sea dashing itself against the sheer, 200-foot sandstone cliffs of The Gap. The walkway that runs along the top of The Gap is famous for its views, and has also gained an unfortunate reputation as a popular suicide spot.

When the sun shines, the 15-minute cliff-top stroll along South Head Walkway between The Gap and the **Macquarie Lighthouse** affords some of

Sydney's most inspiring views. Convict-architect Francis Greenway (jailed for forgery) designed the original lighthouse here, Australia's first, in 1818. Although the present structure dates to 1883, it captures much of the satisfying simplicity and symmetry of the Georgian original. The first light-house keeper was Robert Watson, who sailed to Australia as quarter-master on one of the ships of the First Fleet and who gave his name to Watsons Bay. ⊠ *Old South Head Rd., Vaucluse.*

The Rocks & Sydney Harbour Bridge

The Rocks is the birthplace not just of Sydney but of modern Australia. Here, the 11 ships of the First Fleet, the first of England's 800-plus ships carrying convicts to the penal colony, dropped anchor in 1788, and this stubby peninsula enclosing the western side of Sydney Cove became known simply as The Rocks.

The first crude wooden huts erected by the convicts were followed by simple houses made from mud bricks cemented together by a mixture of sheep's wool and mud. The rain soon washed this rough mortar away, and no buildings in The Rocks survive from the earliest settlement. Most of the architecture dates from the Victorian era, by which time Sydney had become a thriving port. Warehouses lining the waterfront were backed by a row of tradesmen's shops, banks, and taverns, and above them, ascending Observatory Hill, rose a tangled mass of alleyways lined with the cottages of seamen and wharf laborers. By the late 1800s all who could afford to had moved out of the area, and it was widely regarded as a rough, tough, squalid part of town. As late as 1900 bubonic plague swept through The Rocks, prompting the government to offer a bounty for dead rats in an effort to exterminate their disease-carrying fleas.

The character of The Rocks area changed considerably when the Sydney Harbour Bridge was constructed during the 1920s and 1930s, when many old houses, and even entire streets, were demolished to make room for the bridge's southern approach route. The bridge took almost nine years to build and replaced the ferries that once carried passengers and freight across the harbor.

It is only since the 1980s that The Rocks has become appreciated for its historic significance, and extensive restoration has transformed the area. Here you can see the evolution of a society almost from its inception to the present, and yet The Rocks is anything but a stuffy tutorial. History stands side by side with shops, cafés, and museums.

a good walk

Begin at Circular Quay, the lively waterfront area where Sydney's ferry, bus, and train systems converge. Follow the quay toward Harbour Bridge and, as you round the curve, turn left and walk about 20 yards into First Fleet Park. The map on the platform here describes the colony of 1808. The Tank Stream entered Sydney Cove at this very spot. This tiny watercourse, the colony's first source of fresh water, decided the location of the first European settlement on Australian soil.

Return to the waterfront and take the paved walkway toward Harbour Bridge. The massive art deco–style building to your left is the **Museum of Contemporary Art** ⑯, devoted to painting, sculpture, film, video, and performance art from the past 20 years.

Continue on the walkway around Circular Quay West; when you reach the Moreton Bay fig trees in the circular bed, look left. The bronze statue beneath the trees is the figure of **William Bligh** ⑰ of HMS *Bounty* fame. To the right is a two-story, cream-color stone house, **Cadman's Cottage** ⑱. Built in 1816, it is Sydney's oldest surviving house. The futuristic building ahead of you on the waterfront is the **Overseas Passenger Terminal** ⑲, the main mooring for passenger liners in Sydney.

Have a look inside Cadman's Cottage and then climb the stairs leading to George Street. Note the original gas street lamp at the top of these steps. Turn right, and immediately on the right stands the **Sydney Visitors Information Centre** ⑳, which has a bookshop and an information counter with useful leaflets about the city.

After leaving the Information Centre, turn right past the redbrick facade of the Australian Steam Navigation Company. Continue down the hill and steps on the right to **Campbells Cove** ㉑ and its warehouses. The waterfront restaurants and cafés are a pleasant spot for a drink or meal, although you pay for the view.

Walk back up the steps beside the warehouses and cross to Upper George Street, lined with restored 19th-century buildings. Across the road is Atherden Street, Sydney's shortest lane. Note the small garden of staghorn ferns that has been painstakingly cultivated on tiny rock ledges at the end of this street. Just behind the Westpac Bank on the corner of George and Playfair streets is the **Westpac Banking Museum** ㉒, which exhibits early Australian coinage.

Continue up George Street toward the Sydney Harbour Bridge until you are directly beneath the bridge's massive girders. The green iron cubicle standing on the landward side of George Street is a gentleman's toilet, modeled on the Parisian pissoir. Toilets such as this were fairly common in the early 1900s, but they have since been replaced by more discreet brick constructions—such as the modern rest room that stands behind this sole survivor.

Walk under the bridge to **Dawes Point Park** ㉓ for excellent views of the harbor, including the Opera House and the small island of Fort Denison. This park also provides an unusual perspective from underneath the **Sydney Harbour Bridge** ㉔—an unmistakable symbol of the city, and one of the world's widest long-span bridges.

Turn your back on the harbor and walk up **Lower Fort Street** ㉕, which runs to the right of the Harbour View Hotel. Continue to the corner of Windmill Street, where you'll find the wedge-shape Hero of Waterloo, one of the oldest pubs in the city.

Lower Fort Street ends at **Argyle Place** ㉖, built by Governor Macquarie and named after his home county in Scotland. The houses and other buildings here in the minisuburb of Millers Point are worth an inspection—particularly **Holy Trinity Church** ㉗ on the left-hand side and the Lord Nelson Hotel, which lies to one side of the village green.

Argyle Place is dominated by **Observatory Hill** ㉘, the site of the colony's first windmill and, later, a signal station. If you have the energy to climb the steps that lead to the hill, you can reach a park shaded by giant Moreton Bay fig trees, where you will be rewarded with one of the finest views in Sydney. On top of the hill is the **Sydney Observatory** ㉙, now a museum of astronomy. You can also follow the path behind the Observatory to the National Trust Centre and the **S. H. Ervin Gallery** ㉚, which mounts changing exhibitions with Australian themes.

Leave Argyle Place and walk down Argyle Street into the dark tunnel of the **Argyle Cut** ㉛. On the lower side of the cut and to the left, the Argyle Stairs lead up through an archway. Several flights of steps and a 15-minute walk will take you onto Harbour Bridge and to the South East Pylon for a dizzying view of the Opera House and the city. To get

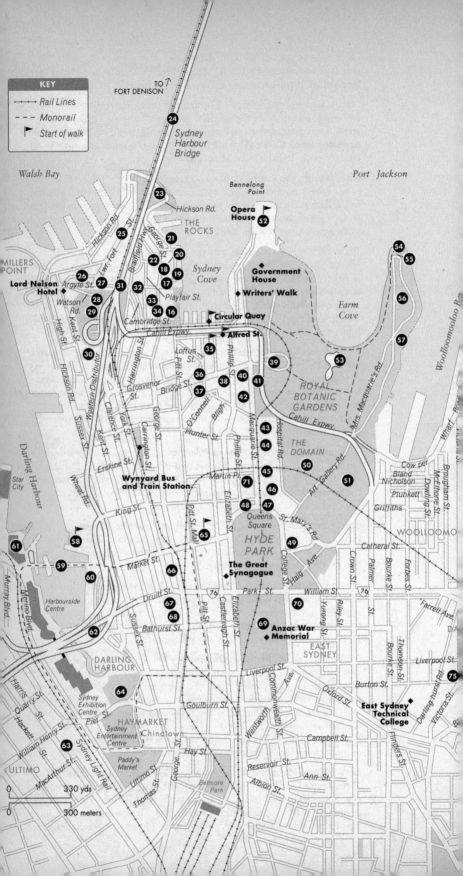

+—+ *Rail Lines*

- - - *Monorail*

⚑ *Start of walk*

TO ↑
FORT DENISON

Walsh Bay

Port Jackson

Sydney
Harbour
Bridge

24

23

Bennelong
Point

Hickson Rd.

THE
ROCKS

Opera
House
52

MILLERS
POINT

25

Lord Nelson
Hotel ◆

26

27

31

32

Argyle St.

Watson
Rd.

28

29

21

22 18 19
20
17
33
34 16

Playfair St.

Sydney
Cove

Cambridge St.

Circular Quay

Government
House ◆

Writers' Walk ◆

Farm
Cove

54
55

56

Cahill Expwy.

Alfred St.

57

High St.

Kent St.

30

Hickson Rd.

Western Distributor

Harrington St.

Grosvenor
St.

35

Loftus
St.

36

37

Bridge St.

38

O'Connell St.

Bligh St.

Pitt St.

Phillip St.

40

42

41

39

53

ROYAL
BOTANIC
GARDENS

Mrs. Macquarie's Rd.

Woolloomooloo Rd.

Clarence St.

Sussex St.

York St.

Kent St.

George St.

Carrington St.

Erskine St.

Wheat Rd.

Star
City

Darling Harbour

Hunter St.

Macquarie St.

43

44

THE
DOMAIN

Cahill Expwy.

Art Gallery Rd.

50

51

Cow per
Bland
Nicholson
Plunkett
Griffiths

WOOLLOOMO

Wynyard Bus
and Train Station ⚑

Martin Pl.

71

45

46

Hospital Rd.

McElhone St.
Broughton St.
Dowling St.
Wharf Road

Elizabeth St.

48

47

St. Mary's Rd.

Catheral St.

61

58

King St.

Market St.

60

59

66

Pitt St. Mall

65

Queens
Square

HYDE
PARK

49

College St.

Haig Ave.

Crown St.

Palmer St.

Bourke St.

Forbes St.

Merino Blvd.

Murray Blvd.

Harbourside
Centre

Druitt St.

67

68

62

Sussex St.

Bathurst St.

The Great
Synagogue ◆

Park St.

76

Castlereagh St.

Elizabeth St.

69 Anzac War
◆ Memorial

William St.

70

76

EAST
SYDNEY

Yurong St.

Riley St.

Oxford St.

Bourke St.

Thomson St.

Liverpool St.

Farrell Ave.

DA

75

Harris St.

Quarry St.

Hackett St.

William Henry St.

64

63

DARLING
HARBOUR

Sydney
Exhibition
Centre

Pier St.

HAYMARKET

Chinatown

Sydney
Light Rail

Sydney
Entertainment
Centre

Paddy's
Market

Goulburn St.

Hay St.

Thomas St.

Ultimo St.

George St.

Belmore
Park

Liverpool St.

Commonwealth St.

Wentworth Ave.

Campbell St.

Reservoir St.

Albion St.

Ann St.

EAST
SYDNEY
Technical
College ◆

Burton St.

Flinders St.

Victoria St.

Darlinghurst Rd.

MacArthur St.

ULTIMO

0 ———— 330 yds

0 ———— 300 meters

Central Sydney

to the Sydney Harbour Bridge walkway from the top of the stairs, cross the road, walk left for 20 yards, and then follow the signs to the walkway and pylon. You should allow at least 1 hour for this detour.

The walk resumes at the foot of the steps on Argyle Street. Continue down the street and turn left under the archway inscribed with the words **Argyle Stores** ㉜. The old warehouses around this courtyard have been converted to upscale fashion shops and galleries. Leave the Argyle Stores and cross onto Harrington Street.

The Gumnut Café is on the left-hand side of this street. Ten yards beyond the café is the **Suez Canal** ㉝, a narrow lane that runs down the incline toward George Street. Turn right at **Nurses Walk** ㉞, another of the area's historic and atmospheric back streets, then left into Surgeons Court and left again onto George Street. On the left is the handsome sandstone facade of the former Rocks Police Station, now a crafts gallery. From this point, Circular Quay is only a short walk away.

TIMING   The attractions of The Rocks are many, so to walk this route—even without lingering in museums or galleries or walking up to the Sydney Harbour Bridge—you should allow about three hours. The Museum of Contemporary Art, Sydney Observatory, and the S. H. Ervin Gallery each require an hour at the very least. The Rocks' numerous souvenir shops can absorb even more time.

The area is often very crowded on weekends, when The Rocks Market on George Street presents a serious distraction from sightseeing. At the end of the workweek, office workers in a TGIF mood flock to the local pubs, which become rowdy after about 10 PM.

What to See

㉛ **Argyle Cut.** Argyle Street links Argyle Place with George Street, and the thoroughfare is dominated by the Argyle Cut and its massive walls. In the days before the cut was made, the sandstone ridge here was a major barrier to traffic crossing between Circular Quay and Millers Point. In 1843, convict work gangs hacked at the sandstone with hand tools for 2½ years before the project was abandoned due to lack of progress. Work restarted in 1857, when drills, explosives, and paid labor completed the job. On the lower side of the Cut, an archway leads to the **Argyle Stairs**, which begin the climb from Argyle Street up to the Sydney Harbour Bridge walkway, and a spectacular view from the South East Pylon.

㉖ **Argyle Place.** With all the traditional requirements of an English green—a pub at one end, a church at the other, and grass in between—this charming enclave in the suburb of Millers Point is unusual for Sydney. Argyle Place is lined with 19th-century houses and cottages on its northern side and overlooked by Observatory Hill to the south.

need a break? While in the west end of Argyle Place, consider the liquid temptations of the **Lord Nelson,** Sydney's oldest hotel, which has been licensed to serve alcohol since 1842. The sandstone pub has its own brewery on the premises. One of its specialties is Quayle Ale, named after the former U.S. vice president, who "sank a schooner" here during his 1989 visit to Australia. ⊠ *19 Kent St., Millers Point* ☎ *02/ 9251–4044* ⊕ *www.lordnelson.com.au.*

㉜ **Argyle Stores.** These solid sandstone warehouses date to the late 1820s and now house chic gift and souvenir shops, clothes boutiques, and cafés. ⊠ *Argyle St. opposite Harrington St., The Rocks.*

⑱ **Cadman's Cottage.** Sydney's oldest building, completed in 1816, has a history that outweighs its modest dimensions. John Cadman was a convict who was sentenced for life to New South Wales for stealing a horse. He later became superintendent of government boats, a position that entitled him to live in the upper story of this house. The water practically once lapped at Cadman's doorstep, and the original seawall still stands at the front of the house. The small extension on the side of the cottage was built to lock up the oars of Cadman's boats, since oars would have been a necessity for any convict attempting to escape by sea. The upper floor of Cadman's Cottage is now a National Parks and Wildlife Service bookshop and information center for Sydney Harbour National Park. ⊠ *110 George St., The Rocks* ☎ *02/9247–8861* ⊕ *www.cityofsydney.nsw.gov.au/hs_hb_cadmans_cottage.asp* ☽ *Mon. 10–3, Tues.–Fri. 9–4:30, weekends 11–4.*

㉑ Campbells Cove. Robert Campbell was a Scottish merchant who is sometimes referred to as the "father of Australian commerce." Campbell broke the stranglehold that the British East India Company exercised over seal and whale products, which were New South Wales's only exports in those early days. The cove's atmospheric sandstone **Campbells Storehouse,** built from 1838 onward, now houses waterside restaurants. The pulleys that were used to hoist cargoes still hang on the upper level of the warehouses.

The cove is also the mooring for Sydney's fully operational tall ships—including the HMAV *Bounty,* an authentic replica of the original 18th-century vessel—which conduct theme cruises around the harbor.

㉓ Dawes Point Park. The wonderful views of the harbor, Fort Denison, and, since the 1930s, the Harbour Bridge have made this park and its location noteworthy for centuries. Named for William Dawes, a First Fleet marine officer and astronomer who established the colony's first basic observatory nearby in 1788, this park was also once the site of a fortification known as Dawes Battery. The cannon on the hillside pointing toward the Opera House came from the ships of the First Fleet.

Harrington Street area. The small precinct around this street forms one of The Rocks' most interesting areas. Many old cottages, houses, and warehouses here have been converted into hotels. Between Harrington Street and George Street are some historical and creatively named alleyways to explore, including Nurses Walk and Suez Canal.

㉗ Holy Trinity Church. Every morning redcoats would march to this 1840 Argyle Place church from Dawes Point Battery (now Dawes Point Park), and it became commonly known as the Garrison Church. As the regimental plaques and colors around the walls testify, the church still retains a close military association. The tattered ensign on the left wall was carried into battle by Australian troops during the Boer War, in which many Australians enlisted to help Great Britain in its war with South Africans of Dutch ancestry. During that conflict, Australian officer Lieutenant Harry Morant was court-martialed and executed by a British firing squad for carrying out reprisals against Boer prisoners. The incident provoked outrage in parts of Australian society, and marked the last time that an Australian soldier would be dealt with by a British military court. ⊠ *Argyle Pl., Millers Point* ☎ *02/9247–1268* ☽ *Daily 9–5.*

㉕ Lower Fort Street. At one time the handsome Georgian houses along this street, originally a rough track leading from the Dawes Point Battery to Observatory Hill, were among the best addresses in Sydney. Elaborate wrought-iron lacework still graces many of the facades. Some residents can trace their family roots to this address for several generations.

Hero of Waterloo, which dates from 1844, is Sydney's second-oldest hotel. Gold fever struck during the middle of the 19th century, and it was not uncommon for an entire ship's crew to desert and head for the goldfields as soon as the ship reached Sydney. Captains often resorted to skul-duggery to recruit a new crew, and legend has it that many a lad who drank with a generous sea captain in the Hero would wake the next morning on a heaving deck, already out of sight of land. ⊠ *81 Lower Fort St., The Rocks* ☎ *02/9252–4553* ⏱ *Daily 10 AM–11 PM.*

16 Museum of Contemporary Art. Andy Warhol, Roy Lichtenstein, Cindy Sherman, and local artists Juan Devila, Maria Kozic, and Imants Tillers are just some of the well-known names whose works hang in this ponderous Art Deco building. The MCA houses one of Australia's most important collections of modern art, as well as two significant collections of Aboriginal art. The museum's café, with outdoor seating beside the harbor, serves breakfast and lunch. ⊠ *Circular Quay W, The Rocks* ☎ *02/9252–4033* ⊕ *www.mca.com.au* ⊡ *Free* ⏱ *Daily 10–5.*

34 Nurses Walk. Cutting across the site of the colony's first hospital, Nurses Walk acquired its name at a time when "Sydney" and "sickness" were synonymous. Many of the 736 convicts who survived the voyage from Portsmouth, England, aboard the First Fleet's 11 ships arrived suffering from dysentery, smallpox, scurvy, and typhoid. A few days after he landed at Sydney Cove, Governor Phillip established a tent hospital to care for the worst cases. Subsequent convict boatloads had even higher rates of death and disease.

Beyond Nurses Walk, the 1882 **Rocks Police Station** on George Street now houses several crafts shops. Note the police truncheon thrust into the lion's mouth above the doorway, an architectural motif that appears on at least one other of Sydney's Victorian police stations.

need a break? At the **Gumnut Café** (⊠ 28 Harrington St., The Rocks ☎ 02/9247–9591) a painless history lesson comes with a delicious lunch. A convict-built well still stands here, in what is The Rock's second-oldest building—originally the 1830 residence of blacksmith William Reynolds. You can still see bits of seashells embedded in the wall where the original mortar remains. The restaurant tucked away in this sandstone cottage serves delicious salads, pasta dishes, sandwiches, rolls, and cakes. The Gumnut has a devoted clientele, who know the best tables are in the shady back garden, and reservations are necessary at lunchtime. If you're staying in the area, breakfast here is a great start to the day. Prices are moderate.

28 Observatory Hill. The city's highest point, at 145 feet, was known originally as Windmill Hill since the colony's first windmill occupied this breezy spot. Its purpose was to grind grain for flour, but soon after it was built, the canvas sails were stolen, the machinery was damaged in a storm, and the foundations cracked. Before it was 10 years old, the mill was useless. Several other windmills were subsequently erected in the area, however, and this part of The Rocks is still known as Millers Point. In 1848 the signal station at the top of the hill was built. This later became an astronomical observatory, and Windmill Hill changed its name to Observatory Hill. Until 1982 the metal ball on the tower of the observatory was cranked up the mast every afternoon and dropped at precisely one o'clock so ship captains could set their chronometers.

19 Overseas Passenger Terminal. Busy **Circular Quay West** is dominated by this multilevel steel and glass port terminal, which is often used by visiting cruise ships. There are a couple of excellent waterfront restaurants at the terminal's northern end, and it's worth taking the escalator to the upper deck for a good view of the harbor and Opera House.

30 **S. H. Ervin Gallery.** This gallery, in the architecturally impressive National Trust Centre just behind Observatory Hill, concentrates on Australian art and architecture from a historical perspective. The changing exhibitions are of a consistently high standard and have shown the work of such well-known Australian artists as Lloyd Rees, Sidney Nolan, Hans Heysen, and Russell Drysdale. The gallery has a bookshop, and there is an outstanding National Trust gift shop next door. ✉ *National Trust Centre, Observatory Hill, Watson Rd., Millers Point* ☎ *02/9258–0123* ⊕ *www.nsw.nationaltrust.org.au/ervin.html* ⊠ *A$6* ⊙ *Tues.–Fri. 11–5, weekends noon–5.*

33 **Suez Canal.** So narrow that two people cannot walk abreast, this alley acquired its name before drains were installed, when rainwater would pour down its funnel-like passageway and gush across George Street. Lanes such as this were once the haunt of the notorious late-19th-century Rocks gangs, when robbery was rife in the area. The "Pushes" (gangs) are remembered in a local wine bar known as The Rocks Push.

24 **Sydney Harbour Bridge.** Sydney's iron colossus, the Harbour Bridge was a monumental engineering feat when it was completed in 1932. The roadway is supported by the arch, not by the massive stone pylons, which were added for aesthetic rather than structural reasons. The 1,650-foot-long bridge is 160-feet wide and contains two sets of railway tracks, eight road lanes, a bikeway, and a footpath on both sides. Actor Paul Hogan worked for several years as a rigger on the bridge, long before he tamed the world's wildlife and lowlifes in *Crocodile Dundee.*

There are several ways to experience the bridge and its spectacular views. The first is to follow the walkway from its access point near the Argyle Stairs to the **South East Pylon** (☎ 02/9247–3408). This structure houses a display on the bridge's construction, and you can climb the 200 steps to the lookout and its unbeatable harbor panorama. The fee is A$2, and the display is open daily 10–5.

Another more expensive option is the ⇨ **Special Interest Tours, Bridge-Climb tour** (☎ 02/9252–0077 ⊕ www.bridgeclimb.com.au), which takes you on a guided walking tour to the very top of the Harbour Bridge.

The third option is to walk to the midpoint of the bridge to take in the views free of charge, but be sure to take the eastern footpath, which overlooks the Sydney Opera House. Access is via the stairs on Cumberland Street, close to the ANA Hotel.

29 **Sydney Observatory.** Originally a signaling station for communicating with ships anchored in the harbor, this handsome building on top of Observatory Hill is now an astronomy museum. Within its sandstone walls, hands-on displays—including constellation charts, talking computers, and games—illustrate principles of astronomy. During evening observatory shows, you can tour the building, watch videos, and, weather permitting, get a close-up view of the universe through a 16-inch mirror telescope. Reservations are required for the evening show, and times vary depending on the season. ⊠ *Observatory Hill, Watson Rd., Millers Point* ☎ *02/9217–0485* ⊕ *www.phm.gov.au/observe* ⊠ *Free; evening show A$10* ⊙ *Daily 10–5.*

20 **Sydney Visitors Information Centre.** Once a mariners' mission, this building now offers insight into the history of The Rocks, with displays of artifacts and a short video. Staff can answer questions and make travel bookings, and the informative Rocks Walking Tours depart from here. The building also contains the very popular Sailor's Thai restaurant and a less-expensive canteen. ⊠ *106 George St., The Rocks* ☎ *02/9255–1788* ⊙ *Mar.–Oct., daily 9–5; Nov.–Feb., daily 9–6.*

Upper George Street. The restored warehouses and Victorian terrace houses that line this part of George Street make this a charming section of The Rocks. The covered **Rocks Market** takes place here on weekends.

㉒ **Westpac Banking Museum.** This museum on a lane off George Street displays a collection of coins from the earliest days of the colony of New South Wales. ⬦ *6–8 Playfair St., The Rocks* ☎ *02/9763–5670* ⬦ *Free* ⊙ *Weekdays 9–5, weekends 10–4.*

⑰ **William Bligh statue.** Although history may have painted him as a tyrant, Captain William Bligh of HMS *Bounty* fame was perhaps more unlucky than cruel. In 1806, almost two decades after the infamous mutiny on the ship he commanded, Bligh became governor of New South Wales. Two years later he faced his second mutiny. Bligh had made himself unpopular with the soldiers of the New South Wales Corps, commonly known as the Rum Corps, who were the real power in the colony. When he threatened to end their lucrative monopoly on the liquor trade, he was imprisoned in an incident known as the Rum Rebellion. He spent the next two years as a captive until his successor, Lachlan Macquarie, arrived. Ironically, the statue's gaze frequently rests on HMAV *Bounty*, a replica of Bligh's ship, as it sails around the harbor on daily sightseeing cruises.

Macquarie Street & the Domain South

Some of Sydney's most notable Victorian-era public buildings, as well as one of its finest parks, can be found in this area. In contrast to the simple, utilitarian stone convict cottages of The Rocks, these buildings were constructed at a time when Sydney was experiencing a long period of prosperity, thanks to the gold rushes of the mid-19th century and an agricultural boom. The sandstone just below the surface of many coastal areas adjacent to the city proved an ideal building material—easily honed into the ornamentation so fashionable during the Victorian era.

The sights here will also acquaint you with two of the most remarkable figures in Australian history: Governor Lachlan Macquarie and his government architect, Francis Greenway.

a good walk

This historical walk roughly follows the perimeter of the Royal Botanic Gardens and the Domain South. A shady park bench is never far.

Begin at Circular Quay. Turn your back on the harbor and cross Alfred Street, which runs parallel to the waterfront. The most notable historic building along Alfred Street is the **Customs House** ㉟ ☞. When it was built in the late 1880s, the sandstone structure was surrounded by warehouses storing the fleeces that were the colony's principal export.

Walk up Loftus Street, which runs to the right of the Customs House. In Customs House Lane at the rear you can still see a pulley that was used to lower the wool bales to the dockyard from the top floor of Hinchcliff's Wool Stores.

Follow Loftus Street to the small triangular park on your right, **Macquarie Place** ㊱, which has a number of historical monuments. The southern side of the park is bordered by busy Bridge Street, lined with a number of grandiose Victorian buildings. Across Bridge Street, the **Lands Department** ㊲ is one of the city's finest examples of Victorian public architecture. Walk up Bridge Street past the facade of the Department of Education. The **Museum of Sydney** ㊳ stands on the next block. Built on the site of the first Government House, the museum chronicles the history of the city between 1788 and 1850.

BUILDING SYDNEY

DESCENDED FROM SCOTTISH clan chieftains, Governor Lachlan Macquarie was an accomplished soldier and a man of vision, the first governor to foresee a role for New South Wales as a free society rather than an open prison. Macquarie, who was governor from 1810 to 1821, laid the foundations for that society by establishing a plan for the city, constructing significant public buildings, and advocating that reformed convicts be readmitted to society. Francis Greenway, his government architect, was himself a former prisoner.

Macquarie's policies of equality may seem perfectly reasonable today, but in the early 19th century they marked him as a radical. When his vision of a free society threatened to blur distinctions between soldiers, settlers, and convicts, Macquarie was forced to resign. He was later buried on his Scottish estate, his gravestone inscribed with the words "the Father of Australia."

Macquarie's grand plans for the construction of Sydney might have come to nothing were it not for Francis Greenway. The governor had been continually frustrated by his masters in the Colonial Office in London, who saw no need for an architect in a penal colony. Then, in 1814, fate delivered Greenway into his hands. Greenway had trained as an architect in England, where he was convicted of forgery and sentenced to 14 years in New South Wales. Macquarie seized this opportunity, gave Greenway a ticket of leave that allowed him to work outside the convict system, and set him to work transforming Sydney.

Over the next few years Greenway designed lighthouses, hospitals, convict barracks, and many other essential government buildings, several of which remain to bear witness to his simple but elegant eye. Yet despite his capability as an architect, Greenway was a difficult and temperamental man. When his patron Macquarie returned to England in 1822, Greenway quickly fell from favor and retired to his farm north of Sydney. Some years later he was charged with misappropriating this property, but he was able to produce a deed giving him title to the land. It is now believed that the signature on the title deed is a forgery. Greenway was depicted on one side of the old $10 notes, which went out of circulation early in the 1990s. Only in Australia, perhaps, would a convicted forger occupy pride of place on the currency.

Continue up Bridge Street to the corner of Macquarie Street. The figure on horseback about to gallop down Bridge Street is Edward VII, successor to Queen Victoria. The castellated building behind him is the **Sydney Conservatorium of Music** ㊴, originally built in 1819 as stables for Government House, which is screened by trees near the Opera House.

Your next stop is the lovely 1870s **History House** ㊵, headquarters of the Royal Australian Historical Society. It's just south of Bridge Street on Macquarie Street, Sydney's most elegant boulevard. Opposite History House are the fine wrought-iron **Garden Palace Gates** ㊶, flanking one of the entrances to the Royal Botanic Gardens. A little farther south along Macquarie Street (Number 145) is the **Royal Australasian College of Physicians** ㊷. The patrician facade of this building gives some idea of the way Macquarie Street looked in the 1840s, when it was lined with the homes of the colonial elite.

The ponderous brown building ahead is the **State Library of New South Wales** ㊸. Cross the road toward this building, passing the Light Horse Monument and the Shakespeare Memorial. Australian cavalrymen fought with distinction in several Middle Eastern campaigns during World War I, and the former statue is dedicated to their horses, which were not allowed to return due to Australian quarantine regulations.

Continue along Macquarie Street toward the gates of **State Parliament House** ㊹, in the north wing of the former Rum Hospital. In a stroke of political genius, Governor Macquarie persuaded two merchants to build a hospital for convicts in return for an extremely lucrative three-year monopoly on the importation of rum.

The next building on the left is the Victorian-style **Sydney Hospital** ㊺, constructed to replace the central section of the Rum Hospital, which began to fall apart almost as soon as it was completed. Beyond the hospital is the **Sydney Mint** ㊻, originally the Rum Hospital's southern wing. Next door is the **Hyde Park Barracks** ㊼, commissioned by Macquarie and designed by Greenway to house prisoners. Opposite Hyde Park Barracks is the 1970s high-rise Law Court building. This area is the heart of Sydney's legal district.

Cross Queens Square to the other side of the road, where the figure of Queen Victoria presides over Macquarie Street. To Victoria's left is another Greenway building, **St. James Church** ㊽, originally designed as a courthouse.

Return to the other side of Macquarie Street and walk along College Street to **St. Mary's Cathedral** ㊾. This is Sydney's Roman Catholic cathedral, based on the design of Lincoln Cathedral in England. Both the pointed door arches and flying buttresses are signatures of the Gothic style.

At the rear of the cathedral, cross St. Mary's Road to Art Gallery Road. You are now in the parklands of **the Domain South** ㊿. Continue past the statue of Robert Burns, the Scottish poet. The large trees on the left with enormous roots and drooping limbs are Moreton Bay figs. Despite their name, their fruit is inedible and poisonous—as Captain James Cook discovered when he fed some to his pigs. Directly ahead is the **Art Gallery of New South Wales** (51), housed in a grand Victorian building with modern extensions. The gallery contains the state's largest art collection. From the Art Gallery, you can return to Macquarie Street by crossing the Domain or wandering for a 1 km (½ mi) through the Royal Botanic Gardens. If you have an Explorer bus pass, you can catch the bus back to the city center from the front of the gallery.

TIMING Half a day is sufficient to complete the outlined itinerary, even with stops to inspect the Museum of Sydney, Hyde Park Barracks, and the Art Gallery of New South Wales. Apart from the initial climb from Circular Quay to Macquarie Street, the terrain is flat and easy.

What to See

51 **Art Gallery of New South Wales.** Apart from Canberra's National Gallery, this is the best place to explore the evolution of European-influenced Australian art, as well as the distinctly different concepts that underlie Aboriginal art. All the major Australian artists of the last two centuries are represented in this impressive collection.

The entrance level, where large windows frame spectacular views of the harbor, exhibits 20th-century art. Below, in the gallery's major extensions, the Yiribana Gallery displays one of the nation's most comprehensive collections of Aboriginal and Torres Strait Islander art. The bookshop on the ground floor stocks an offbeat collection of souvenirs, as well as some excellent alternatives to the standard tourist postcard. ✉ *Art Gallery Rd., the Domain* ☎ *02/9225–1744* ⊕ *www.artgallery. nsw.gov.au* ✑ *Free; special-exhibition fee varies* ☉ *Daily 10–5.*

35 **Customs House.** The last surviving example of the elegant sandstone buildings that once ringed Circular Quay, this former customs house now holds the Centre for Contemporary Craft, a retail crafts gallery, and the Djamu Gallery, Australia's largest permanent exhibition of Aboriginal and Pacific Island artifacts. The rooftop Café Sydney, the standout in the clutch of restaurants and cafés in this late-19th-century structure, overlooks Sydney Cove. The building stands close to the site where the British flag was first raised on the shores of Sydney Cove in 1788. ✉ *Customs House Sq., Alfred St., Circular Quay* ☎ *02/9265–2007.*

50 **The Domain South.** Laid out by Governor Macquarie in 1810 as his own personal "domain" and originally including what is now the Royal Botanic Gardens, this large park is a tranquil area at the city's eastern edge. Office workers flock here for lunchtime recreation, and the park holds free outdoor concerts during the Festival of Sydney in January.

41 **Garden Palace Gates.** These gates are all that remain of the Garden Palace, a massive glass pavilion that was erected for the Sydney International Exhibition of 1879 and destroyed by fire three years later. On the arch above the gates is a depiction of the Garden Palace's dome. Stone pillars on either side of the gates are engraved with Australian wildflowers. ✉ *Macquarie St., between Bridge and Bent Sts., Macquarie Street.*

40 **History House.** You're welcome to visit History House, the home of the Royal Australian Historical Society, and its collection of books and other materials. Note the balconies and the Corinthian columns, all made from iron, which was just becoming popular when this building was constructed in 1872. ✉ *133 Macquarie St., Macquarie Street* ☎ *02/9247–8001* ✑ *Library A$5* ☉ *Weekdays 9:30–4:30.*

47 **Hyde Park Barracks.** Before Governor Macquarie arrived, convicts were left to roam freely at night, and there was little regard for the sanctity of life or property on the streets of Sydney after dark. As the new governor, Macquarie was determined to establish law and order, and he commissioned convict-architect Francis Greenway to design this building to house prisoners. Displaying the restrained, classical lines that typify the architecture of the Georgian era, this 1819 building is considered Greenway's architectural masterpiece. The clock on the tower is the oldest functioning public timepiece in New South Wales.

Today the Barracks houses compelling exhibitions that explore behind the scenes of the prison. For example, a surprising number of relics from this period were preserved by rats, who carried away scraps of clothing and other artifacts for their nests beneath the floorboards. This bizarre detail is graphically illustrated in the foyer. A room on the top floor is strung with hammocks, exactly as it was when the building housed convicts. ⊠ *Queens Sq., Macquarie St., Hyde Park* ☎ *02/9223–8922* ⊕ *www.hht.nsw.gov.au* ⊠ *A$7* ⊙ *Daily 9:30–5.*

need a break? On a sunny day, the courtyard tables of the **Hyde Park Barracks Café** provide one of the city's finest places to enjoy an outdoor lunch. The café serves light, moderately priced meals, salads, and open sandwiches, with a wine list including Australian vintages. ⊠ *Queens Sq., Macquarie St., Hyde Park* ☎ *02/9223–8922.*

37 Lands Department. The figures occupying the niches at the corners of this 1890 sandstone building are early Australian explorers and politicians. James Barnet's building stands among other fine Victorian structures in the neighborhood. ⊠ *Bridge St., near the intersection of Macquarie Pl., Macquarie Street.*

36 Macquarie Place. This park, once a site of ceremonial and religious importance to Aboriginal people, contains a number of important monuments, including the obelisk formerly used as the point from which all distances from Sydney were measured. On a stone plinth at the bottom of the park is the anchor of HMS *Sirius,* flagship of the First Fleet, which struck a reef and sank off Norfolk Island in 1790. The bronze statue with his hands on his hips represents Thomas Mort, who in 1879 became the first to export refrigerated cargo from Australia. The implications of this shipment were enormous. Mutton, beef, and dairy products suddenly became valuable export commodities, and for most of the following century, agriculture dominated the Australian economy.

Bridge Street runs alongside Macquarie Place. Formerly the site of the 1789 Government House and the colony's first bridge, this V-shape street was named for the bridge that once crossed the Tank Stream, which now flows underground. Today several grandiose Victorian structures line its sidewalks.

Macquarie Street. Sydney's most elegant boulevard was shaped by Governor Macquarie, who from 1810 until he was ousted in 1822, planned the transformation of the cart track leading to Sydney Cove into a stylish street of dwellings and government buildings. An occasional modern high-rise breaks up the streetscape, but many of the 19th-century architectural delights here escaped demolition.

38 Museum of Sydney. This museum, built on the site of the original Government House, documents Sydney's early period of European colonization. One of its most intriguing exhibits is outside: the striking Edge of the Trees sculpture, with its 29 columns that "speak," and which contain artifacts of Aboriginal and early European inhabitation. Inside the museum, Aboriginal culture, convict society, and the gradual transformation of the settlement at Sydney Cove are woven into an evocative portrayal of life in the country's early days. The museum has a popular café and a shop that stocks unusual gifts. ⊠ *Bridge and Phillip Sts., City Center* ☎ *02/9251–5988* ⊕ *www.hht.nsw.gov.au* ⊠ *A$7* ⊙ *Daily 9:30–5.*

Near the museum, at the intersection of Bridge Street and Phillip Street, is an imposing pair of sandstone buildings. The most impressive view of the mid-19th-century **Treasury Building,** now part of the Hotel Inter-Continental, is from Macquarie Street. The **Colonial Secretary's Office—**

designed by James Barnet, who also designed the Lands Department—stands opposite the Treasury Building. Note the buildings' similarities, right down to the figures in the corner niches.

42 Royal Australasian College of Physicians. Once the home of a wealthy Sydney family, the building now houses a different elite: some of the city's most eminent physicians. ⊠ *Macquarie St., between Bridge and Bent Sts., Macquarie Street.*

48 St. James Church. Begun in 1822, the Colonial Georgian–style St. James is Sydney's oldest surviving church, and another fine Francis Greenway design. Intended to serve as the colony's first courthouse, the building was half completed when Commissioner Bigge, who had been sent from England to investigate Macquarie's administration, ordered that the structure be converted into a church. At the time, a courthouse for inhabitants of a penal colony was considered frivolous. Now lost among the skyscrapers, the church's tall spire once served as a landmark for ships entering the harbor.

Enter St. James through the door in the Doric portico. Plaques commemorating Australian explorers and administrators cover the interior walls. Inscriptions testify to the hardships of those early days. ⊠ *Queens Sq., Macquarie St., Hyde Park* ☎ *02/9232–3022* ☉ *Daily 9–5.*

49 St. Mary's Cathedral. The first St. Mary's was built here in 1821, but fire destroyed the chapel, and work on the present cathedral began in 1868. The spires weren't added until 2000, which is the reason that they're noticeably lighter in color than the rest of the church. St. Mary's has some particularly fine stained-glass windows and a terrazzo floor in the crypt, where exhibitions are often held. The cathedral's large rose window was imported from England.

At the front of the cathedral stand statues of Cardinal Moran and Archbishop Kelly, two Irishmen who were prominent in Australia's Roman Catholic Church. Due to the high proportion of Irish men and women in the convict population, the Roman Catholic Church was often the voice of the oppressed in 19th-century Sydney, where anti-Catholic feeling ran high among the Protestant rulers. Australia's first cardinal, Patrick Moran, was a powerful exponent of Catholic education and a diplomat who did much to heal the rift between the two faiths. By contrast, Michael Kelly, his successor as head of the church in Sydney, was excessively pious and politically inept; Kelly and Moran remained at odds until Moran's death in 1911. ⊠ *College and Cathedral Sts., Hyde Park* ☎ *02/9220–0400* ⊠ *Tour free* ☉ *Weekdays 6:30–6:30, Sat. 8–7:30, Sun. 6:30 AM–7:30 PM; tour Sun. at noon.*

43 State Library of New South Wales. This large complex is based around the Mitchell and Dixson libraries, which house the world's largest collection of Australiana. The reference collection in the library's modern Macquarie Street extension is generally the most interesting, with an excellent shop for books and gifts, a café, free films, and changing exhibitions with Australian historical and cultural themes in the upstairs gallery.

Enter the foyer of the library through the classical portico to see one of the earliest maps of Australia, a copy in marble mosaic of a map made by Abel Tasman, the Dutch navigator, in the mid-17th century. Beyond the map and through the glass doors lies the vast Mitchell Library reading room, but you need a reader's ticket (establishing that you are pursuing legitimate research) to enter. You can, however, take a free escorted tour of the library's buildings. Inquire at the reception desk of the general reference library on Macquarie Street. ⊠ *Macquarie St., Macquarie Street* ☎ *02/9230–1414* ⊕ *www.slnsw.gov.au* ☉ *Weekdays 9–9, week-*

ends 11–5; General Reference Library tour Tues.–Thurs. at 2:30; Mitchell Library tour Tues. and Thurs. at 11.

44 State Parliament House. The simple facade and shady verandas of this Greenway-designed 1816 building, formerly the Rum Hospital, typify Australian colonial architecture. From 1829, two rooms of the old hospital were used for meetings of the executive and legislative councils, which had been set up to advise the governor. These advisory bodies grew in power until New South Wales became self-governing in the 1840s, at which time Parliament occupied the entire building. The Legislative Council Chamber—the upper house of the parliament, identifiable by its red color scheme—is a prefabricated cast-iron structure that was originally intended to be a church on the goldfields of Victoria.

State Parliament generally sits between mid-February and late May, and again between mid-September and late November. You can visit the public gallery to watch the local version of the Westminster system of democracy in action. On weekdays, generally between 9:30 and 4, you can tour the building's public areas, which contain a number of portraits and paintings. You must reserve ahead. ⊠ *Macquarie St., Macquarie Street* ☎ *02/9230–2111* ⊕ *www.parliament.nsw.gov.au* ☉ *Weekdays, 9:30–4; hrs vary when Parliament is in session.*

39 Sydney Conservatorium of Music. Providing artistic development for talented young musicians, this institution hosts free lunchtime and evening concerts (usually on Wednesday and Friday). The conservatory's turreted building was originally the stables for nearby Government House. The construction cost caused a storm among Governor Macquarie's superiors in London and eventually helped bring about the downfall of both Macquarie and the building's architect, Francis Greenway. ⊠ *Conservatorium Rd., off Macquarie St., Macquarie Street* ☎ *02/9230–1222.*

45 Sydney Hospital. Completed in 1894 to replace the main Rum Hospital building, this institution offered an infinitely better medical option. By all accounts, admission to the Rum Hospital was only slightly preferable to death itself. Convict nurses stole patients' food, and abler patients stole from the weaker. The kitchen sometimes doubled as a mortuary, and the table was occasionally used for operations.

In front of the hospital is a bronze figure of a boar. This is *Il Porcellino,* a copy of a statue that stands in Florence, Italy. According to the inscription, if you make a donation in the coin box and rub the boar's nose, "you will be endowed with good luck." Sydney citizens seem to be a superstitious bunch because the boar's nose is very shiny indeed.

If you're in need of a rest, walk through the arch just to one side of the statue and into the shady courtyard of the hospital, which has a fountain and several benches. ⊠ *Macquarie St. and Martin Pl., Macquarie Street* ☎ *02/9382–7111.*

46 Sydney Mint. The south wing of Greenway's 1816 Rum Hospital became a branch of the Royal Mint after the 1850s Australian gold rushes, which lured thousands of gold prospectors from around the world. Currently in the process of redevelopment, it will ultimately house the headquarters of the Historic Houses Trust, when it will be open for public viewing. ⊠ *Macquarie St., Macquarie Street* ☎ *no phone.*

The Opera House, the RBG & the Domain North

Bordering Sydney Cove, Farm Cove, and Woolloomooloo Bay, this section of Sydney includes the iconic Sydney Opera House, as well as extensive and delightful harborside gardens and parks.

The colony's first farm was established here in 1788, and the botanical gardens were initiated in 1816. The most dramatic change to the area occurred in 1959, however, when ground was broken on the site for the Sydney Opera House at Bennelong Point. This promontory was originally a small island, then the site of 1819 Fort Macquarie, later a tram depot, and finally the Opera House, one of the world's most striking modern buildings. The area's evolution is an eloquent metaphor for Sydney's own transformation.

a good walk

From Circular Quay, walk around Sydney Cove along Circular Quay East. This walkway is also known as Writers' Walk. Brass plaques embedded in the sidewalk commemorate prominent Australian writers, playwrights, and poets. The apartment buildings, cafés, and restaurants along the street's landward side have some of Sydney's best views, yet they caused enormous controversy when they were built in the late 1990s—just as the Sydney Opera House had its own loud critics when it was first built. One look and you'll see why the building closest to the Opera House is known to all as "The Toaster."

Ahead, on the Bennelong Point promontory, is the unmistakable **Sydney Opera House** 52 . Its distinctive white tiled "sails" and prominent position make this the most widely recognized landmark of urban Australia. The Opera House has fueled controversy and debate among Australians, but whatever its detractors may say, the structure leaves few people unmoved.

The **Royal Botanic Gardens** 53 , on the landward side of the Opera House, combines with the rolling Domain park to form the city's eastern border. You can either walk around the Farm Cove pathway or head inland to explore the gardens, including a stop at **Government House,** before returning to the waterfront.

The pathway around the cove leads to a peninsula, **Mrs. Macquarie's Point** 54 , in the northern part of the Domain. It is named for Elizabeth Macquarie, the governor's wife, who planned the road through the park. As you round the peninsula and turn toward the naval dockyard at Garden Island, notice the small bench carved into the rock with an inscription identifying it as **Mrs. Macquarie's Chair** 55 .

Continue through **the Domain North** 56 on Mrs. Macquarie's Road to the **Andrew (Boy) Charlton Pool** 57 , built over Woolloomooloo Bay. From the pool are views of the Garden Island naval base and the suburb of Potts Point, across the bay.

This road eventually takes you to the southern part of the Domain. The once-continuous Domain is divided into north and south sections by the Cahill Expressway, which leads up to the Sydney Harbour Bridge and down into the Sydney Harbour Tunnel.

At the end of the walk, you can return to the city and Macquarie Street by reentering the botanical gardens through the Woolloomooloo Gate near the roadway over the Cahill Expressway.

TIMING A walk around the Sydney Opera House, Royal Botanic Gardens, and the Domain North can easily be completed in a half day. The walk is highly recommended on a warm summer evening. Allow more time if you wish to explore the gardens more thoroughly. These are delightful at any time of year, though they're especially beautiful in spring.

What to See

57 **Andrew (Boy) Charlton Pool.** Since it emerged from a total makeover at the end of 2002, this heated, outdoor, Olympic-size pool overlooking the

navy ships tied up at Garden Island has become a local favorite. Complementing its stunning location is a radical design in glass and steel with timber decking. The pool also has a chic terrace café above Woolloomooloo Bay. ⊠ *Mrs. Macquarie's Rd., the Domain North, the Domain* ☎ *02/9358–6686* ⊡ *A\$4.50* ☉ *Oct.–Mar., daily 6:30 AM–8:30 PM.*

56 **The Domain North.** The northern part of the Domain adjoins the Royal Botanic Gardens and extends from Mrs. Macquarie's Point to the Cahill Expressway. Surrounded by Farm Cove and Woolloomooloo Bay, this is a pleasant, harbor-fringed park.

Government House. Completed in 1843, this two-story, sandstone, Gothic Revival building in the Royal Botanic Gardens served as the residence of the Governor of New South Wales—who represents the British crown in local matters—until the Labor Party Government handed it back to the public in 1996. Prominent English architect Edward Blore designed the building without ever having set foot in Australia. The house's restored stenciled ceilings are its most impressive feature. Paintings hanging on the walls bear the signatures of some of Australia's best-known artists, including Roberts, Streeton, and Drysdale. You are free to wander on your own around Government House's gardens, which lie within the Royal Botanic Gardens, but you must join a guided tour to see the house's interior. ⊠ *Royal Botanic Gardens, the Domain* ☎ *02/9931–5200* ⊡ *Free* ☉ *House Fri.–Sun. 10–3; gardens daily 10–4.*

55 **Mrs. Macquarie's Chair.** During the early 1800s, Elizabeth Macquarie often sat on the point in the Domain at the east side of Farm Cove, at the rock where a seat has been hewn in her name.

54 **Mrs. Macquarie's Point.** The inspiring views from this point combine with the shady lawns to make this a popular place for picnics. The views are best at dusk, when the setting sun silhouettes the Opera House and Harbour Bridge.

★ **53** **Royal Botanic Gardens.** Groves of palm trees, duck ponds, a cactus garden, a restaurant, greenhouses, and acres of lawns are some of the reasons that Sydneysiders are addicted to these gardens, where the convicts of the First Fleet tried to establish a farm. Their early attempts at agriculture were disastrous. The soil was poor and few of the convicts came from an agricultural background, and for the first couple of years the prisoners and their guards teetered on the verge of starvation. The colony was eventually saved by the arrival of a supply ship in 1790, although it was only the establishment of farms on good alluvial soil to the west of the city at Parramatta that ensured its long-term survival.

The gardens were founded in 1816 and greatly expanded during the 1830s. The wonderful collection of plants and trees are both native Australians and exotics from around the world. Garden highlights include the Sydney Tropical Centre, housed in the Pyramid and Arc glass houses, and the lush Sydney Fernery. Also within the gardens is Government House, former residence of the Governor of New South Wales, representative of the British crown in local matters, and the Botanic Gardens Restaurant. The Gardens Shop carries unusual souvenirs. Tours leave from the visitor center, near the Art Gallery of New South Wales. ⊠ *The Domain North, the Domain* ☎ *02/9231–8125* ⊕ *www.rbgsyd.gov.au* ⊡ *Gardens free, Sydney Tropical Centre A\$2.20, tour free* ☉ *Royal Botanic Gardens daily dawn–dusk; Sydney Tropical Centre and Sydney Fernery daily 10–4; tour daily at 10:30.*

⚑ **52** **Sydney Opera House.** Sydney's most famous landmark had such a long
and troubled construction phase that it's almost a miracle that the building was ever completed. In 1954, the state premier appointed a com-

mittee to advise the government on the building of an opera house. The site chosen was Bennelong Point (named after an early Aboriginal inhabitant), which was, until that time, occupied by a tram depot. The premier's committee launched a competition to find a suitable plan, and a total of 233 submissions came in from architects the world over. One of them was a young Dane named Joern Utzon.

His plan was brilliant, but it had all the markings of a monumental disaster. The structure was so narrow that stages would have minuscule wings, and the soaring "sails" that formed the walls and roof could not be built by existing technology.

Nonetheless, Utzon's dazzling, dramatic concept caught the judges' imagination, and construction of the giant podium began in 1958. From the start, the contractors faced a cost blowout; the building that was projected to cost A$7 million and take four years to erect would eventually require A$102 million and 15 years. Construction was financed by an intriguing scheme. Realizing that citizens might be hostile to the use of public funds for the controversial project, the state government raised the money through the Opera House Lottery. For almost a decade, Australians lined up to buy tickets, and the Opera House was built without depriving the state's hospitals or schools of a single cent.

Initially it was thought that the concrete exterior of the building would have to be cast in place, which would have meant building an enormous birdcage of scaffolding at even greater expense. Then, as he was peeling an orange one day, Utzon had a flash of inspiration. Why not construct the shells from segments of a single sphere? The concrete ribs forming the skeleton of the building could be prefabricated in just a few molds, hoisted into position, and joined together. These ribs are clearly visible inside the Opera House, especially in the foyers and staircases of the Concert Hall.

In 1966, Utzon resigned as Opera House architect and left Australia, embittered by his dealings with unions and the government. He has never returned to see his masterpiece. A team of young Australian architects carried on, completing the exterior one year later. Until that time, however, nobody had given much thought to the *interior*. The shells created awkward interior spaces, and conventional performance areas were simply not feasible. It's a tribute to the architectural team's ingenuity that the exterior of the building is matched by the aesthetically pleasing and acoustically sound theaters inside.

In September 1973 the Australian Opera performed *War and Peace* in the Opera Theatre. A month later, Queen Elizabeth II officially opened the building in a ceremony capped by an astonishing fireworks display. Nowadays, the controversies that raged around the building seem moot. The Sydney Opera House, poised majestically on a harbor peninsula, has become a loved and potent national symbol, and a far more versatile venue than its name implies, hosting a wide range of performance arts and entertainment: dance, drama, films, opera, and jazz. It also has four restaurants and cafés, and several bars that cater to its hordes of patrons. Guided one-hour tours depart at frequent intervals from the tour office, on the lower forecourt level, 8:30–5 on most days. Tours can be limited or canceled due to performances or rehearsals. Call in advance. ⊠ *Bennelong Point, Circular Quay* ☎ *02/9250–7111* ⊕ *www. soh.nsw.gov.au* ✆ *Tour A$17.*

Darling Harbour

Until the mid-1980s, this horseshoe-shape bay on the western edge of the city center was a wasteland of disused docks and railway yards. Then, in an explosive burst of activity, the whole area was redeveloped and opened in time for Australia's bicentennial in 1988. Now there's plenty to take in at the Darling Harbour complex: the National Maritime Museum, the large Harbourside shopping and dining center, the Sydney Aquarium, the Cockle Bay waterfront dining complex, the Panasonic IMAX Theatre, and the gleaming Exhibition Centre, whose masts and spars recall the square riggers that once berthed here. At the harbor's center is a large park shaded by palm trees. Waterways and fountains lace the complex together.

The Powerhouse Museum is within easy walking distance of the harbor, and immediately to the south are Chinatown and the Sydney Entertainment Centre. The Star City entertainment complex, based around the Star City Casino, lies just to the west of Darling Harbour.

a good walk

Start at the Market Street end of Pitt Street Mall, Sydney's main pedestrian shopping precinct. Take the monorail—across Market Street and above ground level on the right-hand side of Pitt Street—from here to the next stop (Darling Park), passing the large Queen Victoria Building on your left. Get off at this stop and go down the steps and escalator. On your right is **Sydney Aquarium** 58 ▶.

From here, take the escalator back up to historic **Pyrmont Bridge** 59. Cross below the monorail track to the other side of the walkway. The building immediately below is **Cockle Bay Wharf** 60, a three-level complex that houses some of Sydney's finest restaurants.

On the opposite side of the bridge stands the **Australian National Maritime Museum** 61, the large white-roof building on your right, which charts Australia's vital links to the sea with lively interactive displays. After visiting the museum, grab a bite to eat at the adjacent Harbourside center, then walk through Darling Harbour, where you'll notice a curved building with a checkerboard pattern beside the elevated freeway. This is the **Panasonic IMAX Theatre** 62, with an eight-story movie screen. Cross under the elevated freeway and walk past the carousel.

The intriguing **Powerhouse Museum** 63, inside an old power station with extensive modern additions, makes a worthwhile detour from the amusements of Darling Harbour. Walk west to Merino Boulevard. Then continue south to William Henry Street and turn right. The museum is just south of the intersection of William Henry and Harris streets.

From the Powerhouse, walk back to William Henry Street and follow it east until it becomes Pier Street. Here you'll find the **Chinese Garden of Friendship** 64, a small but serene park amid a sea of concrete and steel.

You can return to the city center by monorail—follow signs to the Haymarket station—or take a short walk around the colorful streets, shops, markets, and restaurants of Chinatown, south of the Chinese Garden.

TIMING You'll need at least a half day to see the best of the area. If you want to skip the museums, a good time to visit is in the evening, when the tall city buildings reflect the setting sun and spill their molten images across the water. You might even pop over to Chinatown for dinner. Later, pubs, cafés, and nightclubs turn on lights and music for a party that lasts well past midnight. Darling Harbour is a family favorite on weekends, when entertainers perform on the water and in the forecourt area.

What to See

🕄 61 **Australian National Maritime Museum.** The six galleries of this soaring, futuristic building tell the story of Australia and the sea. In addition to figureheads, model ships, and brassy nautical hardware, there are antique racing yachts and the jet-powered *Spirit of Australia,* current holder of the water speed record. Among the many spectacular exhibits is the fully rigged *Australia II,* the famous 12-meter yacht with winged keel that finally broke the New York Yacht Club's hold on the America's Cup in 1983. The USA Gallery displays objects from such major U.S. collections as the Smithsonian Institution and was dedicated by President George Bush Sr. on New Year's Day 1992. An outdoor section showcases numerous vessels moored at the museum's wharves, including the HMAS *Vampire,* a World War II destroyer. ⊠ *Darling Harbour* ☎ *02/9298–3777* ⊕ *www.anmm.gov.au* ⊠ *A$20* ⊙ *Daily 9:30–5.*

★ ⑥⑤ **Chinese Garden of Friendship.** Chinese prospectors came to the Australian goldfields as far back as the 1850s, and the nation's long and enduring links with China are symbolized by this tranquil walled enclave, the largest garden of its kind outside China. Designed by Chinese landscape architects, the garden includes bridges, lakes, waterfalls, sculpture, and Cantonese-style pavilions. The garden is a perfect respite from sightseeing and Darling Harbour's crowds. ⊠ *Darling Harbour* ☎ *02/9281–6863* ⊠ *A$4.50* ⊙ *Daily 9:30–5.*

⑥⓪ **Cockle Bay Wharf.** Fueling Sydney's addiction to fine food, most of this sprawling waterfront complex is dedicated to gastronomy. Dining options include a tandoori takeaway, a steak house, a Greek seafood spot, and an Italian-style café. Also here is Sydney's biggest nightclub, Home. If you have a boat you can dock at the marina—and avoid the hassle of parking a car in one of the city's most congested centers. ⊠ *201 Sussex St., Darling Harbour* ☎ *02/9264–4755* ⊕ *www.cocklebaywharf. com* ⊙ *Weekends 10 AM–4 AM.*

☺ ⑥② **Panasonic IMAX Theatre.** Both in size and impact, this eight-story-tall movie screen is overwhelming. One-hour presentations take you on astonishing, wide-angle voyages of discovery into space, through ancient Egypt, or to the summit of Mount Everest. ⊠ *Darling Harbour* ☎ *02/9281–3300* ⊕ *www.imax.com.au* ⊠ *A$15* ⊙ *Daily 10–10.*

☺ ⑥③ **Powerhouse Museum.** Learning the principles of science becomes a painless process with the museum's stimulating, interactive displays, ideal for all ages. Exhibits in the former 1890s electricity station that once powered Sydney's trams include a whole floor of working steam engines, space modules, airplanes suspended from the ceiling, state-of-the-art computer gadgetry, and a 1930s art deco–style movie-theater auditorium. A highlight is the top-level Powerhouse Garden Restaurant, painted in characteristically vibrant colors and patterns by famous local artist Ken Done and his team. ⊠ *500 Harris St., Darling Harbour, Ultimo* ☎ *02/9217–0111* ⊕ *www.phm.gov.au* ⊠ *A$10* ⊙ *Daily 10 AM–5 PM.*

⑤⑨ **Pyrmont Bridge.** Dating from 1902, this is the world's oldest electrically operated swing-span bridge. The structure once carried motor traffic, but it's now a walkway that links the Darling Harbour complex with Cockle Bay and the city. The monorail runs above the bridge, but the center span still swings open to allow tall-masted ships into Cockle Bay, which sits at the bottom of the horseshoe-shape shore.

off the beaten path

SYDNEY FISH MARKET – Second in size only to Tokyo's giant Tsukiji fish market, Sydney's is a showcase for the riches of Australia's seas. Just a five-minute drive from the city, the market is a great place to sample sushi, oysters, octopus, spicy Thai and Chinese fish dishes, and fish and chips at the waterfront cafés overlooking the fishing fleet. It's open daily from 7 AM to about 5. ⊠ *Pyrmont Bridge Rd. and Bank St., Pyrmont West* ☎ *02/9004–1100* ⊕ *www. sydneyfishmarket.com.au.*

🕐 ▶ **58** **Sydney Aquarium.** The larger and more modern of Sydney's two public aquariums presents a fascinating view of the underwater world, with saltwater crocodiles, giant sea turtles, and delicate, multicolor reef fish and corals. Excellent displays highlight Great Barrier Reef marine life and Australia's largest river system, the Murray-Darling, and the marine mammal sanctuary and touch pool are favorites with children. Two show-stealing transparent tunnels give a fish's-eye view of the sea, while sharks and stingrays glide overhead. The aquarium is often crowded on weekends. Although the adult admission price is high, family tickets are a reasonable value. ⊠ *Aquarium Pier, Wheat Rd., Darling Harbour* ☎ *02/9262–2300* ⊕ *www.sydneyaquarium.com.au* 🖃 *A$23* ⊙ *Daily 9 AM–10 PM.*

Sydney City Center

Shopping is the main reason to visit Sydney's city center, but there are several buildings and other places of interest among the office blocks, department stores, and shopping centers.

a good walk

Begin at the Market Street end of Pitt Street Mall. With the mall at your back, turn left onto Market Street and walk a few meters to the entrance to **Sydney Tower** **65** ▶. High-speed elevators will whisk you to the top of the city's tallest structure, and the spectacular view will give you an excellent idea of the lay of the land.

Return to Market Street and walk in the other direction to George Street. Turn left and continue to the Sydney Hilton Hotel, on the left-hand side. For a little refreshment, take the steps down below street level to the Marble Bar, an opulent basement watering hole with florid decor and architecture.

Back up on George Street cross the road to enter the **Queen Victoria Building (QVB)** **66**, a massive Victorian structure that occupies an entire city block. The shops are many and varied, and the meticulous restoration work is impressive. After browsing in the QVB, exit at the Druitt Street end and cross this road to the elaborate **Sydney Town Hall** **67**, the domain of Sydney City Council and a popular performance space. Next door is the Anglican **St. Andrew's Cathedral** **68**.

Cut across George Street and walk east along Bathurst Street to the southern section of **Hyde Park** **69**. This is the city center's largest green space and the location of the Anzac War Memorial, which commemorates Australians who fought and died in the service of their country. Continue through the park to College Street, cross the road, and walk a few more feet to the **Australian Museum** **70**, an excellent natural history museum covering the Australia-Pacific region.

From the museum, cross College Street and then Park Street and follow the shady avenue through the northern half of Hyde Park to the Archibald Memorial Fountain, a focal point of this section of the park. Continue past the fountain and cross the road to Macquarie Street. As you walk north on Macquarie, you'll pass the Hyde Park Barracks, Sydney Mint, and Sydney Hospital. In front of the hospital, cross the road to the large pedestrian precinct of **Martin Place** **71** and walk the length of the plaza to George Street. This is Sydney's banking headquarters and the site of the cenotaph war memorial near the George Street end.

From here you can return to the Pitt Street Mall via Pitt Street, or walk north on George Street to Circular Quay.

TIMING   The walk itself should take no longer than a couple hours. Plan more time for an extended tour of the Australian Museum or for shopping in the Queen Victoria Building. Weekday lunchtimes (generally 1–2) in the city center are elbow-to-elbow affairs, with office workers trying to make the most of their brief break.

What to See

🖑 **70** **Australian Museum.** The strength of this natural history museum, a well-respected academic institution, is its collection of plants, animals, geological specimens, and cultural artifacts from the Asia-Pacific region. Particularly notable are the collections of artifacts from Papua New Guinea and from Australia's Aboriginal peoples. The museum also has a comprehensive gems and minerals display, an excellent shop, and a lively café. ⊠ *6 College St., near William St., Hyde Park* ☎ *02/9320–6000* ⊕ *www.austmus.gov.au* ≊ *A\$8* ⊙ *Daily 9:30–5.*

69 **Hyde Park.** Declared public land by Governor Phillip in 1792 and used for the colony's earliest cricket matches and horse races, this area was turned into a park in 1810. The gardens are formal, with fountains, statuary, and tree-lined walks, and its tranquil lawns are popular with office workers at lunchtime. In the southern section of Hyde Park (near Liverpool Street) stands the 1934 Art Deco **Anzac Memorial** (☎ 02/9267–7668), a tribute to the Australians who died in military service during World War I, when the acronym ANZAC (Australian and New Zealand Army Corps) was coined. The 120,000 gold stars inside the dome represent each man and woman of New South Wales who served. The lower level exhibits war-related photographs. It's open Monday–Saturday 10–4, Sunday 1–4. ⊠ *Elizabeth, College, and Park Sts., Hyde Park.*

> need a
> break?

Stop in the **Marble Bar** for a drink, and to experience a masterpiece of Victorian extravagance. The 1890 bar was formerly located in another building that was constructed on the profits of the horse-racing track, thus establishing the link between gambling and majestic public architecture that has its modern-day parallel in the Sydney Opera House. Threatened with demolition in the 1970s, the whole bar was moved—marble arches, color-glass ceiling, elaborately carved woodwork, paintings of voluptuous nudes, and all—to its present site. By night, it serves as a backdrop for jazz and other live music. ⊠ *Sydney Hilton Hotel, basement level, 259 Pitt St., City Center* ☎ *02/9266–2000* ⊙ *Closed Sun.*

71 **Martin Place.** Sydney's largest pedestrian precinct, flanked by banks, offices, and the MLC Shopping Centre, forms the hub of the central business district. There are some grand buildings here—including the beautifully refurbished Commonwealth Bank and the 1870s Venetian Renaissance–style General Post Office building with its 230-foot clock tower (now a Westin hotel). Toward the George Street end of the plaza the simple 1929 cenotaph war memorial commemorates Australians who died in World War I. Weekdays from about 12:30, the amphitheater near Castlereagh Street hosts free lunchtime concerts with sounds from all corners of the music world, from police bands to string quartets to rock 'n' rollers. ⊠ *Between Macquarie and George Sts., City Center.*

66 **Queen Victoria Building (QVB).** Originally the city's produce market, this vast 1898 sandstone structure had become a maze of shabby offices by the time it disappeared under scaffolding in 1981. When the wraps came off five years later, the building was handsomely restored with sweeping staircases, enormous stained-glass windows, and the 1-ton Royal Clock, which is suspended from the glass roof. Other restoration highlights in this 650-feet-long building include the period-style tiling on the ground floor, the central glass dome, and Victorian-era toilets on the Albert Walk level. The excellent QVB shopping complex includes more than 200 boutiques, with those on the upper floors generally more up-scale and exclusive. The basement level has several inexpensive dining options. ⊠ *George, York, Market, and Druitt Sts., City Center* ☎ *02/ 9264–9209* ⊙ *Daily 24 hrs.*

68 St. Andrew's Cathedral. The foundation stone for Sydney's Gothic Revival Anglican cathedral—the country's oldest—was laid in 1819, although the original architect, Francis Greenway, fell from grace soon after work begun. Edmund Blacket, Sydney's most illustrious church architect, was responsible for its final design and completion—a whopping 50 years later in 1869. Notable features of the sandstone construction include ornamental windows depicting Jesus' life and a great east window with images relating to St. Andrew. ⊠ *Sydney Sq., George St., next to Town Hall, Hyde Park* ☎ *02/9265–1661* ⊙ *Mon., Tues., Thurs., Fri. 7:30–5:30; Wed. and Sun. 7:30 AM–8 PM; Sat. 9–4; tours weekdays at 11 and 1:45, Sun. at noon.*

▶ **65 Sydney Tower.** Short of taking a scenic flight, a visit to the top of this 1,000-foot golden-minaret-topped spike is the best way to view Sydney's spectacular layout. This is the city's tallest building, and the views from its indoor observation deck are astounding. The panorama encompasses the entire Sydney metropolitan area of more than 1,560 square km (600 square mi), and you can often see as far as the Blue Mountains, more than 80 km (50 mi) away. Free guided tours, conducted hourly on the observation deck, cover the major sights and landmarks of the city below as well as details about the tower itself. ⊠ *100 Market St., between Pitt and Castlereagh Sts., City Center* ☎ *02/9223–0933* 🎟 *A$19.80* ⊙ *Sun.–Fri. 9 AM–10:30 PM, Sat. 9 AM–11:30 PM.*

67 Sydney Town Hall. Sydney's most ornate Victorian building—an elaborate, multilayer sandstone structure—is often rather unkindly likened to a wedding cake. It does have some grand interior spaces, especially the vestibule and large Centennial Hall, and a massive Grand Organ, one of the world's most powerful, which is central to lunchtime concerts held here. For building tours, call for details. ⊠ *George and Druitt Sts., City Center* ☎ *02/9265–9007, 02/9231–4629 for tour information* ⊙ *Weekdays 9–5.*

Elizabeth Bay & Kings Cross, Darlinghurst & Paddington

The city's inner east suburbs are truly the people's Sydney—from the mansions of the colonial aristocracy and the humble laborers' cottages of the same period to the modernized terrace houses of Paddington, one of Sydney's most charming suburbs, and one of its most desirable. The tour also passes through Kings Cross and Darlinghurst, the country's best-known nightlife district, and makes a stop at the acclaimed Sydney Jewish Museum.

a good tour

Begin at the bus stop on Alfred Street ▶, just behind Circular Quay, and catch Bus 311, which leaves from the stop on Bridge Street, between Pitt and Gresham streets. (This bus also reads either RAILWAY VIA KINGS CROSS or RAILWAY VIA ELIZABETH BAY.) Ask the driver to drop you off at Elizabeth Bay House and take a seat on the left side of the bus.

You'll wind your way through the city streets to Macquarie Street, past the State Library, the New South Wales Parliament, Hyde Park Barracks, and St. Mary's Cathedral. The bus then follows the curve of Wool-loomooloo Bay, where it passes Harry's Café de Wheels, a unique Sydney institution, and beneath the bows of naval vessels at the Garden Island

Dockyard, the main base for the Australian navy. Visiting ships from other Pacific Ocean navies can often be seen along this wharf.

Just before the Garden Island gates, the bus turns right and climbs through the shady streets of Potts Point and Elizabeth Bay to **Elizabeth Bay House** 72, an aristocratic Regency-style mansion and one of Australia's finest historic homes.

After a spin through Elizabeth Bay House, continue north to the **Arthur McElhone Reserve** 73 for a pleasant resting spot with harbor glimpses. Take the stone steps leading down from the park to Billyard Avenue. Near the lower end of this street is a walled garden with cypress trees and banana palms reaching above the parapets. Through the black iron gates of the driveway, you can catch a glimpse of Boomerang, a sprawling, Spanish-style villa built by the manufacturer of the harmonica of the same name. When it was last traded, in 2002, this was Sydney's second most expensive house, worth just a shade over A$20 million. Just beyond the house, turn left to **Beare Park** 74, overlooking the yachts in Elizabeth Bay.

Return to Billyard Avenue. Wait at the bus stop opposite the first gate of Boomerang for Bus 311, but make sure that you catch one marked RAILWAY, *not* CIRCULAR QUAY. This bus threads its way through the streets of Kings Cross, Sydney's nightlife district, and Darlinghurst. During the day the Cross is only half awake, although the doormen of the various strip clubs are never too sleepy to lure passersby inside to watch nonstop video shows. Ask the driver to deposit you at the stop near the corner of Darlinghurst Road and Burton Street. From here, the moving and thought-provoking **Sydney Jewish Museum** 75 is just across the road.

After leaving the museum, walk along the wall of the former Darlinghurst Jail, now an educational institution, to Oxford Street. Turn left, and on your right about 300 yards up Oxford Street is the long sandstone wall that serves as the perimeter of **Victoria Barracks** 76 and its Army Museum. These barracks were built in the middle of the 19th century to house the British regiments stationed in the colony.

Almost opposite the main entrance to the barracks is the start of **Shadforth Street** 77, which is lined with some of the oldest terrace houses in Paddington. From Shadforth Street turn right onto Glenmore Road, where the terrace houses become far more elaborate. Follow this road past the intersection with Brown Street to the colorful collection of shops known as Five Ways.

Walk up Broughton Street to the right of the Royal Hotel, which has a fine Victorian pub. Turn right at Union Street, left onto Underwood, and right at William Street. You are now among the boutique shops of Paddington, and you may want to spend some time browsing here before completing the walk. On the right is Sweet William, a shop for chocolate lovers. If you're in the mood, don't miss Oxford Street's designer clothing and curio shops. Walking toward the city along Oxford, you'll arrive at the restored colonial mansion of **Juniper Hall** 78.

You can take any bus back to the city from the other side of Oxford Street, but if the sun is shining, consider heading out to Bondi Beach, a mere 20-minute ride on Bus 380.

TIMING   Allow the better part of a day to make your way through these neighborhoods, especially if you want to take a good look around Elizabeth Bay House and the Sydney Jewish Museum. If you wish to tour Victoria Barracks, take this trip on a Thursday and get there by 10, which probably means going there first and visiting the area's other sights in the afternoon. There is an additional diversion on Saturday, when the famous Paddington Bazaar brings zest and color to the upper end of Oxford Street.

The walk around Paddington is not particularly long, but some of the streets are steep. This walk can be shortened by continuing along Oxford Street from Victoria Barracks to Juniper Hall, rather than turning onto Shadforth Street.

What to See

73 Arthur McElhone Reserve. One of the city's welcome havens, the reserve has tree ferns, a gushing stream, a stone bridge over a carp pond, and views up the harbor. ✉ *Onslow Ave., Elizabeth Bay* 🎫 *Free* ⊙ *Daily dawn–dusk.*

74 Beare Park. With its pleasant harbor views, this waterfront park is a favorite recreation spot among Elizabeth Bay locals. The adjoining wharf is often busy with sailors coming and going to their yachts, moored out in the bay. ✉ *Off Ithaca Rd., Elizabeth Bay* 🎫 *Free* ⊙ *Daily dawn–dusk.*

Elizabeth Bay. Much of this densely populated but still-charming harborside suburb was originally part of the extensive Elizabeth Bay House grounds. Wrought-iron balconies and French doors on some of the older apartment blocks give the area a Mediterranean feel. During the 1920s and 1930s this was a fashionably bohemian quarter.

72 Elizabeth Bay House. Regarded in its heyday as the "finest house in the colony," this 1835–39 mansion has retained little of its original furniture, but the rooms have been restored in the style of its early life. The most striking feature is an oval-shape salon, naturally lighted through glass panels in a dome roof, with a staircase that winds its way to the upper floor. The colonial secretary Alexander Macleay lived here for only six years before suffering crippling losses in the colonial depression of the 1840s. In return for settling his father's debts, his son William took possession of the house and most of its contents and promptly evicted his father. ✉ *7 Onslow Ave., Elizabeth Bay* ☎ *02/9356–6302* ⊕ *www. hht.nsw.gov.au* 🎫 *A$7* ⊙ *Tues.–Sun. 10–4:30.*

> **off the beaten path**

HARRY'S CAFE DE WHEELS – The attraction of this dockyard nighttime food stall is not so much the pies and coffee Harry dispenses as the clientele. Famous opera singers, actors, and international rock-and-roll stars have been spotted here rubbing shoulders with shift workers and taxi drivers. Sampling one of the stall's famous meat pies with peas is a must. ✉ *1 Cowper Wharf Rd., Woolloomooloo* ☎ *02/9211–2506* ⊕ *www.harryscafedewheels.com.au.*

78 Juniper Hall. Built in 1824 by gin distiller Robert Cooper, this patrician Paddington residence was named for the juniper berries used to make the potent beverage. Cooper did everything on a grand scale, and that included raising and housing his family. He built Juniper Hall, with its simple and elegant lines typical of the Georgian period, for his third wife, Sarah, whom he married when he was 46 (she was just a teenager) and who bore 14 of his 24 children. The house later became an orphanage. It was renovated at considerable public expense and opened as a museum during the 1980s. Due to lack of funds the house is now closed to the public and contains offices. ✉ *248 Oxford St., Paddington.*

Paddington. Most of this suburb's elegant two-story houses were built during the 1880s, when the colony experienced a long period of economic growth following the gold rushes that began in the 1860s. The balconies are trimmed with decorative wrought iron, sometimes known as Paddington lace, that initially came from England and later was produced in Australian foundries. If you look closely at the patterns, you may be able to distinguish between the rose-and-thistle design that came from England and the flannel-flower, fern, and lyre-bird feather designs made in Australia.

During the depression of the 1890s, Paddington's boom came to an abrupt end. The advent of the automobile and motorized public transportation just a few years later meant that people could live in more distant suburbs, surrounded by gardens and trees, and such inner-city neighborhoods as Paddington became unfashionable. The area declined further during the depression of the 1930s, when many terrace houses were converted into low-rent accommodations and most of the wrought-iron balconies were boarded up to create extra rooms.

In the late 1960s inner-city living became fashionable, and many young couples rushed to buy these quaint but dilapidated houses at bargain prices. Renovated and repainted, the now-stylish Paddington terrace houses give the area its characteristic, villagelike charm. Today, a pretty renovated terrace home can cost close to A$1 million.

77 **Shadforth Street.** Built at about the same time as Elizabeth Bay House, the tiny stone houses in this street were assembled to house the workers who built and serviced the **Victoria Barracks.**

need a break? The **Royal Hotel** (⊠ 237 Glenmore Rd., Paddington ☎ 02/9331–2604) has a fine Victorian pub with leather couches and stained-glass windows. It's a good place to stop for something cool to drink. On the floor above the pub is a balconied restaurant that's popular on sunny afternoons.

75 **Sydney Jewish Museum.** Artifacts, interactive media, and audiovisual displays chronicle the history of Australian Jews and commemorate the 6 million killed in the Holocaust. Exhibits are brilliantly arranged on eight levels, which lead upward in chronological order, beginning with the handful of Jews who arrived on the First Fleet in 1788 to the migration of 30,000 survivors of the camps to Australia. ⊠ *148 Darlinghurst Rd., Darlinghurst* ☎ *02/9360–7999* ⊕ *www.sjm.com.au* ✉ *A$10* ☺ *Sun.–Thurs. 10–4, Fri. 10–2.*

76 **Victoria Barracks.** Built by soldiers and convicts from 1841 on to replace the colony's original Wynyard Barracks—and still occupied by the army—this vast building is an excellent example of Regency-style architecture. Behind the 740-foot-long sandstone facade is mostly a parade ground, where an army band performs Thursdays at 10 AM during the free tours. Dress uniforms have been abolished in the Australian army, so the soldiers wear their parade-ground dress, which includes the famous slouch hat. The brims of these hats are cocked on the left side, allowing soldiers to present arms without knocking them off.

In the former military prison on the parade grounds is the **Army Museum,** with exhibits covering Australia's military history from the early days of the Rum Corps to the Malayan conflict of the 1950s. Its volunteer staff is knowledgeable and enthusiastic, and students of military history will not be disappointed. ⊠ *Oxford St., Paddington* ☎ *02/9339–3000* ☺ *Museum Thurs. 10–noon, Sun. 10–2:30; barracks tour mid-Feb.–early Dec., Thurs. at 10.*

Around Sydney

The Sydney area has numerous activities that are well away from the inner suburbs. These include historic townships, the Sydney 2000 Olympics site, national parks in which to enjoy the Australian bush, and wildlife and theme parks that particularly appeal to children.

Other points of interest are the beaches of Bondi and Manly; the historic city of Parramatta, founded in 1788 and located 26 km (16 mi) to the west; and the magnificent Hawkesbury River, which winds its way around the city's western and northern borders. The waterside suburb of Balmain, 5 km (3 mi) away, has an atmospheric Saturday flea market and backstreets full of character.

Visiting many of these places by public transportation would take a considerable amount of time and effort, so it may be best to rent a car or to go with one of the tour operators that run excursions and day trips.

TIMING   Each of the sights below could easily fill the best part of a day. If you're short on time, try a tour company that combines visits within a particular area—for example, a day trip west to the Olympic Games site, Australian Wildlife Park, and the Blue Mountains.

What to See

☺ **Australian Wildlife Park.** You'll have close encounters with more than 600 Australian native animals here, including koalas, kangaroos, and reptiles, as well as the chance to view crocodiles and rain forest birds. Also in the park is the Outback Woolshed, where sheep are rounded up and shorn, whips are cracked, and hooves thunder in a 30-minute demonstration of a time-honored Australian agricultural tradition. ⊠ *Australia's Wonderland, Wallgrove Rd., Eastern Creek* ☎ *02/9830–9100* 💷 *A$17.60; free with Australia's Wonderland ticket* ☉ *Daily 9–5.*

☺ **86** **Australia's Wonderland.** The largest amusement park in the Southern Hemisphere is landscaped and choreographed for total fun. Action ranges from a Ferris wheel to a roller coaster to the Australian Wildlife Park. Superheros and villains roam the grounds for family photo opps. The complex is in the metropolitan region's west. Admission prices cover all rides and entry fees, including the wildlife park and woolshed. ⊠ *Wallgrove Rd., Eastern Creek* ☎ *02/9830–9100* ⊕ *www.wonderland.com.au* 💷 *A$48.40* ☉ *Daily 10–5.*

81 **Bondi.** Apart from a pleasant day at the beach, Bondi's main appeal is sociological. This is where Sydney sheds its clothes and most of its inhibitions. Many of the city's sporting subcultures congregate here—among them cyclists, anglers, surfers, bodybuilders, and skateboarders—as does a crowd of exhibitionists and eccentrics. The promenade along the back of the beach is the best place to take in the scene.

In spite of its glorious beach and sparkling views, this suburb has not always been fashionable. Bondi—an Aboriginal word meaning "place of breaking waters"—was developed during the 1920s and 1930s. But the spare redbrick architecture, lack of trees, and generally flat terrain did their share to reduce the suburb's appeal. Over the years, Bondi acquired a seedy image fostered by low rents and the free-and-easy lifestyle that the suburb afforded. Author Peter Corris—Australia's version of Raymond Chandler—used Bondi as a tawdry, neon-lighted backdrop for his 1980s thriller, *The Empty Beach.*

Over the past decade, Bondi's proximity to the city and affordable real estate has attracted young and upwardly mobile residents. Most of the old apartment blocks have been smartly renovated or replaced by con-

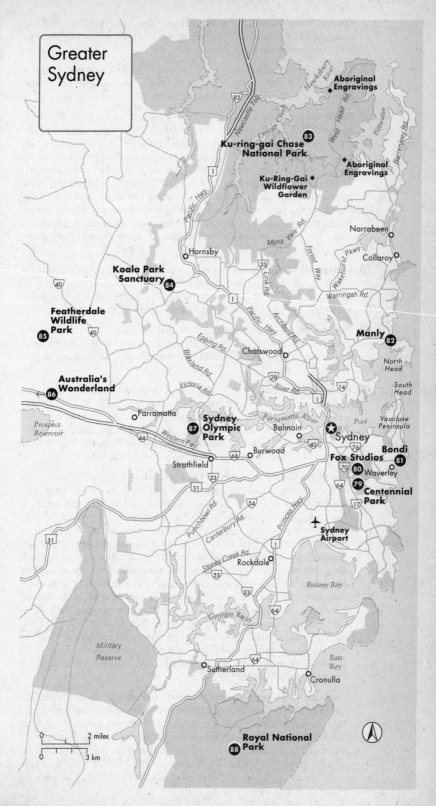

dos that house some of Sydney's wealthiest residents, and Campbell Parade, the beachside street, has been populated with a row of glittering cafés and restaurants.

To get to Bondi, take Bus 380 or 382 from Circular Quay via Elizabeth and Oxford streets, or catch a train to Bondi Junction and then board Bus 380 or 382. A higher-cost option is the Bondi Explorer bus.

79 Centennial Park. More than 500 acres of palm-lined avenues, groves of Moreton Bay figs, paperbark-fringed lakes, and cycling and horse-riding tracks make this a popular park and Sydney's favorite workout circuit. In the early 1800s, the marshy land at the lower end provided Sydney with its fresh water. The park was proclaimed in 1888, the centenary of Australia's foundation as a colony. The Centennial Park Café is often crowded on weekends, but a mobile canteen between the lakes in the middle of the park serves snacks and espresso. Bikes and blades can be rented from the nearby Clovelly Road outlets, on the eastern side of the park. ⊠ *Oxford St. and Centennial Ave., Centennial Park* ⊕ *www.cp. nsw.gov.au* ⊙ *Daily dawn–dusk.*

85 Featherdale Wildlife Park. This park is home to a roll call of Australia's extraordinary fauna in native bush settings. Few Australians will ever see some of these creatures in the wild. ⊠ *217 Kildare Rd., Doonside* ☎ *02/9622–1644* ⊕ *www.featherdale.com.au* ⊡ *A$16* ⊙ *Daily 9–5.*

80 Fox Studios. Australia's largest movie production facility also incorporates a retail center and movie theaters. ⊠ *Driver Ave., Centennial Park, Moore Park* ☎ *1300/369849* ⊕ *www.foxstudios.com.au* ⊡ *Free* ⊙ *Daily 10 AM–11 PM.*

84 Koala Park Sanctuary. At this private park on Sydney's northern outskirts, you can cuddle a koala or hand feed a kangaroo. The sanctuary also has dingoes, wombats, emus, and wallaroos, and there are sheep-shearing and boomerang-throwing demonstrations. Feeding times are 10:20, 11:45, 2, and 3. ⊠ *84 Castle Hill Rd., West Pennant Hills* ☎ *02/ 9484–3141* ⊕ *www.koalaparksanctuary.com.au* ⊡ *A$16* ⊙ *Daily 9–5.*

83 Ku-ring-gai Chase National Park. On a nature hike here, you can see many rock engravings and paintings created and left by the area's originally inhabitants, the Guringai Aboriginal tribe, for which the park is named. The creation of the park in the 1890s also ensured the survival of large stands of eucalyptus trees, as well as small pockets of rain forest in moist gullies. The wildlife here includes swamp wallabies, possums, and goannas, as well as several bird species. The many trails that traverse the park are a delight and mostly designed for easy-to-moderate hikes. The compelling 3-km (2-mi) Garigal Aboriginal Heritage Walk at West Head takes in ancient rock-art sites. There are also many trails in the Bobbin Head area, and from Mt. Ku-ring-gai train station you can walk the 3-km (2-mi) Ku-ring-gai track to Appletree Bay. Another track, the 30-minute Discovery Trail, is wheelchair accessible and provides an excellent introduction to the region's flora and fauna. Leaflets on all of the walks are available at the park's entry stations and from the Kalkari Visitor Centre and the Wildlife Shop at Bobbin Head.

The park is 24 km (15 mi) north of Sydney. Railway stations at Mt. Ku-ring-gai, Berowra, and Cowan, close to the park's western border, provide access to walking trails. On Sunday, for example, you can walk from Mt. Ku-ring-gai station to Appletree Bay and then to Bobbin Head, where a bus can take you to the Turramurra rail station. By car, take the Pacific Highway to Pymble. Then turn into Bobbin Head Road or continue on the highway to Mt. Colah and turn off into the park on

Ku-ring-gai Chase Road. You can also follow the Pacific Highway to Pymble and then drive along the Mona Vale Road to Terry Hills and take the West Head turnoff.

Camping in the park is permitted only at the **Basin in Pittwater** (☎ 02/ 9472–8949). Sites must be booked in advance. The rate is A$9 per night for adults, A$4.50 for children; children under 5 are free. Supplies can be purchased in Palm Beach. For more information on the park, contact Ku-ring-gai Chase National Park Visitors Centre. ✉ *Box 834, Hornsby, 2077* ☎ *02/9472–8949* ⊕ *www.npws.nsw.gov.au.*

⑧② Manly. Until the Sydney Harbour Bridge was built in the 1930s, making the area more accessible, Manly's air of distant enchantment and ease established it as a popular holiday resort. Many Sydneysiders can still recall childhood holidays spent at Manly, embroidered with sand castles, dribbling ice creams, and visits to the Manly Aquarium and the amusement park on Manly Pier.

A sprawling suburb surrounding the base of North Head, the rearing promontory at the northern approach to Sydney Harbour, Manly has an ocean beach as well as a harbor beach. The area was named by Governor Phillip, the colony's first governor, when he noted the "manly behavior" of the local Aborigines. Two years later, in 1790, he might have reconsidered his choice of words when those same Aborigines speared him in the shoulder at Manly Cove.

Manly is more family oriented than Bondi—better mannered, better shaded, and well equipped with cafés—although it does lack its southern sister's sheer entertainment value. If you're thinking about spending the day in Manly, consider visiting the Quarantine Station. To get to Manly, take a ferry or JetCat from Circular Quay. From its landing point the beach is a 10-minute walk.

★ ⑧⑧ Royal National Park. Established in 1879 on the coast south of Sydney, the Royal has the distinction of being the first national park in Australia and the second in the world, after Yellowstone National Park in the United States. Originally set aside as a combination botanical and zoological garden for city dwellers, the park remains popular among Sydneysiders on long weekends and holidays. Surprisingly few foreign travelers visit the national park, however. Those who do are guaranteed great bird-watching—more than 200 species have been recorded. Several times during the past decade large areas of the park have been ravaged by bushfires. Although some of the park's rain forest gullies have been destroyed, most of these burned areas have recovered remarkably, since many of Australia's woodland species have evolved under a regimen of fire that was used as a hunting method by Australia's Aboriginal people.

Several walking tracks traverse the park, most of which require little or no hiking experience. The Lady Carrington Walk, a 10-km (6-mi) trek, is a self-guided tour that crosses 15 creeks and passes several historic sites. Other tracks take you along the coast past beautiful wildflower displays and through patches of rain forest. You can canoe the Port Hacking River upstream from the Audley Causeway; rentals are available at the Audley boat shed on the river. The Illawarra–Cronulla train line stops at Loftus, Engadine, Heathcote, Waterfall, and Otford stations, where most of the park's walking tracks begin. *Royal National Park Visitor Centre ✛ 35 km (22 mi) south of Sydney via the Princes Highway to Farnell Avenue (south of Loftus) or McKell Avenue at Waterfall ✉ mailing address: Box 44, Sutherland, 1499* ☎ *02/9542–0648; National Parks and Wildlife Service district office 02/9542–0666* ✆ *A$10 per vehicle per day.*

87 **Sydney Olympic Park.** The center of the 2000 Olympic and Paralympic Games lies 14 km (9 mi) west of the city center. Sprawling across 1,900 acres on the shores of Homebush Bay, the site was originally a muddy, mangrove-covered backwater on the Parramatta River. By the 1960s, Homebush Bay had served as a racecourse, brick works, armaments depot, and slaughterhouse. During the next decade the bay experienced its ugliest era when it was contaminated through uncontrolled dumping of household and industrial waste, some of it highly toxic.

The transformation, which came about only after Sydney won the bid to host the games, was miraculous. Rising from the shores of the bay is now a series of majestic stadiums, arenas, and accommodation complexes. Among the park's sports facilities are an aquatic center, archery range, athletic center, tennis center, and velodrome, and the centerpiece, an 85,000-seat, A$665 million Olympic Stadium. Since the conclusion of the 2000 Games, it has been mostly used for concerts and sporting events. The Royal Sydney Easter Show, the country's largest agricultural show, with arts displays and demonstrations by craftspersons, takes place here the two weeks before Easter.

The best way to see Sydney Olympic Park is on an Explorer Bus Tour, operated by Sydney Buses. Explorer Buses depart from the Visitors Centre every 30 minutes from just after 9 AM until about 4 PM daily and travel in a circuit. There are ten stops around the site. Your ticket is valid all day and allows you to get on and off the bus as many times as you like. A bus is available between the Centre and Strathfield Station, reached by train from Town Hall or Central stations. A more scenic and relaxing alternative is to take RiverCat from Circular Quay to Homebush Bay. ⊠ *1 Herb Elliot Ave., Homebush Bay* ☎ *02/9714–7888* ⌑ *A$10.*

BEACHES

Sydney is tailor-made for beach lovers. Within the metropolitan area there are more than 30 ocean beaches, all with golden sand and rolling surf, as well as several more around the harbor with calmer water for safe swimming. If your hotel is on the harbor's south side, the logical choice for a day at the beach is the southern ocean beaches between Bondi and Coogee. On the north side of the harbor, Manly is easily accessible by ferry, but beaches farther north involve a long trip by car or public transportation.

Lifeguards are on duty at most of Sydney's ocean beaches during summer months, and flags indicate whether a beach is being patrolled. "Swim between the flags" is an adage that is drummed into every Australian child, with very good reason: The undertow can be very dangerous. Idyllic as it might appear, Sydney's surf claims a number of lives each year, a high proportion of them visitors who are not familiar with local conditions. The flags indicate that a beach is patrolled by lifeguards. If you get into difficulty, don't fight the current. Breathe evenly, stay calm, and raise one arm above your head to signal the lifeguards.

Some visitors to Sydney are concerned about sharks. Although there is no shortage of sharks both inside and outside the harbor, these species are not typically aggressive toward humans. In addition, many Sydney beaches are protected by shark nets, and the risk of attack is very low. A more common hazard is jellyfish, known locally as bluebottles, which inflict a painful sting—with a remote risk of more serious complications (including allergic reactions). Staff at most beaches will supply a spray-on remedy to help relieve the pain, which generally lasts about 24 hours.

Many beaches will post warning signs when bluebottles are present, but you can determine the situation for yourself by looking for the telltale blue bladders washed up along the waterline.

Topless sunbathing is common at all Sydney beaches, but full nudity is permitted only at a couple of locations, including Lady Jane Beach, close to Watsons Bay on the south side of the harbor.

Details of how to reach the beaches by bus, train, or ferry are provided below, but some of the city's harbor and southern beaches are also on the Bondi Explorer bus route. These are Nielsen Park, Camp Cove, Lady Jane, Bondi, Bronte, Clovelly, and Coogee.

Numbers in the margin correspond to beaches on the Sydney Beaches map.

Inside the Harbor

★ 🔟 **Balmoral.** This long, peaceful beach—among the best of the inner-harbor beaches—is one of Sydney's most exclusive northern suburbs. The Esplanade, which runs along the back of the beach, has several snack bars and cafés. You could easily combine a trip to Balmoral with a visit to Taronga Zoo. To reach Balmoral, take the ferry from Circular Quay to Taronga Zoo and then board Bus 238. ✉ *Raglan St., Balmoral.*

🔢 **Camp Cove.** Just inside South Head, this crescent-shape beach is where Sydney's fashionable people come to see and be seen. The gentle slope of the beach and the relatively calm water make it a safe playground for young children. A shop at the northern end of the beach sells salad rolls and fresh fruit juices. The grassy hill at the southern end of the beach has a plaque to commemorate the spot where Captain Arthur Phillip, the commander of the First Fleet, first set foot inside Port Jackson. Parking is limited, and if you arrive by car after 10 on weekends, you'll have a long walk to the beach. Take Bus 324 or 325 from Circular Quay. ✉ *Cliff St., Watsons Bay.*

🔢 **Lady Jane.** Lady Jane—officially called Lady Bay—is the most accessible of the nude beaches around Sydney. It's also a popular beach on Sydney's gay scene, although it attracts a mixed crowd. From Camp Cove, follow the path north and then descend the short, steep ladder leading down the cliff face to the beach.

🔢 **Nielsen Park.** By Sydney standards, this beach at the end of the Vaucluse Peninsula is small, but behind the sand is a large, shady park that's ideal for picnics. The headlands at either end of the beach are especially popular for their magnificent views across the harbor. The beach is protected by a semicircular net, so don't be deterred by the correct name of this beach, Shark Bay. The shop and café behind the beach sell drinks, snacks, and meals. Parking is often difficult on weekends. A 10-minute walk will take you to historic Vaucluse House and a very different harborside experience. Take Bus 325 from Circular Quay. ✉ *Greycliffe Ave. off Vaucluse Rd., Vaucluse.*

South of the Harbor

🔢 **Bondi.** Wide, wonderful Bondi (pronounced *bon*-dye) is the most famous and most crowded of all Sydney beaches. It has something for just about everyone, and the droves who flock here on a sunny day give it a bustling, carnival atmosphere unmatched by any other Sydney beach. Facilities include toilets and showers. Cafés, ice-cream outlets, and restaurants are on Campbell Parade, which runs behind the beach. Families tend to prefer the more sheltered northern end of the beach. Surfing is popular at the south end, where you'll also find a path that winds along the sea-sculpted cliffs to Tamarama and Bronte beaches.

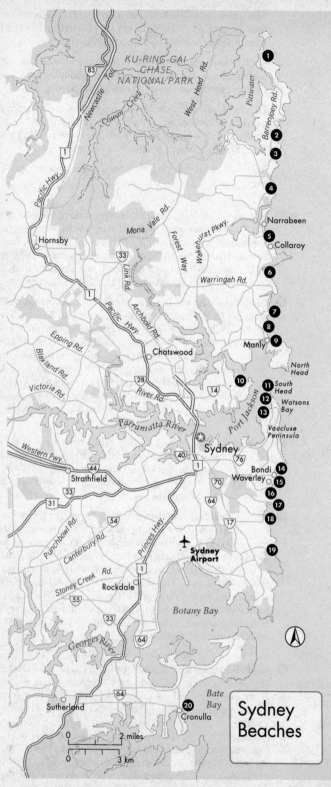

Sydney
Beaches

Take Bus 380 or 382 from Circular Quay via Elizabeth and Oxford streets, or take the train from the city to Bondi Junction and then board Bus 380 or 382. ✉ *Campbell Parade, Bondi Beach.*

★ 16 **Bronte.** If you want an ocean beach that's close to the city, has a choice of sand or grassy areas, and offers a terrific setting, this one is hard to beat. A wooded park of palm trees and Norfolk Island pines surrounds Bronte. The park includes a playground and sheltered picnic tables, and excellent cafés are in the immediate area. The breakers can be fierce, but the sea pool at the southern end of the beach affords safe swimming. Take Bus 378 from Central Station, or take the train from the city to Bondi Junction and then board Bus 378. ✉ *Bronte Rd., Bronte.*

★ 17 **Clovelly.** Swimming is safe at the end of this long, keyhole-shape inlet, even on the roughest day, which makes it a popular family beach. There are toilet facilities but no snack bars or shops in the immediate area. This is also a popular snorkeling spot that usually teems with tropical fish. Take Bus 339 from Argyle Street, Millers Point (The Rocks), or Wynyard bus station; Bus 341 from Central Station; or a train from the city to Bondi Junction. Then board Bus 329. ✉ *Clovelly Rd., Clovelly.*

 18 **Coogee.** A reef protects this lively beach (pronounced *kuh*-jee), creating calmer swimming conditions than those found at its neighbors. A grassy headland overlooking the beach has an excellent children's playground. Cafés in the shopping precinct at the back of the beach sell ice cream, pizza, and the ingredients for picnics. Take Bus 373 from Circular Quay or Bus 372 from Central Station. ✉ *Coogee Bay Rd., Coogee.*

20 **Cronulla.** Even on the hottest days you can escape the crowds by heading to Cronulla, the southernmost and largest beach in the metropolitan area. Good surf is usually running at this beach, and the sand is backed by a grassy park area. Cronulla is a long way from the city by train, however, and its attractions don't justify a long trip if you're not staying nearby. ✉ *Kingsway, Cronulla.*

19 **Maroubra.** This expansive beach is very popular with surfers, although anyone looking for more than waves will probably be unimpressed by the rather scrappy surroundings and the lackluster shopping area. Take Bus 395 from Central Station or Bus 396 from Circular Quay. ✉ *Marine Parade, Maroubra.*

★ 15 **Tamarama.** This small, fashionable beach—it's also known as "Glam-a-rama"—is one of Sydney's prettiest, but the rocky headlands that squeeze close to the sand on either side make it less than ideal for swimming. The sea is often hazardous here, and surfing is prohibited. A café at the back of the beach sells open sandwiches, fresh fruit juices, and fruit whips. Take the train from the city to Bondi Junction. Then board Bus 391, or walk for 10 minutes along the cliffs from the south end of Bondi Beach. ✉ *Tamarama Marine Dr., Tamarama.*

North of the Harbor

3 **Bungan.** If you *really* want to get away from it all, this is the beach for you. Very few Sydneysiders have discovered Bungan, and those who have would like to keep it to themselves. As well as being relatively empty, this wide, attractive beach is one of the cleanest, due to the prevailing ocean currents. Access to the beach involves a difficult hike down a wooden staircase, and there are no facilities. Take Bus 184 or 190 from the Wynyard bus station. ✉ *Beach Rd., off Barrenjoey Rd., Mona Vale.*

5 **Collaroy–Narrabeen.** This is actually one beach that passes through two suburbs. Its main attractions are its size—it's almost 3 km (2 mi) long—and the fact that it's always possible to escape the crowds here. The shops

are concentrated at the southern end of the beach. Take Bus 155 or 157 from Manly or Bus 182, 184, 189, or 190 from the Wynyard bus station. ⊠ *Pittwater Rd., Narrabeen.*

6 Dee Why–Long Reef. Separated from Dee Why by a narrow channel, Long Reef Beach is remoter and much quieter than its southern neighbor. However, Dee Why has better surfing conditions, a big sea pool, and several take-out shops. To get here take Bus 136 from Manly. ⊠ *The Strand, Dee Why.*

7 Freshwater. Sprawling headlands protect this small beach on either side, making it popular among families. The surf club on the beach has good facilities as well as a small shop that sells light refreshments. Take Bus 139 from Manly. ⊠ *The Esplanade, Harbord.*

8 Manly. The Bondi Beach of the north shore, Manly caters to everyone except those who want to get away from it all. The beach is well equipped with changing and toilet facilities, and cafés, souvenir shops, and ice-cream parlors line the nearby shopping area, the Corso. Manly also has several nonbeach attractions. The ferry ride from the city makes a day at Manly feel more like a holiday than just an excursion to the beach. Take a ferry or JetCat from Circular Quay. From the dock at Manly the beach is a 10-minute walk. ⊠ *Steyne St., Manly.*

FodorsChoice ★

2 Newport. With its backdrop of hills and Norfolk Island pines, this broad sweep of sand is one of the finest of the northern beaches. Newport is known for its bodysurfing, and the atmosphere is fairly relaxed. A shopping center within easy walking distance has one of the best selections of cafés and take-out shops of any Sydney beach. Take Bus 189 or 190 from the Wynyard bus station. ⊠ *Barrenjoey Rd., Newport.*

1 Palm Beach. The wide golden sands of Palm Beach mark the northern end of Sydney's beaches. The ocean beach runs along one side of a peninsula separating the large inlet of Pittwater from the Pacific Ocean. Bathers can easily cross from the ocean side to Pittwater's calm waters and sailboats, and you can take a circular ferry trip around this waterway from the wharf on the Pittwater side. The view from the lighthouse at the northern end of the beach is well worth the walk. On a windy day, the southern end of the beach affords some protection. Nearby shops and cafés sell light snacks and meals. The suburb of Palm Beach is a favorite with successful filmmakers and with Sydney's wealthy elite, many of whom own weekend houses in the area. Take Bus 190 from Wynyard bus station. ⊠ *Ocean Rd., Palm Beach.*

9 Shelly. This delightful little beach is protected by a headland rising behind it to form a shady park, and it is well endowed with food options. The snack shop and restaurant on the beach sell everything from light refreshments to elaborate meals, and there are a couple of waterfront cafés at nearby Fairy Bower Bay. On weekends the beach is crowded and parking in the area is nearly impossible. It's best to walk along the seafront from Manly. Take a ferry or JetCat from Circular Quay to Manly. From there the beach is a 1-km (½-mi) walk. ⊠ *Marine Parade, Manly.*

4 Warriewood. Enticing and petite in its cove at the bottom of looming cliffs, Warriewood has excellent conditions for surfers and windsurfers. For swimmers and sunbathers, however, the beach does not justify the difficult journey down the steep cliffs. If you take public transportation here you'll face a long walk from the nearest bus stop. Basic toilet facilities are available on the beach, but there are no shops nearby. Take Bus 184, 189, or 190 from Wynyard bus station or Bus 155 from Manly. ⊠ *Narrabeen Park Parade, Warriewood.*

WHERE TO EAT

Although most Sydney restaurants are licensed to serve alcohol, the few that aren't usually allow you to bring your own bottle (BYOB). Reservations are generally required with a few noticeable exceptions where no bookings at all are taken. Lunch is most often served between noon and 2:30, and dinner is served, usually in a single sitting, between 7 and 10:30. The 10% General Sales Tax is already incorporated in the prices, and a 10% tip is customary. You may pay a corkage fee in BYOB restaurants and some may add a small service surcharge on weekends and holidays. Under the NSW Smoke-Free Environment Act, smoking is prohibited inside all restaurants throughout the state.

WHAT IT COSTS In Australian Dollars					
	$$$$	$$$	$$	$	¢
RESTAURANTS	over A$65	A$46–A$65	A$36–A$45	A$26–A$35	under A$25

Restaurant prices are per person for a main course at dinner.

The Rocks & Circular Quay

Italian

$ ✕ **Aqua Luna.** The restaurant may look out onto the watery charms of Circular Quay, but the food harks back to the gently rolling hills of Tuscany. Little wonder, since Darren Simpson—the youngest cook ever to win Britain's Young Chef of the Year Award—was previously head chef of London's Italianate Sartoria restaurant. Flavors are rustic and authentic, and whenever possible dishes use organic ingredients. Favorites include a salad of artichokes, salted lemons, honey, and almonds and a hearty rabbit-and-borlotti-bean risotto. ⊠ *Opera Quays, No. 2, Shop 18, Macquarie St., East Circular Quay* ☎ *02/9251–0311* ▤ *AE, DC, MC, V* ☺ *No lunch weekends.*

Japanese

$–$$$$ ✕ **Yoshii.** Sydney's finest sushi chef, Ryuichi Yoshii, has moved his eponymous restaurant to The Rocks, where the calm, zenlike decor feels just like Japan. Lunchtime bento boxes start at A$35, but serious sushi fans will want to book the special sushi menus (from A$50 at lunch). For the full Yoshii experience, try the set dinner menu (A$80–A$110), which may include grilled scallop on the half shell under grated apple and glistening salmon roe orbs or *agedashi tofu* (deep-fried tofu in a sweet "dashi," or broth) and foie gras (duck liver with eggplant in broth), a perfect blend of east and west. ⊠ *115 Harrington St., The Rocks* ☎ *02/ 9247–2566* ⚑ *Reservations essential.* ▤ *AE, DC, MC, V* ☺ *Closed Sun. No lunch Mon. and Sat.*

Modern Australian

$$$–$$$$ ✕ **Rockpool.** A meal at Rockpool is a crash course in what modern Australian cooking is all about, conducted in a glamorous, long dining room with a catwalk-like ramp. Chefs Neil Perry and Khan Danis weave Thai, Chinese, Mediterranean, and Middle Eastern influences into their repertoire with effortless flair and originality. Prepare to be amazed by herb- and spice-crusted tuna on braised eggplant salad, stir-fried squid with black-ink noodles, slow-cooked abalone with black fungi and truffle oil, and the luscious stuffed pig's trotter in red curry sauce. If there's room (and there's always room), try the famous date tart. ⊠ *107 George St., The Rocks* ☎ *02/9252–1888* ⚑ *Reservations essential* ▤ *AE, DC, MC, V* ☺ *Closed Sun.–Mon. No lunch.*

Fodor'sChoice
★

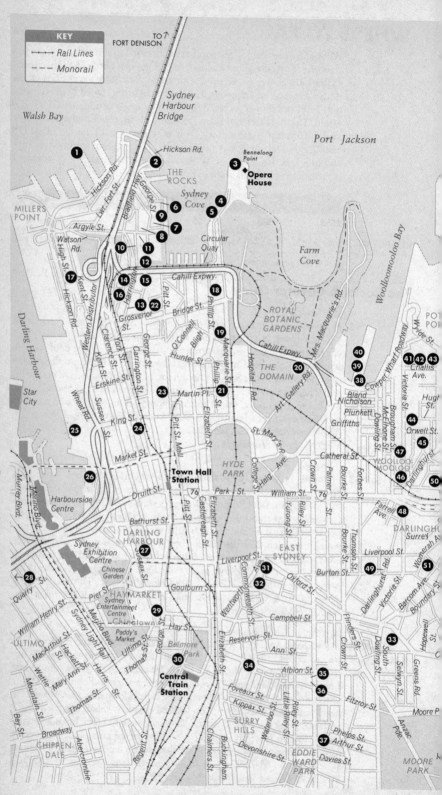

KEY

— Rail Lines

- - - Monorail

TO ↑
FORT DENISON

Sydney
Harbour
Bridge

Walsh Bay

Port Jackson

Hickson Rd.

Bennelong
Point

THE
ROCKS

❸
◆ Opera
House

Sydney
Cove

MILLERS
POINT

❻

❾

❹

❺

Argyle St.

❼

Watson
Rd.

❽

Circular
Quay

Farm
Cove

Woolloomooloo Bay

❿ ⓫

⓬

Cahill Expwy.

⓱

⓮ ⓯

⓲

Darling Harbour

Grosvenor
St.

⓭ ㉒

Bridge St.

ROYAL
BOTANIC
GARDENS

Mrs. Macquarie's Rd.

POT
POI

Cahill Expwy.

⓳

㊵

㊶ ㊷ ㊸
Challis
Ave.

Star
City

Hunter St.

THE
DOMAIN

㊴

㊳

㊹

Orwell St.

㉓

Martin Pl.

⓴

Art Gallery Rd.

Bland
Nicholson
McElhone
Plunkett
Griffiths

㊻

Hugh
St.

⓴

㉑

㉔

King St.

St. Mary's

WOOLLOO
MOOLOO

㊼

㊺

Darlinghurst

㉕

Market St.

HYDE
PARK

College St.

Catheral St.

㊽

Harbourside
Centre

㉖

Town Hall
Station

Druitt St.

Park St.

William St.

DARLINGH
Surrey

Bathurst St.

76

EAST
SYDNEY

Burton St.

DARLINGHU

㉗

Liverpool St.

㊾

㊿

Sydney
Exhibition
Centre

DARLING
HARBOUR

Chinese
Garden

Liverpool St.

㉛

Oxford St.

㉘

Quarry St.

Pier 26
Sydney
Entertainment
Centre

HAYMARKET

Chinatown

㉜

Campbell St.

㉙

Goulburn St.

㉝

William Henry St.

Paddy's
Market

Hay St.

Reservoir St.

Ann St.

ULTIMO

Belmore
Park

㉚

Central
Train
Station

Albion St.

㉞

㉟

Foveaux St.

㊱

Fitzroy St.

Kippax St.

Broadway

SURRY
HILLS

Phelps St.

㊲

Arthur St.

CHIPPEN-
DALE

Devonshire St.

EDDIE
WARD
PARK

Davies St.

MOORE
PARK

MOORE P

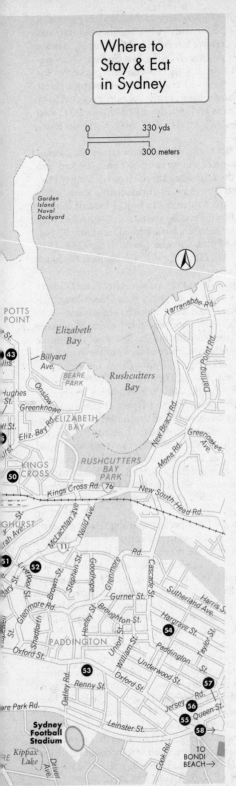

Where to Stay & Eat in Sydney

```
0        330 yds
0        300 meters
```

\$\$–\$\$\$ ✕ **Aria.** From the Mercedes-Benz upholstery to the Limoges porcelain, everything here screams "Big Night Out!" Chef Matthew Moran and partner Peter Sullivan are the creative forces behind this clubby, lavishly appointed restaurant perfectly positioned on the East Circular Quay waterfront, near the Opera House. It's the appropriate backdrop for Moran's baked salmon fillet served with crushed Kipfler potatoes, crème fraîche, broad beans, and lobster bisque, or the succulent roasted baby chicken with sautéed mushrooms and gnocchi. ✉ *1 Macquarie St., East Circular Quay* ☎ *02/9252–2555* ▭ *AE, DC, MC, V* ☻ *No lunch weekends.*

\$\$ ✕ **Guillaume at Bennelong.** Chef Guillaume Brahimi rattles the pans at possibly the most superbly located dining room in town. Tucked into the side of the Opera House, the restaurant affords views of Sydney Harbour Bridge and the city lights. Prices hover at reasonable levels, while Brahimi's creations soar. Try the Moreton Bay bug (a kind of lobster) paired with sauternes-glazed sweetbreads, a satiny slow-poached rack of West Australian lamb, or the signature basil-infused rare tuna. ✉ *Sydney Opera House, Bennelong Point, Circular Quay* ☎ *02/9241–1999* ⌂ *Reservations essential* ▭ *AE, DC, MC, V* ☻ *Closed Sun. No lunch Sat.–Thurs.*

\$\$ ✕ **Quay.** In his take on Modern Australian cuisine, chef Peter Gilmore masterfully crafts such dishes as crisp pork belly with Queensland scallops, and pressed duck confit with star anise. Desserts are sublime—particularly the five-textured Valrhona chocolate cake, which may make you weak at the knees—and the wine list fits the flavors of the cuisine like an old glove. Glass walls afford wonderful views of the bridge and Opera House, right at your fork's tip. ✉ *Upper Level, Overseas Passenger Terminal, West Circular Quay, The Rocks* ☎ *02/9251–5600* ⌂ *Reservations essential* ▭ *AE, DC, MC, V* ☻ *No lunch weekends.*

Fodor's Choice
★

\$–\$\$ ✕ **harbourkitchen & bar.** Dramatic harbor and Opera House views are democratically shared by this one-size-fits-all restaurant and its attendant bar. The food rivals the views of the Opera House and is best described as Modern Rustic, with a produce-driven menu revolving around the rotisserie and wood-fired grill. The long list of dishes includes everything from roasted prawns with green garlic and artichokes to veal scallopini with cassoulet and fusilli. ✉ *Park Hyatt Sydney, 7 Hickson Rd., Circular Quay* ☎ *02/9256–1660* ⌂ *Reservations essential* ▭ *AE, DC, MC, V.*

\$ ✕ **Pavilion on the Park.** A recipe for a perfect morning: After an early stroll through the Botanic Gardens head to this conservatory-style café, shaded by Moreton Bay figs amid the green lawns of the Domain, for a lingering breakfast of muffins with scrambled eggs, Mohr smoked salmon, and hollandaise. Lunch in the adjoining restaurant takes you into more serious territory, with such lively variations as scallops on white polenta or brioche crumbed calves' liver with nuggets of honey and brown roasted cauliflower. ✉ *1 Art Gallery Rd., the Domain* ☎ *02/9232–1322* ⌂ *Reservations essential* ▭ *AE, DC, MC, V* ☻ *No dinner.*

\$ ✕ **The Wharf Restaurant.** At one time only the Wharf's proximity to the Sydney Theatre Company (they share Pier 4) attracted diners, but with Tim Pak Poy of Claude's now one of the owners, the emphasis is firmly on the food. Free-range chicken is spiced with cinnamon and roasted whole, prawns are preserved with butter, and trout is cured with beetroot and served with Waldorf sauce (chopped celery, apples, and walnuts in a mayonnaise-based sauce). You can see Sydney Harbour Bridge from some tables, but it's North Sydney and the ferries that provide the real floor show. Meal times and sizes are flexible to accommodate theatergoers. ✉ *End of Pier 4, Hickson Rd., Walsh Bay* ☎ *02/9250–1761* ⌂ *Reservations essential* ▭ *AE, DC, MC, V* ☻ *Closed Sun.*

Southwestern

¢–$$ ✕ **Wildfire.** Coyote Cafe supremo Mark Miller has brought a touch of Santa Fe and a whole lot more to this house of everything wood-fired right on Circular Quay. As ferries slide out to Manly, tuck into dishes from freshly shucked oysters at the crustacean bar, to the full Churrasco banquet, a meat-fuelled frenzy inspired by the food of Brazil. The decor has turned a hangarlike space underneath the Overseas Passenger Terminal into a buzzy, charm-filled room, but it's the view that usually ends up as eye candy. ⊠ *Lower Level, Overseas Passenger Terminal, West Circular Quay, The Rocks* ☎ *02/9252–5077* ⌚ *Reservations essential* ▤ *AE, DC, MC, V.*

Thai

★ ¢–$ ✕ **Sailor's Thai.** Sydney's most exciting and authentic Thai food comes from this glamorously restored restaurant in the Old Sailors Home. Downstairs, business types rub shoulders with sightseers and hard-core shoppers, devouring delicious red curries and salads fragrant with lime juice and fish sauce. Upstairs is The Sailor's Thai Canteen, a casual first-come, first-served noodle bar, where the long, communal zinc table groans with such offerings as *som dtam* (shredded papaya salad) and *pad thai* (rice noodles stir-fried with shrimp, egg, peanuts, and chili). Reservations essential for main restaurant, not accepted at the Canteen. ⊠ *106 George St., The Rocks* ☎*02/9251–2466* ▤ *AE, DC, MC, V* ☉ *Restaurant closed Sun. (Canteen open daily). No lunch Sat.*

City Center Area

Chinese

¢–$$ ✕ **Golden Century.** For two hours—or as long as it takes for you to consume delicately steamed prawns, luscious mud crab with ginger and shallots, and *pipis* (triangular clams) with black bean sauce—you might as well be in Hong Kong. This place is heaven for seafood lovers, with wall-to-wall fish tanks filled with crab, lobster, abalone, and schools of barramundi, parrot fish, and coral trout. You won't have to ask if the food is fresh. Most of it is swimming around you as you eat. The atmosphere is no-frills and the noise level can be deafening, but the food is worth it. Supper is served late evenings from 10 until 4. ⊠ *393–399 Sussex St., Haymarket* ☎ *02/9212–3901* ▤ *AE, DC, MC, V.*

French

$$ ✕ **Banc.** Dashing restaurateur-about-town Stan Sarris and British-trained chef Liam Tomlin have joined forces to turn a former bank into the city center's most lavish dining room, complete with marblelike columns, high ceilings, and sleek, two-tone banquettes. Throw in a 22-page wine list, a heavily laden cheese trolley, and a legal-eagle lunch crowd, and you have one of the city's most seductive dining scenes. It's made even more enticing by an ethereally light scallop mousse with sautéed scampi or a heavenly filet of beef with potato-and-truffle gnocchi and panfried foie gras. ⊠ *53 Martin Pl., City Center* ☎ *02/9233–5300* ⌚ *Reservations essential* ▤ *AE, DC, MC, V* ☉ *Closed Sun.–Mon. No lunch Sat.*

Malaysian

★ ¢–$$ ✕ **Chinta Ria Temple of Love.** Part-time jazz DJ Simon Goh has put a unique spin on this Malaysian restaurant, with a giant laughing Buddha, miked-up chefs, and retro furniture salvaged from a car-factory canteen. The music is loud and swinging, much like the crowds that flock here. The no-reservations policy for dinner means you need to get here early to be sure of a table. Waits can be lengthy, even on Monday nights. The food is hawker-style Malaysian, which means intense, fierce dishes such as the coconut-rich *laksa* (Malaysian curry), flaky curry puffs, and

CloseUp

AUSTRALIAN CUISINE: WHAT IS IT WHEN IT'S AT HOME?

AUSTRALIA SIMPLY DIDN'T have time to sit back and wait for a homegrown cuisine to evolve in the traditional way. By the time the country was settled by the British 200 years ago, the industrial revolution had already made it virtually impossible for any single region to be isolated enough to gradually develop its own food resources and traditions, without outside influence or interference.

So we borrowed an Anglo-Saxon way of eating that had little to do with where, what, or who we happened to be. We learned, of necessity, to include what was in our natural larder. The incredibly vast landmass of Australia means that somewhere in the country is a microclimate that is suitable for producing whatever we feel like eating, from the tropical fruit and sugarcane fields of northern Queensland, to the grazing pastures and citrus groves of the temperate Riverina and Riverland areas, to the cool-climate dairy products of Victoria and Tasmania. It also didn't take us too long to realize that a country surrounded by water is a country surrounded by oysters, clams, crabs, lobsters, prawns, and fish.

The next great influence came from the Southern Europeans who came to this country as refugees after World War II. Many were Spaniards, Greeks, and Italians, people who had lived with coastal breezes in their veins and whose lives and foods had been warmed by the Mediterranean sun.

But the emergence of a truly identifiable Australian way of eating came when we finally realized in the late '70s that it was actually Asia's doorstep we were on, and not England's. These Asian and Mediterranean influences, together with a continual drive for superior produce and a spirit of experimentation, are the major factors that continue to define Australian cuisine. It's a cuisine that has many faces. Key dishes can immortalize indigenous produce, such as rare-roasted kangaroo with baby beets, or steamed barramundi

with soy and ginger. At the same time, they can totally transform more universal ingredients, such as char-grilled Atlantic salmon with preserved lemon and couscous, or a miraculous checkerboard ice cream flavored with aniseed and pineapple.

But Australian cuisine is no slammed-together grab bag of fusion techniques or East meets West. It's not just about ingredients. It's about attitude. It's brash, easygoing, big-flavored, fresh, and thoroughly natural. It's Japanese-born Tetsuya Wakuda's impossibly silky ocean trout confit with trout roe and konbu seaweed at Tetsuya's in Sydney. Or Malaysian native Cheong Liew's bravely conceived braised chicken with sea scallops, veal sweetbreads, roasted fennel, and black moss at Grange Restaurant in Adelaide. Or Sydneysider Neil Perry's adventure trek of mud crab, sweet pork, and green papaw salad at Rockpool in Sydney. It's also Chris Jackman's delicate snow-pea custard with fresh morel mushrooms at Mit Zitrone in Hobart. Even French Provincial cooking, currently enjoying a revival in Australia, seems somehow sunnier, brighter, and fresher than it ever was in the Left-Bank bistros of Paris.

This is the sort of cooking that has made Australia a modern culinary force, and stamped Sydney as one of the three current food capitals of the world, along with New York and London. Let the academics ponder if it is a true cuisine or just a lifestyle. The rest of us will do the only sensible thing: head off to a great Australian restaurant and make up our own minds.

—Terry Durack

Hokkien mee (Chinese-style noodles)—all worth the wait. ⊠ *Level 2, 201 Sussex St., Cockle Bay Wharf, Darling Park, City Center* ☎ *02/ 9264-3211* ⊟ *AE, DC, MC, V.*

Modern Australian

$$$$ ✕ **Forty One.** The view east over the harbor is glorious, the private dining rooms are plush, and Dietmar Sawyere's Asian-influenced classical food is full of finesse. The set-price dinner menu (A$120) varies, but might include a tantalizing warm salad of Chinese duck and sea scallops, and the cruelly delicious Valrhona-chocolate tart. The vegetarian menu, with the likes of goat's cheese with marinated peppers and kalamata-olive oil, is sublime. The restaurant's decadent Krug Room is a snug haven for those who still believe a glass of champagne and a little foie gras can cure most of the world's ills. ⊠ *Chifley Tower, Level 42, 2 Chifley Sq., City Center* ☎ *02/9221-2500* ⌂ *Reservations essential* ⊟ *AE, DC, MC, V* ☉ *Closed Sun. No lunch Mon. and Sat.*

★ **$$$$** ✕ **Tetsuya's.** It's worth getting on the waiting list—there's always a waiting list—to sample the unique blend of Western techniques and Japanese/French flavors crafted by Sydney's most applauded chef Tetsuya Wakuda. The serene, expansive dining room's unobtrusive Japanese aesthetic leaves the food as the true highlight. Scallop sashimi with duck foie gras and tartare of tuna with olive oil and wasabi jelly are typical items from a pricey set menu (A$185) that never fails to intrigue as much as it dazzles. Views of a Japanese garden complete with bonsai and a waterfall make this place seem miles from the city center. ⊠ *529 Kent St., City Center* ☎ *02/9267-2900* ⌂ *Reservations essential* ⊟ *AE, DC, MC, V* ☉ *Closed Sun.–Mon. No lunch Tues.–Thurs.*

$$–$$$ ✕ **Est.** The elegant, pillared dining room is the perfect setting for showing off chef Peter Doyle's modern, light touch. The *jacqueline* sauce (flavored with cream, carrot, and sherry) on the crisp, skinned John Dory lets the fish shine, while a ragout of beans, tapenade, and rosemary oil complements the lamb. Anything Doyle cooks with scallops is divine. The dessert of mixed berries with rhubarb jelly will test any dieter's resolve. ⊠ *Level 1, Establishment Hotel, 252 George St., City Center* ☎ *02/ 9240-3010* ⌂ *Reservations essential* ⊟ *AE, DC, MC, V* ☉ *Closed Sun. No lunch Sat.*

Steak

$$ ✕ **Prime.** Until Prime came along, steak houses in Sydney were old-fashioned, macho affairs where men in dark suits scoffed down copious quantities of cheap red wine and charred red meat. Inspired by the likes of Smith & Wollensky and Maloney & Porcelli in New York, Stan Sarris, of Banc fame, decided to elevate the image of the Aussie steak. The result is an elegant restaurant in what was once the staff canteen for postal workers, in the basement of the city post office. As well as serving some of the best steaks in town, Prime also has knockout seafood tortellini and poached barramundi with clams. The oysters are also superb. ⊠ *1 Martin Pl., City Centre* ☎ *02/9229-7777* ⌂ *Reservations essential* ⊟ *AE, DC, MC, V* ☉ *Closed Sun. No lunch Sat.*

Darlinghurst & Woolloomooloo

Cafés

★ ¢ ✕ **bills.** This sunny corner café is so addictive it should come with a health warning. It's a favorite hangout of everyone from local nurses to semi-disguised rock stars, and you never know who you might be sitting next to ("Isn't that Nicole Kidman?") at the big communal table. If you're not interested in the creaminess of what must be Sydney's best scrambled eggs, try the ricotta hot cakes with honeycomb butter. At lunch you'll have to decide between the spring-onion pancakes with gravlax and the most famous steak sandwich in town. ⊠ *433 Liverpool St., Darlinghurst* ☎ *02/9360–9631* ⚐ *Reservations not accepted* ▤ *AE, MC, V* ⛏ *BYOB* ☾ *Closed Sun. No dinner.*

Italian

$–$$ ✕ **Otto.** Few restaurants have the pulling power of Otto, a place where radio shock-jocks sit side by side with fashion-magazine editors and foodies, all on the revamped and stylish Finger Wharf. Yes, it's a scene. But fortunately, it's a scene with good Italian food and waiters who have just enough attitude to make them a challenge worth conquering. The homemade pastas are very good, the slow-roasted duck with green lentils benchmark, and the selection of Italian wines expensive but rarely matched this far from Milan. ⊠ *The Wharf at Woolloomooloo, 8 Cowper Wharf Rd., Woolloomooloo* ☎ *02/9368–7488* ⚐ *Reservations essential* ▤ *AE, DC, MC, V* ☾ *Closed Mon.*

Modern Australian

$$ ✕ **Salt.** Are you wearing black? Is your hand in martini position? Do you look like someone groovy and influential? Then you're ready to dine at Salt, the hippest, happiest Mod-Oz bistro. Chef Luke Mangan has worked with three-star chefs in London, and his skills shine in such dishes as baked guinea fowl breast with Parmesan and artichoke puree, and salt-baked salmon with dates and watercress in a smoked tea bisque. ⊠ *229 Darlinghurst Rd., Darlinghurst* ☎ *02/9332–2566* ⚐ *Reservations essential* ▤ *AE, DC, MC, V* ☾ *No lunch weekends.*

★ ¢–$ ✕ **Bayswater Brasserie.** The Bayz, as regulars affectionately call it, has been serving oysters, colorful cocktails, and easygoing Mediterranean- and Asian-influenced cuisine since the early '80s. Start with a drink in the moody back bar. Then try for a table in the front room, styled like a French brasserie. The menu changes regularly, but there's always an excellent selection of oysters opened to order. Blackboard specials may include baked barramundi with grilled witloof and confit tomatoes, or braised lamb shanks with polenta and leeks. ⊠ *32 Bayswater Rd., Kings Cross* ☎ *02/9357–2177* ▤ *AE, DC, MC, V* ☾ *Closed Sun. No lunch Mon.–Thurs. and Sat.*

Seafood

$ ✕ **Manta Ray.** Part of the swank Finger Wharf development, this fine seafood restaurant has a salty sea view to match. Straightforward preparations and garnishes allow the seafood's natural flavors to speak for themselves: salt cod and olive oil, simple shellfish bisque, and a casserole of crab, *yabbie* (a burrowing crustacean similar to crawdads), squid, and fish. Part-owner Tim Connell is a former fish merchant whose day begins in the wee hours with a trip to the Sydney fish markets. The setting is breezy and bistro-style, with glass doors that slide open to let in the sounds of gulls and the slap of rigging in the marina. ⊠ *The Wharf at Woolloomooloo, 7 Cowper Wharf Rd., Woolloomooloo* ☎ *02/9332–3822* ⚐ *Reservations essential* ▤ *AE, DC, MC, V.*

Paddington & Woollahra

French

$$$$ ✕ **Claude's.** This tiny, unprepossessing restaurant proves that good
FodorsChoice things really do come in small packages. Among Chef Tim Pak Poy's
★ startlingly executed and thoughtfully presented creations are grilled breast of Muscovy duck in caramel, crisp battered marron (freshwater lobster), and an ethereal goat's milk soufflé with peaches. This was the first restaurant to serve Australia's cultivated black truffles. ⊠ *10 Ox-*

ford St., Woollahra ☎ 02/9331–2325 ⬧ Reservations essential ☰ AE,
MC, V ☺ Closed Sun.–Mon. No lunch.

$ ✕ **Bistro Moncur.** Chef Damien Pignolet, no stranger to fine dining after
having run nearby Claude's, is the beaming owner of a loud and proud
bistro that spills over with happy-go-lucky patrons who don't mind waiting a half hour for a table. How refreshing to order salmon and get salmon,
to order sausages and get sausages, and to have no disappointments.
Even the coffee at the end of the meal is the ultimate coffee. And the
bill, though not cheap, is appropriate to the bistro nature of the place.
⊠ Woollahra Hotel, 116 Queen St., Woollahra ☎ 02/9363–2519
⬧ Reservations not accepted ☰ AE, DC, MC, V ☺ No lunch Mon.

¢–$ ✕ **Bistro LuLu.** Cozy and intimate, this woody bistro brings a touch of
the Paris boulevards to Sydney's fashion catwalk. The food is essentially
unfussy and unpretentious, but the essentials are all here in such dishes
as seared chicken livers with beetroot, Parmesan, and sherry vinegar;
grilled sardines with spiced cucumbers and feta; and the standout sir-
loin with Café de Paris butter and frites. On the lighter side, there's a
selection of organic salads, which might be a platter of asparagus, avocado, boiled egg, and anchovy croutons dressed with lemon. ⊠ 257
Oxford St., Paddington ☎ 02/9380–6888 ⬧ Reservations essential
☰ AE, DC, MC, V ☺ No lunch Mon.–Wed.

Italian

★ $$ ✕ **Buon Ricordo.** Walking into this happy, bubbly place is like turning
up at a private party in the backstreets of Naples. Host, chef, and sur-
rogate uncle Armando Percuoco invests classic Neapolitan and Tuscan
techniques with inventive personal touches to produce such dishes as
warmed figs with Gorgonzola and prosciutto, truffled egg pasta, and
scampi with saffron sauce and black-ink risotto. Everything comes with
Italian–style touches that you can see, feel, smell, and taste. Leaving the
restaurant feels like leaving home. ⊠ 108 Boundary St., Paddington ☎ 02/
9360–6729 ⬧ Reservations essential ☰ AE, DC, MC, V ☺ Closed
Sun.–Mon. No lunch Tues.–Thurs.

$$ ✕ **Lucio's.** From the Tuscan-style pots to the art-cluttered walls, this smart
restaurant revels in all things Italian. Chef Tim Fisher scrupulously con-
tinues the Latin tradition laid down over two decades by owner Lucio
Galletto. Selections from the menu include a melt-in-the-mouth baked
salmon fillet with grilled zucchini and black olives; delicate grilled quail
with a purée of eggplant, shallots, and sage; and a succulent roast, milk-
fed veal with peppers. The surroundings are elegant, the presentation
is artful, and the service is knowledgeable and in the best Italian tradition. ⊠ 47 Windsor St., Paddington ☎ 02/9380–5996 ⬧ Reservations essential ☰ AE, DC, MC, V ☺ Closed Sun.

Potts Point

Italian

¢ ✕ **Fratelli Paradiso.** Fratelli (meaning brothers) is run by the Paradiso siblings, whose Italian heritage shows in everything from the bomba (like
a donut) in their adjoining bakery to the friendly service. Arrive early
to find local devotees sipping a morning constitutional caffeine hit with
their rice pudding, or at dinner for one of the best pennes with a melting veal ragu. The zucchini flower and fontina risotto is the stuff local
legends are built on. ⊠ 12–16 Challis Ave., Potts Point ☎ 02/9357–1744
⬧ Reservations not accepted ☰ AE, DC, MC, V ☺ No dinner weekends.

Modern Australian

¢–$ ✕ **Lotus.** In the world of fashion, according to one-time clothing design
house Merivale and Mr John, the new glamor is restaurants. That's why

Merivale's and John Hemmes' family now run so many restaurants, including this funky little bistro. With its fabulous back bar and pencil-thin diners, the food probably doesn't have to be as good as it is. Tender pink lamb rack comes on garlic mash, stuffed squid is lifted with a hint of chili, and the richness of duck liver salad is cut through with the pepperiness of watercress. ⊠ *22 Challis Ave., Potts Point* ☎ *02/9326–0488* ⌂ *Reservations not accepted* ▭ *AE, DC, MC, V* ☺ *Closed Mon. No lunch Tues.–Thurs.*

Pan-Asian

¢–$ ✕ **Jimmy Liks.** Everybody who's anybody (and a lot of those who are nobody) clamor for a seat at the long, communal, timber table at this grooviest of groovy restaurants. It's no disappointment to park in the bar while you wait for some of the most fabulous Asian "street food" around. Will Meyrick may have honed his palate on the byways of Asia, but his *keng om* (braised venison shank) or smoked eel on betel leaves are pure restaurant heaven. Lighting is sexy and low, not unlike the jeans on half the diners. ⊠ *188 Victoria St., Potts Point* ☎ *02/8354–1400* ⌂ *Reservations not accepted* ▭ *AE, DC, MC, V* ☺ *Closed Sun. No lunch.*

¢ ✕ **XO.** At the second restaurant of Rockpool's Neil Perry, Asian cuisines are practiced with textbook dexterity. Sure, there are great city views from the multilevel space, but most people come for the tamarind duck, the pipis in a complex version of Hong Kong's sensational XO sauce (made with dried scallops), and the sticky, addictive Yunnan ribs. There's a bar for lingering while you wait for a table, which happens more often than not as the restaurant doesn't take bookings. ⊠ *155 Victoria St., Potts Point* ☎ *02/9331–8881* ⌂ *Reservations not accepted* ▭ *AE, DC, MC, V* ☺ *Closed Sun.–Mon. No lunch.*

Surry Hills

Chinese

¢–$ ✕ **Billy Kwong.** Locals rub shoulders while eating no-fuss Chinese food at chef Kylie Kwong's trendy drop-in restaurant. Kwong prepares the kind of food her family cooks, with Grandma providing not just the inspiration but also the recipes. Even the dumplings are made by specialty chefs from Shanghai. While the table you're occupying is probably being eyed by the next set of adoring fans, staff members never rush you. But you could always play nice and ask for the bill with your last mouthful of braised pork belly or silken tofu. ⊠ *3/355 Crown St., Surry Hills* ☎ *02/9332–3300* ⌂ *Reservations not accepted* ▭ *AE, MC, V* ⌂ *BYOB* ☺ *No lunch.*

French

$–$$ ✕ **Marque.** Back in the mid-1990s, Mark Best won an award as Sydney's most promising young chef. Now that promise has been fulfilled in his sleek and elegant Darlinghurst restaurant. Few chefs approach French flavors with such passion and dedication. Stints with three-star demigods Alain Passard in Paris, and Raymond Blanc in England, haven't done any harm either, and it's impossible not to be impressed when food is this well crafted. Best's boned chicken with pearl barley farce is a triumph, as are the salad of autumn vegetables and the baby madeleines. ⊠ *355 Crown St., Surry Hills* ☎ *02/9332–2225* ⌂ *Reservations essential* ▭ *AE, DC, MC, V* ☺ *Closed Sun. No lunch.*

Modern Australia

★ $$ ✕ **MG Garage Restaurant.** Sydney is all revved up about this glamorous, good-time restaurant, which even has an MG on the floor. High-performance chef Jeremy Strode has moved up from Langton's in Melbourne. He pleases palates with an amazing cauliflower *panna cotta* (silky egg custard) topped with gently smoky slivers of eel, and his parsley soup with poached oysters is a gastronomic feat immersed in deep-green chlorophyll. ✉ *490 Crown St., Surry Hills* ☎ *02/9383–9383* ⌕ *Reservations essential* ▤ *AE, DC, MC, V* ◷ *Closed Sun. No lunch Mon. and Sat.*

¢ ✕ **Bécasse.** Foodies have been falling over each other to eat at this modest dining room of Banc protégé Justin North, and not just because the prices are good. They also come for handcrafted food with more than a touch of classic technique. A salad of beetroot, leek, and lamb's tongue (*mache*) is giddily good and light, while a side dish of fried potatoes served with bone marrow is enough to stop your heart. Roasted barramundi with pippies and mussels should calm the nerves and please the cardiologist. ✉ *48 Albion St., Surry Hills* ☎ *02/9280–3202* ⌕ *Reservations essential* ▤ *AE, MC, V* ◷ *Closed Mon.–Tues. No lunch.*

Thai

★ $–$$ ✕ **Longrain.** Start with a cocktail in the cool, minimalist bar, where Sydney's high life gathers around low-slung tables. Then make for the dining room, where the hip crowd jostles for a position at one of three giant wooden communal tables—it might be trendy, but the food is terrific. Chef Martin Boetz raised this restaurant to become a leader of Sydney's Thais with an enthusiasm that's matched by his intimate knowledge of ingredients. His duck, venison, tuna, beef shin, and pork hock each marry style with substance. Reservations are not accepted for dinner. ✉ *85 Commonwealth St., Surry Hills* ☎ *02/9280–2888* ▤ *AE, DC, MC, V* ◷ *Closed Sun. No lunch weekends.*

Greater Sydney

Italian

$–$$$ ✕ **Icebergs Dining Room and Bar.** The fashionable set just adore being perched like seagulls over Bondi Icebergs swimming pool and Australia's most famous beach. It's not just because former Otto supremo Maurizio Terzini has used his not-inconsiderable talent (and that of designer Carl Pickering) to showcase the waves, the sand, and the sun. Chef Karen Martini's modern Italian food, such as swordfish with salsa verde, or a gorgeous Balmain bug (like a shovel-nosed lobster) salad with peas and tarragon, is equally glorious. ✉ *1 Notts Ave., Bondi Beach* ☎ *02/9365–9000* ⌕ *Reservations essential* ▤ *AE, DC, MC, V* ◷ *Closed Mon.*

Modern Australian

$$ ✕ **Aqua Dining.** At this restaurant perched over North Sydney Olympic Pool, you may feel guilty savoring the food and the incredible views of the harbor while others exercise, but don't let that stop you from enjoying this place. Resign yourself to simply feasting on swordfish on white beans and artichokes, roasted west Australian marron with mustard potato and lemon oil, or caramel pear served with a dentist's nightmare of nougat parfait. Natural light floods the space during the day, and at night it's the twinkles on the harbor that catch your eye. ✉ *Paul and North Cliff Sts., Milsons Point* ☎ *02/9964–9998* ⌕ *Reservations essential* ▤ *AE, DC, MC, V* ◷ *No lunch Sat.*

★ $–$$ ✕ **The Bathers' Pavilion.** Balmoral Beach is blessed. Not only does it possess an inviting sandy beach and great water views, but it also has one of the best eating strips north of Harbour Bridge. Queen of the strip is Bathers' Pavilion, which includes a restaurant, café, and lavish private dining room. Serge Dansereau cooks with one hand on the seasons and the other on the best local ingredients, creating set-price dinner menus (A$87–A$110) that are colorful, light, and thoroughly appropriate to the time and place. Dishes might include ocean trout with seaweed,

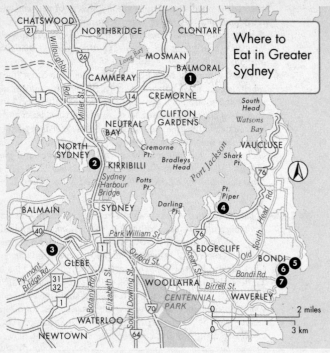

Where to
Eat in Greater
Sydney

spinach, and horseradish sauce, or steamed snapper in pine-nut butter.
⊠ *4 The Esplanade, Balmoral* ☎ *02/9969–5050* ✍ *Reservations essential* 🖃 *AE, DC, MC, V.*

$–$$ ✕ **Sean's Panaroma.** It may look like a cross between a half-finished bomb shelter and a neglected shore house, but this beachside restaurant is home to Sean Moran, one of Sydney's brightest and most innovative chefs. While lunches are easygoing affairs, things get a little more serious at night as Moran cooks up memorable dishes including Barossa Valley chicken with sweet-potato puree and peas, Illabo lamb shoulder with cannellini beans and sugar snap peas; and raspberry, blackberry, and blueberry trifle. ⊠ *270 Campbell Parade, Bondi Beach* ☎ *02/9365–4924* ✍ *Reservations essential* 🖃 *MC, V* 🍶 *BYOB* ⊙ *No lunch weekdays. No dinner Sun.–Tues.*

$ ✕ **Hugo's.** Snappy leisure wear and "cool dude" dispositions are the order of the day at Hugo's—and that's just the waitstaff. Like Bondi itself, this restaurant works effortlessly on many levels, without ever taking itself too seriously. Weekend breakfasts are legendary, especially on one of the outside bench seats, where you can watch the waves as well as the passing parade of gorgeous suntans. At night, things get serious with the justly famous panfried prawn and avocado stack, roasted duck breast on bok choy, and spanner crab linguine. ⊠ *70 Campbell Parade, Bondi Beach* ☎ *02/9300–0900* ✍ *Reservations essential* 🖃 *AE, DC, MC, V* ⊙ *No lunch weekdays.*

Seafood

$$–$$$ ✕ **Pier.** With its wraparound harbor views and shipshape good looks, this wharf restaurant is a highly appropriate place to enjoy Australia's finest seafood. Chefs Steve Hodges and Greg Doyle know their fish and manage to reach beyond the predictable char-grills and fish-and-chips without being gimmicky. The freshness of the produce itself sings in such fish as curried blue-eye cod, pot-roasted rock lobster, and snapper fillets with Jerusalem artichoke. ✉ *594 New South Head Rd., Rose Bay* ☎ *02/9327–6561* ▤ *AE, DC, MC, V.*

$$ ✕ **Boathouse on Blackwattle Bay.** When Sydneysiders talk about "the bridge," they're not necessarily referring to Sydney Harbour. Almost as loved is very much newer Anzac Bridge, which you can see best from a window table at this waterside eatery. You also get a good view of the fish markets, appropriate since seafood is the focus here, with clams, mussels, crabs, and lobsters all coming from live tanks in the kitchen. Meat eaters can console themselves by ordering beef filet with pea puree or suckling pig with grilled figs. ✉ *End of Ferry Rd., Glebe* ☎ *02/9518–9011* ⚓ *Reservations essential* ▤ *AE, DC, MC, V* ☾ *Closed Mon.*

WHERE TO STAY

Sydney has numerous accommodations options, from glamorous hotels to bed-and-breakfasts, the latter of which can be found even close to the heart of the city. The best address in town is undoubtedly The Rocks, which combines harbor views and proximity to major cultural attractions, restaurants, shops, and galleries with a tranquil atmosphere. The area around Kings Cross is the city's second major hotel district. Keep in mind, however, that this is also the city's major nightlife district, and not for the faint-hearted after sunset.

If you arrive in Sydney without a hotel reservation, the best place to start looking is the Tourism New South Wales information counter at the international airport, which acts as a clearinghouse for unsold hotel rooms. It can often obtain a significant saving on published room rates.

WHAT IT COSTS In Australian Dollars				
	$$$$	**$$$**	**$$**	**$**	**¢**
HOTELS	over $450	$301–$450	$201–$300	$151–$200	under $150

Hotel prices are for two people in a standard double room in high season, including tax and service, based on the European Plan (with no meals) unless otherwise noted.

The Rocks & Circular Quay

$$$$ 🏨 **ANA Hotel.** Sydney's largest hotel towering above Sydney Harbour from its prime position in The Rocks is *the* place to grab a room with a view. The north-facing rooms overlooking the harbor are the ones to book; views on the other sides—Darling Harbour, the city, or the eastern suburbs—are less impressive. Rooms are large and modestly opulent but slightly anonymous, and decorated in an inoffensive, autumnal color scheme. On the 36th floor, the glass wall of the Horizons Bar provides terrific views of Sydney Harbour, especially in the evening. ✉ *176 Cumberland St., The Rocks, 2000* ☎ *02/9250–6000* 🖷 *02/9250–6250* 🌐 *www.anahotelsyd.com.au* ⇆ *524 rooms, 39 suites* ⚑ *3 restaurants, room service, in-room data ports, in-room safes, minibars, cable TV, pool, gym, hair salon, sauna, spa, 3 bars, dry cleaning, laundry service, concierge, Internet, business services, convention center, meeting rooms, parking (fee); no-smoking rooms* ▤ *AE, DC, MC, V.*

★ **$$$$** 🏨 **Four Seasons Hotel Sydney.** Formerly the Regent of Sydney, a change of ownership in 2002 breathed new panache and elegance into one of Sydney's finest luxury hotels. Rooms are large, stylish, but soothing, and serviced twice a day. All have butler service. Between the 32nd and 34th floors, Executive Club rooms offer extra services such as meeting rooms and complimentary breakfast, and spectacular views. The spa has original treatments using exotic ingredients and Australian Aboriginal tech-

niques. ⊠ *199 George St., Circular Quay, 2000* ☎ *02/9238–0000*
🖷 *02/9251–2851* ⊕ *www.fourseasons.com/sydney* ↘ *417 rooms, 114
suites* ⬧ *3 restaurants, room service, in-room data ports, in-room safes,
minibars, cable TV, pool, gym, spa, bar, dry cleaning, laundry service,
concierge, Internet, business services, convention center, meeting rooms,
parking (fee); no-smoking rooms* ⊟ *AE, DC, MC, V.*

$$$$ 🏨 **Hotel Inter-Continental Sydney.** This sleek, sophisticated, multistory hotel
rises from the sandstone facade of the historic Treasury Building. It's
also near the harbor and within easy walking distance of Circular Quay,
the Opera House, and the central business district. The best views are
from the rooms facing north, which overlook Harbour Bridge, or from
the rooms on the eastern side of the hotel, which overlook the Botanic
Gardens. Four executive floors offer extra privileges such as meeting
rooms, separate check-in/check-out, and complimentary breakfast and
cocktails. ⊠ *117 Macquarie St., Circular Quay, 2000* ☎ *02/9230–0200*
🖷 *02/9240–1240* ⊕ *www.sydney.interconti.com* ↘ *475 rooms, 28
suites* ⬧ *3 restaurants, room service, in-room data ports, in-room safes,
minibars, cable TV, pool, gym, health club, bar, dry cleaning, laundry
service, concierge, Internet, business services, convention center, meeting rooms, parking (fee); no-smoking rooms* ⊟ *AE, DC, MC, V.*

$$$$ 🏨 **Observatory Hotel.** Oozing with calm, dignity, and style, this small,
Fodor's Choice   elegant hotel, run by the upscale Orient Express hotel group, is a pop-
★   ular choice for those who prefer a less conspicuous city address—and
are willing to pay a bit more for it. Throughout the gorgeous property,
antique reproductions accented by Venetian and Asian touches evoke
the cozy opulence of a country estate. The health club is the finest of
any city hotel, and guest rooms are extremely spacious. The best are the
junior suites. The four-story hotel's single weakness is its lack of views.
⊠ *89–113 Kent St., The Rocks, 2000* ☎ *02/9256–2222* 🖷 *02/9256–2233*
⊕ *www.observatoryhotel.orient-express.com* ↘ *78 rooms, 22 suites*
⬧ *Restaurant, room service, in-room data ports, in-room safes, minibars, cable TV, in-room VCRs, indoor pool, health club, sauna, steam
room, bar, dry cleaning, laundry service, concierge, Internet, business
services, convention center, meeting rooms, parking (fee); no-smoking
rooms* ⊟ *AE, DC, MC, V.*

$$$$ 🏨 **Park Hyatt Sydney.** Moored in the shadow of Harbour Bridge, the city's
Fodor's Choice   most expensive hotel has the finest location of any in Sydney. An extra
★   dash of sophistication—such as butler service—distinguishes the luxurious atmosphere. Sandstone and earth tones dominate the decor, which
combines reproductions of classical statuary with contemporary bronzes
and Australian artwork. Most rooms in the four-story hotel overlook
Campbell's Cove and the Opera House. Most also have balconies.
Don't miss the excellent Australian cuisine at harbourkitchen & bar. ⊠ *7
Hickson Rd., Circular Quay, 2000* ☎ *02/9241–1234* 🖷 *02/9256–1555*
⊕ *www.sydney.hyatt.com* ↘ *120 rooms, 38 suites* ⬧ *Restaurant, room
service, in-room data ports, in-room safes, minibars, cable TV, pool, gym,
hair salon, sauna, spa, 2 bars, dry cleaning, laundry service, concierge,
Internet, business services, convention center, meeting rooms, parking
(fee); no-smoking rooms* ⊟ *AE, DC, MC, V.*

★ **$$$**   🏨 **Quay West.** Bordering The Rocks and the central business and shop-
ping district, this statuesque tower combines the space and comforts of
an apartment with the amenities of a five-star hotel, all at a reasonable
price. Each of these luxurious one- and two-bedroom apartments has
a lounge and dining room, a fully equipped kitchen, and a laundry. Fa-
cilities include 24-hour room service, a well-equipped and glamorous
health club, restaurant, bar, and valet parking. All rooms are on the eighth
floor or higher, and all have either harbor or city views. Some of the
more expensive Harbour View Suites have balconies. ⊠ *98 Gloucester*

St., The Rocks, 2000 ☎ 02/9240–6000 🖷 02/9240–6060 ➳ 135 apartments ♿ Restaurant, room service, in-room data ports, in-room safes, kitchens, minibars, microwaves, in-room VCRs, indoor pool, health club, sauna, bar, dry cleaning, laundry service, concierge, Internet, business services, convention center, meeting rooms, parking (fee); no-smoking rooms ▭ AE, DC, MC, V.

$$ 🏨 **Quest Stafford.** These self-contained studios and terrace-house apartments, in a premium position in The Rocks, have kitchen facilities, making them a good choice if you're looking to prepare your own food during your stay. The terrace houses have a separate bedroom on an upper level and a kitchen and lounge room downstairs, at a much lower price than a five-star hotel room in the same area. Decor and furnishings are functional and somewhat bland. Rooms on the fourth through sixth floors of the main building have views across Circular Quay to the Opera House. ✉ 75 Harrington St., The Rocks, 2000 ☎ 02/9251–6711 🖷 02/9251–3458 ⊕ www.questapartments.com.au ➳ 54 apartments ♿ In-room data ports, in-room safes, kitchenettes, cable TV, in-room VCRs, pool, gym, sauna, spa, dry cleaning, laundry service, business services, parking (fee) ▭ AE, DC, MC, V.

¢–$$ 🏨 **The Russell.** For charm, character, and central location, it's hard to beat this quaint, ornate, Victorian hotel. No two rooms are the same, but all have fresh flowers, down pillows, and Gilchrist & Soames toiletries. The spacious double rooms at the front have views of Circular Quay. There are also somewhat quieter, standard-size double rooms overlooking Nurses Walk or opening onto an internal courtyard. Ceiling fans and windows that open allow for a breeze in all rooms. Winding corridors and the steep and narrow staircase to the hotel's reception desk can be obstacles. Breakfast is included. ✉ 143A George St., The Rocks, 2000 ☎ 02/9241–3543 🖷 02/9252–1652 ⊕ www.therussell.com.au ➳ 26 rooms, 16 with bath; 1 suite, 1 apartment ♿ Restaurant, fans; no a/c, no cable TV in some rooms ▭ AE, DC, MC, V ⊙ CP.

$ 🏨 **Harbour Rocks Hotel.** This converted, historic Rocks wool store offers reasonable value for its location, but the character is confined to the exterior of the 150-year-old building. Rooms are tidy but pared down to the bare necessities, with little concern for charm or style. Top-floor rooms on the eastern side of the four-story building afford glimpses of Circular Quay and the Opera House. There is a luggage elevator but no guest elevator in the three-story hotel. ✉ 34–52 Harrington St., The Rocks, 2000 ☎ 02/9251–8944 🖷 02/9251–8900 ⊕ www.harbourrocks.com.au ➳ 55 rooms ♿ Restaurant, in-room safes, minibars, bar, laundry service; no-smoking rooms ▭ AE, DC, MC, V.

City Center Area

$$$$ 🏨 **Westin Sydney.** Most of the public areas of this striking, city-center hotel were re-created from Sydney's former General Post Office. All but 50 of the guest rooms are in a 31-story atrium tower that rises at the rear of the ornate GPO building; yet, despite its size, this 416-room hotel conveys an impression of warmth and intimacy. Heritage Rooms, in the original GPO, have soaring ceilings and windows, and Tower Rooms provide panoramic city views. Key neighborhoods, the Royal Botanic Gardens, and the historic precinct of Macquarie Street all lie within easy strolling distance. ✉ 1 Martin Pl., City Center, 2000 ☎ 02/8223–1111 🖷 02/8223–1222 ⊕ www.westin.com.au ➳ 366 rooms, 50 suites ♿ 2 restaurants, room service, in-room data ports, in-room safes, minibars, cable TV, indoor pool, gym, hair salon, health club, massage, sauna, bar, dry cleaning, laundry service, concierge, Internet, business services, convention center, meeting rooms, parking (fee); no-smoking rooms ▭ AE, DC, MC, V.

$$$ ⊞ **The Grace Hotel.** Retaining traces of the art deco style of its origins, this modernized city center hotel has spacious, uncluttered rooms—although views have long been compromised by the surrounding buildings. During World War II, the building was used as the Sydney headquarters for General Douglas MacArthur's Pacific campaign. Despite the hotel's location, rooms are quiet. Those that overlook the central well of the building are best if you seek absolute silence. The hotel is especially popular with group travelers. ⊠ *77 York St., City Center, 2000* ☎ *02/9272–6888* ⎙ *02/9229–8189* ⊕ *www.gracehotel.com.au* ⟳ *382 rooms, 6 suites* ♢ *3 restaurants, room service, in-room data ports, in-room safes, indoor pool, gym, sauna, spa, steam room, bar, dry cleaning, laundry service, Internet, business services, convention center, meeting rooms; no-smoking floor* ☰ *AE, DC, MC, V.*

$$$ ⊞ **Medina Grand Harbourside.** Its water views, central location on Darling Harbour's King Street Wharf, and moderate rates make Medina a great choice if you're looking for an apartment-style hotel. Accommodations consist of studios and one-bedroom apartments, and though the furnishings are purely functional, the rooms are large and bright. Each unit has a kitchenette. The one-bedroom apartments, which have a laundry and bath as well as a dining-lounge area, make a good base for an extended stay. ⊠ *55 Shelley St., King Street Wharf, Darling Harbour, 2000* ☎ *02/9249–7000* ⎙ *02/9249–6900* ⊕ *www.medinaapartments. com.au* ⟳ *114 rooms* ♢ *Restaurant, room service, in-room data ports, in-room safes, kitchenettes, pool, gym, sauna, spa, steam room, dry cleaning, laundry service, business services, convention center, meeting rooms, parking (fee); no-smoking rooms* ☰ *AE, DC, MC, V.*

★ ¢ ⊞ **Sydney Central YHA.** Operated by the Australian arm of the Youth Hostels Association, this Chicago-style redbrick opposite Central Railway Station offers a high standard of accommodation for budget travelers. Rooms are either multi-share or doubles, some with en suite bathrooms. The hotel is well equipped for leisure—there's even a rooftop pool—and attracts a lively crowd of international backpackers. Guests must be members of a Hostelling International Association; if you're not, you can pay a one-year membership fee of A$52 (about US$30) when you check in. ⊠ *11 Rawson Pl., Chinatown 2000* ☎ *02/9281–9111* ⎙ *02/9281–9199* ⊕ *www.yha.com.au/hostels/details.cfm?hostelid=29* ⟳ *151 rooms, 54 with bath* ♢ *Restaurant, grocery, pool, sauna, bar, Internet, travel services, parking (fee); no room phones, no room TVs* ☰ *MC, V.*

★ ¢ ⊞ **Y on the Park.** Rooms at the Y, near the corner of Hyde Park and Oxford Street, are often booked months in advance by travelers looking for comfortable and affordable lodgings in a good city location. Rooms have a predictably institutional feel, but come in several configurations, from the four-bed backpacker rooms with shared bathrooms to family rooms and even deluxe and corporate rooms, which are still well within the budget price category. Unexpected are such in-room amenities as king beds, French press coffeemakers, and toiletries. Studios have a kitchenette. Apart from the dormitories, all rooms include a Continental breakfast. ⊠ *5–11 Wentworth Ave., East Sydney, 2010* ☎ *02/9264–2451* ⎙ *02/ 9285–6288* ⊕ *www.ywca-sydney.com.au/hotel.asp?HotelID=1* ⟳ *156 rooms* ♢ *Café, in-room data ports, in-room safes, some refrigerators; no phones in some rooms, no TV in some rooms* ☰ *AE, DC, MC, V* �}◯{ *CP.*

Paddington & Woollahra

$ ⊞ **The Hughenden.** Modern behemoths not your style? Try one of the cozy rooms in this converted Victorian mansion. Most rooms are on the small side but all are individually and prettily decorated in period style with floral-print fabrics and the like. In a prestigious eastern-suburbs address close to many of Sydney's finest antiques shops and art dealers, the hotel offers easy access to Oxford Street, Centennial Park, and Paddington. The city and the eastern beaches are 10–15 minutes by public transportation. A full made-to-order breakfast is included and you can make use of the grounds and porch. If a tub is important to you, ask for a room with one. ✉ *14 Queen St., Woollahra, 2025* ☎ *02/9363–4863* 🖷 *02/9362–0398* 🌐 *www.hughendenhotel.com.au* 🛏 *36 rooms* ♿ *Restaurant, in-room data ports, bar, library, free parking; some pets allowed (fee); no smoking* ▤ *AE, DC, MC, V* ◉❙ *BP.*

¢ ▣ **Sullivans Hotel.** In the heart of Sydney's gay neighborhood, this small, friendly, family-owned and -operated hotel has simple rooms at an outstanding price. Just a 15-minute walk from the city in fashionable Paddington, the hotel is close to the shops, cafés, restaurants, movie theaters, and nightlife of Oxford Street. The recommended Garden Rooms overlook the central courtyard, pool, and the terrace houses at the rear. Those that overlook the city are more likely to be affected by traffic noise. Decor is generic, but rooms score high marks for general cleanliness. ✉ *21 Oxford St., Darlinghurst, Paddington, 2021* ☎ *02/9361–0211* 🖷 *02/9360–3735* 🌐 *www.sullivans.com.au* 🛏 *62 rooms* ♿ *Café, in-room data ports, pool, bicycles, free parking* ▤ *AE, DC, MC, V.*

East of the City

$$$ ▣ **W Sydney.** Recrafted from the historic Finger Wharf, this member of the stylish international chain does little to disguise the fact that it was once a warehouse. Giant trusses and brontosauruslike machinery that once formed the working core of the wharf have been left exposed, creating a funky, neo-gothic interior. There's a background of pumping techno music, and minimalist furnishings in the public spaces are punctuated with splashes of red and chrome. Guest rooms, which have a light, bright, cappuccino-color scheme, are arranged like the cabins on a luxury liner, rising in tiers on the outside of the central cavity. *The Wharf at Woolloomooloo,* ✉ *Cowper Wharf Rd., Woolloomooloo, 2011* ☎ *02/9331–9000* 🖷 *02/9331–9031* 🌐 *www.whotels.com* 🛏 *104 rooms, 36 suites* ♿ *5 restaurants, in-room data ports, in-room safes, minibars, pool, gym, bar, dry cleaning, laundry service, concierge, Internet, business services, convention center, meeting rooms, parking (fee); no-smoking rooms* ▤ *AE, DC, MC, V.*

$$ ▣ **Kirketon.** This is a small hotel elevated to an art form. The strong sense of design is apparent from the moment you step through the big glass doors and into the minimalist foyer. The coffee-and-cream-color rooms are a study in simplicity. Furnishings blend 1950s classics with European imports, but the relentless pursuit of style sometimes intrudes into the comfort zone. For example, rooms lack couches or comfortable chairs. However, if you don't mind suffering slightly in the name of fashion, there's no better address. ✉ *229 Darlinghurst Rd., Darlinghurst, 2010* ☎ *02/9332–2011* 🖷 *02/9332–2499* 🌐 *www.kirketon.com.au* 🛏 *40 rooms* ♿ *Restaurant, in-room data ports, in-room safes, kitchenettes, minibars, cable TV, bar, concierge, Internet business services, meeting rooms, parking (fee); no-smoking rooms* ▤ *AE, DC, MC, V.*

$$ ▣ **Medusa.** If you're tired of the standard traveler's room, this modern hotel could be just the tonic. The converted Victorian terrace house has been widely applauded by the international style arbiters: Colors are brash—blues, yellows, and creams splashed against reds—and furnishings (platform beds, chaise lounges, etc.) might have come direct from a Milan design gallery. Every room is slightly different, and each has a kitchenette. Behind the glamor is a comfortable, well-run hotel with

friendly, attentive staff. This is one of the few city hotels that welcomes people with pets. ⊠ *267 Darlinghurst Rd., Darlinghurst, 2010* ☎ *02/ 9331–1000* ⌨ *02/9380–6901* ⊕ *www.medusa.com.au* ↩ *18 rooms* ⌂ *In-room data ports, in-room safes, kitchenettes, minibars, bar, parking (fee), some pets allowed* ☰ *AE, DC, MC, V.*

★ $$ ⊞ **Regents Court.** Small, elegant, and at the cutting edge of contemporary style, this boutique hotel is one of Sydney's best-kept secrets. The mood is intimate yet relaxed, and the location in a cul-de-sac in Potts Point is quiet. Each room has its own well-equipped kitchenette, and many have an extra pull-down bed in addition to the queen-size bed. Bauhaus chairs and Jorge Pensi uplights provide the accents against a cool, minimalist backdrop. A breakfast basket is available for in-room preparation, but experienced patrons know to head upstairs to eat in splendor amid the glorious rooftop garden. ⊠ *18 Springfield Ave., Potts Point, Kings Cross, 2011* ☎ *02/9358–1533* ⌨ *02/9358–1833* ⊕ *www.regentscourt.com.au* ↩ *30 rooms* ⌂ *Kitchenettes, in-room VCRs, dry cleaning, laundry service, concierge, Internet, parking (fee)* ☰ *AE, DC, MC, V.*

¢–$$ ⊞ **Simpsons of Potts Point.** This historic hotel retains many decorative features from its Victorian origins, including stained-glass windows and a grand cedar staircase. Rooms are comfortable and decorated in a modestly opulent period style. The best is the slightly more expensive Cloud Room, which has a palatial en suite bathroom. If you book via the Internet, however, you'll receive a 10% discount. ⊠ *8 Challis Ave., Potts Point, Kings Cross, 2011* ☎ *02/9356–2199* ⌨ *02/9356–4476* ⊕ *www. simpsonspottspoint.com.au* ↩ *14 rooms* ⌂ *Free parking* ☰ *MC, V* ⑩ *CP.*

¢–$$ ⊞ **Victoria Court Sydney.** A small, smart hotel on a leafy street in Potts Point, the Victoria Court is appealing for more than just its reasonable rates. Hand-painted tiles and etched-glass doors recall the hotel's Victorian ancestry, yet the rooms come with the modern blessings of en suite bathrooms and comfortable beds. Most rooms have marble fireplaces, some have four-poster beds, and some have balconies overlooking Victoria Street. ⊠ *122 Victoria St., Potts Point, Kings Cross, 2011* ☎ *02/ 9357–3200* ⌨ *02/9357–7606* ⊕ *www.victoriacourt.com.au* ↩ *25 rooms* ⌂ *In-room safes* ☰ *AE, DC, MC, V* ⑩ *CP.*

Sydney Area Lodging

$–$$ ⊞ **Ravesi's on Bondi Beach.** This small hotel with a dash of art deco looks out on Australia's most famous beach. All rooms are spacious and uncluttered, decorated in a stylish sand-and-sea color scheme. Oceanfront rooms have the best views. For family-size space, the split-level suites, which have their own terrace, are recommended. Frequent bus service takes 25 minutes to get to the city. ⊠ *Campbell Parade and Hall St., Bondi Beach, 2026* ☎ *02/9365–4422* ⌨ *02/9365–1481* ⊕ *www.ravesis. com.au* ↩ *16 rooms* ⌂ *Restaurant, bar; no a/c* ☰ *AE, DC, MC, V.*

★ $ ⊞ **Trickett's Luxury Bed & Breakfast.** The original Victorian character of this restored mansion is evident in the 13-foot ceilings, the ballroom, and the Oriental rugs and period furnishings. Guest rooms are large and have hardwood floors; each has a bathroom stocked with robes. Although the B&B is in a quiet historic neighborhood, there are many dining options and a waterfront park within walking distance. A substantial Continental breakfast is included. ⊠ *270 Glebe Point Rd., Glebe, 2037* ☎ *02/9552–1141* ⌨ *02/9692–9462* ↩ *7 rooms* ⌂ *Fans, Internet, free parking; no smoking* ☰ *AE, DC, MC, V* ⑩ *CP.*

NIGHTLIFE & THE ARTS

The Arts

The most comprehensive listing of upcoming events is in the Metro section of the *Sydney Morning Herald,* published on Friday. On other days, browse through the entertainment section of the paper. **Ticketek Phone Box Office** (☎ 02/9266–4800 ⊕ www.ticketek.com) is the major ticket reservations agency, covering most shows and performances.

Ballet, Opera, Classical Music

Fodor'sChoice
★
Sydney Opera House (✉ Bennelong Point, Circular Quay ☎ 02/9250–7777 ⊕ www.soh.nsw.gov.au), despite its name, actually showcases all the performing arts: it has five theaters, only one of which is devoted to opera. The Australian Ballet, the Sydney Dance Company, as well as the Australian Opera Company call the Opera House home. The complex also includes two stages for theater and the 2,700-seat Concert Hall, where the Sydney Symphony Orchestra and the Australian Chamber Orchestra perform regularly. The box office is open Monday–Saturday 9–8:30.

Dance

Bangarra Dance Theatre (✉ Wharf 4, 5 Hickson Rd., The Rocks ☎ 02/9251–5333 ⊕ www.bangarra.com.au), an Aboriginal dance company, stages productions based on contemporary Aboriginal social themes, often to critical acclaim. The company usually performs here at its headquarters in The Rocks.

Sydney Dance Company (✉ Pier 4, Hickson Rd., The Rocks ☎ 02/9221–4811 ⊕ www.sydneydance.com.au) is an innovative contemporary dance troupe with an international reputation from its many years under acclaimed director Graeme Murphy. The company generally performs at the Opera House when it's in town.

Theater

Belvoir Street Theatre's (✉ 25 Belvoir St., Surry Hills ☎ 02/9699–3444 ⊕ www.belvoir.com.au) two stages are home to innovative and challenging political and social drama. The smaller downstairs space is the home of "B Sharp," Company B's upstart company of brave, new Australian works. The theater is a 10-minute walk from Central Station.

Capitol Theatre (✉ 13 Campbell St., Chinatown, Haymarket ☎ 02/9266–4800), one of the city's landmarks, is a century-old building that crumbled to ruins but was revived thanks to a recent makeover that included such refinements as fiber-optic ceiling lights that twinkle in time to the music. The 2,000-seat theater specializes in Broadway blockbusters.

Lyric Theatre (✉ 20–80 Pyrmont St., Darling Harbour, Pyrmont ☎ 02/9777–9000 ⊕ www.starcity.com.au), at the Star City Casino complex, is Sydney's most spectacular dedicated performing arts venue. Despite its size, there's no better place to watch the big-budget musicals that are its staple fare. Every seat in the lavishly spacious, 2,000-seat theater is a good one.

Stables Theatre (✉ 10 Nimrod St., Kings Cross ☎ 02/9361–3817) has long been known as a proving ground for up-and-coming talents and plays. The avant-garde works of this small theater sometimes graduate to the big stage.

State Theatre (✉ 49 Market St., City Center ☎ 02/9373–6655) is the grande dame of Sydney theaters, a mid-city venue that demands a dressed-up night to pay homage to a golden era. Built in 1929 and restored to its full-blown opulence in 1980, the theater has a Gothic foyer with a vaulted ceiling, mosaic floors, marble columns and statues, and brass and bronze doors. A highlight of the magnificent theater is the 20,000-piece chandelier that is supposedly the world's second largest. **The Wharf Theatre** (✉ Pier 4, Hickson Rd., The Rocks ☎ 02/9250–1777), on a redeveloped wharf in the shadow of Harbour Bridge, hosts the Sydney Theatre Company, one of Australia's most original and highly regarded companies. Contemporary British and American plays and the latest offerings from leading Australian playwrights such as David Williamson and Nick Enright are the main attractions.

Nightlife

"Satan made Sydney," wrote Mark Twain, quoting a citizen of the city, and to some there can be no doubt that Satan was the principal architect behind Kings Cross. Strictly speaking, Kings Cross refers to the intersection of Victoria Street and Darlinghurst Road, although the name "The Cross" applies to a much wider area. Essentially, it is a ½-km (¼-mi) stretch of bars, burlesque shows, cafés, video shows, and massage parlors. The area does not come to life much before 10 PM, and the action runs hot for most of the night.

Sydneysiders in search of late-night action are more likely to head for Oxford Street, between Hyde Park and Taylor Square, where the choice ranges from pubs to the hottest dance clubs in town. Oxford Street is also the nighttime focus for Sydney's large gay population. Another nightlife district runs along Cockle Bay Wharf in Darling Harbour; the bars, restaurants, and nightclubs here are especially popular during the summer months. Nightlife in The Rocks is focused on the pubs along George Street, which attract a boisterous crowd.

The *Sydney Morning Herald* daily entertainment section is the most informative guide to the city's pubs and clubs. For club scene coverage—who's been seen where and what they were wearing—pick up a free copy of *Beat,* available at just about any Oxford Street café or via the Internet (⊕www.beat.com.au). The CitySearch Web site (⊕www.sydney.citysearch.com.au) is another weekly source of entertainment information.

Bars & Lounges

For a northern Sydney landmark pub, **The Oaks** (✉ 118 Military Rd., Neutral Bay ☎ 02/9953–5515) also encapsulates the very best of the modern pub. The immensely popular pub is big and boisterous. It has a beer garden, a restaurant, and several bars, which offer varying levels of sophistication. The pub is packed on Friday and Saturday nights, although it opens at 10 AM.

FodorsChoice **Hemmesphere** (✉ Level 4, 252 George St., City Center ☎ 02/9240–3040)
★ is where Sydney's hippest pay homage to cocktail culture from low, leather divans. The mood is elegant, sleek, and cultish, and the guest list is usually sprinkled with whichever glitterati happen to be in town. Club members, who pay A$1,500 a year, get priority.

Soho Bar (✉ 171 Victoria St., Kings Cross ☎ 02/9358–6511) is the most civilized cocktail bar in Kings Cross, and the mood on the upper story is relaxed and funky, and still stylish despite its age. Stylish dress is expected. The adjoining pool room is rated one of the city's finest. The bar is open daily 10 AM–3 AM, later on Friday and Saturday.

Comedy Clubs

Sydney's Original Comedy Store (✉ Shop 102, Building 207, Fox Studios, Bent St., Moore Park, Centennial Park ☎ 02/9357–1419), Sydney's oldest comedy club, performs in this plush 300-seat theater in a huge Fox Studios movie production facility. The difficult-to-find theater is at the rear of the studio complex, close to the parking lot. Shows are Tuesday–Saturday at 8, and admission runs from about A$15 to A$27.50.

Dance Clubs

DCM (✉ 31–33 Oxford St., Darlinghurst ☎ 02/9267–7380) revels in its reputation as one of Sydney's hottest dance clubs. "Dress to impress" is practiced here, and minimalist, clingy apparel shows off the gym-hardened crowd to best advantage. The club is also popular with Sydney's gays and lesbians. It's open Thursday and Friday 11–7, Saturday 10 PM–10:30 AM, and Sunday 9–7. The cover charge (up to A$12) varies throughout the week.

Ettamogah Bar and Restaurant (✉ 225 Harbourside, Darling Harbour ☎ 02/9281–3922), based on a famous Australian cartoon series depicting an Outback saloon, has three bars and an open-air restaurant. The atmosphere at this theme pub varies from family-friendly during the day to nightclub in the evening. Hours are weekdays 11 AM–midnight, Saturday 11 AM–3 AM, and Sunday 11 AM–11 PM, with a A$5–A$10 cover charge Thursday–Saturday.

Home (✉ Cockle Bay Wharf, 201 Sussex St., Darling Harbour ☎ 02/9266–0600) is Sydney's largest nightclub, a three-story colossus that holds up to 2,000 party animals. The main dance floor has an awesome sound system, and the top-level terrace bar is the place to go when the action becomes too frantic. Outdoor balconies provide the essential oxygen boost. Arrive early, or prepare for a long wait. It's open weekends 10 PM–4 AM, and there's often a cover charge (up to A$20).

Lizard Lounge (✉ 34 Oxford St., Darlinghurst ☎ 02/9331–1936), the Exchange Hotel's upstairs cocktail lounge/dance club, provides a more refined alternative to the raucous action of the street-level gay bar. Specialty beers are served, as well as the latest cocktails. The lounge is open Monday through Thursday 5 PM–1 AM and Friday through Sunday 5 PM–3 AM, with a A$10–A$15 cover charge.

★ **Tank** (✉ 3 Bridge La., City Center ☎ 02/9251–9933) is the grooviest and best-looking of all Sydney's nightclubs, with a polar-cool clientele and a slick dress code rigidly enforced at the door. The interior is plush and relaxed, despite its space-capsule atmosphere. Hours are 10 PM–5 AM, and be prepared for expensive drinks.

Gambling

Star City Casino (✉ 20–80 Pyrmont St., Darling Harbour, Pyrmont ☎ 02/9777–9000 ⊕ www.starcity.com.au) is a glitzy, 24-hour, Las Vegas–style casino with 200 gaming tables and 1,500 slot machines. Gambling options include roulette, craps, blackjack, baccarat, and the classic Australian game of two-up.

Gay & Lesbian Bars & Clubs

Most of the city's gay and lesbian venues are along Oxford Street, in Darlinghurst. The free *Sydney Star Observer,* available along Oxford Street, has a round-up of Sydney's gay and lesbian goings-on, or check the magazine's Web site (⊕ www.ssonet.com.au). A monthly free magazine, *Lesbians on the Loose,* lists events for women, and the free *SX* (⊕ SXNews.com.au) also lists bars and events.

★ **ARQ** (✉ 16 Flinders St., Darlinghurst ☎ 02/9380–8700 ⊕ www.arqsydney.com.au), Sydney's biggest gay nightclub, attracts a clean-cut crowd who like to whip off their shirts and dance. There's a bar, multiple dance floors, and plenty of chrome and sparkly lighting.

Beauchamp Hotel (✉ 267 Oxford St., Darlinghurst ☎ 02/9331–2575) is a gay and lesbian pub mostly remarkable for what it lacks. There are no floor shows, cruisy lighting, dance floor, or cocktail bar—just a comfortable, unpretentious, traditional Australian pub that appeals mostly to older gays. It's open daily 10 AM–1 AM, and is especially sociable on weekend afternoons.

Beresford (⊠ 354 Bourke St., Surry Hills ☎ 02/9331–1045) is a traditional pub that transforms itself into a total party zone on weekends with the accent on muscles, sweat, and bare skin. It's open Tuesday through Thursday 2 PM–10 PM and Friday through Sunday 2 PM–5 AM, but the action begins at about midnight on Friday and barely skips a beat until Sunday morning. The pub is legendary for its post-Gay Mardi Gras street parties.

Though the atmosphere, the music, and the decor of **The Newtown Hotel** (⊠ 174 King St., Newtown ☎ 02/9557–1329) do not approach the gloss and sophistication of Paddington's glamorous gay scene, you can't beat its laid-back atmosphere and the bawdy, in-your-face drag shows.

Jazz Clubs

The Basement (⊠ 29 Reiby Pl., Circular Quay ☎ 02/9251–2797 ⊕ www.thebasement.com/au) is a Sydney legend, the city's premier venue for top jazz and blues musicians. Dinner is also available. Expect a cover charge of A$10–A$20.

Soup Plus (⊠ 383 George St., City Center ☎ 02/9299–7728), a small, subterranean jazz venue, hosts mainly contemporary jazz. Although it's is too small to attract big-name artists, the cozy, clubby atmosphere has fostered a loyal clientele that helps maintain this as Sydney's longest-running jazz venue. Hours are Monday–Saturday noon–10, and there's a A$5–A$20 cover charge.

Pubs with Music

Mercantile Hotel (⊠ 25 George St., The Rocks ☎ 02/9247–3570), in the shadow of Harbour Bridge, is Irish and very proud of it. Fiddles, drums, and pipes rise above the clamor in the bar, and lilting accents rejoice in song seven nights a week. Hours are Sunday–Wednesday 10 AM–midnight and Thursday–Saturday 10 AM–1 AM. There's no cover charge.

Rose, Shamrock and Thistle (⊠ 193 Evans St., Rozelle ☎ 02/9810–2244), popularly known as the Three Weeds, is a friendly, boisterous pub 5 km (3 mi) from the city center. It's one of the best places to hear live music, generally from Thursday through Saturday for a moderate cover charge of A$5–A$10. Otherwise, come for free noon–midnight Monday–Wednesday and noon–10 Sunday.

SPORTS & THE OUTDOORS

Australian Rules Football

A fast, demanding game in which the ball can be kicked or punched between teams of 22 players, Australian-rules football has won a major audience in Sydney, even though the city has only a single professional team compared to the dozen who play in Melbourne—the home of the sport. The **Sydney Football Stadium** (⊠ Moore Park Rd., Centennial Park, Paddington ☎ 02/9360–6601 ⊕ www.scgt.nsw.gov.au) hosts games April–September.

Beaches

For detailed information on nearby beaches, *see* the Sydney Beaches section.

Cricket

Cricket is Sydney's summer sport, and it's often played at the beach as well as in parks throughout the nation. For Australians, the pinnacle of excitement is The Ashes, when the national cricket team takes the field against the English. It happens every other summer (December–January), and the two nations take turns hosting the event. Cricket season runs from October through March. Some games take place at the **Sydney Cricket Ground** (⊠ Moore Park Rd., Centennial Park, Paddington ☎ 02/9360–6601 ⊕ www.scgt.nsw.gov.au).

Golf

More than 80 golf courses, 35 of which are public, lie within a 40-km (25-mi) radius of the Sydney Harbour Bridge. Golf clubs and carts are usually available for rent.

Bondi Golf Club (⊠ 5 Military Rd., North Bondi ☎ 02/9130–1981) is a 9-hole public course on the cliffs overlooking famous Bondi Beach. Although the par-28 course is hardly a challenge for serious golfers, the views are inspiring. The course is open to the public after noon on most days. The greens fee is A$22.

New South Wales Golf Course (⊠ Henry Head, La Perouse ☎ 02/9661–4455) is a rigorous, challenging, par-72 championship course on the cliffs at La Perouse, overlooking Botany Bay. The course is generally open to nonmembers midweek, but you must make advance arrangements with the pro shop. The greens fee is A$150.

Riverside Oaks Golf Club (⊠ O'Brien's Rd., Cattai ☎ 02/4560–3299), on the bush-clad banks of the Hawkesbury River, is a spectacular 18-hole, par-73 course about a 90-minute drive northwest of Sydney. The greens fee is A$75 weekdays, A$89 weekends.

Rugby

Rugby League, known locally as footie, is Sydney's winter addiction. This is a fast, gutsy, physical game that bears some similarities to North American football, although the action is more constant and the ball cannot be passed forward. The season falls between April and September. The **Sydney Football Stadium** (⊠ Moore Park Rd., Centennial Park, Paddington ☎ 02/9360–6601 ⊕ www.scgt.nsw.gov.au) is the main venue.

Running

The path that connects the **Opera House to Mrs. Macquarie's Chair,** along the edge of the harbor through the Royal Botanic Gardens, is one of the finest in the city. At lunchtime on weekdays, this track is crowded with corporate joggers.

Bondi Beach to Tamarama is a popular and fashion-conscious running path that winds along the cliffs south from Bondi. It's marked by distance indicators and includes a number of exercise stations.

Manly beachfront is good for running. If you have the legs for it, you can run down to Shelly Beach, or pop over the hill to Freshwater Beach and follow it all the way to check out the surf at Curl Curl.

Sailing & Boating

EastSail (⊠ D'Albora Marine, New Beach Rd., Rushcutters Bay, Darling Point ☎ 02/9327–1166 ⊕ www.eastsail.com.au) rents yachts for you to sail or motor yourself around the harbor from about A$325 per half day for a 31-foot sloop. Skippers' rates are around A$40 per hour.

Northside Sailing School (⊠ The Spit, Mosman ☎ 02/9969–3972 ⊕ www.northsidesailing.com.au) at Middle Harbour rents small sailboats. Rates start at A$40 per hour, and you can also book an instructor to show you the ropes.

Scuba Diving

Pro Dive (⊠ 27 Alfreda St., Coogee ☎ 02/9665–6333 ⊕ www.prodive.com.au) is a PADI operator conducting courses and shore- or boat-diving excursions around the harbor and city beaches. Some of the best dive spots are close to the eastern suburbs' beaches of Clovelly and Coogee, where Pro Dive is based. A four-hour boat dive with an instructor or dive master costs around A$169, including rental equipment.

Swimming

Sydney has many heated Olympic-size swimming pools, some of which go beyond the basic requirements of a workout.

Andrew (Boy) Charlton Pool (⊠ Mrs. Macquarie's Rd., the Domain North, the Domain ☎ 02/9358–6686) isn't just any heated, outdoor, and Olympic-size pool. Its stunning location overlooking the ships at Garden Island, its radical glass-and-steel design, and its chic terrace café above Woolloomooloo Bay make it an attraction unto itself. Admission is A$4.50 and it's open October–March, daily 6:30 AM–8:30 PM.

Surfing

All Sydney surfers have their favorite breaks, but you can usually count on good waves on at least one of the city's ocean beaches. In summer, surfing reports are a regular feature of radio news broadcasts.

Manly Surf School (⊠ North Steyne Surf Club, Manly Beach, Manly ☎ 02/9977–6977 ⊕ www.manlysurfschool.com) conducts courses for adults and children and provides all equipment, including wet suits. The cost for adults is A$50 for a day of three two-hour classes. Private instruction costs A$80 per hour.

Surfcam (⊕ www.surfcam.com.au) has surf reports and weather details.

Tennis

Cooper Park Tennis Centre (⊠ Off Suttie Rd., Cooper Park, Double Bay ☎ 02/9389–9259) is a complex of eight synthetic-grass courts in a park surrounded by an expansive area of native bushland, about 5 km (3 mi) east of the city center. Weekday court hire is A$22 per hour from 7 to 5, and A$25 per hour from 6 to 10; on weekends it's A$1 more per hour.

Parklands Sports Centre (⊠ Lang Rd. and Anzac Parade, Moore Park, Centennial Park ☎ 02/9662–7033) has nine courts set in a shady park approximately 2½ km (1½ mi) from the city center. The weekday cost is A$21 per hour from 9–3 and A$22 from 4–9; it's A$24 per hour from 8–6 on weekends.

Windsurfing

Rose Bay Aquatic Hire (⊠ 1 Vickery Ave., Rose Bay ☎ 02/9371–7036 ⊕ www.aquatichire.com.au) rents Windsurfers, catamarans, and Lasers. The cost is from A$16 per hour for a basic Windsurfer, from A$35 per hour for a Maricat suitable for up to four. Windsurfer instruction is also available.

SHOPPING

Sydney's shops range from those carrying high-class international brand names such as Tiffany's and Louis Vuitton to one-of-a-kind Aboriginal art galleries, plus opal shops, crafts galleries, and weekend flea markets. If you're interested in buying genuine Australian products, look carefully at the labels. Stuffed koalas and didgeridoos made anywhere but in Australia have become a standing joke. Business hours are usually about 9 or 10 to 6 on weekdays; Thursday is a later night with stores open until 9. Shops are open Saturday 9–5 and Sunday 11–5, roughly. The sticker price includes the new Goods and Services Tax (GST).

Department Stores

David Jones (⊠ Women's store, Elizabeth and Market Sts., City Center ⊠ men's store, Castlereagh and Market Sts., City Center ☎ 02/

9266–5544 ⊕ www.davidjones.com.au)—or "Dee Jays," as it's known locally—is the city's largest department store, with a reputation for excellent service and high-quality goods. Clothing by many of Australia's finest designers is on display here, and the store also markets its own fashion label at reasonable prices. The basement level of the men's store is a food hall with international treats.

Gowings (⊠ 8 Transvaal Ave., Double Bay ☎ 02/9287–6394 ⊕ www. gowings.com.au) is Australia's answer to L.L. Bean—an old-fashioned store jam-packed with practical everyday items from hats to umbrellas to undergarments, mostly at no-frills prices. It's open Monday–Wednesday and Friday 9–5:30, Thursday 9–9, Saturday 9:30–5, and Sunday 10–4.

Grace Bros (⊠ George and Market Sts., City Center ☎ 02/9238–9111 ⊕ www.gracebros.com.au), opposite the Queen Victoria Building, is the place to shop for clothing and accessories by Australian and international designers. After a tough stretch of shopping you can rest and recover at the café on the bookstore level.

Flea Markets

Balmain Market (⊠ St. Andrew's Church, Darling St., Balmain), set in a leafy churchyard less than 5 km (3 mi) from the city, has a rustic quality that makes it a refreshing change from city-center shopping. Craftwork, plants, handmade furniture, bread, tarot readings, massages, and toys are among the offerings at the 140-odd stalls. Inside the church hall you can buy international snacks, from Indian *samosas* (deep-fried pastries stuffed with meat or vegetables) to Indonesian *satays* (marinated cubes of meat cooked on skewers) to Australian meat pies. The market runs 8:30–4 on Saturday.

Fodor'sChoice
★ **Paddington Bazaar** (⊠ St. John's Church, Oxford St., Paddington), more popularly known as Paddington Market, is a busy churchyard bazaar with more than 100 stalls crammed with clothing, plants, crafts, jewelry, and souvenirs. Distinctly New Age and highly fashion conscious, the market is also an outlet for a handful of avant-garde clothing designers. It also acts as a magnet for buskers and some of the area's flamboyant and entertaining characters. It's open Saturday 10–4. While you're in the neighborhood, check out nearby Oxford Street's cafés and clothing boutiques.

The Rocks Market (⊠ Upper George St., near Argyle St., The Rocks), a sprawling covered bazaar, transforms the upper end of George Street into a multicultural collage of music, food, arts, crafts, and entertainment. It's open weekends 10–5.

Shopping Centers & Arcades

Harbourside (⊠ Darling Harbour), the glamorous, glassy pavilion on the water's edge at Darling Harbour, houses more than 200 clothing, jewelry, and souvenir shops. However, its popularity is not so much due to the stores as to its striking architecture and spectacular location. The shopping center, which is open daily 10–approximately midnight, also has many cafés, restaurants, and bars that overlook the harbor.

Dressed to thrill, **Oxford Street** is Paddington's main artery, lined with boutiques, home furnishing stores, and Mediterranean-inspired cafés that provide a perfect venue for watching the never-ending fashion parade.

Pitt Street Mall (⊠ Between King and Market Sts., City Center), at the heart of Sydney's shopping area, includes the Mid-City Centre, Centrepoint Arcade, Imperial Arcade, Skygarden, Grace Bros, and the charming and historic Strand Arcade—six multilevel shopping plazas crammed with more than 450 shops, from mainstream clothing stores to designer boutiques.

Queen Victoria Building (✉ George, York, Market, and Druitt Sts., City Center ☎ 02/9264–9209) is a splendid Victorian building near Town Hall that has more than 200 boutiques, cafés, and antiques shops. Even if you have no intention of shopping, the meticulously restored 1890s building itself is worth a look. The QVB is open 24 hours, although the shops do business at the usual hours.

Specialty Stores

Aboriginal Art

Aboriginal art includes historically functional items, such as boomerangs, wooden bowls, and spears, as well as paintings and ceremonial implements that testify to a rich culture of legends and dreams. Although much of this artwork remains strongly traditional in essence, the tools and colors used in Western art have fired the imaginations of many Aboriginal artists. Works on canvas are now more common than works on bark, for example. Although the two most prolific sources of Aboriginal art are Arnhem Land and the Central Desert Region (close to Darwin and Alice Springs, respectively), much of the best work finds its way into the galleries of Sydney.

Aboriginal Art Centres (✉ Aboriginal and Tribal Art Centre, 117 George St., Level 1, The Rocks ☎ 02/9247–9625 ✉ Aboriginal Art Shop, Opera House, Upper Concourse, Circular Quay ☎ 02/9247–4344 ✉ 7 Walker La., Paddington ☎ 02/9360–6839) are variously named shops selling Aboriginal work, from large sculpture and bark paintings to such small collectibles as carved emu eggs. The stores are open Monday–Wednesday and Friday 9–5:30, Thursday 9–9, Saturday 9–5, and Sunday 10–4.

Coo-ee Aboriginal Art (✉ 98 Oxford St., Paddington ☎ 02/9332–1544) sells a wide selection of wearable Aboriginal artwork including jewelry and T-shirts painted with abstract designs, sold at moderate prices. The store is open Monday–Saturday 10–6 and Sunday 11–5.

Books

Ariel Booksellers (✉ 42 Oxford St., Paddington ☎ 02/9332–4581 ⊕ www.arielbooks.com.au ✉ 103 George St., The Rocks ☎ 02/9241–5622) is a large, bright, browser's delight and the place to go for literature, pop culture, and anything avant-garde. It also has a terrific selection of art books. The Paddington store is open daily 10 AM–midnight; the store at The Rocks is open daily 10–6.

Dymocks (✉ 424–430 George St., City Center ☎ 02/9235–0155 ⊕ www.dymocks.com.au), a big, bustling bookstore packed to its gallery-level coffee shop, is the place to go for all literary needs. It's open Monday–Wednesday and Friday 9–5:30, Thursday 9–9, and weekends 9–4.

The Travel Bookshop (✉ Shop 3, 175 Liverpool St., Hyde Park ☎ 02/9261–8200) carries Sydney's most extensive selection of maps, guides, armchair travel books, and histories.

Bush Apparel & Outdoor Gear

Mountain Designs (✉ 499 Kent St., City Center ☎ 02/9267–3822 ⊕ www.mountaindesigns.com.au), in the middle of Sydney's "Rugged Row" of outdoor specialists, sells camping and climbing hardware and dispenses the advice necessary to keep you alive and well in the wilderness.

Paddy Pallin (✉ 507 Kent St., City Center ☎ 02/9264–2685 ⊕ www.paddypallin.com.au) is the first stop for serious bush adventurers heading for the Amazon, Annapurna, or wild Australia. You'll find maps, books, and mounds of gear tailored especially for the Australian outdoors.

★ **R. M. Williams** (✉ 389 George St., City Center ☎ 02/9262–2228 ⊕ www.australianoutback.com.au) is the place to get the complete bush look, with accessories such as Akubra hats, Drizabone riding coats, plaited kangaroo-skin belts, and moleskin trousers.

Crafts

Australian Craftworks (✉ 127 George St., The Rocks ☎ 02/9247–7156), in the former Rocks police station, sells superb woodwork, ceramics, knitwear, and glassware, as well as souvenirs made by leading Australian craftspeople. It's open Friday–Wednesday 9–7 and Thursday 9–9.
Object Gallery (✉ 31 Alfred St., Circular Quay ☎ 02/9247–9126 ⊕ www.object.com.au), located inside the refurbished Customs House building, sells beautiful and pricey creations in glass, wood, and ceramic.

Clothing

Belinda (✉ 8 Transvaal Ave., Double Bay ☎ 02/9328–6288) is where Sydney's female fashionistas go when there's a dress-up occasion looming. From her namesake store that scores high marks for innovation and imagination, former model Belinda Seper sells nothing but the very latest designs off the catwalks.
Collette Dinnigan (✉ 33 William St., Paddington ☎ 02/9360–6691 ⊕ www.collettedinnigan.com.au), one of the hottest names on Australia's fashion scene, has dressed Nicole Kidman, Cate Blanchett, and Sandra Bullock. Her Paddington boutique is packed with sensual, floating fashions crafted from silks, chiffons, and lace in soft pastel colors accented with hand-beading and embroidery.
Country Road (✉ 142–144 Pitt St., City Center ☎ 02/9394–1818 ⊕ www.countryroad.com.au) stands somewhere between Ralph Lauren and Timberland, with an all-Australian assembly of classic, countrified his n' hers, plus an ever-expanding range of soft furnishings in cotton and linen for the rustic retreat.
Marcs (✉ Shop 288, Mid City Centre, Pitt Street Mall, City Center ☎ 02/9221–5575 ⊕ www.marcs.com.au) comes from somewhere close to Diesel-land in the fashion spectrum, with a range of clothing, footwear, and accessories for the fashion-conscious. Serious shoppers should look for the Marcs Made in Italy sub-label for that extra touch of style and craftsmanship.
Orson & Blake (✉ 83–85 Queen St., Woollahra ☎ 02/9326–1155) is a virtual gallery dedicated to great modern design, with an eclectic array of housewares, fashions, handbags, and accessories, and even a coffee shop where you can mull over your wares.
Scanlan & Theodore (✉ 443 Oxford St., Paddington ☎ 02/9361–6722) is the Sydney store for one of Melbourne's most distinguished fashion houses. Designs take their cues from Europe, with superbly tailored women's knitwear, suits, and stylishly glamorous evening wear.

KNITWEAR **Artwear by Lara S** (✉ 77 ½ George St., City Center ☎ 02/9247–3668) is Australian knitwear at its best, with the promise of years of warmth and style in every garment. Comfort as well as fashion are the keywords for these soft and luscious pure wool designs, which range from eye-catching to understated, some in ultrafine wool for itch-free wearing.
Dorian Scott (✉ Shop 7, Hotel Inter-Continental, 117 Macquarie St., Circular Quay ☎ 02/9247–1818), specializes in bright, high-fashion Australian knitwear for men, women, and children, and carries sweaters and scarves in natural colors.

T-SHIRTS & **Beach Culture** (✉ 105 George St., The Rocks ☎ 02/9252–4551) is firmly
BEACHWEAR rooted in the sand and surf ethos, and the place for one-stop shopping for Australia's great surf brands, including Billabong and Mambo. As well as board shorts, towels, and T-shirts, there's a totally groovy collection of jewelry, footwear, and essential accessories for the après-surf scene.

Done Art and Design (✉ 123 George St., The Rocks ☎ 02/9251–6099 ⊕ www.kendone.com.au) sells the striking designs of prominent artist Ken Done, who catches the sunny side of Sydney with vivid colors and bold brush strokes. His shop also carries practical products with his distinctive designs, including bed linens, sunglasses, beach towels, beach and resort wear, and T-shirts.

Mambo (✉ 80 Campbell Parade, Bondi Beach ☎ 02/9365–2255 ⊕ www.mambo.com.au) takes its cues from the bold colors and culture of the beach. The shirts, T-shirts, board shorts, and accessories are funky—not for those who prefer their apparel understated.

JEWELRY **Dinosaur Designs** (✉ Strand Arcade, George St., City Center ☎ 02/9223–2953) sells a luminous array of bowls, plates, and vases, as well as fanciful jewelry crafted from resin and Perspex™ in eye-popping color combinations.

★ **Makers Mark** (✉ 72A Castlereagh St., City Center ☎ 02/9231–6800 ⊕ www.makersmark.com.au) has a gorgeous and varied collection of designer jewelry and objects for the home crafted by the very finest artisans. Prices can be surprisingly moderate.

★ **Paspaley Pearls** (✉ 142 King St., City Center ☎ 02/9232–7633) derives its wares from the Paspaley pearl farms, near the remote Western Australia town of Broome, which the family's craftsmen turn into exquisite jewelry. Prices start high and head for the stratosphere, but if you're serious about a high-quality pearl, this gallery requires a visit.

Percy Marks Fine Gems (✉ 60 Elizabeth St., City Center ☎ 02/9233–1355) has an outstanding collection, if you're looking for Australian gemstones of the highest quality, with a dazzling array of black opals, pink diamonds, and pearls from Broome.

Rox Gems and Jewellery (✉ Strand Arcade, George St., City Center ☎ 02/9232–7828) sells serious one-off designs at the cutting edge of lapidary chic, and can be spotted on some exceedingly well-dressed wrists.

LUGGAGE **Luggageland** (✉ 397 George St., City Center ☎ 02/9299–6699 ⊕ www.luggageland.com.au) is the place to go if your shopping has outgrown your suitcase, if you've lost a wheel while on the move, or if your case simply won't survive the trip. This mid-city store sells a complete range of luggage from the best-known brands that will make lugging it all home again a comparative joy. Opening hours are Monday–Wednesday and Friday 9–5:30, Thursday 9–9, Saturday 9–5, and Sunday 11–5.

MUSIC **Birdland Records** (✉ 3 Barrack St., City Center ☎ 02/9299–8527) has an especially strong range of jazz, blues, African, and Latin American music, and authoritative assistance. It's open weekdays 9–6, Saturday 10–5:30.

Folkways (✉ 282 Oxford St., Paddington ☎ 02/9361–3980) sells Australian bush, folk, and Aboriginal recordings. The store is open Monday 9–6; Tuesday, Wednesday, and Friday 9–7; Thursday 9–9; Saturday 9:30–6:30; and Sunday 10–5.

OPALS Australia has a virtual monopoly on the world's supply of this fiery gemstone. The least expensive stones are doublets, which consist of a thin shaving of opal mounted on a plastic base. Sometimes the opal is covered by a quartz crown, in which case it becomes a triplet. The most expensive stones are solid opals, which cost anywhere from a few hundred dollars to a few thousand. You can pick up opals at souvenir shops all over the city, but if you intend to buy a valuable stone you should visit a specialist.

Flame Opals (✉ 119 George St., The Rocks ☎ 02/9247–3446 ⊕ www.flameopals.com.au) sells nothing but solid opals—black, white, and Queensland boulder varieties, which have a distinctive depth and luster—set in either sterling silver or 18-karat gold. The sales staff is very helpful. The shop is open weekdays 9–7, Saturday 10–5, and Sunday 11:30–5.

Gemtec (✉ 51 Pitt St., Circular Quay ☎ 02/9251–1599 ⊕ www.gemtec.com.au) is the only Sydney opal retailer with total ownership of its entire production process—mines, workshops, and showroom—making prices very competitive. In the Pitt Street showroom, you can see artisans at work cutting and polishing the stones. Hours are weekdays 9–5:30 and weekends 10–4.

SOUVENIRS **ABC Shops** (✉ Level 1, Albert Walk, Queen Victoria Building, 455 George St., City Center ☎ 02/333–1635), the retail arm of Australia's national broadcaster, sells an offbeat collection of things Australian in words, music, and print—an unfailing source of inspiration for gifts and souvenirs. Hours are Monday–Wednesday and Friday 9–6, Thursday 9–9, Saturday 9–5, and Sunday 10–5.

Australian Geographic (✉ Centrepoint, Pitt St., City Center ☎ 02/9231–5055) is the retail outlet of the magazine dedicated to Australia's plants, animals, and natural wonders—a virtual museum crammed with games, puzzles, experiments, and environmental science that promises endless fascination for the inquisitive mind, from children to near-fossil.

SYDNEY A TO Z

To research prices, get advice from other travelers, and book travel arrangements, visit www.fodors.com.

AIR TRAVEL

Several international and domestic airlines serve Sydney's Kingsford–Smith International Airport from North America, Europe, and Southeast Asia. Qantas flights with numbers QF1 to QF399 depart from the Kingsford–Smith airport's international terminal. Flights QF400 and higher depart from the domestic terminal.

Air Canada, Air New Zealand, Alitalia, British Airways, Cathay Pacific Airways, Garuda, Japan Airlines, Lauda Air, Malaysia Airlines, Qantas Airways, Singapore Airlines, Thai Airways, and United Airlines all have flights to Sydney.

Qantas Airways and Virgin Blue connect Sydney to other cities in Australia.

🛂 Carriers **Air Canada** ☎ 1300/655767. **Air New Zealand** ☎ 13–2476. **Alitalia** ☎ 02/9244–2400. **British Airways** ☎ 1300/767177. **Cathay Pacific Airways** ☎ 13–1747. **Garuda** ☎ 1300/365330. **Japan Airlines** ☎ 02/9272–1111. **Lauda Air** ☎ 02/9241–4277. **Malaysia Airlines** ☎ 13–2627. **Qantas Airways** ☎ 13–1313. **Singapore Airlines** ☎ 13–1011. **Thai Airways** ☎ 1300/651960. **United Airlines** ☎ 13–1777. **Virgin Blue** ☎ 13–6789.

AIRPORTS

Kingsford–Smith International Airport is Sydney's main airport, 8 km (5 mi) south of the city. Luggage carts are available in the baggage area of the international terminal. You can convert your money to Australian currency at the Travelex offices in both the arrivals and departures areas. These are open daily from about 5 AM–10 PM or later, depending on flight arrival or departure times.

Tourism New South Wales has two information counters in the arrival level of the international terminal. One provides free maps and brochures and handles general inquiries. The other deals with hotel reservations. Both counters are open daily from approximately 6 AM–11 PM.

Kingsford–Smith's domestic and international terminals are 3 km (2 mi) apart. To get from one terminal to the other, you can take a taxi for about A$13, use the Airport Shuttle Bus, or catch the Airport Express bus. The latter departs approximately every 10–15 minutes from the arrivals terminal, between about 5 AM and 11 PM. Both bus services cost A$3.

🏢 **Kingsford–Smith International Airport** ☎ 02/9667-9111 🌐 www.sydneyairport.com.au.

TRANSFERS The green-and-yellow Airport Express bus provides a fast, comfortable link between the airport terminals and the city, Kings Cross, and Darling Harbour. If you're traveling with fewer than four people, the cost compares favorably with that of a taxi—the bus is A$7 one-way, A$12 round-trip. From the international and domestic terminals, the Airport Express Bus stops first at Central Station, then travels along George Street to Circular Quay and The Rocks before making a loop of Kings Cross. Buses depart approximately every 20 minutes on weekdays between 6:30 AM and 8 PM, approximately every 30 minutes on weekends. Refer to timetables outside the airport terminals for full details, or call the State Transit Infoline. A brochure on the service is usually available from the Tourism New South Wales counter at the airport.

The Airport Link rail service is the fastest connection between the city and the airport. Travel time to the city is 13 minutes, and trains depart every 5–10 minutes during peak hours and at least every 15 minutes at other times. One-way fare is A$10. The link meshes with the suburban rail network at Central Station and Circular Quay Station. On the downside, access to the platform is difficult for travelers with anything more than light luggage, trains do not have adequate stowage facilities, and for two traveling together, a taxi is more convenient and costs only slightly more.

Taxis are available outside the terminal buildings. The fare to city hotels is about A$30, about A$28 to Kings Cross.

A chauffeured limousine to the city hotels costs about A$85. Waiting time is charged at the rate of A$60 per hour. Astra Chauffeured Limousines are reliable services.

🏢 **Airport Express** ☎ 13-1500. **Astra Chauffeured Limousines** ☎ 13-2121. **Airport Link** ☎ 13-1500 🌐 www.airportlink.com.au. **State Transit Infoline** ☎ 13-1500.

BOAT & FERRY TRAVEL

Cruise ships call frequently at Sydney as part of their South Pacific itineraries. Passenger ships generally berth at the Overseas Passenger Terminal at Circular Quay. The terminal sits in the shadow of Harbour Bridge, close to many of the city's major attractions as well as to the bus, ferry, and train networks. Otherwise, passenger ships berth at the Darling Harbour Passenger Terminal, a short walk from the city center.

There is no finer introduction to the city than a trip aboard one of the commuter ferries that ply Sydney Harbour. The hub of the ferry system is Circular Quay, and ferries dock at the almost 30 wharves—which span the length and breadth of the harbor—between about 6 AM and 11:30 PM. One of the most popular sightseeing trips is the Manly ferry, a 30-minute journey from Circular Quay that provides glimpses of harborside mansions and the sandstone cliffs and bushland along the north shore. On the return journey, consider taking the JetCat, which skims the waves in an exhilarating 15-minute trip back to the city. But be warned: passengers are not allowed on deck, and the views are obscured.

The one-way Manly ferry fare is A$5.30, and the JetCat costs A$6.70. Fares for shorter inner-harbor journeys start at A$4.20. You can also buy economical ferry-and-entrance-fee passes, available from the Circular Quay ticket office, to such attractions as Taronga Zoo and Sydney Aquarium.

The sleek RiverCat ferries travel west from Circular Quay as far as Parramatta. These ferries are used overwhelmingly by commuters, although they also provide a useful and practical connection to Homebush Bay, site of Sydney Olympic Park. The A$20 fare to the park includes bus service to the Olympic Park Information Centre.

State Transit Authority ☎ 13-1500 ⊕ www.sydneybuses.nsw.gov.au.

BUS TRAVEL TO & FROM SYDNEY
Greyhound Pioneer Australia and McCafferty's bus service is available to all major cities from Sydney. You can purchase tickets for long-distance buses from travel agents, by telephone with a credit card, or at bus terminals. Approximate travel times by bus are: Sydney to Canberra, 4 hours; Sydney to Melbourne, 11 hours; Sydney to Brisbane, 11 hours; Sydney to Adelaide, 13 hours. The main terminal is the Central Station (Eddy Avenue) terminus just south of the City Center. Lockers are available in the terminal.

Greyhound Pioneer Australia ☎ 13-2030 ⊕ www.greyhound.com.au. **McCafferty's** ☎ 13-1499 ⊕ www.mccaffertys.com.au.

BUS TRAVEL WITHIN SYDNEY
Bus travel in Sydney is rather slow due to the city's congested roads and undulating terrain. Fares are calculated by the number of city sections traveled. The minimum two-section bus fare (A$1.50) applies to trips throughout the inner-city area. You would pay the minimum fare, for example, for a ride from Circular Quay to Kings Cross, or from Park Street to Oxford Street in Paddington. Tickets may be purchased from the driver, who will compute the fare based on your destination. Discounted fares are available in several forms, including Travelten passes (valid for 10 journeys), which start at A$11.30 and are available from bus stations and most newsagents.

State Transit Authority ☎ 13-1500 ⊕ www.sydneybuses.nsw.gov.au.

CAR RENTAL
If you rent from a major international company, expect to pay about A$75 per day for a medium-size automatic and about A$65 for a standard compact. However, if you go with a local operator, such as Bayswater, you might pay as little as A$25 per day if you're prepared to drive a slightly older model vehicle with higher mileage (usually one–two years old). Some of these discount operators restrict travel to within a 50-km (30-mi) radius of the city center, and one-way rentals are not possible. A surcharge applies if you pick up your car from the airport.

Agencies **Avis** ☎ 13-6333. **Bayswater** ☎ 02/9360-3622. **Budget** ☎ 13-2727. **Dollar** ☎ 02/9223-1444. **Hertz** ☎ 13-3039. **Thrifty** ☎ 1300/367227.

CAR TRAVEL
With the assistance of a good road map or street directory, you shouldn't have too many problems driving in and out of Sydney, thanks to a decent freeway system. Keep in mind that Australia is almost as large as the United States minus Alaska. In computing your travel times for trips between Sydney and the following cities, allow for an average speed of about 85 kph (53 mph). The main roads to and from other state capitals are: the 982-km (609-mi) Pacific Highway (Highway 1) north to Brisbane; the 335-km (208-mi) Hume Highway (Highway 31) southwest to Canberra, or 874 km (542 mi) to Melbourne; and the 1,038-km (644-mi) Princes Highway (Highway 1) to the NSW south coast and Melbourne. Adelaide is 1,425 km (884 mi) away via the Hume and Sturt

(Highway 20) highways, and Perth is a long and rather tedious 4,132-km (2,562-mi) drive via Adelaide.

Driving a car around Sydney is not particularly recommended. Close to the city, the harbor inlets plus the hilly terrain equal few straight streets. Parking space is limited, and both parking lots and parking meters are expensive. If you do decide to drive, ask your car-rental agency for a street directory or purchase one from a newsstand.

For details on emergency assistance, gasoline, road conditions, and rules of the road, *see* Car Travel *in* Smart Travel Tips A to Z.

CONSULATES

🛂 **British Consulate General** ⊠ Gateway Bldg., 1 Macquarie Pl., Level 16, Circular Quay ☎ 02/9247-7521. **Canadian Consulate General** ⊠ 111 Harrington St., Level 5, The Rocks ☎ 02/9364-3000. **New Zealand Consulate General** ⊠ 55 Hunter St., Level 10, City Center ☎ 02/9223-0222. **U.S. Consulate General** ⊠ 19-29 Martin Pl., Level 59, City Center ☎ 02/9373-9200.

DISCOUNTS & DEALS

For the price of admission to two or three top attractions, the seesyd-neycard, available from the Sydney Visitor Information Centre in The Rocks, through the Web site, and from several other locations listed on the Web site, gets you into numerous Sydney sights and attractions, such as the Opera House, Sydney Aquarium, the Koala Park Sanctuary, and many more. Several different cards are available, including single-day and weekly cards. Cards may also include public transportation. Prices start at A$59 for a single-day adult card without transportation.

SydneyPass (⇨ Transportation Around Sydney) allows unlimited travel on public transportation for between three and seven days.

🛂 **seesydneycard** ☎ 02/9960-3511 ⊕ www.seesydneycard.com.

EMERGENCIES

Dial 000 for an ambulance, the fire department, or the police. Dental Emergency Information Service provides names and numbers for nearby dentists. It's available only after 7 PM daily. Royal North Shore Hospital is 7 km (4½ mi) northwest of the city center. St. Vincent's Public Hospital is 2½ km (1½ mi) east of the city center.

Your best bet for a late-night pharmacy is in the major city hotels or in the Kings Cross and Oxford Street (Darlinghurst) areas. You can also call the Pharmacy Guild 24 hours a day for advice and assistance.

🛂 **Dentist Dental Emergency** ☎ 02/9211-2224.

🛂 **Hospitals Royal North Shore Hospital** ⊠ Pacific Hwy., St. Leonards ☎ 02/9926-7111. **St. Vincent's Public Hospital** ⊠ Victoria and Burton Sts., Darlinghurst ☎ 02/9339-1111.

🛂 **24-hour Pharmacies Pharmacy Guild** ☎ 02/9966-8377.

🛂 **Police Sydney Police Centre** ☎ 02/9281-0000.

MAIL, INTERNET & BUSINESS SERVICES

If you will require business services, such as faxing, using a computer, photocopying, typing, or translation services during your trip, plan to stay in a hotel with a business center, since their services are normally available only to guests.

DHL and Federal Express both ship internationally overnight.

🛂 **Internet Cafés Global Gossip** ⊠ 111 Darlinghurst Rd., Kings Cross ☎ 02/9326-9777. **Internet Cafe** ⊠ Hotel Sweeney, Level 2, 236 Clarence St., City Center ☎ 02/9261-5666. **Phone Net Café** ⊠ 73-75 Hall St., Bondi ☎ 02/9365-0681.

🛂 **Post Office General Post Office** ⊠ Martin Pl., City Center.

🛂 **Overnight Service DHL** ☎ 13-1406 ⊕ www.dhl.com.au. **Federal Express** ☎ 13-2610 ⊕ www.fedex.com.au.

MONEY MATTERS

Any bank will exchange travelers checks and most foreign currencies. ATMs are prevalent in airports, shopping malls, and tourist areas. Cirrus and Plus cards are accepted at most ATMs, but check with your bank to make sure that you'll be able to access your funds overseas and that you have a four-digit PIN.

MONORAIL & TRAM TRAVEL

Sydney Monorail is one of the fastest, most relaxing forms of public transport in the city, but its use is limited to travel between the city center, Darling Harbour, and Chinatown. The fare varies from A$2.60 to A$3.60 per one-way trip, and A$3.90 to A$4.90 for a round-trip ticket. An A$8 Day Ticket is a better value if you intend to use the monorail to explore. You can purchase tickets at machines in the monorail stations. The monorail operates every 2–6 minutes, generally from 7 AM–10 PM, and until midnight on Friday and Saturday. Stations are identified by a large white M against a black background.

The Sydney Light Rail, identifiable by signs with a large black M against a white background, is a limited system that provides a fast, efficient link between Central Station, Darling Harbour, the Star City casino and entertainment complex, Sydney fish markets, and the inner-western suburbs of Glebe and Lilyfield. The modern, air-conditioned tram cars operate at 5- to 11-minute intervals, 24 hours a day. One-way tickets are A$2.60 to A$3.60, and the Day Pass is a comparatively good value at A$8. You can purchase tickets at machines in Light Rail stations.

🔲 **Sydney Light Rail and Monorail information** ☎ 02/8584-5288 ⊕ www.metromonorail.com.au or www.metrolightrail.com.au.

SIGHTSEEING TOURS

Dozens of tour operators lead guided trips through Sydney and the surrounding areas. Options include shopping strolls, tours of the Sydney fish markets, and rappelling the waterfalls of the Blue Mountains. The Sydney Visitors Information Centre and other booking and information centers can provide you with many more suggestions and recommendations. Most suburban shopping plazas have a travel agency—in addition to the many general and specialist travel agents in the city center.

BOAT TOURS A replica of Captain Bligh's *Bounty* is alive and afloat on Sydney Harbour, and Bounty Cruises conducts various harbor excursions. A lunch cruise (A$72 weekdays, A$99 weekends) departs daily at 12:30 and travels east along the harbor. Most of the voyage is made under sail, and all on board are encouraged to take a turn with the ropes and the wheel. A commentary is provided, and the cruise focuses as much on square-rigger sailing and the history of the *Bounty* as on the sights of Sydney Harbour. For photographers, the nightly 7 o'clock dinner cruise (A$109) affords spectacular possibilities. Cruises depart from Campbell's Cove, in front of the Park Hyatt Sydney Hotel.

Fodor'sChoice Captain Cook Cruises is the largest cruise operator on the harbor. Its ★ best introductory trip is the 2½-hour Coffee Cruise, which follows the southern shore of the harbor to Watsons Bay, crosses to the north shore to explore Middle Harbour, and returns to Circular Quay. The Sydney Harbour Explorer cruise allows you to disembark from the cruise boat at the Opera House, Watsons Bay, Taronga Zoo, or Darling Harbour, explore, and catch any following Captain Cook explorer cruise. Four Explorer cruises (A$25) depart daily from Circular Quay at two-hour intervals, beginning at 9:30. Coffee cruises (A$39) depart daily at 10 and 2:15. Dinner, sunset, and show-time cruises are also available. All cruises depart from Wharf 6, Circular Quay.

The State Transit Authority runs several cruises aboard harbor ferries, at lower costs than those of privately operated cruises. Light refreshments are available on board. All cruises depart from Wharf 4 at the Circular Quay terminal. The Morning Harbour Cruise (A$15), a one-hour journey, takes in the major sights of the harbor to the east of the city. The boat departs daily at 10 and 11:15. The Afternoon Harbour Cruise (A$22) is a leisurely 2½-hour tour that takes in the scenic eastern suburbs and affluent Middle Harbour. Tours leave weekdays at 1 and weekends at 1:30. The 1½-hour Evening Harbour Lights Cruise (A$19) takes you into Darling Harbour for a nighttime view of the city from the west, then passes the Garden Island naval base to view the Opera House and Kings Cross. Tours depart Monday through Saturday at 8 PM.
Bounty Cruises ☎02/9247-1789 ⊕ www.thebounty.com. **Captain Cook Cruises** ☎02/9206-1122 ⊕ www.captcookcrus.com.au. **State Transit Authority** ☎13-1500 ⊕ www.sydneybuses.nsw.gov.au.

BUS TOURS The only guided bus tour of the inner city is the Sydney Explorer bus, which makes a 35-km (22-mi) circuit of all the major attractions, including The Rocks, Kings Cross, Darling Harbour, Chinatown, and across Harbour Bridge to Milsons Point. Ticket holders can board or leave the bus at any of the 26 stops along the route and catch any following Explorer bus. The bright red buses follow one another every 20 minutes, and the service operates from 8:40 daily. The last bus to make the circuit departs Circular Quay at 5:20. If you choose to stay on board for the entire circuit, the trip takes around 90 minutes.

The Bondi Explorer bus runs a guided bus tour of the eastern suburbs. The blue bus begins its 30-km (19-mi) journey at Circular Quay and travels through Kings Cross, Double Bay, Vaucluse, and Watsons Bay to the Gap, then returns to the city via Bondi, Bronte, and other beaches; Centennial Park; and Oxford Street. You can leave the bus at any of its 19 stops and catch a following bus, or remain on board for a round-trip of about 90 minutes. Buses follow one another at 30-minute intervals beginning at 9:15. The last bus departs Circular Quay at 4:15.

Tickets for either Explorer bus, valid for one day, cost A$30 and can be purchased on board or from the New South Wales Travel Centre.

Several coach companies run day trips in and around the Sydney region, reaching as far as the Blue Mountains, the Hunter Valley wine region, Canberra, wildlife parks, and the 2000 Olympics site at Homebush Bay. The major operators listed below all have a 24-hour information and reservation service.
Australian Pacific Coaches ☎1800/306306. **Murrays Australia** ☎13-2259. **New South Wales Travel Centre** ✉11-31 York St., City Center ☎13-2077. **State Transit Authority, Explorer Bus routes** ☎13-1500.

NATIONAL PARKS & BUSH TOURS Bush Limousine Tour Company specializes in quality small-group tours. Off-the-shelf and tailor-made tours are available to places such as the Blue Mountains, the Southern Highlands, the Hunter Valley, and the alpine region of southern New South Wales.

Mount 'n Beach Safaris is a four-wheel-drive operator that arranges soft adventures to areas of outstanding beauty around Sydney. The Blue Mountains Wildlife Discovery allows you the chance to see koalas and kangaroos, enjoy morning tea in the bush, take in the scenic highlights of the Blue Mountains, lunch at a historic pub, and return to Sydney in time for a performance at the Opera House. The Mountain Wine and Waves tours of the Hunter Valley wine-growing district and the aquatic playground of Port Stephens are available in two- to five-day options.

Wildframe operates two one-day hiking-and-sightseeing trips to the Grand Canyon area, one of the loveliest parts of the Blue Mountains. Groups are limited to a maximum of 16, and all guides have specialist qualifications. The price is A$65, or A$90 for a slightly less demanding walk (the price includes lunch).

🏠 **Bush Limousine Tour Company** ☎ 02/9418-7222. **Mount 'n Beach Safaris** ☎ 02/9267-5899. **Wildframe** ☎ 02/9314-0658.

SPECIAL INTEREST TOURS BridgeClimb is a unique tour that affords the ultimate view of the harbor and city center. Wearing a special suit and harnessed to a static line, you can ascend the steel arch of the Sydney Harbour Bridge in the company of a guide. The tour lasts for three hours and costs from A$145 per person. Tours depart from 5 Cumberland Street, The Rocks. Night climbs are also available.

Easyrider Motorbike Tours conducts exciting chauffeur-driven (you ride as a passenger) Harley-Davidson tours to the city's beaches, the Blue Mountains, Royal National Park, Hawkesbury River, and the Hunter Valley wineries. A two-hour tour costs A$190 per person, and a full-day excursion starts at about A$400.

🏠 **BridgeClimb** ☎ 02/9252-0077 🌐 www.bridgeclimb.com.au. **Easyrider Motorbike Tours** ☎ 02/9247-2477 🌐 www.easyrider.com.au.

WALKING TOURS The Rocks Walking Tours will introduce you to Sydney's European settlement site, with an emphasis on the neighborhood buildings and personalities of the convict period. The 1½-hour tour costs A$17.50 and involves little climbing. Tours leave weekdays at 10:30, 12:30, and 2:30, and weekends at 11:30 and 2.

Sydney Guided Tours with Maureen Fry are an excellent introduction to Sydney. Standard tours cost A$18 and cover the colonial buildings along Macquarie Street, a ramble through the historic waterside suburbs of Glebe and Balmain, or Circular Quay and The Rocks. Theme tours include art galleries, food and markets, heritage hotels, and a tour of the Opera Centre, where operas are rehearsed before they move to the Sydney Opera House.

🏠 **The Rocks Walking Tours** ✉ Kendall La., off Argyle St., The Rocks ☎ 02/9247-6678. **Sydney Guided Tours** ☎ 02/9660-7157 🖷 02/9660-0805 🌐 www.ozemail.com.au/~mpfry.

TAXIS & LIMOUSINES

Taxis are a relatively economical way to cover short to medium distances in Sydney. A 3-km (2-mi) trip from Circular Quay to the eastern suburbs costs around A$14. Drivers are entitled to charge more than the metered fare if the passenger's baggage exceeds 55 pounds, if the taxi has been booked by telephone, or if the passenger crosses Harbour Bridge, where a toll is levied. Fares are 10% higher between 10 PM and 5 AM, when the numeral "2" will be displayed in the tariff indicator on the meter. At all other times, make sure the numeral "1" is displayed. Taxis are licensed to carry four passengers. Most drivers will accept payment by American Express, Diners Club, MasterCard, and Visa, although a 10% surcharge is applied. Taxis can be hailed on the street, hired from a taxi stand, or booked by phone. Taxi stands can be found outside most bus and railway stations, as well as outside the larger hotels. Complaints should be directed to Taxi Cab Complaints.

Chauffeur-driven limousines are available for trips around Sydney. At your request, the driver will give commentary on the major sights. Limousines can be rented for approximately A$80 per hour.

🏠 Limousine Companies **Astra Chauffeured Limousines** ☎ 13-2121.
🏠 Taxi Companies **ABC Taxis** ☎ 13-2522. **Taxi Cab Complaints** ☎ 1800/648478. **Taxis Combined Services** ☎ 02/8332-8888.

TELEPHONES

The telephone code for Sydney and New South Wales is 02. If you're calling a New South Wales number that is a nonlocal call, you'll need to dial 02 before the eight-digit local number. You can make interstate and international calls from any telephone. To make an interstate call, use the following codes: Australian Capital Territory (ACT), 02; Northern Territory (NT), 08; Queensland (QLD), 07; South Australia (SA), 08; Tasmania (TAS), 03; Victoria (VIC), 03; and Western Australia (WA), 08. Public telephones are located throughout the city. The cost of a local call is 40¢. Some public phones will accept coins; more will accept phone cards, which are available in units of A$5, A$10, A$20, and A$50 from post offices and businesses that display the yellow PHONECARD sign.

TRAIN TRAVEL

The main terminal for long-distance and intercity trains is Central Station, about 2 km (1 mi) south of the city center. Two daily services (morning and evening) operate between Sydney and Melbourne; the trip takes about 10 hours. Three *Explorer* trains make the four-hour trip to Canberra daily. The *Indian-Pacific* leaves Sydney on Monday and Thursday afternoons for Adelaide (26 hours) and Perth (64 hours). The overnight *Brisbane XPT* makes the 15-hour Sydney–Brisbane journey every day. Call the state rail authority, Countrylink, between 6:30 AM and 10 PM daily for information about fares and timetables, or check the Countrylink Web site.

Tickets for long-distance train travel can be purchased from Countrylink Travel Centres at Central Station, Circular Quay, Wynyard Station, and Town Hall Station.

For journeys in excess of 7 km (4 mi), Sydney's trains are considerably faster than buses. However, the rail network has been designed primarily for rapid transit between outlying suburbs and the city. Apart from the City Circle line, which includes the Circular Quay and Town Hall stations and the spur line to Kings Cross and Bondi Junction, the system does not serve areas of particular interest to tourists. If you plan on using the trains, remember the following axioms: all trains pass through Central Station; Town Hall is the "shoppers" station; the bus, ferry, and train systems converge at Circular Quay. Trains generally operate from 4:30 AM to midnight.

As an example of fare prices, a one-way ticket from Town Hall Station to Bondi Junction costs A$2.60. Several discounted fares are also available, including off-peak tickets that apply on weekends and after 9 AM on weekdays.

🚈 **Central Station** ✉ Eddy Ave., City South. **Countrylink Travel Centres** ✉ Eddy Ave., Central Station, City South ✉ Shop W6/W7 Alfred St., Circular Quay, Circular Quay ✉ Shop W15, Wynyard Concourse, Wynyard Station, City Center ✉ Queen Victoria Bldg., lower level, George and Park Sts., Town Hall Station, City Center ☎ 13-2232 ⊕ www.countrylink. nsw.gov.au.

TRANSPORTATION AROUND SYDNEY

Despite its vast size, Sydney packs its primary attractions into a fairly small area. For the most part, public transport is an efficient, economical way to see the city. Getting to and from such areas as The Rocks, Darling Harbour, and the Opera House is simple on Sydney's buses, ferries, and trains, except during rush hours. Once you're there, these areas are best explored on foot.

A TravelPass allows unlimited travel aboard buses, ferries, and trains, but not trams, within designated areas of the city for a week or more.

The most useful is probably the weeklong Blue TravelPass (A$27), which covers the city and eastern suburbs and inner-harbor ferries. (Ferries to Manly and trains will cost extra.) TravelPasses are available from railway and bus stations and from most newsagents on bus routes.

If you're planning on spending three days or fewer in Sydney and taking the Airport Express bus, the guided Sydney Explorer and Bondi Explorer buses, and any of the three sightseeing cruises operated by the State Transit Authority, SydneyPass (A$90 for three days, five- and seven-day passes available) will save you money. In addition to free travel on all these services, the pass also allows unlimited travel on any public bus or harbor ferry and on most suburban train services. Purchase passes from the Tourism New South Wales counter on the ground floor of the international airport terminal or from the driver of any Explorer or Airport Express bus.

For route, timetable, and ticket price information on Sydney's buses, ferries, and trains call the State Transit Infoline, daily 6 AM–10 PM. ✈ **State Transit Infoline** ☎ 13-1500 ⊕ www.sydneybuses.nsw.gov.au.

TRAVEL AGENCIES
The following travel agencies can help you arrange various tours and excursions.
✈ Agencies **American Express Travel Service** ✉ 92 Pitt St., City Center ☎ 02/9239-0666. **Thomas Cook** ✉ 175 Pitt St., City Center ☎ 02/9231-2877.

VISITOR INFORMATION
There are tourist information booths throughout the city, including Circular Quay, Martin Place, Darling Harbour, and the Pitt Street Mall.

The Backpacker's Travel Centre specializes in budget tours, lodging, and information. Countrylink, the state rail authority, is a good source of Sydney and New South Wales travel information.

The Sydney Information Line has useful recorded service and entertainment information. The Sydney Visitors Information Centre is the major source of information, brochures, and maps for Sydney and New South Wales. The Tourist Information Service is a free phone-in facility that provides information on accommodations, tours, and shopping. It also provides other tips on what to see and do in Sydney.

The CitySearch Web site is a great resource for the latest on Sydney's arts, food, and nightlife scene.
✈ Tourist Information **Backpacker's Travel Centre** ✉ Shop 33, Imperial Arcade, off Pitt St. near Market St., City Center ☎ 02/9231-3699. **CitySearch** ⊕ www.sydney. citysearch.com.au. **Countrylink** ✉ Shop W15, Wynyard Concourse, Wynyard Station, City Center ☎ 13-2829. **Sydney Information Line** ☎ 02/9265-9007. **Sydney Visitors Information Centre** ✉ 106 George St., The Rocks ☎ 02/9255-1788 🖶 02/9241-5010 ⊕ www.sydneyvisitorcentre.com.

WATER TAXIS
A fun, fast, but somewhat expensive way to get around is by water taxi. (Circular Quay to Watsons Bay, for example, costs A$50.) These operate to and from practically anywhere on Sydney Harbour that has wharf or steps access.
✈ **Harbour Taxi Boats** ☎ 02/9555-1155. **Taxis Afloat** ☎ 02/9955-3222.

NEW SOUTH WALES

2

FODOR'S CHOICE

Convent Pepper Tree, hotel and winery in Pokolbin

Rae's on Watego's, boutique hotel on Watego's Beach

Robert's at Pepper Tree, restaurant in Pokolbin

Sea Acres Rainforest Centre, park in Port Macquarie

Silks Brasserie, restaurant in Leura

The Snowy Mountains, in Kosciuszko National Park

Three Sisters, rock formation near Katoomba

Vulcan's, restaurant in Blackheath

Zig Zag Railway, in Clarence

HIGHLY RECOMMENDED

RESTAURANTS Ca Marche, in Port Macquarie

Crackenback Cottage, in Thredbo Valley

Fig Tree Restaurant, in Ewingsdale

HOTELS Aanuka Beach Resort, in Coffs Harbour

Avoca House, in Wollombi

Eagles Range, in Jindabyne

Jemby Rinjah Lodge, in Blackheath

Lilianfels Blue Mountains, in Echo Point

Old George and Dragon, in East Maitland

Reynella, in Adaminaby

Vineyard Hill Country Motel, in Pokolbin

Woodbyne, in Jaspers Brush

SIGHTS Dorrigo National Park, near Bellingen

Falls Reserve, near Wentworth Falls

Sublime Point Lookout, in Leura

By Michael
Gebicki, Anne
Matthews,
and David
McGonigal

Updated by
Dominic
O'Grady,
Malcolm
Harding,
Craig Johnston,
and Meredith
Heyward

FOR MANY TRAVELERS, SYDNEY IS NEW SOUTH WALES, and they look
to the other, less-populated states for Australia's famous wilderness experiences. There may be no substitute for Queensland's Great Barrier Reef
or the Northern Territory's Kakadu National Park, but New South Wales
shelters many of Australia's natural wonders within its borders. The state
incorporates the World Heritage areas of Lord Howe Island and the subtropical rain forests of the north coast, as well as desert Outback, the
highest mountain peaks in the country, moist river valleys, warm seas,
golden beaches, and some of the finest vineyards in the country. And all
are within easy reach of the country's largest, most glamorous city.

New South Wales was named by Captain James Cook during his voyage of discovery in 1770: the area's low, rounded hills reminded him of
southern Wales. It was the first state to be settled by the British, whose
plan to establish a penal colony at Botany Bay in 1788 was scrapped in
favor of a site a short distance to the north—Sydney Cove. Successive
waves of convicts helped swell the state's population, but the discovery
in 1850 of gold at Bathurst on the western edge of the Great Dividing
Range sparked a population explosion. The state's economic might was
bolstered by gold and further strengthened by the discovery of huge coal
seams in the Hunter Valley. Timber and wool industries also thrived.

Today, with approximately 6.4 million people, New South Wales is Australia's most populous state. Although this is crowded by Australian standards, it's worth remembering that New South Wales is larger than every
U.S. state except Alaska. The state can be divided into four main regions.
In the east, a coastal plain reaching north to Queensland varies in width
from less than a mile to almost 160 km (100 mi). This plain is bordered
to the west by a chain of low mountains known as the Great Dividing
Range, which tops off at about 7,000 feet in the Snowy Mountains in
the state's far south. On the western slopes of this range is a belt of pas-
ture and farmland. Beyond that are the western plains and Outback, an
arid, sparsely populated region that takes up two-thirds of the state.

Eighty kilometers (50 mi) west of Sydney in the Great Dividing Range
are the Blue Mountains, a domain of tall eucalyptus trees, deep river
valleys, and craggy sandstone outcrops that provide the perfect environment for hiking and adventure activities. The mountains are also famous for their charming guesthouses and lush, cool-climate gardens. About
100 km (60 mi) south of Sydney, the Southern Highlands form a cool
upland region that is geographically similar to the Blue Mountains. The
difference here is a more genteel atmosphere, and the added attraction
of the nearby temperate South Coast beaches. The Hunter Valley region,
about 240 km (150 mi) northwest of Sydney, draws visitors for its
wineries, food, historic towns, and tranquil countryside.

The North Coast stretches almost 600 km (372 mi) up to the Queensland border, and its seaside delights contrast with the rest of the state's
rural splendor. With its sandy beaches, surf, and warm climate, the area
is a perfect holiday playground. Finally, a tiny, remote speck in the Pacific Ocean, Lord Howe Island is the state's tropical island paradise, ringed
with fringing coral, stacked with towering, forested volcanic peaks,
and teeming with seabirds and marine life.

Exploring New South Wales

New South Wales covers a large area that can broadly be divided into
six popular regions. The Blue Mountains lie to the west of Sydney, while
the Southern Highlands and South Coast stretch to the southwest, and
the Hunter Valley dips north of the capital. Also above Sydney is the North

Coast, as is remote Lord Howe Island, a distant offshore environment of its own. At the state's south edge are the Snowy Mountains, part of the Great Dividing Range, which bridges New South Wales from the northern state of Queensland to the southern state of Victoria.

There are excellent highways and paved rural roads connecting these major points, and driving is convenient and easy once you're outside of Sydney. Plenty of tour operators hit all the main points, though, if you want to stay in the capital and make day or overnight trips. A bus network makes exploring an option for budget travelers. Trains run from Sydney north to Brisbane and south to Melbourne and beyond. To explore Sydney's suburbs, you can try the local bus and train networks. Bicycling is also an option along the scenic backroads and valleys, and mountain-biking enthusiasts will enjoy tackling the highland lanes. You can fly to Lord Howe Island in about two hours from Sydney.

About the Restaurants

Dining varies dramatically throughout New South Wales, from superb city-standard restaurants to average country-town fare. As popular weekend retreats for well-heeled Sydneysiders, the Blue Mountains and Southern Highlands have a number of fine restaurants and cozy tearooms that are perfect for light lunches or afternoon teas. In the Hunter Valley, several excellent restaurants show off the region's fine wines. And although the Snowy Mountains area isn't gastronomically distinguished, the succulent trout makes a standout meal.

In spite of the North Coast's excellent seafood and exotic fruits, fine dining is rare away from such major resort centers as Coffs Harbour and Port Macquarie. The small northern town of Byron Bay stands out, however, for its sophisticated cafés and restaurants. Despite its minuscule size and isolation, Lord Howe Island attracts a polished and well-heeled clientele who demand a high standard of dining. At restaurants throughout New South Wales, reservations are always a good idea.

WHAT IT COSTS In Australian dollars					
	$$$$	$$$	$$	$	¢
AT DINNER	over $50	$36–$50	$21–$35	$10–$20	under $10

Prices are per person for a main course at dinner.

About the Hotels

The state's accommodation scene includes everything from run-of-the-mill motels to historic cliff-perched properties in the Blue Mountains and large, glossy seaside resorts in the Southern Highlands. Bear in mind that room rates are often much lower weekdays than weekends, particularly in the areas closest to Sydney—the Blue Mountains, Hunter Valley, and Southern Highlands. In the Snowy Mountains prices are highest during the winter ski season—and are considerably cheaper out of ski season, although a few close. During the off-season (from October through May), some hotels close. Although chains aren't typical, an upscale group of small Peppers resorts are located throughout the state and tend to have particularly lovely settings. Rates in the Snowy Mountains are highest during the winter ski season.

WHAT IT COSTS In Australian dollars					
	$$$$	$$$	$$	$	¢
FOR 2 PEOPLE	over $300	$201–$300	$151–$200	$100–$150	under $100

Prices are for two people in a standard double room in high season.

2

It's wise to decide in advance whether you'd like to cover a lot of ground quickly or choose one or two places to linger a while. If you have four days or fewer, stick close to Sydney in the Blue Mountains or the Southern Highlands, or just hop on a plane to Lord Howe Island for an invigorating contrast to Sydney. In a very busy week you could visit the Blue and Snowy mountains and either the Hunter Valley or Southern Highlands, whereas two weeks would allow a Blue Mountains–North Coast–Lord Howe circuit or brief stops in most of the six regions.

If you have 4 days

Start with a visit to the ⬚ **Blue Mountains.** You could arrange a round-trip itinerary from Sydney in a fairly hectic day or, preferably, spend a night in ⬚ **Katoomba,** ⬚ **Blackheath,** or ⬚ **Leura** and make it a two-day excursion. Return to Sydney, and then head north to the ⬚ **Hunter Valley.** A two-day–one-night driving visit here would allow you enough time to see the main sights and spend time touring the wineries before traveling back to Sydney on the last day. Alternatives could be a quick visit to the Blue Mountains, then a tour of the **Southern Highlands,** or you could fly to ⬚ **Cooma** ㉒ from Sydney for an escape to Australia's highest alpine region, the ⬚ **Snowy Mountains.** Then again, you might want to chuck all of that and fly to ⬚ **Lord Howe Island** for beaches, reefs, soaring mountains, and a relaxing holiday pace.

If you have 7 days

Visit the ⬚ **Blue Mountains** and ⬚ **Hunter Valley** as described above, then continue to the **North Coast.** In three days of driving you wouldn't get much farther than ⬚ **Coffs Harbour** ⑰ (with overnights there and in ⬚ **Port Macquarie** ⑭), and this would be rushing it, but it's possible to fly back to Sydney from Coffs. Of course, if the North Coast holds special appeal, head straight there from the Blue Mountains and give yourself a chance to take in more of it. You could also spend three days in the **Southern Highlands,** then continue south to the ⬚ **Snowy Mountains** for some alpine air, trout fishing, and bushwalking.

If you have 14 days

Divide and conquer: choose three areas and give yourself four days in each, taking into account travel time between them to round out the fortnight. The following combinations would allow for optimal encounters with the varied best of the state: wine, water, and wide-open spaces with the **Hunter Valley–North Coast–Snowy Mountains;** rocks, rain forests, and reefs with the **Blue Mountains–North Coast–Lord Howe Island;** or a watery triad of the **South Coast–North Coast–Lord Howe.**

When to Visit New South Wales

For many visitors the Australian summer (December–February), which complements the northern winter, has great pull. During these months the north and south coast and Lord Howe Island are in full vacation mode, and upland areas as the Blue Mountains and Southern Highlands provide relief from Sydney's sometimes stifling humidity. This is also the ideal season for bushwalking in the cool Snowy Mountains, but be aware that a few of the hotels here close from October through May—the off-season for skiing. The best times to visit the Hunter Valley are during the February–March grape harvest season and the September Hunter Food and Wine Festival.

Although the North Coast resort region is at its peak (and its most crowded) in summer, autumn (March–May) and spring (September–November) are also good times to visit—especially the far north, which is usually quite hot and humid in summer.

On Lord Howe Island, February is the driest and hottest month, and August is the windiest month. Many of the island's hotels and restaurants close for at least part of the June-to-August period. Summer is the best bet, especially for swimming, snorkeling, and diving, but from Christmas through the first half of January the island is booked solid months in advance.

There are some wonderful options if you are in New South Wales in winter (officially June, July, and August). The Snowy Mountains ski season runs from early June to early October. And the "Yulefest" season from June through August is a popular time to visit the Blue Mountains, with blazing log fires and Christmas-style celebration packages.

THE BLUE MOUNTAINS

Sydneysiders have been doubly blessed by nature. Not only do they have a magnificent coastline right at their front door, but a 90-minute drive west puts them in the midst of one of the most spectacular wilderness areas in Australia—Blue Mountains National Park. Standing at 3,500-plus feet high, these "mountains" were once the bed of an ancient sea. Gradually the sedimentary rock was uplifted until it formed a high plateau, which was etched by eons of wind and water into the wonderland of cliffs, caves, and canyons that exists today. Now these richly forested hills, crisp mountain air, gardens that blaze with autumn color, vast sandstone chasms, and little towns of timber and stone are supreme examples of Australia's diversity. The mountains' distinctive blue coloring is caused by the evaporation of oil from the dense eucalyptus forests. This disperses light in the blue colors of the spectrum, a phenomenon known as Rayleigh Scattering.

For a quarter of a century after European settlement, these mountains marked the limits of westward expansion. Early attempts to cross them ended at sheer cliff faces or impassable chasms. For convicts, many of whom believed China lay on the far side, the mountains offered a tantalizing possibility of escape. But not until 1813 did explorers finally forge a crossing by hugging the mountain ridges—the route that the Great Western Highway to Bathurst follows today.

When a railway line from Sydney was completed at the end of the 19th century, the mountains suddenly became fashionable, and guesthouses and hotels flourished. Wealthy Sydney businesspeople built grand weekend homes here, cultivating cool-climate gardens that are among the area's human-made glories. Mountain walking was popular at the time, and the splendid network of trails that crisscrosses the area was created during this period. Now such lower Blue Mountain towns as Glenbrook, Blaxland, and Springwood are commuter territory. Combined with the dramatic natural beauty of the region, the history and charm of local villages make the Blue Mountains one of the highlights of any tour of Australia.

Numbers in the margin correspond to points of interest on the Blue Mountains map.

2

Food

Hunter Valley, the New South Wales wine region, Coffs Harbour and Port Macquarie along the beach-lined coast north of Sydney, Byron Bay, and Lord Howe Island all have stellar restaurants. If you're a foodie, you might want to choose these destinations over others on your visit, as the varieties of regional wines, locally harvested produce, and fresh-caught seafood liven the taste of meals in these areas.

The Great Outdoors

The mountains and national parks of New South Wales are great spots for scenic walks and hikes, horse-back riding, as well as mountain biking, rappelling, canyoning, and rock climbing. Deep in the south of the state, the Snowy Mountains—Australia's winter playground—afford excellent cross-country skiing in particular. The north and south coasts and its popular beaches inspire water sports galore, including surfing, snorkeling, scuba diving, and boating. In the heavily forested Yarrunga Valley, catch a glimpse of a kookaburra or a mysterious lyrebird. The roaring 270-foot Fitzroy Falls are also nearby. Northeast of Kangaroo Valley, Pebbly Beach has hundreds of kangaroos.

Shopping

Byron Bay, the Blue Mountains, and Southern Highlands have terrific locally made crafts shops. It would be difficult to visit the Hunter Valley without purchasing some of its excellent wines, but the area is also full of antiques shops (particularly around Pokolbin and Wollombi), arts-and-crafts shops, and galleries that display the works of local artists and potters.

Wineries

The Hunter Valley, Australia's largest grape-growing region, has more than 70 wineries and an international reputation for producing excellent chardonnay, shiraz, and a dry semillon. Many well-known vineyards are based near the village of Pokolbin, which also has antiques shops and art galleries.

Springwood & the Lower Blue Mountains

79 km (49 mi) northwest of Sydney.

❶ The National Trust–listed **Norman Lindsay Gallery and Museum,** dedicated to the Australian artist and writer, is one of the cultural highlights of the Blue Mountains. Lindsay is best known for his paintings, etchings, and drawings, but he also built model boats, sculpted, and wrote poetry and children's books, among which *The Magic Pudding* has become an Australian classic. Some of his most famous paintings were inspired by Greek and Roman mythology and depict voluptuous nudes. Lindsay lived in this house during the latter part of his life until he died in 1969, and it contains a representative selection of his superb work (featured in the movie *Sirens* starring another famous Australian, Elle MacPherson). The delightful landscaped gardens contain several of Lindsay's sculptures, and you can also take a short but scenic bushwalk beyond the garden. ✉ *14 Norman Lindsay Crescent, Faulconbridge* ☎ *02/4751–1067* ⊕ *www.hermes.net.au/nlg* 🖃 *A$8* ⊙ *Daily 10–4.*

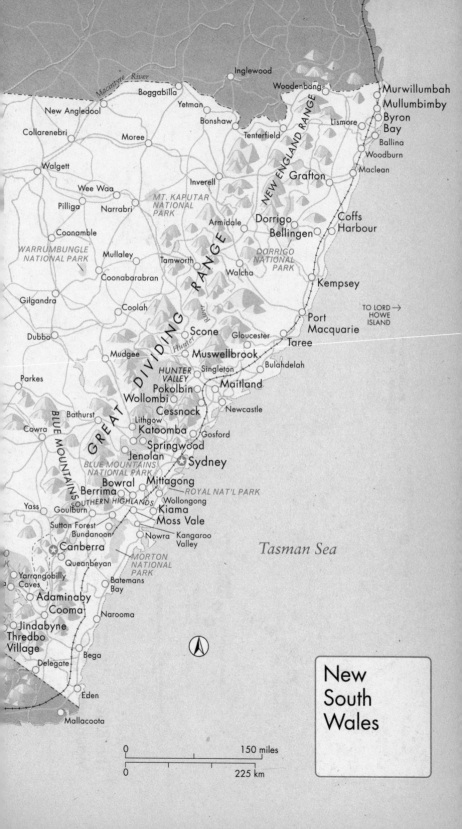

Inglewood

Macintyre River

Boggabilla

New Angledool

Yetman

Bonshaw

Woodenbong

Murwillumbah

Mullumbimby

Byron
Bay

Collarenebri

Moree

Tenterfield

Lismore

NEW ENGLAND RANGE

Ballina

Woodburn

Walgett

Inverell

Grafton

Maclean

Wee Waa

MT. KAPUTAR
NATIONAL
PARK

Pilliga

Narrabri

Armidale

Dorrigo

Bellingen

Coffs
Harbour

Coonamble

WARRUMBUNGLE
NATIONAL PARK

Mullaley

Tamworth

Walcha

DORRIGO
NATIONAL
PARK

Gilgandra

Coonabarabran

Coolah

Scone

Gloucester

Kempsey

Dubbo

Mudgee

Hunter River

Muswellbrook

Port
Macquarie

TO LORD →
HOWE
ISLAND

Parkes

Singleton

Taree

HUNTER
VALLEY

Pokolbin

Bulahdelah

Wollombi

Maitland

Bathurst

Cessnock

Newcastle

Cowra

Lithgow

Katoomba

Gosford

BLUE MOUNTAINS

Springwood

GREAT DIVIDING RANGE

Jenolan

Sydney

BLUE MOUNTAINS
NATIONAL PARK

Yass

Goulburn

Bowral

Berrima

Mittagong

ROYAL NAT'L PARK

SOUTHERN HIGHLANDS

Wollongong

Sutton Forest

Kiama

Moss Vale

Bundanoon

Nowra

Kangaroo
Valley

Tasman Sea

Canberra

Queanbeyan

MORTON
NATIONAL
PARK

Yarrangobilly
Caves

Batemans
Bay

Adaminaby

Cooma

Narooma

Jindabyne

Thredbo
Village

Delegate

Bega

Eden

Mallacoota

0   150 miles

0   225 km

New
South
Wales

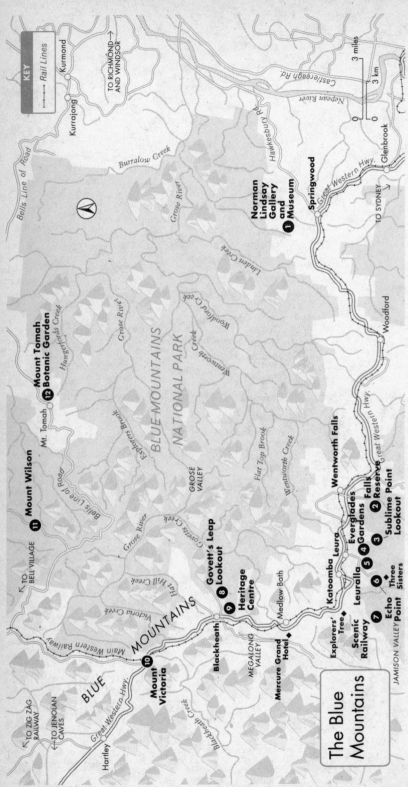

TO RICHMOND AND WINDSOR →

Kurmond

Kurrajong

Bells Line of Road

Burralow Creek

Grose River

Hungerfords Creek

Mount Tomah
Botanic Garden

⑫ Mt. Tomah

Mount Wilson ⑪

← TO
BELL VILLAGE

Bells Line of Road

Explorers Brook

BLUE MOUNTAINS

NATIONAL PARK

Grose River

GROSE
VALLEY

Govetts Creek

Grose River

Govett's Leap
Lookout ⑧

Heritage
Centre ⑨

Hat Hill Creek

Victoria Creek

MOUNTAINS

Blackheath

← TO ZIG ZAG
RAILWAY

← TO JENOLAN
CAVES

BLUE

Mount
Victoria ⑩

Main Western Railway

Hartley

Great Western Hwy.

Blackheath Creek

MEGALONG
VALLEY

Mercure Grand Hotel

Medlow Bath

Explorers'
Tree ◆

Scenic
Railway

Katoomba

Leura

Leuralla

⑤

⑥

⑦ Echo
Three
Point
Sisters

JAMISON VALLEY

Wentworth
Falls

Everglades
Gardens

④

③

Falls
Reserve

② Sublime Point
Lookout

Great Western Hwy.

Woodford

Woodford Creek

Wentworth Creek

Flat Top Brook

Linden Creek

Wentworth Creek

Norman
Lindsay
Gallery
and
Museum ①

Springwood

Great Western Hwy.

TO SYDNEY ↓

Hawkesbury Rd.

Castlereagh Rd.

Nepean River

Glenbrook

0 ——— 3 miles
0 ——— 3 km

The Blue
Mountains

Wentworth Falls

26 km (16 mi) west of Springwood.

This attractive township has numerous crafts and antiques shops, a lake, and a popular golf course. Wentworth Falls straddles both sides of the highway, but most points of interest and views of the Jamison Valley and Blue Mountains National Park are to the south side of the road.

★ ❷ From a lookout in the **Falls Reserve,** south of the town of Wentworth Falls, you can take in magnificent views both out across the Jamison Valley to the Kings Tableland and of the 935-foot-high **Wentworth Falls** themselves. To find the best view of the falls you'll have to follow the trail that crosses the stream and zigzags down the sheer cliff face, signposted NATIONAL PASS. If you continue, the National Pass cuts back across the base of the falls and along a narrow ledge to the delightful Valley of the Waters, where it ascends to the top of the cliffs, emerging at the Conservation Hut. The complete circuit takes at least three hours and is a moderate walk. ⊠ *Falls Rd.*

Where to Eat

$ ⨯ **Conservation Hut.** From its spot on the cliffs overlooking the Jamison Valley, this spacious, mud-brick bistro serves simple, savory fare and satisfying cakes from its prime spot in Blue Mountains National Park. An open balcony is a delight on warm days, and a fire blazes in the cooler months. A hiking trail from the bistro leads down into the Valley of the Waters, one of the splendors of the mountains. It's a wonderful premeal walk. ⊠ *Fletcher St.* ☎ *02/4757–3827* ▭ *AE, MC, V* ⛛ *BYOB* ☾ *No dinner.*

Leura

5 km (3 mi) west of Wentworth Falls.

Leura is one of the prettiest mountain towns, with colonial buildings lining an entire main street that has been classified as an urban conservation area by the National Trust. There are plenty of unusual shops in town, as well as excellent cafés and restaurants.

★ ❸ **Sublime Point Lookout,** just outside Leura, lives up to its name with a great view of the Jamison Valley and the generally spectacular Blue Mountains scenery. This far less crowded vantage point provides a different perspective than that of the famous **Three Sisters** rock formation at nearby Katoomba. ⊠ *Sublime Point Rd.*

❹ Leura's delightful **Everglades Gardens,** one of the best public gardens in the Blue Mountains region, includes native bushland and exotic flora, a rhododendron garden, an alpine plant area, and formal European-style terraces. From the gardens, the views of the Jamison Valley and the rugged escarpment and cliff are magnificent. Everglades also has an interesting art gallery. This National Trust–listed, cool-climate arboretum and nature reserve was established in the 1930s. ⊠ *37 Everglades Ave.* ☎ *02/ 4784–1938* ▭ *A$6* ☾ *Daily 10–4.*

❺ The mansion of **Leuralla** dates from 1911 and still belongs to the family of Dr. H. V. ("Doc") Evatt (1894–1965), the first president of the General Assembly of the United Nations and later the leader of the Australian Labor Party. The historic house contains a collection of 19th-century Australian art and a small museum dedicated to Dr. Evatt. Gardens surround the house, and within the grounds is the **New South Wales Toy and Railway Museum,** an extensive collection of railway memorabilia. The toy display includes tin-plate automobiles, ships, and planes, as well as antique dolls and bears. ⊠ *36 Olympian Parade* ☏ *02/4784–1169* 🎟 *A$8* 🕙 *Daily 10–5.*

Where to Stay & Eat

$$$ ✕ **Silks Brasserie.** Thanks to its Sydney-standard food, wine, and service,
Fodor'sChoice   Silks rates as one of the finest Blue Mountains restaurants. Dishes in-
★   clude fresh fish with Asian-style sauces, osso buco served with couscous, sautéed tiger prawns in champagne vinaigrette with sesame-seed biscuits, and a seafood medley with lemongrass and cardamom cream sauce—plus tempting desserts and a cheese plate. In colder months, a log fire warms the simple but elegant interior. ⊠ *128 the Mall* ☏ *02/4784–2534* 🍴 *AE, DC, MC, V.*

$$ ✕ **Cafe Bon Ton.** If you're looking for a caffeine fix or simply a good meal, head to this bright, elegant café—with terrific coffee—for breakfast, cake, or a three-course Italian dinner. Dishes include pasta, pizza, and a choice of meat, fish, and vegetarian fare. In winter a log fire burns in the grate, and on warm summer days the shady garden in front is ideal for lunch. The café is at the lower end of Leura Mall. ⊠ *192 the Mall* ☏ *02/ 4782–4377* 🍴 *AE, MC, V.*

$$–$$$ 🏨 **Fairmont Resort.** The Fairmont might be the largest hotel in the mountains, but it still has the cozy warmth of a traditional Blue Mountains guesthouse. Perhaps this is due in part to its location, perched on the edge of the cliffs and surrounded by gardens. The well-equipped rooms are a little bit country in style; those facing the valley have the best views. Numerous facilities and activities, such as tennis and a spa, are available, and as a guest you'll have access to the adjoining Leura Golf Course, the finest in the mountains. ⊠ *1 Sublime Point Rd., 2780* ☏ *02/4782–5222* 🖨 *02/4784–1685* ⊕ *www.peppers.com.au* 🛏 *193 rooms, 17 suites* ♨ *2 restaurants, cable TV, 4 tennis courts, 2 pools, gym, sauna, spa, squash, bar, video-game room, meeting rooms; no-smoking rooms* 🍴 *AE, DC, MC, V.*

en route   From Leura, the dazzling 19-km (12-mi) journey along **Cliff Drive** leads to Echo Point at Katoomba and beyond. The road skirts the rim of the Jamison Valley, often only yards from the cliff edge, and provides truly spectacular Blue Mountains views. Begin at the southern end of the Mall on Leura's main street.

Katoomba

2 km (1 mi) west of Leura.

Easily the largest town in the Blue Mountains, Katoomba developed in the early 1840s as a coal-mining settlement, turning its attention to tourism at a later point in the 19th century. The town center has shops, cafés, and places to stay, but the breathtaking local scenery is the real reason to come.

 ❻   The best views around Katoomba are from **Echo Point,** which overlooks the densely forested Jamison Valley and soaring sandstone pillars. These
Fodor'sChoice   formations—the **Three Sisters**—take their name from an Aboriginal leg-
★   end that relates how three siblings were turned to stone by their witch-doctor father to save them from the clutches of a mythical monster. The Three Sisters also illustrate the geological character of the Blue Mountains. The area was once a seabed that rose over a long period and subsequently eroded, leaving behind tall formations of sedimentary rock. From Echo Point you can clearly see the horizontal sandstone bedding in the landscape. At night, floodlighting illuminates the formations.

✉ *Follow Katoomba St. south out of Katoomba to Echo Point Rd., or take Cliff Dr. from Leura.*

Blue Mountains Visitor Information Centre, beside the highway at Glenbrook, provides useful information on bushwalks from Katoomba. Walks, which vary from an easy half-hour stroll to the Three Sisters to a challenging four-hour hike, start from the Echo Point area. ✉ *Echo Point Rd.* ☎ *1300/653408* ⊕ *www.bluemountainstourism.org.au* ☉ *Daily 9–5.*

❼ Far below Echo Point, the **Scenic Railway** was built into the cliff face during the 1880s to haul coal and shale from the mines in the valley. When the supply of shale was exhausted, the railway was abandoned until the 1930s, when the Katoomba Colliery began using the carts to give tourists the ride of their life on the steep incline. Today the carriages are far more comfortable, but the ride down to the foot of the cliffs is no less exciting. Just a few steps from the railway is the **Scenic Skyway,** a cable car that carries passengers for a short ride across the gorge, with a 1,000-foot drop below. If you're going to pick one, the railway is more spectacular. ✉ *Cliff Dr. and Violet St.* ☎ *02/4782–2699* ✆ *Round-trip railway A$12, round-trip skyway A$10* ☉ *Daily 9–5.*

The giant screen at the **Edge Maxvision Cinema** reaches to the height of a six-story building and runs a variety of films. The most worthwhile is *The Edge,* shown daily at 10, an exciting 40-minute movie on the region's valleys, gorges, cliffs, waterfalls, and other dramatic scenery. The large complex includes a café and gift shop, and at night the cinema screens regular feature films. ✉ *225–237 Great Western Hwy.* ☎ *02/4782–8928* ✆ *A$13.50* ☉ *Daily; last show at 5:30.*

Where to Stay & Eat

$ ✕ **Paragon Cafe.** With its chandeliers, gleaming cappuccino machine, and bas-relief figures above the booths, this wood-paneled 1916 restaurant, a traditional area favorite, recalls the Blue Mountains in their heyday. The menu has all-day fare, including waffles for breakfast, homemade soups for lunch, and famous Paragon meat pies for dinner. Their 52 varieties of homemade chocolates are definitely worth sampling. ✉ *65 Katoomba St.* ☎ *02/4782–2928* ▭ *AE, MC, V* ☉ *No dinner.*

★ $$$$ ✕▣ **Lilianfels Blue Mountains.** Since this is one of the upscale Orient-Express hotels, you can expect a certain level of luxury and attention to detail here. Guest rooms are spacious and plush, with silk drapes, down *doonas* (duvets), and marble bathrooms. You can best appreciate the majestic views of Jamison Valley from one of the slightly more expensive Valley View rooms. The restaurant, Darley's, serves exceptional modern Australian country food to both guests and visitors in refined surroundings. ✉ *Lilianfels Ave., Echo Point, 2780* ☎ *02/4780–1200* 🖷 *02/4780–1300* ⊕ *www.lilianfels.com.au* ☝ *Reservations essential* ➪ *81 rooms, 4 suites* ☝ *2 restaurants, cable TV, tennis court, pool, gym, sauna, spa, steam room, mountain bikes, billiards, bar, dry cleaning, laundry service, concierge, Internet, meeting rooms; no-smoking rooms* ▭ *AE, DC, MC, V.*

$$$$ ✕▣ **Echoes.** With an architectural style that the hotel simply calls "eclectic," this striking boutique property perches precipitously above the Jamison Valley, combining great views with traditional Blue Mountains comfort and an excellent restaurant. Rooms are simply furnished with striped drapes and upholstery, which lend a modern yet not austere feel. Wentworth, the top floor corner suite, has particularly good views on two sides. The hotel is close to the Three Sisters and the network of trails that lead down into the Jamison Valley. ✉ *3 Lilianfels Ave., 2780* ☎ *02/4782–1966* 🖷 *02/4782–3707* ⊕ *www.echoeshotel.com.au* ➪ *12* suites ☼ *Restaurant, sauna, spa, bar, Internet; no smoking* ▤ *AE, DC, MC, V* ⑩ *BP.*

$$–$$$ ✕▥ **Mountain Heritage Country House Retreat.** The Mountain Heritage house overlooking the Jamison Valley is steeped in history: it served as a "coffee palace" during the temperance movement, a rest-and-relaxation establishment for the British navy during World War II, and even a religious retreat in the 1970s. Warm and welcoming country-house furnishings make use of Australian motifs in several room styles. The two very private Valley View suites have their own verandas, kitchens, lounge rooms with fireplaces, and Jacuzzis. ✉ *Apex and Lovel Sts., 2780* ☎ *02/4782–2155* 🖷 *02/4782–5323* ⊕ *www.mountainheritage.com.au* ⬎ *37 rooms, 4 suites* ☼ *Restaurant, in-room VCRs, pool, gym, bar, recreation room, Internet, meeting rooms; no smoking* ▤ *AE, DC, MC, V.*

$–$$$ ✕▥ **Carrington Hotel.** It's unlikely you'll find a veranda, piazza, and ballroom elsewhere in the Blue Mountains. Established in 1880, the Carrington was the first of the area's truly grand lodgings, offering high-end facilities of its time. Today its Federation-style furnishings have been authentically employed to make the public rooms and guest rooms graceful reminders of a glorious past. The enormous chandelier-lighted dining room serves modern Australian and traditional dishes. ✉ *15–47 Katoomba St., 2780* ☎ *02/4782–1111* 🖷 *02/4782–7033* ⊕ *www.thecarrington.com.au* ⬎ *63 rooms* ☼ *2 restaurants, billiards, bar, dry cleaning, laundry service, meeting room; no-smoking rooms, no a/c* ▤ *AE, DC, MC, V* ⑩ *BP.*

en route West of Katoomba, Cliff Drive becomes Narrow Neck Road and returns you to the Great Western Highway. From there, the highway winds along the ridge top, passing a couple of points of interest between Katoomba and the next main town of Blackheath. About 1 km (½ mi) beyond where Narrow Neck Road joins the highway, the **Explorers' Tree** on the left marks an important historic site. George Blaxland, William Charles Wentworth, and William Lawson, the men who finally pioneered the route across these mountains in 1813, carved their initials into the trunk of this tree, which in time has grown over the traces of their passing.

At the small village of Medlow Bath, 4 km (2½ mi) beyond the Explorers' Tree, it's impossible to miss the enormous **Mercure Grand Hydro Majestic Hotel** (✉ Great Western Hwy., Medlow Bath ☎ 02/4788–1002 ⊕ www.hydromajestic.com.au) on the left-hand side of the highway. This sprawling art deco building was a fashionable hotel and European-style spa in the 1930s, especially popular with honeymoon couples. During World War II the U.S. Army used the hotel as a hospital for soldiers wounded in the Pacific. The place subsequently fell on hard times, but extensive restoration has recaptured some of its original art deco detail. The view of Megalong Valley from the Casino Lounge is outstanding, making it a good place for coffee, a light lunch, or a sampling of the pastry chef's pretty cakes and delicacies. Arrive at dusk for a drink on the terrace while the sun is still lighting the valley below.

Blackheath

12 km (7½ mi) north of Katoomba.

Magnificent easterly views over the Grose Valley—which has outstanding hiking trails, delightful gardens, and several antiques shops—head the list of reasons to visit Blackheath, at the 3,495-foot summit of the Blue Mountains. The town was named by Governor Macquarie, who visited in 1815 after a rough road had been constructed through here to the town of Bathurst, beyond the mountains.

8 Blackheath's most famous view is from the **Govett's Leap Lookout,** with its striking panorama of the Grose Valley and Bridal Veil Falls to the right. Govett was a surveyor who mapped this region extensively in the 1830s. He calculated that the perpendicular drop near the falls is 528 feet. ⊠ *End of Govett's Leap Rd.*

9 The **Heritage Centre,** operated by the National Parks and Wildlife Service, provides useful information on Aboriginal and European historic sites, as well as helpful suggestions for camping, guided walks, and hiking in Blue Mountains National Park. The center, which is a two-minute stroll from Govett's Leap Lookout, also has videos, interactive educational displays, exhibitions, and a nature-oriented gift shop. The nearby **Blackheath Bakery** has achieved local fame for its delicious sourdough bread. ⊠ *Govett's Leap Rd.* ☎ *02/4787–8877* ⊕ *www.npws.nsw.gov. au* ⊗ *Daily 9–4:30.*

☏ The **Megalong Australian Heritage Centre,** in a deep mountain valley off the Great Western Highway 15 km (9 mi) from Blackheath, is a working sheep and cattle farm with displays of animals and pioneer skills. Events begin at 10:30 and include a cattle show, a Clydesdale horse show, tractor rides, and sheep-shearing. There's also a baby-animal nursery, and both adults and children can go horseback riding around the farm's 2,000 acres. If you'd like to go farther afield, you can join an overnight muster ride. ⊠ *Megalong Rd., Megalong Valley* ☎ *02/4787–8688* ▭ *A\$9.95* ⊗ *Daily 9–5.*

Where to Stay & Eat

\$\$\$ ✕ **Vulcan's.** Don't let the concrete floor and rough redbrick walls fool
Fodor'sChoice   you—they belie this tiny Blackheath café its reputation for outstanding
★   food. Operated by Phillip Searle (formerly one of the leading lights of Sydney's dining scene) and Barry Ross, Vulcan's specializes in slow-roasted dishes, often with Asian or Middle Eastern spices. The restaurant's checkerboard ice cream—with star anise, pineapple, licorice, and vanilla flavors—is a favorite that looks as good as it tastes. There is an outdoor dining area. Smoking is not permitted. ⊠ *33 Govetts Leap Rd.* ☎ *02/4787–6899* ▭ *AE, DC, MC, V* ☖ *BYOB* ⊗ *Closed Mon.–Thurs.*

★ **\$\$–\$\$\$**   ▥ **Jemby Rinjah Lodge.** Designed for urbanites seeking a wilderness experience, these self-contained timber cabins set in bushland sleep up to six and have natural-wood furnishings and a picture window opening onto a small deck. Three tree houses elevate you to the same level as the kookaburra birds. Lodges without kitchens are also available at a lower rate. Activities include free guided walks of the Grose Valley, feeding wild parrots, and spotlighting possums at night. ⊠ *336 Evans Lookout Rd., 2785* ☎ *02/4787–7622* ▭ *02/4787–6230* ⇶ *15 rooms without bath, 10 cabins, 3 tree houses* ⟁ *Restaurant, some kitchenettes, Internet, meeting rooms; no smoking* ▭ *AE, DC, MC, V.*

Horseback Riding

At the foot of the Blue Mountains, 10 km (6 mi) from Blackheath, **Werriberri Trail Rides** (⊠ Megalong Rd., Megalong Valley ☎ 02/4787–9171) conducts reasonably priced half- to two-hour horseback rides through the beautiful Megalong Valley. Everyone is catered to—with quiet horses for beginners, ponies on leads for young children, and frisky mounts for experienced riders. All rides are guided, and hard hats are supplied. Rides range from A\$22 for a half hour to A\$150 for a full day.

Mount Victoria

⓾ *7 km (4½ mi) northwest of Blackheath.*

The settlement of Mount Victoria has a Rip Van Winkle air about it—drowsy and only just awake in an unfamiliar world. A walk around the village reveals many atmospheric houses and stores with the patina of time spelled out in their fading paintwork. Mount Victoria is at the far side of the mountains at the western limit of this region, and the village serves as a good jumping-off point for a couple of out-of-the-way attractions.

Stalactites, stalagmites, columns, and lacelike rock on multiple levels fill **Jenolan Caves,** a labyrinth of underground rivers and vast limestone chasms sculpted by underground rivers. There are as many as 300 caves in the Jenolan area.

The first European to set eyes on the caves was James McKeown, an escaped convict who preyed on the stagecoaches traveling across the mountains and who used the caves as a hideout in the 1830s. A search party eventually followed his horse's tracks, and the capture of McKeown made his secret caves suddenly famous.

Three caves near the surface can be explored without a guide, but to see the very best formations, you need to take a guided tour. Nine of these caves are open to the public: they are graded according to difficulty, and even the easiest entails climbing a total of 300 stairs interspersed throughout the cave. Tours depart every 15 minutes on weekends, approximately every 30 minutes on weekdays, and last from one to two hours. Fascinated? You may also want to inquire about the caves in Abercrombie and Wombeyan to the west and south of Jenolan.

To reach the caves, follow the Great Western Highway north out of Mount Victoria as it winds through rural hill country. Then turn after Hartley southwest toward Hampton. Jenolan Caves is 59 km (37 mi) from Mount Victoria. ⊠ *Jenolan* ☎ *02/6359–3311* ⊕ *www.jenolancaves.org. au* 🖃 *A$15–A$55* ☉ *Daily 9:30–5:30.*

Fodor'sChoice
★ Aboard the huff-and-puff vintage steam engine on the **Zig Zag Railway,** you'll experience dramatic views on the thrilling, cliff-hugging 16-km (10-mi) round-trip ride. Built in 1869, this was the main line across the Blue Mountains until 1910. The track is laid on the cliffs in a giant "Z," and the train climbs the steep incline by chugging back and forth along switchbacking sections of the track—hence its name. The steam engine operates on weekends, public holidays, and weekdays during the school holidays. A vintage self-propelled diesel-powered railcar is used at other times. The railway is 19 km (12 mi) northwest of Mount Victoria. Take the Darling Causeway north out of town, then turn northwest on Bells Line of Road in Bell. ⊠ *Bells Line of Rd., Clarence* ☎ *02/6353–1795* ⊕ *www.zigzagrailway.com.au* 🖃 *A$17* ☉ *Trains depart Clarence Station daily at 11, 1, and 3.*

Where to Eat

¢–$ ✕ **Bay Tree Tea Shop.** When a fire is burning in the grate and scones are pulled piping hot from the kitchen is the best time to arrive at this cozy café, which is particularly welcoming on chilly afternoons, but is delightful anytime. The menu includes hearty soups, salads, a fantastic "meat-pie hot pot," lasagna, and quiche. Almost everything is made on the premises—bread, baked goods, and even the jam that comes with afternoon tea. ⊠ *26 Station St.* ☎ *02/4787–1275* 🗀 *No credit cards* ☉ *Closed Tues.–Wed. No dinner.*

en route The **Bells Line of Road** route back to Sydney is reached by taking the Darling Causeway north out of Mount Victoria and turning right at the village of Bell. Named after explorer Archibald Bell, who discovered a path over the mountains from Richmond, and built by convicts in 1841, this scenic road runs from Lithgow to Richmond and winds its way along the mountain ridges. Along the way you'll pass gardens, apple orchards, small villages, and roadside fruit stalls.

Mount Wilson

⓫ *30 km (19 mi) northeast of Mount Victoria.*

Built more than a century ago by wealthy families seeking a retreat from Sydney's summer heat, this enchanting village was planted with avenues of elms, beeches, and plane trees that give it a distinctly European air. The town is at its prettiest during spring and autumn, when its many gardens are in full splendor. It lies off the Bells Line of Road at the end of Five Mile Road, which snakes along a sandstone ridge.

The cool, shady woodlands of **Cathedral of Ferns** are a great place to take a refreshing stroll. This pretty glen is on Mt. Irvine Road. There is no admission fee, and a jaunt around the circular track takes 15–20 minutes.

Mount Tomah

25 km (16 mi) southeast of Mount Wilson.

The area around the village of Mount Tomah, which lies on the Bells Line of Road, holds strong appeal for garden lovers.

⓬ The cool-climate branch of Sydney's Royal Botanic Gardens, the **Mount Tomah Botanic Garden,** provides a spectacular setting for many native and imported plant species. At 3,280 feet above sea level, the moist, cool environment is perfect for rhododendrons, conifers, maples, and a variety of European deciduous trees. The delightful gardens also have a shop, a visitor center, picnic areas, and a restaurant with modern Australian cuisine. Guided walks are available by arrangement. The family rate (A$8.80) is a good bargain. ⊠ *Bells Line of Rd.* ☎ *02/4567–2154* ⊕ *www.rbgsyd.nsw.gov.au* ⊠ *A$4.40* ☉ *Daily 10–4.*

en route The Bells Line of Road winds past the villages of Bilpin and Kurrajong, with a terrific panorama of the Sydney metropolitan region from the Bellbird Hill Lookout near Kurrajong, and then continues through Richmond and Windsor. These latter settlements were founded in 1810 and contain several historic churches and other buildings from the mid-1800s. If you have time, it's worth having a look around both towns. From Richmond, Sydney is about a 60-minute drive away.

Blue Mountains A to Z

To research prices, get advice from other travelers, and book travel arrangements, visit www.fodors.com.

BUS TRAVEL

Public buses operate between the Blue Mountains settlements, although the areas of greatest scenic beauty are some distance from the towns. If you want to see the best that the Blue Mountains have to offer, take a guided tour or rent a car and drive from Sydney.

CAR RENTAL

Renting a car is the best plan, and you can do so in either Sydney or Katoomba. Distances between Blue Mountains towns are short, roads are generally in good condition, and there are many scenic routes and lookouts that are accessible only by car.

If you plan to rent a car in Katoomba, you can reserve one in advance from Thrifty.

🚗 Thrifty ✉ Unit 2, 19 Edward St. ☎ 02/4782-9488.

CAR TRAVEL

Leave Sydney via Parramatta Road and the M4 Motorway, which leads to Lapstone at the base of the Blue Mountains. From there, continue on the Great Western Highway and follow the signs to Katoomba. The 110-km (68-mi) journey to Katoomba takes between 90 minutes and 2 hours.

EMERGENCIES

In an emergency, dial 000 to reach an ambulance, the fire department, or the police.

🚗 Hospital Blue Mountains District Anzac Memorial Hospital ✉ Great Western Hwy., Katoomba ☎ 02/4784-6500.

MAIL, INTERNET & SHIPPING

You can snack while surfing the Internet at the Barcode 6ix–Internet Caffe in Katoomba. The friendly, relaxed setting and the on-site technical help make this a popular hangout. Log on daily 9–9. Ten minutes costs A$1, a half hour is A$3, and an hour costs A$5.

🚗 Barcode 6ix–Internet Caffe ✉ 6 Katoomba St., Katoomba ☎ 02/4782-6896.

MONEY MATTERS

You can change money and travelers checks at any bank. ATMs are usually found near shopping facilities.

TOURS

Since the Blue Mountains are one of Sydney's most popular escapes, you can take a day trip from there with a coach touring company or make your own way to the mountains and then link up with a guided tour. The region is also great for outdoor adventure and horseback-riding trips.

ADVENTURE-SPORTS TOURS Blue Mountains Adventure Company runs rappelling, canyoning, rock-climbing, and mountain-biking trips. Most outings (from A$119) last one day, and include equipment, lunch, and transportation from Katoomba.

High 'n Wild conducts rappelling, canyoning, rock-climbing, and mountain-biking tours. One-day rappelling trips cost A$119; combination rappelling and canyoning tours cost A$139.

🚗 Blue Mountains Adventure Company 📮 Box 242, Katoomba, 2780 ☎ 02/4782-1271 🖷 02/4782-1277 🌐 www.bmac.com.au. **High'n Wild** ✉ 3–5 Katoomba St., Katoomba 2780 ☎ 02/4782-6224 🖷 02/4782-6143.

BUS TOURS Australian Pacific Tours runs daily bus tours from Sydney to the Blue Mountains (from A$83.50) and Jenolan Caves (from A$92). The company also has daily departures for a two-day Jenolan Caves/Blue Mountains tour, which includes accommodations at Jenolan Caves Guest House (from A$215). Buses depart from the Overseas Shipping Terminal, on the Harbour Bridge side of Circular Quay. Free pickup from central hotels is available.

Fantastic Aussie Tours can arrange a number of tours, including four-wheel-drive tours (call for details) and double-decker bus tours. Weekends and public holidays from 9:30 to 4:30, the Blue Mountains Explorer Bus (A$25) meets trains from Sydney at the Katoomba Railway Station.

The double-decker makes 27 stops on its hourly circuit, including the major attractions around Katoomba and Leura. You are free to leave the tour at any point and join a later bus. At the end of the tour, the buses return to Katoomba Station to reconnect with Sydney-bound trains. **Australian Pacific Tours** ⊠ Circular Quay W, Sydney ☎ 1300/655965. **Fantastic Aussie Tours** ⊠ 283 Main St., Katoomba ☎ 02/4782-1866.

FOUR-WHEEL-DRIVE TOURS The local Blue Mountains company Cox's River Escapes has off-the-beaten-track half-day (A$110) or full-day (A$165) four-wheel-drive tours for a maximum of six people in each air-conditioned vehicle. **Cox's River Escapes** ✈ Box 81, Leura, 2780 ☎ 02/4784-1621 ☎ 02/4784-2450 ⊕ www.bluemts.com.au/coxsriver.

TRAIN TRAVEL

Train services from Sydney stop at most of the many small stations along the railway line from the base of the mountains to Mount Victoria. However, if you're traveling by train only, you'll be very limited in the scope of what you can see.

The Blue Mountains are served by Sydney's Cityrail commuter trains, with frequent services to and from the city between 5 AM and 11 PM. On weekdays it's A$11.20 one-way between Sydney's Central Station and Katoomba, the main station in the Blue Mountains. If you travel on weekends, or begin travel after 9 on weekdays, it's A$13.40 round-trip. **Cityrail** ☎ 13-1500.

VISITOR INFORMATION

Blue Mountains Visitor Information Centres are at Echo Point in Katoomba and at the foot of the mountains on the Great Western Highway at Glenbrook. The Echo Point office is open daily 9–6, and the Glenbrook office is open weekdays 9–5 and weekends 8:30–4:30. Sydney Visitors Information Centre, open daily 9–6, has information on Blue Mountains hotels, tours, and sights. **Blue Mountains Visitor Information Centres** ⊠ Echo Point Rd., beside the highway at Glenbrook, Echo Point ☎ 1300/653408 ⊕ www.bluemountainstourism.org.au. **Sydney Visitors Information Centre** ⊠ 106 George St., The Rocks, Sydney, 2000 ☎ 02/9255-1788 ☎ 02/9241-5010 ⊕ www.sydneyvisitorcentre.com.

THE SOUTHERN HIGHLANDS & COAST

This fertile upland region just over 100 km (62 mi) southwest of Sydney was first settled during the 1820s by farmers in search of grazing lands. Later during the 19th century, wealthy Sydney folk built grand country houses here, primarily to escape the city's summer heat and humidity. Farming still prevails today, but the area's hills, intricate landscape, and aristocratic airs continue to attract visitors. Although the region is often compared with England, Australia's ruggedness manages to dramatize even this picturesque rural scene with the steep sandstone gorges and impenetrable forests of Morton National Park. As a bonus, the South Coast—with its excellent surfing and swimming beaches—is just a short drive away.

Mittagong

103 km (64 mi) southwest of Sydney.

Although it's known as the gateway to the Southern Highlands, the commercial center of Mittagong holds few attractions except for a selection of crafts and antiques shops. Farther afield, at Berrima, Bowral, and Moss Vale, you'll find more antiques shops specializing in the quirky to the highly coveted. The Tourism Southern Highlands Information Centre on Main Street has maps and local brochures.

off the beaten path

WOMBEYAN CAVES – From Mittagong, you can detour through rugged mountain scenery to these spectacular and delicate limestone formations. Five caves are open to the public, although the Fig Tree Cave is the only one where you can look around on your own. Guided tours to the others take place at regular intervals throughout the day. You can also explore the bushwalking trails and look for wildlife. The caves are just 66 km (41 mi) from Mittagong, but the journey along the narrow, winding, and partly unsealed road takes about 1½ hours each way. ✉ *Wombeyan Caves, via Mittagong* ☎ *02/4843–5976* ⊕ *www.goulburn.net.au/wombeyan* ✆ *Self-guided cave tour A$12, guided 1-cave tour A$15, guided 2-cave tour A$21* ⊙ *Daily 8:30–5.*

Shopping

Over 45 individual stalls in **Mittagong Antiques Centre** (✉ 85–87 Main St., Mittagong ☎ 02/4872–3198) deal in antiques, collectibles, fine arts, and secondhand goods. Curiosities might include a pair of blacksmith's farm gates or delicately preserved pond yachts. Photography enthusiasts make a point to visit the photographic equipment collection, where prices range from A$5 to more than A$10,000. A café is on-site, and the center is open daily 10–5.

The Old Shed (✉ Old Hume Hwy., Mittagong ☎ 02/4872–2295), a family-run business based here for more than 40 years, has an eclectic mix of collectibles: old barn doors, rustic wheel barrows, wedding dresses from the 1940s, and upscale English and French antiques. Look for the range of kitchen furniture made from recycled materials. Prices start at 50¢ and rise to around A$3,000. It's open daily 10–5.

Berrima

14½ km (9 mi) southwest of Mittagong.

Founded in 1829, Berrima is an outstanding example of an early Georgian colonial town, preserved in almost original condition. The entire English-style settlement is virtually a museum of early colonial sandstone and brick buildings, many of them built by convicts, such as the National Trust–listed Harpers Mansion and the Holy Trinity Church. The 1839 Berrima Gaol is still in use, and the 1834 Surveyor General Inn claims to be Australia's oldest continuously licensed hotel (one of several in the country that make the same claim). To learn more about the town's history, pick up a copy of the self-guided walking tour at the courthouse, or join one of the extremely knowledgeable local guides.

The 1838 **Berrima Courthouse**, with its grand classical facade, is the town's architectural highlight. The impressive sandstone complex, now a museum, contains the original courtroom and holding cells. Inside is a reenactment—with wax mannequins and an audio track—of an infamous murder trial, as well as audiovisual and conventional displays of such items as iron shackles and cat-o'-nine-tails that were once used on recalcitrant convicts. The courthouse also serves as the local information center. ✉ *Wilshire St.* ☎ *02/4877–1505* ✆ *Museum A$5* ⊙ *Daily 10–4.*

Where to Eat

$–$$ ✕ **White Horse Inn.** This meticulously restored inn is not just a fine example of colonial Australian architecture; the atmospheric 1832 hotel (which is reputed to have a resident ghost) is an ideal spot for lunch and morning or afternoon tea indoors or in the courtyard. The lunch menu lists soups, salads, open sandwiches, excellent focaccia, and many desserts. In the evening, more expensive modern Australian fare is served in the traditionally decorated formal dining rooms. ⊠ *Market Pl.* ☎ *02/4877–1204* ⊟ *AE, DC, MC, V.*

Shopping

The Bell Gallery (⊠ 10 Jellore St. ☎ 02/4877–1267), open Friday–Monday 11–4, is Berrima's classiest shop. Craftwork displays include unusual glassware, pottery, fabrics, and other handmade items.

Among the town's numerous antiques shops, **Peppergreen in Berrima** (⊠ Market Pl. ☎ 02/4877–1488) is outstanding both for its size and its extraordinary selection of old wares. In addition to the expected jewelry, silver, glassware, and china items, Peppergreen stocks buttons, books, old lace and linen, and other intriguing collectibles. It's open daily 10–5.

Bowral

9½ km (6 mi) east of Berrima.

Bowral has been a desirable country address for the wealthy since the 1880s and is famous for its fine old houses, tree-lined streets, and antiques and crafts shops. The parks and private gardens are the focus of the colorful spring **Tulip Time Festival,** held every September and October. For panoramas of Bowral, Mittagong, and the surrounding countryside, don't miss the scenic drive up 2,830-foot-high **Mt. Gibraltar,** which has four short walking trails at the summit.

Bowral's main attraction—at least for cricket fans—is the **Bradman Museum.** Bowral was the childhood home of Australia's legendary cricketer Sir Donald (The Don) Bradman, who played for and captained the Australian team 1928–48. The museum sits next to the town's idyllic cricket oval and has a shop and tearooms. ⊠ *Glebe Park, St. Jude St.* ☎ *02/4862–1247* ⊕ *www.bradman.org.au* ⊠ *A$7.50* ☉ *Daily 10–5.*

Where to Stay & Eat

$$$ ✕ **Grand Bar and Brasserie.** An extensive blackboard menu aims to please just about everyone at this lively city-style brasserie, with seafood dishes and meat dishes such as the winter lamb shanks slow-roasted in red wine. And the modern Australian menu changes seasonally. Some ingredients in the sauces, however, seem more for visual effect than for any gastronomic reason. Wine is available by the glass. ⊠ *The Grand Arcade, 295 Bong Bong St.* ☎ *02/4861–4783* ⊟ *AE, DC, MC, V.*

$ ✕ **Janeks.** One of just a few eateries in Bowral with outdoor seating, Janeks also happens to serve three square meals. You can order waffles or baked goods for breakfast and toasted sandwiches, soups, pastas, and salads at lunch. At dinner, look for such modern Australian dishes as steamed mussels with lemongrass, chili, and coriander; smoked tuna steak accompanied by a salad with wasabi dressing; or a warm wild duck salad. Reservations are essential for dinner. ⊠ *Corbett Plaza, Wingecarribee St.* ☎ *02/4861–4414* ⊟ *AE, MC, V* ☉ *Closed Sun. No dinner Mon.–Thurs.*

$$$$ ✕▦ **Milton Park.** One of Sydney's elite families built this grand hotel with expansive English-style gardens as their country retreat on a forested estate 13 km (8 mi) east of Bowralas. A warm French provincial style permeates the plush hotel. Most guest rooms lead onto an internal courtyard, and the six suites have whirlpool baths. Modern Australian cuisine—such as aged filet of beef with polenta and sautéed spinach, or scallops served on a bed of bok choy and pistachios—is served in the

elegant Hordern Room. ⊠ *Horderns Rd., 2576* ☎ *02/4861–1522*
🖷 *02/4861–7962* ⚲ *34 rooms, 6 suites* ⚐ *2 restaurants, 2 tennis
courts, pool, massage, boccie, croquet, bar, meeting rooms; no a/c*
▱ *AE, DC, MC, V.* ⎟⊙⎟ *BP.*

$$ ⊡ **Links House Country Guest House.** This friendly guesthouse, directly
opposite the Bowral golf course, has been catering to visitors since
1928. Rooms are small but tastefully appointed, and the suites are ideal
for romantic getaways. When you book, try to secure Number 20—a
delightful cottage-style room in the hotel's gardens. A full, cooked
breakfast is included in the rate, and Basil's Restaurant serves Australian
fare. Children are not encouraged. ⊠ *17 Links Rd., 2576* ☎ *02/
4861–1977* 🖷 *02/4862–1706* ⊕ *www.linkshouse.com.au* ⚲ *11 rooms
with shower, 3 suites, 1 cottage* ⚐ *Restaurant, tennis court, Internet;
no a/c, no kids, no smoking* ▱ *AE, DC, MC, V* ⎟⊙⎟ *BP.*

Moss Vale

10 km (6 mi) southeast of Berrima.

Founded as a market center for the surrounding farming districts, which
now concentrate on horses, sheep, and dairy and stud cattle, Moss Vale
is today a township with abundant antiques and crafts shops. It's a nice
place to shop and stroll, and the Leighton Gardens in the center of town
are particularly attractive in spring and autumn.

The lagoon and swamplands of the **Cecil Hoskins Nature Reserve,** on the
banks of the Wingecarribee River north of Moss Vale, have been a
wildlife sanctuary since the 1930s. This important wetland area shel-
ters more than 80 species of local and migratory waterfowl, including
pelicans and black swans. You may even be fortunate enough to see a
reclusive platypus here. The reserve has bird-watching blinds, a picnic
area, and several easy walking tracks with excellent views of the river
and wetlands. ⊠ *Moss Vale–Bowral Rd., Bowral* ☎ *02/4887-7270*
⊠ *Free* ⊙ *Daily dawn–dusk.*

Golf

With its well-groomed greens and on-course accommodation, the 18-
hole, par-71 **Moss Vale Golf Club** (⊠ Arthur St. ☎ 02/4868–1503 or 02/
4868–1811) is regarded as one of the best and most challenging courses
in this golf-mad region. Nonmembers are welcome every day except Sat-
urday, but phone first. Greens fees are A$23 for 9 holes and A$34 for
18 holes.

Sutton Forest & Bundanoon

6–13 km (4–8 mi) south of Moss Vale.

The drive from Moss Vale through the tranquil villages that lie to the
south is particularly rewarding—a meandering journey that winds past
dairy farms and horse stud farms. Although relatively unimportant
today, **Sutton Forest** was the focus of the area's early settlement. In later
years, this small township became the country seat of the governors of
New South Wales, who periodically based themselves at the grand coun-
try house, Hillview. The village, 6 km (4 mi) from Moss Vale, also con-
tains a few shops and the pleasant Sutton Forest Inn. At the nearby hamlet
of **Exeter** you'll find the 1895 St. Aidans Church, complete with a
vaulted timber ceiling and beautiful stained-glass windows.

South of Sutton Forest, **Bundanoon** (Aboriginal for "place of deep gul-
lies") was once an extremely busy weekend getaway for Sydneysiders.

Its popularity was due to its location—on the main rail line to Melbourne, at a bracing elevation of 2,230 feet and perched above the northern edge of spectacular Morton National Park. The tranquil village is still delightful and provides the best access to the park's western section. There are a few antiques and crafts shops, and Bundanoon is also the focus of the annual **Brigadoon Festival,** held in April, a lively event with pipe bands, highland games, and all things Scottish.

Where to Stay & Eat

$$$ ⨉🏨 **Peppers Manor House Southern Highlands.** Adjoining the Mt. Broughton Golf & Country Club and set in 185 acres of gardens and pastureland, this elegant country resort is based around a grand 1920s family home. The baronial great hall has a high vaulted ceiling and leaded windows, and there are five traditionally decorated guest rooms in the main building. Some have a bath, and others a shower. Three suites are available, and the two-bedroom, two-baths Elms Cottages are ideal for families. Both guests and nonguests can dine in the hotel's stylish Kater's Restaurant, which serves Australian country cuisine. ⊠ *Kater Rd., Sutton Forest, 2577* ☎ *02/4868–2355* 🖷 *02/4868–3257* ⊕ *www.peppers. com.au* ↪ *40 rooms, 3 suites* 🔥 *Restaurant, golf privileges, outdoor pool, tennis court, mountain bikes, croquet, volleyball, 2 bars, Internet, meeting rooms; no a/c* ☐ *AE, DC, MC, V* ⦿| *BP.*

Sports & the Outdoors

GOLF The exclusive, Scottish-style **Mt. Broughton Golf & Country Club** (⊠ Kater Rd., Sutton Forest ☎ 02/4869–1597 ⊕ www.mtbroughton.com.au) has a picturesque, 18-hole, par-72 championship course that is considered by pros to be among the top 100 in Australia. Facilities are of a very high standard. Nonmembers are welcome but should call in advance. Greens fees are A$77 weekdays (including cart), A$94 weekends (including cart).

HORSEBACK The superbly equipped **Highlands Equestrian Centre** (⊠ Sutton Farm, RIDING Illawarra Hwy., Sutton Forest ☎ 02/4868–2584) runs cross-country rides and classes for everyone from beginners to advanced riders who are capable of dressage and show jumping. Pony rides cost A$15, and escorted trail rides start at A$30. Reservations are essential. It's also possible to book accommodations in the farm's historic 1830s homestead.

Morton National Park & Fitzroy Falls

19 km (12 mi) southwest of Moss Vale.

With more than 400,000 acres, rugged **Morton National Park** ranks as one of the state's largest national parks. This scenic region encompasses sheer sandstone cliffs and escarpments, scenic lookouts, waterfalls, and densely forested valleys. It is very popular with bushwalkers and birdwatchers. The Bundanoon area has a variety of walks, many of which can be completed in less than an hour.

At **Fitzroy Falls,** the park's eastern highlight, water tumbles 270 feet from the craggy sandstone escarpment. A boardwalk leads to lookouts with spectacular views of the falls and the heavily forested Yarrunga Valley. Several marked bushwalks of varying lengths along the escarpment's eastern and western edges allow further exploration of the area. Bird life is prolific: look for kookaburras, parrots, and even the elusive lyrebird. The **Fitzroy Falls Visitor Centre** (⊠ Nowra Rd. ☎ 02/4887–7270), operated by the National Parks and Wildlife Service, has a shop, information displays, and a café. It's open daily 9–5:30.

off the
beaten
path

BURRAWANG – From Fitzroy Falls you can take a short scenic drive to the northeast via the sleepy hamlets of Myra Vale and Wildes Meadow. Originally an 1860s timber village, Burrawang has retained much of its original charm in its weatherboard houses and buildings, such as the 1870s **Burrawang General Store.** On weekends pay a visit to the **Old School House,** where you'll find an excellent collection of antiques for sale and a dining room that serves delicious lunches, teas, and coffees. Burrawang is 11 km (7 mi) from Fitzroy Falls.

ROBERTSON – The attractive farming area around Robertson, 8 km (5 mi) east of Burrawang, provided the setting for the movie *Babe.* Yes, all those green, English-looking fields were in fact located in Australia's Southern Highlands. You can also explore the temperate rain forest of **Robertson Nature Reserve** on a short walk, then call in at the rustic local pub for a drink.

Kangaroo Valley

18 km (11 mi) southeast of Fitzroy Falls.

After descending the slopes of Barrengarry Mountain, from which there are wonderful views of the plains and coast below, the Moss Vale Road reaches Kangaroo Valley, a lush dairy farming region first settled during the early 1800s. Many old buildings remain, and the entire charming, verdant region is National Trust–classified. The Kangaroo Valley township has several cafés and crafts shops, and you can rent a canoe, golf, swim in the river, or hike. The grand, medieval-style Hampden Bridge, which was erected over the Kangaroo River in 1897, marks the entrance to the village.

The **Pioneer Settlement Reserve,** next to Hampden Bridge, has a unique perspective on the valley's history. The site includes Pioneer Farm, a re-creation of a late 19th-century homestead, and several forest and woodland bushwalks. ⊠ *Moss Vale Rd.* ☎ *02/4465–1306* ✉ *A$3.50* ⊙ *Daily 10–4.*

Where to Stay & Eat

★ $$$ ✕▥ **Woodbyne.** In the manner of other boutique hotels, the all-white timber villa radiates a sense of refined calm. Seven spacious guest rooms, decorated in neutral tones, are sparingly furnished with design-conscious pieces, art, and fabrics. Each room has a garden view, and the garden's design harks back to another era that delighted in precise composition. There's a two-night minimum and children are not encouraged on weekends. ⊠ *4 O'Keefe's La., just off the Prince's Highway south of Berry, Jaspers Brush, 2535* ☎ *02/4448–6200* 🖷 *02/4448–6211* ⊕ *www.woodbyne.com* ⇩ *7 rooms* ⚘ *Restaurant, minibars, outdoor pool, Internet, meeting rooms; no smoking, no a/c* ▤ *AE, MC, V* ꛂ *BP.*

en route

After leaving Kangaroo Valley via Moss Vale Rd., turn left after about 3½ km (2 mi) onto the narrow, precipitous Kangaroo Valley Road, which leads to the delightful town of **Berry.** Styling itself as the "Town of Trees," this roadside settlement has carefully preserved its 19th-century heritage and architecture. The town's 1886 bank now serves as the local history museum, and the main street is lined with craft and gift shops housed in attractive old buildings.

From Berry you can either travel to Kiama along the Princes Highway or you can take a more scenic coastal route via the sands and wild surf of spectacular **Seven Mile Beach,** and the quiet seaside villages of **Gerroa** and **Gerringong.** It is 26 km (16 mi) to Kiama along the latter route.

Kiama

47 km (29 mi) northeast of Kangaroo Valley.

First "discovered" by the intrepid explorer George Bass, who sailed here from Sydney in his small whaleboat in 1797, this attractive coastal township of 23,000 began life as a fishing port. Kiama has long been a popular vacation center due to its mild climate, fine beaches, pleasant walks, and easy rail access from Sydney.

Kiama has preserved several significant 19th-century buildings, such as the National Trust–listed weatherboard cottages on Collins Street, the Presbyterian church, and Manning Street's surprisingly grand post-office. The Kiama Visitors Centre has a "Heritage Walks" brochure that describes points of interest around the town center.

The town's beaches—including Kendalls, Easts, Surf, and Bombo—are excellent for swimming and surfing. Other popular activities around Kiama are fishing and scuba diving. Several boat operators based in the harbor offer game, sports, and deep-sea fishing trips, and others cater to divers.

Two of Kiama's most visited sights are located at Blowhole Point. These are the blowhole itself, through which—given the right conditions—the sea erupts, and the impressive 1887 Kiama Lighthouse.

> off the beaten path

JAMBEROO – One of the Kiama area's highlights is a short excursion to this delightful old settlement 9 km (5½ mi) inland. Settlers first came to this tranquil farming valley in the 1820s. The village contains some interesting shops and several old stone buildings, including the 1875 National Trust–classified schoolhouse. The old-style Jamberoo Pub is a good spot for an ice-cold beer on a hot day.

Where to Eat

$$ ✕ **Chachis.** One of Collins Street's historic 1880s cottages has been converted into a friendly and reasonably priced Italian-style restaurant that serves lunch, dinner, and snacks. Meat, seafood, and vegetarian main courses are available, and the four pastas come with a choice of eight sauces. The dessert menu is extensive and tempting. Dining is either indoors or on the veranda. ⊠ *The Terraces, Collins St.* ☎ *02/4233–1144* ▤ *AE, DC, MC, V* ☯ *Closed Tues.*

> en route

Exploring the lower half of the south coast from Kiama to Eden is one of this region's greatest pleasures. About 39 km (24 mi) past Ulladulla, take the side road 8 km (5 mi) to **Pebbly Beach,** where you'll find hundreds of kangaroos. You might even catch a few playing in the surf. About 110 km (68 mi) farther along the Prince's Highway is **Central Tilba,** a pleasant step back in time where you can visit arts-and-crafts shops or sample locally produced wines and cheeses.

Eden

271 km (168 mi) southwest of Kiama.

On Twofold Bay, Eden is the third-deepest natural harbor in the world. As a result, it's home to one of the state's largest fishing fleets and some of the best whale-watching on the east coast. Visit the **Eden Killer Whale Museum** in the center of town for a glimpse at Old Tom, the skeleton of the last of the killer whale pod that made Eden a famous whaling town more than 100 years ago. ✉ *Imlay St.* ☎ *02/6496–2094* 💵 *A$5.50* 🕓 *Daily 9–4.*

Where to Stay & Eat

$$$$ ✕ **Wheelhouse Restaurant.** You'll find the best of locally caught seafood and spectacular views of the wharf, Twofold Bay, and Mt. Imlay at this casual restaurant. Look for oysters avocado and blackened Cajun fish with mango salad. ✉ *Eden Wharf* ☎ *02/6496–3392* ⊟ *AE, MC, V* 🍴 *BYOB* 🕓 *Closed Tues.–Sun. in winter.*

$–$$ 🏠 **The Crown and Anchor.** This bed-and-breakfast is in Eden's oldest-surviving building, dating from the 1840s—a splendid example of elegant Regency architecture. Carefully restored and filled with antiques by owners Judy and Mauro Maurilli, the B&B is aimed at those looking for a cozy, romantic getaway—with spectacular sea views. Some rooms have fireplaces, but all have access to the twin fireplace in the lounge, where complimentary champagne and port can be enjoyed. ✉ *239 Imlay St., 2551* ☎ *02/6496–1017* 🖨 *02/6496–3878* ⊕ *www.acr.net.au/~crownanchor* 🛏 *4 rooms* ♿ *No smoking, no kids, no a/c, no room phones, no room TVs* ⊟ *AE, MC, V* ⏹ *BP.*

$ 🏠 **Wirrina.** As if a night in this comfortable, Central Tilba B&B weren't rewarding enough, in the morning you'll be treated to a magnificent full breakfast: homegrown fruit, freshly baked bread, and a country-style egg, cheese, and herb soufflé. It's all served on a rustic balcony overlooking hills where eagles dart and dive in the morning updrafts. Rooms have polished wooden floors and simple country-style furniture. ✉ *Blacksmith's La., Central Tilba, 2546* ☎ *02/4473–7279* 🖨 *02/4473–7279* ⊕ *www.naturecoast-tourism.com.au/goodnite* 🛏 *3 rooms* ♿ *Internet. No kids, no a/c, no room phones, no room TVs* ⊟ *AE, MC, V* ⏹ *BP.*

Whale-Watching

Cat Balou Cruises (✉ *Main Wharf* ☎ *02/6496–2027*) runs daily whale-watching trips October–November 7:30–noon. The A$55 fare includes refreshments, and if you don't see any whales you'll receive a refund for half of the fare.

Southern Highlands & South Coast A to Z

To research prices, get advice from other travelers, and book travel arrangements, visit www.fodors.com.

BUS TRAVEL

Greyhound Pioneer Australia and McCaffertys have daily service between Sydney and Mittagong. The journey takes 2½ hours, and the round-trip fare is A$46–A$56. The same companies also run daily buses from Canberra (2 hours) at A$40–A$48 round-trip.

Local buses run among the main Highlands towns, but these will not take you to the out-of-the-way attractions.
🚌 **Greyhound Pioneer Australia** ☎ 13–2030 ⊕ www.greyhound.com.au. **McCaffertys** ☎ 13–1499 ⊕ www.mccaffertys.com.au.

CAR RENTAL

Renting a car is the best way to see most of the area. You can reserve a car through Avis, Hertz, and Thrifty.
🚗 **Avis** ✉ Shell Service Station, Argyle and Yarrawa Sts., Moss Vale ☎ 02/4868–1044. **Hertz** ✉ Highlands Small Business Shop, Unit 4, Sherwood Village, Kirkham Rd., Bowral ☎ 02/4862–1755. **Thrifty** ✉ Mobil Service Station, Hume Hwy., Mittagong ☎ 02/4872–1283.

CAR TRAVEL

From central Sydney, head west along Parramatta Road and follow the signs to the Hume Highway (Highway 5). Join the Hume Highway at Ashfield and drive southwest until you reach the Mittagong exit. Mittagong is 103 km (64 mi) southwest of Sydney, and the drive should take 1½–2 hours.

Distances between towns and attractions are small, and roads are generally in very good condition and scenic—all the more reason to drive them yourself.

EMERGENCIES

In case of any emergency, dial 000 to reach an ambulance, the fire department, or the police.

MAIL, INTERNET & SHIPPING

Most post offices are in the middle of town, on the main street. In Bowral you can surf the Internet and check e-mail at the Great Australian Icecreamery. If you're staying in Mittagong, try Mittagong Mania for Internet access.

Great Australian Icecreamery ⊠ Bong Bong St., Bowral ☎ 02/4861-4628. **Mittagong Mania** ⊠ Albion St., Mittagong ☎ 02/4871-7777.

MONEY MATTERS

You can change money and travelers checks at any bank; ANZ Bank, Commonwealth, and National have many branches in the area. Look for ATMs at banks and shopping centers.

TOURS

The best way to see the old buildings and other attractions of Berrima is on an informative stroll with Historic Berrima Village Guided Walking Tours. Tours cost A$10 and depart from the Berrima Courthouse on Wilshire Street by prior arrangement.

Wild Escapes conducts a full-day tour (A$242) from Sydney that includes Kiama, Kangaroo Valley, and the Southern Highlands. The company specializes in small-group travel, with an emphasis on the natural environment. Prices include lunch and drinks.

Historic Berrima Village Guided Walking Tours ☎ 02/4877-1505. **Wild Escapes** ☎ 02/9980-8799.

TRAIN TRAVEL

Sydney's Cityrail commuter line trains have frequent daily service to Mittagong, Bowral, Moss Vale, and Bundanoon. Trains from Sydney also stop daily at Kiama. Round-trip fares to the Southern Highlands (Bowral) cost A$29.20 during peak hours and A$17.70 for an off-peak ticket. Round-trip fares to Kiama cost A$24.80 for a peak ticket and A$14.80 for an off-peak ticket.

Cityrail ☎ 13-1500.

VISITOR INFORMATION

Kiama Visitors Centre, open daily 9–5, has information on the Kiama, Jamberoo, and Minnamurra areas. Sydney Visitors Information Centre, open daily 9–6, has information on Southern Highlands and South Coast hotels, tours, and sights. Tourism Southern Highlands Information Centre is open daily 8–5:30.

Kiama Visitors Centre ⊠ Blowhole Point, Kiama, 2533 ☎ 02/4232-3322 or 1300/654262. **Sydney Visitors Information Centre** ⊠ 106 George St., The Rocks, Sydney, 2000 ☎ 02/9255-1788 ⎙ 02/9241-5010 ⊕ www.sydneyvisitorcentre.com. **Tourism Southern Highlands Information Centre** ⊠ 62-70 Main St., Mittagong, 2575 ☎ 02/4871-2888 or 1300/657559.

THE HUNTER VALLEY

To almost everyone in Sydney, the Hunter Valley conjures up visions not of coal mines or cows—the area's earliest industries—but of wine. The Hunter is the largest grape-growing area in the state, with more than 70 wineries and a reputation for producing excellent wines. Much of it has found a market overseas, and visiting wine lovers might recognize the Hunter Valley labels of Rosemount, Rothbury Estate, or Lindemans.

The Hunter Valley covers an area of almost 25,103 square km (9,692 square mi), stretching from the town of Gosford north of Sydney to Taree, 177 km (110 mi) farther north along the coast, and almost 300 km (186 mi) inland. The meandering waterway that gives this valley its name is also one of the most extensive river systems in the state. From its source on the rugged slopes of the Mt. Royal Range, the Hunter River flows through rich grazing country and past the horse stud farms around Scone in the upper part of the valley, home of some of Australia's wealthiest farming families. In the Lower Hunter region, the river crosses the vast coal deposits of the Greta seam. Coal mining, both open-cut and underground, is an important industry for the Hunter Valley, and the mines in this area provide the fuel for the steel mills of Newcastle, the state's second-largest city, which lies at the mouth of the Hunter River.

Cessnock

185 km (115 mi) north of Sydney.

The large town of Cessnock is better known as the entrance to the Lower Hunter Valley than for any particular attraction in the town itself. Between 1890 and 1960 this was an important coal-mining area, but when coal production began to decline during the 1950s, the mines gradually gave way to vines.

At **Rusa Park Zoo,** 4½ km (3 mi) north of Cessnock, animals from all over the world mingle with such Australian fauna as koalas, wallabies, kangaroos, wombats, snakes, and lizards in a 24-acre bushland park. There are more than 90 species of animals and birds here, including monkeys, deer, and antelope. Barbecue and picnic facilities are available. ⊠ *Lomas La., Nulkaba* ☎ *02/4990–7714* ✉ *A$10* ☉ *Daily 9:30–4:30.*

Golf

The 18-hole, par-72 **Oaks Golf and Country Club** (⊠ Lindsay St. ☎ 02/4990–1633) is one of the Hunter Valley's more notable courses. The club welcomes visitors on most days, but it's best to check beforehand. Greens fees are A$19 weekdays and A$22 weekends.

Wollombi

31 km (19 mi) northwest of Cessnock.

Nothing seems to have changed in the atmospheric town of Wollombi since the days when the Cobb & Co. stagecoaches rumbled through town. Founded in 1820, Wollombi was the overnight stop for the coaches on the second day of the journey from Sydney along the convict-built Great Northern Road—at that time the only route north. The town is full of delightful old sandstone buildings and antiques shops, and there's also a museum in the old court house with 19th-century clothing and bushranger memorabilia. The local hotel, the Wollombi Tavern, serves its own exotic brew, which goes by the name of Dr. Jurd's Jungle Juice. The pub also scores high marks for its friendliness and local color.

Lodging

★ ¢–$ 🖬 **Avoca House.** Overlooking the Wollombi Brook just outside of town, this charming century-old house, with its vine-covered verandas and central courtyard, is a country classic with a layout that guarantees privacy. The owners, Russell and Kay Davies, pay great attention to detail to ensure that their guests have a comfortable and memorable stay. The largest of the three tasteful rooms is a self-contained suite with a queen bed and a sitting room. Rates include a hearty country-style breakfast, and dinner is available by arrangement. ✉ *Wollombi Rd., 2325* 🕾 *02/ 4998–3233* 🖷 *02/4998–3319* 🖘 *2 rooms, 1 suite* ⚲ *Kitchenettes, billiards, laundry service, some pets allowed; no a/c in some rooms, no room phones, no room TVs* ☰ *MC, V* ⦿ *BP.*

Pokolbin

10 km (6 mi) northwest of Cessnock.

The Lower Hunter wine-growing region is centered around the village of Pokolbin, where there are antiques shops, good cafés, and dozens of wineries.

Any tour of the area's vineyards should begin at Pokolbin's **Wine Country Visitor Information Centre.** The center can provide free maps of the vineyards, brochures, and a handy visitor's guide. ✉ *111 Main Rd., Pokolbin, 2325* 🕾 *02/4990–4477* ⏱ *Mon.–Sat. 9–5, Sun. 9:30–4.*

In a delightful rural corner of the Mt. View region, **Briar Ridge Vineyard** is one of the Hunter Valley's most outstanding small wineries. It produces a limited selection of sought-after reds, whites, and sparkling wines. The semillon, chardonnay, shiraz, and superbly intense cabernet sauvignon are highly recommended. The vineyard is on the southern periphery of the Lower Hunter vineyards, about a five-minute drive from Pokolbin. ✉ *Mt. View Rd., Mount View* 🕾 *02/4990–3670* ⊕ *www.briarridge. com.au* ⏱ *Daily 10–5.*

On the lower slopes of Mt. Bright, one of the loveliest parts of the Lower Hunter region, is **Drayton's Family Wines.** Wine making is a Drayton family tradition dating from the mid-19th century, when Joseph Drayton first cleared these slopes and planted vines. Today, the chardonnay, semillon, and shiraz made here are some of the most consistent award-winners around. ✉ *Oakey Creek Rd.* 🕾 *02/4998–7513* ⊕ *www. draytonswines.com.au* ⏱ *Weekdays 8:30–5, weekends 10–5.*

The **Lindemans Hunter River Winery** has been one of the largest and most prestigious wine makers in the country since the early 1900s. In addition to its Hunter Valley vineyards, the company also owns property in South Australia and Victoria, and numerous outstanding wines from these vineyards can be sampled in the tasting room. Try the red burgundy, semillon, or chardonnay. The winery has its own museum, displaying vintage wine-making equipment, as well as two picnic areas, one near the parking lot and the other next to the willow trees around the dam. ✉ *McDonalds Rd.* 🕾 *02/4998–7684* ⊕ *www.lindemans.com.au* ⏱ *Daily 10–5.*

The **Rothbury Estate,** set high on a hill in the heart of Pokolbin, is one of the Lower Hunter Valley's premier wineries, established in 1968 by Australian wine-making legend Len Evans. Rothbury grows grapes in many areas of New South Wales, but grapes grown in the Hunter Valley go into the Brockenback Range wine, its most prestigious. The fine semillon and earthy shiraz wines that make this vineyard famous are available in a delightful tasting room sample. The on-site café has good food and, of course, a terrific wine list. ⊠ *Broke Rd.* ☎ *02/4998–7672* ⊕ *www.rothburyestate.com.au* 🎫 *Tour A$4* ☉ *Daily 9:30–4:30; guided tour daily at 10:30.*

Founded in 1858, **Tyrrell's Wines** is the Hunter Valley's oldest family-owned vineyard. This venerable establishment crafts a wide selection of wines and was the first to produce chardonnay commercially in Australia. Its famous Vat 47 Chardonnay is still a winner. Enjoy the experience of sampling fine wines in the old-world tasting room, or take a picnic lunch to a site overlooking the valley. ⊠ *Broke Rd.* ☎ *02/4993–7000* ⊕ *www.tyrrells.com.au* ☉ *Mon.–Fri. 8–5, Sat. 8–4:30; guided tour Mon.–Sat. at 1:30.*

The low stone and timber buildings of the **McGuigan Hunter Village** are the heart of the Pokolbin wine-growing district. This large complex includes a resort and convention center, gift shops, restaurants, and two tasting rooms, those of the **McGuigan Brothers Winery** and the underground rooms of **Hunter Cellars.** At the **Hunter Valley Cheese Company**'s shop you can taste superb Australian cheeses before you buy. At the far end of the complex you'll find a large, shady picnic area with barbecues and an adventure playground. ⊠ *Broke and McDonalds Rds.* ☎ *02/4998–7700* ⊕ *www.mcguiganwines.com.au* ☉ *Daily 9:30–5.*

Where to Stay & Eat

$$$$ ✕ **Robert's at Pepper Tree.** Built around a century-old pioneer's cottage
Fodor's Choice and surrounded by grapevines, this stunning restaurant matches its sur-
★ roundings with creative fare by chef Robert Molines. The modern Australian menu draws inspiration from regional French and Italian cooking, which is applied to local hare, scallops, and lamb. In the airy, country-style dining room—with antique furniture, bare timber floors, and a big stone fireplace—first courses might include char-grilled quail and a seafood salad of octopus, tuna, prawns, and mussels. Head for the cozy fireside lounge for after-dinner liqueurs. ⊠ *Halls Rd.* ☎ *02/4998–7330* 🍴 *AE, DC, MC, V.*

$$ ✕ **Il Cacciatore Restaurant.** Serving up a vast array of Italian specialties, the outdoor terrace at Il Cacciatore is the perfect place for a leisurely weekend lunch. Don't be put off by the building, which is unattractive; once inside the restaurant your senses will be overwhelmed by the wonderful aromas wafting from the kitchen. Italian favorites crowd this menu. Try the veal involtini, or the chicken encrusted in *gremolata* (a rub of parsley, lemon peel, and garlic), and make sure you leave plenty of room for the long list of *dolci* (desserts). An extensive list of local and imported wines complements the menu. ⊠ *McDonald and Gillard Rds.* ☎ *02/4998–7639* 🍴 *AE, MC, V* ☉ *No lunch weekdays.*

$$$–$$$$ ✕🏠 **Peppers Guest House Hunter Valley.** This cluster of long, low buildings, in a grove of wild peppercorn trees and surrounded by flagstone verandas, imitates the architecture of a classic Australian country homestead. The atmosphere extends to the luxurious guest rooms, which have scrubbed-pine furnishings and floral-print fabrics, and to the Chez Pok restaurant's fine country-style fare with French, Asian, and Italian influences. The hotel has a devoted following and is booked well in advance for weekends. ⊠ *Ekerts Rd., 2320* ☎ *02/4998–7596* 📠 *02/4998–7739* ⊕ *www.peppers.com.au* ⇨ *47 rooms with shower, one 4-bedroom homestead* ♿ *Restaurant, tennis court, pool, sauna, spa, bar, Internet, meeting rooms; no-smoking rooms, no a/c in some rooms* 🍴 *AE, DC, MC, V* ⦿ *BP.*

$$$–$$$$ ✕🏠 **Casuarina Country Inn.** There's a powerful sense of fantasy about this luxurious country resort lapped by a sea of grapevines. Each of the palatial guest suites is furnished according to particular themes, such as the famous French Bordello suite, with its four-poster canopy bed; the Victorian suite, with its stunning period furnishings; the Chinese imperial suite, with its opium couch for a bed; or the movie-inspired Moulin Rouge suite. The nearby Casuarina Restaurant specializes in flambéed dishes theatrically prepared at your table. There is a minimum two-night booking on weekends. ⊠ *Hermitage Rd., 2320* ☎ *02/4998–7888* 🖷 *02/4998–7692* ⊕ *www.casuarinainn.com.au* ➷ *9 suites, 2 cottages* ♣ *Restaurant, cable TV, tennis court, pool, sauna, billiards, Internet, meeting rooms; no smoking* ☰ *AE, DC, MC, V.*

$$$$
Fodor'sChoice
★
Convent Pepper Tree. This former convent, the most luxurious accommodations in the Hunter Valley, was transported 605 km (375 mi) from its original home in western New South Wales. There's a maximum of 34 guests at any given time, which creates a friendly, intimate atmosphere despite the imposing two-story timber building. Rooms are cozy, spacious, and elegantly furnished, each with doors that open onto a wide veranda. The house is surrounded by the vineyards of the Pepper Tree Winery and is adjacent to Robert's at Pepper Tree, which has delicious meals. Rates include a full country breakfast plus predinner drinks and canapés. ⊠ *Halls Rd., 2320* ☎ *02/4998–7764* 🖷 *02/4998–7323* ⊕ *www.peppers.com.au* ➷ *17 rooms* ♣ *Tennis court, pool, spa, bicycles, meeting rooms; no smoking* ☰ *AE, DC, MC, V.*

$–$$$
The Carriages Guest House. Set on 36 acres at the end of a quiet country lane is a rustic-looking but winsome guesthouse. Each of its very private suites has antique country pine furniture and a large sitting area, and many have open fireplaces. The more expensive Gatehouse Suites also come with whirlpool baths and full kitchen facilities. Breakfast—a basket of goodies delivered to your door or served in the Gatehouse Suites—is included. ⊠ *Halls Rd., 2321* ☎ *02/4998–7591* 🖷 *02/4998–7839* ➷ *10 suites* ♣ *Kitchenettes, tennis court, saltwater pool, Internet; no kids* ☰ *AE, MC, V* ⦿ *BP.*

$$
Glen Ayr Cottages. Tucked away in the Pokolbin bushland, these trim, colonial-style timber cottages have marvelous views from their verandas. The cottages, which sleep between four and eight people, are built on a ridge with vineyards on one side and eucalyptus forest on the other. The furnishings are comfortable but simple: no televisions or telephones are allowed to compete with the songs of birds. ⌂ *Box 188, Cessnock, 2325* ☎ *02/4998–7784* 🖷 *02/4998–7476* ➷ *6 cottages* ♣ *Kitchens; no room phones, no room TVs* ☰ *MC, V.*

★ $$
Vineyard Hill Country Motel. The smart and modern motel suites, on a rise in a secluded part of the Hunter Valley, have views across the vineyards to the Pokolbin State Forest. One- and two-bedroom lodgings are an exceptional value. Each pastel-color suite has its own high-ceiling lounge area, a private deck, and a kitchenette. The best views are from Rooms 4 through 8. Full, cooked breakfasts are available. There is a minimum stay of two nights on weekends. ⊠ *Lovedale Rd., 2320* ☎ *02/4990–4166* 🖷 *02/4991–4431* ⊕ *www.vineyardhill.com.au* ➷ *8 suites* ♣ *Kitchenettes, pool, spa* ☰ *AE, MC, V.*

Muswellbrook

111 km (69 mi) northwest of Pokolbin.

First settled in the 1820s as cattle farming land, the Upper Hunter Valley town of Muswellbrook is an agricultural and coal mining center with few attractions other than tranquil hills and rich farmlands, some historic buildings, and the Regional Art Gallery. There are numerous wineries around the nearby village of Denman, however, including Arrowfield Wines and the excellent Rosemount Estate.

Scone

26 km (16 mi) north of Muswellbrook.

The delightful Upper Hunter farming town of Scone contains some historic mid-19th-century buildings and a local museum, and there are particularly fine accommodations in the area. Sometimes called the horse capital of Australia, the town is also known for its high-quality horse and cattle stud farms and its penchant for playing polo.

Where to Stay & Eat

$$–$$$$ ✕🖼 **Belltrees Country House.** On a working cattle and horse ranch that dates from the 1830s, this outstanding rural retreat offers a taste of the finer side of Australian country life. Activities abound, including horseback riding, polo, archery, and clay pigeon shooting, or take a four-wheel-drive spin into the surrounding mountains. Accommodations are in a modern building surrounded by gardens; two self-contained cottages; and the secluded, romantic Mountain Retreat, with unparalleled views from atop its 5,000-foot mountain perch. Belltrees is a two-hour drive from the Lower Hunter wineries on paved roads. ⊠ *Gundy Rd., 2337* ☎ *02/6546–1123* 🖷 *02/6546–1193* ⊕ *www. belltrees.com* ⇆ *4 rooms, 3 cottages* ⚭ *Dining room, kitchenettes, tennis court, saltwater pool, Internet, meeting rooms; no smoking, no a/c, no room phones* ⊟ *AE, MC, V.*

Maitland

121 km (75 mi) southeast of Scone.

Maitland was one of Australia's earliest European settlements, and you can best explore the town's history by strolling along High Street, which has a number of colonial buildings and is classified by the National Trust as an urban conservation area. Leading off this thoroughfare is Church Street, with several handsome two-story Georgian homes, a couple of which are open to the public.

In one of Church Street's Georgian houses, the **Maitland City Art Gallery** contains both a permanent collection and changing exhibitions. ⊠ *Brough House, Church St.* ☎ *02/4933–1657* 🖾 *A$2* ⊘ *Daily 9–4.*

The National Trust's **Grossman House** adjoins Maitland's art gallery. The restored 1870 home is furnished as a Victorian merchant's town house with an interesting collection of colonial antiques. ⊠ *Church St.* ☎ *02/ 4933–6452* 🖾 *A$2* ⊘ *Thurs.–Sun. 10–3; also by appointment.*

off the
beaten
path

MORPETH – This riverside village is a scenic 5-km (3-mi) country drive from Maitland (take the New England Highway to Melbourne Street, which leads to Morpeth). Due to the settlement's comparative isolation, its quaint shop fronts, wharves, and even the hitching posts have survived from the time when this was an important trading station for the Hunter River Steam Navigation Company. Today the hamlet is a backwater of the best possible kind: a place for browsing through crafts shops or just sitting under a tree by the riverbank.

Where to Stay & Eat

★ $$$$ ✕🖼 **Old George and Dragon.** With its sumptuous colors, green baize walls, oil paintings, Asian curios, and plush furnishings, this former coaching inn comes undiluted from the full-blown opulence of the Victorian era. The four period-style rooms have enclosed courtyards brimming with greenery. The rate includes a traditional country-style dinner. The menu changes seasonally but always lists classics: roast partridge with apples and calvados, or filet of beef. The extensive wine list highlights Australia's finest. ✉ *48 Melbourne St., East Maitland, 2323* ☎ *02/4933–7272* 🖷 *02/4934–1481* ⚓ *Reservations essential* ⇔ *4 rooms* ♨ *Restaurant, bar; no room phones, no room TVs, no kids under 12, no smoking* ⊟ *AE, DC, MC, V* ⦿ *BP* ☺ *Restaurant closed Sun.–Mon.*

Golf

The 18-hole, par-71 **Maitland Golf Club** (✉ Sinclair St., East Maitland ☎ 02/4933–7512 or 02/4933–4141) is one of the Hunter Valley's notable courses. The club welcomes nonmembers on most days, but it's best to check beforehand. Greens fees are A$14 for 9 holes and A$18 for 18 holes.

Hunter Valley A to Z

To research prices, get advice from other travelers, and book travel arrangements, visit www.fodors.com.

BUS TRAVEL

Daily Keans Express Travel buses depart at 3 PM for the 2½-hour journey to Cessnock from Sydney's Central Coach Terminal on Eddy Avenue (near Central Station). The fare is A$27 one-way.

An excellent alternative to the dangerous combination of driving and sampling too many wines is to hop aboard one of the minibuses operated by Cessnock-based Vineyard Shuttle Service. The buses travel between area hotels, wineries, and restaurants. A day pass (good 9–5) with unlimited stops is A$27, or A$35 with evening transportation to and from the restaurant of your choice. The dinnertime shuttle service is A$10 without purchase of a day pass.

🚌 **Keans Express Travel** ☎ 02/4990–5000 or 1800/043339. **Vineyard Shuttle Service** ☎ 0409/32–7193 or 02/4991–3655.

CAR RENTAL

🚗 **Hertz** ✉ 191 Wollombi Rd., Cessnock ☎ 02/4991–2500.

CAR TRAVEL

If you plan to spend several days exploring the area, you will need a car. Other than taking a guided tour on arrival, this is the most convenient way to visit the wineries and off-the-beaten-path attractions, such as Wollombi and Morpeth.

To reach the area, leave Sydney by the Harbour Bridge or Harbour Tunnel and follow the signs for Newcastle. Just before Hornsby this road joins the Sydney–Newcastle Freeway. Take the exit from the freeway signposted HUNTER VALLEY VINEYARDS VIA CESSNOCK. From Cessnock, the route to the vineyards is clearly marked. Allow 2½ hours for the 185-km (115-mi) journey from Sydney.

EMERGENCIES

In case of any emergency, dial **000** to reach an ambulance, the fire department, or the police.

TOURS

Several Sydney-based bus companies tour the Hunter Valley. Alternate ways to explore the region are by horse-drawn carriage, bicycle, motorbike, or even in a hot-air balloon. Full details are available from the Wine Country Visitor Information Centre.

AAT Kings operates a one-day bus tour of the Hunter Valley and Wollombi from Sydney on Tuesday, Wednesday, Thursday, and Sunday.

Buses depart from the Overseas Passenger Terminal on the Harbour Bridge side of Circular Quay at 8:45 and return at 7:15. Free hotel pickup is available on request. Tours cost A$117 and include lunch and wine tasting.

Drifting across the valley while the vines are still wet with dew is an unforgettable way to see the Hunter Valley. Balloon Aloft runs hour-long flights for A$250.

Paxton Brown, based in Pokolbin, conducts half-day (from A$52.50) and full-day (from A$79) horse-drawn carriage tours of the wineries. The full-day tour includes a champagne picnic.

🚩 **AAT Kings** ☎ 02/9252-2788. **Balloon Aloft** ☎ 02/4938-1955 or 1800/028568. **Paxton Brown** ☎ 02/4998-7362.

VISITOR INFORMATION

Scone (Upper Hunter) Tourist Information Centre is open daily 9–5. Sydney Visitors Information Centre, open daily 9–6, has information on Hunter Valley accommodations, tours, and sights. Wine Country Visitor Information Centre is open weekdays 9–5, Saturdays 9:30–5, and Sundays 9:30–3:30.

🚩 **Scone (Upper Hunter) Tourist Information Centre** ✉ Kelly and Susan Sts., Scone, 2337 ☎ 02/6545-1526. **Sydney Visitors Information Centre** ✉ 106 George St., The Rocks, Sydney, 2000 ☎ 02/9255-1788 🖷 02/9241-5010 ⊕ www.sydneyvisitorcentre.com. **Wine Country Visitor Information Centre** ✉ Turner Park, Aberdare Rd., Cessnock, 2325 ☎ 02/4990-4477 ⊕ www.winecountry.com.au.

THE NORTH COAST

The North Coast is one of the most glorious and seductive stretches of terrain in Australia. An almost continuous line of beaches defines the coast, with the Great Dividing Range rising to the west. These natural borders frame a succession of rolling green pasturelands, mossy rain forests, towns dotted by red-roof houses, and waterfalls that tumble in glistening arcs from the escarpment.

A journey along the coast leads through several rich agricultural districts, beginning with grazing country in the south and moving into plantations of bananas, sugarcane, mangoes, avocados, and macadamia nuts. Dorrigo National Park, outside Bellingen, and Muttonbird Island, in Coffs Harbour, are two parks good for getting your feet on some native soil and for seeing unusual bird life.

The North Coast is a major vacation playground, sprinkled with resort towns that offer varying degrees of sophistication. In addition to surfing, swimming, and boating, which are popular throughout this region, Coffs Harbour and Byron Bay both have excellent diving and several notable dive operators who provide trips and instruction. White-water rafting is a popular sport in the Coffs Harbour region.

The tie that binds the North Coast is the Pacific Highway. Crowded, slow, and deadly dull, this highway rarely affords glimpses of the Pacific Ocean. You can drive the entire length of the North Coast in a single day, but allow at least three—or, better still, a week—to properly sample some of its attractions.

Numbers in the margin correspond to points of interest on the North Coast map.

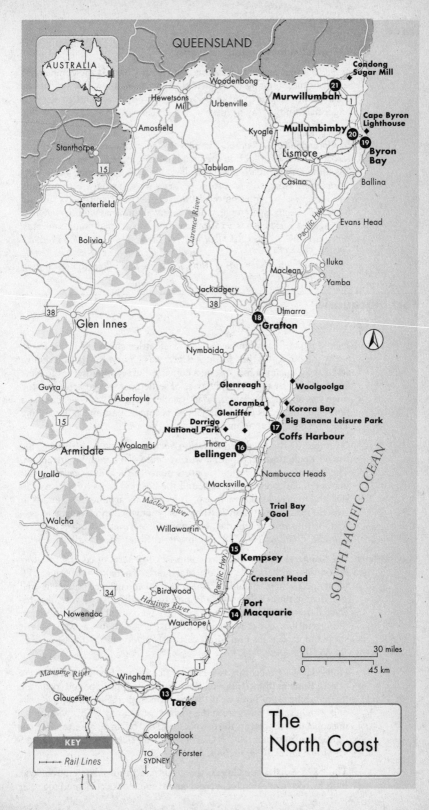

AUSTRALIA

QUEENSLAND

Woodenbong

Condong
Sugar Mill

Hewetsons
Mill

Urbenville

21

Murwillumbah

Amosfield

Kyogle

Mullumbimby

Cape Byron
Lighthouse

Stanthorpe

Lismore

20

19

Byron
Bay

15

Tabulam

Casina

Ballina

Tenterfield

Evans Head

Bolivia

Maclean

Iluka

Yamba

Jackadgery

38

Ulmarra

38

Glen Innes

18

Grafton

Nymboida

Guyra

Aberfoyle

Glenreagh

Woolgoolga

Coramba
Gleniffer

Korora Bay

Big Banana Leisure Park

15

Dorrigo
National Park

17

Coffs Harbour

Armidale

Woolombi

Thora

16

Bellingen

Uralla

Nambucca Heads

Walcha

Macksville

Trial Bay
Gaol

Willawarrin

Kempsey

15

Crescent Head

Birdwood

Port
Macquarie

14

Nowendoc

34

Wauchope

0   30 miles

0   45 km

Wingham

Gloucester

13

Taree

Coolongolook

KEY

Rail Lines

TO
SYDNEY

Forster

SOUTH PACIFIC OCEAN

Clarence River

Pacific Hwy

Macleay River

Hastings River

Manning River

The
North Coast

Taree

⑬ *335 km (208 mi) northeast of Sydney.*

Taree, the first major town along the North Coast, is the commercial center of the Manning River district. Apart from a few fine beaches in the area, or perhaps to make an overnight stop, there is little reason to linger here on the way north.

Lodging

$$$ ⊡ **Clarendon Forest Retreat.** The private self-contained cottages at this resort provide affordable luxury in a forest setting. Each cottage is spotless and equipped with a kitchen, laundry, two bedrooms, and a loft. Three more-expensive sandstone cottages have sunken whirlpool tubs and antiques. Activities on the 1,000-acre beef-cattle property include horseback riding, swimming, tennis, bushwalking, and wildlife-viewing. The nearest surf beach is a 15-minute drive. A two-night minimum stay is required. ⊠ *Coates Rd., Failford via Taree, 2430* ☎ *02/6554–3162* 🖷 *02/6554–3242* ⊕ *www.cfr.com.au* 🛏 *6 cottages* ♿ *Kitchens, tennis court, pool, horseback riding, Internet, some pets allowed; no smoking* ⊟ *AE, DC, MC, V.*

Port Macquarie

⑭ *82 km (51 mi) north of Taree.*

Port Macquarie was founded as a convict settlement in 1821. The town, set at the mouth of the Hastings River, was chosen for its isolation to serve as an open jail for prisoners convicted of second offenses in New South Wales. By the 1830s the pace of settlement was so brisk that the town was no longer isolated, and its usefulness as a jail had ended. Today's Port Macquarie has few reminders of its convict past and is flourishing as a vacation and retirement area.

☙ Operated by the Koala Preservation Society of New South Wales, the town's **Koala Hospital** is both a worthy cause and a popular attraction. The Port Macquarie region supports many of these extremely appealing but endangered marsupials, and the hospital cares for 150 to 250 sick and injured koalas each year. You can walk around the grounds to view the recuperating animals. Try to time your visit during feeding times— 8 in the morning or 3 in the afternoon. ⊠ *Macquarie Nature Reserve, Lord St.* ☎ *02/6584–1522* 🖾 *Donation requested* ☉ *Daily 9–4:30.*

Fodor'sChoice The **Sea Acres Rainforest Centre** comprises 178 acres of coastal rain for-
★ est on the southern side of Port Macquarie. There are more than 170 plant species here, including 300-year-old cabbage tree palms, as well as native mammals, reptiles, and prolific bird life. An elevated boardwalk allows you to stroll through the lush environment without disturbing the vegetation. The center has informative guided tours, as well as a gift shop and a pleasant rain forest café. ⊠ *Pacific Dr.* ☎ *02/6582–3355* 🖾 *A$10* ☉ *Daily 9–4:30.*

Housed in a 19th-century two-story shop near the Hastings River is the eclectic **Hastings District Historical Museum,** which displays period costumes, memorabilia from both world wars, farm implements, antique clocks and watches, and relics from the town's convict days. This wide-ranging collection represents the town's social history in an entertaining, enlightening manner. ⊠ *22 Clarence St.* ☎ *02/6583–1108* 🖾 *A$5* ☉ *Mon.–Sat. 9:30–4:30, Sun. 1–4:30.*

The 1828 **St. Thomas Church,** the country's third-oldest church, was built by convicts using local cedar and stone blocks cemented together with powdered seashells. The church is in the same area as the Hastings District Historical Museum. ⊠ *Hay and William Sts.* ☎ *02/6584–1033* 🎫 *A$3* ☉ *Weekdays 9:30–noon and 2–4.*

Where to Stay & Eat

★ **$$** ✕ **Ca Marche.** Cassegrain Winery, 20 minutes from town, has a terrific lunch spot serving French-inspired Australian cuisine. Start with a spicy serving of Dukkar Tucker, crusty bread served with olive oil, nuts, and herbs. Continue with such traditional fare as roasted, corn-fed chicken with garlic, or Niçoise salad with fresh-caught fish fillets. The dining room has views of the vineyards and formal gardens. Cassegrain's cellar door is open for tastings daily from 9–5. ⊠ *764 Fernbank Creek Rd.* ☎ *02/6582–8320* 🎫 *AE, DC, MC, V* ☉ *No dinner.*

$–$$ ✕ **Portabellos.** The dining room is deceptively casual, given the sophisticated mix of cuisines coming from the kitchen. Breakfast can be a simple affair, with good coffee and homemade pastries, but lunch and dinner move up a notch with spicy Jamaican-inspired chicken salad or cashew, coriander, and saffron gnocchi served with roasted tomato and Parmesan. The inventive food and reasonable prices bring in locals and visitors. ⊠ *124 Horton St.* ☎ *02/6584–1171* 🔊 *Reservations essential* 🎫 *AE, DC, MC, V* ☉ *Closed Sun.–Mon.* 🍴 *BYOB.*

$$$–$$$$ ✕🛏 **Four Points by Sheraton.** Located on the river, in the center of town, the interiors of the hotel are painted in soothing tones and feature dark mahogany wood. Most of the spacious rooms have balconies, but be sure to book a room with river or beach views. The Four Points is within easy walking distance of all Port Macquarie's attractions. The hotel's restaurant, Compass, serves such contemporary cuisine as grilled rib-eye filet with an olive tapenade and potato rosti, as well as freshly caught local seafood. Deep discounts are often available. ⊠ *2 Hay St., 2444* ☎ *02/6589–2888* 🖨 *02/6589–2899* 🌐 *www.fourpoints.com/portmacquarie* 🛏 *99 rooms, 18 apartments, 6 studios* 🍴 *Restaurant, in-room data ports, in-room safes, minibar, refrigerators, cable TV with movies, pool, gym, bar, laundry service, concierge, meeting rooms; no-smoking rooms* 🎫 *AE, DC, MC, V.*

$$–$$$ 🛏 **HW Boutique Motel.** This is not your average motel. Some of the perks: designer furnishings, high-quality bed linens, marble bathrooms, and private balconies with views looking north along the New South Wales coast. Chichi Molton Brown bath products are supplied and, in many rooms, so are spa baths. The HW is a five-minute walk into town and is directly opposite Town Beach. Breakfast is available. ⊠ *1 Stewart St., 2444* ☎ *02/6583–1200* 🖨 *02/6584–1439* 🌐 *www.hwescape.com.au* 🛏 *44 rooms, 4 apartments* 🍴 *Kitchenettes, minibars, refrigerators, cable TV, pool, laundry facilities, Internet, airport shuttle; no smoking rooms* 🎫 *AE, DC, MC, V.*

$ 🛏 **Azura Beach House B&B.** An almost stylish bed-and-breakfast opposite Shelley Beach, this is an easy walk to Sea Acres and coastal walking tracks. The in-room furnishings are rather minimalist, with some reproduction arts-and-crafts pieces, accented by a splash of bright beach colors. There's a shared lounge area and hot tub. Because of its small, two-bedroom size, the inn can be booked by two couples traveling together. Azura is a five-minute drive to the town center. ⊠ *109 Pacific Dr., 2444* ☎ *02/6582–2700* 🌐 *www.azura.com.au* 🛏 *2 rooms* 🍴 *Fans, kitchenettes, microwaves, refrigerators, VCRs, pool, outdoor hot tub, Internet; no a/c* 🎫 *MC, V.*

en route | A rough but scenic alternative to taking the Pacific Highway north from Port Macquarie is the unpaved Maria River Road that runs through forests and farmland to **Crescent Head**—a beach renowned in the surfing world. Take the vehicular ferry across the Hastings River from Port Macquarie to reach the road, then rejoin the highway near Kempsey.

Kempsey

⑮ *48 km (30 mi) north of Port Macquarie.*

Several historic buildings, the Macleay River Historical Society Museum and Settlers Cottage, an Aboriginal theme park, and various arts-and-crafts shops are among the attractions of this Pacific Highway town, inland on the Macleay River. The nearby coastline also merits a look. Kempsey is the business center for a large farming and timber region, as well as the place where Australia's famous Akubra hats are made.

> **off the beaten path**

TRIAL BAY GAOL – This jail occupies a dramatic position on the cliffs above the sea. The purpose of the jail, built in the 1870s and 1880s by convicts, was to teach prisoners useful skills, but the project proved too expensive and was abandoned in 1903. During World War I, the prison served as an internment camp for some 500 Germans. To get here, follow the well-marked Plummer's Road northeast from Kempsey to the village of South West Rocks and Trial Bay Gaol, 37 km (23 mi) from town. ☎ 02/6566–6168 ⊠ A$4.50 ⊗ Daily 9–4.30.

Bellingen

⑯ *100 km (62 mi) north of Kempsey.*

In a river valley a few miles off the Pacific Highway, Bellingen is one of the prettiest towns along the coast, and the detour here will probably come as a welcome relief if you've been droning along the Pacific Highway. Many of Bellingen's buildings have been classified by the National Trust, and the picturesque town has a museum and plenty of cafés, galleries, and crafts outlets. Bellingen is a favored hangout for artists and other creative types.

From Bellingen, a meandering and spectacular road circles inland to meet the Pacific Highway close to Coffs Harbour. This scenic route first winds along the river, then climbs more than 1,000 feet up the heavily wooded escarpment to the **Dorrigo Plateau.** At the top of the plateau is ★ **Dorrigo National Park** (☎ 02/6657–2309), a small but outstanding subtropical rain forest that is included on the World Heritage list. Signposts along the main road indicate walking trails. The Satinbird Stroll is a short rain forest walk, and the 6-km (4-mi) Cedar Falls Walk leads to the most spectacular of the park's many waterfalls. The excellent **Dorrigo Rainforest Centre,** open daily from 9 to 5, has information, educational displays, and a shop, and from here you can walk out high over the forest canopy along the Skywalk boardwalk. The national park is approximately 31 km (19 mi) from Bellingen.

> **off the beaten path**

GLENIFFER – If you have an hour to spare, cross the river at Bellingen and take an 18-km (11-mi) excursion on the Bellingen–Gleniffer Road to the village of Gleniffer. This tranquil, rambling journey leads through farmlands and wooded valleys and across Never Never Creek to—believe it or not—the Promised Land, a peaceful, pastoral region. Author Peter Carey once lived in this vicinity, and the river and its surroundings provided the backdrop for his novel *Oscar and Lucinda*. Several swimming holes and picnic areas are along this road.

Lodging

$ ⊡ **Koompartoo.** These self-contained, open-plan cottages, on a hillside overlooking Bellingen, are superb examples of local craftsmanship, particularly in their use of timbers from surrounding forests. Each has a complete kitchen and family room. Bathrooms have showers instead of tubs. Breakfast is available by arrangement. ✉ *Rawson and Dudley Sts., 2454* ⊕ *www.midcoast.com.au/koompart* ☎☎ *02/6655–2326* 📠 *4 cottages* ⌂ *In-room VCRs, kitchenettes, outdoor hot tub; no room phones, no smoking* ▭ *MC, V.*

en route Beyond Dorrigo township, a gravel road completes the loop to the towns of Coramba and Moleton, the latter of which is the location for **George's Gold Mine** (✉ Bushmans Range Rd. ☎ 02/6654–5355). Perched on a ridge high above the Orara Valley, this 250-acre cattle property still uses the slab huts and mustering yards built in the region's pioneering days. Owner George Robb is one of the legendary old-timers of the area, and his tour of his gold mine is a vivid account of the personalities and events from the days when "gold fever" gripped these hills. In addition to the mine and its historic equipment, the property has its own rain forest, mountain springs, stand of rare red cedars, and a barbecue-picnic area. Admission, which includes a tour, is A$10. George's Gold Mine is open Wednesday–Sunday 10–5, daily during school holidays; the last tour of the property departs at about 3.

Coffs Harbour

⑰ *35 km (22 mi) northeast of Bellingen via the Pacific Hwy., 103 km (64 mi) from Bellingen via the inland scenic route along the Dorrigo Plateau.*

The area surrounding Coffs Harbour is the state's "banana belt," where long, neat rows of banana palms cover the hillsides. Set at the foot of steep green hills, the town has great beaches and a mild climate. This idyllic combination has made it one of the most popular vacation spots along the coast. Coffs is also a convenient halfway point in the 1,000-km (620-mi) journey between Sydney and Brisbane.

The town has a lively and attractive harbor in the shelter of **Muttonbird Island,** and a stroll out to this nature reserve is delightful in the evening. To get here follow the signs to the Coffs Harbour Jetty, then park near the marina. A wide path leads out along the breakwater and up the slope of the island. The trail is steep, but the views from the top are worth the effort. The island is named after the muttonbirds (also known as shearwaters) that nest here between September and April, spending their days at sea and returning to their burrows in the evening. In late April, the birds begin their annual migration to New Zealand, the Philippines, and past Japan to the Aleutian Islands between eastern Siberia and Alaska. Between June and September Muttonbird Island is also a good spot from which to view migrating whales.

Ⓒ Near the port in Coffs Harbour, the giant **Pet Porpoise Pool** aquarium includes sharks, colorful reef fish, turtles, seals, and dolphins. A 90-minute sea-circus show takes place at 10:30 or 2:15. Children may help feed the dolphins and seals. ✉ *Orlando St.* ☎ *02/6652–2164* 💲 *A$17* ☉ *Daily 9–5.*

Just north of the city, impossible to miss, is the Big Banana—the symbol of Coffs Harbour. This monumental piece of kitsch is part of the **Big Banana Leisure Park** complex, which takes a fascinating look at the past, present, and future of horticulture. Three tours are available: one by minibus and another on a 2-km (1-mi) elevated railway. The guided walking tour travels through a hydroponic growing area, packing shed, and plantation filled with an incredible selection of tropical fruits. Other attractions include the toboggan run and an ice-skating rink. At the end of the tour, you can wander down the hill to the Nut House and the Banana Barn to purchase the park's own jams, pickles, and fresh tropical fruit. ⊠ *Pacific Hwy.* ☎ *02/6652–4355* ⊕ *www.bigbanana.com* ✉ *A$12* ⊙ *Daily 9–5; last tour departs at 3.*

off the beaten path

THE GOLDEN DOG – The Golden Dog, in the tiny village of Glenreagh about 35 km (22 mi) northwest of Coffs Harbour, is a fine example of an atmospheric bush pub, full of character and old local memorabilia. The Golden Dog is also famous for its eccentricities. You might see a horse or even motorbike in the bar. The bistro is open daily for lunch, as well as dinner on Friday and Saturday, but a particularly good time to visit is for Sunday lunch, when jazz, bush, or folk bands often perform in the beer garden. ⊠ *Coramba Rd., Glenreagh* ☎ *02/6649–2162.*

Where to Stay & Eat

$$ ✕ **Blue Fig Espresso Bar.** Despite its minuscule dimensions, this restaurant south of Coffs Harbour has won a devoted clientele for its passionate, innovative food. Parmesan-crusted smoked sardines with eggplant jam, roast quail with roasted pumpkin and verjus sauce, and ox fillet with a tomato-and-lime chutney are typical selections from a menu that does nothing by the book. ⊠ *23 First Ave., Sawtell* ☎ *02/6658–4334* ▭ *MC, V* ⊙ *Closed Sun.–Mon.*

$–$$ ✕ **Shearwater Restaurant.** Interesting and inventive flavor combinations characterize the menu at Shearwater. For lunch, try the Moroccan spiced wild barramundi with lime mayonnaise or duck salad with sesame noodles, shiitake mushrooms, and eggplant cress. After dark, the chef serves up peppered kangaroo fillet on a bed of garlic *kumara* (locally grown sweet potatoes) and ratatouille chutney, and Asian-inspired fare such as Szechwan duck with bok choy and ginger relish. The room is relaxed, and the service friendly and attentive. ⊠ *321 Harbour Dr.* ☎ *02/ 6651–6053* ▭ *AE, MC, V* ⊙ *No dinner Mon.–Tues.*

★ **$$$–$$$$** ▣ **Aanuka Beach Resort.** Clustered in cabanas amid palms, frangipani, and hibiscus are cedar suites, each with its own lounge, kitchen facilities, private laundry, and private two-person whirlpool tub set in a glass-ceiling bathroom. Teak furniture and antiques collected from Indonesia and the South Pacific fill the suites. The landscaping is highly imaginative. The pool, for example, is immersed in a miniature rain forest with a waterfall and hot tub. The resort borders a secluded white-sand beach and the blue waters of the Pacific Ocean. Rates include a tropical buffet breakfast. ⊠ *Firman Dr.* ☎ *02/6652–7555* 🖷 *02/ 6652–7053* ⊕ *www.aanuka.breakfree.com.au* ⇥ *48 suites* ⌂ *Restaurant, kitchenettes, cable TV, 3 tennis courts, 3 pools, gym, hot tub, 2 bars, Internet, meeting rooms* ▭ *AE, DC, MC, V* ⊚ *BP.*

$$–$$$$ ▣ **Pelican Beach Resort Australis.** You can bring the kids to this terraced beachfront complex, which has a striking North Coast setting that adults appreciate. Pastel colors decorate the spacious yet somewhat generic guest rooms, each of which has a private balcony or patio that faces either the sea or the mountains to the west. Facilities, however, are rather stylish and include a huge saltwater swimming pool resembling a tropical lagoon. Children have their own outdoor junior gym and miniature golf course. ⊠ *Pacific Hwy., 2450* ☎ *02/6653–7000* 🖷 *02/6653–7066* ⊕ *www.australishotels.com* ⇥ *112 rooms* ⌂ *Restau-*

*rant, in-room VCRs, minibars, miniature golf, 3 tennis courts, saltwa-
ter pool, gym, hot tub, sauna, beach, bar, playground, meeting rooms;
no-smoking rooms* ⊟ *AE, DC, MC, V.*

Sports & the Outdoors

SCUBA DIVING The warm seas around Coffs Harbour make this particular part of the
coast, with its moray eels, manta rays, turtles, and gray nurse sharks, a
scuba diver's favorite. Best are the Solitary Islands, 7 km–21 km (4 mi–13
mi) offshore. The following companies provide equipment, dive tours,
snorkeling trips, and an instruction course for novice scuba divers. **Island Snorkel & Dive** (☎ 02/6654–2860). **Dive Quest** (☎ 02/6654–1930).

WHITE-WATER The highly regarded **Wildwater Adventures** (✉ 754 Pacific Hwy., Boam-
RAFTING bee ☎ 02/6653–3500) conducts one-, two-, and four-day rafting trips
down the Nymboida River. Trips begin from Bonville, 14 km (9 mi) south
of Coffs Harbour on the Pacific Highway, but pickups from the Coffs
Harbour and Bellingen region can be arranged. One-day trips start at
A$135, including meals.

Shopping

Hidden by gum trees 16 km (10 mi) north of Coffs Harbour, the four-
level **Lake Russell Gallery** (✉ Smiths Rd. and Pacific Hwy. ☎ 02/
6656–1092) houses a first-rate collection of contemporary Australian
art and craftwork. Prices are low, and the complex includes pleasant tearooms. The gallery is open daily 10–5.

en route   A few miles north of the Big Banana, the Pacific Highway loops
through banana plantations toward the sea. A short detour off this
road will take you to **Korora Bay,** a small crescent of sand cradled
between rocky headlands. About 10 km (6 mi) north of Korora Bay,
a wide, shallow lagoon formed by **Moonee Creek** provides safe,
sheltered bathing that's particularly good for children. Note that the
beaches between Korora Bay and Moonee are often unsafe for
swimming because of wild pounding surf and the absence of
lifeguards outside of school holiday periods.

About 15 km (9 mi) north is the town of **Woolgoolga**—"Woopi" to
locals—known for its large Sikh population, whose ancestors came to
Australia from India at the end of the 19th century. The **Guru
Nanak Sikh Temple** is the town's main attraction. Request entrance
at the Temple View Restaurant opposite. Woolgoolga is 58 km (36
mi) from Grafton.

Grafton

⑱ *84 km (52 mi) north of Coffs Harbour.*

This sizable city is at the center of the Clarence Valley, a rich agricultural district of sugarcane farms. The highway bypasses Grafton, but
it's worth detouring to see some of the notable Victorian buildings on
Fitzroy, Victoria, and Prince streets. The **Grafton Regional Gallery** museum displays traditional and contemporary Australian arts and crafts.
✉ *158 Fitzroy St.* ☎ *02/6642–3177* ⊙ *Tues.–Sun. 10–4.*

Grafton is famous for its jacaranda trees, which erupt in a mass of purple flowers in the spring. During the last week of October, when the
trees are at their finest, Grafton holds its **Jacaranda Festival.** The celebration includes arts-and-crafts shows, novelty races, children's rides,
and a parade.

en route Between Grafton and the far north coast, the Pacific Highway enters sugarcane country, where tiny sugarcane trains and thick, drifting smoke from burning cane fields are ever-present. The highway passes the fishing and resort town of **Ballina,** where beaches are the prime feature.

Byron Bay

19 *176 km (109 mi) north of Grafton (exit right from the highway at Bangalow or Ewingsdale).*

Byron Bay is the easternmost point on the Australian mainland and perhaps earns Australia its nickname, the "Lucky Country." Fabulous beaches, storms that spin rainbows across the mountains behind the town, and a sunny, relaxed style cast a spell over practically everyone who visits. For many years Byron Bay lured surfers with abundant sunshine, perfect waves on Wategos Beach, and tolerant locals who allowed them to sleep on the sand. These days a more upscale crowd frequents Byron Bay, but the beachfront has been spared from high-rise resorts. There are many art galleries and crafts shops to explore, and local folk offer sea-kayaking and hang-gliding tours. The town is at its liveliest on the first Sunday of each month, when Butler Street becomes a bustling market.

Cape Byron Lighthouse, the most powerful beacon on the Australian coastline, dominates Byron Bay. The headland above the parking lot near the lighthouse is a launching point for hang gliders, who soar for hours on the warm thermals. This is also a favorite place for whale-watching between June and September, when migrating humpback whales often come close inshore. ✉ *Lighthouse Rd.* ☎ *02/6685–8565* ◔ *Lighthouse grounds daily 8–5:30.*

Cape Byron Walking Track circuits a 150-acre reserve and passes through grasslands and rain forest. The headland is the highlight of the route. From several vantage points along the track you may spot dolphins in the waters below.

Beaches
Several superb beaches lie in the vicinity of Byron Bay. In front of the town, Main Beach provides safe swimming, and Clarks Beach, closer to the cape, has better surf. The most famous surfing beach, however, is Wategos, the only entirely north-facing beach in the state. To the south of the lighthouse, Tallow Beach extends for 6 km (4 mi) to a rocky stretch of coastline around Broken Head, which has a number of small sandy coves. Beyond Broken Head is lonely Seven Mile Beach.

Where to Stay & Eat
★ **$$$** ✕ **Fig Tree Restaurant.** In its century-old farmhouse with distant views of Byron Bay and the ocean, the Fig Tree serves up creative Mod-Oz (Modern Australian) cuisine in magnificently forested surroundings. Produce fresh from the owners' farm stands out on a regularly changing menu that usually includes pasta dishes, seafood, and salads served with homemade bread. Ask for a table on the splendid veranda. The restaurant is 5 km (3 mi) inland from Byron Bay. ✉ *4 Sunrise La., Ewingsdale* ☎ *02/6684–7273* ♦ *Reservations essential* ▤ *AE, DC, MC, V* ☖♈ *BYOB* ◔ *Closed Sun.–Tues. No lunch Wed.*

$$–$$$ ✕ **The Raving Prawn.** As you would expect from a restaurant with a name like this, Australia's tasty little crustaceans are featured prominently on the menu. Seared, pan-tossed, or cold, the prawns here are fantastic. Salmon also makes an appearance, served with citrus couscous, caramelized lime, and tzatziki. Other main courses include an inventive surf and turf—a steak filet filled with creamy garlic seafood sauce and double-cooked duckling. The atmosphere is relaxed and casual and the waitstaff is friendly. ⊠ *Shop 10, Feros Arcade, Johnson St.* ☎ *02/ 6685–6737* ☐ *AE, DC, MC, V* ☾ *No lunch Mon.–Tues.*

$ ✕ **Beach Café.** A Byron Bay legend, this outdoor café is a perfect place to sit in the morning sun and watch the waves. It opens at 7:30 daily, and breakfasts are wholesome and imaginative. The fresh juices and tropical fruits alone are worth the 10-minute stroll along the beach from town. ⊠ *Clarks Beach* ☎ *02/6685–7598* ☐ *MC, V* ☾ *No dinner.*

$$$$ ✕☐ **Rae's on Watego's.** If a high-design boutique hotel is your cup of
Fodor's Choice tea, you'd be hard-pressed to do better than at Rae's luxurious Mediter-
★ ranean-style villa, surrounded by a tropical garden. Each suite is individually decorated with an exotic collection of antiques, Indonesian art, and furnishings. Expect gorgeous four-poster beds, tile floors, huge windows, in-room fireplaces, and private terraces. This is the ultimate in service and seclusion—with a top-notch restaurant serving creative Australian and Thai dishes made with fresh and local ingredients. ⊠ *8 Marina Parade, Watego's Beach, 2481* ☎*02/6685–5366* ☐*02/6685–5695* ⊕*www. raes.com.au* ⤶*7 suites* ☾ *Restaurant, room service, in-room VCRs, massage, Internet; no kids under 13* ☐*AE, DC, MC, V.*

$–$$$ ☐ **Julian's Apartments.** It would be shame to call these studio apartments opposite Clarks Beach "well designed"—they border on tastefully adorable. Apartments have either a balcony or courtyard, and have a simple, modern kitchen table and Tivoli chairs, a comfy yet streamlined sofa, and other pale-wood pieces—nothing ostentatious. All are fully equipped with kitchen and laundry. Each apartment sleeps up to three people; some are suitable for small families. There is no pool in the complex, but with the beach so close, you don't need one. ⊠ *124 Lighthouse Rd., 2481* ☎ *02/6680–9697* ☐ *02/6680–9695* ⊕ *www. juliansbyronbay.com* ⤶ *11 apartments* ☾ *Kitchens, microwaves, laundry facilities, cable TV, in-room VCRs, laundry facilities, free parking* ☐ *AE, MC, V.*

Nightlife

With several good-size venues, the small town of Byron Bay has an unusually wide choice of music and entertainment every night of the week. **Cocomangas Bar, Restaurant, and Nightclub** (⊠ 32 Jonson St. ☎ 02/ 6685–8493) serves up tropical cocktails and live dance music into the wee hours Monday through Saturday. **The Railway Friendly Bar** (⊠ Jonson St. ☎ 02/6685–7662) is a nightclub and restaurant with modern Australian food and live bands.

Scuba Diving

The **Byron Bay Dive Centre** (⊠ 109 Jonson St. ☎ 02/6685–7149) has snorkeling and scuba-diving trips for all levels of experience, plus gear rental and instruction. The best local diving is at Julian Rocks, some 3 km (2 mi) offshore, where the confluence of warm and cold currents supports a profusion of marine life.

Shopping

Byron Bay is one of the state's arts-and-crafts centers, with many innovative and high-quality items for sale, such as leather goods, offbeat designer clothing, essential oils, natural cosmetics, and ironware.

The **Colin Heaney Hot Glass Studio** (⊠ 6 Acacia St., Industrial Estate ☎ 02/ 6685–7044) sells exquisite handblown glass goblets, wineglasses, paperweights, and sculpture. The shop is open weekdays 9–5 and weekends 10–4. An additional attraction is watching the glassblowers at work on weekdays.

Mullumbimby

20 *23 km (14 mi) northwest of Byron Bay.*

Mullumbimby, affectionately known as "Mullum," is a peaceful inland town with several historic buildings, interesting arts-and-crafts shops, and a reputation for attracting alternative-lifestyle types. The town sits at the center of a fertile banana and subtropical fruit-growing region, well worth a short detour off the Pacific Highway.

Where to Stay & Eat

$$$$ ✕⃞ **Sakura Farm.** Owner Genzan Kosaka is a Zen Buddhist priest, and a stay at his farm is a unique way to experience Japanese culture. Guest quarters are Western-style, either in a three-bedroom house or in a newer, cozier two-bedroom lodge. The chance to sample authentic Japanese cooking is a big attraction, but chef Seiko Kosaka also prepares French meals from time to time. Other options include shiatsu massage, instruction in Buddhist meditation, and using the Japanese-style bath facilities. Rates include all meals. ⊠ *Left Bank Rd., Lot 5, 2482* 🏠🏠 *02/ 6684–1724* ➲ *2 cottages* ♨ *Dining room, massage, hiking; no smoking, no a/c, no room phones, no room TVs* ➧ *No credit cards* ⊙⃝ *AP.*

Murwillumbah

21 *53 km (33 mi) northwest of Byron Bay.*

The towering, cone-shape peak of 3,800-foot Mt. Warning dominates pleasant, rambling Murwillumbah, which rests amid sugarcane plantations on the banks of the Tweed River. Apart from the seaside resort of Tweed Heads, Murwillumbah is the last town of any size before the Queensland border.

At the **Condong Sugar Mill,** on the banks of the Tweed River 5 km (3·mi) north of town, you can take an informative tour during the crushing season, July–November. The one-hour visit includes a video and a hands-on tour of the mill, during which you are invited to sample sugar and some of the other products manufactured at the complex. ⊠ *Pacific Hwy., Murwillumbah* 🏠 *02/6670–1700* 🖂 *A$7* ⊙ *July–Nov., Tues.–Thurs. 9–3, weather permitting.*

North Coast A to Z

To research prices, get advice from other travelers, and book travel arrangements, visit www.fodors.com.

AIR TRAVEL

From Sydney, Kendall Airlines Regional Express (Rex) services Ballina (close to Byron Bay). Qantas Airways and its subsidiary Eastern Australia Airlines fly into Taree, Port Macquarie, Kempsey, Coffs Harbour, Grafton, and Coolangatta.

🇫 **Regional Express (Rex)** 🖀 13–1713 ⊕ www.regionalexpress.com.au. **Qantas Airways** 🖀 13–1313 ⊕ www.quantas.com.au.

BUS TRAVEL

Greyhound Pioneer Australia, McCafferty's, and Pioneer Motor Service frequently run between Sydney and Brisbane, with stops at all major North Coast towns. Sydney to Coffs Harbour is a nine-hour ride. Sydney to Byron Bay takes 12.

Long-distance buses are more than adequate for travel among the coast's main centers, and all of the larger towns provide local bus services. Bus travel, however, is not recommended for getting off the beaten track or exploring beyond the major towns.

🚌 **Greyhound Pioneer Australia** ☎ 13-2030 ⊕ www.greyhound.com.au. **McCaf-**ferty's ☎ 13-1499 ⊕ www.mccaffertys.com.au. **Pioneer Motor Service** ☎ 02/9281-2233.

CAR RENTAL

A car is essential for touring the North Coast's off-highway attractions and traveling at your own pace. Avis, Budget, and Hertz offices are in Coffs Harbour, while Avis has another office in Ballina and Hertz has more in Port Macquarie and Byron Bay.

🚗 **Avis** ☎ 02/6686-7650 Ballina, 02/6651-3600 Coffs Harbour. **Budget** ☎ 02/6651-4994 Coffs Harbour. **Hertz** ☎ 02/6621-8855 Byron Bay, 02/6651-1899 Coffs Harbour, 02/6583-6599 Port Macquarie.

CAR TRAVEL

From Sydney, head north via the Harbour Bridge or Harbour Tunnel and follow the signs to Hornsby and Newcastle. Join the Sydney–Newcastle Freeway, then continue up the Pacific Highway (Highway 1), the main route along the 604-km (375-mi) Taree-to-Queensland coast. Taree is 335 km (208 mi) north of Sydney.

EMERGENCIES

In case of any emergency, dial 000 to reach an ambulance, the fire department, or the police.

MAIL, INTERNET & SHIPPING

You'll find post offices in the middle of most towns, on the main street. You can hook up to the Internet at the public library in Coffs Harbour, at Port Pacific in Port Macquarie, and at Computer Solutions in Murwillumbah.

🖥 Internet **Coffs Harbour Public Library** ✉ Coffs Harbour ☎ 02/6648-4900. **Computer Solutions** ✉ Tweed Valley, Murwillumbah ☎ 02/6672-8300. **Port Pacific** ✉ Clarence St., Port Macquarie ☎ 02/6583-8099.

MONEY MATTERS

You can change money and traveler's checks at any bank—look for ANZ, Commonwealth, National, and Westpak. In more populated towns, you'll find ATMs in any shopping area.

TOURS

Wilay Bijar Aboriginal Tours takes small four-wheel-drive tours of Aboriginal sites around Port Macquarie and Kempsey. Tours include a smoke ceremony and a walk on which your guide will identify local bush foods. Half-day tours start at A$60 including morning tea and lunch. Mountain Trails four-wheel-drive tours conducts half- and full-day tours of the rain forests and waterfalls of the Great Dividing Range to the west of Coffs Harbour in style—a seven-seat Toyota Safari or a 14-seat, Australian-designed four-wheel-drive vehicle. The half-day tour costs A$56 and the full-day tour is A$83, including lunch and morning and afternoon snacks.

🚙 **Mountain Trails 4WD Tours** ☎ 02/6658-3333. **Wilay Bijar Aboriginal Tours** ☎ 02/6562-5959.

TRAIN TRAVEL

Trains stop at Taree, Kempsey, Coffs Harbour, Grafton, Byron Bay, and Murwillumbah, but much of the Sydney–Brisbane railway line runs inland and the service is not particularly useful for seeing the North Coast. Call Countrylink, the New South Wales rail operator, for fare and service details.

🚆 Train Information **Countrylink** ☎ 13-2232.

VISITOR INFORMATION

Byron Bay Visitor Information Centre and Coffs Harbour Visitor Information Centre are open daily 9–5. Murwillumbah Visitors Centre is open Monday through Saturday 9–4, and Sunday 9–3. Port Macquarie Visitor Information Centre is open weekdays 8:30–5 and weekends 9–4. Sydney Visitors Information Centre, open daily 9–6, has information on North Coast accommodation, tours, and sights.

🚩 Tourist Information **Byron Bay Visitor Information Centre** ⊠ Jonson St., Byron Bay ☎ 02/6685-8050. **Coffs Harbour Visitor Information Centre** ⊠ Rose Ave. and Marcia St., Coffs Harbour ☎ 02/6652-1522 or 1800/025650 ⊕ www.coffs.tv. **Murwillumbah Visitors Centre** ⊠ Pacific Hwy. and Alma St., Murwillumbah ☎ 1800/674414 or 02/6672-1340. **Port Macquarie Visitor Information Centre** ⊠ Clarence and Hays Sts., Port Macquarie ☎ 1800/025935 or 02/6581-8000. **Sydney Visitors Information Centre** ⊠ 106 George St., The Rocks, Sydney, 2000 ☎ 02/9255-1788 🖷 02/9241-5010 ⊕ www.sydneyvisitorcentre.com.

LORD HOWE ISLAND

A tiny crescent of land 782 km (485 mi) northeast of Sydney, Lord Howe Island is the most remote and arguably the most beautiful part of New South Wales. With the sheer peaks of Mt. Gower (2,870 feet) and Mt. Lidgbird (2,548 feet) richly clad in palms, ferns, and grasses; golden sandy beaches; and the clear turquoise waters of the lagoon, this is a remarkably lovely place. Apart from the barren spire of Ball's Pyramid, a stark volcanic outcrop 16 km (10 mi) across the water to the southeast, the Lord Howe Island Group stands alone in the South Pacific. The island has been placed on UNESCO's World Heritage list as a "natural area of universal value and outstanding beauty."

Not only is the island beautiful, but its history is fascinating. It may be that the first ship to sight it did so in 1788, when it passed by on the way to the Norfolk Island penal settlement farther out in the Pacific. And evidence, or lack of it, suggests that Lord Howe was uninhabited by humans until three Europeans and their Maori wives and children settled it in the 1830s. English and American whaling boats then began calling in for supplies, and by the 1870s the small population included a curious mixture of people from America (including whalers and a former slave), England, Ireland, Australia, South Africa, and the Gilbert Islands. Many of the descendants of these early settlers still live on Lord Howe. In the 1870s, when the importance of whale oil declined, islanders set up an export industry of the seeds of the endemic Kentia (*Howea forsteriana*), the world's most popular indoor palm. It's still a substantial business, but rather than seeds, seedlings are now sold.

Lord Howe is a remarkably safe and relaxed place, where cyclists and walkers far outnumber the few cars, and where locals and visitors alike leave doors unlocked and bags unattended. There are plenty of walks, both flat and rather precipitous, and fine beaches. Among the many bird species is the rare, endangered, flightless Lord Howe woodhen (*Tricholimnas sylvestris*). In the sea below the island's fringing reef is the world's southernmost coral reef, with more than 50 species of hard corals and more than 500 fish species. For its size, the island has enough to keep you alternately occupied and unoccupied for at least five days. Even the dining scene is of an unexpectedly high quality.

Fewer than 300 people live here, which is part of the reason that much of the island shows so little impact from its 150-plus years of sustained human habitation. Visitor numbers are limited to 400 at any given time, though at present hotel beds can only accommodate 393 tourists.

The allocation of those remaining seven tourists is the subject of local controversy.

Exploring Lord Howe Island

The first view of Lord Howe Island rising sheer out of the South Pacific is spectacular. The sense of wonder only grows as you set out to explore the island, which, at a total area of 3,220 acres (about 1 mi by 7 mi), is pretty manageable. You don't have to allow much time to see the town. Most of the community is scattered along the hills at the northern end of the island. There are a few shops, a hospital, a school, and three churches. Everything else is either a home or lodge.

As one of the very few impediments to winds sweeping across the South Pacific, the mountains of Lord Howe Island create their own weather. Visually, this can be amazing as you stand in sunshine on the coast watching cap clouds gather around the high peaks. The average annual rainfall of about 62 inches mostly comes down in winter. Note that, except during the period of Australia's summer daylight savings time (when Lord Howe and Sydney are on the same time), island time is a curious half hour ahead of Sydney. Additionally, many of the lodges, restaurants, and tour operators close in winter—generally from June through August—and accommodation prices are reduced considerably during that period.

What to See

Lord Howe Museum makes a good first stop in town. The sign on the door is typical of the island's sense of time: "The museum is staffed entirely by volunteers . . . if there is no one in attendance by 2:15 PM it should be assumed that the museum will not be open on that day." Inside there's an interesting display of historical memorabilia and a less impressive collection of marine life and stuffed land animals. ⊠ *Lagoon Rd.* ☎ *No phone* ✍ *A$4* ☼ *Daily 2–4.*

A very enjoyable way of filling a sunny day is to take a picnic down to **Neds Beach,** on the eastern side of the island, where you'll find green lawns sloping down to a sandy beach and clear blue waters. This is a fantastic place for swimming and snorkeling. Fish swim close to the shore, and the coral is just a few yards out.

Several **walks**—short, moderate, and considerable—can take you around the island. The short-to-moderate category includes a flat, easy walk around forested Stevens Reserve, right in the heart of town; trips to surf-pounded Blinky Beach, to great views from Clear Place and at Middle Beach; and to a good snorkeling spot under the heights of Mt. Gower by Little Island. The moderate climbs up Mt. Eliza and Malabar at the island's northern end are more strenuous than the other walks, although much less so than Mt. Gower. They afford tremendous views of the island, including its hulking, mountainous southern end and the waters and islets all around.

The ultimate challenge on Lord Howe is the climb up the southernmost peak of **Mt. Gower,** which rises straight out of the ocean to an astonishing 2,870 feet above sea level. The hike is rated medium to hard, so you should be in good physical condition if you plan to climb the peak. National park regulations require that you use a guide when climbing Mt. Gower. **Jack Shick** (☎ 02/6563–2218) is a highly recommended guide who makes the climb on Monday and Thursday in summer. The cost is A$25. Meet at Little Island Gate at 7:30 AM sharp. Reservations are not required, but you'll need to bring lunch and drinks, and wear a jacket and sturdy walking shoes. After a scramble along the shore, the ascent into the forest begins. There's time for a break at the Erskine River crossing by some pretty cascades. Then it's a solid march to the summit. The views, the lush vegetation, and the chance to see the rare island wood-hen all make the hike worthwhile.

Where to Stay & Eat

$$ ✕ **Beachcomber Lodge.** The Beachcomber serves up traditional home-cooked fare at a good-value buffet of hot and cold dishes on Thursday evening, as well as a popular "island fish fry" dinner on Sunday and Wednesday. The locally caught fish is cooked in beer batter and accompanied by chips and salads. Desserts, a cheese platter, and coffee follow the main courses. ⊠ *Anderson Rd.* ☎ *02/6563–2032* ▤ *AE, DC, MC, V.*

$$ ✕ **Blue Peters Cafe.** Many patrons drop in for cake and coffee or tea. Others come for the beer, wine, and cocktails. The meals at this bright, modern, indoor-outdoor café are generous: Salads and antipasto plates are available, as are fish-and-chips, enormous burgers, and Tex Mex fare. ⊠ *Lagoon Rd.* ☎ *02/6563–2019* ▤ *AE, MC, V* ☺ *No dinner.*

$$$$ ✕▣ **Capella Lodge.** Lord Howe's most luxurious accommodation may seem a bit out of the way on the island's south end, but you'll be rewarded by truly dramatic views. The lodge's veranda overlooks beaches, the ocean, and the lofty peaks of Mt. Lidgbird and Mt. Gower. The nine high-ceiling guest suites make use of unique textiles, such as hand-printed bedspreads, and shuttered doors that let light in while maintaining privacy. The equally stylish White Gallinule Restaurant serves all meals, often using local seafood. Presentation is excellent, and the menu changes daily. Nonguests are welcome, but call ahead for reservations. ⊠ *Lagoon Rd., 2898* ☎ *02/6563–2008 or 02/9544–2273 restaurant reservations; 02/9544–2387 for Sydney booking office* ☎ *02/6563–2180* ⊕ *www.lordhowe.com* ⤏ *9 suites* ↺ *Restaurant, in-room VCRs, snorkeling, boating, mountain bikes, bar, airport shuttle; no-smoking rooms, no a/c* ▤ *AE, MC, V* ◉ *BP.*

$$$$ ✕▣ **Arajilla.** This intimate retreat is tucked away at the north end of the island amid tropical gardens. The spacious suites and two-bedroom apartments have well-equipped kitchens, separate lounge areas, and private decks. You can rent mountain bikes, and a complimentary transportation service is also available. The excellent restaurant serves fine wine and light modern cuisine nightly for guests and nonguests. ⊠ *Old Settlement Beach, 2898* ☎ *02/6563–2002* ☎ *02/6563–2022* ⊕ *www.arajilla.com.au* ⤏ *10 suites, 2 apartments* ↺ *Restaurant, snorkeling, fishing, mountain bikes, bar; no a/c* ▤ *AE, DC, MC, V* ◉ *BP.*

$$$–$$$$ ✕▣ **Pinetrees.** Descendants of the island's first settlers run the largest resort on the island, one of the few that stays open year-round. The original 1884 homestead forms part of this central resort, but most accommodations are in undistinguished motel-style units, which have verandas leading into pleasant gardens. Five Garden Cottages and two luxury suites are a cut above the other rooms. At Pinetrees Restaurant, a limited, changing menu might include seared local tuna with snow pea and celeriac salad, or grilled kingfish with roast tomatoes and salsa verde. Credit cards are accepted for advance reservations only. ⊠ *Lagoon Rd., 2898* ☎ *02/9262–6585, 02/6563–2177 for restaurant* ☎ *02/9262–6638* ⊕ *www.pinetrees.com.au* ⤏ *31 rooms with shower, 2 suites, 5 cottages* ↺ *Restaurant, tennis court, billiards, bar, meeting rooms; no a/c, no room phones, no room TVs, no smoking* ▤ *AE, DC, MC, V* ◉ *AP.*

$$$–$$$$ ▣ **Somerset.** Although not overly luxurious, the spacious cottage suites at this lodge have separate living rooms and private verandas. Subtropical gardens surround the grounds, which contain barbecue areas. You can

rent bikes, helmets, and snorkeling gear. The lodge is in an ideal location, close to town and walking distance from excellent beaches. ✉ *Neds Beach Rd., 2898* ☎ *02/6563–2061* 🖷 *02/6563–2110* ⊕ *www. lordhoweisle.com.au* ⇔ *25 suites* ⚭ *Kitchenettes, bicycles, laundry service; no a/c, no room phones* ▤ *MC, V.*

Sports & the Outdoors

Fishing

Fishing is a major activity on Lord Howe. Several well-equipped boats regularly go out for kingfish, yellowfin tuna, marlin, and wahoo. A half-day trip with **Oblivion Sports Fishing** (☎ 02/6563–2185) includes tackle and bait, for around A$65. It's best to arrange an excursion as soon you arrive on the island.

Golf

Nonmembers are welcome at the spectacularly located—between the ocean on one side and two mountains on the other—9-hole, par-36 **Lord Howe Island Golf Club** (☎ 02/6563–2179), and you can rent clubs. The greens fee is A$20 for 9 or 18 holes.

Scuba Diving

The reefs of Lord Howe Island provide a unique opportunity for diving in coral far from the equator. And, unlike many of the Queensland islands, superb diving and snorkeling is literally just offshore, rather than a long boat trip away. Even though the water is warm enough for coral, most divers use a 5mm wet suit. Dive courses are not available in June and July. If you're heading to Lord Howe specifically for diving, contact **Pro Dive Travel** (☎ 02/9232–5733 🖷 02/9281–0660) in Sydney, which has packages that include accommodations, airfares, and diving.

Snorkeling

The best snorkeling spots are on the reef that fringes the lagoon, at Neds Beach and North Bay, and around the Sylph Hole off Old Settlement Beach—a spot that turtles frequent. You can likely rent snorkeling gear from your lodge. A good way to get to the reef, and view the coral en route, is on a glass-bottom boat trip. The *Coral Empress/Coral Princess* (☎ 02/6563–2326) runs two-hour cruises that include snorkeling gear in the A$25 charge.

Lord Howe Island A to Z

To research prices, get advice from other travelers, and book travel arrangements, visit www.fodors.com.

AIR TRAVEL

Unless you have your own boat, the only practical way of getting to Lord Howe Island is by Qantas from Brisbane or Sydney. In both cases, the flying time is about two hours. Your hosts on Lord Howe Island will pick you up from the airport. Note that the baggage allowance is only 31 pounds per person. Special discounts on airfares to the island are often available if you're coming from overseas and you purchase tickets outside of Australia.

🛈 Qantas ☎ 13-1313 ⊕ www.quantas.com.au.

BIKE TRAVEL

Despite the island's hills and high peaks, much of the terrain is fairly flat, and bicycles, usually available at your lodge, are the ideal form of transportation. Helmets, which are supplied with the bikes, must be worn by law. If your hotel doesn't have free bikes, **Wilson's Hire Service** (✉ Lagoon Rd. ☎ 02/6563–2045) rents them for about A$8 a day.

CAR RENTAL

There are just six rental cars on the island. Your lodge can arrange one for you (if any are available) for about A$50 per day. However, with 24 km (15 mi) of roads on the island, even cutting the 24 kph (15 mph) maximum permissible driving speed in half, you'll soon run out of places to go.

EMERGENCIES

In case of any emergency, dial 000 to reach an ambulance, the fire department, or the police.
🗗 **Doctor** Dr. Frank Reed ☎ 02/6563–2000, 02/6563–2056 after hours. **Hospital** ✉ Lagoon Rd. ☎ 02/6563–2000.

MONEY MATTERS

Although most major credit cards are accepted, there are no ATMs on the island. Be sure to carry adequate cash or traveler's checks in addition to credit cards.

TELEPHONES

International and long-distance national calls can be made from public phones, which you can find in tourist areas around the island. There are also four phones at the post office.

TOURS

Islander Cruises conducts several tours around the island, including ferries and cruises to North Bay for snorkeling, a two-hour sunset cocktail cruise on the lagoon, and a morning and evening cappuccino cruise around the lagoon. Prices range from A$22 to A$45 and private charters are also available.

Ron's Ramble is a scenic and highly informative three-hour stroll (A$15) around a small section of the island, with knowledgeable guide Ron Matthews explaining much about Lord Howe's geology, history, and plant and animal life. The rambles take place on Monday, Wednesday, and Friday afternoons starting at 2.

Whitfield's Island Tours runs a half-day air-conditioned bus tour (A$25) that provides a good overview of the island's history and present-day life. The tours include morning or afternoon tea at the Whitfield home.
🗗 **Islander Cruises** ☎ 02/6563–2021. **Ron's Ramble** ☎ 02/6563–2010. **Whitfield's Island Tours** ☎ 02/6563–2115.

VISITOR INFORMATION

Contact the Lord Howe Island Board for advance information on the island. Although Lord Howe has a visitor center, open weekdays from 9 to 12:30, with general information, most of the tours and activities should be arranged through Thompson's Store on Neds Beach Road, the Blue Peters Cafe on Lagoon Road, or Joy's Shop on Middle Beach Road. A notice board outside the visitor center indicates which trips should be booked where. The Sydney Visitors Information Centre, open daily 9–6, also has information on Lord Howe Island.
🗗 **Lord Howe Island Board** ✉ Lord Howe Island, 2898 ☎ 02/6563–2066 🖷 02/6563–2127. **Lord Howe visitor center** ☎ 02/6563–2114. **Sydney Visitors Information Centre** ✉ 106 George St., The Rocks, Sydney, 2000 ☎ 02/9255–1788 🖷 02/9241–5010 ⊕ www.sydneyvisitorcentre.com.

THE SNOWY MOUNTAINS

Down by Kosciuszko, where the pine-clad ridges raise
Their torn and rugged battlements on high,
Where the air is clear as crystal, and the white stars fairly blaze,
At midnight in the cold and frosty sky . . .

Fodor'sChoice
★
Banjo Paterson's 1890 poem, "The Man from Snowy River," tells of life in the Snowy Mountains—the hard life, to be sure, but with its own beauty and great reward. It's still possible to experience the world that Paterson described by visiting any of the hundred-odd old settlers' huts scattered throughout the Snowys. Hike the mountains and valleys with camera in hand, and breathe deeply the crystal-clear air.

Reaching north from the border with Victoria, this section of the Great Dividing Range is an alpine wonderland. The entire region is part of Kosciuszko (pronounced "koh-*shoosh*-ko") National Park, the largest alpine area in Australia, which occupies a 6,764-square-km (2,612-square-mi) chunk of New South Wales. The national park also contains Australia's highest point in Mt. Kosciuszko, which reaches a modest—on a worldwide scale—7,314 feet. Mountain peaks and streams, high meadows, forests, caves, glacial lakes, and wildflowers provide for a wealth of outdoor activities.

This wilderness area lends itself to cross-country skiing in winter and, in other seasons, walking and all kinds of adventure activities. The many self-guided walking trails are excellent, especially the popular Mt. Kosciuszko summit walk. In addition, local operators, and others based in Sydney, offer hiking, climbing, mountain biking, white-water rafting, and horseback riding tours and excursions.

A number of lakes—Jindabyne, Eucumbene, Tooma, and Tumut Pond reservoirs—and the Murray River provide excellent trout fishing. Khancoban's lake is a favorite for anglers, and Adaminaby is another fishing center. Tackle can be rented in a few towns, and a local operator conducts excursions and instruction. The trout fishing season extends from the beginning of October to early June.

Although the downhill skiing isn't what Americans and Europeans are used to, the gentle slopes and relatively light snowfalls are perfect for cross-country skiing. Trails from Cabramurra, Kiandra, Perisher Valley, Charlotte Pass, and Thredbo are very good; don't hesitate to ask locals about their favorites. The ski season officially runs from the June holiday weekend (second weekend of the month) to the October holiday weekend (first weekend).

Après-ski action in the Snowys is focused on the hotels in Thredbo, the large Perisher Blue resort, and the subalpine town of Jindabyne. Most hotel bars host live music in the evenings during the ski season, ranging from solo piano to jazz to rock bands. Thredbo tends toward the cosmopolitan end of the scale, and Jindabyne makes up with energy what it lacks in sophistication. Note, however, that many of the hotels close from October through May (room rates are considerably cheaper during these months in hotels that stay open), and nightlife is much quieter outside of the ski season.

Numbers in the margin correspond to points of interest on the Snowy Mountains map.

Cooma

㉒ *419 km (260 mi) southwest of Sydney, 114 km (71 mi) south of Canberra.*

The gateway to the Snowy Mountains and the ideal place to gather some information on the region (from the visitor center), Cooma is a relatively attractive town with an interesting history as the capital of the Snowy Mountains region. Cooma is the headquarters for the **Snowy Mountains Hydroelectric Authority.** Between 1949 and 1974, more than 100,000 people from more than 30 different countries were employed in the construction of the Snowy Mountains Hydroelectric Scheme. The 16 major dams, seven power stations, lakes, tunnels, and pipelines that make up the extensive scheme can generate almost 4 million kilowatts of electricity, which is distributed to Victoria, South Australia, New South Wales, and the Australian Capital Territory.

The Snowy Mountains Hydroelectric Authority's Snowy Information Centre has films and displays that explain the technical workings of this huge, complicated project—one of the world's modern engineering wonders. There are also three power stations in the Snowy Mountains region (including those at Khancoban and Cabramurra) that are open for visits and tours; bookings can be made at the center in Cooma. ⊠ *Monaro Hwy.* ☎ *02/6453–2004 or 1800/623776* ⊙ *Weekdays 8–5, weekends 8–1.*

Fishing

Based in Cooma, the **Alpine Angler** (⊠ Snowy Mountains Hwy. ☎ 02/ 6452–5538) has trout fly-fishing excursions for novices and advanced anglers throughout the Snowy Mountains region. Lessons, equipment, transportation, and even accommodations are available. Prices start at A$250 per person.

Jindabyne

㉓ *63 km (39 mi) southwest of Cooma.*

This picturesque, mountain-surrounded resort town, with European-style architecture and a village air, was built in the 1960s on the shores of Lake Jindabyne, a human-made lake that flooded the original town when the Snowy River was dammed. In summer, several outdoor activities center on the lake, and plenty of hiking, boating, and fishing equipment is available to rent or buy. For information on park trails and activities, stop in at the **Snowy Region Visitor Centre** (☎ 02/6450–5600), open daily 8–6, in the center of Jindabyne on the main Kosciuszko Road. Here you can find information on hikes, flora and fauna, and all that Kosciuszko National Park has to offer. In winter, Jindabyne becomes a major base for budget skiers, with plenty of inexpensive local chalets and apartments.

Where to Stay & Eat

$$ ✕ **Balcony Bistro.** Huge steaks and seafood platters are the house specials at this very popular small, dark, and intimate bistro. The balcony above the dining area serves as a bar, with some tables on a covered deck overlooking Lake Jindabyne. During ski season, Balcony Bistro doubles as a nightclub. ⊠ *Old Town Centre, Level 3* ☎ *02/6456–2144* ▱ *AE, DC, MC, V* ⊙ *No lunch.*

★ **$$** ✕ **Crackenback Cottage.** This stone-and-timber bistro, on the road to Thredbo on the outskirts of Jindabyne, glows with rustic warmth. Expect generous servings of traditional favorites—soup, salad, roasts, pie, and mountain trout—as well as wood-fired pizzas with innovative toppings such as local smoked trout or goat cheese. The restaurant also serves scones and afternoon tea, but it's famous for its *gluhwein* (mulled wine) and Australia's largest selection of schnapps. Call ahead as the summer

schedule varies. ⊠ *Alpine Way, Thredbo Valley* ☎ *02/6456–2198* 🖩 *AE, DC, MC, V* ⊘ *No dinner Sun.–Thur. in summer.*

$ ✕**Brumby Bar and Bistro.** Only the lighting is subdued at this hopping bistro, where the live entertainment—from duets to rock bands—is as popular as the food. The menu includes grilled steaks, chicken, beef Stroganoff, panfried trout and other seafood, lasagna, and schnitzels. You can help yourself to the salad and vegetable bar. ⊠ *Alpine Gables Motel, Kalkite St. and Kosciuszko Rd.* ☎ *02/6456–2526* ⌣ *Reservations not accepted* 🖩 *AE, MC, V.*

$$$ 🏨**Station Resort.** The largest resort in the Snowy Mountains accommodates more than 1,400 guests on its 50 tranquil rural acres. Relatively inexpensive lodging, spacious and comfortable rooms, and several dining options make this hotel a popular choice with families and the under-35 set. Guest rooms sleep from two to seven people. A daily shuttle service connects the hotel with the Skitube Terminal. Rates can include meals and ski-lift tickets. The resort is 6 km (4 mi) from Jindabyne. ⊠ *Dalgety Rd., 2627* ☎ *02/6456–2895* 🖷 *02/6456–2544* ⊕ *www.perisherblue.com.au* ⇺ *250 rooms with shower* ⌣ *Restaurant, grill, pizzeria, downhill skiing, ski shop, 2 bars, nightclub, shops; no-smoking rooms, no a/c, no room phones* 🖩 *AE, DC, MC, V* ⋈ *AP.*

$$ 🏨**Alpine Gables Motel.** These split-level suites each have a kitchenette, a lounge, and a separate bedroom in an upstairs loft. The modern decor makes extensive use of wood and glass, and some rooms have bunks for kids. Suites can accommodate up to six people. The Brumby Bar and Bistro is one of the town's most popular watering holes. ⊠ *Kalkite St. and Kosciuszko Rd., 2627* ☎ *02/6456–2555* 🖷 *02/6456–2815* ⊕ *www.alpinegables.com.au* ⇺ *42 suites* ⌣ *Restaurant, kitchenettes, room TVs with movies, sauna, spa, bar, recreation room; no a/c, no smoking* 🖩 *AE, DC, MC, V.*

★ ¢ 🏨**Eagles Range.** The two cedar lodges on this 300-acre sheep ranch combine the best of comfort and value in the Snowys. A stay at the two-story Homestead guesthouse includes dinner, bed, and breakfast. A three-bedroom, self-catering lodge is ideal for groups. Both options are charmingly rustic, with exposed wood rafters, country-style furniture, and views of the surrounding ranges. The larger building has an open fireplace, and the smaller one has a wood-burning stove. The property is about 12 km (7½ mi) from Jindabyne. ⊡ *Box 298, Dalgety Rd., Jindabyne, 2627* 🕿🕿 *02/6456–2728* ↩ *4 rooms, one 3-bedroom lodge* ☐ *Spa, mountain bikes, horseback riding* ⊟ *MC, V* �‖❘ *MAP.*

Nightlife

The nightclub at **Balcony Bistro** is popular. The **Lake Jindabyne Hotel** (⊠ Kosciuszko Rd. 🕿 02/6456–2203) has a long-standing reputation for its party atmosphere. In winter, the nightclub and bars inside the **Station Resort** usually rock until at least 1 AM.

Sports & the Outdoors

BP Ski Hire (⊠ BP Service Station, Kosciuszko Rd., Jindabyne 🕿 02/6456–1959) rents snowboards and downhill or cross-country skis and equipment.

Paddy Pallin (⊠ Kosciuszko Rd., Thredbo turnoff 🕿 02/6456–2922) specializes in clothing and equipment for outdoor adventurers. In addition to retail sales, the shop rents out everything needed for a week in the wilderness, from Gore-Tex jackets to mountain bikes and all kinds of ski gear. The shop also conducts guided expeditions of all kinds.

en route
From Jindabyne, divergent roads lead to two major destinations for walking, skiing, and generally exploring magnificent Kosciuszko National Park. One is Kosciuszko Road, which takes you to the northern route and Perisher Blue, and the other is the Alpine Way to the Skitube Terminal and Thredbo Village.

Kosciuszko Road heads north to Sawpit Creek, from which point you need snow chains between June 1 and October 10. Rent chains from gas stations in Cooma and Jindabyne. This road continues to the vast Perisher Blue ski region (including the resorts of Smiggin Holes, Perisher Valley, Mt. Blue Cow, and Guthega), as well as the less-commercial skiing area around Charlotte Pass, which is at the very end of the road but accessible by over-snow transport during winter. There are several excellent walks from Charlotte Pass, including a particularly scenic 10-km (6-mi) round-trip walk to Blue Lake, part of a 21-km (13-mi) loop that connects a number of peaks and a couple of other glacial lakes, and a more strenuous 18-km (11-mi) round-trip walk to the summit of Mt. Kosciuszko.

In the other direction from Jindabyne, the **Alpine Way** runs southwest to Thredbo Village and past the Skitube Terminal at Bullocks Flat, approximately 21 km (13 mi) from Jindabyne. The 8-km (5-mi) **Skitube** (🕿 02/6456–2010) has an underground-overground shuttle train that transports skiers to the terminals at Perisher (10 minutes) and Mt. Blue Cow (19 minutes). The service operates 24 hours daily in winter, and is open year-round.

Perisher Blue

❷❹ *30 km (19 mi) west of Jindabyne.*

The four adjoining skiing areas of Smiggin Holes, Perisher Valley, Mt. Blue Cow, and Guthega have merged to become the megaresort of **Perisher Blue** (🕿 1300/655822 for general information). This is the largest snowfield in Australia, with 50 lifts and T-bars that serve all standards of slopes, as well as more than 100 km (62 mi) of cross-country trails. Because it is a snowfield area—at 5,575 feet above sea level—Perisher Blue virtually closes down between October and May. Some lodges and cafés do stay open, especially around the Christmas holidays.

Where to Stay & Eat

$$$$ ✕🏨 **Perisher Valley Hotel.** With a location on the slopes of Perisher Blue, this is a true "ski-in and ski-out" hotel, renowned for its outstanding service and facilities. Each of the 31 luxurious suites accommodates between two and six people, and delicious meals are served in its Snowgums Restaurant, which has stunning views of the mountain scenery. The hotel is open only during the ski season, and rates include breakfast, dinner, and over-snow transport to the hotel. ⊠ *Mt. Kosciuszko Rd., Perisher Valley, 2624* ☎ *02/6459–4455* 🖷 *02/6457–5177* ↵ *31 suites* ♿ *2 restaurants, sauna, spa, ski shop, ski storage, 2 bars, shops, dry cleaning, laundry service; no smoking* ▤ *AE, DC, MC, V* ⊗ *Closed Oct.–May* ◯ *MAP.*

$$–$$$$ 🏨 **Perisher Manor.** Rooms at this ski-in, ski-out hotel vary from budget level to stylish, deluxe accommodations with views. All rooms are centrally heated and very comfortable, and the hotel has 24-hour reception, a lobby lounge with an open fireplace, drying rooms, and ski lockers. It's open only in ski season. ⊠ *Perisher Valley Rd., Perisher Valley, 2624* ☎ *02/6457–5291* 🖷 *02/6457–5064* ↵ *49 rooms* ♿ *Restaurant, café, ski storage, 2 bars; no phone in some rooms, no TV in some rooms* ▤ *AE, DC, MC, V* ⊗ *Closed Oct.–May.*

Nightlife

Perisher Manor stages rock bands throughout the ski season. If you want to join the after-ski set, drop in at the cocktail bar of the **Perisher Valley Hotel.**

Skiing

Lift tickets for use at any of the **Perisher Blue** (☎ 02/6459–4495) ski areas are A$77 per day, A$324 for five days. From the Bullocks Flat Skitube Terminal, combined Skitube and lift tickets are A$92 per day. From here, skiers can schuss down the mountain to a choice of four high-speed quad chairlifts and a double chair. Blue Cow has a good choice of beginner- and intermediate-level runs, but no accommodations are available.

Thredbo Village

㉕ *32 km (20 mi) southwest of Jindabyne.*

Nestled in a valley at the foot of the Crackenback Ridge, this resort has a European feeling that is unique on the Australian snowfields. In addition to some of the best skiing in the country, this all-seasons resort has bushwalking, fly-fishing, canoeing, white-water rafting, tennis courts, mountain-bike trails, a 9-hole golf course, and a 2,300-foot alpine slide. The altitude at Thredbo Village is 5,000 feet above sea level. The pollution-free, high-country environment is home to the **Australian Institute of Sport's Thredbo Alpine Training Centre** (⊠ Friday Dr. ☎ 02/6459–4138), which was primarily designed for elite athletes but is now open to the public. Facilities include an Olympic-size swimming pool; a running track; squash, basketball, badminton, volleyball, and netball courts; and a well-equipped gymnasium. It's open 7 AM–7 PM in summer, 10 AM–8 PM in winter.

The **Crackenback Chairlift** provides easy access to Mt. Kosciuszko, Australia's tallest peak, with great views of the Aussie alps. From the upper chairlift terminal at 6,447 feet, the journey to the 7,314-foot summit is a relatively easy 12-km (7½-mi) round-trip hike in beautiful alpine country. You can also take a mile walk to an overlook. Be prepared for unpredictable and sometimes severe weather.

Where to Stay & Eat

$$$–$$$$ ✕▥ **Bernti's Mountain Inn.** Bernti's is a unique, boutique-style mountain inn with friendly service and superb food, all within walking distance of the chairlifts. Most rooms have delightful mountain views and king-size beds, and the lounge welcomes you with a fire, bar, and pool table. Outside, whirlpools, saunas, and plunge pools overlook the mountains. The popular terrace café serves snacks and drinks in the day, and innovative dishes alongside a comprehensive wine list at night. The inn is open year-round, and rates are considerably cheaper out of ski season. ✉ *Mowamba Pl., Thredbo, 2625* ☎ *02/6457–6332* 🖷 *02/6457–6348* ↩ *27 rooms* ⚭ *Restaurant, sauna, billiards, ski storage, bar, laundry service, meeting room; no smoking* ▭ *AE, DC, MC, V* ⦿*| AP.*

$$$$ ▥ **Novotel Lake Crackenback Resort.** Poised on the banks of a lake that mirrors the surrounding peaks of the Crackenback Range are these luxury apartments, which make great family accommodations. Apartments in this all-season resort include one-bedroom-plus lofts, which sleep four, and two- and three-bedroom units. Each has a modern kitchen, a laundry with drying racks, under-floor heating, a fireplace, and such thoughtful extras as under-cover parking and lockable ski racks outside the rooms. ✉ *Alpine Way, via Jindabyne, 2627* ☎ *02/6456–2960* 🖷 *02/6456–1008* ⊕ *www.novotellakecrackenback.com.au* ↩ *46 apartments* ⚭ *Restaurant, kitchens, cable TV with movies, 3 tennis courts, pool, gym, sauna, bar, meeting rooms, Internet; no-smoking rooms, no a/c* ▭ *AE, DC, MC, V.*

$$–$$$$ ▥ **Thredbo Alpine Hotel.** Warm autumn colors and contemporary wood and glass furnishings fill the rooms at this spacious and comfortable hotel within easy reach of the ski lifts at Thredbo. You have a choice of several restaurants and après-ski facilities. You can also arrange to rent private apartments in the village through the hotel. ✉ *Friday Dr., Thredbo Village, 2625* ☎ *02/6459–4200* 🖷 *02/6459–4201* ⊕ *www.thredbo. com.au* ↩ *65 rooms* ⚭ *3 restaurants, in-room VCRs, tennis court, pool, sauna, spa, ski storage, 3 bars, nightclub, Internet, meeting rooms; no a/c* ▭ *MC, V* ⦿*| CP.*

Nightlife

The **Thredbo Alpine Hotel,** at the center of the village, has a popular nightclub, open September–January, and a choice of three bars.

Skiing

Among downhill resorts of the area, **Thredbo** (☎ 02/6459–4119) has the most challenging runs—with the only Australian giant-slalom course approved for World Cup events—and the most extensive snowmaking in the country. Lift tickets are A$77 per day, A$324 for five days.

Thredbo Sports (✉ Ski-lift terminal, Thredbo Village ☎ 02/6459–4100) rents downhill and cross-country skis and snowboards.

en route | Between Thredbo and Khancoban, the Alpine Way turns south and then west as it skirts the flanks of **Mt. Kosciuszko.** This 40-km (25-mi) gravel section of the highway, often impassable in winter but reasonable at other times, leads through heavily forested terrain, with pleasant views to the south. Nineteen kilometers (12 mi) past Dead Horse Gap is the turnoff to **Tom Groggin,** the highest point of the Murray River accessible by road. Australia's longest river travels west for another 2,515 km (1,560 mi) before it meets the sea south of Adelaide.

Khancoban North to Yarrangobilly

81 km (50 mi) northwest of Thredbo.

26 Once a dormitory town for workers on the Snowy Mountains Hydro-electric Scheme—it's close to a dam and two of the project's power stations—**Khancoban** is now a favorite with anglers who try their luck in the lake created by the damming of the Swampy Plain River.

27 In a picturesque valley outside Khancoban is the Snowy Mountains Hydroelectric Authority's **Murray 1 "Inflowmation Station."** Interactive displays demonstrate the importance of water in Australia, the driest inhabited continent. From here you can see the power station's 10 turbine generators. ⊠ *Alpine Way, via Khancoban* ☎ *02/6453–2004 or 1800/623776* ⊠ *Free* ☉ *Weekdays 8–5, weekends 8–1.*

28 The road north (known as the KNP5) from Khancoban leads past the Tooma and Tumut Pond reservoirs and Round Mountain to **Cabramurra.** At 4,890 feet this is the highest town in Australia. The scenic Goldseekers Track is a pleasant 3 km (2 mi) return walk that starts at Three Mile Dam, approximately 8 km (5 mi) north of Cabramurra on Link Road.

29 Just north of Cabramurra stands a major component of the Snowy Mountains Hydroelectric Scheme—the **Tumut 2 Power Station.** You can tour the station, read informative displays about the Snowy Scheme's construction, and go inside the mountain to explore some of the scheme's workings. Reserve ahead for tours. ⊠ *Elliot Way, via Cabramurra* ☎ *02/6453–2004* ⊠ *A$10* ☉ *Weekdays 9–5, weekends 8–1.*

30 Stalactites, stalagmites, and other rock formations fill **Yarrangobilly Caves** (☎ 02/6454–9597), a network of limestone grottoes. A few of the caves are open to the public. One of them, South Glory Cave, has a self-guided tour. Four other caves must be toured with a guide. You can also bathe in 27°C (80°F) thermal pools, an enjoyable complement to the 12°C (53°F) chill inside the passages. The caves are within Kosciuszko National Park and the area contains pristine wilderness, including the spectacular Yarrangobilly Gorge. The caves are about 21 km (13 mi) north of Kiandra. The self-guided tour costs A$8.80, the guided tour A$11. The caves are open daily from 9 to 5 (subject to winter road conditions).

en route A long but very scenic route along the Snowy Mountains Highway will take you to Adaminaby and eventually Cooma. First you'll pass through **Kiandra,** a small, now-tranquil village that was the site of a frantic early 1860s gold rush.

Adaminaby

31 *40 km (25 mi) southeast of Kiandra, 50 km (31 mi) northwest of Cooma.*

Halfway between Kiandra and Cooma, this is the town closest to **Lake Eucumbene,** the main storage dam for the Snowy Mountains Hydroelectric Scheme. The lake holds eight times as much water as Sydney Harbour. Adaminaby was moved to its present site in the 1950s, when the lake was created, and the area is now best known for its horseback holidays and recreational fishing. The town's most famous structure is a 54-foot-long fiberglass trout.

Lodging

★ ¢–$$ 🏠 **Reynella.** Set in undulating country near the highest point in Australia, this small sheep and cattle all-inclusive resort lets you saddle up and head off into "The Man from Snowy River" country. Reynella is renowned for its multiday horseback safaris into Kosciuszko National Park. All levels of riding ability are welcome. The homestead provides basic but comfortable lodge-style accommodations with shared facilities. In winter, the property makes a good base for both downhill and cross-country skiing. It is 9 km (5½ mi) south of Adaminaby. ⊠ *Kingston Rd., 2630* ☎ *02/6454–2386* ☐ *02/6454–2530* ⊕ *www.reynellarides.com.au* ⇨ *20 rooms without bath* ⊘ *Dining room, tennis court, fishing, horseback riding; no a/c, no room phones, no TV in rooms* ☰ *AE, MC, V* ⦿ *AI.*

Snowy Mountains A to Z

To research prices, get advice from other travelers, and book travel arrangements, visit www.fodors.com.

AIR TRAVEL
Impulse Airlines (reservations through Qantas) operates daily flights between Sydney and Cooma. From Cooma's airport, it is a half-hour drive to Jindabyne.
🛈 Qantas ☎ 13–1313 ⊕ www.quantas.com.au.

BUS TRAVEL
During ski season, Greyhound Pioneer Australia makes daily runs between Sydney and the Snowy Mountains via Canberra. The bus stops at Cooma, Berridale, Jindabyne, Thredbo, the Skitube Terminal, and Perisher Blue. It's a seven-hour ride to Thredbo from Sydney, three hours from Canberra.

In winter, shuttle buses connect the regional towns with the ski fields. At other times of the year, the only practical way to explore the area is by rental car or on a guided tour.
🛈 Greyhound Pioneer Australia ☎ 13–2030 ⊕ www.greyhound.com.au.

CAR RENTAL
Rent cars in Cooma from Thrifty Car Rental, which also has an office at Cooma's airport.
🛈 Thrifty Car Rental ⊠ Sharpe St., Cooma ☎ 02/6452–5300.

CAR TRAVEL
Take Parramatta Road from Sydney to the juncture with the Hume Highway at Ashfield, about 8 km (5 mi) from the city center. Follow the highway to just south of Goulburn and then turn onto the Federal Highway to Canberra. The Monaro Highway runs south from Canberra to Cooma. The 419-km (260-mi) journey takes at least five hours.

To visit anything beyond the main ski resort areas, a car is a necessity. Be aware, however, that driving these often steep and winding mountain roads in winter can be hazardous, and you must carry snow chains from June through October.

EMERGENCIES
In case of any emergency, dial 000 to reach an ambulance, the fire department, or the police.
🛈 Cooma District Hospital ⊠ Bent St., Cooma ☎ 02/6252–1333.

MAIL & SHIPPING
Post offices can usually be found in the middle of town, on the main street. It's best to mail outgoing letters and packages from post offices, as it's unusual for hotels to handle these transactions. Most hotels can, however, help organize delivery of skiing equipment before you arrive.

MONEY MATTERS

Most banks will cash traveler's checks and exchange money, as will tourist hotels and the visitor center in Jindabyne. The most common banks in the region include National and Commonwealth. You can find ATMs at the larger banks and in popular shopping areas, and ski resorts. Credit cards are widely accepted.

SKITUBE TRAVEL

The Skitube shuttle train—running from the Alpine Way, between Jindabyne and Thredbo, to the Perisher Blue area—operates year-round and is a useful means of reaching either of these resorts. For full details of services and fares, contact the Skitube information office.
🔳 **Skitube** ☎ 02/6456-2010.

TOURS

In addition to joining up with one of the tour operators listed here, you can also, if you are an experienced walker, undertake one of the area's many fine walks without a guide. Talk to staff at the Snowy Region Visitor Centre for suggestions and trail maps.

Local operator Morrell Adventure Travel runs various guided hiking and mountain-biking trips in the Snowy Mountains between November and April. Trips range from three to 15 days and start at A$425, including all meals. Jindabyne's Paddy Pallin arranges bushwalking, mountain biking, white-water rafting and canoeing, and horseback riding. Outstanding cross-country ski programs are also available, from introductory weekends to snow-camping trips.

Murrays Australia operates both skiing/accommodation packages and a transportation service (during the ski season only) to the Snowy Mountains from Canberra. These depart from Canberra's Jolimont Tourist Centre at Alinga Street and Northbourne Avenue.
🔳 **Morrell Adventure Travel** ✉ 62 Jindabyne St., Berridale, 2628 ☎ 02/6456-3681. **Murrays Australia** ☎ 13-2251 or 02/6295-3611. **Paddy Pallin** ✉ Kosciuszko Rd., Thredbo turnoff, Jindabyne, 2627 ☎ 02/6456-2922 or 1800/623459.

VISITOR INFORMATION

Cooma Visitors Centre is open June through September, daily 7–6, and October through May, daily 9–5. Snowy Region Visitor Centre is open daily 8–6. Sydney Visitors Information Centre is open daily 9–6.
🔳 Tourist Information **Cooma Visitors Centre** ✉ 119 Sharpe St., Cooma ☎ 02/6450-1742 or 02/6450-1740. **Snowy Region Visitor Centre** ✉ Kosciuszko Rd., Jindabyne ☎ 02/6450-5600 ⊕ www.snowymountains.com.au. **Sydney Visitors Information Centre** ✉ 106 George St., The Rocks, Sydney, 2000 ☎ 02/9255-1788 🖨 02/9241-5010 ⊕ www.sydneyvisitorcentre.com.

BROKEN HILL

1160 km (720 mi) west of Sydney, 295 km (183 mi) north of Mildura, 508 km (316 mi) northeast of Adelaide.

Nicknamed the "Silver City," Broken Hill began as an isolated mining town, founded in the desert Outback in 1883. Boundary rider Charles Rasp discovered silver ore here at a broken hill jutting out into the arid plain, in land that originally belonged to the Wiljali people. Miners arrived not long after. They dug into the hill using both open-cut and tunneling methods, exploiting a lode that was 220 m (720 feet) wide and over 7 km (4.3 mi) long. They took the high-grade ore and left the rest behind, using the rock pile to fill in some of the open cut. This hill of mullock (iron ore waste) now dominates the town's skyline.

Broken Hill is no longer the boomtown that it once was, but it still has a population of around 20,000, and sights here reflect the area's mining heritage and culture. Many of the old mines are now museums and art galleries abound. The **Pro Hart Gallery** (✉ Wyman St.) features the work of well-known contemporary Australian artist Pro Hart, famous for his depictions of the Outback. The **Mutawintji National Park** (✣ 120 km/74 mi northeast of Broken Hill ☎ 08/8088–5933 ⊕ www.npws.nsw.gov.au.) has one of the most important collections of Aboriginal rock art in New South Wales and has been managed by the Mutawintji Aboriginal Land Council since 1998. Because of its cultural and environmental value, access is with ranger-led tours only (Wed. and Sat., Apr.– Nov.).

Where to Stay & Eat

$ ✕ **MacGregor's Cafe.** This café with the best view in town is set on top of Mullock Hill. Dining on Australian and continental grub—like red snapper and grilled feta cheese, or pasta, steak, and burgers—you can take in a vista of the Line of Load Miners Memorial and Visitors Centre. ✉ *Federation Way* ☎ *08/8087–1345* ▭ *AE, DC, MC, V.*

$$ **Imperial Fine Accommodation.** This handsome, two-story hotel is two blocks from Broken Hill's town center. Large rooms are furnished in style, with timber fittings and art deco nightstands. A nifty games room includes a full-size billiards table, and you can meet fellow travelers around the large pool or guest lounge. An attractive garden surrounds the property. Children are not encouraged. ✉ *88 Oxide St.* ☎ *08/8087–7444* 📠 *08/8087–7234* ✍ *imperial@pcpro.net.au* *5 rooms* *Pool, billiards, recreation room; no kids, no smoking* ▭ *AE, DC, MC, V* 🍽 *BP.*

$$ **Old Willyama Motor Inn.** Actors often stay here when they're filming in the region, as the desert to the northwest of town is a popular setting for movies, TV shows, and commercials. It's not fancy, but it's friendly and comfortable, with rooms decorated in a simple, casual style. ✉ *30 Iodide St.* ☎ *08/8088–3355* 📠 *08/8088–3956* ✍ *oldwilly@pcpro.net.au* *Refrigerators, free parking* ▭ *AE, DC, MC, V.*

¢ **Mulberry Vale Bush Cabins.** This gathering of modern, self-contained cabins is set in the wilderness. The location is about 5 km (3 mi) from Broken Hill. ✉ *Menindee Rd.* ☎ *08/8088–1597* ✍ *mulberry@ruralnet.net.au* *No phones in some rooms* ▭ *MC, V.*

¢ **Palace Hotel.** Fans of the 1994 camp Australian classic, *The Adventures of Priscilla, Queen of the Desert,* shouldn't leave Broken Hill without visiting this grand, old-style motel. In its famous foyer is a colorful collection of mind-blowing murals—one of which (a copy of Boticelli's *Birth of Venus*) was painted by long-time owner, Mario Celotto. The largest room, the Priscilla, was used in a scene for the film. Note only some rooms have private baths, and children are not encouraged. ✉ *227 Argent St.* ☎ *08/8088–1699* ✍ *mariospalace@bigpond.com.au* *20 rooms* *Dining room, refrigerators, pool, some pets allowed, no-smoking rooms* ▭ *AE, MC, V.*

Broken Hill A to Z

AIR TRAVEL

To reach this remote Outback town, you can fly from Sydney with Hazelton, from Melbourne and Adelaide with Kendall.

Hazelton ☎ 13-1713. **Kendall** ☎ 13-1300.

VISITOR INFORMATION

Broken Hill Visitor Information Centre ✉ Bromide and Blende Sts. ☎ 08/8088-6077 ⊕ www.murrayoutback.org.au.

CANBERRA AND THE A.C.T.

3

FODOR'S CHOICE

Aubergine, restaurant in Griffith

Australian War Memorial, in Campbell

Boat House by the Lake, restaurant in Barton

The Chairman and Yip, restaurant in Canberra City

Hyatt Hotel Canberra, in Yarralumla

National Museum of Australia, on the Acton Peninsula

Parliament House, in Capital Hill

Rydges Capital Hill, hotel in Forrest

Saville Park Suites, in Canberra City

HIGHLY RECOMMENDED

RESTAURANTS The Fig Café, in Griffith

The Tryst, in Manuka

HOTELS Argyle Executive Apartments, in Reid

By Michael
Gebicki
Updated by
Roger Allnutt

THE NATION'S CAPITAL is the city that Australians most like to dislike. In the national consciousness, "Canberra" stands for politicians and bureaucrats who spend and sometimes squander the national wealth, conceive overly ambitious projects for their own personal aggrandizement, make unreasonable decisions, and ride around in taxpayer-funded cars while ordinary citizens roll up their sleeves and work. The reality is vastly different. Canberra is typically Australian through and through. Those who live here will tell you that to know Canberra is to love it, although a significant proportion of its residents seem to flee their home city at every opportunity, to judge by the number of vehicles with Canberra registration plates on Sydney's streets every weekend.

The need for a national capital arose only in 1901, when the Australian states—which had previously operated separate and often conflicting administrations—united in a federation. An area of about 2,330 square km (900 square mi) of undulating sheep-grazing country in southeastern New South Wales was set aside and designated the Australian Capital Territory (A. C. T.). The inland site was chosen partly for reasons of national security and partly to end the bickering between Sydney and Melbourne, both of which claimed to be the country's legitimate capital. The name Canberry—an Aboriginal word meaning "meeting place" that had been previously applied to this area—was changed to Canberra for the new city. Like everything else about it, the name was controversial, and debate has raged ever since over which syllable should be stressed. These days, you'll hear *Can-*bra more often than Can-*ber*-ra.

From the very beginning this was to be a totally planned city. Walter Burley Griffin, a Chicago architect and associate of Frank Lloyd Wright, won an international design competition. Griffin arrived in Canberra in 1913 to supervise construction, but progress was slowed by two world wars and the Great Depression. By 1947 Canberra, with only 15,000 inhabitants, was little more than a country town.

Development increased during the 1950s, and the current population of more than 300,000 makes Canberra by far the largest inland city in Australia. The wide tree-lined avenues and spacious parkland of present-day Canberra have largely fulfilled Griffin's original plan. The major public buildings are arranged on low knolls on either side of human-made Lake Burley Griffin, the focus of the city. Satellite communities—using the same radial design of crescents and cul-de-sacs employed in Canberra, but each with a shopping center at its nucleus—house the city's growing population.

Canberra gives an overall impression of spaciousness, serenity, and almost unnatural order. There are no advertising billboards, no strident colors, and very few buildings more than a dozen stories high. It is paradoxically unlike anywhere else in Australia—the product of a brave attempt to create an urban utopia—and its success or failure has fueled many a pub debate.

EXPLORING CANBERRA & THE A. C. T.

Canberra's most important public buildings stand within the Parliamentary Triangle, formed by Lake Burley Griffin on the north side and two long avenues, Commonwealth and Kings, which radiate from Capital Hill, the city's political and geographical epicenter. The triangle can be explored comfortably on foot, but you'll need to use transportation for the rest of your stay in the city.

Most of Canberra's galleries, museums, and public buildings can be seen in a couple of days, but the capital's parks and gardens, and Namadgi National Park to the south, can easily delay you for another day or so. Several lesser-known attractions, such as Lanyon Homestead, also warrant a visit.

If you have
2 days

In two busy days you will be able to see most of the main city attractions. You could start day one with the spectacular view from the **Telstra Tower** ⑮, and then visit the **National Capital Exhibition** ④ for a good look into Canberra's planning and history. Your next stop should be the Parliamentary Triangle, where you might spend the remainder of the day visiting the **National Gallery of Australia** ⑧, **Questacon** ⑥, **Old Parliament House** ⑨, and **Parliament House** ⑩. Fill in the city-center gaps on the second day with the **National Museum of Australia** ⑭, **Australian National Botanic Gardens** ⑯, the **Australian War Memorial** ❶, and **ScreenSound Australia.**

If you have
4 days

After seeing all of the above, spend days three and four visiting the **Australian Institute of Sport, St. John the Baptist Church and the Schoolhouse Museum,** and the **Royal Australian Mint** ⑫. Then take a drive around the pleasant suburb of Yarralumla and the **Yarralumla Diplomatic Missions** ⑪ en route to the **National Zoo and Aquarium** ⑬. You should also be able to fit in a visit to **Lanyon Homestead** and **Tidbinbilla Nature Reserve,** to the city's south.

If you have
6 days

With six days your itinerary could easily cover the above suggestions, plus a gentle bicycle ride around **Lake Burley Griffin** ②, a day hike in **Namadgi National Park,** and perhaps a visit to the **Canberra Deep Space Communications Complex** at Tidbinbilla. You could also take a trip a few miles north of the city to **Cockington Green.** Or spend a couple of days in **Kosciuszko National Park,** in southern New South Wales. The main summer activities are hiking, fishing, and horseback riding; in winter (June–October), both cross-country and downhill skiing are options.

Although locals maintain otherwise, Canberra can be difficult to negotiate by car, given its radial roads, erratic signage, and often large distances between suburbs. The best solution is to buy a good street map and try to relax about missing turnoffs and ending up on the wrong radial roads. Maps highlighting scenic drives are available from the Canberra Visitor Centre for A$2.20. Canberra's ACTION buses can get you around town comfortably and without stress.

Numbers in the text correspond to numbers in the margin and on the Canberra map.

When to Visit

February to April, when autumn leaves paint the city parks with amber, is a particularly good time to visit Canberra. This time also coincides with the theater, dance, musical productions, open-air film festival, and jazz and rock concerts of the February Canberra National Multicultural Festival. This event, which incorporates the international Hot Air Balloon Fiesta, is just one of the celebrations leading up to Canberra Days festivities in March. The spring flower celebration, Floriade, lasts from mid-September to mid-October.

CENTRAL CANBERRA

This self-drive tour takes in virtually all of central Canberra's major attractions, including the Parliamentary Triangle buildings, the lakeside sights, and the Australian War Memorial.

a good tour

From the city center, head first to the **Australian War Memorial ❶** ▶, at the top of Anzac Parade, one of the nation's most popular attractions. Next, stop at Regatta Point for excellent views of **Lake Burley Griffin ❷** and the **Captain Cook Memorial Jet ❸**, a spectacular fountain that rockets a plume of water far above the lake. This is also the location for the **National Capital Exhibition ❹**, which not only explains how the city was planned and built, but also reveals the civic secrets of Canberra's present and future with videos, models, and audiovisual displays.

There is plenty to see at the next stop, over Commonwealth Avenue Bridge to the lake's southern shore and the Parliamentary Triangle: the **National Library of Australia ❺**, the interactive **Questacon—The National Science and Technology Centre ❻**, the **High Court of Australia ❼**, and the **National Gallery of Australia ❽**, the country's premier art gallery. You could easily spend an entire morning or afternoon exploring Questacon and the National Gallery, but for most visitors, the National Library and High Court deserve only a quick glance.

The nearby **Old Parliament House ❾** once served as the hub of national politics, but this gracious old building now houses the National Portrait Gallery. Farther up Capital Hill, sprawling **Parliament House ❿**, a striking contrast to its humble predecessor, merits an extended visit.

After visiting Parliament House circle the **Yarralumla Diplomatic Missions ⓫** before stopping at the **Royal Australian Mint ⓬**. Next head to the **National Zoo and Aquarium ⓭**, a must-see if you have not yet experienced Australia's unique indigenous birds, animals, and marine life. Allow plenty of time for the **National Museum of Australia ⓮**, which explores the culture, history, and landscape that make Australia unique.

Finally, climb to the summit of Black Mountain, capped by the 600-foot-high **Telstra Tower ⓯**, which commands spectacular views of the city, lake, and surrounding countryside. At the foot of the mountain are the **Australian National Botanic Gardens ⓰**, which contain superb displays of native flora.

TIMING
You could squeeze this entire tour into one very busy day, but it would not do justice to Parliament House or any of the major museums or galleries. To accommodate these, split the tour into two parts. Wind up the first day with a visit to the National Gallery of Australia and resume your sightseeing on the following day at Old Parliament House.

The major galleries and museums—particularly the Australian War Memorial, the National Museum of Australia, the National Gallery, and Questacon—draw large crowds on weekends, so explore these on a weekday if you can.

What to See

Australian-American Memorial. This slender memorial with an eagle at its summit was unveiled in 1954 to commemorate the role of American forces in the defense of Australia during World War II. The monument stands near the northern side of Kings Avenue Bridge, surrounded by

3

In its academies, museums, galleries, and public buildings, Canberra eloquently symbolizes the modern, sophisticated, technologically advanced nation that it leads. And yet, buried among tall forested hills that ring with the sounds of wild Australia, Canberra can frustrate the best intentions. The pristine lawns that lap against the brick villas of suburbia are still singed when the Australian summer turns on its blast-furnace heat and water restrictions come into force. Canberra makes the most of its situation with local parks, cycle paths, state-of-the-art sporting facilities, and nearby national parks with easy access.

City Dining
Despite the city's modest size, Canberra's dining scene has been spurred to culinary heights by the youth, affluence, and sophisticated tastes of its inhabitants. Canberra now claims to have more restaurants per person than any other city in Australia, and the very best would fare well against restaurants in Sydney or Melbourne.

Hotels & Homesteads
Until the past decade or so, Canberra's hotels for the most part offered only modern utilitarian facilities. Today's accommodations, however, meet the highest standards in comfort and amenities, particularly with the trend toward serviced apartment-style hotels with kitchen facilities. Country homesteads tucked away in the surrounding mountain ranges also provide a chance to experience life on working sheep and cattle farms—often in magnificently rugged surroundings—without sacrificing creature comforts. Generally, however, these lodgings are too distant from Canberra to serve as a practical base for exploring the national capital.

Galleries, Museums & Public Buildings
With more than 30 national institutions, Canberra has an impressive array of museums, art galleries, and public buildings to visit. The vast, modern Parliament House is the most famous of these, but the National Gallery of Australia, Questacon—the National Science and Technology Centre, the Australian Institute of Sport, and the Australian War Memorial provide no less fascinating glimpses into the nation's history, character, and aspirations.

Parks, Reserves & the Great Outdoors
Canberra's surrounding mountain ranges and river valleys, combined with the crisp spring and autumn weather, allow for several invigorating outdoor pursuits. Within the A. C. T. itself lie a national park, a nature reserve, and vast areas of bush- and parkland that are great for walks. Lake Burley Griffin and its environs provide a scenic backdrop for walking and cycling. Kosciuszko National Park and the New South Wales snowfields are also within easy reach of the capital, far closer than they are to Sydney.

---

the government departments in charge of Australia's armed services. ⊠ *Russell Dr., Russell.*

🔟 **Australian National Botanic Gardens.** Australian plants and trees have evolved in isolation from the rest of the world, and these delightful gardens on the lower slopes of Black Mountain display the continent's best

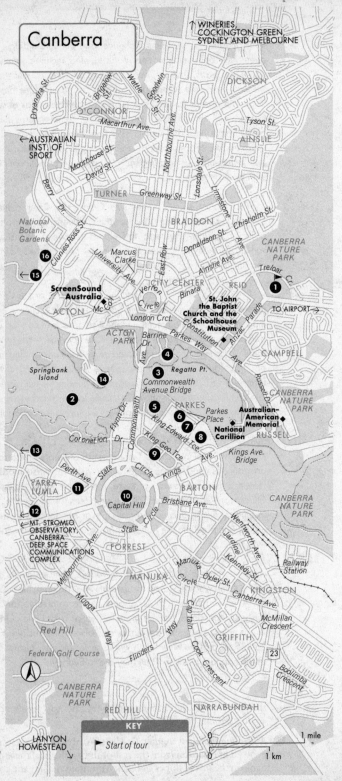

Canberra

WINERIES,
COCKINGTON GREEN,
SYDNEY AND MELBOURNE

←AUSTRALIAN
INST. OF
SPORT

KEY

▶ Start of tour

collection of this unique flora. The rain forest, rock gardens, Tasmanian alpine garden, and eucalyptus lawn—with more than 600 species of eucalyptus—number among the 125-acre site's highlights. Two self-guided nature trails start from the rain-forest gully, and free guided tours depart from the visitor center at 11 on weekdays, 11 and 2 on weekends. It costs A$1.10 per hour or A$4.40 per day to park. If you like to walk, you'll find free parking along the nearby streets. ☒ *Clunies Ross St., Black Mountain, Acton* ☎ *02/6250–9540* ⊕ *www.anbg.gov.au* ☒ *Free* ☉ *Gardens Jan.–Feb., daily 9–8; Mar.–Dec., daily 9–5. Visitor center daily 9:30–4:30.*

⬤ 1 Australian War Memorial. Both as a memorial to Australians who served

Fodor's Choice ★ their country in wartime and as a military museum, this is a shrine of great national importance and the most popular attraction in the national capital. Exhibits in the museum, which is built roughly in the shape of a Byzantine church, cover the period from the Sudan campaign of the late 19th century to the Vietnam War. Displays include a Lancaster bomber, a Spitfire, tanks, landing barges, the giant German Amiens gun, and sections of two of the Japanese midget submarines that infiltrated Sydney Harbour during World War II. The memorial is the focus of Canberra's powerful Anzac Day ceremony, honoring fallen members of Australia's armed forces, held on April 25. Free guided tours take place daily at 10, 10:30, 11, 1:30, and 2.

You can best appreciate the impressive facade of the War Memorial from the broad avenue of **Anzac Parade.** Anzac is an acronym for the Australian and New Zealand Army Corps, formed during World War I. The avenue is flanked by several memorials commemorating the army, navy, air force, and nursing corps, as well as some of the campaigns in which Australian troops have fought, including the Vietnam War. The red gravel used on Anzac Parade symbolizes the blood of Australians spilled in war. ☒ *Anzac Parade at Limestone Ave., Campbell* ☎ *02/6243–4211* ⊕ *www.awm.gov.au* ☒ *Free* ☉ *Daily 10–5.*

❸ Captain Cook Memorial Jet. This water jet in ⇨ **Lake Burley Griffin,** off Commonwealth Park's Regatta Point, commemorates James Cook's discovery of the east coast of Australia in 1770. On windless days the jet spurts a 6-ton plume of water 490 feet into the sky—making this one of the world's highest fountains.

❼ High Court of Australia. As its name implies, this gleaming concrete-and-glass structure is the ultimate court of law in the nation's judicial system. The court of seven justices convenes only to determine constitutional matters or major principles of law. Inside the main entrance of the building, the public hall contains a number of murals depicting various constitutional and geographic themes. Each of the three courtrooms over which the justices preside has a public gallery, and you can observe the proceedings when the court is in session. ☒ *King Edward Terr., Parkes* ☎ *02/6270–6811 or 02/6270–6850* ☒ *Free* ☉ *Daily 9:45–4:30.*

❷ Lake Burley Griffin. At the very heart of the city, this large lake is one of Canberra's most captivating features. The parks that surround the lake are ideal for walking and cycling, and you can hire bikes and boats from Acton Park on the northern shore.

❹ National Capital Exhibition. Photographs, plans, audiovisual displays, and a laser model inside this lakeside pavilion illustrate the past, present, and future development of the national capital. Exhibits cover the time of the early settlers, Walter Burley Griffin's winning design for the city, and city plans for the coming decades. From the pavilion's terrace there are sweeping views of the Parliamentary Triangle across the lake: the

National Library on the right and the National Gallery on the left form the base of the Parliamentary Triangle, which rises toward its apex at Parliament House on Capital Hill. The terrace makes a great spot from which to photograph the lakeside buildings and the Captain Cook Memorial Jet. The restaurant and kiosk on the terrace serve full meals and light snacks. If the sun is shining you can sit down at a table, relax, and enjoy the scenery. ⊠ *Regatta Point, Commonwealth Park* ☎ *02/ 6257–1068* ⧆ *Free* ⊙ *Daily 9–5.*

National Carillon. The tall, elegant bell tower on Lake Burley Griffin's Aspen Island was a gift from the British government to mark Canberra's 50th anniversary in 1963. The carillon consists of 53 bells, and 45-minute recitals are played at 12:45 every weekday December–February (Wednesday only June–August), 2:45 weekends and public holidays, and 5:45 Thursdays during summer. The music ranges from popular songs to hymns and special carillon compositions. ⊠ *Aspen Island, off Wendouree Dr., Parkes* ☎ *02/6271–2888.*

❽ **National Gallery of Australia.** The nation's premier art gallery contains a sprinkling of works by the masters, including Rodin, Picasso, Pollock, and Warhol, but its real strength lies in its Australian artwork. The gallery houses the most comprehensive collection of Australian art in the country, with superlative works of Aboriginal art as well as paintings by such famous native sons as Arthur Streeton, Sir Sidney Nolan, Tom Roberts, and Arthur Boyd. An excellent bookshop stocks an extensive selection of Australian art postcards, and you can grab a bite to eat at the restaurant or café. Free guided tours commence from the foyer at 11 and 2 each day. Although admission is free, there's usually a fee for special-interest exhibitions, which often display artwork from around the world. ⊠ *Parkes Pl., Parkes* ☎ *02/6240–6502* ⊕ *www.nga.gov.au* ⧆ *Free; fee for special exhibits* ⊙ *Daily 10–5.*

need a break? There are a couple of good spots to catch your breath amid the Parliamentary Triangle's mix of history, culture, and science. **Bookplate** (⊠ Parkes Pl., Parkes ☎ 02/6262–1154), in the foyer of the National Library, serves breakfast, lunch, and great coffee weekdays 8:30–6 and weekends 11–3. The **Juniperberry Café** (⊠ Parkes Pl., Parkes ☎ 02/6240–6666), on the ground floor of the National Gallery, serves snacks daily 10–4.

❺ **National Library of Australia.** A treasury of knowledge, constructed loosely on the design of the Parthenon in Athens, the library houses more than 5 million books and 500,000 aerial photographs, maps, drawings, and recordings of oral history. Changing exhibitions are displayed in the ground floor gallery. ⊠ *Parkes Pl., Parkes* ☎ *02/6262–1111* ⊕ *www. nla.gov.au* ⧆ *Free* ⊙ *Mon.–Thurs. 9–9, Fri.–Sun. 9–5; guided 1-hr tour Tues. at 12:30.*

❿❹ **National Museum of Australia.** This comprehensive museum is spectacularly located on Acton Peninsula, thrust out over the calm waters of Lake Burley Griffin. The museum highlights the stories of Australia and Australians by exploring the key people, events, and issues that shaped and influenced the nation. The numerous exhibitions focus on rare and unique objects that illustrate the continent's complex origins. Memorabilia include the carcass of the extinct Tasmanian tiger, the old Bentley beloved by former Prime Minister Robert Menzies, and the black baby garments worn by dingo victim Azaria Chamberlain. ⊠ *Acton Peninsula* ☎ *02/6208–5000 or 1800/026132* ⊕ *www.nma.gov.au* ⧆ *Free; fee for special exhibits* ⊙ *Daily 9–5.*

FodorsChoice ★

National Zoo and Aquarium. Display tanks alive with coral, sharks, rays, and exotic fish let you take a fish-eye's view of the underwater world. An adjoining 15-acre wildlife sanctuary is a bushland park that provides a habitat for the more remarkable species of Australia's fauna: emus, koalas, penguins, dingoes, kangaroos, and Tasmanian devils. ⊠ *Lady Denman Dr., Scrivener Dam, Yarralumla* ☎ *02/6287–1211* ⊕ *www. zooquarium.com.au* ✆ *A$18.50* ⊙ *Daily 9–5.*

Old Parliament House. Built in 1927, this long white building was meant to serve only as a temporary seat of government, but it was more than 60 years before its much larger successor was finally completed on the hill behind it. Now that the politicians have moved out, the renovated building is open for public inspection. Guided tours, departing from Kings Hall on the half-hour, take you through the legislative chambers, party rooms, and suites that once belonged to the prime minister and the president of the Senate. Old Parliament House also contains the expanding **National Portrait Gallery**, which displays likenesses of important Australians past and present. In the old House of Representatives, you can watch a 45-minute sound-and-light show entitled, appropriately, *Order! Order!* While you're in the area, take a stroll through the delightful **Senate Rose Gardens**. ⊠ *King George Terr., Parkes* ☎ *1300/652020* ✆ *A$2, including sound-and-light show* ⊙ *Daily 9–5; sound-and-light show at noon and 4:15.*

Parliament House. Much of this vast futuristic structure is submerged, covered by a domed glass roof that follows the contours of Capital Hill. From a distance, the most striking feature of the building is its 250-foot flagpole. Although it might look from afar only as big as a postage stamp, the Australian flag that flies night and day from the top is actually the size of a double-decker bus.

Fodor'sChoice
★

The design for the Parliament House was chosen in an international contest that attracted more than 300 entries. The New York firm of Mitchell, Giurgola & Thorp won the contest with a design that merged structural elegance with the natural environment. Work commenced in 1980, and the building was completed for the Australian Bicentennial in 1988.

You approach the building across a vast courtyard with a central mosaic entitled *Meeting Place,* designed by Aboriginal artist Nelson Tjakamarra. Native timber has been used almost exclusively throughout the building, and the work of some of Australia's finest contemporary artists hangs on the walls.

Parliament generally sits Monday–Thursday mid-February–late June and mid-August–mid-December. Both chambers have public galleries, but the debates in the House of Representatives, where the prime minister sits, are livelier and more newsworthy than those in the Senate. The best time to observe the House of Representatives is during **Question Time** (☎ 02/6277–4889 sergeant-at-arms' office), starting at 2, when the government and the opposition are most likely to be at each other's throats. To secure a ticket for Question Time, contact the sergeant-at-arms' office. Book a week in advance, if possible. Guided tours take place every half hour from 9 to 4. ⊠ *Capital Hill* ☎ *02/6277–5399* ⊕ *www.aph. gov.au* ✆ *Free* ⊙ *Daily 9–5 (later when Parliament is sitting).*

Questacon—The National Science and Technology Centre. This interactive science facility is the city's most entertaining museum. With several display halls built around a central gallery, Questacon entertains and educates with about 200 hands-on exhibits. High-tech computer gadgetry is used along with anything from pendulums to feathers to illustrate principles of mathematics, physics, and human perception. Staff members are on hand to explain the scientific principles behind the exhibits, and intriguing science shows take place regularly. This stimulating, participative environment is highly addictive and great fun—you're likely to have trouble getting out in less than a couple of hours. ⊠ *King Edward Terr., Parkes* ☎ *02/6270–2800* ⊕ *www.questacon.edu.au* ⊠ *A$10* ⊙ *Daily 9–5.*

⑫ **Royal Australian Mint.** If you really want to know how to make money, this is the place to visit. The observation gallery inside the mint has a series of windows where you can watch Australian coins being minted. Blanks are brought from the basement storage level up to the furnaces, where they are softened and finally sent to the presses to be stamped. The foyer has a display of rare coins, and silver and gold commemorative coins are for sale. There is no coin production on weekends or from noon to 12:40 on weekdays. ⊠ *Denison St., Deakin* ☎ *02/6202–6819* ⊕ *www.ramint.gov.au* ⊠ *Free* ⊙ *Weekdays 9–4, weekends 10–4.*

St. John the Baptist Church and the Schoolhouse Museum. These are the oldest surviving buildings in the Canberra district. When they were constructed in the 1840s, the land was part of a 4,000-acre property that belonged to Robert Campbell, a well-known Sydney merchant. The homestead, Duntroon, remained in the Campbell family until it was purchased by the government as a site for the Royal Military College. The schoolhouse is now a small museum with relics from the early history of the area. ⊠ *Constitution Ave., Reid* ☎ *02/6249–6839* ⊠ *Museum A$2.20, church free* ⊙ *Museum Wed. 10–noon, weekends 2–4; church daily 9–5.*

ScreenSound Australia. Australia's movie industry was booming during the early years of the 20th century, but it ultimately couldn't compete with the sophistication and volume of imported films. Concern that film stock and sound recordings of national importance would be lost prompted the construction of this edifice to preserve Australia's movie and musical heritage. The archive contains an impressive display of Australian moviemaking skills, including a short film that was shot on Melbourne Cup Day in 1896—the oldest film in the collection. Special exhibitions focus on aspects of the industry ranging from rock music to historic newsreels. ⊠ *McCoy Circuit, Acton* ☎ *02/6248–2000* ⊕ *www. screensound.gov.au* ⊠ *Free* ⊙ *Weekdays 9–5, weekends 10–5.*

⑮ **Telstra Tower.** The city's tallest landmark, this 600-foot structure on the top of Black Mountain is one of the best places to begin any tour of the national capital. Three observation platforms afford breathtaking views of the entire city as well as the mountain ranges to the south. The tower houses an exhibition on the history of telecommunications in Australia and a revolving restaurant with a spectacular nighttime panorama. The structure provides a communications link between Canberra and the rest of the country and serves as a broadcasting station for radio and television networks. The tower's massive scale and futuristic style caused a public outcry when it was built in 1980. ⊠ *Black Mountain Dr., Acton* ☎ *02/6219–6111 or 1800/806718* ⊠ *A$3.30* ⊙ *Daily 9 AM–10 PM.*

⑪ **Yarralumla Diplomatic Missions.** The expensive, leafy suburb of Yarralumla, west and north of Parliament House, contains many of the city's 70 or so diplomatic missions, most of which have been built in styles that reflect the home country's architecture. Some of these were established when Canberra was little more than a small country town, and it was only with great reluctance that many ambassadors and their staffs were persuaded to transfer from the temporary capital in Melbourne.

The Williamsburg-style **U.S. Embassy** occupies a commanding position on a hilltop across from Parliament House. Other embassies of architectural interest include the handsome white neoclassical building of the **South African Embassy** on State Circle, the **Indian High Commission** on Turrana Street, the unmistakable **Chinese Embassy** on Coronation Drive, the **High Commission of Papua New Guinea** on Forster Crescent, the **Embassy of Indonesia** and the **Embassy of Finland** on Darwin Avenue, and the **Embassy of Thailand** on Empire Circuit. Some of these embassies and high commissions open their doors for public inspection on special occasions. For more details, contact the Canberra Visitor Centre.

Around Canberra & the A. C. T.

Canberra's suburbs and the rural regions of the A. C. T. provide a variety of lesser attractions. These include the Australian Institute of Sport, a nature reserve with native animals, two national parks, a historic homestead, and Canberra's important contribution to the space race. You will need a car to reach these attractions.

TIMING Don't try to cram all of these sights into one outing; instead, choose a few places to visit over the course of a day or two. The Australian Institute of Sport and Cockington Green are within 15 minutes of the city. The Canberra Deep Space Communications Complex and Lanyon Homestead are twice as far. Namadgi National Park and Tidbinbilla Nature Reserve are 45–60 minutes south and west, respectively. A trip to Kosciuszko National Park warrants at least a couple of days in itself.

What to See

Australian Institute of Sport (AIS). Established to improve the performance of Australia's elite athletes, this 150-acre site north of the city comprises athletic fields, a swimming center, an indoor sports stadium, and a sports-medicine center. Olympic and other athletes train here for archery, gymnastics, swimming, soccer, and other sports. You'll need to join one of the daily 1½-hour tours, some guided by AIS athletes, to explore the institute, but you're welcome to use some of the facilities, including the swimming pool and tennis courts, for a reasonable fee. Half of the tour takes in visits to the various facilities, where you may be able to watch some of the institute's squads in training. The remaining time is spent in the **Sports Visitors Centre.** Here displays and a video wall focus on AIS athletes and the achievements of Australian sporting stars, and there are many fun hands-on exhibits. ⊠ *Leverrier Crescent, Bruce* ☏ *02/ 6214–1010* ⊕ *www.aisport.com.au* ✉ *Guided tour A$12* ⊙ *Weekdays 8:30–4:45, weekends 9:45–4:15. Tours daily at 10, 11:30, 1, and 2:30.*

Canberra Deep Space Communications Complex. Managed and operated by the Commonwealth Scientific and Industrial Research Organization (CSIRO), this is one of just three tracking stations in the world linked to the Deep Space control center, the long-distance arms of the U.S. National Aeronautics and Space Administration (NASA). The function of the four giant antennae at the site is to relay commands and data between NASA and space vehicles or orbiting satellites. The first pictures of men walking on the moon were transmitted to this tracking station. The station, located 40 km (25 mi) southwest of Canberra, is not open to the public, but the visitor information center houses models, audio-visual displays, and memorabilia from space missions. ⊠ *Off Paddy's River Rd., Tidbinbilla* ☏ *02/6201–7880* ⊕ *www.cdscc.nasa.gov* ✉ *Free* ⊙ *Apr.–Oct., daily 9–5; Nov.–Mar., daily 9–8.*

Cockington Green. Thatch-roof houses, castles, and canals have been reproduced in small scale to create a miniature slice of England on this 5-acre site. The display also has the Heritage Rose Walk, with its splendid display of roses, and the Torquay Restaurant, which serves contemporary cuisine as well as such suitably British dishes as steak-and-kidney pie and roast beef with Yorkshire pudding. The park is about 11 km (7 mi) north of the city center, off the Barton Highway. ⊠ *11 Gold Creek Rd., Gold Creek Village, Nicholls* ☎ *02/6230–2273 or 1800/627273* ⊕ *www.cockington-green.com.au* ✏ *A$11.50* ⊙ *Daily 9:30–4:30.*

Kosciuszko National Park. Kosciuszko is a wonderful alpine park, and Australia's largest. It's actually in New South Wales, although a segment of its boundary does touch the A. C. T. The gateway city, Cooma, is only 114 km (71 mi) from Canberra.

Lanyon Homestead. When it was built in 1859 on the plain beside the Murrumbidgee River, this classic homestead from pioneering days was the centerpiece of a self-contained community. Many of the outbuildings and workshops have been magnificently restored and preserved. The adjacent **Nolan Gallery** (☎ 02/6237–5192) displays a selection of the well-known Ned Kelly paintings by the famous Australian painter Sir Sidney Nolan. The property is 30 km (19 mi) south of Canberra off the Monaro Highway. ⊠ *Tharwa Dr., Tharwa* ☎ *02/6237–5136* ✏ *Homestead A$7, combined with gallery A$8* ⊙ *Tues.–Sun. 10–4.*

Mt. Stromlo Observatory. Australia has been a leader in the field of astronomy, and the telescope at Mt. Stromlo Observatory was the first in the country, built in 1924. The observatory is a hands-on astronomy-and-science center enabling you to explore the universe through telescopes and interactive exhibits. ⊠ *Cotter Rd., Weston Creek* ☎ *02/ 6125–0232* ✏ *A$6* ⊙ *Daily 9:30–4:30.*

Namadgi National Park. Covering almost half the total area of the Australian Capital Territory's southwest, this national park has a well-maintained network of walking trails through mountain ranges, trout streams, and some of the most accessible subalpine forests in the country. The park's boundaries are within 30 km (19 mi) of Canberra, and its former pastures, now empty of sheep and cattle, are grazed by hundreds of eastern gray kangaroos in the early mornings and late afternoons. There are 150 km (93 mi) of marked walking tracks, and at Yankee Hat, off the Naas/ Boboyan Road, you can visit an Aboriginal rock-art site.

The remote parts of the park have superb terrain, but you must be an experienced navigator of wild country to explore them. Snow covers the higher altitudes June–September. The Namadgi Visitors Centre (open weekdays 9–4, weekends 9–4:30) is on the Naas/Boboyan Road, 3 km (2 mi) south of the village of Tharwa. ⊠ *Namadgi National Park, via Tharwa* ☎ *02/6207–2900.*

Tidbinbilla Nature Reserve. Set in eucalyptus forests in the mountain ranges 40 km (25 mi) southwest of Canberra, this 12,000-acre reserve has large walk-through enclosures, where you can observe kangaroos, wallabies, and koalas in their native environment. The walking trails cross rocky mountaintops, open grassland, and gullies thick with tree ferns. The reserve also has some unusual rock formations, including Hanging Rock, a granite outcrop once used as a shelter by the Aboriginal inhabitants of the area. Bird-watchers should plan to visit during the 2:30 feeding time, when many colorful species can be seen and photographed at close quarters. Ranger-guided walks—including evening wildlife-spotlighting tours and strolls in search of koalas and platypuses—take place on weekends and during school holidays. The visitor center has a slide show and nocturnal animals exhibit. ⊠ *Paddy's River Rd., Tidbinbilla* ☎ *02/6205–1233* ✏ *A$9.20* ⊙ *Nov.–Mar., daily 9–8; Apr.–Oct., daily 9–6. Visitor center weekdays 9–4:30, weekends 9–5:30.*

Wineries. In the past decade or so, the Canberra region has seen a huge growth in the number of wineries, which produce a range of quality cool-climate chardonnays, Rieslings, cabernets, and merlots to rival the very best Australian medal winners. Most of the wineries are open for touring and tastings. Collect a tour planner of the wineries from the Canberra Visitor Centre, or from the **Kamberra Wine Centre** (✉ Flemington Rd. at Northbourne Ave., Lyneham, ☎ 02/6262–2333) at the northern entrance to Canberra overlooking the Canberra Racecourse. Among the well-respected wineries are Helms, Brindabella Hills, Madews, Doonkuna Estate, Jeir Creek, Clonakilla, Pialligo Estate, and Lark Hill.

WHERE TO EAT

Based on its population, Canberra has more restaurants per person than any other city in Australia, and the variety reflects the city's cosmopolitan nature. In addition to eclectic Australian and fusion restaurants, you'll find authentic French, Italian, Turkish, Vietnamese, and Chinese dining options, among many others. Overall the standards for food and service can compete with the larger cities, and while the look can be stylish—particularly at the latest upstarts—the feeling is generally casual.

The main restaurant precincts are around the city center and in the trendy suburbs of Manuka and Kingston. However, you'll find many fine eateries tucked away in such small suburban centers as Dickson (Canberra's Chinatown), Griffith, and Woden.

WHAT IT COSTS In Australian Dollars					
	$$$$	$$$	$$	$	¢
RESTAURANTS	over $50	$36–$50	$21–$35	$10–$20	under $10

Restaurant prices are per person for a main course at dinner.

Central Canberra & Northern Suburbs

ITALIAN
$$
✕ **Mezzalira on London.** Sleek and glossy, this city-center Italian restaurant is the fashionable gathering place for Canberra's smart set. The menu varies from robust pasta dishes and pizzas to char-grilled salmon with arugula and balsamic vinegar, grilled Italian sausages with truffle-oil mash, and grilled vegetables in a red-wine sauce. Pizzas from the wood-fired oven make for good casual dining at a modest price. The espresso enjoys a reputation as Canberra's finest. ✉ *Melbourne Building, West Row and London Circuit, Canberra City* ☎ *02/6230–0025* ▤ *AE, DC, MC, V* ⊘ *Closed Sun.*

$
✕ **Tosolini's.** A long-standing favorite with Canberra's café society, this Italian-accented brasserie offers a choice of indoor or sidewalk-table eating and a menu that works hard from breakfast through dinner. Among the items you can order are fresh fruit juices, fruit shakes, focaccia, and a small selection of main meals of pasta, risotto, and pizzas. The coffee is particularly good, and the cakes have an enthusiastic following. Try to plan lunch for before or after the noon–2 crush. The owners also have a more upscale branch in Manuka. ✉ *East Row and London Circuit, Canberra City* ☎ *02/6247–4317* ✉ *2 Furneaux St., Manuka* ☎ *02/6232–6600* ▤ *AE, DC, MC, V* ⊟ *BYOB (bottled wine only)* ⊘ *No dinner Sun.–Tues.*

MODERN
AUSTRALIAN
$$–$$$
Fodor'sChoice
★
✕ **Boat House by the Lake.** There is something restful about looking out over the water of Lake Burley Griffin as you dine on the superb food of this modern, airy restaurant. High ceilings give the restaurant a spacious, open feel, and tall windows provide lovely views of the lake. Choices are unusual and innovative, such as rare roasted kangaroo fillet with

emu crouton, served with lemon balm salad and a spicy garlic sauce. There is a variety of excellent wines to go with your meal—and save room for the scrumptious desserts. ⊠ *Grevilliea Park, Menindie Dr., Barton* ☎ *02/6273–5500* ⌲ *Recommended* ⊟ *AE, DC, MC, V* ☉ *Closed Sun. No lunch Sat.*

$$ ✕ **Anise.** Here you'll find a calm, relaxing haven amid the many restaurants and bars of Canberra's West Row dining strip. Have a drink at the quiet bar before being seated at one of the well-spaced, damask-covered tables. Filling selections include the roast veal rump with baby artichokes, peas, pancetta, and roasted garlic. ⊠ *20 West Row* ☎ *02/6257–0700* ⊟ *DC, MC, V* ☉ *Closed Sun. and Mon. No lunch Sat.*

$$ ✕ **Fringe Benefits.** Creative food served in spacious, stylish surroundings is the specialty of this top Canberra restaurant located on the city's outer edge. The menu plunders freely from East and West to concoct dishes such as duck sausages with lentils, deep-fried quail with coriander jam, ginger-cured salmon with saffron risotto, and a decadent chocolate mousse. The wine cellar here is impressive, and you can sample vintages by the bottle or by the glass. ⊠ *54 Marcus Clarke St., Canberra City* ☎ *02/6247–4042* ⊟ *AE, DC, MC, V* ☉ *Closed Sun. No lunch Sat.*

PAN-ASIAN ✕ **The Chairman and Yip.** The menu garners universal praise for its in-
$$ novative mix of Asian and Western flavors against a backdrop of arti-
Fodor'sChoice facts from Maoist China. Among other items on the menu, you'll find
★ duck pancakes and steamed barramundi with kumquats, ginger, and shallots. Finish with a delicious dessert, such as cinnamon-and-star-anise crème brûlée. The service and wine list are outstanding. ⊠ *108 Bunda St., Canberra City* ☎ *02/6248–7109* ⌲ *Reservations essential* ⊟ *AE, DC, MC, V* ᵇ *BYOB (bottled wine only)* ☉ *No lunch weekends.*

TURKISH ✕ **Ottoman.** Occupying an expansive space in the Parliamentary Trian-
$$ gle, this unique restaurant offers plush comfort amid Turkish decor. Though you'll be tempted to feast on the wonderful dips and appetizers, focus on the excellent entrees. Try the tender slices of veal, cooked in mild spices and served with a piquant lemon sauce on eggplant and baby spinach. ⊠ *Cnr. Broughton and Blackall Sts., Barton* ☎ *02/6273–6111* ⊟ *AE, DC, MC, V* ☉ *No lunch Sat.–Mon. No dinner Sun. and Mon.*

STEAK ✕ **Charcoal Restaurant.** Practically unchanged since it opened for busi-
$–$$ ness in the 1960s, this restaurant still serves the capital's best beef. Wooden panels and wine racks line the walls, and at night soft lights and maroon upholstery provide a romantic glow. The superb steaks vary from a half-pound sirloin to a monster 2-pounder. A limited selection of fish and poultry dishes is also available. The wine list has more than 100 varieties of Australian reds, including some local wines. ⊠ *61 London Circuit, Canberra City* ☎ *02/6248–8015* ⊟ *AE, DC, MC, V* ☉ *Closed Sun. No lunch Sat.*

VIETNAMESE ✕ **Little Saigon.** A relaxed, breezy atmosphere pervades the indoor and out-
$ door tables at this popular Vietnamese eatery. You'll find all the traditional favorites—including noodle dishes and salads—cooked with fresh ingredients and authentic spices. Groups often book banquets here, while locals grab quick, tasty take-away lunch boxes for A$5. ⊠ *Novotel Building, Alinga St., Canberra City* ☎ *02/6230–5003* ⊟ *DC, MC, V.*

Southern Suburbs

ECLECTIC ✕ **Rubicon.** The menu may be limited, but the ambience is cozy and friendly,
$$ and everything about this restaurant speaks of attention to detail. Take, for example, the organic, pan-roasted lamb rump, served with crisp parsnip and grilled pear, along with brandied kumquats and mint jus. Savor the

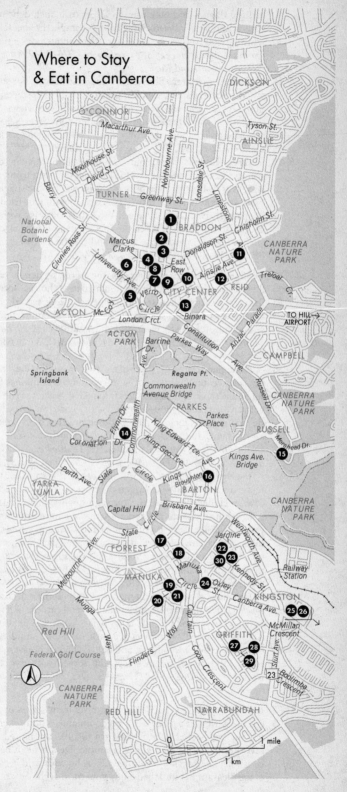

Where to Stay & Eat in Canberra

melting flavors and take time to linger over such delicious desserts as ginger- and lime-infused crème brûlée. Sample the cheese board and the wines, if you can, as the extensive selection includes a number of local varieties. ⊠ *6A Barker St., Griffith* ☎ *02/6295–9919* ▭ *DC, MC, V* ⊗ *Closed Sun. and Mon.*

★ **$$** ✕ **The Tryst.** Selections here suit all moods and tastes. For something spicy, try Moroccan pan-fried lamb, prepared with rich spices, a hint of balsamic oil, and served with couscous. You'll have views of the elegant, tree-lined lawns whether you dine inside or on the terrace. Stroll through the surrounding shops after your meal. ⊠ *Bougainville St., Manuka* ☎ *02/ 6239–4422* ▭ *AE, DC, MC, V* ⊗ *No dinner Sun.*

$–$$ ✕ **Verve.** Tables spill out onto the sidewalk of this hip, casual café, or you can view the passing parade through the open front. Pasta, curries, and meat dishes form the bulk of the menu. Try the spaghetti *pescatore* (with seafood) with al dente pasta, served with pan-fried seafood, garlic, parsley, basil, and olive oil. Weekends are busy with locals during breakfast and brunch, when the special menu lists a selection of old favorites: eggs, pancakes, waffles, and meats. ⊠ *Cnr. Franklin St. and Flinders Way, Manuka* ☎ *02/6239–4666* ▭ *MC, V.*

MODERN   ✕ **Atlantic.** As the name suggests, the emphasis here is on fish, but the
AUSTRALIAN   diverse menu lists plenty of other imaginative choices. Specialties include
$$ the stars of Australian seafood: blue-eyed cod, served with marinated artichoke salad and a soft poached egg, and salmon scallops, served with seared bug (crayfish) meat and dill potatoes. ⊠ *20 Palmerston La., Manuka* ☎ *02/6232–7888* ▭ *AE, DC, MC, V* ⊗ *Closed Sun. No lunch Sat.*

$$ ✕ **Aubergine.** The large, plate-glass windows of this cozy restaurant look
Fodor'sChoice   out onto relaxing parkland. A seasonal menu combines fresh produce,
★   subtle spices, and pungent sauces into such delicacies as pan-seared salmon with crusted prawn mousse, served with tomato and avocado salsa. Calorie-rich desserts include date pudding drizzled with Bailey's ice cream and caramel fudge sauce. The wine list includes some rare vintages from wineries around Australia. ⊠ *18 Barker St., Griffith* ☎ *02/ 6260–8666* ▭ *AE, DC, MC, V* ⊗ *No lunch weekends.*

★ **$$** ✕ **The Fig Café.** Despite its city-slick decor, this small local restaurant is relaxed and friendly—although the prices are far more serious than the café label might suggest. But the high-quality, highly imaginative food is worth it: fig game pie, served with olive mint and cannellini beans; yellow-fin tuna, served with fennel and *salade niçoise* (salad with egg, tuna, green beans, olives, and tomatoes); and lamb loin, served in a parsley-feta crust with a spinach tartlet. If the sun is shining, the courtyard is especially recommended for lunch. ⊠ *Shop 2, 4 Barker St., Griffith* ☎ *02/6295–6915* ▭ *AE, DC, MC, V* ⊗ *Closed Sun.–Mon.*

$–$$ ✕ **First Floor.** A spacious dining room and modern decor add spunk to this lively restaurant overlooking the peaceful gardens of Kingston's Green Square. Here, Mod Oz food takes Asian twists that tingle the taste buds. Among the excellent choices are garlic-and-chili squid sautéed in olive oil with parsley and onions, and baked chicken breast marinated in the house mixture of Indian spices and served with dal. ⊠ *Jardine St., Kingston* ☎ *02/6260–6311* ▭ *AE, DC, MC, V* ⊗ *Closed Sun. No lunch Sat.*

SOUTHWESTERN   ✕ **Tu Tu Tango.** This lively Manuka restaurant serves up southwestern
$ cuisine with flair and draws a predominantly youthful crowd. Specialties such as beef chili and blue-corn tortillas are paired with such old favorites as corn bread and guacamole. Desserts can be outrageously lavish; try the peach-and-orange gazpacho with wild berries. Sip drinks at the pleasant bar and then enjoy your meal at the outdoor dining area.

✉ *36–38 Franklin St., Manuka* ☎ *02/6239–4322* 🖃 *AE, DC, MC, V*
🍴 *BYOB.*

WHERE TO STAY

Canberra and its surrounding neighborhoods have comfortable, modern accommodations with a variety of room facilities and on-site activities. Standard in most rooms are color TVs, coffee- and tea-making equipment, and refrigerators. Most hotels have laundry and dry cleaning services; those that don't usually have laundry facilities. You can usually request hair dryers, irons, and other implements for personal grooming. Most hotels also have no-smoking rooms or floors, which you should be sure to reserve ahead of time.

WHAT IT COSTS In Australian Dollars				
$$$$	**$$$**	**$$**	**$**	**¢**
HOTELS over $300	$201–$300	$151–$200	$100–$150	under $100

Hotel prices are for two people in a standard double room in high season, including tax and service, based on the European Plan (with no meals) unless otherwise noted.

Canberra City & Northern Suburbs

$$ 🏨 **Chifley on Northbourne.** The rooms and facilities here rival those of some of Canberra's more expensive hotels. Dark timber furnishings, a piano, and an open fire create a cozy, clublike atmosphere in the reception area, while the olive-and-cinnamon color scheme and gum-leaf motif in the rooms provide a very Australian feel. The hotel is close to the city center, but it unfortunately overlooks one of the city's major arteries, so light sleepers should request a poolside room at the back of the hotel. ✉ *102 Northbourne Ave., Braddon, 2601* ☎ *02/6249–1411 or 1800/065064* 🖨 *02/6249–6878* ⊕ *www.chifleyhotels.com* 🛏 *68 rooms, 10 suites* ⚒ *Restaurant, in-room data ports, refrigerators, pool, gym, bar, dry cleaning, laundry service, business services, free parking* 🖃 *AE, DC, MC, V.*

$$ 🏨 **Crowne Plaza Canberra.** This atrium-style hotel, in a prime location between the city center and the National Convention Centre, has modern facilities and a moderate level of luxury. Decorated in cream and honey tones, guest rooms are large, comfortable, and well equipped. Public areas have a cool, contemporary style, with plenty of chrome and glass, giant potted plants, and fresh flowers. ✉ *1 Binara St., Canberra City, 2601* ☎ *02/6247–8999 or 1800/020055* 🖨 *02/6257–4903* ⊕ *www. crowneplazacanberra.com.au* 🛏 *287 rooms, 6 suites* ⚒ *2 restaurants, refrigerators, pool, gym, sauna, 2 bars, dry cleaning, laundry service, concierge, business services, free parking* 🖃 *AE, DC, MC, V.*

$$ 🏨 **Saville Park Suites.** Most of the accommodations at this hotel a block
FodorśChoice away from the city center are self-contained one- and two-bedroom suites
★ with spacious lounge and dining areas, full kitchens, and private balconies. Standard rooms are available for a lower price. Head down to the Zipp Restaurant and Wine Bar for delicious Mod Oz fare—or enjoy it in the luxury of your room. ✉ *84 Northbourne Ave., Canberra City, 2612* ☎ *02/6243–2500 or 1800/630588* 🖨 *02/6243–2599* ⊕ *www. savillesuites.com.au* 🛏 *52 rooms, 123 suites* ⚒ *Restaurant, in-room data ports, refrigerators, indoor pool, gym, sauna, bar, meeting rooms, free parking* 🖃 *AE, DC, MC, V.*

★ **$-$$** 🏨 **Argyle Executive Apartments.** Small groups enjoy the good value of these smart, comfy, fully self-contained two- and three-bedroom apartments barely a five-minute walk from the city center. Each unit has a large living and dining area, a separate kitchen with a microwave and dishwasher, a secure garage, and free laundry facilities. Set amid gardens, units have either a balcony or a private courtyard. Rates are available with and without maid service. ⊠ *Currong and Boolee Sts., Reid, 2612* ☎ *02/ 6275–0800* 🖷 *02/6275–0888* ⊕ *www.argyleapartments.com.au* ⌦ *30 apartments* ⚹ *Kitchens, refrigerators, laundry facilities, free parking* ⊟ *AE, DC, MC, V.*

$ 🖵 **Comfort Inn Downtown.** Travelers on a budget appreciate this excellent-value motel. Facilities are modern, and it's close to the city center. There are three types of rooms, some of which have kitchenettes, and the place is kept absolutely spotless. ⊠ *82 Northbourne Ave., Braddon, 2601* ☎ *02/6249–1388* 🖷 *02/6247–2523* ⊕ *www.comfortinn.com.au* ⌦ *61 rooms, 4 suites* ⚹ *Restaurant, some kitchenettes, gym, laundry facilities, free parking* ⊟ *AE, DC, MC, V.*

$ 🖵 **Olims Canberra Hotel.** Inside its original National Heritage–listed building and a modern addition built around a landscaped courtyard, this former pub—one of the city's first—has double rooms, split-level suites with kitchens, and two- and three-bedroom suites. Guest rooms and public spaces are contemporary in style, with laminated, pinelike wood finishes, fabrics and carpets tinged with red ocher, and beige walls. Rates are reduced Friday–Sunday. The hotel is about 1 km (½ mi) east of the city center, close to the Australian War Memorial. ⊠ *Ainslie and Limestone Aves., Braddon, 2601* ☎ *02/6248–5511* 🖷 *02/6247–0864 or 1800/020016* ⊘ *olimcanb@fc-hotels.com.au* ⌦ *77 rooms, 49 suites* ⚹ *2 restaurants, kitchenettes, refrigerators, bar, dry cleaning, laundry service, free parking* ⊟ *AE, DC, MC, V.*

Canberra South

$$$–$$$$ 🖵 **Hyatt Hotel Canberra.** This elegant hotel, the finest in the city, occu-
Fodor's Choice pies a 1924 National Heritage building that has been restored to its orig-
★ inal art deco style. Warm peaches and earth tones decorate the large, luxurious rooms and spacious suites. Enormous marble bathrooms will appeal to anyone who enjoys a good soak in the tub. The hotel has extensive gardens and is within easy walking distance of the Parliamentary Triangle. Afternoon tea, held daily between 2:30 and 5 in the gracious Tea Lounge, is one of Canberra's most popular traditions. ⊠ *Commonwealth Ave., Yarralumla, 2600* ☎ *02/6270–1234* 🖷 *02/ 6281–5998* ⊕ *www.canberra.hyatt.com* ⌦ *231 rooms, 18 suites* ⚹ *3 restaurants, room service, in-room data ports, in-room safes, minibars, refrigerators, tennis court, saltwater pool, gym, sauna, spa, 2 bars, dry cleaning, laundry service, concierge, business services, free parking* ⊟ *AE, DC, MC, V.*

$$–$$$ 🖵 **Rydges Capital Hill.** Rooms are spacious, airy, and comfortable at the
Fodor's Choice Rydges, one of Canberra's most luxurious hotels and a magnet for a
★ largely business clientele. Contemporary furnishings fill the standard rooms; the 38 Spa Suites and two Premier Suites are particularly sumptuous. The atrium ceiling is composed of immense fabric sails. The hotel is close to Parliament House, and in the evening its bar always has a stimulating flow of political gossip from parliamentary staff and members of the press, who drop in regularly. ⊠ *Canberra Ave. and National Circle, Forrest, 2603* ☎ *02/6295–3144* 🖷 *02/6295–3325* ⊕ *www. rydges.com.au* ⌦ *146 rooms, 40 suites* ⚹ *Restaurant, room service, refrigerators, pool, health club, sauna, spa, bar, dry cleaning, laundry service, concierge, business services, free parking* ⊟ *AE, DC, MC, V.*

$$–$$$ 🖵 **The York.** You'll find comfort and convenience at this family-owned boutique hotel in the heart of the trendy Kingston café area. Choose from roomy one-bedroom and two-bedroom suites or attractive studios that include a fully equipped kitchen, an en-suite bathroom, and a separate

dining and living room. All of the rooms have balconies, some overlooking a quiet garden courtyard. The chic Artespresso restaurant is also an art gallery displaying quality contemporary exhibitions. ✉ *Cnr. of Giles and Tench Sts., Kingston, 2603* ☎ *02/6295–2333* 🖷 *02/6295–9559* ⊕ *www.yorkcanberra.com.au* ⟿ *9 studios, 16 suites* ♨ *Restaurant, kitchens, laundry service, free parking* ▭ *AE, DC, MC, V.*

$–$$ ▥ **Manuka Park Apartments.** The comfortable one- and two-bedroom apartments and interconnecting suites in this low-rise building all have cooking facilities, a living room, and a laundry area. Fully carpeted, open-plan rooms have a clean, contemporary feel. In a leafy suburb, the units are within easy walking distance of the restaurants, boutiques, and antiques stores of the Manuka shopping district. Landscaped gardens surround the apartments, all of which have a private balcony or courtyard. ✉ *Manuka Circle and Oxley St., Manuka, 2603* ☎ *02/6239–0000 or 1800/688227* 🖷 *02/6295–7750* ⊕ *www.manukapark.com.au* ⟿ *40 apartments* ♨ *Kitchens, refrigerators, saltwater pool, free parking* ▭ *AE, DC, MC, V.*

¢–$ ▥ **Telopea Inn on the Park.** This motel lies in a tranquil, leafy southern suburb bordered by parklands and close to Parliament House. Though small, rooms are a good value, and the larger ones with kitchenettes appeal to families. ✉ *16 New South Wales Crescent, Forrest, 2603* ☎ *02/6295–3722* 🖷 *02/6239–6373* ⊕ *www.telopeainn.com.au* ⟿ *45 rooms* ♨ *Restaurant, some kitchenettes, refrigerators, pool, sauna, spa, bar, free parking* ▭ *AE, MC, V.*

Outside Canberra

$$$$ ▥ **Avalanche Homestead.** Perched on a hillside in the Tinderry Mountains, this large, modern homestead offers a taste of the "real" Australia. Rooms are spacious and comfortable, and dinners are splendid banquets served in a vast baronial hall. Daily activities include horseback riding, cattle mustering, sheep shearing, trout fishing, and bushwalking. The property is 45 km (28 mi) south of Canberra and adjoins an 80,000-acre nature reserve that abounds with kangaroos, wallabies, wombats, and colorful birds. Rates include all meals and activities. ✑ *Box 544, Burra Creek, Queanbeyan, 2620* ☎ *02/6236–3245* 🖷 *02/6236–3302* ⊕ *www.avalanchehomestead.com.au* ⟿ *6 rooms with shower, 1 with bath* ♨ *Pool, hiking, fishing, horseback riding, laundry service, free parking* ▭ *AE, DC, MC, V* ⊙ *All-inclusive.*

$ ▥ **Elmslea Homestead.** Surrounded by ancient elm trees and filled with a lifetime of history, this classic 1910 Federation-style homestead combines charm, grace, and character. The original dining room, kitchen, maid's room, laundry, and dairy, decorated in their original themes, have been transformed into guest quarters. Breakfast is included, and dinner can be provided by prior arrangement. Winery tours and balloon flights can be arranged, and there are several fine craft shops in nearby Bungendore, a small, rustic village 25 minutes downroad from Canberra. ✉ *80 Tarago Rd., Bungendore, 2621* ☎ *02/6238–1651* ⊕ *www.elmslea.com.au* ⟿ *5 rooms.* ♨ *Dining room, laundry service, free parking* ▭ *DC, MC, V* ⊙ *CP.*

NIGHTLIFE & THE ARTS

Canberra after dark has a reputation for being dull. Actually, the city isn't quite as boring as the rest of Australia thinks, nor as lively as the citizens of Canberra would like to believe. Most venues are clustered in the city center and the fashionable southern suburbs of Manuka and Kingston. Except on weekends, few places showcase live music. The Thursday edition of the *Canberra Times* has a "What's On" section.

The Arts

Canberra Theatre Centre. The city's premier arts and theater venue hosts productions by the local opera company, theatrical troupe, and symphony orchestra. Performances by such major national companies as the Australian Ballet are frequently held here. For a listing of current events check the entertainment pages of the *Canberra Times.* ⊠ *Civic Sq., London Circuit, Canberra City* ☎ *02/6257–1077* ⊕ *www.canberratheatre.org.au.*

Nightlife

Nightspots in the city center offer everything from laser light shows and noisy bands to dance and comedy clubs. Many waive cover charges except for special events.

Bobby McGee's. The party atmosphere at this flamboyant American-style restaurant and entertainment lounge appeals to a varied group. Service is slick and professional, and the staff is gregarious and spontaneous. ⊠ *Rydges Canberra Hotel, London Circuit, Canberra City* ☎ *02/6257-7999* 🖃 *No cover charge except for special events* ☉ *Weekdays 5 PM–3 AM, Sat. 7 PM–4 AM.*

Casino Canberra. An attempt was made to create a European-style facility by leaving out slot machines in favor of the more sociable games of roulette, blackjack, poker, minibaccarat, pai gow, and keno. There are 40 gaming tables here, and the complex includes a restaurant and two bars. ⊠ *21 Binara St., Canberra City* ☎ *02/6257-7074* ☉ *Daily noon–6 AM.*

Corvo's Wine and Oyster Bar. The amazing Beer Mountain—a pyramid-shape stack of beer bottles—behind the bar should be the first thing to grab your attention at this stylish bar in the heart of the city. The menu lists various oyster concoctions together with cocktails. This is *the* place to start the evening. A jazz band plays on some nights. ⊠ *Melbourne Building, West Row, Canberra City* ☎ *02/6262-7898* ☉ *Mon.–Thurs. 11 AM–11 PM, Fri. 11 AM–1 AM, Sat. 3 PM–1 AM, Sun. noon–8 PM.*

FMs. This modern club attracts a twentysomething crowd to hip DJ-spun music on weekends. ⊠ *40–42 Manuka Franklin St.* ☎ *02/6295-1845* 🖃 *No cover* ☉ *Tues.–Sat. 9 PM–3 AM.*

Holy Grail. With locations in the city center and south in Kingston, Holy Grail not only serves fabulous salads, pastas, and grills, but it also has great rhythm and blues bands playing Thursday through Sunday at 9 PM. Grab a comfortable table and meet friends over a glass of wine. ⊠ *Bunda St., Canberra City* ☎ *02/6257-9717* ⊠ *Green Sq., Kingston* ☎ *02/6295-6071* 🖃 *A$5 cover.*

ICBM and Insomnia. Professionals and students in their 20s and 30s dance to Top 40 hits at this loud, modern bar. Wednesday is Comedy Night, and a DJ spins tunes on Saturday. ⊠ *50 Northbourne Ave.* ☎ *02/6248-0102* 🖃 *A$5 Comedy Night show, A$5 Saturday DJ dance* ☉ *Wed.–Sat. 9 PM–2 AM.*

In Blue. Downstairs you'll you can step up to the cocktail and vodka bar while sampling terrific tapas and a variety of cigars. Then head upstairs to the nightclub, where DJs mix everything from dance to rhythm and blues. ⊠ *Cnr. Mort and Alinga Sts.* ☎ *02/6248-7405* 🖃 *No cover* ☉ *Daily 4 PM–3 AM.*

Minque. This relaxing bar is a great place to sit back and groove to the nightly music theme, which can range from rock to rhythm and blues.

✉ 17 *Manuka Franklin St.* ☎ *02/6295–8866* ✉ *No cover* ☉ *Tues.–Sun. 3–midnight.*

Tilley's Devine Café Gallery. This 1940s-style club was once for women only, but today anyone can sit at the wooden booths and listen to live bands, poetry readings, or comedy acts. Performances are held several times weekly, and you can either buy a ticket or catch one while you have a meal and a drink. ✉ *Wattle St., Lyneham* ☎ *02/6249–1543.*

SPORTS & THE OUTDOORS

Bicycling

Canberra has almost 160 km (100 mi) of cycle paths, and the city's relatively flat terrain and dry, mild climate make it a perfect place to explore on two wheels. One of the most popular cycle paths is the 40-km (25-mi) circuit around Lake Burley Griffin.

Mr. Spokes Bike Hire rents several different kinds of bikes as well as tandems and baby seats. Bikes cost A$12 for the first hour, including helmet rental, A$30 for a half day, and A$40 for a full day. ✉ *Barrine Dr., Acton Park* ☎ *02/6257–1188* ☉ *Closed Mon.–Tues. except during school holidays.*

Boating

Sit back and relax aboard the *MV Southern Cross* while cruising Lake Burley Griffin. Apart from seeing the important buildings, parks, and foreshore areas of the parliamentary Triangle, the A$14 cruise provides an insight into the history, culture, and ecology of the national capital. **Southern Cross Cruises** ✉ *Mariner Pl., Alexandrina Dr.* ☎ *02/6273–1784.*

You can rent aquabikes, surf skis, paddleboats, and canoes daily (except May–July) for use on Lake Burley Griffin from **Burley Griffin Boat Hire.** Rates start at A$12 for a half hour. ✉ *Barrine Dr., Acton Park* ☎ *02/6249–6861.*

Golf

On the lower slopes of Red Hill, the 18-hole, par-73 **Federal Golf Course** is regarded as the most challenging of the city's greens. Nonmembers are welcome on most weekdays provided they make advance bookings. ✉ *Red Hill Lookout Rd., Red Hill* ☎ *02/6281–1888* ✉ *Greens fee A$50.*

Among the top four courses in Canberra, the 18-hole, par-72 **Gold Creek Country Club** is a public course—with the added bonus of three practice holes and a driving range. Prices include a golf cart. ✉ *Harcourt Hill, Curran Dr., Nicholls* ☎ *02/6241–9888* ✉ *Greens fees A$40 weekdays, A$55 weekends.*

Another highly rated course is at the **Yowani Country Club,** 3 km (2 mi) north of the city. The club also has three first-class bowling greens, as well as convenient motel units for visitors. Built on flat terrain, the course is deceptively challenging, with heavily wooded fairways, water storage lakes, and tricky bunkers all coming into play. ✉ *Northbourne Ave., Lyneham* ☎ *02/6241–2303* ✉ *A$25 daily.*

Hiking

Namadgi National Park, Tidbinbilla Nature Reserve, and Kosciuszko National Park have excellent bushwalking tracks.

Hot-Air Ballooning

A spectacular way to see Canberra is on a hot-air balloon flight at dawn, which includes panoramas over Lake Burley Griffin and Parliament House. Prices start from A$170. **Balloon Aloft** (☎ 02/6285–1540). **Dawn Drifters** (☎ 02/6285–4450).

Running

A favorite running track is the 3-km (2-mi) circuit formed by Lake Burley Griffin and its two bridges, Kings Avenue Bridge and Commonwealth Avenue Bridge.

Tennis

The **National Sports Club** offers play on synthetic grass courts. ⊠ *Mouat St., Lyneham* ☎ *02/6247–0929* ✈ *A\$16 per hr during daylight, A\$20 per hr under lights* ⊘ *Daily 9 AM–10 PM.*

At the **Australian Institute of Sport** you can play on one of the establishment's six outdoor courts. ⊠ *Leverrier Crescent, Bruce* ☎ *02/6214–1281* ✈ *A\$12 per hr* ⊘ *Weekdays 8 AM–9 PM, weekends 8–7.*

SHOPPING

Canberra is not known for its shopping, but there are a number of high-quality arts-and-crafts outlets where you are likely to come across some unusual gifts and souvenirs. The city's markets are excellent, and the galleries and museums sell interesting and often innovative items designed and made in Australia. In addition to the following suggestions, there are several malls and shopping centers in Canberra City and the major suburban town centers.

Cuppacumbalong Craft Centre. A former pioneering homestead near the Murrumbidgee River, this is now a crafts gallery for potters, weavers, painters, and woodworkers, many of whom have their studios in the outbuildings. The quality of the work is universally high, and you can often meet and talk with the artisans. The center is about 34 km (21 mi) south of Canberra, off the Monaro Highway. ⊠ *Naas Rd., Tharwa* ☎ *02/6237–5116* ⊘ *Wed.–Sun. 11–5.*

Gold Creek Village. Next to Cockington Green on the city's northern outskirts, this complex of more than 20 specialty shops includes clothes, crafts, pottery, and gift stores. The large shopping center also has a restaurant, coffee shop, children's playground, and walk-in aviary. ⊠ *O'Hanlon Pl., Gold Creek Village, Gungahlin* ☎ *02/6230–2273* ⊘ *Daily 10–5.*

Old Bus Depot Markets. This old bus depot, south of the lake in the suburb of Kingston, now hosts a lively Sunday market. Handmade crafts are the staples here, and exotic, inexpensive food and buskers add to the shopping experience. ⊠ *Wentworth Ave., Kingston Foreshore, Kingston* ☎ *02/6292–8391* ⊘ *Jan.–Nov., Sun. 10–4; Dec., weekends 10–4.*

CANBERRA & THE A. C. T. A TO Z

To research prices, get advice from other travelers, and book travel arrangements, visit www.fodors.com.

AIR TRAVEL

Several domestic airlines connect the rest of Australia with the capital city.

Canberra is served by Qantas and its subsidiaries Eastern, Southern, and Airlink; Regional Express (Rex); and Virgin Blue. There are regular (about hourly) flights to Sydney and Melbourne, as well as frequent services to Brisbane. Connections can be made to other Australian destinations as well.

Canberra has only one airport, which is used by large commercial liners, small private planes, and the Air Force alike. Early flights may be fogged in, so plan for delays. It's about ½ hour to Sydney, an hour to

Melbourne, and two hours to Brisbane. There are no direct flights to distant points like Perth or Darwin.

CARRIERS **🖪 Carriers Qantas Airways** ☎ 13–1313. **Regional Express** ☎ 13–1713. **Virgin Blue** ☎ 13–6789.

AIRPORTS
Canberra International Airport is 7 km (4 mi) east of the city center. Taxis are available from the line at the front of the terminal. The fare between the airport and the city is about A$16.

Canberra International Airport (☎ 02/6275–2236).

BUS TRAVEL
The main terminal for intercity coaches is the Jolimont Tourist Centre. Canberra is served by two major coach lines, McCafferty's/Greyhound Pioneer and Murrays Australia, both of which have at least three daily services to and from Sydney. Fares to Sydney start from A$25 one-way.
🖪 Bus Information Jolimont Tourist Centre ⊠ 65–67 Northbourne Ave. **McCafferty's/Greyhound Pioneer** ☎ 02/6249–6006, 13–1499, or 13–2030. **Murrays Australia** ☎ 13–2251.

BUS TRAVEL WITHIN CANBERRA
Canberra's public transportation system is the ACTION bus network, which covers all of the city. Buses operate weekdays 6:30 AM–11:30 PM, Saturday 7 AM–11:30 PM, and Sunday 8–7. There is a flat fare of A$2.40 per ride. If you plan to travel extensively on buses, purchase an Off-Peak Daily ticket for A$6, which allows unlimited travel on the entire bus network. Tickets, maps, and timetables are available from the Canberra Visitor Centre and the Bus Information Centre.
🖪 Bus Information Centre ⊠ East Row, Civic ☎ 13–1710.

CAR RENTAL
National car-rental operators with agencies in Canberra include Avis, Budget, Hertz, and Thrifty. Rumbles Rent A Car is a local operator that offers discount car rentals.
🖪 Agencies Avis ⊠ 17 Lonsdale St., Braddon ☎ 02/6249–6088 or 13–6333. **Budget** ⊠ Shell Service Station, Cnr. Mort St. and Girrahween St., Braddon ☎ 02/6257–2200 or 13–2727. **Hertz** ⊠ 32 Mort St., Braddon ☎ 02/6257–4877 or 13–3039. **Rumbles Rent A Car** ⊠ 11 Paragon Mall, Gladstone St., Fyshwick ☎ 02/6280–7444. **Thrifty** ⊠ 29 Lonsdale St., Braddon ☎ 02/6247–7422 or 1300/367227.

CAR TRAVEL
From Sydney, take the Hume Highway to just south of Goulburn and then turn south onto the Federal Highway to Canberra. Allow 3 to 3½ hours for the 300-km (186-mi) journey. From Melbourne, follow the Hume Highway to Yass and turn right beyond the town onto the Barton Highway. The 655-km (406-mi) trip takes around 8 hours.

Canberra is not an easy city to drive in, and you may well find yourself confused by the radial-road system and its turnoffs. Still, because sights are scattered about and not easily connected on foot or by public transport, a car is a good way to see the city itself, as well as the sights in the Australian Capital Territory. You can purchase maps with clearly marked scenic drives at the Canberra Visitor Centre for A$2.20.

EMBASSIES
The British High Commission is open weekdays 8:45–5, the Canadian High Commission is open weekdays 8:30–12:30 and 1:30–4:30, the New

Zealand High Commission is open weekdays 8:45–5, and the U.S. Embassy is open weekdays 8:30–12:30.

⚑ Canada **Canadian High Commission** ⊠ Commonwealth Ave., Yarralumla ☎ 02/6270–4000.

⚑ New Zealand **New Zealand High Commission** ⊠ Commonwealth Ave., Yarralumla ☎ 02/6270–4211.

⚑ United Kingdom **British High Commission** ⊠ Commonwealth Ave., Yarralumla ☎ 02/6270–6666.

⚑ United States **U.S. Embassy** ⊠ Moonah Pl., Yarralumla ☎ 02/6214–5600.

EMERGENCIES

In case of an emergency, dial 000 to reach an ambulance, the fire department, or the police. Canberra Hospital has a 24-hour emergency department.

If medical or dental treatment is required, seek advice from your hotel reception desk. There are doctors and dentists on duty throughout the city but their office hours vary. Many pharmacies in the city have extended hours.

⚑ Hospital **Canberra Hospital** ⊠ Yamba Dr., Garran ☎ 02/6244–2222. **Calvary Hospital** ⊠ Belconnen Way, Bruce ☎ 02/6201–6111.

MAIL & SHIPPING

The main post office is open weekdays 8:30 to 5:30. To send mail Post Restante, address it with the recipient's name c/o GPO Canberra, ACT. Mail is held for one month. You'll find post offices at suburban shopping centers throughout the city, or look in the phone book under Australia Post.

Most larger hotels have rooms with data ports or Internet service on site. You can have free Internet access at any public library in Canberra. Internet cafés abound throughout town, including in the Canberra Centre shopping mall. Rates are about A$2 for 15 minutes.

⚑ **Main Post Office** ⊠ 53–73 Alinga St. ☎ 13–1318.

MONEY MATTERS

All banks can exchange checks and cash. ATMs are everywhere, and most take credit cards as well as bank cards. There are money-changing facilities at Canberra Airport, and American Express and Thomas Cook have offices in the city.

TAXIS

You can phone for a taxi, hire one from a stand, or flag one down in the street. Taxis in Canberra have meters, and fees are set based on the mileage. There's an extra fee for booked rides called in by phone. You can bargain an hourly rate for a day tour of the area. Tipping isn't customary, but drivers appreciate it when you give them the change.

⚑ **Canberra Cabs** ☎ 13–2227.

TOURS

A convenient (and fun!) way to see the major sights of Canberra is atop the double-decker Canberra Tour bus, operated by City Sightseeing, which makes a regular circuit around the major attractions. Tickets are A$25 and valid 24 hours, so you can hop on and off all day.

Idol Moments can tailor private chauffeur-driven tours to meet your interests. Prices range from A$38 to A$68.

Murrays conducts half- and full-day tours that stop at the major tourist attractions. The full-day tour includes lunch at the Parliament House. Rates are A$34.10 for a half-day tour and A$75.90 for a full-day tour.

🔁 Tour Operators **City Sightseeing** ☎ 0500/505012 for cost of local call. **Idol Moments** ☎ 02/6295-3822. **Murrays** ☎ 13-2251.

TRAVEL AGENCIES
Reliable travel agencies include American Express Travel and Thomas Cook.
🔁 Local Agents **American Express Travel** ✉ Centrepoint Building, City Walk and Petrie Plaza ☎ 02/6247-2333. **Thomas Cook** ✉ Canberra Centre, Bunda St. ☎ 02/6257-2222.

TRAINS
The Canberra Railway Station is on Wentworth Avenue, Kingston, about 5 km (3 mi) southeast of the city center. EXPLORER trains make the 4-hour trip between Canberra and Sydney three times daily. A daily coach-rail service operates on the 10-hour run between Canberra and Melbourne. Passengers must travel the 60 km (37 mi) between Canberra and Yass Junction by bus.
🔁 **Canberra Railway Station** ☎ 02/6295-1198 or 13-2232 ⊕ www.countrylink.nsw.gov.au.

VISITOR INFORMATION
The Visitor Information desk in the large Canberra Centre shopping arcade has pamphlets on many Canberra attractions.

The Canberra Visitor Centre, open daily 9–6, is a convenient stop for those entering Canberra by road from Sydney or the north. The staff makes accommodation bookings for Canberra and the Snowy Mountains. The ground-floor kiosk in the Canberra Centre, open during shopping hours, is another useful source of information on attractions and shops.

The Kamberra Wine Centre not only offers tastings of its own wines, but also provides maps detailing the locations of other wineries in the area. It's open daily 10–5.
🔁 Tourist Information **Canberra Centre** ✉ Bunda and Akuna Sts. ☎ no phone. **Canberra Visitor Centre** ✉ 330 Northbourne Ave., Dickson ☎ 02/6205-0044 ⊕ www.canberratourism.com.au. **Kamberra Wine Centre** ✉ Flemington Rd. at Northbourne Ave., Lyneham, ☎ 02/6262-2333.

MELBOURNE

4

FODOR'S CHOICE

Café di Stasio, in St. Kilda

Chapel Street shopping, in South Yarra

Federation Square, landmark in the City Center

Flower Drum, restaurant in the City Center

The Park Hyatt, in the City Center

Hotel Como, in South Yarra

Victoria Market, bazaar in the City Center

HIGHLY RECOMMENDED

RESTAURANTS Caffe e Cucina, in South Yarra

Chinta Blues, in St. Kilda

Dog's Bar, in St. Kilda

Langton's, in the City Center

Melbourne Wine Room Restaurant, in St. Kilda

HOTELS King, in Fitzroy

Oakford Gordon Place, in the City Center

Robinson's by the Sea, in St. Kilda West

Sheraton Towers Southgate, in Southbank

The Tilba, in South Yarra

Windsor Hotel, in the City Center

SIGHTS Lygon Street, in Carlton

Southgate, in Southbank

SHOPPING Little Collins Street, in the City Center

By Terry Durack, Walter Glaser, Michael Gebicki, and Josie Gibson

Updated by Dan Cash

MELBOURNE (SAY *MEL*-BURN) IS THE cultivated sister of brassy Sydney. To the extent that culture is synonymous with sophistication—except when it comes to watching Australian-rules football or the Melbourne Cup—some call this city the cultural capital of the continent. Melbourne is also known for its rich migrant influences, particularly those expressed through food: the espresso cafés in Lygon Street, Melbourne's "little Italy," or the Greek district of the city central.

Named after then-British Prime Minister Lord Melbourne, the city of 3 ½ million was founded in 1835 when the Englishman John Batman and a group of businessman bought 243,000 hectares of land from the local Aborigines for a few trinkets. After gold was discovered in Victoria in the 1850s, Melbourne soon became the fastest-growing city in the British empire, and a number of its finer buildings were constructed during this period.

If, like its dowager namesake, Victoria is a little stuffy and old-fashioned, then the state capital of Melbourne is positively old world. For all the talk of Australia's egalitarian achievements, Melbourne society displays an almost European obsession with class. The city is the site of some of the nation's most prestigious schools and universities, and nowhere is it more important to have attended the right one. In a country whose convict ancestors are the frequent butt of jokes, Melburnians pride themselves on the fact that, unlike Sydney, their city was founded by free men and women who came to Victoria of their own accord.

Whatever appearances they maintain, Melburnians do love their sports, as evidenced by their successful bid to host the 2006 Commonwealth Games. The city is sports mad—especially when it comes to the glorious, freewheeling Melbourne Cup. On the first Tuesday of each November, everyone heads to Flemington for the horse race that brings the entire nation to a grinding halt. Gaily dressed in all manner of outrageous costume, from Christmas trees to tiaras, blue-collar workers and society dames converge to sip champagne, picnic, and cheer on their favorite thoroughbreds before making the rounds of Cup parties. The city also comes alive during the Australian Tennis Open, one of the four tennis Grand Slam events, which is held every January at Melbourne Park.

For years Melbourne's city central region was seen as an inferior tourist attraction compared with Sydney's sparkling harbor and eye-catching Opera House. But a large-scale building development along the Yarra River in the early '90s transformed what was once an eyesore into a vibrant entertainment district known as Southgate. Starting from the old-world charm of Alexandria Bridge behind Flinders Street Station, pedestrians can tour through Southgate's myriad of bars, shops, and restaurants on the south side of the Yarra River. An assortment of unusual water displays farther along serve to mark the entrance to the Southbank's brash Crown Casino. Its towers fueled with gasoline shoot bursts of flames every hour on the hour after dark.

As if that wasn't enough, the Victorian government commissioned a A$430 million construction of Federation Square, a large civic landmark in the heart of the city. Completed in 2002, it houses the Victorian National Gallery, the Centre for the Moving Image, and a wine hall showcasing local vintages and other attractions.

EXPLORING MELBOURNE

When Ava Gardner came to Melbourne in 1956 to make the film *On the Beach,* she was credited with quipping that the city *would* be a great place to make a movie about the end of the world. As it turns out, an enterprising journalist invented the comment, but these days Melburnians recall the alleged remark with wry amusement rather than rancor, which shows how far this city of 3.5 million has come. And, considering that Melbourne is consistently rated among the "world's most livable cities" in quality-of-life surveys, Melburnians seem to have opinion on their side.

The symbol of Melbourne's civility, as in turn-of-the-20th-century Budapest or in Boston, is the streetcar. Solid, dependable, going about their business with a minimum of fuss, trams are an essential part of the city. For a definitive Melbourne experience, climb aboard a tram and proceed silently and smoothly up the "Paris end" of Collins Street.

As escapes from the rigors of urban life, the parks and gardens in and around Melbourne are among the most impressive features of the capital of the Garden State. More than one-quarter of the inner city has been set aside as recreational space. The profusion of trees, plants, and flowers creates a rural tranquillity within the thriving city.

Melbourne is built on a coastal plain at the top of the giant horseshoe of Port Phillip Bay. The City Center is an orderly grid of streets where the state parliament, banks, multinational corporations, and splendid Victorian buildings that sprang up in the wake of the gold rush now stand. This is Melbourne's heart, which you can explore at a leisurely pace in a couple of days.

In Southbank, one of the "neighborhoods" (suburbs) outside of the city center, the Southgate development has refocused Melbourne's vision on the Yarra River. Once a blighted stretch of factories and run-down warehouses, the southern bank of the river is now a vibrant, exciting part of the city, and the river itself is finally taking its rightful place in Melbourne's psyche. Stroll along the Esplanade in the suburb of St. Kilda, amble past the elegant houses of East Melbourne, enjoy the shops and cafés in Fitzroy or Carlton, rub shoulders with locals at the Victoria Market, nip into the Windsor for afternoon tea, or hire a canoe at Studley Park to paddle along one of the prettiest stretches of the Yarra—and you may discover Melbourne's soul as well as its heart.

When to Visit Melbourne

Melbourne is at its most beautiful in fall, March–May. Days are crisp, sunny, and clear, and the foliage in parks and gardens is glorious. Melbourne winters can be gloomy, but by September the weather clears up, the football finals are on, and spirits begin to soar. Book early if you want to spend time in Melbourne in late October or early November when the Spring Racing Carnival and the Melbourne International Festival are in full swing. The same advice goes for early March when the city hosts a Formula 1 car racing grand prix and in mid-January during the Australian Tennis Open.

City Center

Melbourne's center is framed by the Yarra River to the south and a string of parks to the east. On the river's southern bank, the Southgate development, the arts district around the National Gallery, and the King's Domain–Royal Botanic Gardens areas also merit attention.

Numbers in the text correspond to numbers in the margin and on the Melbourne City Center map.

If you have 1 day

If you're low on time, set your priorities: For those seeking boutique shopping, take a two-block tour down **Little Collins Street,** from Elizabeth Street to Russell Street in the city central. For a hipster's day of urban exploring, journey east to **Chapel Street** in South Yarra for shopping and eating. Or, if you prefer natural sights, go marvel at the city's **Royal Botanic Gardens** or for a stroll along the bay on Kerford Road south of the city and continue along The Boulevarde to neighboring ⌖ **St. Kilda.**

4

If you have 3 days

Have a few days to do a little more exploring? Take a walk along the Southgate promenade to see the **Crown Casino.** Then jump aboard a Yarra River cruise boat, or take the kids to see the sharks at the **Melbourne Aquarium** opposite Southgate. On your third day, stroll through the **Royal Botanic Gardens** and see the **Shrine of Remembrance.** Then take a cable car on St. Kilda Road to the hip Acland Street area, in the suburb of ⌖ **St. Kilda,** for dinner.

If you have 5 days

Take in the farther-flung sights just outside the city. Head to Belgrave aboard the **Puffing Billy** steam railway through the fern gullies and forests of the Dandenongs, for example. On the way back, stop at a teahouse in **Belgrave** or **Olinda** to hand-feed the beautifully colored local bird life. Or take an evening excursion to ⌖ **Phillip Island** for the endearing sunset penguin parade at Summerland Beach. For these and other nearby activities and destinations, *see the Victoria chapter.*

a good walk

One of the finest vistas of the city is from Southbank Promenade, looking across the Yarra River and its busy water traffic to the city's sparkling towers. Start with a stroll around the shops, bars, cafés, and buskers of **Southgate** ❶ ⌖ and a visit to the **Victorian Arts Centre** ❷ before crossing the ornate Princes Bridge to the city proper. Take a look to the east from the bridge. The Melbourne Cricket Ground and the Melbourne Park tennis center dominate the scene. On the green banks of the Yarra, boathouses edge toward the water and rowers glide across the river's surface.

At the corner of Swanston and Flinders streets are four major landmarks: **Flinders Street Station** ❸, with its famous clocks, **Young and Jackson's Hotel** ❹ and its infamous *Chloe* painting, **St. Paul's Cathedral** ❺, and **Federation Square** ❻, a boldly designed landmark that took four years to complete. This corner also marks the beginning of Swanston Street, a pedestrian roadway intended to bring people off the sidewalks and onto the street. Ironically, though, once there, you have to dodge trams, tour buses, and even service and emergency vehicles. So it's better to keep to the sidewalk after all. **City Square** ❼ has been pretty much overshadowed by an adjacent development, but the witty statues along this stretch of road are worth examining in some detail. Fifty yards up the Collins Street hill on the City Square side is the Regent Theatre, a fabulous 1930s picture palace transformed into a live theater and the latest in a series of rebirths in Melbourne's classic theater life. Go west on the north side of Collins Street to the **Block Arcade** ❽, the finest example of the many arcades that Melbourne planners built to defy the strictness of the grid pattern. Turn right between the Hunt Leather and Weiss clothing shops, cross Little Collins Street, and bear right to enter the airy, graceful **Royal Arcade** ⑨. Standing guard over the shops are Gog and Magog, the mythical giants that toll the hour on either side of Gaunt's Clock.

Bourke Street Mall ⑩ is a cluttered, lively pedestrian zone—although trams run through here, too—busy with buskers and sidewalk artists. From here, you can climb the Bourke Street hill to the east to reach the **State Houses of Parliament** ⑪ and adjacent **Parliament Gardens** ⑫ at the end. Or, head across the street from the gardens to take a peek in the **Princess Theatre** ⑬, and then walk southeast for two blocks to the venerable **Windsor Hotel** ⑭, an ideal spot for high tea. Walk south to the **Old Treasury Building Museum** ⑮ and its Melbourne Exhibition, then cross the Treasury Gardens to the **Fitzroy Gardens** ⑯ and **Cook's Cottage** ⑰. Head along Lansdowne Street to see the towering **St. Patrick's Cathedral** ⑱.

You can call it quits now and visit the remaining historical sights on another day. If you've got the stamina, however, walk west along Albert Street, which feeds into Lonsdale Street, and then turn right at Russell Street. Two blocks north is the **Old Melbourne Gaol** ⑲, where you can briefly consort with assorted scoundrels. Backtrack down Russell Street, turning right into La Trobe Street. At the next corner is the **State Library** ⑳. This was once also the site of Melbourne's excellent (if overcrowded) Museum of Victoria, now relocated to controversial premises in the Carlton Gardens. Next, try a little shopping under the inverted glass cone of Lonsdale Street's Melbourne Central Complex. If you're there on the hour, make your way to the center of the cone and look for the massive clock, which turns into a tableau of twittering birds and native animals to the tune of "Waltzing Matilda." Walk past Lonsdale to Elizabeth Street, where you can peek in the **Church of St. Francis** ㉑. Then turn and head south on Elizabeth for three blocks, past the general post office, and make a left on Collins Street. The **Athenaeum Theater and Library** ㉒ is on the left side of the second block, and the **Paris End** ㉓ area is on the next block at Alfred Place.

TIMING From Southgate to St. Patrick's Cathedral—with time for the Victorian Arts Center, the Old Treasury Building Museum, the State Houses of Parliament, and refreshments—takes a good part of the day. It's possible to do a whirlwind walk, with a nod to all the sights in a couple of hours. However, plan a longer stroll if you can—perhaps also incorporating elements of the Golden Mile heritage trail, which traces 150 years of Melbourne's history in a trek around the central business district.

WHAT TO SEE
㉒ **Athenaeum Theater and Library.** The present building, which includes a theater and library, was built in 1886. These days, the Athenaeum is used mainly for live theatrical performances, yet it's also remembered as the venue for the first talking picture show ever screened in Australia. ✉ *188 Collins St., City Center* ☎ *03/9650–3504.*

⑧ **Block Arcade.** Melbourne's most elegant 19th-century shopping arcade was restored in 1988; 100 years of grime was scraped back to reveal a magnificent mosaic floor. The arcade was built during the 1880s, when the city was flushed with the prosperity of the gold rushes, a period recalled as "Marvelous Melbourne." ✉ *282 Collins St., City Center* ☎ *03/9654–5244.*

need a break?
The **Hopetoun Tea Room** (✉ Block Arcade, City Center ☎ 03/9650–2777) has been serving delicate sandwiches, refined cakes, and perfectly poured cups of tea for a century. It's a slice of 1890s Melbourne time-warped into the present without too many modern intrusions.

The Arts Melbourne regards itself as the artistic and cultural capital of Australia. It's home to the Australian Ballet and opera, theater, and dance companies—from the traditional to the avant-garde.

4

Food Melbourne's dining scene is a vast smorgasbord of cuisines and dining experiences. Chinese restaurants on Little Bourke Street are the equal of anything in Hong Kong. The neighborhood of Richmond's Victoria Street convincingly reincarnates Vietnam. The central business district now has so many hole-in-the-wall Italian cafés that you could almost be in Rome. And a stroll down Fitzroy Street in St. Kilda is a racy, cosmopolitan walk on the wild side, where you can find everything from sushi and Singapore *laksa* (spicy Malaysian noodle soup) to spaghetti and *som tum* (Thai green papaya salad).

Markets London has Portobello Road, and Melbourne has Victoria Market, a fantastic assortment of new and used goods—not to mention a ton of food items. In fact, whereas most cities consider themselves lucky to have one major fresh-food market, Melbourne has nearly a dozen, from Prahran to South Melbourne. Fine cheeses and palate-pleasing wines are made right on Melbourne's doorstep, while a caring band of butchers, bakers, and wholesalers keep chefs stocked with the latest, the freshest, and the best.

Nightlife Many Melburnians content themselves with a night at the movies, but nightclubs, live music venues, pubs, and cocktail lounges are always full of action. Melbourne's nightlife centers around King Street and Flinders Lane, with dozens of retro-style bars and clubs. The chic hotels tend to have hip cocktail lounges with an A-list clientele.

Sports Melburnians, like Aussies in general, do love a good match. The Melbourne Cup horse race in November brings the entire city to a standstill. The same is true of Australian-rules football, one of a few varieties of "footy." This, the nation's number-one spectator sport, has its stronghold in Melbourne. The season begins in March and reaches its climax at the Grand Final, held in September, when crowds of 100,000 are commonplace. Scenic Albert Park Lake in South Melbourne is also home to the Australian Grand Prix, which hosts the first round of the Formula One season in March.

The Great Outdoors Melbourne is an excellent jumping-off point for outdoor adventures, including bushwalking, a surf-and-turf trip down the Great Ocean Road, or a foray to one of Victoria's outstanding national parks. For details on these activities and destinations, *see* the *Victoria* section in chapter 5.

🔟 **Bourke Street Mall.** Once the busiest east–west thoroughfare in the city, Bourke is now a pedestrian zone (but watch out for those trams!). Two of the city's biggest department stores are here, **Myer** (No. 314) and **David Jones** (No. 310). An essential part of growing up in Melbourne is being taken to Myer's at Christmas to see the window displays. ✉ *Bourke St. between Elizabeth St. and Swanston Walk, City Center.*

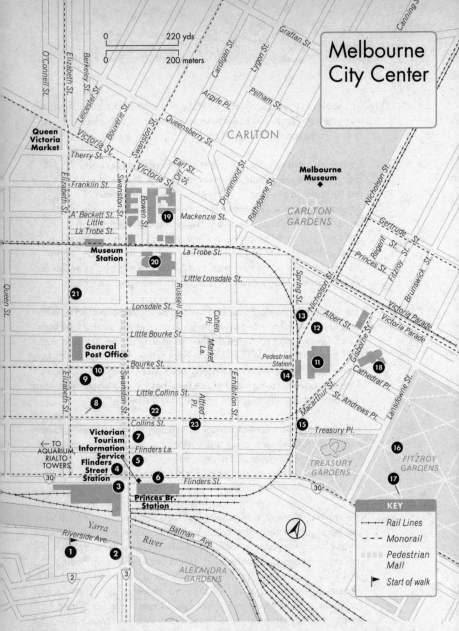

Melbourne City Center

O'Connell St.

Elizabeth St.

Berkeley St.

Leicester St.

Bouverie St.

Swanston St.

Cardigan St.

Lygon St.

Grattan St.

Canning St.

Argyle Pl.

Pelham St.

Queensberry St.

CARLTON

Queen Victoria Market

Victoria St.

Therry St.

Victoria St.

Earl St.

Drummond St.

Rathdowne St.

Melbourne Museum ◆

Franklin St.

Elizabeth St.

A' Beckett St.
Little
La Trobe St.

Bowen St.

Swanston St.

Mackenzie St.

CARLTON GARDENS

Gertrude St.

Nicholson St.

Regent St.

Princes St.

Fitzroy St.

Brunswick St.

Victoria Parade

La Trobe St.

Museum Station

⑲

⑳

Queen St.

㉑

Russell St.

Little Lonsdale St.

Spring St.

Nicholson St.

⑬

Albert St.

Gisborne St.

Lansdowne St.

Victoria Parade

Lonsdale St.

Cohen Pl.

Market La.

⑫

⑱

General Post Office

Little Bourke St.

Pedestrian Station

Cathedral Pl.

⑨ ⑩

Bourke St.

⑪

Elizabeth St.

Swanston St.

Little Collins St.

Exhibition St.

⑭

Macarthur St.

St. Andrews Pl.

⑧

Alfred Pl.

㉒

⑮

Treasury Pl.

⑯

FITZROY GARDENS

㉓

Collins St.

Victorian Tourism Information Service

⑦

Flinders La.

TREASURY GARDENS

⑰

← TO AQUARIUM, RIALTO TOWERS

Flinders Street Station

⑤

④

⑥

Flinders St.

㉚

㉚

③

Princes Br. Station

Yarra

Riverside Ave.

River

Batman Ave.

ALEXANDRA GARDENS

KEY

①

②

②

③

‡‡‡ Rail Lines
--- Monorail
▦▦▦ Pedestrian Mall
⚑ Start of walk

Carlton Gardens. Forty acres of tree-lined paths, artificial lakes, and flower beds in this English-style 19th-century park form a backdrop for the Exhibition Buildings that were erected in 1880 and are still used for trade shows. The gardens are on the northeast edge of the city center, bounded by Victoria Parade and Nicholson, Carlton, and Rathdowne streets. The outstanding Museum of Victoria was relocated here from its former home next to the State Library.

㉑ **Church of St. Francis.** This Roman Catholic church was constructed in 1845, when the city was barely a decade old. The simple, frugal design starkly contrasts with the Gothic exuberance of St. Paul's, built 40 years later. The difference illustrates just what the gold rush did for Melbourne. ⊠ *Elizabeth and Lonsdale Sts., City Center* ☎ *no phone.*

❼ **City Square.** Bronze statues emerge from the crowd along this shopping area: a series of tall, thin men striding across the mall, or a snarling dog reaching for some unfortunate's ankles. The square also has the statue of Robert Burke and William Wills, whose 1860–61 expedition was the first to cross Australia from south to north. You can admire the parade from a stylish café on the square. ⊠ *Swanston St. between Collins St. and Flinders La., City Center.*

⓱ **Cook's Cottage.** Once the property of the Pacific navigator Captain James Cook, the modest home was transported stone by stone from Great Ayton in Yorkshire and re-erected in the lush Fitzroy Gardens in 1934. It's believed that Cook lived in the cottage between voyages. The interior is simple and sparsely furnished, a suitable domestic realm for a man who spent much of his life in cramped quarters aboard small ships. ⊠ *Fitzroy Gardens, near Lansdowne St. and Wellington Parade, East Melbourne* ☎ *no phone* 💰 *A\$3* 🕑 *Apr.–Oct., daily 9–5; Nov.–Mar., daily 9–5:30.*

Crown Casino. Melbourne's first casino has blackjack, roulette, and poker machines. There are also dozens of restaurants and retail shops. Look for the impressive water and lighting displays on the first floor. The casino is on the south bank of the Yarra. ⊠ *Riverside Ave., Southbank* ☎ *03/9292–8888* ⊕ *www.crowncasino.com.au* 🕑 *Daily 24 hrs.*

off the beaten path

EAST MELBOURNE – The harmonious streetscapes in this historic enclave of Victorian houses, which date from the boom following the gold rushes of the 1850s, are a great excuse for a stroll. Start at the southeast corner of Fitzroy Gardens and head north on Clarendon to George Street. Turn right and take in the procession of superb terrace houses and mature European trees as you walk down the gentle slope of the street. Two blocks ahead, turn left on Simpson, then again on wide, gracious Hotham Street. On either side of the grassy median that divides the roadway, the mix of terrace houses and freestanding mansions includes some of the suburb's finest architecture. Back at Clarendon, turn north. Bishopscourt, the bluestone residence of the Anglican Archbishop of Melbourne, occupies the next block. Wind right again down Gipps Street and make your way to pretty Darling Square. For different scenery on the way back, take Simpson Street south and turn right on Wellington Parade.

❻ **Federation Square.** Encompassing a whole city block, the A\$430 million, award-winning construction of Federation Square was completed in 2002 after four years of work. The bold, abstract-styled landmark was designed to house the new National Gallery of Victoria, featuring only Australian art. The square also incorporates the Centre for the Moving Image; the BMW Edge amphitheater, a contemporary music and theater per-

Fodor's Choice
★

formance venue; the Victorian Wine Precinct, showcasing the best of local wine; the Melbourne Visitor Centre; and restaurants, bars, and gift shops. ⊠ *Flinders St., between Swanston and Russell Sts., City Center* ☎ *03/9658–9658* ⊕ *www.fedsq.com* ⊙ *Mon.–Thur. 10–5, Fri. 10–9, weekends 10–6.*

⑯ Fitzroy Gardens. This 65-acre expanse of European trees, manicured lawns, garden beds, statuary, and sweeping walks is Melbourne's most popular central park. Among its highlights is the **Avenue of Elms**, a majestic stand of 130-year-old trees that is one of the few in the world that has not been devastated by Dutch elm disease. ⊠ *Lansdowne St. and Wellington Parade, East Melbourne* ☒ *Free* ⊙ *Daily sunrise–sunset.*

❸ Flinders Street Station. Melburnians use the clocks on the front of this grand Edwardian hub of Melbourne's suburban rail network as a favorite meeting place. When it was proposed to replace them with television screens an uproar ensued. Today, there are both clocks and screens. ⊠ *Flinders St. and St. Kilda Rd., City Center.*

off the beaten path

MELBOURNE AQUARIUM – Become part of the action as you stroll through tubes surrounded by water and the denizens of the deep at play. Or take a ride on an electronic simulator. The aquamarine building illuminates a previously dismal section of the Yarra bank, opposite Crown Casino. ⊠ *Flinders St. and King St., City Center* ☎ *03/9620–0999* ⊕ *www.melbourneaquarium.com.au* ☒ *A$22* ⊙ *Feb.–Dec., daily 9:30–6; Jan., daily 9:30–9.*

⑲ Old Melbourne Gaol. A museum run by the Victorian branch of the National Trust is housed in the city's first jail. The building has three tiers of cells with catwalks around the upper levels. Its most famous inmate was the notorious bushranger Ned Kelly, who was hanged here in 1880. His death mask and one of the four suits of armor used by his gang are displayed in a ground-floor cell. Evening candlelight tours are a popular, if macabre, facet of Melbourne nightlife. These depart Wednesday, Friday, Saturday, and Sunday at 8:30 September–May, and 7:30 June–August. reservations are essential. ⊠ *Russell St., at Mackenzie St., City Center* ☎ *03/9663–7228* ⚠ *Reservations essential* ☒ *Self-guided day tours A$12.50, candlelight tours A$20* ⊙ *Daily 9–5.*

⑮ Old Treasury Building Museum. The neoclassical bluestone and sandstone building was built in 1862 to hold the gold that was pouring into Melbourne from mines in Ballarat and Bendigo—architect J. J. Clark designed the building when he was only 19—with subterranean vaults protected by iron bars and foot-thick walls. The Melbourne Exhibition, occupying the entire ground floor, takes you from Aboriginal times to the present with relics from Melbourne's past borrowed from public and private collections. Not to be missed is the Built on Gold show staged in the vaults themselves. ⊠ *Treasury Pl. and Spring St., City Center* ☎ *03/ 9651–2233* ⊕ *www.oldtreasurymuseum.org.au* ☒ *A$5* ⊙ *Weekdays 9–5, weekends 10–4.*

㉓ Paris End. Beyond the cream and red Romanesque facade of St. Michael's Uniting Church, the eastern end of Collins Street takes on a name coined by Melburnians to identify the elegance of its fashionable shops as well as its general hauteur. Alas, modern development has stolen some of the area's architectural appeal, but shoppers still frequent the venerable **Le Louvre** salon (No. 74), favored by Melbourne's high society.

⑫ Parliament Gardens. Stop here for a breath of cool green air in the center of the city. The gardens have a modern fountain and an excellent view of the handsome yellow Princess Theatre across Spring Street. The gardens are also home to the lovely St. Peter's Church. ✉ *Parliament, Spring, and Nicholson Sts., East Melbourne* ⊙ *Daily dawn–dusk.*

Pellegrini's Espresso Bar (✉ 66 Bourke St., East Melbourne ☎ 03/9662–1885) serves industrial-strength coffee and bargain-price cakes, sandwiches, and pasta dishes. At lunchtime, the narrow bar draws a mixed crowd of students, shoppers, and businesspeople.

⑬ Princess Theatre. The ornate, 1886 wedding cake–style edifice was re-furbished in the late 1980s for a production of *Phantom of the Opera*, which was a blockbuster success. The theater, across from Parliament Gardens, is one of Melbourne's Broadway-style venues, along with the Regent Theatre on Collins Street. ✉ *163 Spring St., East Melbourne* ☎ *03/9299–9800.*

off the beaten path

RIALTO TOWERS OBSERVATION DECK – If you want a bird's-eye view of Melbourne, there's no better—or more popular—place than from the 55th floor of the city's tallest building. The 360-degree panorama is superb, with views on a clear day extending to the Dandenong Ranges and far out into Port Phillip Bay. Admission includes a 20-minute film and use of high-powered binoculars. ✉ *Level 55, 525 Collins St., at King St., City Center* ☎ *03/9629–8222* ▦ *Observation deck A$10.50* ⊙ *Sun.–Thurs. 10–10, Fri. and Sat. 10–11.*

❾ Royal Arcade. Built in 1869, this is the city's oldest shopping arcade and, despite alterations, it retains an airy, graceful elegance notably lacking in more modern shopping centers. Walk about 30 feet into the arcade, turn around, and look up to see the statues of Gog and Magog, the myth-ical monsters that toll the hour on either side of **Gaunt's Clock.** At the far end is a wrought-iron portico from the same period, one of the few remaining examples of the verandas that used to grace the city center. ✉ *355 Bourke St., City Center* ☎ *no phone.*

⑱ St. Patrick's Cathedral. Ireland supplied Australia with many of its early immigrants, especially during the Irish potato famine in the middle of the 19th century. Melbourne's Roman Catholic cathedral is closely as-sociated with Irish Catholicism in Australia. A statue of the Irish pa-triot Daniel O'Connell stands in the courtyard. Construction of the Gothic Revival building began in 1858 and took 82 years to finish. St. Pat's lacks the exuberant decoration of St. Paul's, Melbourne's Anglican cathedral. ✉ *Cathedral Pl., East Melbourne* ☎ *03/9662–2233* ⊙ *Week-days 6:30–5, weekends 7:15–7.*

❺ St. Paul's Cathedral. This 1892 headquarters of Melbourne's Anglican faith is regarded as one of the most important works of William But-terfield, a leader of the Gothic Revival style in England. The interior is highly decorative, right down to the patterned floor tiles. The English organ is particularly noteworthy. Outside the cathedral is the Statue of Matthew Flinders, the first seaman to circumnavigate the Australian coast-line, between 1801 and 1803. ✉ *Flinders and Swanston Sts., City Cen-ter* ☎ *03/9650–3791* ⊙ *Weekdays 7–6, Sat. 8:30–5, Sun. 8–7:30.*

St. Peter's Church. Two years after St. Peter's was built in 1846, Melbourne was proclaimed a city from its steps. The church, one of Melbourne's oldest buildings, is at the top end of Parliament Gardens. ✉ *Albert and Nicholson Sts., East Melbourne.*

★ ▶ ❶ **Southgate.** On the river's edge next to the Victorian Arts Center, the development of Southgate successfully refocused Melbourne's attention on the scenic Yarra River and revitalized a sadly neglected part of the city. It's a prime spot for a walk and for lingering in general—designer shops, classy restaurants, bars, and casual eating places help locals and visitors while away the hours. It's especially vibrant, with throngs of people and street theater performers, on weekends. The Southgate promenade links with the forecourt of Crown Casino. ⊠ *Maffra St. and City Rd., Southbank* ☎ *03/9699–4311* ⊕ *www.southgate-melbourne. com.au.*

⓫ **State Houses of Parliament.** Dating to 1856, this building was used as the National Parliament from the time of federation in 1900 until 1927, when the first Parliament House was completed in Canberra. Today, the commanding building houses the Victoria State Parliament. To view the chambers, simply ask at the reception desk inside the front door. Parliament usually sits Tuesday to Thursday March–July and again August–November. ⊠ *Spring St., East Melbourne* ☎ *03/9651–8911* ☞ *Free* ◷ *Weekdays 9–4; guided tour at 10, 11, noon, 2, 3, and 3:45 when parliament is not in session.*

⓴ **State Library.** The library stocks more than 1.5 million volumes, one of Australia's finest collections of manuscripts, and a vast number of maps, prints, and paintings. On a rise behind lawns and heroic statuary, this handsome 1853 building was constructed during the gold rush boom. It's currently undergoing a major phased renovation, due to finish in 2005. ⊠ *328 Swanston St., City Center* ☎ *03/8664–7000* ⊕ *www. statelibrary.vic.gov.au* ☞ *Free* ◷ *Mon.–Thurs. 10–9, Fri.–Sun. 10–6.*

off the
beaten
path

FodorsChoice
★

VICTORIA MARKET – You don't have to be a shopper to enjoy this sprawling, spirited bazaar. The century-old market is the prime produce outlet, and it seems that most of Melbourne comes here to buy its strawberries, fresh flowers, and imported cheeses. On Sunday, you can find deals on jeans, T-shirts, bric-a-brac, and secondhand goods. The Gaslight Night Market, open from December to mid-February nightly from 5:30 to 10, has over 20 prepared food stalls offering a variety of international cuisines and entertainment. Foodies Dream Tours (A$22) and cooking classes (fee) are also available. ⊠ *Queen and Victoria Sts., City Center* ☎ *03/9320–5822* ⊕ *www. qvm.com.au* ◷ *Tues. and Thurs. 6–2, Fri. 6–6, Sat. 6–3, Sun. 9–4.*

❷ **Victorian Arts Centre.** Although it lacks the architectural grandeur of Sydney's Opera House, the Southbank Arts Centre is Melbourne's most important cultural landmark and the venue for performances by the Australian Ballet, Australian Opera, and Melbourne Symphony Orchestra. It also encompasses the Melbourne Concert Hall, Arts Complex, and National Gallery of Victoria. One-hour tours begin from the information desk at noon and 2:30, Monday through Saturday. On Sunday, a 90-minute backstage tour begins at 12:15. At night, look for the center's spire. Lit with brilliant fiber-optic cables, it creates a magical spectacle. ⊠ *100 St. Kilda Rd., Southbank* ☎ *03/9281–8000* ⊕ *www. vicartscentre.com.au* ☞ *Tour A$10, backstage tour (no children) A$13.50* ◷ *Mon.–Sat. 9 AM–11 PM, Sun. 10–5.*

★ ⓮ **Windsor Hotel.** Not just a grand hotel, the Windsor is home to one of Melbourne's proudest institutions—the ritual of afternoon tea (from A$30), served daily 3:30–5:30. Ask about theme buffet teas served on weekends, such as the Chocolate Indulgence, available June–October (A$45), with a vast selection of chocolates and chocolate cakes and

desserts. Although the Grand Dining Room—a belle-epoque extravaganza with a gilded ceiling and seven glass cupolas—is open only to private functions, try to steal a look anyway. ⊠ *103 Spring St., City Center*
☎ *03/9633–6000* ⊕ *www.thewindsor.com.au.*

❹ Young and Jackson's Hotel. Pubs are not generally known for their artwork, but climb the steps to the bar here to see *Chloe,* a painting that
has scandalized and tititlated Melburnians for many decades. The larger-
than-life nude, painted by George Lefebvre in Paris in 1875, has hung
on the walls of Young and Jackson's Hotel for most of the last century.
⊠ *1 Swanston St., City Center* ☎ *03/9650–3884.*

South Melbourne & Richmond

These two riverside neighborhoods are home to King's Domain Gardens (which includes the Royal Botanic Gardens and a number of other
interesting sights), some great restaurants, and, for sports lovers, the Melbourne Cricket Ground.

King's Domain Gardens. This expansive stretch of parkland includes
Queen Victoria Gardens, Alexandra Gardens, the Shrine of Remembrance,
Pioneer Women's Garden, the Sidney Myer Music Bowl, and the Royal
Botanic Gardens. The floral clock in Queen Victoria Gardens talks and
tells time, providing a brief recorded history of the gardens in and
around Melbourne. It's opposite the Victorian Arts Centre on St. Kilda
Road in one of the Domain's many informal gardens. ⊠ *Between St.
Kilda and Domain Rds., Anderson St., and Yarra River, South Melbourne.*

Melbourne Cricket Ground. A visit here to tour its outstanding museums
is essential for an understanding of Melbourne's sporting obsession. Get
the scoop on a tour, which covers the Australian Gallery of Sport and
Olympic Museum; the famous Long Room, usually accessible only
through membership in the Melbourne Cricket Club (for which there
is a *20-year* waiting list); the MCC Cricket Museum and Library; a view
of the Great Southern Grandstand; and pictorial walkways. The memorabilia, especially the cricket-related bits, are some of the best in the
world. The ground is a pleasant 10-minute walk from the city center or
a tram ride to Jolimont Station. ⊠ *Jolimont Terr., Jolimont* ☎ *03/
9657–8867* ⊕ *www.mcg.org.au* 🎟 *A$16* ☉ *Tours daily on the hr 10–3
(except on event days).*

National Gallery of Victoria. A massive, moat-encircled, bluestone and
concrete edifice houses works from renowned international painters, including Picasso, Renoir, and Van Gogh. (Australian art is displayed at
the gallery in Federation Square.) ⊠ *180 St. Kilda Rd., South Melbourne* ☎ *03/9208–0222* ⊕ *www.ngv.vic.gov.au* 🎟 *Free* ☉ *Daily 10–5.*

Royal Botanic Gardens. The present design and layout were the brain-
child of W. R. Guilfoyle, curator and director of the gardens from 1873
to 1910. Within its 100 acres are 12,000 species of native and imported
plants and trees, sweeping lawns, and ornamental lakes populated with
ducks and swans that love to be fed. You can discover the park on your
own or by joining guided walks that leave from the visitor center. A highlight is the Aboriginal Heritage Walk, led by an Aboriginal cultural in-
terpreter, which explores the culture of the indigenous people of
Melbourne. The main entrance to the gardens is on Birdwood Avenue,
opposite the Shrine of Remembrance. During summer there are alfresco
performances of classic plays, usually Shakespeare, along with children's classics such as *Wind in the Willows* and the highly popular *Moonlight Cinema* series. ⊠ *King's Domain Gardens S, Birdwood Ave.,
South Yarra* ☎ *03/9252–2429* ⊕ *www.rbgsyd.gov.au* 🎟 *Free* ☉ *Apr.,*

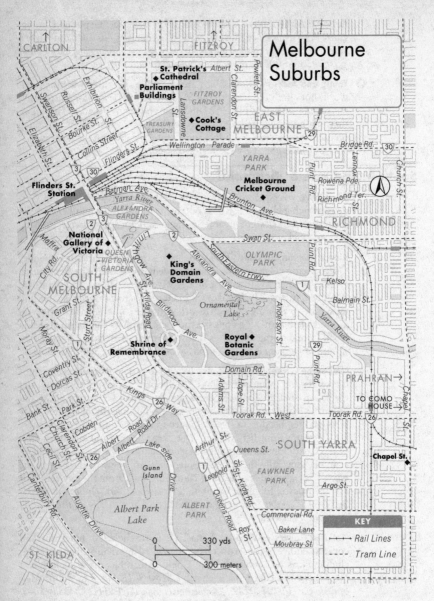

daily 7:30–6; May–Aug., daily 7:30–5:30; Sept.–Oct., daily 7:30–6; Nov.–Mar., daily 7:30–8:30.

Shrine of Remembrance. Melbourne's War Memorial, in the King's Domain Gardens, was dedicated in 1934 to commemorate the fallen in World War I and has since grown to recognize service in World War II, Korea, Malaya, Borneo, Vietnam, and the Gulf War. The temple-style structure is designed so that at 11 AM on Remembrance Day—the 11th day of the 11th month, when in 1918 armistice for World War I was declared—a beam of sunlight passes over the Stone of Remembrance in the Inner Shrine. In the forecourt is an eternal flame. ⊠ *St. Kilda Rd., South Melbourne* ☎ *03/9654–8415* ⊕ *www.shrine.org.au* ✉ *Donations accepted* ☉ *Daily 10–5.*

St. Kilda

The cosmopolitan bayside suburb of St. Kilda, 6 km (4 mi) south of the city center, is to Melbourne what seaside Bondi is to Sydney. Whatever St. Kilda lacks in surf, it more than makes up for with culinary offerings. Sunday afternoon half of Melbourne comes here to eat ice cream, have a stroll, and watch the world go by. The St. Kilda experience begins at the pier on Lower Esplanade, a good spot from which to watch sailboats.

By night, St. Kilda becomes Melbourne's red-light district, although it pales in comparison with Sydney's Kings Cross. To reach the suburb from the city, take Tram 16, 69, 79, 96, or 12.

Acland Street. St. Kilda's restaurant row, Acland (AK-land), is an alphabet soup of restaurants and cuisines, including Chinese, French, Italian, Jewish, and Lebanese.

Esplanade. The walkway which parallels the beach is the scene of a lively and entertaining Sunday market crowded with arts-and-crafts stalls, which form a backdrop for performances by buskers and street-theater troupes. To the south, the Esplanade curves around the Luna Park amusement area.

off the beaten path

LUNA PARK – The main attraction of this faded amusement park, modeled after New York's Coney Island, is the old-fashioned Big Dipper roller coaster. A less stomach-churning option is the slower Scenic Railway, named for the great view it provides of the city. The park also has a Ferris wheel, bumper cars, and a ghost train. ⊠ *Lower Esplanade, St. Kilda* ☎ *1300–888-272* ⊕ *www.lunapark. com.au* ⊠ *Park admission free, major rides A$6.50 each, A$32.95 unlimited rides* ⊙ *Dec.–Mar., Fri. 7 PM–11 PM, Sat. 11–11, Sun. 11–7; Apr.–Nov., weekends 11–6.*

Scheherazade. St. Kilda is the center for Melbourne's Jewish population, and the best-known nook to nosh in is Scheherazade, opened in 1958 by Polish émigrés Masha and Avram Zeliznikow. The avenue's famous cake shops also make for sumptuous window-shopping. ⊠ *99 Acland St., St. Kilda* ☎ *03/9534–2722.*

Fitzroy

Melbourne's bohemian quarter is 2 km (1 mi) north of the city center. If you're looking for an Afghan camel bag or a secondhand paperback, or yearn for a café where you can sit over a plate of tapas and watch Melbourne go by, Fitzroy is the place.

Brunswick Street. Along with Lygon Street in nearby Carlton, Brunswick is one of Melbourne's favorite eat streets. Guernica (No. 257) is a smart, highly regarded modern Australian restaurant. Mario's Restaurant (No. 303) is an old favorite among locals and serves some of Melbourne's best pasta in a fun atmosphere. A little farther up, Rhumbarella (No. 342) dispenses coffee and cocktails to the hip and hungry. Babka Bakery Café (No. 358) serves everything from great breads and cheesecake to Russian breakfast blintzes.

The street also has galleries such as Roar Studios (No. 115) and the Woman's Gallery (No. 375), which specialize in the work of up-and-coming Australian artists. On Shore (No. 267) sells only Australian-made arts and crafts, which make excellent souvenirs. Port Jackson Press (No. 397) publishes and sells prints by Australian artists. The Brunswick

Street Bookstore (No. 305) has a good selection of modern Australian literature.

Carlton

To see the best of Carlton's Victorian-era architecture, venture north of Princes Street, paying particular attention to Drummond Street, with its rows of gracious terrace houses, and Canning Street, which has a mix of workers' cottages and grander properties.

★ **Lygon Street.** Known as Melbourne's Little Italy, Lygon Street is a perfect example of Melbourne's multiculturalism—where once you'd have seen only Italian restaurants, there are now Thai, Afghan, Malay, Caribbean, and Greek eateries. Toto's Pizza House (No. 101) claims to be Australia's first pizzeria. Whether or not the boast is true, Toto's has served cheap pizza for more than 45 years. Jamaica House (No. 106) is a local haunt. At Casa del Gelato (No. 161) you can enjoy some of the city's best ice cream. For Southeast Asian fare, Lemongrass Restaurant (No. 189) serves a more sophisticated and understated strain of Thai food than the boisterous curries of other Thai restaurants. Nyonya Malaysian Restaurant (No. 191) is good for reasonably priced, well-prepared dishes.

Near Grattan Street is a local institution, the University Café (No. 257). Tiamo (No. 303) has been a trysting place for generations of Melbourne lovers, who come for the coziness, wholesome food, and good coffee. The legendary Jimmy Watson's Wine Bar (No. 333) is the spot for a convivial glass or two downstairs, or a more formal meal upstairs. The area has great color, particularly at night when the sidewalks are thronged with diners and strollers and a procession of high-revving muscle cars rumbling along the strip.

🕭 **Melbourne Museum.** The State Government of Victoria committed A$290 million for this spectacular building, which hosts such exhibits as Bunjilaka, the Aboriginal Centre; the Forest Gallery (an actual, live forest); and a children's museum. The Australia Gallery focuses on Victoria's heritage and includes memorabilia from the television show *Neighbours,* as well as the preserved body of Australia's greatest racing horse Phar Lap. The beautiful Pasifika Gallery has displays of Pacific islands' cultures and lifestyles, including traditional boatmaking, housing, and hunting techniques from Polynesia, Melonesia, and Micronesia. There's also a wide-screen IMAX cinema on-site. ⊠ *Carlton Gardens, Carlton* ☎ *03/8341–7777* ⊕ *www.melbourne.museum.vic.gov.au* ✉ *A$15* ⊙ *Daily 10–5.*

South Yarra/Prahran

One of the coolest spots to be on any given night is in South Yarra and Prahran. If you're feeling alternative, head for Greville Street, which runs off Chapel near the former Prahran Town Hall and has more bars and eateries, groovy clothes, and music shops.

Fodor'sChoice **Chapel Street.** The heart of the trendy South Yarra/Prahran area is this ★ long road packed with pubs, bars, notable restaurants, upscale boutiques, cinemas, and even army surplus stores and pawnshops. One of the classiest places to stop for a bite, if you can get in, is Caffe e Cucina (No. 581). Kasbah (No. 481) is a casual option for eats.

Como House. A splendid white Victorian mansion overlooking the Yarra, Como is Melbourne's finest example of an early colonial house. The main part of the mansion was built around 1855, and the kitchen wing predates that by 15-odd years. Come to stroll the five acres of gardens; a café serves lunch and snacks. ⊠ *Lechlade Ave. and Williams Rd., South Yarra* ☎ *03/9827–2500* ⊕ *www.nattrust.com.au* ✉ *A$10* ⊙ *Daily 10–5.*

Around Melbourne

↺ **Melbourne Zoological Gardens.** Flourishing gardens and open-environment animal enclosures are hallmarks of this world-renowned zoo. Of particular interest are animals unique to Australia, such as the koala, kangaroo, wombat, emu, and echidna. A lion park, reptile house, and butterfly pavilion are also on-site, as is a simulated African rain forest where the only group of gorillas in the country resides. Friends of the Zoo distribute free guides from 10 to 3. Jazz bands occasionally serenade visitors (and the animals) on summer evenings. The zoo is 4 km (2½ mi) north of Melbourne city center. ⊠ *Elliot Ave., Parkville* ☎ *03/ 9285–9300* ⊕ *www.zoo.org.au* ✉ *A$15.80* ⊙ *Daily 9–5.*

Rippon Lea. Begun in the late 1860s, Rippon Lea is a sprawling polychrome brick mansion built in the Romanesque style. By the time of its completion in 1903, the original 15-room house had swollen into a 33-room mansion. Notable architectural features include a grotto, a tower that overlooks the lake, a fernery, and humpback bridges. In summer, plays are performed on the grounds. Take the Sandringham subway line 15 minutes south of the city center. ⊠ *192 Hotham St., Rippon Lea Elsternwick* ☎ *03/9523–6095* ✉ *A$10* ⊙ *Daily 10–5.*

↺ **Scienceworks Museum.** A former sewage-pumping station in suburban Spotswood has been transformed into a much more glamorous place. This hands-on museum of science-related activities entertains while it educates. A perennially popular permanent exhibit is Sportsworks, where you can test your speed against an Olympic sprinter and perform other sporting feats. The **Melbourne Planetarium** here uses a super computer and projection system to simulate 3D travel through space and time on a 15-meter (49-foot) domed ceiling. ⊠ *2 Booker St., Spotswood* ☎ *03/9392–4800* ⊕ *www.scienceworks.museum.vic.gov.au* ✉ *A$15* ⊙ *Daily 10–4:30.*

WHERE TO EAT

Reservations are generally advised in the city. Although most restaurants are licensed to sell alcohol, the few that aren't usually allow you to bring your own. Wine lists range from encyclopedic to small and selective, often specializing in Australian wines, which show unequaled freshness and fruit. Lunch is served noon–2:30, and dinner—usually a single seating—is 7–10:30. A 10%–12% tip is customary, and there may be a corkage fee in BYOB restaurants. There is no sales tax or service charge.

WHAT IT COSTS In Australian Dollars				
	$$$$	$$$	$$	$	¢
AT DINNER	over $50	$36–$50	$21–$35	$10–$20	under $10

Prices are per person for a main course at dinner.

City Center

CHINESE
$$–$$$
Fodor'sChoice
★

✕ **Flower Drum.** Under meticulous owner Gilbert Lau, Flower Drum has blossomed as one of the country's truly great Chinese restaurants, serving superb Cantonese cuisine. The restrained elegance of the decor, deftness of the service, and intelligence of the wine list puts most other restaurants to shame. Simply ask your waiter for the day's special and prepare yourself for a feast: perhaps crisp-skinned Cantonese roast duck served with plum gravy, succulent dumplings of prawn and flying fish roe, a perfectly steamed Murray cod, or huge Pacific oysters with black bean sauce. ⊠ *17 Market La., City Center* ☎ *03/9662–3655* ⚖ *Reservations essential* ▭ *AE, DC, MC, V* ⊗ *No lunch Sun.*

FRENCH
★ **$$**

X **Langton's.** Both the upscale restaurant and the easygoing wine bar have excellent values, considering chef Walter Trupp's London pedigree and sommelier Stewart Langton's epic wine list. In the wine bar, tuck into a sensational spit-roasted Barossa Valley chicken with confit potatoes and roasted ratatouille. In the restaurant, choose between the rotisserie of duck with creamed polenta, a shellfish lasagne with basil veloute, or a parsley cappuccino with ham Pithivier. ⊠ *Sargood House, 61 Flinders La., City Center* ☎ *03/9663–0222* ⚖ *Reservations essential* ▭ *AE, DC, MC, V* ⊗ *Closed Sun. No lunch Sat.*

ITALIAN
$$–$$$

X **Grossi Florentino.** For more than 80 years, to dine at Florentino has been to experience the height of Melbourne hospitality. Upstairs, in the famous mural room with its wooden panels, Florentine murals, and hushed conversation, everything conspires to make you feel special. So, too, does Guy Grossi's full-bodied Italian cooking, running from a delicious braised rabbit with muscatel and *farro* (a speltlike Tuscan grain) to a tender veal shank with basil broth and black cabbage. Downstairs, the Grill Room has more businesslike fare, while the cellar bar is perfect for a glass of wine and pasta of the day. ⊠ *80 Bourke St., City Center* ☎ *03/9662–1811* ⚖ *Reservations essential* ▭ *AE, DC, MC, V* ⊗ *Closed Sun. No lunch Sat.*

$$

X **Becco.** Every city center needs a place like Becco, with its drop-in bar, lively dining room, and attached food store full of great cheeses, imported pastas, and preserves. At lunchtime, no-time-to-dawdle business types tuck into whitebait fritters, tagliolini with fresh tuna, and ricotta cake. Things get a little moodier at night, when a Campari and soda at the bar is an almost compulsory precursor to dinner. ⊠ *11–25 Crossley St., City Center* ☎ *03/9663–3000* ⚖ *Reservations essential* ▭ *AE, DC, MC, V* ⊗ *Closed Sun.*

¢–$$

X **Basso.** Owners of St. Kilda's Café a Taglio have brought their winning formula to this subterranean space in the city. Order at the counter then join the crowds at long communal tables eating the finest Roman-style pizza, perhaps Gorgonzola and radicchio. Or save yourself for heartier options courtesy of standout local Italian chef Marco Lori (ex-Becco). His char-grilled rib-eye filet with mustard mash is divine, even better than the roasted duck with dolcetto sauce. The prices look like typos (in your favor). ⊠ *Georges Bldg., rear, 195 Little Collins St., City Center* ☎ *03/9650–0077* ▭ *AE, DC, MC, V* ⊗ *No dinner weekends.*

JAPANESE
¢

X **Yu.u.** This hard to find, must-reserve, very modern Japanese restaurant with barely a sign is tucked behind a graffiti-covered door. But find it you should, because awaiting your undivided attention are all the grills, salads, and nabe hot-pots (simmering one-pot dishes with fish, tofu, and vegetables) you'd find in a Tokyo restaurant—other than sushi, that is. From gleamingly fresh soy beans (*edamame*) with sake, to the lotus root salad, Yu.u. is a little bento box in the back lanes of Melbourne. ⊠ *137 Flinders La., City Center* ☎ *03/9639–7073* ⚖ *Reservations essential* ▭ *AE, DC, MC, V* ⊗ *Closed weekends.*

MIDDLE EASTERN
$$

X **Mo Mo.** One of the defining features of modern Melbourne dining is the Middle Eastern theme. This pillow-laden basement restaurant nails the flavors completely by using a pungent mix of spices in such entrées as *bastourma* (cured beef) salad with wild arugula and goat cheese, and *tagine* (Moroccan stew). ⊠ *115 Collins St., basement (enter from*

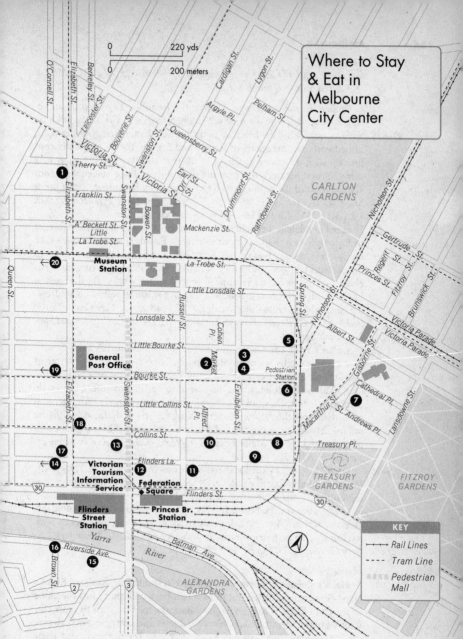

Where to Stay & Eat in Melbourne City Center

KEY

+—+ Rail Lines
- - - Tram Line
Pedestrian Mall

George Parade), City Center 🕿 *03/9650–0660* 🖃 *AE, DC, MC, V* 🕑 *Closed Sun. No lunch Sat.*

MODERN   ✕ **Ondine.** In this swish space below the Republic Tower, you can pe-
AUSTRALIAN   ruse the encyclopedic wine list while Chefs Donovan Cooke and Philipa
$$–$$$ Sibley-Cooke whip up delicacies in the kitchen. Using their gourmet skills,
honed with the three stars of France and Britain, they'll magically con-
jure up such delicacies as tortellini of Moreton Bay bugs (similar to a
shovel-nosed lobster), roast saddle of rabbit, and pot-au-feu with root
vegetables and dumplings. 🖂 *Republic Tower, basement, 299 Queen
St., City Center* 🕿 *03/9602–3477* 🖄 *Reservations essential* 🖃 *AE,
DC, MC, V* 🕑 *Closed Sun.–Mon. No lunch Sat.*

$$ ✕ **ezard at adelphi.** Few chefs build slicker bridges between the flavors
of East and West than Melbourne's Teage Ezard. His adventurous take
on fusion is pushing boundaries. Some combinations may appear to verge
on the reckless—crème brûlée flavored with roasted Jerusalem arti-
choke and truffle oil, for example—yet everything works. Try the roasted
barramundi with Chinese broccoli, fragrant rice, and yellow curry dress-
ing, and baby bamboo shoot salad. 🖂 *187 Flinders La., City Center* 🕿 *03/
9639–6811* 🖄 *Reservations essential* 🖃 *AE, DC, MC, V* 🕑 *Closed Sun.
No lunch Sat.*

$$ ✕ **Walter's Wine Bar.** Smack in the middle of Melbourne's lively Southgate complex, this is one nonstop party. Nibble on a classy platter of
local cheeses, sip a lively Mornington Peninsula pinot or a well-raised
Yarra Valley chardonnay, and dine on simple grills and other bistro-style
dishes such as duck, smoked salmon, and upscale burgers. Whether you
sit outside on the balcony overlooking the river or inside with the
milling throng, it's an essential Melbourne experience. 🖂 *Southgate Complex, Level 3, South Melbourne* 🕿 *03/9690–9211* 🖄 *Reservations essential* 🖃 *AE, DC, MC, V.*

$–$$ ✕ **Verge.** Beloved by the local arts set for its brains as much as its body,
Verge fits Melbourne like a glove. Office workers drop in for a mid-morning coffee, or for after-work drinks and dinner. The split-level space's
hard edges are warmed considerably by Simon Denton's impeccable service and Karen White's modern bistro food. Try the roast chicken with
parsnips or angel hair pasta with prawns and chili. 🖂 *1 Flinders La.,
City Center* 🕿 *03/9639–9500* 🖃 *AE, DC, MC, V.*

Melbourne Suburbs

CAFÉS   ✕ **Blake's Cafeteria.** Former Southbank restaurateur Andrew Blake's
$$ latest venture has turned out to be a laid-back café that raids the globe
in search of flavor. From an Afghani pancake for breakfast to spare ribs
with Vietnamese–inspired coleslaw for dinner and everything in between,
it's a please-all, open-all-day kind of venue. Try the succulent baby
chicken with eggplant pickle, the roasted veal with hummus, or sweet
Piquillo peppers stuffed with tuna tartare. 🖂 *132 Greville St., Prahran*
🕿 *03/9510–3900* 🖃 *AE, DC, MC, V* 🕑 *Closed weekends.*

$$ ✕ **Richmond Hill Café and Larder.** Leading chef and food writer Stephanie
Alexander is the force behind this bright and buzzy café–cum–produce
store. The bistro fare brims with wonderful flavors, from the chicken,
almond, and mushroom pie to a "hamburger as it should be." After you've
eaten, pick up some marvelous cheese and country-style bread from the
adjoining cheese room and food store. 🖂 *48–50 Bridge Rd., Richmond*
🕿 *03/9421–2808* 🖃 *AE, DC, MC, V* 🕑 *No dinner Sun.*

FRENCH   ✕ **Circa the Prince.** Circa, at the swank Prince Hotel, feels somewhat like
$$ an Arabian dream, all Egyptian tea lights, white leather lounges, and
walls masked with organza and silk. In one of the best-looking dining
rooms in Australia, former British chef Michael Lambie is serving the

kinds of dishes that made Leed's chef Marco Pierre White so famous in Britain, particularly the rabbit cappuccino with white bean. The U. K.–French inspired fare is a very good match for the exhaustive and very tempting wine list. ✉ *2 Acland St., St. Kilda* ☎ *03/9536–1122* ◬ *Reservations essential* ▭ *AE, DC, MC, V.*

ITALIAN
$$–$$$
Fodor'sChoice
★

✕ **Café di Stasio.** This café treads a very fine line between mannered elegance and decadence. A sleek marble bar and modishly ravaged walls contribute to the sense that you've stepped into a scene from *La Dolce Vita*. Happily, Café di Stasio is as serious about its food as its sense of style. Crisply roasted duck is now a local legend, char-grilled baby squid is a sheer delight, and the pasta is always al dente. If the amazingly delicate lobster omelet is on the menu, do yourself a favor and order it. ✉ *31 Fitzroy St., St. Kilda* ☎ *03/9525–3999* ◬ *Reservations essential* ▭ *AE, DC, MC, V.*

★ $$–$$$ ✕ **Melbourne Wine Room Restaurant.** Although the Wine Room itself buzzes day and night with young, black-clad types, the adjoining restaurant is far less frenetic. Elegantly whitewashed, with a moody glow that turns dinner for two into a romantic tête-à-tête, it possesses a gloriously down-at-the-heels sense of glamour. Despite Chef Karen Martini's move to Sydney, she remains in charge of menus. The Italianate fare, at once confident and determinedly single-minded, runs from powerful risottos to forceful pastas and grills that make you sit up and take notice. ✉ *125 Fitzroy St., St. Kilda* ☎ *03/9525–5599* ◬ *Reservations essential* ▭ *AE, DC, MC, V* ☉ *No lunch Mon.–Thurs.*

★ $$ ✕ **Caffe e Cucina.** Close your eyes and think of Italy. This always-packed café set the standards for Melbourne's many atmospheric espresso stops. It draws the fashionable, look-at-me crowd for a quick coffee and pastry downstairs, or for a more leisurely meal upstairs in the warm, woody dining room. Order melt-in-the-mouth gnocchi, calamari *San Andrea* (lightly floured and deep fried), prosciutto with figs, and a glass of Victorian pinot noir. For dessert, the tiramisu is even better looking than the crowd. Reservations are essential upstairs, but not accepted downstairs. ✉ *581 Chapel St., South Yarra* ☎ *03/9827–4139* ▭ *AE, DC, MC, V.*

¢–$ ✕ **Café a Taglio.** Rarely has pizza been this delicious, or this groovy. Although there is a blackboard menu of very good pastas and other Italian dishes, regulars prefer to cruise the counter, choosing from the giant squares of pizza on display. Toppings include bright-orange pumpkin, strikingly pretty rosemary and potato, tangy anchovy and olives, beautifully bitter radicchio, pancetta, tomato, and more. ✉ *157 Fitzroy St., St. Kilda* ☎ *03/9534–1344* ◬ *Reservations not accepted* ▭ *AE, MC, V.*

MALAYSIAN
★ $

✕ **Chinta Blues.** This is a curious, beckoning sort of place that manages to combine both the charms of a Malaysian-style coffeehouse with the vibe and cool of a modern street-smart café, with barely a seam showing. Tables are simple plywood, seating is by way of communal benches, and the walls are covered in dark wooden shelves stocked with Asian groceries. Curry laksa—a bathtub of noodles, chicken, and prawns in a spicy broth—is heaven in a bowl, and spinach *blachan* (with fermented, dried shrimp paste) and spicy wok-fried noodles satisfy most hotheads. ✉ *6 Acland St., St. Kilda* ☎ *03/9534–9233* ▭ *AE, MC, V.*

MEDITERRANEAN
★ $–$$

✕ **Dog's Bar.** With its blazing fires, artfully smoky walls, and striking wrought-iron chandeliers, the Dog's Bar has a lived-in, neighborly look. The regulars at the bar look as if they grew there, while the young, artistic-looking groups who mooch around the front courtyard seem so satisfied you can practically hear them purr. They take their wines seriously here, and you can find some particularly fine local pinot noir and sauvignon blanc at prices that won't break the bank. Put together a selection

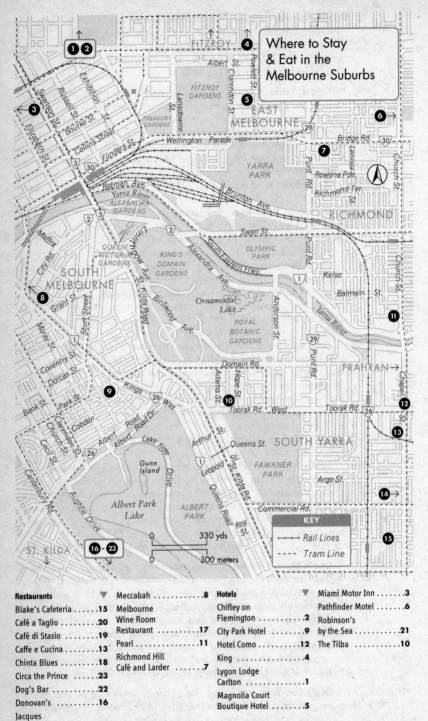

Where to Stay & Eat in the Melbourne Suburbs

KEY
+—+ Rail Lines
– – – Tram Line

Restaurants ▼

Blake's Cafeteria	15
Café a Taglio	20
Café di Stasio	19
Caffe e Cucina	13
Chinta Blues	18
Circa the Prince	23
Dog's Bar	22
Donovan's	16
Jacques Reymond	14
Meccabah	8
Melbourne Wine Room Restaurant	17
Pearl	11
Richmond Hill Café and Larder	7

Hotels ▼

Chifley on Flemington	2
City Park Hotel	9
Hotel Como	12
King	4
Lygon Lodge Carlton	1
Magnolia Court Boutique Hotel	5
Miami Motor Inn	3
Pathfinder Motel	6
Robinson's by the Sea	21
The Tilba	10

of antipasto from the tempting counter display, or opt for one of the daily pasta specials. ✉ *54 Acland St., St. Kilda* ☎ *03/9525–3599* ⚸ *Reservations not accepted* ▤ *AE, DC, MC, V.*

MIDDLE EASTERN ✕ **Meccabah.** One-time Greg Malouf (Mo Mo) protégé Cath Claring-
$ bold has opened her new place with a bang down at the rejuvenated Docklands. With its water views and harborfront position, the crowds have given her please-all menu a big thumbs up. Claringbold's food is gloriously redolent of the Middle East. Delicious chicken and green olive tagine, lemony grills, and sumac dusted salads are good, honest food that mum would've served . . . if she were from Lebanon. It's a terrific, energetic place to migrate in the evening, when you can dine to splendid sunset views of the city skyline and the bay. ✉ *NewQuay Promenade, Docklands* ☎ *03/9642–1300* ⚸ *Reservations not accepted* ▤ *AE, DC, MC, V.*

MODERN ✕ **Jacques Reymond.** French discipline and an Asian palette delightfully
AUSTRALIAN intertwine in this glamorous, century-old Victorian mansion with its re-
$$$–$$$$ cently modernized interior. The wine list is the stuff an oenophile dreams of, and service is intelligent, intuitive, and informed. The Burgundian-born chef uses the finest Australian produce to create such classics as roasted veal loin with ginger and soy butter, and fillet of barramundi hot-pot with fresh rice noodles as part of set menus (A$65–A$115). A selection of killerby wines complements each course, including such richly prepared desserts as millefeuilles of blue cheese with walnuts and grapes. Also available is the highly acclaimed six-course vegetarian option. ✉ *78 Williams Rd., Prahran* ☎ *03/9525–2178* ⚸ *Reservations essential* ▤ *AE, DC, MC, V* ⊙ *Closed Sun.–Mon. No lunch Sat.*

$$ ✕ **Donovan's.** This bay-side hot spot has all the allure of a smart beach house that's straight out of *Martha Stewart Living* magazine. As you enter, pause to watch the chefs at work in the immaculate kitchen, then get a window table and enjoy wide-open views of St. Kilda beach and its passing parade of rollerbladers, skateboarders, dog walkers, and ice-cream lickers. Owners Kevin and Gail Donovan are such natural hosts you may feel like bunking down overnight. Homespun decor, like plump and plush pillows, graceful flower arrangements, and a cozy, open fireplace, make the atmosphere even more relaxing. Chef Robert Castellani serves up wonderful pasta and risotto, a thoroughly delicious fish soup, and dishes for two, including a memorable baked Alaska. ✉ *40 Jacka Blvd., St. Kilda* ☎ *03/9534–8221* ⚸ *Reservations essential* ▤ *AE, DC, MC, V.*

$$ ✕ **Pearl.** Geoff Lindsay's Pearl may be mostly white and shimmery inside, a glittering gem beloved by Melbourne's beautiful folk. But it's also home to one of the best local chefs, whose menu balances on the fork's tip, making the clear distinction between cutting edge and pure novelty. Some of his best flavors include a watermelon and feta salad with satiny tomato jelly, and a sour yellow curry of Queensland scallops. Pure culinary wizardry. ✉ *631–633 Church St., Richmond* ☎ *03/9421–4599* ▤ *AE, DC, MC, V* ⊙ *No lunch Sat.*

WHERE TO STAY

	WHAT IT COSTS In Australian Dollars				
	$$$$	$$$	$$	$	¢
FOR 2 PEOPLE	over $300	$201–$300	$151–$200	$100–$150	under $100

Prices are for two people in a standard double room in high season.

$$$$ 🏨 **Hotel Sofitel Melbourne.** Half of the twin-towered Collins Place complex, the Sofitel was designed by architect I. M. Pei, and it combines glamor and excellent facilities with a prime location. Guest rooms, which begin on the 35th floor of the 50-story building, are built around a mirrored central atrium, and views are exceptional. The Atrium bar on the 35th floor is a good place to enjoy the scenery. The hotel's rooms and views are among the best in town, although service standards are patchy. ✉ *25 Collins St., City Center, 3000* ☎ *03/9653–0000* 📠 *03/9650–4261* ⊕ *www.sofitelmelbourne.com.au* ⬱ *311 rooms, 52 suites* ⚭ *2 restaurants, in-room data ports, in-room safes, cable TV with movies, health club, spa, 2 bars, dry cleaning, laundry service, business services; no-smoking floors* ⊟ *AE, DC, MC, V.*

$$$$ 🏨 **The Park Hyatt.** This elegant, boutique-style hotel fits perfectly in its
Fodor'sChoice   location next to Fitzroy Gardens, opposite Saint Patrick's cathedral and
★   overlooking some of the city's most beautiful historic Victorian buildings. Warm colors and rich wood paneling add softness to the art deco stylings inside the rooms, which all have a walk-in wardrobe, king-size bed, Italian marble bathroom, and roomy, modern work space. Suites are even more luxurious, some with fireplaces, terraces, and spa baths. The five-level radii restaurant and bar headlines the hotel's artsy beat with its front panel of hand-sculptured, sapphire-color glass and circular bar. Commissioned contemporary artworks by international talents are on exhibition throughout the hotel—and some are for sale. ✉ *1 Parliament Sq., City Center, 3000* ☎ *03/9224–1234* 📠 *03/9224–1200* ⊕ *www.melbourne.hyatt.com* ⬱*216 rooms, 24 suites* ⚭ *2 restaurants, café, room service, in-room data ports, in-room safes, cable TV with movies and video games, indoor pool, health club, hair salon, hot tub, massage, sauna, spa, steam room, bar, baby-sitting, dry cleaning, laundry service, concierge, Internet, business services, meeting rooms, airport shuttle, car rental, travel services, parking (fee)* ⊟ *AE, DC, MC, V.*

★ $$$$ 🏨 **Sheraton Towers Southgate.** In the bustling Southgate river district, the Sheraton has a terrific vantage point—the Melba Brasserie—from which to view passing pedestrian and Yarra River traffic. Autumn tones decorate the rooms, and a cascading fountain bubbles in the hotel's beautiful marbled foyer. The hotel is popular with a business clientele and has the usual business-oriented facilities. ✉ *1 Southgate Ave., Southbank, 3006* ☎ *03/9696–3100* 📠 *03/9690–5889* ⊕ *www.sheraton-towers.com.au* ⬱ *385 rooms, 11 suites* ⚭ *Restaurant, in-room data ports, in-room safes, cable TV with movies, pool, health club, bar, dry cleaning, laundry service, business services; no-smoking floors* ⊟ *AE, DC, MC, V.*

★ $$$$ 🏨 **Windsor Hotel.** The aristocrat of Melbourne hotels, century-old Windsor combines the character of the Victorian era with the modern blessings of first-rate food and comfortable beds. Guest rooms are plushly decorated with Laura Ashley–style wall coverings and rosewood furnishings. The marble bathrooms are, however, modest in size compared with those in modern hotel rooms of the same price. Standard rooms are rather small, but the two-room executive suites provide good value, and the Victorian suites are vast. The hotel commands a position opposite the Parliament House, close to theaters, parks, and fine shops. ✉ *103 Spring St., City Center, 3000* ☎ *03/9633–6000* 📠 *03/9633–6001* ⊕ *www.thewindsor.com.au* ⬱ *160 rooms, 20 suites* ⚭ *Restaurant, gym, spa, in-room data ports, in-room safes, cable TV with movies, 2 bars, dry cleaning, laundry service, business services; no-smoking floors* ⊟ *AE, DC, MC, V.*

$$$ 🏨 **The Adelphi.** This design-driven boutique hotel breaks new ground with its contemporary style: functionalist maple and matte-finish-metal surfaces and clean, cool lines. The best rooms are those at the front (room

numbers ending in 01). The Adelphi's pièce de résistance is an 80-foot lap pool on the top floor, which has a glass bottom that juts out from the edge of the building. Bathers literally swim into space. The view from the bar on the same floor, framed by the Gothic spires of St. Paul's, is heavenly, and ezard at adelphi serves daring, memorable Mod Oz fusion fare. ⊠ *187 Flinders La., City Center, 3000* ☎ *03/9650–7555* 🖷 *03/9650–2710* ⊕ *www.adelphi.com.au* ↪ *24 rooms with shower, 10 with bath* ⚭ *Restaurant, in-room data ports, cable TV with movies, pool, gym, 2 bars, dry cleaning, laundry service; no-smoking floors* ⊟ *AE, DC, MC, V* ¶◯¶ *CP.*

$$$ 🏨 **Hotel Causeway.** Among fashion boutiques, restaurants, and a host of hip cafés in the alleyways off Little Collins Street is this stylish small hotel. Rooms are simply yet stylishly decorated and each has its own bathroom. The dark red upholstery and deep walnut furnishings are offset with light, cream-color walls. There are three split-level suites for a family of up to four. ⊠ *275 Little Collins St., City Center, 3000* ☎ *03/9660–8888* 🖷 *03/ 9660–8877* ⊕ *www.causeway.com.au* ↪ *42 rooms, 3 duplexes* ⚭ *Satellite TV with movies, gym, steam room, bar, laundry facilities, business services; no-smoking floors* ⊟ *AE, DC, MC, V* ¶◯¶ *CP.*

★ $$$ 🏨 **Oakford Gordon Place.** This historic 1883 structure is one of the most interesting and comfortable apartment hotels in the city. It's just a stone's throw from the Parliament Building and is surrounded by excellent restaurants and theaters. It's also a good value. Modern, comfortable apartments contain washing machines, dryers, and dishwashers. Breakfast is served on a covered terrace. The studio and one- and two-bedroom apartments face a vine-covered courtyard with a 60-foot saltwater pool and a century-old palm tree. ⊠ *24 Little Bourke St., City Center, 3000* ☎ *03/9663–2888* 🖷 *03/9639–1537* ⊕ *www.oakford. com* ↪ *82 apartments* ⚭ *Restaurant, kitchens, cable TV, saltwater pool, gym, sauna, spa, dry cleaning, laundry facilities; no-smoking floors* ⊟ *AE, DC, MC, V* ¶◯¶ *BP.*

$$ 🏨 **Grand Mercure Hotel Melbourne.** The Grand Mercure is the smallest of the city's upscale hotels, with only 58 one- and two-bedroom suites. Rooms are tastefully decorated in apricot, burgundy, lemon, and pale green, and are beautifully furnished. All have kitchenettes with a microwave oven and a refrigerator. Guests have use of a small private courtyard, inspired by the Renaissance gardens of Italy. The central location is a bonus. ⊠ *321 Flinders La., City Center, 3000* ☎ *03/9629–4088* 🖷 *03/9629–4066* ⊕ *www.mercure.com* ↪ *58 suites* ⚭ *Restaurant, in-room data ports, kitchenettes, refrigerators, cable TV with movies, health club, bar, dry cleaning, laundry service; no-smoking floors* ⊟ *AE, DC, MC, V.*

$ 🏨 **Hotel Y.** Built in 1975 for budget travelers, this hotel has comfortable rooms simply furnished in an Ikealike style. If you need Internet access, the licensed café has a kiosk. The city center and Victoria Market are within walking distance. ⊠ *489 Elizabeth St., City Center, 3000* ☎ *03/ 9329–5188* 🖷 *03/9329–1469* ⊕ *www.asiatravel.com/australia/ prepaidhotels/hotely* ↪ *60 rooms* ⚭ *Cafeteria, pool, room TVs, laundry facilities, dry cleaning, meeting rooms* ⊟ *AE, DC, MC, V.*

¢–$ 🏨 **Kingsgate Hotel.** Built in 1926, the Kingsgate provides value-for-money accommodation in the heart of the city. Rooms are simple yet thoughtfully furnished, and each has its own bathroom and color TV. The hotel is just a minute's walk from Spencer Street train station and within walking distance of other city attractions, such as Crown Casino and Southgate. The hotel also has its own lounge bar and French-style restaurant. Half the rooms have a shared bathroom and are even cheaper. ⊠ *131 King St., between Bourke and Little Collins Sts., City Center, 3000* ☎ *03/9629–4171* 🖷 *03/9629–7110* ⊕ *www.holidaycity.com/*

kingsgate-melbourne ⇨ *200 rooms, 100 with bath* ⌂ *Restaurant, bar, Internet, dry cleaning, laundry, business services* ▭ *AE, DC, MC, V.*

Melbourne Suburbs

$$$
Fodor'sChoice
★

🏨 **Hotel Como.** With its opulence and funky modern furnishings, this luxury hotel is as popular with business travelers as it is with visiting artists and musicians. Gray marble and chrome are prominent throughout the Pop Art–meets–art-deco interior. Rooms have king-size beds, bathrobes, and Jacuzzis. Some suites on the third and sixth floors have access to private Japanese gardens, and some suites have fully equipped kitchenettes. The Como enjoys a reputation for outstanding service and a swank clientele. ✉ *630 Chapel St., South Yarra, 3141* ☎ *03/9825–2222* 🖷 *03/ 9824–1263* ⊕ *www.mirvachotels.com.au* ⇨ *30 rooms, 77 suites* ⌂ *In-room data ports, in-room safes, some kitchenettes, cable TV with movies and video games, pool, health club, massage, sauna, bar, dry cleaning, laundry service, meeting rooms; no-smoking floors* ▭ *AE, DC, MC, V.*

★ **$$–$$$**
🏨 **The Tilba.** Built as a grand residence at the turn of the 20th century, the Tilba became a hotel in 1920, and staying here feels like a sojourn in a luxurious private house. During World War II it was occupied by Ladies for the Armed Services and later fell on hard times until it was renovated in the mid-1980s. Now it's a small hotel with genuine charm, filled with antiques and eclectic pieces of furniture. In one room, for example, a bedstead was once the gate on a Queensland cattle ranch. The hotel overlooks Fawkner Park and is a short stroll from the chichi Toorak Road shops and restaurants. ✉ *30 Toorak Rd., South Yarra, 3141* ☎ *03/ 9867–8844* 🖷 *03/9867–6567* ⊕ *www.thetilba.com.au* ⇨ *2 rooms with bath, 12 rooms with shower* ⌂ *Dry cleaning, laundry service, meeting rooms; no-smoking rooms, no a/c in some rooms* ▭ *AE, DC, MC, V.*

$–$$$
🏨 **Magnolia Court Boutique Hotel.** Although its name might imply modernity, the rooms and furnishings are slightly Victorian (and spotless) at this small B&B–like inn. Standard rooms are modest in size, but the suites have more space and comfort at just a moderately higher rate. A family suite with a kitchen and space for six is also available. The hotel is separated from the city center by Fitzroy Gardens and is about a 12-minute walk from Spring Street. ✉ *101 Powlett St., East Melbourne, 3002* ☎ *03/9419–4222* 🖷 *03/9416–0841* ⊕ *www.magnolia-court. com.au* ⇨ *23 rooms, 3 suites* ⌂ *Dry cleaning, laundry service, meeting rooms, in-room data ports, in-room safes, café, some kitchenettes, meeting rooms* ▭ *AE, DC, MC, V.*

$$
🏨 **Chifley on Flemington.** Wrought-iron balconies and a cobblestone central courtyard mimic New Orleans architecture at this hotel a few minutes north of the central business district by car or tram. There's a small reception area instead of a traditional lobby, and the comfortable, spacious Victorian-style guest rooms are decorated with warm colors and brass beds. ✉ *5–17 Flemington Rd., at Blackwood St., Carlton, 3053* ☎ *03/9329–9344* 🖷 *03/9328–4870* ⊕ *www.constellationhotels.com* ⇨ *217 rooms, 8 suites* ⌂ *2 restaurants, pool, gym, sauna, 2 bars, dry cleaning, laundry service; no-smoking floors* ▭ *AE, DC, MC, V.*

$–$$
🏨 **City Park Hotel.** Close to the parks on the south side of the city, this ultramodern, four-story motel is ideal for travelers on limited budgets. Rooms have coffeemakers and small refrigerators, and those in the front of the redbrick building have balconies. The executive-honeymoon suite has a spa bath and sauna. There are relatively few amenities, but the city is about 1½ km (1 mi) away and frequent tram service is available on St. Kilda Road, a two-minute walk from the hotel. ✉ *308 Kings Way, South Melbourne, 3205* ☎ *03/9699–9811* 🖷 *03/9699–9224* ⊕ *www.cityparkhotel.com.au* ⇨ *38 rooms, 6 suites* ⌂ *Restaurant, refrigerators, bar, Internet, meeting rooms* ▭ *AE, DC, MC, V.*

★ $–$$ 🏨 **King.** Behind the boom-style Italianate facade is a modern B&B establishment that combines elegant, grandly proportioned rooms with minimalist interiors. The 1867 building is listed on Melbourne's Historic Buildings Register. The architect and original occupier, J. B. Denny, was the supervising architect for St. Patrick's Cathedral. Each of the spacious first-floor bedrooms has its own marble bathroom, and the attic is equipped with an en suite shower. ⊠ *122 Nicholson St., at King William St., Fitzroy, 3065* 📞*03/9417–1113* 📠*03/9417–1116* ⊕*www.kingaccomm. com.au* 🛏*3 rooms* ⚲ *No-smoking rooms, no a/c in some rooms, no room phones, no room TVs, no kids under 14* ⊟ *AE, DC, MC, V* ⑩*BP.*

$ 🏨 **Lygon Lodge Carlton.** In the heart of Melbourne's Little Italy and just a short tram ride from the city center, this motel is close to some of the city's best ethnic restaurants—the perfect place for the budget-conscious traveler who appreciates a colorful, lively neighborhood. Some deluxe rooms have kitchenettes, only a few dollars more than standard rooms. Also here are a penthouse, a full apartment suite, and three suites large enough to accommodate a family. ⊠ *220 Lygon St., at Gratton St., Carlton, 3053* 📞 *03/9663–6633* 📠 *03/9663–7297* ✉ *lygonlodgemotel@bigpond.com* 🛏*41 rooms, 17 suites* ⚲ *Restaurant, some kitchenettes, room TVs with movies, some in-room safes, in-room data ports, dry cleaning, laundry facilities* ⊟ *AE, DC, MC, V.*

$ 🏨 **Pathfinder Motel.** Built in the early 1960s in quiet, residential Kew, this relaxed, comfortable motel is on a direct tram line to the city, 7 km (4½ mi) away. The reception area and lobby, furnished with antiques, face a courtyard with a small waterfall and fishpond. Rooms are cream-color brick, with polished wood furniture and floral fabrics. ⊠ *Burke and Cotham Rds., Kew, 3101* 📞 *03/9817–4551* 📠 *03/9817–5680* 🛏 *21 rooms, 3 apartments* ⚲ *Some microwaves, pool, laundry facilities, meeting rooms; no smoking* ⊟ *AE, DC, MC, V.*

★ $ 🏨 **Robinson's by the Sea.** This lovely terrace house overlooks Port Phillip Bay, a five-minute stroll from the nightlife of Fitzroy Street, St. Kilda. The sitting room is warm, inviting, and furnished with excellent antiques and objets d'art. The prize front bedroom has a large balcony, a king-size bed, and its own sitting area. Other rooms are smaller but quieter. This, one of Melbourne's best bed-and-breakfasts, is run by Wendy Robinson, a virtual one-woman B&B industry: she also writes guides to inns and B&Bs around the country and conducts hospitality-training courses. Mrs. Robinson's famous breakfasts are a treat. ⊠ *335 Beaconsfield Parade, at Cowderoy St., St. Kilda West, 3182* 📞 *03/9534–2683* 📠 *03/9534–2683* ⊕ *www.babs.com.au* 🛏 *5 rooms without bath* ⚲ *Free parking; no-smoking rooms* ⊟ *AE, DC, MC, V* ⑩*BP.*

¢ 🏨 **Miami Motor Inn.** Like a Motel 6, only fancier, Miami Motor Inn is an excellent value for the budget- and style-conscious. The first two levels contain standard motel rooms with large wardrobes and private, streamlined bathrooms. The top floor has well-kept "economy rooms" with shared bathroom facilities. The staff are very helpful and can provide breakfast at good rates. ⊠ *13 Hawke St., at Spencer St., West Melbourne, 3003* 📞 *1800/132333 or 03/9321–2444* 📠 *03/9328–1820* ⊕ *www.themiami.com.au* 🛏 *78 rooms, 38 with shared bath* ⚲ *TVs, in-room data ports, laundry facilities* ⊟ *MC, V.*

NIGHTLIFE & THE ARTS

The Arts

Melbourne Events, available from tourist outlets, is a comprehensive monthly guide to what's happening in town. For a complete listing of performing arts events, galleries, and film, consult the "EG" (Entertainment Guide) supplement in the Friday edition of *The Age* newspaper. *Brother Sister* is the local gay paper.

Dance

In the 2,000-seat State Theatre at the Arts Centre, the **Australian Ballet** (✉ Victorian Arts Centre, 100 St. Kilda Rd., Southbank ☎ 03/9669–2700 Ballet, 13–6166 Ticketmaster) stages five programs annually and frequently presents visiting celebrity dancers from around the world.

Music

The **Melbourne Concert Hall** (✉ Victorian Arts Centre, 100 St. Kilda Rd., Southbank ☎ 03/9281–8000) stages classy concerts. Big-name, crowd-drawing contemporary artists perform at **Melbourne Park** (✉ Batman Ave., City Center ☎ 03/9286–1234).

The **Melbourne Symphony Orchestra** (✉ Victorian Arts Centre, 100 St. Kilda Rd., Southbank ☎ 13–6166 Ticketmaster) performs virtually year-round in the 2,600-seat Melbourne Concert Hall.

Open-air summertime (December–March) concerts can be seen at the **Sidney Myer Music Bowl** (✉ King's Domain near Swan St. Bridge, South Melbourne ☎ 13–6166 Ticketmaster).

Opera

The **Opera Australia** (✉ Victorian Arts Centre, 100 St. Kilda Rd., Southbank ☎ 03/9686–7477) has regular seasons, often with performances by world-renowned stars. The length and time of seasons vary, but all performances take place in the Melbourne Concert Hall.

Theater

Half-Tix (✉ Melbourne Town Hall, Swanston St., City Center ☎ 03/9650–9420) ticket booth in the Bourke Street Mall sells tickets to theater attractions at half price on performance days. It's open Monday 10–2, Tuesday–Thursday 11–6, Friday 11–6:30, and Saturday 10–2. Sales are cash only.

The **Melbourne Theatre Company** (✉ 19 Russell St., City Center ☎ 03/9684–4510) is the city's first and most successful theater company, and has two seasons yearly, during which classical, international, and Australian works are performed at the Russell Street Theatre. The city's second-largest company, the **Playbox at the CUB Malthouse Company** (✉ 113 Sturt St., Southbank ☎ 03/9685–5111), stages about 10 new or contemporary productions a year. The theater, the CUB Malthouse, is a flexible space designed for drama, dance, and circus companies.

Revues and plays are staged at the **Comedy Theatre** (✉ 240 Exhibition St., City Center ☎ 03/132–849). **Her Majesty's Theatre** (✉ 219 Exhibition St., City Center ☎ 03/9663–3211) hosts international musicals like *Cats* and *Chicago*. **La Mama** (✉ 205 Faraday St., Carlton ☎ 03/9347–6142) puts on innovative and contemporary productions in a bohemian theater. The **Princess Theatre** (✉ 163 Spring St., City Center ☎ 03/9299–9800) is the home of Broadway-style blockbusters. The **Regent Theatre** (✉ 191 Collins St., City Center ☎ 03/9299–9500) presents mainstream productions. **Theatreworks** (✉ 14 Acland St., St. Kilda ☎ 03/9534–3388) concentrates on contemporary Australian plays.

Nightlife

Bars & Cocktail Lounges

There has been a relative explosion in the number of bars, cocktail lounges, and nightclubs within the downtown area; the best ones are located in Flinders Lane and Little Collins Street. Many swank hotels have equally swank cocktail lounges. Bars not in major hotels tend to be more casual. The bubbling gay district along Commercial Road, in Prahran, also has many bars and restaurants.

The Atrium (✉ 25 Collins St., City Center ☎ 03/9653–0000), a cocktail bar on the 35th floor of the Hotel Sofitel, has spectacular views. Find old-world charm in the heart of the Windsor Hotel at the **The Cricketeer's Bar** (✉ 103 Spring St., City Center ☎ 03/9633–6170). The Grand Hyatt's **Deco Bar** (✉ 123 Collins St., City Center ☎ 03/9657–1234) is a sophisticated spot. The faithful patrons of **Dog's Bar** (✉ 54 Acland St., St. Kilda ☎ 03/9525–3599) are laid-back and supercool—they'd have to be to hang out at a bar advertising itself as a canine hot spot.

The George Hotel Bar (✉ Fitzroy and Grey Sts., St. Kilda ☎ 03/9525–5599) is in a superbly renovated 19th-century building. Reminiscent of Hollywood opulence, **Gin Palace** (✉ 190 Little Collins St., City Center ☎ 03/9654–0533) has more than enough types of martinis to satisfy any taste. Enter from Russell Street. **The Hairy Canary** (✉ 212 Little Collins St., City Center ☎ 03/9654–2471) is one of the grooviest places in the city, but it's standing-room-only unless you get here early. Stop by the **Park Lounge** (✉ 192 Wellington Parade, East Melbourne ☎ 03/9419–2000), at the Hilton on the Park, for drinks before or after the football or cricket match at the nearby Melbourne Cricket Ground. **Revolver** (✉ 229 Chapel St., Prahran ☎ 03/9521–5985) caters to the young. Antique leather sofas and cigars characterize the classy milieu at the **Supper Club** (✉ 161 Spring St., City Center ☎ 03/9654–6300).

Comedy Clubs

Comedy Club Melbourne (✉ 380 Lygon St., Carlton ☎ 03/9348–1622) is a popular place to see top-class Australian and international acts. In addition to being a hallowed live music venue, the **Esplanade Hotel** (✉ 11 Upper Esplanade, St. Kilda ☎ 03/9534–0211) is a testing ground for local comedians.

Dance Clubs

Most of the central city's dance clubs are along the King Street strip. Popularity is a fickle thing. Follow the crowds and ask your hotel concierge if you want the latest and hippest. The clubs usually open at 9 or 10 weekends and some weeknights and stay open until the early morning hours. Expect to pay a small cover at most clubs—between A$5 and A$15. Take note that King Street has a reputation for late-night violence. Authorities and club owners have improved the situation, but be cautious.

The action ranges from fast to furious at the multilevel, high-tech **Metro** (✉ 20–30 Bourke St., City Center ☎ 03/9663–4288), which has eight bars, a glass-enclosed café, and three dance floors. This nightclub is one of the hottest clubs in town for Melbourne's twentysomethings. The city's enduring night spot, previously known as Chasers, **Zos** (✉ 386 Chapel St., Prahran ☎ 03/9827–7379) is a good bet for anyone under 35. Music varies from night to night.

Jazz Clubs

Bennetts Lane (✉ 25 Bennetts La., City Center ☎ 03/9663–2856) is one of the city center's jazz mainstays, and cutting-edge cabaret acts are featured at **45 Downstairs** (✉ 45 Flinders La., City Center ☎ 03/9662–9966). **The Night Cat** (✉ 141 Johnston St., Fitzroy ☎ 03/9417–0090) hosts jazzy evening shows most nights of the week.

Music Clubs

At the **Crown Casino** (✉ Crown Entertainment Complex, Level 3, Riverside Ave., Southbank ☎ 03/9292–8888), the Showroom and the Mer-

cury Lounge attract big international and Australian headliners. For rock
and roll, punk, and grunge, head to the **Prince of Wales** (✉ 29 Fitzroy
St., St. Kilda ☎ 03/9536–1166), which also has a gay bar downstairs.
The Hi-Fi Bar (✉ 125 Swanston St., City Center ☎ 03/9654–7617) is a
popular venue for live local and less-known international rock bands.

SPORTS & THE OUTDOORS

Australian-Rules Football

Tickets for Aussie rules football (AFL) are available through **Ticketmaster** (☎ 13–6166) or at the playing fields. The **Melbourne Cricket Ground**
(✉ Brunton Ave., Yarra Park ☎ 03/9657–8867) is the prime venue for
AFL games.

An ambitious multimillion dollar residential and commercial redevelopment of the docks and former factory sites at the city's western edge,
Docklands has as its centerpiece the high-tech, indoor **Colonial Stadium**
(✉ Bourke St. W, Docklands ☎ 03/8625–7700). It's home to a number of Australian-rules football clubs. You can reach the district on foot
from Spencer Street.

Bicycling

Melbourne and its environs contain more than 100 km (62 mi) of bike
paths, including scenic routes along the Yarra River and Port Phillip Bay.
Bikes can be rented for about A$25 per day from the bike rental outposts (trailers) alongside the bike paths.

Bicycle Victoria (✉ Level 10, 446 Collins St., City Center ☎ 03/9328–3000)
can provide information about area bike paths.

Boating

At the **Studley Park Boathouse** (✉ Boathouse Rd., Kew ☎ 03/9853–1972),
canoes, kayaks, and rowboats are available for hire on a peaceful, delightful stretch of the Lower Yarra River, about 7 km (4½ mi) east of
the city center. Rentals cost from A$22 per hour for a two-person kayak
or rowboat to A$28 per hour for a four-person rowboat. The boathouse
is open daily from 9 until sunset.

Car Racing

Australian Formula 1 Grand Prix (✉ Albert and Canterbury Rds., Albert
Park ☎ 03/9258–7100 ⊕ www.grandprix.com.au) is a popular fixture
on Melbourne's calendar of annual events. It's held in the suburb of Albert Park, a small neighborhood 4 km (2½ mi) south of the city that encompasses the area surrounding Albert Park Lake.

Cricket

All big international and interstate cricket matches in Victoria are played
at the **Melbourne Cricket Ground** (✉ Brunton Ave., Yarra Park ☎ 03/
9657–8867 Stadium, 13–6166 Ticketmaster) from October to March.
The stadium has lights for night games and can accommodate 100,000
people. Tickets are available at the gate or through Ticketmaster.

Golf

Melbourne has the largest number of championship golf courses in
Australia.

Four kilometers (2½ mi) south of the city, **Albert Park Golf Course**
(✉ Queens Rd., South Melbourne ☎ 03/9510–5588) is an 18-hole,
par-72 course that traverses Albert Park Lake, near where the Formula
1 Grand Prix is held in March. The 18-hole, par-67 **Brighton Golf Links**
(✉ Dendy St., Brighton ☎ 03/9592–1388) has excellent scenery but is
quite busy on weekends and on midweek mornings. Club rental is avail-

AUSTRALIAN-RULES FOOTBALL

DESPITE ITS NAME, *novice observers frequently ask the question: "What rules?" This fast, vigorous game, played between teams of 18, is one of four kinds of football down under. Aussies also play Rugby League, Rugby Union, and soccer, but Aussie Rules, widely known as "footy," is the one to which Victoria, South Australia, the Top End, and Western Australia subscribe. It's the country's most popular spectator sport.*

Because it is gaining an international television audience, the intricacies of Aussie-rules football are no longer the complete mystery they once were to the uninitiated: the ball can be kicked or punched in any direction, but never thrown. Players make spectacular leaps vying to catch a kicked ball before it touches the ground, for which they earn a free kick. The game is said to be at its finest in Melbourne, and any defeat of a

Melbourne team—particularly in a grand final, as happened a few years ago—is widely interpreted as a sign of moral lassitude in the state of Victoria.

New South Wales and Queensland devote themselves to two versions of rugby. Rugby League, the professional game, is a faster, more exciting version of Rugby Union, the choice of purists.

able. **Ivanhoe Public Golf Course** (⊠ Vasey St., East Ivanhoe ☎ 03/9499–7001), an 18-hole, par-68 course, is well suited to the average golfer and is open to the public every day except holidays. Just five minutes from the beach, **Sandringham Golf Links** (⊠ Cheltenham Rd., Sandringham ☎ 03/9598–3590) is one of the better public courses. The area is known as the golf links because there are several excellent courses in the vicinity. Sandringham is an 18-hole, par-72 course.

Horse Racing
Melbourne is the only city in the world to declare a public holiday for a horse race—the Melbourne Cup—held on the first Tuesday in November since 1861. The Cup is also a fashion parade, and most of Melbourne society turns out in full regalia. The rest of the country comes to a standstill, with schools, shops, offices, and factories tuning in to the action.

The city has four top-class racetracks. **Flemington Race Course** (⊠ Epsom Rd., Flemington ☎ 03/9371–7171), 3 km (2 mi) outside the city, is Australia's premier race course and home of the Melbourne Cup. **Moonee Valley Race Course** (⊠ McPherson St., Moonee Ponds ☎ 03/9373–2222) is 6 km (4 mi) from town and holds the Cox Plate race in October. **Caulfield Race Course** (⊠ Station St., Caulfield ☎ 03/9257–7200), 10 km (6 mi) from the city, runs the Blue Diamond in February and the Caulfield Cup in October. **Sandown Race Course** (⊠ Racecourse Dr., Springvale ☎ 03/9518–1300), 25 km (16 mi) from the city, hosts the Sandown Cup in November.

Running
Some of the more popular local running trails include the 4-km (2½-mi) Tan, beginning at Anderson Street and Alexandra Avenue and looping around the perimeter of the Royal Botanic Gardens; the 5-km (3-mi)

Albert Park Lake Run in Albert Park; and the Bay Run, an 18-km (11-mi) round-trip run along Port Phillip Bay, starting at Kerford Road and Beaconsfield Parade in Albert Park and continuing on to Bay Street in Brighton.

Soccer

Pick-up or local league games are played in all seasons but summer in **Olympic Park** (⊠ Ovals 1 and 2, Swan St., Richmond ☎ 03/9286–1600).

Tennis

The **Australian Open** (☎ 03/9286–1175 ⊕ www.ausopen.com.au), held in January at the Melbourne Park National Tennis Centre, is one of the world's four Grand Slam events. You can buy tickets at the event.

Brought your racket? **Australian Open Tennis–Melbourne Park** (⊠ Batman Ave., City Center ☎ 03/9286–1244) has 22 outdoor and four hard indoor Rebound Ace courts. Play is canceled during the Australian Open in January. **East Melbourne Tennis Centre** (⊠ Powlett Reserve, Albert St., East Melbourne ☎ 03/9417–6511) has five synthetic-grass outdoor courts. **Fawkner Park Tennis Center** (⊠ Fawkner Park, Toorak Rd. W., South Yarra ☎ 03/9820–1551) has six synthetic-grass outdoor courts.

SHOPPING

Melbourne has firmly established itself as the nation's fashion capital. Australian designer labels are available on High Street in Armadale, on Toorak Road and Chapel Street in South Yarra, and on Bridge Road in Richmond. High-quality vintage clothing abounds on Greville Street in Prahran. Most shops are open Monday through Thursday 9–5:30, Friday until 9, and Saturday until 5. Major city stores are open Sunday until 5.

Department Stores

David Jones (⊠ 310 Bourke St., City Center ☎ 03/9643–2222), in the Bourke Street Mall, is one of the city's finer department stores.

Myer Melbourne (⊠ 314 Bourke St., City Center ☎ 03/9661–1111) is a vast department store with a long-standing reputation for quality merchandise.

Markets

Chapel Street Bazaar (⊠ 217–223 Chapel St., Prahran ☎ 03/9529–1727) has wooden stalls selling everything from stylish secondhand clothes to sunglasses and knickknacks.

Essential Ingredient (⊠ Elizabeth St., Prahran ☎ 03/9520–3287) stocks raw ingredients, a lot of pre- and semiprepared foods, and packaged goods from around the world.

Prahran Market (⊠ 177 Commercial Rd., Prahran ☎ 03/8290–8220) sells nothing but food—a fantastic, mouthwatering array imported from all over the world. Committed foodies seek out everything from star fruit and lemongrass to emu eggs and homemade relishes.

South Melbourne Market (⊠ Cecil St., cnr., of Coventry St., South Melbourne ☎ 03/8290–8220), open Wednesday, Friday, and weekends from 8 AM, thrives on its huge variety of fresh produce and foodstuffs.

Shopping Centers, Arcades & Malls

Australia on Collins (⊠ 260 Collins St., City Center ☎ 03/9650–4355) offers fashion, homewear, beauty, and an abundance of food. Fashion labels include Gazman, Made in Japan, Country Road, and Siricco Leather.

Block Arcade (⊠ 282 Collins St., City Center ☎ 03/9654–5244), an elegant 19th-century shopping plaza, contains the venerable Hopetoun Tea Rooms, The French Jewel Box, Orrefors Kosta Boda, Dasel Dolls and Bears, and Australian By Design.

Bridge Road, in the suburb of Richmond at the end of Flinders Street, east of the city, is a popular shopping strip for women's retail fashion that caters to all budgets.

Burke Road, in the leafy eastern suburb of Camberwell, has coffee shops, boutiques, and stores selling top Australian men's and women's labels.

Fodor'sChoice **Chapel Street,** in South Yarra between Toorak and Dandenong Roads,
★ is where you can find some of the ritziest boutiques in Melbourne, as well as cafés, art galleries, bars, and restaurants.

Crown Entertainment Complex (⊠ Riverside Ave., Southbank ☎ 03/9292–8888), the mall adjacent to the casino, sells Versace, Donna Karan, Gucci, Armani, and Prada, among others.

High Street, between the suburbs of Prahran and Armadale, to the east of Chapel Street, has the best collection of antiques shops in Australia.

The Jam Factory (⊠ 500 Chapel St., South Yarra ☎ 03/9860–8500) consists of a group of historic bluestone buildings that house cinemas, fashion, food, and gift shops, as well as a branch of the giant Borders book and music store.

★ **Little Collins Street,** in the heart of the city, has an excellent range of boutique and designer-label stores. A host of quality cafés and eateries can be found in neighboring laneways.

Melbourne Central (⊠ 300 Lonsdale St., City Center ☎ 03/9922–1100) is a dizzying complex huge enough to enclose a 100-year-old shot tower (used to make bullets) in its atrium.

Royal Arcade (⊠ 355 Bourke St., City Center ☎ no phone), built in 1846, is Melbourne's oldest shopping plaza. It remains a lovely place to browse, and it's home to the splendid Gaunt's Clock, which tolls away the hours.

Southgate (⊠ 4 Southbank Promenade, Southbank ☎ 03/9699–4311) has a spectacular riverside location. The shops and eateries here are a short walk both from the city center across Princes Bridge and from the Victorian Arts Center. There's outdoor seating next to the Southbank promenade.

Specialty Stores

Books

Borders (⊠ The Jam Factory, Chapel St., South Yarra ☎ 03/9824–2299) is a gigantic book and music emporium.

Brunswick Street Bookstore (⊠ 305 Brunswick St., Fitzroy ☎ 03/9416–1030) sells modern Australian literature, art and design-orientated books.

Hill of Content (⊠ 86 Bourke St., City Center ☎ 03/9662–9472), with a knowledgeable staff and an excellent selection of titles, is a Melbourne favorite.

Clothing

Andrea Gold (✉ 110 Bridge Rd., Richmond ☎ 03/9428–1226) stocks a wide selection of women's wear, including dresses, suits, jewelry, and handbags.

Anthea Crawford (✉ 205 Bridge Rd., Richmond ☎ 03/9428–1670) attracts women who want high-quality dresswear, hats, and accessories.

Cose Plus (✉ 3/286 Toorak Rd., South Yarra ☎ 03/9826–5788) is a popular women's shop.

Endo-D (✉ 123 Toorak Rd., South Yarra ☎ 03/9866–2248) carries women's fashions and accessories.

Jean Pascal (✉ 1023 High St., Armadale ☎ 03/9822–8144) is a local favorite of women shoppers.

Trappings Gallery (✉ 1025 High St., Armadale ☎ 03/9822–9433) sells a combination of women's working clothes and dress garments, with all the stylish accoutrements available.

Sam Bear (✉ 225 Russell St., City Center ☎ 03/9663–2191), a Melbourne institution, sells everything from Aussie outerwear to Swiss Army knives.

Gifts

Aboriginal Handcrafts (✉ Mezzanine, 130 Little Collins St., City Center ☎ 03/9650–4717) stocks handcrafts created by Aborigines, including paintings, drawings, cooking implements, and more.

Australiana General Store (✉ 20–45 Collins St., City Center ☎ 03/9650–2075) sells all kinds of Australian-made goods.

National Trust Gift Shop (✉ 493 Toorak Rd., Toorak ☎ 03/9827–9385) has Australian-made goods, including cards, pottery, clothes, and natural medicines.

Jewelry

Altmann and Cherny (✉ 120 Exhibition St., City Center ☎ 03/9650–9685) sells opals at tax-free prices to overseas tourists.

Craft Victoria (✉ 31 Flinders La., City Center ☎ 03/9650–7775) has the best selection of international and local pottery and jewelry.

Makers Mark Gallery (✉ Shop 9, 101 Collins St., City Center ☎ 03/9654–8488) showcases the work of some of the country's finest jewelers.

Music

Batman Records (✉ 277 Little Lonsdale St., City Center ☎ 03/9639–3777) has a vast collection of old hits and contemporary music.

Discurio (✉ 105 Elizabeth St., City Center ☎ 03/9600–1488) carries a good cross section of traditional pop, rock, and contemporary music by Australian artists.

MELBOURNE A TO Z

To research prices, get advice from other travelers, and book travel arrangements, visit www.fodors.com.

AIR TRAVEL

Melbourne is most easily reached by plane, as it—like many places in Australia—is hours by car from even the nearest town. International airlines flying into Melbourne include Air New Zealand, British Airways, Qantas, and United. Domestic carriers serving Melbourne are Qantas and Virgin Blue.

🛪 Carriers **Air New Zealand** ☎ 13/2476. **British Airways** ☎ 03/9656–8133. **Virgin Blue** ☎ 13/6789. **Qantas Airways** ☎ 13/1313. **United** ☎ 13/1777.

AIRPORTS

Melbourne Airport is 22 km (14 mi) northwest of the central business district and can be reached easily from the city on the Tullamarine Freeway. The international terminal is in the center of the airport complex. Domestic terminals are on either side.

🚻 **Melbourne Airport** ☎ 03/9297-1600 ⊕ www.melbourne-airport.com.au.

TRANSFERS Skybus, a public transportation bus service, runs between the airport and city center, making a loop through the city before terminating at Spencer Street Station. The A$13 shuttle departs every 15 minutes from 6 AM to midnight, then every half hour afterward. Airport-bound buses depart from Spencer Street at half-hour intervals from 6 AM to 12 PM, and then at hourly intervals after that.

For three or more people traveling together, a taxi is a better value to or from the airport. You can catch a taxi in front of the building. The cost into town is approximately A$30. Limousines to the city cost about A$160. Limousines Australia is one of the larger companies.

🚻 **Limousines Australia** ☎ 03/9486-6527. **Skybus** ☎ 03/9335-3066 ⊕ www.skybus.com.au.

BUS TRAVEL TO & FROM MELBOURNE

McCaffertys Greyhound links the city with all Australian capital cities and with major towns and cities throughout Victoria. The terminal is on the corner of Swanston and Franklin streets. From Melbourne, it's about 10 hours to Adelaide, about 12 hours to Sydney, about 50 hours to Perth (consider flying), and about 8 hours to Canberra.

🚻 **Travel Coach** ☎ 13-2030 ⊕ www.greyhound.com.au, www.mccaffertys.com.au.

BUS & TRAM TRAVEL WITHIN MELBOURNE

The city's privately operated public transport system includes buses, trains, and trams (streetcars). In fact, Melbourne has one of the world's largest tram networks, with 365 km (226 mi) of track in the inner city and suburbs. By and large, the system is a delight—fast, convenient, and cheap.

The city's public transport system is operated by Metropolitan Transit, which divides Melbourne into three zones. Zone 1 is the urban core, where you will likely spend most of your time. The basic ticket is the one-zone ticket, which can be purchased on board the bus or prepurchased from news agents for A$2.60 and is valid for travel within that zone on any tram, bus, or train for a period of two hours after purchase. For travelers, the most useful ticket is probably the Zone 1 day ticket, which costs A$5 and is available on board any tram. A free route map is available from the Victoria Tourism Information Service.

Trams run until midnight and can be hailed wherever you see a green and gold tram-stop sign. A free City Circle tram operates every 10 minutes daily 10–6 on the fringe of the Central Business District, with stops in Flinders, Spencer, La Trobe, Victoria, and Spring streets. Look for the burgundy-and-cream trams.

🚻 **Metropolitan Transit** ☎ 13-1638 ⊕ www.victrip.com.au. **Victoria Tourism Information Service** ☎ 13-2842 ⊕ www.visitvictoria.com.

CAR RENTAL

Avis, Budget, and Hertz have branches at Melbourne Airport as well as downtown. If you rent from a major company, expect to pay about A$60 per day for a compact standard model. If you don't mind an older model and can return the car to the pick-up point, consider a smaller local rental agency, such as Eurocar and Rent-a-Bomb.

🚻 **Avis** ☎ 13-6333. **Budget** ☎ 13-2727. **Eurocar** ☎ 13-1390. **Hertz** ☎ 13-3039. **Rent-a-Bomb** ☎ 03/9428-0088.

CAR TRAVEL

The major route into Melbourne is Hume Highway, which runs northeast to Canberra, 646 km (400 mi) distant, and Sydney, which is 868 km (538 mi) away. Princes Highway follows the coast to Sydney in one direction and to Adelaide, 728 km (451 mi) northwest of Melbourne, in the other. The Western Highway runs northwest 111 km (69 mi) to Ballarat, and the Calder Highway travels north to Bendigo, a journey of 149 km (92 mi). From Melbourne, it takes 10 to 12 hours to reach Sydney, about 9 hours to Adelaide, and about 1½ hours to Bendigo and Ballarat. The Royal Automobile Club of Victoria (RACV) is the major source of information on all aspects of road travel in Victoria.

Melbourne's regimented layout makes it easy to negotiate by car, but two unusual rules apply because of the tram traffic on the city's major roads. Trams should be passed on the *left,* and when a tram stops to allow passengers to disembark, the cars behind it also must stop unless there is a railed safety zone for tram passengers.

At some intersections within the city, drivers wishing to turn *right* must stay in the *left* lane as they enter the intersection, then wait for the traffic signals to change before proceeding with the turn. The rule is intended to prevent traffic from impeding tram service. For complete directions, look for the black-and-white traffic signs suspended overhead as you enter each intersection where this rule applies. All other right-hand turns are made from the center. It's far easier to understand this rule by seeing it in action rather than reading about it.

Royal Automobile Club of Victoria (RACV) ☎ 13-1955 ⊕ www.racv.com.au.

CONSULATES

Most embassies are in Canberra, but many countries also have consulates or honorary consuls in Melbourne, including the American Consulate-General and the British Consulate-General. Others are usually listed in the telephone directory under the specific country.

American Consulate-General ✉ 553 St. Kilda Rd., St. Kilda ☎ 03/9526-5900. **British Consulate-General** ✉ 90 Collins St., City Center ☎ 03/9652-1600.

EMERGENCIES

In an emergency, dial **000** to reach an ambulance, the fire station, or the police. The Collins Place Pharmacy is open 9–6.

Doctors & Dentists Swanston Street Medical Centre ✉ 393 Swanston St., City Center ☎ 03/9654-2722. **Royal Dental Hospital** ✉ Elizabeth St. and Flemington Rd., Parkville ☎ 03/9341-0222. **The Medical Center** ✉ 115-125 Victoria Rd., Northcote ☎ 03/9482-2866.

Hospitals Alfred Hospital ✉ Commercial Rd., Prahran ☎ 03/9276-2000. **Royal Women's Hospital** ✉ 132 Grattan St., Carlton ☎ 03/9344-2000. **St. Vincent's Hospital** ✉ Victoria Parade, Fitzroy ☎ 03/9288-2211.

Pharmacy Collins Place Pharmacy ✉ 45 Collins St., City Center ☎ 03/9650-9034.

MAIL, BUSINESS & INTERNET SERVICES

The general post office is open from 8:15 to 5:30 weekdays and 10 to 3 on Saturday. The post office's Express Post can send mail overnight within Australia; Federal Express handles 24-hour overseas packages.

Melbourne's larger hotels have business services and can recommend local businesses for any additional necessities. If you prefer an Internet café, Melbourne has them, too.

Internet Cafés Internet Café St. Kilda ✉ 9 Grey St., St. Kilda ☎ 03/9534-2666. **ProGamer Internet and Games Cafés** ✉ 208-210 Latrobe St., City Center ☎ 03/9639-7171.

Mail Services General Post Office ✉ Bourke St. and Elizabeth St., City Center ☎ 03/9203-3076. **MBE Business Service Centre** ✉ 439 Little Bourke St., City Center.

MONEY MATTERS

Money changers in Melbourne are not as common as in other major international cities—try along Collins, Elizabeth, or Swanston streets. ATMs are plentiful throughout Victoria and accept CIRRUS, Maestro, PLUS, and credit cards. Other places to get and change money include large hotels, American Express, and Thomas Cook. If heading into regional Victoria, it's wise to cash up beforehand rather than relying on regional banking outlets, which may or may not cater to international travelers.

🏦 Banks **ANZ** ✉ 6/530 Collins St., City Center ☎ 13-1314. **Commonwealth** ✉ 225 Bourke St., City Center ☎ 03/9675-1220 ✉ 385 Bourke St., City Center ☎ 03/9675-7000 ✉ 21 Swanston St., City Center ☎ 03/9675-1496 ✉ 231 Swanston St., City Center ☎ 03/9663-3901. **National Australia** ✉ 164 Bourke St., City Center ✉ 500 Bourke St., City Center ✉ 271 Collins St., City Center ✉ 203 Elizabeth St., City Center ☎ 13-2265. **Westpac** ✉ 447 Bourke St., City Center ✉ 360 Collins St., City Center ✉ Collins and Swanston Sts., City Center ✉ 555 Collins St., City Center ☎ 13-2032.

🏦 Exchange Services **American Express** ✉ 233 Collins St., City Center ☎ 03/9633-6333. **Thomas Cook** ✉ 257 Collins St., City Center ✉ 99 Williams St., City Center ✉ 188 Swanston St., City Center ✉ 261 Bourke St., City Center ☎ 13-1771.

SIGHTSEEING TOURS

BOAT TOURS The *Wattle* is a restored steam tug that cruises Port Phillip Bay. The boat runs from Melbourne September–May, and is available for charter. Five one-hour cruises also leave from Gem Pier in Williamstown from around noon on. Tickets are A$5 for adults.

The modern, glass-enclosed boats of the Melbourne River Cruises fleet take one, two, and two-and-a-half-hour cruises daily (A$17, A$25, and A$30 respectively) on the Yarra River, either west through the commercial heart of the city or east through the parks and gardens, or a combination of the two. There's also a trip to the port town of Williamstown, west of Melbourne. The boat departs from Berth 1, Princes Walk, on the opposite side of Princes Bridge from Flinders Street Station, or Berth 5 and 6 at Southgate. Look for the blue kiosk. Daily tours run every half hour from 10 to 4.

Yarra Yarra Water Taxis use a 1950s mahogany speedboat. The size of the boat makes it possible to follow the Yarra as far as Dight's Falls, passing some of Melbourne's larger houses in the wealthiest suburbs on the way. It costs A$100 per hour and can carry up to six passengers. If you want to plan a barbecue, the boat stops at a small island where you can cook your own.

Gray Line (➪ *see* Bus Tours) also has boat tours.

🚤 **Melbourne River Cruises** ✉ Vault 18, Banana Alley and Queensbridge St., City Center ☎ 03/9614-1215. *Wattle* ✉ 20 Victoria Dock, West Melbourne ☎ 03/9328-2739 🌐 www.baysteamers.com.au. **Yarra Yarra Water Taxis** ☎ 0411/255179.

BUS TOURS Gray Line has guided tours of Melbourne and its surroundings by coach and boat. On the Melbourne Experience tour, you'll visit the city center's main attractions and some of the surrounding parks. The A$50 tour departs daily at 8:45 from the company's headquarters and is three hours.

AAT Kings, Australian Pacific Tours, Great Sights, and Melbourne Sightseeing all have similar general-interest trips and prices.

Melbourne Explorer has a do-it-yourself tour of the city on a bus that circles past major attractions, including the zoo, art galleries, museums, and the parks to the east. The tour ticket (A$32) is valid for 21 stops along the circuit. The tour begins at the Town Hall on Swanston Street (near Little Collins Street).

🚌 **AAT Kings** ✉ 180 Swanston St., City Center ☎ 03/9663-3377. **Australian Pacific Tours** ✉ 180 Swanston St., City Center ☎ 03/9663-1611. **Gray Line** ✉ 180 Swanston

St., City Center ☎03/9663-4455 ⊕ www.grayline.com.au. **Great Sights** ✉180 Swanston St., City Center ☎ 03/9639-2211. **Melbourne Explorer** ✉ 180 Swanston St., City Center ☎ 03/9650-7000. **Melbourne Sightseeing** ✉ 180 Swanston St., City Center ☎ 03/9663-3388 ⊕ www.ozhorizons.com.au.

SHOPPING TOURS Serious shoppers might want to take advantage of a Shopping Spree Tour, which includes lunch and escorted shopping at some at Melbourne's best manufacturers and importers. Tours depart Monday through Saturday at 8:30. The cost is A$65 per person.

🚩 **Shopping Spree Tours** ☎ 03/9596-6600.

SPORTS TOURS Melbourne's excellent bicycle path network and flat terrain makes cycling pleasurable. For around A$12 per hour, rent a bike from Bicycles For Hire, which is on the Yarra River near Princes Bridge in the city. For more information about cycling around Melbourne—with or without help—contact Bicycle Victoria.

Journey Events Travel specializes in sporting tours of Melbourne. Headed by ex-AFL football star Paul Salmon, the company organizes packages for major sporting events including Aussie-rules football games, tennis, golf, cricket, and the Formula 1 Grand Prix. Tours include accommodations and admission.

🚩 **Bicycle Victoria** ✉ Level 10, 446 Collins St., City Center ☎ 03/9328-3000 🖷 03/8636-8800. **Hire A Bicycle** ✉ Under Batman Ave. at Yarra River, South Yarra ☎ 04/1261-6633. **Journey Events Travel** ✉ Level 7, 420 St. Kilda, Melbourne ☎ 03/9639-6022 🖷 03/9639-7055.

TOWN HALL TOUR Learn about the history and the architectural significance of the Town Hall throughout Melbourne's development. Some tours visit the refurbished Town Hall Organ; it's available Monday–Friday at 11 AM and 1 PM. Tours are free but reservations are essential.

🚩 **Melbourne Town Hall** ✉ Swanston and Little Collins Sts., City Center ☎ 03/9658-9658.

WALKING TOURS Guided walking tours (A$20) taking in Melbourne's architectural and historical sites are available through Golden Mile Heritage Trail. Tours are 2½ to 3½ hours.

🚩 **Golden Mile Heritage Trail** ☎ 1300/130152 ⊕ www.melbournesgoldenmile.com.

TELEPHONES

The code for Victoria (and Tasmania) is 03. If you're in Melbourne, you don't need to dial the 03 before numbers in regional Victoria, but you must use the 03 for Tasmanian numbers. Public telephones are everywhere. Most accept coins as well as phone cards that can be purchased in certain denominations from newsagents and post offices.

TAXIS

Melbourne's taxis are gradually adopting a yellow color scheme, and drivers are required to wear uniforms. Taxis are metered, and can be hailed on the street and at taxi stands or ordered by phone. Major taxi companies include Yellow Cabs, Embassy, North Suburban, and Silver Top.

🚩 **Embassy** ☎ 13-1755. **North Suburban** ☎ 13-1119. **Silver Top** ☎ 13-1008. **Yellow Cabs** ☎ 13-2227.

TRAIN TRAVEL

Spencer Street Railway Station is at Spencer and Little Collins streets. The country-wide V-Line service has eight-hour trips to Sydney. Public transportation is available here, but if you've got cumbersome luggage, you'd do better to head for the taxi stand outside the station.

🚩 **Spencer Street Railway Station** ✉ Spencer St. ☎ 03/9691-2001. **V Line** ✉ Spencer St. ☎ 13-6196.

VISITOR INFORMATION

The Melbourne Information Centre at Federation Square provides information in six languages with large-screen videos, touch screens, permanent displays, and daily newspapers, and there is access to the Melbourne Web site as well. The Centre is open daily 9–6. The Best of Victoria Booking Service here can help if you're looking for accommodations. It also has cheap Internet access.

Want a free personalized tour? The Melbourne Greeters service, a Melbourne Information Centre program, pairs you with a local volunteer who shares your interests. You can spend two to four hours with the volunteer visiting relevant parts of the city and talking about subjects such as Aboriginal culture, Australian film, parks and gardens, shopping, gay culture, history, theater, and sports. At least three days' notice, preferably more, is required.

City Ambassadors provided by the City of Melbourne rove the central retail area providing directions and information for anyone who needs their assistance (Monday–Saturday 10–5).

🚹 **Best of Victoria Booking Service** ☎ 1300/780045 or 03/9642-1055. **City of Melbourne Ambassadors Program** ☎ 03/9658-9658. **Melbourne Greeters** ✉ Federation Square, Flinders and Swanston Sts., City Center ☎ 03/9658-9524 🖷 03/9654-1054. **Melbourne Information Centre** ✉ Federation Square, Flinders and Swanston Sts., City Center ☎ 03/9658-9658 ⊕ www.melbourne.vic.gov.au.

VICTORIA

5

FODOR'S CHOICE
Arthurs, restaurant in Sorrento
Boroka Downs, hotel in Halls Gap
Gardiwerd (Grampians National Park), at Halls Gap
Hepburn Springs Spa Centre, near Hepburn Springs
La Baracca, restaurant in Main Ridge
Port Campbell National Park, at Port Campbell
Stefano's, restaurant in Mildura
T'Gallant, winery in Main Ridge
Trentham Estate, winery in Trentham Cliffs

HIGHLY RECOMMENDED

RESTAURANTS The Boatshed, in Ballarat
Kosta's Taverna, in Lorne

HOTELS The Ansonia, in Ballarat
Howqua Dale Gourmet Retreat, in Howqua
Kinross, in Beechworth
Lake House Restaurant, in Daylesford
Quamby Homestead, in Woolsthorpe

SIGHTS Logan's Beach, near Warrnambool
Phillip Island
Wilson's Promontory National Park, at Tidal River

By Terry
Durack, Walter
Glaser,
Michael
Gebicki, and
Josie Gibson

Updated by
Liza Power

IT'S NOT JUST CITIES THAT TRAVELERS LOVE; it's often the roads between them, and many of Victoria's best sights are within a day's drive of Melbourne. You can follow the spectacular western coastline to reach the stunning rock formations known as the Twelve Apostles, or watch the sunrise over the northern Yarra Valley vineyards from the basket of a hot-air balloon—glass of champagne in hand. Take in a sunset over the Murray River, accompanied by laughing kookaburras, from the deck of a meandering paddle steamer. Taste local wines on the Mornington Peninsula, or spend a day at the beach in charming Queenscliff.

Separated from New South Wales by the mighty Murray River and fronted by a rugged and beautiful coastline, Victoria's terrain is as varied as any in the country. If you're expecting an Australian norm of big sky and vast desert horizons, you may be surprised by lush farms, vineyards, forests, and mountain peaks. And though it's younger than its rival, New South Wales, Victoria possesses a sense of history and continuity often missing in other Australian states, where humanity's grasp on the land appears temporary and precarious. Even the smallest rural communities in Victoria erect some kind of museum.

In Australian terms, Victoria is a compact state, astonishing in its contrasts and all the more exciting for them. Beyond the urban sprawl of Melbourne, which now extends its tentacles as far as the Mornington Peninsula, the great oceanscapes of the West Coast are among the most seductive elements of Victoria's beauty. The romantic history of the gold rushes pervades central Victoria, while paddle steamers still ply the waters of the mighty Murray River. The long stretch of the Murray region is also known for its wineries. From the Grampians in the west to the sprawling alpine parks in the east, the great Victorian outdoors is reason enough itself to plan a trip.

Exploring Victoria

A collection of sweeping landscapes has been quilted together to make up this beautiful state. Along the West Coast, rugged, cliff-lined seascapes alternate with thick forests and charming resort towns. Inland are historic goldfields communities, river towns along the Murray, and esteemed vineyards. However, the contrasting landscape is best represented in Victoria's national parks: the weathered offshore rock formations of Port Campbell; the waterfalls, flora, and fauna of Gardiwerd; the high-country solitude of Alpine National Park; and the densely forested mountains and white-sand beaches of Wilson's Promontory.

The best way to explore Victoria is by car. The state's road system is excellent, with clearly marked highways linking the Great Ocean Road to Wilson's Promontory, the Yarra Valley, the Murray River region, and the Mornington Peninsula. Although distances can be great, the changing scenery is entertainment in itself—and you'll always discover new corners of the state as you go. From Melbourne, the capital, you can travel to Geelong in the Bellarine Peninsula, as well as the northwest settlements of Ballarat and Bendigo. If you're exploring the Murray River region, head for the towns of Echuca, Wodonga, Swan Hill, and Mildura. Buses and trains, which cost less but take more time, also run between most regional centers.

About the Restaurants
You'll eat extremely well in Victoria, where chefs take pride in their trend-setting preparations of fresh local produce. A range of international flavors are found in casual and fine dining spots—and you can have your fill without breaking your budget, as prices are far less than in Sydney.

On Sunday, join Victorians for their beloved all-day brunch, when café menus feature "brekky" until as late as 4 PM.

WHAT IT COSTS In Australian dollars				
	$$$$	$$$	$$	$	¢
AT DINNER	over $50	$36–$50	$21–$35	$10–$20	under $10

Prices are for a main course at dinner.

About the Hotels

Accommodations in Victoria include grand country hotels, simple roadside motels, secluded bushland or seaside cabins, and backpacker hostels. Although you won't find large, modern resorts in this state, most of the grand old mansions and simple homes offering rooms have hot water, air conditioning, and free parking. Also, as at the larger international hotel chains, rates are usually reduced after school and national holidays. The Victorian Tourism Information (www.visitvictoria.com) has a list of the state's accommodations to help you plan.

WHAT IT COSTS In Australian dollars				
	$$$$	$$$	$$	$	¢
FOR 2 PEOPLE	over $300	$201–$300	$151–$200	$100–$150	under $100

Prices are for two people in a standard double room in high season, including tax and service, based on the European Plan (with no meals) unless otherwise noted.

Timing

Victoria is at its most beautiful in fall, March through May, when days are crisp, sunny, and clear, and the foliage in parks and gardens is glorious. Winter, with its wild seas and leaden skies, stretches May through August in this region, providing a suitable backdrop for the dramatic coastal scenery. It's dry and sunny in the northeast, however, thanks to the cloud-blocking bulk of the Great Dividing Range. Northeast summers, November through February, are extremely hot, so it's best to travel here and through gold country in spring and fall.

Festivals abound throughout the state, starting with Warrnambool's Wunta Fiesta in February, which entertains thousands with whale-boat races, a seafood and wine festival, and a carnival. The Rutherglen Wine Festival, which celebrates the year's harvest with music, parades, and parties, is a major event during Labor Day weekend in March. The Begonia Festival in Ballarat is held annually in February or March, also when Port Fairy hosts the popular Port Fairy Folk Festival. The annual Maldon Festival and Queenscliff Music Festival, both in November, draw hundreds of visitors to town. Accommodations are also hard to find between Christmas and New Year's, during school holidays, and during events at the Phillip Island Grand Prix Circuit.

Victorians love the great outdoors, hence the many mountain biking, hiking, and four-wheel-drive trails throughout the state. The best whitewater rafting, abseiling, rock climbing, hang-gliding, and bushwalking options are in the high country around Bright and Mount Buffalo. Wilson's Promontory, Warburton, and the Upper Yarra region around Marysville also have beautiful trails. Victoria's mostly mild weather means that you can participate in outdoor activities from skiing to hiking almost whenever you visit.

5

Victoria's relatively compact size makes the state's principal attractions appealingly easy to reach. Another region, another taste of this richly endowed state, is never too far away. Head off to the Melbourne suburbs for antiquing and nightlife, drive along the Great Ocean Road, explore Phillip Island, take a wine-tasting tour, hike through the forested mountains, or settle back into the Hepburn Springs spas. The longer you stay, the more you'll find to keep you in this fascinating state of myriad outdoor settings.

If you have
3 days

Tour ⊡ **Melbourne** the first day, spend the night, and on the next morning head for **Belgrave.** Here you can ride on the Puffing Billy through the fern gullies and forests of the ⊡ **Dandenongs.** In the afternoon, travel to ⊡ **Phillip Island** for the endearing sunset penguin parade at Summerland Beach. Stay the night, and on the third morning meander along the coastal roads of the **Mornington Peninsula** through such stately towns as Sorrento and Portsea. Stop at a beach, or pick a Melbourne neighborhood or two to explore in the afternoon.

If you have
5 days

The first day tour ⊡ **Melbourne** and spend the night, then on day two make your way west along the Great Ocean Road. This is one of the world's finest scenic drives, offering stops at the irresistible beaches of the **West Coast Region** and at the National Wool Museum in **Geelong.** Overnight in ⊡ **Lorne,** beneath the Otway Ranges, then drive west to **Port Campbell National Park** on day three. Here you can view the Twelve Apostles rock formation, take a walk to the beach, and continue to ⊡ **Warrnambool** for the night. On day four, take a morning tour of Flagstaff Hill Maritime Village, then drive northeast to the goldfields center of ⊡ **Ballarat.** This evening you can explore the town's 19th-century streetscapes, then catch the sound-and-light show at Sovereign Hill Historical Park. Spend the night here, and in the morning revisit Sovereign Hill and its entertaining re-creation of the 1851 gold diggings before returning to Melbourne.

If you have
10 days

Spend your first day and night in ⊡ **Melbourne,** and on day two explore ⊡ **Phillip Island.** After sunset, watch the penguin parade at Summerland beach, then stay on the island or return to Melbourne for the night. On day three, take a drive along the West Coast, overnighting in ⊡ **Lorne.** Spend day four discovering the delights of **Port Campbell National Park** and ⊡ **Warrnambool,** then drive to ⊡ **Port Fairy** for the night. Start day five early with a drive via **Grampians National Park,** where you can pet the tame kangaroos at Zumstein. Overnight in ⊡ **Ballarat,** then on day six take your time wandering through **Daylesford** and the spa town of **Hepburn Springs** toward ⊡ **Bendigo,** where you'll stay the night. On day seven tour the Golden Dragon Museum, examining the history of the Chinese on the goldfields. In the afternoon, drive to ⊡ **Echuca,** a Murray River town, stopping in a couple of wineries on your way to ⊡ **Beechworth.** Stay here two nights, taking days eight and nine to discover **Alpine National Park.** On the last day, revisit your favorite regional highlights as you make your way back to the capital.

AROUND MELBOURNE

Beaches and vineyards, mountains and wild parks, and gardens and grand estates are just a few hours outside of the city. To the east, in the Dandenong Ranges, the narrow, winding Mount Dandenong Tourist Road takes you on a scenic journey through rain forests and flower-filled towns of timber houses. South of Melbourne, the Bellarine Peninsula to the west and the Mornington Peninsula to the east form a horseshoe around Port Phillip Bay. While the Mornington Peninsula offers myriad wineries, horseback riding, and scenic walking trails, the Bellarine offers a pathway to the Great Ocean Road, one of the country's most spectacular ocean drives. Phillip Island's rugged coastline surrounds wildlife parks populated with koalas, seals, and thousands of fairy penguins. Further west, Wilson's Promontory and the Gippsland Lakes are two more of the state's remarkable natural areas.

The Dandenongs/Yarra Valley

Melburnians come to the Dandenong Ranges for a breath of fresh air, especially in autumn when the deciduous trees turn golden, and in spring when the gardens explode into color with tulip, daffodil, azalea, and rhododendron blooms. The vine-carpeted Yarra Valley—home of many top-class wines—is a favorite at all times of the year, although local reds always taste better by a crackling open fire in autumn or winter.

Healesville
60 km (37 mi) northeast of Melbourne.

The township of Healesville began its days in the 1860s as a coach stop along the road to the Gippsland and Yarra Valley goldfields. Two decades later, when the region's gold mining declined, Healesville became a logging center that grew by leaps and bounds, especially after it was linked by rail with Melbourne in 1889. The town was soon a popular mountain retreat for wealthy Melburnians, whose descendents still arrive to visit the famous Yarra Valley wineries and to see the wildlife in the Healesville Sanctuary.

Healesville's main street, lined with antique dealers, two old art deco hotels, and a huddle of shops, makes for a pleasant wander after lunch at a nearby winery. From here, you can travel to Marysville, where picturesque pathways lead past the Steavensons Falls and through forests of beech and mountain ash trees. Another option is to take the spectacular Acheron Way drive, which circles back to Warburton.

The most popular way to sample the wines and see the vineyards of the Yarra Valley is on a winery tour. Most depart from Melbourne and include four to five wineries and lunch; alternately, you could concoct your own leisurely wine tour of the region. If you haven't time for touring, head to the Healesville Hotel, which has a fantastic wine list with labels from many smaller boutique vineyards. One of the best times to visit the Yarra Valley is during February, when the Grape Grazing Festival features wine tastings, music, and fine cuisine. On Grape Grazing Day 21, wineries present two meals designed by top regional chefs—and matched by two superb wines—to an accompaniment of live music.

Take one of the daily tours at **De Bortoli** (✉ Pinnacle La., Dixon's Creek ☎ 03/5965–2271) and you'll follow the wine-making process through vineyards and barrel sheds. Chardonnays and Rieslings are specialties, and tastings are offered. The restaurant, which has stunning views of the surrounding vines, landscaped gardens, and mountains, serves such

The Amazing Outdoors

Victoria has outstanding national parks: coastal, mountain, rain forest, and riparian environments that are havens for remarkable plant and animal life. Bushwalking, canoeing, fishing, hiking, rafting, and riding are all choices here—it's a great state for getting out. Alpine National Park, Mt. Buffalo National Park, and others throughout the state show off the vast wilderness so near to the capital. Even on a day trip from Melbourne you can see some of Australia's best outdoor sights: the seascapes of Port Campbell, the rock spires and waterfalls in Grampians National Park, and the fairy penguin and sea lion colonies on Phillip Island.

5

Tasteful Dining

You'll eat well in this state of natural beauty and bounty, especially in Victoria's wine country. Regional specialties include kangaroo steaks, Gippsland cheeses, smoked meats, apples, organic blueberries from the Mornington Peninsula, and sun-dried citrus fruits and pistachios from Mildura. If you love seafood, head for Queenscliff and to towns along the Great Ocean Road, where lobster and prawns are particularly succulent. Also, don't miss the restaurants and wineries of the Yarra Valley and the Mornington Peninsula, which usually have a bountiful selection of labels to match their exquisite cuisine.

An exciting form of Victorian cooking is evolving at such restaurants as Arthurs on the Mornington Peninsula. For excellent Greek food, head along the famous Great Ocean Road to Kosta's, in Lorne. City-smart dining stops continue to spring up all around the state. Two examples are Mietta's Queenscliff Hotel, in the seaside village of Queenscliff, and at the Lake House Restaurant in the spa town of Daylesford.

Old-Fashioned Lodging

Gracious bed-and-breakfasts, host farms, and old-fashioned guesthouses are Victoria's welcome alternatives to hotel and motel accommodations. Bed-and-breakfasts are particularly good options, as they're run by locals who can advise you about regional history, activities, and attractions. Motels are best for those passing through towns quickly; travelers who want to linger should book a gracious historic hotel, where such Old World charms as silver tea service are combined with the luxuries of a modern resort. Queenscliff, Ballarat, and Mildura in particular have numerous charming bed-and-breakfasts, but you'll need to book early in December and January.

Spas

Victoria's spa center is Hepburn Springs, in the central-west region. Resorts offers massage, hydrotherapy, homeopathy, and beauty treatments. Other areas to look for spas are in St. Kilda, 10 minutes from Melbourne, where you'll find the famous Sea Baths. The Mornington Pensinsula has outdoor Japanese spas set amid rolling green hills.

Wineries

Victoria now has hundreds of wineries, particularly in the Yarra Valley and on the Mornington Peninsula. Vineyards have also flourished in the Pyrenees Ranges, and you'll find numerous boutique wineries along the Bellarine Peninsula. Travel agencies in Melbourne and the larger towns throughout the state have package tours that cover a range of wineries and regions.

You can plan your own wine-tasting circuit as well with help from the regional tourist offices, which have maps of the wineries and details about tour times and labels.

---

special dishes as Yarra Valley goat's-cheese panna cotta with pink grapefruit and spice; slow-roasted Yarra Valley kid goat served with sage, oregano, and pumpkin; and double-roasted duck with braised chicory and a Campari–blood orange sauce.

Domaine Chandon (✉ Maroondah Hwy., Green Point ☎ 03/9739–1110) schedules tours that take visitors through the step-by-step production of sparkling wine, including visits to the vines, the bottling area, and the riddling room. Tastings are in the beautiful Green Point Room, where huge glass windows overlook the vines. Platters of regional cheeses and fruits are available to accompany your vintage choices.

Eyton on Yarra (✉ Cnr. Maroondah Hwy. and Hill Rd., Coldstream ☎ 03/5962–2119) is set in an unusual structure that contains a wine tasting bar and an award-winning restaurant. Live music is played in the vineyard soundshell from December through March. Tastings are 10 to 5 daily except Christmas.

A variety of pungent reds and whites are ready for sampling at **Kellybrook Winery** (✉ Fulford Rd., Wonga Park ☎ 03/9722–1304), where visitors can attend tastings and then wander through the vineyards. The restaurant serves such delicacies as home-cured gravlax of Yarra Valley trout fillets, served with avocado salsa; seafood salad, poached in an herb-and-wine broth; and porterhouse steak, served with wild mushroom ragout and Kellybrook Shiraz jus.

Set amid the vineyards, **St. Huberts** (✉ Cnr. Maroondah Hwy. and St. Huberts Rd., Healesville ☎ 03/9739–1118) produces a wide selection of highly regarded wines. There's a picnic area and barbecue facilities, as well as free jazz performances on summer Sundays.

Take a walk through the tranquil bush exhibits at the **Healesville Sanctuary** and you'll come face-to-face with wedge-tailed eagles, grumpy wombats, nimble sugar-gliders, and shy platypus. ✉ *Badger Creek Rd., Healesville* ☎ *03/5957–2800* 🎫 *A$15.80* ⏰ *Daily 9–5.*

Belgrave
43 km (27 mi) southeast of Melbourne, 40 km (24 mi) from Healesville.

Belgrave is an unexceptional town at its heart, but it's the home of a favorite regional attraction: the Puffing Billy steam train. To assist pioneers at the turn of the 20th century, the Australian government carved four narrow-gauge railway tracks through the Dandenong mountains. Today the train still runs, and it's a prime way to experience the cool fern gullies and damp forests that blanket the foothills.

Nestled into a green valley at the center of the Upper Yarra, about 30 km (18 mi) from Healesville, Warburton's pretty main street makes a lovely stroll. You can spend a relaxed Sunday browsing through the antiques shops and snacking at small cafés. Get up early and you might spot a native platypus paddling about in the river.

Also near Belgrave, Yarra Ranges National Park offers the chance to walk through the Rainforest Gallery. This series of platforms extends beneath the rain-forest canopy, allowing visitors to see exactly what's in the trees. Mt. Donna Buang, 20 km (12 mi) from Warburton, has a snow-capped peak and lovely walking trails.

⟲ **Puffing Billy,** the sole survivor from the narrow-gauge era, is a gleaming little steam engine that hauls passenger wagons between Belgrave and Emerald Lake. It's the perfect way to take in the picture-book scenery of forests and trestle bridges. The 13-km (8-mi) trip takes an hour each way. The annual Great Train Race, held in May, is a local contest where runners have to beat the train on its journey through the forests. ✉ *Old Monbulk Rd.* ☎ *03/9754–6800, 1900/937069 for timetable details* ⊕ *www.puffingbilly.com.au* ✍ *A$24.50 one way, A$38 round-trip.*

Sherbrooke

47 km (29 mi) east of Melbourne, 8 km (5 mi) north of Belgrave.

The mountain roads near the little settlement of Sherbrooke loop through towering mountain ash trees and giant ferns. Stop and listen; bellbirds and whipbirds commonly echo calls through the forest. The flightless lyrebird, an accomplished mimic, also resides in the woods.

Deep in the lush expanse of the Dandenong Ranges National Park, the six-acre **George Tindale Memorial Garden** has azaleas, camellias, and hydrangeas that spill down the hillside, depending on the season. ✉ *Sherbrooke Rd.* ☎ *13–1963* ✍ *Donations accepted* ⊙ *Daily 10–5.*

Olinda

48 km (30 mi) east of Melbourne, 10 km (6 mi) north of Belgrave, 8 km (5 mi) from Sherbrooke.

The **National Rhododendron Gardens** are a sight to behold during October, when you'll see acres of white, mauve, and pink blooms and spectacular countryside vistas. Combine a visit with tea and scones in one of the many quaint cafés dotting this part of the Dandenongs. A small train provides transport throughout the garden. ✉ *The Georgian Rd., off Olinda-Monbulk Rd.* ☎ *13–1963* ✍ *A$8.60* ⊙ *Daily 10–5.*

Where to Eat

$$ ✕ **Kenloch.** The old mansion is surrounded by vast, shaded gardens painted with fern gullies and rhododendrons. It's the perfect setting for this stately, somewhat old-fashioned restaurant where you can dine on appropriately traditional English meals. Barbecued rack of lamb and beef rib-eye are among the heartier choices, but you can also stop in for finger sandwiches, small appetizers, and Devonshire teas. ✉ *Mt. Dandenong Tourist Rd., Olinda* ☎ *03/9751–1008* ▭ *AE, DC, MC, V* ⊙ *No dinner Sun.–Thurs.*

$$ ✕ **Sacrebleu.** Succulent bistro fare is the specialty of this moderately priced restaurant, which is colorfully named for a mild, 14th-century expletive. Dig into beef in red wine or tangy prawn salad. The wine list mixes French and Australian labels. ✉ *Shop 5, 1526 Mt. Dandenong Tourist Rd., Olinda* ☎ *03/9751–2520* ▭ *AE, DC, MC, V.*

$$ **Wild Oak Café.** Settle beneath the shady oak tree and nibble on such delicate dishes as crab and pawpaw salad, accompanied by a glass of crisp chardonnay. Local musicians perform Friday nights and Sunday afternoons. ✉ *232 Ridge Rd., Olinda* ☎ *03/9751–2033* ▭ *AE, DC, MC, V* ⊙ *Closed Sun.–Wed.*

Mornington Peninsula

The Mornington Peninsula circles the southeastern half of Port Phillip Bay. Along the coast, a string of seaside villages stretches from the larger towns of Frankston and Mornington to the summer holiday towns of Mount Martha, Rosebud, Rye, Sorrento, and Portsea. On the Western Port Bay side, the smaller settlements of Flinders, Somers, and Hastings have prettier, and quieter, beaches without the crowds.

NEW SOUTH WALES

Lake Victoria

Murray R.

Sturt Hwy.

Darling R.

Merbein

Mildura

Red Cliffs

20

79

MALLEE CLIFFS NATIONAL PARK

MURRAY-KULKYNE PARK

Murrumbidgee R.

Balranald

20

20

Hay

Cobb Hwy.

75

HATTAH-KULKYNE NATIONAL PARK

Hattah

Murray

Valley

Hwy.

PINK LAKES STATE PARK

Ouyen Hwy.

Underbool

12

Ouyen

Calder Hwy.

16

Swan Hill

Murray R.

Cohuna

Gunbower

16

BIG DESERT WILDERNESS AREA

WYPERFELD NATIONAL PARK

Lake Albacutya

79

Birchip

Kerang

Avoca R.

Loddon R.

Loddon Valley

Echuca

Shepparton

Midland Hwy.

Goulburn R.

Lake Hindmarsh

Sunraysia Hwy. 121

Western Hwy.

8

Nhill

Borung Hwy.

Warracknabeal

Charlton

Wedderburn

79

Eaglehawk

Bendigo

Maldon

Northern Hwy.

Mitchellstown

Seymour

Hume Hwy.

Dimboola

Henty Hwy.

Wimmera Hwy.

LITTLE DESERT NAT'L PARK

Horsham

Wartook

Wimmera Hwy.

Edenhope

Glenelg R.

Halls Gap

Zumstein

GRAMPIANS NATIONAL PARK

GARDIWERD

Sunraysia Hwy.

Maryborough

Stawell

Avoca

Pyrenees

Ararat

8

Hepburn Springs

Castlemaine

Daylesford

39

75

Midland Hwy.

Calder Hwy.

79

Casterton

Glenelg Hwy.

Hamilton

Western Hwy.

Ballarat

Yarra Valley

31

Yarra R.

Maroondah Hwy.

Melbourne

Werribee

1

Dandenong

Macarthur

Mortlake

Hamilton Hwy.

Darlington

OTWAY RANGES

Geelong

Port Phillip Bay

Mornington

Nelson

LOWER GLENELG NATIONAL PARK

Woolsthorpe

Camperdown

Princes Hwy.

Torquay

Barwon R.

Bellarine Peninsula

Queenscliff

Portsea

Frei

Portland

Port Fairy

Warrnambool

1

Colac

Lorne

MORNINGTON PENINSULA

PHILLIP I.

Sa Rem

Peterborough

Port Campbell

Apollo Bay

PORT CAMPBELL NAT'L PARK

Princetown

OTWAY NAT'L PARK

Bass Strait

AUSTRALIA

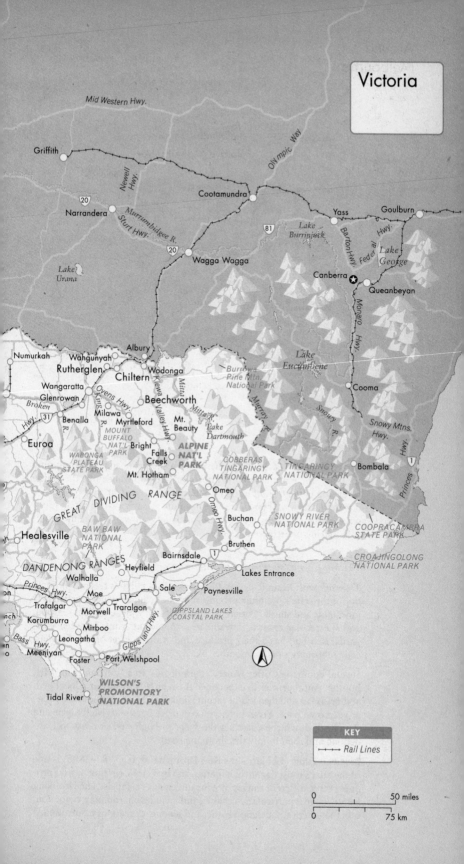

Victoria

Mid Western Hwy.

Griffith

Newell Hwy.

20

Narrandera

Murrumbidgee R.

Sturt Hwy.

20

Lake Urana

Cootamundra

Olympic Way

81

Wagga Wagga

Lake Burrinjuck

Yass

Goulburn

Barton Hwy.

Federal Hwy.

Canberra ★

Queanbeyan

Lake George

Monaro Hwy.

Numurkah

Wahgunyah

Albury

Rutherglen

Chiltern

Wodonga

Lake Eucumbiene

Burrowa Pine Mtn National Park

Cooma

Wangaratta

Glenrowan

Ovens Hwy.

King R.

Kiewa Valley Hwy.

Mitta R.

Beechworth

Broken R.

Hwy.

31

Benalla

Milawa

Myrtleford

Mt. Beauty

Mitta R.

Snowy R.

Snowy Mtns. Hwy.

Euroa

MOUNT BUFFALO NAT'L PARK

Bright

Falls Creek

Lake Dartmouth

WABONGA PLATEAU STATE PARK

ALPINE NAT'L PARK

Murray R.

Bombala

Princes Hwy.

1

Mt. Hotham

COBBERAS TINGARINGY NATIONAL PARK

TINGARINGY NATIONAL PARK

GREAT DIVIDING RANGE

Omeo

Omeo Hwy.

SNOWY RIVER NATIONAL PARK

COOPRACAMBRA STATE PARK

Healesville

BAW BAW NATIONAL PARK

Buchan

CROAJINGOLONG NATIONAL PARK

DANDENONG RANGES

Bruthen

Bairnsdale

1

Heyfield

Lakes Entrance

Walhalla

Princes Hwy.

Moe

Sale

Paynesville

Trafalgar

Morwell

Traralgon

1

GIPPSLAND LAKES COASTAL PARK

Korumburra

Mirboo

Leongatha

Bass Hwy.

Gippsland Hwy.

Meeniyan

Foster

Port Welshpool

Tidal River

WILSON'S PROMONTORY NATIONAL PARK

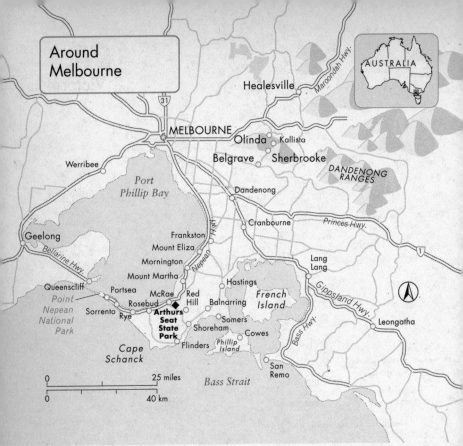

Around Melbourne

AUSTRALIA

Set aside at least a day for a drive down the peninsula, planning time for lunch and wine tasting. An afternoon cliff-top walk along the bluffs, or even a game of golf at Cape Schank, is the perfect way to finish a day in this region. If you'll be here in summer, pack a swimsuit and sunscreen for impromptu ocean dips as you make your way around the peninsula's string of attractive beaches.

Red Hill
121 km (75 mi) southeast of Melbourne.

Together with Main Ridge and Merricks, Red Hill has recently become one of the state's premium producers of cool-climate wines, particularly pinot noir and shiraz. For an afternoon of fine wine, excellent seafood, and spectacular coastal views, plan a route that winds between vineyards. Red Hill has a busy produce and crafts market on the first Saturday morning of each month.

Several companies offer winery tours of this area, starting from Melbourne. Another way to experience the region is to stay at a local bed-and-breakfast and then journey from Flinders to Merricks and Main Ridge at your own pace. From here, you can drive back into Melbourne and then head down the coast via the Nepean Highway, or cross to Dandenong and then follow the shoreline road.

Dromana Estate (⊠ Harrisons Rd., Dromana ☎ 03/5987–3800) is one of the area's most beautiful wineries, run by Gary Crittenden, who produces three different ranges of wine under several labels. The Dromana Estate range is particularly notable, and includes chardonnay, pinot noir, cabernet, merlot, sauvignon blanc, and schinus-chardonnay. Surrounded by rolling hills, the Vineyard Cafe overlooks a picturesque lake. Tastings are scheduled daily.

Red Hill Estate (⊠ Shoreham Rd., Red Hill South ☎ 03/5989–2838) is famous for its award-winning Max's Restaurant, perched on a hillside with sweeping views over the 30-acre vineyards to Westernport and Phillip Island. Dishes include coconut and coriander king prawns served on mango salsa, and Tuscan duck and red-wine sauce served with angel-hair pasta. Don't miss the rich chocolate tart, served with Red Hill strawberries and double cream.

Fodor'sChoice **T'Gallant Winemakers** (⊠ Cnr. Mornington, Flinders, and Shand Rds., Main
★ Ridge ☎ 03/5989–8660) produces such interesting wines as the Imogen pinot gris, pinot noir, chardonnay, and muscat a petits grains. La Baracca Restaurant is always buzzing—and the food is exceptional, with dishes that draw from local ingredients (and the house herb garden). Try the tiny baked parcels of pecorino cheese wrapped in T'Gallant grape vine; piadina with proscuitto, tallegio, and rocket; or the spinach ricotta cannelloni drenched in zesty tomato sauce and shaved parmesan.

Established nearly a quarter-century ago, **Stonier Winery** (⊠ Frankston–Flinders Rd., Merricks ☎ 03/5989–8300) is one of the peninsula's oldest vineyards. Wines include chardonnay, pinot noir, and cabernet. Although there's no restaurant, platters accompany the daily tastings.

Where to Eat

$$$ ✕ **Bittern Cottage.** Influenced by their adventures to northern Italy and southern France, Jenny and Noel Burrows show off their provincial-style cooking skills using regional Australian produce. The set menu includes a trio of patês, plus wine-simmered duck breasts. Blueberry *bavarois* (whipped cream and gelatin) rounds out the meal. ⊠ *2385 Frankston–Flinders Rd., Bittern* ☎ *03/5983–9506* ▭ *AE, DC, MC, V* ✆ *Closed Mon.–Thurs.*

$$–$$$ ✕ **Poff's.** On a hillside with views across a vineyard to the valley below, this modern restaurant is consistently rated one of the area's best. The menu is brief, and dishes are described with an austerity that downplays their caliber. Chef Sasha Esipoff's approach is to work with the best local ingredients in season, resulting in dishes such as mussels in a spicy broth and other Asian-inspired creations. The crème caramel is fantastic. ⊠ *Red Hill Rd., 7 km (4½ mi) from McCrae, Red Hill* ☎ *03/5989–2566* ▭ *AE, DC, MC, V* ✆ *Closed Mon.–Wed.*

Arthurs Seat

76 km (47 mi) south of Melbourne, 10 km (6 mi) from Red Hill.

Sweeping views of the surrounding countryside and Port Phillip Bay are the attractions of a trip to **Arthurs Seat State Park.** Walking tracks, a public garden, and a marked scenic drive make this a draw both for local families and tourists. A chairlift sometimes runs from the base of the mountain to the summit. Note that the road from Mornington is open at all times, so you can enjoy the spectacular mountaintop view even when the park is closed. ⊠ *Arthurs Seat Rd. at Mornington Peninsula Hwy.* ☎ *03/5987–2565* ▭ *Free* ✆ *Sept.–June, daily 11–5; July–Aug., weekends 11–5:30.*

Where to Eat

$–$$ ✕ **Arthurs.** Considered the Mornington Peninsula's best dining experi-
Fodor'sChoice ence, Arthurs has three eateries, all with fine views of Port Phillip Bay.
★ The poached ocean trout at The Peak is delicious, perfectly topped off with the Armagnac-marinated figs for dessert. High-profile locals, including a few politicians, frequent the place. The less formal, and less

216 < **Victoria**

expensive, Vineyard Bar and Coffee Shop serves snacks daily, and an ice cream and snack kiosk satisfies cravings between meals. ⊠ *Arthurs Seat Scenic Rd., Arthurs Seat* ☎ *03/5981–4444* ▭ *AE, DC, MC, V* ⊙ *No lunch Sun.–Thurs.*

<table>
<tr><td>en route</td><td>At the end of the Nepean Highway, in Portsea, turn left into Back Beach Road and make a right to London Bridge, a fantastic natural span carved by the ocean. The bridge itself actually collapsed years ago, but a rock formation remains. The sole of the Mornington Peninsula boot runs in a straight line for 28 km (17 mi), forming a long, narrow coastal park that ends at Cape Schanck. Here you can visit the Cape Schanck Lighthouse and Museum (⊠ Borneo Rd., Cape Shank ☎ no phone). The sea can be violent along this coastline—in 1967, Australian prime minister Harold Holt drowned at Cheviot Beach just west of London Bridge. Swimming is advisable only where the beach is patrolled by lifeguards. Cape Schank is also one of Victoria's largest golfing centers. The Moona Links course hosts the annual Australian Open Championships.</td></tr>
</table>

Sorrento

93 km (58 mi) southwest of Melbourne, 25 km (16 mi) west of Arthurs Seat.

Sorrento, with its evocative Italian name, is one of the region's prettiest bayside beach towns—and most exclusive resorts. It's also the peninsula's oldest settlement, and thus is dotted with numerous historic buildings and National Trust sites. In summer months, the town transforms from a sleepy seaside village into a hectic holiday gathering place. Sorrento back beach, with its rock pools and cliffside trails, and Point King, with its piers and boathouses, are the two most popular hangouts.

You can still visit Sorrento in the cooler months, when the attractions are its art galleries and its antiques, arts, and crafts shops. The main street is lined with little cafés, albeit with fish-and-chips vendors tucked in between. From Sorrento, you can catch the ferry to Queensliff and spend an afternoon on the other side of the bay, or drive down to the Great Ocean Road. Or you can just lie on the sand, soaking in the balmy air in front of the waves, while munching on hot, newspaper-wrapped fish-and-chips and watching the crowd.

Swim with the Dolphins is just what the name says—a chance to swim with the large, gentle creatures. Visitors travel by boat out into the bay, where the dolphins await; you can still take the boat ride if you don't want to swim. A wetsuit, snorkel, and flippers are supplied, and the company offers round-trip bus tours from Melbourne. ⊠ *Sorrento Pier* ☎ *03/5984–5678* ▭ *A$33 sightseeing, A$66 dolphin swim, A$112 tour from Melbourne* ⊙ *Pier 24 hrs, boat departures daily at 8, 12, and 4.*

The **Sorrento Marine Aquarium** has more than 200 fish species living in tanks with myriad underwater environments. Sea lion feedings are Sunday and Monday at noon. ⊠ *St. Aubin's Way* ☎ *03/5984–4478* ▭ *A$5.50 individual, A$13.50 family (2 adults, 2 kids)* ⊙ *Daily 9–4.*

Phillip Island

★ *125 km (78 mi) south of Melbourne.*

The nightly waddle of the miniature fairy penguins from the sea to their burrows in nearby dunes is the island's main draw, attracting throngs of onlookers on summer weekends and holidays. However, the island's unusual coastline is another reason to explore Phillip Island for longer than a day.

At the end of the Summerland Peninsula, out past the penguin parade, two rock formations are particularly captivating. At low tide, you can walk across a basalt causeway to the **Nobbies** and take in the splendid views along the island's wild northern coast. Thousands of shearwaters (muttonbirds) nest here from September to April, when they return north to the Bering Strait in the Arctic. Farther out, **Seal Rocks** is Australia's largest colony of fur seals, with 5,000 or more creatures basking on rocky platforms and capering in the sea in midsummer.

To reach Phillip Island by car, drive from Melbourne along the B420. You can also catch a ferry to Phillip Island from Stony Point on the Mornington Peninsula.

The most memorable part of visiting **Summerland Beach** is the sight of the fluffy young fairy penguins standing outside their burrows, waiting for their parents to return from the sea with their dinner. Unlike the large, stately emperor penguins of the Antarctic, fairy penguins rarely grow much bigger than a large duck. The daily spectacle is hardly a back-to-nature experience. The penguins emerge from the surf onto a floodlit beach, while a commentator in a tower describes their progress over a public address system. Spectators, who watch from concrete bleachers, may number several thousand on a busy night. Camera flashbulbs are forbidden. The "parade" begins at approximately 8 PM. If you don't mind rising at the crack of dawn, you can have breakfast with the penguins, too. ⊠ *Summerland Beach* ☎ *03/5956–8300 or 03/5956–8691, breakfast bookings 1300/ 366422* ⊕ *www.penguins.org.au* ✉ *A$13* ☉ *Daily sunrise–sunset.*

The **Phillip Island Grand Prix Circuit** continues the island's long involvement with motor sport, dating back to 1928 when the Australian Grand Prix (motor racing) was run on local unpaved roads. The circuit was completely redeveloped in the 1980s, and in 1989 hosted the first world-class Australian Motorcycle Grand Prix, which has made its home there. The circuit hosts regular club car and motorcycle races as well as big-ticket events, and the museum and restaurant are surprisingly good. Tours of the track are held every hour and are well worth joining. ⊠ *Back Beach Rd.* ☎ *03/5952–9400* ✉ *Tour and museum A$12, self-guided tour A$11* ☉ *Daily 9–5, tours at 11.*

The seaside town of **Cowes** is a pretty, unpretentious place with the usual beachwear stores, pizzerias, and a few decent eateries, most within walking distance of accommodations. Restaurant and hotel bookings are essential during the busy summer months.

Where to Stay & Eat

Phillip Island Vineyard and Winery (⊠ Berrys Beach Rd., Phillip Island ☎ 03/5956–8465) serves gourmet platters and has wine tastings. For lunch, try the **Clock Café by the Bay** (⊠ 4 The Esplanade, Cowes ☎ 03/ 5952–2856). You can also grab a tasty meal at **The Jetty** (⊠ Cnr. The Esplanade and Thompson Ave., Cowes ☎ 03/5952–2060), which overlooks the bay and offers fresh seafood, steaks, pizzas, and snacks. The best fine-dining option is **Carmichaels** (⊠ 17 The Esplanade, Cowes ☎ 03/5952–2060), where main courses drawing on local produce include pepper-flavored duck, and lobster medallions served with lime and coriander sauce. For dessert, there's rich chocolate and Grand Marnier cake, served with raspberry ice cream and toffee shavings. The large balcony overlooking the water is popular for balmy summer dinners and sunshine-filled Sunday lunches.

$–$$$ ⬚ **Rothsaye and Abaleigh on Lovers Walk.** Whether for the fine beach on the doorstep or the outstanding accommodations, these self-contained apartments, cottage, and suites have great appeal. The suites hold up to six and include thoughtful touches: breakfast baskets, beach chairs and umbrellas, fishing lines, and even sunscreen. Two apartments, with up to four bedrooms and four bathrooms each, are charmingly decorated with local antiques and have tranquil views. Each can be closed off to create a self-contained studio. Lovers Walk leads into the center of the town of Cowes from the front door. ☒ *2 and 6 Roy Ct., Cowes, 3922* ☎ *03/5952–2057 Rothsaye; 03/5952–5649 Abaleigh* ⚡ *2 suites, 1 cottage, 2 apartments* ⚿ *Kitchens, outdoor hot tub, beach, fishing, laundry facilities, free parking; no kids* ▤ *MC, V* ⍾ *CP.*

$–$$ ⬚ **Kaloha Resort.** A few minutes' walk from the beach and the center of Cowes, this quiet, leafy resort has one- and two-bedroom suites and a five-room apartment. Twelve of the suites have spas. The restaurant, with an imaginative, Asian-inspired menu, is surprisingly good, and the prices are refreshingly moderate. Bookings are essential. ☒ *Steele and Chapel Sts., Cowes, 3922* ☎ *03/5952–2179* ☎ *03/5952–2723* ⚡ *34 suites, 1 apartment* ⚿ *Restaurant, picnic area, some microwaves, pool, beach, bar, playground, laundry service, free parking; no room phones in some rooms* ▤ *AE, MC, V.*

Around Melbourne A to Z

To research prices, get advice from other travelers, and book travel arrangements, visit www.fodors.com.

CAR RENTAL
Renting a car in Melbourne and driving south is the most practical way of seeing the Mornington Peninsula, although there are daily V/Line bus services from Melbourne to much of regional Victoria.

EMERGENCIES
In case of an emergency, dial 000 to reach an ambulance, the police, or the fire department.

TOURS
Day trips from Melbourne are run by local tour operators, including Australian Pacific Tours, Gray Line, and AAT Kings. Tours of the Dandenongs cost from about A$56, and those to the penguin parade cost around A$96.

🚩 Tourist Information **AAT Kings** ☒ 180 Swanston St., City Center ☎ 1300/556100. **Australian Pacific Tours** ☒ 180 Swanston St., City Center ☎ 03/9663–1611. **Gray Line** ☒ 180 Swanston St., City Center ☎ 03/9663–4455.

VISITOR INFORMATION
The Victoria Information Centre is open weekdays 9 to 6, weekends 9 to 5. The Phillip Island Information Centre, which has a branch in Wonthaggi, is open daily 9 to 5. All other information centers are open daily 9 to 5 as well.

🚩 Tourist Information **Melbourne Visitor Information Centre** ☒ Cnr. Flinders St. and St. Kilda Rd., Melbourne ☎ 03/9658–9658 ☎ 03/9650–6168. **Mornington Peninsula Visitor Centre** ☒ 3598 Point Nepean Rd., Dromana ☎ 03/5987–3078. **Phillip Island Information Centre** ☒ Tourist Rd., Newhaven ☎ 03/5956–7447 or 1300/366422 ☎ 03/5956–7905 ☒ Watt St., Wonthaggi 3995 ☎ 03/5671–2444. **Victoria Visitor Information Centre** ☒ Town Hall, Swanston and Little Collins Sts., City Center, Melbourne ☎ 03/132842. **Yarra Valley Visitor Information Centre** ☒ The Old Courthouse, Harker St., Healesville ☎ 03/5962–2600 ☎ 03/5962–2040.

WEST COAST REGION

Victoria's Great Ocean Road is arguably the country's most dramatic and spectacular coastal drive, heading west from Melbourne along rugged, windswept beaches. The road, built during the Great Depression atop majestic cliffs, occasionally dips down to sea level. Here in championship surfing country, some of the world's finest waves pound mile after mile of uninhabited golden sandy beaches. As you explore the coastline, don't miss Bell's Beach, site of the Easter Surfing Classic, one of the premier events of the surfing world. But be careful because the fierce undertow along this coastline can be deadly.

Although this region is actually on the southeast coast of the Australian mainland, it lies to the west of Melbourne, and to Melburnians it is therefore known as the "West Coast." From the city, you should allow two or more days for a West Coast sojourn.

Werribee

32 km (20 mi) southwest of Melbourne, 157 km (97 mi) west of Phillip Island.

Once a country town, now a generally undistinguished outer suburb of Melbourne, Werribee is notable for the glorious Werribee Park Mansion and its attendant safari-style zoo.

Victoria's Open Range Zoo, part of the original Werribee Park property, is a 200-acre safari-style zoo of the highest caliber. Safari buses travel through a landscape that replicates southern Africa, passing among giraffe, rhinoceros, zebra, and hippopotamus. Australian animals also live in the park. A walk-through section houses cheetahs, apes, meerkats, and other African animals in natural conditions. ⊠ *K Rd.* ☎ *03/ 9731–9600* ⊕ *www.zoo.org.au* ⊠ *A$15.95* ⊘ *Daily 9–5; tours 10–3:40.*

The 60-room Italianate **Werribee Park Mansion,** dating from 1877, is furnished with period antiques. More than 25 acres of formal gardens surround the mansion. This was one of the grandest homes in the colony, built by wealthy pastoralists Thomas and Andrew Chirnside. Part of the mansion is now the luxurious Mansion hotel, winery, and day spa. Wine tasting, musical performances, and special events are held most weekends. ⊠ *K Rd.* ☎ *03/9741–2444* ⊠ *A$11* ⊘ *Daily 10–4:45.*

Geelong

72 km (45 mi) southwest of Melbourne, 40 km (25 mi) west of Werribee.

Victoria's second-largest city, Geelong relies on heavy industry—notably automobile construction—for its prosperity. Its proximity to the great surf beaches of the West Coast is one of its greatest appeals. The scenic foreshore along the Esplanade is decorated with some of the city's most gracious homes. It's a good place to stretch your legs by the water and have lunch as you're headed down the Great Ocean Road.

The **National Wool Museum** tells the story of this major Australian industry. Three galleries highlight the harvesting of wool, its manufacture into textiles, and the methods by which it is sold. Exhibits include a reconstructed shearers' hut and a 1920s mill worker's cottage. Audiovisual displays tell the story in an entertaining, informative manner. ⊠ *Moorobool and Brougham Sts.* ☎ *03/5227–0701* ⊠ *A$8* ⊘ *Daily 9:30–5.*

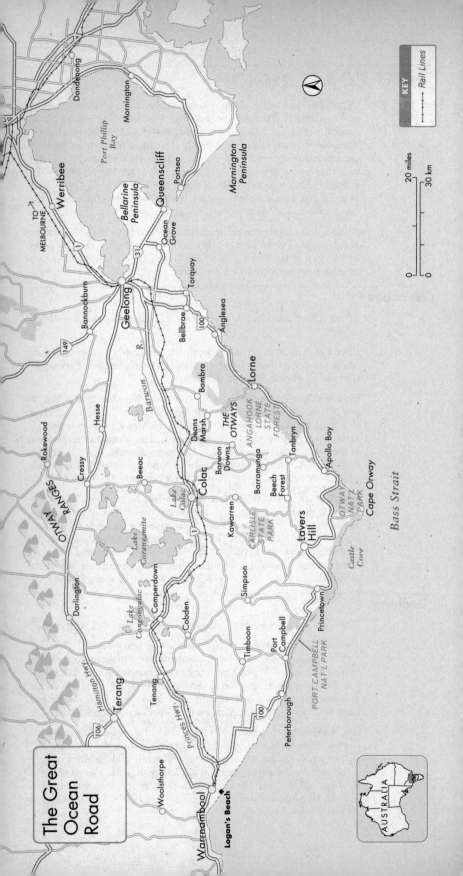

Queenscliff

103 km (64 mi) southwest of Melbourne, 31 km (19 mi) south of Geelong.

The lovely coastal village of Queenscliff, and nearby sibling Point Lonsdale, make for a worthy—and well-signposted—detour on the drive between Geelong and Lorne. During the late 19th century Queenscliff was a favorite weekend destination for well-to-do Melburnians, who traveled on paddle steamers or by train to stay at the area's grand hotels. Some, like the Grand, Ozone, and the Queenscliff Hotel, draw tourists to this day.

Good restaurants and quiet charm are also traits of Queenscliff. The best beach is at Lonsdale Bay. Point Lonsdale, once a sleepy little village known primarily for its lighthouse, is now a busy summer resort. The annual Queenscliff Music Festival, on the last weekend in November, draws hundreds of visitors to town.

Where to Stay & Eat

$–$$$ ✕⊞ **Queenscliff Hotel.** Gloriously restored to its original state, the Queenscliff has fine dining in either a small formal room, a leafy conservatory, or an outdoor courtyard. Fish and game are favored, with main-dish choices including braised rabbit leg with parsnip. A separate menu is available for vegetarians. Rooms are simply furnished and decorated in 19th-century style. ⊠ *16 Gellibrand St., 3225* ☎ *03/5258–1066* ☞ *21 rooms, 2 with bath* ⚭ *Restaurant, library, laundry facilities, free parking; no room phones, no room TVs* ⊟ *AE, DC, MC, V.*

$–$$ ✕⊞ **Athelstane House.** Charming and welcoming are the words for this old, comfortable local home, which has been a guesthouse since 1860. Nine rooms include four standards, three balcony rooms, one deluxe balcony room (with a corner jetted tub), and one apartment. The restaurant is famed for such innovative dishes as butter lettuce and scallop salad, and paella with local mussels, scallops, chorizo, and fresh fish. Meals are best enjoyed when accompanied by a local wine from the Bellarine vineyards. Take your breakfast outside to one of the large courtyards. Children are not encouraged. ⊠ *4 Hobson St., 3225* ☎ *03/5258–1024* ☞ *9 rooms* ⚭ *Restaurant, room service, some in-room hot tubs, in-room VCRs, free parking; no kids* ⊟ *AE, DC, MC, V.*

en route From Queenscliff, follow signs toward the Great Ocean Road for 45 km (28 mi) to **Torquay,** Australia's premier surfing and windsurfing resort. Here is Bell's Beach, famous for its Easter surfing contests and its October international windsurfing competitions. Great Ocean Road, a positively magnificent coastal drive, officially begins at Eastern View, 10 km (6 mi) east of Lorne.

Lorne

140 km (87 mi) southwest of Melbourne, 95 km (59 mi) southwest of Queenscliff, 50 km (31 mi) southwest of Torquay.

A little town at the edge of the Otway Range, Lorne is the site of both a wild celebration every New Year's Eve and the popular Pier-to-Pub Swim held shortly thereafter. Some people make their reservations a year in advance for these events. It's also the home of the Great Otway Classic, a footrace held annually on the second weekend in June.

Just before the road enters Lorne, it crosses the Erskine River. From a campsite near the bridge, an 8-km (5-mi) trail winds up the **Erskine River**

Valley. This lush, green haven of eucalyptus, tree ferns, waterfalls, and rustic bridges is delightful, but keep an eye out for leeches if you're bare-legged. The track passes the Sanctuary, a rock amphitheater where early pioneers gathered for religious services. If you're not in the mood for a walk, Erskine Road, which exits Lorne to the north, passes close to Erskine Falls.

Where to Stay & Eat

★ $$-$$$ ✗ **Kosta's.** Lively, bright, informal, and noisy, especially in peak season, Kosta's is one of Lorne's most popular restaurants. The menu is heavily Greek-influenced, with lots of local seafood and Moroccan-style stews, as well as homemade *tsatziki* (a yogurt, cucumber, and garlic dip), and char-grilled lamb. Fresh local specialties include char-grilled fish and lobster. ⊠ *48 Mountjoy Parade* ☎ *03/5289–1883* ⊟ *AE, MC, V.*

$$-$$$$ 🏠 **Erskine on the Beach.** The 1868 house was built in a 12-acre property and fully restored in 1930. The guesthouse, which has a shared bathroom, is surrounded by gracious gardens and perfectly manicured croquet lawns. Inside are cozy open fireplaces and comfortable, if simple, rooms without modern trimmings. Grass tennis courts and a beach are nearby. The adjoining Erskine Resort is more upscale and is priced accordingly—although guesthouse patrons can use the facilities at no charge. Rates include breakfast and use of facilities. ⊠ *Mountjoy Parade, 3232* ☎ *03/5289–1209* ⊕ *www.erskinehouse.com.au* ⌂ *55 rooms, 26 suites* ⚑ *Restaurant, putting green, 8 tennis courts, beach, croquet, laundry service, free parking; no phones in some rooms, no TV in some rooms* ⊟ *AE, DC, MC, V* ⫶⊙⫶ *BP.*

en route — Forty-five kilometers (28 mi) after Lorne, the Great Ocean Road passes the charming, historic fishing town of Apollo Bay. The highway then weaves in and out of the rain forest until it reaches the coastal town of Wattle Hill, where a dead-end side road leads you to the shore at Moonlight Head, part of **Otway National Park** (☎ 13–1963). The coastal formation was named by Matthew Flinders, the first circumnavigator of Australia, who saw the headland during a fierce storm when the moon broke through the clouds for a moment. Other ships, not his, have foundered here. The cliffs are among the highest in the country.

The Great Ocean Road heads inland slightly after Otway National Park, coming back to the coast at **Princetown.** This is the beginning of Port Campbell National Park, the most dazzling section of the drive. For the next 32 km (20 mi), the road snakes along the cliff tops for a heart-stopping, roller-coaster ride.

Port Campbell National Park

FodorśChoice ★ — *225 km (140 mi) southwest of Melbourne, 56 km (35 mi) west of Lorne.*

Stretching some 30 km (19 mi) along the southern Victoria coastline, Port Campbell National Park is the site of some of the most famous geological formations in Australia. Along this coast the ferocious Southern Ocean has gnawed at limestone cliffs for ages, creating a sort of badlands-by-the-sea, where columns of resilient rock stand offshore. The most famous formation is the Twelve Apostles, as much a symbol for Victoria as the Sydney Opera House is for New South Wales. Equally dramatic are the formations at Bay of Martyrs and Bay of Islands Coastal Reserve.

The level of the sea was much higher 25 million years ago, and as the water receded, towering sediments of sand, mud, limestone, and seashells were left standing to face the waves. The ocean is continuously carving these massive towers into strange shapes, even as they slowly crumble into the sea.

The best time to visit the park is January–April, when you can also witness events on nearby Muttonbird Island. Toward nightfall, hundreds of hawks and kites circle the island in search of hungry, impatient baby muttonbirds emerging from their protective burrows. The hawks and kites beat a hasty retreat at the sight of thousands of adult shearwaters approaching with food for their chicks as the last light fades from the sky. ⊠ *Park Office: Tregea St., Port Campbell* ☎ *03/1319–63.*

Generally speaking, you don't come to Port Campbell to bushwalk, but if you want to explore the area on foot, pick up a pamphlet for the self-guided Discovery Walk at the **Port Campbell Visitors Centre** (⊠ 26 Morris St., Port Campbell ☎ 03/5598–6089), open daily 9 to 5. The walk begins near Port Campbell Beach and takes about 1½ hours to complete. It's safe to swim only at this beach. The pounding surf and undertow are treacherous at other nearby beaches.

Where to Stay

¢ ⛺ **Port Campbell National Parks and Cabins.** Campsites in the town of Port Campbell start at A$16 per day for a site without electricity, A$18 with power. Cabins with bath are available from A$72 to A$95 a day. The campground has hot water and showers, as well as river and beach swimming areas and a TV room. Advance reservations are suggested. From here, it's just 10 minute's drive to the Twelve Apostles. ⊠ *Morris St., Port Campbell* ☎ *03/5598–6492* ⊕ *www.12apostlestourism.org* ⤳ *15 cabins, 70 power campsites, 60 nonpower campsites* ♨ *Flush toilets, laundry facilities, showers, fire pits, grills, swimming* ▤ *AE, DC, MC, V.*

Warrnambool

262 km (162 mi) southwest of Melbourne, 122 km (76 mi) west of Lorne, 66 km (41 mi) west of Port Campbell.

A friendly settlement of hardy souls who earn their living on both land and sea, Warrnambool makes the most of its location in between the beaches and the big country farms. It's also the closest big town to Port Campbell National Park, and thus attracts tourists who come for the area's myriad swimming, surfing, and fishing opportunities. The February Wunta Fiesta is the town's main event, which includes whale boat races, a seafood and wine festival, a carnival, and children's activities.

★ The sheltered bay at **Logan's Beach**, 3 km (2 mi) from the center of Warrnambool, has a beautiful setting and smooth sands for strolling. Winter holds the added fascination of watching southern right whales swim close to shore, where they give birth to their calves. They take up residence here for a considerable stretch of time and are easily observed from a cliffside viewing platform.

☾ The staff at the **Warrnambool Visitor Information Centre** can advise you of the southern right whales' presence and direct you to the best observation points. While here, you can collect a Kid's Country Treasure Hunt Guide kit. Children who answer the questions on the "treasure map," which is designed to introduce them to Warrnambool and its surroundings, get a free badge, book, or decal. ⊠ *600 Raglan Parade* ☎ *03/5564–7837* ☾ *Daily 9–5.*

🔅 A highlight in Warrnambool is **Flagstaff Hill Maritime Village,** a re-created 19th-century village built around a fort constructed in 1887 during one of the Russian scares that intermittently terrified the colony. In the village, visit an 1853 lighthouse, wander through the old fort, or board the *Reginald M,* a trading ship from the South Australian Gulf. ⊠ *Merri and Banyan Sts.* ☎ *03/5564–7841* 💷 *A$12* 🕓 *Daily 9–5.*

🔅 **Lake Pertobe Adventure Playground** is an 86-acre children's paradise. Facilities include lakes with children's powerboats, paddleboats, kayaks, canoes, pleasure boats, and junior sailing craft. Land attractions include a playground, barbecue facilities, and walking tracks. ⊠ *Pertobe Rd.* ☎ *03/5564–7837* 💷 *Free* 🕓 *Daily 24 hrs.*

Hopkins Falls, 13 km (8 mi) northeast of Warrnambool on Wangoom Road, makes for a pleasant side trip. After parking your car you can inspect the waterfall comfortably on foot (it's about 2 minutes away).

Tower Hill State Game Reserve, on an extinct volcano now green with vegetation, is a half-hour drive northwest of Warrnambool. The reserve is an attempt to return part of the land to a native state by introducing local flora and fauna. Spend some time at the park's natural history center and then walk around the trails. It's 14 km (8 ½ mi) from Warrnambool. ⊠ *Princes Hwy., Koroit* ☎ *03/5565–9202* 💷 *Free* 🕓 *Reserve daily 8–5, natural history center daily 9:30–4:30.*

Where to Stay & Eat

$$ ✕ **Mahogany Ship.** Decorated in a loosely nautical theme, this restaurant above the Flagstaff Hill Maritime Village has splendid views of Lady Bay harbor and the ocean beyond. Local crayfish (spiny lobsters) are a specialty. Steak and poultry dishes are also available. Children can order from a separate menu, which includes that Australian favorite, fish-and-chips. The tavern next door serves less expensive meals. ⊠ *Flagstaff Hill Maritime Village, Merri St.* ☎ *03/5561–1833* 🖃 *AE, DC, MC, V.*

★ ¢–$ ✕🏠 **Quamby Homestead.** Australian antiques fill this magnificent century-old homestead, an ideal base from which to explore the Warrnambool area. Modern rooms in former staff quarters are set apart from the homestead and surrounded by an English-style garden, where native birdcalls compete with the shrieks of resident peacocks. The dining room, in the homestead, serves fine country meals, which are available to nonresident guests on weekends. Rates include breakfast and dinner. It's 26 km (16 mi) north of Warrnambool. ⊠ *Caramut Rd., Woolsthorpe, 3276* ☎ *03/5569–2395* 🖷 *03/5569–2244* 📧 *7 rooms* ♨ *Dining room, free parking; no room phones, no room TVs, no kids* 🖃 *AE, DC, MC, V* ❑ *MAP.*

$ 🏠 **Central Court Motel.** On Princes Highway opposite the Tourist Information Centre, this clean, contemporary two-story motel is a 10-minute walk from the main shopping center. The Maritime Museum and the beach are just a short walk away. ⊠ *581 Raglan Parade, 3280* ☎ *03/ 5562–8555* 🖷 *03/5561–1313* 📧 *36 rooms, 2 suites* ♨ *Restaurant, room service, minibars, pool, bar, baby-sitting, laundry service, meeting rooms, free parking, no-smoking rooms* 🖃 *AE, DC, MC, V.*

$ 🏠 **Sundowner Mid City Motor Inn.** Set along the Great Ocean Road, this modern, two-story motel fronted by a neatly manicured garden is within walking distance of the town center and the beach. Exceptionally clean, large rooms have all the modern conveniences. Jukes Restaurant has a seasonal à la carte menu listing top-quality local produce and seafood. Meeting rooms, a pool, hot tub, and barbecue area make it a great place to congregate. Breakfast is included in the price. ⊠ *525 Raglan Parade, 3280* ☎ *03/5562–3866* 🖷 *03/5562–0923* 📧 *60 rooms, 9 suites* ♨ *Restaurant, room service, in-room data ports, some in-room hot* *tubs, some microwaves, minibars, refrigerators, room TVs with movies, pool, outdoor hot tub, bar, baby-sitting, laundry service, meeting rooms, free parking* ⊟ *AE, DC, MC, V* ⦶ *BP.*

Sports & the Outdoors

BICYCLING   The **Melbourne to Warrnambool Road Race** is a cycling classic held annually on the second Saturday in October. The race starts at 7:15 AM at Port Melbourne and finishes at Raglan Parade in Warrnambool at approximately 2:30.

Bikes can be rented from **Warrnambool Cycles** (⊠ 184 Fairy St., Warrnambool ☎ 03/5561–5225).

CAR RACING   The **Grand Annual Sprintcar Classic** (☎ 03/5562–8229) is held at Premier Speedway in Allansford east of Warrnambool during the last weekend in January.

FISHING   Warrnambool and the surrounding district have great river and surf fishing. A 28-day fishing license costs A$10 and is required for fishing the rivers and streams of Victoria. Contact **Warrnambool Shooters and Anglers Shop** (⊠ 101 Liebig St. ☎ 03/5562–3502) for information.

GOLF   The **Warrnambool Golf Course** (⊠ off Younger St. ☎ 03/5562–2108) is a first-class 18-hole, par-72 course. Greens fees are A$27. Club rental is A$15, and a motorized cart for 18 holes costs A$33.

Shopping

The Warrnambool **Saturday Market** (⊠ Warrnambool Showgrounds, Koroit St. ☎ no phone) is held on the first Saturday of each month in the Safeway parking lot. For crafts and homegrown produce, visit the **Warrnambool Town and Country Crafts Community Market** (⊠ Swan Reserve, Raglan Parade ☎ no phone), which takes place on the second Saturday morning of each month.

Port Fairy

291 km (180 mi) southwest of Melbourne, 29 km (18 mi) west of Warrnambool.

Port Fairy wins the vote of many a Victorian as the state's prettiest village. The second-oldest town in Victoria, it was originally known as Belfast, and there are indeed echoes of Ireland in the landscape and architecture. Founded during the whaling heyday in the 19th century, Port Fairy was once a whaling station with one of the largest ports in Victoria. The town still thrives as the base for a fishing fleet, and as host to the Port Fairy Folk Festival, one of Australia's most famous folk festivals, every March. More than 50 of the cottages and sturdy bluestone buildings that line the banks of the River Moyne have been classified as landmarks by the National Trust, and few towns repay a leisurely stroll so richly.

The **Historical Society Museum** contains relics from whaling days and from the many ships that have foundered along this coast. ⊠ *Old Courthouse, Gipps St.* ☎ *no phone* ▨ *A$2* ☉ *Wed. and weekends 2–5.*

Mott's Cottage is a restored limestone-and-timber cottage built by Sam Mott, a member of the whaling crew that discovered the town in the cutter *Fairy.* ⊠ *5 Sackville St.* ☎ *03/5568–2682* ▨ *A$2* ☉ *Wed. and weekends 1–4, or by appointment.*

Where to Stay & Eat

¢–$$$ ✕ **Dublin House Inn.** This solid stone building dates from 1855 and is furnished in period style. Chef Glenn Perkins uses the freshest local produce, creating dishes that incorporate everything from seafood to free-range chicken, duckling, and local beef. Lobster is available, but call ahead. The 32-seat dining room opens for dinner daily during summer. Dublin House Inn also has rooms for an overnight stay—functional rather than luxurious, but no less pleasant for their period style—and a two-bedroom cottage with a dishwasher, queen-size bed, washing machine and dryer, fold-out couch, and coffee-making facilities. ⊠ *57 Bank St., 3284* ☎ *03/5568–2022* 🖷 *03/5568–2158* ⊕ *www.dublin@standard.net.au* 🛏 *3 rooms, 1 cottage* ⚭ *Restaurant, laundry service, free parking* 🖃 *AE, MC, V.*

$–$$ 🏠 **Goble's Mill House.** An imaginative refurbishment of an 1865 flour mill on the banks of the Moyne River transformed its levels into six guest rooms with en suite bathrooms and a spacious sitting area, all furnished with antiques. The upper-story loft bedroom is especially appealing, with a balcony overlooking the ever-active river. The open fire makes the sitting room cozy, and a separate guest pantry is stocked with juices and freshly baked shortbreads. You can also enjoy fishing off the Mill House's private jetty. Breakfast is included. ⊠ *75 Gipps St., 3284* ☎ *03/ 5568–1118* 🖷 *03/5568–1178* 🛏 *6 rooms* ⚭ *Dock, fishing, free parking* 🖃 *MC, V* ⑩ *BP.*

Hamilton

290 km (180 mi) west of Melbourne, 82 km (51 mi) north of Port Fairy.

One of western Victoria's principal inland cities, Hamilton is rich grazing country. It has a lovely botanical garden and a lake made from damming the Grange Burn. There is a beach on the lake, and the water is full of trout. The town is the original seat of the Ansett family, and there is evidence of their fortune in and around town. Consider heeding the call of the Grampians Mountains, visible along the skyline north of Hamilton, and heading the 100-odd km (60-odd mi) into forested, craggy Grampians National Park.

The **Hamilton Art Gallery** has a highly respected collection of watercolors, engravings, pottery, antique silver, and porcelain from the Mediterranean. ⊠ *Brown St.* ☎ *03/5573–0460* 📧 *Free* ⊙ *Weekdays 10–5, Sat. 10–noon and 2–5, Sun. 2–5.*

Where to Stay

¢–$ 🏠 **Arrandoovong Homestead Bed and Breakfast.** Amid the tranquillity of a 500-acre grazing property, this 1850s bluestone homestead has 2,500 sheep as well as an increasingly popular B&B. Owners Jeanie and Bill Sharp, who bought Arrandoovong in 1952, lead guests upstairs to spacious, lovingly maintained, antiques-furnished rooms. Dinner is available on request at A$40 per person. The homestead is 20 minutes from Hamilton, ideal for day trips to South Australia's famed Coonawarra wine region, the Shipwreck Coast, and the Grampians. ⊠ *Chrome Rd., Branxholme, 3302* ☎ *03/5578–6221* 🖷 *03/5578–6249* 🛏 *3 rooms, 1 with bath* 🖃 *AE, MC, V* ⑩ *BP.*

West Coast Region A to Z

To research prices, get advice from other travelers, and book travel arrangements, visit www.fodors.com.

CAR TRAVEL

Driving is the most convenient way to see the region, and the only way to really enjoy the Great Ocean Road. Distances are considerable, and the going may be slow on the most scenic routes, especially during the summer holiday period.

Take the Princes Highway west from Melbourne to Geelong. From there, follow signs to Queenscliff and Torquay, where you connect with the Great Ocean Road. For an alternative inland route to Warrnambool, much quicker but vastly less interesting, take the Princes Highway.

EMERGENCIES

In case of an emergency, dial 000 to reach an ambulance, the police, or the fire department.

TOURS

AAT Kings has a day tour of the Great Ocean Road from Melbourne for A$110. Passengers can stay overnight from a selection of accommodations before returning to Melbourne on a bus the next day.

The Wayward Bus is a minibus that takes 3½ days to meander from Melbourne to Adelaide via the Great Ocean Road, Mount Gambier, and the Coorong, with overnight stops at Port Fairy, Apollo Bay, and Beachport. Passengers can leave the bus at either overnight stop and catch the following bus. Tours depart Melbourne on Tuesday, Thursday, and Saturday from October–April. The cost is A$310 per person, including three nights' accommodation and picnic lunches.

 AAT Kings ⊠ 180 Swanson St., City Center, Melbourne ☎ 03/9663-3377. **The Wayward Bus** ⊠ 180 Swanson St., City Center, Melbourne ☎ 1800/882823.

TRAIN TRAVEL

Geelong is fed by small, fast, and frequent Sprinter trains from Melbourne on the V-Line. The West Coast Railway serves points farther west and operates daily services between Melbourne and Warrnambool. Although the trains provide restful means of getting to main centers, they run inland and don't provide the extraordinary views you can see by car.

 Train Lines **V-Line** ☎ 1800/800120. **West Coast Railway** ☎ 03/5226-6500.

VISITOR INFORMATION

The Geelong Great Ocean Road Visitor Information Centre and the Port Fairy Tourist Information Centre are open daily 9–5. The Warrnambool Visitor Information Centre is open weekdays 9–5 and weekends 10–4. Contact the Department of Natural Resources and Environment for more information on area parks.

 Tourist Information **Department of Natural Resources and Environment** ⊠ 240 Victoria Parade, East Melbourne, Melbourne ☎ 03/9412-4011. **Geelong Great Ocean Road Visitor Information Centre** ⊠ Stead Park, Princes Hwy., Geelong ☎ 03/5275-5797. **Port Fairy Tourist Information Centre** ⊠ Bank St., Port Fairy ☎ 03/5568-2682. **Warrnambool Visitor Information Centre** ⊠ 600 Raglan Parade, Warrnambool ☎ 03/5564-7837.

GARDIWERD

Fodor'sChoice
★

260 km (163 mi) west of Melbourne, 100 km (62 mi) from Hamilton.

Formerly called The Grampians, the lands now known as *Gardiwerd* (the Aboriginal name) combine stunning mountain scenery, abundant native wildlife, and invigorating outdoor activities. Close to the western border of Victoria, this 412,000-acre region of sharp sandstone peaks was forced up from an ancient seabed, sculpted by eons of wind and rain, then carpeted with fantastic wildflowers part of the year. The park has more than 160 km (99 mi) of walking trails, as well as some 900 wildflower species, 200 species of birds, and 35 species of native mammals. The best time to visit is October–December, when wildflowers are in bloom, the weather is mild, and summer crowds have yet to arrive.

Don't miss the **Brambuk Cultural Centre.** Owned and operated by Aboriginal people, it provides a unique living history of Aboriginal culture in this part of Victoria. The **Dreaming Theatre** brings local legends to life on stage ($4.40). ✉ *Dunkeld Rd., Halls Gap* ☎ *03/5356–4452* ✆ *Free* ⊙ *Daily 9–5.*

Where to Stay & Eat

The national park base is Halls Gap, which has motels, guesthouses, host farms, and caravan parks. Eleven campgrounds exist within the national park. The fee is A$8.60 per site for up to six people, and the rule is first come, first served. Pick up a permit at the park's visitor center or at the campground.

$$ ✕ **Kookaburra.** This is the best local bet for good food. Try the venison in steak, sausage, or pie. Or choose duckling, milk-fed veal, or pork fillet smoked over cherry-wood embers. Finish with a traditional bread-and-butter pudding. ✉ *Grampians Rd., Halls Gap* ☎ *03/5356–4222* ▭ *AE, DC, MC, V.*

$$$$ ▨ **Boroka Downs.** At this stunning boutique hotel, guests stay in elegantly
Fodor$Choice decorated suites with balconies overlooking paddocks grazed by kan-
★ garoos, emus, and wallabies. Each room has its own fireplace, spa tub, CD player, and kitchen. Bedside views of Gardiwerd are exceptional. ✉ *Birdswing Rd., Halls Gap, 3381* ☎ *03/5356–6243* 🖷 *03/5356–6343* ⊕ *www.borokadowns.com.au* ⇄ *5 rooms* ⌂ *In-room VCRs, kitchens, microwaves, free parking* ▭ *AE, MC, V.*

$ ▨ **Glenisla Homestead.** For an atmospheric alternative to motel accommodation, this 1842 B&B on the western side of the national park is highly recommended. On an active sheep station, the homestead has three large colonial suites with their own lounge areas and bathrooms. There is also a large dining room and open courtyard. ✉ *Off Hamilton-Horsham Rd., Cavendish, 3314* ☎ *03/5380–1532* 🖷 *03/5380–1566* ⊕ *www. grampians.net.au/glenisla/* ⇄ *3 suites* ⌂ *Dining room, fishing, horseback riding, laundry service, free parking* ▭ *AE, MC, V* ⦿ *BP.*

Gardiwerd A to Z

To research prices, get advice from other travelers, and book travel arrangements, visit www.fodors.com.

CAR TRAVEL

Halls Gap is reached via Ballarat and Ararat on the Western Highway (Highway 8). The town is 260 km (161 mi) northwest of Melbourne, 97 km (62 mi) northeast of Hamilton, 146 km (91 mi) west of Ballarat.

TOURS

Gray Line operates a one-day tour of Gardiwerd (A$103) that departs Melbourne on Monday and Thursday

🚩 **Gray Line** ✉ 180 Swanson St., City Center, Melbourne ☎ 03/9663–4455.

VISITOR INFORMATION

🚩 Tourist Information **Stawell and Grampians Visitor Information Centre** ✉ 50–52 Western Hwy., Stawell, Melbourne ☎ 03/5358–2314. **Halls Gap Visitor Information Centre** ✉ Grampians Rd., Halls Gap ☎ 03/5356–4616.

GOLD COUNTRY

Victoria was changed forever in the mid-1850s by the discovery of gold in the center of the state. Fantastic news of gold deposits caused immigrants from every corner of the world to pour into Victoria to seek their fortunes as "diggers"—a name that has become synonymous with Australians ever since. Few miners became wealthy from their searches, however. The real money was made by those supplying goods and services to the thousands who had succumbed to gold fever.

Gold towns that sprang up like mushrooms to accommodate these fortune seekers prospered until the gold rush receded, when they became ghost towns or turned to agriculture to survive. Today, Victoria's gold is again being mined in limited quantities, while these historic old towns remain interesting relics of Australia's past.

Ballarat

106 km (66 mi) northwest of Melbourne, 146 km (91 mi) east of Halls Gap in Grampians National Park.

In the local Aboriginal language, the name Ballarat means "resting place," since a plentiful supply of food was around Lake Wendouree, to the north of the present township. The town flourished when gold was discovered here in 1851, but it was not Australia's first major gold strike. That honor belongs to Bathurst, in western New South Wales. However, Victoria in 1851 *was* El Dorado. During the boom years of the 19th century, 90% of the gold mined in Australia came from the state. The biggest finds were at Ballarat and then Bendigo, and the Ballarat diggings proved to be among the richest alluvial goldfields in the world. In 1854, Ballarat was the scene of the battle of the Eureka Stockade, a skirmish that took place between miners and authorities, primarily over the extortionate gold license fees that miners were forced to pay. More than 20 men died in the battle, the only time that Australians have taken up arms in open rebellion against their government.

Montrose Cottage and Eureka Museum of Social History, built in 1856 by a Scottish miner, was the first bluestone house in Ballarat. Inside you can see furniture and handiwork of the period. Adjoining the cottage is a museum with impressive displays of artifacts from Ballarat's gold-mining days and the women of Eureka. The tours conducted by Laurel Johnson, the owner of the museum, are lively and informative. ✉ *111 Eureka St.* ☎ *03/5332–2554* 🎫 *A$6.50* ⊘ *Daily 9–5.*

The prosperity of the gold rush left Ballarat well endowed with handsome buildings, and the short stretch of **Lydiard Street** around Sturt Street has a number of notable examples.

One of the historic edifices of Lydiard Street is the **Ballarat Fine Arts Gallery.** A large Australian collection includes exhibitions of contemporary works. One impressive exhibit is the tattered remains of the original Southern Cross flag that was flown defiantly by the rebels at the Eureka Stockade. ✉ *40 Lydiard St.* ☎ *03/5331–5622* 🎫 *A$5* ⊘ *Daily 10:30–5.*

On the shores of Lake Wendouree, Ballarat's **Botanic Gardens** are identifiable by the brilliant blooms and classical statuary. At the rear of the gardens, the Begonia House is the focus of events during the town's Begonia Festival, held annually in February or March. ✉ *Wendouree Parade* 🎫 *no phone* 🎫 *Free* ⊘ *Daily sunrise–sunset.*

Sovereign Hill Historical Park is built on the site of the Sovereign Hill Quartz Mining Company's mines. This is an authentic re-creation of life, work, and play on the gold diggings at Ballarat following the discovery of gold here in 1851. Sovereign Hill is the backdrop for Blood on the Southern Cross, a 90-minute sound-and-light spectacular that focuses on the Eureka uprising. The story is told with passion and dramatic technical effects, although the sheer wealth of historical detail clouds the story line. The climax of the show is the battle of the Eureka Stockade. Be prepared for chilly nights, even in midsummer. Numbers are limited and advance bookings are recommended.

Near the entrance to the historical park is the **Voyage to Discovery,** a museum designed to provide an overview of society and the world at large at the time of the gold rush. The museum is excellent, with imaginative dioramas and computer terminals that encourage you to become an active participant in the gold-discovery process.

Included in Sovereign Hill Historical Park admission is the **Gold Museum,** across Bradshaw Street. It displays an extensive collection of nuggets from the Ballarat diggings as well as some examples of finished gold in the form of jewelry. There's an excellent souvenir shop on-site. ⊠ *Bradshaw St.* ☎ *03/5331–1944* ☒ *A$25, Blood on the Southern Cross show A$30, Sovereign Hill and Blood on the Southern Cross A$51* ⊙ *Daily 10–5. Sometimes closed for maintenance Aug. and Dec. No sound-and-light show Sun.*

○ **Ballarat Wildlife and Reptile Park** shelters native Australian wildlife from different habitats. Animals include saltwater crocodiles, snakes, lizards, wombats, echidnas, and kangaroos. Daily tours are at 11, with a koala show at 2 and a wombat show at 2:30. The park also has a café, and barbecue and picnic areas. ⊠ *Fussel and York Sts., East Ballarat* ☎ *03/5333–5933* ☒ *A$14.50* ⊙ *Daily 9–5:30.*

Where to Stay & Eat

★ $$–$$$ ╳ **The Boatshed.** This restaurant has knockout views of Lake Wendouree and a light, airy environment ideal for a light breakfast, leisurely brunch, afternoon tea, or a romantic interlude at dinnertime. The Caesar salad is tasty, as is the borscht made with locally grown ingredients. ⊠ *View Point, Lake Wendouree* ☎ *03/5333–5533* ☐ *AE, DC, MC, V.*

$–$$ ╳ **Europa Cafe.** Italian, Middle Eastern, and Asian dishes are served with flair at this hip, yet relaxed dining spot. The all-day breakfast is legendary, and lunches include such savory treats as tarts with roma tomato, feta cheese, olive tapenade, and spinach; chicken-liver pâté; and smoked salmon bruschetta. For dinner, go for the delicious Moroccan chicken, served on lemon and pine-nut couscous. Lamb lovers should order the slow-cooked shanks in tomato, onion, garlic, and white-wine sauce, served with creamy mashed potatoes and gremolata beans. Note that the restaurant closes at 6:30 Monday through Wednesday. ⊠ *411 Sturt St.* ☎ *03/5331–2486* ☐ *AE, DC, MC, V.*

★ $–$$$ ╳☐ **The Ansonia.** Built in the 1870s as professional offices—and rescued by new owners, who refurbished a derelict shell—the Ansonia is now an excellent boutique hotel and restaurant. Open from 7 AM, the restaurant serves sumptuous breakfast and lunch, in addition to an eclectic dinner. For example, linguine with baby beets sits alongside Caesar salad and steaks. There are four different styles of accommodation, from two-room apartments to studios, all of which are beautifully furnished and appointed. ⊠ *32 Lydiard St. S, Ballarat, 3350* ☎ *03/5332–4678* ╞ *03/5332–4698* ☞ *20 rooms* ○ *Restaurant, dry cleaning, laundry service, meeting rooms, free parking* ☐ *AE, DC, MC, V.*

$–$$$ ☐ **Ravenswood.** Tucked behind a garden brimming with peach trees, pussy willows, fuchsias, and climbing roses, this three-bedroom timber cottage is ideal for anyone looking for family-size accommodation with kitchen facilities. The house, a bit less than 1½ km (1 mi) from the center of Ballarat, has been decorated with contemporary furniture and carpeting to a high standard of comfort. Breakfast supplies are provided. ⊕ *Box 1360, Ballarat Mail Center, 3354* ☎ *03/5332–8296* ╞ *03/5331–3358* ☞ *1 cottage* ○ *Dining room, free parking* ☐ *AE, DC, MC, V* ⊙| *CP.*

Golf

At **Ballarat Golf Club** (✉ Sturt St., West Ballarat ☎ 03/5334–1023) greens fees are A$19 for the 18-hole, par-70 course. Clubs are available.

Daylesford & Hepburn Springs

109 km (68 mi) northwest of Melbourne, 45 km (28 mi) northeast of Ballarat.

Nestled in the slopes of the Great Dividing Range, Daylesford and its nearby twin, Hepburn Springs, constitute the spa capital of Australia. The water table here is naturally aerated with carbon dioxide and rich in soluble mineral salts. This concentration of natural springs was first noted during the gold rush, and a spa was established at Hepburn Springs by Swiss-Italian immigrants in 1875, when spa resorts were fashionable in Europe. After a long decline, this spa was revived in a health-conscious style. Lake Dayelsford is a favorite area for locals to visit in autumn, when the deciduous trees turn bronze and the nights are enjoyed warming up next to an open fire with a glass of local red.

FodorśChoice ★ Mineral baths and treatments are available at the bright, modern **Hepburn Springs Spa Centre,** where the facilities include communal spa pools, private aerospa baths, float tanks, and saunas. Massages, facials, and other body treatments are on the menu. Services generally run under A$100, although rates are slightly higher on weekends. ✉ *Main Rd., Mineral Springs Reserve* ☎ *03/5348–2034* ⊕ *www.hepburnspa.com. au* ✍ *A$25 full access, A$10 pool and spa only* ⊗ *Weekdays 10–7, Sat. 9–10, Sun. 9–7.*

Above the Hepburn Springs Spa Centre, a path winds through a series of mineral springs at the **Mineral Springs Reserve.** Each spring has a slightly different chemical composition—and a significantly different taste. Empty bottles are filled free with the mineral water of your choice.

Perched on a hillside overlooking Daylesford, the **Convent Gallery** is a former nunnery that has been restored to its lovely Victorian state. It displays contemporary Australian pottery, glassware, jewelry, sculpture, and prints, all for sale. At the front of the gallery is Bad Habits, a sunny café that serves light lunches and snacks. ✉ *Daly St.* ☎ *03/ 5348–3211* ✍ *A$3.50* ⊗ *Daily 10–6.*

Where to Stay & Eat

★ $$$ ✕▦ **Lake House Restaurant.** Consistently rated one of central Victoria's best restaurants, this rambling lakeside pavilion brings glamor to spa country. The seasonal menu, which utilizes fresh Australian produce, lists such delicacies as hot gravlax of Atlantic salmon, as well as a selection of imaginative Asian-accented and vegetarian dishes. Guest rooms in the lodge are breezy and contemporary: those at the front have better views, but slightly less privacy, than those at the back, which are screened by rose-entwined trellises. Three-night packages are available, with higher rates for waterfront rooms. Breakfast is included. ✉ *King St., Daylesford 3460* ☎ *03/5348–3329* 🖷 *03/5448–3995* ⊕ *www. lakehouse.com.au* ⌨ *33 rooms* ⚒ *Restaurant, dining room, tennis court, pool, sauna, bicycles, bar, laundry service, meeting rooms, free parking; no a/c in some rooms* ▭ *AE, DC, MC, V* ⦿❘ *BP.*

$$$ ▦ **Holcombe Homestead.** Stay in a century-old farmhouse that's one of the architectural glories of rural Victoria, complete with nearby kangaroos, kookaburras, and trout fishing. The house has been furnished in keeping with its Victorian character. The view from the top of the hillside is idyllic, with beautiful sunsets. Owners John and Annette Marshall live in a neighboring house and will prepare box lunches and

dinner on request. ⊠ *Holcombe Rd., Glenlyon, 3461, 15 km (9 mi) from Daylesford* ☎ *03/5348-7514* 🖷 *03/5348-7742* ⊕ *www.holcombe. com.au* 🛏 *6 rooms, 3 with bath* ⚘ *Dining room, tennis court, fishing, mountain bikes, laundry service, meeting rooms, free parking; no a/c in some rooms, no kids* ▭ *AE, DC, MC, V* ¶ *BP.*

$–$$ 🏠 **Dudley House.** Behind a neat hedge and picket gate, this fine example of timber Federation architecture sits on Hepburn Springs' main street. Rooms have been restored and furnished with antiques. A full English breakfast and afternoon tea with scones is included. The town's spa baths are within walking distance. Spa packages and dinner are available by arrangement. ⊠ *101 Main St., Hepburn Springs, 3460* ☎ *03/5348-3033* ⊕ *www.netconnect.com.au/~dudley* 🛏 *4 rooms* ⚘ *Dining room, free parking; no room phones, no room TVs, no kids under 16, no smoking* ▭ *AE, MC, V* ¶ *BP.*

Castlemaine

119 km (74 mi) northwest of Melbourne, 38 km (24 mi) north of Daylesford.

Castlemaine is another gold-mining town, yet the gold here was mostly on the surface. Lacking the deeper reef gold where the real riches lay, the town never reached the prosperity of Ballarat or Bendigo, as is evidenced by its comparatively modest public buildings.

Castlemaine Information Centre, built as the town market in 1862, resembles an ancient Roman basilica and is an exception among the town's generally unadorned public buildings. The statue on top of the building is Ceres, Roman goddess of the harvest. The center has a gold rush history display. ⊠ *Mostyn St., Castlemaine* ☎ *03/5470-6200* 🎟 *Free* ⊙ *Daily 9–5.*

Buda House is a tribute to the diversity of talents drawn to Australia's gold rush. Built in 1861, the house was purchased two years later by Ernest Leviny, a Hungarian jeweler who established a business on the Castlemaine goldfields. It was the last of his six daughters, Hilda, who left the house and its contents to the state when she died in 1981. Within this delightful building you can see a century's worth of the Leviny family's personal effects, including furniture, silver, and art. ⊠ *42 Hunter St.* ☎ *03/5472-1032* 🎟 *A$7* ⊙ *Wed.–Sat. noon–5, Sun. 10–5.*

The **Castlemaine Art Gallery,** built in 1913, displays works by many of the region's artists. ⊠ *Lyttleton St.* ☎ *03/5472-2292* 🎟 *A$4* ⊙ *Weekdays 10–5, weekends 12–5.*

Maldon

137 km (85 mi) northwest of Melbourne, 16 km (10 mi) northwest of Castlemaine.

Relative isolation has preserved Maldon, a former mining town, almost intact, and today the entire main street is a magnificent example of vernacular goldfields architecture. Notice the bull-nose roofing over the verandas, a feature now back in architectural vogue. Maldon's charm has become a marketable commodity. Now the town is busy with tourists and thick with tea shops and antiques sellers. Take it all in during a short stroll along the main street. The town's main event is the Maldon Festival, held each year in November.

Three kilometers (2 mi) south of Maldon is **Carman's Tunnel,** a gold mine that has remained unaltered since it closed in 1884. The mine, which can be seen only on a candlelight tour, provides a glimpse of the ingenious techniques used by early gold miners. The 1,870-foot tunnel is dry, clean, and spacious. Tours are given every half hour and are suitable for all ages. ⊠ *Parkin's Reef Rd.* ☎ *03/5475–2667* 🖅 *A$4* ⊙ *Weekends 1:30–4.*

🔄 **Castlemaine & Maldon Railway.** This 45-minute loop aboard a historic steam train winds through forests of eucalyptus and wattle, which are spectacular in spring. Check for specials, such as the lovers' fling on Valentine's Day. ⊠ *Hornsbury St., Maldon* ☎ *03/5475–2966* 🖅 *A$13* ⊙ *Feb.–Dec., Wed. 11:30 and 1; Sun. 11:30, 1, 2:30; Jan., daily, departs hourly 10–4.*

Bendigo

150 km (93 mi) northwest of Melbourne, 36 km (22 mi) northeast of Maldon, 92 km (57 mi) south of Echuca.

Gold was discovered in the Bendigo district in 1851, and the boom lasted well into the 1880s. The city's magnificent public buildings bear witness to the richness of its mines. Today Bendigo is a bustling, enterprising small city—not as relaxing as other goldfield towns, but its architecture is noteworthy. Most of Bendigo's distinguished buildings are arranged on either side of Pall Mall in the city center. These include the **Shamrock Hotel, General Post Office,** and **Law Courts,** all majestic examples of late-Victorian architecture.

The refurbished **Bendigo Art Gallery** houses a notable collection of contemporary Australian painting, including the work of Jeffrey Smart, Lloyd Rees, and Clifton Pugh. Pugh once owned a remote Outback pub infamous for its walls daubed with his own pornographic cartoons. The gallery also has some significant 19th-century French Realist and Impressionist works, bequeathed by a local surgeon. ⊠ *42 View St.* ☎ *03/5443–4991* 🖅 *Free* ⊙ *Daily 10–5.*

Central Deborah Gold-Mine, with a 1,665-foot mine shaft, yielded almost a ton of gold before it closed in 1954. To experience life underground, take a guided tour of the mine. An elevator descends 200 feet below ground level. ⊠ *Violet St.* ☎ *03/5443–8322* 🖅 *A$16.50, combined entry with Vintage Talking Tram A$26.50* ⊙ *Daily 9:30–5; last tour at 4:05.*

A good introduction to Bendigo is a tour aboard the **Vintage Talking Tram,** which includes a taped commentary on the town's history. The tram departs on its 8-km (5-mi) circuit every hour between 10 and 3 from the Central Deborah Gold-Mine. ⊠ *Violet St.* ☎ *03/5443–8322* 🖅 *A$12.90* ⊙ *Daily 9–5.*

Joss House (Temple of Worship) was built in gold-rush days by Chinese miners on the outskirts of the city. At the height of the boom in the 1850s and 1860s, about a quarter of the miners were Chinese. These men were usually dispatched from villages on the Chinese mainland, and they were expected to work hard and return as quickly as possible to their villages with their fortunes intact. The Chinese were scrupulously law-abiding and hardworking—qualities that did not always endear them to other miners—and anti-Chinese riots were common. ⊠ *Finn St., Emu Point* ☎ *03/5442–1685* 🖅 *A$3.30* ⊙ *Daily 10–5.*

The superb **Golden Dragon Museum** evokes the Chinese community's role in Bendigo life, past and present. Its centerpieces are the century-old Loong imperial ceremonial dragon and the Sun Loong dragon, which, at more than 106 yards in length, is said to be the world's longest. When carried in procession, it requires 52 carriers and 52 relievers—the head alone weighs 64 pounds. Also on display are other ceremonial objects, costumes, and historic artifacts. ⊠ *5–9 Bridge St.* ☎ *03/5441–5044* 💷 *A$6.50* 🕙 *Daily 9–5.*

Where to Stay & Eat

$$–$$$ ✕ **Bazzani.** This restaurant fuses a mainly Italian menu with Asian influences under the capable stewardship of a second generation of Bazzanis. Try the ravioli with a tomato, chili, and coriander broth, or the wild mushroom risotto. A good selection of local and Pyrenées wines is very well priced. Lighter alternatives fill the lunch menu, plus coffee and snacks. ⊠ *Howard Pl.* ☎ *03/5441–3777* ▤ *AE, DC, MC, V.*

$$–$$$ ✕ **Whirrakee.** This stylish, family-run restaurant and wine bar in one of Bendigo's many grand old buildings serves Mediterranean- and Asian-inspired dishes. Try the char-grilled baby octopus, or the tasty arugula salad with pesto and balsamic vinegar. The relatively small wine list showcases local wineries. ⊠ *17 View Point* ☎ *03/5441–5557* ▤ *AE, DC, MC, V.*

¢–$$ 🏨 **Shamrock Hotel.** This landmark Victorian hotel at the city center has a choice of accommodation, from simple, traditional guest rooms with shared facilities to large suites. If you're looking for reasonably priced luxury, ask for the Amy Castles Suite. Rooms are spacious and well maintained, but furnishings are dowdy and strictly functional. The hotel's location and character are the real draws. ⊠ *Pall Mall and Williamson St., 3550* ☎ *03/5443–0333* 🖷 *03/5442–4494* ➥ *26 rooms, 2 with bath; 4 suites* ♻ *Restaurant, 3 bars, laundry facilities, meeting rooms, free parking; no a/c in some rooms* ▤ *AE, DC, MC, V.*

$ 🏨 **Nanga Gnulle Garden Cottages.** On a hillside on the outskirts of town, Rob and Peg Green have created a haven in mud brick and timber, surrounded by a superb garden. Pronounced "nanga-nully," the name means small stream in the local Aboriginal language. The couple built the luxurious Waroona (Aboriginal for resting place) garden cottage for visitors as well as a two-bedroom cottage. Each cottage has a self-contained kitchen and washer/dryer. The staff is extremely laid-back and friendly. Wood furniture and natural fabrics fill the rooms. Breakfast provisions are included. ⊠ *40 Harley St., 3550* ☎ *03/5443–7891* 🖷 *03/5442–3133* ➥ *2 cottages* ♻ *Kitchens, hot tub, laundry facilities, free parking* ▤ *MC, V* ❯❮ *CP.*

Sports & the Outdoors

GOLF   You can rent clubs for A$10 per round at **Bendigo Golf Club** (⊠ Golf Links Rd., Epsom ☎ 03/5448–4206). Greens fees for the 18-hole, par-72 course are A$16.50.

TENNIS   **Bendigo Outdoor Grass Tennis** (⊠ Edwards Rd. ☎ 03/5442–2411) has five Rebound Ace hard courts, which are open daily. Courts are A$14 per hour 9–6, A$18 per hour 6 PM–10 PM.

Shopping

Bendigo Mohair Farm (⊠ Maryborough Rd., Lockwood ☎ 03/5435–3400) is a working Angora-goat stud farm. The showroom displays hand-knit sweaters, mohair rugs, scarves, hats, ties, and toys for purchase. The farm also has barbecue and picnic facilities.

Gold Country A to Z

To research prices, get advice from other travelers, and book travel arrangements, visit www.fodors.com.

CAR TRAVEL

For leisurely exploration of the Gold Country, a car is essential. Although public transport adequately serves the main centers, access to smaller towns is less assured, and even in the bigger towns, attractions tend to be widely dispersed.

To reach Bendigo, take the Calder Highway northwest from Melbourne;
for Ballarat, take the Western Highway. The mineral springs region and
Maldon lie neatly between the two main cities.

EMERGENCIES
In an emergency, dial 000 to reach an ambulance, the police, or the fire
department.

TOURS
Operators who cover this area include Gray Line, Australian Pacific Tours,
and AAT Kings; all three depart from 180 Swanston Street in Melbourne.
🚩 **AAT Kings** ☎ 03/9663-3377. **Australian Pacific Tours** ☎ 03/9663-1611. **Gray Line**
☎ 03/9663-4455.

TRAIN TRAVEL
Rail service to Ballarat or Bendigo is available. For timetables and rates,
contact CountryLink or the Royal Automobile Club of Victoria (RACV).
🚩 Train Information **CountryLink** ☎13-2232. **Royal Automobile Club of Victoria (RACV)**
☎ 13-1955.

VISITOR INFORMATION
The visitor center in Ballarat is open weekdays 9–5 and weekends 10–4,
the one in Bendigo is open daily 9–5, and the one in Daylesford is open
daily 10–4.
🚩 Tourist Information **Ballarat Tourist Information Centre** ✉ 39 Sturt St., Ballarat
☎ 03/5332-2694. **Bendigo Tourist Information Centre** ✉ Old Post Office, Pall Mall,
Bendigo ☎ 03/5444-4445. **Daylesford Regional Visitor Information Centre** ✉ 49 Vincent St., Daylesford ☎ 03/5348-1339 🖶 03/5321-6193 ⊕ www.visitdaylesford.com.

MURRAY RIVER REGION

From its birthplace on the slopes of the Great Dividing Range in southern New South Wales, the Mighty Murray winds 2,574 km (1,596 mi)
in a southwesterly course before it empties into Lake Alexandrina,
south of Adelaide. On the driest inhabited continent on earth, such a
river, the country's largest, assumes great importance. Irrigation schemes
that tap the river water have transformed its thirsty surroundings into
a garden of grapevines and citrus fruits.

Once prone to flooding and droughts, the river has been laddered with
dams that control the floodwaters and form reservoirs for irrigation. The
lakes created in the process have become sanctuaries for native birds.
In the pre-railroad age of canals, the Murray was an artery for inland
cargoes of wool and wheat, and old wharves in such ports as Echuca
bear witness to the bustling and colorful riverboat era.

Victoria, Tasmania, New South Wales, and Western Australia were
planted with vines during the 1830s, fixing roots for an industry that
has earned international repute. One of the earliest sponsors of Victorian viticulture was Charles LaTrobe, the first Victorian governor. La-
Trobe had lived at Neuchâtel in Switzerland and married the daughter
of the Swiss Counsellor of State. As a result of his contacts, Swiss wine
makers emigrated to Australia and developed some of the earliest Victorian vineyards in the Yarra Valley, east of Melbourne.

Digging for gold was a thirst-producing business, and the gold rushes
stimulated the birth of an industry. By 1890 well over half the total Australian production of wine came from Victoria. But just as it devastated
the vineyards of France, the strain of tiny plant lice, phylloxera, arrived
from Europe and wreaked havoc in Victoria. In the absence of wine,

Australians turned to beer, and not until the 1960s did wine regain national interest. Although most wine specialists predict that Victoria will never recover its preeminence in the Australian viticulture, high-quality grapes are grown in parts of the state, best known for muscat, Tokay, and port. The Rutherglen area produces the finest fortified wine in the country, and anyone who enjoys the after-dinner "stickies" (dessert wines) is in for a treat when touring here.

Euroa

140 km (87 mi) northeast of Melbourne.

Maygars Hill (✉ 3665 Longwood Mansfield Rd., Longwood East ☎ 03/5798–5417 ⊕ www.strathbogieboutiquewines.com) is a small, 6-acre estate boutique winery consisting of 2 acres of cabernet sauvignon and 4 acres of shiraz. Vineyard walks are available, as well as cellar-door wine tasting by appointment. There's also a cottage with bed-and-breakfast accommodation. It's 14 km (8 mi) from Euroa.

Balloon Flights Victoria (☎ 03/5798–5417 🖷 03/5798–5457 ⊕ www.balloonflightsvic.com) has hot-air balloon flights over farmland near Strathbogie Ranges. A one-hour flight costs A$225 per person, including a champagne breakfast upon touchdown. Flights are available year-round and depart from a Longwood farm near Euroa, on the Hume Highway, a 90-minute drive from Melbourne.

Beechworth

131 km (82 mi) northeast of Euroa, 271 km (168 mi) northeast of Melbourne, 96 km (60 mi) northwest of Alpine National Park.

One of the prettiest towns in Victoria, Beechworth flourished during the gold rush. When gold ran out, the town was left with all the apparatus of prosperity—fine Victorian banks, imposing public buildings, breweries, parks, prisons, and hotels wrapped in wrought iron—but with scarcely two nuggets to rub together. However, poverty preserved the town from such modern amenities as aluminum window frames, and many historic treasures that might have been destroyed in the name of progress have been restored and brought back to life.

A stroll along **Ford Street** is the best way to absorb the character of the town. Among the distinguished buildings are **Tanswell's Commercial Hotel** and the government buildings. Note the jail, antiques shops, and sequoia trees in **Town Hall Gardens.** Much of Beechworth's architecture is made from the honey-color granite quarried outside of town.

Burke Museum takes its name from Robert Burke, who, with William Wills, became one of the first white explorers to cross Australia from south to north in 1861. Burke was superintendent of police in Beechworth, 1856–59. Paradoxically, but not surprisingly, the small area and few mementos dedicated to Burke are overshadowed by the Ned Kelly exhibits, which include letters, photographs, and memorabilia that give genuine insight into the man and his misdeeds. The museum also displays a reconstructed streetscape of Beechworth in the 1880s. ✉ *Loch St.* ☎ *03/5728–1420* 🖃 *A$5* ⊙ *Daily 10:30–3:30.*

The **Carriage Museum** is in a corrugated-iron building that was once a stable. Displays range from simple farm carts and buggies to Cobb & Co. stagecoaches, some of which were modeled on U.S. designs. ✉ *Railway Ave.* 🖃 *A$1.50* ⊙ *Daily 10:30–12:30 and 1:30–4:30.*

NED KELLY: AN EXTRAORDINARY LIFE

S UCH IS LIFE." With those words Ned Kelly plunged to his death, hanged for murder at the age of 24.

Although it's been more than a century since his hanging, Ned Kelly continues to provoke controversy. Many Australians revere him, although his critics consider him a common criminal. But thanks to a mere two-year reign as a bushranger, he has been immortalized in film, art, and through countless works of song, poetry, and prose.

The English had Robin Hood, the Americans Jesse James. People love a notorious hero, and Ned Kelly was a natural: a tall, tough, idealistic youth who came to symbolize the struggle against an uncaring ruling class. Ned's attitudes were shaped by the prevailing forces of the time: corrupt local politics and the unscrupulous actions of some squatters who tried to force small landholders—like members of the Kelly clan—off their land.

Like many other lads from Irish working-class families, Ned got to know the police at a young age. At 15 he was charged with the assault of a pig and fowl dealer named Ah Fook and with aiding another bushranger, but was found not guilty on both charges. A year later, as a result of a friend's prank, he was convicted of assault and indecent behavior and sentenced to six months' hard labor. Within weeks of his release he was back in Melbourne's notorious Pentridge Prison serving three years for allegedly receiving a stolen horse. After this, Ned was determined to stay out of prison, but events were to dictate otherwise. It was matriarch Ellen Kelly's arrest—on what some claim were trumped-up charges—that was the turning point in the story. Warrants were issued for sons Ned and Dan, and a subsequent shoot-out left three policemen dead.

The heat was soon on the Kelly boys and their friends Joe Byrne and Steve Hart, whose occasional raids netted them thousands of pounds and worked the police into a frenzy. The gang's reputation was reinforced by their spectacular crimes, which were executed with humanity and humor. In 1878 they held scores of settlers hostage on a farm near Euroa en route to robbing the local bank, but they kept the folks entertained with demonstrations of horsemanship. The following year they took control of the town of Jerilderie for three days, dressing in police uniforms and captivating the women. According to one account, Joe Byrne took the gang's horses to the local blacksmith and charged the work to the NSW Police Department.

The final showdown was ignited by the murder of a police informer and former friend, Aaron Sherritt. The gang fled to Glenrowan, where Ned ordered a portion of the train line derailed and telegraph wires cut to delay the police. Among other aims, the plan was to take the survivors prisoner and use them as pawns to secure the release of Mrs. Kelly. Meanwhile, the gang holed up in a local pub, where they played cards and danced. The police were warned of the plan by a captive who had managed to escape, and the scene was set for a bloody confrontation.

Although the gang had their trademark heavy body suits made from plow mould boards and boilerplate, all were shot and killed except Ned, who took a bullet in his unprotected legs and was eventually captured. In hastily arranged proceedings in Melbourne, Ned appeared before Judge Redmond Barry, the same man who had sentenced his mother to three years' imprisonment. Barry ordered Ned Kelly to be hanged, a sentence carried out on November 11, 1880—despite a petition of 60,000 signatures attempting to have him spared. As the judge asked the Lord to have mercy on Ned's soul, the bushranger defiantly replied that he would meet him soon in a fairer court in the sky.

Twelve days after Ned Kelly's death, Judge Redmond Barry died.

—Josie Gibson

off the beaten path

MT. BUFFALO NATIONAL PARK – You can visit this beautiful, much-loved corner of the Victorian Alps, about 50 km (31 mi) south of Beechworth, and see many of the same natural wonders you'd find at the better-known (but more distant) Alpine National Park. Anderson Peak and the Horn both top 5,000 feet, and the park is full of interesting granite formations, waterfalls, animal and plant life, and more miles of walking tracks than you're likely to cover. The gorge walk is particularly scenic. Lake Catani has swimming and a camping area. Primary access to the park is from Myrtleford and Porepunkah. Both towns have hotels and motels.

Where to Stay & Eat

★ $$$$ ✕▭ **Howqua Dale Gourmet Retreat.** Owners Marieke Brugman and Sarah Stegley fully pamper their guests in this gem of rural Victoria. Marieke's cooking is wonderful, and Sarah has an encyclopedic knowledge of wine, especially Victorian vintages. Accommodations are luxurious, with splendid views. Each room is decorated and furnished in a particular theme—Asian, Victorian, modern, and Balinese—with appropriate art, and each has its own access to the garden. Horseback riding, boating on nearby Lake Eildon, or fishing can be arranged. Prices include meals, which vary seasonally. Brugman also conducts cooking classes on-site. ⊠ *Howqua River Rd., 140 km (87 mi) southwest of Beechworth, Howqua, 3722* ☎ *03/5777–3503* 🖷 *03/5777–3896* 🛏 *6 rooms* ⚅ *Restaurant, tennis court, pool, bar, meeting rooms, free parking; no a/c, no room phones, no room TVs* ⊟ *AE, DC, MC, V* ¶◎¶ *FAP.*

$–$$ ✕▭ **The Bank.** The restaurant's refined, dignified ambience befits its status as a former Bank of Australasia. The food, based on local produce like high-country beef, duck, and quail, is proficiently prepared and presented with style. Dinner is semiformal and à la carte. Four luxurious garden suites are in what was originally the carriage house and stables. Rates include breakfast. ⊠ *86 Ford St., 3747* ☎ *03/5728–2223* 🖷 *03/5728–2883* 🛏 *4 suites* ⚅ *Restaurant, dining room, laundry facilities, free parking* ⊟ *AE, DC, MC, V* ¶◎¶ *BP.*

★ $ ✕▭ **Kinross.** This former manse hosts a wealth of creature comforts. Chintz fabrics and dark-wood antiques fill the rooms. Sink into one of the plush armchairs and enjoy the fireplace. Each room has one, as well as electric blankets and eiderdown pillows on the beds. Room 2, at the front of the house, is the largest. Rates include breakfast. Hosts Christine and Bill Pearse's Saturday night dinners are a highlight. It's a two-minute walk from the center of Beechworth. ⊠ *34 Loch St., 3747* ☎ *03/5728–2351* 🖷 *03/5728–5333* 🛏 *5 rooms* ⚅ *Dining room, laundry facilities, free parking* ⊟ *AE, MC, V* ¶◎¶ *BP.*

¢ ▭ **Country Rose.** In a quiet backstreet about 1 km (½ mi) from the center of Beechworth, this retreat adjoining a family home is large and an extremely good value for anyone looking for comfort, privacy, and tranquillity. The decorations are frilly, with antique iron bedsteads, and there are kitchen facilities. The house is surrounded by a commercial rose garden, through which you're welcome to wander. ⊠ *Malakoff St., 3747* ☎ *03/5728–1107* 🛏 *2 rooms* ⚅ *Kitchen, free parking* ⊟ *No credit cards* ¶◎¶ *CP.*

¢ ▭ **Rose Cottage.** A small timber guesthouse, Rose Cottage oozes country charm. Guest rooms are comfortable, with French doors that open onto the garden. The house is filled with antiques, accented with Tiffany-style stained-glass lamps, and draped with lace, which might be a bit overpowering for some. Children are accommodated by prior arrangement. Reserve far in advance. ⊠ *42 Camp St., 3747* ☎ *03/5728–1069* 🛏 *4 rooms* ⚅ *Dining room, recreation room, free parking; no room phones* ⊟ *AE, DC, MC, V* ¶◎¶ *BP.*

Shopping

Buckland Gallery (✉ Ford and Church Sts. ☎ 03/5728–1432) sells Australian crafts and souvenirs that are far superior to the average, including soft toys, hats, woolen and leather items, edible Australiana, turned-wood candlesticks, pottery, and children's wear.

Chiltern

274 km (170 mi) northeast of Melbourne, 31 km (19 mi) north of Beechworth.

Originally known as Black Dog Creek, Chiltern is another gold rush town that fell into a coma when gold ran out. The main street of this tiny village is an almost perfectly preserved example of a 19th-century rural Australian streetscape, a fact not unnoticed by contemporary filmmakers. Notable buildings include the **Athenaeum Library and Museum,** the **Pharmacy,** the **Federal Standard Office,** and the **Star Hotel,** which has in its courtyard the largest grapevine in the country, with a girth of almost 6 feet at its base.

Lake View House is the childhood home of Henry Handel Richardson, the pen name of noted 19th-century novelist Ethel Florence, whose best-known works are *The Getting of Wisdom* and *The Fortunes of Richard Mahony.* In *Ultima Thule,* one of Richardson's characters reflects on Chiltern, which the author fictionalized as Barambogie: "Of all the dead-and-alive holes she had ever been in, this was the deadest." Among the memorabilia on display is a Ouija board the author used for séances. ✉ *Victoria St.* ☎ *03/5726–1391* 🖂 *A$2* ☉ *Weekends 10:30–noon and 1–4.*

off the beaten path

YACKANDANDAH – From Chiltern, you might find the 40-km (25-mi) drive southeast, through hilly countryside to the picturesque gold mining town of Yackandandah, worth a two-hour detour. The town has interesting old buildings, contemporary shops, a couple of pubs, and places to have Devonshire teas.

Rutherglen

274 km (170 mi) northeast of Melbourne, 18 km (11 mi) northwest of Chiltern.

The surrounding red loam soil signifies the beginning of the Rutherglen wine district, the source of Australia's finest fortified wines. If the term conjures up visions of cloying ports, you're in for a surprise. In his authoritative *Australian Wine Compendium,* James Halliday says, "Like Narcissus drowning in his own reflection, one can lose oneself in the aroma of a great old muscat."

The main event in the region is the Rutherglen Wine Festival, held during Labor Day weekend in March. The festival is a celebration of food, wine, and music—in particular jazz, folk, and country. Events are held in town and at all surrounding wineries. For more information on the wine festival, contact the **Rutherglen Tourist Information Centre** (✉ Walkabout Cellars, 84 Main St., Rutherglen ☎ 02/6032–9166).

All Saints Vineyards & Cellars has been in business since 1864. Owned and operated by Peter Brown (one of the famous Brown Brothers of Milewain) the property features a National Trust–classified castle, which was built in 1878 and modeled on the castle of Mey in Scotland. Products include the Museum Muscat and Museum Tokay, both made from 50-year-old grapes. The Terrace restaurant is on-site. ✉ *All Saints Rd., Wah-*

gunyah, 9 km (5½ mi) from Rutherglen ☎ *02/6033–1922* 🎫 *Free* ⊘ *Daily 9–5.*

Another long-established winery, **Buller's Calliope Vineyard,** has many vintage stocks of muscat and fine sherry distributed through its cellar outlet. Also on the winery's grounds is **Buller Bird Park,** an aviary. ✉ *Three Chain Rd. and Murray Valley Hwy.* ☎ *02/6032–9660* 🎫 *Free* ⊘ *Mon.–Sat. 9–5, Sun. 10–5.*

Despite the slick image proffered by **Campbell's Rutherglen Winery,** this is a family business that dates back more than 120 years. You can wander freely through the winery on a self-guided tour. Campbell's Merchant Prince Brown Muscat, Second Edition, is highly regarded by connoisseurs. Campbell Family Vintage Reserve is available only at the cellar door. ✉ *Murray Valley Hwy.* ☎ *02/6032–9458* 🎫 *Free* ⊘ *Mon.–Sat. 9–5:30, Sun. 10–5:30.*

Chambers Rosewood Winery was established in the 1850s and is one of the heavyweight producers of fortified wines. Bill Chambers's muscats are legendary, with blending stocks that go back more than a century. Don't miss the chance to sample the vast tasting range. ✉ *Off Corowa Rd.* ☎ *02/6032–8641* 🎫 *Free* ⊘ *Mon.–Sat. 9–5, Sun. 11–5.*

Along with exceptional fortified wine, **Pfeiffer Wines** has fine varietal wine, such as its Pfeiffer Chardonnay. It also has one of the few Australian plantings of gamay, the classic French grape used to make beaujolais. At this small, rustic winery, you can order a picnic basket stuffed with crusty bread, pâté, cheese, fresh fruit, wine, and smoked salmon, but be sure to reserve in advance. Wine maker Chris Pfeiffer sets up tables on the old wooden bridge that spans Sunday Creek, where you can take your picnic provisions. Phone ahead to book a table. ✉ *Distillery Rd., Wahgunyah, 9 km (5½ mi) from Rutherglen* ☎ *02/6033–2805* 🎫 *Free* ⊘ *Mon.–Sat. 9–5, Sun. 11–4.*

Where to Stay & Eat

$–$$ ✕ **Shamrock Cafe.** This small lunchtime favorite serves pastas and stir-fries, as well as such local specialties as the Murray cod. ✉ *121 Main St.* ☎ *02/6032–8439* 🖃 *AE, DC, MC, V.*

$–$$ ✕ **The Terrace.** Part of the All Saints estate, the restaurant is a welcome place to rest after a heavy wine-tasting itinerary. The menu lists light fare such as Mediterranean eggplant or more exotic choices like emu osso buco and smoked Lake Hume trout. Desserts are excellent, especially when combined with a formidable northeast fortified wine. ✉ *All Saints Rd., Wahgunyah* ☎ *02/6033–1922* 🖃 *AE, DC, MC, V* ⊘ *No dinner.*

¢ 🏨 **Wine Village Motor Inn.** In the heart of Rutherglen, this basic motel has a pool for relaxing during hot northeastern summer days. ✉ *217 Main St., 3685* ☎ *02/6032–9900* 🖷 *02/6032–8125* 🛏 *16 rooms* ♨ *Pool, free parking; no smoking* 🖃 *AE, DC, MC, V.*

Echuca

206 km (128 mi) north of Melbourne, 194 km (120 mi) west of Rutherglen, 92 km (57 mi) north of Bendigo.

Echuca's name derives from a local Aboriginal word meaning "meeting of the waters," a reference to the town's location at the confluence of the Murray, Campaspe, and Goulburn rivers. When the railway from Melbourne reached Echuca in 1864, the town became the junction at which wool and wheat cargo were transferred to railroad cars from barges on the Darling River in western New South Wales. During the second half of the 19th century, Echuca was Australia's largest inland port. River trade languished when the railway network extended into the interior, but reminders of Echuca's colorful heyday remain in the restored paddle steamers, barges, historic hotels, and the Red Gum Works, the town's sawmill, now a working museum.

Echuca's importance was recognized in the 1960s, when the National Trust declared the port a historic area. Nowadays it's a busy town of almost 10,000, the closest of the river towns to Melbourne. High Street, the main street of shops and cafés, leads to the river. Paddle steamer trips along the Murray are especially relaxing if you've been following a hectic touring schedule.

A tour of the **Historic River Precinct** begins at the Port of Echuca office, where you can purchase a ticket (with or without an added river cruise) that gives admission to the Star and Bridge hotels and the Historic Wharf area. The **Bridge Hotel** was built by Henry Hopwood, ex-convict father of Echuca, who had the foresight to establish a punt and later to build a bridge at this commercially strategic point on the river. The hotel is sparsely furnished, however, and it takes great imagination to re-create what must have been a roistering, rollicking pub frequented by river men, railway workers, and drovers. Built in the 1860s, the **Star Hotel** has an underground bar and escape tunnel, which was used by after-hours drinkers in the 19th century to evade the police. It also contains displays and memorabilia from the era. In the **Historic Wharf,** the heavy-duty side of the river trade business is on view, including a warehouse, old railroad tracks, and riverboats. Unlike those of the Mississippi or the Danube, the small, squat, utilitarian workhorses of the Murray are no beauties. Among the vessels docked at the wharf, all original, is the PS *Adelaide,* Australia's oldest operating paddle steamer. The Adelaide cannot be boarded, but it occasionally is stoked up, with the requisite puff-puffs, chug-chugs, and toot-toots. ⊠ *Murray Esplanade* ☎ *03/5482–4248* ✉ *A$10, A$20 with river cruise* ⊙ *Daily 9–5.*

Port of Echuca Woodturners is an old sawmill where timber from the giant river red gums that flourish along the Murray was once brought. Stop and watch the wood turners, blacksmith, and local businesses ply their trade today. Their work is for sale in the adjacent gallery. ⊠ *Murray Esplanade* ☎ *03/5480–6407* ✉ *Free* ⊙ *Daily 9–5.*

Sharp's Movie House and Penny Arcade is a nostalgic journey back to the days of the penny arcades. Have your fortune told; test your strength, dexterity, and lovability; or watch a peep show that was once banned in Australia. There are 60 machines here, the largest collection of operating penny arcade machines in the country. The movie house shows edited highlights of Australian movies that date back to 1896. A visit is highly recommended. ⊠ *Bond Store, Murray Esplanade* ☎ *03/ 5482–2361* ✉ *A$11* ⊙ *Daily 9–5.*

Life-size wax effigies of U.S. presidents may be the last thing you would expect to find in Echuca, but the **World in Wax Museum** has a Washington, Lincoln, and Kennedy—along with Fidel Castro, T. E. Lawrence (of Arabia), Queen Elizabeth II, Prince Charles, Lady Diana, and Australian celebrities and native sons. ⊠ *630 High St.* ☎ *03/5482–3630* ✉ *A$9* ⊙ *Daily 9–5.*

Riverboat trips along the Murray are especially relaxing if you've been following a hectic touring schedule. Several riverboats make short, one-hour excursions along the river, including the PS *Pevensey* and the PS *Canberra.* River traffic is limited to a few speedboats, small fishing skiffs, and an occasional kayak. The banks are thickly forested with river red gums, which require as much as half a ton of water per day. ⊠ *PS Pevensey tickets, Port of Echuca, Murray Esplanade* ☎ *03/5482–4248* ☜ *A$15.50* ⊙ *Departs five times daily* ⊠ *PS Canberra tickets, Bond Store, Murray Esplanade* ☎ *03/5482–2711* ☜ *A$12.50* ⊙ *Departs daily at 10, 11:30, 12:45, 2, and 3:15.*

Where to Stay & Eat

$$ ✕ **Oscar W's.** Named after the last paddle steamer ever made in this once-busy port, this is one of Echuca's finest restaurants. With a beautiful, tree-fringed view of the Murray River, it's a comfortable, relaxed establishment with dishes as diverse as grilled flat bread with tomato tapenade and an intriguing fillet of ostrich with red onion jam. ⊠ *Murray Esplanade* ☎ *03/5482–5133* ⊟ *AE, DC, MC, V.*

$$$$ ⊡ **PS Emmylou.** The perfect end to a trip to Echuca is an overnight cruise on the PS *Emmylou*. Departing Echuca around sunset, the paddle steamer shuffles downriver during a three-course dinner, a night in a cabin, and breakfast the following morning. The boat can accommodate 18 guests in 8 bunk rooms and one double-bed cabin, all with shared showers and toilets. Sunrise over the river, the boat churning past mist-cloaked gum trees and laughing kookaburras, is a truly memorable experience. ⊠ *57 Murray Esplanade* ☎ *03/5480–2237* 🖷 *03/5480–2927* ⊕ *www.emmylou.com.au* 🛏 *9 rooms* ⚸ *Dining room, bar; no a/c, no room phones, no room TVs.*

$$–$$$ ⊡ **River Gallery Inn.** In a renovated 19th-century building around the corner from the historic port precinct, this hotel has large, comfortable rooms at moderate prices. Each is decorated and furnished in a different theme: pretty and French provincial, opulent and Victorian, and mock-rustic, early Australia. An arts-and-crafts gallery is below the hotel. Four rooms overlook the street, but it's still quiet. Five rooms have whirlpool tubs. Rates include breakfast. ⊠ *578 High St., 3564* ☎ *03/5480–6902* 🛏 *6 rooms, 2 suites* ⚸ *Dining room, meeting rooms, free parking; no room phones* ⊟ *AE, MC, V* ⊙| *BP.*

Sports & the Outdoors

BOATING   **Echuca Boat and Canoe Hire** (⊠ Victoria Park Boat Ramp ☎ 03/5480–6208) rents one-person kayaks, canoes, and motorboats. Combination camping/canoeing trips are also available. A canoe costs A$18 per hour, A$60 per day. A kayak is A$15 per hour, A$30 per day.

FISHING   No license is required to fish the Murray River on the Victorian side. Rods and bait are available from Echuca Boat and Canoe Hire.

GOLF   **Rich River Golf Club** (⊠ West of Moama, across Murray River from Echuca ☎ 03/5482–2444), with two superb 18-hole, par-72 championship courses, charges A$30 greens fees for 18 holes on weekends, A$25 weekdays, and A$22 for clubs and cart rental.

WATERSKIING   The **Southern 80 Water-Ski Race,** held during the first weekend in February, is best viewed from the Echuca Boat Ramp. The race consists of high-power boats that pull two skiers apiece for 80 km (50 mi) through the twists and turns of the Murray River.

Swan Hill

350 km (217 mi) northwest of Melbourne, 97 km (60 mi) northwest of Echuca, 251 km (156 mi) southeast of Mildura.

Named in 1836 by the explorer Major Thomas Mitchell for the creatures that kept him awake at night, Swan Hill is a prosperous town surrounded by rich citrus groves and vineyards.

The **Swan Hill Pioneer Settlement** evokes life in a 19th-century Victorian river port with its replica pioneer homes, operational stores, machinery, and the landlocked paddle wheeler *Gem*, once the largest cargo-passenger boat on the Murray. Today you can relive the experience of the river trade with a cruise aboard the century-old paddleboat *PYAP*, which departs twice a day. At night, the settlement becomes the backdrop for the Pioneers sound-and-light show, which uses state-of-the-art lighting effects to bring the history of Swan Hill to life. Note that bookings are essential for the show. ⊠ *Horseshoe Bend,* ☎ *03/5036–2410* ☎ *A$16, sound-and-light show A$10* ☉ *Daily 9–5, show begins 1 hr after sunset.*

Where to Stay & Eat

$$–$$$ ╳ **Riverview Cafe.** This casual eatery overlooking the picturesque Maraboor River serves up hearty breakfasts, light lunches, and morning and afternoon teas. Beer, wine, and spirits are also available. ⊠ *Pioneer Settlement* ☎ *03/5036–2412* ⊟ *AE, DC, MC, V* ☉ *No dinner.*

$ ▦ **Lady Augusta Motor Inn.** This two-story motel, which surrounds a tree-lined courtyard, has large doubles, two-bedroom suites, and spa suites. All are well maintained. It's a short stroll from the town center. ⊠ *375 Campbell St., 3585* ☎ *03/5032–9677* ☒ *03/5032–9573* ↘ *24 rooms* ⬙ *Restaurant, cable TV with movies, pool, bar, meeting rooms, free parking* ⊟ *AE, DC, MC, V.*

en route | From Swan Hill, the Murray Valley Highway traverses farm country that has seen many years of irrigation. The only green in this rust-color semidesert is that of the citrus crops and vineyards. After passing the south end of Hattah-Kulkyne National Park, which is full of kangaroos and interesting bird life, turn right onto the Calder Highway (Highway 79) and proceed north through Red Cliffs, which has a Sunday market, into Mildura.

Mildura

557 km (345 mi) northwest of Melbourne, 251 km (156 mi) northwest of Swan Hill.

Claiming more hours of sunshine per year than Queensland's Gold Coast, Mildura is known for dried fruit, wine, citrus, and avocados, as well as its hydroponic vegetable-growing industry. The town was developed in 1885 by two Canadians, George and William Chaffey, who were persuaded to emigrate by Victorian premier Alfred Deakin. The Chaffey brothers were world pioneers in irrigation, and the irrigated vineyards of the Riverland region are enormously productive. However, though they provide Australians with much of their inexpensive cask wines, a premium table wine rarely bears a Riverland label.

At the **Pioneer Cottage,** you can get a good idea of what life was like in the days when Mildura was one antipodean frontier of European settlement. ⊠ *3 Hunter St.* ☎ *03/5023–3742* ☎ *A$2.50* ☉ *Tues., Fri.–Sat. 10–4.*

It's worth a peek into the **Workingman's Club** just to see the bar: at 300 feet, it's one of the world's longest. All of Mildura turns out to drink at its 27 taps, including local arts groups and rotary clubs, who come to nosh on lunch and dinner specials in the large new bistro restaurant. (⊠ Deakin Ave. ☎ 03/5023–0531 ☎ Free ☉ Daily 11–10)

↻ On the banks of the Murray, the **Golden River Fauna Gardens** has an extensive collection of native and exotic birds in walk-through aviaries. Daily shows feature dingos, wombats, and monkeys. You can hand-feed native animals, such as kangaroos and wallabies. Train rides along the river come with the entry price. Sample the selection of locally produced boutique wines at the café. ⊠ *Flora Ave.* ☎ *03/5023–5540* 🖃 *A$12* ⊙ *Daily 9–5.*

Fodor'sChoice **Trentham Estate Winery** is worth visiting as much for seeing the delight-
★ ful vistas from a picturesque bend of the Murray River as for tasting its medal-winning wines. Notable dishes at the on-site restaurant include yabbies (small, freshwater lobsterlike crustaceans), Murray perch, and kangaroo, which team admirably with the prize-winning wines available for tasting. In fine weather, you can eat on the veranda or under towering gums overlooking the river. The restaurant serves lunch Tuesday–Sunday and dinner on Saturday. To find Trentham, head across the Murray and follow the Sturt Highway through Buronga until you see the Trentham Estate sign on the right. ⊠ *Sturt Hwy., Trentham Cliffs, 15 km (9 mi) from Mildura* ☎ *03/5024–8888* 🖃 *Free* ⊙ *Daily 9–5.*

🄲 A popular option for kids, the **Aquacoaster** is a big complex of pools that includes an enormous water slide. ⊠ *18 Orange Ave.,* ☎ *03/5023–6955* 🖃 *A$9.50* ⊙ *Weekdays 2–6, weekends 1:30–6, school holidays 10–9.*

Where to Stay & Eat

$$–$$$ ✕ **Stefano's.** This restaurant became nationally known with the Australian
Fodor'sChoice television series *A Gondola on the Murray,* which showcased the skills
★ and personality of Stefano de Pieri. His northern Italian cuisine is tasty and prepared primarily from the Riverland's bountiful local produce. The extensive menu includes seasonal specialties like yabbies on a kipfler potato and caper salad, chicken and prosciutto tortellini, fresh vegetarian fettuccine, and a sumptuous European selection of desserts and cakes. ⊠ *Grand Hotel, 7th St. (enter from Langtree Ave.)* ☎ *03/5023–0511* 🖃 *AE, DC, MC, V* ⊙ *No dinner Sun.*

¢ 🏨 **Chaffey International Motor Inn.** Rooms and facilities at this fresh, central motel are well above average for country Victoria—and certainly better than those at any other motel in town. Modern rooms are simply decorated with a floral motif. Room service is available until 9 PM. ⊠ *244 Deakin Ave., 3500* ☎ *03/5023–5833* 🖶 *03/5021–1972* ✎ *32 rooms* ⌂ *Restaurant, room service, pool, spa, bar, dry cleaning, laundry facilities, meeting rooms, free parking* 🖃 *AE, DC, MC, V.*

¢ 🏨 **Mildura Country Club Resort.** What really sets the place apart is the surrounding golf course. Pleasantly decorated rooms all open onto the 18-hole greens. Spacious grounds and a large swimming pool add to the resort. ⊠ *12th St. Ext., 3500* ☎ *03/5023–3966* 🖶 *03/5021–1751* ✎ *40 rooms* ⌂ *Restaurant, 18-hole golf course, pool, sauna, bar, meeting rooms, free parking* 🖃 *AE, DC, MC, V.*

Murray River Region A to Z

To research prices, get advice from other travelers, and book travel arrangements, visit www.fodors.com.

CAR TRAVEL

The wide-open spaces of the northeast wineries and Murray River districts make driving the most sensible and feasible means of exploration. There is enough scenic interest along the way to make the long drives bearable, especially if you trace the river route. The direct run from Melbourne to Mildura is quite daunting (557 km [345 mi]). However, those towns accessed by the Hume Highway are easily reached from the capital city.

Beechworth and Rutherglen are on opposite sides of the Hume Freeway, the main Sydney–Melbourne artery. Allow four hours for the journey from Melbourne, twice that from Sydney. Echuca is a three-hour drive from Melbourne, reached most directly by the Northern Highway (Highway 75).

EMERGENCIES

In an emergency, dial 000 to reach an ambulance, the police, or the fire department.

⚑ Echuca and District Hospital ✉ Francis St., Echuca ☎ 03/5482-2800.
⚑ Amcal Pharmacy ✉ 192 Hare St., Echuca ☎ 03/5482-6666.

TOURS

The Gray Line operates one-day bus tours of Echuca, departing Melbourne on Friday and Sunday at 8:45 AM. The cost is A$103.

⚑ Gray Line ✉ 180 Swanson St., City Center, Melbourne ☎ 03/9663-4455.

TRAIN TRAVEL

V-Line trains run to most of the major towns in the region, including Echuca, Rutherglen, Swan Hill, and Mildura—but not Beechworth. This reasonable access is most useful if you do not have a car or want to avoid the long-distance drives. As with most country Victorian areas, direct train access from Melbourne to the main centers is reasonable, but getting between towns isn't as easy. The train to Swan Hill or Mildura may be an appealing option for those utterly discouraged by the long drive.

⚑ V-Line ☎ 1800/800120.

VISITOR INFORMATION

The information centers in Beechworth, Rutherglen, and Swan Hill are open daily 9–5:30; the center in Echuca is open daily 9–5; and the Mildura center is open weekdays 9–4 and weekends 10–4, but they close for lunch weekdays 12:30–1.

⚑ Tourist Information Beechworth Tourist Information Centre ✉ Ford and Camp Sts., Beechworth ☎ 03/5728-1374. **Echuca Tourist Information Centre** ✉ Leslie St. and Murray Esplanade, Echuca ☎ 03/5480-7555. **Mildura Tourist Information Centre** ✉ Langtree Mall, Mildura ☎ 03/5023-3619. **Rutherglen Tourist Information Centre** ✉ Walkabout Cellars, 84 Main St., Rutherglen ☎ 02/6032-9166. **Swan Hill Regional Information Office** ✉ 306 Campbell St., Swan Hill ☎ 03/5032-3033.

ALPINE NATIONAL PARK

323 km (200 mi) northeast of Melbourne.

The name Alpine National Park actually applies to three loosely connected areas in eastern Victoria that follow the peaks of the Great Dividing Range. This section covers the area, formerly called Bogong National Park, that contains the highest of the Victorian Alps. Its many outdoor activities include excellent walking trails among the peaks, fishing (license required), horseback riding, mountaineering, and skiing.

The land around here is rich in history. *Bogong* is an Aboriginal word for "big moth," and it was to Mount Bogong that Aborigines came each year after the winter thaw in search of bogong moths, considered a delicacy. Aborigines were eventually displaced by cattlemen who brought their cattle here to graze. Since the creation of the park in the mid-1980s, grazing has become more limited.

Stately snow gums grace the hills throughout the year, complemented by alpine wildflowers in bloom October–March. There are half- and full-day trails for bushwalkers, many of them in the Falls Creek area south of Mount Beauty. In winter the area is completely covered in snow, and bushwalkers put on cross-country skis, especially at Falls Creek and Mount Hotham.

For more information and a list of all walks and parks in the area, contact the **Department of Natural Resources and Environment** (✉ 240 Victoria Parade, East Melbourne ☎ 03/9412–4011 ⊕ www.parkweb.vic. gov.au).

Where to Stay & Eat

Old cattlemen's huts are scattered throughout the park and may be used by hikers free of charge. These, however, are often occupied, and shelter is never guaranteed. Bush camping is permitted throughout the park, and there is a basic campground at Raspberry Hill.

Hotels, motels, commercial camping, and caravan parks are in the major towns around the park, including Bright, Mount Beauty, Harrietville, Anglers Rest, Glen Valley, and Tawonga, as well as in the ski resorts of Falls Creek, Mount Buller, and Mount Hotham year-round.

The town of Bright is reasonably well supplied with dining possibilities. **Cafe Bacco** (✉ 2D Anderson St., Bright ☎ 03/5750–1711) has an informal Italian flavor. Try the prawns with saffron mayonnaise. The tiramisu is delicious.

Simone's (✉ Ovens Valley Motel Inn, Great Alpine Rd. and Ashwood Ave., Bright ☎ 03/5755–2022) is a remarkable find with its classic osso buco, gnocchi, and panna cotta.

Skiing

Ski resorts are open at Falls Creek, Mount Buller, Mount Buffalo, and Mount Hotham in winter.

Alpine National Park A to Z

To research prices, get advice from other travelers, and book travel arrangements, visit www.fodors.com.

BUS TRAVEL

Bus services operate from Albury on the New South Wales border in the north. During ski season, Pyles Coaches depart from Mount Beauty for Falls Creek and Mount Hotham, and depart from Melbourne for Falls Creek.

🚌 **Pyles Coaches** ☎ 03/5754–4024.

CAR TRAVEL

Alpine National Park is 323 km (200 mi) northeast of Melbourne, and you can reach it two ways. If you want to go to the park taking a short detour through the historic town of Beechworth, take the Hume Freeway (Route 31) north out of Melbourne and turn southeast onto the Ovens Highway at Wangaratta. Beechworth is about a 30-km (19-mi) detour off the Hume. You can also follow the Princes Highway east from Melbourne through Sale and Bairnsdale. Pick up the Omeo Highway north from here to Omeo, and then head west to Cobungra and Mount Hotham. The turnoff for Falls Creek is another 39 km (24 mi) north of Omeo.

VISITOR INFORMATION

The ranger station for the Alpine National Park is on Mount Beauty, and there are information centers in Bright, Omeo, and Falls Creek. The station at Mount Beauty has ranger-led programs.

🚌 Tourist Information **Alpine National Park** ✉ Kiewa Valley Hwy., Tawonga South ☎ 03/5754–4693. **Bright Visitor Center** ✉ 119 Gavan St., Bright ☎ 03/5755–2275. **De-**

partment of Natural Resources and Environment ✉ 240 Victoria Parade, East Melbourne ☎ 03/9412–4011. **Falls Creek Visitor Center** ✉ 1 Bogong High Plains Rd., Falls Creek ☎ 1800/033079. **Omeo Visitor Center** ✉ 199 Day Ave., Omeo ☎ 0500/877477.

WILSON'S PROMONTORY NATIONAL PARK

★ *231 km (144 mi) southeast of Melbourne.*

This southernmost granite peninsula once connected Tasmania with mainland Australia, and there are botanical and geological odds and ends common both to the mainland and the wayward island. More than 180 species of bird have been sighted here, and Corner Inlet, along Five Mile Beach, is a seabird sanctuary. Near the visitor center at Tidal River, you may sight tame marsupials, including kangaroos, wombats, and koalas.

There are more than 20 well-marked trails here, some meandering past pristine beaches and secluded coves excellent for swimming, others more strenuous. One tough but popular trail is the 9½-km (6-mi) **Sealer's Cove Walk,** which traverses the slopes of Mount Wilson Range before descending through Sealer's Swamp to the tranquil Sealer's Cove. The **Lilly Pilly Gully Nature Walk,** a 5-km (3-mi) trip among tree ferns and giant mountain ash, gives a good introduction to the park's plant and animal life with the aid of informative signs posted along the way. And from the top of Mount Oberon on a good day, you can see across the Bass Strait all the way to Tasmania.

Although Wilson's Promontory is perhaps the best-known sight in the Gippsland region, there are also notable seaside towns and inland parks also worth visiting. **Tarra Bulga National Park,** about an hour's drive from Wilson's Promontory, has numerous walking tracks that wind through fern gullies and towering forests where rainbow parrots flit through the branches. Drive along the spectacular, winding **Grand Ridge Road** through the Strzelecki Ranges, and stop in the historic towns of **Port Albert** and **Yarram.** Further east of the Prom, Gippsland's **Lakes District** is a boater's paradise, particularly around the pretty towns of Metung and Painsville. Nearby, **Lakes Entrance** is a popular summer holiday resort where boats and water sports are easy to arrange.

Where to Stay & Eat
A few quality lodging establishments have sprung up in this once-rugged area. Dining is a bit more problematic: There's not much to be said about food in this particular corner unless you catch it and cook it yourself. The Foster Motel has a dining room, and the Exchange Hotel serves good pub dinners.

In Foster, north of the national park, the **Hillcrest Farmhouse** (✉ Ameys Track, Foster, 3960 ☎ 03/5682–2769) is a B&B in an 1880s farmhouse on 10 acres with a vineyard. Overlooking the sea and mountains at Wilson's Promontory is the **Larkrise Pottery and Farm** (✉ Fish Creek-Foster Rd., Foster, 3960 ☎ 03/5682–2953), with two B&B rooms on 40 acres of land.

⚠ **Tidal River Campground.** With 480 campsites, the well-known Tidal River Campground is among Australia's largest. During the January–February peak season, sites cost A$18.60 per night for up to three persons, A$3.90 for each additional person. Single-room motor trailers (A$49), known as "huts," contain two double bunk beds, hot plates, a small refrigerator, heaters, and cold water. Heated cabins accommodate two to six people and start at A$81 during peak season. Due to popularity, ballot forms must be lodged by June for a chance to secure a camping site during peak months. Huts and cabins must also be prebooked, up to 12 months ahead. ⊠ *Park Office, Wilson's Promontory National Park* ☎ *03/5680–9555* ↪ *480 campsites* ☆ *Flush toilets, pit toilets, full hook-ups, drinking water, laundry facilities, showers, fire pits, grills, picnic tables, electricity, public telephone, general store, ranger station.*

Wilson's Promontory National Park A to Z

To research prices, get advice from other travelers, and book travel arrangements, visit www.fodors.com.

CAR TRAVEL
To get to Wilson's Promontory National Park, 231 km (144 mi) south of Melbourne, take the Princes Highway to Dandenong, and then the South Gippsland Highway south to Meeniyan or Foster. Tidal River is another 70 km (43 mi) from there. There is no public transportation to the park.

VISITOR INFORMATION
Wilson's Promontory National Park headquarters sells guidebooks. Prom Country Information Centre handles all accommodation inquiries. Both are open daily 9–5.

🛈 Tourist Information **Department of Natural Resources and Environment** ⊠ 240 Victoria Parade, East Melbourne ☎ 03/9412–4011. **Prom Country Information Centre** ☎ 1800/630704 ⊕ www.promcountry.com.au. **Wilson's Promontory National Park** ⊠ Tidal River ☎ 03/5680–9555.

TASMANIA

FODOR'S CHOICE

Brickendon, historic accommodations in Longford

Fee and Me, restaurant in Launceston

Franklin–Gordon Wild Rivers National Park, near Strahan

Freycinet Lodge, in Coles Bay

Freycinet National Park, near Coles Bay

Hatherley House, in Launceston

Kelleys, restaurant in Hobart

Mit Zitrone, restaurant in Hobart

Port Arthur Historic Site, in Port Arthur

Salamanca Place, market in Hobart

HIGHLY RECOMMENDED

RESTAURANTS Elbow Room, in Hobart

Mures Fish House Complex, in Hobart

Stanley's on the Bay, in Stanley

Stillwater, in Launceston

Synergy, in Launceston

HOTELS Beachside Retreat West Inlet, in Stanley

Cradle Mountain Lodge, in Sheffield

Corinda's Cottages, in Hobart

Franklin Manor, in Strahan

Lemonthyme Lodge, in Mona

Matilda's of Ranelagh, in Ranelagh

Oakford on Elizabeth Pier, in Hobart

Waratah on York, in Launceston

SIGHTS Antarctic Adventure, in Hobart

Cradle Mountain–Lake St. Clair National Park

Richmond colonial village, near Hobart

Updated by
Roger Allnutt

SEPARATED FROM THE MAINLAND by the rough Bass Strait, the island of Tasmania holds a bounty of natural diversity and old-fashioned hospitality. It's a hiker's dream, rich with untracked wilderness along its southwest and west coasts. Elegant English settlements with vast gardens fringe the east and north edges. Remnants of the island's volatile days as a penal colony await exploration in an abundance of museums and historic sites that preserve the lore of this fascinating piece of Australia.

About the size of West Virginia, and with a population of less than a half million, the Tasmania is an unspoiled reminder of a simpler, slower lifestyle. It has been called the England of the south, as it, too, is richly cloaked in mists and rain, glows with russet and gold shades in the fall, and has the chance of an evening chill year-round. Where the English tradition of a Christmas roast may strike you as strange during a steamy Sydney summer, such rites appear natural amid Tasmania's lush quilt of lowland farms and villages. Many towns retain an English ambience, with their profusion of Georgian cottages and commercial buildings, the preservation of which attests to Tasmanians' attachment to their past.

Aborigines, who crossed a temporary land bridge from Australia, first settled the island some 45,000 years ago. Europeans discovered it in 1642, when Dutch explorer Abel Tasman arrived at its southwest coast, but not until 1798 was Tasmania (then called Van Diemen's Land, after the Governor of the Dutch East Indies) thought to be an island. Much of Tasmania's subsequent history is violent, however, and there are episodes that many residents may wish to forget. The entire population of full-blooded Aborigines was wiped out by English troops and settlers, or exiled to the Bass Strait islands. The establishment in 1830 of a penal settlement at Port Arthur for the colony's worst offenders ushered in a new age of cruelty.

Today, walking through the lovely grounds in Port Arthur or the unhurried streets of Hobart, it's difficult to picture Tasmania as a land of turmoil and tragedy—in fact, it's one of Australia's safest places for travel. But that is the great dichotomy of this island, for, in many ways, Tasmania is still untamed. This is one of the most mountainous islands in the world, and tracts of its southwest remain unexplored, their access barred by impenetrable rain forests and deep river gorges. Of all Australia's states, Tasmania has set aside the greatest percentage of land—28%—as national parks, and the island's extreme southern position results in a wild climate that's often influenced by Antarctica. Thus, if you're planning a trip into the alpine wilderness, be prepared for sudden and severe weather changes. A snowstorm in summer isn't unusual.

Exploring Tasmania

Tasmania is compact—the drive from southern Hobart to northern Launceston takes little more than two hours. Although the hilly terrain and winding roads make exploration of some areas more time-consuming, the scenes usually are more breathtaking as well. In the great, untrammeled southwest, there are very few roads and just a handful of bushwalking trails. Elsewhere, the landscape ranges from perfectly tame to entirely wild—from classic rural farmland tableaux to the most formidable mountain ranges in Australia.

The easiest way to see the state is by car, as you can plan a somewhat circular route around the island. Begin in Hobart or Launceston, where car rentals are available from the airport city agencies, or in Devonport if you arrive on the ferry from Melbourne. Although distances seem small, allow plenty of time for stops along the way—and bring a sturdy pair of shoes

If you have 3 days

Spend your first morning in ⊡ **Hobart,** where you can stroll around the docks, Salamanca Place, and Battery Point, and take a cruise on the Derwent River. After lunch, drive to ⊡ **Richmond** and explore its 19th-century streetscape, then stay in a local bed-and-breakfast. On the second day head for ⊡ **Port Arthur** and spend the morning exploring the town's historic park, the site of the island's former penal colony. Take the afternoon to drive through the dramatic scenery of the Tasman Peninsula, noting the tessellated pavement and Tasman Arch blowhole near Eaglehawk neck. Return to Hobart for the night, then on the third morning take a leisurely drive round the scenic ⊡ **Huon Valley.** On return to Hobart, finish your tour with a trip to the summit of Mt. Wellington.

If you have 5 days

Explore ⊡ **Hobart** on foot the first morning, then head for the Cadbury chocolate factory in Claremont, wandering through historic ⊡ **Richmond** on the way back. Spend the night in Hobart, then on the second day drive through the scenic **Huon Valley.** Return to Hobart for the night, and on the third day drive to ⊡ **Port Arthur,** taking in the beauty of the Tasman Peninsula on the way. Spend the night in Port Arthur, then drive early on the fourth day to ⊡ **Freycinet National Park.** Climb the steep path to the outlook over Wineglass Bay, then descend to the sands for a picnic and swim. Stay the night in the park, then on day five meander back to Hobart via ⊡ **Ross** and **Oatlands.** Return to the capital, topping off the day with city views from Mt. Wellington.

If you have 10 days

Take a walking tour of ⊡ **Hobart** on the first morning, then take an afternoon drive to ⊡ **Richmond** before returning for the night. On the second day, drive to the Tasman Peninsula, enjoying the scenic backroads before heading to ⊡ **Port Arthur** for the night. On the third day, head back southwest through Hobart toward the bucolic orchards of the ⊡ **Huon Valley** and the Tahune Forest Airwalk. Stay the night, then depart early on the fourth morning for ⊡ **Strahan,** stopping at Lake St. Clair, Donaghy's Hill Lookout, and Nelson Falls. Spend the night, take an all-day cruise on the Gordon River, and stay another night. On day six make the long drive north via Zeehan and Marrawah to ⊡ **Stanley,** a lovely village set beneath the rocky majesty of the Nut. Have lunch here, then head back east to ⊡ **Devonport,** where you'll stay the night. On day seven, turn inland via Sheffield or Wilmot to reach ⊡ **Cradle Mountain National Park.** Here you'll stay two nights, using day eight to fully explore the region's natural beauty. On the ninth day, leave early for ⊡ **Launceston,** spend the night, then head back to Hobart through **Ross** and **Oatlands.**

---

for impromptu mountain and seaside walks, when you'll have huge patches of forest and long expanses of white beaches all to yourself.

About the Restaurants

Restaurants in Tasmania lean toward the compact and casual. Although you can definitely dine finely in the larger towns, eateries more commonly serve filling, casual meals in a familial atmosphere. Local seafood, steaks, hearty meat pies, produce, and wines are usually menu highlights; ask your waiter, or even the restaurant owner, for recommendations. Hobart, in particular, has recently made its own high marks on the food scene with innovative delicacies cooked up at several up-and-coming restaurants. When dining out at more upscale places, the dress code is still comfortable, but more stylish and conservative. Wineries are particularly good places to sample the wonders grown or produced on the island. Also look for cheese and produce specialists in the wine regions. Some even set up roadside stalls where you can sample their wares.

WHAT IT COSTS In Australian Dollars				
$$$$	**$$$**	**$$**	**$**	**¢**
AT DINNER over $50	$36–$50	$21–$35	$10–$20	under $10

Restaurant prices are for a main course at dinner.

About the Hotels

In Tasmania, hotels of all levels usually include tea- and coffee-making facilities, room refrigerators, TVs, heating, electric blankets, irons and hair dryers on request, and laundry facilities. Apart from a few hotels right in the main city center, most Hobart accommodations have free parking. In many smaller places, especially the colonial-style cottages, no smoking is allowed inside.

WHAT IT COSTS In Australian Dollars				
$$$$	**$$$**	**$$**	**$**	**¢**
FOR 2 PEOPLE over $300	$201–$300	$151–$200	$100–$150	under $100

Hotel prices are for two people in a standard double room in high season, including tax and service, based on the European Plan (with no meals) unless otherwise noted.

Timing

Winter can draw freezing blasts from the Antarctic. This is not the time of year for the highlands or wilderness areas. It's better in the colder months to enjoy the cozy interiors of colonial cottages and the open fireplaces of welcoming pubs. The east coast is generally mild and more protected from the weather than the west, which is struck by the "roaring 40s," weather-bearing winds that blow across the southern 40s latitudes, unobstructed by landmasses for thousands of miles. Summer can be surprisingly hot—bushfires are common—but temperatures are generally lower than on the Australian mainland. Early autumn is beautiful, with deciduous trees in full color. Spring, with its wildflowers, is a splash of pastel hues and the season for rainbows.

Tasmania is a relaxing island with few crowds, except during the mid-December to mid-February school holiday period and at the end of the annual Sydney-to-Hobart yacht race. Remember that Australian seasons are the reverse of those in the northern hemisphere, and those here are more extreme, as it sits to the south of the continent. Local festivals celebrate events throughout the year, so check the tourism web site when planning your trip. Most attractions and sights, including the national parks, are open year-round; however, November through March is the best time to hike in the Cradle Mountain area or the South West.

HOBART

Straddling the Derwent River at the foot of Mt. Wellington's forested slopes, Hobart rivals Sydney as Australia's most beautiful state capital. Founded as a penal settlement in 1803, Hobart is the second-oldest city in the coun-

Tassie Tastes Tasmania's clean air, unpolluted waters, and temperate climate provide a pristine environment in which fresh seafood, beef, dairy goods, fruits and vegetables, and wine are produced year-round. In particular, the island's culinary fame is based on its superb, bountiful seafood. Tasmanian dairy products are worth the indulgence, notably King Island's cheese and thick double cream. With more than 100 vineyards, Tasmania is also establishing itself as a force in Australian wine making, and the quality reds and whites from small producers are gaining accolades locally and overseas. And no one should miss a tour of the famous Cadbury–Schweppes chocolate and cocoa factory near Hobart, where you can sample from the richly flavored treats that have long been an Australian favorite.

6

Colonial Homes & Cottages Tasmania nurtures the architectural gems that have survived its colonial past. With only a small population to support, the state has rarely found it necessary to demolish the old to make way for the new. Many cottages built during the first days of the colony are now bed-and-breakfasts, guesthouses, and self-catering apartments. They are in the best-preserved towns and villages, as well as in the major cities of Hobart and Launceston. Georgian mansions, country pubs, colonial cottages, charming boutique hotels, and welcoming motels are all part of the quality accommodation network ready to invite you in for some real "Tassie" hospitality.

Outdoor Adventures Tasmania is an explorer's playground, with some of Australia's best and most challenging walking terrain. Large sections of mountains and coasts are incorporated into regulated natural areas like Mt. Field, Southwest, and Franklin Gordon Wild Rivers national parks in the southwest, and Rocky Cape National Park on the north coast. The state's western wilderness is still virtually untouched, and it's the domain of serious trekkers. You can find less strenuous and relatively pristine walking around Cradle Mountain, in the center of Tasmania, and the Freycinet Peninsula on the east coast. The island has myriad opportunities for cycling, diving, bushwalking (hiking), rafting, sailing, sea kayaking, and game and trout fishing.

---

try after Sydney, even though it feels as though it's the oldest. Many of the colonial brick and sandstone, convict-built structures have been restored and now define the atmosphere of this small city of 185,000.

As in Sydney, life here revolves around the port. The Derwent River has one of the deepest harbors in the world, the broad, deep estuary making it a great spot for sports. It was the Derwent that attracted the original settlers, who quickly capitalized on the natural treasure. Many of the converted warehouses that still line the wharf were formerly used to store Hobart's major exports—fruit, wool, and corn—as well as the products of the whaling fleet that used the city as a base.

Hobart sparkles between Christmas and the New Year, summer Down Under, during the annual Sydney-to-Hobart yacht race. The event dominates conversations among Hobart's citizens, who descend on Constitution Dock to welcome the yachts and join in the boisterous festivities

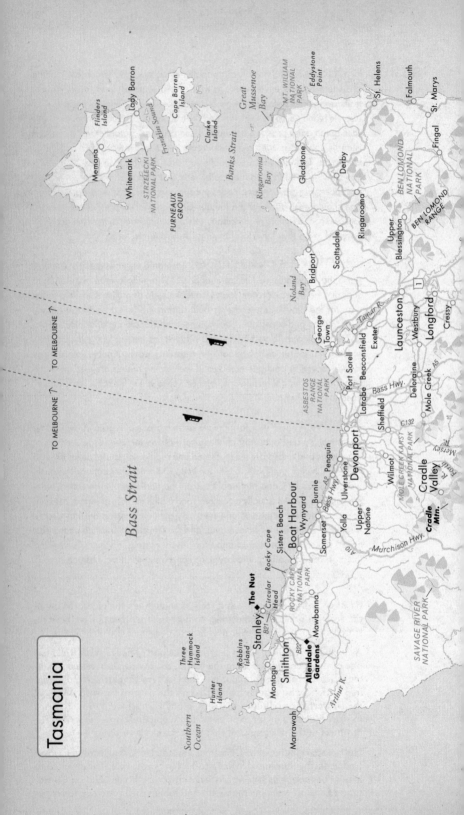

Tasmania

of the crews. The New Year also coincides with the Tastes of Tasmania Festival, when the dockside area comes alive with the best of Tasmanian food and wine on offer in numerous cafés, bars, and waterfront stalls. Otherwise, Hobart *is* a placid city whose nightlife is largely confined to excellent restaurants, jazz clubs, and the action at the Wrest Point Casino in Sandy Bay.

Exploring Hobart

Numbers in the text correspond to numbers in the margin and on the Downtown Hobart map.

a good walk

Begin by the city's focal point at the docks, the old warehouses of Macquarie Street and Franklin Wharf. Spend a couple of hours at the **Tasmanian Museum and Art Gallery** ❶ ▶ and the **Maritime Museum of Tasmania** ❷, opposite **Constitution Dock** ❸, before following the line of the wharves to **Parliament House** ❹ and **Salamanca Place** ❺. This is Hobart's most vibrant shopping district and gathering place, where the colorful Salamanca morning market opens on Saturday. The **Antarctic Adventure** ❻ museum is here and deserves a visit of at least two hours. After your visit, climb Montpelier Road onto Hampden Road, which leads to the **Narryna Heritage Museum** ❼ and antiques shops, charming cottages, and other historic buildings. Head back toward Castray Esplanade, but this time turn left into Runnymede Street and walk by the delightful homes of **Arthur's Circus** ❽ before returning to Salamanca Place.

TIMING   You should allow two hours or more for this walk, depending on how long you like to linger and watch local life. The dock and wharf areas are always busy with fishing vessels, pleasure craft, and sightseeing ferries. Saturday is the liveliest time for Salamanca Place, when the area's market is set up, although the craft and art galleries are more pleasant on weekdays, when crowds are smaller.

What to See

★ � ❻   **Antarctic Adventure.** Hobart is Australia's Antarctic exploration capital, home to the Australian Antarctic Division, and this museum brilliantly captures the feel of life in the "frozen" south. Exhibits inform you about Antarctic and Macquarie Island wildlife, explorers, and weather, but this is no dry, sober display. You can visit a re-created authentic Antarctic field camp, learn of the exploits of heroes such as Mawson and Shackleton, experience subzero temperatures in the cold room, and ski down a French alpine mountainside on the "Blizzard" simulator ride. ✉ *2 Salamanca Sq., Battery Point* ☎ *03/6220–8220 or 1800/350028* 💲 *A$16* ☉ *Daily 10–5.*

❽   **Arthur's Circus.** Hobart's best-preserved street is an enchanting collection of tiny houses and cottages set in a circle around a village green on Runnymede Street, in the heart of historic Battery Point. Most of these houses, which were built in the 1840s and 1850s, have been nicely restored.

Bonorong Wildlife Park. Situated 25 km (16 mi) north of Hobart on the highway to Launceston, the park has a wide selection of Australian species, including koalas, wombats, quolls (indigenous cats), and the notorious Tasmanian devil. ✉ *Briggs Rd., Brighton* ☎ *03/6268–1184* 💲 *A$11* ☉ *Daily 9–5.*

Brooke Street Pier. The busy waterfront at Brooke Street Pier is the departure point for harbor cruises. Nearby **Elizabeth Street Pier** has trendy restaurants and bars. ✉ *Franklin Wharf, Hobart City.*

☺ **Cadbury-Schweppes Chocolate Factory.** Very few children (or adults!) can resist a tour of the best chocolate and cocoa factory in Australia. Book

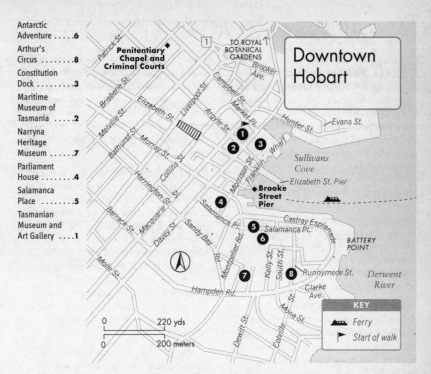

Downtown
Hobart

KEY
Ferry
Start of walk

0   220 yds
0   200 meters

well in advance through the visitor information center. ⊠ *Cadbury Estate, Claremont, 12 km (7½ mi) north of Hobart* ☎ *03/6249–0333 or 1800/627367* ☞ *A$12.50* ⊙ *Tours weekdays at 9, 9:30, 10:30, and 1.*

❸ Constitution Dock. Yachts competing in the annual Sydney-to-Hobart race moor at this colorful marina dock from the end of December through the first week of January. Buildings fronting the dock are century-old reminders of Hobart's trading history. ⊠ *Argyle and Davey Sts., Hobart City.*

❷ Maritime Museum of Tasmania. The old state library building houses one of the best museum maritime collections in Australia, including figureheads, whaling implements, models, and photographs dating as far back as 1804. ⊠ *Argyle and Davey Sts., Hobart City* ☎ *03/6234–1427* ☞ *A$7* ⊙ *Daily 10–4:30.*

❼ Narryna Heritage Museum. Museum exhibits in this gracious old town house depict the life of Tasmania's pioneers. A collection of colonial relics is displayed. ⊠ *103 Hampden Rd., Battery Point* ☎ *03/6234–2791* ☞ *A$5* ⊙ *Aug.–June, weekdays 10:30–5, weekends 2–5.*

❹ Parliament House. Built by convicts in 1840 as a customs house, this building did not acquire its present function until 1856. Although it's closed to the general public, you can take a tour of the building on weekdays. Contact the Clerk of the House if you'd also like to watch a session of parliament from the viewing gallery. The grounds of Parliament House are maintained by the Royal Botanic Gardens. ⊠ *Morrison St., between Murray St. and Salamanca Pl., Hobart City* ☎ *03/6233–2374* ☞ *Free* ⊙ *Guided tours weekdays 10–2.*

Penitentiary Chapel and Criminal Courts. Built and used during the early convict days, these buildings vividly portray Tasmania's penal, judicial, and religious heritage in their courtrooms, old cells, and underground

CloseUp

TASMANIA'S CONVICT PAST

THEY CAME IN CHAINS to this hostile island where the seasons were all the wrong way around and the sights and smells unfamiliar. They were the men and women that Great Britain wanted to forget, the desperately poor refuse of an overcrowded penal system that considered seven years of transportation an appropriate penalty for stealing a loaf of bread that might have meant the difference between survival and starvation. They were mostly young, usually uneducated, and often—from 1830 onward—they were Irish. Sending "troublemakers" halfway around the world was one good way of ridding the land of voices calling for its freedom.

When Lieutenant John Bowen inaugurated the first permanent incursion into Van Diemen's Land in September 1803, he brought with him as servants 21 male convicts and three female prisoners. In just under 50 years, when the last convict ship arrived, that total had soared to 57,909 male prisoners, and 13,392 women prisoners. Tasmania, Governor George Arthur observed, had become an island prison.

Port Arthur, established in 1830, was—contrary to today's legend—never the most ghastly hellhole of the convict gulag. That dubious honor was shared by Sarah Island on Tasmania's west coast and Norfolk Island in the South Pacific. There was a classification system to keep hardened felons apart from those who had strayed a bit. The latter worked at Maria Island or as domestic servants on Midlands estates. Repeat offenders and the violent miscreants, though, ended up on the Tasman Peninsula.

First established as a timber-getting site for Hobart, the Port Arthur penal settlement opened with 68 prisoners and soon became Australia's main convict center. Its natural advantages—two narrow necks and steep cliffs pounded by surging surf—could hardly be overlooked. With the closure of the Maria Island colony in 1832 and Macquarie Harbour a year later, numbers at Port Arthur increased to 675 prisoners in 1833. More buildings went up, and a semaphore system

advising of escapes linked Port Arthur with Hobart via numerous hilltop stations. The penal colony became a self-sufficient industrial center where prisoners sawed timber, built ships, laid bricks, cut stone, and made tiles, shoes, iron castings, and clothing.

Soon Port Arthur was ranked as the "best" of the British Empire's 35 colonial prisons. It was even regarded as excessively permissive by some critics because of the reformist philosophy behind the Model Prison, where punishments, including floggings, took place. Completed in 1852, the goal of this pinwheel-shape prison was penance with reform. Thus, some criminals were isolated from all human contact, held in silence (except for Sunday services) to contemplate their misdeeds.

Female prisoners were shipped off as domestic workers or to the female factories, where they sewed, knitted, and tended animals in often dank conditions. Not surprisingly, male guards took cruel advantage of the women and there were hundreds of unplanned pregnancies.

Convict banishment to Van Diemen's Land ceased in 1853. Most of the Port Arthur inmates were given tickets of leave or were sent to the countryside as agricultural laborers. Insane convicts (and there were many who had gone quite mad here) were incarcerated in the old wooden barracks until a special asylum was finished in 1868.

The settlement closed in 1877 after some 12,000 sentences had been served. For a while the authorities tried to expunge all memories of the peninsula's shame. They even changed the name for a time to Carnarvon. This halfhearted cover-up failed. Today, memories of Tasmania's convict past burn brighter than ever as society once again wrestles with the same dilemmas of good and evil, crime and punishment.

—Steve Robertson

tunnels. If you want to get spooked, come for the nighttime ghost tour (reservations recommended). ⊠ *Brisbane and Campbell Sts., Hobart City* ☎ *03/6231–0911* ✉ *A$7.70, ghost tour A$8.80* ⏱ *Tour weekdays 10–3, ghost tour daily 7:45 PM.*

❺ **Salamanca Place.** Old whaling ships used to dock at Salamanca Place.
Fodor'sChoice Today many of the warehouses that were once used by whalers along
★ this street have been converted into crafts shops, art galleries, and restaurants. On Saturday, a boisterous market takes place, where dealers of Tasmanian arts and crafts, antiques, old records, and books—and a fair bit of appalling junk—display their wares between 8 and 3. Keep an eye open for items made from beautiful Tasmanian timber, particularly Huon pine.

> **need a break?** The **Retro Cafe** (⊠ 31 Salamanca Pl., Battery Point ☎ 03/6223–3073) is among the most stylish and coolly casual of Salamanca Place's busy cafés with sidewalk tables. It's a great place to get a quick, light bite of quiche or focaccia with a coffee or glass of local wine.

Shot Tower. Built in the 1860s, this structure today is the only remaining circular sandstone tower in the world. Lead bullets were once manufactured here for use in the firearms of the day. You reach the breathtaking views of the Derwent estuary from the top of the 160-foot tower by climbing an internal staircase. ⊠ *Channel Hwy., Taroona* ☎ *03/6227–8885* ✉ *A$4.50* ⏱ *Daily 9–4.*

❶ **Tasmanian Museum and Art Gallery.** The museum and gallery, which overlook Constitution Dock, have many exhibits on Tasmania's history. It's the best place in Hobart to learn about the island's Aborigines and the unique wildlife. ⊠ *40 Macquarie St., Hobart City* ☎ *03/6211–4177* ✉ *Free* ⏱ *Daily 10–5.*

> **off the beaten path** **ROYAL TASMANIAN BOTANICAL GARDENS –** The largest area of open land in Hobart, these well-tended gardens are rarely crowded and provide a welcome relief from the city. Exotic plants represent the English horticultural tradition, and there are interesting native Tasmanian species as well. One section has been specially designed for wheelchairs. The Japanese Garden is dominated by a miniature Mt. Fuji. Children love the flower clock. ⊠ *Lower Domain Rd., Queen's Domain* ☎ *03/6234–6299* ✉ *Free* ⏱ *Daily 8–4:45, education center noon–4.*

Where to Eat

Constitution Dock is the perfect place for yacht-watching, as well as for gobbling fresh fish-and-chips from one of the *punts* (small diners) moored on the water. Ask for the daily specials, such as local blue grenadier or trevalla, which cost A$5–A$8. The city's main restaurant areas include the docks and around Salamanca Place. Excellent seafood and steaks are local highlights, but a recent influx of talented young chefs has expanded Hobart's culinary horizons.

★ **$$** ✕ **Elbow Room.** The chef–proprietor of this stylish basement restaurant earns his reputation for innovative cuisine. Tablecloths and silverware add to the feeling of elegance and refinement. Filling meals include *tournedos* (a small beef-tip fillet) topped with red wine and shallot butter—savory enough to melt in your mouth. The restaurant is noted for its excellent wine list. ⊠ *9–11 Murray St. (entrance off Despard St.), Hobart City* ☎ *03/6224–4254* ▤ *AE, DC, MC, V.*

$$ ✕ **Meehan's.** Plan to splurge for a big night out at the Grand Chancellor Hotel's signature restaurant, which has superb views of Hobart's bustling waterfront. The menu is seasonal and highlights local produce. Options might include aged King Island porterhouse steak with artichoke mash, grilled onion, and red wine au jus; or barbecued, boned quail marinated in lemon, garlic, herbs, and wine and served with couscous and Mediterranean vegetables. The wine list is excellent. ⊠ *1 Davey St., Hobart City* ☎ *03/6235–4535 or 1800/222229* ⚲ *Reservations essential* ⋔ *Jacket and tie* ▤ *AE, DC, MC, V* ⊗ *No lunch Sun. or Mon.*

$$ ✕ **The Point.** Breathtaking views of the city easily justify a visit to this revolving restaurant atop one of Hobart's tallest buildings. Luckily, the food is equally rewarding. Tables are widely spaced around a mirrored central column and all have views. Sample the savory smoked Tasmanian salmon appetizer; or, to impress, order prawns flambéed at your table. ⊠ *Wrest Point Hotel, 410 Sandy Bay Rd., Sandy Bay* ☎ *03/6225–0112* ⚲ *Reservations essential* ⋔ *Jacket required* ▤ *AE, DC, MC, V.*

$–$$ ✕ **Ball and Chain Grill.** If you like your beef, game, poultry, or seafood cooked on a wood fire burned down to real charcoal, then this is the place to go. The huge, succulent hunks of beef served here test even the heartiest appetite. ⊠ *87 Salamanca Pl., Battery Point* ☎ *03/6223–2925* ▤ *AE, DC, MC, V* ⊗ *No lunch Sat. or Sun.*

$–$$ ✕ **Cornelian Bay Boat House.** This restaurant on the edge of the River Derwent settles diners into calm, relaxing surroundings. Large windows in this former boathouse and bathing pavilion provide a panorama of the river looking down to the Tasman Bridge. Bite into the crisp-skin Tasmanian salmon, served with green split-pea soup, and oven-dried tomato puree with a dill and olive oil dressing. Vegetarians will love the eggplant au gratin, with mushroom, baby onions, fresh pasta, and goat's cheese. ⊠ *Queens Walk Cornelian Bay* ☎ *03/6228–9289* ▤ *AE, MC, V* ⊗ *No dinner Sun.*

$–$$ ✕ **Drunken Admiral.** With all the naval kitsch cluttering the walls, you might expect the food to be second-rate, but each nautically named dish is well prepared. Try the Deck Hands seafood platter, a combination of hot and cold delicacies. Or you can sample the seafood extravaganza of the Drunken Admiral set dinner. Afterward, if you're up to it, indulge in freshly baked sticky almond pudding. ⊠ *17–19 Hunter St., Hobart City* ☎ *03/6234–1903* ⚲ *Reservations essential* ▤ *AE, MC, V.*

$–$$ ✕ **Kelleys.** In an old fisherman's cottage, the place is perfectly suited for
Fodor'sChoice dining on some of the best seafood in Hobart. Baked fillets of sea trout
★ are wrapped in prosciutto, and served with peas, walnut and rocket (arugula) salad, shaved Parmesan, and a sherry vinaigrette. ⊠ *5 Knopwood St., Battery Point* ☎ *03/6224–7225* ⚲ *Reservations essential* ▤ *AE, MC, V* ⊗ *No lunch weekends.*

$–$$ ✕ **Mit Zitrone.** A couple of miles north of the city center, among other
Fodor'sChoice restaurants reflecting Hobart's ethnic influences, Mit Zitrone draws a
★ discerning following with its quality offerings best described as Modern Australian with flair. Twice-cooked eggs and poached eye filet of beef are popular specialties. ⊠ *333 Elizabeth St., North Hobart* ☎ *03/6234–8113* 🖶 *03/6231–9150* ⚲ *Reservations essential* ▤ *AE, MC, V* ⛾ *BYOB* ⊗ *Closed Sun. and Mon.*

★ $–$$ ✕ **Mures Fish House Complex.** On the top floor of this complex on the wharf, Mures Upper Deck Restaurant has superb indoor and alfresco views of the harbor. Try the flathead—a house version of the local fish, trevalla, panfried with smoked trout pâté and Brie. Downstairs, Mures Lower Deck is a less expensive alternative: you order, take a number, pick up your food, and eat it at tables outside. Also in the complex, Orizuru has Hobart's best and freshest sushi and sashimi. ⊠ *Victoria Dock, Hobart City* ☎ *03/6231–1999 Upper Deck, 03/6231–2121*

Lower Deck, 03/6231–1790 Orizuru ▤ AE, DC, MC, V; no credit cards Lower Deck.

$–$$ ✗ **Rockerfellers.** This cheerful, inexpensive restaurant and bar, two blocks from the wharf, has tasty, filling tapas-style dishes for around A$7. The main menu includes hearty fare: chicken, calamari, and vegetarian dishes. Come Sunday or Monday night for smooth, melodic jazz music on the small stage. ⊠ *11 Morrison St., Hobart City* ☎ *03/6234–3490* ▤ *AE, DC, MC, V.*

¢ ✗ **Jackman and McRoss.** This lively café makes a perfect refueling stop when you're exploring Battery Point and Salamanca Place. Fantastic breads, pies, cakes, and pastries are accompanied by a selection of hearty coffees. The hearty, slow-cooked beef pie is a Tasmanian classic. For a sandwich with an unusual flavor twist, try the pastrami and spiced pear with mustard on sunflower rye bread. ⊠ *57–59 Hampden Rd., Battery Point* ☎ *03/6223–3186* ▤ *No credit cards* ☉ *No dinner.*

Where to Stay

Area accommodations include hotels, guesthouses, bed-and-breakfasts, and self-catering cottages. Although there are several new hotels in Hobart, as well as many chain accommodations, the greatest attractions are the lodgings in old, historic houses and cottages, most of which have been beautifully restored and renovated.

★ $$–$$$$ ⌧ **Hotel Grand Chancellor.** Across the street from the old wharf and steps from some of the best restaurants in Hobart, this monolith seems a bit out of place amid Hobart's quaint colonialism. What it lacks in period charm, however, it more than makes up for in luxury. All rooms have large wooden desks and thick white guest bathrobes. Some rooms overlook the harbor. ⊠ *1 Davey St. (Box 1601), Hobart City, 7001* ☎ *03/6235–4535 or 1800/222229* 🖶 *03/6223–8175* ⊕ *www.hotelchancellor.com.au* ⤻ *212 rooms, 12 suites* � ᕈ *2 restaurants, pool, hair salon, health club, massage, sauna, bar, laundry service, airport shuttle, car rental, free parking* ▤ *AE, DC, MC, V.*

$$$ ⌧ **Moorilla Vineyard Chalets.** The stylish cottages, built in 1958, make for charming photos amid a lush, private peninsula along the River Derwent. Four spacious and light self-contained chalets—two with two bedrooms and two with one bedroom—have views of the Derwent River and the estate's vineyard. Day guests can still enjoy a complimentary wine tasting. Moorilla is 13 km (8 mi) north of Hobart. ⊠ *655 Main Rd., Berridale 7011* ☎ *03/6277–9900* 🖶 *03/6249–4093* ⊕ *www.moorilla.com.au* ⤻ *4 chalets* ᕈ *Restaurant, in-room data ports, kitchens, free parking* ▤ *AE, DC, MC, V.*

$$–$$$ ⌧ **Hadley's Hotel.** Utterly steeped in history, this venerable city center gem dates from 1834. In 1912, Hadley's played host to South Pole discoverer Roald Amundsen upon his return from the icy wasteland. Legend has it that at first he was turned away because in his bearded, bedraggled state he looked like a penniless bum. Today the rooms reflect early Tasmanian style with plush carpets and soaring ceilings. The food at the Ritz Atrium Restaurant is contemporary Australian with an emphasis on seafood. ⊠ *34 Murray St., Hobart City, 7000* ☎ *03/6223–4355 or 1800/131689* 🖶 *03/6224–0303* ⤻ *67 rooms* ᕈ *Restaurant, room service, bar, laundry facilities, free parking* ▤ *AE, DC, MC, V.*

$$–$$$ ⌧ **Lenna of Hobart.** This 19th-century hotel, a short stroll from Battery Point and Salamanca Place, is an eclectic mix of old-world charm and Australian colonial furnishing. Inside the 1874 Italianate mansion, soft lights glow through stained-glass walkways that are lined with urns and Greek statuary. Rooms have flower-upholstered wicker chairs, canopy beds, and antique-style telephones. Alexander's Restaurant serves fine

Continental cuisine on a seasonal menu, and there's often tasteful live piano music. ✉ *20 Runnymede St., Battery Point, 7000* ☎ *03/6232–3900 or 1800/030633* 🖷 *03/6224–0112* ⊕ *www.lenna.com.au* 🛏 *45 rooms, 4 suites* ♨ *Restaurant, bar, laundry service, business services, free parking* ⊟ *AE, DC, MC, V.*

$$–$$$ 🏨 **Salamanca Inn.** These elegant, self-contained apartments blend in well with the surrounding historic district. Queen-size sofa beds, modern kitchens, and free laundry facilities make the accommodations perfect for families. Ask for a room on the sunny western side, but don't expect great views from a three-story building. All apartments are serviced by housekeepers. ✉ *10 Gladstone St., Battery Point, 7000* ☎ *03/6223–3300 or 1800/030944* 🖷 *03/6223–7167* ⊕ *www.salamancainn. com.au* 🛏 *68 rooms* ♨ *Restaurant, kitchens, pool, spa, laundry facilities, free parking* ⊟ *AE, DC, MC, V.*

$–$$$ 🏨 **Corus Hotel.** This bright, breezy hotel on the edge of the central business district is ideally situated for both work and pleasure. Large rooms have plenty of light, while suites include king-size beds, whirlpool tubs, and luxury fittings. A modern bistro, with Tasmanian flavors, is part of the food and beverage facilities. ✉ *156 Bathurst St., Hobart City, 7000* ☎ *03/6232–6255 or 1800/030003* 🖷 *03/6234–7884* 🛏 *126 rooms, 14 suites* ♨ *Restaurant, bar, laundry facilities, free parking* ⊟ *AE, DC, MC, V.*

$–$$$ 🏨 **Wrest Point Hotel and Casino.** This 17-floor hotel earned its fame in 1973 when it opened the first legalized gambling casino in Australia. The more expensive rooms in the tower and on the water's edge have grand views over Mt. Wellington and the Derwent River; some have whirlpool baths. The motor inn overlooks relaxing gardens and has access to the main hotel and casino facilities. Regine's nightclub (Wednesday through Sunday) is a major entertainment spot in Hobart. ✉ *410 Sandy Bay Rd., Sandy Bay, 7005* ☎ *03/6225–0112* 🖷 *03/6225–2424* ⊕ *www.wrestpoint.com.au* 🛏 *Tower: 184 rooms, 13 suites; motor inn: 81 rooms* ♨ *2 restaurants, room service, tennis court, pool, hair salon, health club, cabaret, casino, nightclub, car rental, travel services, free parking* ⊟ *AE, DC, MC, V.*

$$ 🏨 **Barton Cottage.** Built in 1837, this refurbished lodge still maintains its colonial grace while offering modern conveniences. Seven rooms with such names as Footman, Pantrymaid, and Chambermaid are simply decorated with antiques, and all have private baths. An old coach house has been restored into a private hideaway. ✉ *72 Hampden Rd., Battery Point, 7000* ☎ *03/6224–1606* 🖷 *03/6224–1724* ⊕ *www. bartoncottage.com.au* 🛏 *7 rooms* ♨ *Dining room, some kitchens, free parking* ⊟ *AE, DC, MC, V* ⫢ *BP.*

$$ 🏨 **Colville Cottage.** From the moment you pass through the white picket fence into the garden surrounding this cottage, you can't help but feel relaxed. The interior exudes warmth and welcome with hardwood floors, fireplaces, and antique furniture. Fresh flowers and bay windows trimmed with iron lace add to the sense of coziness. Children are welcome to stay. ✉ *32 Mona St., Battery Point, 7000* ☎ *03/6223–6968* 🖷 *03/6224–0500* ⊕ *www.salamanca.com.au/colvillecottage* 🛏 *6 rooms* ♨ *Lounge, free parking; no smoking* ⊟ *MC, V* ⫢ *BP.*

★ $$ 🏨 **Corinda's Cottages.** This charming residence was built in the 1880s for Alfred Crisp, a wealthy timber merchant who later became Lord Mayor of Hobart. Three historic outbuildings—including a gardener's residence, servants' quarters, and coach house—have been lovingly converted into delightful self-contained cottages. The B&B is close to the woodlands, yet it's only a few minutes from the city center. ✉ *17 Glebe St., Glebe, 7000* ☎ *03/6234–1590* 🖷 *03/6234–2744* ⊕ *www. corindascottages.com.au* 🛏 *3 cottages* ♨ *Kitchens, laundry service, free parking* ⊟ *AE, MC, V* ⫢ *BP.*

$$ ⊞ **Islington Elegant Private Hotel.** A converted 1845 mansion, this hotel exudes good taste from the moment you enter its spacious, black-and-white tile foyer. Colonial-style rooms are graced with antiques, and matching curtains and bedspreads. Although minutes from the city center, the hotel seems comfortably isolated, with a lush garden, outdoor pool, and stunning view of Mt. Wellington. Ask for a room with garden access. A large complimentary Continental breakfast is served in a sunny conservatory. ⊠ *321 Davey St., South Hobart, 7000* ☎ *03/6223–3900* 🖷 *03/6224–3167* 🖎 *8 suites* ⟐ *Pool, laundry service, free parking* ⊟ *AE, DC, MC, V* ⦶ *CP.*

★ **$$** ⊞ **Oakford On Elizabeth Pier.** Well positioned on a historic pier extending into the harbor, this all-suite apartment and hotel complex is only a five-minute walk from the city or Salamanca Place. Several restaurants, the extremely popular T42 bar, and even a conference facility, are all next door. All rooms are fully self-contained and have the bedroom on a mezzanine floor, and many have balconies. ⊠ *Elizabeth St. Pier, Hobart City, 7000* ☎ *03/6220–6600 or 1800/620462* 🖷 *03/6224–1277* ⊕ *www.oakford.com* 🖎 *56 rooms* ⟐ *Restaurant, room service, room TVs with movies, sauna, gym, bar, free parking* ⊟ *AE, DC, MC, V.*

$$ ⊞ **Warwick Cottages.** Annie's Room and Pandora's Box, identical cottages built by convicts in 1854, are filled with an assortment of colonial bric-a-brac that lends individual charm. Pandora's Box, for example, has an antique meat grinder and old-style carriage lanterns. A winding staircase in each cottage leads to a double bed upstairs, and the ground floor has two single beds. ⊠ *119–121 Warwick St., North Hobart, 7000* ☎ *03/6254–1264* 🖷 *03/6254–1527* 🖎 *2 cottages* ⟐ *Kitchens, free parking* ⊟ *DC, MC, V.*

$–$$ ⊞ **The Lodge on Elizabeth.** Bask in the opulence of this grand manor, which was built by convicts in 1829. It's within walking distance of the city center, but far enough removed to make you feel that you're in an earlier century. Complimentary port is served fireside, from which you can head upstairs to luxuriate in a spa room. ⊠ *249 Elizabeth St., Hobart 7000* ☎ *03/6231–3830* 🖎 *13 rooms* ⟐ *Refrigerators, some in-room hot tubs, laundry facilities, free parking* ⊟ *MC, V.*

$ ⊞ **Cromwell Cottage.** This simple 1873 guesthouse is remarkable for its colorful rooms, including all-red, all-yellow (the sunniest), or all-blue quarters. Otherwise, ask for the garden room. Wonderful old brass beds and antique furnishings complete the decor. Some rooms have a view of the Derwent River. ⊠ *6 Cromwell St., Battery Point, 7000* ☎ *03/6223–6734* 🖷 *03/6223–6605* ⊕ *www.view.com.au/cromwell* 🖎 *5 rooms* ⟐ *Dining room, free parking* ⊟ *No credit cards* ⦶ *BP.*

Nightlife & the Arts

Hobart's nightlife is tame. Consult the Friday or Saturday editions of the local newspaper, the *Mercury,* for the latest in evening entertainment. *This Week in Tasmania,* available at most hotels, is a comprehensive guide to current performances and rock and jazz concerts.

Casino

In the Wrest Point Hotel, the **Wrest Point Casino** (⊠ 410 Sandy Bay Rd., Sandy Bay ☎ 03/6225–0112) has blackjack, American roulette, mini-baccarat, keno, minidice, craps, federal wheel, federal poker and stud poker, and two-up. Maximum stakes are A$500, and a special suite on the ground floor caters to high rollers. The Wrest Point also stages late-night comedy and cabaret. It's open from Monday through Thursday 1 PM to 3 AM, Friday and Saturday 1 PM to 4 AM, and Sunday noon to 3 AM.

Music

For something relaxing, try the piano bar at the **Grand Chancellor** (⊠ 1 Davey St., Hobart City ☎ 03/6235–4535).

For the serious bop-till-you-drop set, head for **Round Midnight** (⊠ 39 Salamanca Pl., Battery Point ☎ 03/6223–2491). **Syrup** (⊠ 39 Salamanca Pl., Battery Point ☎ 03/6224–8249), in the same building, is another rocking dance club.

Bar Celona (⊠ 24 Salamance Sq. ☎ 03/6224–7557), a wine bar, has a good selection of local vintages by the glass or bottle. **Isobar** (⊠ 11 Franklin Wharf ☎ 03/6231–6600) is a colorful and cool place to listen to live bands while relaxing over a drink.

Pubs with live music include **Bakers** (⊠ Cnr. Barrack and Macquarie Sts. ☎ 03/6223–5206). The contemporary crowd heads for the raucous, Art Deco **Republic Bar and Cafe** (⊠ 299 Elizabeth St. ☎ 03/6234–6954). There's lively jazz at **Temple Bar** (⊠ 121 Macquarie St. ☎ 03/6223–2883). The world-acclaimed Tasmanian Symphony Orchestra performs in its permanent home, **Federation Concert Hall** (⊠ 1 Davey St., Hobart City ☎ 03/6235–4535), adjacent to the Hotel Grand Chancellor. Seating 1,100, the auditorium doubles as a concert venue for touring artists and an upscale lecture hall.

Theater

Playhouse Theatre (⊠ 106 Bathurst St., Hobart City ☎ 03/6234–1536) stages traditional, locally cast plays in addition to more cutting-edge work.

Theatre Royal (⊠ 29 Campbell St., Hobart City ☎ 03/6233–2299) is an 1834 architectural gem. Notice the portraits of composers painted on the magnificent dome. Classic and contemporary plays by Australian and international playwrights are in the company's repertoire.

Sports & the Outdoors

Walking is excellent around Mt. Wellington, which has a number of well-marked trails. However, you'll find the best hiking a bit further away in South West National Park or in Mt. Field National Park.

Bushwalking

Many hiking trails are within easy reach of Hobart, including several routes around Mt. Wellington, which you need a car to reach. There are many shops that stock outdoor equipment; however, if you're planning to do any serious bushwalking, you should really bring your own gear. Sneakers are adequate for walking around Mt. Wellington and along beaches. Stop in at the Tasmanian Travel and Information Centre for more details on hiking opportunities.

Fishing

Tasmania's well-stocked lakes and streams are among the best places in the world for trout fishing. The season runs from August through May, and licensed trips can be arranged through the Tasmanian Travel and Information Centre.

There are several professional fishing guides on the island. For further information, contact **Tasmanian Professional Trout Guides Association** (⊠ 2/13 Jindabyne Rd., Kingston, 7050 ☎ 03/6229–5896).

Golf

Several excellent golf courses are within the Hobart area and usually have club rental available. Prices and accessibility vary; some courses require visitors to belong to an overseas club or to be introduced by a member. Greens fees run about A$60 for 18 holes; it's around A$25 for equipment. Check with the tourist office for a complete list of courses.

Built in the 1930s, the nine-hole **Bothwell Golf Course** (☎ 03/6259–1210 for secretary) is the oldest golf course in Australia. It's in the village of Bothwell, about 75 km (47 mi) north of Hobart. The fences around the greens are mainly for protection from sheep, as the course is part of a working farm. Although the course doesn't have a number to call for bookings (you just turn up at the edge of the village and follow the instructions on the clubhouse door), you can phone the secretary at home for more information.

Skiing

Tasmania's premier snowfield is at Ben Lomond, east of Launceston. The other snowfield is at Mt. Field, 81 km (50 mi) northwest of Hobart. Contact the Tasmanian Travel and Information Centre for information on conditions, accommodations, and equipment rental.

Spectator Sports

You can watch cricket, soccer, and Australian-rules football in Hobart. Buy tickets (A$10–A$40) at the gates.

Cricket matches take place November to March at the **Bellerive Oval** (⊠ Derwent St., Bellerive ☎ 03/6244–7099) on the scenic Eastern Shore. Football matches are Saturday afternoons in winter (April to August) at **North Hobart Sports Ground** (⊠ Ryde St., North Hobart ☎ 03/6234–3203).

Shopping

Tasmania is noted for its artisans and craftspeople, who work with a diverse range of materials to fashion unusual souvenirs. Pottery, metalwork, and wool garments are all locally made. However, the key find is items made from regional timber, which includes myrtle, sassafras, and the unique Huon Pine.

The Salamanca Place market is Hobart's hub of arts and crafts activities on Saturdays. Many other shops and outlets are located throughout the city. Look for antiques, particularly larger items like tables and chairs, which can be packaged and shipped to your home country.

Aspect Design (⊠ 79 Salamanca Pl., Battery Point ☎ 03/6223–2642) stocks blown glass, wooden products, pottery, and jewelry. **Handmark Gallery** (⊠ 77 Salamanca Pl., Battery Point ☎ 03/6223–7895) sells Hobart's best wooden jewelry boxes as well as Art Deco jewelry, pottery, painting, and sculpture. **Tasmania Shop** (⊠ 120A Liverpool St., Hobart City ☎ 03/6231–5200) specializes in products made in Tasmania, including wood, pottery, food, and wine. The **Wilderness Society Shop** (⊠ 33 Salamanca Pl., Battery Point ☎ 03/6234–9370) sells prints, cards, books, and T-shirts, all made in Australia.

Hobart A to Z

To research prices, get advice from other travelers, and book travel arrangements, visit www.fodors.com.

AIR TRAVEL

Hobart International Airport is one hour by air from Melbourne or two hours from Sydney. Hobart is served by Qantas and Virgin Blue. On the island, TasAir can get you to the northwest, to bucolic King Island, and to Flinders Island (charter flights only). Tickets can also be booked through Tasmanian Travel and Information Centre in cities around the island.

🗐 Carriers **Qantas** ☎ 13-1313 ⊕ www.qantas.com.au. **TasAir** ☎ 03/6248-5088 ⊕ www.tasair.com.au. **Virgin Blue** ☎ 13-6789 ⊕ www.virginblue.com.au.

AIRPORTS

Hobart International Airport is 22 km (14 mi) east of Hobart.

🗐 **Hobart International Airport** ✉ Strachan St., Cambridge ☎ 03/6216-1600

TRANSFERS The trip between the airport and Hobart along the Eastern Outlet Road should take no more than 20 minutes by car. Tasmanian Redline Coaches has regular airport shuttle service for A$9 per person between the airport and its downtown depot at 199 Collins Street. Depending on how busy they are, the driver may even drop you off close to your hotel in the city area. For small groups, taxis are an economical way to travel to the city. Metered taxis are available at the taxi stand in front of the terminal. The fare to downtown Hobart is approximately A$30.

🗐 **Tasmanian Redline Coaches** ✉ 199 Collins St., Hobart City ☎ 03/6231-3233 or 1300/360000 ⊕ www.tasredline.com.au.

BUS TRAVEL TO & FROM HOBART

Tasmanian Redline Coaches run daily to towns and cities across the state. Buses also meet the ferry from Victoria that comes into Tasmania's northern port city, Devonport.

TassieLink also has daily services around the state. The TassieLink Explorer Pass is a one-week ticket (to be used within 10 days) for unlimited travel around Tasmania (A$160). A two-week pass (to be used in 20 days) costs A$220, and other passes are also available.

The "Metro," operated by Metropolitan Tasmania, runs a bus system from downtown Hobart to the surrounding suburbs daily from 6 AM to midnight. Special "Day Rover" tickets for A$4 permit unlimited use of buses for a day from 9 AM onward.

🗐 Bus Lines **Metro** ✉ GPO Bldg., 9 Elizabeth St., Hobart City ☎ 03/6233-4232 or 13-2201. **Tasmanian Redline Coaches** ✉ 199 Collins St., Hobart City ☎ 03/6231-3233 or 1300/360000. **TassieLink** ✉ Hobart Transit Ctr., 199 Collins St., Hobart City ☎ 1300/300520 ⊕ www.tassielink.com.au.

CAR RENTALS

Cars, campers, caravans, and minibuses are available for rent. The largest companies are Autorent Hertz, Avis, Budget, Curnow's, and Thrifty, all of which have airport locations. Lower-priced rental companies include Lo-Cost Auto Rent. Many companies can arrange delivery to your hotel.

🗐 Agencies **Autorent Hertz** ☎ 03/6237-1111 or 13-3039. **Avis** ☎ 03/6234-4222 or 13-6333. **Budget** ☎ 03/6234-5222 or 13-2727. **Curnow's** ☎ 03/6236-9611. **Lo-Cost Auto Rent** ☎ 03/6231-0550. **Rent-a-Bug** ☎ 03/6231-0300. **Thrifty** ☎ 03/6234-1341.

CAR TRAVEL

If you're arriving in Devonport on the *Spirit of Tasmania* ferry from Melbourne, Hobart is about four hours south by car.

Unlike mainland Australia, most places in Tasmania are within easy driving distance, rarely more than three or four hours in a stretch. Hobart itself is extremely compact. Most sights are easily visited on a walking tour. If you do drive in the city, watch the one-way street system in the city center, which takes some getting used to.

EMERGENCIES

In case of any emergency, dial **000** to reach an ambulance, the fire department, or the police.

🛈 Hospitals **Calvary Hospital** ✉ 49 Augusta Rd., Lenah Valley ☎ 03/6278-5333. **Royal Hobart Hospital** ✉ 48 Liverpool St., Hobart City ☎ 03/6222-8308. **St. Helen's Private Hospital** ✉ 186 Macquarie St., Hobart City ☎ 03/6221-6444.

MONEY MATTERS

You can cash traveler's checks and change money at ANZ Bank, Commonwealth Bank (two locations), and National Bank in downtown Hobart.

🛈 Banks **ANZ Bank** ✉ 22 Elizabeth St., Hobart City ☎ 03/6221-2601. **Commonwealth Bank** ✉ 81 Elizabeth St., Hobart City ☎ 13-2221 or 03/6238-0673. **National Bank** ✉ 76 Liverpool St., Hobart City ☎ 13-2265. **Westpac** ✉ 28 Elizabeth St., Hobart City ☎ 13-2032.

TAXIS

You can hail metered taxis in the street or find them at designated stands and major hotels. Cabs for hire have lighted signs on their roofs. Contact City Cabs or Taxi Combined.

🛈 Taxi Companies **City Cabs** ☎ 13-1008. **Taxi Combined** ☎ 13-2227.

TOURS

AIRPLANE TOURS Par Avion Tours has some of the most exciting ways to see Hobart and its surroundings. One flight goes to Melaleuca Inlet on the remote southwest coast and includes a boat trip with Wilderness Tours around Bathurst Harbour, with stops for bushwalking. The all-inclusive cost is A$275, including lunch and afternoon tea. Shorter, less-expensive flights cover just as much territory but don't include time for walking or meals.

🛈 **Par Avion Tours** ✉ Hobart International Airport ☎ 03/6248-5390 ⊕ www.paravion.com.au.

BIKE TOURS Island Cycle Tours has a range of trips around Tasmania, including 3-, 4-, 6-, and 7-day coastal tours. Prices include equipment, accommodations, meals, guides, van service, and entry to nearby attractions and activities. The exhilarating descent from the top of Mt. Wellington into Hobart (A$48) is a must.

🛈 **Island Cycle Tours** ✉ Box 2014, Lower Sandy Bay 7005 ☎ 1300/880334 ⊕ www.islandcycletours.com.

BOAT TOURS Captain Fell's Historic Ferries runs the MV *Emmalisa,* an old-fashioned ferry, daily around Derwent Harbour. Cruises (1¼ hours, A$12) include an excellent commentary on Hobart and its environs. The lunch trip is A$22 with a hot meal, and the dinner cruise (A$25) includes wine with the meal.

The MV *Cartela,* built in 1912, plies the harbor and cruises to Cadbury's and to a winery in the morning, at lunch, and in the afternoon. Fares start at A$12. The *Lady Nelson* sailing ship takes 90-minute cruises around the harbor on Saturday and Sunday for A$6.

🛈 Tour Operators **Captain Fell's Historic Ferries** ✉ Franklin Wharf Pier, Hobart Waterfront ☎ 03/6223-5893. *Lady Nelson* ✉ Elizabeth Wharf, Hobart Waterfront ☎ 03/6234-3348. **MV *Cartela*** ✉ Franklin Wharf Ferry Pier, Hobart Waterfront ☎ 03/6223-1914.

BUS TOURS Hobart Explorer runs half-day city sightseeing tours on Tuesday, Thursday, and Saturday mornings, including visits to Battery Point and Salamanca Place. The cost is A$26. Tigerline Coaches operates full-day tours to destinations including Salamanca Place, Bruny Island, Bonorong Wildlife Center, Port Arthur, and Richmond.

🛈 Tour Operators **Hobart Explorer** Tasmanian Travel and Information Centre ✉ 20 Davey St., at Elizabeth St., Hobart City ☎ 03/6230-8233. **Tigerline Coaches** ✉ Roche O'May Terminal, Pier One, Hobart Waterfront ☎ 1300/653633.

CELEBRITY TOUR Errol Flynn was born and educated in Hobart—and was reportedly expelled from several schools—before becoming a heartthrob of the 1940s and '50s. The Errol Flynn Tour (A$40) takes you to places in Hobart associated with his life in the city.
🎬 **Errol Flynn Tours** ✉ Drifters Internet Café, 9/33 Salamanca Pl., Hobart City ☎ 03/6224-6286.

WALKING TOURS Walks led by the National Trust provide an excellent overview of Battery Point, including visits to mansions and 19th-century houses. Tours leave the wishing well (near the post office in Franklin Square) every Saturday at 9:30, and the A$12 cost includes morning tea. The National Trust also conducts daily tours (hourly 10–2) of the old penitentiary (there's also a spooky night tour), courthouse, and chapel on Campbell Street.
🎬 **National Trust** ✉ 6 Brisbane St., Hobart City ☎ 03/6223-5200.

VISITOR INFORMATION

The Tasmanian Travel and Information Centre hours are weekdays 9–5 and Saturday 9–noon, often longer in the summer.
🎬 **Tasmanian Travel and Information Centre** ✉ 20 Davey St., at Elizabeth St., Hobart City, 7000 ☎ 03/6230-8233 ⊕ www.tourism.tas.gov.au.

SIDETRIPS FROM HOBART

Hobart is a perfect base for short trips to some of Tasmania's most historic and scenic places. Although you can visit them in a day, it's best to stay the night and experience their delights at a leisurely pace.

Huon Valley

En route to the vast wilderness of Southwest National Park you'll pass through the tranquil Huon Valley. Sheltered coasts and sandy beaches are pocketed with thick forests and small farms. Vast orchards cover the undulating land; in fact, William Bligh planted the first apple tree here, thus founding one of the region's major industries. Lush pastures shelter plump vegetables, succulent berries, and rows of fruit trees. Farmed salmon and trout caught fresh from churning blue rivers are other delicious regional delicacies.

The valley is also famous for the Huon pine, much of which has been logged over the decades. The trees that remain are strictly protected, so other local timbers are used by the region's craftspeople.

The **Forest and Heritage Centre** (✉ Church St., Geeveston ☎ 03/6297-1836 ☑ A$5 ☉ Daily 9–5) has fascinating displays on the history of forestry in the area, as well as items crafted from the beautiful timbers. At the **Shipwrights Point School of Wooden Boatbuilding** (✉ Franklin ☎ 03/6266-3586 ☑ Free ☉ Weekdays 10–4) you can watch Tasmania's fine timbers being crafted into beautiful wooden boats.

Beyond Geeveston, the cantilevered, 1,880-foot-long **Tahune Forest Airwalk** (✉ Arve Rd. ☎ 03/6297-0068 ☑ A$9 ☉ Daily 9–5) rises to 150 feet above the forest floor, providing a stunning panorama of the Huon and Picton rivers and the Hartz Mountains. The best views are from the platform at the end of the walkway.

Spectacular cave formations and thermal pools amid a fern glade await at the **Hastings Caves and Thermal Springs** (☎ 03/6298-3209 ☑ A$14.50 ☉ Daily 9–5) beyond Southport, at the southern end of the region. You can take a tour of the chambers, or just relax at the well-equipped picnic areas. The route to the sight is well-marked.

Where to Stay

★ **$–$$** ⊞ **Matilda's of Ranelagh.** The official greeters at this delightful, 1850 Heritage-listed bed-and-breakfast are five golden retrievers. Elegant Victorian and Edwardian furnishings and spa baths in all rooms provide the ultimate in elegance and comfort. The house is set in beautiful English-style gardens. ⊠ *44 Louisa St., Ranelagh 7109* ☎ *03/6264–3493* 🖷 *03/6264–3491* ⊕ *www.matildasofranelagh.com.au* 🛏 *5 rooms* ♨ *Dining room, laundry facilities, free parking* ▤ *MC, V* ⊙ *BP.*

Bruny Island

From the village of Kettering, a ferry crosses the D'Entrecasteaux Channel to reach Bruny Island, one of Tasmania's little-publicized island gems. Names here reflect the influence of the French explorers who sailed through this region in the 1770s and 1780s. At Bruny's southern tip is a convict-built lighthouse and magnificent coastal scenery.

Richmond

★ A half-hour's drive northeast of Hobart and a century behind the big city, this colonial village is a major tourist magnet. On weekends parking is tight, and you'll jostle with crowds strolling and browsing through the crafts shops, antiques stores, and quaint cafés along the main street. Thus, you'll need to wander a bit outside town to get the best sense of Richmond's character and historic importance.

Richmond Bridge, Australia's oldest bridge and a picturesque counterpoint to the town's church-spired skyline, is a convict-built stone structure dating from 1823. You can stroll over the bridge any time. It's located at one end of the small town's main street. ⊠ *Richmond.*

The well-preserved **Richmond Jail,** built in 1825, has eerie displays of chain manacles, domestic utensils, and instruments of torture. ⊠ *37 Bathurst St., Richmond* ☎ *03/6260–2127* 🎟 *A$3.50* ⊙ *Daily 10–5.*

Where to Stay

$–$$ ⊞ **Millhouse on the Bridge.** Originally built in 1853, this lovely restored mill overlooking the Richmond Bridge is now a cozy B&B. Comfortable guest rooms have homespun touches, such as homemade preserves, and you can gather with the family in the large sitting room after a meal. The quiet garden, blossoming orchard, and river trails make for peaceful morning and afternoon strolls. ⊠ *2 Wellington St., Richmond, 7000* ☎ *03/6260–2428* 🖷 *03/6260–2148* ⊕ *www.millhouse.com.au* 🛏 *4 rooms* ♨ *Dining room, laundry service, free parking* ▤ *MC, V* ⊙ *BP.*

PORT ARTHUR

102 km (63 mi) southeast of Hobart.

When Governor Arthur was looking for a site to dump his worst convict offenders in 1830, the Tasman Peninsula was a natural choice. Joined to the rest of Tasmania only by the narrow Eaglehawk Neck, the spit was easy to isolate and guard. And so evolved Port Arthur, a penal colony whose name became a byword for vicious horror and cruelty. Between 1830 and 1877, more than 12,000 convicts served sentences in Britain's equivalent of Devil's Island, and nearly 2,000 of them died here. Few men escaped. Dogs were used to patrol the narrow causeway and guards spread rumors that sharks infested the waters. Reminders of those dark days remain in some of the area names—Dauntless Point, Stinking Point, Isle of the Dead. In an effort to eliminate references to its notorious past, the penal settlement's name was changed to Carnarvon a few years after it closed in 1877; however, out of familiarity, the name Port Arthur was reinstated in 1927.

The main penal colony was at Port Arthur, but a number of outstations were also established at other strategic locations around the Tasman Peninsula. The "Convict Trail," which you can follow by car, takes in seven such sites, including the remains of a coal mine. In the tiny village of Koonya, you can also view the Cascades, the name given to a collection of historic buildings that have been restored as a B&B. This once-foreboding peninsula has become Tasmania's major tourist attraction, filled with beautiful scenery and historic sites that recapture Australia's difficult beginnings.

Exploring Port Arthur

FodorsChoice **Port Arthur Historic Site,** on the grounds of the former Port Arthur Penal
★ Settlement, now comprises one of the nicest large parks in Tasmania. Be prepared to do some walking among widely scattered sites. Begin at the excellent visitor center, which introduces you to the experience by "sentencing, transporting, and assigning" you before you ever set foot on the colony. Most of the original buildings were damaged by bushfires in 1895 and 1897, shortly after the settlement was abandoned, but you can still see the beautiful church, round guardhouse, commandant's residence, model prison, hospital, and government cottages.

The old **lunatic asylum** is now an excellent museum with a scale model of the Port Arthur settlement, a video history, and a collection of tools, leg irons, and chains. Along with a walking tour of the grounds and entrance to the museum, admission includes a harbor cruise, of which there are eight scheduled daily in summer. There is a separate twice-daily cruise to and tour of the **Isle of the Dead,** which sits in the middle of the bay. It's estimated that 1,769 convicts and 180 others are buried here, mostly in communal pits. Ghost tours (reservations are essential) leave the visitor center at dusk and last about 90 minutes. ⊠ *Arthur Hwy.* ☎ *03/6251–2310 or 1800/659101* ✉ *Penal Settlement tour A$22; Isle of the Dead tour A$8.80 (48-hr, multiple-entry pass); ghost tour A$14.30* ☉ *Daily 8:30–dusk.*

☾ **Bush Mill Steam Railway and Settlement** is a great place to learn about a timber worker's life at the turn of the 20th century. Highlights are a replica steam-powered bush sawmill, settlement, and narrow-gauge passenger steam railway. ⊠ *Arthur Hwy.* ☎ *03/6250–2221* ✉ *A$15* ☉ *Daily 9–5.*

A wildlife refuge for injured animals of many species, **Tasmanian Devil Park** is probably the best place in the state to see Tasmanian devils (burrowing carnivorous marsupials about the size of a dog), as well as quolls, boobooks (a small, spotted brown owl), masked owls, eagles, and other native fauna. Watch the live "Kings of the Wind" show, which stars birds of prey and other species in free flight. ⊠ *Arthur Hwy., 11 km (7 mi) north of Port Arthur, Taranna* ☎ *03/6250–3230* ✉ *A$11* ☉ *Daily 9–5.*

Where to Stay & Eat

$–$$ ✕ **Felons.** This restaurant in the visitor center at the Port Arthur Historic Site serves fresh Tasmanian seafood and game. You won't be disappointed by the ever-succulent local fish of the day, cooked New Orleans style (with a spicy Cajun coating), oven-baked with lemon butter, or deep-fried tempura-style in a light batter. If it's tea time, pop in for one of the exceedingly rich desserts. ⊠ *Arthur Hwy.* ☎ *03/6251–2314 or 1800/659101* ✉ *AE, DC, MC, V.*

$ ✕ **Good Onya.** This small, colonial-style café specializes in salads and delicious home-baked scones during the day. At night, the adjacent Bush Mill Grill opens for such hearty dinners as Bushman's steak (marinated Scotch fillet) and vegetable stockpot. Save room for the tasty apple crumble and ice cream. ⊠ *Arthur Hwy.* ☎ *03/6250–2221* ⊟ *AE, DC, MC, V.*

$–$$ ⌂ **Cascades Colonial Accommodation.** Part of a onetime convict outstation that dates to 1841, these cottages are comfortable and full of character. Each has kitchen facilities, and breakfast provisions are included in the room rate. A small museum related to the property is also on-site. ⊠ *531 Main Rd., 20 km (12 mi) north of Port Arthur, Koonya, 7187* ☎ *03/6250–3873* 🖶 *03/6250–3013* 🛏 *4 cottages* ⚘ *Kitchens, laundry facilities, free parking* ⊟ *No credit cards* �‖ *CP.*

$ ⌂ **Port Arthur Motor Inn.** On a ridge behind an old church, this motel overlooks the entire historic penal settlement site. The comfortable but somewhat old-fashioned guest rooms have small bathrooms and look like they are straight out of the 1960s. Although no rooms have good views, the hotel's main restaurant, the Commandant's Table, overlooks the prison ruins and has a particularly lovely vista at sunset. ⊠ *Arthur Hwy., Port Arthur, 7182* ☎ *03/6250–2101 or 1800/030747* 🖶 *03/6250–2417* 🛏 *35 rooms* ⚘ *Restaurant, bar, laundry facilities, free parking* ⊟ *AE, DC, MC, V.*

$ ⌂ **Port Arthur Villas.** A 10-minute walk from the penal colony, these modern apartments have verandas, old-fashioned brickwork, and pleasant cottage gardens typical of Port Arthur dwellings. Studio and two-bedroom units are well appointed and have fully equipped kitchens. Barbecue facilities are also on-site. ⊠ *52 Safety Cove Rd., Port Arthur, 7182* ☎ *03/6250–2239 or 1800/815775* 🖶 *03/6250–2589* 🛏 *9 apartments* ⚘ *Kitchens, playground, laundry facilities, free parking* ⊟ *AE, DC, MC, V.*

Port Arthur A to Z

To research prices, get advice from other travelers, and book travel arrangements, visit www.fodors.com.

CAR TRAVEL
Port Arthur is an easy 90-minute drive from Hobart via the Arthur Highway. Sights include the Tessellated Pavement, an interesting geological formation; the Blowhole, spectacular in wild weather; and Tasman Arch, a naturally formed archway. At the peninsula's far northwest corner is the fascinating Coal Mines Historic Site where convicts mined Australia's first coal in dreadful conditions.

A private vehicle is essential if you want to explore parts of the Tasman Peninsula beyond the historic settlement.

EMERGENCIES
In case of any emergency, dial **000** to reach an ambulance, the fire department, or the police.

TOURS
You can visit Port Arthur on a tour run by the Port Arthur Historic Site, take a sea kayak through the surrounding waters, or fly above the cliffs by plane.

AIRPLANE TOURS Choose from two scenic flights over the massive sea cliffs of the Tasman Peninsula and its national park with Tasmanian Seaplanes, based in Port Arthur. Fares begin at A$82.

🛦 **Tasmanian Seaplanes** ☎ 03/6227-8808.

BUS TOURS The Tasmanian Travel and Information Centre organizes day trips from Hobart to Port Arthur by bus. The Port Arthur Historic Site conducts daily tours around Port Arthur. The popular torchlight ghost tour has guides who recount stories of apparitions and supposed hauntings at the site. Tigerline Coaches conducts full-day tours of the penal settlement and Bush Mill.

⚑ Tour Operators **Port Arthur Historic Site** ✉ Arthur Hwy., Port Arthur ☎ 1800/659101. **Tasmanian Travel and Information Centre** ✉ 20 Davey St., at Elizabeth St., Hobart City ☎ 03/6230-8233. **Tigerline Coaches** ✉ 199 Collins St., Hobart City ☎ 1300/653633.

FREYCINET NATIONAL PARK

Fodor'sChoice *238 km (149 mi) from Port Arthur, 214 km (133 mi) southwest of Launceston, 206 km (128 mi) northeast of Hobart.*

It took the early European explorers of Van Diemen's Land four voyages and 161 years to realize that the Freycinet Peninsula, a thickly forested wedge of granite jutting east into the Southern Ocean, was not an island. In 1642 Abel Tasman saw it through fierce squalls and, thinking it separate from the mainland, named it Van Der Lyn's Island, after a member of the Dutch East India Company's council of governors. In 1773, Tobias Furneaux of the HMS *Adventure,* part of Captain Cook's second world expedition, passed by far enough out to sea to believe Tasman's theory. Twenty-five years later, explorer Matthew Flinders—who at age 25 circumnavigated Tasmania in the *Tom Thumb* with his cat— agreed. It was not until 1803, when Nicolas Baudin's hydrographer, Pierre Faure, took a longboat and crew into what is now Great Oyster Bay, that Van Der Lyn's Island was proven to be attached. It was named the Freycinet Peninsula after the expedition's chief cartographer.

Now a 24,700-acre slice of land halfway along Tasmania's east coast, Freycinet is renowned for it scenery. The road onto the peninsula halts just beyond the township of **Coles Bay,** where serious hikers strap on their backpacks and day-trippers eye the steep, 30-minute climb to the lookout platform above **Wineglass Bay.** Others visitors head down the rocky, precipitous slope to the ocean, where talcum-soft sand meets turquoise water and the hulking granite bluffs of **Mt. Graham** and **Mt. Freycinet** loom above a mantle of trees. A round-trip walk from the parking lot to Wineglass Bay takes about 2½ hours. In three hours you can scramble up the huge granite rock face of **Mt. Amos,** where you'll be rewarded with incredible views over the bay.

The park's many trails are well signposted. On a day trip, you can walk the **Isthmus Track** to cross the peninsula at its narrowest point, hiking past swamps and waterbird colonies to sheltered Hazards Beach. Return on the **Hazards Beach Track,** beneath the mighty bulk of the snaggle-toothed Hazards, daunting granite towers that glower over the national park. This walk takes about 4½ hours.

Daily entry to the park is A$10 per car or A$3.50 for pedestrians and bus passengers. Accommodation are at Coles Bay and Freycinet Lodge.

Where to Stay & Eat

$$–$$$$ ✕🏨 **Freycinet Lodge.** Wooden one- and two-bedroom cabins are unob-
Fodor'sChoice trusively nestled into a densely treed forest above Great Oyster Bay. Simple, comfortable rooms and furnishings are enriched with handsome Tasmanian timber. Secluded balconies are ideal for drinking in the views. Local seafood on the menu is particularly good. ✉ *Freycinet National Park, Coles Bay, 7215* ☎ *03/6257-0101* 🖷 *03/6257-0278* ⊕ *www.freycinetlodge.com.au* 🛏 *60 cabins* ⚘ *Restaurant, tennis court,*

recreation room, laundry facilities, free parking; no room phones, no room TVs ⊟ *AE, DC, MC, V.*

$–$$$ ✕⊡**Edge of the Bay.** Beachfront locations and spectacular views across Great Oyster Bay to The Hazards make these suites and cottages coveted vacationer hideaways. The restaurant uses Tasmanian produce and has local wines. There's a minimum stay of two nights. ✉ *2308 Main Rd., Coles Bay, 7215* ☎ *03/6257–0102* 🖷 *03/6257–0102* ⊕ *www.edgeofthebay. com.au* ⤳ *8 suites, 11 cottages* ♿ *Restaurant, kitchenettes, beach, boating, hiking, bar, laundry facilities, free parking* ⊟ *AE, MC, V.*

Freycinet National Park A to Z

To research prices, get advice from other travelers, and book travel arrangements, visit www.fodors.com.

BUS TRAVEL
Tasmanian Redline Coaches runs between Hobart and Bicheno, where you can connect with a local bus that runs twice daily on weekdays, and once on Saturday, to Coles Bay. A shuttle bus runs from Coles Bay to the parking lot within the national park.
🚌 **Tasmanian Redline Coaches** ☎ 1300/360000.

CAR TRAVEL
From Hobart or Launceston it's about a 2½-hour drive to the park.

TOURS
Freycinet Adventures has sports tours ranging from a half day to five days in length. This is an energetic and enriching way to appreciate what many believe is Tasmania's most scenic coastline. Choose from sea kayaking, rappelling, or rock climbing. You can even try them all. Adventures around lovely Maria Island are also available. Costs range from A$75 to A$935 per person.

Freycinet Experience runs excellent four-day walks in the park. Accommodation is in high-quality tent camps and a timber lodge overlooking the stunning sands of Friendly Beaches. The cost is A$1,350 per person, including round-trip transportation from Hobart, meals, wine, and park fees.

Other ways to experience the wonders of the Freycinet Peninsula include cruises on the MV *Kahala* with Freycinet Sea Charters, which cost from A$75 per person for a half-day trip and A$132 for a full-day adventure, including lunch. A scenic flight with Freycinet Air starts at A$82 per person.
🚌 **Tour Operators Freycinet Adventures** ☎ 03/6257-0500 🖷 03/6257-0447. **Freycinet Air** ☎ 03/6375-1694. **Freycinet Experience** ☎ 03/6334-4615 🖷 03/6334-5525. **Freycinet Sea Charters** ☎ 03/6257-0355.

VISITOR INFORMATION
Contact Freycinet National Park directly for information about hiking, camping, and wildlife. The office is open daily from 9 to 5.
🚌 **Freycinet National Park** ✉ Park Office ☎ 03/6256-7000.

EAST COAST RESORTS

From Hobart the road to Coles Bay passes through beautiful coastal scenery with spectacular white sandy beaches, usually completely deserted. Coles Bay is reached via a side road from the main highway just before Bicheno, another fishing and holiday town. Further north, around St. Helens, are quiet holiday retreats and sheltered harbors.

Swansea

60 km (37 mi) from Freycinet National Park, 135 km (84 mi) from Hobart, 134 km (83 mi) from Launceston.

The township contains many old stone colonial buildings, some of which are now used for hotels and restaurants. South of town is the unusual "Spiky Bridge," so named because many of the sandstone blocks on the top layer of the construction were placed vertically, thus creating a spiky effect. Nearby is the convict-built Three Arch Bridge; both crossings date from 1845.

New vineyards such as Freycinet and Coombend Vineyards are popping up every year in this region, producing excellent cool-climate wines. In summer, stop for fresh berries and ice cream at **Kate's Berry Farm** (⊠ Addison St., Swansea ☎ 03/6257–8428), about 2 km (1 mi) south of town.

need a break?

Step behind the red door of a former bank building into the **Left Bank Café** (⊠ Maria St., Swansea ☎ 03/6257–8896) for simple, tasty food in a cheerful, funky setting. Bright curtains surround picture windows that look out towards Great Oyster Bay. Cool salads and hot treats, including quiche and lasagne, grace the menu. Be sure to sample the wonderful cakes served with local berry sauces.

Where to Stay

$$ ⬚ **Meredith House.** The 1853 glory shines through this refurbished residence in the center of town. Exquisite red cedar furnishings and antique touches add to the old-world ambience. The central location and serene atmosphere make this a favorite of travelers. You can request morning and evening meals in the dining room. ⊠ *15 Noyes St., Swansea, 7190* ☎ *03/6257–8119* 🖷 *03/6257–8123* ⤶ *11 rooms* ♨ *Dining room, free parking* ▭ *AE, MC, V* ⦿⦿ *BP.*

$–$$ ⬚ **Wagners Cottages.** Four beautifully furnished stone cottages, two of which date from the 1850s, sit amid rambling gardens in rural surroundings. There are also two country-style guest rooms in the main house. A full complimentary breakfast is served in the sunny atrium. ⊠ *Tasman Hwy., Swansea, 7190* ☎ *03/6257–8494* 🖷 *03/6257–8267* ⤶ *4 cottages, 2 rooms* ♨ *Some in-room hot tubs, some kitchens, laundry facilities, free parking* ▭ *AE, DC, MC, V* ⦿⦿ *BP.*

$ ⬚ **Kabuki by the Sea.** Look out over Schouten Island and The Hazards from the terraces of this cliff-top inn for some of the most stunning coastal views in the state—then watch the moon rise over Great Oyster Bay while dining at the outstanding Japanese restaurant. Cottages have all the comforts of a true Japanese *ryokan* (a traditional style of Japanese inn), including a sitting and dining room and kitchen facilities. The hotel is 10 minutes south of Swansea. ⊠ *Tasman Hwy., Rocky Hills, 7190* ☎🖷 *03/6257–8588* ⊕ *www.view.com.au/kabuki* ⤶ *5 rooms* ♨ *Restaurant, laundry service, free parking* ▭ *AE, MC, V.*

$ ⬚ **Schouten House.** This attractive Georgian mansion makes for a comfortable, stylish B&B that shows off original antiques in every room. You can also dine on Provençal fare in the restaurant, which serves fresh seafood, farm produce, and local wines. The central location means you're just a block from Great Oyster Bay. ⊠ *1 Waterloo Rd., Swansea, 7190* ☎ *03/6257–8564* 🖷 *03/6257–8767* ⤶ *4 rooms* ♨ *Restaurant, bar, free parking* ▭ *AE, MC, V* ⦿⦿ *BP.*

St. Helens

119 km (74 mi) from Swansea, 265 km (164 mi) from Hobart, 163 km (101 mi) from Launceston

The fishing port of St. Helens nestles into a sheltered inlet set back about 8 km (5 mi) from the main northeast coastline. Here you'll find the artist village of Binalong Bay, as well as the end point of the four-day Bay of Fires walk. Top-rated cheeses are produced at the factory in nearby Pyengana. For dramatic views, head for St. Columba Falls.

Where to Stay

$$ ⌂ **Wybalenna Lodge.** English-style gardens welcome you to this lodge above Georges Bay. Enter and you'll embark on a journey of gracious living in a mansion with lofty ceilings and elegant decor. With a day's notice, you can take a private dinner in the formal dining room, where a full set menu of local seafood is cooked to perfection. ⌂ *56 Tasman Hwy., St. Helens, 7216* ☎ *03/6376–1611* ⎙ *03/6376–2612* ⋈ *4 rooms* ♨ *Dining room, laundry facilities, free parking* ⊟ *MC, V.*

THE MIDLANDS

The Great Western Tiers mountains on the Midlands' horizon form a backdrop to verdant, undulating pastures that are strongly reminiscent of England. Off the beaten trail you can discover trout-filled streams and lakes, snow-skiing slopes, grand Georgian mansions, and small towns redolent with colonial character.

The first real road to the isolated Midlands appeared more than 175 years ago, blazed by brave explorers who linked Hobart with Launceston, near Tasmania's north coast. Journeys back then stretched to eight days, but today you can speed between the cities on the 200-km (124-mi) Highway 1 (Midlands Highway; locals sometimes call it Heritage Highway) in less than 2½ hours. To do so, however, would mean bypassing many of Tasmania's appealing historic sites and English-style villages.

Oatlands

85 km (53 mi) north of Hobart.

Situated alongside Lake Dulverton, Oatlands is an 1820s Georgian town built as a garrison for the local farming community. The settlement was also a center for housing the convicts building the Hobart to Launceston highway. It was named in June 1821 by Governor Macquarie for what he predicted would be the best use for the surrounding fertile plains.

Oatlands has the greatest concentration of sandstone buildings in Australia, all clustered on or just off of High Street. More than 150 are within a 2-km (1-mi) radius. A charming row of workers' cottages is at the end of High Street.

The most outstanding structure in Oatlands is the sandstone **Council Chambers and Town Hall**, erected in 1880. The building is not open to the public.

The oldest building here is the **Court House.** The large room at its core was reputedly built in 1829 by two convicts in four months.

Callington Mill, which used wind power to grind grain, was completed in 1837. With the surrounding mill buildings, it gives a glimpse into early

Tasmanian industry. There's also a doll collection on-site. ⊠ *Mill La., off High St.* ☎*03/6254–1212* ⊠*Mill: free; doll collection: A$2* ⊘ *Weekdays 9–5.*

Of **Oatlands' churches,** Georgian **St. Peter's Anglican** was built in 1838 from a design by John Lee Archer, the colony's civil engineer, who also designed the bridge at Ross. **St. Paul's Catholic** was built in 1848, again of the mellow golden sandstone prevalent in Oatlands. The **Presbyterian Campbell Memorial Church** was erected in 1856 and rebuilt in 1859 after the original steeple collapsed.

Where to Stay

$$ 🏠 **Amelia Cottage.** Convict-built in 1838, this cottage was once a changing station for horses riding the dusty road between Hobart and Launceston. It contains many of its original features, including shutters, a fuel stove, a baker's oven, and a flagstone kitchen floor, with modern amenities cleverly concealed. Forget-me-not Cottage, built in the old stables, is run by the same owners as Waverley and Croft cottages just outside Oatlands. ⊠ *104 High St., 7120* ☎ *03/6254–1264* 🖷 *03/6254–1527* 🛏 *4 cottages* ♨ *Kitchens, free parking* ⊟ *AE, MC, V.*

$ 🏠 **Oatlands Lodge.** The two-story, 1830 guesthouse has convict-split sandstone interior walls complemented by attractive and comfortable country furnishings and quilts. This building stands right in the middle of Oatlands, but as the village is no longer on the highway, it's a blessedly tranquil place with a pretty cottage garden. The lodge once served as a shop and a girls' school. A complete English-style breakfast is included; dinners and picnic lunches are available. ⊠ *92 High St., 7120* ☎ *03/ 6254–1444* 🛏 *3 rooms* ♨ *Dining room, laundry facilities, free parking* ⊟ *AE, MC, V* ⧖ *BP.*

Ross

55 km (34 mi) northeast of Oatlands, 140 km (87 mi) north of Hobart.

This pretty village of some 500 residents is Tasmania's most historic town, with several structures dating from the mid-19th century. Historic buildings in Ross include the Macquarie Store, the Old Ross General Store, and the old Scotch Thistle Inn, built around 1840.

The 1836 **Ross Bridge** (⊠ Bridge St.) is architect John Lee Archer's best-loved work. Graceful arches are highlighted by local sandstone and the decorative carvings of a convicted highwayman, Daniel Herbert, who was given freedom for his efforts. Herbert's work can also be seen throughout the graveyard where he's buried.

The buildings at the intersection of **Church Street,** the main road, and Bridge Street are often said to summarize life neatly. They include the **Man-O-Ross Hotel** (temptation), the **Town Hall** (recreation), the **Catholic Church** (salvation), and the **Old Gaol** (damnation).

The **Tasmanian Wool Centre** details the region's famous industry, which produces Australia's top-rated superfine wool and some of the best fibers in the world. To feel the difference between various wools and their divergent thicknesses—and to leave with hands soft from lanolin—is worth the admission alone. ⊠ *Church St.* ☎ *03/6381–5466* ⊠ *Donations accepted* ⊘ *Daily 9–4:30.*

Where to Stay & Eat

The Man-O-Ross is a good option for food of the basic counter-meal variety. For great American-style dishes (try the pancakes and maple syrup or BLTs), stop by Oppy's on Church Street.

$ ⊡ **Colonial Cottages of Ross.** Four self-contained cottages, built between 1830 and 1880, provide charming and historic accommodation. Apple Dumpling Cottage (circa 1880) and Hudson Cottage (circa 1850) each sleep four adults. Church Mouse Cottage (circa 1840) is just for two. Captain Samuel's Cottage (circa 1830) accommodates six or more people. Bathroom and kitchen facilities are modern. ⊠ *12 Church St., 7209* ☎ *03/6381–5354* ⊟ *03/6381–5408* ⊷ *4 cottages* ♢ *Kitchens, laundry service, free parking* ⊟ *AE, MC, V.*

$ ⊡ **Ross Bakery Inn.** Right next to St. John's Church of England, this 1832 sandstone colonial building served as the Sherwood Castle Inn. It's now a very comfortable four-room guesthouse with a bakery on the premises. At breakfast you get to taste the daily bread straight from the wood-fired oven. ⊠ *Church St., 7209* ☎ *03/6381–5246* ⊟ *03/6381–5360* ⊷ *3 rooms* ♢ *Dining room, free parking* ⊟ *AE, MC, V* ⏀ *BP.*

$ ⊡ **Somercotes.** Snuggled into a bucolic pasture and riverside setting just outside town, this 1823 National Trust property has a blacksmith shop and gorgeous gardens. Stay in original colonial cottages once occupied by families who emigrated from England. Don't worry—the amenities are up-to-date. Historic tours of the property are available. ⊠ *Mona Vale Rd., 7209* ☎ *03/6381–5231* ⊟ *03/6381–5356* ⊷ *4 cottages* ♢ *Kitchens, fishing, free parking* ⊟ *AE, MC, V.*

---

en route   North of Ross, **Campbell Town** has a couple of notable firsts. In 1877, Alfred Barret Biggs, a local schoolteacher who had read of Alexander Graham Bell's invention of the telephone in 1876, built his own telephone, partly out of Huon pine. Using the telegram line at Campbell Town railway station, Biggs called Launceston, which may have been the first telephone call in Australia—or, for that matter, in the Southern Hemisphere. Some of his prototype telephones are in Launceston's Queen Victoria Museum. Then, in 1931, local lad Harold Gatty joined American flyer Wiley Post on his record-breaking world circumnavigation, making him the first navigator on a round-the-world flight. A metal globe in the town park commemorates his achievement.

Like Ross, Campbell Town has a famous and beautiful crossing. The Red Bridge was built in 1836–38 with locally made red bricks. The structure carries more than 1 million vehicles annually—and has had no major repair work since its construction. Campbell Town also has many fine examples of colonial architecture. The free Heritage Highway Museum, in the old Court House on the main street, merits a visit.

Longford

72 km (45 mi) northwest of Ross, 212 km (131 mi) north of Hobart.

It's worth taking a short detour from the highway to visit this town, a National Trust historic site. Settled in 1813, Longford was one of northern Tasmania's first towns. The Archer family name is all over Longford, and their legacy is in the town's buildings.

Of particular early historic interest is **Christ Church** (⊠ Archer St.), built in 1839 and set on spacious grounds. William Archer, the first Australian-born architect (of European descent), designed the west window of the church, which is regarded as one of the country's finest. Currently, the building is only open on Sunday.

There are a number of other **historic villages** in the vicinity of Longford that are worth a visit. Hadspen, Carrick, Hagley, Perth, and Evandale all have charm. Near Evandale, Clarendon House is one of the great Georgian houses of Australia.

Where to Stay

$–$$ ☒ **Brickendon.** More than just a historic farm accommodation, this
Fodor'sChoice   1824 site near Longford has been in the Archer family for seven gener-
★   ations. It's also a true colonial village, with 20 National Trust classified buildings on site. After you've toured the lovingly restored chapel and barns, try your luck at trout fishing in the Macquarie River while the kids frolic with the animals. Enjoy the romance and history of the quaint cottages, which spoil you with open fires, deep baths, antique furnishings, and private gardens. ☒ *Woolmers La., 7301* ☏ *03/ 6391–1383 or 03/6391–1251* 🖷 *03/6391–2073* ⊕ *www.brickendon. com.au* ↦ *5 cottages* ♿ *Kitchens, playground, laundry service, free parking* ▤ *AE, DC, MC, V.*

$$ ☒ **Woolmers.** Imagine being transported back to a farm estate perfectly preserved in time. Woolmers is one of the nation's most significant rural properties, owned by the another branch of the Archer family from 1816 until the administration was taken over by a public trust. The collections, family possessions, and farming lifestyle are a genuine reflection of Australia's past. The original fireplace has one duplicate outside of Tasmania—at the White House. You can tour the estate on a day visit (A$12) or spend the night in a superbly restored worker's cottage on the property. Plan time to stroll through the National Rose Garden and have a picnic—packed to order—by the river. ☒ *Woolmers La., 7301* ☏ *03/ 6391–2230* 🖷 *03/6391–2270* ⊕ *www.vision.net.au/~woolmers* ↦ *7 cottages* ♿ *Kitchens, picnic grounds, free parking* ▤ *AE, DC, MC, V.*

Midlands A to Z

To research prices, get advice from other travelers, and book travel arrangements, visit www.fodors.com.

CAR TRAVEL

Highway 1 (Midland Highway) bypasses the heart of Oatlands, Ross, and Longford, which is one reason they've kept their old-fashioned characters. Oatlands is only an hour's drive from Hobart. These towns can be seen as part of a day trip from the capital or as stops along the drive between Hobart and Launceston.

TOURS

Fielding's Historic Tours has a daytime Convict Tour (A$7), available by appointment, and an evening Ghost Tour at 9 (A$8), which inspects Oatlands' jails and other historic buildings by lamplight.

Specialty Tours of Ross is operated by the informative and genial Tim Johnson, a local history buff who also runs Colonial Cottages of Ross. His Ross Historic Tour has a minimum rate of A$25 for up to five people. Reservations are essential.

🚩 Tour Operators **Fielding's Historic Tours** ☏ 03/6254–1135. **Specialty Tours of Ross** ☏ 03/6381–5354.

LAUNCESTON

20 km (12 mi) from Longford.

Nestled in a fertile agricultural basin where the South and North Esk rivers join to form the Tamar, the city of Launceston (pronounced *Lonscss-tun*) is the commercial center of Tasmania's northern region. Its abundance of unusual markets and shops is concentrated downtown, unlike Hobart's gathering of shops in its historic center, set apart from the commercial district. Launceston is far from bustling, and is remarkable for its pleasant parks, late 19th-century homes, historic mansions, and private gardens. Perhaps its most compelling asset is the magnificent scenery on which it verges: rolling farmland and the rich loam of English-looking landscapes powerfully set off by the South Esk River meandering through towering gorges.

Exploring Launceston

Aside from its parks and gardens, Launceston's main appeal lies in the sumptuous surrounding countryside. However, refurbished restaurants, shops, and art galleries along the banks of the Tamar and North Esk Rivers have turned rundown railway yards into a glitzy new social scene.

The **Queen Victoria Museum,** opened in 1891, combines items of Tasmanian historical interest with natural history. The museum has a large collection of stuffed birds and animals (including the now-extinct thylacine, or Tasmanian, tiger), as well as a joss house (a Chinese shrine) and a display of coins. ✉ *Wellington and Paterson Sts.* ☏ *03/6323–3777* 🎫 *Free* 🕓 *Mon.–Sat. 10–5, Sun. 2–5.*

Almost in the heart of the city, the South Esk River flows through **Cataract Gorge** on its way toward the Tamar River. A 1½-km (1-mi) path leads along the face of the precipices to the **Cliff Gardens Reserve,** where there are picnic tables, a pool, and a restaurant. Take the chairlift in the first basin for a thrilling aerial view of the gorge—at just over 900 feet, it's the longest single chairlift span in the world. Self-guided nature trails wind through the park. ✉ *Paterson St., at Kings Bridge* ☏ *03/6331–5915* 🎫 *Gorge: free; chairlift: A$7* 🕓 *Daily 9–4:40.*

Along both sides of the Tamar River north from Launceston the soil is perfect for grape cultivation. A brochure on the **Wine Route of the Tamar Valley and Pipers Brook Regions,** available from Tasmanian Travel and Information Centre, can help you to plan a visit to St. Matthias, Ninth Island, Delamere, Rosevears, and Pipers Brook wineries. Many establishments serve food during the day so you can combine your tasting with a relaxing meal.

Notley Fern Gorge, about 25 km (16 mi) northwest of Launceston near Exeter, is a captivating remnant of the verdant forests that once covered the western hills overlooking the Tamar River. A short walking track winds down to a deep gorge lorded over by towering tree ferns, a species that has been growing in Tasmania for 350 million years. ✉ *Notley Hills* ☏ *03/6223–6191* 🎫 *Free* 🕓 *Year-round.*

off the beaten path

WAVERLY WOOLLEN MILLS – Opened in 1874, these mills on the North Esk River are still powered by a waterwheel. They take pride in using only the finest Tasmanian wool. A store on the premises sells products made in the mills. ✉ *Tasman Hwy. and Waverly Rd.* ☏ *03/6339–1106* 🎫 *A$4* 🕓 *Weekdays 9–5.*

Where to Eat

$$–$$$ ✕ **Fee and Me.** One of Tasmania's top dining venues, Fee and Me has
Fodor'sChoice won more culinary accolades than you could poke a mixing spoon at.
★ "Fee" is the talented chef, Fiona Hoskin, who creates the wonderful food served here. You might begin with Tasmanian Pacific oysters or chicken dumplings in a fragrant broth. Delectable main courses include steamed

mussels in a rich tomato broth, roasted quail on potato straws with honeyed chili sauce, and roasted loin of Tasmanian venison. The licensed restaurant serves wine from Australia's top vineyards. ⊠ *190 Charles St.* ☎ *03/6331–3195* ⌕ *Reservations essential* 🏛 *Jacket required* ☰ *AE, MC, V* ☾ *Closed Sun.*

$$ ✕ **Fluid.** Sit outside on the boardwalk overlooking the North Esk River while indulging in a light snack. Or, you can let the savory entrées tempt you. Richest of all is the duck breast on buckwheat noodles, double roasted with a soured blackcurrant jus. Meals are easily paired with choices from the long list of local wines. ⊠ *Launceston Seaport Blvd., Launceston City* ☎ *03/6334–3220* ☰ *AE, MC, V.*

★ $$ ✕ **Stillwater.** Part of Ritchie's Mill and directly across from the Penny Royal World, this restaurant serves scrumptious, casual fare during the day. The dinner menu adds local seasonal produce complemented by an extensive list of Tasmanian wines. The seafood is particularly recommended. ⊠ *Paterson St.* ☎ *03/6331–4153* ☰ *AE, MC, V.*

★ $$ ✕ **Synergy.** A casual café by day and a relaxed, contemporary restaurant by night, Synergy serves up modern, innovative cuisine at all hours. Tingle your taste buds with the unusual wallaby fillet, which comes with preserved lemon and roast capsicum couscous, as well as pine nut, currant, and spinach salad beneath a tahini and yogurt dressing. ⊠ *135 George St.* ☎ *03/6331–0110* ☰ *No credit cards* ☾ *Closed Sun.*

$–$$ ✕ **Hallams.** This restaurant overlooking the Tamar River has a menu that highlights the town's fresh seafood. To sample it all, order the hot antipasto platter, which comes with rice-wrapped sea-run trout, oysters, marinated mussels, banana noodle prawns, BBQ calamari, and grilled scallops. The friendly, exuberant crowd instantly makes you feel part of the waterfront scene. ⊠ *13 Park St.* ☎ *03/6334–0554* ☰ *AE, MC, V.*

$–$$ ✕ **Jailhouse Grill.** Go directly to jail, and have a delectable steak when you get there. Surrounded by chains and bars, diners feast on prime beef steaks (or fish and chicken), vegetable dishes, and a salad bar. The wine list—all Tasmanian—is comprehensive. ⊠ *32 Wellington St.* ☎ *03/ 6331–0466* ☰ *AE, DC, MC, V* ☾ *No lunch Sat.–Thurs.*

¢–$ ✕ **Fresh on Charles.** Step into this casual, busy place for a quick snack or meal. Don't stop at the rich coffee—order one of the thick open sandwiches, hearty hot dishes, or tasty desserts. ⊠ *178 Charles St.* ☎ *03/ 6331–4299* ☰ *No credit cards* ☾ *Closed Sun.*

Where to Stay

$$–$$$ 🏨 **Alice's Cottages.** Constructed from the remains of three buildings erected during the 1840s, this delightful bed-and-breakfast is a place for whimsical touches. Antique furniture drawers might contain old-fashioned eyeglasses or books; an old turtle shell and a deer's head hang on the wall; and an old Victrola and a four-poster canopy bed lend colonial charm to a room. Modern conveniences are cleverly tucked away among the period furnishings. ⊠ *129 Balfour St., 7250* ☎ *03/6334–2231* 🖷 *03/6334–2696* ⇥ *9 rooms* ⌕ *Some in-room hot tubs, minibars, laundry facilities, free parking* ☰ *AE, MC, V* ⧉ *BP.*

$$–$$$ 🏨 **Country Club Resort and Villas.** Soft gray, blue, and pink pastels color this luxury property on the outskirts of Launceston. The curved driveway to the club is lined with flowers and manicured gardens, and the championship golf course is one of the best in Australia. Gamble in the Casino, dance, and watch evening cabaret shows. The Terrace Restaurant serves specialties such as smoked duck breast and local scallops. Choose between resort rooms and villas, some of which have fully equipped

kitchens. ☒ *Country Club Ave., Prospect Vale, 7250* ☎ *03/6335–5777 or 1800/030211* 🖷 *03/6343–1880* ⊕ *www.countryclubcasino.com.au* 🛏 *88 rooms, 16 suites* ⚒ *Restaurant, dining room, room service, 18-hole golf course, tennis court, pool, sauna, spa, horseback riding, squash, cabaret, casino, dance club, Internet, free parking* ▤ *AE, DC, MC, V.*

$$–$$$ 🏨 **Hatherley House.** This magnificent 1830s mansion has been transformed
FodorsChoice into a hip, intimate hotel. Brazenly high-tech spa bathrooms, with
★ gleaming glass and stainless steel, are juxtaposed against gracious European furnishings and modern works of art. The expansive, lush gardens are like an English parkland. ☒ *43 High St., Launceston 7250* ☎ *03/6334–7727* 🖷 *03/6334–7728* ⊕ *www.hatherleyhouse.com.au* 🛏 *9 rooms* ⚒ *Minibars, Internet, laundry facilities, free parking* ▤ *AE, DC, MC, V.*

$$–$$$ 🏨 **Launceston International Hotel.** This modern, six-story building in the city center has big rooms that blend old-world charm with modern conveniences. Sample fresh Tasmanian produce at the Avenue Restaurant, or join the crowds at Jackson's Tavern and the Lobby Bar. ☒ *29 Cameron St., 7250* ☎ *03/6334–3434 or 1800/642244* 🖷 *03/6331–7347* 🛏 *162 rooms, 7 suites* ⚒ *3 restaurants, room service, 2 bars, laundry service, free parking* ▤ *AE, DC, MC, V.*

★ $$–$$$ 🏨 **Waratah on York.** Built in 1862, this grand Italianate mansion has been superbly restored. Spacious, modern rooms are tastefully decorated to reflect the era in which the building was constructed; six rooms have spa baths. Enjoy panoramas over the Tamar and just a quick walk to the city center. Breakfast is served in the elegant dining room. ☒ *12 York St., 7250* ☎ *03/6331–2081* 🖷 *03/6331–9200* ⊕ *www.waratahonyork. com.au* 🛏 *9 rooms* ⚒ *Dining room, laundry service, free parking; no smoking* ▤ *AE, MC, V* ⎪⊚⎪ *BP.*

$$–$$$ 🏨 **York Mansions.** Luxurious 19th-century elegance is the lure of these self-contained, serviced apartments. Room names like The Gamekeeper, The Countess, and The Duke of York hint at their opulence; indeed, each room has its own theme and style—and a fireplace. The cottage garden at the rear, where you can sip drinks beneath a 130-year-old oak tree, enriches this sumptuous 1840 National Trust property. ☒ *9 York St., 7250* ☎ *03/6334–2933* 🖷 *03/6334–2870* ⊕ *www.yorkmansions.com. au* 🛏 *5 apartments* ⚒ *Some in-room hot tubs, kitchens, laundry facilities, laundry service, free parking* ▤ *AE, DC, MC, V.*

$–$$$ 🏨 **Prince Albert Inn.** First opened in 1855, the Prince Albert still shines like a gem in the lackluster downtown. Crossing the threshold of an Italianate facade, you enter a Victorian time warp, where wall-to-wall portraits of British royalty hang in the plush dining room. Renovations in seven of the guest rooms have not broken the spell. Lace curtains, velvet drapery, and fluffy comforters maintain the atmosphere and maximize comfort. ☒ *22 Tamar St., 7250* ☎ *03/6331–7633* 🖷 *03/6334–1579* ⊕ *www.princealbertinn.com.au* 🛏 *17 rooms* ⚒ *Some in-room hot tubs, lounge, travel services, free parking; no smoking* ▤ *AE, DC, MC, V.*

$ 🏨 **Old Bakery Inn.** You can choose from three areas at this colonial complex: a converted stable, the former baker's cottage, or the old bakery. A loft above the stables is also available. All rooms reflect colonial style, with antique furniture and lace curtains. One room in the old bakery was actually the oven. Its walls are 2 feet thick. ☒ *York and Margaret Sts., 7250* ☎ *03/6331–7900 or 1800/641264* 🖷 *03/6331–7756* 🛏 *23 rooms* ⚒ *Restaurant, free parking* ▤ *AE, MC, V.*

Nightlife & the Arts

The local newspaper, the *Examiner,* is the best source of information on local nightlife and entertainment. The **Country Club Casino** (⊠ Country Club Ave.· ☎ 03/6335–5777) has blackjack, American roulette, minibaccarat, keno, minidice, federal and stud poker, federal wheel, and two-up. There's also late-night dancing. The casino is open daily until early morning.

Live bands and jazz are a feature of the entertainment at the **Royal on George** (⊠ 90 George St. ☎ 03/6331–2526), a refurbished 1852 pub. The **Lounge Bar** (⊠ 63 St. John St. ☎ 03/6334–6622) in a 1907 ex-bank building offers live bands upstairs as well as a vodka bar in the old vault.

The curtain at the **Princess Theatre** (⊠ 57 Brisbane St. ☎ 03/6323–3666) rises for local and imported stage productions. The **Silverdome** (⊠ 55 Oakden Rd., ☎ 03/6344–9988) holds regular music concerts—everything from classical to heavy metal.

Shopping

Launceston is a convenient place for a little shopping, with most stores central on George Street and in nearby Yorktown Mall. **Design Centre of Tasmania** (⊠ Brisbane and Tamar Sts. ☎ 03/6331–5506) carries wonderful items made from Tasmanian timber, including custom-design furniture. Other choice products are the high-quality woolen wear, pottery, and glass. One of the best arts-and-crafts stores is **National Trust Old Umbrella Shop** (⊠ 60 George St. ☎ 03/6331–9248), which sells umbrellas and gifts such as tea towels and toiletries. **The Sheep's Back** (⊠ 53 George St. ☎ 03/6331–2539) sells woolen products exclusively.

Launceston A to Z

To research prices, get advice from other travelers, and book travel arrangements, visit www.fodors.com.

AIR TRAVEL
The Launceston airport is served by several domestic airlines, including Southern Australia Airlines, Island Airlines, Virgin Blue, and Qantas.
🖪 Airlines **Australia Airlines** ☎ 13-1313. **Island Airlines** ☎ 1800/645875. **Quantas** ☎ 13-1313. **Virgin Blue** ☎ 13-6789.

BUS TRAVEL
TassieLink Route Services and Tasmanian Redline Coaches serve Launceston from Devonport, Burnie, and Hobart.
🖪 Bus Information **Tasmanian Redline Coaches** ⊠ 16-18 Charles St. ☎ 03/6336-1444 or 1300/360000. **TassieLink Route Services** ⊠ Gateway Tasmania, St. John and Bathurst Sts. ☎ 1300/300520.

CAR RENTAL
Cars, campers, caravans, and minibuses are available for rent from the airport at several agencies in Launceston: Autorent Hertz, Avis, Budget, and Thrifty.
🖪 Agencies **Autorent Hertz** ⊠ 58 Paterson St. ☎ 03/6335-1111. **Avis** ⊠ 29 Cameron St. ☎ 03/6334-7722. **Budget** ⊠ Launceston Airport ☎ 03/6391-8566. **Thrifty** ⊠ 151 St. John St. ☎ 03/6333-0911.

CAR TRAVEL
Highway 1 connects Launceston with Hobart 2½ hours to the south and with Devonport 1½ hours to the northwest.

EMERGENCIES

In case of any emergency, dial 000 to reach an ambulance, the fire department, or the police.

🛈 Hospitals Launceston General Hospital ✉ Charles St. ☎ 03/6348-7111. **St. Luke's Hospital** ✉ 24 Lyttleton St. ☎ 03/6335-3333. **St. Vincent's Hospital** ✉ 5 Frederick St. ☎ 03/6331-4999.

MONEY MATTERS

You can cash traveler's checks and change money at ANZ Bank, Commonwealth Bank, and National Bank.

🛈 Banks ANZ Bank ✉ 69 Brisbane St. ☎ 13-1314. **Commonwealth Bank** ✉ 97 Brisbane St. ☎ 03/6337-4444. **National Bank** ✉ 130 Brisbane St. ☎ 13-2265.

TAXIS

Central Cabs and Taxi Combined can be hailed in the street or booked by phone.

🛈 Taxi Companies Central Cabs ☎ 13-1008. **Taxi Combined** ☎ 13-2227.

TOURS

You can book a city sights tour of Launceston by replica tram through the Coach Tram Tour Company or at the Tasmanian Travel and Information Centre. Tours run November through April twice daily. Launceston Historic Walks conducts a leisurely stroll through the historic heart of the city. Walks leave from the Tasmanian Travel and Information Centre weekdays at 9:45 AM.

Tasmanian Wilderness Travel leads day and multiday tours to Cradle Mountain, the breathtakingly dramatic Walls of Jerusalem, and the Tamar Valley. Tigerline Coaches runs similar tours. Tamar River Cruises conducts informative and relaxing trips on the Tamar as far as the Batman Bridge, past many wineries and into Cataract Gorge.

🛈 Tour Operators Coach Tram Tour Company ☎ 03/6336-3133. **Launceston Historic Walks** ☎ 03/6331-3679. **Tamar River Cruises** ☎ 03/6334-9900. **Tasmanian Wilderness Transport and Tours** ☎ 03/6334-4442. **Tigerline Coaches** ☎ 1300/653633.

VISITOR INFORMATION

The Tasmanian Travel and Information Centre is open weekdays 9–5 and Saturday 9–noon.

🛈 Tasmanian Travel and Information Centre ✉ St. John and Paterson Sts. ☎ 03/6336-3122.

NORTHWEST COAST

The northwest coast of Tasmania is one of the most exciting and least known areas of the state. Most of the local inhabitants are farmers, fisherfolk, or lumberjacks. They're a hardy bunch and some of the friendliest folk in Tasmania. The rugged coastline here has long been the solitary haunt of abalone hunters, and from the area's lush grazing land comes some of Australia's best beef and cheese. Tasmanian farmers are the only legal growers of opium poppies (for medicinal use) in the Southern Hemisphere, and fields in the northwest are blanketed with their striking white and purple flowers.

Devonport & Environs

89 km (55 mi) northwest of Launceston, 289 km (179 mi) northwest of Hobart.

In the middle of the north coast, Devonport is the Tasmanian port where the ferry from Melbourne docks. Visitors from the ferry often dash off to other parts of Tasmania without realizing that the town and its surroundings have many interesting attractions.

In the Old Harbour Master's residence, the **Maritime Museum** contains a fascinating collection of local and maritime history. ⊠ *Victoria Parade* ☎ *03/6424–7100* ⊠ *A\$3* ⊙ *Tues.–Sun. 10–4.*

Stop at the **Tiagarra Aboriginal Cultural and Art Centre** to see remnants of Tasmania's Aboriginal past, including more than 250 images of rock engravings. ⊠ *Mersey Bluff* ☎ *03/6424–8250* ⊠ *A\$3.30* ⊙ *Daily 9–5.*

The **Don River Railway** re-creates the atmosphere of a working passenger railway by using both steam and diesel traction in a pleasant journey along the banks of the Don River. ⊠ *Forth Main Rd.* ☎ *03/ 6424–6335* ⊠ *A\$8* ⊙ *Daily 10–5.*

South from Devonport along the Bass Highway toward Launceston are two places to stir the taste buds. The **House of Anvers** specializes in making exquisite chocolates—you can even watch the staff in action. (⊠ Bass Hwy. Latrobe ☎03/6426–2703 ⊠Entry free; museum A\$2 ⊙Daily 7–5)

The **Ashgrove Farm Cheese Factory** makes delicious, English-style cheeses like Cheddar, Lancashire, and Cheshire. (⊠ 6173 Bass Hwy. Elizabeth Town ☎ 03/6368–1105 ⊠ Free ⊙ Daily 9–5)

The small village of **Sheffield** has more than 30 murals depicting local history painted on the walls of buildings.

Where to Stay & Eat

\$–\$\$ ✕ **Essence.** Settle back and dig into some interesting dishes in this intimate restaurant and wine bar. Fresh local produce is featured throughout the menu. Take a stroll afterward, since the restaurant is just a few streets from the town center. ⊠ *28 Forbes St., Devonport* ☎ *03/ 6424–6431* ⊟ *DC, MC, V* ⊙ *Closed Sun. and Mon.*

\$ ✕ **Pedro's.** Tasty seaside bounty is caught fresh daily and cooked up in this kitchen on the edge of the Leven River. Relax above the flowing water while sampling local crayfish, calamari, Tasmanian scallops, flounder, or trevalla. Can't stay? Try the building's take-away fish-and-chips outlet. ⊠ *Wharf Rd., Ulverstone* ☎ *03/6425–5181* ⊟ *MC, V.*

\$ ✕ **Rialto Gallery.** Simple pasta dishes are the order of the day at this Venetian Italian restaurant. Cream-base sauces are favored. Other entrées include such classics as veal scallopini. ⊠ *159 Rooke St. Devonport* ☎ *03/6424–6793* ⊟ *AE, DC, MC, V* ⊙ *No lunch weekends.*

\$ ⌷ **Birchmore.** This elegant bed-and breakfast is set in a beautifully renovated old mansion in the heart of Devonport. Rooms are luxuriously appointed, and have writing desks and faxes (on request) for business travelers. ⊠ *10 Oldaker St., Devonport, 7310* ☎ *03/6423–1336* 🖷 *03/ 6423–1338* ⊕*www.view.com.au/birchmore* ⇥*6 rooms* ⌂ *Some in-room faxes, laundry service, meeting rooms, free parking* ⊟ *DC, MC, V.*

\$ ⌷ **Rannoch House.** A spacious, early 1900s Federation-style home is the setting for this tranquil hotel. Walk through the rambling gardens—and on to the ferry terminal nearby. Country-style cooked breakfasts are served up each morning. ⊠ *5 Cedar Court, East Devonport, 7310* ☎ *03/ 6427–9818* 🖷 *03/6427–9181* ⇥ *5 rooms* ⌂ *Dining room, free parking* ⊟ *MC, V.*

\$ ⌷ **Westella House.** This charming 1885 period homestead has stunning sea views. Log fires, hand-crafted banisters and mantles, and antique furnishing draw you into the cozy ambience. A hearty, home-cooked breakfast starts the day. ⊠ *68 Westella Dr., Ulverstone, 7315* ☎ *03/ 6425–6222* 🖷*03/6425–6276* ⊕*www.westella.com* ⇥*3 rooms* ⌂ *Laundry facilities, free parking* ⊟ *MC, V.*

en route   Just 40 minutes east of Devonport is **Narawntapu National Park,** which contains coastal vegetation, heath, and beaches. It's an ideal spot to see native animals like wallabies and wombats grazing insouciantly in the wild. **Lillicoe Beach,** just west of Devonport, is perfect at dusk on a summer's night for seeing little fairy penguins emerge from the surf and waddle to their burrows. Heading west on Bass Highway toward Burnie, stop in briefly at **Penguin,** a charming little town with small penguin statues for litter baskets on its sidewalks. The railway line along the foreshore is usually a blaze of color thanks to verdant gardens maintained by the local homeowners. From Penguin the road leads through the Table Cape region to Burnie, Wynyard, and Boat Harbour, passing through rich farm country and gentle hills. The Rocky Cape National Park is an attractive stopover before arriving in Stanley.

Where to Stay

$–$$ Killynaught Spa Cottages. Five cozy, decorative cottages comprise this relaxed vacation option. Two are self-contained spa apartments in an 1800s family home; there's also an executive spa apartment. Open fires add touches of warmth and romance. Although kitchen facilities are included, you can order a platter from the Violet's Cafe. ⊠ *17266 Bass Hwy., Boat Harbour, 7321* ☎ *03/6445–1041* 🖷 *03/6445–1556* ⊕ *www. killynaught.com.au* ⤶ *8 rooms* ⌂ *Café, kitchens, laundry, free parking* ▤ *DC, MC, V.*

Stanley

140 km (87 mi) northwest of Devonport, 430 km (267 mi) northwest of Hobart.

Stanley is one of the prettiest villages in Tasmania and a must for anyone traveling in the northwest. A gathering of historic cottages at the foot of the Nut, Tasmania's version of Uluru (Ayers Rock), it's filled with friendly tea rooms, interesting shops, and old country inns. Stop by the **Highfield Historic Site** (A$2), the fully restored house and grounds that once held the Van Diemen's Land Company.

The **Nut** (☎ 03/6458–1286 Nut Chairlifts), a sheer volcanic plug some 12½ million years old, rears up right behind the village. It's almost totally surrounded by the sea. You can either tackle the steep 20-minute climb or take a chairlift (A$7 round-trip, A$4 for trip down) to the summit. At the top, walking trails lead in all directions.

Where to Stay & Eat

$–$$ ✕ **Julie and Patrick's.** Some say this restaurant serves the best fish-and-chips in Tasmania. Formal diners stay upstairs, while noshers head to the casual downstairs café, and those on the run grab meals from the take-out counter. You can choose your fish and shellfish from tanks at the shop. Try muttonbird (shearwater), a local specialty—and be prepared for its oily, slightly gamey taste. ⊠ *2 Alexander Terr.* ☎ *03/ 6458–1103* ▤ *MC, V.*

★ $–$$ ✕ **Stanley's on the Bay.** Set on the waterfront in the fully restored old Bond Store, the restaurant specializes in fine steaks and seafood. Try the eye fillet of beef topped with prawns, scallops, and fish fillets, served in a creamy white wine sauce. ⊠ *15 Wharf Rd.* ☎ *03/6458–1404* ▤ *DC, MC, V* ☉ *Closed July and Aug.*

★ $–$$ **Beachside Retreat West Inlet.** These contemporary, ecologically conscious cabins are set on frontal sand dunes overlooking the sea. Luxurious fittings use local timbers (made by a wood-turning son of owners whose work is available at Stanley Artworks). Set on farmland adjacent to wetlands and the sea, the retreat is perfect for bird-watching or just strolling on the beach. ✉ *253 Stanley Hwy., 7331* ☎ *03/6458–1350* 🖷 *03/6458–1350* 🗪 *3 rooms* ⚴ *Kitchens, laundry facilities, travel services, free parking* 🚍 *DC, MC, V.*

$ 🖃 **Touchwood Cottage.** Built in 1840, this is one of Stanley's oldest homes, and it's furnished with plenty of period pieces. The product of an architect's whimsy (or incompetence), the cottage is known for its doorways of different sizes and oddly shaped living room. Rooms are cozy, with open fires that add a romantic ambience. Afternoon tea is served on arrival. The cottage is near the Nut and the popular Touchwood crafts shop, where guests receive a discount. ✉ *31 Church St., 7331* ☎ *03/6458–1348* 🗪 *3 rooms with shared bath* ⚴ *Dining room, free parking* 🚍 *MC, V* 🍽 *BP.*

Shopping

Touchwood Quality Crafts (✉ Church St. ☎ 03/6458–1348) carries one of the finest selections of Tasmanian crafts in the state.

Smithton

140 km (87 mi) northwest of Devonport, 510 km (316 mi) northwest of Hobart.

Travelers come here to get away, to venture outdoors in remote places, and to explore the rugged northwest coast. Two rain forest–clad nature reserves in the area, Julius River and Milkshakes Hills, are worth visiting.

Around each corner of the private **Allendale Gardens** is a surprise: a cluster of native Tasmanian ferns or a thicket of shrubs and flowers. Forest walks of 10 to 25 minutes take you past trees more than 500 years old. The gardens shelter more birds than you're likely to see in other areas of Tasmania. ✉ *Eurebia, Edith Creek, 14 km (9 mi) from Smithton* ☎ *03/6456–4216* 🎟 *A$7.50* ⊙ *Oct.–Apr., daily 10–4.*

About 65 km (40 mi) west of Smithton the road reaches the wild west coast. **Arthur River Cruises** (☎ 03/6457–1158 ⊕ www.arthurrivercruises. com) runs boat trips on the serene waterway, which take you through pristine rain forest that has remained unchanged for centuries. Half-day excursions start at A$60. Call for directions.

Join in an evening of spotting Tasmanian devils in their natural habitat on Joe King's **Tasmanian Devil Tour** (✉ Marrawah ☎ 03/6457–1191). An old "shack" on the windswept coast provides shelter from which to watch the Tasmanian devils fight over food, perhaps warding off other intruders, such as quolls. Stay the night at the self-contained rural retreat Glendonald Cottage.

Where to Stay & Eat

$$ ✕🖃 **Tall Timbers.** This lodge is one of the finest establishments in the northwest. Built with Tasmanian wood, the main house has a cozy bar and two restaurants, one for formal dining and the other a huge bistro. In a separate Tasmanian-wood building, rooms are simply decorated. Specialties in Grey's Fine Dining restaurant include rock crayfish, chicken breast, rabbit hot pot, Atlantic salmon, and crêpes suzette for dessert. ✉ *Scotchtown Rd. (Box 304), Smithton, 7330* ☎ *03/ 6452–2755* 🖷 *03/6452–2742* 🗪 *59 rooms* ⚴ *2 restaurants, tennis court, bar, playground, laundry service, convention center, free parking* 🚍 *AE, DC, MC, V.*

Northwest Coast A to Z

To research prices, get advice from other travelers, and book travel arrangements, visit www.fodors.com.

AIR TRAVEL

Devonport is served by QantasLink, TasAir, and Kendell Airlines.
🛪 Carriers **Kendell** ☎ 13-1300. **QantasLink** ☎ 13-1313. **TasAir** ☎ 03/6427-9777 or 1800/062900 ⊕ www.tasair.com.au.

BOAT & FERRY TRAVEL

Spirit of Tasmania I and *II* operate in reverse directions across Bass Strait. The ferries make the 10-hour, overnight crossing daily. In peak periods, extra daylight sailings are added to meet the demand. Each ferry carries a maximum of 1,400 passengers and up to 600 vehicles. Cabin rates range from A$173–A$278 per adult each way in low season (April 30–August 31) and from A$201–A$364 the rest of the year. Airline-style cruise seats are available for A$94 to A$125. A standard-size car is free except during the December–January summer school holiday period. Facilities include children's playrooms, a games arcade, gift shops, and several restaurants and bars. Advance bookings are essential.
🛥 Boat & Ferry Lines **Spirit of Tasmania** ⊠ Station Pier, Port Melbourne ☎ 13-2010 or 1800/811580 ⊕ www.spiritoftasmania.com.au ⊠ Berth 1, The Esplanade, Devonport ☎ 13-2010

BUS TRAVEL

Tasmanian Redline Coaches has offices in Devonport, Burnie, and Smithton.
🚌 **Tasmanian Redline Coaches** ⊠ 9 Edward St., Devonport ☎ 03/6421-6490 ⊠ 117 Wilson St., Burnie ☎ 03/6434-4488 ⊠ 19 Smith St., Smithton ☎ 03/6452-1262.

CAR RENTAL

Cars, campers, and minibuses are available for rent in Devonport.
🚗 Agencies **Autorent Hertz** ⊠ 26 Oldaker St. ☎ 03/6424-1013. **Avis** ⊠ Devonport Airport ☎ 03/6427-9797. **Budget** ⊠ Airport Rd. ☎ 03/6427-0650 or 13-2727. **Thrifty** ⊠ 10 The Esplanade ☎ 03/6427-9119.

CAR TRAVEL

Many of the northwest roads are twisty and even unpaved in the more remote areas. A few may require four-wheel-drive vehicles. However, two-wheel drive is sufficient for most touring. Be prepared for sudden weather changes. This is one of the colder parts of Tasmania, and snow in the summertime is not uncommon in the highest areas.

EMERGENCIES

In case of any emergency, dial **000** to reach an ambulance, the fire department, or the police.

TOURS

Seair Adventure Charters conducts scenic flights that depart from Cradle Valley Airstrip and take you over the valley and across to Barn Bluff, Mt. Ossa, the Acropolis, Lake St. Clair, Mt. Olympus, and other sights in the area. Doors on the planes are removable for photography. Thirty- to 90-minute flights are available. Flights are also available from Wynyard Airport.
🛩 **Seair Adventure Charters** ⊠ Cradle Valley Airstrip, Cradle Valley ☎ 03/6492-1132 ⊠ Wynyard Airport, Wynyard ☎ 03/6442-1220.

VISITOR INFORMATION

Tasmanian Travel and Information Centre has offices in Devonport and Burnie. Hours are usually weekdays 9–5 and Saturday 9–noon, and often longer in the summer.

🔲 Tasmanian Travel and Information Centre ✉ 92 Formby Rd., Devonport ☎ 03/6424-4466 ✉ 48 Civic Sq., off Little Alexander St., Burnie ☎ 03/6434-6111.

WEST COAST

The wildest and least explored countryside in Australia lies on Tasmania's west coast. Due to the region's remoteness from the major centers of Hobart and Launceston, as well as its rugged terrain, the intrepid pioneers who developed this part of the island endured incredible hardships and extremely difficult living conditions. Communities were quickly established and abandoned as the search for mineral wealth continued, and even today the viability of towns depends on the fluctuations in the price of the metals. The region still seems like part of the frontier.

Much of the land lies in protected zones or conservation areas, and there are lingering resentments among conservationists, loggers, and local, state, and federal government agencies. Strahan is the major center for tourism, and the departure point for cruises along the pristine Gordon River and Macquarie Harbour. The area's rich mining history is kept alive in smaller towns such as Queenstown and Zeehan, and you should allow time to enjoy their attractions.

In the heyday of mining in Queenstown at the beginning of the 20th century, ore was taken by train to be loaded at ports on Macquarie Harbour. A former rack and pinion train line carrying ore is now the restored **Westcoast Wilderness Railway** (✉ Macquarie Harbour ☎ 03/6471–1700 ⊕ www.abtrailway.com.au), which makes the 35-km (22-mi) journey from Queenstown to Strahan. Check the Web site for current prices. The line passes through one of the world's last pristine wilderness areas, as well as through historic settlements and abandoned camps, across 40 bridges and wild rivers, and up and down steep gradients.

| off the beaten path | **WEST COAST PIONEERS' MEMORIAL MUSEUM** – The West Coast is internationally recognized as one of the world's richest mineral provinces, with vast deposits of tin, gold, silver, copper, lead, and zinc. This museum, in the old Zeehan School of Mines and Metallurgy, was established in 1894. Displays include a remarkable selection of minerals, historical items, and personal records of the region. Some exhibits are in a re-created underground mine. ✉ *Main St., Zeehan, 7469* ☎ *03/6471–6225* 🎟 *A$6* ⏱ *Daily 8:30–5.* |

Strahan

265 km (164 mi) southeast of Smithton, 305 km (189 mi) northwest of Hobart.

This lovely, lazy fishing port has one of the deepest harbors in the world and a population under 750. It used to be a major port for mining companies. The brown color that sometimes appears on the shoreline is not pollution but naturally occurring tannin from surrounding vegetation. The town sits on the edge of Macquarie Harbour, and mixes a still-active fishing industry with tourism. The foreshore walking track gives an excellent view of the Strahan area. Don't overlook the short easy walk from the foreshore through rain forest to Hogarth Falls.

The main reason to visit Strahan is to join a cruise from majestic Macquarie Harbour to the tranquil waters of the Gordon River and the World **FodorsChoice** Heritage Site of **Franklin–Gordon Wild Rivers National Park.** The return journey includes a stop at Sarah Island, once one of the harshest ★ penal settlements in Tasmania. Half- and full-day cruises run daily; some include a smorgasbord lunch and other refreshments.

Other worthwhile destinations, if you have some extra time, include the towering Henty Dunes north of town, the lush forest along the walk to Teepookana Falls, and—for the adventurous—a true rain-forest trek along the Bird River Track to some eerie, overgrown ruins on the shores of Macquarie Harbour.

Strahan Visitor Centre is also a museum that concentrates on local subjects and is not afraid to tackle such controversial issues as past conservation battles over the Gordon River and the fate of Tasmania's Aborigines. Its striking architecture has won it several awards. Don't miss performances of the play *The Ship That Never Was,* based on a true story of convict escape and a loophole in British justice. ⊠ *Strahan Rd.* ☎ *03/6471–7622* ✉ *A$10* ⊙ *Daily 10–6.*

Where to Stay & Eat

$ ✕ **Hamers Hotel.** This basic, bar-style restaurant specializes in seafood and steak, and the food is better than most pub counter meals for about the same price. Dessert includes a choice of fresh cakes. ⊠ *The Esplanade* ☎ *03/6471–7191* ▭ *MC, V.*

$$$ ▥ **Ormiston House.** Utterly luxurious, this mansion has been faithfully restored to ultimate elegance. Four-poster beds, spacious rooms, and cozy fireplaces (a necessity about 10 months of the year) make this the best romantic hideaway on the west coast. You can still keep in touch with the modern world, though, as the hotel provides fax and e-mail services. ⊠ *The Esplanade, 7468* ☎ *03/6471–7077 or 1800/625745* 🖷 *03/ 6471–7007* ⊕ *www.ormistonhouse.com.au* ➴ *4 rooms* ♨ *Restaurant, bar, free parking* ▭ *AE, DC, MC, V.*

★ $$-$$$ ▥ **Franklin Manor.** Set in gardens near the harbor, Franklin Manor is an exquisite wilderness retreat with delightful food and hospitality. This century-old mansion has open fires and a relaxing lounge. An added perk is that rooms have heated towel rails. The restaurant is known for its refined, comfortable ambience. An à la carte menu includes lobster, oysters, pot-roasted quail, and sea trout. ⊠ *The Esplanade, 7468* ☎ *03/ 6471–7311* ⊕ *www.strahanaccommodation.com* ➴ *18 rooms* ♨ *Restaurant, room service, outdoor hot tub, bar, lounge, free parking* ▭ *AE, DC, MC, V* ⑩ *BP.*

$$ ▥ **Risby Cove.** High-class accommodations meet a stunning waterfront at this elegant lodging. Art is a main theme—there's even a gallery of contemporary paintings, sculpture, and weaving. Ecotourism is another focus, and sea kayaking is available. The room furnishings are bright and modern, made of native woods. Whirlpool tubs add to the comfort. The restaurant, with a menu that lists Tasmanian wines and such seafood delicacies as ocean trout risotto, overlooks the marina. ⊠ *The Esplanade, 7468* ☎ *03/6471–7572* 🖷 *03/6471–7582* ⊕ *www.risby. com.au* ➴ *4 rooms* ♨ *Restaurant, boating, marina, mountain bikes, free parking* ▭ *AE, MC, V.*

$-$$ ▥ **Strahan Village.** Waterfront and hilltop cottage, terraces, and hotel rooms make up this extensive property. Family-style units with self-catering facilities and hot tubs are available. Dining options range from the spectacular, cliff-top Macquarie Restaurant to the more casual Hamers Hotel and waterside Fish Cafe. ⊠ *The Esplanade, 7468* ☎ *03/6471–4200*

🖩 *03/6471–4389* 🖘 *103 rooms* 🛆 *3 restaurants, laundry facilities, travel services* 🖃 *AE, DC, MC, V.*

West Coast A to Z

To research prices, get advice from other travelers, and book travel arrangements, visit www.fodors.com.

CAR TRAVEL

A vehicle is absolutely essential for moving from place to place on the west coast. The road from Hobart travels through the Derwent Valley and past lovely historic towns such as Hamilton before rising to the plateau of central Tasmania, famous for its lake and stream fishing. At Derwent Bridge, you can make a short detour to Lake St. Clair. Craggy mountain peaks and dense forest are scenic highlights along the road to Queenstown; the denuded hillsides resemble a moonscape. The road from Queenstown to Strahan twists and turns through stands of native timber.

The north highway snakes down from Burnie (a link road joins Cradle Mountain with the highway) to the mining towns of Rosebery and Zeehan. From here, a newer link road to Strahan passes the Henty Dunes and Ocean Beach, which is often battered by the storms of the Roaring Forties. The adventurous can take the unsealed link road north from Zeehan, which crosses the Pieman River (by barge) and then tracks through pristine forest and open plateau to rejoin the coast at the Arthur River and hence to Marrawah and Smithton.

EMERGENCIES

In case of any emergency, dial **000** to reach an ambulance, the fire department, or the police.

TOURS

Wilderness Air flies seaplanes from Strahan Wharf over Frenchman's Cap, the Franklin and Gordon rivers, Lake Pedder, and Hells Gates, with a landing at Sir John Falls. It's a great way to see the area's peaks, lakes, coast, and rivers. Seair Adventures Charters has similar tours by helicopter and small plane.

Gordon River Cruises has half- and full-day tours on Macquarie Harbour and the Gordon River; the full-day tour includes a smorgasbord lunch. An informative commentary accompanies the trip to historic Sarah Island, and you can disembark at Heritage Landing and take a half-hour walk through the vegetation to a 2,000-year-old Huon pine tree. Reservations are essential.

World Heritage Cruises has the MV *Wanderer,* which sails daily from Strahan Wharf. Meals and drinks are available on board. The leisurely journey pauses at Sarah Island, Heritage Landing, and the Saphia Ocean Trout Farm on Macquarie Harbour. From October through April they also operate a half-day cruise.

West Coast Yacht Charters has daily twilight cruises on Macquarie Harbour aboard the 60-foot ketch *Stormbreaker* that include a dinner of the famed local crayfish (A$55). The company also operates a two-day/two-night sailing excursion (A$390, meals included), a morning fishing trip (A$45), and overnight cruises on the Gordon River (A$275, all meals included).

Offices of all tour operators are located on Strahan Wharf.

🎏 Air Tours **Wilderness Air** ☎ 03/6471-7280. **Seair Adventure Charters** ☎ 03/6471-7718.

🖪 Boat Tours **Gordon River Cruises** ☎ 03/6471–4300 ⊕ www.strahanvillage.com.au.
West Coast Yacht Charters ☎ 03/6471–7422. **World Heritage Cruises** ☎ 03/6471–7174
🖶 03/6471–7431 ⊕ www.worldheritagecruises.com.au.

TASMANIA NATIONAL PARKS

Cradle Mountain–Lake St. Clair National Park

★ *173 km (107 mi) northwest of Hobart to Lake St. Clair at the southern end of the park, 85 km (58 mi) from Devonport, 181 km (113 mi) from Launceston.*

Cradle Mountain–Lake St. Clair National Park contains the most spectacular alpine scenery in Tasmania and the top mountain trails in Australia. Popular with hikers of all ability, the park has several high peaks, including Mt. Ossa, the highest in Tasmania (more than 5,300 feet). The Cradle Mountain section of the park lies in the north. The southern section of the park, Lake St. Clair, is popular for boat trips and hiking.

One of the most famous trails in Australia, the **Overland Track** traverses 85 km (53 mi) between the park's north and south boundaries. Tasmania's Parks and Wildlife Service has provided several basic sleeping huts that are available on a first-come, first-served basis. Because space in the huts is limited, hikers are advised to bring their own tents. If you prefer to do the walk in comfort, you can use well-equipped, heated private structures managed by Cradle Mountain Huts.

Several of Cradle Mountain's most alluring natural attractions can be enjoyed on short (20-minute to three-hour) walks. The best include the Enchanted Walk, Wombat Pool, Lake Lilla, Dove Lake Loop, and Marion's Lookout. In late April you can make your way up the Truganini Track to see the native fagus bushes turn the hillsides a dazzling yellow and orange. It's the closest thing Australia has to Vermont in autumn.

Where to Stay

Caravan, car, and bus campgrounds at the northern end of ⚠ **Cradle Mt. Tourist Park** (☎ 03/6492–1395) have showers, toilets, laundry facilities, and cooking shelters with electric barbecues. Tent sites cost A\$8–A\$10 per person, per night. Bunkhouse accommodations are A\$18–A\$30 per person, per night. Sites with electrical hookup are A\$10–A\$12 per person, per night. Self-contained cabins cost from A\$75–A\$95 per double. Advance booking is essential.

★ \$\$\$–\$\$\$\$ 🏨 **Cradle Mountain Lodge.** This wilderness lodge gave birth to a genre in Australia, and it's the most comfortable place to stay at Cradle Mountain. Accommodations are not luxurious, but they are homey. The environment is what counts here, and it is magnificent. The high-ceiling guest rooms, two per cabin, are cheerfully decorated. A couple of walking trails begin at the lodge door. Breakfast is included in room rates, and there's a minimum two-night stay. ✚ *60 km (37 mi) from Sheffield* 🕮 *Box 153, Sheffield, 7306* ☎ *03/6492–1303* 🖶 *03/6492–1309* ⊕ *www.cradlemountainlodge.com.au* 🛏 *98 rooms* ⚘ *Dining room, business services, travel services* ▭ *MC, V* ¶◯¶ *BP.*

★ \$\$\$ 🏨 **Lemonthyme Lodge.** Perhaps the largest log cabin in the Southern Hemisphere, this huge lodge lies about 12 km (7 mi) east of the park, near the tiny village of Mona, and is set in a lush wood. Guided walks let you view the towering trees and native wildlife. With its huge stone fireplace and soaring ceiling, this hotel has a grander look than Cradle Mountain Lodge but is not as close to the park. 🕮 *Locked Bag 158, Devonport, 7310* ☎ *03/6492–1112* 🖶 *03/6492–1113* ⊕ *www.*

lemonthyme.com.au ⤴ *31 rooms* ⚭ *Dining room, kitchenettes, hiking, laundry service, free parking* ▭ *AE, MC, V.*

Mt. Field National Park

70 km (43 mi) northwest of Hobart.

One of the first two national parks created in Tasmania in 1917, Mt. Field National Park still ranks as the most popular among Tasmanians and visitors alike. The park's easily navigable trails, picnic areas, and well-maintained campsites are ideal for family outings. Animals, including wallabies and possums, are often out and about around dusk.

Some 80 km (50 mi) northwest of Hobart, **Mt. Mawson** is the most popular ski area in southern Tasmania. Walkers can take the 20-minute, 1-km (½-mi) **Russell Falls Nature Walk**, which is paved and suitable for wheelchairs. It winds up a hill to the gorgeous Horseshoe Falls, then to the fascinating Tall Trees Walk, then another 20 minutes to Lady Barron Falls.

Where to Stay

Wilderness huts, on certain trails throughout the park, cost A$20 for two adults.

⚠ **Land of the Giants Services Caravan Park** (✉ Park Access Rd. ☎ 03/6288–1526) is a campground and caravan park with toilets, hot water, showers, free firewood, and laundry facilities. It's conveniently located near the entrance to Mt. Field. Fees per person are A$12 for a campsite and A$17 for a powered site. Minimal grocery supplies can be purchased at the kiosk near the caravan park.

Southwest National Park

Maydena is 98 km (61 mi) northwest of Hobart, Geeveston is 60 km (37 mi) southwest of Hobart.

The largest park in Tasmania, Southwest encompasses the entire southwestern portion of the state, connecting with Franklin-Gordon Wild Rivers, Cradle Mountain–Lake St. Clair, and the Walls of Jerusalem national parks to create an unsurpassed World Heritage wilderness area. This is one of the few virgin land tracts in Australia, and its five mountain ranges and more than 50 lakes were unknown to all but the most avid bushwalkers until the 1970s. Although the park holds the greatest appeal for the hardy and adventurous, within its boundaries are some pleasant but quite underpublicized easy-access locales.

The two main ways to access the park are through Maydena north of Hobart and via Geeveston in the Huon Valley. After entering the park through Maydena, turn south off the Gordon River Road a mile along Scott's Peak Road to the **Creepy Crawly Nature Trail,** a 15-minute duckboard stroll through extremely dense rain forest that evokes the ancient supercontinent of Gondwana. At the end of Scott's Peak Road is a knoll where you can park and look out onto the rugged peaks of the **Western Arthurs Range.** Beyond Geeveston and Dover you can walk to the park's southeastern corner on a flat, two-hour track that starts near the tiny village of Cockle Creek and leads to **South Cape Bay.**

Where to Stay

Campsites are available at Lake Pedder, Scott's Peak Dam, and Edgar Dam. Gas, food, and accommodations are available in Strathgordon.

Tasmania National Parks A to Z

To research prices, get advice from other travelers, and book travel arrangements, visit www.fodors.com.

AIR TRAVEL

Two companies provide air service into the Southwest National Park at Cox Bight and Melaleuca: Par Avion Tours and TasAir.

♠ Carriers Par Avion Tours ☎ 03/6248-5390. **TasAir** ☎ 03/6248-5088 ⊕ www. tasair.com.au.

BUS TRAVEL

Tasmanian Wilderness Transport and Tours runs to Cradle Mountain from Devonport, Strahan, and Launceston. It also serves Lake St. Clair from Launceston, Devonport, and Hobart. TassieLink operates buses daily (except Sunday) from Hobart and Queenstown to Derwent Bridge near the park's southern entrance, and also from Launceston and Devonport to Cradle Mountain at the northern entrance to the park.

A regularly scheduled minibus is available to Southwest National Park from Tasmanian Wilderness Travel in Hobart on Tuesday, Thursday, and weekends from December through March. Scheduled buses also leave Hobart for the Mt. Field National Park weekdays, except public holidays.

♠ Bus Lines Tasmanian Wilderness Transport and Tours ☎ 03/6334-4442. **Tasmanian Wilderness Travel** ☎ 03/6288-1445. **TassieLink** ☎ 1300/300520.

CAR TRAVEL

Lake St. Clair is 173 km (107 mi) from Hobart and can be reached via the Lyell Highway, or from Launceston via Deloraine or Poatina. Cradle Mountain is 85 km (53 mi) south of Devonport and can be reached by car via Claude Road from Sheffield or via Wilmot. Both lead 30 km (19 mi) along Route C132 to Cradle Valley. The last 10 km (6 mi) are unpaved, but the road is in very good condition.

To get to Mt. Field National Park from Hobart, drive north on the Lyell Highway and then west on Maydena Road.

VISITOR INFORMATION

The Tasmanian National Parks office in Hobart has information on all the state's national parks.

♠ Tourist Information Cradle Mountain Visitor Center ✉ Park Rd. ☎ 03/6492-1133. **Lake St. Clair Visitor Center** ✉ Park Rd. ☎ 03/6289-1172. **Mt. Field National Park** ✉ Park Rd. ☎ 03/6288-1149. **Southwest National Park** ✉ Park Rd., Maydena ☎ 03/6288-1283. **Tasmanian National Parks** ✉ 134 Macquarie St., Hobart City ☎ 03/6233-6191 ⊕ www.parks.tas.gov.au.

QUEENSLAND

7

FODOR'S CHOICE

Cape Tribulation National Park, in Cape Tribulation

Catalina, restaurant in Port Douglas

Coconut Beach Rainforest Resort, in Cape Tribulation

Dreamworld, theme park in Coomera

e'cco, restaurant in Brisbane

Eumundi Markets, in Eumundi

The Great Green Way, highway near Cairns

Hilton Cairns, in Cairns

Kingfisher Bay Resort and Village, on Fraser Island

Lone Pine Koala Sanctuary, in Brisbane

Magnetic Mango, budget hotel on Magnetic Island

Mossman Gorge, in Mossman

O'Reilly's Rainforest Guesthouse, in the Gold Coast Hinterland

Palazzo Versace, hotel in Southport

Red Ochre Grill, in Cairns

Sabai Sabai, restaurant in Sunshine Beach

Silky Oaks Lodge and Restaurant, in Mossman

Skyrail Rainforest Cableway, in Smithfield

Spirit House, restaurant in Yandina

Vineyard Cottages and Café, in Ballandean

Whitsunday Moorings Bed and Breakfast, in Airlie Beach

So many wonderful hotels, restaurants, nightclubs, and shops can be found in Queensland that there's not enough space to list them all on this page. To see what Fodor's editors and contributors highly recommend, please look for the black stars as you leaf through this chapter.

Updated by
Alia Levine

A FUSION OF FLORIDA, LAS VEGAS, AND THE CARIBBEAN, Queensland attracts crowd lovers and escapists alike. Name your outdoor pleasure and you'll probably find it here, whether you want to soak in the Coral Sea, stroll from cabana to casino with your favorite cocktail, or cruise rivers and rain forests with crocs and other intriguing creatures of the tropics.

At 1,727,999 square km (667,180 square mi) and more than four times the size of California, Queensland has enormous geographic variety. Its eastern seaboard stretches 5,200 km (3,224 mi)—about the distance from Rome to Cairo—from the subtropical Gold Coast to the wild and steamy rain forests of the far north. Up until the 1980s the northern tip and the Cape York Peninsula had not yet been fully explored, and even today crocodiles still claim a human victim once in a while. Away from the coastal sugar and banana plantations, west of the Great Dividing Range, Queensland looks as arid and dust-blown as any other part of Australia's interior. Few paved roads cross this semidesert, and, as in the Red Centre, communication with remote farms is mostly by radio and air. Not surprisingly, most of the state's 3.6 million inhabitants reside on the coast.

Local license plates deem Queensland the "Sunshine State," a sort of Australian Florida—a laid-back stretch of beaches and sun where many Australians head for their vacations. The state has actively promoted tourism, and such areas as the Gold Coast in the south and Cairns in the north have exploded into mini-Miamis, complete with high-rise buildings, casinos, and beachfront amusements. The major attraction for Australians and foreign tourists alike is the Great Barrier Reef, the 1,900-km (1,178-mi) ecological masterpiece that supports thousands of animal species. With such an abundance of marine life, it's not surprising that Queensland is a popular fishing spot. Cairns and Lizard Island in the far north are renowned for big-game fishing; black marlin can weigh in at more than a half ton. For more information on the reef, an integral part of any trip to the state, *see* Chapter 8.

Queensland was thrust into the spotlight with the Commonwealth Games in 1982 and World Expo '88. In 2000, Brisbane (*briz*-bin) and surrounding areas were used as training bases by several nations before the Sydney Olympics, and Olympic soccer matches were held at the world-famous Gabba—Queensland's center for cricket and Australian Rules Football. In 2001, the city hosted the Goodwill Games, the biggest multisport invitational of its kind in the world, making Brisbane the first city outside of the United States and Russia to hold the event. Such big-name competitions have exposed Brisbane to the wider world and helped bring the city, along with other provincial capitals, to full-fledged social and cultural maturity. Consequently, Queensland is a vibrant place to visit, and Sunshine Staters are far more likely to be city kids who work in modern offices than stereotypical "bushies" who work the land. Whatever their background, Queenslanders are known for their friendliness and hospitality. As with so many other lands blessed with hot weather and plenty of sunshine, the pace of life here is relaxed.

Exploring Queensland

Queensland is the huge northeast section of the Australian continent that stretches from the northern point of the Cape York Peninsula south through Brisbane and Lamington National Park. The Great Barrier Reef parallels most of the state's edge, all the way south to Hervey Bay, but there are many other underwater sites to explore even just around Brisbane. A coastal road makes for easy travel between the major cities of Brisbane, Townsville, Cairns, and Port Douglas, as well as the little towns that are jumping-off points to such vacation spots as Fraser Island, the Whitsundays, and Magnetic Island. Vast distances between major hubs make flying the best option between mainland cities and to the off-shore resorts if you're short on time. Otherwise, the drive along the coastal route is gorgeous, with hundreds of opportunities for boat journeys out to the Great Barrier Reef and its islands.

The southern end of the state bordering New South Wales is known as the Gold Coast, where sprawling beach towns mimic Miami Beach and Waikiki. North of Brisbane is the quieter Sunshine Coast, where you can kick back on nearly deserted beaches or take four-wheel-drive expeditions into beautiful rain forests. The northern Cape York Peninsula is all tropical terrain, where you can hike and camp in the jungle to the sounds of wild birds—and the grunts of enormous crocodiles. Don't dismiss the western hinterlands, either, where mountains stretch into the central deserts that border the country's Northern Territory and South Australia. Here, the stark, dusty landscape, rushing rivers, and roads with such names as The Adventure Way beckon hardy travelers who truly wish to get off the beaten path and experience Australia at its most challenging.

About the Restaurants

After only a few days in Queensland, you'll find that the concept of specialized rural cuisines is virtually unknown here. Steak and seafood predominate once you leave city limits behind. Brisbane, however, has its share of new, Mediterranean-Asian–influenced menus, and in Noosa people argue about dishes and spices and the merits of the special local ingredients of "Noosa Cuisine" with a fervor that others reserve for horse races or football.

WHAT IT COSTS In Australian Dollars				
$$$$	**$$$**	**$$**	**$**	**¢**
RESTAURANTS over $50	$36–$50	$21–$35	$10–$20	under $10

Restaurant prices are per person for a main course at dinner.

About the Hotels

Queensland accommodations range from rain-forest lodges, Outback pubs, colonial "Queenslander" bed-and-breakfasts, and backpacker hostels to deluxe beachside resorts and big-city hotels. The luxury resorts are clustered around the major tourist areas of Cairns, the islands, and the Gold Coast. In the smaller coastal towns, accommodation is mostly in motels and bed-and-breakfasts.

WHAT IT COSTS In Australian Dollars				
$$$$	**$$$**	**$$**	**$**	**¢**
HOTELS over $300	$201–$300	$151–$200	$100–$150	under $100

Hotel prices are for two people in a standard double room in high season, in the European Plan (with no meals) unless otherwise noted.

When to Visit Queensland

North of Cairns, the best time for visiting is May to September, when the daily maximum temperature averages around 27°C (80°F) and the water is comfortably warm. During the wet season up there, from about December through March, expect monsoon conditions. Elsewhere in the state, the tropical coast is besieged from October through April by deadly box jellyfish and the tiny transparent *Irukandji*, which make ocean

**If you have
3 days**

Fly into ▣ **Cairns** and take a boat out to one of the reef islands for a day, then head up to ▣ **Cape Tribulation** for the next two days to take in the sights and sounds of the rain forest. If you'd rather have a Miami Beach–style trip, fly into ▣ **Brisbane** and head straight for the glitzy **Gold Coast,** overnighting in ▣ **Surfers Paradise.** You could end the spree with a final night and day in ▣ **Lamington National Park** for its sub-tropical wilderness and bird life.

**If you have
5 days**

Spend three days on shore and two days on the reef. Stay the first night in ▣ **Brisbane,** then head up the **Sunshine Coast** for a hike up one of the **Glass House Mountains** ⑯ on the way to ▣ **Noosa Heads.** ㉘ Apart from beach and surf time, take in the Sunshine Coast's monument to kitsch, **Big Pineapple** ㉒ and indulge in one of their famous ice-cream sundaes. Then make your way back to Brisbane for a flight to ▣ **Cairns** and either a boat to the reef or a drive to the **rain forest** north of Cairns for cruising the rivers, listening to the jungle, relaxing on the beach, and looking into the maw of a crocodile.

**If you have
7 or
more
days**

Unless you're keen on seeing everything, limit yourself to a couple of areas, such as **Brisbane,** its surrounding **Sunshine and Gold Coasts,** and the rain forests **north from Cairns,** and take three to four days in each—Queensland's warm climate is conducive to slowing down. Extended stays will also allow you to take a four-wheel-drive trip all the way to the top of **Cape York Peninsula** from **Cairns,** go for overnight bushwalks in national parks, spend a few days on a **dive boat** exploring islands and reefs north of Cairns, trek inland to the Outback's **Carnarvon National Park** and **Undara lava tubes,** take the **Matilda Highway** through the Outback, or just lie back and soak in the heat.

---

swimming impossible. Because of school holidays, sea- and reef-side Queensland tends to fill up around Christmas and into January. When making travel plans, remember that there is no daylight saving time in the state; consequently, summertime air schedules can be confusing.

BRISBANE

Brisbane was founded as a penal colony for prisoners who had committed crimes after their arrival in Australia. The waterway across which the city sprawls was discovered by two escaped convicts in 1823, and the penal settlement was established on its banks the following year, 32 km (20 mi) from Moreton Bay.

Few historic buildings have survived the wrecker's ball, and today's city is very much a product of enthusiastic and ongoing development. Far surpassing the architecture are the open spaces: Brisbane is beautifully landscaped, brimming with jacarandas, tulip trees, flame trees, oleanders, frangipani, and the ever-stunning bougainvillea. In summer the city broils, and although the climate is pleasant at other times of the year, there is never any doubt that this is a subtropical region.

Many of Brisbane's inner suburbs have places to find fabulous food and quieter accommodations. Most are only a 5- to 10-minute drive or a 15- to 20-minute walk from the city center, a cheap cab or bus ride. Fortitude Valley combines Brisbane's Chinatown with a cosmopolitan influx of clubs, restaurants, and boutiques. Spring Hill has several high-quality accommodations, and suburbs such as Paddington, New Farm, and the West End in South Brisbane are full of restaurants and bars.

Brisbane is also a convenient base from which to explore the Sunshine Coast, the Gold Coast, and Surfers Paradise. From here, you can also reach the stunning, mountainous hinterlands (with their cooler climates), as well as the islands of Moreton Bay. All are at most a couple of hours' drive away from the city center.

Exploring Brisbane

City Center

Brisbane's inner-city landmarks—a combination of Victorian, Edwardian, and slick high-tech architecture—are best explored on foot. Most of them lie within the triangle formed by Ann Street and the bends of the Brisbane River. Hint: The streets running toward the river are named after female (British) royalty, and those streets running parallel to the river are named after male royalty.

Numbers in the text correspond to numbers in the margin and on the Brisbane map.

a good walk

Start at **St. John's Anglican Cathedral** ❶ ☞, near the corner of Wharf and Ann streets. Like so many other grand edifices in Australia, this building was never completed. Inside the cathedral grounds, look for the Deanery, where the proclamation declaring Queensland separate from New South Wales was read in 1859.

Walk southeast along Wharf Street, across Queen Street, south on Eagle Street, and southwest on Elizabeth Street to **Old St. Stephen's Church** ❷, which stands in the shadow of St. Stephen's Catholic Cathedral. Both buildings are in Gothic Revival style.

One block northwest of the church, and worlds away in terms of style, is the **National Bank Building** ❸, on Queen Street. Note the doors and interior of this classical palazzo. Continue southwest along Queen Street for one block to **MacArthur Chambers** ❹, General Douglas MacArthur's main Pacific office during World War II and one of Brisbane's earliest office blocks, now housing **Dymocks,** one of Australia's largest chain bookstores, and **MacArthur Central Mall.**

At the corner of Elizabeth and Edward streets, head northwest along Edward Street and turn right onto Adelaide Street. On the left look for **Anzac Square and the Shrine of Remembrance** ❺, built in memory of Australian casualties in World War I. The circular Doric Greek Revival cenotaph is particularly handsome. The lawns around the memorial are a good place to take a break.

Return to Edward Street and head northwest to Wickham Terrace. Turn left and follow the street as it curves to the **Old Windmill** ❻. This is one of only two remaining convict-built buildings from the days when Brisbane was a penal settlement, called Moreton Bay, set up to take Sydney's particularly recalcitrant convicts.

Back on Edward Street, walk two blocks southeast and turn right onto Adelaide Street. Past David Jones department store and abutting King George Square is the classical, bell-towered **Brisbane City Hall** ❼. Consider taking the lift to the bell tower for great views of the city.

7

Diving

Cairns makes a great base for divers. The cognoscenti may argue about whether the Great Barrier Reef or the Red Sea provides better diving, but the fact remains that the reef is one of the certified wonders of the world.

Ecotourism

Guided rain-forest nature walks in the Gold Coast Hinterland, among other places, provide the opportunity to experience first-hand Queensland's unique flora and fauna while learning a little something about it.

Fishing

If you're a serious deep-sea angler, head to Cairns. Scores of char-ter boats leave the city in pursuit of black marlin, tuna, and reef fish.

The Outback

Follow the Matilda Highway, Queensland's very own Route 66. This meandering roadway stretches from the coastal town of Rockhampton through the pioneer gemfield towns of Sapphire and Rubyvale, deep into the state's Outback, where you can meet real Crocodile Dundee types and drink a beer in a pub with the locals.

Parks

From the varied ecosystems of Lamington National Park on the New South Wales Border, to the gorges and Aboriginal rock paintings of Carnarvon National Park northwest of Brisbane, to the rain forests of Daintree north of Cairns, Queensland has one of the most extensive and organized park systems in Australia.

Reef Visits

Snorkeling, scuba diving, and glass-bottom boat trips on the Great Barrier Reef are essential parts of any trip to Queensland.

Wild Queensland

If you have the time, an explorer's curiosity, or just wish to see one of the world's last wild jungles, take a trip north from Cairns. The remaining pockets of ancient, untouched wilderness that warrant the area's listing as a World Heritage Site provide one of the most archetypal Australian adventures you can have.

From City Hall, walk over to the Queen Street Mall between George and Edward streets for a choice of places to grab lunch or a drink. There's often free entertainment at lunch hour.

Head southwest to George Street and the **Treasury Building** 8, alias the Conrad Treasury Casino. Walk southeast on William Street, which runs behind the Treasury Building, to the **Old Commissariat Store** 9, which is the city's other surviving convict-built structure. Today it houses the Royal Historical Society of Queensland along with its museum and library. Farther along William Street, turn left onto Margaret Street and then right onto George Street. The **Mansions on George Street** 10, built of brick and sandstone just before the turn of the 20th century, are former town houses now occupied by offices, a restaurant, a bookshop, and the National Trust gift shop.

For a break from the city streets, cross Alice Street and on your right will be the splendid French Renaissance **Parliament House** 11. If Queens-

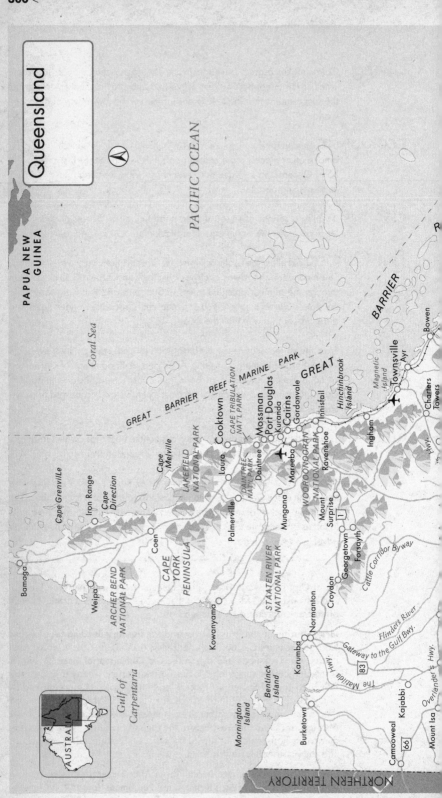

Queensland

PAPUA NEW GUINEA

PACIFIC OCEAN

Coral Sea

Gulf of Carpentaria

AUSTRALIA

NORTHERN TERRITORY

GREAT BARRIER REEF MARINE PARK

CAPE TRIBULATION NAT'L PARK

GREAT BARRIER R

Cape Grenville
Iron Range
Cape Direction
Bamaga
Weipa
Coen
Cape Melville
LAKEFIELD NATIONAL PARK
ARCHER BEND NATIONAL PARK
CAPE YORK PENINSULA
Kowanyama
Palmerville
Laura
Cooktown
DAINTREE NAT'L PARK
Daintree
Mossman
Port Douglas
Kuranda
Cairns
Gordonvale
Mareeba
Mungana
WOOROONOORAN NATIONAL PARK
Innisfail
Ravenshoe
Mount Surprise
Hinchinbrook Island
Ingham
Magnetic Island
Townsville
Ayr
Bowen
Charters Towers
Hwy.
STAATEN RIVER NATIONAL PARK
Normanton
Croydon
Georgetown
Forsayth
Cattle Corridor Byway
Karumba
Flinders River
Gateway to the Gulf Bwy.
The Matilda Hwy.
83
Bentinck Island
Mornington Island
Burketown
Camooweal
Kajabbi
Mount Isa
Overlander's Hwy.
66

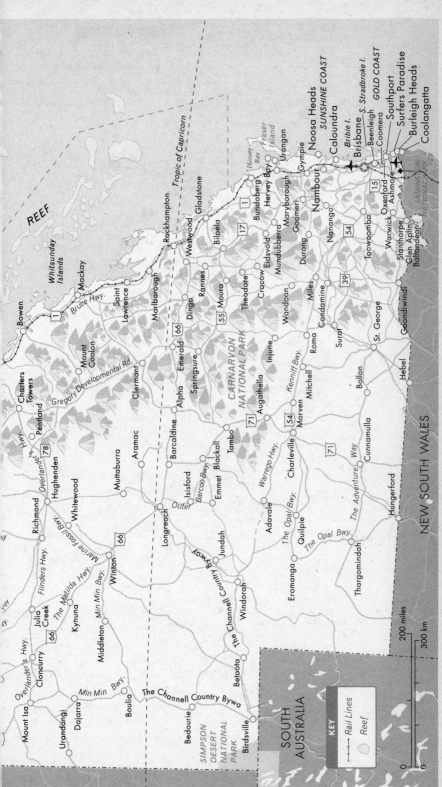

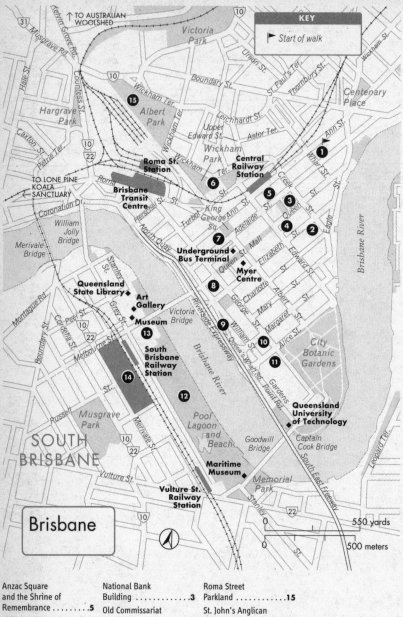

KEY

▶ Start of walk

Brisbane

550 yards

500 meters

land's Parliament is in session, you can look in on the proceedings from a visitor's gallery. Now step into the City Botanic Gardens, which stretch over to the river. There are some venerable trees in the garden that are well worth extending your walk to see, as well as a charming restaurant-cum-café tucked away at the back of the property.

From the south end of the Botanic Gardens, by the Queensland University of Technology campus, the pedestrian- and cycle-only Goodwill Bridge crosses the Brisbane River. Across the river lies **South Bank Parklands** ⑫, an enormously popular destination for Brisbane folk and visitors alike. It contains a sprawling beach lagoon, weekend markets, cafés, restaurants, and plenty of places for a picnic or to sit and relax. Adjacent to South Bank Parklands is the **Queensland Cultural Centre** ⑬, extending for a block on either side of Melbourne Street. Explore the Queensland Art Gallery or the Queensland Museum's natural history exhibits, then pick up a souvenir of your visit at one of the shops. At South Bank's northwest corner is the imposing **Brisbane Convention and Exhibition Centre** ⑭.

Follow Melbourne Street northeast and walk back to the heart of the city across Victoria Bridge. Head northwest along George Street until you hit Roma Street, which will lead you to the **Roma Street Parkland** ⑮.

TIMING   Without pausing at any of the attractions, this walk takes about two hours and includes a hike up a small hill to get to the Old Windmill. South Bank Parklands will require the most exploring, especially if you visit when the markets are operating. During Brisbane's blistering summer it's a good idea to carry water, as the humidity can be draining. Winter is quite pleasant. The boardwalk along the river at South Bank is a great place to enjoy the city views.

WHAT TO SEE   **Anzac Square and the Shrine of Remembrance.** Walking paths through Anzac ❺ Square stretch across green lawns, directing all eyes toward the Doric Greek Revival shrine, constructed of Queensland sandstone. An eternal flame burns within the shrine for Australian soldiers who died in World War I. Equally spine-tingling is the **Shrine of Memories,** a crypt below the flame that stores soil samples labeled "forever Australian"; the soil was collected from battlefields on which Australian soldiers perished. On April 25, Anzac Day, a moving dawn service is held here in remembrance of Australia's fallen soldiers. ⊠ *Adelaide St. between Edward and Creek Sts., City Center* ☒ *Free* ⊙ *Shrine weekdays 11–3.*

❼   **Brisbane City Hall.** Once referred to as the "million-pound town hall" because of the massive funds poured into its construction, this community center built in 1930 has been a major symbol of Brisbane's civic pride. Visitors and locals "ooh" and "aah" at the grand pipe organ and circular concert hall inside this substantial Italianate structure. Other features include an observation platform affording superb city views and a ground-floor museum and art gallery, where you can tour both the building and its huge clock tower, home to one of Australia's largest civic clocks. ⊠ *King George Sq., Adelaide St., City Center* ☎ *07/3403–8888* ☒ *Free* ⊙ *Mon.–Fri. 10–3, Sat. 10–2.*

⑭   **Brisbane Convention and Exhibition Centre.** This imposing, modern building covers 4½ acres and is equipped with four exhibition halls, a 4,000-seat Great Hall, and a Grand Ballroom. ⊠ *Glenelg and Merivale Sts., South Brisbane* ☎ *1800/036308* ⊕ *www.brisconex.com.au.*

❹   **MacArthur Chambers.** As commander-in-chief of the Allied Forces fighting in the Pacific, General Douglas MacArthur came to Australia from the Philippines, leaving the Japanese in control there with his famous

vow, "I shall return." This present-day bookstore, mall, and apartment block was MacArthur's World War II headquarters. ✉ *Queen St., entrance at 201 Edward St., City Center.*

need a break?

Duck around the corner from MacArthur Chambers, taking a right on Elizabeth Street, and stop in at the locally owned **American Bookstore.** Work your way to the back, where you'll find ✕ **Café Libri,** a small, well-stocked café serving coffee, savory cakes (try the Dutch Apple), and extravagantly filled sandwiches. Sample the traditional English afternoon tea sandwiches: paper-thin slices of cucumber, watercress, ham, and smoked salmon on white bread—with the crusts cut off, of course. ✉ *173 Elizabeth St.* ☎ *07/ 3229–4677* ☐ *AE, DC, MC, V* ⊘ *Closed Sun.*

⑩ **Mansions on George Street.** Constructed in 1890 as six fashionable town houses, these splendid Victorian terrace homes are well worth a visit. The exterior is garnished with elegant, wrought-iron lace trim, while inside are the National Trust gift shop, restaurants, bookshops, and professional offices. ✉ *40 George St., City Center.*

❸ **National Bank Building.** Brisbane's National Bank went up in 1885 and is one of the country's finest Italian Renaissance–style structures. Aside from the majestic entrance hall with its ornate ceilings and eye-catching dome, the most interesting features are the front doors, which were crafted from a single cedar trunk. ✉ *308 Queen St., City Center* ⊘ *Weekdays 9–4.*

❾ **Old Commissariat Store.** Convict-built in 1829, this was the first stone building in Brisbane, erected over the location of the city's original timber wharf. It has served variously as a customs house, storehouse, and immigrants' shelter and is currently the headquarters of the Royal Historical Society of Queensland. ✉ *115 William St., City Center* ☎ *07/ 3221–4198* ☐ *A$4* ⊘ *Tues.–Sat. 10–4.*

❷ **Old St. Stephen's Church.** The tiny old 1850 church that adjoins St. Stephen's Catholic Cathedral is Brisbane's oldest house of worship, a particularly fine example of Gothic Revival architecture. The church is believed to have been designed by Augustus Pugin, a noted English architect who designed much of London's Houses of Parliament. The church is not open to the public. ✉ *Elizabeth St. near Creek St., City Center.*

❻ **Old Windmill.** This is the oldest of the two remaining convict buildings in Brisbane. The poorly designed 1828 windmill never worked very well. Whenever the wind died down, convicts were forced to power a treadmill to crush grain for the colony's bread, thus tagging this landmark the "Tower of Torture." When fire erupted across the city in 1864, scorching almost everything in its path, the windmill survived with only minimal damage. Stripped of its blades, the tower now looks a lot like a lighthouse. The interior of the building is not open to the public. ✉ *Wickham Park, Wickham Terr., City Center.*

⑪ **Parliament House.** Opened in 1868, this splendid stone-clad, French Renaissance building, with a Mount Isa–copper roof, earned its colonial designer a meager 200-guinea salary. A legislative annex was added in the late 1970s. The interior is fitted with polished timber, brass, and frosted and engraved glass. On weekdays, building tours take place. Afterward, wander through the adjacent **City Botanic Gardens.** ✉ *George and Alice Sts., City Center* ☎ *07/3406–7111* ☐ *Free* ⊘ *Weekdays 9–5; tour Tues., Wed., Thurs., 10:30 and 2:30; Fri. on request, last tour at 4:15.*

> **need a break?** The **Queen Street Mall**, a two-block pedestrian boulevard, stretches from George Street to Edward Street. It has a fine selection of shops and eateries. The **David Jones** department store (on Queen Street Mall) has a well-stocked food hall, where you can assemble your own picnic to eat in nearby **King George Square**.

⑬ Queensland Cultural Centre. The Queensland Art Gallery, Queensland Museum, State Library, Performing Arts Complex, and a host of restaurants, cafés, and shops are all here. On weekdays at noon there are free tours of the Performing Arts Complex. Backstage peeks at the 2,000-seat Concert Hall and Cremorne Theatre are often included. ✉ *Melbourne St., South Brisbane* ☎ *07/3840–7303 art gallery, 07/3840–7555 museum, 07/3840–7810 library, 13–6246 Performing Arts Complex* 🎫 *Free* ☉ *Gallery daily 10–5, museum daily 9:30–5, library Mon.–Thurs. 10–8 and Fri.–Sun. 10–5.*

⑮ Roma Street Parkland. At the world's largest subtropical garden within a city, you can wander through a maze garden or the Lilly Pilly Garden, which displays native evergreen rain-forest plants; past a huge lake; and along forest paths. Unique Queensland artwork is on display throughout the park. Pack a picnic or grab lunch at the Tomoko café. ✉ *1 Parkland Blvd., City Center* ☎ *07/3006–4545* ⊕ *www.romastreetparkland. com* ☉ *Daily 24 hrs.*

▶ **❶ St. John's Anglican Cathedral.** Built in 1901 with porphyry rock, this is a fine example of Gothic Revival architecture. Guided tours are available on weekdays. Inside the cathedral grounds is the **Deanery,** which predates the construction of the cathedral by almost 50 years. This building, originally constructed as a doctor's residence, became a temporary government house when Queensland was proclaimed a separate colony from New South Wales in 1859. The proclamation of separation was read from the building's east balcony on June 6, 1859. ✉ *373 Ann St., City Center* ☎ *No phone* ☉ *Guided cathedral tours weekdays at 10 and 2.*

⑫ South Bank Parklands. One of the most appealing urban parks in Australia, and the former site of Brisbane's World Expo '88, the 40-acre complex includes gardens, a Maritime Museum, an IMAX theater, foot- and cycling paths, a sprawling beach lagoon (complete with lifeguards), and a Nepalese-style carved-wood pagoda. You'll also find shops and restaurants, as well as excellent views of the city. The parklands, which host Friday-night Lantern Markets and a weekend Crafts Village, lie alongside the river just south of the Queensland Cultural Centre. ✉ *Grey St., South Brisbane* ☎ *07/3867–2000, 07/3867–2020 for entertainment information* 🎫 *Maritime Museum A$5* ☉ *Parklands daily 5 AM–midnight, Lantern Markets Fri. 5–10 PM, Crafts Village Sat. 11–5 and Sun. 9–5.*

❽ Treasury Building. This massive Edwardian baroque edifice overlooking the river stands on the site of the officers' quarters and military barracks from the original penal settlement. Bronze figurative statuary surrounds the structure. Constructed between 1885 and 1889, the former treasury reopened as **Conrad Treasury Casino.** In addition to floors of game rooms, the Casino also houses five restaurants and seven bars. ✉ *William and Elizabeth Sts., City Center* ☎ *07/3306–8888* ☉ *Daily 24 hrs.*

Around Brisbane

🐾 **Australian Woolshed.** In a one-hour stage show, eight rams from the major sheep breeds found in Australia perform, giving an insight into the dramatically different appearances—and personalities—of sheep. There's also a koala sanctuary, where for A$13 you can be photographed holding a koala. Also on-site are water slides, miniature golf, an animal nursery, and a crafts shop. Barbecue lunches are available. Take the train or a taxi (A$20) to Ferny Grove Station (about a 10-minute walk from the station). ⊠ *148 Samford Rd., Ferny Hills* ☎ *07/3872–1100* ⊕ *www. auswoolshed.com.au* ◪ *A$16.50* ☉ *Daily 8:30–5; shows daily at 9:30, 11, 1, and 2:30.*

🅒 **Lone Pine Koala Sanctuary.** Queensland's most famous fauna park, FodorsChoice founded in 1927, claims to be the oldest animal sanctuary in the world.
★ The real attraction for most people are the koalas, although emus, wombats, and kangaroos also reside here. You can pet and feed some of the animals, and for A$13 you can have a quick cuddle and a photo with a koala. The MV *Mirimar* (☎ 07/3221–0300), a historic 1930s ferry, travels daily to the Lone Pine Koala Sanctuary from North Quay at the Victoria Bridge in Brisbane proper at 10 and returns at 2:50. The A$25 round-trip ferry fee includes entry to the park. Buses No. 430 from the Myer Centre and No. 445 from outside City Hall also stop here. ⊠ *Jesmond Rd., Fig Tree Pocket* ☎ *07/3378–1366* ⊕ *www.koala.net* ◪ *A$15* ☉ *Daily 8:30–5.*

Where to Eat

Australian

$–$$ ✕ **The Breakfast Creek Hotel.** A Brisbane institution, this enormous hotel perched right on the wharf at Breakfast Creek is renowned for its superb steaks. Just choose your cut, the method of cooking, and a sauce to go with it. Vegetarians also have options, such as spinach-and-feta lasagna and several kinds of salad. ⊠ *2 Kingsford Smith Dr., Albion* ☎ *07/3262–5988* ☰ *AE, DC, MC, V.*

Contemporary

$$–$$$$ ✕ **Siggi's at The Port Office.** Socialites rub shoulders with visiting celebrities and high-powered businesspeople at this comfortable no-smoking restaurant in the Stamford Plaza hotel. The service is impeccable, and the dining and bar areas make full use of the architecture of the 19th-century Port of Brisbane Office in which they are placed. Each month a set menu based on a theme such as seafood or Greek cooking supplements the Continental menu, which changes frequently. Look for cappuccino of lobster bisque with chestnuts and porcini dust, or the glazed truffle honey double roasted duckling over Lyonnaise-scented potatoes, a garlic confit, and a reduction sauce with truffle oil. Desserts are just as worthy. ⊠ *Edward and Margaret Sts., City Center* ☎ *07/ 3221–4555* ◬ *Reservations essential* ☰ *AE, DC, MC, V* ☉ *Closed Sun.–Mon. No lunch.*

Eclectic

$$–$$$ ✕ **Oxley's on the River.** By day the dining room at the only restaurant in Brisbane built right on the river is sunny and has a bird's-eye view of river traffic; by night, light from the city and the moon dimple the water and lend an intimate, romantic feel. The sirloin steak with mustard and red-wine jus, Queensland barramundi, mud crab, and a whole reef fish stuffed with rice, shallots, and ginger are all rightly famed. Oxley's is a five-minute taxi ride from the city center. ⊠ *330 Coronation Dr., Milton* ☎ *07/3368–1866* ☰ *AE, DC, MC, V.*

Italian

$$ ✕ **Il Centro.** No expense has been spared in fitting this handsome Eagle Street Pier eatery with gleaming wood floors, terra-cotta tiles, enormous windows that take advantage of the river view, and covered outdoor seating. Wondrous aromas spill out of an open kitchen into the stylish din-

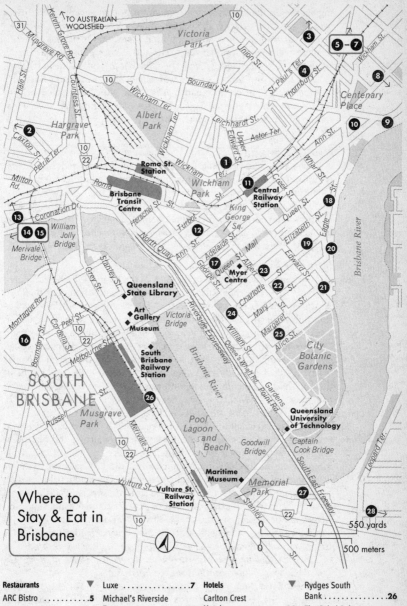

ing room. On the seasonal menu watch for potato gnocchi with Torres Strait lobster tail, sand-crab lasagna, and duck with tarragon jus, mustard fruits, and caramelized sweet-potato frittata. Or try the Moreton bay bug grilled with summer vegetables and a sweet potato salsa. Throw your diet out the window and try *semifreddo* (chilled dessert) with varying fruits and sauces, or the warm chocolate tart with gelato and caramel sauce. The predominantly Australian wine list is excellent, and there's a vegetarian menu. ⊠ *Eagle Street Pier, 1 Eagle St., City Center* ☎ *07/3221–6090* ⊕ *www.ilcentro.com.au* ⊟ *AE, DC, MC, V* ☺ *No lunch Sat.*

Mediterranean

$–$$ ✕ **Grape Wine and Food Bar.** Creative fare such as roasted duck breast with fondant potatoes, beet purée, and caramelized radicchio has people returning again and again to this bar in the hopping New Farm district. If you just want a snack, try the grazing menu, which holds such treats as sand crab cakes on a blue-cheese fromaggio. The superb wine list has plenty of varieties by the glass, and exotic cheeses are available. ⊠ *85 Merthyr Rd., New Farm* ☎ *07/3358–6500* ⊟ *AE, DC, MC, V.*

Modern Australian

$$–$$$ ✕ **Armstrongs.** Tucked away in the back of the boutique Inchcolm Hotel, well-known local chef Russell Armstrong creates French-influenced Australian dishes for serious foodies. The small, ground-floor restaurant only seats about 30, but lucky diners are treated to seared Queensland scallops on crisp fried potatoes, beanettes, and a fennel cream sauce; or loin of Victorian lamb carved over a gallette of Moroccan-spiced couscous with sheep's yogurt and coriander. Another meal includes warm salad of roasted veal sweetbreads, smoked hock, and confit of duck with *salade niçoise* (salad with egg, tuna, green beans, olives, and tomatoes). ⊠ *73 Wickham Terr., City Center* ☎ *07/3832–4566* ⊟ *AE, DC, MC, V* ☺ *Closed Sun. No lunch Sat.*

$$ ✕ **e'cco.** The excellent food in this petite dining place has earned a loyal
Fodor'sChoice following. The white-columned entry leads into a maroon-and-black din-
★ ing room with an open bar and kitchen, where the menu lists a wide range of seasonally changing, Mediterranean- and Asian-inspired dishes using local produce and beautifully presented. The field mushrooms on olive toast with arugula, truffle oil, and lemon is superb, as is the seared Atlantic salmon with salad of green papaya, coriander, chili, lime, and cashews. For dessert, try the upside-down pear-and-caramel cake with vanilla ice cream, and pay close attention to the bartender's suggestions of accompanying wines. ⊠ *100 Boundary St., City Center* ☎ *07/ 3831–8344* ⊕ *www.eccobistro.com* ⌂ *Reservations essential* ⊟ *AE, DC, MC, V* ☺ *Closed Sun.–Mon. No lunch Sat.*

$$ ✕ **Summit Restaurant.** Perched beside the lookout on the slopes of Mt. Coot-tha, this restaurant affords unbeatable views of the city, especially at night. The original building dates from 1925 and has been patronized by such lights and dignitaries as Katharine Hepburn, Princess Alexandra, and King Peter of Yugoslavia. Treat yourself to grilled kangaroo loin on rosemary skewers followed by iced mango-and-coconut parfait with mango coulis and crisp macaroons. Taxi fare to the Summit from the city is about A$15. ⊠ *Sir Samuel Griffith Dr.* ☎ *07/ 3369–9922* ⊟ *AE, DC, MC, V.*

$$ ✕ **Telegraph Restaurant.** The old, ornate General Post Office of Fortitude Valley houses two bars, a wine cellar–cum–café, and this restaurant, where meals have a Mediterranean kick while still retaining the flavors of Brisbane's subtropical climate. Try the corn-fed chicken with date and pistachio couscous, stewed tomatoes, and tahini yogurt; or fresh prawns with red papaya, toasted coconut, green chili, peanut, and lime. Finish

with the cherry frangipani tart with cream and maple syrup. The bistro's modern, minimalist decor makes use of blacks, browns, reds, and creams. ⊠ *740 Ann St., Fortitude Valley* ☎ *07/3252–1322* ⊕ *www. gpohotel.com.au* ⊟ *AE, DC, MC, V.*

$–$$ ✕ **Luxe.** This casual restaurant–cum–bar serves delicious tapas-style starters and modern Australian meals with a Euro-Mediterranean edge. Sample smoked sardines with kipfler potatoes, French beans, and a grain mustard dressing; or oxtail ravioli with wild mushrooms, baby spinach *duxelles* (chopped mushrooms, shallots, and onions sautéed in butter), and sweet port eschallots. Stacked char-grilled asparagus and artichokes with Parmesan crackling and tomato jelly is one of the many vegetarian options. The wine and cocktail lists are impressive. Glass doors open to allow dining to spill outside onto the pavement. ⊠ *39 James St., New Farm* ☎ *07/3854–0671* ⊟ *AE, DC, MC, V.*

★ ¢–$ ✕ **Freestyle.** Tucked away in the inner-city suburb of Rosalie, this café and gallery is known for its artfully designed sundaes (served in vases) and such classic Australian dishes as sticky date pudding. You may also arrive in time for a tea-leaf reading, a tea-tasting, or the monthly *soirée*, where owner Martin Duncan holds court amidst live music, flamboyant flowers, and modern Australian artwork. An extensive assortment of teas and coffees, as well as a large, predominantly Australian and New Zealand wine list is also available. ⊠ *19 Nash St., Rosalie* ☎ *07/3876–2288* ⊕ *www.freestyle-online.com* ⊟ *AE, DC, MC, V* ♥ *No dinner.*

¢–$ ✕ **The Gunshop Cafe.** Named for the gun shop it once was, this West End café is one of many good places to eat in a one-mile radius. Although you can still see where the guns used to hang on the unfinished brick walls, there is now a constantly changing exhibit of local art. Tin buckets of lilies fill the arches separating the dining area from the open kitchen. Watch for the grilled haloumi cheese with apple, green beans, walnuts, and balsamic-drizzled mesclun greens; or fish of the day with lemon risotto, asparagus, crab oil, and roast lemon. Finish with a slice of fig, pistachio, and ginger tart. Dine at the wooden tables indoors, or in the back garden, either on the deck or amid the ferns. ⊠ *53 Mollison St., West End* ☎ *07/3844–2241* ⊟ *AE, DC, MC, V* ♥ *Closed Mon. and Tues.*

Seafood

★ $$–$$$ ✕ **Pier Nine Restaurant.** The city's most stylish seafood restaurant prepares everything from fish-and-chips to lobsters. Only the best catches from the Northern Territory to Tasmania appear here, and several types of fresh oysters are delivered daily and shucked to order. Try the wok-seared king prawns or the barbecued Moreton Bay bugs if they're available. The sizable Australian wine list has a selection available by the glass. The dining room's glass walls admit plenty of sunshine and afford fine river views. ⊠ *Eagle Street Pier, 1 Eagle St., City Center* ☎ *07/3229–2194* ⊟ *AE, DC, MC, V.*

$$ ✕ **Michael's Riverside Restaurant.** Michael Platsis owns four very different restaurants, all in the Riverside Centre, and the jewel of the bunch is this silver-service establishment. You'll encounter sweeping views of the Brisbane River and the Story Bridge while you enjoy a menu that changes daily and focuses on Queensland seafood. Raspberry Drambuie crème brûlée is one possible dessert. Michael's has what just might be the best wine cellar in town. ⊠ *123 Eagle St., City Center* ☎ *07/ 3832–5522* ⊕ *www.michaelsrestaurant.com.au* ♙ *Reservations essential* ⊟ *AE, DC, MC, V* ♥ *No lunch weekends.*

Thai

¢–$ ✕ **Caxton Thai.** This traditional Thai restaurant, where you dine between red and yellow walls and amid Thai art and sculptures, is popular with both locals and tourists. The most-requested dish is the pork chop with basil—a bit of Aussie fusion, perhaps? In this otherwise traditional Thai restaurant, you can find a warm Thai salad, a mixture of chicken, prawn, glass noodles, and vegetables. There's a generous vegetarian menu. ⊠ *47B Caxton St., Paddington* 🕾 *07/3367–0300* ⊕ *www.caxtonthai. com.au* 🖃 *AE, DC, MC, V.*

Vietnamese

$–$$ ✕ **The Green Papaya.** The simple dishes here employ traditional North Vietnamese cooking techniques. The selection is less extensive than in most Asian restaurants, but what's served is very good, thus ensuring the restaurant's local popularity. Try grilled chicken with lemon leaves or prawns in coconut juice. The dining room is modest yet bright, with chrome-and-wooden chairs and yellow walls. Lunches are available by appointment on Fridays. ⊠ *898 Stanley St., East Brisbane* 🕾 *07/ 3217–3599* ⊕ *www.greenpapaya.com.au* 🖃 *AE, DC, MC, V* ☉ *Closed Mon. No lunch Sat.–Thurs.*

Where to Stay

★ $$$$ 🏨 **Conrad Treasury Brisbane.** Like the Conrad Treasury Casino one block to the north, this National Heritage–listed hotel represents a beautiful sandstone example of Edwardian baroque architecture. Rooms have antique furniture and large, luxurious bathrooms. The hotel has five very different restaurants to suit all budgets and tastes. ⊠ *130 William St., City Center, 4000* 🕾 *07/3306–8888* 🖷 *07/3306–8880* ⊕ *www.conrad. com.au* ➪ *114 rooms, 16 suites* ♨ *5 restaurants, room service, in-room safes, minibars, refrigerators, gym, sauna, 7 bars, casino, laundry service, business services, free parking* 🖃 *AE, DC, MC, V.*

$$$–$$$$ 🏨 **Sheraton Brisbane Hotel and Towers.** Despite its position above the city's main rail station, this hotel is a quiet and pleasant place to stay. Brass and natural timber complement the travertine marble floor of the mezzanine lobby, and there's a spectacular skylit atrium. Floors 26 through 29 constitute the pricier Towers, where service and comfort are extended to include use of the exclusive Towers Club lounge. Decorated in soft beige and brown tones, the rooms in both sections of the hotel are spacious and elegant, with marble bathrooms. ⊠ *249 Turbot St., City Center, 4000* 🕾 *07/3835–3535* 🖷 *07/3835–4960* ⊕ *www.starwood.com/ sheraton* ➪ *385 rooms, 25 suites* ♨ *3 restaurants, room service, in-room fax, in-room safes, minibars, pool, gym, hair salon, hot tub, massage, sauna, 2 bars, lounge, nightclub, laundry service, business services, meeting room, free parking, no-smoking rooms* 🖃 *AE, DC, MC, V.*

★ $$$–$$$$ 🏨 **Stamford Plaza Brisbane.** On the riverfront next to the City Botanic Gardens, this is arguably Brisbane's finest hotel. The soaring lobby, full of artwork, flower arrangements, and an expanse of natural woods, is warm and inviting. Guest rooms, decorated in neoclassical style in muted yellow and beige, enjoy clear views over the river. The room service menu allows you to choose from the hotel's three restaurants—including its signature restaurant, Siggi's. ⊠ *Edward and Margaret Sts., City Center, 4000* 🕾 *07/3221–1999 or 1800/773700* 🖷 *07/3221–6895 or 1800/773900* ⊕ *www.stamford.com.au* ➪ *232 rooms, 20 suites* ♨ *4 restaurants, room service, in-room fax, pool, gym, sauna, spa, 2 bars, shops, baby-sitting, laundry service, business services, free parking, no-smoking floors* 🖃 *AE, DC, MC, V.*

$–$$$$ 🏨 **Royal Albert Boutique Hotel.** This Heritage-listed building is right in the heart of Brisbane and offers more than you might expect from a standard hotel. Each larger-than-average room has a self-contained kitchen and laundry. The reproduction antique furniture and cream and plum plush carpets add elegant finishing touches. This is a small hotel where staff members are very friendly and take pride in greeting guests by name. There is a licensed brasserie on the ground floor. ⊠ *Elizabeth and Albert Sts., City Center, 4000* ☎ *07/3291–8888, 1800/655054* 🖷 *07/ 3229–7705* ⊕ *www.atlantisproperties.com.au* ⤵ *28 rooms, 25 suites, 3 apartments* ⟁ *Restaurant, kitchenettes, laundry facilities, parking (fee), no-smoking rooms* ☰ *AE, DC, MC, V.*

$–$$$$ 🏨 **The Point Brisbane.** Across the Brisbane River from the central business district, this modern hotel lets guests in many rooms view the city lights from afar. Accommodations range from studios to one- and two-bedroom apartments with fully equipped kitchens and private laundry facilities. The hotel provides a courtesy shuttle bus to the city. ⊠ *21 Lambert St., Kangaroo Point, 4169* ☎ *07/3240–0888 or 1800/088388* 🖷 *07/3392–1155* ⊕ *www.thepointbrisbane.com.au* ⤵ *43 rooms, 3 suites, 60 apartments* ⟁ *Restaurant, room service, tennis court, pool, gym, bar, baby-sitting, dry cleaning, laundry facilities, laundry service, business services, meeting room, travel services, free parking, no-smoking rooms* ☰ *AE, DC, MC, V.*

$$$ 🏨 **Quay West.** This modern hotel opposite Brisbane's Botanic Gardens exudes good taste with pressed-metal ceilings, sandstone columns, hammered-iron decorations, and white louvered shutters. The warm, earthy tones complement the sandstone floors. The suites are fitted with plantation teak furniture and include fully equipped kitchens and laundry facilities. The first floor of the hotel has a tropically landscaped area surrounding the heated pool. Intricately carved early 19th-century teak columns from South Africa support a poolside pergola. ⊠ *132 Alice St., City Center, 4000* ☎ *07/3853–6000 or 1800/672726* 🖷 *07/3853–6060* ⊕ *www.mirvachotels.com.au* ⤵ *74 suites* ⟁ *Restaurant, in-room data ports, in-room fax, kitchens, minibars, TV with movies, pool, gym, sauna, spa, bar, laundry facilities, free parking* ☰ *AE, DC, MC, V.*

$$–$$$ 🏨 **Country Comfort Lennons Hotel.** A feature of Brisbane's skyline for many years, this hotel has a winning location in front of the Queen Street Mall at the river end. Most of the spacious rooms have city views; those on floors 15 to 20 afford river panoramas. The hotel's ground level opens onto the mall. ⊠ *66–76 Queen St., City Center, 4000* ☎ *07/3222–3222* 🖷 *07/3221–9389* ⊕ *www.lennonshotel.com* ⤵ *118 rooms, 34 suites* ⟁ *Restaurant, room service, refrigerators, pool, sauna, spa, 2 bars, baby-sitting, laundry facilities, laundry service, business services, meeting room, travel services, parking (fee)* ☰ *AE, DC, MC, V.*

$$–$$$ 🏨 **The Sebel Suites Brisbane.** The minimalist furnishings here create an uncluttered ambience that is refreshing and elegant. Rooms are decorated in navy, cream, and red with light wood furniture, and the suites have kitchens as well as washers and dryers. Its central city location— two blocks from the Queen Street Mall—is a winning feature. Palettes Brasserie and Bar, a popular dining and bar venue for city workers, serves breakfast, lunch, and dinner. ⊠ *Albert and Charlotte Sts., City Center, 4000* ☎ *07/3224–3500 or 1800/888298* 🖷 *07/3211–0277* ⊕ *www. mirvachotels.com.au* ⤵ *46 rooms, 110 suites* ⟁ *Restaurant, room service, in-room data ports, some kitchenettes, pool, wading pool, sauna, bar, meeting room, parking (fee), no-smoking floors* ☰ *AE, DC, MC, V.*

$–$$$ 🏨 **Rydges South Bank.** Sandwiched between the Brisbane Convention and Exhibition Centre and South Bank Parklands, the Rydges is an excellent choice for business and leisure travelers. The rooms are predominantly olive green and pale yellow and have modern furnishings and computer workstations. Although there is no pool in the complex, the beach at South Bank Parklands is very close. Parking is available, but depending on your accommodations package you may have to pay a fee for it. ✉ *9 Glenelg St., South Brisbane, 4101* ☎ *07/3255–0822* 🖷 *07/3255–0899* ⊕ *www.rydges.com* 🛏 *244 rooms, 61 suites* ⚒ *Restaurant, café, room service, in-room data ports, gym, sauna, spa, 2 bars, laundry service, business services, parking (fee)* 🖃 *AE, DC, MC, V.*

$–$$ 🏨 **Carlton Crest Hotel.** At this hotel, ideally situated opposite City Hall and close to the center of town, two towers surround a central lobby that is elegantly furnished with French-style sofas and carpets. Crest Tower rooms are on the small side, but the bathrooms are spacious. Executive rooms are furnished in earthy tones. Picasso's, on the ground level, serves Mediterranean cuisine. ✉ *Ann and Roma Sts., City Center, 4000* ☎ *07/3229–9111 or 1800/777123* 🖷 *07/3229–9618* ⊕ *www.carltoncrest-brisbane.com.au* 🛏 *432 rooms, 6 suites* ⚒ *2 restaurants, room service, in-room data ports, in-room VCRs, pool, gym, sauna, 3 bars, laundry service, concierge, business services, meeting room, free parking; no-smoking floors* 🖃 *AE, DC, MC, V.*

$–$$ 🏨 **Inchcolm All Suites Hotel.** Converted from Heritage medical chambers, this boutique hotel now serves up doses of personalized service amid intimate oak surroundings. The spacious rooms are fitted with timber louvers, hand-carved fretwork, and cream fabrics. Some one- and two-bedroom suites have spa baths. A lounge chair by the rooftop lilliputian pool is an ideal place to enjoy the Brisbane skyline. Armstrongs restaurant serves French-influenced Australian cuisine. ✉ *73 Wickham Terr., City Center, 4000* ☎ *07/3226–8888* 🖷 *07/3226–8899* ⊕ *www.inchcolmhotel.com.au* 🛏 *35 suites* ⚒ *Restaurant, kitchenettes, pool, bar, free parking* 🖃 *AE, DC, MC, V.*

¢–$ 🏨 **Ridge Haven.** This late 19th-century bed-and-breakfast is for travelers who want to experience suburban Brisbane. In the southern suburb of Annerley, Ridge Haven is still just 4 km (2½ mi) from the center of town. With high ceilings, ornate cornices, and reproduction antiques, the rooms exude both comfort and old-fashioned romance. Breakfast is served in the dining room or on a patio with a view of the suburbs. Proprietors Peter and Morna Cook allow guests to use the kitchen or barbecue for lunch or dinner. Complimentary homemade aromatherapy toiletries are a nice touch. ✉ *374 Annerley Rd., Annerley, 4103* ☎ *07/3391–7702* 🖷 *07/3392–1786* ⊕ *www.uqconnect.net/ridgehaven* 🛏 *3 rooms with shower* ⚒ *Dining room* 🖃 *MC, V* ⊗ *BP.*

¢–$ 🏨 **Thornbury House.** Buttermilk-color walls, polished floors, thick carpets, and wooden furniture give this three-level 19th-century merchant's house a sense of old-world charm. The price includes breakfast, which you can enjoy in the garden courtyard. A more formal sitting room, where you'll find complimentary port on a sideboard, is for quiet evenings. A self-contained apartment is also available on a weekly basis. ✉ *1 Thornbury St., Spring Hill, 4000* ☎ *07/3832–5985* 🖷 *07/3832–7756* ⊕ *www.babs.com.au/thornbury* 🛏 *5 rooms, 1 apartment* 🖃 *AE, MC, V* ⊗ *BP.*

¢ 🏨 **La Torretta.** A 10-minute walk from the Southbank gardens takes you to this sprawling, early 1900s West End Queenslander. There are two simple, comfortable rooms, and a large guest lounge looks out onto a tropical Brisbane garden. The price includes a breakfast of strong Italian coffee with homemade bread and jam. The owners, Charles and Dorothy Colman, speak Italian, French, and German. If you're lucky, you may hear Dorothy singing opera upstairs while you're eating breakfast. ✉ *8 Brereton St., West End 4101* ☎ *07/3846–0846* 🖷 *07/3846–0846* ⊕ *www.users.bigpond.com/colmanwilliams* 🛏 *2 rooms* ⚒ *Dining room, library, free parking* 🖃 *MC, V* ⊗ *CP.*

Nightlife & the Arts

The Arts

The Saturday edition of *The Courier–Mail* newspaper lists concerts, ballet, opera, theater, jazz, and other events. Thursday's paper includes a free *What's On* magazine, which is a comprehensive entertainment guide for Brisbane.

The Brisbane Powerhouse (✉ 119 Lamington St., New Farm ☎ 07/3358–8600 ⊕ www.brisbanepowerhouse.com), built in a former power plant, hosts avant-garde live performances in flexible 200- and 400-seat theaters. Cafés, restaurants, bikeways, boardwalks, and picnic areas complement the funky art space.

At the **Queensland Art Gallery** (✉ Melbourne St., South Brisbane ☎ 07/3840–7333) you can check out interesting permanent and visiting exhibitions.

The **Queensland Performing Arts Complex** (✉ Melbourne St., South Brisbane ☎ 07/3840–7444 or 13–6246 ⊕ www.qpac.com.au), the city's cultural heart, hosts both international and Australian entertainers and performing troupes.

Nightlife

Adrenalin Sports Bar (✉ 127 Charlotte St., City Center ☎ 07/3229–1515) is a large American-style haunt with pool tables, 40 television screens broadcasting sporting events, and a large open bar surrounded by tables and chairs. It's open Sunday through Thursday 11:30 AM–midnight, and until 2:20 AM on Friday and Saturday.

Conrad Treasury Casino (✉ Queen St., City Center ☎ 07/3306–8888)—with a "neat and tidy" dress code geared toward securing an upscale clientele—is a 24-hour, European-style casino. It has three levels of gaming, with 104 tables and more than 1,000 machines, plus four restaurants and five bars.

Empire Hotel (✉ 339 Brunswick St., Fortitude Valley ☎ 07/3852–1216 ⊕ www.empirehotel.com.au) packs in four bars under one roof. Make yourself at home in the Family Bar, or relax with a cocktail and cool jazz at the ultra-hip Press Club, fitted with leather sofas, arty lamps, and silver fans. Dance-music fans flock to the Empire Bar, whereas those who fancy alternative and rock music mingle upstairs in the Moonbar. It's open daily until 5 AM, except Sunday.

R Bar (✉ 235 Edward St., City Center ☎ 07/3220–1477) is a café, bar, club, and tavern all rolled into one in the historic Rowes Arcade. The establishment, which caters to a sophisticated clientele of thirtysomethings, is open Tuesday–Saturday 10 AM until the wee hours of the morning. There's a A$6 cover charge after 7 PM.

Sports & the Outdoors

Biking

An extensive network of bicycle paths crisscrosses Brisbane, making pedal power one of the most rewarding ways to see the city, though hills can be challenging. A highlight is to follow the Bicentennial Bikeway southeast along the Brisbane River, across the Goodwill Bridge, and then along to South Bank Parklands or the Kangaroo Point cliffs.

Brisbane's "Bicycle Guide," detailing more than 400 km (250 mi) of cycling paths, is available from the **Brisbane City Council** (✉ 69 Ann

St., City Center, ☎ 07/3403–8888 ⊕ www.brisbane.qld.gov.au). **Brisbane Bicycle Sales and Hire** (✉ 87 Albert St., City Center ☎ 07/3229–2433 ⊕ www.brizbike.com) rents out bikes from the heart of the city. **Valet Cycle Hire and Tours** (☎ 0408–003198 ⊕ www.valetcyclehire.com) conducts guided bike tours and will deliver a rental bike right to your hotel.

Cricket
Queensland Cricketers' Club (✉ Vulture St., East Brisbane ☎ 07/3896–4533) provides playing schedules and ticket information for the nation's favorite sport, which is played during the Australian summer.

Golf
Indooroopilly Golf Club (✉ Meiers Rd., Indooroopilly ☎ 07/3721–2173) is one of Brisbane's premier golf courses. Although there are two courses here, only the East—an 18-hole, par-72 course—is open to visitors.

St. Lucia Golf Links (✉ Indooroopilly Rd. and Carawa St., St. Lucia ☎ 07/3870–2556) is an 18-hole, par-71 course open to visitors. You can dine at one of two stylish options: the Clubhouse or the 19th Café, overlooking the 18th green.

Rugby
Rugby League, a professional variation of rugby, is played in winter in Australia. Call **Queensland Rugby Football League** (☎ 1900/934212) for match programs and information. Call **Queensland Rugby Union** (☎ 07/3214–3333 ⊕ www.qru.com.au) for details on Rugby Union, the popular—and more familiar—international game.

Tennis
Contact **Tennis Queensland** (✉ 83 Castlemaine St., Milton ☎ 07/3368–2433) for information about playing at Brisbane's municipal or private courts and for details on upcoming tournaments.

Shopping

Department Stores
The renowned David Jones and Myer department stores are downtown on the Queen Street Mall.

Discount Stores
Stones Corner (✉ Logan and Old Cleveland Rds., Stones Corner), a business and residential area about 10 km (6 mi) south of the city center, is a popular shopping area where stores have opened discount outlets selling goods that are either seconds or end-of-season styles. Houseware stores are also represented.

Malls & Arcades
The historic and aesthetically pleasing **Brisbane Arcade** (✉ City Center) joins Queen Street Mall and Adelaide Street and has elegant designer boutiques and jewelry shops. **Broadway on the Mall,** which runs between the Queen Street Mall and Adelaide Street, connects via a walkway to David Jones department store, and it has a very good food center on the lower ground floor. **Chopstix** (✉ 249 Brunswick St., Fortitude Valley ☎ no phone) is a collection of 20 Asian shops and restaurants in the heart of Chinatown. **MacArthur Central** (✉ Edward and Queen Sts. City Center ☎ 07/3221–5977) also houses boutiques and specialty shops, a bookstore, as well as a food court.

Myer Centre (✉ Queen, Elizabeth, and Albert Sts., City Center ☎ no phone) houses the national department store of the same name, as well as boutiques, specialty shops, delis, restaurants, and cinemas. **The Pavilion** (✉ Queen and Albert Sts., City Center) has two levels of exclusive shops. **Queen Street Mall** (✉ City Center ☎ no phone) is considered the best downtown shopping area, with numerous buskers and a generally festive atmosphere. **Rowes Arcade** (✉ 235 Edward St., City Center ☎ no phone) is a renovated 1920s ballroom and banquet hall with boutique clothing stores. **Savoir Faire** (✉ 20 Park Rd., Milton ☎ no phone) is an upscale shopping and dining complex 10 minutes from the business district. **Tattersalls Arcade** (✉ Queen and Edward Sts., City Center ☎ no phone) caters to discerning shoppers with a taste for upscale designer labels. **Wintergarden Complex** (✉ Queen Street Mall, City Center ☎ no phone) houses boutiques and specialty shops, as well as a food court.

Markets

The Brisbane Powerhouse (✉ 119 Lamington St., New Farm ☎ 07/3358–8600 ⊕ www.brisbanepowerhouse.com) hosts a farmers' market with fresh local produce from 6 AM to noon on the second Saturday of the month. The **Riverside Markets** (✉ 123 Eagle St., City Center), an upscale arts-and-crafts market, is housed in the Riverside Centre, which is open Sunday 8–4. **South Bank Parklands** hosts a Friday-night Lantern Market that is open 5–10, and a Crafts Village that sells good-quality homemade clothing and arts and crafts on Saturday 11–5, Sunday 9–5.

Specialty Stores

ABORIGINAL CRAFTS

Aboriginal Art Culture Craft Centre (✉ South Bank Parklands, Southbank ☎ 07/3844–0255) sells genuine Aboriginal hunting paraphernalia and boomerangs, woomeras, didgeridoos, bark paintings, pottery, and carvings. Books, T-shirts, and other Australian-made gifts and souvenirs are also for sale.

ANTIQUES

Brisbane Antique Market (✉ 791 Sandgate Rd., Clayfield ☎ 07/3262–1444), near the airport, collects more than 40 dealers of antiques, collectibles, and jewelry under one roof.

Cordelia Street Antique and Art Centre (✉ Cordelia and Glenelg Sts., South Brisbane ☎ 07/3844–8514), housed inside an old church, purveys an interesting selection of antiques and jewelry.

Paddington Antique Centre (✉ 167 Latrobe Terr., Paddington ☎ 07/3369–8088) is a converted theater filled with antiques and bric-a-brac. More than 50 dealers operate within the center.

AUSTRALIAN PRODUCTS

Greg Grant Country Clothing (✉ Myer Centre, Queen St., City Center ☎ 07/3221–4233) specializes in the legendary Driza-Bone oilskin coats, Akubra and leather hats, whips, R. M. Williams boots, and moleskins.

My Country Clothing Collection (✉ Level 1, Broadway on the Mall, Queen Street Mall, City Center ☎ 07/3221–2858) sells country-style clothing for the whole family, plus stock whips, moleskins, and steer-hide belts, all made in Australia.

OPALS

Quilpie Opals (✉ Lennons Plaza Bldg., 68 Queen Street Mall, City Center ☎ 07/3221–7369) carries a large selection of Queensland boulder opals as well as high-grade opals, available as individual stones or already set.

SOUVENIRS

Australia The Gift (✉ 150 Queen Street Mall, City Center ☎ 07/3210–6198 ⊕ www.australiathegift.com.au) sells quality Australian-made handicrafts, plus postcards, books, and novelty items.

Brisbane A to Z

To research prices, get advice from other travelers, and book travel arrangements, visit www.fodors.com.

AIR TRAVEL

Flight time from Brisbane to Bundaberg is 45 minutes; to Cairns, 2 hours; to Coolangatta, 30 minutes; to Emerald, 1 hour 40 minutes; to Gladstone, 1 hour 15 minutes; to Hamilton Island, 1 hour 45 minutes; to Hervey Bay, 55 minutes; to Mackay, 1 hour 35 minutes; to Maroochydore, 25 minutes; to Maryborough, 45 minutes; to Rockhampton, 1 hour 10 minutes; and to Townsville, 1 hour 50 minutes.

CARRIERS Brisbane is Queensland's major travel crossing point. Many international airlines have head offices in the city center as well as information booths at the airport. Qantas flies to all major Australian cities; Virgin Blue links a number of major cities; and smaller airlines connect the rest of the state. Flight West Airlines flies to Gladstone and Townsville.

Air Nauru flies to a number of islands in the south and central Pacific Ocean. Air New Zealand flies from Brisbane to Auckland five times a week, with connecting flights to Los Angeles and London. Air Pacific is Fiji's international airline. Air Vanuatu flies from Brisbane to Vanuatu three times a week. All Nippon Airways flies daily from Brisbane to Japan via Sydney. Cathay Pacific Airways links Brisbane to most major cities throughout the world. EVA Airways is the international airline for Taiwan. Garuda Indonesia is the airline of Indonesia. Malaysian Airlines flies from Brisbane to countries all around the world. Norfolk Jet Express flies from Brisbane to Norfolk Island in the South Pacific three times a week. Qantas flies from Brisbane to countries around the world and domestically within Australia. Royal Brunei Airlines flies from Brisbane to Brunei four times a week. Singapore Airlines flies from Brisbane to more than 30 countries via Singapore. Solomon Airlines flies from Brisbane to the Solomon Islands and other South Pacific islands. Thai Airways is the international airline of Thailand.

🛫 Carriers **Air Nauru** ⊠ Level 4, 97 Creek St., City Center, Brisbane ☎ 07/3229-6455. **Air New Zealand** ⊠ 63 Adelaide St., City Center, Brisbane ☎ 13-2476. **Air Pacific** ⊠ Level 10, 313 Adelaide St., City Center, Brisbane ☎ 1800/230150. **Air Vanuatu** ⊠ Level 5, 293 Queen St., City Center, Brisbane ☎ 07/3221-2566. **All Nippon Airways** ⊠ 217 George St., CBD, Brisbane ☎ 07/3407-7200. **Cathay Pacific Airways** ⊠ Level 1, Brisbane International Airport, Airport Dr., Eagle Farm, Brisbane ☎ 13-1747 ⊕ www.cathaypacific.com.au. **EVA Airways** ⊠ 127 Creek St., City Center, Brisbane ☎ 07/3229-8000. **Flight West** ⊠ Pandanus Ave., Eagle Farm, Brisbane ☎ 07/3212-1212 or 1300/130092. **Garuda Indonesia** ⊠ 288 Edward St., City Center, Brisbane ☎ 1300/365330. **Malaysian Airlines** ⊠ Level 17, 80 Albert St., City Center, Brisbane ☎ 13-2627. **Norfolk Jet Express** ⊠ Level 4, 97 Creek St., City Center, Brisbane ☎ 07/3221-6677. **Qantas** ⊠ 247 Adelaide St., City Center, Brisbane ☎ 07/3238-2700 or 13-1313 ⊕ www.qantas.com. **Royal Brunei Airlines** ⊠ 60 Edward St., City Center, Brisbane ☎ 07/3017-5000. **Singapore Airlines** ⊠ Level 19, 344 Queen St., City Center, Brisbane ☎ 13-1011 ⊕ www.singaporeair.com.au. **Solomon Airlines** ⊠ Level 5, 217 George St., City Center, Brisbane ☎ 07/3407-7266. **Thai Airways** ⊠ Level 4, 145 Eagle St., City Center, Brisbane ☎ 07/3215-4700. **Virgin Blue** ⊠ Level 7, Centenary Sq., 100 Wickham St., Fortitude Valley, Brisbane ☎ 13-6789 ⊕ www.virginblue.com.

AIRPORTS & TRANSFERS

🛫 **Brisbane International Airport** ⊠ Airport Dr., Eagle Farm ☎ 07/3406-3190.

AIRPORT TRANSFERS Brisbane International Airport is 9 km (5½ mi) from the city center. Coachtrans provides a daily bus service, called SkyTrans Shuttle, to and from city hotels every 30 minutes between 5 AM and 8:30 PM. The fare is A$9 per person one way, A$15 round-trip.

Airtrain has train services to Central Station and other stations throughout Brisbane and the Gold Coast. The fare is A$9 per person one way to Central Station, A$18 round-trip. Trains depart up to four times an hour and it takes 18 minutes to reach the City Center.

Taxis to downtown Brisbane cost approximately A$30.
🚕 **Coachtrans** ☎ 07/3860-6999.
🚕 **Airtrain** ☎ 07/3211-2855 or 13-1230 🌐 www.airtrain.com.au.

BOAT & FERRY TRAVEL
Speedy CityCat ferries, run by the Brisbane City Council, call at 13 points along the Brisbane River, from Bretts Wharf to the University of Queensland. They run daily 6 AM–10:30 PM about every half hour. The CityCat ferries are terrific for taking a leisurely look at Brisbane river life. From the city skyline to the homes of the well-heeled, there's always something of interest to see.
🚢 **CityCat ferries** ☎ 13-1230.

BUS TRAVEL
Greyhound Pioneer Australia travels to all parts of Australia from Brisbane. McCafferty's Express Coaches offers a number of bus passes including "Follow the Sun" passes for travel from Brisbane to Cairns in North Queensland.

Buses are a good way to get around, as stops are well signposted and the buses mostly run on schedule. The main travel points are Brisbane and Cairns. It's 1,716 km (1,064 mi) and 25 hours by bus between them. For routes, schedules, and fares, call Trans Info.
🚌 Bus Information **Greyhound Pioneer Australia** ✉ Brisbane Transit Centre, Roma St., City Center ☎ 07/3258-1670 or 13-2030 🌐 www.greyhound.com.au. **McCafferty's Express Coaches** ✉ Brisbane Transit Centre, Roma St., City Center ☎ 07/3236-3035 or 13-1499 🌐 www.mccaffertys.com.au. **Trans Info** ☎ 13-1230 🌐 www.transinfo.qld.gov.au.

BUSINESS SERVICES
You can send faxes, make photocopies, retrieve e-mail, and find other business services at most major hotels, including the Conrad Treasury Brisbane, Stamford Plaza Brisbane, and Sheraton. You can also send faxes and make photocopies at the General Post Office.

CAR RENTAL
All major car-rental agencies have offices in Brisbane, including Avis, Budget, Hertz, and Thrifty. Four-wheel-drive vehicles are available.
🚗 Agencies **Avis** ✉ 275 Wickham St., Fortitude Valley ☎ 07/3252-7111. **Budget** ✉ 105 Mary St., City Center, Brisbane ☎ 13-2727. **Hertz** ✉ 55 Charlotte St., City Center, Brisbane ☎ 13-3039. **Thrifty** ✉ 49 Barry Parade, Fortitude Valley ☎ 1300/367227.

CAR TRAVEL
Brisbane is 1,002 km (621 mi) from Sydney along coastal Highway 1. An inland route from Sydney follows Highway 1 to Newcastle and then heads inland on Highway 15. Either drive can be made in a day; however, two days are recommended for ample time to sightsee.

It takes about 20 hours to drive between Brisbane and Cairns, slightly less than by bus.

EMERGENCIES
In an emergency, dial 000 for an ambulance, the fire department, or the police.

Travellers Medical Service is a 24-hour medical center. Services include a travel health clinic, a women's health clinic, and 24-hour hotel visits. The staff can also recommend dentists and pharmacies to suit your needs.
🏠 **Royal Brisbane Hospital** ⊠ Herston Rd., Herston ☎ 07/3636-8111. **Travellers Medical Service** ⊠ Level 1, 245 Albert St., City Center ☎ 07/3211-3611.

MAIL, SHIPPING & INTERNET

The general post office is open weekdays 7 AM–6 PM. Australia Post, located on-site, provides overnight mail services.

Federal Express has international door-to-door mail services and is open weekdays 9 AM–5:30 PM.

The following are Internet Cafés in the Brisbane area: International Youth Service Centre (not only for youth); Dialup Cyber Lounge, open Monday–Saturday 10 AM–7 PM and Sunday 10–6.
🏠 Internet Cafés **International Youth Service Centre (IYSC)** ⊠ 2/69 Adelaide St., City Center ☎ 07/3229-9985. **Dialup Cyber Lounge** ⊠ 126 Adelaide St., City Center ☎ 07/3211-9095. **Purrer Cyber Space Café** ⊠ 751 Stanley St., Woolloongabba ☎ 07/3392-1377.
🏠 Major Services **Federal Express** ⊠ 11-15 Gould Rd., Herston ☎ 13-2610.
🏠 Post Office **General Post Office** ⊠ 261 Queen St., City Center ☎ 13-1318.

MONEY MATTERS

You can cash traveler's checks and change money at most banks and financial institutions around town. ATMs, usually located next to banks, are reliable and will accept most cards that are enabled for international access. ANZ Bank is one of the biggest banks in Australia. Commonwealth Bank of Australia is easily recognizable due to its distinctive black-and-yellow logo. National Australia Bank has several branches in the heart of Brisbane.
🏠 Banks **ANZ Bank** ⊠ 324 Queen St., City Center ☎ 07/3228-3228. **Commonwealth Bank of Australia** ⊠ 240 Queen St., City Center ☎ 13-2221. **National Australia Bank** ⊠ 225 Queen St., City Center ☎ 13-2265.

TAXIS

Taxis are metered and relatively inexpensive. They are available at designated taxi stands outside hotels, downtown, and at the railway station, although it is usually best to phone for one.

Black and White Cabs, like its name suggests, has a fleet of black-and-white taxis. Yellow Cabs has the largest taxi fleet in Brisbane. The taxis are easily recognizable due to their orange color.
🏠 Taxi Companies **Black and White Cabs** ⊠ 11 Dryandra Rd., Eagle Farm ☎ 13-1008 ⊕ www.blackandwhitecabs.com.au. **Yellow Cabs** ⊠ 116 Logan Rd., Woolloongabba ☎ 13-1924.

TOURS

Australian Day Tours conducts half- and full-day tours of Brisbane, as well as trips to the Gold Coast, Noosa Heads, and the Sunshine Coast.

City Nights tours depart daily from the Brisbane City Hall, City Sights Bus Stop 2 (Adelaide Street), at 6:30 PM for a trip up scenic Mt. Coot-tha. After enjoying the city's lights you are taken on a CityCat ferry ride down the Brisbane River before joining the bus for a ride back to town through the historic Valley precinct. The A$18 tour finishel at 9 PM.

City Sights open tram-style buses, run by the Brisbane City Council, make half-hourly circuits of city landmarks and other points of interest. They leave from Post Office Square every 40 minutes, starting at 9 AM, with a break from 12:20 to 1:40. You can buy tickets on the bus, and you can get on or off at any of the 19 stops. The A$18 ticket is also valid for use on the CityCat ferries and commuter buses.

Kookaburra River Queens is a paddle wheeler that runs lunch and dinner cruises on the Brisbane River. The lunch cruise includes scenic and historic commentary; live entertainment and dancing are highlights of the dinner cruise. Tours run A$38–A$65 per person.

Historic Walks is an informative brochure by The National Trust, available from the Queensland Government Travel Centre and hotels. ⚑ Tour Operators **Australian Day Tours** ✉ Brisbane Transit Centre, Roma St., Level 3, City Center ☎ 07/3236-4155 or 1300/363436. **City Nights** ✉ Brisbane City Council, 69 Ann St., City Center ☎ 13-1230. **City Sights** ✉ Brisbane City Council, 69 Ann St., City Center ☎ 13-1230. **Kookaburra River Queens** ✉ Eagle Street Pier, 1 Eagle St., City Center ☎ 07/3221-1300. **National Trust** ✉ Edward and Adelaide Sts., City Center ☎ 13-1801.

TRAIN TRAVEL

Railways of Australia runs nightly service between Sydney and Brisbane (14 hours). Regular service from 5:30 AM until midnight connects Brisbane and the Gold Coast. The *Sunlander* and the luxurious *Queenslander* trains make a total of four runs a week between Brisbane and Cairns in the north. Other long-distance passenger trains are the *Spirit of the Tropics* (twice per week) between Brisbane and Townsville, the *Spirit of Capricorn* (once per week) between Brisbane and Rockhampton, the high-tech *Tilt Train* between Brisbane and Rockhampton (six times per week), the *Inlander* between Townsville and Mount Isa (twice per week), the *Westlander* between Brisbane and Charleville (twice per week), and the *Spirit of the Outback* between Brisbane and Longreach (twice per week). Packages, such as Reef and Rail or Outback Aussies Adventures, are also available. Trains depart from the Roma Street Station. For details contact Queensland Rail's Traveltrain or the City Booking Office.

The Great South Pacific Express offers first-class "Orient Express"–type luxury rail service among Sydney, Brisbane, and Cairns. The train runs twice weekly each way and can be combined with numerous sightseeing tours, such as an air excursion to a coral cay on the Great Barrier Reef to snorkel and enjoy a picnic lunch. ⚑ Train Information **City Booking Office** ☎ 13-2232. **Great South Pacific Express** ☎ 1800/627655 ⊕ www.gspe.com. **Queensland Rail's Traveltrain** ✉ 305 Edward St., City Center ☎ 07/3235-2222 or 13-2232 ⊕ www.traveltrain.qr.com.au.

VISITOR INFORMATION

⚑ Tourist Information **Brisbane Tourism** ⌂ Elizabeth St., Box 12260, 4001 ✉ Brisbane City Hall, Adelaide St., City Center ☎ 07/3006-6200 ⊕ www.brisbanetourism.com.au. **Queensland Travel Centre** ⌂ 243 Edward St., Box 9958, 4001 ☎ 13-8833 ⊕ www.queenslandtravel.com.au.

CARNARVON NATIONAL PARK

Despite its remote location 700 km (434 mi) northwest of Brisbane— *way* off the beaten path—Carnarvon National Park is one of the most popular parks in central Queensland. Its 21 km (13 mi) of walking trails are suitable for the whole family, with only a few side trails that involve difficult ascents. Even on hot days, the park's shady gorges are cool and refreshing.

Carnarvon is famous for its ancient Aboriginal paintings, particularly those in the Art Gallery and Cathedral Cave. Both galleries span more than 165 feet of sheer sandstone walls covered with red ocher stencils of ancient Aboriginal life—among them weapons and hands. An extensive boardwalk system with informational plaques allows easy access to the fragile paintings. Carnarvon is best visited during the dry season, late April through October, when most roads to the park are passable. ☎ 07/4984–4505.

Where to Stay

$–$$ ⊡ **Carnarvon Gorge Wilderness Lodge.** Waterfalls, wildlife, and bush-walking tracks envelop you at this ecologically friendly lodge at the entrance to Carnarvon Gorge. Timber and canvas Safari Cabins, each with a veranda, a refrigerator, and air-conditioning, blend in with the surrounding bush. You can swim in a free-form rock pool at the lodge—or walk over to the nearby swimming holes—and dine at an on-site restaurant. ⊠ *Carnarvon Gorge, 4702* ☎ *07/4984–4503 or 1800/ 644150* ⊟ *07/4984–4500* ⊕ *www.carnarvon-gorge.com* ⇌ *30 cabins* ⌂ *Restaurant, refrigerators, pool, hiking, bar, laundry facilities* ⊟ *AE, DC, MC, V.*

¢   ⚠ **Takarakka Bush Resort.** Just outside of Carnarvon National Park, Takarakka has powered and unpowered sites, as well as canvas cabins. Unpowered sites start from A$8 per night, powered campsites run A$22 for two adults, and canvas cabins, with refrigerators and fans, cost A$65 per night. Facilities include fresh water, hot communal showers, a communal kitchen, and a small grocery shop. Note that no fuel is available at the National Park. Bookings must be made about one year in advance if you want to stay during the peak season (June through July), and you must bring your own linen, cutlery, and cookware. ⊠ *Takarakka, Carnarvon Gorge, via Rolleston, 4702* ☎ *07/4984–4535* ⊟ *07/ 4984–4556* ⊕ *www.takarakka.com.au* ⇌ *14 cabins, 44 powered sites, 17 unpowered sites* ⌂ *Flush toilets, pit toilets, full hook-ups, partial hook-ups, drinking water, showers, fire pits, electricity, general store, pond* ⊟ *AE, MC, V.*

Carnarvon National Park A to Z

AIR TRAVEL

Two-hour direct flights depart from Brisbane on Thursdays and Sundays in association with Carnarvon Gorge Wilderness Lodge. Flights are included in three-, four-, and seven-night packages. Bookings can be made through the lodge or through Queensland Travel Centre. Private air charters can be arranged with Five Star Aviation.

🖪 Carriers **Five Star Aviation** ☎ 1800/643700. **Queensland Travel Centre** ⊠ 243 Edward St., 4001 ☎ 13-8833 ⊕ www.queenslandtravel.com.au.

CAR TRAVEL

A four-wheel-drive vehicle is recommended for travel to Carnarvon, especially right after the wet season (January–late April), when many roads may still be flooded. From Brisbane, take the Warrego Highway 486 km (301 mi) west to Roma, then 271 km (168 mi) north toward Injune and Carnarvon. Be sure to bring food for at least two extra days in case of road flooding. If you are driving up or down the coast, head in through Central Queensland, by way of Rockhampton, along route 66 for 263 km (164 mi) until you reach Emerald, then head 242 km (150 mi) south of Emerald along route 55.

TOURS

Australian Pacific Tours travels to Carnarvon Gorge five times a year—stopping at the Gorge for two nights—as a part of several Queensland tours. Northern Highland Travel travels from Sydney in New South Wales up to Carnarvon Gorge twice a year (April and May), stopping at Carnarvon Gorge for four days each trip. A separate tour visiting Longreach and the Gorge runs three times a year (June, July, and August). Scenic Tours Australia runs tours to Carnarvon Gorge five to six times a year, stopping at the Gorge for two nights each trip.

⚑ Tour Operators Australian Pacific Tours ⊠ Brisbane Transit Centre ☎ 07/3236–4088 or 1800/675222 ⊕ www.aptours.com.au. **Northern Highland Travel** ⊠ 5 Spotted Gum Grove, Thornton ☎ 1800/623068 ⊕ www.nht.com.au. **Scenic Tours Australia** ☎ 1300/136001 ⊕ www.scenictours.com.

THE GOLD COAST

Three hundred days of sunshine a year and an average temperature of 24°C (75°F) ensure the popularity of the Gold Coast, the most developed tourist destination in Australia, with plenty of amusement complexes and resorts. Christmas, Easter, and December through February are peak seasons. An hour south of Brisbane, the Gold Coast officially comprises the 32 km (20 mi) from Southport to Coolangatta, and has now sprawled as far inland as Nerang. It has 35 patrolled beaches and 446 km (277 mi) of canals and tidal rivers, which is nine times longer than the canals of Venice.

Unless you're intending to access your inner teenager, you may wish to steer clear of Surfers Paradise during "Schoolies Week," an approximately month-long graduation festival celebrated by post–high schoolers. From mid-November to mid-December, expect throngs of teenagers, many of whom are on vacation without their families for the first time. Vacationing Queensland locals tend to avoid this part of the Gold Coast during this time.

Coomera

48 km (30 mi) south of Brisbane.

In just one day at **Dreamworld,** a family theme park, you can thrill on the fastest, tallest ride in the world, the Tower of Terror, and the tallest high-speed gravity roller coaster in the southern hemisphere, the Cyclone. You can also watch Bengal tigers play and swim with their handlers on Tiger Island, cuddle a koala in Koala Country, cool off in a water park, or cruise the park on a paddle wheeler. The park is 40 minutes outside Brisbane and 20 minutes from Surfers Paradise along the Pacific Highway. ⊠ *Dreamworld Pkwy.* ☎ *07/5588–1111 or 1800/073300* ⊕ *www.dreamworld.com.au* 💰 *A$56* ⊗ *Daily 10–5.*

FodorsChoice ★

Oxenford

2 km (1 mi) south of Coomera.

At **Warner Bros. Movie World,** one of the few movie theme parks outside the United States, you can wander through the set re-creations of the *Harry Potter Movie Magic Experience,* laugh at the antics of the *Police Academy* stunt show, or rocket through the *Lethal Weapon* roller coaster. Young children enjoy Looney Tunes Village, while shoppers take heart at the numerous shops selling Warner Bros. souvenirs. ⊠ *Pacific Hwy.* ☎ *07/5573–3999 or 07/5573–8485* ⊕ *www.movieworld.com.au* 💰 *A$56* ⊗ *Daily 10–5:30.*

When you're looking for **Wet 'n' Wild Water Park,** keep your eyes peeled for Matilda, the giant kangaroo mascot of the 1982 Brisbane Commonwealth Games. The park has magnificent water slides, as well as a

The Gold Coast

wave pool with a 3-foot-high surf. There's also Calypso Beach, a tropical island fringed with white-sand beaches, surrounded by a slow-moving river where you can laze about in brightly colored tubes. For a little more excitement, plunge down a thrilling water-slide ride on a tandem tube at Terror Canyon. ⊠ *Pacific Hwy.* ☎ *07/5573–6233* ⊕ *www. wetnwild.com.au* ☜ *A$35* ☺ *Daily 10–4:30.*

Hope Island

6 km (4 mi) east of Oxenford.

Home to a Hyatt Regency hotel, **Sanctuary Cove** is a resort with two golf courses, an outstanding marina, and a shopping center with boutiques, restaurants, a movie theater, a health club, and a brewery.

Where to Stay

★ $$$–$$$$ 🏨 **Hyatt Regency Sanctuary Cove.** Set amid landscaped tropical gardens, this opulent low-rise hotel resembles a monumental Australian colonial mansion. Five three-story guest courts are luxuriously appointed, each with its own large, private balcony. The main lobby building, known as the Great House, leads past a cascading waterfall to the courtyard and swimming pool–hot tub area. There's also a sandy beach lagoon fed with filtered saltwater next to the resort's main harbor. A walkway from the hotel leads directly into the village. ⊠ *Manor Circle, Sanctuary Cove, 4212* ☎ *07/5530–1234* 🖷 *07/5577–8234* ⊕ *www. sanctuarycove.hyatt.com* ⟿ *223 rooms, 24 suites* ♨ *2 restaurants, room service, in-room data ports, refrigerators, room TVs with movies, driving range, 2 18-hole golf courses, 9 tennis courts, 2 pools, health* club, hair salon, hot tub, massage, sauna, beach, boating, marina, fishing, bowling, 2 bars, baby-sitting, children's programs (ages 4–12), laundry service, meeting rooms, travel services, free parking ⊟ AE, DC, MC, V.

South Stradbroke Island

1 km (½ mi) east of the Gold Coast.

White-sand beaches, diverse flora and fauna, and a peaceful interior draw visitors to South Stradbroke Island, which is just 20 km (12 mi) long and 2 km (1 mi) wide. It's also a good spot for outdoor activities, especially fishing and boating. The first white settlers—cane farmers—arrived on the island during the 1870s, followed by oystermen in the 1880s. Old oyster beds can still be seen in the waters on the boat ride to Couran Cove Resort.

Where to Stay

$$$–$$$$ ⊞ **Couran Cove Resort.** Just 15 minutes by boat from the glitz of the Gold Coast, this ecotourism resort is a haven of peace and harmony. The vision of Olympic athlete Ron Clarke, a long-distance runner, the property has an amazing array of sporting facilities: biking, swimming, tennis, rock climbing, baseball, basketball, and more. Spacious, self-contained rooms, a restaurant, and two cafés are also on-site. Lodgings vary, from standard rooms and suites to cabins and lodges, but every accommodation has a view over the beach, bush, or lagoon. Many are built over the water so you can fish right off the balcony. ⊙ *South Stradbroke Island, Box 224, Runaway Bay, Gold Coast, 4216* ☎ 07/5597–9000 or 1800/632211 ⊞ 07/5597–9090 ⊕ *www.courancove. com* ⇄ *100 rooms, 92 suites, 91 cabins, 29 lodges, 10 villas* ⌂ *Restaurant, 2 cafés, in-room safes, kitchenettes, putting green, 3 tennis courts, 2 pools, health club, massage, spa, beach, snorkeling, windsurfing, boating, jet skiing, parasailing, waterskiing, fishing, bicycles, basketball, bar, shops, children's programs (ages 3–12), Internet, business services, convention center, travel services* ⊟ AE, DC, MC, V.

Southport

16 km (10 mi) southeast of Oxenford.

In Southport, look for the turnoff to the **Spit**, a natural peninsula pointing north. This is where you'll find fine dining, exclusive shops, and the town's top attraction. **Seaworld** is Australia's largest marine park. Six daily shows highlight whales, dolphins, sea lions, and waterskiing. Rides include a monorail, a corkscrew roller coaster, and water slides. Dolphin Cove, the largest natural dolphin lagoon in the world, allows limited numbers of visitors, age 14 years or more, to swim with the dolphins. All rides except helicopter and parasailing flights and swimming with the dolphins are included in the ticket price. ⊠ *Seaworld Dr.* ☎ 07/5588–2222 ⊕ *www.seaworld.com.au* ⊠ *A$54* ⊙ *Daily 10–5.*

Where to Stay & Eat

$–$$$ ✕ **Cafe Romas.** At this stylish restaurant overlooking the Southport Marina, you can sit at tables under an awning on the boardwalk, one level up on the veranda, or inside the café itself, decorated in European style and lit by Parisian lamps. The seaside setting dovetails nicely with a menu that draws on the ocean's bounty, including oysters, snapper, mussels, and tempura prawns. The café consistently wins "Best Café" awards from local judges. ⊠ *Marina Mirage Shopping Center, Seaworld Dr., the Spit* ☎ 07/5531–2488 ⊟ AE, DC, MC, V.

$$$$
Fodor's Choice
★ ▦ **Palazzo Versace.** The house of Versace lent its fashion flair to the design and decor of this regal, opulent hotel. Pure class and elegance sum up the style, with European architecture, water views, and a state-of-the-art spa. All rooms are elegantly fitted and have a private spa bathroom. The signature restaurant, Vanitas, serves contemporary Australian cuisine in a dining room overlooking the stunning lagoon pool. The hotel's name attracts the rich and famous, and its facilities and charm live up to all expectations. ⊠ *Seaworld Dr., 4217* ☎ *07/5509–8000* 🖷 *07/5509–8889* ⊕ *www.palazzoversace.com* ⇨ *205 rooms, 72 condos* ৬ *3 restaurants, room service, in-room hot tubs, pool, health club, spa, beach, dock, marina, bar, shops, baby-sitting, laundry service, concierge, business services, convention center, meeting rooms, car rental, travel services, no-smoking rooms* ▤ *AE, DC, MC, V.*

★ **$$$$** ▦ **Sheraton Mirage.** A low-rise building nestled amid lush gardens and fronting a secluded beach, this resort has a distinctly Australian look. The tasteful rooms make use of soft colors and overlook gardens, the Pacific Ocean, or vast saltwater lagoons. A suspension bridge over the road links the resort with the elegant Marina Mirage Shopping Center, although you would be wise to sample the excellent fare at the resort's own restaurants first. ⊠ *Seaworld Dr., 4217* ☎ *07/5591–1488* 🖷 *07/5591–2299* ⊕ *www.starwood.com/sheraton* ⇨ *284 rooms, 10 suites, 39 villas* ৬ *2 restaurants, room service, in-room data ports, kitchenettes (some), 4 tennis courts, pool, health club, hot tub, spa, beach, bar, baby-sitting, laundry service, concierge, business services, convention center, meeting room, car rental, travel services, free parking, no-smoking rooms* ▤ *AE, DC, MC, V.*

Sports & the Outdoors

BOATING Rent yachts and cabin cruisers from **Popeye's Boat Hire** (⊠ Mariner's Cove, 212 Seaworld Dr. ☎ 07/5591–2553 or 07/5532–5822).

FISHING **Gold Coast Fishing Tackle** (⊠ 15 Nind St. ☎ 07/5531–0755) can provide tackle and advice about the best local fishing spots.

Shopping

One of the most elegant shopping centers on the Gold Coast is the **Marina Mirage** (⊠ Seaworld Dr., the Spit ☎ 07/5577–0088 ⊕ www.marinamirage.com.au), where you'll find such designer boutiques as Nautica, Aigner, Louis Vuitton, and Hermès, along with fine antiques, beach- and leisure wear, perfume, and duty-free goods. There are fine restaurants, a medical center, and marina facilities as well.

Main Beach

6 km (4 mi) south of Southport.

A residential area full of high-rise apartments and houses, Main Beach is also a popular swimming spot for Brisbane residents looking for good surf without the crowds of nearby Surfers Paradise. Tedder Avenue at Main Beach is one of the local haunts. It has a strip of elegant coffee shops, cafés, restaurants, bars, and clubs separate from the tourist areas, which makes it the spot to get the measure of real-time Gold Coast life.

Surfers Paradise

8 km (5 mi) south of Southport, 72 km (45 mi) south of Brisbane.

The heart of town, around Cavill Avenue, is an eclectic collection of high-rises overlooking the beach, where bodies bake in the sand under signs warning of the risks of skin cancer. Surfers Paradise may be kitschy and commercial, but the nightlife is the best on the Gold Coast.

If your thirst for the bizarre isn't satisfied by the crowds in Surfers Paradise, the displays at **Ripley's Believe It or Not! Museum** may give you that extra thrill. This is the home of the renowned African fertility statues: more than 500 women claim they became pregnant soon after rubbing them. ⊠ *Raptis Plaza, Cavill Ave.* ☎ *07/5592–0040* ⊕ *www.ripleys. com.au* ☑ *A$12.50* ⊘ *Daily 9 AM–11 PM.*

Surfers Paradise hosts the annual **Indy Car Race** (☎ 07/5588–6800 Gold Coast Indy Office ⊕ www.indy.com.au). The date changes each year, but when it occurs it's a big event, with streets blocked off to create a challenging course for the world's top speed demons. The race is usually held in the month of October.

On Friday nights, the beachfront promenade spills over with crafts and gifts at the **Surfers Paradise Friday Night Beachfront Lantern Market,** held throughout the year. ⊠ *Promenade* ☎ *07/5538–3632* ☑ *Free* ⊘ *Daily 5:30–10.*

Where to Stay & Eat

$–$$$ ⨉ **Mango's.** The Nerang River fronts this tropically inspired restaurant with a thatched roof, exposed beams, palm trees, and a waterfall. Even though the establishment seats 250, the candlelit tables and clever layout create a sense of intimacy. The menu includes delicious seafood and Italian dishes. Try grilled springwater barramundi or grilled lobster with brandy butter. ⊠ *Tiki Village, Cavill Ave.* ☎ *07/5531–6177* ▭ *AE, DC, MC, V* ⊘ *Closed Mon. No lunch.*

★ $$ ⨉ **Cristel's.** The chefs here have a considerable reputation for their innovative approach to food style and presentation. Expect such dishes as Atlantic salmon, served with spinach and red pepper salad drizzled in an olive and basil dressing. Save room for mango cheeks in lemongrass syrup, served with raspberry sorbet. Seating is in an open kitchen, versatile bar, and a private dining room. ⊠ *Parkroyal Surfers Paradise, 2807 Gold Coast Hwy.* ☎ *07/5592–9900* ▭ *AE, DC, MC, V* ⊘ *Closed Sun.–Mon. No lunch.*

$–$$ ⨉ **Hard Rock Cafe Surfers.** Packed with the usual rock memorabilia, this is one of the hottest spots on the coast. The menu lists American favorites such as hamburgers and deli sandwiches. The Pray for Surf bar and Hard Rock Shop are on the ground floor; the main restaurant and bar are on the second floor. ⊠ *Cavill Ave. and Gold Coast Hwy.* ☎ *07/5539–9377* ▭ *AE, DC, MC, V.*

$–$$ ⨉ **Omeros Bros. Seafood Restaurant Sayas.** A magnificent Inca-style bungalow sets a tone of resort elegance for this seafood restaurant. Cast-iron chairs, blue-and-yellow walls, and crisp white tablecloths complement the flavorful cuisine, which ranges from grilled fish to veal and steaks. ⊠ *Ocean Ave. and Gold Coast Hwy.* ☎ *07/5584–6060* ▭ *AE, DC, MC, V* ⊘ *No lunch.*

★ $$$–$$$$ ▤ **Marriott Surfers Paradise Resort.** The lobby's giant columns and grand circular staircase—cooled by a colorful Indian punkah—typify this hotel's opulent style. The large guest rooms, decorated in gentle hues of beige, light plum, and moss green, have walk-in closets, marble bathrooms, balconies, and ocean views. The hotel beach, on a saltwater lagoon stocked with brilliantly colored fish, is deep enough for scuba lessons. There are dive and water-sports shops on the premises, and you can rent windsurfing equipment, water skis, and catamarans on the river. ⊠ *158 Ferny Ave., 4217* ☎ *07/5592–9800* 🖷 *07/5592–9888* ⊕ *www.marriott. com* ⇆ *300 rooms, 30 suites* ⌂ *3 restaurants, room service, in-room data ports, in-room fax, in-room safes, in-room VCRs, 2 tennis courts,* *pool, gym, health club, hair salon, sauna, spa, steam room, dive shop, dock, windsurfing, boating, marina, waterskiing, 2 bars, shops, baby-sitting, children's programs (ages 4–14), playground, dry cleaning, laundry facilities, laundry service, concierge, business services, meeting room, travel services, free parking, no-smoking floor* ⊟ *AE, DC, MC, V.*

$$$–$$$$ 🏨 **The Moroccan Beach Resort.** Opposite a lifeguard-patrolled section of the beach, these white Mediterranean-style apartments create a stark contrast to the blue skies and water. The pick of the development's three towers is the Esplanade, which faces the beach. The hotel-style rooms are quite small—but comfortable—and the one- and two-bedroom apartments are spacious and luxurious. Apartments come with a well-equipped kitchen and laundry facilities. Outside, there is a common barbecue area. ⊠ *14 View Ave., 4217* ☎ *07/5526–9400 or 1800/811454* 🖷 *07/5555–9990* ⊕ *www.moroccan.com.au* ⇗ *30 rooms, 150 apartments* ⚭ *Kitchens (some), 3 pools, wading pool, gym, 3 hot tubs, babysitting, free parking* ⊟ *AE, DC, MC, V.*

$$–$$$ 🏨 **Royal Pines Resort.** Nestled beside the Nerang River, 7 km (4½ mi) west of Surfers Paradise, this resort has the best of just about everything: 500 acres of manicured gardens, two championship golf courses, a PGA-accredited golf school, tennis courts, small lakes, a native wildlife sanctuary, and a marina with access to the Nerang River. The resort hosts major golf events, including the Australian Ladies Masters, which takes place in late February or early March. Pastel colors and natural-wood furnishings decorate the rooms. Junior suites have hot tubs and overlook the golf courses. ⊠ *Ross St., Ashmore, 4214* ☎ *07/5597–1111 or 1800/074999* 🖷 *07/5597–2277* ⊕ *www.royalpinesresort.au-hotels. com* ⇗ *285 rooms, 45 suites* ⚭ *6 restaurants, driving range, 2 18-hole golf courses, putting green, 7 tennis courts, pro shop, 3 pools, health club, hair salon, 2 bars, business services, convention center, meeting room, travel services, free parking* ⊟ *AE, DC, MC, V.*

$–$$ 🏨 **Gold Coast International Hotel.** In the heart of Surfers Paradise and just one block from the beach, this hotel sets a high standard of service for its guests. The grand marble foyer leads to the stylish lobby bar, where a pianist plays nightly. Pastel colors and cane furniture make for relaxed and beachy—but still luxurious—guest rooms. The rooms all have views of the Pacific Ocean or the Gold Coast Hinterland. You can lounge by the pool with a cocktail, or if you're looking for a little more activity, work up a sweat in the hotel's health club. The entertaining chefs at the Yamagen Japanese Restaurant will cook your food right in front of you. ⊠ *Gold Coast Hwy. and Staghorn Ave., 4217* ☎ *07/5584–1200* 🖷 *07/ 5584–1280* ⊕ *www.gci.com.au* ⇗ *296 rooms, 24 suites* ⚭ *2 restaurants, café, room service, in-room data ports, room TVs with movies and video games, 2 tennis courts, pool, health club, hair salon, sauna, spa, steam room, 2 bars, shops, laundry service, concierge, meeting rooms, travel services, free parking* ⊟ *AE, DC, MC, V.*

Nightlife

New nightspots spring up in Surfers Paradise all the time. Whether you're looking to have a game of pool or dance the night away, the town has many options.

The Drink (⊠ 4 Orchid Ave. ☎ 07/5570–6155) claims to be "the sexiest club on the coast." Popular with the rich and famous—especially during the Indy Car festival in October—the club mainly plays commercial dance music. It's open daily 9 PM to 5 AM.

Having operated for more than two decades, **Melba's** (⊠ 46 Cavill Ave. ☎ 07/5538–7411) is one of Surfers Paradise's oldest clubs. It attracts an upscale crowd and plays the latest dance and pop music. A café, open 7 AM to 3 AM daily, is also on-site.

Shooters Saloon Bar (✉ Mark Complex, Orchid Ave. ☎ 07/5592–1144), with an American saloon theme, has a nightclub, sports bar, and pool hall. The action begins at 10 PM and continues until 5 AM.

Shopping

The enormous **Chevron Renaissance** (✉ 3240 Gold Coast Hwy. ☎ 07/5592–5188), one of the most stylish shopping centers in Surfers Paradise, has more than 50 stores and commercial offices throughout its modern, spacious layout. Numerous eateries and an Irish pub are here as well.

The Paradise Centre (✉ Cavill Ave. ☎ 07/5592–0155) houses 120 shops and restaurants, as well as an extensive amusement arcade and a Woolworth's variety store.

Raptis Plaza (✉ 4 The Esplanade ☎ 07/5592–2123), in the heart of town, is filled with enticing boutiques and cafés.

Broadbeach

8 km (5 mi) south of Southport.

With clean beaches, great cafés, and trendy nightspots, Broadbeach is one of the most popular areas on the Gold Coast. It's also home to Pacific Fair, one of Australia's leading shopping centers.

Where to Stay & Eat

$–$$ ✕ **Sopranos.** Wooden tables spill out onto the terra-cotta–tile sidewalk of Surf Parade, Broadbeach's restaurant strip. With a well-stocked bar, a frequently changing menu that takes advantage of the coast's supply of seafood, and a generous display of desserts, the restaurant is rarely empty. The menu combines Mediterranean styles with a pan-Asian blend of seasonings; try marinated barramundi in lemongrass, cilantro, garlic, chili, and lime, grilled and topped with tempura prawns, or the barbecued octopus tossed with chili, garlic, and olive oil, served on scented rice. ✉ *Shop 11, Surf Parade* ☎ *07/5526–2011* ▭ *AE, DC, MC, V.*

$$–$$$ ✕▣ **Hotel Conrad and Jupiter's Casino.** This hotel-casino, aligned with the Hilton chain, always seems to be bustling—especially in the sprawling lobby, where people meet to head into a restaurant, bar, or the main gambling rooms. The casino has 100 gaming tables and more than 100 gaming machines. High rollers should head straight for the lavishly appointed Club Conrad. The restaurants include Andiamo, a local Italian star, as well as the Prince Albert, a traditional English pub. ✉ *Broadbeach Island, Gold Coast Hwy., 4218* ☎ *07/5592–1133 or 1800/074344* 🖨 *07/5592–8219* ⊕ *www.conrad.com.au* ➥ *609 rooms, 29 suites, 2 penthouses* ⚿ *6 restaurants, coffee shop, in-room data ports, 4 tennis courts, pool, hair salon, sauna, squash, 8 bars, casino, pub, shops, baby-sitting, laundry service, concierge, business services, convention center, meeting room, car rental, travel services, free parking* ▭ *AE, DC, MC, V.*

$ ▣ **Antigua Beach Resort.** Less than a minute's walk from the beach and around the corner from Broadbeach's shopping centers and restaurants, this three-story, bright peach and blue hotel has balconies on all sides. Self-contained suites are decorated in bright, tropical colors. The pool and terrace outside are ringed by landscaped gardens with barbecues. ✉ *6 Queensland Ave., 4218* ☎ *07/5526–2288* 🖨 *07/5526–2266* ✑ *antigua@onthenet.com.au* ➥ *23 rooms* ⚿ *Kitchens, microwaves, refrig-*

*erators, pool, hot tub, sauna, laundry facilities, travel services, free
parking* ⊟ *AE, DC, MC, V.*

Nightlife

Jupiter's Casino (⊠ Broadbeach Island, Gold Coast Hwy. ☎ 07/
5592–1133) in Broadbeach provides flamboyant around-the-clock entertainment. The casino has 100 gaming tables on two levels, and includes blackjack, baccarat, craps, sic bo, pai gow, and keno, plus more
than 100 gaming machines that operate 24 hours daily. The 950-seat
showroom hosts glitzy Las Vegas–style productions.

Shopping

Oasis Shopping Centre (⊠ Victoria Ave. ☎ 07/5592–3900) is the retail
heart of beachside Broadbeach, with more than 100 shops and an attractive mall where open-air coffee shops stand umbrella-to-umbrella
along the edge. A monorail runs from the center to Jupiters Casino.

Pacific Fair (⊠ Hooker Blvd. ☎ 07/5539–8766), a sprawling outdoor
shopping center, is Queensland's largest. Its major retailers and 260 specialty stores should be enough to satisfy even die-hard shoppers. There
are also undercover malls, landscaped grounds with three small lakes,
a children's park, movie theaters, and a village green. The shopping center is adjacent to Jupiters Casino.

Burleigh Heads

9 km (5½ mi) south of Surfers Paradise.

Presented to the Queensland Department of Environment by wildlife naturalist David Fleay, **David Fleay's Wildlife Park** consists of wetlands and
rain forests in their natural states. These can be viewed from boardwalks
through the park. You'll see koalas, kangaroos, dingoes, platypuses, and
crocodiles. The animals are grouped together in separate zones according to their natural habitat. The park is 2 km (1 mi) west of town.
⊠ *W. Burleigh Rd.* ☎ *07/5576–2411* ⊠ *A$13* ☉ *Daily 9–5.*

Where to Eat

$$ ✕ **Oskars on Burleigh.** The magnificent view toward Surfers Paradise makes
this beachfront restaurant worth a visit. Two of the tropically inspired
delights on the menu are glazed Bowen mango and prawns with coconut,
macadamia nuts, and curry mayonnaise. Dine inside the restaurant, where
glass walls ensure an unhindered view of the coastline, or on the large
open deck on the surf side. Terra-cotta tiles, charcoal and stainless-steel
fittings, and simple wooden furniture complete the experience. ⊠ *43
Goodwin Terr.* ☎ *07/5576–3722* ⊕ *www.oskars.com.au* ⌂ *Reserva-
tions essential.* ⊟ *AE, DC, MC, V.*

Currumbin

6 km (4 mi) south of Burleigh Heads.

Across the creek from Palm Beach on the Gold Coast Highway is the
community of Currumbin and the **Currumbin Wildlife Sanctuary.** What
started off as a bird park in 1947 is now a 70-acre National Trust Re-
serve that shelters huge flocks of Australian lorikeets, other exotic birds,
bilbies, kangaroos, and koalas. Aboriginal dancers also perform daily.
Come between 8 and 9 or 4 and 5 when the lorikeets are fed. The park's
lovely grounds are ideal for picnics, and there is a café-restaurant on-
site. ⊠ *28 Tomewin St., off Gold Coast Hwy.* ☎ *07/5534–1266* ⊕ *www.
currumbin-sanctuary.org.au* ⊠ *A$18.40* ☉ *Daily 8–5.*

Coolangatta

25 km (16 mi) south of Surfers Paradise, 97 km (60 mi) south of Brisbane.

This southernmost Gold Coast border suburb blends into its New South Wales neighbor, Tweed Heads. It's a pleasant town, with a state-line lookout at the Captain Cook memorial at Point Danger. Coolangatta is also the home of the glorious Greenmount and Kirra beaches with their great surf breaks.

Gold Coast Hinterland

A visit to the Gold Coast wouldn't be complete without a short journey to the nearby **Gold Coast Hinterland**. Be forewarned, however, that this can induce culture shock: the natural grandeur of this area contrasts dramatically with the human-made excesses of the coastal strip.

The two main areas, Mt. Tamborine and Springbrook, can be reached from a number of exits off the main Gold Coast Highway or via Beaudesert from Brisbane. From the Gold Coast itself, follow the signs from Nerang or Mudgeeraba.

Tamborine National Park consists of several smaller parks. Queensland's first national park, **Witches Falls** (☎ 07/5545–1171), is a good spot for families, with picnic facilities and a 4-km (2½-mi) walk. The 1-km (½-mi) walk to Curtis Falls and back in the **Joalah National Park** (☎ 07/5545–1171) is part of a larger circuit and is accessed via the parking lot in Dapsang Street. **MacDonald National Park** (☎ 07/5545–1171) at Eagle Heights has a flat, easy 1½-km (1-mi) walk.

Springbrook National Park (☎ 07/5533–5147) is the vista that dominates the skyline west of the Gold Coast. Apart from ancient Antarctic beech trees, the park has many waterfalls and walking trails. Natural Bridge is a lovely waterfall that cascades through the roof of a cave into an icy pool, making a popular swimming spot. This cave is also home to Australia's largest glowworm colony, and at night hundreds of them light up the cavern to stunning effect. Purling Brook Falls, the area's largest waterfall, can be reached via a 4-km (2½-mi) walking track that takes hikers under the cliff face. It includes some stairs and uphill walking.

Lamington National Park (☎ 07/5533–3584) is an interesting tropical-subtropical-temperate ecological border zone with a complex abundance of plant and animal life that's astounding. Its 50,600-acre expanse is made up of two sections: Binna Burra and Green Mountains. Lamington National Park is listed as part of the Central Eastern Rainforest Reserves World Heritage Area, which protects the park's extensive and varied rain forest regions.

Where to Stay & Eat

Two lodges in the hinterland provide both budget and higher-price accommodations. Binna Burra also has a campground at the entrance to Lamington National Park that charges A$10 per person per night, and 17 on-site tents cost A$40 per night for two people, A$60 per night for four. Amenities include shower and toilet facilities, coin-operated gas barbecue stoves and hot plates, coin-operated laundry facilities, and a café. The views across the hinterland from this campground are spectacular. If camping, you must bring your own linens, as Binna Burra lodge does not provide this service.

$–$$$$ 🏨 **Governor's Retreat Resort.** On the banks of Guanaba Creek, toward the top of Mount Tamborine, is this luxurious hotel. Villas are decorated with Balinese and Javanese furniture, including king-size canopy beds. The lounge and restaurant has an enormous stone fireplace, making it a popular place when temperatures dip. Terraced gardens have miniature waterfalls, and rain-forest plants bloom among the boulders. The resort offers several spa packages. ✉ *123 Alpine Terr., Mount Tamborine, 4272* ☎ *07/5545–1522* 🖷 *07/5545–1622* ⊕ *www. governorsretreat.com.au* ➲ *6 villas* ☖ *Restaurant, in-room hot tubs, kitchenettes, in-room VCRs, massage, spa, free parking; no kids* ☰ *AE, DC, MC, V.*

$–$$$$
Fodor'sChoice
★
🖽 **O'Reilly's Rainforest Guesthouse.** The O'Reilly family has been welcoming guests onto their land since 1926. Originally a farm, the guesthouse is still family-run, with an O'Reilly present every morning making toast for guests in the dining room. There are four types of cabins, ranging from a 1930s-style house with shared bathroom up to a spacious suite with recycled timber flooring and four balconies that have spectacular views of the rain forest and Canungra Valley. Nearby is the canopy walk, a suspension bridge that lets you stroll high above the rain-forest floor. Most rates include all meals and activities, such as guided forest walks, children's activities, four-wheel-drive trips, and flying fox (zip-line) rides. ✉ *Green Mountains, via Canungra, 4275* ☎ *07/5544–0644 or 1800/ 688722* ⊕ *www.oreillys.com.au* ➲ *70 rooms* ☖ *Restaurant, café, refrigerators, pool, outdoor hot tub, massage, sauna, hiking, bar, library, recreation room, theater, shop, children's programs (all ages), laundry facilities, free parking; no room TVs* ☰ *AE, DC, MC, V.*

$–$$
🖽 **Binna Burra Mountain Lodge.** The cozy and secluded cabins at tranquil Binna Burra Mountain Lodge, founded in 1933, afford sweeping views across the hinterland to the Gold Coast. Rates include all meals and guided activities, such as the highly informative guided bushwalks and rappelling. There are also kids-only bushwalks, picnics, and rain-forest adventures, as well as the Discovery Forest educational environmental playground. The lodge also operates a Binna Burra bus that makes a daily round-trip to the Surfers Paradise Transit Centre. ✉ *Binna Burra Rd., Beechmont, 4211* ☎ *07/5533–3622 or 1800/074260* ⊕ *www. binnaburralodge.com.au* ➲ *40 cabins* ☖ *Restaurant, mountain bikes, hiking, bar, children's programs (all ages), laundry facilities, free parking* ☰ *AE, DC, MC, V* ⫯⊙⫯ *All-inclusive.*

¢
🖽 **Canungra Hotel.** In the middle of Canungra Valley, surrounded by vineyards, is this sprawling, two-story Tudor-style house with a wraparound veranda. Locals drink and play the poker machines downstairs, while upstairs are sunny suites lined with old photographs of the area. ✉ *18 Kidston St., Canungra 4275* ☎ *07/5543–5233* 🖷 *07/5543–5617* ➲ *9 rooms* ☖ *Restaurant, bar, casino* ☰ *AE, DC, MC, V.*

Gold Coast A to Z

To research prices, get advice from other travelers, and book travel arrangements, visit www.fodors.com.

AIR TRAVEL
Flight times from the Gold Coast are 30 minutes to Brisbane, 2 hours 10 minutes to Melbourne, and 1 hour 25 minutes to Sydney. Qantas operates out of Gold Coast Airport.

CARRIERS 🛈 **Qantas** ☎ 13–1313.

AIRPORTS
Also known as Coolangatta Airport, Gold Coast Airport is the region's main airport.
🛈 **Gold Coast Airport** ✉ Gold Coast Hwy., Bilinga ☎ 07/5589-1100.

BUS TRAVEL

Long-distance buses traveling between Sydney and Brisbane stop at Coolangatta and Surfers Paradise.

Allstate Scenic Tours leaves Brisbane for O'Reilly's Rainforest Guesthouse in the Gold Coast Hinterland (A$44 round-trip) Sunday–Friday at 9:30 AM from the Brisbane Transit Centre.

Greyhound Pioneer Australia runs an express coach from the Gold Coast to Brisbane International Airport and Coolangatta (Gold Coast) Airport, as well as day trips that cover southeast Queensland with daily connections to Sydney and Melbourne.

McCafferty's Express Coaches operates between Brisbane's Roma Street transit center and the Gold Coast.

From the Gold Coast, Mountain Coast Company buses pick passengers up from the major bus depots, most of the major hotels, and from Coolangatta Airport for O'Reilly's Rainforest Guesthouse in the Gold Coast Hinterland (A$39 round-trip).

Surfside Buslines runs every 15 minutes between Gold Coast attractions, along the strip between Tweed Heads and Southport.
🚌 Bus Information **Allstate Scenic Tours** ✉ Brisbane Transit Centre, Roma St., Brisbane ☎ 07/3003-0700. **Greyhound Pioneer Australia** ✉ 6 Beach Rd., Surfers Paradise ☎ 13-2030 ⊕ www.greyhound.com.au. **McCafferty's Express Coaches** ✉ 6 Beach Rd., Surfers Paradise ☎ 07/5538-2700 or 13-1499 ⊕ www.mccaffertys.com.au. **Mountain Coast Company** ☎ 07/5524-4249. **Surfside Buslines** ☎ 13-1230.

CAR RENTAL

All major car-rental agencies have offices in Brisbane, Surfers Paradise, and at Gold Coast Airport. Companies operating on the Gold Coast include Avis, Budget, and Thrifty. Four-wheel-drive vehicles are available.
🚗 Agencies **Avis** ✉ Ferny and Cypress Aves., Surfers Paradise ☎ 07/5539-9388. **Budget** ✉ Gold Coast Airport, Gold Coast Hwy., Bilinga ☎ 07/5536-5377. **Thrifty** ✉ 3006 Gold Coast Hwy., Surfers Paradise ☎ 07/5570-9999 ✉ Gold Coast Airport, Gold Coast Hwy., Bilinga ☎ 07/5536-6955.

CAR TRAVEL

The Gold Coast begins 65 km (40 mi) south of Brisbane. Take the M1 highway south. The highway bypasses the Gold Coast towns, but there are well-marked signs to guide you to your destination. From Brisbane International Airport take the Toll Road over the Gateway Bridge to avoid having to drive through Brisbane, then follow the signs to the Gold Coast. Driving distances and times from the Gold Coast are 859 km (533 mi) and 12 hours to Sydney via the Pacific Highway, 105 km (65 mi) and 1 hour to Brisbane, and 1,815 km (1,125 mi) and 22 hours to Cairns.

EMERGENCIES

In an emergency, dial 000 for an ambulance, the fire department, or the police.
🚑 **Gold Coast Hospital** ✉ 108 Nerang St., Southport ☎ 07/5571-8211.

MAIL, INTERNET & SHIPPING

Internet Express Café is a good place to retrieve e-mail and surf the Web. The Gold Coast Mail Centre has Australia Post overnight services; it's open weekdays 8:30 to 5.
📧 **Internet Express Café** ✉ Australia Fair Shopping Centre, Level 1, Marine Parade, Southport ☎ 07/5527-0335.
📧 **Gold Coast Mail Centre** ✉ 26 Crombie Ave., Bundall ☎ 13-1318.

MONEY MATTERS

You can cash traveler's checks and change money at most banks and financial institutions on the Gold Coast. Commonwealth Bank of Australia and ANZ have ATMs that accept Cirrus and Maestro cards, as well as others that are enabled for international access.

🏦 Banks **ANZ** ✉ 3171 Gold Coast Hwy. ☎ 13-1314. **Commonwealth Bank of Australia** ✉ Pacific Fair Shopping Center, Hooker Blvd. ☎ 07/5526-9071.

TOURS

Coachtrans provides theme-park transfers and has several day tours of the Gold Coast. Terranora Coach Tours conducts a variety of day tours of the Gold Coast.

🏦 Tour Operators **Coachtrans** ✉ 64 Ourimbah Rd., Tweed Heads ☎ 07/5506-9700. **Terranora Coach Tours** ✉ 85 Anne St., Southport ☎ 07/5538-7113.

TRAIN TRAVEL

Regular service from 5:30 AM until midnight connects Brisbane and the Helensvale, Nerang, and Robina stations on the Gold Coast. Contact Queensland Rail.

🏦 Train Information **Queensland Rail** ✉ 305 Edward St. Brisbane ☎ 07/3235-1323 or 13-2232 ⊕ www.qr.com.au.

VISITOR INFORMATION

🏦 Tourist Information **Gold Coast Information Centres** ✉ Beach House Plaza, Marine Parade, Coolangatta ☎ 07/5536-7765 ✉ Cavill Mall Kiosk, Surfers Paradise ☎ 07/5538-4419. **Gold Coast Tourism Bureau** ✉ 64 Ferny Ave., Level 2, Surfers Paradise, 4217 ☎ 07/5592-2699 ⊕ www.goldcoasttourism.com.au.

SOUTHERN DOWNS

A two-hour drive west of Brisbane, the Southern Downs is a popular weekend escape for those keen to head for the hills. This area ranges from Cunninghams Gap in the east to Goondiwindi in the west, to Allora in the north and Wallangarra in the south. During summer, the trees of the area known as the Granite Belt, named after the large granite formations scattered throughout the area, bear peaches, plums, cherries, and apricots. In autumn, the many vineyards are ripe for harvesting. Winter invites wine-tasting tours, and spring brings the scent of peach and apple blossoms to the air.

The Southern Downs is one of Queensland's premier wine-producing areas, with 25 or so wineries scattered around the town of Stanthorpe. Although they only produce a fraction of Australia's wine, the area is forging a name for itself with highly regarded vintages.

Stanthorpe

225 km (140 mi) southwest of Brisbane.

This is the coldest town in Queensland, and it has been known to have snow in winter. It is also the center of Queensland's first boutique wine region, as well as the hub for the local fruit producers. The name Stanthorpe is derived from two English words: *stannum,* meaning tin, and *thorpe,* meaning village or town. It was so named because in the early 1870s tin was discovered in the area, which spurred a mining boom that lasted 15 years. When the resources ran out, the land was used for grazing until after World War II, when the first vineyards were established by Italian migrants.

Glen Aplin

10 km (6 mi) south of Stanthorpe.

Glen Aplin is a tiny blink-and-you'll-miss-it town, but it is also the home of **Felsberg Winery** (✉ Townsends Rd., Glen Aplin ☎ 07/4683–4332), known for its red wines and honey mead, a fermented honey wine. To reach the winery, you must drive up a winding road to a German-inspired château perched on top of a hill. The tasting room affords views over the Severn River Valley and the Granite Belt area. The winery is open daily 9:30–4:30.

Ballandean

8 km (5 mi) south of Glen Aplin.

Ballandean is perhaps the most famous town in the wineries region, mostly due to the **Ballandean Estate Wines,** winners of numerous wine awards. The property includes the oldest family-owned and -operated vineyard and winery in Queensland; the first grapes were grown on the site in 1931. The tasting room is the original brick shed built in 1950. The Barrel Room Cafe behind it—complete with huge, wine-filled, 125-year-old wooden barrels lining one wall—serves light lunches and coffee. ✉ *Sundown Rd., Ballandean* ☎ *07/4684–1226* ⊕ *www. ballandean-estate.com.au* 🖾 *Free* 🕙 *Daily 9–5; free tours at 11, 1, 3, and by request.*

Girraween National Park is one of the most popular parks in southeast Queensland. At the end of the New England Tableland, it has massive granite outcrops, boulders and precariously balanced rocks, eucalyptus forests, and wildflowers in spring. There are also about 17 km (10½ mi) of walking tracks. Campers must obtain permits from the park's ranger. ✉ *Ballandean, 4382, 11 km (7 mi) north of Wallangarra or 26 km (16 mi) south of Stanthorpe on the New England Hwy.* ☎ *07/4684–5157.*

Where to Stay & Eat

\$\$–\$\$\$ ✕🏠 **Vineyard Cottages and Café.** Built around a turn-of-the-20th-cen-
Fodor'sChoice   tury church that is now the Vineyard Café, this place has earned a rep-
★   utation for quality and attention to detail. Wood furnishings, cream-color carpets, and fresh flowers decorate the cottage interiors. The café, open on weekends for nonguests, serves superb meals in a country atmosphere. You can also order dinner from the menu and have it delivered to your room—complete with a white linen tablecloth and a scented candle. Breakfast is included, and deluxe picnic hampers are available. ✉ *New England Hwy., Ballandean, 4382* ☎ *07/4684–1270* 🖶 *07/4684–1324* ⊕ *www.vineyard-cottages.com.au* 🛏 *4 cottages* ⚭ *Restaurant, room service, bar* 🖃 *AE, MC, V* ⑩ *CP.*

\$–\$\$\$ 🏠 **Vacy Hall.** This redbrick mansion set in verdant gardens was built in the 1880s as a private home for the landed gentry. With wraparound verandas and balconies, high ceilings, antique furnishings, and fireplaces in almost every room, this Heritage-listed house has successfully retained an air of languid, old-world charm. The hotel was in fact the first inn in Toowoomba—a town of beautiful parks and public gardens. ✉*135 Russell St., Toowoomba 4350* ☎*07/4639–2055* 🖶*07/4632–0160* ✉*mandersen@bigpond.com* 🛏*12 rooms* ⚭ *In-room fax, in-room data ports, minibar, dry cleaning, laundry facilities, free parking* 🖃 *AE, DC, MC, V.*

Southern Downs A to Z

To research prices, get advice from other travelers, and book travel arrangements, visit www.fodors.com.

BUS TRAVEL
Crisps Coaches operates regular daily service from Brisbane.
▪ **Crisps Coaches** ☎ 07/3236-5266.

CAR TRAVEL
The Southern Downs is an easy two-hour drive west of Brisbane via the Cunningham Highway. This is the best way to travel to this area, as the picturesque drive takes you through hills and small country towns.

EMERGENCIES
In an emergency, dial 000 for an ambulance, the fire department, or the police.
▪ **Stanthorpe Hospital** ✉ 6 McGregor Terr., Stanthorpe ☎ 07/4681-5222.

TOURS
The Grape Escape runs winery and progressive dinner tours, including overnight excursions, in Stanthorpe and from Brisbane or the Gold Coast. The full-day winery tour (A$60–A$80) visits five wineries and includes lunch. The overnight winery tour (A$198, including accommodation) visits eight wineries. The progressive dinner tours (A$85) include three courses, each at a different winery, and run every Saturday night June through August.
▪ **The Grape Escape** ☎ 07/4681-4761 or 1800/361150 ⊕ www.grapeescape.com.au.

VISITOR INFORMATION
▪ Tourist Information **Southern Downs Tourist Association** ✉ Albion St., Warwick ☎ 07/4661-3401 ⊕ www.qldsoutherndowns.org.au. **Stanthorpe Tourist Information Centre** ✉ Leslie Parade, Stanthorpe ☎ 07/4681-2057.

SUNSHINE COAST

One hour from Brisbane by car to its southernmost point, the Sunshine Coast is a 60-km (37-mi) stretch of white-sand beaches, inlets, lakes, and mountains. It begins at the Glass House Mountains and extends to Rainbow Beach in the north. Kenilworth is its inland extent, 40 km (25 mi) from the ocean. For the most part, the Sunshine Coast has avoided the high-rise glitz of its southern cousin, the Gold Coast. Although there are plenty of stylish restaurants, endearing bed-and-breakfasts, and luxurious hotels, the Sunshine Coast is best loved for its abundant national parks, secluded coves, and picturesque mountain villages.

en route
The Bruce Highway runs north from Brisbane through flat eucalyptus country and past large stands of pine, which are slowly retreating as Brisbane housing sprawls northward. Shortly after the Caboolture turnoff, 44 km (27 mi) north of Brisbane, you will come to a region that was once home to a large Aboriginal population but is now a prosperous dairy center. Here also is the turnoff to **Bribie Island,** 25 km (16 mi) to the east, which has magnificent beaches, some with glass-calm waters and others with rolling Pacific surf.

Numbers in the margin correspond to points of interest on the Sunshine Coast map.

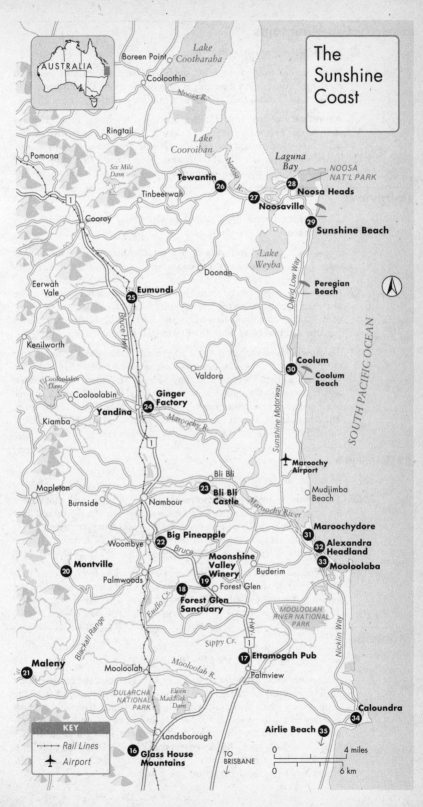

AUSTRALIA

The Sunshine Coast

Boreen Point

Lake Cootharaba

Cooloothin

Noosa R.

Ringtail

Lake Cooroiban

Laguna Bay

NOOSA NAT'L PARK

Pomona

Six Mile Dam

Tewantin 26

Noosa R.

27 **Noosaville**

28 **Noosa Heads**

Tinbeerwah

Cooroy

29 **Sunshine Beach**

Lake Weyba

Eerwah Vale

25 **Eumundi**

Doonan

David Low Way

Peregian Beach

Kenilworth

Bruce Hwy.

Cooloolabin Dam

Ginger Factory 24

Valdora

30 **Coolum**

Coolum Beach

Cooloolabin

Yandina

Maroochy R.

SOUTH PACIFIC OCEAN

Kiamba

Sunshine Motorway

✈ **Maroochy Airport**

Mapleton

Bli Bli 23 **Bli Bli Castle**

Maroochy River

Mudjimba Beach

Burnside

Nambour

Big Pineapple 22

Bruce

Maroochydore

31

32 **Alexandra Headland**

Woombye

Montville 20

Moonshine Valley Winery

19

Buderim

33 **Mooloolaba**

Palmwoods

18

Forest Glen Sanctuary

Forest Glen

Eudlo Cr.

MOOLOOLAH RIVER NATIONAL PARK

Blackall Range

Maleny 21

Mooloolah

Mooloolah R.

Sippy Cr.

17 **Ettamogah Pub**

Palmview

Nicklin Way

DULARCHA NATIONAL PARK

Ewen Maddock Dam

Caloundra 34

Landsborough

Airlie Beach 35

KEY

┼─┼─┼─ *Rail Lines*

✈ *Airport*

16 **Glass House Mountains**

TO BRISBANE

0 — 4 miles

0 — 6 km

Glass House Mountains

16 *65 km (40 mi) north of Brisbane.*

More than 20 million years old, the Glass House Mountains consist of nine dramatic, conical outcrops. The cones lie along the old main road about a half hour outside Brisbane to the west of the Bruce Highway.

Australia Zoo, Crocodile Hunter Steve Irwin's home base, displays Australian animals: pythons, taipans, adders, kangaroos, eagles, wallabies—and crocodiles. ⊠ *Glass House Mountains Tourist Route, 5 km (3 mi) north of Glass House Mountains, Beerwah* ☎ *07/5494–1134* ⊕ *www.crocodilehunter.com* ⊠ *A$21* ☉ *Daily 8:30–4.*

Palmview

21 km (13 mi) north of Glass House Mountains, 82 km (51 mi) north of Brisbane.

There's a large, red-roof parody of a classic Australian pub on the left side of the Bruce Highway a few kilometers north of Palmview. A vintage car perches precariously on the roof, and the whole building appears on the verge of collapse. This is the **Ettamogah Pub,** whose name and design are based on the famous pub featured for decades in the work of Australian cartoonist Ken Maynard. It has an upstairs bistro, a beer garden, and bar. Next door, the **Ettamogah Bakery** sells excellent pies.

The **Aussie World** amusement area adjacent to Ettamogah Pub has a large shed with pool tables, as well as long wooden tables that form the pub's beer garden. There are also pony rides, a Ferris wheel, a roller coaster, a merry-go-round, a small lake with motorized boats, a luge ride, a souvenir outlet that sells Ettamogah-brand beverages, and an opal shop. The **Aboriginal Cultural Centre** displays Aboriginal art. ⊠ *Bruce Hwy.* ☎ *07/5494–5444* ⊠ *Free; rides extra* ☉ *Daily 9–5.*

Forest Glen

10 km (6 mi) northwest of Palmview.

18 The expansive **Forest Glen Sanctuary** is a drive-through park that covers 60 acres of forest and pastures where rusa, fallow, chital, and red deer will come right up to your car, especially if you have purchased a 50¢ feed bag. Koala shows take place daily at 11 and 2. ⊠ *Tanawha Tourist Dr., off Bruce Hwy.* ☎ *07/5445–1274* ⊠ *A$13.90* ☉ *Daily 9–5.*

19 The **Moonshine Valley Winery** produces quality wines from Queensland-grown fruit. It offers free tastings of its wines and liquors, including the genuine Australian spirit Captain John. ⊠ *374 Mons Rd.* ☎ *07/5445–1198* ⊠ *A$13.90* ☉ *Weekdays 10–4, weekends 10–5.*

Montville

20 *16 km (10 mi) northwest of Forest Glen.*

This quaint mountain village, settled in 1887, is called the creative heart of the Sunshine Coast. There are panoramic views of the coast from the main street, which was built with a blend of Tudor, Irish, and English cottages of log or stone; Bavarian and Swiss houses; and old Queenslanders. Shops in town are filled with a browser's delight of curiosities and locally made crafts. **Kondalilla National Park** (⊠ Kondalilla Falls Rd.), with its swimming hole, waterfall, picnic grounds, and walking trails, is also a popular local attraction.

ABORIGINAL ART & MUSIC

ABORIGINES CAN LAY CLAIM to one of the oldest art and music traditions in the world. Traditionally a hunter-gatherer society with an oral lore, Aborigines used these modes to impart knowledge and express beliefs. The underlying sacred and ritual themes were based primarily upon the Dreaming (an oral history that established the pattern of life for each clan). Pictures were drawn in sand, painted on trees or implements, and carved or painted onto rock surfaces. Similarly, songs and music were used to portray events such as sacred rituals, bushfires, or successful hunts. Traditionally only men created works of art—painted or carved—while women expressed themselves through body decoration and by making artifacts such as bags or necklaces. Today, however, there are many female Aboriginal artists, some of whom follow the traditional styles and others who have adapted their own style of art.

There are several different and easily recognizable types of Aboriginal art. X-ray art reveals the exterior of the creatures as well as their internal organs and skeleton. Mimi art is myriad small matchlike figures of men, women, and animals engaged in some obvious activity such as a hunt. This art resembles that found in many Pacific Islands as well as South Africa and Spain. Another type is stenciling, especially of the hands, but also of feet and sometimes entire bodies; the body part is placed on a surface and paint is sprayed around it to leave an impression on the object. Symbolic art uses diagonal, parallel, or concentric lines painted or carved onto surfaces of the body art.

The oldest form of Aboriginal art is painting or engraving on rocks. Archaeologists have evidence that the marks made in Koonalda cave, beneath the Nullarbor Plain in South Australia, are up to 20,000 years old. Rock art is predominately magical-cum-religious expression in haunting red or white figures.

Like visual art, music also had a purpose and followed regional or song lines. For example, a clan might sing about a bushfire in different ways according to their song line—how and where the fire started, how it spread, and how it eventually died down. Music was also used to recount stories of travels made by animal or human ancestors, often in minute detail describing each place and event, to define tribal lands and boundaries.

The didgeridoo is possibly the world's oldest musical instrument, originally found in Northern Australia. It is made from tree trunks hollowed out by termites and is used to accompany chants and songs. In most tribal groups, men, women, and children can play the instrument. It is played by sealing your mouth at one end and vibrating your lips. The didgeridoo acts as an amplifier to produce a haunting, hollow sound.

Today there is not only a resurgence of Aboriginal art and music, but also an acceptance of it in contemporary mainstream Australian art. Young Aborigines who may not have had a strong religious or tribal upbringing are learning about their ancestors through art and music. An example of this are the Aborigines who formed Tjapukai Aboriginal Cultural Park near Cairns. Through the park, the local Aborigines were able to resurrect their tribal language and culture and then present it to the public through music and art. They can present contemporary artworks that are connected with their Dreaming, and keep their ancestral connection alive to pass on to future generations.

—Jane Carstens

Where to Stay & Eat

$–$$ ✕ **Montville Views.** Both the large veranda and stylish enclosed dining area overlook the rain forest and the coast at this restaurant tucked below Montville's main street. The modern Australian fare borrows freely from other cuisines in such dishes as barramundi dusted in Cajun seasoning and served with a flambéed banana and salad. The signature dish is the creole salad, seasoned with cayenne pepper and known as "the firecracker." ⊠ *171–183 Main St.* ☎ *07/5442–9204* ▭ *MC, V* ☉ *No dinner Mon.–Wed.*

¢–$ ✕ **Poets Café.** The wood and wrought-iron veranda surrounds a dining room entirely enclosed by French doors, which are usually swung wide open to let in views of the rain forest. The menu focuses on open sandwiches, seafood platters, and meat and pasta dishes. Save room for *Utopia*, the chocolate macadamia tart. ⊠ *167 Main St.* ☎ *07/5478–5479* ▭ *AE, DC, MC, V.*

$$$ ⊡ **The Falls Cottages.** Adjacent to the forest of Kondalilla Falls National Park and built in the style of traditional Queensland houses, these secluded cottages make for a lovely romantic getaway. Hardwood floors, floral patterns, country furnishings, and wood fires fill the spacious cottages, which also have whirlpool tubs and cooking facilities. The getaway-from-it-all atmosphere means no room phones. A breakfast basket each morning is included in the price. ⊠ *20 Kondalilla Falls Rd., 4560* ☎ *07/5445–7000* ⊕ *www.thefallscottages.com.au* ↝ *6 cottages* ☐ *In-room hot tubs, kitchenettes, free parking; no room phones* ▭ *AE, DC, MC, V* ◎ *CP.*

¢–$$$ ⊡ **Clouds of Montville.** This two-tiered colonial-style motel is set on five acres of rain forest on the Blackall Range, overlooking the lush valleys leading to the Sunshine Coast. Generously-sized rooms and self-contained cottages, all with internal brick walls, floral furnishings, and verandas, are scattered amid the trees. A free-form saltwater pool is surrounded by rocks and tropical plants. ⊠ *166 Balmoral Rd., 4560* ☎ *07/ 5442–9174* ⊟ *07/5442–9475* ⊕ *www.cloudsofmontville.com.au* ↝ *10 rooms, 4 cottages* ☐ *Tennis court, saltwater pool, laundry facilities, free parking* ▭ *AE, DC, MC, V.*

Shopping

Jasmin Cottage (⊠ 169 Main St. ☎ 07/5442–9420) showcases arts and crafts from local and international designers, including pottery, vases, jewelry, leatherwork, and picture frames.

Natures Image Photography (⊠ Main St. ☎☎ 07/5442–9564 ⊕ www. nature.artdata.net.au) sells beautiful photographs of Australian animals and landscapes.

Maleny

㉑ *14 km (8.7 mi) west of Montville.*

The tiny hinterland village of Maleny is a lively mix of rural life, the arts, wineries, and cooperative community ventures. First settled around 1880, Maleny is now a working dairy town; each week calves are led up the main street to the sale yards, handily situated next door to the local pub. Maleny is also known for its large number of arts and crafts galleries and festivals, such as the Scarecrow Carnival and the Spring Festival of Color, held during the second weekend in November. **Lake Baroon,** accessible from Maleny's main street, offers sailing, canoeing, fishing, and swimming, as well as walking trails along the banks to where the Obi Obi Creek flows into the lake.

Where to Stay & Eat

¢–$ ✕ **Maple 3 Café.** A covered veranda and courtyard surround this local favorite. The menu changes daily, but there are always salads, foccacias, and a lot of dessert options. Come in for brunch, grab a sandwich and huge slice of cake, and head down to Lake Baroon for a picnic, or just sit out front and watch the eclectic mix of Maleny townsfolk go about their day. ✉ *3 Maple St.* ☎ 07/5499–9177 ☐ *AE, DC, MC, V.*

$–$$ ☐ **Maleny Tropical Retreat.** At the end of a steep, winding driveway is a dense, misty rain-forest valley; in its midst is this this Balinese-style bed-and-breakfast. Tropical gardens surround the small, two-story house furnished with Balinese touches—right down to the music. Each room has a balcony overlooking the rain forest and a glassed-walled spa-bath, both of which provide fabulous views of Lake Baroon. Hiking trails from the house lead to the creek. ✉ *304 Maleny-Montville Rd., 4552* ☎ *07/5435–2113* 🖷 *07/5435–2114* ⊕ *www.malenytropicalretreat.com* ⏎ *2 rooms* ⚬ *In-room hot tubs, in-room VCRs, hiking, free parking; no kids, no smoking* ☐ *AE, DC, MC, V.*

Shopping

Peace of Green (✉ 38 Maple St. ☎ 07/5499–9311) is a collective of local artists and craftspeople who share a rambling old gallery on Maleny's main street. Staffed by the artists, the gallery showcases paintings, pottery, vases, jewelry, clothing, woodwork, and glasswork.

Bold in Gold (✉ 43 Maple St. ☎ 07/5499–9299 ⊕ www.boldingold.com.au) sells handcrafted jewelry and a wide selection of art by local artists.

Nambour

9 km (5½ mi) northwest of Forest Glen, 101 km (63 mi) north of Brisbane.

★ ☾ ㉒ Sunshine Plantation is home to the impossible-to-miss **Big Pineapple.** The 50-foot fiberglass monster towers over the highway, and you can climb inside to learn how pineapples are grown. The plantation is a tourist-oriented operation, incorporating a large souvenir shop, jewelry store, arts-and-crafts shop, restaurants (with impressive ice-cream sundaes), flume rides, train rides, and an animal nursery. It's also a good place to see how macadamia nuts and other tropical fruits are cultivated. ✉ *Nambour Connection Rd., 6 km (4 mi) south of Nambour* ☎ 07/5442–1333 ⊕ *www.bigpineapple.com.au* ✉ *Free; rides extra* ☾ *Daily 9–5.*

☾ ㉓ Children love **Bli Bli Castle,** a surprisingly realistic 1973 replica of a Norman castle. The castle is starting to show its age but still has everything necessary for a rousing game of make-believe, including dungeons and a torture chamber. The turnoff for Bli Bli is at the north end of Nambour, opposite a Toyota dealership. ✉ *David Low Way, Bli Bli* ☎ 07/5448–5373 ✉ *A$10* ☾ *Daily 9–4.*

Yandina

9 km (5½ mi) north of Nambour.

☾ ㉔ The **Ginger Factory** is one of the legendary establishments of Queensland tourism. It now goes far beyond its original factory-door sale of ginger, although you can still observe the factory at work. A restaurant and a large shop sell ginger in all forms—from crystallized ginger to ginger incorporated into jams, chocolates, and herbal products. There's also a miniature train ride (A$6). ✉ *50 Pioneer Rd. (Coolum Rd.) 1 km (½ mi) east of Bruce Hwy.* ☎ 07/5446–7100 ⊕ *www.buderimginger.com* ✉ *Free* ☾ *Daily 9–5.*

Where to Stay & Eat

$$ ✕ **Spirit House.** The owners, who lived in Thailand for five years, have
Fodor'sChoice done a remarkable job rendering Thai cuisine on Queensland soil. The
★ menu changes seasonally, but a worthy signature dish is the whole
crispy fish with tamarind, chili, and garlic sauce. Save plenty of room
for desserts such as fresh mango with sticky rice, or tropical ice creams
and sorbet. The tropical garden setting is complete with a lagoon and
Buddhist shrines. A hydroponic farm and cooking school are on-site.
✉ *4 Ninderry Rd.* ☎ *07/5446–8994* ⊕ *www.spirithouse.com.au* ▭ *AE,
DC, MC, V* ⌘ *Reservations essential* ⊘ *No dinner Sun.–Tues.*

$–$$ ⌂ **Ninderry Manor.** Bright but homey furnishings, beds romantically
draped with nets, and personal service make this luxury bed-and-break-
fast worth every cent. On the ridge of Mt. Ninderry in the Sunshine Coast
hinterland, this 1850s manor house has excellent views of the coastline.
You'll be treated to chocolates on arrival and a leisurely full breakfast.
At dusk, enjoy cocktails and canapés while listening to the wildlife from
the courtyard, or set off to one of several excellent restaurants nearby.
✉ *12 Karnu Dr., Ninderry, 7 km (4½ mi) outside Yandina, 4561* ☎ *07/
5472–7255* ⌨ *07/5446–7089* ⊕ *ninderrymanor.com.au* ▭ *3 rooms*
⌂ *Pool, business services, meeting rooms, free parking; no kids, no smoking* ▭ *AE, DC, MC, V* ⊠ *BP.*

Eumundi

㉕ *18 km (11 mi) north of Nambour, 21 km (13 mi) southwest of Noosa
Heads.*

Fodor'sChoice The **Eumundi Markets,** the best street markets on the Sunshine Coast, take
★ place on Saturday from 7 to 2 on Memorial Drive in Eumundi. Local
craftspeople sell colorful wares in more than 250 stalls.

Where to Stay

$ ⌂ **Taylor's Damn Fine Bed and Breakfast.** Taylor's lives up to its name with
a gracious old Queenslander filled with an eclectic but harmonious
blend of Australian and Asian furnishings. The spacious guest rooms,
four with double beds and one with twin beds, have private baths. Two
are adjacent to the main house in a restored railway carriage. The house
overlooks 4 acres of lush paddock that borders the North Maroochy
River, where you can take a short rain-forest walk. Also on the property are a pool and a 190-yard golf-driving range. The B&B is a short
stroll from Eumundi's main street, and a 15-minute drive from Noosa.
Dinner is available by prior arrangement for groups of eight or more.
✉ *15 Eumundi–Noosa Rd., 4562* ☎ *07/5442–8685* ⌨ *07/5442–8168*
⊕ *www.taylorsbandb.com.au* ▭ *5 rooms, 1 3-bedroom cottage* ⌂ *Dining room, driving range, pool, free parking, some pets allowed; no a/c,
no room phones* ▭ *AE, DC, MC, V.*

Tewantin

㉖ *18 km (11 mi) northeast of Eumundi, 7 km (4½ mi) west of Noosa Heads.*

Originally a timber and fishing town, Tewantin now draws visitors
with its relaxed and welcoming atmosphere. You can fish or boat in the
peaceful Noosa River, or enjoy a tranquil riverside dinner.

Where to Eat

$ ✕ **Amici's.** An open, informal restaurant with tables on the deck overlooking
the marina, this Italian restaurant highlights veal steaks, woodfired pizzas, and hand-made pasta. The casual waitstaff and generous portions ensure its popularity with both locals and tourists. ✉ *Noosa Harbour
Marine Village, Tewantin* ☎ *07/5449–0515* ▭ *MC, V.*

Sports & the Outdoors

BOATING You can rent canoes, catamarans, windsurfers, paddle skis, and motorboats at **Everglades Tourist Park and Boat Hire** (☎ 07/5485–3164) at Boreen Point, north of Tewantin on the western side of Lake Cootharaba. They also run a water taxi to the Everglades, where you can hire a canoe to explore.

GUIDED TOURS **Everglades Water Bus Co.** conducts combined boat and four-wheel-drive tours from Harbour Town Jetty in Tewantin to the Everglades, Cooloola National Park, Cherry Venture, Bubbling Springs, and the Coloured Sands. Another boat takes you to the Jetty Restaurant in Boreen Point. ☒ *Harbour Town Marina* ☎ *07/5447–1838.*

Noosaville

27 *4 km (2½ mi) east of Tewantin, 3 km (2 mi) west of Noosa Heads.*

A snug little town dotted with small hotels and apartment complexes, Noosaville is the access point for trips to the **Teewah Coloured Sands,** an area of multicolored sands that were created by natural chemicals in the soil. Dating from the Ice Age, some of the 72 different hues of sand form cliffs rising to 600 feet.

Where to Eat

$–$$ ✕ **Gusto.** Terra-cotta and Turkish tiles pave this open-air dining room looking out onto the Noosa River. Marble tables are surrounded by oil paintings of lilies and frangipani hung on butterscotch walls. The house specials are the pan-seared scallops with artichoke fritters, and the char-grilled Mooloolaba king prawns with avocado, feta, and lime salad. For dessert, try the pear tart tartin, or the vanilla pannacotta with summer berries. ☒ *257 Gympie Terr.* ☎ *07/5449–7144* ▭ *AE, DC, MC, V.*

★ $–$$ ✕ **Max's Native Sun Cuisine.** This small indoor-outdoor Cajun-creole restaurant has a devoted following, thanks to owner-chef Max Porter's formidable reputation. The specialty is duck; the six-course tasting menu includes a layered dish of pâtés and duck-leg confit. There are also six-course seafood and vegetarian set menus. Entrées rotate, but expect dishes similar to creole prawn chowder. Finish with a Grand Marnier and passion-fruit soufflé. ☒ *Thomas St. at No. 1 Island Resort* ☎ *07/5447–1931* ▭ *AE, MC, V* ☉ *Closed Sun.–Mon. No lunch.*

¢ ✕ **The Nourish Bar.** This riverside café specializes in fresh fruit smoothies and juices. Take it to sit on the riverbank, or stay on the patio with a "Noosaville Tropics" blend of pineapple, strawberries, banana, honey, and coconut cream. The café also serves fresh fruit gelati, espresso, and such delicacies as panini, pumpkin-and-chickpea salad, and pancakes with caramelized apple. ☒ *Shop 1, 253 Gympie Terr.* ☎ *07/5449–9449* ▭ *AE, DC, MC, V.*

Sports & the Outdoors

GOLF The **Noosa Valley Country Club** (☒ 92 Valley Dr., Doonan ☎ 07/5449–1411) accepts visiting players. A 9-hole course is open daily, but tee times must be booked in advance.

RIVER CRUISES **Beyond Noosa's Great Escape** (☒ Jetty 67, Gympie Terr. ☎ 07/5449–9177 ⊕ www.beyondnoosa.com.au) trips take in the Everglades and the Noosa River and Lakes. The Everglades Cruise and Coloured Sands Safari is the most comprehensive tour, combining a cruise with a four-wheel-drive trip to Coloured Sands, Cherry Venture, and the rain forest, and including barbecue lunch and morning and afternoon teas.

Noosa Heads

28 *39 km (24 mi) northeast of Nambour, 17 km (11 mi) north of Coolum, 140 km (87 mi) north of Brisbane.*

Set beside the calm waters of Laguna Bay at the northern tip of the Sunshine Coast, Noosa Heads is one of the most stylish resort areas in Australia. The town once consisted of nothing more than a few shacks until the mid-1980s. Surfers discovered it first, lured by the spectacular waves that curl around the sheltering headland of Noosa National Park. Today, Noosa Heads is a charming mix of surf, sand, and sophistication, with a serious reputation for its unique and evolving cuisine. Views along the trail from Laguna Lookout to the top of the headland take in miles of magnificent beaches, ocean, and dense vegetation.

Where to Stay & Eat

$$ ✕ **Cato's Restaurant and Bar.** Cato's, in the Sheraton Noosa Resort, has a downstairs bar with windows thrown open onto bustling Hastings Street and a relaxed upstairs dining section. Seafood predominates; the Caesar salad with seared scallops and prosciutto is a constant favorite, as is the spiced tuna steak with baby beets. A fantastic seafood buffet on Friday and Saturday nights costs A$52.50. ⊠ *Hastings St.* ☎ *07/5449–4787* ▤ *AE, DC, MC, V.*

$–$$ ✕ **Aromas.** Café culture is a big part of the Noosa scene; this coffee shop was one of the first on Hastings Street and is still one of the best and most popular. The loyal clientele comes for the film-noir ambience and great people-watching. The menu has a modern Mediterranean slant, with an impressive array of cakes, biscuits, and coffees also on offer. ⊠ *32 Hastings St.* ☎ *07/5474–9788* ▤ *AE, DC, MC, V.*

$–$$ ✕ **Ricky Ricardo's River Bar and Restaurant.** A glassed-in dining room overlooking the Noosa River makes this restaurant perfect for anything from a relaxed lunch to a romantic dinner. The menu has a loose Mediterranean theme, with an emphasis on the best local, organic produce. Start off with a few tapas and a drink before moving on to a main course of a tagine of whitefish, fennel, pumpkin, and green chili over couscous and cilantro relish. ⊠ *Noosa Wharf, Quamby Pl.* ☎ *07/5447–2455* ⊕ *www.rickyricardos.com* ▤ *AE, DC, MC, V.*

$–$$ ✕ **Berardo's on the Beach.** Ex-pat. New Yorker Jim Berardo came to Noosa to retire and ended up with two restaurants. Berardo's on the Beach is the more casual of the two, and its prime location open to Noosa beach gives it a constant stream of customers. Quirky fish sculptures line the walls, and hand-blown chartreuse carafés are on every table. The weekly changing menu lists extravagant open sandwiches and light meals such as steamed mussels with *gremolata* (Italian seasonings), oregano, tomato, and toasted sourdough. You can also order cocktails and fresh juices, making it a lively place to take a break from the beach. ⊠ *Hastings St.* ☎ *07/5448–0888* ⊕ *www.berardos.com.au* ▤ *AE, DC, MC, V.*

$–$$ ✕ **Bistro C.** Spectacular views of the bay from the open dining area make a stunning backdrop for a meal of modern Australian cuisine. The menu highlights seafood, though landlubbers can partake of several vegetarian and meat dishes. Try the seafood antipasti plate, the justly famous egg-fried calamari, or grilled prawn skewers on a mango, snowpea, and cherry-tomato salad, served with ginger syrup and lime oil. ⊠ *Hastings St.* ☎ *07/5447–2855* ⊕ *www.bistroc.com.au* ▤ *AE, DC, MC, V.*

$–$$ ✕ **Sails.** "Super fresh and super simple" could be the motto at Sails, where modern Australian cuisine and an emphasis on seafood are the order of the day. Try the sushi platter, char-grilled Moreton Bay bugs, or smoked salmon with marinated feta. The open dining pavilion backs straight onto Noosa's famous beach. ⊠ *Corner Park Rd. and Hastings St.* ☎ *07/5447–4235* ⊕ *sailsnoosa.citysearch.com.au* ⊟ *AE, DC, MC, V.*

★ **$$$$** ✕⊡ **Sheraton Noosa Resort.** This six-story, horseshoe-shape complex faces fashionable Hastings Street on one side and the river on the other. There are various themes at play here, from the hard-to-miss apricot exterior to the luxury poolside villas. It's hard to find fault with the spacious rooms: each has a kitchenette, balcony, and Jacuzzi. Cato's Restaurant and Bar serves tropical fare. ⊠ *Hastings St., 4567* ☎ *07/5449–4888* 🖷 *07/5449–2230* ⊕ *www.sheratonnoosa.com.au* 🗝 *140 rooms, 19 suites, 8 villas, 2 penthouses* ♿ *Restaurant, kitchenettes, cable TV with movies and video games, pool, health club, massage, sauna, spa, bar, baby-sitting, laundry service, concierge, Internet, business services, meeting room, travel services, free parking; no-smoking floor* ⊟ *AE, DC, MC, V.*

$$$–$$$$ ⊡ **Netanya Noosa.** Most of the airy suites in this low-rise beachfront complex look straight over the main beach; a few are in a garden wing. Guests are pampered with soft bathrobes. Most suites have verandas large enough for room-service dining. The Presidential suite has a private terrace with an outdoor Jacuzzi, and a magnificent dining room in which a local chef will serve specially prepared dinners on request. ⊠ *75 Hastings St., 4567* ☎ *07/5447–4722 or 1800/072072* 🖷 *07/5447–3914* ⊕ *www.netanyanoosa.com.au* 🗝 *48 suites* ♿ *Kitchenettes, pool, outdoor hot tub, gym, sauna, spa, laundry service, travel services, free parking* ⊟ *AE, DC, MC, V.*

¢ ⊡ **Halse Lodge.** If you're looking for cheap accommodations in Noosa, look no further than this Heritage-listed guesthouse with colonial-style furnishings. Pictures of Noosa from yesteryear decorate the large utility rooms. The rooms are clean, the shared bathrooms modern. Choose from double rooms, twin rooms, and bunk rooms that sleep either four or six people. A short walk from Hastings Street, right on the edge of Noosa National Park, the complex is set in 2 acres of garden overlooking town. ⊠ *Halse La., 4567* ☎ *07/5447–3377 or 1800/242567* 🖷 *07/5447–2929* ⊕ *www.halselodge.com.au* 🗝 *26 rooms with shared bath* ♿ *Cafeteria, billiards, Ping-Pong, bar, travel services, free parking; no a/c, no room phones, no room TVs* ⊟ *MC, V.*

Shopping

Hastings Street has the best shopping in Noosa Heads, with chic boutiques, basic beach shops, bookshops, and jewelry and gift shops.

Sports & the Outdoors

Sea Wind Charters of Noosa (⊠ 10 Cooloosa St., Sunshine Beach ☎ 07/5447–3042) rents yachts and Jet Skis. The company also has a half-day cruise (A$75) that includes jet skiing, sailing, and boomnetting (being trailed behind a boat by a net).

Sunshine Beach

㉙ *4 km (2.5 mi) south of Noosa Heads.*

Ten minutes away from the bustle and crowds of Hastings Street and Noosa Beach is the serene suburb of Sunshine Beach, home to a number of good restaurants, a small shopping village and 16 km (10 mi) of beachfront leading to Noosa National Park.

Where to Stay & Eat

$–$$ ✕ **Sabai Sabai.** A long, winding bench with scattered Thai silk cushions
Fodor'sChoice leads to a terra-cotta–tile courtyard lined with bougainvillea, banana
★ palms, and bamboo. Inside, terra-cotta walls are teal and watermelon-colored, and the floor is decorated with piles of coconuts, sculptures, and huge potted tropical blossoms. The mostly Vietnamese and Thai

menu changes seasonally, but signature dishes remain: whole crispy fish with sweet-and-sour ginger-and-lime sauce, and *phrik king tofu* (stir-fried kaffir lime leaves, garlic, and chili, served with coconut rice and pickled green papaya relish). An extensive Australian and New Zealand wine list is on hand, as is a vegetarian menu. Desserts include the tropical parfait, with layers of fresh mango and raspberry couli, served with passion fruit brûlée and meringue. ⊠ *46 Duke St.* ☎ *07/5473–5177* 🖃 *AE, DC, MC, V.*

$–$$$ 🏨 **La Mer.** Across the street from the beach, every apartment-style suite in this two-story hotel has balconies facing the water. Rooms are large, with woven cane furniture and tile floors. Sunrise views from the balconies are gorgeous. La Mer is walking distance to Sunshine Beach's shopping village and restaurants, and you can book most tours in the hotel lobby. ⊠ *5-7 Belmore Terr. 4567* ☎ *07/5447–2111* 🖷 *07/5449–2483* ⊕ *www.lamersunshine.com.au* ➷ *18 units* ⚲ *Kitchens, in-room VCRs, pool, recreation room, baby-sitting, laundry facilities, travel services, free parking* 🖃 *AE, DC, MC, V.*

Coolum

③⓪ *17 km (11 mi) south of Noosa Heads, 25 km (16 mi) northeast of Nambour.*

At the center of the Sunshine Coast, Coolum makes an ideal base for exploring the surrounding countryside. It has what is probably the finest beach along the Sunshine Coast, and a growing reputation for good food.

Where to Stay & Eat

$–$$ ✕ **Beachhouse Restaurant and Bar.** Across the street from Coolum Beach and beneath the Baywatch Resort, this laid-back restaurant reflects the nature of the town. Windows are thrown wide open to bring in sea breezes over the terra-cotta–tile floor. Indoor and outdoor tables host local seasonal produce with Asian and Mediterranean flavors: seared scallops with smoked eggplant purée; cucumber and tzaztiki salad; and soy-glazed duck with roasted sweet potatoes and baby bok choy. ⊠ *172 David Low Way* ☎ *07/5446–4688* 🖃 *AE, DC, MC, V.*

¢ ✕ **Mojo's on the Beach.** If you're looking for a quick snack, a vegetarian bite, or a simple sandwich to take to the beach, this is the spot to get the best. Freshly squeezed or blended juices and smoothies, as well as coffee, are on hand to accompany the meal. For offbeat choices, try the souvlaki or a lentil burger. ⊠ *Shop 3, The Esplanade* ☎ *07/5473–9877.*

$$$–$$$$ 🏨 **Coolum Seaside.** These spacious, sunny apartments have excellent views of the coast, and are just around the corner from the beach and the town's main restaurant drag. Each unit has a large balcony or terrace, and some have a private roof garden. Bright seaside prints line the off-white walls, and tropically colored furniture stands atop bleached terra-cotta tiles. Several apartments can accommodate 10 guests. ⊠ *23 Beach Rd.,Coolum Beach, 4573* ☎ *07/5455–7200, 1800/809062* 🖷 *07/5455–7288* ⊕ *www.coolumseaside.com* ➷ *30 apartments* ⚲ *Cable TV, in-room VCRs, kitchens, 2 pools, hot tub, spa, laundry facilities, free parking* 🖃 *MC, V.*

★ $$$–$$$$ 🏨 **Hyatt Regency Resort.** Spread out at the foot of Mount Coolum, this is one of the best health spa–resorts in Australia. The spa has everything a fitness fanatic could want: pools, an aerobics room, a supervised gym, hot tubs, a hair and beauty salon, and dozens of beauty, pampering, and health treatments. Accommodations consist of one-bedroom studio suites and two-bedroom villas. The Ambassadors Club has two-bedroom luxury villas and three-bedroom residences. A boutique, wine shop, and restaurants are arranged around the complex's village square. A shuttle will transport you around the 370-acre resort. ✉ *Warran Rd., Coolum Beach, 4573* ☎ *07/5446–1234* 🖷 *07/5446–2957* ⊕ *www. coolum.hyatt.com* ⇨ *156 suites, 168 villas* ☖ *4 restaurants, in-room safes, kitchenettes, some microwaves, cable TV with movies, 18-hole golf course, 7 tennis courts, pro shop, 8 pools, wading pool, hot tub, aerobics, gym, health club, hair salon, massage, spa, beach, 4 bars, dance club, nightclub, shops, baby-sitting, children's programs (ages 6 wks–2), dry cleaning, laundry service, Internet, business services, convention center, meeting rooms, travel services, free parking; no smoking* 🖃 *AE, DC, MC, V* ⦿ *CP.*

Maroochydore

③① *18 km (11 mi) south of Coolum, 21 km (13 mi) north of Caloundra, 18 km (11 mi) east of Nambour.*

Maroochydore has been a popular beach resort for years and suffers its fair share of high-rise towers. Nevertheless, with its location at the mouth of the Maroochy River, the town has excellent surfing and swimming beaches.

Where to Stay & Eat

$$$–$$$$ ✕⊡ **Novotel Twin Waters Resort.** Nestled amid 660 private acres 9 km (5½ mi) north of Maroochydore, this hotel was built around a 15-acre saltwater lagoon bordering the Maroochy River and Mudjimba Beach (a boardwalk joins the resort and the beach). The family-style resort has a golf club with one of Queensland's finest courses, where kangaroos and ducks make their home. There are resident golf, surfing, and tennis pros. The lagoon is the site of activities such as catamaran sailing, windsurfing, and canoeing, all of which are free for guests. The excellent restaurant, Lily's-on-the-Lagoon, perches over one section of the lake. ✉ *Ocean Dr., 4558* ☎ *07/5448–8000* 🖷 *07/5448–8001* ⊕ *www. twinwatersresort.com.au* ⇨ *244 rooms, 120 suites* ☖ *4 restaurants, room service, some microwaves, refrigerators, room TVs with movies, driving range, 18-hole golf course, 6 tennis courts, pool, hair salon, massage, spa, beach, windsurfing, boating, bicycles, volleyball, 3 bars, baby-sitting, children's programs (ages 2–12), Internet, business services, convention center, meeting room, travel services, free parking* 🖃 *AE, DC, MC, V.*

Sports & the Outdoors

FISHING Rods and reels are available at **Maroochydore Fishing World** (✉ 22 1st Ave. ☎ 07/5443–2714).

GOLF The **Headland Golf Club** (✉ Golf Links Rd., Buderim ☎ 07/5444–5800), an 18-hole, par-72 course only a few km inland from Maroochydore, is open on Sunday, Monday, and Friday.

Shopping

One of the best shopping centers on the Sunshine Coast is **Sunshine Plaza** (✉ Aerodrome Rd. ☎ 07/5443–4133).

Alexandra Headland

③② *4 km (2½ mi) south of Maroochydore, 1 km (½ mi) north of Mooloolaba.*

The development between Maroochydore, Alexandra Headland, and Mooloolaba is continuous, so you're often unaware of passing through different townships. Alexandra Headland is the smallest of the three and has a very good surf beach.

Where to Stay

$–$$$$ ⊡ **Alexandra Beach Resort.** This sprawling complex overlooks the patrolled beach of Alexandra Headland and is a popular place for families and couples. The resort centerpiece is a huge 150-meter (492-foot) pool with a hot tub at either end, and a lagoon with two water slides and some rapids. In addition to 28 standard rooms, there are one-, two-, and three-bedroom units as well as a penthouse. Rooms are simply furnished with cane furniture and have kitchen and laundry facilities. Lagoon rooms have steps from the balcony straight into the pool. ⊠ *Alexandra Parade and Pacific Terr., 4572* ☎ *07/5475–0600 or 1800/ 640377* 🖷 *07/5475–0611* ⊕ *www.alexbeach.com* ➷ *28 rooms, 7 suites, 171 apartments* ⚌ *Restaurant, café, room service, in-room safes, cable TV with movies, 3 pools, gym, 2 outdoor hot tubs, bar, shops, baby-sitting, playground, laundry service, meeting room, free parking* ⊟ *AE, DC, MC, V.*

Mooloolaba

❸❸ *5 km (3 mi) south of Maroochydore.*

In a clear underwater tunnel you'll come face-to-face with giant sharks, stingrays, and other local marine species at **Underwater World.** Seal shows take place three times a day. ⊠ *Parkyn Parade* ☎ *07/5444–8488* 🖾 *A$22.50* ⊙ *Daily 9–5.*

Where to Stay & Eat

★ $–$$ ✕ **Bella Venezia Italian Restaurant.** A large wall mural of Venice, simple wooden tables, and terra-cotta floor tiles decorate this popular establishment at the back of an arcade. You can eat in or take out traditional and modern Italian cuisine, such as manicotti rolled with spinach, ricotta cheese, and shaved ham, and topped with tomato sauce and *bocconcini* cheese. ⊠ *Pacific Bldg., 95 The Esplanade* ☎ *07/5444–5844* ⊟ *MC, V* ⊗ *No lunch.*

¢–$ ✕ **The Coffee Club.** Although it's part of a national restaurant chain, this open-air, centrally located, combination restaurant–bar–café has top-flavor coffees and desserts that shouldn't be disregarded. Try the *affogatto,* a long, black espresso with ice cream, paired with a slice of Coffee Club mudcake or a piece of mango-and-macadamia strudel. Open sandwiches, salads, and light meals can be ordered any time. The dinner menu highlights such tasty offerings as spinach-ricotta ravioli, and cajun-seasoned chicken breast, served with garlic mayonnaise, on a vegetable salsa. ⊠ *The Esplanade* ☎ *07/5478–3688* ⊟ *DC, MC, V.*

$$$–$$$$ ⊡ **Sirocco Resort.** The stylish, futuristic curves of this apartment complex stand out on Mooloolaba's main drag, just across the road from the beach. Apartments have two- to five-bedroom plans, but each has sleek modern furniture, a whirlpool tub, a balcony, and magnificent beach views. Several smart restaurants are just outside the resort's front doors. ⊠ *59–75 The Esplanade* 🕮 *Box 798, 4557* ☎ *07/5444–1400 or 1800/ 303131* ⊕ *www.sirocco-resort.com* ➷ *51 apartments* ⚌ *In-room hot tubs, cable TV, pool, wading pool, gym, spa, car rental, travel services, free parking* ⊟ *MC, V.*

$–$$$$ ⊡ **Landmark Resort.** Floor-to-ceiling windows with balconies looking out onto the water are the memorable traits of this lovely resort. Rooms have wood and wicker furniture, tropical floral prints, marble breakfast bars, and whirlpool tubs. ⊠ *The Esplanade and Burnett St. 4557* ☎ *07/5444–5555 or 1800/888835* 🖷 *07/5444–5055* ⊕ *www. landmarkresorts.au.com* ➷ *132 rooms* ⚌ *In-room hot tubs, cable TV, pool, gym, sauna, recreation room, car rental, travel services, free parking* ⊟ *AE, DC, MC, V.*

Nightlife
Friday's on the Wharf (✉ Parkyn Parade and River Esplanade ☎ 07/5444–8383) is a popular nightspot.

Sports & the Outdoors
BOATING You can hire canopied motorboats from **Swan Boat Hire** (✉ 59 Bradman Ave., Maroochydore ☎ 07/5443–7225).

FISHING Deep-sea fishing charters can be arranged through **Mooloolaba Reef and Game Charters** (✉ 33 Jessica Blvd. ☎ 07/5444–3735).

Caloundra

㉞ *21 km (13 mi) south of Maroochydore, 56 km (35 mi) south of Noosa Heads, 91 km (56 mi) north of Brisbane.*

It's not just its excellent beaches that make Caloundra so popular: the town is also free of much of the glitz of the more touristy Queensland resorts. King's Beach and calm Bulcock Beach attract families.

Where to Stay

$–$$ 🏨 **Rolling Surf Resort.** Set amid tropical gardens, the Rolling Surf fronts the white sand of King's Beach. Wooden blinds, cane furniture, and beach prints fill the well-equipped apartments, which have between one and three bedrooms. All rooms have whirlpool tubs, and most come with balconies overlooking the beach. The resort has its own café and a restaurant with white-linen service. ✉ *Levuka Ave., King's Beach, 4551* ☎ *07/5491–9777* ⊕ *www.rollingsurfresort.com* ⇖ *74 rooms* ⚭ *Restaurant, café, cable TV, pool, gym, sauna, laundry facilities, travel services, free parking* ⊟ *MC, V.*

¢ 🏨 **City Centre Motel.** True to its name, this motel is within walking distance from Caloundra's main streets and the beach. Rooms in this two-story, somewhat innocuous building are small and simple but brightly decorated, with mauve walls, tile floors, and pastel prints. ✉ *20 Orsova Terr., 4551* ☎ *07/5491–3301* 🖷 *07/5491–2481* ✎ *caloundracitycentre@bigpond.com* ⇖ *7 rooms* ⚭ *Refrigerators* ⊟ *DC, MC, V.*

Sunshine Coast A to Z

To research prices, get advice from other travelers, and book travel arrangements, visit www.fodors.com.

AIR TRAVEL
By air from Maroochydore, it's 25 minutes to Brisbane, 2 hours 25 minutes to Melbourne, and 1 hour 35 minutes to Sydney.

CARRIERS Qantas operates out of Maroochy Airport (also known as Sunshine Coast Airport).
🛈 **Qantas** ☎ 13-1313.

AIRPORTS
Maroochy Airport is the main airport for the Sunshine Coast.
🛈 **Maroochy Airport** ✉ Friendship Dr., Mudjimba ☎ 07/5448-9672.

BUS TRAVEL
SunCoast Pacific offers daily bus service from Brisbane Airport and the Roma Street Transit Centre in Brisbane. Distances are short: from Brisbane to Caloundra takes 1½ hours; from Caloundra to Mooloolaba takes 30 minutes; from Mooloolaba to Maroochydore takes 10 minutes; from Maroochydore to Noosa takes 30 minutes; and from Noosa to Tewantin takes 10 minutes.
🛈 **SunCoast Pacific** ☎ 07/3236-1901.

CAR RENTAL

Several international companies have offices on the Sunshine Coast. Avis has offices in Maroochydore, Maroochy Airport, and Noosa Heads. Budget has one of the biggest rental car fleets on the Sunshine Coast. Hertz has offices in Noosa Heads and at Maroochy Airport. Thrifty has an office at Maroochy Airport.

🔢 Agencies **Avis** ✉ Shop 6, corner Beach Rd. and Ocean St., Maroochydore ☎ 07/5443-5055 ✉ Maroochy Airport, Friendship Dr., Mudjimba ☎ 07/5443-5055 ✉ Shop 1, corner Hastings St. and Noosa Dr., Noosa Heads ☎ 07/5447-4933. **Budget** ✉ 146 Alexandra Parade, Alexandra Headland ☎ 07/5443-6555. **Hertz** ✉ 16 Noosa Dr., Noosa Heads ☎ 07/5447-2253 ✉ Maroochy Airport, Friendship Dr., Mudjimba ☎ 07/5448-9731. **Thrifty** ✉ Maroochy Airport, Friendship Dr., Mudjimba ☎ 07/5443-1733.

CAR TRAVEL

A car is a necessity on the Sunshine Coast. The traditional route to the coast has been along the Bruce Highway (Highway 1) to the Glass House Mountains, with a turnoff at Cooroy. This makes for about a two-hour drive from Brisbane to Noosa, the heart of the area. However, the motorway may be marginally faster. Turn off the Bruce Highway at Tanawha (toward Mooloolaba) and follow the signs. The most scenic route is to turn off the Bruce Highway to Caloundra and follow the coast to Noosa Heads.

EMERGENCIES

In an emergency, dial 000 to reach an ambulance, the fire department, or the police.

🔢 **Caloundra Hospital** ✉ West Terr., Caloundra ☎ 07/5491-1888. **Nambour General Hospital** ✉ Hospital Rd., Nambour ☎ 07/5470-6600.

MAIL, SHIPPING & INTERNET

Internet Arcadia in Noosa is open weekdays 9–7 and 9–5 on Saturday. The Australian post office is open weekdays 8:30–5:30.

🔢 **Internet Arcadia** ✉ Shop 3, Arcadia Walk, Noosa Junction ☎ 07/5474-8999.
🔢 **Australia Post** ✉ 21 Ocean St., Maroochydore ☎ 13-1318.

MONEY MATTERS

Commonwealth Bank of Australia will cash traveler's checks and change money. ATMs are plentiful and reliable.

🔢 **Commonwealth Bank of Australia** ✉ 166 Horton Parade, Maroochydore ☎ 07/5443-8693 ✉ 25 Brisbane Rd., Mooloolaba ☎ 07/5444-3166 ✉ 24 Sunshine Beach Rd., Noosa Heads ☎ 07/5447-5555.

TOURS

Adventures Sunshine Coast offers one-day trips from Noosa Heads and Caloundra that take you walking, canoeing, rock climbing, and/or rappelling among rain forests and mountains.

Clip Clop Treks conducts various horse riding treks, ranging from half-day excursions to weeklong camping expeditions.

Southern Cross Motorcycle Tours provides one of the best ways to get a feel for the Sunshine Coast. Ride a Harley-Davidson motorcycle from the beach to the Blackall Range. Southern Cross Motorcycle Tours has a team of experienced guides who know the area and will take you on a half- or full-day's excursion.

🔢 Tour Operators **Adventures Sunshine Coast** ✉ 69 Alfriston Dr., Buderim ☎ 07/5444-8824. **Clip Clop Treks** ☎ 07/5449-1254. **Southern Cross Motorcycle Tours** ☎ 07/5445-0022.

TRAIN TRAVEL

Trains, including the high-tech *Tilt Train,* leave regularly from Roma Street Transit Centre in Brisbane en route to Nambour, the business hub of the Sunshine Coast. Once in Nambour, however, you'll need a car, so it may make more sense to drive from Brisbane.

🚆 **Roma Street Transit Centre** ✉ Roma St. ☎ 13-2232.

VISITOR INFORMATION

🛈 Tourist Information **Caloundra Tourist Information Centre** ✉ 7 Caloundra Rd., Caloundra ☎ 07/5491-2125. **Maroochy Tourist Information Centre** ✉ 6th Ave., Maroochydore ☎ 07/5479-1566. **Noosa Information Centre** ✉ Hastings St., Noosa Heads ☎ 07/5447-4988 or 1800/448833 ⊕ www.tourismnoosa.com.au.

FRASER ISLAND

Some 200 km (124 mi) north of Brisbane, Fraser is both the largest of Queensland's islands and the most unusual. Originally known as K'gari to the local Butchulla Aboriginal people, the island was later named after Eliza Fraser, who in 1836 was shipwrecked here and lived with local Aborigines for several weeks. It's the world's largest sand island—instead of coral reefs and coconut palms, it has wildflower-dotted meadows, freshwater lakes, a teeming bird population, dense stands of rain forest, towering sand dunes, and sculpted, multicolor sand cliffs along its east coast. That lineup has won the island a place on UNESCO's World Heritage list. The surf fishing is legendary, and humpback whales and their calves can be seen wintering in Hervey Bay between May and September. The island also has interesting Aboriginal sites dating back more than a millennium.

Hervey Bay is the name given to the expanse of water between Fraser Island and the Queensland coast. It's also the generic name given to a conglomeration of four nearby coastal towns—Urangan, Pialba, Scarness, and Torquay—that have grown into a single settlement. This township is the jumping-off point for most excursions to Fraser Island. (Note that maps and road signs usually refer to individual town names, not Hervey Bay.)

Fraser's east coast marks the intersection of two serious Australian passions: an addiction to the beach and a love affair with the motor vehicle. Unrestricted vehicle access has made this coast a giant sandbox for four-wheel-drive vehicles during busy school holiday periods. All vehicles entering the island must have a Vehicle Access Permit (A$30 on mainland, A$40 if bought on the island). These permits are valid for one month. There are a number of places in southeast Queensland where you can obtain these and camping permits for the island. (If you prefer your wilderness *sans* dune-buggying, head for the unspoiled interior of the island.) For the name of the closest center contact **Naturally Queensland** (✉ 160 Ann St., Brisbane ☎ 07/3227-8186).

Exploring Fraser Island

Note that swimming in the ocean off the east coast is not recommended because of the rough conditions and large number of sharks that hunt close to shore.

Highlights of a drive along the east coast include **Eli Creek,** a great freshwater swimming hole. North of this popular spot lies the rusting hulk of the *Maheno,* half buried in the sand, a roost for seagulls and a prime hunting ground for anglers when the tailor are running. North of the *Maheno* wreck are the **Pinnacles**—dramatic, deep-red cliff formations.

Great Sandy National Park (☎ 07/4121–1800) covers the top third of the island. Beaches around Indian Head are known for their shell middens—basically attractive rubbish heaps that were left behind after Aboriginal feasting. The head's name is another kind of relic: Captain James Cook saw Aborigines standing on the headland as he sailed past, and he therefore named the area after inhabitants he believed to be "Indians." Farther north, past Waddy Point, is one of Fraser Island's most magnificent variations on sand: wind and time have created enormous dunes.

The center of the island is a quiet, natural garden of paperbark swamps, giant satinay and brush box forests, wildflower heaths, and 40 freshwater lakes—including the spectacularly clear **Lake McKenzie**, ringed by a beach of incandescent whiteness. This is the perfect place for a refreshing swim.

The island's excellent network of walking trails converges at **Central Station**, a former logging camp at the center of the island. Services here are limited to a map board, parking lot, and campground. It's a promising place for spotting dingoes, however. Comparative isolation has meant that Fraser Island's dingoes are the most purebred in Australia. They're also wild animals, so remember: don't feed them, watch from a distance, and keep a close eye on children.

A boardwalk heads south from Central Station to **Wanggoolba Creek**, a favorite spot of photographers; this little stream snakes through a green palm forest, trickling over a bed of white sand between clumps of the rare angiopteris fern. One trail from Central Station leads through rain forest—incredibly growing straight out of the sand—to **Pile Valley**, where you'll find a stand of giant satinay trees.

Where to Stay & Eat

You must have a permit (A$3.85 per person per night) to camp on Fraser Island, except in private campsites. The Department of Environment and Heritage manages the island, and you can obtain a permit from a number of places in southeast Queensland. For the closest center, contact **Naturally Queensland** (⊠ 160 Ann St., Brisbane ☎ 07/3227–8186).

$$$–$$$$
Fodor'sChoice
★

✕⬚ **Kingfisher Bay Resort and Village.** This stylish, high-tech marriage of glass, stainless steel, dark timber, and corrugated iron nestles in the tree-covered dunes on the edge of the calm waters of Fraser Island's west coast. Accommodations include well-appointed hotel rooms with balconies, villas, and wilderness lodges for groups. Rangers conduct informative four-wheel-drive tours and free nature walks, and children can join junior ranger programs. The first-class menu at Seabelle's incorporates kangaroo, emu, and crocodile, as well as local island fruits, herbs, nuts, and vegetables. ⬚ *Box 913, Brisbane, 4001* ☎ *07/4120–3333 or 1800/072555* ⬚ *07/3221–3270* ⊕ *www.kingfisherbay. com* ⬚ *152 rooms, 110 villas, 180 beds in lodges* ⬚ *3 restaurants, 2 tennis courts, 4 pools, beauty salon, massage, spa, boating, fishing, hiking, volleyball, 4 bars, shops, baby-sitting, children's programs (ages 6–14), dry cleaning, laundry facilities, business services, convention center, meeting rooms, car rental, travel services, free parking, no-smoking rooms; no a/c in some rooms* ⊟ *AE, DC, MC, V.*

$–$$$
⬚ **Fraser Island Retreat.** At this pick of the east-coast accommodations you'll find breezy one-bedroom and family-size bungalows with polished timber floors and bamboo furnishings. The on-site restaurant serves good food in pleasant surroundings, and a small store sells groceries, gas, and diesel. ⬚ *Box 5224, Torquay, 4655* ☎ *07/4127–9144 or 1800/446655*

🏠 07/4127–9131 🛏 *9 rooms* 🍴 *Restaurant, grocery, cable TV, pool, bar, free parking; no a/c, no room phones* 💳 *AE, MC, V.*

Fraser Island A to Z

To research prices, get advice from other travelers, and book travel arrangements, visit www.fodors.com.

AIR TRAVEL

Qantaslink has several flights daily between Brisbane and Hervey Bay Airport on the mainland.

📶 **Qantaslink** ☎ 13-1313.

BOAT & FERRY TRAVEL

Fraser Island Ferry Service connects Rainbow Beach (between Brisbane and Hervey Bay via the Bruce Highway) to Inskip Point, at the southern end of the island. The round-trip fare is A$30 per vehicle, including driver and passengers; ferries run every 20 minutes between 6 AM and 5:30 PM.

Kingfisher vehicle ferries run 12 km (7 mi) south of Urangan to Fraser Island from Mary River Heads and Inskip Point. Fare is A$82 round-trip including the driver, plus A$5.50 for each additional passenger. Ferries depart for Fraser at 7:15 AM, 11 AM, and 2:30 PM.

📶 **Boat & Ferry Information Fraser Island Vehicle Ferry Service** ✉ Rainbow Beach Wharf ☎ 07/5486-3120. **Kingfisher** ☎ 07/4125-5155.

BUS TRAVEL

McCafferty's Express Coaches travels between Brisbane and Hervey Bay and throughout Queensland. Greyhound Pioneer Australia travels from Hervey Bay north and south along the Queensland coast.

📶 **Bus Lines Greyhound Pioneer Australia** ✉ Bay Central Coach Terminal, First Ave., Pialba ☎ 13-2030 🌐 www.greyhound.com.au. **McCafferty's Express Coaches** ✉ Bay Central Coach Terminal, First Ave., Pialba ☎ 07/4124-4000 or 13-1499 🌐 www.mccaffertys. com.au.

CAR RENTAL

You can rent four-wheel-drive vehicles at Kingfisher Bay Resort and Village and Fraser Island Retreat.

📶 **Agencies Fraser Island Retreat** ☎ 07/4127-9144. **Kingfisher Bay Resort and Village** ☎ 07/4120-3333.

CAR TRAVEL

The southernmost tip of Fraser Island is 200 km (124 mi) north of Brisbane. The best access is via vehicle ferry from Rainbow Beach, or from the Hervey Bay area, another 90 km (56 mi) away. For Rainbow Beach, take the Bruce Highway toward Gympie then follow the signs to Rainbow Beach. For Hervey Bay, head farther north to Maryborough, then follow signs to Urangan.

Despite the island's free-range feeling, the rules of the road still apply. Wear seat belts, drive on the left, and obey the speed limit. The island has a serious accident rate of about one per week. Watch out for creek crossings, which are often deeper than they look and can be quite dangerous, and keep an eye on the tide. Tide tables are available from ranger stations or from any shop on the island. It is generally advised to keep your vehicle off the beach for three hours before high tide and four hours after.

Four-wheel-drive rentals may be cheaper on the mainland, but factoring in the ferry ticket makes it less expensive to get your rental on-island.

EMERGENCIES

In an emergency, dial 000 to reach an ambulance, the fire department, or the police.

TOURS

Air Fraser Island operates whale-watching flights of 45 minutes or more across Hervey Bay between July and October, and scenic flights and day trips to the island year-round. Prices start at A$50 per person. You can also get packages that include renting a four-wheel-drive vehicle for A$110 per person.

For day-trippers, the Kingfisher passenger ferry runs between Urangan and North White Cliffs, near Kingfisher Bay Resort. The A$35 fare includes morning tea, lunch, and a ranger-led walking tour.

Whale Connections has daily whale-watching tours July–November. These begin at Urangan Boat Harbour in Hervey Bay.

🔊 Tour Operators **Air Fraser Island** ☎ 07/4125-3600. **Kingfisher** ☎ 07/4125-5155. **Whale Connections** ☎ 07/4124-7247.

VISITOR INFORMATION

Fraser Coast Tour Booking Office and Whale Watch Centre, on the mainland, is a good source of information, maps, and brochures. The center will also help you with tour and accommodations bookings.

🔊 Tourist Information **Fraser Coast Tour Booking Office and Whale Watch Centre** ✉ Buccaneer Ave., Urangan ☎ 07/4128-9800. **Hervey Bay Tourist and Visitors Centre** ✉ 353 The Esplanade, Hervey Bay ☎ 07/4124-4050.

THE OUTBACK

Queensland's Outback region is an exciting place to visit, filled with real Crocodile Dundee types and people used to relying on each other in isolated townships. It can also be a hazardous place, especially for independent travelers who want to experience it at their own pace in their own car. Always carry spare water, a first-aid kit, and sufficient fuel to get to the next town—and always know how far away the next town is. If you're traveling into remote areas, advise the local police or another responsible person of your travel plans and report back to them when you return. The **Matilda Highway** has made life easier for Outback travelers. This is a combination of existing highways from the Queensland–New South Wales border south of Cunnamulla with Karumba in the Gulf of Carpentaria. Eighteen marked **Matilda Byways** link various small towns.

If you choose to tour this vast, rugged region, there are several popular routes. You can travel north-west from Brisbane on the **Warrego Highway,** or head inland from Rockhampton along the **Capricorn Highway,** stopping at the frontier gemfield towns of **Sapphire** and **Rubyvale** to try your hand at fossicking. Spend a night or two at **Carnarvon Gorge** before continuing on to **Longreach** and **Winton.** If you're based in Cairns, you can head west from Townsville along the **Overlander's Highway,** stopping at the once-prosperous gold-mining town of **Charters Towers** and **Ravenswood** before heading south toward Longreach or further west toward **Tennant Creek.**

The Outback is not known for its finely tuned, delicately seasoned cuisine; rather, it's a place for digging into hearty steak, beef, and damper (bread cooked in a cast iron pot or in the coals of a campfire). Most pubs and hotels serve a filling steak platter—such as the "dinosaur" steaks at Torren's Creek's Exchange Hotel.

One of the highlights of the Queensland Outback, ★ **Stockman's Hall of Fame** brings to life the early days of white Australian settlement. Exhibits, on everything from Aboriginal history to droving, mustering, and bush crafts, pay tribute to the pioneers who sought to tame the Australian Outback. ⊠ *Off Matilda Hwy., Longreach* ☎ 07/4658–2166 ⊕ *www.outbackheritage.com.au* ⊠ *A$19.80* ☼ *Daily 9–5.*

Longreach is the birthplace of Qantas, Australia's first national airline. The **Qantas Founders' Outback Museum** here has displays about Australia's first days of flight. ⊠ *Qantas Hangar, Longreach Airport, Longreach* ☎ 07/4658–3737 ⊠ *A$7* ☼ *Daily 9–5.*

The low-framed rustic **Walkabout Creek Hotel** (⊠ Middleton St., Mackinlay ☎ 07/4746–8424), made famous in the original *Crocodile Dundee* movie, offers both accommodations and drinks at the pub.

Dip your toes in **Combo Waterhole**, where A. B. "Banjo" Peterson wrote the lyrics for **Waltzing Matilda,** Australia's informal national anthem. The song was based on one of Banjo Peterson's experiences in the Outback. Around 13 km (8 mi) southeast of the small town of Kyuna, the waterhole is easily found off the Matilda Highway. A 20-minute walk will take you straight to the site.

In Winton, you can visit the interactive **Waltzing Matilda Centre,** which has an art gallery, history museum, restaurant, and sound-and-light show. The center also houses the Qantilda Museum, a diverse collection of Outback pioneering memorabilia. ⊠ *Elderslie St., Winton* ☎ 07/ 4657–1466 ⊠ *A$14* ☼ *Daily 9–5.*

The Outback isn't all arid, dusty plains; the town of Mitchell—with its wide, tree-lined streets of classic colonial architecture—boasts **The Great Artesian Spa.** Two billabong-like large pools in landscaped grounds provide welcome relief from the sweltering heat. One pool is naturally warm, while the other is cool. ⊠ *4 Cambridge St., Mitchell* ☎ 07/ 4623–1073 ⊠ *A$5* ☼ *Daily 9–5.*

The **gemfields** of Central Queensland are found near Rubyvale, Sapphire, Anakie, and the Willows, towns with a Wild-West, frontier feel. This 10,000-hectare (25,000-acre) area comprises one of the world's richest sapphire fields, which since the 1870s has attracted amateur fossickers worldwide. Commercial and tourist mines are scattered throughout the fields, and once you make a find you can choose from 100-plus gemcutters. The second week of August is Gemfest, when miners, merchants, and traders swap, sell, and barter their wares.

Miner's Heritage is Australia's largest underground sapphire mine. Guided tours run through the hand-hewn tunnels, and you can try your luck with the fossicking facilities. A gemcutter and an impressive showroom are also on the premises. ⊠ *Main Rd., Rubyvale* ☎ 07/4985–4444 ⊠ *A$4* ☼ *Daily 9–5.*

Where to Stay

¢ ▦ **Hotel Corones.** Built in the 1920s by Greek immigrant Harry (Poppa) Corones, this block-size hotel became a hub for wealthy sheep and cattle property owners. Among its attractions are a ladies' drawing room, a large ballroom, a dining room, and a wide first-floor balcony that runs the length of the building. The hotel has motel and hotel rooms, as well as heritage rooms furnished in 1920s style. ⊠ *33 Willis St., Charleville, 4470* ☎ 07/4654–1022 🖷 07/4654–1756 ⤶ *25 rooms* ☖ *Bar; no a/c in some rooms, no room phones* ▭ *AE, MC, V.*

¢ ▣ **The Rubyvale Hotel and Cabins.** Constructed of corrugated iron, logs, and "billy boulders" from the mines, this hotel looks like it has been around since the first miners. The cabins, however, are spacious and comfortable. Wood-paneled walls and wood furnishings remain in keeping with the rustic atmosphere, while large potted plants throughout the cabin and terraced gardens outside are relaxing and lush. ⌧ *Keilambete Rd., 4702* ☎ *07/4985–4754* ⌕ *4 cabins* ♻ *Restaurant, in-room hot tubs, bar, free parking* ▭ *AE, MC, V.*

The Outback A to Z

To research prices, get advice from other travelers, and book travel arrangements, visit www.fodors.com.

AIR TRAVEL

CARRIERS Qantas services such Outback towns of Blackall, Charleville, Longreach, and Mount Isa.
▣ Qantas ☎ 13-1313.

BUS TRAVEL

Coral Coaches travels between Mount Isa and Karumba via Cloncurry, Quamby, Burke, Wills Road House, and Normanton. It departs Mount Isa on Tuesday and Karumba on Wednesday. It also runs a line from Cairns to Karumba.

Greyhound Pioneer Australia services all of the towns on the Finders Highway between Townsville and Mount Isa with connections to the Northern Territory.

McCafferty's Express Coaches services all of the towns on the Warrego and Landsborough highways between Brisbane, Charleville, Longreach, and Mount Isa; on the Capricorn Highway between Rockhampton and Longreach; and on the Flinders Highway between Townsville and Mount Isa, with connections to the Northern Territory.
▣ Bus Lines **Coral Coaches** ☎ 07/4031-7577. **Greyhound Pioneer Australia** ☎ 13-2030 ⊕ www.greyhound.com.au. **McCafferty's Express Coaches** ☎ 13-1499 ⊕ www. mccaffertys.com.au.

EMERGENCIES

In an emergency, dial 000 to reach an ambulance, the fire department, or the police.

TRAIN TRAVEL

Queensland Rail runs the *Westlander* from Brisbane to Charleville, the *Inlander* between Townsville and Mount Isa, the *Spirit of the Outback* between Brisbane and Longreach, and the *Gulflander* between Normanton and Croydon.
▣ **Queensland Rail** ☎ 13-2232 ⊕ www.qr.com.au.

VISITOR INFORMATION

▣ Tourist Information **Barcaldine Tourist Information Centre** ☎ 07/4651-1724. **Birdsville Wirrarri Centre** ☎ 07/4656-3300. **Blackall Tourist Information Centre** ☎ 07/4657-4637. **Boulia Library and Tourist Information Centre** ☎ 07/4746-3386. **Charleville Information Centre** ☎ 07/4654-3057. **Cloncurry John Flynn Place** ☎ 07/4742-1251. **Cunnamulla Tourist Information Centre** ☎ 07/4655-2481. **Hughenden Visitor Information Centre and Dinosaur Display** ☎ 07/4741-1021. **Kynuna Roadhouse and Caravan Park** ☎ 07/4746-8683. **Longreach Tourist Information Centre** ☎ 07/4658-3555. **McKinlay Walkabout Creek Hotel** ☎ 07/4746-8424. **Mitchell Tourist Information Centre** ☎ 07/4623-1133. **Mount Isa Riversleigh Centre** ☎ 07/4749-1555. **Quilpie Tourist Information Centre** ☎ 07/4656-2166. **Richmond Marine Fossil Mu-**

seum ☎ 07/4741-3429. Torrens Creek Information Centre ☎ 07/4741-7272. Winton Waltzing Matilda Centre ☎ 07/4657-1466.

AIRLIE BEACH

③⑤ *635 km (395 mi) south of Cairns, 1,130 km (702 mi) north of Brisbane*

Like Noosa and other towns along the Pacific Coast, Airlie (pronounced "Ellie") Beach enjoys great weather throughout the year. A small seaside town, perhaps best known as a jumping-off point to the Whitsunday Islands and the Great Barrier Reef, it has one main street packed with cafés and bars, travel agencies, and hotels. Although it's clearly a resort town, it is significantly more relaxed than those along the Gold and Sunshine coasts. Airlie Beach Esplanade, with its boardwalk, landscaped gardens, sculpted swimming lagoon, and Saturday morning craft markets, is a pleasant place to enjoy the mainland.

Shute Harbour, 11 km (7 mi) from Airlie Beach, is the main ferry terminal and gateway to the islands and the reef. **Conway National Park,** a 10-minute drive away, has 150 acres of forest surrounding Mount Rooper, with spectacular views of Whitsunday Passage. Follow the trails on foot or horseback through the rain forest to Cedar Creek Falls, or take a walk along Swamp Bay, a coral-strewn beach.

At **The Barefoot Bushman's Wildlife Park** you can view a comprehensive collection of Australian wildlife, including cassowaries, crocodiles, koalas, kangaroos, and wombats. Wildlife shows are at 11:30, noon, 1, 1:30, and 2 daily. ⊠ *Shute Harbour Rd.* ☎ *07/4946-1480* 🖃 *A$19.80* 🕐 *Daily 9-4:30.*

Where to Stay & Eat

$-$$ ✕ **Capers at the Beach Bar and Grill.** Tables spill out across bleached terracotta tiles at this busy, beachside restaurant. The menu leans toward Asian and Mediterranean flavors, served in coconut-crusted fish braised in Thai curry, and char-grilled spatchcock with garlic, chili, and lemon zest served with saffron, pepper, and tomato rice. End with the warm, chocolate sticky date pudding, served with Kahlua-and-pistachio caramel sauce and *bacio* gelati. There's live music on Friday nights. ⊠ *The Esplanade* ☎ *07/4964-1777* 🖃 *AE, DC, MC, V.*

¢-$ ✕ **Airlie Thai.** Overlooking the water, this traditional Thai restaurant has a wide range of well-seasoned dishes and vegetarian options. Start with hot-and-sour coconut soup, followed by jungle curry spiced with *kachai*, lime leaves, red curry paste, and fresh chilies. The sweet sticky rice wrapped in banana leaf is the only dessert, but it's perfect. ⊠ *Beach Plaza, The Esplanade* ☎ *07/4946-4683* 🖃 *AE, DC, MC, V.*

¢-$$ 🏨 **Airlie Beach Hotel.** With the beach directly opposite and the main street directly behind it, this hotel is arguably the most convenient base from which to explore the region. Spacious rooms are decorated with photographs of the reef, ocean, and islands, and each opens onto a balcony overlooking the palm-lined beachfront. ⊠ *Cnr. The Esplanade and Coconut Grove, 4802* ☎ *07/4964-1999, 1800/466233* 🖷 *07/4964-1988* 🌐 *www.airliebeachhotel.com.au* 🛏 *80 rooms.* ⚖ *2 restaurants, in-room dataports, minibars, cable TV, saltwater pool, laundry facilities, free parking* 🖃 *AE, DC, MC, V.*

¢-$ 🏨 **Whitsunday Moorings Bed and Breakfast.** Overlooking Abel Point Marina, the view from the patio is fantastic at dusk. The house is framed in mango and frangipani trees, with an abundance of lorikeets. While Peter, host of this bed-and-breakfast, is extraordinarily helpful with regard to activities in the area (and an excellent breakfast chef), the lure of his poolside hammock can overcome even the most energetic guest. Rooms are tiled

FodorśChoice
★

in terra-cotta, with bamboo mat ceilings and cedar blinds. Breakfast is a five-course affair, combining white linen with tropical fruits and flowers, homemade jams, freshly squeezed juice, and a wide choice of dishes. ⊠ 37 *Airlie Crescent, 4802* ☎ *07/4946–4692* ⊕ *www.whitsundaymooringsbb. com.au* ⤴ *2 rooms* ♨ *Kitchens, pool* ⊟ *DC, MC, V.*

Airlie Beach A to Z

AIR TRAVEL

The nearby Whitsunday Coast Airport in Proserpine, 25 km (16 mi) from Airlie Beach, has daily flights by Qantas from Brisbane, Cairns, interstate cities, and overseas destinations.
🗊 **Qantas** ☎ 13-1313.

BUS TRAVEL

Greyhound Pioneer, McCafferty's Express Coaches, and Oz Experience offer approximately twelve services daily into Airlie Beach.

TRAIN TRAVEL

Queensland Rail operates approximately eight trains weekly into the Proserpine Railway Station. The Great South Pacific Express also stops in Proserpine.

VISITOR INFORMATION

🗊 **Whitsunday Information Centre** ⊠ Airlie Beach, 4802 ☎ 07/4945-3711, 1800/801252 ⊕ www.whitsundayinformation.com.au.

TOWNSVILLE & MAGNETIC ISLAND

Australia's largest tropical city, with a population of 127,000, is the commercial capital of the north and a major center for education, scientific research, and defense. The city developed around the pink granite outcrop of Castle Hill, the first feature one notices about the place, which rises from otherwise featureless coastal plains to just under 1,000 feet. On the banks of the boat-filled Ross Creek, Townsville is a pleasant city, an urban sprawl of palm-fringed malls, white-lattice verandas on historic colonial buildings, and lots of parkland and gardens. Townsville is also the stepping-off point for Magnetic Island, one of the largest Queensland islands and a haven for wildlife.

Townsville

The summit of **Castle Hill,** 1 km (½ mi) from the city center, provides great views of the city as well as the islands of the Great Barrier Reef. While you're perched on top, think about the proud local resident who, along with various scout troops, spent years in the 1970s piling rubble onto the peak to try to add the 23 feet that would officially make it Castle Mountain. Technically speaking, a rise has to exceed 1,000 feet to be called a mountain, and this one tops out at just 977 feet. Most people walk to the top, along a steep walking track that doubles as one of Queensland's most scenic jogging routes.

Reef HQ, on the waterfront, only a few minutes' walk from the city center, has the largest natural-coral aquarium in the world—a living slice of the Great Barrier Reef. There are more than 100 species of hard coral, 30 soft corals, and hundreds of fish. Also here are an enclosed underwater walkway, touch pool, theater, café, and shop. ⊠ *Flinders St. E* ☎ *07/4750–0800* 🕾 *A$19.50* ☉ *Daily 9–5.*

The **Museum of Tropical Queensland,** next door to Reef HQ, displays relics of the HMS *Pandora,* which sank in 1791 while carrying 14 crew members of the *Bounty* to London to stand trial for mutiny. Also on display are Australian dinosaur fossils and cultural exhibits about the Torres Strait Islands and Aboriginal peoples. ✉ *Flinders St. E* ☎ *07/4726–0600* 🖃 *A$9* ☉ *Daily 9–5.*

A stroll along **Flinders Street** will show you some of Townsville's turn-of-the-20th-century colonial architecture. **Magnetic House, The Bank** (now a lounge bar), and other buildings have been beautifully restored. The old **Queens Hotel** is in Classical Revival style, as is the 1885 **Perc Tucker Regional Gallery,** which was originally a bank. The apparently immovable **masonry clock tower** (✉ Flinders and Denham Sts.) of the post office was erected in 1889 but taken down during World War II so it wouldn't be a target for air raids. It was put up again in 1964.

The National Trust has placed three very different dwellings alongside each other at the **Castling Street Heritage Centre.** The 1884 worker's cottage, 1921 farmhouse, and Currajong, a grand residence built in 1888, have been completely restored and furnished. ✉ *5 Castling St., West End* ☎ *07/4772–5195* 🖃 *A$5* ☉ *Feb.–Nov., Wed. 10–2, weekends 1–4.*

⟲ **The Strand**—a promenade along 3 km (2 mi) of sandy beach with swimming enclosures, restaurants, water-sports facilities, barbecue and picnic areas, and a water playground for children—runs northwest along Cleveland Bay. Kissing Point, at the far end, has a rock pool, military museum, and a coconut-palm-shaded park with impressive views.

Townsville Common, also known as Townsville Environment Park, is an important bird sanctuary. Spoonbills, jabiru storks, pied geese, herons, and ibis, plus occasional wallabies, goannas, and even echidnas make their home here. Most of the birds leave the swamplands from May through August, the dry months, but they're all back by October. To get to the Common, take a taxi past the airport. Access is free.

On Gregory Street, **Queen's Gardens** is a popular spot for weddings, as well as a lovely place to spend a cool couple of hours away from the scorching coast. The park is bordered with frangipani and towering Moreton Bay Fig trees, whose unique hanging roots and branches create a mysterious veiled entryway to the grounds. Access is free. ✉ *Gregory St.* ☎ *No phone* 🖃 *Free* ☉ *Daily dawn to dusk.*

off the beaten path

BILLABONG SANCTUARY – This 22-acre nature park shelters crocodiles, koalas, wombats, dingoes, and wallabies, as well as a range of bird life, including cassowaries, kookaburras, and beautiful red-tailed black cockatoos. Educational shows throughout the day give you the chance to learn more about native animals and their habits and include koala and crocodile feeding and snake handling. ✉ *Bruce Hwy., Nome, 17 km (11 mi) south of Townsville* ☎ *07/ 4778–8344* 🖃 *A$22* ☉ *Daily 8–5.*

Where to Stay & Eat

★ **$–$$$** ✕ **Gauguin Restaurant and Bar.** French painter Paul Gauguin's use of color and the similarities between Tahiti, where he lived for a time, and tropical Townsville influenced this stylish restaurant. The dining room consists of wood paneling, cane furniture, and glass doors opening onto a covered patio area. The food is contemporary with French influences. Start off with the poppy-and-sesame-crumbed calamari with honey and garlic dressing. Move on to Moroccan braised lamb shanks or the salad of sautéed seafood and sun-dried tomatoes. ✉ *Gregory St. Headland, The Strand* ☎ *07/4724–5488* ⊕ *www.gauguin.com.au* 🖃 *AE, DC, MC, V.*

$-$$ ✕ **Flutes Restaurant.** This popular local eatery makes up for its plain decor with good service and excellent fare. Try such starters as Black River barramundi panfried with mild spices, or chicken breast filled with bacon-wrapped Camembert cheese. Then tickle your taste buds with the banana fritters with custard for dessert. Although there's no lunch inside the restaurant on weekdays, the terrace is open for lunch daily. ✉ *Townsville Reef International, 63 The Strand* ☎ 07/4721–1777 ⊟ *AE, DC, MC, V.*

$-$$ ✕ **Yotz Watergrill + Bar.** Old-fashioned ceiling fans, boat-themed artwork, wicker furniture, and bleached wood floorboards set the nautical theme of this restaurant. A seafood-filled menu offers fresh-caught choices: seafood chowder, fish and chips, grilled barramundi. Add the pumpkin-and-mascarpone cheesecake to finish. ✉ *Gregory St. Headland, The Strand* ☎ 07/4724–5488 ⊕ *www.yotz.com.au* ♨ *Reservations essential* ⊟ *AE, DC, MC, V.*

¢-$ ✕ **The Australian Hotel Café.** This 1888 two-story hotel is a classic example of Townsville colonial architecture. The café doesn't take up much of the building, and you can eat outside on the street or inside on modern chrome tables over a black-and-white tile floor. Try the rib fillet or fish and chips—then head next door for a pint of lager in the pub. ✉ *11 Palmer St.* ☎ 07/4722–6910 ⊕ *www.australianhotel.com.au* ⊟ *AE, DC, MC, V.*

$-$$$$ ▦ **Jupiter's Townsville Hotel and Casino.** Dominating Townsville's waterfront vista, the hotel's bland, block shape still looks sophisticated against the adjacent marina. This location translates into great views across to Magnetic Island from all 11 floors. Rooms have bright tropical reds, blues, and greens and are larger than standard hotel rooms. This is a busy hotel—with North Queensland's first casino—but rooms are pleasantly quiet. ✍ *Box 1223, Sir Leslie Thiess Dr., 4810* ☎ 07/4722–2333 ⊟ 07/4772–4741 ⊕ *www.jupiterstownsville.com.au* ➘ *193 rooms, 16 suites* ♨ *3 restaurants, room service, room TVs with movies, 2 tennis courts, pool, gym, massage, sauna, spa, 5 bars, casino, baby-sitting, laundry service, business services, meeting room, travel services, free parking; no-smoking rooms* ⊟ *AE, DC, MC, V.*

$ ▦ **Seagull's Resort on the Seafront.** Three acres of palm tree–studded tropical gardens form the backdrop for this very pleasant, two-story brick complex. Cane furniture and tropical color schemes decorate the spacious hotel rooms. Self-contained apartments and suites with kitchenettes are available. Seagull's restaurant serves generous portions of local seafood. The resort is 2½ km (1½ mi) from the city center (with free shuttle service) and about a 10-minute walk to the beach. ✉ *74 The Esplanade, 4810* ☎ 07/4721–3111 ⊕ *www.seagulls.com.au* ➘ *55 rooms, 11 suites, 4 apartments* ♨ *Restaurant, room service, some kitchenettes, room TVs with movies, tennis court, 2 pools, bar, playground, dry cleaning, laundry facilities, Internet, business services, convention center, meeting room, travel services, free parking* ⊟ *AE, DC, MC, V.*

$ ▦ **Townsville Reef International.** This four-story beachfront hotel overlooking Cleveland Bay is a modern property with a high standard of service. It has typical Queensland decor, with lots of lattice, tropical prints, and muted grays and greens. With Flutes Restaurant, a palm-tree-shaded pool, and private balconies overlooking the bay and Magnetic Island, this is a fine place to stay. ✉ *63 The Strand, 4810* ☎ 07/4721–1777 ⊟ 07/4721–1779 ⊕ *www.bestwestern.com.au/reefinternational* ➘ *45 rooms* ♨ *Restaurant, room service, room TVs with movies, pool, hot tub, bar, laundry service, Internet, meeting room, free parking* ⊟ *AE, DC, MC, V.*

¢-$ ▦ **The Rocks Guesthouse.** In its past incarnations this 1886 Victorian-style home has been a hospital, upscale guesthouse, and army house.

Today it ís an elegant bed-and-breakfast with a vast dining room, billiard room, polished wood floors, and bric-a-brac everywhere, thanks to collectors and owners Joe Sproats and Jenny Ginger. Complimentary sherry is provided on the veranda evenings at 6. You can walk to the city and surrounding attractions. ⊠ *20 Cleveland Terr., 4810* ☎ *07/ 4771–5700* 🖷 *07/4771–5711* ⊕ *www.therocksguesthouse.com* ⤴ *9 rooms, 2 with bath; 1 self-contained apartment* ⟡ *Dining room, billiards, croquet, bar, meeting room, free parking; no TV in some rooms* ⊟ *MC, V* ⦿ *CP.*

¢–$ ✕🖼 **Historic Yongala Lodge.** This late 19th-century lodge was originally the home of building magnate Matthew Rooney, whose family was shipwrecked along with 119 others on S.S. *Yongala,* which sank off the coast of Townsville in 1911. Rooms are decorated with antiques, old photographs, and wrought-iron ceiling fittings. The dining room turns out traditional Greek food and eclectic fusions on large communal tables above a black-and-white-tile floor, or you can eat outside on the wide, colonial-style veranda. Friday and Saturday nights, there's lively Greek music and entertainment. ⊠ *11 Fryer St., 4810* ☎ *07/4772–4633* 🖷*07/4721–1074* ⊕*www.historicyongala.com.au* ⤴*18 rooms* ⟡ *Restaurant, room service, refrigerators, in-room VCRs, saltwater pool, bar, laundry facilities, meeting rooms, free parking* ⊟ *AE, DC, MC, V.*

Nightlife & the Arts

THE ARTS **Civic Theatre** (⊠ Boundary St. ☎ 07/4727–9797) hosts some of the state's finest performing artists.

Townsville Entertainment and Convention Centre (⊠ Entertainment Dr. ☎ 07/4771–4000) can seat 4,000 and has hosted such international acts as Tom Jones and Tina Turner. The center is also the home of the Townsville Crocodiles National Basketball League team.

NIGHTLIFE For gamblers, the main attraction in Townsville is the **Jupiters Townsville Hotel and Casino** (⊠ Sir Leslie Thiess Dr. ☎ 07/4722–2333), which has a full range of gaming opportunities including minibaccarat, sic bo, blackjack, roulette, keno, and slot machines, as well as the Australian game of two-up.

The Brewery (⊠ 252 Flinders St. ☎ 07/4724–2999), once the original Townsville Post Office, now houses a bar that also serves light meals and a micro-brewery. The owners have done a fine job of combining ultra-modern wood and chrome finishing with the original design and furnishings from its days as a post office; the bar itself is the old stamp counter. It's open 7 AM–2 AM every day.

Sports & the Outdoors

BEACHES Townsville is blessed with a golden, 2-km (1-mi) strand of beach along the northern edge of the city. Four human-made headlands jut into the sea, and a long pier is just the spot for fishing. There is no surf, as the beach is sheltered by the reef and Magnetic Island.

DIVING Surrounded by tropical islands and warm waters, Townsville is an important diving center. Diving courses and excursions here are not as crowded as in the hot spots of Cairns or the Whitsunday Islands.

The wreck of the *Yongala,* a steamship that sank just south of Townsville in 1911, lies in 99 feet of water about 16 km (10 mi) offshore, 60 km (37 mi) from Townsville. Now the abode of marine life, it is one of Australia's best dive sites and can be approached as either a one- or two-day trip. All local dive operators conduct trips out to the site.

Adrenalin Dive (⊠ 121 Flinders St. ☎ 07/4724–0600 ⊕ www.adrenalindive.com.au) offers dive trips to a number of popular sites in the region.

Pro-Dive (⊠ Reef HQ, Flinders St. E ☎ 07/4721–1760) arranges day trips and overnight trips. Sites include *Yongala* and the outer Barrier Reef.

FISHING **Barnacle Bill Guided Fishing Tours** (⊠ Pacific Dr., Horseshoe Bay ☎ 07/4758–1237) will organize fishing trips around the Townsville and Magnetic Island areas.

GOLF **Rowes Bay Golf Course** (⊠ Cape Pallarenda Rd., Pallarenda ☎ 07/4774–1188) has an 18-hole and a par-3, 9-hole course.

Willows Golf Tourist and Sports Resort (⊠ 19th Ave., Kirwan ☎ 07/4773–4777) has an 18-hole championship course.

Shopping

Castletown Shoppingworld (⊠ 35 Kings Rd., Pimlico ☎ 07/4772–1699) houses shops as well as a supermarket, a post office, and a medical center. **Flinders Street Mall,** a bright and sunny street closed to vehicular traffic, has been the main shopping area of Townsville in years past. Recently, locals have all headed for the suburban centers.

Magnetic Island

The bulk of Magnetic Island's 52 square km (20 square mi) is national parkland, laced with miles of walking trails and rising to a height of 1,640 feet on Mount Cook. The terrain is punctuated with huge granite boulders and softened by tall hoop pines, eucalypt forest, and small patches of rain forest. A haven for wildlife, the island shelters rock wallabies, koalas, and an abundance of bird life.

The 2,500-odd residents live on the eastern shore, with the main settlements at Picnic Bay, Arcadia, Nelly Bay, and Horseshoe Bay. Magnetic Island is also home to many artists and craftspeople, so plan time to explore the local studios and galleries around the island. You can also escape to 23 bays and beaches.

Alma Bay's beach near Arcadia is good for swimming and snorkeling. Near the northeastern corner of the island, Radical Bay has a small, idyllic beach surrounded by tree-covered rock outcrops. Horseshoe Bay has the largest beach, with boat rentals and a campground. There is good snorkeling at Nelly Bay, and Geoffrey Bay has a well-marked snorkel trail. You can pick up free, self-guiding trail cards that identify various corals and sea life from the information center adjacent to the Picnic Bay Jetty.

There are 24 km (15 mi) of hiking trails on the island, most of which are relatively easy. The most popular walk leads to World War II gun emplacements overlooking Horseshoe and Florence bays. At a leisurely pace it takes 45 minutes each way from the Horseshoe–Radical Bay Road. The best views are on the 5-km (3.2-mi) Nelly Bay to Arcadia walk, which is rewarding if you take the higher ground. Carry plenty of water, sunscreen, and insect repellent.

The walking trails of the island run under gum trees that are home to many koalas. At the **Koala and Wildlife Park** in Horseshoe Bay you can see several Australian animals, including koalas, kangaroos, and wombats. ⊠ *Horseshoe Bay* ☎ *07/4778–5260* 🖅 *A$10* ⊙ *Daily 9–5.*

One way to get an overview of Magnetic Island is to ride the **Magnetic Island Bus Service,** whose drivers provide commentary. Your A$10 ticket allows one day of unlimited travel to different points on the island, enabling you to return to the places you like most. A three-hour guided tour is also available, with a driver, commentary, and morning or afternoon tea for A$30. Reservations for the guided tour are essential. They depart daily at 9 and 1. ⊠ *44 Mandalay Ave., Nelly Bay* ☎ *07/ 4778–5130.*

Where to Stay & Eat

Magnetic Island's lodgings are geared largely to the needs of Australians on vacation rather than to those of international visitors. As a result they tend to be less expensive.

¢–$$
Fodor'sChoice
★
✕ **Magnetic Mango.** A mango plantation since the 1920s, the farm is now entirely organic, growing 60 different varieties of mango as well as citrus trees and coconut palms. The very basic, open-air restaurant seats guests at picnic tables, relying instead on the excellent food for its appeal. Pan-Asian and tropical influences are woven through the choices: herb-encrusted kangaroo in white wine *jus,* king prawn and mango salad, and pork, mango, and banana curry. Baked cheesecake with mango sorbet, fresh cream, and mango coulis tops off the meal, or try the equally decadent macadamia-nut cake. A store, a playground, minigolf, lagoon boardwalk, and old gold mine make for explorations after you dine. Devonshire tea is served in the afternoon. ⊠ *Horseshoe Bay* ☎ *07/477– 5018* ⊟ *No credit cards* ☉ *Closed Thurs. and Fri.*

¢–$
✕⊞ **Magnetic Island International Resort.** This comfortable resort nestles amid 11 acres of lush gardens 2 km (1 mi) from the beach. Rooms follow a pastel-yellow color scheme, with kitchenettes, tile floors, and cane furniture. At the resort's terrace restaurant, MacArthur's, beef and seafood are the mainstays; try grilled coral trout on a bed of crisp snow peas, topped with tiger prawns and finished with a lemon and chive beurre blanc. Hiking trails into the national parkland are nearby, and the energetic can take advantage of floodlit tennis courts in the cool evenings. Courtesy coach transfers from Picnic Bay to the resort are available. ⊠ *Mandalay Ave., Nelly Bay, 4819* ☎ *07/4778–5200 or 1800/079902* 🖷 *07/4778–5806* ⊕ *www.magneticresort.com* 🗘 *80 rooms, 16 suites* ⚐ *Restaurant, room service, fans, kitchenettes, refrigerators, 2 tennis courts, pool, wading pool, gym, volleyball, bar, baby-sitting, playground, dry cleaning, laundry service, convention center, meeting room, travel services, free parking* ⊟ *AE, DC, MC, V.*

¢
⊞ **Beaches at Arcadia.** A stone's throw from the beach, this hotel run by hosts Judith and Malcolm equally accommodates the ambitious and guests intent on relaxing. Breezy, sunny rooms have wooden floors and wrought-iron furniture. Sip a cold drink on your private veranda, or laze by a pool surrounded by rainbow lorikeets and black cockatoos. ⊠ *39 Marine Parade, Arcadia, 4819* ☎ *07/4778–5303* 🖷 *07/4778–5303* ✍ *beachesbandb@iprimus.com.au* 🗘 *2 rooms* ⚐ *Dining room, saltwater pool, free parking; no kids* ⊟ *MC, V.*

Sports & the Outdoors

HORSEBACK
RIDING
With ★ **Bluey's Horseshoe Ranch Trail Rides** you can take a one-hour bush ride, or a more extensive two-hour bush and beach ride with a chance to take the horses swimming. Half-day rides are also offered. ⊠ *38 Gifford St., Horseshoe Bay* ☎ *07/4778–5109.*

TOAD RACES
One of the more unusual evening activities on Magnetic Island are the weekly toad races at Arkie's Backpacker Resort. Held every Wednesday night at 8 PM for 20 years, the event raises funds for local charities. The crowd is generally a mix of tourists and locals. Once the race has been won, the winning owner kisses his or her toad and collects the proceeds. ⊠ *7 Marine Parade, Arcadia* ☎ *07/4778–5177.*

WATER SPORTS **Adrenalin Jet Ski Tours** (✉ 46 Gifford St. ☎ 07/4778–5533) provides half-day tours around Magnetic Island on two-seater sports boats. **Horseshoe Bay Watersports** (✉ 97 Horseshoe Bay Rd. ☎ 07/4758–1336) offers sailing, parasailing, waterskiing, aquabikes, and canoes for hire.

You can sail to hard-to-reach beaches and bays with **Jazza's Sailing Tours** (✉ 97 Horseshoe Bay Rd. ☎ 07/4778–5530), which depart Horseshoe Bay daily, for a A$50 trip including lunch, afternoon tea, boomnetting, snorkeling, and live jazz. **Ocean Runner** (✉ Horseshoe Bay ☎ 07/4778–5144 ⊕ www.oceanrunner.com.au) tours take you to Magnetic Island's many bays, allowing time for snorkeling and other water activities.

Townsville & Magnetic Island A to Z

To research prices, get advice from other travelers, and book travel arrangements, visit www.fodors.com.

AIR TRAVEL

CARRIERS Qantas flies frequently from Townsville Airport to Brisbane, Cairns, interstate cities, and overseas destinations. Virgin Blue also connects Townsville to Brisbane.

🛃 Carriers **Qantas** ☎ 13-1313. **Virgin Blue** ☎ 13-6789.

AIRPORTS & TRANSFERS

AIRPORT Airport Transfers and Tours runs shuttle buses that meet each flight. The
TRANSFERS cost of the transfer to Townsville is A$7 one-way, A$11 round-trip. Townsville Taxis are available at the airport. The average cost of the journey to a city hotel is A$16.

🛃 **Townsville Airport** ☎ 07/4774-6302.

🛃 Taxis & Shuttles **Airport Transfers and Tours** ☎ 07/4775-5544. **Townsville Taxis** ✉ 11 Yeatman St., Hyde Park ☎ 07/4772-1555 or 13-1008.

BIKE & MOPED TRAVEL

Townsville's flat terrain is well suited to cycling. You can rent a bike for A$10 a day at Coral Sea Skydiving Company, which also offers tandem sky dives.

Magnetic Island Holiday Photos rents bicycles for A$14 a day. Road Runner Scooter Hire rents scooters and trail bikes, and also conducts Harley-Davidson tours.

🛃 Bike Rentals **Coral Sea Skydiving Company** ✉ 14 Plume St., South Townsville ☎ 07/4772-4889. **Magnetic Island Holiday Photos** ✉ The Esplanade, Picnic Bay ☎ 07/4778-5411. **Road Runner Scooter Hire** ✉ The Esplanade, Picnic Bay ☎ 07/4778-5222.

BOAT & FERRY TRAVEL

Capricorn Barge Company runs a car and passenger ferry service to Magnetic Island with three to six departures daily.

Sunferries has 20-minute catamaran service every day from Townsville (leaving from 168–192 Flinders Street East and from the Breakwater Terminal on Sir Leslie Thiess Drive) to Nelly Bay on Magnetic Island. Bus and island transfers meet the ferry during daylight hours. There are up to 15 departures daily; a round-trip ticket costs A$16.95.

🛃 Boat & Ferry Information **Capricorn Barge Company** ☎ 07/4772-5422. **Sunferries** ☎ 07/4771-3855.

BUS TRAVEL

Greyhound Pioneer and McCafferty's Express Coaches travel regularly to Cairns, Brisbane, and other destinations throughout Australia from the Townsville Transit Center.

Magnetic Island Bus Service meets each boat at Picnic Bay in the south and travels across to Horseshoe Bay in the north of the island. An unlimited day pass costs A$11.

🚌 Bus Lines **Greyhound Pioneer** ✉ Palmer and Plume Sts., South Townsville ☎ 13-2030 ⊕ www.greyhound.com.au. **Magnetic Island Bus Service** ☎ 07/4778-5130. **McCafferty's Express Coaches** ✉ Palmer and Plume Sts., South Townsville ☎ 07/4772-5100 13-1499 ⊕ www.mccaffertys.com.au.

CAR RENTAL

Avis, Budget, Hertz, and Thrifty all have rental cars available in Townsville.

The tiny Mini Moke, a soft-top version of the Minor Mini car, provides an ideal means of exploring Magnetic Island. Magnetic Mokes rents Mini Mokes for A$65 for 24 hours.

🚗 Agencies **Avis** ✉ 81-83 Flinders St. E, Townsville ☎ 07/4721-2688. **Budget** ✉ 251 Ingham Rd., Townsville ☎ 07/4725-2344. **Hertz** ✉ Stinson Ave., Townsville ☎ 07/4775-5950. **Magnetic Mokes** ✉ 4 The Esplanade, Picnic Bay ☎ 07/4778-5377. **Thrifty** ✉ 289 Ingham Rd., Townsville ☎ 1800/658959.

CAR TRAVEL

Townsville is 1,400 km (868 mi) by road from Brisbane—a colossal, dull drive. The 370-km (230-mi) journey from Townsville to Cairns, with occasional Hinchinbrook Island views, is more appealing.

EMERGENCIES

In an emergency, dial 000 to reach an ambulance, the fire department, or the police.

🚑 **Aitkenvale Medical Centre** ✉ 295 Ross River Rd., Aitkenvale ☎ 07/4775-7444. **Townsville General Hospital** ✉ Eyre St., Townsville ☎ 07/4781-9211.

MAIL, INTERNET & SHIPPING

The Australia Post office is open weekdays 8:30 to 5:30.

📮 **Australia Post** ✉ Shaws Arcade, Sturt St., Townsville ☎ 07/4760-2020.

MONEY MATTERS

ANZ Bank can change money and cash traveler's checks. Commonwealth Bank of Australia accepts most overseas cards. Westpac is one of Australia's largest banks.

🏦 Banks **ANZ Bank** ✉ 298 Ross River Rd., Aitkenvale ☎ 13-1314. **Commonwealth Bank of Australia** ✉ 370 Flinders Mall, Townsville ☎ 07/4721-1290. **Westpac** ✉ 153 Charters Towers Rd., Hermit Park ☎ 07/4775-9777.

TAXIS

You can flag Townsville Taxis on the street or find one at stands or hotels. Magnetic Island Taxi has a stand at the ferry terminal at Picnic Point.

🚕 Taxi Companies **Magnetic Island Taxi** ☎ 07/4772-1555 or 13-1008. **Townsville Taxis** ✉ 11 Yeatman St., Hyde Park ☎ 07/4772-1555 or 13-1008.

TOURS

Coral Princess has several three- to seven-night cruises that leave from Townsville and Cairns. The comfortable, 54-passenger, minicruise ship stops for snorkeling, fishing, and exploring resort islands. The crew includes marine biologists who give lectures and accompany you on excursions. Divers can rent equipment on board. Lessons are also available.

Reef and Island Tours runs catamaran trips from the Wonderland wharf to its pontoon at Kelso Reef on the outer edge of the Great Barrier Reef. Once there, you have the choice of fishing, snorkeling, diving, or viewing coral through a glass-bottom boat. Morning and afternoon tea and a tropical buffet lunch are included in the A\$136 cost. The boat departs daily (except Monday and Thursday) at 9 and returns at 6.

🚩 Tour Operators **Coral Princess** ✉ Breakwater Marina, Townsville ☎ 07/4040-9999 ⊕ www.coralprincess.com.au. **Reef and Island Tours** ✉ Flinders St., Townsville ☎ 07/4721-3555.

TRAIN TRAVEL

The *Queenslander* travels between Brisbane and Townsville once a week, the *Spirit of the Tropics* travels twice a week, and the *Sunlander* travels the route three times a week. For more information call the Railways Booking Office in Brisbane.

🚩 **Railways Booking Office** ☎ 13-2232 ⊕ www.traveltrain.qr.com.au.

VISITOR INFORMATION

The Environmental Protection Agency has an office in Picnic Bay on Magnetic Island with information on walking trails. Magnetic Island Tourist Bureau is the island's primary oracle.

Townsville Enterprise has the widest range of material and information on all local attractions and is open weekdays 8:30–5. Townsville Tourism Information Centre has a kiosk in Flinders Mall.

🚩 Tourist Information **Environmental Protection Agency** ✉ Picnic Bay ☎ 07/4778-5378. **Magnetic Island Tourist Bureau** ✉ 10 Endeavour Rd., Arcadia, 4819 ☎ 07/4778-5256. **Townsville Enterprise** ✉ Enterprise House, 6 The Strand, Townsville, 4810 ☎ 07/4726-2728. **Townsville Tourism Information Centre** ✉ Flinders Mall, Townsville ☎ 07/4721-3660.

CAIRNS

Cairns is the capital of the region known as Tropical North Queensland. The city is closer to Papua New Guinea than it is to most of Australia, although its sense of isolation has decreased with its role as an international gateway. Built on Trinity Inlet, Cairns is bordered by the Coral Sea to the east and the rain-forest–clad mountains of the Great Dividing Range to the west.

A walk along the promenade often provides views of a variety of bird life, including night herons, blue cranes, giant sea eagles, and white egrets. At low tide, you may even see saltwater crocodiles basking themselves on the mangrove-bordered mudflats. Many older homes are built on stilts to catch ocean breezes, and overhead fans are ubiquitous. High-rise hotels, motels, and cheap hostels abound, and most people use the town as a base for exploring the surrounding ocean and rain forest.

Fodor'sChoice ★ A beautiful drive is along what locals call **The Great Green Way** (⊕ www.greatgreenway.com), the main road connecting Townsville to Cairns. The road heads through sugarcane, papaya, and banana plantations, passing dense rain forest, white beaches, and bright blue water dotted with tropical islands. The 345-km (215-mi) drive takes around four hours, but you'll want to stop to explore one or more towns, parks, waterfalls, and rain-forest tracts along the way.

Exploring Cairns

The **Esplanade,** fronting Trinity Bay, and the waterfront are the focal points of life in Cairns. Many of the town's best stores and hotels are found on The Esplanade, and this is also where many of the backpackers who throng to Cairns like to gather, giving it a lively, slightly bohemian feel. Trinity Bay is a shallow stretch of hundreds of yards of mangrove flats, uncovered at low tide, that attract interesting bird life. In the late 1980s,

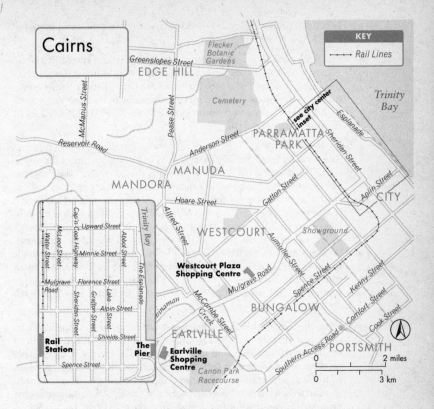

some of the waterfront was filled in, and **Pier Market Place,** a shopping-hotel complex, was constructed.

Cairns can trace its beginnings to the point where The Esplanade turns into **Wharf Street.** In 1876 this small area was a port for the gold and tin mined inland. The area later became known as the Barbary Coast because of its criminal element. Today, it's once again a thriving port.

Charter fishing boats moor at **Marlin Marina.** Big-game fishing is a major industry, and fish weighing more than 1,000 pounds have been caught in the waters off the reef. The docks for the catamarans that conduct Great Barrier Reef tours are found here at Marlin Marina and at nearby Trinity Wharf.

The actual center of Cairns is **City Place,** a quaint pedestrian mall where you can watch the passing parade. Some of the town's few authentic pubs, as well as the major shopping area, are around the square.

The **Cairns Museum** houses a collection of artifacts and photographs of the city's history, including a fascinating exhibit on the life of Aborigines in the rain forest. The museum is next to City Place on Shields Street. ⊠ *Lake and Shields Sts., CBD* ☎ *07/4051–5582* ✉ *A$4* ⊙ *Mon.–Sat. 10–3.*

★ The largest regional gallery in Queensland, the **Cairns Regional Gallery,** is housed in the former Public Office building. Designed and built in the early 1930s, the magnificent, two-story edifice has high-ceilinged, maple-panel rooms with native timber floors. A diverse range of media by local, national, international, and indigenous artists is on display. One-hour guided tours are on Wednesdays and Fridays. Workshops are often held in conjunction with exhibits. ⊠ *City Place, Cnr. Shields and Ab-*

bott Sts., CBD ☎ *07/4031–6865* ⊕ *www.cairnsregionalgallery.com.
au* ⊠ *A$4* ⊙ *10–5.*

Reef Teach presents informative and entertaining lectures six nights a week.
A marine biologist uses slides and samples of coral to inform prospec-
tive divers and general sightseers about the Great Barrier Reef's evolu-
tion and the unique inhabitants of this delicate marine ecosystem.
⊠ *Bolands Centre, 14 Spence St., CBD* ☎ *07/4031–7794* ⊠ *A$13*
⊙ *Mon.–Sat. 6:15–8:30.*

Around Cairns

The **Kuranda Scenic Railway** from Cairns to Kuranda is one of the loveliest rail journeys in the world. Kuranda is the gateway to the Atherton
Tablelands, an elevated area of rich volcanic soil that produces some of
Australia's finest beef, dairy, and produce. Between this tableland and
the narrow coastal strip is a rugged dividing range filled with waterfalls,
lakes, caves, and gorges. The train makes the 40-minute ascent through
the rain forest via the Barron River Gorge and 15 hand-hewn tunnels.
Several tours are available, from full-day rain-forest safaris to simple
round-trip train and bus rides. Tickets are A$31 one-way and A$44 round-
trip. Many visitors take the train out to Kuranda and return via the Skyrail
Rainforest Cableway. ⊠ *Cairns Railway Station, Bunda St., CBD* ☎ *07/
4031–3636.*

Fodor'sChoice From the remarkable **Skyrail Rainforest Cableway,** six-person cable cars
★ carry you on a 7½-km (5-mi) journey across the top of the rain-forest
canopy to the tiny highland village of Kuranda. Here you'll find daily
markets and the **Australian Butterfly Sanctuary,** where you'll see thousands
of tropical butterflies in a rain-forest environment. At the second stop
you can walk to Barron Falls or into the rain forest. Some conservationists
protested the construction of the cable car in the mid-1990s, but the Skyrail
today does provide a unique perspective on this astonishingly rich area.
The base station is 15 km (9 mi) north of Cairns. The cableway is open
daily 8–5, but 3:30 is the last time to board for a round-trip. Tickets
are A$30 one-way, A$46 round-trip. Many visitors take the Kuranda
Scenic Railway out to Kuranda and the cableway on the return trip.
⊠ *Caravonica Lakes, Kamerunga Rd. and Cook Hwy., Smithfield*
☎ *07/4038–1555* ⊕ *www.skyrail.com.au.*

The **Tjapukai Aboriginal Cultural Park,** at the base of the Skyrail Rain-
forest Cableway, has three theaters, one of which draws on state-of-the-
art holographic technology. A surrounding encampment vignettes aspects
of tribal life, including fire making, didgeridoo playing, preparation of
bush foods and medicines, and instruction on how to throw a boomerang
and spear. Aboriginal elders oversaw development of the Cultural Park.
Aboriginal artworks are on display and for sale. ⊠ *Kamerunga Rd., Smithfield, 15 km (9 mi) north of Cairns* ☎ *07/4042–9999* ⊕ *www.tjapukai.
com.au* ⊠ *A$28* ⊙ *Daily 9–5.*

Wooroonooran National Park, which extends from just south of Gordonvale
and stretches to the Palmerston Highway between Innisfail and Milla
Milla, is one of the most densely vegetated areas in Australia. Rain forest dominates Wooroonooran—from lowland tropical rain forest to
the stunted growth on Mt. Bartle Frere, at 5,287 feet the highest point
in Queensland, where you'll find Australia's largest remaining area of
upland rain forest. The largely undeveloped park encompasses both the
eastern and western slopes of the Bellenden Ker range.

The park has many trails, including a short, paved path that leads from
the parking area to Josephine Falls, which is a fine place to swim. Picnic facilities and toilets are here as well. The more adventurous can fol-

low a 15-km (9-mi) return trail that leads from the parking area to the summit of Mt. Bartle Frere.

Bush camping is allowed, with ranger permission, throughout the park, except at Josephine Falls. Permits cost A$3.50 per person per night. Bring supplies with you. To reach the park, look for signs south of Cairns along the Bruce Highway. ⊠ *Off of Bruce Hwy., Box 93, Miriwinni, 4871* ☎ *07/4067–6304.*

off the beaten path

UNDARA VOLCANIC NATIONAL PARK – The lava tubes here are a fascinating geological oddity in the Outback, attracting an ever-increasing number of visitors for day visits and overnight trips. A volcanic outpouring 190,000 years ago created the hollow basalt tubes. There are several places where you can walk into the tubes. Leaving the ferns, vines, and wallabies at the entrance, you'll step onto the smooth, dry tunnel floor. Above, horseshoe bats twitter and flitter in the crannies. Patterns etched in the ceiling by water seepage create an incongruous cathedral effect.

You must take a guided tour in order to visit the tubes. **Undara Experience** (⊠ Mt. Surprise ☎ 07/4097–1411 🖷 07/4097–1450 ⊕ www.undara.com.au) conducts two-hour (A$33), half-day (A$63), and full-day (A$93) tours of the tubes. The company can also organize bus transfers from Cairns.

Australian Pacific Tours (⊠ 278 Hartley St., City Center, Cairns ☎ 07/4041–9419) runs daily tours to Undara from Cairns May–October and Tuesday, Wednesday, and weekends November–April. Tours cost A$116 and include lunch.

Old railway cars have been converted into comfortable (if compact) motel rooms at the **UNDARA LAVA LODGE** (⊠ Mt. Surprise ☎ 07/4097–1411 🖷 07/4097–1450 ⊕ www.undara.com.au) – The lodge, set amid savanna and woodlands, supplies the complete Outback experience: bush breakfasts, campfires, and evening wildlife walks. Packages start at A$119 per night.

Where to Eat

$–$$$$ ✕ **The Raw Prawn Café.** A statue of a Balinese war god greets you at the entryway of this colorful, open-air restaurant. Yellow-and-blue tables sit on orange-and-blue tiles under a canopy of netting. Inside, white linen-covered tables lead to a mauve bar and an open kitchen. The menu is heavily seafood-oriented: mud crab, bugs, prawns, and the house special, "Hop, Skip, Hump, and Jump," a platter of ostrich, crocodile, camel, and kangaroo. Hold out for the mango parfait for dessert. ⊠ *103 The Esplanade CBD* ☎ *07/4031–5400* ⊟ *AE, DC, MC, V.*

$$–$$$ ✕ **Red Ochre Grill.** This restaurant uses about 40 different native foods
Fodor's Choice to create modern Australian cuisine. A warm red and terra-cotta din-
★ ing room features a large, freshwater tank displaying local red-claw yabbies (freshwater crayfish) and rainbow fish. Try the Australian antipasto platter of emu pâté, crocodile wontons, and smoked ostrich for starters, followed by kangaroo sirloin with quandong-chili glaze. The hot Turkish doughnuts with lemon-myrtle coconut ice cream and wild lime syrup are hard to resist. There is a good Australian wine list with selections available by the glass or bottle. ⊠ *43 Shields St., CBD* ☎ *07/4051–0100* ⊕ *www.redochregrill.com.au* ⊟ *AE, DC, MC, V* ☉ *No lunch Sun.*

★ **$$** ✕ **Breezes Brasserie.** Floor-to-ceiling windows overlooking Trinity Inlet and the distant mountains set the mood in this attractive restaurant in the Hilton Cairns. The decor is bright, with tropical greenery, white table-cloths, and candles. You can feast on anything—from quick sandwiches to full-course dinners. The modern Australian fare includes such delights as smoked Tasmanian salmon served with a bug mush (Australian lobster mixed with mashed potato), accompanied by red-wine jus. A spectacular seafood and Mediterranean buffet is available nightly. ⊠ *Hilton Cairns, Wharf St., CBD* ☎ *07/4052–6786* ⊟ *AE, DC, MC, V* ⊙ *No lunch.*

$$ ✕ **Sirocco Restaurant.** Many of the innovative, modern Australian dishes served at this waterfront restaurant have tropical and Asian undertones. Witness baked Moreton Bay bugs with finger lime, coconut butter, and a ginger-rhubarb relish; or char-grilled Atlantic salmon, herb, and wasabi mash with wok-fried Tableland vegetables and a tamarind and cilantro sauce. The dessert tray has to be seen to be believed. The interior of the restaurant is gracious and elegant, and tables are set with silver cutlery. ⊠ *Radisson Plaza Hotel, Pierpoint Rd., CBD* ☎ *07/4031–1411* ⊟ *AE, DC, MC, V* ⊙ *No lunch.*

$$ ✕ **Tawny's on the Jetty.** The extensive menu at this waterfront restaurant highlights local seafood and fresh produce from the nearby Atherton Tablelands. Desserts, such as banana and macadamia-nut pudding, are tropically inspired. ⊠ *Marlin Parade, Waterfront* ☎ *07/4051–1722* ⊟ *AE, DC, MC, V* ⊙ *No lunch.*

$–$$ ✕ **Roma Roulette.** Popular with locals and tourists alike, this Italian restaurant has an easygoing, informal atmosphere. Smiling chef Jimmy often personally advises customers on what to order. The scallopini and seafood dishes are popular. ⊠ *48A Aplin St., CBD* ☎ *07/4051–1076* ⊟ *AE, DC, V* ⛽ *BYOB* ⊙ *Closed Mon.–Tues.*

¢–$$ ✕ **Perrotta's at the Gallery.** Curved, galvanized steel tables and chairs from a local designer line the deck of the stately Cairns Regional Art Gallery. Completely outdoors, this café, restaurant, and winebar is open every day from 8 AM until late. For breakfast, try the french toast with star anise-scented pineapple and lime marscapone. Lunch fare includes yellowfin tuna burger with spiced avocado, shallots, feta, and wasabi aïoli. Desserts like pear and almond tart with rosemary anglaise are a memorable finish. ⊠ *Gallery Deck, Cairns Regional Gallery, Abbott and Shields Sts., CBD* ☎ *07/4031–5899* ⊕ *www.cairnsregionalgallery.com* ⊟ *AE, DC, MC, V.*

Where to Stay

$$$$ ▦ **Hilton Cairns.** The seven-story hotel curves along the shoreline and affords wonderful sea views. The lobby, which looks out past lush gardens to the ocean, is distinctly tropical, with ceramic floor tiles and an atrium filled with rain-forest palms and ferns. Plants from a rooftop garden dangle in the long external walkways, and rooms on the lowest level open onto a palm forest. Rooms are tastefully appointed and furnished. The hotel is near the business district and a famous game-fishing club. ⊠ *Wharf St., CBD, 4870* ☎ *07/4050–2000* 🖷 *07/4050–2001* ⊕ *www. hilton.com* ⇥ *258 rooms, 5 suites* ♨ *2 restaurants, room service, in-room data ports, in-room safes, room TVs with movies, pool, health club, hot tub, sauna, marina, 2 bars, baby-sitting, laundry service, Internet, concierge, car rental, travel service, no-smoking rooms, business services, meeting room, free parking* ⊟ *AE, DC, MC, V.*

★ **$$$$** ▦ **Hotel Sofitel Reef Casino.** The Reef is part of an entertainment complex in the heart of Cairns. A rooftop conservatory is a tropical hot-house by day, at night turning into a candlelighted dinner theater within a rain forest. Along with a coffee shop, casino, nightclub, and several bars, you'll also find Pacific Flavours Brasserie and Tamarind, a Thai-Australian restaurant. ✉ *35–41 Wharf St., CBD, 4870* ☎ *07/4030–8888 or 1800/808883* 🖷 *07/4030–8788* ⊕ *www.reefcasino.com.au* 🛏 *128 suites* ⚓ *2 restaurants, room service, in-room data ports, in-room safes, room TVs with movies, pool, gym, hot tub, massage, sauna, 4 bars, lounge, casino, nightclub, baby-sitting, laundry service, business services, meeting room, car rental, travel services, free parking* ▭ *AE, DC, MC, V.*

$$–$$$$ 🏨 **Radisson Plaza Hotel at the Pier.** The Radisson overlooks Trinity Wharf and Marlin Marina, the main Cairns terminals for cruises to the Barrier Reef. The hotel's conservative, low-rise design is typical of northern Queensland, but its lobby atrium is spectacular—a replica of a rain forest with real and artificial plants, a boardwalk, and an aquarium resembling a miniature tropical reef. Rooms are sunny and spacious; keep an eye out for the parrots on your balcony. Next door is Pier Marketplace, with numerous shops and restaurants. ✉ *Pierpoint Rd., CBD, 4870* ☎ *07/4031–1411 or 1800/333333* 🖷 *07/4031–3226* ⊕ *www.radisson.com* 🛏 *216 rooms, 22 suites* ⚓ *2 restaurants, room service, in-room safes, room TVs with movies, pool, wading pool, health club, hot tub, sauna, billiards, Ping-Pong, 2 bars, baby-sitting, laundry service, concierge, business services, travel services, free parking* ▭ *AE, DC, MC, V.*

$$$ 🏨 **Holiday Inn Cairns.** This seven-story hotel affords views of Trinity Bay and the Coral Sea. A marble floor, luxurious rugs, and cane sofas decorate the glass-wall lobby, which overlooks the hotel gardens. Guest rooms are done in muted shades of blues and yellows, with cane chairs and wood tables. The hotel is within walking distance of shops, restaurants, and the business district. ✉ *The Esplanade and Florence St., CBD, 4870* ☎ *07/4050–6070* 🖷 *07/4050–3770* ⊕ *www.holiday-inn.com* 🛏 *226 rooms, 6 suites* ⚓ *Restaurant, room service, in-room data ports, in-room safes, room TVs with movies, pool, wading pool, hot tub, bar, baby-sitting, laundry service, business services, meeting room, travel services, free parking; no-smoking floor* ▭ *AE, DC, MC, V.*

$$–$$$ 🏨 **Il Palazzo Boutique Hotel.** A 6½-foot Italian marble replica of Michelangelo's *David* greets you in the foyer, and other intriguing objets d'art appear throughout this boutique hotel serving luxury in a smaller package. The suites are spacious, with a soft-green color scheme, forged-iron and glass tables, and cane furniture. They all have fully equipped kitchens and laundry machines. Try Matsuri, the hotel's Japanese-style cafeteria. ✉ *62 Abbott St., CBD, 4870* ☎ *07/4041–2155 or 1800/813222* 🖷 *07/4041–2166* ⊕ *www.ilpalazzo.com.au* 🛏 *38 suites* ⚓ *Cafeteria, room service, kitchens, pool, hair salon, dry cleaning, free parking* ▭ *AE, DC, MC, V.*

★ $$–$$$ 🏨 **Pacific International Cairns.** A soaring three-story lobby makes for an impressive entrance to this hotel facing the waterfront and the marina. Cane-and-rattan chairs, soft pastels, tropical plants, and Gauguin-style prints fill the guest rooms, all of which have private balconies. Within the hotel are three restaurants and a coffee shop. ✉ *The Esplanade and Spence St., CBD, 4870* ☎ *07/4051–7888 or 1800/079001* 🖷 *07/4051–0210* ⊕ *www.pacifichotelcairns.com* 🛏 *163 rooms, 13 suites* ⚓ *3 restaurants, coffee shop, in-room data ports, minibars, room TVs with movies, pool, spa, bar, baby-siting, laundry service, meeting room, travel services* ▭ *AE, DC, MC, V.*

$$ 🏨 **RIHGA Colonial Club Resort Cairns.** More than 10 acres of tropical gardens surround this colonial-style resort built around three lagoonlike swimming pools. The public areas and rooms are simply furnished with cane furniture, ceiling fans, and vivid tropical patterns. Apartments with some cooking facilities are available. A free shuttle makes the 7-km (4½-mi) run to the city center hourly, and courtesy airport transfers are provided. ⊠ *18–26 Cannon St., Manunda, 4870* ☎ *07/4053–5111* 🖷 *07/4053–7072* ⊕ *www.cairnscolonialclub.com.au* 🛏 *264 rooms, 82 apartments* 🍴 *3 restaurants, room TVs with movies, refrigerators, tennis court, 3 pools, gym, sauna, 2 spas, bicycles, 4 bars, shops, baby-sitting, playground, dry cleaning, laundry service, Internet, business services, car rental, free parking* 🖃 *AE, DC, MC, V.*

¢–$ 🏨 **Lilybank.** In the early 1900s this was the home of the Mayor of Cairns, as well as the homestead of North Queensland's first tropical fruit plantation. This two-story Queenslander has a wooden wraparound veranda, and white, high-ceilinged rooms, each with its own private veranda. Stratford is less than 10 minutes from the town center and the airport. Hosts Pat and Mike are happy to book tours and share the affections of their poodles and cockatoo. The saltwater pool, surrounded by a brick patio and trees, is particularly pleasant. ⊠ *75 Kamerunga Rd., Stratford, 4870* ☎ *07/4055–1123* 🖷 *07/4058–1990* ⊘ *hosts@lilybank.com.au* 🛏 *5 rooms* 🍴 *Dining room, pool, library, laundry facilities, free parking* 🖃 *AE, MC, V.*

¢ 🏨 **Club Crocodile Hides Hotel.** This 1880s building with breezy verandas is a superb example of colonial Outback architecture. An adjoining motel has modern rooms with tropical decor, and you can choose between rooms with shared facilities or those with private baths. Rates include Continental breakfast. The hotel is in the center of the Cairns Mall. ⊠ *Lake and Shields Sts., CBD, 4870* ☎ *07/4051–1266* 🖷 *07/4031–2276* 🛏 *72 rooms* 🍴 *Restaurant, in-room safes, refrigerators, pool, hot tub, 5 bars, baby-sitting, laundry facilities, travel services* 🖃 *AE, DC, MC, V* ⦿ *CP.*

Nightlife

1936 (⊠ 35–41 Wharf St., CBD ☎ 07/4030–8888), a mixed retro and modern club in the Hotel Sofitel Reef Casino, isn't exactly the place to go for a quiet chat. However, the live nightly shows and "underworld" feel of Manhattan in the 1930s actually work quite well. It's open Thursday–Saturday from 8 PM until the wee hours of the morning. There's a A$5 cover—but hotel guests get in free.

The Pier Tavern (⊠ The Pier Marketplace, Pierpoint Rd., CBD ☎ 07/4031–4677), overlooking the waterfront, is a lively, upscale watering hole and a good place to meet locals.

Mondo on the Waterfront (⊠ Cairns Hilton, The Esplanade, CBD ☎ 07/4052–6780), looking out onto Trinity Inlet, is open all day for coffee, light lunches, and dinners (and a huge range of homemade ice cream), but it is really ideal in the evenings, where the outdoor tables surrounded by palm and flaming red poinsiana trees are the perfect place to drink cocktails and relax.

Sports & the Outdoors

Adventure Trips

Raging Thunder (⊠ 52–54 Fearnley St., CBD ☎ 07/4030–7990) conducts adventure packages that take in the Great Barrier Reef, white-water rafting through the rain forest, the Tjapukai Aboriginal Cultural Park, Kuranda Scenic Railway or Skyrail, and hot-air ballooning over the Atherton Tablelands—the best of Cairns in one package.

RNR Rafting (⊠ 4 Shields St., CBD ☎ 07/4051–7777) runs very exciting one-, two-, and five-day white-water expeditions that are suitable only for the physically fit.

Beaches

Cairns has no beaches of its own. Most people head out to the reef to swim and snorkel. Just north of the airport, however, are **Machans Beach, Holloways Beach, Yorkey's Knob, Trinity Beach,** and **Clifton Beach.** Do not swim in these waters from October through May, when deadly box jellyfish, called marine stingers, and invisible-to-the-eye *Irukandji* float in the water along the coast. Some beaches have small netted areas, but it's advisable to stick to hotel pools during this time. These jellyfish stay closer to shore and are usually not found around the Great Barrier Reef or any nearby islands.

Diving

Several diving schools in Cairns provide everything from beginner's lessons to equipment rentals and expeditions for experienced divers.

Deep Sea Divers Den (✉ 319 Draper St., CBD ☏ 1800/612223) offers day trips that include three dives, equipment, and lunch.

Mike Ball Dive Expeditions (✉ 143 Lake St., CBD ☏ 07/4031–5484) has dive trips to a number of locations along the Queensland coastline.

Pro Dive (✉ 116 Spence St., CBD ☏ 07/4031–5255) conducts three-day, two-night trips to the Great Barrier Reef.

Quicksilver (✉ Pier Marketplace, The Esplanade, CBD ☏ 07/4031–4299 ⊕ www.quicksilver-cruises.com) runs sightseeing, snorkeling, and diving tours on their sleek catamarans to the outer Barrier Reef. Scenic helicopter flights over the reef are also available.

Reef Magic Cruises (✉ 13 Shields St., CBD ☏ 07/4031–1588) runs day trips to 10 different locations on the Great Barrier Reef.

Reef Teach (✉ 9 Spence St., CBD ☏ 07/4031–7794) offers several dive trips to various locations.

Tusa Dive (✉ Shield St. and The Esplanade, CBD ☏ 07/4031–1448 ⊕ www.tusadive.com) runs daily snorkeling and dive trips 90 minutes from shore.

Shopping

Malls

Cairns Central (✉ McLeod and Spence Sts., CBD ☏ 07/4041–4111), adjacent to the Cairns railway station, houses 180 specialty stores, a Myer department store, an international food court, and cinemas. **Orchid Plaza** (✉ 79–87 Abbott St., CBD ☏ 07/4051–7788) has clothing stores, cafés, record stores, a pearl emporium, an art gallery, and a post office. **Pier Marketplace** (✉ Pierpoint Rd., CBD ☏ 07/4051–7244), on The Esplanade, houses such international chains as Brian Rochford and Country Road, and the offices of yacht brokers and tour operators. Many of the cafés, bars, and restaurants open onto verandas on the waterside. **Trinity Wharf** (✉ Wharf St., CBD ☏ 07/4031–1519) has everything from designer clothes and souvenirs to resort wear, hairdressers, restaurants, and a coach terminal. You can request complimentary transportation from your hotel to this waterfront shopping spot.

Markets

You can buy souvenir items, arts and crafts, and T-shirts at the nightly **Cairns Night Markets** (✉ The Esplanade at Aplin St., CBD).

Held Friday afternoon, all day Saturday, and Sunday morning, **Rusty's Bazaar** (✉ Grafton and Sheridan Sts., CBD) is the best street market in Cairns. Everything from homegrown fruit and vegetables to secondhand items and antiques is on sale.

Specialty Stores

Australian Craftworks (⊠ Shop 20, Village La., Lake St., CBD ☎ 07/4051–0725) sells one of the city's finest collections of local crafts. **Jungara Gallery** (⊠ 89 The Esplanade, CBD ☎ 07/4051–5355) has Aboriginal and New Guinean arts and artifacts on display and for sale. **The Queensland Aborigine** (⊠ Shop 4, Tropical Arcade, Shield St., CBD ☎ 07/4041–2800) has Aboriginal art and crafts for sale, weaving workshops, and a fascinating museum. The well-respected **Original Dreamtime Gallery** (⊠ Orchid Plaza, Lake St., CBD ☎ 07/4051–3222) carries top-quality artwork created by the Aborigines of the Northern Territory. **Reef Gallery** (⊠ The Pier Marketplace, CBD ☎ 07/4051–0992) sells paintings by leading local artists.

Cairns A to Z

To research prices, get advice from other travelers, and book travel arrangements, visit www.fodors.com.

AIR TRAVEL

Domestic airlines based at Cairns Airport include Qantas and Virgin Blue. Among the international airlines based at the airport are Air New Zealand, Cathay Pacific, Continental Micronesia, Garuda Indonesia, Malaysian Airlines, and Singapore Airlines.

🛪 Carriers **Air New Zealand** ☎ 13-2476. **Cathay Pacific** ☎ 1300/361060. **Continental Micronesia** ☎ 07/4034-9122. **Garuda Indonesia** ☎ 1300/365330. **Malaysian Airlines** ☎ 13-2627. **Qantas** ☎ 07/4050-4054. **Singapore Airlines** ☎ 13-1011. **Virgin Blue** ☎ 13-6789.

AIRPORTS & TRANSFERS

Cairns Airport is a hub for both domestic and international airlines.
🛪 **Cairns Airport** ⊠ Airport Rd., ☎ 07/4052-9703.
🛪 **Express Chauffeured Coaches** ⊠ 5 Opal St., Port Douglas ☎ 07/4098-5473.

BUS TRAVEL

Greyhound Pioneer Australia operates daily express buses from major southern cities to Cairns. By bus, Cairns to Brisbane takes 25 hours, to Sydney it's 42 hours, and to Melbourne it's 50 hours. McCafferty's Express Coaches stops in Cairns at the Trinity Wharf Center.
🛪 Bus Lines **Greyhound Pioneer Australia** ⊠ Trinity Wharf Center, Wharf St., CBD ☎ 13-2030 ⊕ www.greyhound.com.au. **McCafferty's Express Coaches** ⊠ Wharf St., CBD ☎ 07/4051-5899 or 13-1499 ⊕ www.mccaffertys.com.au.

CAR RENTAL

Avis, Budget, Hertz, and Thrifty all have rental cars and four-wheel-drive vehicles available in Cairns.
🛪 Agencies **Avis** ⊠ Lake and Aplin Sts., CBD ☎ 07/4035-9100. **Budget** ⊠ 153 Lake St., CBD ☎ 07/4051-9222. **Hertz** ⊠ 147 Lake St., CBD ☎ 07/4051-6399 or 13-3039. **Thrifty** ⊠ Sheridan and Aplin Sts., CBD ☎ 1300/367227.

CAR TRAVEL

The 1,712-km (1,061-mi), 20-hour route from Brisbane to Cairns runs along the Bruce Highway (Highway 1), which later becomes the Captain Cook Highway. Throughout its length, the road rarely touches the coast and is often not even picturesque. Unless you're planning to spend time in Central Queensland, Airlie Beach, and the Whitsundays, or exploring the Fraser Island, Hervey Bay, and South Burnett region, it's best to fly to Cairns and rent a car instead.

EMERGENCIES

In an emergency, dial 000 to reach an ambulance, the fire department, or the police.

🏥 **Cairns Base Hospital** ✉ The Esplanade, CBD ☎ 07/4050-6333.

INTERNET

You can retrieve e-mail and check the Internet at Inbox Café, which is open every day from 7 AM until midnight.

🏥 **Inbox Café** ✉ 119 Abbott St., CBD ☎ 07/4041-4677 ⊕ www.inboxcafe.com.au.

MONEY MATTERS

Commonwealth Bank will cash traveler's checks and change money. National Bank of Australia is one of Australia's largest banks. Westpac has automatic teller machines that accept most overseas cards.

🏥 **Banks Commonwealth Bank** ✉ 76 Lake St., CBD ☎ 07/4041-2760. **National Bank of Australia** ✉ 14 Shields St., CBD ☎ 07/4080-4111. **Westpac** ✉ 63 Lake St., CBD ☎ 13-2032.

TOURS

BOAT TOURS Coral Princess has a range of three- to seven-night cruises that leave from Cairns and Townsville on a comfortable, 54-passenger minicruise ship. There are plenty of stops for snorkeling, fishing, and exploring resort islands. The crew includes marine biologists who give lectures and accompany you on excursions. Divers can rent equipment on board; lessons are also available.

Great Adventures Outer Barrier Reef and Island Cruises runs a fast catamaran daily to Green Island and the outer Barrier Reef, where diving, snorkeling, and helicopter overflights are available. Some trips include a buffet lunch and coral viewing from an underwater observatory and a semisubmersible.

Ocean Spirit Cruises conducts a full-day tour aboard the *Ocean Spirit*, the largest sailing vessel of its type in the world, and the smaller *Ocean Spirit II*. A daily trip to Michaelmas or Upolo Cay includes four hours at the Great Barrier Reef, coral viewing from a semisubmersible or a glass-bottom boat at Upolo Cay, swimming and snorkeling, and a fresh seafood lunch. Introductory diving lessons are available.

🏥 **Tour Operators Coral Princess** ✉ 5/149 Spence St., CBD Cairns, 4870 ☎ 07/4031-1041 or 1800/079545 ⊕ www.coralprincess.com.au. **Great Adventures Outer Barrier Reef and Island Cruises** ✉ Wharf St., CBD ☎ 07/4044-9944 or 1800/079080. **Ocean Spirit Cruises** ✉ 33 Lake St., CBD ☎ 07/4031-2920.

EXCURSIONS Reef and Rainforest Connections organizes several day trips and excursions out of Cairns and Port Douglas. One day trip includes visits to the Kuranda Scenic Railway, Skyrail Rainforest Cableway, and Tjapukai Aboriginal Cultural Park. Excursions are also available to Cape Tribulation and Bloomfield Falls, the Daintree River and Mossman Gorge, and the Low Isles on the Great Barrier Reef. Another tour operator is Down Under Tours, organizing day trips to Kuranda, Cape Tribulation, and the Daintree and four-wheel-drive excursions, picking you up from your hotel.

🏥 **Reef and Rainforest Connections** ✉ 40 Macrossan St., Port Douglas ☎ 07/4099-5777 ⊕ www.reefandrainforest.com.au. **Down Under Tours** ✉ 26 Redden St., Cairns ☎ 07/4035-5566 ⊕ www.downundertours.com.

HORSEBACK-RIDING TOURS Blazing Saddles offers half-day horse rides through the rain forest and to lookouts over the northern beaches. Trips cost A$79.

🏥 **Blazing Saddles** ✉ Captain Cook Hwy., Palm Cove ☎ 07/4059-0955.

NATURE TOURS Daintree Wildlife Safari runs 1½-hour tours down the Daintree River.

Daintree Rainforest River Trains run full-day and half-day tours through mangrove swamps and thick rain forest to see native orchids, birds, and crocodiles.

Wilderness Challenge runs trips to the top of the Cape York Peninsula from June through November.

⚡ Tour Operator Daintree Rainforest River Trains ☎ 07/4090-7676. **Daintree Wildlife Safari** ☎ 07/4098-6125. **Wilderness Challenge** ✉ 15 Panguna St., Trinity Beach, 4870 ☎ 07/4055-6504 🖶 07/4057-7226 ⊕ www.wilderness-challenge.com.au.

TRAIN TRAVEL

Trains arrive at the Cairns Railway Station on Bunda Street. The *Sunlander* and *Queenslander* trains make the 32-hour journey between Brisbane and Cairns. The *Sunlander* runs three times a week to Cairns. The *Queenslander* has been refurbished to the level of most luxury cruise ships, making the journey equal in comfort to that of the world's great deluxe trains. It runs once a week; contact the railway station to find out which day it's running. The *Savannahlander* leaves Cairns each Wednesday and winds its way to Forsayth in the heart of the Gulf of Savannah.

The Great South Pacific Express offers first-class "Orient Express"–type luxury between Sydney, Brisbane, and Cairns. It's 22 hours by train from Sydney to Brisbane, and three days from Brisbane to Cairns. The train runs twice weekly each way and includes many extra sightseeing tours during the journey.

⚡ Train Information Cairns Railway Station ✉ Bunda St., City Center ☎ 07/4036-9250. **The Great South Pacific Express** ☎ 1800/627655.

VISITOR INFORMATION

⚡ Tourism Tropical North Queensland ✉ Fogarty Rd. and The Esplanade, CBD ☎ 07/4051-3588.

NORTH FROM CAIRNS

The Captain Cook Highway runs from Cairns to Mossman, a relatively civilized stretch known mostly for the resort town of Port Douglas. Past the Daintree River, wildlife parks and sunny coastal villages fade into one of the most sensationally wild corners of the continent. If you came to Australia in search of high-octane sun, empty beaches and coral cays, steamy jungles filled with exotic bird noises and rioting vegetation, and a languid, beachcomber lifestyle, then head straight for the coast between Daintree and Cooktown.

The southern half of this coastline lies within Cape Tribulation National Park, part of the Greater Daintree Wilderness Area, a region named to UNESCO's World Heritage list because of its unique ecology. If you want to get a peek at the natural splendor of the area, there's no need to go past Cape Tribulation. However, the Bloomfield Track does continue on to Cooktown, a destination that will tack two days onto your itinerary. This wild, rugged country breeds some notoriously maverick personalities and can add a whole other dimension to the Far North Queensland experience.

Prime time for visiting the area is from May through September, when the daily maximum temperature averages around 27°C (80°F) and the water is comfortably warm. During the wet season, which lasts from about December through March, expect monsoon conditions. Toxic box and transparent *Irukandji* jellyfish make the coastline unsafe for swimming during this time, but the jellies don't drift out as far as the reefs, so you're safe there.

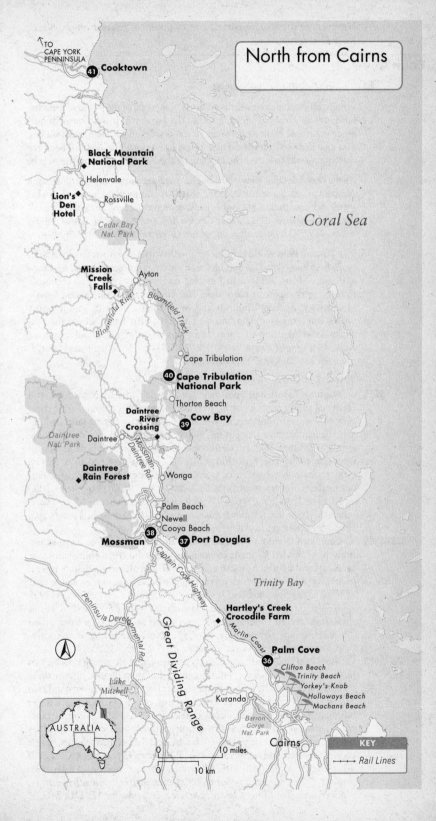

North from Cairns

Coral Sea

Trinity Bay

41 Cooktown

TO CAPE YORK PENNINSULA

Black Mountain National Park

Helenvale

Lion's Den Hotel

Rossville

Cedar Bay Nat. Park

Mission Creek Falls

Ayton

Bloomfield River

Bloomfield Track

Cape Tribulation

40 **Cape Tribulation National Park**

Thorton Beach

Daintree River Crossing

39 **Cow Bay**

Daintree Nat. Park

Daintree

Mossman-Daintree Rd.

Daintree Rain Forest

Wonga

Palm Beach
Newell
Cooya Beach

Mossman **38**

37 **Port Douglas**

Captain Cook Highway

Peninsula Developmental Rd.

Great Dividing Range

Hartley's Creek Crocodile Farm

Marlin Coast

Palm Cove

36

Clifton Beach
Trinity Beach
Yorkey's Knob
Holloways Beach
Machans Beach

Lake Mitchell

Kuranda

Barron Gorge Nat. Park

Cairns

AUSTRALIA

0   10 miles

0   10 km

KEY

Rail Lines

Numbers in the margin correspond to points of interest on the North from Cairns map.

Palm Cove

36 *23 km (14 mi) north of Cairns.*

A mere 20-minute drive north of Cairns, this is one of the jewels of Queensland and an ideal base for exploring the far north. It is an oasis of quietude that those in the know seek out for its magnificent trees, calm waters, and excellent restaurants. The loudest noises you are likely to hear are the singing of birds and the lapping of the Pacific Ocean on the beach.

At the **Outback Opal Mine** you can glimpse huge specimens of this unique Australian gemstone and opalized seashells and fossils. The owners, who were once opal miners at Coober Pedy, demonstrate how an opal is formed, cut, and polished. ✉ *Captain Cook Hwy., next to Wild World* ☎ *07/ 4055–3492* ⊕ *www.outbackopalmine.com.au* ✆ *Free* ☉ *Daily 8–6.*

The 10-acre **Wild World** is home to a wide variety of Australian wildlife, including kangaroos, crocodiles and other reptiles, pelicans, and cassowaries. Most distinguished among its residents is Sarge, a crocodile that the park claims is more than 100 years old and the largest female in captivity. At 1,540 pounds and more than 17 feet in length, Sarge won't leave many unconvinced. The park also has a snake show, a snake-handling demonstration, and a giant North Queensland cane-toad race. ✉ *Captain Cook Hwy.* ☎ *07/4055–3669* ⊕ *www.wildworld-aus.com.au* ✆ *A$24* ☉ *Daily 8:30–5.*

Where to Stay

$$$$ ⊡ **Angsana Resort and Spa.** Fine landscaping, pools, barbecues, and plenty of sunny areas in which to relax enhance this colonial-style complex of vacation apartments, which opens directly onto a large, white-sand beach. Each apartment has a large private veranda, a comfortable sitting and dining area, two bathrooms, and two or three bedrooms with king-size beds. The furnishings are all custom-designed in a cheery, modern style. Kitchens have granite-top counters, and there are laundry facilities in every apartment. ✉ *1 Veivers Rd., 4879* ☎ *07/4055–3000 or 1800/672236* 🖷 *07/4055–3090* ⊕ *www.angsana.com* ⇆ *69 apartments* ⚶ *Restaurant, room service, in-room safes, kitchens, 3 pools, spa, shop, dry cleaning, laundry facilities* ⊟ *AE, DC, MC, V.*

$$$–$$$$ ⊡ **Courtyard Great Barrier Reef Resort.** Built around a free-form swimming pool shaded by giant melaleucas and palm trees, this complex is an escapist's delight. You can enjoy all the amenities of a deluxe resort, including plush rooms with private balconies, at a more reasonable rate. ⌖ *Box 122, Veivers Rd. and Williams Esplanade, 4879* ☎ *07/4055–3999* 🖷 *07/4055–3902* ⊕ *www.courtyard.com* ⇆ *185 rooms, 4 suites* ⚶ *Restaurant, in-room data ports, in-room safes, refrigerators, room TV with movies, tennis court, pool, spa, bar, baby-sitting, laundry service, business services, meeting room* ⊟ *AE, DC, MC, V.*

★ **$$$–$$$$** ⊡ **Sebel Reef House.** Set amid lovely gardens, this charming hotel seems more like a private club, with a waterfall that spills into one of three swimming pools. The lobby, along with its mural of the Queensland rain forest, is decorated with a superb collection of New Guinea Sepik River handicrafts. The main building dates to 1885, and the comfortable rooms have a turn-of-the-20th-century atmosphere characterized by mosquito netting, whitewashed walls, and pastel furnishings. Some rooms have bars and refrigerators. ✉ *99 Williams Esplanade, 4879* ☎ *07/ 4055–3633* 🖷 *07/4059–3305* ⊕ *www.reefhouse.com.au* ⇆ *63 rooms, 4 suites* ⚶ *Restaurant, in-room VCRs, kitchenettes, some refrigerators, 3 pools, spa, bar, library, laundry service, Internet* ⊟ *AE, DC, MC, V.*

$$ ⊞ **Novotel Palm Cove Resort.** The villagelike buildings and 100 acres of gardens and golf fairways here are just a five-minute walk from the beach. The one-, two-, and three-bedroom guest quarters incorporate a tropical color scheme and a harmonious mixture of cane and wood furniture. You can tuck into barramundi, prawns, reef fish, and crabs at the resort's Paperbark Restaurant. Palm Cove jetty, where tour operators pick up passengers for trips to the Great Barrier Reef, is just a five-minute walk from the resort. ⊠ *Coral Coast Dr., 4879* ☎ *07/4059–1234* ⊟ *07/ 4059–1297* ⊕ *www.novotel-pcr.com.au* ☞ *152 rooms, 72 suites, 119 apartments* ♿ *2 restaurants, in-room data ports, refrigerators, room TVs with movies, 9-hole golf course, 3 tennis courts, 10 pools, dive shop, windsurfing, boating, jet skiing, squash, baby-sitting, children's programs (ages 5–12)* ⊟ *AE, DC, MC, V.*

en route — North of Palm Cove, where the Captain Cook Highway swoops toward the sea, a sign announces the beginning of the **Marlin Coast,** and for the next 30 km (19 mi) the road plays hide-and-seek with a glorious stretch of shoreline, ducking inland through tunnels of coconut palm and curving back to the surf.

★ **Hartley's Creek Crocodile Farm** shelters hundreds of crocodiles plus many native animals, such as koalas, kangaroos, dingoes, snakes, lizards, and such native birds as the rare cassowary, which is a large and colorful bird found only in New Guinea and parts of northern Australia. ⊠ *Cook Hwy., 40 km (25 mi) north of Cairns* ☎ *07/ 4055–3576* ⊕ *www.hartleyscreek.com* 🖾 *A$24* ⊙ *Daily 8:30–5, crocodile show at 3, crocodile photos at 4, koalas and dingoes show at 1, snake show at 2.*

Port Douglas

❸ *61 km (38 mi) northwest of Cairns.*

In the early '80s Port Douglas was a sleepy little fishing village, but today it's one of the "in" places to go in Australia, drawing international stars looking to get away from it all as well as locals. The road into town passes through sugarcane fields, then widens and is flanked by palm trees that were planted elsewhere during World War II for palm oil, then moved here to create this avenue. Known simply as the "Port" to locals, the town has an indefinable mystique. Enough of the old Queensland colonial buildings remain to give it an authentic feel, despite the growing presence of modern resorts and hotels.

Port Douglas also serves as a good base for exploring Daintree rain forest, Cape Tribulation, and the Great Barrier Reef. High-speed cruises leave the Port for the Outer Reef.

The Rainforest Habitat Wildlife Sanctuary is a wonderful park that houses more than 180 species of native rain forest wildlife, including cassowaries, parrots, wetland waders, kangaroos, and crocodiles. You can eat a sumptuous buffet breakfast with the birds for A$34, which includes admission and an informative guided tour of the habitat. ⊠ *Port Douglas Rd.* ☎ *07/4099–3235* ⊕ *www.rainforesthabitat.com.au* 🖾 *A$20* ⊙ *Daily 8–5:30, breakfast with the birds daily 8–11.*

Where to Stay & Eat

$$–$$$$ ✕ **Catalina.** Huge bird of paradise plants greet you at the entrance of
Fodor'sChoice this sprawling restaurant built to resemble the veranda and dining room
★ of a gracious old Queenslander. Diners sit surrounded by tall, wrought-iron candelabras and plants. Try the coral trout steamed in banana leaf

with capsicum, cilantro, lemon, and coconut salsa, or the seared More-ton Bay bugs with avocado, grapefruit, papaya, and French–Asian aïoli. Finish with the flourless chocolate cake and homemade banana ice cream. ☒ *22 Wharf St.* ☎ *07/4099–5287* ⌂ *Reservations essential.* ▭ *AE, DC, MC, V* ☉ *Closed Mon.*

$$–$$$ ✕ **Ironbar.** Built like a ramshackle, corrugated-iron shack, this restaurant has a menu scattered with Aussie colloquialisms. But don't be fooled into thinking the food is as slap-happy as the atmosphere. "Dip your lid" to a taste of the prime rib-eye fillet served with a red wine and garlic sauce, or kangaroo marinated in garlic and olive oil on roasted vegetables with bush tomato dust and a semi-dried tomato pesto. If you time it right, you may see the cane toad races held in the backroom bar. ☒ *5 Macrossan St.* ☎ *07/4099–4776* ▭ *AE, DC, MC, V.*

$$–$$$ ✕ **Macrossans.** This modern, glass-walled restaurant in the Sheraton Mirage is a study in opulence. High-quality antiques, floor-length white tablecloths, and elegant silver settings complement the cuisine: dishes prepared with fresh seafood and local produce. The food is artfully presented, usually with a garnish of exotic fruit. Try Mossman prawns if they are available, and save some room for dessert, especially the soufflé of the day. ☒ *Davidson St.* ☎ *07/4099–5888* ▭ *AE, DC, MC, V* ☉ *Closed Tues. and Wed. No lunch.*

★ $$ ✕ **Nautilus Restaurant.** Pull up one of the high-back cane chairs outside under a canopy of magnificent coconut palms. The modern Australian cuisine is fresh and original, with plenty of seafood on the menu, and all dishes are beautifully presented. The Nautilus is famous for its mud crabs cooked to order. Try the lightly fried whole coral trout, the leeks and sweet peppers with coconut-and-lemon dressing, or Thai chicken curry with steamed rice. For dessert, you can't go wrong ordering the mango soufflé. ☒ *17 Murphy St.* ☎ *07/4099–5330* ▭ *AE, DC, MC, V* ⌂ *Reservations essential* ☉ *No lunch.*

$–$$ ✕ **Salsa Bar and Grill.** Locals look on the lively seaside Salsa Bar and Grill as a Port Douglas institution. The contemporary Australian dishes run the gamut from seafood and steaks to fresh salads and light snacks. The interior is bright and beachy, and a huge wooden deck becomes an intimate dinner setting once the sun goes down. There's a happy hour daily 3–5. ☒ *Wharf St.* ☎ *07/4099–5390* ▭ *AE, DC, MC, V.*

$–$$ ✕ **Sardi's Italian Seafood Restaurant and Bar.** Cool terra-cotta tiles and warm brown-and-cream stucco walls set the mood for a wonderfully Italian experience. The mouthwatering *bruschetta al pomodoro* combines fresh tomatoes, herbs, and olive oil on crispy toasted bread. The lightly crumbed, grilled calamari comes with a parsley sauce and a green salad, and the lasagna incorporates Moreton Bay bugs. You can dine at formal tables, in relaxed lounge suites, or next to a small pool in a peaceful garden. A well-stocked bar lines two sides of the restaurant. ☒ *123 Davidson St.* ☎ *07/4099–6585* ⊕ *www.sardisrestaurant. com.au* ▭ *AE, DC, MC, V* ☉ *Closed Sun. (may be open some Sun. July–Nov.; phone ahead). No lunch.*

★ $$$–$$$$ ▦ **Sheraton Mirage Port Douglas.** Elegant guest rooms at this deluxe resort have tropical-print bedspreads and cane furniture upholstered in blues and greens. Rooms overlook the hotel gardens, golf course, or 5 acres of swimmable saltwater lagoons that surround the Mirage. Valets are available 24 hours a day to assist with everything from replenishing ice buckets to arranging special candlelight dinners in your room. You're free to use the gym and tennis courts at the neighboring Mirage Country Club. The modern Macrossans seafood restaurant is a local favorite. ☒ *Davidson St., 4871* ☎ *07/4099–5888* ▤ *07/4099–4424* ⊕ *www.sheraton-mirage.com* ↪ *291 rooms, 3 suites, 100 villas* ⌂ *4 restaurants, coffee shop, room service, in-room hot tubs (some), minibars, room TVs with* *movies, 18-hole golf course, 9 tennis courts, 3 pools, health club, hair salon, beach, 3 bars, shops, baby-sitting, dry cleaning, laundry service, concierge, business services, convention center, meeting room, helipad, travel services; no-smoking rooms* ▤ *AE, DC, MC, V.*

★ **$$–$$$$**   **Rydges Reef Resort.** This relaxing resort has an extensive choice of accommodation styles, from standard hotel rooms to self-contained villas, all set against a backdrop of rain forest. Cane furniture and brightly colored bedspreads fill standard rooms, while villas have modern furnishings. Water enthusiasts can take advantage of the snorkeling and dive lessons available on weekdays. Excellent amenities for children include baby-sitting, miniature golf, a games room, toddler-friendly pools, and a kid's club. ⊠ *87–109 Port Douglas Rd., 4871* ☎ *07/4099–5577 or 1800/445644* 🖷 *07/4099–5559* ⊕ *www.rydges.com/portdouglas* ⇴ *285 rooms, 14 suites, 180 villas* ♨ *2 restaurants, in-room safes, kitchens (some), minibars, room TVs with movies, miniature golf, 2 tennis courts, 5 pools, gym, 2 bars, recreation room, baby-sitting, children's programs (ages 5–12), laundry service, meeting rooms* ▤ *AE, DC, MC, V.*

$–$$$$ **Hibiscus Gardens Resort Apartments.** The breathtaking beauty of Four Mile Beach is just a short walk from this breezy, Balinese-inspired resort. Cool, terra-cotta-tile floors work nicely with the warmth of teak and cedar in each apartment. Most private balconies afford spectacular views of Mossman Gorge and the mountains of the Daintree rain forest. ⊠ *22 Owen St., 4871* ☎ *07/4099–5315 or 1800/995995* 🖷 *07/4099–4678* ⊕ *www.hibiscusportdouglas.com.au* ⇴ *34 apartments* ♨ *In-room data ports, in-room fax, kitchens, cable TV, pool, spa, laundry service* ▤ *AE, DC, MC, V.*

Shopping

Unquestionably the best and most elegant shopping complex in northern Queensland, the **Marina Mirage** (⊠ Wharf St. ☎ 07/4099–5775) contains 40 fashion and specialty shops for souvenirs, jewelry, accessories, resort wear, and designer clothing.

Sports & the Outdoors

Poseidon Diving (⊠ Marina Mirage ☎ 07/4099–4772 ⊕ www.poseidon-cruises.com.au) conducts snorkeling and diving trips to the Great Barrier Reef. A marine naturalist will explain the biology and history of the reef before you dive down to see it yourself. Prices range from A$130 to A$310 and include a buffet lunch.

Quicksilver (⊠ Marina Mirage ☎ 07/4087–2100 ⊕ www.quicksilver-cruises.com) runs high-speed, sleek catamarans to the outer Barrier Reef for sailing, snorkeling, and diving trips. Prices start at A$156. Also available are scenic helicopter flights over the spectacular coastline, starting at A$98.

Mossman

38   *14 km (9 mi) northwest of Port Douglas, 75 km (47 mi) north of Cairns.*

Mossman is a sugar town with a population of less than 2,000. Its appeal lies not in the village itself but 5 km (3 mi) out of town where you find the beautiful waterfalls and river at **Mossman Gorge.**

Fodor'sChoice
★

Where to Stay & Eat

$ ✕ **High Falls Farm.** 14 km (9 mi) from Mossman Gorge, a tropical fruit display and orchard overlooking Whyanbeel Creek is an excellent place to stop and have lunch after hiking and swimming at Mossman Gorge.

Tables are on a veranda overlooking the rain forest, and you can also take yourself on a tour through the orchards, market gardens, and tree nursery, where you will be given a tasting plate of around 10 different kinds of tropical fruit (A\$4). The house special is baked barramundi, served with tropical fruit. High Falls Farm is open from 9 AM–5 PM. ⊠ *Lot 1 Old Forestry Rd., Whyanbeel* ☎ *07/4098–8148* ⊟ *AE, DC, MC, V.*

$$$$ 🏨 **Silky Oaks Lodge and Restaurant.** On a hillside surrounded by national
Fodor'sChoice parkland, this hotel is reminiscent of the best African safari lodges. Air-
★ conditioned, tropically inspired villas on stilts overlook either the rain forest and the river below or a natural rock swimming pool. Views from the verandas are stunning. The lodge is the starting point for four-wheel-drive, cycling, and canoeing trips into otherwise inaccessible national park rain forest. ⊠ *Finlayvale Rd., Mossman Gorge, 4871* ☎ *07/ 4098–1666* 🖶 *07/4098–1983* ⊕ *www.poresorts.com.au* ⇌ *60 rooms* ♨ *Restaurant, in-room hot tubs, minibars, tennis court, pool, spa, bar, lounge, library, shops, laundry facilities, laundry service, travel services, free parking* ⊟ *AE, DC, MC, V.*

en route New species of fauna and flora are still being discovered in the **Daintree Rainforest,** and the tropical vegetation is as impressive as anything found in the Amazon Basin. Collect information and maps for exploring from park rangers, since you'll need to detour off the main road to find the best areas for walking. You can also arrange guided four-wheel-drive tours, which include walking within the rain forest, or a ride on a riverboat. The national park is 35 km (22 mi) northwest of Mossman off the Mossman–Daintree Road.

The intrepid can follow the Mossman–Daintree Road as it winds through sugarcane plantations and towering green hills to the **Daintree River crossing,** which leads to Cape Tribulation National Park. The Daintree is a relatively short river, yet it's fed by heavy monsoonal rains that make it wide, glossy, and brown—and a favorite inland haunt for saltwater crocodiles. On the other side of the river a sign announces the beginning of Cape Tribulation National Park. The road beyond the ferry crossing is paved. ☎ *07/ 4098–7536* 🖃 *A\$7 per car, A\$1 per walk-on passenger* ⊙ *Ferry crossings every 20 mins daily 6 AM–midnight.*

Cow Bay

㊴ *17 km (11 mi) northeast of the Daintree River crossing, 47 km (29 mi) north of Mossman.*

The sweep of sand at Cow Bay is fairly typical of the beaches north of the Daintree, with the advantage that the fig trees at the back of the beach provide welcome shade. Follow Buchanans Creek Road north from the Daintree River crossing, which after about 10 km (6 mi) turns toward the sea and Cow Bay.

Where to Stay

¢ 🏨 **Crocodylus Village.** Adventurous and budget-conscious travelers appreciate the Village, set in a rain forest clearing about 3 km (2 mi) from Cow Bay. Accommodations are in fixed-site tents, which resemble cabins more than tents because they are raised off the ground and enclosed by a waterproof fabric and insect-proof mesh. Some tents are set up as dormitories with bunk beds, others are private with showers. Both styles are basic, but the entire complex is neat and well maintained, and it has an excellent activities program. ⊠ *Buchanan Creek Rd., 4873* ☎ *07/ 4098–9166* 🖶 *07/4098–9131* ⇌ *5 dormitory tents, 10 private tents*

♿ *Restaurant, pool, snorkeling, fishing, bicycles, bar, library, laundry facilities, travel services* ▭ *MC, V.*

¢ 🏠 **Epiphyte Bed and Breakfast.** Set in a tropical garden and orchard, Epiphyte is a traditional Queenslander pole-house run entirely on solar energy and mostly on rainwater. The veranda, complete with hammocks and couches, provides gorgeous views of Thornton's peak, especially at sunset. Rooms have private verandas, and there is a guest library and lounge with videos, CDs, and books. Breakfast highlights are the fabulous homemade jams. ✉ *22 Silkwood Rd., 4873* ☎ *07/4098–9039* 🌐 *www.rainforestbb.com* 🛏 *4 rooms* ♿ *Free parking* ▭ *No credit cards.*

Cape Tribulation

27 km (17 mi) north of Cow Bay, 34 km (21 mi) north of the Daintree River crossing, 139 km (86 mi) north of Cairns.

Cape Tribulation was named by Captain James Cook, who was understandably peeved after a nearby reef inflicted a gaping wound in the side of his ship, HMS *Endeavour,* forcing him to seek refuge at the present-day site of Cooktown. The Cape Tribulation settlement, small enough to shoot past in a blink, is the activities and accommodations base for the surrounding national park. You'll find a shop, a couple of lodges, and that's about it. All of the regional tours—including rain-forest walks, reef trips, horseback riding, and fishing—can be booked through the village shop.

To reach the tiny settlement, set dramatically at the base of Mt. Sorrow, proceed north from Cow Bay along a road that plays a game of hide-and-seek with the sea, climbing high over the Noah Range before reaching town. Note that north of the Daintree River, there are no banks; while most outlets in the region do accept credit cards, it's worthwhile to know that Mossman is the last town with ATM facilities.

need a break? Drive by orchards of unnameable fruits to a little shack and some plastic tables and you've found the **Daintree Icecream Company** (✉ Cape Tribulation Rd., Alexandra Bay ☎ 07/4098–9114). The café sells nothing but local herb tea, freshly squeezed tropical fruits, and delicious homemade ice cream. Try wattleseed flavor, which tastes uncannily like cappuccino, or the unusual black sapote.

❹⓿ **Cape Tribulation National Park** is an ecological wonderland, a remnant
Fodor'sChoice of the forests in which flowering plants first appeared on Earth—an evolutionary leap that took advantage of insects for pollination and provided an energy-rich food supply for the early marsupials that were replacing the dinosaurs. Experts can readily identify species of angiosperms, the most primitive flowering plant, many of which are found nowhere else on the planet.

The park stretches along the coast and west into the jungle from Cow Bay to Aytor. The beach is usually empty, except for the tiny soldier crabs that move about by the hundreds and scatter when approached. If you hike among the mangroves you're likely to see an incredible assortment of small creatures that depend on the trees for survival. Most evident are mudskippers and mangrove crabs, but keen observers may spot green-backed herons crouched among mangrove roots.

The best time to see the rain forest is May through September. Walking along dry creek beds is the best way to explore. Bring plenty of insect repellent.

Where to Eat

$$ ✕ **The Long House.** In an A-frame wooden building with 30-foot ceilings, this restaurant at Coconut Beach Rainforest Resort has floor-to-ceiling windows and a (free) pool surrounded by rain forest. Wicker tables and chairs surround a giant palm growing up through a hole in the floor, a classic tropical environment in which to sample lamb baked in a fig-and-pistachio rosti (crusty potato cake) and served with tamarillo chutney and rosemary jus. The signature dish may well be the tropics platter for two: garlic lobster tails, emu, crocodile and kangaroo satay, asparagus wrapped in prosciutto, crab-stuffed mushrooms, and macadamia-nut-crumbed Camembert. ⊠ *Cape Tribulation Rd.,* ☎ *07/4098–0033* 🖃 *AE, DC, MC, V.*

¢–$ ✕ **Dragonfly Gallery Café.** Amid rain-forest gardens and overlooking barramundi pools, the gallery was constructed by local craftspeople from native timber and stone. The café is open all day for coffee, sweets, and lunch, as well as for dinner or drinks. A book and gift store and Internet service are also on-site. The gallery showcases local artists working in timber, stone, oils, watercolor, photography, and weaving. ⊠ *Camelot Close* ☎ *07/4098–0121* 🖃 *AE, DC, MC, V.*

Where to Stay

Camping is permitted at **Noah's Beach** (☎ 07/4098–2188), about 8 km (5 mi) south of Cape Tribulation, for a nominal fee. Privately run campgrounds and small resorts can be found along the Daintree Road at Myall Creek and Cape Tribulation.

$$$–$$$$ 🏨 **Coconut Beach Rainforest Resort.** The most dignified of accommoda-
Fodor'sChoice tions at Cape Tribulation sits in a jungle of fan palms, staghorn ferns,
★ giant melaleucas, and strangler figs, about 2 km (1 mi) south of the cape itself. The resort makes much of its eco-awareness, so the villas are fan-cooled rather than air-conditioned. The beach is a two-minute walk away, and there's an elevated walkway set into the nearby rain-forest canopy. The resort offers a nightly "rain-forest orientation," as well as night walks, day hikes, four-wheel-drive tours, and trips out to the reef. ⊠ *Cape Tribulation Rd., 4873* ☎ *07/4098–0033* 🖷 *07/4098–0047* ⊕ *www. coconutbeach.com.au* ↩ *27 rooms, 40 villas* ♨ *Restaurant, 3 pools, beach, mountain bikes, bar, recreation room, baby-sitting, laundry service, travel services; no a/c* 🖃 *AE, DC, MC, V.*

$$$–$$$$ 🏨 **Ferntree Rainforest Resort.** Large, split-level villas and bungalows hunker down in the rain forest, close to the beach, at this comfortable resort. The restaurant is actually two dining huts built into the rain forest. ⌂ *Box 334H, Edge Hill, 4870* ☎ *07/4098–0000* 🖷 *07/4098–0011* ✉ *reservations@ferntree.com.au* ↩ *17 bungalows, 20 villas, 8 suites* ♨ *Restaurant, 2 pools, laundry service, meeting room, travel services, free parking* 🖃 *AE, DC, MC, V.*

¢–$ 🏨 **Cape Trib Beach House.** A range of cabins are set right on the border of the beach and rain forest. Rooms are simple but airy, cooled either by ceiling fans or air-conditioning, with verandas that lead right down to the beach. Much of the hotel is set outdoors, including the bistro, partially under a human-made canopy and partially under the rain forest's own ceiling of Fan Palms. ⊠ *Cape Tribulation Rd., 4873* ☎ *07/ 4098–0030* 🖷 *07/4098–0120* ⊕ *www.capetribbeach.com.au* ↩ *130 rooms* ♨ *Restaurant, kitchens, pool, bar, shop, laundry facilities, Internet* 🖃 *AE, DC, MC, V.*

¢–$ 🏨 **Jungle Treehouse Bed and Breakfast and Farmstay.** Built on poles into the rain forest, this is an eco-friendly bed-and-breakfast, running on renewable solar and hydro-electricity. Rooms consist of slate-tile floors,

native red cedar, silky oak, and red tulip wood furnishings, and walls fashioned from river rock. Each has their own veranda and is cooled by ceiling fans. Boardwalks through the rain forest, the beach as well as restaurants and bars are all within walking distance. **Jungle Adventures Cape Trib** operates out of Jungle Treehouse Bed and Breakfast. ⊠ *Camelot Close, 4873* ☎ *07/4098–0900* 🖷 *07/4098–0065* ⊕ *www. jungletreehousecapetrib.com.au* 🛏 *2 bedrooms* ⛏ *Hiking, travel services; no a/c, no room TVs* 🖃 *AE, DC, MC, V.*

Sports & the Outdoors

Several tour companies in Cairns conduct day trips to the rain forest in four-wheel-drive buses and vans. Try **BTS Tours** (⊠ 49 Macrossan St., Port Douglas, 4871 ☎ 07/4099–5665 ⊕ www.btstours.com.au).

Cape Trib Horse Rides offers two rides per day. If you're staying in Cape Tribulation, they'll pick you up from your accommodation at around 8 or 1:30. Rides take you through rain forest, along Myall beach, and through open paddocks, with opportunities to swim in the rain forest. Morning or afternoon tea is provided. (☎ 1800/111124).

Daintree Rainforest River Trains has what's billed as the world's only floating river train, the *Spirit of Daintree*, which cruises down the Daintree River. There are stops for strolls down the rain forest and mangrove boardwalk for tropical fruit tasting at High Falls Tropical Farm and at Daintree Village for lunch. You can book a number of different cruises, with the river train as the main mode of transportation. Keep an eye out for estuarine (saltwater) crocodiles. There's free pick-up at your accommodation, from Cairns through to Port Douglas. The full-day tour (A$114) departs Cairns at 7:30 AM and Port Douglas at 9. The 2½-hour river cruise (A$28), which includes a guided boardwalk tour and tea, departs at 10:30 and 1:30. The 90-min river cruise (A$22) also departs at 10:30 and 1:30. The one-hour river cruise (AA$17) departs at 9:1 and 4. (⊠ Daintree River Ferry Crossing, Daintree River ☎ 4099–5665, 1800/808309 ⊕ www.daintreerivertrain.com).

en route | The **Bloomfield Track** leads north from Cape Tribulation. Less 30 km (19 mi) long, it is one of the most controversial strips roadway in Australia, and it still generates powerful passion decision in the early '80s to carve a road through the Daint wilderness provoked a bitter conservation battle. The roa through, but the ruckus was instrumental in securing a V Heritage listing for the Daintree, thereby effectively shu logging operations. At Cape Tribulation a sign warn open only to four-wheel-drive vehicles, and although you from driving through in a conventional vehicle, passage over the Cowie Range essentially closes th the most rugged machines.

Bloomfield River

22 km (14 mi) north of Cape Tribulation.

Crossing the Bloomfield River will allow y take in some interesting sights, such as The river is subject to tides at the ford, just before the town of Wujal Wujal dropped sufficiently to allow safe cr cause the submerged causeway can common for vehicles to topple off

Where to Stay

$$$$ 🏨 **Bloomfield Rainforest Lodge.** The lodge sits in rugged surroundings near the Bloomfield River and consists of timber bungalows, each with a balcony at the front, lots of open latticework, and a ceiling fan. Activities include guided walks, fishing, beachcombing along small but deserted beaches, and croc-spotting cruises. The most convenient access is by plane from Cairns—there's a 15½-pound luggage restriction—with the final trip by boat from the Bloomfield River (arranged by the lodge). There's a two-night minimum stay, and rates include all meals and flight transfers from Cairns. 🕮 *Box 966, Cairns, 4870* ☏ *07/4035–9166* 🖷 *07/ 4035–9180* ⊕ *www.bloomfieldlodge.com.au* ⇔ *17 rooms* ⚭ *Restaurant, fans, pool, beach, snorkeling, fishing, bar; no kids under 12* ▤ *AE, DC, MC, V* ⦿ *All-inclusive.*

en route At the Aboriginal settlement of Wujal Wujal on the north bank of the river along the Bloomfield Track, make the short detour inland to **Bloomfield Falls,** where the river is safe for swimming. Some 20 minutes' drive north of the Bloomfield River is a great swimming spot: Pull over to the left where a sign identifies the Cedar Bay National Park and walk down the steep gully to a creek. At the bottom of a small cascade is possibly one of the most perfect swimming holes you're ever likely to find.

About 33 km (20 mi) north of Wujal Wujal, at the junction of the rain forest and an area of open woodland, is the **Lion's Den Hotel** (☏ *07/4060–3911*), a pub whose corrugated-iron walls and tree-stump chairs ooze unself-conscious character. The walls are covered in graffiti, from the simple KILROY WAS HERE variety to the totally scandalous, and for the price of a donation to the Royal Flying Doctor Service, you can add your own wit to the collection.

At the junction of Northern Road (called the Bicentennial National Trail on some maps) and the Cooktown Development Road, jumbled piles of rock beside the road identify **Black Mountain National Park.** The distinctive coloration of these granite boulders is caused by a black algae. Climbing the rocks is difficult and dangerous, and there are stinging trees in the area.

Cooktown

㊶ *96 km (60 mi) north of Cape Tribulation, 235 km (146 mi) north of Cairns.*

The last major settlement on the east coast of the continent, Cooktown is a frontier town on the edge of a difficult wilderness. Its wide main street consists mainly of two-story pubs with four-wheel drives parked out front. Despite the temporary air, Cooktown has a long and impressive history. It was here in 1770 that Captain James Cook beached HMS *Endeavour* to repair her hull. Any tour of Cooktown should begin at the waterfront, where a statue of Captain Cook gazes out to sea, overlooking the spot where he landed.

A town was established a hundred years after Cook's landfall when gold was discovered on the Palmer River. Cooktown mushroomed and quickly became the largest settlement in Queensland after Brisbane, but as in many other mining boomtowns, life was hard and often violent. Chinese miners flooded into the goldfields, and anti-Chinese sentiment flared into race riots, echoing events that had occurred at every other goldfield in the country. Further conflict arose between miners and local

Aborigines, who resented what they saw as a territorial invasion and the rape of the region's natural resources; such place-names as Battle Camp and Hell's Gate testify to the pattern of ambush and revenge.

Cooktown is a sleepy shadow of those dangerous days—when it had 64 pubs on a main street 3 km (2 mi) long—but a significant slice of history has been preserved at the **James Cook Historical Museum**, formerly a convent of the Sisters of Mercy. The museum houses relics of the gold-mining era, Chinese settlement, and both world wars, as well as Aboriginal artifacts, canoes, and a notable collection of seashells. The museum also contains mementos of Cook's voyage, including the anchor and one of the cannons that were jettisoned when the HMS *Endeavour* ran aground. ⊠ *Helen and Furneaux Sts.* ☎ *07/4069–5386* ▱ *A$5.50* ☯ *Daily 9:30–4.*

Where to Stay

$–$$ ▦ **Sovereign Resort.** This attractive, colonial-style hotel in the heart of town is the best bet in Cooktown. With verandas across the front, terracotta tiles, and soft colors, the two-story timber-and-brick affair has the air of a plantation house. Appealing guest rooms trimmed with rustic wooden doors, terra-cotta floor tiles, and soft blues and reds overlook tropical gardens at the rear of the building. The hotel also overlooks the Endeavour River. ⊠ *Charlotte St., 4871* ☎ *07/4069–5400* ▤ *07/4069–5582* ⊕ *www.sovereign-resort.com.au* ⇋ *24 rooms, 5 suites* ⚭ *Restaurant, minibars, pool, bar, meeting room* ▭ *AE, DC, MC, V.*

en route   From Cooktown, the northern tip of the Australian mainland is still some 800 km (496 mi) distant via the road that runs along the middle of Cape York. Although road access to Cape York Peninsula from Cooktown is possible by four-wheel-drive vehicles, weather sometimes limits access right to the tip of the Cape. Check road and weather conditions before heading out.

North from Cairns A to Z

To research prices, get advice from other travelers, and book travel arrangements, visit www.fodors.com.

AIR TRAVEL

Hinterland Aviation links Cairns with Cow Bay—the airport for Cape Tribulation—and the Bloomfield River. Flights to Cow Bay or Bloomfield are A$93.50 per person each way, with a minimum of two people required. Both airfields are isolated dirt strips, and passengers must arrange onward transport to their destination in advance. It's 30 minutes to Cow Bay and 35 minutes to Bloomfield; the in-flight coastal views are spectacular.

🛈 **Hinterland Aviation** ☎ 07/4035-9323 ⊕ www.hinterlandaviation.com.au.

BUS TRAVEL

Coral Coaches runs buses from Cairns to Port Douglas (1½ hours), Cape Tribulation (4 hours), and Cooktown (5½ hours).

The Coral Coaches bus travels the 1½-hour run between the Daintree Ferry crossing and Cape Tribulation twice daily in each direction.
🛈 **Coral Coaches** ☎ 07/4031-7577.

CAR RENTAL

Avis has four-wheel-drive Toyota Land Cruisers for rent from Cairns. The cost varies daily depending on availability of vehicles.
🛈 **Avis** ⊠ Lake and Aplin Sts., Cairns ☎ 07/4035-9100 or 07/4035-5911.

CAR TRAVEL

To head north by car from Cairns, take Florence Street from The Esplanade for four blocks and then turn right onto Sheridan Street, which is the beginning of northbound Highway 1. Highway 1 leads past the airport and forks 12 km (7 mi) north of Cairns. Take the right fork for Cook Highway, which goes as far as Mossman. From Mossman, the turnoff for the Daintree River crossing is 29 km (18 mi) north on the Daintree–Mossman Road. The road north of the river winds its way to Cape Tribulation, burrowing through dense rain forest and onto open stretches high above the coast, with spectacular views of the mountains and coastline.

EMERGENCIES

Be advised that doctors, ambulances, firefighters, and police are scarce to nonexistent between the Daintree River and Cooktown.

In an emergency, dial 000 to reach an ambulance, the fire department, or the police.

🖪 **Cooktown Hospital** ⊠ Hope St., Cooktown ☎ 07/4069-5433. **Mossman District Hospital** ⊠ Hospital St., Mossman ☎ 07/4098-2444. **Mossman Police** ☎ 07/4098-1200. **Port Douglas Police** ☎ 07/4099-5220.

MAIL, INTERNET & SHIPPING

The main post office in Port Douglas is open weekdays 9–5, Saturday 9–noon. You can retrieve e-mail and check the Internet at a number of locations.

Port Douglas Cyberworld Internet Café is open Monday–Saturday 9–5. Uptown Internet Café is open daily 10–10.

🖪 **Main post office** ⊠ Owen and Macrossan Sts., Port Douglas ☎ 07/4099-5210.

🖪 Internet Cafés **Port Douglas Cyberworld Internet Café** ⊠ 38A Macrossan St., Port Douglas ☎ 07/4099-5661. **Uptown Internet Café** ⊠ 48 Macrossan St., Port Douglas ☎ 07/4099-5568.

MONEY MATTERS

ANZ Bank can change money and cash traveler's checks. National Australia Bank accepts most overseas cards. Westpac is one of Australia's largest banks.

🖪 Banks **ANZ Bank** ⊠ Macrossan St., Port Douglas ☎ 13-1314. **National Australia Bank** ⊠ Port Douglas Shopping Center, Macrossan St., Port Douglas ☎ 07/4099-5688. **Westpac** ⊠ Charlotte St., Cooktown ☎ 13-2032.

TOURS

ABORIGINAL TOURS Kuku-Yalanji Aborigines are the indigenous inhabitants of the land between Cooktown in the north, Chillagoe in the west, and Port Douglas in the south. Kuku-Yalanji Dreamtime Tours has guides from this tribe who will take you on a one-hour walk through stunning rain forest and point out such significant features as cave paintings and important Aboriginal sites. They also tell you about traditional bush tucker (food) and medicine. Afterward, tea and damper (camp bread) are served under a bark *warun* (shelter), where you can chat with your guide and ask questions. They are open weekdays 8:30–5; walks leave at 10, 11:30, 1, and 2:30, and cost A$15.

Hazel Douglas, an Aboriginal woman, conducts Native Guide Safari Tours, and her knowledge and passion for her ancestral homeland—which extends from Port Douglas to Cape Tribulation—set this one-day tour apart. After departing from Port Douglas, you'll sample some of the edible flora of the Daintree region, learn how Aboriginal people maintained the balance of the rain-forest ecosystem, and hear legends that have been passed down for thousands of years. Be sure to pack swimwear, insect repellent, and good walking shoes. A maximum of 11 passengers is allowed on each tour. Half-day tours (minimum three people) or private charters (minimum four people) are also available by appointment. The price—A$120 (A$130 from Cairns)—includes pickup in Port Douglas, Quicksilver Catamaran ride from Cairns to Port Douglas (for Cairns passengers), picnic lunch, and Daintree River Ferry crossing.

Tour Operators **Kuku-Yalanji Dreamtime Tours** ⊠ Gorge Rd., 24 km (15 mi) northwest of Port Douglas ☎ 07/4098-1305. **Native Guide Safari Tours** ⊠ 58 Pringle St., Mossman, 4873 ☎ 07/4098-2206 🖷 07/4098-1008 ⊕ www.nativeguidesafaritours.com.au.

BOAT TOURS   *Crocodile Express,* a flat-bottom boat, cruises the Daintree River on crocodile-spotting excursions. The boat departs from the Daintree River crossing at 10:45 and midday for a one-hour cruise. Trips also depart from the Daintree Village regularly from 10 to 4 for a 1½-hour cruise. The one-hour cruise costs A$17, and the 1½-hour cruise costs A$20.

Crocodile Express ☎ 07/4098-6120 or 1800/658833.

EXCURSIONS   BTS Tours captures the best of northern Queensland with several day tours: you can glide over the Daintree rain-forest canopy in a six-person cable car, swim in the natural spas of the Mossman Gorge, or zip up to Cape Tribulation in a four-wheel-drive vehicle. Prices range from A$60 to A$275.

Reef and Rainforest Connections organizes several day trips and excursions out of Cairns and Port Douglas. One day trip includes visits to the Kuranda Scenic Railway, Skyrail Rainforest Cableway, and Tjapukai Aboriginal Cultural Park. Excursions are also available to Cape Tribulation and Bloomfield Falls, the Daintree River and Mossman Gorge, and the Low Isles on the Great Barrier Reef.

Tour Operators **BTS Tours** ⊠ 49 Macrossan St., Port Douglas ☎ 07/4099-5665 ⊕ www.btstours.com. **Reef and Rainforest Connections** ⊠ 40 Macrossan St., Port Douglas ☎ 07/4099-5777 ⊕ www.reefandrainforest.com.au.

FOUR-WHEEL-
DRIVE TOURS   Australian Wilderness Safari has a one-day Daintree and Cape Tribulation Safari aboard air-conditioned four-wheel-drive vehicles. All tours depart from Port Douglas or Mossman, are led by naturalists, and include a Daintree River Cruise, barbecue lunch at Myall Creek, and afternoon tea. Groups are limited to 12 people. This A$140 rain-forest tour is one of the longest-established and one of the best.

Deluxe Safaris conducts three day-long safaris in luxury four-wheel-drive vehicles. You can visit Mossman Gorge and Cape Tribulation, rough it on the rugged track to the magnificent Bloomfield River Falls, or spot kangaroos and other wildlife in the Outback region of Cape York. Lunch and refreshments, included in the A$135–A$150 price, keep your strength up for these energetic journeys.

Tour Operators **Australian Wilderness Safari** ☎ 07/4098-1766. **Deluxe Safaris** ⊠ Port Douglas ☎ 07/4099-6406 ⊕ deluxesafaris.com.au.

VISITOR INFORMATION

Tourist Information **Cape Tribulation Tourist Information Centre** ⊠ Cape Tribulation Rd., Cape Tribulation ☎ 07/4098-0070. **Cooktown Travel Centre** ⊠ Charlotte St., Cooktown ☎ 07/4069-5446.

THE GREAT BARRIER REEF

8

FODOR'S CHOICE

Bedarra Island Resort, in northern Queensland

Hayman Island, in the northern Whitsundays

Heron Island, off Gladstone

Lady Elliot Island, in the Mackay–Capricorn Islands

Lizard Island Lodge, in northern Queensland

HIGHLY RECOMMENDED

RESORTS Contiki Great Keppel Island Resort, on Great Keppel Island

Dunk Island Resort, on Dunk Island

Updated by
Jad Davenport

THE GREAT BARRIER REEF is Queensland's indigo answer to the Red Center. Known as Australia's "Blue Outback," the reef isn't a single entity, but instead a maze of 3,000 individual reefs and 900 islands—most of which are populated exclusively by seabirds and turtles. In 1975, the government established the southern sections of the reef as a marine park. In 1981, the United Nations took this a step farther and designated the Great Barrier Reef a World Heritage Site.

Even if you've only come for fun in the sun, you still can't help but be impressed that coral polyps, some no larger than a pencil tip, have created something so immense. The reef fringes the Queensland coast and its offshore islands north from Brisbane to Papua New Guinea. Altogether it covers an area bigger than Great Britain, forming the largest living feature on earth and the only one visible from space.

Most visitors explore this section of Australia from one of the 26 resorts necklaced along the southern half of the marine park. Although most are closer to the mainland than the true reef, all offer chartered boats out to the real Great Barrier waters. Liveaboard dive boats ply the more remote sections of the northern reef and Coral Sea atolls, exploring large cartographic blank spots on maritime charts that simply read, in bold purple lettering, "Area unsurveyed."

Exploring the Great Barrier Reef

This chapter is arranged in three geographical sections covering islands off the mid-Queensland coast from south to north. The sections group together islands that share a common port or jumping-off point. Addresses for resorts often include the word "via" to indicate which port town to use to reach the island.

If you had the time, money, and patience, you could string together a long holiday that would take you to all the major island resorts. The map linking these various coastal ports and offshore resorts would look like a lace-up boot 1,600 km (1,000 mi) long—but it would also take most of a month even if you only spent one night in each place. Just from Lady Elliot Island north to Lizard Island you'd only see half the reef, which continues north along the roadless wilderness of Cape York to the shores of Papua New Guinea.

About the Restaurants
Many resort rates include all meals, which are served in the dining room, at outdoor barbecues, and at seafood buffets. Some resorts have several restaurants, as well as a premium dining option for which you pay extra. Most restaurants on each island are part of its main resort.

WHAT IT COSTS In Australian Dollars				
$$$$	$$$	$$	$	¢
RESTAURANTS over $65	$46–$65	$36–$45	$25–$35	under $25

Restaurant prices are per person for a main course at dinner.

About the Hotels
You can't pick and choose hotels on the Great Barrier Reef islands—a resort and its base are usually one entity. Islands generally have one resort, though it may have several levels of accommodations. Some cater to those wanting peace and tranquillity, whereas others attract a crowd wanting just the opposite—so choose based on your budget and taste.

With some exceptions, such sporting activities as sailing, snorkeling, and tennis are included in basic rates. However, reef excursions, fishing charters, scuba diving, and other sports requiring fuel usually cost extra.

Dress in general is casual chic, the next step up from T-shirts and jeans. Some upscale restaurants, however, require closed shoes and sports jackets—for example, on Hayman Island. All but the most rustic resorts have air-conditioning, telephones, televisions, tea- and coffeemakers, and refrigerators.

WHAT IT COSTS In Australian Dollars				
$$$$	**$$$**	**$$**	**$**	**¢**
HOTELS over $450	$301–$450	$201–$300	$150–$200	under $150

Hotel prices are for two people in a standard double room in high season, including tax and service, based on the European Plan (with no meals) unless otherwise noted.

When to Visit the Great Barrier Reef

The majority of Barrier Reef islands lie north of the tropic of Capricorn and have a distinctly monsoonal climate. In summer, expect tropical downpours that can mar underwater visibility for days. It's hot everywhere—hotter the farther north you go. However, the warm days, clear skies, and balmy nights of winter are ideal for traveling around Cairns and above. If you choose an island on the southern end of the chain, keep in mind that some winter days are too cool for swimming.

Millions of deadly jellyfish congregate along the coast from October to May. These transparent stingers, no larger than your thumbnail, can kill within minutes; hence, mainland swimming is banned. Offshore islands, however, don't suffer from this blight, and you can swim safely year-round.

MACKAY–CAPRICORN ISLANDS

Lady Elliot Island

Fodor's Choice
★
Lady Elliot Island is a 100-acre coral cay on the southern tip of the Great Barrier Reef, positioned within easy reach of Bundaberg on the Queensland coast. Wildlife easily outnumbers the maximum 105 guests, an atmospheric detail underscored by the ammoniac odor of thousands of nesting seabirds.

Fringed on all sides by the reef and graced with a white coral beach, this oval isle seems to have been made for diving—there's even a budding reef education center complete with saltwater fish exhibits. The land is often battered by waves, which can sometimes cancel dives and wash out underwater visibility. However, when the waters are calm, you'll see turtles, morays, sharks, and millions of tropical fish. Many divers visit Lady Elliot specifically for the large population of manta rays that feed off the wall.

From October to April, Lady Elliot becomes a busy breeding ground for crested and bridled terns, silver gulls, lesser frigate birds, and the rare red-tailed tropic bird. Between November and March, green and loggerhead turtles emerge from the water to lay their eggs; hatching takes place after January. During the hatchling season, staff biologists host guided turtle-watching night hikes. From June through November, pods of humpback whales are visible from the restaurant.

8

Most visits to the Great Barrier Reef combine time on an island with time in Queensland's mainland towns and parks. With a week or more, you could stay at two very different resorts, perhaps at a southern coral cay and a mountainous northern island, allowing a day to travel between them. For the good life, try Hayman, Bedarra, or Lizard islands. If you want to resort-hop, pick the closely arranged Whitsundays.

To fully experience the Great Barrier Reef, divers should jump on one of the many liveaboards that run from Port Douglas to Lizard Island and back, or those that explore the uncharted reefs of the far north and the Coral Sea. Liveaboard trips, which can be surprisingly affordable, run from two days to 10. For land-based diving, consider such islands as Heron or Lizard, which have fringing reefs.

If you have 1 day   Take a boat from Cairns or Port Douglas to a pontoon on the outer reef for a day on the water. A helicopter flight back will provide an astounding view of the reef and islands from above. Or, catch an early boat from Cairns to **Fitzroy Island,** or from Shute Harbour to **Daydream Island.** Spend a couple of hours snorkeling, take a walk around the island to get a look at its wilds, then find a quiet beach for a daydream afternoon.

If you have 3 days   Pick one island that has the water sports and on-land attractions you appreciate—flora and fauna, beaches and pools, or resort nightlife—and give yourself a taste of everything.

If you have 7 or more days   Planning a full week on an island probably means that you're a serious diver, a serious lounger, or both. Divers should hop on one of the Lizard Island–Port Douglas liveaboards for several days, then recuperate on an island that has fringing coral, such as ▣ **Lady Elliot, Heron,** or ▣ **Lizard.** Beach lovers can skip the boat altogether and simply concentrate on exploring one or two islands with great beaches and hiking terrain.

Lady Elliot is one of the few islands in the area where camping—albeit modified—is part of the resort. There are no televisions, and only one guest phone is available. Social activities revolve around diving, reef walking, and the lively bar and restaurant.

Where to Stay & Eat

$–$$ ✕▣ **Lady Elliot Island Resort.** At Lady Elliot, you'll feel more like a marine biologist at an island field camp than a tourist at a luxury resort. Sparsely decorated waterfront cabins have plastic chairs, pine furniture, and wood floors. Campers stay in permanent safari tents and share facilities. Rooms and suites are oceanfront, affording great views. Dinner and breakfast, included in the basic price, are served buffet-style in the dining room. Meals emphasize seafood, grilled dishes, and salads. ⌂ *Box 5206, Torquay, QLD 4655* ☎ *07/5536–3644 or 1800/072200* ⊟ *07/5536–3644* ⊕ *www.ladyelliot.com.au* ⇆ *24 rooms with shower, 5 suites, 12 tents* ⚓ *Restaurant, miniature golf, pool, dive shop, snorkeling, boating, fishing, hiking, baby-sitting, playground, laundry facilities, airstrip; no room TVs* ⊟ *AE, DC, MC, V* ◎| *MAP.*

Sports & the Outdoors

Most divers come to Lady Elliot in hopes of seeing the swirling schools of manta that are often seen feeding near the offshore walls. Certified divers can rent equipment at the resort's dive shop. You can arrange scuba-diving courses through the resort's dive school; costs run A$27.50 for a refresher course to A$485 for an open-water course. Note that diving is very weather-dependent, so this actually isn't a great spot to pursue advanced courses requiring multiple dive days. Boat dives begin at A$39 for a two-tank trip. The resort also offers snorkeling, reef walks, glass-bottom boat rides (A$11), and hiking.

Arriving & Departing

BY PLANE Lady Elliot is the only coral cay with its own airstrip. Small aircraft make the 80-km (50-mi) flight from Hervey Bay, Bundaberg, and Coollangata, coastal towns about 320 km (200 mi) north of Brisbane. Daily flights run from Bundaberg, Hervey Bay, and Brisbane. The 30-minute round-trip flight from Bundaberg or the 35-minute flight from Hervey Bay to Lady Elliot on **Seair Pacific** (☎ 07/4125–5344 or 1800/072200) costs A$219 from the mainland and A$168 for island guests. Strict luggage limits allow 10 kg (22 pounds) per person (the sum of both hand and checked baggage). If your bags exceed this limit, you have the choice of repacking at the ticket counter scale or waving good-bye as the plane departs without you.

Day Trips

A day trip to **Lady Elliot** (☎ 07/4125–5344 or 1800/072200)—including the scenic flight, buffet lunch, glass-bottom boat ride, reef walk (if tides are appropriate), and free snorkeling lesson—is A$219 per person from Bundaberg or Hervey Bay.

Lady Musgrave Island

Lady Musgrave Island sits at the southern end of the Great Barrier Reef Marine Park about 40 km (25 mi) north of Lady Elliot Island. Five kilometers (3 mi) of coral reef and a massive yet calm 3,000-acre lagoon surround the island, a true coral cay of 35 acres—just 500 yards wide. When day-trippers, yachties, divers, and campers converge, traffic on Lady Musgrave gets heavy, but the island has some of the best diving and snorkeling in Queensland. In quiet times, campers have a chance to view a variety of sea life surrounding this tiny speck of land in the Pacific.

In summer (November through March), the island is a bird and turtle rookery. You can expect to find such species as white-capped noddies, wedge-tailed shearwaters, and green and loggerhead turtles. There is also an abundance of flora, including casuarina and pisonia trees.

Camping

The island is uninhabited and has only basic facilities (one toilet block and emergency radio equipment) for campers. Commercial tour operators transport all camping equipment, including a small dinghy, and deliver fresh water, ice, milk, and bread. Camping permits are available from the **Environmental Protection Agency** (☎ 07/4972–6055) for A$4 per person per night, or a maximum of A$16 per family (children under 5 free). No more than 40 campers may visit the island at any one time, and camping reservations must be made 11 months in advance.

Arriving & Departing

BY BOAT You can reach the island on the catamaran MV *Lady Musgrave*, or the trimaran MV *Spirit of Musgrave*, both run by **Lady Musgrave Cruises** (☎07/4159–4519 or 1800/072110 ⊕ www.lmcruises.com.au). The boats de-

Deep Blue Views
Visiting any of these islands requires a journey across the water, which is a prime opportunity to view the vast reefs and coral cays layered in blue and turquoise. The trip may be a ferry ride or flight of just a few minutes—or it could be a highlight of the whole vacation. That's particularly true if you elect to fly by helicopter to Heron Island, or to take the seaplane to Orpheus Island.

Diving
The Great Barrier Reef has literally thousands of spectacular dive sites scattered up and down its coral spine. Some of the most famous, like Briggs Reef off Cairns, might have several hundred divers a day threading through the reefs, admiring moray eels, stingrays, and the occasional white-tipped reef shark. More remote dive sites, like the famous Cod Hole off Lizard Island, will only see 30 divers a day. Still other dive sites, like those in the far north of the Coral Sea, are only accessible after a week-long journey by live-aboard dive boat. In the truly wild reefs, you could run into anything from a pod of Dwarf Minke whales to a graceful tiger shark.

Food
The seas and shoals surrounding the Great Barrier Reef islands deliver a munificent bounty of crayfish, scallops, shrimp, and countless fish that appear on most resort menus. And whether you're in the mood for casual dining or dress-up, you can find a resort restaurant to match your style. They'll fill your cravings as well, with expertly prepared cuisine ranging from fine European delicacies to down-home contemporary cooking.

Island Time
Life in and around the water is why most people visit the Great Barrier Reef, but flora and fauna on the islands themselves can be fascinating. Some have rain forests, or hills and rocky areas, or postcard-perfect beaches. Island resorts can be havens of sports and sociability, or hideaways of solitude and natural splendor. The vast surrounding reef is a true wilderness filled with diverse wildlife, and huge stretches—particularly north of the diving gateway, Cairns—have only a handful of visitors a year and are just a boat ride away

---

part from Port Bundaberg, 20 minutes northeast of Bundaberg, Monday–Thursday and Saturday at 8:30 AM, returning at 5:45 PM. The trip takes 2½ hours in each direction and costs A$135 for day-trippers, A$270 for campers (to secure return passage). There are no transfers on Wednesdays or Fridays. Scuba diving (including equipment) is an extra A$58 for one dive, A$80 for two dives, or A$70 for an introductory lesson. Round-trip coach pickup from accommodations in Bundaberg is available for A$9 per person.

Heron Island

Fodor'sChoice ★ Whereas most resort islands lie well inside the shelter of the distant reef, Heron Island, some 70 km (43 mi) northwest of the mainland port of Gladstone, is actually part of the reef. Heron is a national park and bird sanctuary, which makes it the ideal place to learn about indigenous life on a coral island.

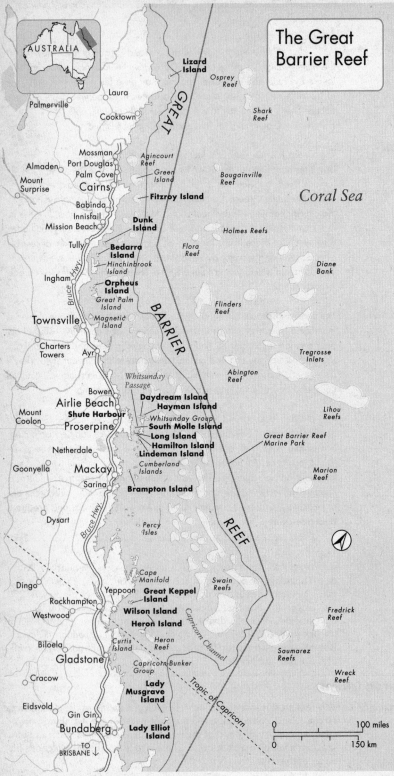

AUSTRALIA

The Great Barrier Reef

Palmerville

Laura

Cooktown

Lizard Island

Osprey Reef

Shark Reef

GREAT

Almaden

Mount Surprise

Mossman
Port Douglas
Palm Cove
Cairns

Agincourt Reef

Green Island

Bougainville Reef

Fitzroy Island

Coral Sea

Babinda
Innisfail
Mission Beach

Dunk Island

Holmes Reefs

Tully

Bedarra Island

Hinchinbrook Island

Flora Reef

Diane Bank

Ingham

Orpheus Island

BARRIER

Great Palm Island

Flinders Reef

Townsville

Magnetic Island

Tregrosse Inlets

Charters Towers

Ayr

Abington Reef

Whitsunday Passage

Bowen

Lihou Reefs

Mount Coolon

Airlie Beach

Daydream Island
Hayman Island

Shute Harbour

Proserpine

Whitsunday Group

South Molle Island

Long Island
Hamilton Island
Lindeman Island

Great Barrier Reef Marine Park

Netherdale

Cumberland Islands

Goonyella

Mackay

Brampton Island

Marion Reef

Sarina

REEF

Dysart

Percy Isles

Dingo

Cape Manifold

Swain Reefs

Yeppoon

Great Keppel Island

Fredrick Reef

Rockhampton

Westwood

Wilson Island

Heron Island

Biloela

Curtis Island

Heron Reef

Gladstone

Saumarez Reefs

Capricorn Channel

Cracow

Capricorn-Bunker Group

Wreck Reef

Eidsvold

Gin Gin

Lady Musgrave Island

Tropic of Capricorn

Bundaberg

Lady Elliot Island

TO BRISBANE ↓

0   100 miles

0   150 km

From November through March, hundreds of migrating green turtles and a number of loggerhead turtles arrive to mate and lay their eggs on the sandy foreshores, mere steps away from Heron's beachside suites. Each turtle returns three or four times during the nesting season to lay clutches of up to 120 eggs, and thousands of tiny hatchlings emerge from the nests from December through April. Between July and October (September is best), humpback whales pass here on their journey from the Antarctic.

The waters are spectacular, teeming with fish and coral, and ideal for snorkeling and scuba diving. The water is clearest in June and July and cloudiest during the rainy season, January and February.

Heron Island also shelters thousands of birds, including noddy terns, silver eyes, rails, and gray and white herons—hence the island's name. From September through March the indigenous bird life is joined by large numbers of migrating birds, some from as far away as the Arctic.

You won't find a lot of activities and entertainment on Heron, as on some other islands. Heron Island Resort, the island's only accommodation, accepts a cozy maximum of only 250 people, and there are no day-trippers. But these might be reasons why you decide to come here.

You can visit uninhabited **Wilson Island**, a Great Barrier Reef Marine Park coral cay, on a day trip from Heron Island. Ten kilometers (6 mi) to the north, it's an attractive adjunct of the Heron Island Resort, which controls access to it. In January and February, Wilson Island becomes the breeding ground for roseate terns and green and loggerhead turtles. The island also now hosts a small, luxury camp run by P&O Australian Resorts.

Where to Stay

$$–$$$$ ☒ **Heron Island Resort.** Set among palm trees and connected by sand paths, accommodations range from simple cabins with shared bathrooms to large, comfortable suites. With private balconies, cane furniture, and pastel or vibrant reef-inspired decor, the modern suites merit the extra expense. Among the activities are guided walks, kids' programs, and cruises. Rates include three daily meals; breakfast and lunch are served buffet style. Dinner usually consists of a four-course set menu, and there's a weekly seafood smorgasbord. The five-day Wilson Island escape package (A$1,690 to A$1,750), with two nights on Heron Island and three nights at a luxury camp on Wilson Island, includes room, board, and transfers. The island closes in February to protect nesting birds. ⌖ *P&O Australian Resorts, Box 478, Sydney, NSW 2001* ☎ *1800/737678, 1800/225–9849 in North America* ⊕ *www.poresorts.com.au/heron* ➯ *1 beach house, 76 suites, 32 cabins.* ☁ *Coffee shop, dining room, tennis court, 2 pools, dive shop, snorkeling, fishing, paddle tennis, bar, recreation room, children's programs (ages 7–12), laundry service, Internet, meeting rooms; no room TVs* ☰ *AE, DC, MC, V* ⧄ *AP.*

Sports & the Outdoors

You can book snorkeling, scuba diving, and fishing excursions through the dive shop. Open-water diving courses are available for A$525, and resort diving costs A$142 for one day. Excursions for experienced divers range from one to five days, starting at A$48 for a single dive.

Nondivers who want to explore the reef's underwater world can board semisubmersible tours that run twice daily from Heron Island. Also available are guided reef walks, a turtle-watching tour, or a visit to the island's Marine Research Station.

Arriving & Departing

BY BOAT　Transfers are booked through the resort with the accommodations. *Reef Adventurer II,* a high-speed catamaran, (☎ 07/4972–5166 or 13–2469) makes a 2½-hour run to Heron Island from Gladstone, a town on the Queensland coast, for A$82 one-way. The journey can be rough, and some people have problems with gas fumes and seasickness. The boat staff have seasickness tablets on hand, but by the time you feel it coming on, it's probably already too late.

BY HELICOPTER　**Marine Helicopters** (☎ 07/4978–1177) runs a 25-minute helicopter flight to Heron Island from Gladstone for A$274 one-way or A$466 round-trip. The baggage restriction is 15 kilograms (33 pounds) per person and one piece of hand luggage. Lockup facilities for excess baggage are free.

Great Keppel Island

Over the years the Contiki Great Keppel Island Resort has garnered a reputation similar to Fort Lauderdale at spring break. It's a party place, especially as most guests are ages 18 to 35, and there are several private residences in addition to the resort. Although the island is large, at 8 km (5 mi) wide and 11 km (7 mi) long, it lies 40 km (25 mi) from the Great Barrier Reef, which makes for a long trip from the mainland. There's lots to do, though, both on- and offshore: walking trails, 17 stunning beaches, dozens of sports activities, and excellent coral growth in many sheltered coves. An underwater observatory at nearby Middle Island allows you to watch marine life without getting wet. A confiscated Taiwanese fishing boat has been sunk alongside the observatory to provide shelter for tropical fish.

Where to Stay

¢–$$　🏨 **Contiki Great Keppel Island Resort.** The villas and two-story accomFodor'sChoice　modations of this Contiki chain resort stand among gardens and extend
★　up the island's hills. Bright tropical colors and terra-cotta tiles decorate many of the rooms and villas. Choose from garden rooms, beachfront rooms, or villas. The villas are air-conditioned and have wonderful views but are some distance from the beach. Room rates include breakfast and dinner at the buffet-style restaurant. Otherwise, you can dine on wood-fired pizzas or à la carte dishes on your own dime. 🏠 *Contiki Resort, Great Keppel Island, QLD, 4700* ☎ *1/300–305005* 🖷 *02/9770–0093* 🌐 *www.contikiresorts.com* 🛏 *60 villas, 122 rooms with shower* ☖ *3 restaurants, 4 bars, nightclub, 9-hole golf course, 3 tennis courts, 5 pools, hair salon, 2 outdoor hot tubs, snorkeling, windsurfing, boating, jet skiing, parasailing, waterskiing, fishing, aerobics, archery, badminton, basketball, paddle tennis, racquetball, squash, volleyball, Internet; no a/c in some rooms* ▱ *AE, DC, MC, V* 🍴 *MAP.*

¢　🏨 **Great Keppel Island Holiday Village.** Tucked in among the welcome shade of gum trees is this modest, quiet alternative to the youthful party scene at the nearby Contiki Resort. The village, centered around a reception hall that doubles as a grocery store, has a house, several simple cabins, double and single rooms, tents, and a range of dorm accommodations. There are barbecues for cooking out, and you can hike or take a canoe or kayak tour of the island. Note that since the store carries only basic food and supplies, you'll need to bring any favorite munchies or luxury items. ✉ *Community Mailbag, Great Keppel Island, 4700* ☎ *07/4939–8655 or 1800/180235* 🖷 *07/4939–8755* 🌐 *www.gkiholidays.com.au* 🛏 *1 house, 2 cabins, 8 tents, 4 rooms, 2 dormitories* ☖ *Café, pizzeria, snorkeling, boating, hiking; no a/c* ▱ *AE, DC, MC, V.*

Sports & the Outdoors

Great Keppel Island has almost every conceivable sport, and most are included in the basic rate. You'll pay extra for any activity that requires fuel. Camel rides along the beach at sunset, tandem skydiving, and scuba-diving lessons are also available.

Arriving & Departing

BY BOAT **Contiki Great Keppel Island Resort** (☎ 1/300–305005) transfers guests to the island from Rockhampton Airport or Yeppoon Marina. A taxi and launch service from the airport costs A$64 round-trip; the launch alone costs A$31 round-trip. **Keppel Bay Marina** (☎ 07/4933–6244) operates daily island launch services, for A$31 round-trip, from Rosslyn Bay aboard the catamaran *Freedom Flyer*. Departures are at 9, noon, and 3. Return trips are at 10, 2, and 4. **Keppel Tourist Services** (☎ 07/4933–6744) operates the *Spirit of Keppel, Reef Cat,* and *Keppel Kat* from Rosslyn Bay Harbour. Trips alternate between the three craft and depart daily at 7:30, 9:15, 11:30, and 3:30. Return trips depart at 8:15, 2, and 4:30. Trips cost A$22 each way or A$30 round-trip. A tour of the underwater observatory costs A$48 for guests and nonguests alike. **Rotherys Coaches** (☎ 07/4922–4320) operates round-trip coach pickup between the Leichardt Hotel and the airport in Rockhampton with Rosslyn Bay. The cost is A$15.50 one-way, A$27.50 for a round-trip.

BY PLANE **Contiki Great Keppel Island Resort** (☎ 1/300–305005) can arrange flights to the island from Rockhampton. The fare is A$240 round-trip per person, with a minimum of two people. You can also fly to Great Keppel from Brisbane with one of the resort's package tours.

Brampton Island

Seven coral-and-white sandy beaches encircle Brampton Island, and kangaroos, colorful rainbow lorikeets, and butterflies populate the hilly interior's rain forests. Part of the Cumberland Islands near the southern entrance to the Whitsunday Passage, this 195-acre island is one of the prettiest in the area. Most of the island is a designated national park. The resort area, however, is lively, with nightly entertainment in a variety of themes, dances, and floor shows. The biggest attraction, of course, is the water—especially snorkeling over the reef between Brampton and adjoining Carlisle islands.

Where to Stay & Eat

$$$–$$$$ ╳⊡ **Brampton Island Resort.** Choose between a fast-paced, energy-filled holiday or relaxed island experience at this Polynesian-style resort on the beach. High ceilings and verandas lend an airiness to the rooms, which are furnished with rattan furniture and fabrics in soft blues and corals. Some rooms sit as high as 10 feet off the ground, allowing ocean breezes to waft underneath. The Bluewater Restaurant serves a buffet breakfast, smorgasbord lunch, and a set four-course dinner highlighting local seafood. Three meals a day are included in the price. ⌂ *P&O Australian Resorts, Box 478, Sydney, NSW 2001* ☎ *1800/737678, 1800/225–9849 in North America* ⊕ *www.poresorts.com.au/brampton* ⇗ *106 rooms* ⌂ *Restaurant, bar, lounge, cable TV, minibars, refrigerators, 2 pools, 6-hole golf course, 3 tennis courts, massage, beach, snorkeling, jet skiing, waterskiing, aerobics, archery, badminton, basketball, boccie, gym, volleyball, bar, lounge, baby-sitting, laundry service* ⊟ *AE, DC, MC, V* ⎰⎱ *All-inclusive.*

Sports & the Outdoors

Brampton Island's resort has extensive facilities and activities included in the rate. For an extra charge, you can also take boomnetting cruises (being trailed behind a boat by a net), guided walks, Jet Ski island tours, fishing trips, flights to the Great Barrier Reef, island and sunset cruises, waterskiing, tube rides (a tube pulled along behind the ski boat), and guided snorkeling safaris.

Arriving & Departing

BY BOAT   The *Heron II* (☎ 13–2469), a modern, high-speed monohull, leaves Mackay Outer Harbour Thursday through Monday at 11:30. Fare is A$45 one-way and A$90 round-trip. Complimentary coach transfers from Mackay airport are available.

BY PLANE   **Macair Airlines** (☎ 13–1313 ⊕ www.macair.com.au) runs several daily flights from Mackay in an 18-seat Twin Otter plane. Prices start at A$233 round-trip. Flights are also available from Hamilton Island.

Tour Operators

Brampton Island lies 50 km (31 mi) from the Great Barrier Reef. A tour to Hardy Reef involves flying to Hamilton Island and catching a small boat to a pontoon where you can snorkel above the reef. This tour can be chartered for A$400 per person, with a minimum of four persons. A two- to three-hour fishing trip also departs twice weekly. The cost is A$60 per person, which includes bait, tackle, and, in the evening, a chef's preparation of your catch. Book tours through the resort.

THE WHITSUNDAY ISLANDS

Lindeman Island

More than half of Lindeman Island, one of the largest bits of land (2,000 acres) in the **Whitsunday** group, is national park, with 20 km (12 mi) of walking trails that wind through tropical growth and up hills that reward a climb with fantastic views. Bird-watching is excellent here, and, yet, the blue tiger butterflies that you can see in Butterfly Valley may be even more impressive than the birds. With its nature viewing and sporting possibilities, the island draws lots of families. The island lies 40 km (25 mi) northeast of Mackay at the southern entrance to the Whitsunday Passage.

Where to Stay & Eat

$$–$$$ ✕⊡ **Club Med Lindeman Island.** This three-story, palm-tree-filled resort sits on the southern end of the island. Rooms overlook the sea and have a balcony or patio, and all border the beach and pool. Away from the main village are the golf clubhouse, sports center, dance club, and restaurant. Prices include meals, nonmotorized sports, and entertainment, and Club Med even offers packages that cover round-trip airfares within Australia. ⊠ *Lindeman Island via Mackay, QLD 4741* ☎ *07/4946–9776 or 1800/646933* 🖶 *07/4946–9776* ⊕ *www.clubmed.com.au* 🛏 *218 rooms* 🕭 *2 restaurants, 3 bars, in-room safes, 9-hole golf course, 5 tennis courts, 2 pools, beach, snorkeling, windsurfing, boating, jet skiing, fishing, aerobics, archery, badminton, basketball, hiking, volleyball, cabaret, dance club, theater, children's programs (ages 1–12), laundry facilities, Internet, airstrip, travel services* 🖃 *AE, DC, MC, V* ⦿ *All-inclusive.*

Sports & the Outdoors

Club Med's basic price includes most activities, although you have to pay for motorized water sports. Lindeman also has one of the most picturesque 9-hole golf courses anywhere. You can take refresher scuba-diving courses for an additional fee. Dive excursions to the outer reef by air are 30 minutes each way. By boat it's two hours each way.

Arriving & Departing

BY BOAT Boats regularly serve the island from the small port at **Shute Harbour** (36 km [22 mi] east of Proserpine), which is the major coastal access point for all the resorts in the Whitsunday region. The trip takes about an hour and costs A$24 one-way or A$48 round-trip. There are also direct half-hour water-taxi transfers from **Hamilton Island Airport** (☎ 07/4946–9499).

BY PLANE **Island Air Taxis** (☎ 07/4946–9933) fly to the Lindeman airstrip on demand. The one-way cost is A$114 from Proserpine, A$60 from Shute Harbour, A$60 from Hamilton Island, and A$120 from Mackay.

Long Island

This aptly named narrow island lies just off the coast south of Shute Harbour. Although it's 9 km (5½ mi) long, and no more than 1½ km (1 mi) wide, it has walking trails through large areas of thick, undisturbed rain forest, which is protected as national parkland.

Where to Stay

$$$–$$$$ 🏠 **Palm Bay Hideaway.** Tropical, Melanesian-style bungalows and cabins are set on a beach lined by slender coconut palms. Fan-cooled rooms have a refreshing island feel. Packages include restaurant meals, or you can pay a room-only rate. ✉ *Palm Bay Hideaway, PMB 28, via Mackay, QLD 4740* ☎ *07/4946–9233 or 1800/095025* 🖷 *07/4946–9309* ⊕ *www.palmbay.com.au* 🛏 *14 bungalows, 7 cabins* ⚲ *Restaurant, fans, kitchenettes, pool, outdoor hot tub, snorkeling, boating, fishing, hiking, laundry facilities; no a/c* ▭ *AE, DC, MC, V.*

$$$ 🏠 **Club Crocodile Long Island Resort.** This is not the place to commune quietly with nature, because Club Crocodile focuses on outdoor activities, particularly on water sports such as jet skiing and windsurfing. Air-conditioned beachfront and garden-view rooms have ensuite bathrooms and private balconies; budget lodge rooms are fan cooled and have shared bathrooms. With its child-care facilities, the resort attracts lots of families. A constant stream of guests flies into the Hamilton Island airport, then takes the transfer boat to this resort. ✉ *PMB 26, via Mackay, QLD 4740* ☎ *07/4946–9400 or 1800/075125* 🖷 *07/4946–9555* ✉ *longislandres@clubcroc.com.au* 🛏 *156 rooms with shower* ⚲ *Restaurant, café, tennis court, 2 pools, sauna, spa, snorkeling, windsurfing, boating, jet skiing, waterskiing, fishing, basketball, nightclub, baby-sitting, children's programs (ages 4–14), laundry facilities, Internet* ▭ *AE, DC, MC, V* ❐ *MAP.*

$$$ 🏠 **Whitsunday Wilderness Lodge.** This intimate lodge, accessible only by helicopter, is free of TVs, phones, and electric outlets. Private waterfront cabins hold only 20 guests, who take meals and drinks in a breezy beachfront gazebo. The lodge owns and operates a sailing catamaran; excursions with lunch are included. The tariff includes meals, snorkeling equipment, wet suits, and helicopter transfers. ✑ *Box 409, Paddington, QLD 4064* ☎ *07/4946–9777* ⊕ *www.southlongisland.com* 🛏 *10 cabins with shower* ⚲ *Dining room, bar, beach, snorkeling, boating, hiking, shop, helipad; no a/c, no room phones, no room TVs, no kids under 15* ▭ *MC, V* ❐ *All-inclusive.*

Arriving & Departing

BY BOAT You can reach Long Island (but not Whitsunday Wilderness Lodge) by **Whitsunday All Over and Water Taxi** (☎ 07/4946–9499) from either Shute Harbour or Hamilton Island. Boats leave Shute Harbour for Club Crocodile and Palm Bay daily at 7, 8:30, 11, 1:30, 3:30, and 5:30. The 20-minute journey costs A$32 round-trip. A water taxi meets each flight into Hamilton Island, and the 30- to 45-minute transfer to either resort costs A$77 round-trip.

Hamilton Island

Despite the large-scale development on Hamilton, more than 80% of this Whitsunday-group island has been carefully preserved in its natural state, which translates into beautiful beaches, native bush trails, and spectacular lookouts.

The island has the greatest selection of activities and amenities of any Queensland resort. In addition to an extensive sports complex and Barrier Reef excursions, there are six different types of accommodation, nine restaurants, numerous shops and boutiques, and a 200-acre fauna park.

The **Clownfish Club** (☎ 07/4946–8941) caters to children of three age groups: 6 weeks to 2 years, 2 to 5 years, and 5 to 14 years. Each has age-appropriate organized activities, such as sand castle–making, snorkeling, water polo, and beach olympics. Programs are included in the rates, but are subject to availability. It's A\$15 for a half day and A\$35 for a full day for children under 5.

Where to Eat

Hamilton Island Resort has more than a dozen dining options, including several casual cafés, as well as a few formal options.

\$\$–\$\$\$ ✕ **The Beach House.** This is Hamilton Island's signature restaurant, set right on Catseye Beach, where women dress up in chic tropical skirts and men don savvy sports jackets. Fresh, innovative Australian and international flavors are used in extravagant, seven-course lunches and à la carte dinners. The menu, which focuses on seafood, changes daily, but might include barramundi served with roast-capsicum salsa and tomato oil, or char-grilled chicken breast with ratatouille and balsamic syrup. ⊠ *Main resort complex* ☎ *07/4946–8580* ▭ *AE, DC, MC, V* ☉ *Closed Mon.*

\$\$–\$\$\$ ✕ **Romanos Italiano Restaurant.** With polished wood floors and a balcony overlooking the harbor, Romanos is the place to come for a quiet meal. The kitchen produces traditional Italian favorites such as *amatriciana* (pasta with tomato, bacon, onion, and chili), and many dishes highlight the local seafood. ⊠ *Marina Village, Harbourside* ☎ *07/4946–9999* ▭ *AE, DC, MC, V* ☉ *Closed Tues. No lunch.*

\$–\$\$ ✕ **Toucan Tango Café and Bar.** Vibrant summer colors, high ceilings, timber furniture, an Italian terrazzo floor, and potted palms characterize this tropical-theme restaurant overlooking the waters of both Catseye Beach and the main resort. This is the island's relaxed all-day dining option, with a large menu of snacks and a seafood buffet on Friday and Saturday nights. The cocktail bar, with live entertainment nightly, makes the Toucan Tango the hub of activity until late. ⊠ *Main resort complex* ☎ *07/4946–9999* ▭ *AE, DC, MC, V.*

Where to Stay

Make reservations for all accommodations on Hamilton Island with the **Hamilton Island Resort** (⊠ Hamilton Island, Whitsunday Islands, QLD 4803 ☎ 1800/075110 ⊕ www.hamiltonisland.com.au).

\$\$\$\$ ▥ **Beach Club Resort.** This two-story boutique hotel, the island's flagship property, has beachfront views from many rooms. Wooden floors and modern wooden furniture fill the rooms, which have stereos and VCRs. Special touches include airport pickup, exclusive butler service, and personal hosts to arrange everything from restaurant and tour bookings to flight tickets, room service, and specific housekeeping needs. ⊠ *Hamilton Island, Whitsunday Islands, QLD 4803* ☎ *1800/075110* ⊕ *www.hamiltonisland.com.au* ⊅ *55 rooms* ⌂ *Room service, in-room safes, in-room VCRs, minibars, refrigerators, pool, beach, laundry service; no kids* ▭ *AE, DC, MC, V.*

$$$–$$$$ ☷ **Reef View Hotel.** The Reef View lives up to its name with spectacular vistas of the Coral Sea from some rooms. Other rooms overlook the garden. Whichever room you choose, you'll have a private balcony to better enjoy the view. Tile floors, bright walls, and floral-print furnishings fill the rooms. ✉ *Hamilton Island, Whitsunday Islands, QLD 4803* ☎ *1800/075110* ⊕ *www.hamiltonisland.com.au* ↘ *370 rooms, 16 suites* ⚏ *Restaurant, room service, minibars, refrigerators, pool, spa, laundry facilities, concierge, no-smoking floor* ▤ *AE, DC, MC, V.*

$$$–$$$$ ☷ **Whitsunday Holiday Apartments.** These twin 13-story towers, which overlook the Coral Sea toward Whitsunday Island, have the only self-contained apartments on Hamilton Island. One- and two-bedroom accommodations have pastel walls, comfortable wooden and cane furniture, large balconies, fully equipped kitchens, and dining and sitting areas. ✉ *Hamilton Island, Whitsunday Islands, QLD 4803* ☎ *1800/075110* ⊕ *www.hamiltonisland.com.au* ↘ *176 apartments* ⚏ *Kitchens, refrigerators, 2 pools, outdoor hot tub, laundry facilities* ▤ *AE, DC, MC, V.*

$$–$$$ ☷ **Palm Bungalows and Terrace.** The steep roofs and small balconies of this complex resemble Polynesian huts. The theme extends to the décor, with grass mattings and bright floral bedspreads. Each of the small, individual units contains a king-size bed, a small bar, and a furnished patio. The Terrace caters to budget-minded travelers with inexpensive contemporary hotel rooms. ✉ *Hamilton Island, Whitsunday Islands, QLD 4803* ☎ *1800/075110* ⊕ *www.hamiltonisland.com.au* ↘ *50 bungalows, 60 rooms* ⚏ *Minibars, pool, outdoor hot tub* ▤ *AE, DC, MC, V.*

Nightlife

At **Boheme's Bar & Nightclub** (✉ Main resort complex ☎ 07/4946–9990)you can dance or shoot a round of pool. The bar opens Wednesday to Sunday from 9 PM until late, while the nightclub is open 11 PM–3 AM. Try the relaxing **Mantaray Café** (✉ Main resort complex ☎ 07/4946–9990)for light snacks, desserts, and wood-fired pizzas.

Sports & the Outdoors

Hamilton Island Resort has the widest selection of activities on the Whitsunday Islands. Activities include bushwalking, go-carts, a golf driving range, miniature golf, a health and racquet club, a target-shooting range, parasailing, game fishing, scuba diving, waterskiing, speed boats, Jet Skis, catamarans, sea kayaking, and windsurfing, as well as 10 swimming pools and floodlighted tennis courts. Reserve ahead through the **Tour Booking Desk** (☎ 07/4946–8305).

FISHING   The island's 40-foot deep-sea game-fishing boat, *Balek III*, and the smaller catamaran, *Drag-n-Fly*, will take you on a two-hour trip to the outer reef in search of marlin, sailfish, Spanish mackerel, and tuna. Charters can be arranged through Hamilton Island's **Tour Booking Desk** (☎ 07/4946–8305) year-round. Private charters of the larger boat are A$1,600, or a shared charter for A$225 for a full day on *Balek III*,

SCUBA DIVING   Hamilton runs a complimentary introductory scuba course, which includes pool instruction, equipment rental, and a dive with a qualified instructor. If you are already qualified, all equipment can be rented and diving trips arranged. A single dive with **H2O** (☎ 07/4946–8217) runs A$55; a two-tank dive costs A$70.

Shopping

Hamilton Island's Marina Village houses many shops selling resort wear, children's clothes, souvenirs, and gifts. An art gallery, art studio, florist, small supermarket, pharmacy, realtor, medical center, video store, and beauty salon are also on the premises.

Arriving & Departing

BY BOAT **Blue Ferries** (☎ 1800/650851) makes the 35-minute journey from Shute Harbour eight times daily for A$44 round-trip.

BY PLANE **Qantas** (☎ 13–1313) flies directly to the island daily from Sydney, Brisbane, and Cairns, and six days a week from Townsville. Flight connections from other interstate capitals are also available. Boat transfers to all other Whitsunday resort islands can be made from the wharf adjoining the airport.

Tour Operators

The resort's **Tour Booking Desk** (☎07/4946–8305) can organize scenic flights over the Whitsunday Islands and reef by plane or helicopter, plus seaplane flights to the reef. Transfers to the other islands are also available.

Fantasea Cruises (☎ 07/4946–8305 tour booking desk) runs reef trips daily from Hamilton and other islands, as well as from all mainland Whitsunday resorts. From Hamilton it's a 75-km (47-mi) trip to the company's own pontoon on magnificent **Hardy Reef Lagoon.** Every tour gives you four hours on the reef to swim, snorkel, ride in a semisubmersible, or simply relax. Cost is A$145 with a buffet lunch. It's also possible to overnight on Fantasea's floating Reefworld.

Fantasea also sails a high-speed catamaran daily to **Whitehaven Beach,** a 6½-km (4-mi) stretch of glistening sand. The catamaran leaves the harbor at 12:30 for the 30-minute trip to the beach, returning to Hamilton about 4:15. Cost is A$69 with lunch.

Sunsail Australia (✉ Front St. ☎07/4946–9900 or 1800/803988 ⊕ www.sunsail.com.au) has a fleet of 29 boats available for charter and group trips.

South Molle Island

South Molle, a 1,040-acre (416-hectare) island close to Shute Harbour, was originally inhabited by Aborigines, who collected basalt here to use for their axes. Much later, it became the first of the Whitsundays to be used for grazing, hence its extensive grassy tracts. Now the island is a national park with a single, family-oriented resort settled on sheltered Bauer Bay in the north. Protected between two headlands, the bay often remains calm when wind rips through the rest of the Whitsundays.

Where to Stay

$$ ⊞ **South Molle Island Resort.** This resort nestles in a bay at the northern end of the island, with a long jetty reaching out beyond the fringing reef. From offshore it doesn't look very large. Only when you explore the complex do you realize that there are 200 guest rooms. Every room has a balcony, a whirlpool tub, and air-conditioning. Rooms with sea views are more expensive than those fronting the garden. All dining-room meals and most activities are included in the rate; only sports requiring fuel cost extra. This is one of the most pleasant resorts in the Whitsundays. ✉ *South Molle Island, via Shute Harbour, QLD 4741* ☎ *07/4946–9433 or 1800/075080* ⊟ *07/4946–9580* ⇖ *200 rooms* ⚥ *2 restaurants, refrigerators, 9-hole golf course, 2 tennis courts, pool, wading pool, outdoor hot tub, massage, beach, dive shop, snorkeling, windsurfing, jet skiing, waterskiing, archery, gym, volleyball, baby-sitting, children's programs (ages 6–12), laundry service* ⊟ *AE, DC, MC, V* ¶◯¶ *All-inclusive.*

Arriving & Departing

BY BOAT South Molle Island Resort's own boats will pick you up from Shute Harbour. Boats depart daily at 8:30, 10, 11:30, 2, and 4:30, and the 30-

THE REEF

T'S HARD TO IMAGINE that the Great Barrier Reef, which covers an area about half the size of Texas, is so fragile that even human sweat can cause damage. However, despite its size, the Reef is a finely balanced ecosystem sustaining zillions of tiny polyps, which have been building on top of each other for thousands of years. So industrious are these critters that the reef is more than 1,640 feet thick in some places. These polyps are also fussy about their living conditions and only survive in clear, salty water around 18°C (64°F) and less than 98 feet deep.

Closely related to anemones and jellyfish, marine polyps are primitive, sacklike animals with a mouth surrounded by tentacles. Coral can consist of just one polyp (solitary) or many hundreds (colonial), which form a colony when joined together. These polyps create a hard surface by producing lime; as they die, their coral "skeletons" remain, which form the reef's white substructure. The living polyps give the coral its colorful appearance.

The Great Barrier Reef begins south of the tropic of Capricorn around Gladstone and ends in the Torres Strait below Papua New Guinea, making it about 2,000 km (1,240 mi) long and 356,000 square km (137,452 square mi) in area. Declared a World Heritage Site in 1981, it is managed by the Great Barrier Reef Marine Park Authority, which was itself established in 1976. Consequently, detailed observations and measurements of coral reef environments only date back to around this time. Thus, annual density bands in coral skeletons, similar to rings formed in trees, are important potential storehouses of information about past marine environmental conditions.

The reef is a living animal. Early scientists, however, thought it was a plant, which is forgivable. Soft corals have a plantlike growth and a horny skeleton that runs along the inside of the stem. In contrast, the hard, calcareous skeletons of stony corals are the main building blocks of the reef. There are also two main classes of reefs: platform or patch reefs, which result

from radial growth, and wall reefs, which result from elongated growth, often in areas of strong water currents. Fringing reefs occur where the growth is established on subtidal rock, either on the mainland or on continental islands.

Like any living creature, corals must reproduce to survive. They can bud or split from the original polyp, fertilize their eggs internally before releasing them, or shed eggs and sperm into the water for external fertilization. To ensure a better-than-average reproduction rate for the latter method, many corals spawn together on one night of the year, about five days after the full moon in late spring (October–November).

The Great Barrier Reef attracts thousands of divers and snorkelers every year. Apart from the coral, divers can swim with 2,000 species of fish, dolphins, dugongs, sea urchins, and turtles. There are also about 400 species of coral and 4,000 species of mollusk, as well as a diversity of sponges, anemones, marine worms, and crustaceans.

Dive sites are unlimited, with about 3,000 individual reefs, 300 coral cays, 890 fringing reefs, and 2,600 islands (including 618 continental islands that were once part of the mainland) from which to choose. Despite the vast amount of water surrounding the islands, though, freshwater is nonexistent here and thus is a precious commodity; self-sufficiency is particularly important for explorers and campers. Removing or damaging any part of the reef is a crime, so divers are asked to take home only photographs and memories of one of the world's great natural wonders.

—Jane Carstens

minute trip costs A$30 round-trip. **Whitsunday All Over and Water Taxi** (☎ 07/4946–9499) meets each flight into Hamilton Island. The 30-minute ride costs A$77 round-trip.

Daydream Island

Just a short hop from the mainland, Daydream is popular with day-trippers looking to relax or pursue outdoor activities such as hiking and snorkeling. The resort's lush gardens blend into a rain forest, which is surrounded by clear blue water and fringing coral reef.

Where to Stay

$$–$$$$ ☒ **Daydream Island Resort.** Spacious garden- or ocean-view condo-style apartments have modern cane and wooden furniture, terra-cotta–tile floors, and brightly colored beach-theme fabrics. Activities—all free except boating—vary from snorkeling the sunny reef to catching an open-air movie under the stars. Breakfast is the only meal included, but you can dine at the à la carte Mermaids Restaurant or the Tavern restaurant-bar. ☒ *Daydream Island, PMB 22, via Mackay, QLD 4740* ☎ *07/ 4948–8488 or 1800/075040* 🖷 *07/4948–8479* ⊕ *www.daydream.net. au* ⌨ *296 rooms, 9 suites* ⚐ *3 restaurants, coffee shop, miniature golf, 3 pools, sauna, spa, 2 tennis courts, dive shop, snorkeling, windsurfing, jet skiing, waterskiing, badminton, gym, 3 bars, cinema, recreation room, baby-sitting, children's programs (ages 5–12), laundry service, travel services* ▤ *AE, DC, MC, V* ⍐ *CP.*

Sports & the Outdoors

Most sports are included in room rates. Parasailing, fishing, snorkeling, waterskiing, jet skiing, and miniature golf are provided for an additional charge. Day excursions to the surrounding islands and the Great Barrier Reef are also available. The resort also offers introductory dives for A$110 and one-tank dives for A$70.

Arriving & Departing

BY BOAT **Whitsunday All Over and Water Taxi** (☎ 07/4946–9499) runs regularly to Daydream from Shute Harbour (A$32 round-trip). The company also runs boats to Hamilton Island for A$77 round-trip.

BY PLANE Although most people come by boat from Hamilton Airport, an alternative is to fly to **Proserpine Airport** on the mainland. From the airport you can catch a bus to Shute Harbour and a boat from here to the island. Boat transport can be booked through the island's reservations office. **Qantas** (☎ 13–1313) operates flights to and from Proserpine Airport.

Hayman Island

Fodor'sChoice Hayman Island, in the northern Whitsunday Passage, is a 900-acre ★   crescent with a series of hills along its spine. From these peaks, the view of the Whitsunday Passage is unbeatable.

Hayman Island Resort is one of the finest resorts in the world. The area around the resort is arid, but beautiful walking trails crisscross the island. The main beach sits right in front of the hotel, but more secluded sands, as well as fringing coral, can be reached by boat. The architecture is first-class—with reflecting pools, sandstone walkways, manicured tropical gardens, and sparkling waterfalls—and the atmosphere more closely resembles an exclusive club than a resort.

Where to Eat

Reservations are recommended for all restaurants and can be booked through the resort's concierge.

$$$–$$$$ ✕ **La Fontaine.** With Waterford chandeliers and Louis XVI furnishings, this elegant French restaurant is the resort's culinary showpiece. The cuisine rivals the finest restaurants on the mainland and highlights such innovative dishes as chicken breast and wing stuffed with lobster in cream sauce, and roast medallions of lamb with compote of shallots and red-capsicum coulis. Live music usually accompanies dinner. A private dining room, where you can design your own menu in consultation with the chef, is available. ⚜ *Jacket required* 🚬 *AE, DC, MC, V* ⊘ *No lunch.*

$$$ ✕ **La Trattoria.** With its red-and-white–checkered tablecloths and casual furnishings, "Tratt's" is a classic provincial Italian restaurant that could easily be in Sorrento or Portofino. The resident band adds to the Italian-village atmosphere. Seated either inside or outdoors, you can choose from an extensive list of pastas and traditional Italian dishes. 🚬 *AE, DC, MC, V* ⊘ *No lunch.*

$$$ ✕ **The Oriental Restaurant.** This Asian establishment overlooks a teahouse and Japanese garden complete with soothing rock pools and waterfalls. Black lacquer chairs, shoji screens, and superb Japanese artifacts fill this outstanding restaurant. Try *hoi man poo* (Thai-style mussels in black bean sauce), shark-fin soup, or jellyfish vinaigrette. 🚬 *AE, DC, MC, V* ⊘ *No lunch.*

$$–$$$ ✕ **Azure.** Right in front of the island's main beach, this casual restaurant affords gorgeous views. Dining is indoors or alfresco, with seating extending to the sand. There's a splendid buffet breakfast each morning, with tropical fruits and juices, and contemporary Australian cuisine throughout the day and night. The specialty is fresh local seafood. 🚬 *AE, DC, MC, V.*

$–$$ ✕ **Beach Pavilion.** Stop by during a day at the beach or the pool for lunch or sunset cocktails. This casual restaurant serves snacks, hamburgers, steaks, and other simple dishes in a pleasantly informal setting. 🚬 *AE, DC, MC, V.*

Where to Stay

$$$$ ⌂ **Hayman Island Resort.** Asian and Australian artifacts, European tapestries, Persian rugs, and exquisite objets d'art enliven the lobby, restaurants, and rooms, where footsteps and voices echo between the marble walls and floor. Choose from Lagoon, Pool, Beach Garden, or Beach-front Suites, which are all beautifully appointed but overlook different areas of the resort. For utter luxury, nothing tops the 11 penthouse suites, each decorated with a different theme such as French Provincial or Italian Palazzo. ✉ *Hayman Island, QLD 4801* ☎ *07/4940–1234 or 1800/075175* 🖷 *07/4940–1567* ⊕ *www.hayman.com.au* ⬚ *216 rooms, 18 suites, 11 penthouses* ♿ *5 restaurants, room service, in-room safes, minibars, refrigerators, putting green, 6 tennis courts, 3 pools, hair salon, sauna, spa, steam room, beach, dive shop, snorkeling, windsurfing, parasailing, waterskiing, fishing, badminton, health club, volleyball, 2 bars, billiards, Internet, library, baby-sitting, children's programs (ages 5–15), laundry service, business services, convention center, helipad* 🚬 *AE, DC, MC, V.*

Sports & the Outdoors

All nonmotorized water sports on Hayman Island are included in the rates. The resort's water-sports center has a training tank for diving lessons, and a dive shop sells everything from snorkel gear to complete wet suits and sports clothing. The marina organizes parasailing, waterskiing, sailing, boating, fishing, coral-viewing, windsurfing, and snorkeling, as well as dive trips. Contact the hotel's **Recreation Information Centre** (☎ 07/4940–1725) for reservations and information.

Arriving & Departing

BY PLANE   Hayman does not have an airstrip of its own, but you can fly into Hamilton Island on Qantas and transfer onto one of Hayman's luxury motor yachts. Australian sparkling wine is served during the 60-minute trip to the island. Upon your arrival at the wharf, a shuttle conducts you to the resort about 1 km (½ mi) away. Make sure you are ticketed all the way to Hayman Island, including the motor-yacht leg, as purchasing the round-trip yacht journey from Hamilton Island to Hayman separately will cost upward of A$300.

BY BOAT   **Whitsunday All Over and Water Taxi** (☎ 07/4946–9499) runs water taxis to Hayman Island from Shute Harbour. The trip takes about one hour and costs A$90 round-trip.

Tour Operators

The Hayman Island Resort's **Recreation Information Centre** (☎ 07/4940–1725) provides information on all guided tours from or around the island.

A 90-minute coral-viewing trip aboard the *Reef Dancer* (A$66 per person) departs three to four times daily. The coral is viewed from a semisubmersible sub. A Whitehaven Beach Picnic Cruise (A$152) departs Tuesday and Friday at 9:45; the price includes lunch.

Reef Goddess, Hayman Island's own boat, makes Great Barrier Reef excursions Monday, Wednesday, Thursday, and Saturday from 9:15 to 3:30. The A$178 per-person charge includes snorkeling, some drinks, and a light lunch. There is a dive master on board, and the day-trip cost for divers is A$310, which includes weight belt, two tanks, and lunch. Additional equipment can be hired.

You can take a **scenic flights** over or to the Great Barrier Reef by seaplane or helicopter. At the reef, activities include snorkeling, coral viewing from a semisubmersible sub, and refreshments.

CAIRNS ISLANDS

Orpheus Island

Volcanic in origin, this narrow island—11 km (7 mi) long and 1 km (½ mi) wide—uncoils like a snake in the waters between Halifax Bay and the Barrier Reef. Although patches of rain forest exist in the island's deeper gullies and around the sheltered bays, Orpheus is a true Barrier Reef island, ringed by seven unspoiled sandy beaches and superb coral. Incredibly, 340 of the known 350 species of coral inhabit Orpheus's waters.

Where to Stay & Eat

$$$$ ✕▦ **Orpheus Island Resort.** This quiet resort, which books a maximum of 46 guests, is a cross between a South Seas island and an elegant Italian hotel. Accommodations vary from beachfront studios and bungalows to luxury Mediterranean villas. The restaurant, which emphasizes seafood, delivers the tastes of tropical Queensland with deviled king prawns, broiled barramundi with capers, beets, and ginger, and an extensive list of Australian wines. ✉ *Orpheus Island, PMB 15, Townsville Mail Centre, QLD 4810* ☎ *07/4777–7377* 🖷 *07/4777–7533* ⊕ *www. orpheus.com.au* 🛏 *4 bungalows, 17 villas* ♿ *Restaurant, tennis court, 2 pools, hot tub, spa, beach, snorkeling, boating, fishing, gym, 2 bars, recreation room, Internet; no room phones, no room TVs, no kids under 15* ⊟ *AE, DC, MC, V* ⦿ *All-inclusive.*

Sports & the Outdoors

The resort has two freshwater swimming pools, a hot tub, a tennis court, and walking trails. Snorkeling and diving from the island's beaches are spectacular. Resort dive courses cost A$150; two-tank dives are A$120. Most non-boating activities are included in the room rate. For an additional fee, outer-reef fishing charters can be arranged. Trips are subject to weather conditions, and a minimum of six passengers is required.

Arriving & Departing

BY PLANE   Orpheus Island lies 24 km (15 mi) offshore opposite the town of Ingham, about 80 km (50 mi) northeast of Townsville and 190 km (118 mi) south of Cairns. The 25-minute flight from Townsville to Orpheus aboard a Nautilus Aviation seaplane costs A$380 per person round-trip. Book flights when you make your reservation with Orpheus Island Resort.

Tour Operators

The coral around Orpheus is some of the best in the area, and cruises to the outer reef can be arranged through the resort. Whereas most of the islands are more than 50 km (31 mi) from the reef, Orpheus is just 15 km (9 mi) away.

Dunk Island

Dunk Island, which provided the setting for E. J. Banfield's 1908 escapist classic *Confessions of a Beachcomber,* is divided by a hilly spine that runs its entire length. The eastern side consists mostly of national park, with dense rain forest and secluded beaches accessible only by boat. Beautiful paths have been tunneled through the rain forest, along which you might see the large blue Ulysses butterfly, whose wingspan can reach 6 inches.

The resort is family-oriented and informal. It sits on the western side of the island overlooking the mainland, 5 km (3 mi) away.

Where to Stay & Eat

$$$$ ✕🖭 **Dunk Island Resort.** Coconut palms, flowering hibiscus, and frangi-
Fodor'sChoice   pani surround this bay-side resort. With latticed balconies, cool tile floors,
★   wicker furniture, and pastel color schemes, the Beachfront Units offer the best value and the most privacy. The airy Garden Cabanas lack beach views but do sit among tropical gardens. Wood beams, cane furniture, and potted plants fill the Beachcomber Restaurant, which serves pasta and seafood. BB's on the Beach serves snacks, burgers, and pizzas. *P&O Australian Resorts, Box 478, Sydney NSW 2001 ☎ 13–2469, 1800/737678, 800/225–9849 in North America ⊕ www.poresorts. com.au/dunk ➬ 144 rooms, 24 suites, 32 cabanas ᐧ 2 restaurants, 2 cafés, 18-hole golf course, 3 tennis courts, 2 pools, hair salon, spa, beach, boating, jet skiing, parasailing, waterskiing, aerobics, archery, badminton, basketball, boccie, croquet, gym, horseback riding, squash, volleyball, 2 bars, baby-sitting, children's programs (ages 3–14), playground, laundry service, Internet, airstrip ⊟ AE, DC, MC, V ⍰ MAP.*

Sports & the Outdoors

In addition to reef cruises and fishing charters, the resort has a full range of water sports. Resort rates include all sports except horseback riding, scuba diving, and activities requiring fuel. The resort also provides a bushwalking map, which will guide you throughout the island along well-maintained trails.

Arriving & Departing

BY BOAT   Catamarans **MV *Quickcat I and II*** (☎ 07/4068–7289) depart the mainland from Clump Point Jetty in Mission Beach daily at 9:30 and 4:30 for the

20-minute ride to Dunk Island, returning at 10 and 5. Round-trip fare costs A$29. Coach connections to and from Cairns are available.

The **Dunk Island Express water taxi** (☎ 07/4068–8310) departs Mission Beach for Dunk Island five times daily. The trip takes 10 minutes. It's necessary to disembark in shallow waters, so you should take care to keep your luggage from getting wet. The round-trip fare costs A$22 for a day trip, A$26 if you are staying on the island.

BY PLANE Dunk Island has its own landing strip. **Macair Airlines** (☎ 13–1313 🌐 www.macair.com.au) serves the island three times daily from Cairns for A$355 round-trip.

Tour Operators

The **MV *Quickcat*** (☎ 1800/654242), a large passenger catamaran, runs daily (weather permitting) to the reef some 35 km (22 mi) away, leaving Dunk Island at 11:30 and returning at 4:30. The trip includes snorkeling, a glass-bottom boat ride, morning and afternoon tea, and a buffet lunch. The round-trip fare costs A$148. On Sundays and Wednesdays they offer full-day reef cruises with lunch for A$88.

Bedarra Island

Within the confines of this tiny 247-acre island 5 km (3 mi) off the northern Queensland coast, you'll come across natural springs, a dense rain forest, and eight separate beaches. Bedarra Island is a tranquil getaway popular with affluent executives and entertainment glitterati who want complete escape. It's the only Great Barrier Reef resort with an open bar, and the liquor—especially champagne—flows freely. Bedarra accommodates only 30 people, and you stay in freestanding villas hidden amid thick vegetation but still just steps from golden beaches.

Where to Stay & Eat

$$$$ Fodor's Choice ★ ✕🏨 **Bedarra Island.** Elevated on stilts, these two-story, open-plan, tropical-style villas blend into the island's dense vegetation. Polished wood floors, ceiling fans, and exposed beams set the tone for bright, airy accommodations that bear little resemblance to standard hotel rooms. Each villa has a balcony with a double hammock, a view of the ocean, a king-size bed, and a complimentary minibar. Two secluded pavilions featuring private reflecting pools for ocean-view soaking are a short walk from the main compound. All meals and drinks are included in the price—but note that there's no room service. The restaurant emphasizes seafood and tropical fruit, and despite the full à la carte menu, you are urged to request whatever dishes you like. 📫 *P&O Australian Resorts, Box 478, Sydney NSW 2001* ☎ *13–2469, 1800/737678, 800/225–9849 in North America* 🌐 *www.poresorts.com.au/bedarra* ⇨ *14 villas* 👍 *Restaurant, in-room safes, 6-hole golf course, tennis court, pool, spa, beach, dock, snorkeling, laundry service, Internet; no kids under 16* 💳 *AE, DC, MC, V* 🍽 *All-inclusive.*

Sports & the Outdoors

Snorkeling around the island is good, although the water can get cloudy during the rainy season (January and February). In addition, you can windsurf, scuba dive, sail, fish, or boat. A swimming pool, 6-hole golf course, and floodlighted tennis court are on-site. Fishing charters can be organized.

Arriving & Departing

BY BOAT Bedarra Island lies just a few minutes away by boat from Dunk Island. Round-trip fare is included in the accommodation price.

Tour Operators

To get to the Barrier Reef from Bedarra you have to return to Dunk Island, from which all reef excursions depart.

Fitzroy Island

This rugged, heavily forested national park has vegetation ranging from rain forest to heath, and an extensive fringing reef that is excellent for snorkeling and diving. A mere 45-minute cruise from Cairns, Fitzroy is a popular destination for day-trippers. The camping facilities, cabins, and dormitory-style rooms also make it an affordable overnight option.

Where to Stay & Eat

¢–$$ ✕🏨 **Fitzroy Island Resort.** Eight two-bedroom cabins with showers are furnished in natural woods and bright prints, and dormitory-style bunkhouses cater primarily to a young crowd. Lodging can be inexpensive—from A$31 per person in the four-bed bunkhouses to A$110 per person in the cabins—and campsites are A$6 each. The Raging Thunder Beach Bar and Restaurant serves stylish meals, the Flare Grill provides barbecue lunches, and the kiosk sells take-away foods. *🗺 Fitzroy Island Resort, Box 1109, Cairns, QLD 4870 ☎ 07/4051–9588 📠 07/ 4052–1335 ⊕ www.fitzroyislandresort.com.au ➷ 8 cabins, 32 bunkhouses, 6 campsites ⚓ Restaurant, grill, snack bar, pool, dive shop, snorkeling, boating, fishing, hiking, bar, laundry facilities; no a/ c, no room phones, no TV in some rooms ▤ AE, DC, MC, V.*

Arriving & Departing

BY BOAT The **Fitzroy Island Ferry** (☎ 07/4051–9588) departs daily at 8:30, 10:30, and 4 from Trinity Wharf in Cairns. Round-trip fare is A$36 for adults, A$18 children 14 and under. Return trips are at 9:30, 3, and 5.

Sports & the Outdoors

The resort rents catamarans, snorkeling gear, and fishing bait and tackle, and also arranges paddle skiing and guided snorkeling tours. The A$88 sea-kayaking tour is a great way to see the island. An introductory scuba dive costs A$65; a guided certified dive costs A$50. Visit between June and August to see mantas and humpback whales gathering off the coast.

Lizard Island

Safely protected from business pressures and prying eyes, the small, upscale resort on secluded Lizard Island is the farthest north of any Barrier Reef hideaway. At 2,500 acres (1,000 hectares), Lizard is larger and quite different from other islands in the region. Composed mostly of granite, Lizard has a remarkable diversity of vegetation and terrain, where grassy hills give way to rocky slabs interspersed with valleys of rain forest.

Ringed by stretches of white-sand beaches, the island is actually a national park with some of the best examples of fringing coral of any of the resort areas. Excellent walking trails lead to key lookouts with spectacular views of the coast. The highest point, Cook's Look (1,180 feet), is the historic spot from which, in August 1770, Captain James Cook of the *Endeavour* finally spied a passage through the reef that had held him captive for a thousand miles. Large monitor lizards, for which the island is named, often bask in this area.

Diving and snorkeling in the crystal-clear waters off Lizard Island are a dream. Cod Hole, 20 km (12 mi) from Lizard Island, ranks as one of the best dive sites in the world. Here massive potato cod swim right up to you like hungry puppies—an awesome experience, considering these fish weigh 300-pounds and are more than 6 feet long. In the latter part of the year, when black marlin are running, Lizard Island becomes the focal point for big-game anglers.

There is also a lesser-known, and more haunting, part of the island's history. In October 1881, while her husband was away fishing, Mary Watson, her baby daughter, and a Chinese workman vanished from the island. The only clues left behind were signs of an Aborigine attack and a missing iron kettle. It wasn't until three months later that the trio's remains—along with Mary's poignant diary recounting their last days—was discovered on another deserted island where they had died of thirst.

Where to Stay & Eat

$$$$ ✕⊡ **Lizard Island Lodge.** This is one of Australia's premier resorts, with
Fodor'sChoice beachside suites and sumptuous villas with sail-shaded decks and views
★ of the turquoise bay. Pastel blues, greens, and whites decorate the large, comfortable rooms, each with its own veranda, polished wood floors and blinds, and soft furnishings with Balarinji Aboriginal motifs. Meals, which are included in the base rate, emphasize seafood and tropical fruits and include such dishes as fresh coral trout panfried and served with a passion-fruit sauce. An excellent wine list complements the menu. ✉ *Lizard Island, PMB 40, via Cairns, QLD 4871* ☎ *07/4060–3999, 1800/737678, 800/225–9849 in North America* ⊕ *www.poresorts. com.au/lizard* 🛏 *6 rooms, 18 suites, 16 villas* ⚒ *Restaurant, minibars, tennis court, pool, beach, snorkeling, windsurfing, boating, waterskiing, fishing, boccie, bar, laundry service, Internet; no room TVs* ▤ *AE, DC, MC, V* ❘⊙❘ *All-inclusive.*

Sports & the Outdoors

The lodge has an outdoor pool, a tennis court, catamarans, outboard dinghies, Windsurfers, paddle skis, and fishing supplies. There is superb snorkeling around the island's fringing coral. Arrange a picnic hamper with the kitchen staff ahead of time and you can take one of several dinghies out for an afternoon on your own private beach.

DEEP-SEA GAME Lizard Island is one of the big-game fishing centers in Australia: several
FISHING world records have been set here in the last decade. Fishing is best between August and December, and a marlin weighing more than 1,200 pounds is no rarity here. A day on the outer reef, including tackle, costs A$1,550. Inner reef and night fishing are also available. One day's inner reef fishing with light tackle costs A$1,420.

SCUBA DIVING The resort arranges supervised scuba-diving trips to both the inner and outer reef, as well as local dives and night dives. Introductory and refresher courses are available. An introductory, one-dive course, including classroom and beach sessions, is A$175. One-tank boat dives are A$70. If you have a queasy stomach, take seasickness tablets before heading out for an afternoon on the reef, as crossings between dive sites in the exposed ocean can make for a bumpy ride.

Arriving & Departing

BY PLANE Lizard Island has its own small airstrip served by **Macair Airlines** (☎ 13–1313 ⊕ www.macair.com.au). One-hour flights depart twice daily from Cairns and cost from A$614 round-trip.

Tour Operators

The reefs around the island have some of the best marine life and coral anywhere. The 16-km (10-mi), full-day snorkeling and diving trip to the outer reef, which takes you to the world-famous Cod Hole, is A$180. Half-day inner reef trips are A$130. Glass-bottom boat and snorkeling trips and the use of motorized dinghies are included in guests' rates.

GREAT BARRIER REEF A TO Z

To research prices, get advice from other travelers, and book travel arrangements, visit www.fodors.com.

AIR TRAVEL

Regular boat and air services are available to most of the Great Barrier Reef resorts, but because all of the destinations are islands, they require extra travel time. Schedule the last leg of your trip for the early morning, when most charters and launches depart.

Airplane and helicopter pilots follow strict weight guidelines, usually no more than 7 or 10 kg (15 or 22 pounds) permitted per person (including hand baggage). To avoid repacking at the ticket counter where your gear is weighed, travel light. Divers could just bring masks and snorkels, then rent the rest of the gear from the resort dive shop. For information about reaching the various islands, *see* Arriving and Departing *under* individual island headings.

BOAT TRAVEL

Several operators provide uncrewed charters to explore the Great Barrier Reef. Australian Bareboat Charters has a fleet of more than 50 vessels. Cumberland Charter Yachts has a five-day minimum for all charters. Queensland Yacht Charters has been operating for more than 20 years. Whitsunday Rent a Yacht has a fleet of 58 vessels including yachts, catamarans, and motor cruisers.

Crewed charters can be booked through several operators. Whitsunday Private Yacht Charters has a minimum of five nights/six days for all charters. Sunsail Australia has a fleet of 29 boats.

Boat Information Australian Bareboat Charters ⊠ Shute Harbour Jetty, Airlie Beach, QLD 4802 ☎ 07/4946-9232 or 1800/075000. **Cumberland Charter Yachts** ⊠ Abel Point Marina, Airlie Beach, QLD 4802 ☎ 07/4946-7500 or 1800/075101 ⊕ www.ccy.com.au. **Queensland Yacht Charters** ⊠ Abel Point Marina, Airlie Beach, QLD 4802 ☎ 07/4946-7400. **Sunsail Australia** ⊕ Box 65, Hamilton Island, QLD 4803 ☎ 07/4946-9900 or 1800/803988 ⊕ www.sunsail.com.au. **Whitsunday Private Yacht Charters** ⊠ Abel Point Marina, Airlie Beach, QLD 4802 ☎ 07/4946-6880 or 1800/075055. **Whitsunday Rent a Yacht** ⊠ Shute Harbour, Airlie Beach, QLD 4802 ☎ 07/4946-9232 or 1800/075111.

BUSINESS SERVICES

Only the resorts on Hayman and Hamilton islands offer comprehensive business facilities such as meeting rooms and convention spaces. However, most resorts provide basic business services such as faxing and photocopying.

CAMPING

You can camp on many uninhabited islands lying within national parks as long as you have permission from the Queensland Parks and Wildlife Service. The office is open weekdays 8:30-5.

The myriad islands of the Whitsunday group are especially popular with young campers. For more information, contact the Whitsunday Information Centre of the Queensland Parks and Wildlife Service. It is 3 km (2 mi) from Airlie Beach toward Shute Harbour, open weekdays 9-5 and Saturday 9-1.

Queensland Parks and Wildlife Service ⊠ Naturally Queensland Information Centre, Dept. of Environment, 160 Ann St., Brisbane, QLD 4002 ☎ 07/3227-8186. **Whitsunday Information Centre** ⊕ Box 83, Whitsundays, QLD 4802 ☎ 07/4945-3711 or 1800/801252 ⊕ 07/4945-3182.

EMERGENCIES

Emergencies are handled by the front desk of the resort on each island. Each resort can summon aerial ambulances or doctors. Hamilton Island has its own doctor.

MAIL, INTERNET & SHIPPING

Club Croc on Long Island and Hayman, Lindeman, Bedarra, Lizard, and Orpheus islands have e-mail and Internet access. There is a cyber-café kiosk on Fitzroy Island. However, because Internet connections are usually through satellite phone links, they're frequently down.

Australia Post has an official outlet on Hamilton Island. The other islands offer postal services from the reception desk at each resort. You can also arrange special mail services, such as DHL and Federal Express, but it might not be sent overnight.

▶ Post Office **Australia Post** ✉ Hamilton Island ☎ 07/4946-8238.

MONEY MATTERS

Resorts on the following islands have money-changing facilities: Daydream, Fitzroy, Hamilton, Hayman, Lindeman, Lizard, Long, Orpheus, and South Molle. However, you should change money before arriving on the island, as rates are better elsewhere. Hamilton Island has a National Australia Bank branch with an ATM. Bedarra, Brampton, Dunk, and Heron islands have limited currency exchange facilities and no ATMs.

▶ Bank **National Australia Bank** ✉ Hamilton Island ☎ 13-2265.

TELEPHONES

There is only one area code (07) for Queensland and the Great Barrier Reef islands. You don't need to use the code when dialing in-state. International direct-dial telephones are available throughout the islands, and you can make local, national, and international calls on these. All resorts have a set dialing charge, which varies depending on where you're calling. You can use calling cards at any resort.

TOURS

FROM CAIRNS Divers can't do any better than hopping on Explorer Venture's *Nimrod Explorer*. The 72-foot dive boat can take up to 18 passengers on five-day trips between Port Douglas and Lizard Island (A$595 per diver). The fare includes a return flight. The *Nimrod Explorer* is also one of only two boats willing to venture north into the Coral Sea for exploratory diving on 10-day trips that skirt the north Queensland coastline.

Coral Princess runs cruises from three to seven nights that leave from either Cairns or Townsville on a comfortable 54-passenger minicruise ship. Divers can rent equipment on board. Lessons are also available.

Great Adventures operates fast catamaran service daily from Cairns to Green and Fitzroy islands and to the outer Barrier Reef. Some trips include barbecue luncheon and coral viewing from an underwater observatory and a semisubmersible.

Ocean Spirit Cruises conducts full-day tours aboard the *Ocean Spirit* and the smaller *Ocean Spirit II*. A daily trip from Cairns to Michaelmas or Upolu Cay includes four hours at the Great Barrier Reef, coral viewing in a semisubmersible at Upolu Cay only, swimming and snorkeling, and a fresh seafood lunch. Introductory diving lessons are available. Ocean Spirit Cruises also has a three-hour dinner cruise, with live entertainment and a seafood buffet.

Quicksilver Connections operates tours to the reef from Cairns, Palm Cove, and Port Douglas.

🖪 Tour Operators **Explorer Ventures** ☎ 07/4031-5566 ⊕ www.explorerventures.com. **Coral Princess** ☎ 07/4031-1041 or 1800/079545 ⊕ www.coralprincess.com.au. **Great Adventures** ☎ 1800/079080 ⊕ www.greatadventures.com.au. **Ocean Spirit Cruises** ☎ 07/4031-2920 ⊕ www.oceanspirit.com.au. **Quicksilver Connections** ☎ 07/4087-2100 ⊕ www.quicksilver-cruises.com.

FROM MISSION BEACH
The Quick Cat Cruise catamaran travels to Dunk Island and continues on to the Great Barrier Reef for snorkeling and coral viewing. Cruises leave at 10 AM Monday through Saturday. Special reef cruises operate during busy periods. **Quick Cat Cruise** (☎ 07/4068–7289).

FROM PORT DOUGLAS
Quicksilver Connections runs day trips aboard their high-speed catamaran MV *Quicksilver* to their large floating dual-level pontoon on Agincourt Reef. Once there, you can swim, snorkel, or scuba dive around the reef or board the *Quicksilver Sub,* a semisubmersible with superb underwater views through its keel windows. Ten-minute helicopter flights over the reef are also available, as is a fly-cruise helicopter adventure that includes a 30- to 40-minute scenic flight, lunch, and snorkeling on Agincourt Reef.

🖪 Quicksilver Connections (☎ 07/4087-2100 ⊕ www.quicksilver-cruises.com).

FROM TOWNSVILLE
Coral Princess operates cruises to Cairns. Reef and Island Tours runs from the Reef HQ wharf to its pontoon at Kelso Reef on the outer edge of the Great Barrier Reef. The trip takes 2½ hours by high-speed catamaran. Morning and afternoon tea and a full Australian barbecue lunch are included in the A$136 cost. The boat departs daily (except Monday and Thursday) at 8:45 AM, returning at 5:45 PM.

🖪 Coral Princess (☎ 07/4721-1673 or 1800/079545). Reef and Island Tours (☎ 07/4721-3555 or 1800/079797).

VISITOR INFORMATION
🖪 Queensland Travel Centre (✉ Roma and Makerston Sts., Brisbane, QLD 4000 ☎ 13-8833 ⊕ www.tq.com.au).

ADELAIDE AND SOUTH AUSTRALIA

9

FODOR'S CHOICE

Bridgewater Mill Restaurant, in Bridgewater

Chloe's, French restaurant in Kent Town

Grange Restaurant, in Adelaide

Medina Grand Adelaide Treasury, hotel in Adelaide

P. S. Federal, bed-and-breakfast in Goolwa

Seal Bay Conservation Park, on Kangaroo Island

Skillogalee Winery, restaurant in Sevenhill

Thorn Park Country House, bed-and-breakfast in Sevenhill

HIGHLY RECOMMENDED

RESTAURANTS   Blake's Restaurant and Wine Bar, in Adelaide

Grange Jetty Kiosk, in Grange

Market 190, in McLaren Vale

Summit, in Mt. Lofty

Universal Wine Bar, in Adelaide

Vintners Bar and Grill, in Angaston

HOTELS   Adelaide Hills Country Cottages, in Oakbank

Collingrove, in Angaston

Hyatt Regency, in Adelaide

Lawley Farm, in Tanunda

Lodge Country House, in Seppeltsfield

Miners Cottage, near Lyndoch

North Adelaide Heritage Group, in Eastwood

SIGHTS   Banrock Station, in Kingston-on-Murray

Heading Cliff Lookout, near Renmark

Sevenhill Cellars, in Sevenhill

Warrawong Sanctuary, near Mylor

By Michael
Gebicki and
Jacquie van
Santen
Updated by
Melanie Ball

EMBRACED BY PARKS, Adelaide is the capital of the Festival State renowned for celebrations of the arts, multiple cultures, and bountiful harvests from vines, land, and sea. Taste Australia's most celebrated wines, unwind on wildlife-rich Kangaroo Island, or cruise the Murray River. Trek through national parks or live underground like opal miners in the vast Outback. Folksy, casual, yet sometimes sophisticated, South Australia has the nation's most diverse terrain and unusual travel adventures.

Often called the city of pubs and churches, or the Festival City (a reference to the biennial Adelaide Festival of Arts), Adelaide is easy to explore. For this, residents thank William Light, the first surveyor-general of the colony. In 1836, on a flat saucer of land between the Mt. Lofty Ranges and the sea, Light laid out the city center—1½ square km (1 square mi) divided into a grid of broad streets running north to south and east to west—and surrounded it with parks. It's the only early capital not built by English convict labor.

Today Light's plan is recognized as far ahead of its time. This city of a million people moves at a leisurely pace, free of the typical urban menace of traffic jams and glass canyons. The rest of South Australia gives even more reason to cherish this poise and gentility, for Adelaide stands on the very doorstep of the harshest, driest land in the most arid of the earth's populated continents.

Nearly 90% of South Australia's residents live in the fertile south around Adelaide. Hugging the shoreline—wary of moving too close to the barren, jagged hills and stony deserts of the parched interior—they've left the northern half of the state virtually unchanged since the first settlers arrived. Heat and desolate desert terrain have thwarted all but the most determined efforts to conquer the land. Indeed, "conquer" is too strong a word for what is often little better than subsistence. In Coober Pedy, the world's opal capital in the far north, residents live underground to avoid temperatures that top 48°C (118°F).

The scorched, ruggedly beautiful Flinders Ranges north of Adelaide hold Aboriginal cave paintings and fossil remains from the ages when the area was an ancient seabed. Lake Eyre, a great salt lake, in 2000 filled with water for only the fourth time in its recorded history. The Nullarbor ("treeless") Plain stretches west across state lines in its tirelessly flat, ruthlessly arid march into Western Australia.

By comparison, Adelaide is an Eden, but reminders of harsh land beyond the city abound. Poles supporting electric wires are made from steel and cement, not wood: timber is precious. Toward the end of summer, it's common to find trees in the city parks crowded with brilliantly colored parrots, which have fled to these oases from the desert. For many residents, the most urgent concern is not rising crime nor property taxes but bushfire. The city is still haunted by the memory of the Ash Wednesday bushfires that devastated the Adelaide Hills at the end of the long, hot summer of 1983 and cast a pall of smoke over the city that blotted out the sun.

Yet South Australia is, perhaps ironically, gifted with the good life. It produces most of the nation's wine, and the sea ensures a plentiful supply of lobster, famed King George whiting, and tuna. Cottages and guesthouses tucked away in the countryside around Adelaide are among the most charming and relaxing in Australia. Although the state doesn't have attractions on the scale of Sydney Harbour or the Great Barrier Reef, and it draws far fewer visitors than the eastern states, you're likely to come away from here feeling that you've discovered one of Australia's best-kept secrets.

Exploring Adelaide & South Australia

South Australia comprises the dry hot north and the greener, more temperate south. The green belt includes Adelaide and its surrounding hills and orchards, the Barossa Region and Clare Valley vineyards, the beautiful Fleurieu Peninsula, and the Murray River's cliffs and lagoons. Offshore, residents of Kangaroo Island live in a delightfully cocooned way. Heading up to the almost extraterrestrial Coober Pedy is one way to glimpse life in the Outback.

The best way to experience this diverse state is by road. The wine regions, the southern coast, the Murray River, and most other major sights are within a few hours' drive of Adelaide. Longer journeys to Coober Pedy and the ancient Flinders Ranges will emphasize Australia's vastness. In general, driving conditions are excellent, although minor roads in the far north are unpaved.

The most direct route to the Flinders Ranges is via the Princes Highway and Port Augusta, but a more interesting route takes you through the Clare Valley vineyards and Burra's copper-mining towns. Travelers with limited time can enjoy aerial views of the Outback on a flight from Adelaide to Coober Pedy. Two classic train journeys also wind through this state: the Ghan, which runs north to Alice Springs, and the Indian Pacific, which crosses the Nullarbor Plain to reach Perth. Kangaroo Island is served by regional airlines and vehicular ferries.

About the Restaurants

Cafés are the favorite dining spots of South Australians, and inexpensive, bustling casual eateries—with occasionally quirky service—abound in Adelaide and the regional towns. However, there are also many fine-dining establishments where prim-and-proper service includes starched napkins and polished wine glasses. Friday and Saturday are the preferred nights for eating out across the state, although most restaurants draw a good business every evening. Reservations are recommended for weekend nights and during major city festivals—and you'll need to book weeks ahead for such upscale establishments as The Grange.

Restaurants in Adelaide and the surrounding regions favor trendy "Mod Oz" cuisine, where main dishes showcase oysters, crayfish, and whiting prepared with Asian flavors. Bush foods are also popular; look for *quandongs* (native plums), wattle seed, and kangaroo (delicious served as a rare steak). The ubiquitous metwursts and sausages stem from the region's influx of German immigrants in the 19th century.

WHAT IT COSTS In Australian Dollars				
	$$$$	**$$$**	**$$**	**$**	**¢**
AT DINNER	over $50	$36–$50	$21–$35	$10–$20	under $10

Prices are for a main course at dinner.

About the Hotels

South Australia has a delightful variety of lodgings. The most prevalent accommodations are bed-and-breakfasts, which can be found in contemporary studios, converted cottages and stables, restored homesteads, and grand mansions. Outside Adelaide there are few large hotels, although you'll find modern resorts in coastal suburbs, the Barossa Valley, and other tourist centers. Budget hotels have basic rooms with a bed and coffee-making facilities, while upscale places pamper you with or-

Many of the state's attractions are within an easy half-day's journey of Adelaide. The nearby Adelaide Hills capture the essence of South Australia's character, whereas a longer Outback expedition provides an intense contrast—wide horizons, trackless deserts, and barren, starkly beautiful mountains.

9

If you have
3 days

Spend a leisurely day in ⊡ **Adelaide,** with a tram-car excursion to the beach suburb of Glenelg. Spend the night, then take day two to tour the ⊡ **Adelaide Hills,** strolling the historic streets of ⊡ **Hahndorf** and taking in the panorama from atop ⊡ **Mt. Lofty.** Stay the night here, or in a charming bed-and-breakfast in one of the region's small towns. Save day three for wine tasting in the ⊡ **Barossa Region.**

If you have
5 days

The pleasures of ⊡ **Adelaide** and its suburbs, including a walk around the 19th-century streets of North Adelaide, will fill a day. Stay the night in the big city, then on day two drive to the ⊡ **Adelaide Hills.** Sleep in one of the lovely colonial cottages, then meander through the ⊡ **Barossa Valley** wineries and historic villages on day three. Spend the night on a vineyard estate, and on day four cross to ⊡ **Kangaroo Island.** After a night here, you can use day five to explore and appreciate its wildlife and untamed beauty.

If you have
7 days

Spend day one in ⊡ **Adelaide,** nosing through museums and picnicking in a park or on the banks of the Torrens River. After a night in the city, head into the leafy ⊡ **Adelaide Hills,** where car buffs love the National Motor Museum. Stay the night in a local bed-and-breakfast, then on day three travel to the ⊡ **Barossa Region,** where German and English influences are strong and the dozens of wineries offer tempting free tastings. Spend the evening on a vineyard estate, then on day four cross to ⊡ **Kangaroo Island.** Here you'll stay two nights, giving you day five to fully explore the island's remote corners and unwind. On day six, plunge into the Outback at extraordinary ⊡ **Coober Pedy** (consider flying to maximize your time). There you can eat, shop, and stay the night underground as the locals do and *noodle* (rummage) for opal gemstones. If you're a hiker, consider heading for **Flinders Ranges National Park** on day seven to explore one of the country's finest Outback parks.

---

ganic soaps and lotions, plush bath robes, multiple pillows, premium bed linens, and space-age audiovisual equipment.

The best accommodation deals in Adelaide are usually during the weekends, when corporate guests have departed. In regional South Australia, however, weekend nights are usually more expensive than weekday nights, and two-night minimum bookings often apply. On Kangaroo Island, lodgings outside the major towns emphasize conservation; hence, there are few hot tubs or in-house restaurants, and water is often limited. Reservations for all accommodations are recommended during the summer school holidays (December and January), Easter weekend, and during major festivals and sporting events.

WHAT IT COSTS In Australian Dollars				
	$$$$	$$$	$$	$	¢
FOR 2 PEOPLE	over $300	$201–$300	$151–$200	$100–$150	under $100

Prices are for a standard double room in high season, including tax and service, based on the European Plan (with no meals) unless otherwise noted.

Timing

Adelaide has the least rainfall of all Australian capital cities, and the midday summer heat should be avoided throughout the state. The Outback in particular is too hot for comfortable touring during this time, but Outback winters are pleasantly warm. South Australia's national parks are open year-round, and the best times to visit are in spring and autumn. During summer, extreme fire danger may close walking tracks, and in winter heavy rain can make some roads impassable. However, hiking after the rains can be particularly rewarding, as wildlife often gathers around watering holes after a dry spell. Boating on the Murray River and Lake Alexandrina are best from October to March, when the long evenings are bathed in soft light. The ocean is warmest here December to March.

Culture lovers can plan their South Australia visit around Adelaide's two big events: the Adelaide Festival of Arts and Womadelaide, both in February or March. Also, in autumn, you can appreciate wine, gourmet food, and local music at harvest festivals and the Barossa Vintage Festival of wines, held in non-Adelaide Festival years. The annual International Barossa Music Festival is held in October. A totally different experience, held every second October, is the formal Curdimurka Outback Ball, an all-night party at a remote, abandoned railway station on the northern desert fringes.

For sports fans, the annual, six-day Jacob's Creek Tour Down Under cycling race through South Australia is held each January. The Milang-Goolwa Freshwater Classic, held on January 26, is Australia's largest freshwater sailing regatta. The Clipsal 500 in March has V8 Supercars roaring a circuit around Adelaide's streets, and the Oakbank Easter Racing Carnival in the Adelaide Hills is one of the world's biggest horse races.

ADELAIDE

Central Adelaide's grid pattern of streets makes for easy exploration, and the streetscapes are appealing. The entire city center is like an island surrounded by parks, with the meandering Torrens River flowing through the heart of the green belt—at its finest passing the Festival Centre.

Exploring Adelaide

City Center

Numbers in the text correspond to numbers in the margin and on the Adelaide map.

a good walk

Victoria Square ❶ ▶ is Adelaide's geographical heart and a perfectly appropriate place to begin a walking tour. Head north along King William Street, with the **General Post Office ❷** on your left. A short distance away is the **Town Hall ❸**, built to designs by Edmund Wright, mayor of Adelaide in 1859.

9

Arts & Music

Adelaide's Festival Centre is the focus of the city's cultural life. Its name hints at the highlight of South Australia's arts calendar—the biennial Adelaide Festival of Arts, a tremendously successful celebration that was the forerunner to other artistic festivities throughout Australia. Beginning a week before, but concluding the same day, is the Fringe Festival, presenting all that's new in the independent arts. Adelaide also hosts the internationally acclaimed youth festival, Come Out, in off-festival years, and the annual Womadelaide celebration of world music. Country towns and regions have their own festivals, the most notable of which are the biennial Barossa Music Festival and Barossa Vintage (wine) Festival, which both alternate years with the Adelaide Festival of Arts.

Bush Tucker

South Australia, along with the Northern Territory, led the way in educating the Australian palate in the pleasures of bush tucker—the wild foods in the Australian countryside that have been used for millennia by the Aboriginal people. Kangaroo, crocodile, emu, and other regional fare were introduced to a skeptical public who now embrace it and seek ever more inventive preparations of native ingredients. Many menus also have local seafood, especially tuna, King George whiting, and oysters from the waters of Spencer Gulf and the Great Australian Bight.

Historic Homes

Adelaide's accommodations are bargains compared with those in any other Australian capital city. Even so, you might consider staying outside the city in the Adelaide Hills, to have the best of both worlds: easy access to the pleasures of the city as well as to the vineyards, orchards, and rustic villages that are tucked away in this idyllic, rolling landscape. Wonderfully restored historic homes and guesthouses are plentiful in Adelaide and throughout the state.

Outdoor Escapes

Kangaroo Island's Flinders Chase and the Outback's Flinders Ranges national parks are great places to take in South Australia's geographical diversity. Coastal expanses and seascapes stretch into lowland meadows and open forests toward rugged Outback mountain terrain. Australian creatures abound at Cleland Wildlife Park. Carry water in this dry state, and drink it often.

Wonderful Wines

South Australia is considered Australia's premium wine state and produces more than half the total Australian vintage. The premier wines of the Barossa Region, Clare Valley, McLaren Vale, Adelaide Hills, and Coonawarra are treasured by connoisseurs worldwide, and many South Australian producers and wines have been awarded international honors. Whether or not you make it to any vineyard's free tasting rooms, be sure to schedule a trip to the National Wine Centre in Adelaide to get a good working knowledge of Australian wines.

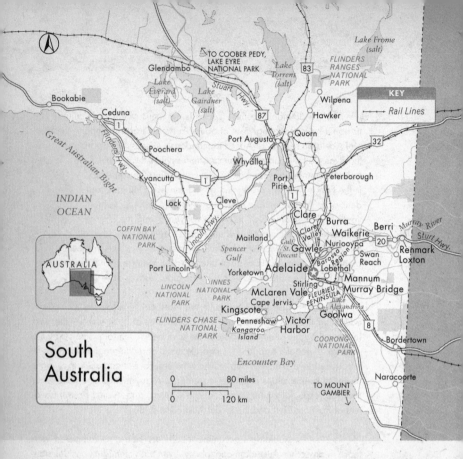

KEY

—⊢— Rail Lines

South
Australia

INDIAN
OCEAN

Great Australian Bight

AUSTRALIA

| 0 | 80 miles |
| 0 | 120 km |

Walk north on King William Street to North Terrace. Dominating this busy corner is the formidable Greco-Roman facade of **Parliament House** ④. To its left is Old Parliament House, the historic rooms of which are open to the public on Parliament House tours. The **South African War Memorial** ⑤, a bronze statue of a mounted trooper commemorating the Boer War, stands opposite. Walk up Kintore Avenue, past the white marble City of Adelaide Lending Library to the **Migration Museum** ⑥, one of Australia's most evocative museums.

Return to North Terrace, walk past the Royal Society of the Arts and the library, and turn left at the grassy courtyard to the **South Australian Museum** ⑦, which holds a particularly rich collection of Aboriginal artifacts. Next along North Terrace is the **Art Gallery of South Australia** ⑧, with its neoclassical exterior. Continue on North Terrace and cross to **Ayers House** ⑨, once the scene for the highlights of Adelaide's social calendar and the home of seven-time state premier Sir Henry Ayers.

Two blocks south on East Terrace, the **Tandanya Aboriginal Cultural Institute** ⑩ showcases the work of Australia's indigenous people. Head north again on East Terrace. If you need a rest, take a detour onto Rundle Street, to the left, which is lined with restaurants and bars, most with pavement tables and chairs. This becomes Rundle Mall, Adelaide's main shopping strip.

Continue straight across North Terrace and walk east along Botanic Road, the shady avenue that leads to the magnificent **Botanic Gardens** ⑪. To the north, off Frome Road, is the **Zoological Gardens** ⑫. The zoo conducts breeding programs for such threatened species as the red panda and the Persian leopard. From here you can follow the riverside trail back to Festival Centre.

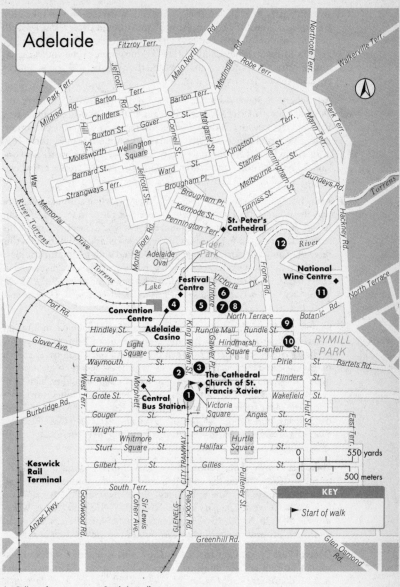

Adelaide

Fitzroy Terr.

Park Terr.

Jeffcott Terr.

Main North Rd.

Medindie Rd.

Robe Terr.

Northcote Terr.

Walkerville Terr.

Torrens

Mildred Rd.

Barton Terr.

St.

Barton Terr.

Kingston Terr.

Stanley St.

Jerningham St.

Melbourne St.

Bundeys Rd.

Park Terr.

Childers St.

Buxton St.

Gover St.

O'Connell St.

Margaret St.

Mann Terr.

Hill St.

Moleworth

Wellington Square

Terr.

Hackney Rd.

Barnard St.

Ward St.

Brougham Pl.

Finniss St.

Strangways Terr.

Jeffcott St.

Brougham Pl.

Kermode St.

St. Peter's Cathedral

River

War Memorial Drive

Monte fiore Rd.

Pennington Terr.

12

Torrens

River Torrens

Adelaide Oval

Elder Park

Victoria Dr.

Frome Rd.

National Wine Centre

Lake

Festival Centre

6

Kintore

11

North Terrace

Port Rd.

Glover Ave.

Convention Centre

4

5

7 **8**

North Terrace

Botanic Rd.

9

Hindley St.

Adelaide Casino

Rundle Mall

Rundle St.

10

RYMILL PARK

Currie St.

Light Square

St.

Hindmarsh Square

Grenfell St.

Bartels Rd.

Waymouth St.

Franklin St.

Morphett St.

King William St.

Gawler Pl.

Pirie St.

Flinders St.

West Terr.

2

3

The Cathedral Church of St. Francis Xavier

Grote St.

Central Bus Station

1

Wakefield St.

Hutt St.

East Terr.

Gouger St.

Victoria Square

Angas St.

Wright St.

Carrington St.

Sturt St.

Whitmore Square

Halifax St.

Hurtle Square

St.

Gilbert St.

Gilles St.

0   550 yards

Keswick Rail Terminal

CITY TRAMWAY

Goodwood Rd.

Sir Lewis Cohen Ave.

South Terr.

Peacock Rd.

GLENELG

Pulteney St.

0   500 meters

KEY

▶ *Start of walk*

Anzac Hwy.

Greenhill Rd.

Glen Osmond Rd.

TIMING A walk past, rather than through, Adelaide's attractions will take only a couple of hours. The South Australian Museum deserves at least 90 minutes, as does the Art Gallery. The more eclectic contents of the Migration Museum repay detailed viewing. In summer, time your visits to indoor attractions such as museums and the art gallery so you are under cover at the hottest time of day.

WHAT TO SEE **Art Gallery of South Australia.** Many famous Australian painters, including Tom Roberts, Margaret Preston, Clifford Possum Tjapaltjarri, Russell Drysdale, and Sidney Nolan, are represented in this collection. Extensive Renaissance and British artworks are on display, and a separate room houses Aboriginal pieces. A café and bookshop are also onsite. ⊠ *North Terr., City Center* ☎ *08/8207–7000* ⊕ *www.artgallery. sa.gov.au* ✉ *Free* ⊙ *Daily 10–5.*

⑨ **Ayers House.** Between 1855 and 1897, this sprawling colonial structure was the home of Sir Henry Ayers, the premier of the state and the man for whom Uluṟu was originally named Ayers Rock. Sir Henry made his fortune from the copper mines at Burra, which enabled him to build this huge mansion. Most rooms have been restored with period furnishings, and the state's best examples of 19th-century costumes are displayed in changing exhibitions. Admission includes a one-hour tour. ⊠ *288 North Terr., City Center* ☎ *08/8223–1234* ✉ *A$8* ⊙ *Tues.–Fri. 10–4, weekends 1–4.*

⑪ **Botanic Gardens.** These magnificent formal gardens include an international rose garden, giant water lilies, an avenue of Moreton Bay figs, an Italianate garden, acres of green lawns, and duck ponds. There's a palm house and the Bicentennial Conservatory—the largest glass house in the Southern Hemisphere—which provides a high-humidity, high-temperature environment for rain-forest species. Free guided tours leave from under the plane trees at the Botanic Gardens Restaurant Monday, Tuesday, Friday, and Sunday at 10:30. ⊠ *North Terr., City Center* ☎ *08/ 8222–9311* ⊕ *www.environment.sa.gov.au/botanicgardens* ✉ *A$3.40* ⊙ *Weekdays 8–sunset, weekends 9–sunset.*

Cathedral Church of St. Francis Xavier. This church faced a bitter battle over construction after the 1848 decision to build a Catholic cathedral. Developed slowly, it is now a prominent, decorative church. ⊠ *Cnr. Wakefield St. and Victoria Sq., City Center* ☎ *08/8210–8123* ✉ *Free* ⊙ *Weekdays 7:30–6:30, Sat. 7:30–7:30, Sun. 6:30 AM–7 PM; services Sat. 6 PM, Sun. 7, 9, 11, and 6; youth mass last Sunday of each month at 6 PM.*

❷ **General Post Office.** Constructed in 1867, this is one of a series of historic Victorian-era buildings on King William Street. ⊠ *Franklin and King William Sts., City Center* ☎ *13–1318* ✉ *Free* ⊙ *Weekdays 9–5.*

need a break? Many locals insist that you haven't been to Adelaide unless you've stopped at a curbside **pie cart** near Adelaide Casino (open 6 PM to 1 AM) or outside the General Post Office on Franklin Street. The floater, a meat pie submerged in pea soup, is South Australia's original contribution to the culinary arts.

❻ **Migration Museum.** Chronicled in this converted 19th-century Destitute Asylum are the origins, hopes, and fates of some of the millions of immigrants who settled in Australia during the past two centuries. The museum is starkly realistic, and the bleak welcome that awaited many migrants is graphically illustrated in the reconstructed quarters of a migrant hostel. ⊠ *82 Kintore Ave., City Center* ☎ *08/8207–7570* ⊕ *www. history.sa.gov.au* ✉ *Free* ⊙ *Weekdays 10–5, weekends 1–5.*

National Wine Centre. The bold design and hi-tech presentation rooms here make the perfect showcase for Australian wines. Taste test some of the best vintages from more than 50 wine-growing areas in the country. ⊠ *Yarrabee House, Cnr. Hackney and Botanic Rds., City Center* ☎ *08/8222-9222* ⊕ *www.wineaustralia.com.au* ⊙ *Daily 10–6.*

4 Parliament House. Ten Corinthian columns are the most striking features of this classical parliament building. It was completed in two stages, 50 years apart, the west wing in 1889 and the east wing in 1939. Alongside is **Old Parliament House,** which dates from 1843. There's a free guided tour of both houses on nonsitting days (generally Fridays) at 10 and 2. ⊠ *North Terr. between King William and Montefiore Sts., City Center* ☎ *08/8237-9100* ⊠ *Free* ⊙ *Daily 8:15–5.*

PopEye launch. Boats travel between Elder Park, in front of the Adelaide Festival Centre, and the rear gate of the Zoological Gardens. There are hourly departures on weekdays; weekends it's every 20 minutes. ⊠ *Elder Park* ☎ *no phone* ⊠ *One-way A$4.50, round-trip A$7.50* ⊙ *Weekdays 11–3, weekends 11–5.*

St. Peter's Cathedral. The spires and towers of this cathedral, founded in 1869 and completed in 1904, dramatically contrast with the nearby city skyline. St. Peter's is the epitome of Anglican architecture in Australia and an important example of grand Gothic Revival. Free 45-minute guided tours are available Wednesday at 11 and Sunday at 3. ⊠ *1–19 King William St., North Adelaide* ☎ *08/8267-4551* ⊠ *Free* ⊙ *Mon.–Sat. 9:30–4, Sun. 12–4.*

5 South African War Memorial. This statue was unveiled in 1904 to commemorate the volunteers of the South Australian Bushmen's Corps who fought with the British in the Boer War. Through the gates behind the statue you can glimpse **Government House,** the official residence of the state governor, which was completed in 1878. The building is not open to visitors. ⊠ *King William St. and North Terr., City Center* ☎ *no phone.*

7 South Australian Museum. The Australian Aboriginal Cultures Gallery in this museum houses 3,000 items in an interactive, high-tech, six-theme exhibition. It's the world's largest collection of its kind. Aboriginal guides lead daily tours and share personal insights. There's also an Indigenous Information Center, an Antarctic explorer Mawson Exhibition, a Pacific Cultures gallery, and a café. ⊠ *North Terr., City Center* ☎ *08/8207-7500* ⊕ *www.samuseum.sa.gov.au* ⊠ *Museum: free; tours A$10* ⊙ *Daily 10–5; tours 11:30, and 1:30.*

10 Tandanya Aboriginal Cultural Institute. The first major Aboriginal cultural facility of its kind in Australia, Tandanya houses a high-quality changing exhibition of works by Aboriginal artists, a theater for dance and music performances, a café, and an excellent gift shop. ⊠ *253 Grenfell St., City Center* ☎ *08/8224-3200* ⊕ *www.tandanya.com.au* ⊠ *A$4* ⊙ *Daily 10–5.*

3 Town Hall. An imposing building, constructed in 1863 in Renaissance style, the Town Hall was modeled after buildings in Genoa and Florence. Free guided tours take place Monday from 10 to noon; reservations are required. ⊠ *King William St., City Center* ☎ *08/8203-7203* ⊠ *Free* ⊙ *By appointment Mon. 10–noon.*

▶ **1 Victoria Square.** This is the very heart of Adelaide. The fountain in the square represents the three rivers that supply Adelaide's water, the Torrens, Onkaparinga, and Murray. Surrounding the square are several stone colonial buildings. Note the three-story **Torrens Building** on the east side.

Zoological Gardens. Adelaide's zoo is small but a world leader in the preservation of endangered species and a pleasant place to see Australian fauna. ⊠ *Frome Rd., City Center* ☎ *08/8267–3255* ⊕ *www.adelaide-zoo.com.au* ⊠ *A$14.50* ⊘ *Daily 9:30–5.*

Around Adelaide

National Railway Museum. Steam-train buffs delight in the collection of locomotive engines and rolling stock in the former Port Adelaide railway yard. The finest of its kind in Australia, the collection includes enormous "Mountain"-class engines and the historic "Tea and Sugar" train, once the lifeline for camps scattered across the deserts of South and Western Australia. Miniature trains run inside the grounds, and an interesting exhibition depicts the social history of the regional railways. ⊠ *Lipson St., Port Adelaide* ☎ *08/8341–1690* ⊕ *www.natrailmuseum.org.au* ⊠ *A$9* ⊘ *Daily 10–5.*

South Australian Maritime Museum. Inside a restored stone warehouse, this museum brings maritime history vividly to life with ships' figureheads, relics of shipwrecks, intricate scale models, a full-size sailing coaster, and slot machines from a beachside amusement park. Lists of past passengers and vessel arrivals in South Australia can be accessed for a small fee. In addition to the warehouse displays, the museum also includes a lighthouse and a steam tug tied up at the wharf nearby. ⊠ *126 Lipson St., Port Adelaide* ☎ *08/8207–6255* ⊕ *www.history.sa.gov.au* ⊠ *A$8.50* ⊘ *Daily 10–5.*

Where to Eat

From gracious restaurants to casual pubs, Adelaide has more eateries per capita than any of the country's state capitals. The city represents all international cuisines and, surprisingly, does so inexpensively. Fresh produce—including fish, local cheeses, asparagus, and olives—is accompanied by world-acclaimed wines. And South Australia's chefs are at the forefront in developing innovative regional cuisine. Hence, menus often change seasonally, and even weekly or daily.

Melbourne, Gouger, O'Connell, and Rundle streets, Norwood Parade, and Glenelg are the six main eating strips. In any one of them, it's fun just strolling around until a restaurant or café takes your fancy.

Cafés

$—$$ ✕ **Paul's on Gouger.** For the finest King George whiting, locals flock to Paul's. Hailed as one of Adelaide's best seafood restaurants, the café serves delicious fare at reasonable prices. Try deep-fried baby prawns with sweet chili sauce as an appetizer before a fish-and-chips lunch. Sit at one of the outdoor tables to enjoy the passing parade. ⊠ *79 Gouger St., City Center* ☎ *08/8231–9778* ▤ *AE, DC, MC, V* ⊘ *No lunch Sun.*

★ **$–$$** ✕ **Universal Wine Bar.** This high-gloss, split-level bar-café with giant mirrors and exposed wine racks along one wall is a favorite of Adelaide's fashionable café society. Stop in for coffee or organic tea, or for a tasty lunch or dinner. The seasonal menu—contemporary Australian cuisine with Asian and European influences—is based on local produce. Wines are sold by the glass. ⊠ *285 Rundle St., City Center* ☎ *08/8232–5000* ▤ *AE, DC, MC, V* ⊘ *Closed Sun.*

$ ✕ **Garage Bar.** Gilded nudes adorn raw brick walls and mirrors reflect exposed beams and pipes in this reborn garage facing Light Square. Asian meets European meets Australian fare in the open kitchen, and the specials blackboard sits on an easel. There's an extensive wine list with quirky descriptions and a pitch out back for playing boccie with a glass in hand. Funky background music by day hints at the after-dark transformation,

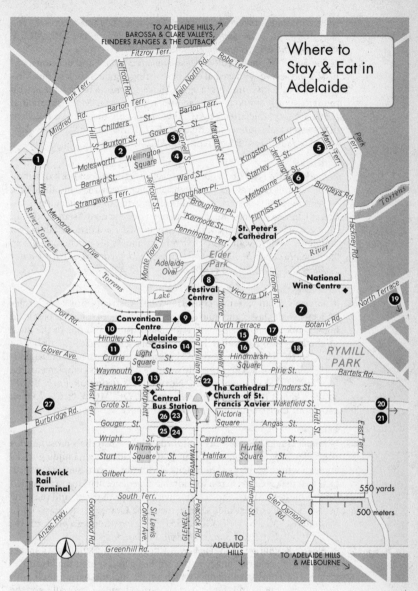

Where to Stay & Eat in Adelaide

when corporate drinkers and diners make way for DJs and dancers. ✉ *163 Waymouth St., City Center,* ☎ *08/8212–9577* ▤ *AE, DC, MC, V* ◷ *No lunch Sat. No dinner Tues.–Sun.*

¢–$ ✕ **The Store.** Aromatic coffee, fresh-squeezed juices, and delicious, un-fussy food served with casual efficiency bring regulars back to this Melbourne Street favorite. It's a great place for brunch—try the bacon sandwich with smoked cheddar and tomato jam. More substantial meals are available after 11 AM. The corner café includes an excellent delicatessen and gourmet supermarket. ✉ *157 Melbourne St., North Adelaide* ☎ *08/8361–6999* ▤ *AE, DC, MC, V.*

Chinese

¢   ✕ **Market Plaza Food Court.** Don't expect sweet-and-sour pork or lemon chicken in this Central Market neighbor. Spicy Vietnamese noodle soups, Korean *bulgogi* (seasoned broiled beef), curries, and challenging traditional Chinese fare elevate it well above your average Asian food hall. Office workers, shoppers, and tourists crowd the Formica tables, yet you never have to wait more than a few minutes for a delicious, cheap meal. ✉ *Moonta St., between Gouger and Grote Sts., City Center* ☎ *08/8212–8866* ▤ *No credit cards.*

Continental

$$ ✕ **Jarmer's.** In an elegantly converted villa, Austrian-born Peter Jarmer perfectly weds classic and nouvelle cuisine techniques using the best local ingredients. Jarmer is a no-shortcuts perfectionist and one of the most original chefs in Australia. Try the scallops galette with carrot beurre blanc, or the juniper berry–glazed kangaroo fillet with herb bread-and-butter pudding. The exceptionally well-priced wine list complements the food. ✉ *297 Kensington Rd., Norwood, Kensington Park* ☎ *08/ 8332–2080* ⌂ *Reservations essential* ▤ *AE, DC, MC, V* ◷ *Closed Sun. and Mon. Lunch by appointment only.*

Eclectic

$$$ ✕ **Magill Estate.** Near the city vineyards where Australia's most famous wine, Penfolds Grange, was created, this pavilion-style building looks across a working vineyard to the city skyline and coast. Sunset is a spectacle that makes eating here a memorable experience. The menu is a showcase of modern Australian cooking with European tones, and the wine list is a museum of Penfolds's finest, including Grange by the glass. ✉ *78 Penfold Rd., Magill* ☎ *08/8301–5551* ⌂ *Reservations essential.* ▤ *AE, DC, MC, V* ◷ *Closed Sun. and Mon. No lunch.*

★ $$–$$$ ✕ **Blake's Restaurant and Wine Bar.** Rustic timber and small, cozy spaces create a wine-cellar intimacy in this sophisticated spot at the Hyatt Regency. The innovative menu—which might include barramundi with orange, cinnamon, and star anise couscous—changes seasonally, and the highly regarded wine list includes some of the finest labels in the country. ✉ *Hyatt Regency Adelaide, North Terr., City Center* ☎ *08/ 8238–2381* ⌂ *Reservations essential* ▤ *AE, DC, MC, V* ◷ *Closed Sun. and Tues. No lunch.*

$–$$ ✕ **The Oxford.** One of the city's most stylish and celebrated restaurants is in the midst of a burgeoning café scene. Light and modern, the Oxford specializes in inventive, beautifully presented Australian dishes with Asian and Mediterranean influences. The menu changes monthly. ✉ *101 O'Connell St., North Adelaide* ☎ *08/8267–2652* ▤ *AE, DC, MC, V* ◷ *Closed Sun. No lunch Sat.*

French

$$ ✕ **Chloe's.** Grand dining, an extensive wine list, and the omnipresent owner and maître d' Nick Papazahariakis define this elegant yet unpretentious restaurant. Georgian chairs, crystal decanters, Lalique chandeliers, and

gleaming silver make every meal an occasion—and often at surprisingly modest prices. The menu is a fusion of French cooking with Australia's best produce; for example, grilled barramundi on sautéed greens, mushrooms, and miso beurre blanc. ⌧ *36 College Rd., Kent Town* ☎ *08/8362–2574* ⌔ *Reservations essential* ▭ *AE, DC, MC, V* ☉ *Closed Sun.*

$–$$ ✕ **Le Zinc Restaurant and Wine Bar.** Opposite the central market, this city restaurant takes its name from the zinc-topped bar. Cuisine is French contemporary—with a changing menu that highlights fresh market produce. And although the aperitifs may be French, the wines are emphatically Australian and available by the glass. ⌧ *41 Gouger St., City Center* ☎ *08/8212–2345* ▭ *AE, DC, MC, V* ☉ *Closed Mon.*

Indian

$ ✕ **Jasmin.** Traditional Indian wood carvings and statuettes, and works by Australian artist Tom Gleghorn, color this celebrated restaurant. Jasmin specializes in Punjabi cooking, and it cellars more than 100 wines from some of Australia's smaller vineyards. The Goan fish curry and butter chicken are highly recommended. ⌧ *31 Hindmarsh Sq., City Center* ☎ *08/8223–7837* ▭ *AE, DC, MC, V* ☉ *Closed Sun.–Mon. No lunch Sat.*

Italian

$–$$ ✕ **Marcellina Pizza Bar Restaurant.** A busy, fun place, this restaurant was the first to introduce South Australia to pizza. Generous seafood, steak, chicken, and Italian specials are also available at reasonable prices. Pizzas can be delivered within the metropolitan district. The restaurant is open daily from 10 AM until 3–5 AM. ⌧ *273 Hindley St., City Center* ☎ *08/8211–7560 restaurant, 13–1967 deliveries* ▭ *AE, DC, MC, V.*

$ ✕ **Amalfi Pizzeria Ristorante.** Along with low prices, bustle, and no-frills setup, this popular bistro holds a few surprises. Specials boards might list risotto, linguine with cockles and mussels, or local oysters baked with chili salsa. Pasta dishes are hearty, and the pizza is fantastic. ⌧ *29 Frome St., City Center* ☎ *08/8223–1948* ▭ *AE, DC, MC, V* ☉ *Closed Sun. No lunch Sat.*

Japanese

$–$$$$ ✕ **Shiki.** Japanese sculptures and elaborate floral arrangements decorate this Japanese restaurant at the Hyatt Regency Adelaide. Four set menus are available in addition to à la carte dining. Unusual dishes include smoked and seared kangaroo fillet served with *ponsu* sauce (a tangy blend of soy sauce and balsamic vinegar), and tempura of barramundi, but you will also find sushi, sashimi, and teriyaki dishes. At *teppanyaki* (grill) and tempura tables, chefs put on a show as they cook—the hot plate on which they prepare the food is part of the table itself. ⌧ *Hyatt Regency Adelaide, North Terr., City Center* ☎ *08/8238–2382* ⌔ *Reservations essential* ▭ *AE, DC, MC, V* ☉ *Closed Sun.–Mon. No lunch.*

Modern Australian

$$$$ ✕ **Grange Restaurant.** World-renowned chef Cheong Liew, who pioneered East–West fusion cuisine in Australia in the early 1970s, works
Fodor'sChoice culinary magic in this establishment at the Hilton Adelaide. It is the best
★ in-house restaurant of any hotel in town. The sometimes surprising meeting of Asian and European flavors, and a complete set of Grange Hermitage wines, creates a set menu experience to delight the most discriminating of palates. ⌧ *233 Victoria Sq., City Center* ☎ *08/8217–2000* ⌔ *Reservations essential.* ▭ *AE, DC, MC, V* ☉ *Closed Jan. and Sun.–Mon. No lunch.*

$$–$$$ ✕ **Botanic Gardens Restaurant.** Decorative fretted timber frames tranquil lake and lawn views from this delightful, century-old place in the Adelaide Botanic Gardens. Some of the finest vintages from South Australia's

smaller wineries partner modern Australian cuisine with Asian and southern European flavors. The set menus include two or three courses with six choices. In addition to lighter lunches, a traditional afternoon tea of scones, jam, and cream is served at the upscale kiosk in the same building. ⊠ *North Terr., City Center* ☏ *08/8223–3526* ⚔ *Reservations essential* ☲ *AE, DC, MC, V* ⊗ *No dinner.*

$$ ✕ **Jolley's Boathouse.** Blue canvas directors' chairs and white-painted timber create a relaxed, nautical air, befitting this restaurant's position overlooking the Torrens River. The modern Australian menu is innovative and eclectic, and changes every eight weeks. Executives with clients make up most lunch crowds, and warm evenings attract couples. ⊠ *Jolley's La., City Center* ☏ *08/8223–2891* ☲ *AE, DC, MC, V* ⊗ *No dinner Sun.*

★ $–$$ ✕ **Grange Jetty Kiosk Restaurant.** Sunlight upon sky-blue and sandy hues blurs the boundary between this restaurant and the suburban beach it overlooks. Couples and families cross town to enjoy the modern Australian fusion treatments of local seafood. Dishes include tiger prawn salad with mango and snow pea shoots, and Tasmanian salmon with goat's cheese pomme purée. This is just the place to discover the joy of South Australian oysters. Breakfast is served on Sunday. ⊠ *The Esplanade and Jetty Rd., Grange* ☏ *08/8235–0822* ⚔ *Reservations essential* ☲ *AE, DC, MC, V* ⊗ *Closed Tues. No dinner Sun.–Mon. June–Aug.*

Where to Stay

Adelaide's accommodations are a mix of traditional mid-rise hotels, backpacker hostels, self-contained apartments, and charming bed-and-breakfasts—many in historic sandstone buildings. City-center hotels are near galleries, shops, museums, gardens, and restaurants, but North Adelaide, a short walk across the Torrens, is quieter. If you're driving, you could base yourself in a beach house or resort apartment around Glenelg, or escape to a bed-and-breakfast in the Adelaide Hills, just a half-hour from the city.

Rates reflect a hotel's proximity to the Adelaide—the more central, the more expensive—and its facilities. Rooms range from clean, comfortable dorms near the nightclub strip to stylish, contemporary lodgings with business services, computers, and health clubs. Adelaide hotels and apartments, in particular, tend to offer specials at weekends. Accommodations should be prebooked for visits coinciding with major festivals and sporting events.

$$$$ 🏨 **Hilton Adelaide.** Overlooking Victoria Square in Adelaide's shopping, theater, and business district, this prestigious hotel exemplifies the Hilton brand. It has two restaurants, including the superb Grange, and a stylish café. Nineteen rooms are fitted for people with mobility problems, and two executive floors have private use of the club lounge, where complimentary Continental breakfast and evening aperitifs and canapés are served. ⊠ *233 Victoria Sq., City Center, 5001* ☏ *08/8217–2000* 🖷 *08/ 8217–2001* ⊕ *www.hilton.com* ⇄ *380 rooms, 10 suites* ⚅ *2 restaurants, café, room service, cable TV with movies, tennis court, pool, gym, hair salon, sauna, spa, 2 bars, dry cleaning, laundry service, in-room data ports, Internet, business services, convention center, car rental, travel services, parking (fee); no-smoking floors* ☲ *AE, DC, MC, V* ❚❘ *CP.*

$$$–$$$$ 🏨 **The Embassy.** Cool modern design is the backdrop for efficient service with a smile at this central hotel. The well-appointed studio apartments all have balconies. Stylish, polished-steel accents set the stage for the contemporary Australian fare in the restaurant. ⊠ *96 North Terr., City Center, 5000* ☏ *1300/551111 or 08/8124–9900* 🖷 *08/8124–9901*

⊕ *www.pacifichotelscorporation.com.au* ⟲ *105 rooms* ⌂ *Restaurant, café, room service, in-room data ports, kitchen, cable TV, pool, gym, wine bar, laundry facilities, car rental, travel services, parking (fee); no-smoking rooms* ▭ *AE, DC, MC, V.*

★ $$$–$$$$ ▦ **North Adelaide Heritage Group.** In the city's leafy historic quarters, luxury meets Australian character in 18 unique properties. Antiques dealers Rodney and Regina Twiss have converted State Heritage–listed cottages, mews, and a manor house into apartments and suites, and filled them with a mix of Australian antiques and contemporary furnishings. Each one- to four-bedroom unit has a bath or spa, sitting room, and kitchen. Most intriguing are the romantic Friendly Meeting Chapel and the Fire Station Inn, where you can sleep near a fire engine. ⊠ *109 Glen Osmond Rd., Eastwood, 5063* ☎ *08/8272–1355* ⊕ *www. adelaideheritage.com* ⟲ *9 cottages, 3 suites, 6 apartments* ⌂ *Some cable TVs, kitchens, in-room data ports, laundry facilities, laundry service; no smoking* ▭ *AE, DC, MC, V.*

$$$–$$$$ ▦ **Novotel Adelaide.** Comfortably furnished rooms, decorated in soft colors, keep within the rich style of the Novotel chain. A cocktail bar in the elegant lobby invites you to enjoy this oasis of calm before stepping outside into the heart of Adelaide's nightlife precinct. Most other attractions are within easy walking distance. ⊠ *65 Hindley St., City Center, 5000* ☎ *08/8231–5552* 🖷 *08/8237–3800* ⊕ *www.accorhotel.com* ⟲ *140 rooms, 41 suites* ⌂ *Restaurant, room service, in-room data ports, room TVs with movies, pool, gym, sauna, spa, bar, Internet, business services, convention center, car rental, travel services, free parking; no-smoking floors* ▭ *AE, DC, MC, V.*

★ $$–$$$$ ▦ **Hyatt Regency Adelaide.** Service, comfort, varied facilities, and a convenient location make this statuesque, atrium-style building Adelaide's premier hotel. Octagonal towers create unusual room shapes—a welcome change from the uniformity of most other accommodations. The best view is from the riverside rooms above the eighth floor. Rooms have high-speed direct Internet access. Extra amenities on the four Regency Club floors include separate concierge service and a complimentary Continental breakfast. The hotel also has three first-rate restaurants: Blake's, Shiki, and Riverside. ⊠ *North Terr., City Center, 5000* ☎ *08/ 8231–1234* 🖷 *08/8231–1120* ⊕ *www.adelaide.hyatt.com* ⟲ *346 rooms, 21 suites* ⌂ *3 restaurants, room service, in-room data ports, cable TV with movies, pool, gym, sauna, spa, bar, nightclub, baby-sitting, dry cleaning, laundry service, Internet, business services, convention center, car rental, travel services, parking (fee); no-smoking floors* ▭ *AE, DC, MC, V* ⦿ *CP.*

$$ ▦ **Medina Grand Adelaide Treasury.** Contemporary Italian furnishings in white, slate grey, and ocher juxtapose 19th-century Adelaide architecture in this stylish hotel on Victoria Square. Cast-iron columns, archways, and barrel-vault ceilings—original features of the former Treasury building—add texture to clean lines in the studio rooms and apartments. The lobby lounge incorporates an 1839 sandstone wall, one of the oldest remaining colonial structures in South Australia. ⊠ *2 Flinders St., City Center, 5000* ☎ *1300/300232 or 08/8112–0000* 🖷 *08/8112–0199* ⊕ *www.medinaapartments.com.au* ⟲ *80 rooms* ⌂ *Restaurant, room service, in-room data ports, in-room safes, kitchens, refrigerators, room TVs with movies, pool, gym, bar, dry cleaning, laundry facilities, laundry service, car rental, travel services, parking (fee); no smoking.* ▭ *AE, DC, MC, V.*

FodorśChoice ★

$–$$$ ▦ **Quest Mansions.** In a handsome, Heritage-listed building between North Terrace and Rundle Mall, these self-catering studios, one-bedroom serviced apartments, and suites are spacious, comfortable, and equipped with complete kitchen facilities. A barbecue and sauna are on the rooftop terrace. The Mansions Tavern in the basement serves counter meals and can provide room service. You can also charge meals back to your room at several local restaurants. ⊠ *21 Pulteney St., City Center, 5000* ☎ *08/8232–0033* 🖷 *08/8223–4559* ⊕ *www.questapartments. com.au ⤴ 6 suites, 6 studios, 33 apartments* ♿ *Room service, kitchens, in-room data ports, room TVs with movies, sauna, pub, baby-sitting, laundry facilities, business services, parking (fee); no-smoking* 🖃 *AE, DC, MC, V.*

¢–$ 🏨 **Adelaide Shores Holiday Village.** The breeze is salty, the lawns are green, and white sand is only a few lazy steps from this resort on the city's coastal fringe. Beyond the dunes is a beach that is rarely crowded, even in holiday season. Accommodations range from two-bedroom stand-alone stilted villas with private balconies to cabin-vans with shared facilities. Adelaide airport is five minutes away, and the city is a 20-minute drive. ⊠ *Military Rd., West Beach 5045* ☎ *08/8353–2655* 🖷 *08/8353–3755* ⊕ *www.adelaideshores.com.au ⤴ 30 villas, 32 apartments, 32 cabins* ♿ *Kitchens, tennis court, pool, wading pool, beach, basketball, billiards, Ping-Pong, volleyball, recreation room, playground, laundry facilities, Internet, free parking; no-smoking rooms, no room phones* 🖃 *AE, DC, MC, V.*

¢ 🏨 **Adelaide Central YHA.** Mostly young people come and go from this purpose-built, city-center hostel like bees around a hive. The bright and airy rooms—family, double, and dorm (6 beds maximum), some with en suites—have metal-frame beds and individual luggage lockers. Cooking is fun in the large, well-equipped communal kitchen, and doors off the huge dining area open onto a balcony overlooking the trees of Light Square. There are TV rooms, recreation areas, and a smoking lounge. Nightclubs, restaurants, and city attractions are close by. YHA members receive discounts off accommodation, tours, and some entertainment. ⊠ *135 Waymouth St.* ☎ *08/8414–3010* 🖷 *08/8414–3015* ⊕ *www. yha.com.au ⤴ 63 rooms* ♿ *Grocery, mountain bikes, billiards, Ping-Pong, shop, laundry facilities, Internet, travel services, parking (fee); no-smoking rooms, no room TVs, no room phones* 🖃 *AE, DC, MC, V.*

Nightlife & the Arts

The Arts

The oldest arts festival in the country, and one that's still groundbreaking, the three-week Adelaide Festival of Arts takes place in February and March of even-numbered years. It's a cultural smorgasbord of outdoor opera, classical music, jazz, art exhibitions, comedy, and cabaret presented by some of the world's top artists. The South Australian Government Visitor and Travel Centre has more information..

The annual, three-day Womadelaide Festival of world music, arts, and dance takes place in early March on stages in Botanic Park and other near-city venues. Crowds can number upward of 65,000.

For a listing of performances and exhibitions, look to the entertainment pages of *The Advertiser,* Adelaide's daily newspaper. *The Adelaide Review,* a free monthly arts paper, reviews exhibitions, galleries, and performances and lists forthcoming events. Tickets for most live performances can be purchased from **BASS Ticket Agency** (⊠ Adelaide Festival Centre, King William St., City Center ☎ 13–1246 Dial 'N Charge).

The **Adelaide Festival Centre** (⊠ King William St., City Center ☎ 13–1246) is the city's major venue for the performing arts. The State Opera, the South Australian Theatre Company, and the Adelaide Symphony Orchestra perform here regularly. Performances are in the Playhouse, Festival, and Space theaters, the outdoor amphitheater, and the Majestic

Theatre at 58 Grote Street. The box office is open Monday–Saturday 9–8 and Sunday 10–6. The Backstage Bistro at the Centre serves modern Australian food.

Nightlife

CASINO Compared with Las Vegas, the action inside **SkyCity** is sedate. All the major casino games are played here, as well as a highly animated Australian two-up, in which you bet against the house on the fall of two coins. The casino complex includes three bars and three restaurants. ⊠ *North Terr., City Center* ☎ *08/8212–2811* ⊗ *Sun.–Thurs. 10 AM–4 AM, Fri. and Sat. 10 AM–6 AM.*

CLUBS Adelaide has a vibrant nightclub and live music scene. Clubs are open weekends and some weeknights from 9 or 10 until the wee hours. Cover charges vary according to the night and time of evening. Nightlife for the coming week is listed in *The Guide,* a pull-out section of the Thursday edition of *The Advertiser,* and *Rip It Up,* a free weekly music and club publication aimed at the younger market.

Adelaide's bright young things generally go nightclubbing along Hindley Street or relax in the trendy cafés of Rundle Street and Gouger Street.

Cargo Club (⊠ 213 Hindley St., City Center ☎ 08/8231–2327) attracts a stylish clientele with funk, acid rock, jazz, and house music. It's open Wednesday, Friday, and Saturday from 9 PM to 5 AM; covers are A$8, A$5, and A$10, respectively.

Heaven (⊠ Cnr. North and West Terrs., City Center ☎ 08/8211–8533) is where the young party crowd dances to contemporary music. Live bands play some weeknights. Doors open Wednesday at 8 PM, Thursday and Friday at 10 PM, and Saturday at 9 PM, and don't close until around 6 AM. Cover charges are A$7 on Wednesday, A$8 on Thursday and Friday, and A$10 on Saturday.

Garage Bar (⊠ 163 Waymouth St., City Center ☎ 08/8212–9577), which is always free, draws well-dressed 25s–35s with funk, groove, and dance music. It's open Monday 10 PM to 2 AM, Thursday 9 PM–2 AM, Friday 10 PM to 5 AM, Saturday 9 PM to 5 AM, and Sunday 4 PM to 10 PM.

Sports & the Outdoors

Participant Sports

BEACHES Adelaide's 25-km (15-mi) coastline from North Haven to Brighton is practically one long beach. There is no surf, but the sand is clean. The most popular spots are west of the city, including **Henley Beach** and **West Beach.** Farther south, **Glenelg** has a carnival atmosphere that makes it a favorite with families.

GOLF One short (par-3) and two 18-hole courses are run by the **City of Adelaide Golf Links** (⊠ Entrance to par-3 course is off War Memorial Dr.; 18-hole courses are off Strangways Terr., War Memorial Dr., North Adelaide ☎ 08/8267–2171). You can hire clubs and carts from the pro shop. Greens fees are from A$15 weekdays and A$18.60 weekends for the north course, A$18 weekdays and A$21.70 weekends for the south course. Daily hours are 6 to 6 April through November, 7 to 6 December through March.

RUNNING The parks north of the city have excellent running routes, especially the track beside the Torrens River.

TENNIS & Just across the Torrens from the city, the **Next Generation Complex** SWIMMING (⊠ War Memorial Dr., North Adelaide ☎ 08/8110–7777) has hard, grass, synthetic, and clay tennis courts, two pools, and a gym, spa, and sauna. Admission is A$55 per day, and it's open weekdays 6 AM–11 PM, weekends 7 AM–10 PM.

Spectator Sports

Venue*Tix (✉ Shop 24, Da Costa Arcade, 68 Grenfell St., City Center ☎ 08/8223–7788) sells tickets for test and international cricket, major sporting events, and concerts.

CRICKET The main venue for interstate and international competition is the Adelaide Oval. During cricket season October–March, the **Cricket Museum** (✉ Adelaide Oval, War Memorial Dr. and King William St., North Adelaide ☎ 08/8300–3800) has 2½-hour tours (A$10) Monday to Friday at 10 and Sunday at 2 (except on match days).

FOOTBALL Australian-rules football is the most popular winter sport in South Australia. Games are generally played on weekends at **AAMI Stadium** (✉ Turner Dr., West Lakes ☎ 08/8268–2088). The Adelaide Crows and Port Power teams play in the national AFL competition on Friday, Saturday, or Sunday. The season runs March to August. Finals are in September.

Shopping

Shops in Adelaide City Center are generally open Monday through Thursday 9 to 5:30, Friday 9 to 9, and Saturday 9 to 5. In the suburbs, shops are often open until 9 PM on Thursday night instead of Friday. Rundle Mall, the main city shopping precinct, and some suburban retailers are open 11 to 5 on Sunday. As the center of the world's opal industry, Adelaide has many opal shops, which are generally in and around King William Street. Other good buys in town are South Australian regional wines and crafts, including excellent Aboriginal artwork.

Specialty Stores

CHOCOLATE Australia's oldest chocolate manufacturer is **Haigh's Chocolates** (✉ 2 Rundle Mall, cnr. King William St., City Center ☎ 08/8231–2844). This family-owned South Australian company has tempted people with its corner shop displays since 1915. Try truffles, pralines, and creams, or Haigh's answer to the Easter rabbit—the chocolate Easter bilby (an endangered Australian marsupial). Hours are Monday through Thursday 8:30 to 6, Friday 8:30 AM to 9:30 PM, Saturday 9 to 5:30, and Sunday 11 to 5:30. You can see chocolates being handmade and taste more produce at **Haigh's Visitor Centre** (✉ 154 Greenhill Rd., Parkside ☎ 08/8372–7077). Free tours run Monday through Saturday at 1 and 2; bookings are essential.

HOME A contemporary craft and design center, **Jam Factory** (✉ 19 Morphett
FURNISHING St., City Center ☎ 08/8410–0727) exhibits and sells unique Australian glassware, ceramics, wood, and metal designs. Creations in the making can be observed in small studios on the premises. For quirky locally made jewelry, pottery, glass, and sculptures, visit **Urban Cow Studio** (✉ 11 Frome St., City Center ☎ 08/8232–6126).

ANTIQUES Antique furniture and decorative arts are for sale at **Megaw and Hogg Antiques** (✉ 118 Grote St., City Center ☎ 08/8231–0101).

JEWELRY & GEMS For high-quality antique jewelry, try **Adelaide Exchange** (✉ 10 Stephens Pl., City Center ☎ 08/8212–2496), near the Myer Center, off Rundle Mall. An excellent selection of opals and other gems is available at **Opal Field Gems Mine and Museum** (✉ 33 King William St., City Center ☎ 08/8212–5300). In addition to an authentic opal-mining display, the museum also has an Aboriginal art gallery and video screenings of opal production. It's open daily and it's free. **The Opal Mine** (✉ 30 Gawler Pl., City Center ☎ 08/8223–4023), a family-run establishment, sells a fine selection of opals and gems.

Malls
Adelaide's main shopping area is **Rundle Mall** (✉ Rundle St., between King William and Pulteney, City Center ☎ 08/8203–7611), a pedestrian plaza lined with boutiques, department stores, and arcades.

Markets
One of the largest produce markets in the Southern Hemisphere, **Central Market** (✉ Gouger St., City Center ☎ 08/8203–7494) also has stalls that sell T-shirts, records, and electrical goods. Hours are Tuesday 7–5:30, Thursday 9–5:30, Friday 7 AM–9 PM, and Saturday 7–3.

Adelaide A to Z

To research prices, get advice from other travelers, and book travel arrangements, visit www.fodors.com.

AIR TRAVEL
International airlines serving Adelaide are Singapore Airlines, Malaysia Airlines, Cathay Pacific, and Garuda Indonesia. Qantas serves both international and domestic destinations. Other major domestic airlines flying into Adelaide include Emu Airways, Regional Express, and Virgin Blue.

🛈 Carriers **Cathay Pacific Airways** ☎ 13-1747 or 08/8234-4737. **Emu Airways** ☎ 08/8234-3711. **Garuda Indonesia** ☎ 1300/365330 or 08/8231-1666. **Malaysia Airlines** ☎ 13-2627 or 08/8231-6171. **Qantas Airways** ☎ 13-1313. **Regional Express** ☎ 13-1713. **Singapore Airlines** ☎ 13-1011 or 08/8203-0800. **Virgin Blue** ☎ 13-6789.

AIRPORT
Adelaide Airport is 6 km (4 mi) west of the city center. The international and domestic terminals are not far apart.

🛈 **Adelaide Airport** ✉ 1 James Schofield Dr., Airport ☎ 08/8308-9211.

TRANSFERS The Skylink Bus costs A$7 and links the airport terminals with city hotels, Keswick country and interstate rail, and central bus stations. The bus leaves hourly from the terminals between 6:30 AM and 9:45 PM and from the city between 6 AM and 9 PM. An extra half hourly service operates from 8 AM to 1 PM Monday to Saturday. Taxis are available from the stands outside the air terminal buildings. The fare to the city is about A$15.

🛈 **Skylink Bus** ☎ 08/8332-0528.

BIKE TRAVEL
Adelaide's parks, flat terrain, and wide, uncluttered streets make it a perfect city for two-wheel exploring. Linear Park Mountain Bike Hire rents 21-speed mountain bikes by the hour or for A$20 per day and A$80 per week, including a helmet, lock, and maps. They're open daily 9–5 in winter, 9–6 in summer, or by appointment.

🛈 **Linear Park Mountain Bike Hire** ✉ Elder Park, adjacent to Adelaide Festival Centre, City Center ☎ 08/8223-6271.

BUS TRAVEL
The Central Bus Station, open daily 7 AM–9 PM, is near the city center. From here, Premier Stateliner operates buses throughout South Australia. V-Line runs interstate and some local services from this terminal. Adjacent to the Central Bus Station at 101 Franklin Street is the terminal for Travel Coach Australia, which is open daily 6:30 AM–9 PM.

🛈 Bus Depot **Central Bus Station** ✉ 111 Franklin St., City Center ☎ 08/8415-5533.

▐ Bus Lines **Premier Stateliner** ☎ 08/8415-5555 ⊕ www.premierstateliner.com.au.
Travel Coach Australia ☎ 08/8231-1701 ⊕ www.mccaffertys.com.au. **V-Line** ☎ 08/
8231-7620 ⊕ www.vlinepassenger.com.au.

BUS TRAVEL WITHIN ADELAIDE

Fares on the public transportation network are based on morning peak
and off-peak travel 9:01–3. A single-trip peak ticket is A$3.20, off-peak
A$1.90. Tickets are available from most railway stations, newsstands,
post offices, and the Passenger Transport Information Centre. If you plan
to travel frequently you can economize with a multitrip ticket (A$20.60),
which allows 10 rides throughout the three bus zones. Off-peak multitrip tickets are A$11.50. Another economical way to travel is with the
day-trip ticket, which allows unlimited bus, train, and tram travel
throughout Adelaide and most of its surroundings from first until last
service. It costs A$6 for adults.

The CityFree buses make about 30 stops in downtown Adelaide and
are free of charge. The Bee Line Bus runs on five-minute intervals around
King William Street Monday–Thursday 7:40 AM–6 PM and Friday 7:40
AM–9:20 PM every 15 minutes; Saturday 8:30 AM–5:30 PM; and Sunday
10 AM–5:30 PM. The City Loop Bus runs every 15 minutes in two central city directions, Monday–Friday 8 AM–8:45 PM, and every 30 minutes Saturday 8:15 AM–5:45 PM and Sunday 10 AM–5:15 PM. Buses have
ramp access for wheelchairs and baby carriages, and they stop at most
major attractions.

Wandering Star is a late-night bus service that operates on Fridays and
Saturdays. From 12:30–4:30 AM you can travel from the city to your
door (or as near as possible) in 11 suburban zones for A$6.

Information about Adelaide's public bus lines is available from the Passenger Transport Information Centre, open Monday through Saturday
8–6 and Sunday 10:30–5:30. Pick up your free metro-guide booklets here.
▐ **Passenger Transport Information Centre** ⊠ Currie and King William Sts., City Center ☎ 08/8210-1000 ⊕ www.adelaidemetro.com.au.

CAR RENTAL

Most of the major car-rental agencies have offices both at the airport
and downtown Adelaide.
▐ Agencies **Avis** ⊠ 136 North Terr., City Center ☎ 08/8410-5727 or 13-6333. **Budget**
⊠ 274 North Terr., City Center ☎ 13-2727 or 08/8223-1400. **Thrifty** ⊠ 296 Hindley St.,
City Center ☎ 08/8211-8788 or 1300/367227.

CAR TRAVEL

Adelaide has excellent road connections with other states. Highway 1
links the city with Melbourne, 728 km (451 mi) southeast, and with Perth,
2,724 km (1,689 mi) to the west, via the vast and bleak Nullarbor Plain.
The Stuart Highway provides access to the Red Centre. Alice Springs is
1,542 km (956 mi) north of Adelaide.

EMERGENCIES

In an emergency, dial 000 to reach an ambulance, the police, or the fire
department.
▐ **Royal Adelaide Hospital** ⊠ North Terr. and Frome Rd., City Center ☎ 08/8222-4000.

TAXIS

Taxis can be hailed on the street, booked by phone, or collected from
a taxi stand. It's often difficult to find a cruising taxi beyond the central business district. Most taxis accept some credit cards. Suburban Taxi
Service is reliable.
▐ **Suburban Taxi Service** ☎ 13-1008.

TOURS

Mary Anne Kennedy, the owner and chief guide of A Taste of South Australia, is one of the most knowledgeable regional food and wine guides. Her private tours are a taste treat and entirely satisfactory. For a behind-the-scenes guided tour (A$30) of the central market, contact Adelaide's Top Food and Wine Tours and ask for the Market Adventure. You can meet stall holders, share their knowledge, and taste the wares. Tours are scheduled Tuesday and Thursday at 10:30 and 1:30, Friday at 10 and 2, and Saturday at 8:30 AM. This is one of several adventures run by Adelaide's Top Food and Wine Tours, which showcase Adelaide's food and wine lifestyle. Tailor-made, high-caliber, private epicurean experiences hosted by respected food authority Graeme Andrews can also be arranged.

The Adelaide Explorer is a replica tram (a bus tricked up to look like a tram) that takes passengers on a city highlights tour, which can be combined with a trip to Glenelg. Passengers may leave the vehicle at any of the attractions along the way and join a following tour. Trams depart every 90 minutes and cost A$25 for just the city, A$30 for the city and Glenelg.

Adelaide Sightseeing operates a morning city sights tour for A$39. The company also has trips to other nearby attractions. For A$42, Gray Line Adelaide provides morning city tours that take in all the highlights. They depart from 101 Franklin Street at 9:30 AM.

Tourabout Adelaide has private tours with itineraries tailored for each traveler. Sandy Pugsley, the owner and chief tour guide, can arrange almost anything you can dream of.

Rundle Mall Information Centre hosts 45-minute free guided walks. The *First Steps Tour* points out the main attractions, facilities, and transport in central Adelaide. Tours depart Monday to Friday at 9:30 AM from outside the booth. Bookings are not required.

🔝 Food & Wine Tours **Adelaide's Top Food and Wine Tours** ☎ 0412/842242 ⊕ www.food-fun-wine.com.au. **A Taste of South Australia** ⌂ Box 250, Adelaide, 5001 ☎ 08/8276-4807 ⊕ www.tastesa.com.au.

🔝 Van Tours **Adelaide Explorer** ✉ 101 Franklin St., next to Central Bus Station, City Center ☎ 08/8231-7172 ⊕ www.adelaideexplorer.com.au. **Adelaide Sightseeing** ✉ 101 Franklin St., City Center ☎ 08/8231-4144 ⊕ www.adelaidesightseeing.com.au. **Gray Line Adelaide** ✉ 101 Franklin St., City Center, ☎ 1300/858687 ⊕ www.grayline.com. **Tourabout Adelaide** ⌂ Box 1033, Kent Town, 5071 ☎ 08/8333-1111 ⊕ www.touraboutadelaide.com.au.

🔝 Walking Tour **Rundle Mall Information Centre** ✉ Rundle Mall and King William St., City Center ☎ 08/8203-7611.

TRAIN TRAVEL

Four suburban train lines serve north and south coast suburbs, the northeast ranges, and Adelaide Hills. Trains depart from Adelaide station. The station for interstate and country trains is the Keswick Rail Terminal, west of the city center. The terminal has a small café and taxis are available from the rank outside. The *Overland* connects Melbourne and Adelaide on Thursday through Sunday. The *Ghan* makes the 20-hour journey to Alice Springs on Sunday and Friday, continuing north to Darwin on Mondays. The *Indian Pacific* links Adelaide with Perth (37½ hours) and Sydney (25 hours) twice a week.

🔝 **Keswick Rail Terminal** ✉ Keswick, 2 km (1 mi) west of city center ☎ 13-2147 ⊕ www.gsr.com.au.

TRAM TRAVEL

The city's only surviving tram route runs between Victoria Square and beachside Glenelg. Ticketing is identical to that of city buses.

TRAVEL AGENTS

American Express and Thomas Cook are two reliable travel agents where you can arrange tour packages, exchange money, and book flights.

🔲 Local Agent Referrals **American Express Travel** ⊠ 122 Pirie St., City Center ☎ 08/8359-2295. **Thomas Cook** ⊠ 45 Grenfell St., City Center ☎ 08/8212-3354.

VISITOR INFORMATION

South Australian Visitor and Travel Centre has specialist publications and tourism brochures on South Australia and especially good hiking and cycling maps.

Sightseeing South Australia is a comprehensive monthly newspaper with features on current events, destinations, and experiences throughout the whole state. It's free at most tourist outlets, hotels, and transportation centers.

🔲 **South Australian Visitor and Travel Centre** ⊠ 18 King William St., City Center ☎ 1300/655276 ⊕ www.southaustralia.com.

THE ADELAIDE HILLS

The green slopes, wooded valleys, and flowery gardens of the Adelaide Hills are a pastoral oasis in this desert state. Orchards, vineyards, avenues of tall conifers and gums, and town buildings of rough-hewn stone give this region a distinctly European look. During the steamy summer months these hills, barely 15 km (9 mi) from the heart of Adelaide, are consistently cooler than the city. To reach the Adelaide Hills, head toward Melbourne along the South Eastern Freeway or drive down Pulteney Street, which, at South Terrace, becomes Unley and then Belair Road. From there, you see the signs to Crafers and the freeway.

Birdwood

44 km (27 mi) east of Adelaide.

☾ Birdwood's historic flour mill, built in 1852, houses Australia's best motoring museum. The **National Motor Museum** is a must for automobile enthusiasts, and it even captivates those usually unmoved by motor vehicles. This outstanding collection includes the first vehicle to cross Australia (1908); the first Holden, Australia's indigenous automobile, off the production line (1948); and hundreds of other historic autos and motorcycles. An interpretative exhibition conveys the impact of the automobile on Australian society. There are picnic facilities and a tearoom. ⊠ *Main St., Birdwood* ☎ *08/8568-5006* ⊕ *www.history.sa. gov.au* ⊠ *A$9* ⊙ *Daily 9-5.*

Mt. Lofty

30 km (19 mi) southwest of Birdwood, via Mount Torrens and Lobethal; 16 km (10 mi) southeast of Adelaide.

There are splendid views of Adelaide from the lookout at the 2,300-foot peak of Mt. Lofty. Much of the surrounding area was devastated during the Ash Wednesday bushfires of 1983.

Mt. Lofty Botanic Gardens, with its rhododendrons, magnolias, ferns, and exotic trees, is glorious in fall and spring. Free guided walks leave the lower parking lot on Thursday at 10:30 during spring and autumn. ⊠ *Picadilly entrance off Lampert Rd.* ☎ *08/8370-8370* ⊕ *www. environment.sa.gov.au/botanicgardens* ⊠ *Free* ⊙ *Weekdays 8:30-4, weekends 10-5.*

A short drive from Mt. Lofty Summit brings you to one of Australia's most unusual parks, **Cleland Wildlife Park.** The main attraction is the native wildlife area, developed in the 1960s, which is divided into five environments with free-roaming animals. You're guaranteed to see wombats, emus, and kangaroos, and swampy billabongs contain waterfowl otherwise difficult to spot. Enclosures protect such endangered species as yellow-footed rock wallabies and Cape Barren geese. Bushwalking trails abound in the park and its surroundings, and guided tours (maximum 20 participants) and two-hour night walks (minimum 12 participants) are available. The daytime tours, in particular, are well worth the fee, as knowledgeable guides show you the area's highlights and share wisdom about the park's plants and animals. Reservations are essential for tours. Note that the park is closed when a fire ban is in effect. ⊠ *Summit Rd.* ☎ *08/8339–2444, 08/8231–4144 Adelaide Sightseeing tours* ⊕ *www.environment.sa.gov.au/parks/cleland* ✉ *A\$12, night walks A\$20, guided tours A\$50* ☉ *Daily 9:30–5.*

Where to Stay & Eat

★ **\$–\$\$** ✕ **Summit.** Spectacular views of the hills, city, and coast across to Yorke Peninsula complement delicious meals in the glass-fronted building atop Mt. Lofty. Chef Paul Cox draws on the surrounding market gardens, farms, and bakeries for his ingredients. The wine list similarly promotes Adelaide Hills wineries. The cuisine, a fusion of modern Australian, French, and Asian, includes such treats as panfried duck breast on sweet potato with fig compote. ⊠ *Mt. Lofty Lookout, Mt. Lofty* ☎ *08/ 8339–2600* ⊟ *AE, DC, MC, V* ☉ *No dinner Mon.–Tues.*

\$\$\$–\$\$\$\$ ⊞ **Grand Mercure Hotel Mt. Lofty House.** This is country living at its finest; a place to enjoy the pleasures of relaxed dining and thoughtful service in an English-garden setting. From a commanding position just below the summit of Mt. Lofty, this refined country house overlooks a distant patchwork of vineyards, farms, and bushland. Guest rooms are large and elegantly furnished. Some have open fires. ⊠ *74 Summit Rd., Crafers, 5152* ☎ *08/8339–6777* 🖷 *08/8339–5656* ⊕ *www.mtloftyhouse. com.au* ⇆ *26 rooms, 3 suites* ⚘ *Restaurant, some in-room hot tubs, cable TV with movies, tennis court, pool, billiards, volleyball, bar, 2 lounges, convention center, free parking* ⊟ *AE, DC, MC, V.*

Mylor

10 km (6 mi) south of Mt. Lofty via the town of Crafers, the South Eastern Freeway, and Stirling; 25 km (16 mi) southeast of Adelaide.

Mylor is a picturesque little village, merely a speck on the map. The wildlife sanctuary in its midst is devoted to the preservation of native animals.

★ ☙ **Warrawong Sanctuary** has no koalas to cuddle, but there's a chance to spot kangaroos, wallabies, bandicoots, and platypuses in their native habitat. To see them, take the daily guided dawn walk or dusk walk (times vary) around this protected 85-acre property of rain forest, gurgling streams, and black-water ponds. Because most of the animals are nocturnal, the evening walk is more rewarding. A seasonal walk-and-dinner package is available, and facilities include a café-restaurant and bush cabin accommodations. Reservations for walks are essential. ⊠ *Stock Rd.* ☎ *08/8370–9197* ⊕ *www.warrawong.com* ✉ *By tour: morning and evening walks A\$22, walk and dinner A\$52.* ☉ *Daily dawn–late.*

Bridgewater

6 km (4 mi) north of Mylor, 22 km (14 mi) southeast of Adelaide.

Bridgewater came into existence in 1841 as a place of refreshment for bullock teams fording Cock's Creek. It was officially planned in 1859 by the builder of the first Bridgewater mill.

The handsome, 143-year-old **stone flour mill** with its churning waterwheel stands at the entrance to the town. These days the mill houses the first-class Bridgewater Mill Restaurant and serves as the shop front for Petaluma Wines, one of the finest labels in Australia. The prestigious Croser champagne is matured on the lower level of the building, and you can tour the cellars by appointment. ⊠ *Mt. Barker Rd.* ☎ *08/ 8339–3422* ⊠ *Free* ☽ *Daily 10–5.*

Where to Stay & Eat

$$ ✕ **Bridgewater Mill Restaurant.** A stylish and celebrated restaurant in a con-
Fodor'sChoice verted flour mill, Bridgewater is one of the best places to dine in the state.
★ Using local produce, chef Le Tu Thai creates a classical Australian menu of fresh, imaginative food as well presented as the surroundings. In summer, book ahead to get a table on the deck beside the waterwheel. If you're feeling flush, ask to see the special wine list. ⊠ *Mt. Barker Rd.* ☎ *08/ 8339–3422* ⊟ *AE, DC, MC, V* ☽ *Closed Tues.–Wed. No dinner.*

$–$$ ✕ **Aldgate Pump.** This friendly, country pub has a lengthy, eclectic menu. The restaurant, warmed by log fires in winter, overlooks a shady beer garden. ⊠ *1 Strathalbyn Rd., 2 km (1 mi) from Bridgewater, Aldgate* ☎ *08/8339–2015* ⊟ *AE, DC, MC, V.*

$$ ⊡ **The Orangerie.** French provincial is the tone of this delightful old stone residence. Gardens filled with statuettes, gazebos, and fountains surround the two self-contained suites. The sunlit one-bedroom suite has an elegantly furnished garden sitting room, which opens onto a private vine-covered terrace. Large gilt mirrors, chandeliers, and antiques furnish the classic Parisian two-bedroom suite. There's an extensive library, and you can star gaze from the hideaway rooftop terrace. ⊠ *4 Orley Ave., Stirling, 5152* ☎ *08/8339–5458* ☐ *08/8339–5912* ⊕ *www.firstpage.com. au/orangerie* ⏎ *2 suites* ♢ *Kitchens, in-room VCRs, saltwater pool, tennis court, boccie, library, free parking; no smoking rooms* ⊟ *AE, MC, V* ⦿ *BP.*

$$$$ ⊡ **Thorngrove Manor.** A romantic Gothic fantasy, Thorngrove deserves its place on the country's prestigious list of luxury hotels. Set amid glorious gardens are seven suites, each with a different configuration and decorative theme. Bejeweled queens, knights, and forest sprites would feel at home amid the antiques and custom-made period pieces. Private entrances ensure you need never seen another guest. Butler service is available, and children receive special attention. ⊠ *2 Glenside La., Stirling, 5152* ☎ *08/8339–6748* ☐ *08/8370–9950* ⊕ *www.slh.com/thorngrove* ⏎ *7 suites* ♢ *Dining room, room service, in-room data ports, in-room safes, some microwaves, refrigerators, room TVs with movies, boccie, croquet, laundry service, Internet, airport shuttle, free parking* ⊟ *AE, DC, MC, V.*

¢ ⊡ **Geoff & Hazel's.** Rough timber doors in a corrugated-iron wall open into three simple double rooms in this hills hideaway designed for backpacker couples and like-minded travelers. Narrow, tree-top balconies invite guidebook reading and there's a colorful shared bathroom. Slab timber tables and bench tops bring the surrounding forest into the communal kitchen-lounge, where you can cook with seasonal vegetables and herbs from the garden. Hosts Geoff and Hazel supply breakfast provisions. ⊠ *19 Kingsland Rd., Aldgate 5154* ☎ *08/8339–8360* ⊕ *www.*

geoffandhazels.com.au 🖵 *3 rooms* 🛁 *Kitchen, laundry facilities, free parking; no-smoking rooms; no room phones, no room TVs* 🖃 *No credit cards* 🍴 *CP.*

Hahndorf

7 km (4½ mi) east of Bridgewater, 29 km (18 mi) southeast of Adelaide.

Hahndorf is a picturesque village that might have sprung to life from the cover of a chocolate box. Founded in 1839 by German settlers, Hahndorf consists of a single shady main street lined with stone-and-timber shops and cottages. Most old shops have become arts-and-crafts galleries, antiques stores, and souvenir outlets; however, German traditions survive in bakeries and a butcher's shop. The village is extremely crowded on Sundays.

The Cedars is the original home, studio, and gardens of Sir Hans Heysen, a famous Australian landscape artist who lived in this area at the turn of the 20th century. Beautifully preserved, the 1920s house is filled with original artifacts, antiques, and an impressive array of the artist's work. The surrounding gardens, where his studio can be seen, inspired many of his paintings. Entrance to the studio and house is by guided tour only. In summer months, daily tours take place at 11, 1, and 3. In June, July, and August, tours take place at 11 and 2. ✉ *Heysen Rd.* ☎ *08/8388–7277* ⊕ *www.visitadelaidehills.com.au/thecedars* 💲 *A$8* ☉ *Sun.–Fri. with tour.*

The **Hahndorf Academy** contains 10 works by Sir Hans Heysen, and holds exhibitions by local artists. ✉ *68 Main St.* ☎ *08/8388–7250* 💲 *Free* ☉ *Mon.–Sat. 10–5, Sun. noon–5.*

Named after the famous landscape painter, the **Heysen Trail** is Australia's longest dedicated walking track. Beginning—or ending—at Cape Jervis, on the Fleurieu Peninsula, the trail wends north for about 1,200 km (750 mi) to Parachilna Gorge, in the Flinders Ranges. Suitable for day walkers and long-distance hikers, the trail passes through national and state parks, and tourist destinations such as the Barossa Valley and Hahndorf. Most sections are closed from December to April because of the high fire danger. For details on routes, equipment, and events, contact Friends of the Heysen Trail (✉ 10 Pitt St., Adelaide 5000 ☎ 08/8212–6299 ⊕ www.heysentrail.asn.au).

Where to Stay & Eat

$–$$ ✕ **Cafe Bamburg.** Cow bells, antlers, and lederhosen festoon this tiny German settler's cottage. Delicious *wurst* (sausage), *kassler* (smoked pork cutlet), meatballs, and other hearty fare fill the plates brought to dark wood tables in the front room and on the narrow veranda overlooking the main street. The choice of German beers is huge, the wine list short. ✉ *81 Main St.,* ☎ *08/8388–1797* 🖃 *No credit cards* ☉ *Closed Mon.–Tues.*

★ $$–$$$ 🏠 **Adelaide Hills Country Cottages.** Amid 200 acres of orchards and cattle pastures near historic Hahndorf, these secluded luxury hideaways are idyllic refuges from the city. Spend an afternoon rowing a boat on the lake beside Apple Tree, an 1860s English cottage. Enjoy the golden glow of Baltic pine in Gum Tree, a pioneer-style stone cottage overlooking a water hole and valley. There's room for just two in Lavender Fields Cottage, a French country-style gem nestled in rolling lavender gardens. All cottages have log fires and whirlpool tubs. Breakfast provisions are supplied. Bookings have a two-night minimum. ✆ *Box 100, Oakbank, 5243, 8 km (5 mi) northeast of Hahndorf* ☎ *08/8388–4193* 🖷 *08/*

8388–4733 ⊕ *www.ahcc.com.au* ⤴ *5 cottages* ⚷ *Kitchens, in-room VCRs, lake, hiking, free parking; no smoking, no room phones* ⊟ *AE, DC, MC, V* ⦿ *BP.*

Adelaide Hills A to Z

To research prices, get advice from other travelers, and book travel arrangements, visit www.fodors.com.

BUS TRAVEL
The Adelaide Hills are served by the Adelaide suburban network, but buses, particularly to some of the more remote attractions, are limited.

CAR TRAVEL
A car gives you the freedom to discover country lanes and villages that are worth exploring.

TOURS
Adelaide Sightseeing runs a daily afternoon coach tour of the Adelaide Hills and historic Hahndorf village (A$43). The tour departs from their offices on Franklin Street.
🚩 **Adelaide Sightseeing** ✉ 101 Franklin St., City Center, Adelaide ☎ 08/8231-4144.

VISITOR INFORMATION
The Adelaide Hills Visitor Information Centre is open daily 9–4.
🚩 **Adelaide Hills Visitor Information Centre** ✉ 41 Main St., Hahndorf ☎ 08/8388-1185 ⊕ www.visitadelaidehills.com.au.

BAROSSA REGION

Some of Australia's most famous vineyards are in the Barossa Region, an hour's drive northeast of Adelaide. Across the two wide, shallow valleys that make up the region are 50 wineries that produce numerous wines, including aromatic Rhine Riesling, Seppelt's unique, century-old Para Port—which brings more than A$1,000 a bottle—and Penfolds Grange, Australia's most celebrated wine.

Cultural roots set the Barossa apart. The area was settled by Silesian immigrants who left the German-Polish border region to escape religious persecution. These conservative, hardworking farmers brought traditions that you can't miss in the solid bluestone architecture, the tall slender spires of the Lutheran churches, and the *kuchen*, a cake that is as popular as the Devonshire tea introduced by British settlers. Together, these elements give the Barossa a charm that no other Australian wine-growing area possesses.

Every winery in the Barossa operates sale rooms, which usually have 6 to 12 varieties of wine available for tasting. Generally, you begin with a light white, such as Riesling, move on through a light, fruity white like a semillon, and then repeat the process with reds like merlot, grenache, and the full-bodied shiraz. Sweet and fortified wine should be left until last. You are not expected to sample the entire range; to do so would overpower your taste buds. It's far better to give the tasting-room staff some idea of your personal preferences and let them suggest wine for you to sample.

Numbers in the margin correspond to points of interest on the Barossa Region map.

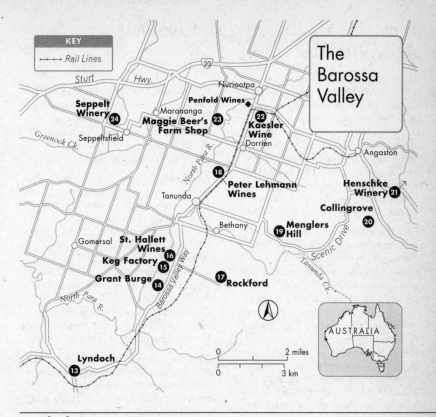

The
Barossa
Valley

Lyndoch

13 *58 km (36 mi) northeast of Adelaide.*

This pleasant little town, surrounded by vineyards—as are most in the Barossa—owes the spelling of its name to a draftsman's error. It was meant to be named Lynedoch, after the British soldier Lord Lynedoch. The town makes a good base for visiting the nearby vineyards.

Where to Stay

$$$ 🏨 **Novotel Barossa Valley Resort.** This complex of one- and two-bedroom apartments nestles in a natural amphitheater overlooking Jacobs Creek and the North Para River. The well-equipped quarters are comfortable and functional, and all have private balconies with vineyard views. Tanunda Golf Course is next door. ⊠ *Golf Links Rd., Roland Flat, 5352, 8 km (5 mi) from Lyndoch* ☎ *1300/657697* 🖷 *08/8524–0100* ⊕ *www. novotelbarossa.com* ➭ *140 apartments* ♨ *Restaurant, café, room service, some in-room hot tubs, cable TV with movies, kitchens, tennis court, pool, health club, sauna, spa, archery, badminton, basketball, billiards, boccie, croquet, Ping-Pong, volleyball, 2 bars, dry cleaning, laundry service, Internet, business services, convention center, travel services, free parking* ⊟ *AE, DC, MC, V.*

$$–$$$ 🏨 **Belle Cottages.** Gardens full of roses surround these classic Australian accommodations. Open fires invite the sampling of a bottle of red after a day in the Barossa region, and brass beds and four posters discourage early rising next morning. In Christabelle Cottage, an 1849 Heritage-listed former chapel, sunlight filters through lead-light windows and a spiral staircase winds up to a mezzanine bedroom. The other cottages have two or three bedrooms, country kitchens, spas, and lounge areas. ⌂ *Box 481, 5351* ☎ *08/8524–4825* 🖷 *08/8524–4046* ⊕ *www.*

CloseUp

THE SHOCKING TRUTH ABOUT AUSTRALIAN WINE

PREPARE TO BE *thoroughly taken aback, or at least a touch startled, as Australia's wine makers meet the challenge of chefs who need wines to work magic with the feisty, spice- and herb-laden flavors of Asia and the Mediterranean in their cooking. Today's lighter, more refreshing wine styles have left traditional wine-and-food–pairing theories dragging their heels in the dust.*

From the wineries of Northeast Victoria, an area known for its full-bodied reds, come some truly remarkable fortified tokays and muscats, all with a delicious, wild, untamed quality that is so rich and sticky you don't know whether to drink them or spread them. Among the more notable varieties are the All Saints Classic Release Tokay, Campbell's Liquid Gold Tokay, and Bailey's Old Muscat. Believe it or not, these are perfect with Australia's distinctive farmhouse cheeses, such as Milawa Gold (North East Victoria), Yarra Valley Persian Fetta, and Meredith Blue (from Victoria's Western District).

Practically unknown beyond these shores is what was once affectionately but euphemistically known as sparkling burgundy, an effervescent red made mainly from shiraz grapes using the traditional méthode champenoise. A dense yet lively wine with fresh, fruity tones, it's suited to game and turkey and is now an integral part of a festive Australian Christmas dinner. Look for labels such as Seppelts Harpers Range, Yalumba, and Peter Lehmann's Black Queen.

Then there are the classic Rieslings of the Barossa Region and Clare Valley of South Australia, first introduced by German and Silesian settlers. Today, wines such as Heggies Riesling, Petaluma Riesling, and Wirra Wirra Hand Picked Riesling are just as much at home with Middle Eastern merguez sausage and couscous as they are with knockwurst and sauerkraut.

Also very Australian in style are the big, oaky semillons of the Hunter Valley (try Tyrrell's Vat 1 Semillon and Lindeman's Hunter River Semillon) and the powerful steak-and-braised-meat–loving cabernets from the rich, red "terra rossa" soil of the Coonawarra district in South Australia. These wines, including Petaluma Coonawarra, Lindeman's Pyrus, and Hollick Coonawarra, have a habit of knocking first-timers' socks off.

As a breed, the Australian shiraz style has delicious pepper-berry characteristics and food-friendly companionability. Not all Australian shiraz carries the now astronomic Grangelike price tags. In fact, other Schubert-inspired wines, such as Penfolds's Bins 128 and 389, are far more accessible, as are a clutch of worthy labels that includes Elderton Shiraz from the Barossa Region, Brokenwood Graveyard Vineyard from the Hunter Valley, and Seppelts Great Western Shiraz from the Grampians in Victoria.

Shiraz is very much at home with modern Australian cooking, working beautifully with Moroccan-inspired lamb, Mediterranean roasted goat, pasta, and yes, even kangaroo with beetroot. Also worth a mention are the elegant, berry-laden pinot noirs of Tasmania and Victoria's Mornington Peninsula (perfect with Peking duck); the fresh, bright-tasting unwooded chardonnays of South Australia (fabulous with fish); and the fragrant sauvignon blancs of Margaret River (excellent with Sydney Rock oysters).

So there you have it. Australian wines have been stopping people in their tracks ever since the first grapes were grown in the first governor's garden back in 1788. If you are about to embark on your own personal discovery of Australian wine and food pairing, get ready to be amazed, astonished, and shocked—into having another glass.

—Terry Durack

bellescapes.com 🖘 *4 cottages* ♨ *Kitchens, in-room VCRs, pool, indoor hot tubs, laundry service, travel services, free parking, some pets allowed* 🖃 *AE, MC, V* 🍴 *BP.*

★ **$$** 🏠 **Miners Cottage.** Among giant gum trees above a billabong, this small, century-old stone cottage consists of a slate-floored kitchen–cum–sitting room, a bedroom, and a bath. Lace drapes the antique bed and trims the tiny windows. A back veranda overlooks a swimming pool in the garden below. The cottage sits on a 66-acre farm in rolling country with a number of fine walks close by. Dinner is available by prior arrangement, and breakfast provisions are included. 🖂 *Box 28, Cockatoo Valley, 5351* ✛ *10 km (6 mi) from Lyndoch* ☎ *08/8524–6213* 🖷 *08/8524–6650* 🌐 *www.minerscottage.com.au* 🖘 *1 cottage* ♨ *Dining room, pool, laundry service, Internet, free parking; no smoking* 🖃 *AE, MC, V* 🍴 *BP.*

Tanunda

13 km (8 mi) north of Lyndoch, 70 km (43 mi) north of Adelaide.

The cultural heart of the Barossa, Tanunda is its most German settlement. The four Lutheran churches in the town testify to its heritage, which is reinforced by the proliferation of shops selling German pastries, breads, and wursts—not to mention the wine—on Tanunda's main street. Many of the valley's best wineries are close by.

🅭 **Grant Burge** is one of the most successful of the Barossa's young, independent wine labels. Wines range from impressive chardonnays and crisp Rieslings to powerful reds such as Meshach. Don't miss the Holy Trinity—a highly acclaimed Rhone blend of grenache, shiraz, and mourvedre. 🖂 *Jacobs Creek, 5 km (3 mi) from Tanunda* ☎ *08/8563–3700* 🌐 *www.grantburgewines.com.au* 🎫 *Free* 🕙 *Daily 10–5.*

🅯 **Keg Factory** uses traditional methods to repair oak casks for wineries. You can watch coopers (barrel makers) working the American and French oak staves inside the iron hoops. Small, handmade port kegs make wonderful souvenirs of the Barossa. 🖂 *St. Halletts Rd.* ☎ *08/8563–3012* 🎫 *Free* 🕙 *Daily 8–5.*

🅰 **St. Hallett Wines** harvests 100-year-old vines for its signature Old Block Shiraz, a classic and fantastic Australian red. This is one of the area's best wineries. Tastings are in the comfortable Old Block Cellar, where a log fire encourages wintertime lingering. Poacher's Blend Semillon and cabernet sauvignon are also good choices. 🖂 *St. Halletts Rd.* ☎ *08/8563–7000* 🌐 *www.sthallett.com.au* 🎫 *Free* 🕙 *Daily 10–5.*

🅱 **Rockford,** nestled in a cobbled stable yard, is a small winery with a tasting room in an old stone barn. The specialties are heavy, rich wines made from some of the region's oldest vines. Several notable labels have appeared under the Rockford name—be sure to try the cabernet sauvignon and the Basket Press Shiraz, outstanding examples of these most traditional of Australian varieties. 🖂 *Krondorf Rd.* ☎ *08/8563–2720* 🌐 *www.rockfordwines.com.au* 🎫 *Free* 🕙 *Mon.–Sat. 11–5.*

🅲 **Peter Lehmann Wines** is owned by a larger-than-life Barossa character whose wine consistently wins international awards and medals. Stone work and an open fire make the tasting room one of the most pleasant in the valley. This is the only place to find Black Queen sparkling shiraz; look for semillon, shiraz, Riesling, and flagship wines. Wooden tables on a treed lawn encourage picnicking on Barossa lunch platters, served daily. 🖂 *Para Rd.* ☎ *08/8563–2500* 🌐 *www.peterlehmannwines.com.au* 🎫 *Free* 🕙 *Weekdays 9:30–5, weekends 10:30–4:30.*

Where to Stay & Eat

$–$$ ✕ **1918 Bistro and Grill.** Housed in a restored villa, this pretty, rustic restaurant makes exemplary use of the Barossa's distinctive regional produce, which ranges from olive oil to almonds to sausages. Don't miss the cleanskin (unlabeled) local house wines. Dine by open fires during winter, or al fresco in the garden in summer. ⊠ *94 Murray St.* ☎ *08/8563–0405* ▭ *AE, DC, MC, V.*

¢–$ ✕ **Die Barossa Wurst Haus & Bakery.** For a hearty German lunch at a reasonable price, no place beats this small, friendly restaurant. The wurst is fresh from the German butcher down the street, the sauerkraut is direct from Germany, and the potato salad is made on-site using a secret recipe. ⊠ *86A Murray St.* ☎ *08/8563–3598* ▭ *No credit cards* ☺ *No dinner.*

★ $$ ⌂ **Lawley Farm.** Built around a courtyard shaded by peppercorn trees, the charming stone cottages here were assembled from the remains of barns dating from the Barossa's pioneering days. The Para Suite—former stables with old ceiling beams from Adelaide shearing sheds—and the sunny Bethany Suite are particularly appealing. A wood-burning stove warms the Krondorf Suite, in the original 1852 cottage with low-beam doors. ⌂ *Box 103, Krondorf Rd., 5352* ☎ *08/8563–2141* ⊕ *www.lawleyfarm.com.au* 🛏 *4 cottages* ♨ *Some in-room data ports, refrigerators, dry cleaning, laundry service, Internet, free parking; no smoking; no room phones* ▭ *AE, DC, MC, V* ⦿ *BP.*

$–$$ ⌂ **Blickinstal Vineyard Retreat.** Its name means "view into the valley," which understates the breathtaking panoramas from this delightful B&B on 20 acres. Amid vineyards in foothills five minutes from the Barossa's heart, the retreat is a tranquil base for exploring. Gardens surround the self-contained lodge apartments and studios, and breakfast is served under the almond tree, weather permitting. You can also indulge in afternoon tea. ⌂ *Box 17, Rifle Range Rd., 5352* ☎ *08/8563–2716* ⊕ *www.users.bigpond.com/blickinstal* 🛏 *6 apartments* ♨ *Kitchenettes, laundry facilities, Internet, free parking; no smoking, no room phones* ▭ *MC, V* ⦿ *BP.*

Shopping

In a double-fronted main-street shop, **Country Cupboard Antiques** (⊠ 69 Murray St. ☎ 08/8563–3155) is a trove of old treasures sourced locally and across South Australia. Time passes quickly among the embroideries, crockery, kitchen implements, baskets, bottles, and countless other collectibles. Hours are Friday through Sunday 10–5.

Bethany

4 km (2½ mi) southeast of Tanunda, 70 km (43 mi) northeast of Adelaide.

The village of Bethany was the Barossa's original German settlement. After establishing the town in 1842, pioneers divided the land as they did in Silesia—with farmhouses side by side at the front of long, narrow strips of land that run down to Bethany Creek. Today Bethany is a Sleepy Hollow, its appearance and character frozen in a past century, and its size and importance eclipsed by the nearby towns.

⑲ Menglers Hill is the best spot from which to view a panorama of the Barossa. Like so much of South Australia, the Barossa suffers from a shortage of rain; in summer the landscape is scorched brown. Only the vineyards, most of which are irrigated, stand out as bright-green rectangles.

Angaston

17 km (11 mi) northeast of Bethany, 86 km (53 mi) northeast of Adelaide.

This area was settled largely by immigrants from the British Isles, and the architecture of Angaston differs noticeably from the low stone buildings of the German towns.

㉑ Collingrove was until 1975 the ancestral home of the Angas family, the descendants of George Fife Angas, one of the founders of modern South Australia. The family carved a pastoral empire from the colony and at the height of their fortunes controlled 14.5 million acres from this house. Today the property is administered by the National Trust, and you can inspect the Angas family portraits and memorabilia, including Dresden china, a hand-painted Louis XV cabinet, and Chippendale chairs. You can also stay overnight at Collingrove. ⊠ *Eden Valley Rd.* ☎ *08/8564–2061* ⊕ *www.collingrovehomestead.com.au* ☞ *A$5* ⊙ *Weekdays 1–4:30, weekends 11–4:30.*

Stephen and Prue Henschke, respective wine maker and viticulturist of **㉒ Henschke Winery,** were named International Red Wine Makers of the Year (1994–95) at London's International Wine Challenge. Taste the magnificent Hill of Grace, a superb red by any standards, and you will understand why Henschke is the Barossa's premium winery. Other great reds include Cyril Henschke Cabernet Sauvignon and Mount Edelstone Shiraz. Their semillon is also excellent. The winery is 4 km (2½ mi) from Keyneton on a passable dirt road. ⊠ *Henschke Rd., 11 km (7 mi) southeast of Angaston, Keyneton* ☎ *08/8564–8223* ⊕ *www.henschke. com.au* ☞ *Free* ⊙ *Weekdays 9–4:30, Sat. 9–noon.*

For a pleasant **drive** from Henschke Winery, turn right into the dirt road and left at the second lane, Gnadenberg Road, along which is the Hill of Grace vineyard opposite the pretty 1860 Gnadenberg Zion Church. Turn left into Lindsay Park Road, passing the famous Lindsay Park horse stud farm, and return to Angaston.

Where to Stay & Eat

★ **\$\$** ✕ **Vintners Bar and Grill.** Top vignerons often meet in this relaxed yet sophisticated restaurant. Its modern, seasonal menus are proudly Barossan and Australian, and complement wines made two minutes from the restaurant. This is the Barossa Region at its confident best. ⊠ *Nuriootpa Rd.* ☎ *08/8564–2488* ⊟ *AE, DC, MC, V* ⊙ *No dinner Sun.*

★ **\$\$\$** ⊡ **Collingrove.** When you wake up in the servants' quarters of this historic homestead, you won't have to do any chores. Antique iron bedsteads, cane chairs, and pine wardrobes give the large, comfortable rooms at the back of the house a delightfully rustic feel. Four of the six rooms have a private bath. The house operates under the auspices of the National Trust and is a museum during the day. Dinner is available by prior arrangement, and breakfast is included. ⊠ *Eden Valley Rd.* ☎ *08/8564–2061* ⊟ *08/8564–3600* ⊕ *www.collingrovehomestead.com.au* ⇆ *6 rooms* ⚲ *Tennis court, library, laundry facilities, Internet, free parking; no smoking, no a/c, no room phones, no room TVs* ⊟ *AE, DC, MC, V* ⊙ *BP.*

Nuriootpa

6 km (4 mi) northwest of Angaston, 74 km (46 mi) northeast of Adelaide.

Long before it was the Barossa's commercial center, Nuriootpa was used as a place of bartering by local Aboriginal tribes, hence its name: Nuriootpa means "meeting place."

㉒ **Kaesler Wine** is one of the area's boutique wineries. Century-old vines underpin the establishment's shiraz and sparkling shiraz, and the cellar door (tasting room) was originally a farm stable. This remarkable little enterprise also has a restaurant serving lunch and dinner and cottage accommodations. ✉ *Barossa Valley Way* ☎ *08/8562–4488* ⊕ *www. kaesler.com.au* ✉ *Free* ⊗ *Daily 10–5.*

Renowned cook, restaurateur, and food writer Maggie Beer is a Barossa personality and an icon of Australian cuisine. Burnt fig jam, quince paste, *verjus* (made from unfermented grape juice), and her signature Pheas-
㉓ ant Farm Pâté are some of the delights you can taste and buy at **Maggie Beer's Farm Shop.** Light lunches are served 12:30–2:30. Wine and coffee are also available. The shop and café area overlook a tree-fringed dam full of fish and turtles. ✉ *Pheasant Farm Rd. (off Samuel Rd.)* ☎ *08/ 8562–4477* ⊕ *www.maggiebeer.com.au* ✉ *Free* ⊗ *10:30 AM–5 PM.*

Marananga

6 km (4 mi) west of Nuriootpa, 68 km (42 mi) northeast of Adelaide.

The tiny hamlet of Marananga inhabits one of the prettiest corners of the Barossa. This area's original name was Gnadenfrei, which means "freed by the grace of god"—a reference to the religious persecution the German settlers suffered under the Prussian kings before they emigrated to Australia. Marananga, the Aboriginal name, was adopted in 1918, when a wave of anti-German sentiment spurred many name changes in the closing days of World War I. The barn at the lower end of the parking lot is one of the most photogenic in the Barossa.

Marananga marks the beginning of a 3-km (2-mi) avenue of date palms planted during the depression of the 1930s as a work-creation scheme devised by the Seppelts, a wine-making family. Look for the Doric temple on the hillside to the right—it's the Seppelt family mausoleum.

㉔ The avenue of date palm trees ends at **Seppelt Winery,** one of the most magnificent in the Barossa. Joseph Seppelt was a Silesian farmer who purchased land in the Barossa after arriving in Australia in 1849. Under the control of his son, Benno, the wine-making business flourished, and today the winery and its splendid grounds are a tribute to the family's industry and enthusiasm. Fortified wine is a Seppelt specialty. This is the only winery in the world that has vintage ports for every year as far back as 1878. Most notable is the 100-year-old Para Vintage Tawny. The grenache, chardonnay, cabernet, and sparkling shiraz are also worth tasting. Seppelt runs a tour of the distillery and its wine-making artifacts. ✉ *Seppeltsfield Rd., 3 km (2 mi) south of Marananga, Seppeltsfield* ☎ *08/8568–6217* ⊕ *www.seppelt.com* ✉ *Free, tour A$7* ⊗ *Weekdays 10–5, weekends 11–5; tour weekdays at 11, 1, 2, and 3; weekends at 11:30, 1:30, and 2:30.*

Where to Stay & Eat

$$$ ✕ **Barossa Picnic Baskets.** Baskets stuffed with meat, pâté, cheese, salad, and fruit make for a perfect lunch outdoors. Each comes with directions to the best picnic spots. A choice of feasts is available, including a vegetarian basket. Phone 24 hours ahead to order. ✉ *Gnadenfrei Estate Winery, Seppeltsfield Rd., Marananga* ☎ *08/8562–2522* ▤ *AE, MC, V.*

★ $$$$ ▥ **Lodge Country House.** Rambling and aristocratic, this bluestone homestead 3 km (2 mi) south of Marananga was built in 1903 for one of the 13 children of Joseph Seppelt, founder of the showpiece winery opposite. Barossa vintages fill the wine cellar, polished timber gleams in the formal dining room, and big, comfortable sofas encourage relaxing in the sitting room, perhaps with a book from the library. The four large guest rooms, off a rear lounge room, are luxuriously equipped and furnished in period style. A bay window seat in each looks out at the garden. Meals make good use of local produce, and breakfast is included. Children are discouraged. ⊠ *Seppeltsfield Rd., Seppeltsfield, 5355* ☎ *08/8562–8277* 🖷 *08/8562–8344* ⊕ *www.thelodgecountryhouse. com.au.* ↘ *4 rooms ⚐ Dining room, tennis court, pool, boccie, library, laundry service, free parking; no smoking, no room TVs, no kids under 16 ⊟ AE, MC, V* ⏣ *BP.*

$$$–$$$$ ▥ **Peppers Hermitage of Marananga.** On a quiet back road with glorious valley views, this deluxe country house hotel has large, modern rooms furnished with style. Each room is named after a different wine grape variety, which influences the color scheme. Four luxury suites have whirlpool tubs and wood stoves. The restaurant, serving innovative regional cuisine, spills onto a garden terrace. ⊠ *Seppeltsfield Rd. at Stonewell Rd., 5352* ☎ *08/8562–2722* 🖷 *08/8562–3133* ⊕ *www. peppers.com.au* ↘ *10 suites, 1 apartment ⚐ Restaurant, room service, in-room data ports, in-room safes, some microwaves, refrigerators, room TVs with movies, pool, lounge, dry cleaning, laundry service, Internet, free parking; no smoking ⊟ AE, DC, MC, V.*

Barossa Region A to Z

To research prices, get advice from other travelers, and book travel arrangements, visit www.fodors.com.

CAR TRAVEL

The most direct route from Adelaide to the Barossa Region is via the town of Gawler. From Adelaide, drive north on King William Street. About 1 km (½ mi) past the Torrens River Bridge, take the right fork onto Main North Road. After 6 km (4 mi) this road forks to the right—follow signs to the Sturt Highway and the town of Gawler. At Gawler, leave the highway and follow the signs to Lyndoch on the southern border of the Barossa. The 50-km (31-mi) journey should take about an hour. A more attractive, if circuitous, route travels through the Adelaide Hills' Chain of Ponds and Williamstown to Lyndoch.

The widespread nature of the Barossa wineries means a car is by far the best way to get around. But keep in mind that there are stiff penalties for driving under the influence of alcohol, and random breath testing occurs throughout the state.

EMERGENCIES

In an emergency, dial 000 to reach an ambulance, the police, or the fire department.

TOURS

Gray Line Adelaide operates a full-day tour of the Barossa Region (A$82) from Adelaide, including lunch at a winery. Tours depart from 101 Franklin Street. Mirror Image Touring Company operates "Classic Times amongst the Vines," a personalized tour of the Barossa. The full-day tour (A$199), hosted by knowledgeable local guides, includes visits to wineries and a three-course lunch. Hotel pickups can be arranged, and one- and two-night packages are available. The Barossa Wine Train is a restored 1950s luxury chartered train that runs thrice weekly from Adelaide to Tanunda. A full-day tour (A$139) is in conjunction with selected coach trips in the Barossa. The day includes lunch and a professional wine guide.

Fruits of Inheritance has private tours with itineraries tailored for each traveler. Rae Grierson, the owner and chief tour guide, can arrange almost anything.

Wine Tours The Barossa Wine Train ⊠ 18–20 Grenfell St., City Center, Adelaide ☎ 08/8212-7888 ⊕ www.barossawinetrain.com.au. **Fruits of Inheritance** ⊡ Box 601, Tanunda, 5352 ☎ 08/8361-8181. **Gray Line Adelaide** ⊠ 101 Franklin St., City Center ☎ 1300/858687. **Mirror Image Touring Company** ⊡ Box 2461, Kent Town, 5071 ☎ 08/8362-1400 ⊕ www.mirror-image.com.au.

VISITOR INFORMATION

The Barossa Wine and Visitor Centre has a small theater, interactive models, and displays. Admission is A$2.50. The center is open weekdays 9–5, weekends 10–4. South Australian Bed & Breakfast Town and Country Association arranges B&B stays in the Barossa Region and other areas across the state.

Tourist Information Barossa Wine and Visitor Centre ⊠ 66–68 Murray St., Tanunda ☎ 08/8563-0600 ⊕ www.barossa-region.org. **South Australian Bed & Breakfast Town and Country Association** ⊡ Box 314, Walkerville, 5081 ☎ 08/8342-1033 ⊟ 08/8342-2033 ⊕ www.sabnb.org.au.

THE CLARE VALLEY

Smaller and less well known than the Barossa, the Clare Valley nonetheless holds its own among Australia's wine-producing regions. Its robust reds and delicate whites are among the country's finest, and the Clare is generally regarded as the best area in Australia for fragrant, flavorsome Rieslings. Almost on the fringe of the vast inland deserts, the Clare is a narrow sliver of fertile soil about 30 km (19 mi) long and 5 km (3 mi) wide, with a microclimate that makes it ideal for premium wine making.

The first vines were planted here as early as 1842, but it took a century and a half for the Clare Valley to take its deserved place on the national stage. The mix of small family wineries and large-scale producers, historic settlements and grand country houses, snug valleys and dense native forest has rare charm. And beyond the northern edge of the valley, where the desert takes hold, there is the fascinating copper-mining town of Burra, which is a natural adjunct to any Clare Valley sojourn.

Auburn

110 km (68 mi) north of Adelaide.

Auburn, the southern gateway to the Clare Valley, initially developed as an overnight halt for wagon trains carting Burra copper ore down to Port Wakefield. The historic buildings of the St. Vincent Street and Main North Road precinct are worth a look for their superb stonework. Auburn was the birthplace of Australian poet C. J. Dennis—the town's Heritage walk passes the home in which he was born. The town's pub serves excellent food.

Jeffrey Grosset established his small, highly regarded **Grosset Wines** in 1981 in an old butter factory. His wines include Polish Hill and Watervale Rieslings, as well as Gaia, a blend of cabernet sauvignon, cabernet franc, and merlot grapes. The vineyard, at 1,870-foot elevation, is the highest in the Clare Valley. ⊠ *King St.* ☎ *08/8849–2175* ⊕ *www.grosset.com.au* ▣ *Free* ⊙ *Sept. (until vintage is sold out), Wed.–Sun. 10–5.*

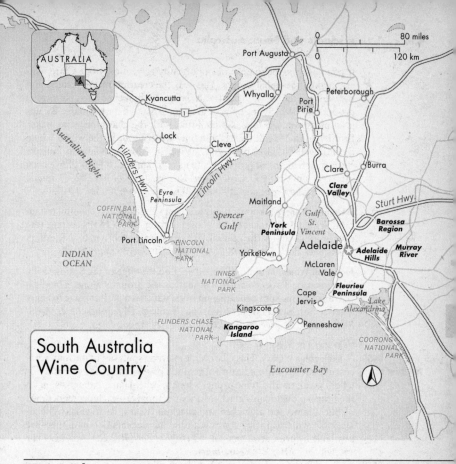

Watervale

8 km (5 mi) north of Auburn, 118 km (73 mi) north of Adelaide.

This tiny hamlet amid acres of vines has a number of Heritage-listed buildings.

🐾 **Crabtree of Watervale** winery, perhaps uniquely among Australian wineries, welcomes children, who are encouraged to explore the property and make friends with its many animals while adults enjoy tasting the vineyard's produce. Tastings and sales are in the original cellars (1870s). The Riesling is especially good, as are the shiraz and cabernet sauvignon. ⊠ *North Terr.* 🕿 *08/8843–0069* ✉ *Free* ⊙ *Daily 11–5, vineyard and winery tour by appointment.*

The cellar buildings of historic **Annie's Lane at Quelltaler** date from 1863. There's a lovely picnic area in front of the cellar. Of greatest interest is the small wine museum, which includes early wine-making equipment. Try the fruity Riesling and full-flavor reds. ⊠ *Quelltaler Rd.* 🕿 *08/8843–0003* ✉ *Free* ⊙ *Weekdays 8:30–5, weekends 11–4.*

Sevenhill

8 km (5 mi) north of Watervale, 126 km (78 mi) north of Adelaide.

Sevenhill is the geographic center of the Clare Valley, and the location of the region's first winery, established by Jesuit priests in 1851 to produce altar wine. The area had been settled by Austrian Jesuits three years earlier, who named their seminary after the seven hills of Rome. They also, rather optimistically, named a local creek the Tiber.

★ If you have the inclination or opportunity to visit only one Clare winery, make it **Sevenhill Cellars.** This was the creation of the Jesuits, and they still run the show. In the 1940s the winery branched into commercial production, which today accounts for 75% of its business. By appointment you can take a guided tour with the charming wine maker Brother John May; it may be the only winery tour in the world where the farewell is "God bless you." Visit St. Aloysius Church, built of stone quarried on the property, and its crypt, in which Jesuits have been interred since 1865. ⊠ *College Rd.* ☎ *08/8843–4222* ⊕ *www. sevenhillcellars.com.au* ⊠ *Free* ☉ *Weekdays 9–4:30, Sat. 10–4.*

Skillogalee Winery is known for its excellent wines and its wonderful restaurant. Wine tasting takes place in a small room in the 1850s cottage (the restaurant occupies the others). Try the shiraz, cabernet, and Riesling. ⊠ *Hughes Park Rd.* ☎ *08/8843–4311* ⊠ *Free* ☉ *Daily 10–5.*

Jeanneret Wines, in a heavily treed area on the edge of the Spring Gully Conservation Park, is worth visiting for the grounds alone. There's a charming picnic spot beneath gum trees, which is a perfect place to enjoy a newly purchased bottle of Riesling or shiraz. ⊠ *Jeanneret Rd.* ☎ *08/ 8843–4308* ⊠ *Free* ☉ *Weekdays 11–5, weekends 10–5.*

Where to Stay & Eat

$–$$ ✕ **Skillogalee Winery.** This Clare Valley darling spills out of the mid-19th-
Fodor's Choice   century cottage onto a beautiful veranda overlooking the vineyard. For
★   a light meal, try the "vine pruner's lunch," chef Diana Palmer's spin on the British ploughman's lunch. More substantial fare includes tender rack of Burra lamb and a chicken and zucchini risotto. Rich whisky chocolate cake with raspberry coulis is a total indulgence. Group dinners are available by prior arrangement. ⊠ *Hughes Park Rd.* ☎ *08/8843–4311* ⊟ *AE, DC, MC, V* ☉ *No dinner.*

$$$$ ⌂ **Thorn Park Country House.** Saved from ruin by owners David Hay and
Fodor's Choice   Michael Speers, Thorn Park is one of Australia's finest dining retreats.
★   Gorgeous antiques fill the mid-19th-century sandstone house and open fires warm the sitting room and small library on wintry days. Bay windows look out on hawthorns, elms, and heritage roses. The cooked breakfasts and dinners define indulgence. David also runs cooking classes. ⊠ *College Rd., 5453* ☎ *08/8843–4304* ⊟ *08/8843–4296* ⊕ *www. thornpark.com.au* ⇨ *6 rooms* ⚹ *Dining room, some in-room VCRs, library, laundry service, Internet, free parking; no smoking, no room phones, no TV in some rooms* ⊟ *AE, DC, MC, V* ⨀ *BP.*

Mintaro

10 km (6 mi) southeast of Sevenhill, 126 km (78 mi) north of Adelaide.

Originally a stop on the Burra–Port Wakefield copper ore route, Mintaro later became known for its enormous slate deposit, which was used internationally for pool tables and locally for building. The tiny town is beautifully preserved; its one street, lined with shops and houses, is Heritage-listed.

More grand than the cottages in Mintaro hamlet is **Martindale Hall.** This gracious manor house, which dates from 1879, was built by Edmund Bowman in an attempt to lure his fiancée from England to the colonies. He failed. Bowman subsequently spent his time buying property and enjoying sport and society, but debt and drought wiped out his fortune, and he was forced to sell the hall in 1891. Decades later in 1965, Martindale Hall was willed to the University of Adelaide. Today it's furnished in period style and doubles as an upscale B&B. The building is featured in director Peter Weir's first film, *Picnic at Hanging Rock.* ⊠ *Mintaro*

Rd. ☎ *08/8843–9088* ⊕ *www.martindalehall.com* ✉ *A$5.50* ⊙ *Weekdays 11–4, weekends noon–4.*

Clare

20 km (12 mi) northeast of Mintaro, 136 km (84 mi) north of Adelaide.

The bustling town of Clare is the Clare Valley's commercial center. Unusual for ultra-English South Australia, many of its early settlers were Irish—hence the valley's name, after the Irish county Clare, and place-names such as Armagh and Donnybrook.

The **Old Police Station Museum** has an interesting collection of memorabilia from Clare's early days, as well as Victorian furniture and clothing, horse-drawn vehicles, and agricultural machinery. The 1850 stone building was Clare's first courthouse and police station. ✉ *Neagles Rock Rd.* ☎ *08/8842–2376* ✉ *A$2* ⊙ *Weekends 10–noon and 2–4.*

On Clare's fringe is **Leasingham Wines,** among the biggest producers in the valley. The winery began operation in 1893, which also makes it one of the oldest vineyards. The tasting room is in an attractive old still house. Leasingham's reputation of late has been forged by its red wines, particularly the peppery shiraz. ✉ *7 Dominic St.* ☎ *08/8842–2785* ⊕ *www. leasingham-wines.com.au* ✉ *Free* ⊙ *Weekdays 8:30–5, weekends 10–4.*

Where to Stay

$–$$ ⊞ **Quality Resort Clare Country Club.** Overlooking the fairways of Clare Golf Course and a tranquil lake, the country club is a place for active travelers who want to sample sports facilities. Several types of rooms are available, from two-bedroom family apartments with kitchenettes to executive units. All have high-quality furnishings and whirlpool tubs. ✉ *White Hutt Rd., 5453* ☎ *08/8842–1060* 🖷 *08/8842–1042* ⊕ *www.countryclubs. com.au/clare* ⇄ *28 rooms, 13 one-bedroom suites, 3 two-bedroom suites, 1 two-bedroom apartment* ⌕ *Restaurant, room service, in-room data ports, in-room hot tubs, some kitchenettes, minibars, cable TV, tennis court, pool, health club, sauna, spa, billiards, bar, laundry facilities, laundry service, free parking; no smoking* ⊟ *AE, DC, MC, V.*

Burra

44 km (27 mi) northeast of Clare, 156 km (97 mi) north of Adelaide.

Burra isn't strictly part of the Clare Valley, but it's an important adjunct to any visit. Burra, like many Australian towns, developed because of mineral wealth. In this case it was copper, which for a time in the early 1850s made Burra Australia's largest inland town, and its seventh-largest settlement overall. The ore ran out quickly, however—the biggest mine closed just 32 years after it opened—and Burra settled into a comfortable existence as a service town.

Today the Heritage Trail leads you to historical sites related to Burra's mining past. The innovative Burra Passport, available at the **Burra Visitor Centre** (✉ Market Sq. ☎ 08/8892–2154 ⊕ www.weblogic.com.au/ burra) makes touring the 11-km (7-mi) Heritage Trail simple and enjoyable. The Basic Passport (A$15 per person) includes a guidebook, map, and key, the latter of which gives access to historic sites, including the Enginehouse Museum, along the Heritage Trail. A Full Passport (A$24)—in addition to the above—allows admission to four museums. The Visitor Center is open daily 9–5.

The **Enginehouse Museum** is in the **Burra Mine Historic Site.** The open-cut, so-called Monster Mine contains many relics of the early days, including a powder magazine, machinery, and chimneys. ⊠ *West and Link-son Sts.* ☎ *08/8892–2154* ✉ *A$4.50* ☉ *Mon., Wed., and Fri. 11–1, weekends 11–2.*

The **Bon Accord Mine**, unlike the phenomenally successful Monster Mine, was a failure. However, the canny Scottish owners made the best of a bad lot by selling the mine shaft, which hit the water table, to the town as a water supply. The old mine is now an interesting museum. ⊠ *Link-son St.* ☎ *08/8892–2154* ✉ *A$3.50* ☉ *Tues., Wed., and Thurs. 1–3; weekends 1–4.*

Redruth Gaol, a colonial prison that later served as a girls' reformatory, houses an informative display on its checkered history. The jail appeared in the Australian film *Breaker Morant.* ⊠ *Tregony St.* ☎ *08/ 8892–2154* ✉ *Part of Passport Key Ticket from visitor center A$15* ☉ *Daily 9–5:30.*

The village of **Hampton** was built for English miners with separate Cornish, Scottish, Welsh, and colonial settlements. The old buildings represent distinct architectural styles. To get here, drive north on Tregony Street from Redruth Gaol and take the first right turn. At the T-junction, turn left into the Hampton parking lot.

Malowen Lowarth is one of several dozen cottages at Paxton Square built between 1849 and 1852 as housing for miners who had moved from the creek dugouts. It's now owned by the National Trust and operates as a museum showcasing period furniture and fittings. ⊠ *Paxton Sq.* ☎ *08/8892–2154* ✉ *A$4.50* ☉ *Sat. 2–4, Sun. 9:30–11:30 AM, and by appointment.*

Market Square Museum re-creates a typical general store and residence circa 1880–1920. ⊠ *Market Sq.* ☎ *08/8892–2154* ✉ *A$3.50* ☉ *Weekends 1–3 and by appointment.*

The **Unicorn Brewery Cellars** are cool and inviting in the desert heat of a Burra summer, even though there's no longer any beer in the house. The 1873 brewery operated for 30 years and was regarded as one of Australia's best producers. ⊠ *Bridge Terr.* ☎ *08/8892–2154* ✉ *Part of Passport Key Ticket from visitor center A$15* ☉ *Daily 9–5:30.*

Clare Valley A to Z

To research prices, get advice from other travelers, and book travel arrangements, visit www.fodors.com.

CAR TRAVEL
The Clare Valley is about a 90-minute drive from Adelaide via Main North Road. From the center of Adelaide, head north on King William Street through the heart of North Adelaide. King William becomes O'Connell Street. After crossing Barton Terrace, look for Main North Road signs on the right. The road passes through the satellite town of Elizabeth, bypasses the center of Gawler, and then runs due north to Auburn, the first town of the Clare Valley when approaching from the capital. Main North Road continues down the middle of the valley to Clare. From Clare town, follow signs to Burra, on the Barrier Highway.

As with the Barossa, a car is essential for exploring the Clare Valley in any depth. Taste wine in moderation if you'll be at the wheel later; penalties are severe for drunk driving.

EMERGENCIES
In an emergency, dial 000 to reach an ambulance, the police, or the fire department.

VISITOR INFORMATION
The Clare Valley Visitor Information Centre is open Monday–Saturday
9–5 and Sunday 10–4.
🖪 **Clare Valley Visitor Information Center** ✉ Town Hall, 229 Main North Rd., Clare
☎ 08/8842-2131.

FLEURIEU PENINSULA

The Fleurieu has traditionally been seen as Adelaide's backyard. Generations of Adelaide families have vacationed in the string of beachside resorts between Victor Harbor and Goolwa, near the mouth of the Murray River. McLaren Vale wineries attract connoisseurs, and the beaches and bays bring in surfers, swimmers, and sun seekers. The countryside, with its dramatic cliff scenery, is a joy to drive through.

Although the region is within easy reach of Adelaide, an overnight stay is recommended to leisurely enjoy all that the Fleurieu has to offer.

You can also easily combine a visit here with one or more nights on Kangaroo Island. The ferry from Cape Jervis, at the end of the peninsula, takes less than an hour to reach Penneshaw on the island, and there are coach connections from Victor Harbor and Goolwa.

McLaren Vale

39 km (24 mi) south of Adelaide.

There are more than 60 wineries in and around this town. The first vines were planted at northern Reynella in 1838 by Englishman John Reynell, who had collected them en route from the Cape of Good Hope. The McLaren Vale region has always been known for its big reds, shiraz, white varietals, and softer reds.

Chapel Hill Winery is a small, somewhat exclusive vineyard, with the tasting room in an old hilltop chapel. Wines include rich shiraz and cabernet sauvignon, as well as a notable chardonnay and verdelho. ✉ *Chapel Hill Rd.* ☎ *08/8323-8429* ⊕ *www.chapelhillwine.com.au* ✉ *Free* ⊙ *Daily noon-5.*

At **d'Arenberg Wines,** family-run since 1912, excellent wine is complemented by a fine restaurant. Wine maker Chester d'Arenberg Osborn is known for his quality whites, including the Noble Riesling (botrytis affected)—a luscious dessert wine—and powerful reds and fortified wines. Reservations are recommended for dining at D'Arry's Verandah restaurant, which overlooks the vineyards, the valley, and the sea. The menu uses local produce and changes seasonally. Lunch is served daily. ✉ *Osborn Rd.* ☎ *08/8323-8206* ⊕ *www.darenberg.com.au* ✉ *Free* ⊙ *Daily 10-5.*

McLaren Vale's most historic winery is **Rosemount Estates,** which has vines dating from 1850. You can stroll around the winery, its historic buildings, and the old, carved vats lining the large tasting room, but there are no organized tours. A superb selection of reds and whites, including fantastic sparkling wines, are on sale. ✉ *Chaffey's Rd.* ☎ *08/8323-8250* ⊕ *www.rosemountestates.com* ✉ *Free* ⊙ *Mon.–Sat. 10-5, Sun. 11-4.*

The cellars at **Wirra Wirra Vineyards** were built in 1894, and they couldn't be more appealing than in winter, when a roaring fire is burning. Try Riesling, cabernet sauvignon, shiraz, the good-value Church Block Dry Red, and a *méthode champenoise* white. ✉ *McMurtrie Rd.* ☎ *08/8323-8414* ⊕ *www.wirra.com.au* ✉ *Free* ⊙ *Mon.–Sat. 10-5, Sun. 11-5.*

Where to Stay & Eat

$$ ✕ **Salopian Inn.** First licensed in 1851, this former inn and celebrated restaurant overlooks rolling vineyards in the heart of McLaren Vale. Fresh local produce is used to create such seasonal treats as roasted duck with spiced cherries and salted spinach, and blue cheese soufflé with caramelized figs and walnuts. There's no wine list—pick from the well-stocked basement cellar. ✉ *Corner Willunga and McMurtrie Rds.* ☎ *08/8323–8769* ⊟ *AE, DC, MC, V* ⊘ *No lunch Wed. No dinner Sun.–Thurs.*

★ ¢–$ ✕ **Market 190.** With its worn floorboards and pressed metal ceilings, this café-shop feels like a country corner store. Bottled olive oil and relishes line the shelves, and cakes and cheeses fill the glass-fronted counter. You can read a magazine over coffee and buy a bunch of flowers on the way out. The menu shows off the Fleurieu Peninsula produce: for a taste of McLaren Vale, order a regional platter. To finish, try a raspberry tartlet served with cream and shredded lime rind. ✉ *190 Main Rd.,* ☎ *08/ 8323–8558* ⊟ *AE, DC, MC, V.*

$–$$$ ▦ **Willunga House B&B.** This grand, State Heritage–listed Georgian stone residence was once the town's post office and general store. Polished parquet floors, pressed metal ceilings, and marble fireplaces are among the restored, original features. Five bedrooms have old brass and iron beds. In winter, a fire blazes in the large, communal sitting room, which opens onto the first-floor balcony. Come hungry to the hearty complimentary breakfast, made with produce fresh from the organic garden. This is an excellent base for touring the region, as it's 7 km (4½ mi) south of McLaren Vale. ✉ *1 St. Peter's Terr., Willunga, 5172,* ☎ *08/8556–2467* ⊟ *08/8556–2465* ⊕ *www.willungahouse.com.au* ⊃ *5 rooms* ⟳ *Dining room, pool, massage, laundry service, Internet, free parking; no smoking, no a/c in some rooms, no room phones, no kids* ⊟ *MC, V* ⊗ *BP.*

Shopping

Old barrels, masterpieces of the cooper's trade, lend character to the **Dridan Fine Arts & Fleurieu Showcase** (✉ Main Rd. ☎ 08/8323–9866). On show in this cavernous shed at Hardy's Tintara winery are paintings, handmade musical instruments, wood and metal sculptures, glass platters, colorful ceramics, painted silk, and glorious bejeweled cats. Hours are 10–5 daily.

Goolwa

44 km (27 mi) southeast of McLaren Vale, 83 km (51 mi) south of Adelaide.

Beautifully situated near the mouth of the mighty Murray River, Goolwa grew fat on the river paddle-steamer trade in the 19th century. At one point it boasted 88 pubs. Today its envious position close to the sea, Lake Alexandrina, and the lovely Coorong National Park has seen tourist business replace river trade as the main source of income. South Australia's first railway line was built to Port Elliott, Goolwa's seaport, in 1854.

Today **Goolwa Wharf** is the launching place for daily tour cruises. The MV *Aroona* departs Goolwa on three-hour trips (A$29) to the Murray mouth. You can add on an optional lunch (A$12), or take a pelican-feeding cruise (A$19). The *Spirit of the Coorong*, a fully equipped motorboat, has an all-day cruise (A$84) to Coorong National Park that includes a guided walk, lunch, and afternoon tea. ✉ *Goolwa Wharf* ☎ *08/ 8555–2203, 1800/442203 for tour cruises.*

The *Wetlands Explorer,* a modern shallow-draft boat with an aft deck, has three day tours, including one to Coorong National Park (A$85).

It departs from Hindmarsh Island. ☒ *Marina Hindmarsh Island* ☎ *08/ 8555–1133.*

Goolwa is also the home port of paddle steamer *Oscar W.* Built in 1908, this boat holds the record for bringing the most bales of wool (2,500) down the Darling River, which flows into the Murray River. When not participating in commemorative cruises and paddleboat races (no public passengers), the boat is open for touring. ☒ *Goolwa Wharf* ☎ *08/ 8555–1144 tourist office* ☒ *Donations accepted.*

Signal Point is an excellent interpretive center that uses audiovisual techniques, artifacts, models, and interactive displays to demonstrate historical and environmental aspects of the Murray River. Other exhibits include stories of the indigenous Ngarrindjeri people and the river trade. There is also a Tourist and Information Booking Centre and a café. ☒ *Goolwa Wharf* ☎ *08/8555–1144 tourist office* ☒ *A$5.50* ☻ *Daily 9–5.*

Coorong National Park (☒ 34 Princes Hwy., Meningie ☎ 08/8575–1200), a sliver of land stretching southeast of the Fleurieu Peninsula and completely separate from it, hugs the South Australian coast for more than 150 km (93 mi). Most Australians became aware of the Coorong's beauty from the 1970s film *Storm Boy,* which told the story of a boy's friendship with a pelican. These curious birds are one reason why the Coorong is a wetland area of world standing. The mainland side of the park, which you can reach driving straight from Adelaide, is off of Princes Highway south of the fishing town of Meningie.

This conservation area and national park is under the jurisdiction of the National Parks and Wildlife South Australia. Thus, there are no opening and closing times—you can visit anytime as long as you drive on the designated tracks. If you'd like to camp, you must first get a permit (A$6 per vehicle per night) from the park office.

Where to Stay

$$ 🏨 **PS** *Federal.* Nestled among reeds beside a bird sanctuary south of town,
Fodor's Choice this century-old paddle steamer could be moored miles from anywhere.
★ Swallows nest under the eaves and pelicans cruise by the deck, while picture windows in the main lounge frame tranquil views of Goolwa and Hindmarsh Island. Louvred windows let cooling breezes into the two tiny top-deck bedrooms, once the domain of the captain. A blue-and-white theme extends into the kitchen, where you'll find full breakfast provisions. Power is limited—there is a TV, CD player, and radio, but hairdryers and electric shavers drain the batteries. The wind generator beside the boat can be noisy on gusty days. ☒ *Off Barrage Rd.* ☎ *08/ 8223–3330 or 0414/821613* 🖶 *08/8223–3330* ⊕ *www.weblogic.com. au/goolwagetaways* ☞ *2 rooms* ♨ *Kitchen, free parking; no a/c, no phones, no room TVs* ▤ *MC, V* ⦿ *BP.*

$ 🏨 **Hays Street Cottage.** Calico curtains, *coir* (coconut-fiber) mats, and sky-blue furniture bring the sea inside this airy house opposite Goolwa's historic wharf. Stripped timbers lend the kitchen a weathered charm; the old fridge could have washed up in a storm. A potbelly stove in the adjoining sitting room provides winter warmth. Off the sitting room are two simply furnished double bedrooms that share a bathroom. ☒ *4 Hays St.* ☎ *08/8555–5557* ☞ *liz@granite.net.au* ☞ *2 rooms* ♨ *Kitchen, free parking; no a/c, no room phones, no room TVs* ▤ *MC, V* ⦿ *BP.*

Victor Harbor

16 km (10 mi) west of Goolwa, 83 km (51 mi) south of Adelaide.

In some ways, Victor Harbor has come full circle. In the 1830s the site was a major whaling center, from which whalers set out to hunt the southern right whale. The species was so named because it was considered the "right" whale to kill—it was slow and easy to target, and its flesh had a high oil content that caused the whale to float after being harpooned. The leviathans came to Encounter Bay, named for the meeting here in 1802 of English and French explorers Matthew Flinders and Nicolas Baudin, to breed in the winter and early spring. Their great numbers made whaling a profitable trade, but the last whale was killed in the bay in 1878. Within that 50-year period the southern right was hunted nearly to extinction. Now the majestic creatures are back—as many as 60 in a season—and Victor Harbor is again capitalizing on their presence, this time for tourism purposes.

The **South Australian Whale Center** tells the often graphic story of the whaling industry along the South Australia coast, particularly in Encounter Bay. Excellent interpretive displays spread over three floors focus on dolphins, seals, penguins, and whales—all of which can be seen in these waters. In whale-watching season (May–October), the center has a 24-hour information hot line on sightings. Children enjoy the Discovery Trail and craft area. ⊠ *2 Railway Terr.* ☎ *08/8552–5644, 1900/931223 whale information* ⊕ *www.webmedia.com.au/whales* ⊠ *A$5.50* ☉ *Daily 11–4:30.*

Visit the **Bluff,** a few km west of Victor Harbor, to see where whalers once stood lookout for their prey. Today the granite outcrop, also known as Rosetta Head, serves the same purpose in very different circumstances. To enjoy views from the Bluff, it's a steep climb to the top. Cycling enthusiasts should try the **Encounter Bikeway,** a track that runs from the Bluff along a scenic coastal route to Goolwa.

Granite Island is linked to the mainland by a causeway, along which trundles a double-decker tram pulled by Clydesdale horses. A self-guided walk leads to the island's summit. Inside Granite Island Nature Park, a penguin interpretive center runs guided tours to view the large, native colony of little penguins. There are also dolphin cruises, whale-watching cruises (from May–October), a shark oceanarium, a kiosk, and a bistro with deck dining overlooking the harbor and ocean. Access to the oceanarium is by boats that depart hourly. Penguin Centre tours depart daily at dusk and take 1½ hours. The Dolphin Cruise departs daily at 2 and lasts 1½ hours. The 2½-hour whale-watching cruises operate daily May–October. ⊠ *Granite Island* ☎ *08/8552–7555* ⊠ *Return tram trip A$6, penguin tours A$10, oceanarium A$15, dolphin cruises A$40, whale-watching cruises A$55* ☉ *Interpretive center daily 11:30–dusk, oceanarium weekdays noon–dusk, weekends 1–dusk (subject to weather).*

The steam-powered **Cockle Train** travels the original route of South Australia's first railway line on its journey to Goolwa. Extended from Port Elliot to Victor Harbor in 1864, the line traces the lovely Southern Ocean beaches on its 16-km (10-mi) route. The train runs by steam power daily during Easter and school holidays. A diesel locomotive pulls the heritage passenger cars Sundays and public holidays. ⊠ *Railway Terr.* ☎ *08/8231–4366* ⊕ *www.steamranger.org.au* ⊠ *Round-trip A$22.*

Head to **Urimbirra Wildlife Park** if you feel like gawking at a menagerie of native Ozzie animals and birds, more than 70 species in all. Among the collection at this open-range zoo are kangaroos, saltwater and freshwater crocodiles, Cape Barren geese, and pelicans. ⊠ *Adelaide Rd.* ☎ *08/8554–6554* ⊕ *http://users.chariot.net.au/~wildlife* ⊠ *A$8* ☉ *Daily 9–6.*

Where to Stay

¢ ⌦ **Hotel Grosvenor.** This quintessential Australian country hotel is a welcome port of call after a day of maritime adventures. Neatly renovated first-floor bedrooms—double, family, and backpacker-sizes—share four basic bathrooms. Club chairs encourage socializing over free tea and coffee in the communal TV lounge. From the balcony you can look down Victor Harbor's main street to Encounter Bay. Locals often crowd the public bar and restaurant downstairs. ⊠ *Cnr. Coral and Ocean Sts.* ☎ *08/8552–1011* ⓕ *08/8552–7274* ✍ *grosvenor@granite. net.au* ↪ *32 rooms* ⌂ *Restaurant, bar, free parking; no a/c, no room phones, no room TVs* ⊟ *MC, V.*

Fleurieu Peninsula A to Z

To research prices, get advice from other travelers, and book travel arrangements, visit www.fodors.com.

CAR TRAVEL

Renting a car in Adelaide and driving south is the best means by which to visit the Fleurieu Peninsula, especially if you wish to tour the wineries, which aren't served by public transport.

The Fleurieu is an easy drive south from Adelaide. McLaren Vale itself is less than an hour away. Leave central Adelaide along South Terrace or West Terrace, linking with the Anzac Highway, which heads toward Glenelg. At the intersection with Main South Road, turn left. This road takes you almost to McLaren Vale. After a detour to visit the wineries, watch for signs for Victor Harbor Road. About 20 km (12 mi) south, the highway splits. One road heads for Victor Harbor, the other for Goolwa. Those two places are connected by a major road that follows the coastline. Drivers heading to Cape Jervis and the Kangaroo Island ferry should stay on Main South Road.

EMERGENCIES

In an emergency, dial **000** to reach an ambulance, the police, or the fire department.

VISITOR INFORMATION

Inside the Victor Harbor Visitor Information Center, open daily 9–5, try the Fleurieu and Kangaroo Island Booking Centre for planning tours and accommodations. The large, open-plan McLaren Vale and Fleurieu Visitor Centre in the heart of the vineyards resembles a winery. In addition to tourist information, it has a café and wine bar, and a wine interpretative counter. The center is open daily 9–5.

🖪 Tourist Information **Fleurieu and Kangaroo Island Booking Centre** ⊠ The Causeway, Victor Harbor ☎ 08/8552–7000 or 1800/088552. **McLaren Vale and Fleurieu Visitor Centre** ⊠ Main St., McLaren Vale ☎ 08/8323–9944. **Victor Harbor Visitor Information Centre** ⊠ The Causeway, Victor Harbor ☎ 08/8552–5738.

KANGAROO ISLAND

Kangaroo Island, Australia's third largest (next to Tasmania and Melville), is barely 16 km (10 mi) from the Australian mainland. Yet the island belongs to another age—a folksy, friendly, less sophisticated time when you'd leave your car unlocked and wave to other drivers as they passed.

The island's interior is stark and barren, interspersed with bush and farmland, but the coastline is sculpted into a series of bays and inlets teeming with bird and marine life. Wildlife is probably the island's greatest attraction. In a single day you can stroll along a beach crowded with sea lions and watch kangaroos, koalas, pelicans, sea eagles, and little penguins in their native environment.

Many people treasure Kangaroo Island for what it lacks. Although it's just two-hour's drive from Adelaide (30 minutes by air), there are few resorts and virtually no nightlife. Its main luxuries are salty sea breezes, sparkling clear water, solitude, and food—local marron (crayfish), yabbies, seafood, corn-fed chicken, lamb, honey, and cheese. Eucalyptus oil–based products are also produced here, and the island has several wineries.

The towns and most of the accommodations are in the eastern third of the island. The most interesting sights are on the southern coast, so it's advisable to tour the island in a clockwise direction, leaving the beaches of the north coast for later in the day. Before heading out, fill your gas tank and pack a picnic lunch.

At the start of your journey, purchase an Island Parks Pass (A$32), available from any National Parks and Wildlife site on the island, or from the **National Parks and Wildlife SA Office** (⊠ 37 Dauncey St., Kingscote ☎ 08/8553–2381 ⊕ www.environment.sa.gov.au/parks/parks.html). The pass covers a selection of guided tours and park entry fees (except camping) and is valid for a year.

Kingscote

121 km (75 mi) southwest of Adelaide.

The largest town on Kangaroo Island, Kingscote is a good travel base. Reeves Point, at the northern end of town, marks the beginning of South Australia's colonial history. Settlers landed here in 1836 and established the first official town in the new colony. Little remains of the original settlement except Hope Cottage, now a small museum with a huge mulberry tree—locals still use the fruit to make jam. The settlement was abandoned barely three years after it began, due to poor soil and a lack of fresh water. The town comes alive in mid-February for a weekend of horse races.

Where to Stay & Eat

$–$$ ✕ **Samphire.** This sun-filled, minimalist restaurant near Cape Willoughby Lightstation overlooks the spectacular northeast coastline and Backstairs Passage. Fresh local produce, simply prepared, is an extra delight. Try the Kangaroo Island *marron* (freshwater crayfish) roasted with lemon butter. A set-menu dinner reigns on Saturday nights. ⊠ *Willoughby Rd., 44 km (28 mi) from Kingscote, Cape Willoughby* ☎ *08/8553–1333* ⌂ *Reservations essential for Sat. dinner.* ▤ *No credit cards* ⊘ *Closed Mon.–Wed. No dinner Sun.–Fri.*

$–$$ ✕▥ **Kangaroo Island Lodge.** The island's oldest resort faces beautiful Eastern Cove at American River. Rooms overlook open water or the saltwater pool; the most attractive are the "water view" rooms, which have rammed earth walls, warming terra-cotta tones, and king-size beds. The restaurant, one of the island's best, makes use of fresh seafood and other local produce. It's 39 km (24 mi) southeast of Kingscote. ⊡ *Box 232, American River, 5221* ☎ *1800/355581 or 08/8553–7053* ▤ *08/ 8553–7030* ⊕ *www.kilodge.com.au* ⬌ *38 rooms* ⌂ *Restaurant, some kitchens, tennis court, pool, sauna, bar, playground, laundry facilities, travel services, free parking; no smoking* ▤ *AE, DC, MC, V.*

$–$$ ✕▥ **Kangaroo Island Seafront.** This hotel near the ferry terminal sits in an ideal position overlooking Penneshaw Bay. Stay in an ocean-view room, or amid tropical gardens in free-standing chalets and two- and three-bedroom, self-contained cottages. The restaurant, which spills out onto a seafront terrace, serves fresh, local produce. ✉ *49 North Terr., Penneshaw, 5222* ☎ *08/8553–1028* 🖷 *08/8553–1204* ⊕ *www.seafront.com.au* ☞ *12 rooms, 6 chalets, 3 cottages* ⚘ *Restaurant, some kitchenettes, tennis court, pool, sauna, bar, laundry facilities, free parking* ▤ *AE, DC, MC, V.*

$ ✕▥ **Ozone Seafront Hotel.** The handsome Victorian exterior hides surprisingly modern rooms above either the ocean or the pool. One popular room is supposedly haunted by the original publican, who died just after his beloved premises burned down in 1918. Seafront views and a 15-minute journey to the airport make it a favorite. ✉ *The Foreshore, 5223* ☎ *08/8553–2011 or 1800/083133* 🖷 *08/8553–2249* ⊕ *www.ozonehotel.com* ☞ *37 rooms* ⚘ *Restaurant, café, room TVs with movies, pool, sauna, spa, 3 bars, laundry facilities, car rental, travel services, free parking; no-smoking rooms* ▤ *AE, DC, MC, V.*

$$–$$$ ▥ **Acacia Apartments.** Self-contained one- and two-bedroom units are available at this Reeve's Point complex. Additional facilities are available for families, travelers with disabilities, senior citizens, and those with allergies. There is convention space for up to 60 guests. Four-wheel-drive tours can be arranged. The state's first British colonial settlement, Reeve's Point, is ½ km (¼ mi) down the hill. Book two nights or more for reduced rates. ✉ *3–5 Rawson St., 5223* ☎ *08/8553–0088 or 1800/247007* 🖷 *08/8553–0008* ⊕ *www.acacia-apartments.com.au* ☞ *8 apartments, 2 suites* ⚘ *Kitchens, some in-room hot tubs, in-room VCRs, indoor pool, spa, playground, laundry facilities, travel services, free parking; no smoking* ▤ *AE, DC, MC, V.*

$$–$$$ ▥ **Correa Corner.** Named after an indigenous flowering plant, this luxurious, owner-hosted B&B nestles in a rambling mix of native and formal gardens. Lace and lead lights add romantic touches to the deluxe rooms. You can even book dinner by candlelight. Enjoy the company of wallabies in the garden. It's 2 km (1 mi) from Kingscote. ✉ *The Parade and 2nd St. (Box 232), Brownlow, 5223* ☎ *08/8553–2498* 🖷 *08/8553–2355* ⊕ *www.correacorner.com.au* ☞ *3 rooms* ⚘ *Dining room, bicycles, bar, library, laundry service, Internet, travel services, free parking; no smoking, no kids (under 12)* ▤ *MC, V* ⦿| *BP.*

$$ ▥ **The Kings.** This hillside boutique B&B captures the style and natural beauty of its surroundings. The spacious, modern suite has three bright rooms. Its private entrance opens into a lush garden courtyard and veranda; there's also a secluded pool. Traditional, full breakfasts are served in the sunny conservatory, from where you can take in stunning river views. ⌂ *Bayview Rd., Box 33, American River, 5221* ☎ *08/8553–7003* 🖷 *08/8553–7277* ⊕ *www.users.on.net/thekings* ☞ *1 suite* ⚘ *Fans, in-room VCRs, pool, free parking; no smoking, no room phones, no kids* ▤ *MC, V* ⦿| *BP.*

$$ ▥ **Wanderers Rest.** Marvelous local artworks festoon the stylish motel units at this aptly named country inn. The elevated veranda and à la carte restaurant, where breakfast is served, have splendid views across American River to the mainland. ⌂ *Bayview Rd., Box 34, American River, 5221* ☎ *08/8553–7140* 🖷 *08/8553–7282* ⊕ *www.wanderersrest.com.au* ☞ *9 rooms* ⚘ *Restaurant, minibars, pool, bar, free parking; no smoking, no room phones, no kids* ▤ *AE, DC, MC, V* ⦿| *BP.*

$ ▥ **Matthew Flinders Terraces.** Glorious gardens surround this circular retreat; 180-degree sea views from the balconied, two-bedroom suites and the elevated restaurant are a bonus. Delicious picnic hampers and add-on breakfast packages are available. ⌂ *Box 42, American River, 5221* ☎ *08/8553–7100* 🖷 *08/8553–7250* ⊕ *www.kangaroo-island-au.com/matthewflinders* ☞ *8 suites* ⚘ *Restaurant, fans, minibars, pool, spa, bar, Internet, free parking; no smoking, no room phones, no kids* ▤ *AE, DC, MC, V.*

Seal Bay Conservation Park

★ *60 km (37 mi) southwest of Kingscote via the South Coast Rd.*

This top Kangaroo Island attraction gives you the chance to visit one of the state's largest sea lion colonies. About 200 animals usually lounge on the beach, except on stormy days, when they shelter in the sand dunes. You can only visit the beach on a tour with an interpretive officer; otherwise, you can follow the self-guided boardwalk. Two-hour sunset tours depart on varied days from Christmas through January 10; bookings are essential. There's also a shop and an information center. ⊠ *Seal Bay* ☎ *08/8559–4207* ✍ *Group tour A$10.50, sunset tour A$20; boardwalk only $7* ☉ *Tours Dec.–Jan., daily 9–7, every 15–45 min; Feb.–Nov., daily 9–4:15, every 30–45 min.*

Little Sahara

7 km (4½ mi) west of Seal Bay Conservation Park, 67 km (42 mi) southwest of Kingscote.

Towering white-sand dunes cover several square miles here, and a short walk is hard to resist. To get here from Seal Bay Road, turn left onto the South Coast Highway and continue until just before a one-lane bridge. Turn left onto the rough track that leads to Little Sahara.

Vivonne Bay

60 km (37 mi) southwest of Kingscote.

A jetty, a few crayfish boats, and a beach that disappears into the distance are all you'll find at Vivonne, but continue to **Point Ellen** for superb views of the bay and Vivonne Bay Conservation Park.

Hanson Bay

20 km (12 mi) west of Vivonne Bay, 80 km (50 mi) southwest of Kingscote.

A narrow, winding road ends at Hanson Bay, a perfect little sandy cove. The gentle slope of the beach and the rocky headlands on either side provide safe swimming. Beyond the headland to the east are several secluded beaches; these are more exposed and riptides make swimming dangerous. You can catch salmon from these beaches. Limestone caves are nearby.

Where to Stay

$ 🖼 **Hanson Bay Cabins.** A wildlife sanctuary adjoins these neat, self-contained, two-bedroom log cabins between Flinders Chase National Park and Kelly Hill Caves. A pristine white-sand beach is within easy walking distance. ✉ *Box 614, Kingscote, 5223* ☎ *08/8853–2603* 🖷 *08/ 8853–2673* ⊕ *www.esl.com.au/hansonbay* ⇆ *6 cabins* ⚠ *Kitchens, beach, fishing, bicycles, laundry facilities, free parking; no smoking, no a/c, no room phones, no room TVs* ⊟ *MC, V.*

Sports & the Outdoors

Fishing is excellent on the island's beaches, bays, and rivers. Crayfish can be caught from the rocks, sea salmon and mullet from the beaches, and bream in the rivers. The island's deep-sea fishing fleet holds several world records for tuna. No permit is required, although restrictions do apply to the size and quantity of fish you can keep.

American River General Store (⊠ The Wharf, American River ☎ 08/ 8553–7051) sells bait and fishing equipment. **American River Rendezvous**

(✉ The Wharf, American River ☎ 08/8553–7150) sells tackle and can arrange fishing trips. You can rent fishing equipment from **Grimshaw's Corner Store & Cafe** (✉ Cnr. Third St. and North Terr., Penneshaw ☎ 08/ 8553–1151).

Flinders Chase National Park

80 km (50 mi) west of Kingscote.

Some of the most beautiful coastal scenery in Australia is on the western end of Kangaroo Island at Flinders Chase National Park. Much of the island was widely cultivated and grazed, but the park has maintained its original vegetation since it was declared a national treasure in 1919.

The seas crashing onto Australia's southern coast are merciless, and their effects are visible in the oddly shaped rocks off Kangaroo Island's shores. A limestone promontory was carved from underneath at Cape du Couedic on the island's southwestern coast, producing what is now known as **Admiral's Arch.** About 4 km (2½ mi) further east are **Remarkable Rocks,** huge boulders balanced precariously on the promontory of Kirkpatrick Point.

Starting in the 1920s, animals from the mainland were introduced to the island. Today large populations of koalas and Cape Barren geese live in the park. Much of the wildlife is so tame that a barricade had to be constructed at the Rocky River Campground to keep humans in and kangaroos and geese out.

Flinders Chase has several 3- to 7-km (2- to 4-mi) walking trails, which take one to three hours to complete. The trails meander along the rivers to the coast, passing mallee scrub and sugar gum forests. The 3-km (2-mi) Rocky River Walking Trail leads to a powerful waterfall before ending on a quiet sandy beach.

The park is on the western end of the island, bounded by the Playford and West End highways.

Where to Stay

Accommodations within the National Park and Cape Willoughby (on the island's east coast) are controlled by the **Flinders Chase National Park Office** (✉ Rocky River HQ ☎ 08/8559–7235 ⊕ www.environment.sa. gov.au/parks/flinderschase). Rustic sofas, chairs, and tables furnish Heritage-listed lighthouse lodgings, huts, cottages, and homesteads (bring sheets and towels). All have cooking facilities. Camping is allowed only at designated sites at Rocky River and bush campgrounds.

Snellings Beach

50 km (31 mi) west of Kingscote.

Surrounded by high, rolling pastures off North Coast Road, Snellings is broad and sandy, one of the best beaches on the island. Swimming is safe.

Where to Stay

$$$ 🏠 **Cape Forbin Retreat.** About 40 km (24 mi) west of Snellings Beach is Cape Forbin. On an isolated headland abundant with wildlife, this snug, self-contained retreat with two bedrooms can accommodate up to six people. Catch a fish, snorkel, comb the beach for shells, or photograph sunsets from the precipitous cliffs. Then spend the evening doing a jigsaw puzzle or curled up beside the wood-burning stove. There is a two-night minimum booking. ✉ *RSD 404, Newland Service, Kingscote, 5223* ☎🖶 *08/8559–3219* ⊕ *www.capeforbinretreat.com.au* ⤶ *1 house*

      ⚐ *Kitchen, beach, snorkeling, fishing, hiking, free parking; no smoking, no a/c, no room TVs* ☲ *MC, V.*

Kangaroo Island A to Z

To research prices, get advice from other travelers, and book travel arrangements, visit www.fodors.com.

AIR TRAVEL

Regional Express flies twice daily between Adelaide and Kingscote, the island's main airport. Ask about 14-day advance-purchase fares and holiday packages in conjunction with SeaLink. Flights to the island take about 30 minutes. Emu Airways also operates daily flights.

📧 Carriers **Emu Airways** ☎ 08/8234-3711 ⊕ www.emuair.mtx.net. **Regional Express** ☎ 13-1713 ⊕ www.regionalexpress.com.au.

BOAT & FERRY TRAVEL

Vehicular ferries allow access for cars through Penneshaw. The most popular option is the SeaLink ferry from Cape Jervis at the tip of the Fleurieu Peninsula, a 90-minute drive from Adelaide.

SeaLink operates the passenger ferry, *Sea Lion 2000,* and MV *Island Navigator,* a designated freight boat with limited passenger facilities. These ferries make respective 40-minute and one-hour crossings between Cape Jervis and Penneshaw. There are usually two to three daily sailings each way, but in peak times there are up to 10 crossings. This is the most popular means of transport between the island and the mainland, and reservations are advisable during the holidays.

Adelaide Sightseeing operates coaches in conjunction with the ferry services from Cape Jervis and Penneshaw, linking Adelaide, Victor Harbor, and Goolwa with Cape Jervis.

📧 Boat & Ferry Information **Adelaide Sightseeing** ✉ 101 Franklin St., City Center, Adelaide ☎ 08/8231-4144. **SeaLink** ☎ 13-1301 ⊕ www.sealink.com.au.

BUS TRAVEL

Public transport on Kangaroo Island is limited to the KI Bus, which loops clockwise around Kangaroo Island daily, leaving Kingscote at 12:30 PM and making five stops at villages and Flinders Chase National Park before returning at 3:30 PM. The bus connects with the SeaLink Island Shuttle, which runs between the ferry terminal in Penneshaw and Kingscote twice a day. Single-sector KI Bus tickets are available onboard (or by booking). More economic is the 14-day KI Bus Pass, which allows unlimited transport and stopovers. Passes are available for travel from Adelaide (A\$139), Cape Jervis (A\$107), and island-only (A\$45).

📧**SeaLink Kangaroo Island** ✉ 440 King William St., Adelaide 5000 ☎ 13-1301 ⊕ www.kibuspass.com.au.

CAR TRAVEL

Kangaroo Island's main attractions are widely scattered; you can see them best on a guided tour or by car. The main roads form a sealed loop, which branches off to such major sites as Seal Bay, and Admirals Arch and Remarkable Rocks in Flinders Chase National Park. Stretches of unsealed road lead to historic lighthouses at Cape Borda and Cape Willoughby, South Australia's oldest. Roads to the island's northern beaches, bays, and camping areas are also unsealed. These become corrugated in summer, but they can be driven carefully in a conventional vehicle. Be alert for wildlife, especially at dawn, dusk, and after dark. Slow down and dip your lights so you don't blind the animals you see.

CAR RENTAL
🚗 **Budget Rent-a-Car** ✉ 1 Commercial St., Kingscote, 5223 ☎ 08/8553-3133.

EMERGENCIES
In an emergency, dial **000** to reach an ambulance, the police, or the fire department.

TOURS
Adventure Charters of Kangaroo Island has quality wildlife and nature four-wheel-drive tours. These range from one to two days, as well as a three-day trip that can combine bushwalking. Tailor-made itineraries, including sea fishing, kayaking, and diving, can also be arranged—day tours cost A$463; one-night tours run A$640; two-day, one-night tours are A$873; and three-day, two-night tours are A$1,050. Kangaroo Island Odysseys operates luxury four-wheel-drive nature tours from one to three days. Prices run from A$279 per person for a day tour to A$1,376 per person for a three-day, two-night tour. Kangaroo Island Wilderness Tours has four fully accommodated and personalized four-wheel-drive wilderness tours, ranging from one to four days. Day tours cost A$270–A$290; overnight tours run A$478–A$503; three-day, two-night tours cost A$1,150–A$1,200; and four-day, three-night tours are A$1,590–A$1,665, depending on your choice of accommodations.

Regional Express also packages its air services in conjunction with the tours led by various travel operators on the island. Choices include a standard one-day island bus tour or a four-wheel-drive tour with the emphasis on adventure. You can construct individual itineraries.

SeaLink Kangaroo Island operates one-day (A$179) and half-day (A$53) coach tours of the island, departing from Adelaide, in conjunction with the ferry service from Cape Jervis. They also can arrange fishing and self-drive tours and extended coach tour packages. Two-day, one-night tours are A$289 and up per person; two-day, one-night self-drive tours start at A$155 per person.

🚗 Adventure Tours **Adventure Charters of Kangaroo Island** 📮 Box 169, Kingscote, 5223 ☎ 08/8553-9119 🖷 08/8553-9122 ⊕ www.adventurecharters.com.au. **Kangaroo Island Odysseys** 📮 Box 494, Penneshaw, 5222 ☎ 08/8553-0386 🖷 08/8553-0387 ⊕ www.kiodysseys.com.au. **Kangaroo Island Wilderness Tours** 📮 Box 84, Parndana, 5220 ☎ 08/8559-5033 🖷 08/8559-5088 ⊕ www.wildernesstours.com.au.
🚌 Bus Tour **SeaLink Kangaroo Island** ✉ 7 North Terr., Penneshaw, 5222 ☎ 13-1301 or 08/8553-1122.

VISITOR INFORMATION
ℹ Tourist Information **Flinders Chase National Park (Department of Environment and Heritage)** ✉ Rocky River HQ ☎ 08/8559-7235. **Gateway Visitor Information Centre** ✉ Howard Dr., Penneshaw ☎ 08/8553-1185 🖷 08/8553-1255 ⊕ www.tourkangarooisland.com.au.

THE MURRAY RIVER

The "Mighty Murray" is the longest river in Australia and among the longest rivers on the planet. From its source in the Snowy Mountains of New South Wales, it travels some 2,415 km (1,500 mi) through 11 locks before it enters the ocean southeast of Adelaide. As European pioneers settled the interior, the river became a major artery for their cargoes of wool and livestock. During the second half of the 19th century, the river reverberated with the churning wheels and shrieking whistles of paddle steamers. This colorful period ended when railways shrank the continent at the turn of the 20th century, easing the difficulty of overland transport and reducing dependence on the river. Today the Murray is ideal for waterskiers, boaters, and anglers.

The Murray's role as an industrial waterway may be over, but it remains a vital part of the economy and life of South Australia. It provides water for the vast irrigation schemes that turned the desert into a fruit bowl, and it supplies Adelaide with its domestic water. The Riverland region is one of the country's largest growers of citrus fruits and produces most of the nation's bulk wine. Also note that Riverland brandy is superior.

In spite of what the railroads did to river traffic, or perhaps because of it, the only way to see the river properly is to spend a few days on a boat. Along this stretch of the Murray, a car is a less efficient and less appealing way to travel through the countryside. A trip down the broad brown river is still an adventure; the history of the little towns on its banks, along with river culture and its importance to South Australia, merits some study. Most rewarding, however, is the area's natural beauty. Couched within high ocher cliffs, the Murray is home to river red gums, still lagoons, and abundant bird life.

Renmark

256 km (159 mi) east of Adelaide.

On a willow-lined bend in the river, Renmark is a busy town, one of the most important on the Murray—a center for the fruit industry, the mainstay of the Riverland region. Fruit growing began here in 1887, when the Canadian Chaffey brothers were granted 250,000 acres to test their irrigation plan. One of the original wood-burning water pumps they devised can still be seen on Renmark Avenue.

Upstream from Renmark toward Wentworth in Victoria, the Murray River is at its tranquil best, gliding between tall cliffs and spilling out across broad lakes teeming with bird life. No towns lie along this section of the river, so this is the route to take for peace and quiet. Downstream from Renmark the river is more populated, although only during peak summer periods does the Murray become even remotely crowded.

★ Sunset turns the Murray Cliffs fiery red and one of the best vantage points for the show is **Heading Cliff Lookout,** 14-km (9-mi) northeast of Renmark on Murno Road.

Olivewood, the original homestead of Charles Chaffey and now run by the National Trust, is a museum. Take time for tea at the café. ✉ *21st St.* ☎ *08/8586–6175* ✉ *A$4* ⊙ *Tues. 2–4, Thurs.–Mon. 10–4.*

Berri

52 km (32 mi) downstream from Renmark, 236 km (146 mi) northeast of Adelaide.

Berri was once a refueling station for the river steamers and today is the economic heart of the Riverland. Wine production is the major industry—the town's Berri Estates is one of the largest single wineries in the Southern Hemisphere.

For anyone who wants to see what the Riverland is all about, **Berri Limited's** showroom has an 8-minute video on various stages of the fruit-growing process. ✉ *Sturt Hwy.* ☎ *08/8582–3321* ✉ *Free* ⊙ *Mon.–Wed. 8:30–4:30, Thurs. and Fri. 8–5, Sat. 9–3, Sun 10–3.*

Loxton

43 km (27 mi) downstream from Berri, 255 km (158 mi) east of Adelaide.

Loxton is a hardworking town, one of the most attractive on the river. It's surrounded by orchards and the vineyards of the Penfold Winery, one of Australia's premier producers. It's also an idyllic spot for canoeists, walkers, campers, and lovers of arts and crafts. In East Terrace, the Loxton Community Hotel-Motel serves counter meals at the bar or in the à la carte bistro.

In **Loxton Historical Village,** many of the town's 19th-century buildings have been reconstructed beside the river. ⊠ *East Terr.* ☎ *08/8584–7194* 🖼 *A$8* ⊙ *Weekdays 10–4, weekends 10–5.*

en route ★ Downstream from Loxton, where the Murray turns west again, the floodplain is patched with salt scrub, trees, and reedy lagoons that attract thousands of birds. Overlooking these waters is **Banrock Station Wine & Wetland Centre.** In this stilted, rammed-earth building you can select a wine to accompany lunch—bush tomato soup, or hot peach and *quandong* (a native fruit) slices—on the deck above the vineyard. Storyboards along the 2.5-km (1.6-mi) Mallee Meets The Valley Trail explain how land clearing, feral animals, Aborigines, and river regulation have shaped the land. The 4.5-km (2.8-mi) Boardwalk Trail (bookings essential) highlights the winery's ongoing work to restore the wetlands. There are several bird hides around the lagoon. The Centre is just off the Sturt Hwy. ⊠ *Holmes Rd., Kingston-on-Murray* ☎ *08/8583–0299 information and Boardwalk Trail bookings* ⊕ *www.banrockstation. com.au* 🖼 *Wine & Wetland Centre free; Boardwalk Trail A$5; Mallee Meets The Valley Trail A$2* ⊙ *Daily 10–5.*

Waikerie

120 km (74 mi) downstream of Loxton, 177 km (110 mi) northeast of Adelaide.

The teeming bird life in this part of the river gave the town of Waikerie its name—the Aboriginal word means "many wings." Surrounded by irrigated citrus orchards and vineyards overlooking the river red gums and cliffs of the far bank, the town is also a center for airplane gliding.

Waikerie is Australia's gliding capital. Taking a scenic flight in a glider from **Waikerie International Soaring Centre** is a great way to see the river and the rich farmland along its banks. Flights run daily November through March and every second weekend from April through October. It's A$300 per day for a two- or seven-day pilot course. ⊠ *Sturt Hwy.* ☎ *08/8541–2644* ⊕ *www.waikerieglidingclub.com.au* 🖼 *20-min flight A$75* ⊙ *Nov.–Mar. daily 8:30–5, Apr.–Oct. weekdays 8:30–5.*

en route Cruising downstream between Waikerie and Swan Reach you approach the tiny settlement of **Morgan.** When you round the bend in the river and catch a glimpse of this sleepy little backwater, it's hard to believe that it was once the state's second-busiest port. In Morgan's heyday at the end of the 19th century, freight from the upper reaches of the Murray was unloaded here and sent by train to Port Adelaide. The demise of river traffic put an end to its prosperity. The towering wharves, railway station, tiny redbrick morgue, and the shops and hotels along Railway Terrace have been preserved largely in their original state.

Swan Reach, not surprisingly named for its bird population, lies 51 km (32 mi) downstream from Morgan. This quiet town overlooks some of the prettiest scenery on the Murray. Below town, the river makes a huge curve—known as Big Bend—where you can see vistas of gold cliffs at sunset.

Mannum

195 km (121 mi) downstream from Waikerie, 84 km (52 mi) east of Adelaide.

Murray River paddle steamers had their origins in Mannum when the first riverboat, the *Mary Ann,* was launched in 1853. The town has a number of reminders of its past at the **Mannum Dock Museum,** including the 1897 paddle steamer *Marion.* You can also take cruises and book overnight cabins on the fully restored boat. When not operating, it's open for exploring. ⊠ *6 Randell St.* ☎ *08/8569–1303* ⊕ *www.psmarion.com/museum.htm* 🖻 *A$5* ☉ *Weekdays 9–5, weekends 10–4.*

Where to Eat

Mannum Club, off Randell Street, has river views from its dining room. Captain Randell's Restaurant has a fine position above the wharf, overlooking the river and the ferry traffic. Willow-edged Mary Ann Reserve by the river is a perfect picnic place.

Murray Bridge

35 km (22 mi) downstream from Mannum, 78 km (48 mi) east of Adelaide.

Murray Bridge is the largest town on the South Australian section of the river, and its proximity to Adelaide makes it a popular spot for fishing, waterskiing, and picnicking. Crowds get heavy on weekends. Dining alternatives are reasonably extensive in Murray Bridge.

The Amorosa (⊠ Bridge St. ☎ 08/8531–0559) serves European food. **The Happy Gathering** (⊠ 1st St. ☎ 08/8532–5888) has Chinese fare.

Murray River A to Z

To research prices, get advice from other travelers, and book travel arrangements, visit www.fodors.com.

BUS TRAVEL

Premier Stateliner operates a twice-daily service between Adelaide and Renmark. The one-way fare from Adelaide is A$34.70, with stops at major Riverland towns. The trip takes four hours.

🚩 **Premier Stateliner** ⊠ 111 Franklin St., City Center, Adelaide, 5000 ☎ 08/8415–5555.

CAR TRAVEL

Leave Adelaide by Main North Road and follow signs to the Sturt Highway and the town of Gawler. This highway continues east to Renmark. Allow 3½ hours for the 295-km (183-mi) trip to Renmark.

Although the Sturt Highway crosses the river several times between Waikerie and Renmark, and smaller roads link more isolated towns along the river, the most impressive sections of the Murray can be seen only from the water. If you've rented a car, drive to Mannum or Murray Bridge and hook up with a river cruise or rent a houseboat to drive yourself along the river.

EMERGENCIES

In an emergency, dial 000 to reach an ambulance, the police, or the fire department.

TOURS

PS *Murray Princess* is a replica Mississippi River paddle wheeler that cruises the Outback. The two-, three-, and five-night voyages depart from Mannum. All cabins are air-conditioned and have bathrooms. Passengers have access to spas, saunas, and nightly entertainment onboard.

Proud Australia Nature Cruises has two- to five-night cruises on the *Proud Mary,* a boutique paddle steamer. Departing upstream from Murray Bridge, you travel in comfortable, air-conditioned cabins with en suite bathrooms and river views. You can even join in free ecological onshore excursions.

Cruise vacations on the river are available aboard large riverboats or in rented houseboats. The latter sleep 2 to 12 people and range in quality from basic to luxurious. During peak summer holiday season, a deluxe eight-berth houseboat starts at around A$1,500 per week, and a four-berth boat starts at around A$800. Off-peak prices drop by as much as 40%. Water and power for lights and cooking are carried onboard. No previous boating experience is necessary—the only requirement is a driver's license.

Houseboats are supplied with basic safety equipment, such as life preservers, with which you should familiarize yourself before departure. Treat your houseboat as your home, and safeguard personal effects by locking all doors and windows before going out.

Liba-Liba has a fleet of 19 houseboats for rent and is based in Renmark. Swan Houseboats are among the most comfortable, well-equipped, and luxurious accommodations on the river. For a free booklet listing prices, layouts, and other details for more than 150 houseboats from Murray Bridge to Renmark, call Houseboat Hirers Association Inc.

🚩 Boat Tours **Houseboat Hirers Association Inc.** ☎ 08/8395-0999 ⊕ www.houseboat-centre.com.au. **Liba-Liba** ☎ 1800/810252 ⊕ www.murray-river.net/houseboats/liba. **Proud Australia Nature Cruises** ✉ 18–20 Grenfell St., Level 4, City Center, Adelaide ☎ 08/8231-9472 ⊕ www.proudmary.com.au. **PS** *Murray Princess* ✉ 96 Randell St., Mannum ☎ 1800/804843 or 08/8569-2511 ⊕ www.captaincook.com.au/murray/index.htm. **Swan Houseboats** ☎ 1800/083183 ⊕ www.swanhouseboats.com.au.

VISITOR INFORMATION

The Berri Interpretive Visitor Centre is open weekdays 9–5 and weekends 10–4. The Renmark Paringa Visitor Centre is open weekdays 9–5, Saturday 9–4, and Sunday 10–4.

🚩 Tourist Information **Berri Interpretive Visitor Centre** ✉ Riverview Dr. ☎ 08/8582-5511. **Renmark Paringa Visitor Centre** ✉ 84 Murray Ave. ☎ 08/8586-6704.

THE OUTBACK

South Australia is the country's driest state, and its Outback is an expanse of desert vegetation. But this land of scrubby saltbush and hardy eucalyptus trees is brightened after rain by wildflowers—including the state's floral emblem, the blood-red Sturt's desert pea, with its black, olivelike heart. The terrain is marked by geological uplifts, abrupt transitions between plateaus broken at the edges of ancient, long-inactive fault lines. Few roads track through this desert wilderness—the main highway is the Stuart, which runs all the way to Alice Springs in the Northern Territory.

The people of the Outback are as hardy as their surroundings. They are also often eccentric, colorful characters who will happily bend your ear over a drink in the local pub. Remote, isolated communities attract loners, adventurers, fortune-seekers, and people simply on the run. In this unyielding country, you must be tough to survive.

Coober Pedy

850 km (527 mi) northwest of Adelaide.

Known as much for the way most of its 3,500 inhabitants live—underground in dugouts gouged into the hills—as for its opal riches, Coober Pedy is arguably Australia's most singular place. The town is ringed by mullock heaps, pyramids of rock and sand left over after mining shafts are dug. Opals are Coober Pedy's reason for existence—this is the world's richest opal field.

Opal was discovered here in 1915, and soldiers returning from World War I introduced the first dugout homes when the searing heat forced them underground. In midsummer, temperatures can reach 48°C (118°F), but inside the dugouts the air remains a constant 22°C–24°C (72°F–75°F). Australia has 95% of the world's opal deposits, and Coober Pedy has the bulk of that wealth. Working mines are off-limits to visitors, although if you befriend a miner in the pub you may be invited for an off-the-record tour.

Coober Pedy is a brick and corrugated-iron settlement propped unceremoniously on a scarred desert landscape. It's a town built for efficiency, not beauty. However, its ugliness has a kind of bizarre appeal. With about 45 different nationalities in residence, there are now clubs, restaurants, and entertainment venues for all backgrounds.

Exploring

Noodling—fossicking (rummaging) for opal gemstones—requires no permit at the Jewelers Shop mining area at the edge of town. Take care in unmarked areas and never walk backwards, as the area is littered with abandoned opal mines down which you might fall.

Although most of Coober Pedy's underground devotions are decidedly secular in nature, the town does have underground churches. **St. Peter and St. Paul's Catholic Church** is a National Heritage–listed building, and the **Catacomb Anglican Church** is notable for its altar fashioned from a windlass (a winch) and lectern made from a log of mulga wood. The **Serbian Orthodox church** is striking, with its scalloped ceiling, rock-carved icons, and brilliant stained-glass windows.

The **Revival Fellowship Underground Church**, adjacent to the Experience Motel, has lively gospel services.

Umoona Opal Mine and Museum is an enormous underground complex with an original mine, a noteworthy video on the history of opal mining, an Aboriginal Interpretive Centre, and clean, underground bunk camping and cooking facilities. Guided tours of the mine are available. ⊠ *Hutchison St.* ☎ *08/8672–5288* ▭ *Tour A$8* ☉ *Daily 8–7; tours at 10, 2, and 4.*

The **Old Timers Mine** is a genuine opal mine turned into a museum. Two underground houses, furnished in 1920s and 1980s styles, are part of the complex, where mining equipment and memorabilia are exhibited in an extensive network of hand-dug tunnels and shafts. Tours are self-guided. ⊠ *Crowders Gully Rd.* ☎☎ *08/8672–5555* ▭ *A$10* ☉ *Daily 9–5.*

Goanna Land (✉ Post Office Hill Rd. ☎ 08/8672–5965), an arts-and-crafts shop at Underground Books, rents clubs for A$10 and arranges play at the 18-hole, par-72 Coober Pedy Golf Club for A$10 per round.

Around Town

Breakaways, a striking series of rock formations, centered on the Moon Plain, is reminiscent of the American West, with its buttes and jagged hills. There are fossils and patches of petrified forest in this strange landscape, which has appealed to filmmakers of apocalyptic films. *Mad Max 3—Beyond Thunderdome* was filmed around here, as was *Ground Zero.* The scenery is especially evocative early in the morning. The Breakaways area is 30 km (19 mi) northeast of Coober Pedy.

An extraordinary measure designed to protect the valuable sheep-grazing land to the south from marauding dingoes, the **Dog Fence** runs 5,600 km (3,500 mi)—9,600 km (6,000 mi) by some people's reckoning—from faraway Queensland. It's a simple wire fence in the Breakaways area, running arrow-straight across this barren country.

The hour-long **Martin's Star Gazing Tour** (☎ 08/8672–5223 ⊕ www. martinsnightsky.com.au) takes place at the Moon Plain Desert, about 6 km (4 mi) outside of Coober Pedy. Daily trips are A$22.

Where to Stay & Eat

$–$$ ✕ **Umberto's.** Perched atop the monolithic Desert Cave Hotel, this restaurant serves the town's most upscale fare. The Outback's softer hues and more colorful wildlife are seen in prints of native birds that decorate the walls. Try the Pacific Island raw fish salad, or the kangaroo fillet with Pernod and brandy *jus.* Although it's the town's best restaurant, there's no need to dress up—no one does in Coober Pedy. ✉ *Hutchison St.* ☎ *08/8672–5688* ▤ *AE, DC, MC, V* ☺ *No lunch.*

¢–$ ✕ **Ampol Restaurant.** This is no ordinary station diner. Hearty food and top wines and beer are served in an airy, glass-fronted restaurant. There's even a shaded beer garden in which to wash down the desert dust. The restaurant is open from 6 AM until late. It's right by the bus station. ✉ *Hutchison St.* ☎ *08/8672–5199* ▤ *MC, V.*

$$ ▦ **Desert Cave Hotel.** What may be the world's only underground hotel presents a contemporary, blocky face to the desert town. In the 19 spacious, subsurface rooms, luxurious furnishings in Outback hues complement and constrast the red striated rock walls that protect sleepers from sound and heat. Aboveground rooms are also available. The hotel has an excellent interpretive center. ✉ *Hutchison St. 5723* ☎ *08/ 8672–5688* 🖶 *08/8672–5198* ⊕ *www.desertcave.com.au* ⤳ *50 rooms* ♣ *Restaurant, café, room service, minibars, refrigerators, room TVs with movies, pool, health club, sauna, spa, bar, shops, baby-sitting, laundry facilities, Internet, convention center, travel services, free parking; nosmoking rooms, no a/c in some rooms* ▤ *AE, DC, MC, V.*

¢–$ ▦ **Mud Hut Motel.** Rammed earth is the building method used here, and desert hues in the guest rooms extend the earthy theme. Two-bedroom apartments have cooking facilities. One unit is available for travelers with disabilities. The à la carte restaurant has outside dining and serves international fare. ✉ *St. Nicholas St., 5723* ☎ *08/8672–3003 or 1800/ 646962* 🖶 *08/8672–3004* ⊕ *www.mudhutmotel.com.au* ⤳ *24 rooms, 4 apartments* ♣ *Restaurant, room service, some kitchenettes, refrigerators, bar, shop, laundry facilities, Internet, travel services, free parking; no-smoking rooms* ▤ *AE, DC, MC, V.*

¢–$ ▦ **Underground Motel.** The Breakaways rock formations sometimes seem close enough to touch at this motel, a step back from town. Each room is uniquely shaped, comfortably furnished, and decorated with Aboriginal designs. Two secluded suites have kitchenette facilities, and main rooms share a communal kitchen. A complimentary light breakfast is provided. ✉ *1185 Catacomb Rd., 5723* ☎ *1800/622979 or 08/ 8672-5324* 🖷 *08/8672-5911* ✎ *elsaunderground@sa86.net* ⇲ *6 rooms, 2 suites* ♻ *Some kitchenettes, some in-room VCRs, playground, laundry facilities, Internet, travel services, free parking, some pets allowed; no-smoking rooms, no a/c* ▤ *AE, DC, MC, V* ❙◯❙ *CP.*

¢ ▦ **Opal Inn.** This combined hotel and motel is the place to meet Coober Pedy characters and opal buyers. Chat with them over a drink in the bistro, a favorite spot for locals to gather, or play a game of pool on one of two tables. Choose from the in-house pub-style rooms with shared bathrooms, the courtyard budget rooms with private baths, the standard motel rooms, or the family suites. You can also pitch a tent or bring your camper. ✉ *Hutchison St. 5723* ☎ *1800/088523 or 08/ 8672-5054* 🖷 *08/8672-5501* ⊕ *www.opalinn.com.au* ⇲ *55 powered camp sites, 10 tent sites, 12 hotel rooms, 12 budget rooms, 75 motel rooms, 2 family rooms* ♻ *Restaurant, some in-room data ports, bar, shop, laundry facilities, Internet, business services, convention center, travel services, free parking; no-smoking rooms, no phones in some rooms, no TV in some rooms* ▤ *AE, DC, MC, V.*

Shopping

More than 30 shops sell opals in Coober Pedy. **The Opal Cave** (✉ Hutchison St. ☎ 08/8672-5028) has a huge opal display, arts and crafts, and adjoining B&B accommodations within one neat, self-contained unit. The **Opal Cutter** (✉ Post Office Hill Rd. 🖷 08/8672-3086) has stones valued from A$7 to A$25,000. Displays of opal cutting can be requested. You can see the world's largest opal matrix at the **Opal Factory** (✉ Hutchison St. ☎ 08/8672-5300).

Underground Books (✉ Post Office Hill Rd. ☎ 08/8672-5558) has an excellent selection of reading material, arts, and crafts, but the best buy is a postcard by local photographer Peter Caust, who captures the essence of the desert landscape. This is also the booking office for the Coober Pedy–Oodnadatta Mail Run Tours.

At **Underground Potteries** (✉ off 17 Mile Rd., adjacent to the golf course 🖷 08/8672-5226) you can watch potters in basement studios creating handmade products. Then walk up and buy them in the main gallery. It's open daily 8:30–6.

Flinders Ranges National Park

690 km (430 mi) from Coober Pedy, 460 km (285 mi) northeast of Adelaide.

Extending north from Spencer Gulf, the mountain chain of the Flinders Ranges includes one of the most impressive Outback parks in the country. These dry, craggy mountain peaks, once the bed of an ancient sea, have been cracked, folded, and sculpted by millions of years of rain and sun. This furrowed landscape of deep valleys is covered with cypress pine and casuarina, which slope into creeks lined with river red gums. The area is utterly fascinating—both for geologists and for anyone else who revels in wild, raw scenery and exotic plant and animal life.

The scenic center of the Flinders Ranges is **Wilpena Pound,** an 80-square-km (31-square-mi) bowl ringed by hills that curve gently upward, only to fall off in the rims of sheer cliffs. The only entrance to the Pound is a narrow cleft through which Wilpena Creek sometimes runs. An impressive **visitor center** (✉ Wilpena Rd. ☎ 08/8648-0048), part of the Wilpena Pound Resort, has more information.

The numerous steep trails in the Flinders Ranges make them ideal for bushwalking, even though the park has few amenities. Water in this region is scarce and should be carried at all times. The best time for walking is during the relatively cool months between April and October. This is also the wettest time of year, so you should be prepared for rain. Wildflowers, including the spectacular Sturt's desert pea, are abundant between September and late October.

The park's most spectacular walking trail leads to the summit of 3,840-foot **St. Mary's Peak,** the highest point on the Pound's rim and the second-tallest peak in South Australia. The more scenic of the two routes to the summit is the outside trail; give yourself a full day to get up and back. The final ascent is difficult, but views from the top—including the distant white glitter of the salt flats on Lake Frome—make the climb worthwhile. ✉ *Off the Princes Hwy.* ☎ *08/8648–4244* ⊕ *www.flinders. outback.on.net.*

Where to Stay

$–$$ 🏨 **Wilpena Pound Resort.** This popular resort at the entrance to Wilpena Pound has chalets (10 with kitchenettes) and sizable motel-style rooms. Here, too, is a campground with 24 powered and 300 unpowered sites, all with shared showers. Units are available for those with disabilities. A licensed restaurant serves meals throughout the day, and you can stock up on goods at the small supermarket. There is also a gas pump. The resort runs four-wheel-drive tours and scenic flights, and the visitor center is a major attraction. ✉ *Wilpena Rd., Wilpena Pound, via Hawker, 5434* ☎ *08/8648–0004* 🖷 *08/8648–0028* ⊕ *www.wilpenapound.com. au* ⇨ *34 rooms, 26 chalets, 324 campsites* ⚴ *Restaurant, café, some kitchenettes, pool, hiking, bar, shops, laundry facilities, Internet, free parking* ⊟ *AE, DC, MC, V.*

¢ ⚠ **Cooinda Campsite.** Follow the signs along the trails to reach the only established wilderness campsite within Wilpena Pound. You can, however, also camp with a permit throughout Flinders Ranges National Park. It's A$10.50 per car per night, and there are no weekly permits, though you can buy a yearly pass. Carry water into your site, and look for water in small rock holes to replenish your supply.

The Outback A to Z

To research prices, get advice from other travelers, and book travel arrangements, visit www.fodors.com.

AIR TRAVEL
Regional Express flies direct to Coober Pedy from Adelaide four times a week.

🛈 **Regional Express** ☎ 13-1713 ⊕ www.regionalexpress.com.au.

BUS TRAVEL
Premier Stateliner buses leave Adelaide's Central Bus Terminal for Wilpena Pound at Flinders Ranges National Park via Quorn on Wednesday at 8:30 AM and Friday at 11 AM, returning from the Pound at 2:30 PM Thursday, 7:15 PM Friday, and 2:30 PM Sunday.

🛈 **Premier Stateliner** ☎ 08/8415-5555 ⊕ www.premierstateliner.com.au.

CAR TRAVEL
The main road to Coober Pedy is the Stuart Highway from Adelaide, 850 km (527 mi) to the south. Alice Springs is 700 km (434 mi) north of Coober Pedy. The drive from Adelaide to Coober Pedy takes about nine hours. To Alice Springs, it is about seven hours.

A rental car is the best way to see Coober Pedy and its outlying attractions. Although some roads are unpaved—those to the Breakaways and the Dog Fence, for example—surfaces are generally suitable for conventional vehicles. Check on road conditions with the police if there has been substantial rain.

To get to Flinders Ranges National Park from Adelaide take the Princes Highway north to Port Augusta, and then head east toward Quorn and Hawker. A four-wheel-drive vehicle is highly recommended for traveling on the many gravel roads in the area.

EMERGENCIES
In an emergency, dial 000 to reach an ambulance, the police, or the fire department.

TOURS
The Coober Pedy–Oodnadatta Mail Run tour is a bona fide Australian classic. You'll join the Outback postman in town in his four-wheel-drive car or bus for a 600-km (372-mi) odyssey to tiny Outback settlements and cattle stations. The route passes historic ruins and monuments, such as part of the Overland Telegraph Line and the original line of the Ghan railway. You visit South Australia's smallest town (William Creek, population 10) and its biggest cattle station, Anna Creek. This is a journey not to be missed. The trip, on Monday and Thursday, costs A$110.
🗺 **Coober Pedy-Oodnadatta Mail Run** ☎ 08/8672-5558 or 1800/069911.

VISITOR INFORMATION
The Coober Pedy Visitor Information Centre is open weekdays 9–5. More information about national parks can be obtained through the Department for Environment and Heritage, or contact Flinders Ranges National Park directly.
🗺 Tourist Information **Coober Pedy Visitor Information Centre** ✉ Coober Pedy District Council Bldg., Hutchison St., Coober Pedy ☎ 08/8672-5298 or 1800/637076 ⊕ www. opalcapitaloftheworld.com.au. **Department for Environment and Heritage** ✉ 77 Grenfell St., City Center, Adelaide ☎ 08/8204-1910 ⊕ www.environment.sa.gov.au/parks/ parks.html. **Flinders Ranges National Park** ✉ Park Rd. ☎ 08/8648-4244.

THE RED CENTRE

FODOR'S CHOICE

Hanuman Thai, restaurant in Alice Springs

Kata Tjuṯa, near Ayers Rock Resort

Kings Canyon, in Watarrka National Park

Kings Canyon Resort, in Watarrka National Park

Kuniya Restaurant, at Ayers Rock Resort

Longitude 131°, resort at Ayers Rock Resort

Sounds of Silence Dinner in the Desert, at Ayers Rock Resort

Uluṟu, near Ayers Rock Resort

HIGHLY RECOMMENDED

RESTAURANTS Bojangles Saloon and Restaurant, in Alice Springs

Red Ochre, in Alice Springs

HOTELS Crowne Plaza Resort, in Alice Springs

Desert Rose Inn, in Alice Springs

Glen Helen Resort, near Alice Springs

MacDonnell Ranges Holiday Park, near Alice Springs

Mercure Inn Diplomat Hotel, in Alice Springs

Outback Pioneer Hotel, at Ayers Rock Resort

SIGHTS Alice Springs Cultural Precinct, near Alice Springs

Alice Springs Desert Park, near Alice Springs

Caroline
Gladstone

THE LUMINESCENT LIGHT OF THE RED CENTRE—named for the deep color of its desert soils—has a purity and vitality that photographs only begin to approach. For tens of thousands of years, this vast desert territory has been home to Australia's indigenous Aboriginal people. Uluru, also known as Ayers Rock, is a great symbol in Aboriginal traditions, as are so many sacred sites among the Centre's mountain ranges, gorges, dry riverbeds, and spinifex plains. At the center of all this lies Alice Springs, Australia's only desert city.

The Red Centre appears at first sight to be harsh and unforgiving—it is, after all, at the heart of some of the world's largest deserts in the middle of the driest continent in the world. The apparent desolation of the spinifex plains conceals a richness and beauty of plant and animal life that has adapted over millennia to survive and thrive in an environment of extremes. Nights in winter can reach the freezing point, and summer days can soar above 43°C (110°F). And with little rain, the pockets of water to be found in isolated gorges and salt pans are precious indicators of surprisingly varied life forms. As with so many deserts, when you stop to look at the Red Centre closely, you'll find that it is full of beauty and tremendous vitality.

The essence of this land of contrasts is epitomized in the paintings of the renowned Aboriginal landscape artist Albert Namatjira and his followers. Viewed away from the desert, their images of the MacDonnell Ranges may appear at first to be garish and unreal in their depiction of mountain ranges of purples and reds and stark-white ghost gum trees. To see the real thing makes it difficult to imagine executing the paintings in any other way.

Uluru (pronounced *oo-loo-roo*), dubbed Ayers Rock by Anglos, that magnificent stone monolith that rises above the surrounding plains, is but one focus in the Red Centre. The rounded forms of Kata Tjuta (*ka*-ta *tchoo*-ta) are another. Watarrka National Park and Kings Canyon, Mt. Conner, and the cliffs, gorges, and mountain chains of the MacDonnell Ranges are other worlds to explore as well.

Exploring the Red Centre

The primary areas of interest are Alice Springs, which is flanked by the intriguing eastern and western MacDonnell Ranges; Kings Canyon; and Ayers Rock Resort and Uluru–Kata Tjuta National Park. Unless you have more than three days, focus on only one of these areas.

To reach the Red Centre, you can fly from most large Australian cities into either Alice Springs or Ayers Rock, or fly the 440 km (275 mi) between these two cities. Coach tours run between all Red Centre sites, as well as between Alice and Ayers Rock Resort. If you like to travel by rail, the Ghan train travels from Adelaide to Alice Springs in about 12 hours; trains from Sydney and Melbourne to Adelaide also connect with the Ghan. You can transport your car by train for an extra charge.

The best way to get around, though, is by car, and two- and four-wheel-drive vehicles can be hired at both Alice Springs and Ayers Rock Resort. Most roads are sealed and in good condition, so a conventional car is adequate. However, roads such as the Mereenie Loop, which links Kings Canyon to Hermannsburg, require a four-wheel-drive vehicle. The Central Australian Tourism Visitors Centre in Alice Springs provides motoring information and books tours and rental cars.

It doesn't take long for the beauty of the desert to capture your heart. Still, allow yourself enough time in the Red Centre to really let it soak in. If you don't fly right into the Ayers Rock Resort, start in Alice Springs, around which you'll find some spectacular scenery. Poke in and around town for a couple of days, then head out to the nearby hills.

10

If you have 3 days

You can hardly ignore one of Australia's great icons: Uluru. Drive straight down from Alice Springs to ▦ **Ayers Rock Resort** for lunch, followed by a circuit of the Rock and a look at the **Uluru–Kata Tjuta Cultural Centre** near its base. Spend the night, then make an early start to catch dawn at **Kata Tjuta** for an exploration of its extraordinary domes. End the day with sunset at the Rock, then return to Alice Springs for the second night via the **Henbury Meteorite Craters.** If you fly in and out of Ayers Resort and have more time, take the final day for a Mala or Uluru Experience walk and a flightseeing tour of the area.

If you opt to spend your days around ▦ **Alice Springs,** stay in town the first morning to walk around the city center and shops. In the afternoon, head out to the **Alice Springs Telegraph Station Historical Reserve** ❾ or **MacDonnell Siding** to look at the *Old Ghan* train. Spend the night, then drive out into either the eastern or western MacDonnell Ranges to explore the gorges and gaps and dip into a water hole. Overnight at the ▦ **Glen Helen Resort.** Make your way back to town through the mountain scenery on the third day.

If you have 5 days

Combine the two itineraries above, taking in the best of Alice Springs and the MacDonnell Ranges before heading down to the Rock. If you want to take in more of the desert, start out in Uluru as above but head west to ▦ **Watarrka National Park** for a day and two nights exploring **Kings Canyon** by yourself or with one of the Aboriginal guided tours. Surprisingly little-visited, Kings Canyon is one of the hidden wonders of central Australia. Stop by **Mt. Conner,** which looks like Uluru except that it's flat on top.

If you have 7 days

Start with three days in and around ▦ **Alice Springs,** then two days and a night in ▦ **Watarrka National Park.** For the remaining two days, knock around ▦ **Uluru–Kata Tjuta National Park,** leaving yourself at least a few hours for absorbing the majesty of the desert. Fly out from the resort to your next destination.

About the Restaurants

Restaurants in Alice Springs and at Ayers Rock Resort surprise visitors with innovative cuisine, fabulous produce, and such unusual Australian dishes as crocodile, kangaroo, and camel. And whatever your dining style, you'll find it here, from fast-food chains and pubs to stylish cafés and high-quality hotel restaurants. Do try to taste "bush tucker," a variety of native meats served with local fruits, berries, and plants. You'll find bush tucker at many saloons and steak houses, usually amid a Northern Territory pioneer atmosphere where Australian cowboys reign and huge steaks are the main draw. Picnics are another dining style in the

Red Centre, where national parks provide scenic backdrops for outdoor meals. Buy picnic foods in Alice Springs or from roadside stores, then head out into the wilds.

Ayers Rock Resort is a gathering of six different hotels and a camp site, all of which are managed by Voyages Hotels and Resorts. Most of these hotels have their own restaurant, painted in the red, ochre, green, and blue shades of the Red Centre and dotted with Aboriginal artifacts. The resorts also have barbecue areas where you can cook your own meals. Ayers Rock Resort and Kings Canyon Resort take bookings for those who want to dine out in style under the stars. Known as the Sounds of Silence Dinner, the meal takes place in the desert near Uluṟu and is an experience not to be missed.

WHAT IT COSTS In Australian Dollars				
	$$$$	$$$	$$	$	¢
AT DINNER	over $50	$36–$50	$21–$35	$10–$20	under $10

Prices are for a main course at dinner.

About the Hotels

Until the late 1970s the Red Centre was the domain of overland travelers, whether independent explorers or tour bus passengers, who favored simple accommodations in campsites and caravans. Over the past two decades, however, tourism to this region has gained solid momentum by attracting a new breed of traveler: the sophisticated Australian. A concurrent rise in overseas visitors resulted in quickly expanding accommodations in Alice Springs and Yulara, the site of the Ayers Rock Resort complex. Note that most of the newer and more upscale hotels are out of walking distance from downtown Alice Springs.

Alice Springs has a everything from youth hostels and comfortable motels to casinos and five-star resorts. Caravan and camping parks are popular, and have numerous facilities and even entertainment. Ayers Rock Resort, a hotel complex in the desert, has seven different accommodations managed by Voyages Hotels and Resorts. Some are amazing and innovative—such as the Longitude 131 ° resort, a collection of stylish, permanent tents with floor-to-ceiling windows, the closest accommodations to Uluṟu. Homesteads and cattle stations also abound, and you can stay on the ranch or camp on the property.

The high season runs from April to September, so make sure to book ahead during this time. The Central Australian Tourism Visitors Centre in Alice Springs has hotel details, and Voyages Hotels & Resorts handles Ayers Rock Resort bookings. Ask about low-season discounts.

WHAT IT COSTS In Australian Dollars				
	$$$$	$$$	$$	$	¢
FOR 2 PEOPLE	over $300	$201–$300	$151–$200	$100–$150	under $100

Hotel prices are for two people in a standard double room in high season, including tax and service, based on the European Plan (with no meals) unless otherwise noted.

Timing
Winter, May through September, is the best time to visit, as nights are crisp and cold, and days are pleasantly warm. Summer temperatures—which can rise to 35°C (95°F)—make hiking and exploring uncomfortable.

10

Aborigine Art & Legends
Virtually all the natural features of the Red Centre—and particularly around Uluṟu, Kata Tjuṯa, and Kings Canyon—play a part in the Aboriginal creation legend, often referred to as The Dreamtime. The significance of these sacred sites is best discovered on a walking tour led by Aboriginal guides, who will also introduce you to such true Outback bush tucker as witchetty grubs. You'll find ancient Aboriginal rock paintings inside some of the caves at the base of Uluṟu itself, as well as rock carvings in the Ewaninga Rock Carvings Conservation Reserve 39 km (24 mi) south of Alice Springs, and at the Corroboree Rock Conservation Reserve 47 km (29 mi) east of Alice. Aboriginal crafts include beautiful dot paintings (in which images are created by a series of colorful dots), woodcarvings, baskets, sculptures, and didgeridoos.

Amazing Geology
The most amazing geological features of the Red Centre are Uluṟu (Ayers Rock) and Kata Tjuṯa (The Olgas). The gorgeous West MacDonnell Ranges are another highlight of the region, where you'll find crystal-clear water holes, gorges, oasis-style palm trees, plunging chasms, and even the 140-million-year-old, 20-km-wide (12-mi-wide) Gosse Bluff meteorite crater. The East MacDonnell Ranges also have gaps and gorges with ancient rock art, while Kings Canyon has sensational views and the rocky domes of the Lost City. Other impressive landforms are the Mt. Connor mesa near Ayers Rock Resort, and the 50-meter (164-foot), red-and-yellow sandstone Chambers Pillar 160 km (99 mi) south of Alice Springs.

Desert Camping
Camping out in the desert under a full moon and the Milky Way is an experience that you will carry with you for the rest of your life. Few travelers realize that there are far more stars and other astronomical sights, like the fascinating Magellanic Clouds, visible in the Southern Hemisphere than in the north. Nights can be very cold in winter, but happily the native mulga wood supplies the best fire in the world, burning hot and long for cooking and for curling up next to in your sleeping bag—a tent is unnecessary. To avoid ants, make your campsite in a dry, sandy riverbed, preferably near a grove of tall ghost gums for shade in the daytime.

Gorges & Canyons
The West MacDonnell Ranges include the amazing gorges of Finke Gorge National Park, where you'll find an oasis of thousands of red cabbage palms in Palm Valley. Glen Helen Gorge is a gap in the ranges through which the Finke River flows, while the Serpentine Gorge has a series of water holes. Ormiston Gorge is surrounded by towering red walls and a deep water hole, and the Standley Chasm also has red, cathedral-like rock walls. The East MacDonnells have the N'Dhala Gorge, renowned for its prehistoric Aboriginal rock paintings, and the Trephina Gorge, where sheer quartzite cliffs make spectacular hiking scenery. Kings Canyon is the region's biggest and most impressive chasm, and the breathtaking, four-hour walk around the rim offers views into an area aptly called the Garden of Eden.

Outback Grub
"Bush tucker" and "Territory tucker" best describe the unique dishes found on Red Centre menus—be they concoctions of native animals

such as kangaroo or emu, or traditional meats prepared with desert fruits and flavorings. Huge steaks, big burgers, and tasty barramundi fish are usually on the menus of restaurants with a frontier theme. The region's fine dining options are at Ayers Rock Resort's two premier hotels, Sails in the Desert and Longitude 131 °. And where else but the Red Centre can you ride a camel along a dry creek bed or across desert sands and then dine around a campfire, or take an historic train from Alice into the desert and dine under the stars?

Many hotels and campgrounds have picnic areas and free barbecues where you can cook your own tucker, and the national parks are full of beautiful spots where you can eat in the shade of a gum tree or by a water hole. If you're staying at Ayers Rock Resort, book the Sounds of Silence Dinner, a four-course fine-dining experience (with beer and wine) served under the stars. Kings Canyon has the similar Sounds of Starlight, designed for couples only.

Photo Opportunities Landscape photography in the Red Centre is challenging and rewarding. Amazing light and intense colors change through the day, and sunset at Uluṟu is but one of hundreds of panoramic sights that will inspire you to pick up your camera. Heat and dust can be a problem, so be sure to bring insulated, dust-proof bags for your cameras and film stock. Also bring a good UV filter to deflect the fierce light of midday.

If you'll be traveling in September, try to see the Henley-On-Todd Regatta in Alice Springs, which takes place on the third Saturday. The highlight of the all-day event is a race of boaters, dressed in bottomless watercraft, scampering across a dry riverbed. The Alice Springs Camel Cup Carnival, on the second Saturday in July, has camel jockeys racing around a track. The Bangtail Muster cattle and float parade wanders along the main street of Alice Springs on May Day.

The vast Red Centre has myriad opportunities for hiking, four-wheel driving, camel riding, horseback riding, water-hole swimming, and hot-air ballooning. National parks are open daily year-round from 8 to 8, but a handful of attractions close during the hot summer months.

ALICE SPRINGS

Once a ramshackle collection of dusty streets and buildings, Alice Springs—known colloquially as "the Alice"—is today an incongruously suburban tourist center with a population of 27,000 in the middle of the desert. The ancient sites of the town, which are a focus of ceremonial activities for the Arrernte Aboriginal tribe, lie cheek by jowl with air-conditioned shops and hotels. The MacDonnell Ranges dominate Alice Springs, changing color according to the time of day from brick red to purple. Another striking feature of the town is the Todd River. Water rarely runs in the desert, and the deep sandy beds of the Todd, fringed by majestic ghost gum trees, suggest a timelessness far different from the bustle of the nearby town.

Until the 1970s the Alice was a frontier town servicing the region's pastoral industry, and life was tough. During World War II it was one of the few (barely) inhabited stops on the 3,024-km (1,875-mi) supply lines between Adelaide and the front line of Darwin. First established at the

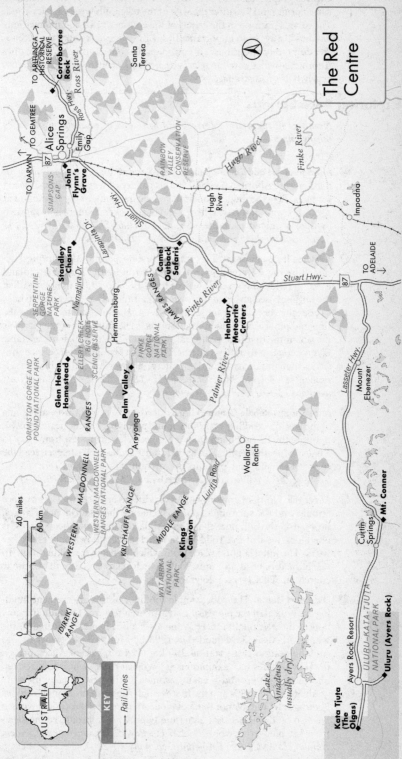

The Red Centre

TO ARLTUNGA HISTORICAL RESERVE →

Corroboree Rock

TO GEMTREE ↑

Santa Teresa

Ross River

Ross Hwy.

TO DARWIN ←

Alice Springs

87

Emily Gap

Hugh River

Finke River

RAINBOW VALLEY CONSERVATION RESERVE

John Flynn's Grave

SIMPSONS GAP

Hugh River

Impadna

Stuart Hwy.

Standley Chasm

Larapinta Dr.

Namatjira Dr.

TO ADELAIDE ↓

87

Camel Outback Safaris

JAMES RANGES

Stuart Hwy.

SERPENTINE GORGE NATURE PARK

Finke River

Hermannsburg

Henbury Meteorite Craters

Lasseter Hwy.

Glen Helen Homestead

ELLERY CREEK BIG HOLE SCENIC RESERVE

FINKE GORGE NATIONAL PARK

Palm Valley

Palmer River

Mount Ebenezer

ORMISTON GORGE AND POUND NATIONAL PARK

RANGES

Areyonga

Wallara Ranch

Luritja Road

Mt. Conner

40 miles

60 km

WESTERN

MACDONNELL

WESTERN MACDONNELL RANGES NATIONAL PARK

KRICHAUFF RANGE

MIDDLE RANGE

Curtin Springs

ULURU-KATA-TJUTA NATIONAL PARK

WATARRKA NATIONAL PARK

Kings Canyon

/DIRRIKI RANGE

Ayers Rock Resort

Uluru (Ayers Rock)

AUSTRALIA

KEY

Rail Lines

Lake Amadeus (usually dry)

Kata Tjuta (The Olgas)

Old Telegraph Station as the town of Stuart, it was moved and renamed Alice Springs in 1933 after the wife of the telegraph boss, Charles Todd. The town's position in the center of the continent as a communications link has always been important. Today the Alice hosts both the U.S. secret-communications base of Pine Gap, just out of town, and the only Aborigine-owned satellite television network, which broadcasts across nearly half of Australia.

Exploring Alice Springs

Numbers in the margin correspond to points of interest on the Alice Springs map.

City Center

⓭ Aboriginal Art and Culture Centre. Learn about the culture and music of the Arrernte Aboriginal people in this gallery of western art and desert artifacts. Play the didgeridoo at the music museum, or try your hand at spear throwing and taste billy tea and bush tucker. Explore on your own or take a guided tour for A$5. ✉ *86 Todd St.,* ☎ *08/8952–3408* ⊕ *www.aboriginalart.com.au* ✆ *A$5* ⊘ *Daily 9–6.*

➋ Adelaide House Museum. This was the first hospital in Alice Springs, designed by the Reverend John Flynn and run by the Australian Inland Mission (which Flynn established) from 1926 to 1939. In hot weather, the hospital used an ingenious system of air tunnels and wet burlap bags to cool the rooms. The building is now a museum devoted to the mission and pioneering days in Alice Springs. The stone hut at the rear was the site of the first field radio transmission in 1926, which made viable Flynn's concept of a flying doctor. The Royal Flying Doctor Service continues to maintain its "mantle of safety" all over Australia's remote settlements. ✉ *Todd Mall* ☎ *08/8952–1856* ✆ *A$4* ⊘ *Mar.–Nov., weekdays 10–4, weekends 10–noon.*

⓬ Alice Springs Reptile Centre. Thorny devils, frill-neck lizards, and some of the world's deadliest snakes are found at this park in the heart of town, opposite the Royal Flying Doctor Service. Viewing is best from May to August when the reptiles are at their most active. You can even feed the snakes by hand and pick up the pythons. ✉ *9 Stuart Terr.* ☎ *08/ 8952–8900* ⊕ *www.reptilecentre.com.au* ✆ *A$7* ⊘ *Daily 9:30–5.*

➊ Anzac Hill. North of downtown, Anzac Hill has an excellent view of Alice Springs and the surrounding area, including the MacDonnell Ranges. From atop the hill, note that Todd Mall, the heart of Alice Springs, is one block west of the Todd River, which at best flows only every few years. The hill is a good place from which to begin a walking tour. To reach the top, head up Lions Walk, which starts opposite the Catholic church on Wills Terrace downtown.

➌ Old Court House. The wide, simple rooflines of this government building are typical of the pioneering style of architecture. The building now houses the National Pioneer Women's Hall of Fame, dedicated to the women of Australia. Founded in 1993 by Molly Clark, owner of Old Andado Station cattle station 200 km (124 mi) east of Alice Springs, the Hall includes such exhibitions as "Women First," which features 100 photos of such ground-breaking women as the first female university graduate in the 1880s and the first woman Anglican priest in the 1990s. Photographs and memorabilia of pioneering Central Australian women are also on display, as is a Signature Quilt with embroidered messages from 350 pioneering women. ✉ *27 Hartley St.* ⊕ *www.pioneerwomen. com.au* ✆ *A$2.20* ⊘ *Feb.–mid-Dec. daily 10–2.*

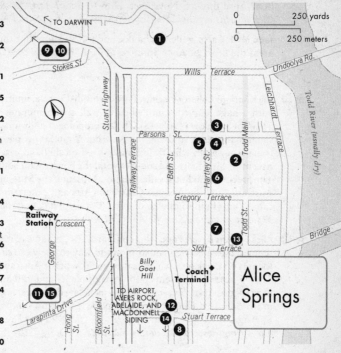

6 **Old Hartley Street School.** Alas, little remains here that recalls the black-boards and lift-top desks in use in 1929, when Miss Pearl Burton was the school's first teacher, but it's worth a peek anyway. The school is also the headquarters of the Alice Springs National Trust branch, and brochures on local sights are available. ⊠ *Hartley St.* ☎ *08/8952–4516* ▦ *Free* ⊙ *Weekdays 10:30–2:30.*

5 **Old Stuart Town Gaol.** The 1908 jail is the oldest surviving building in Alice Springs—and it looks it. With almost no air coming through the jail's tiny barred windows, imprisonment here on a long, hot summer day must have been punishment indeed. ⊠ *Parsons St.* ▦ *A$2.20* ⊙ *Weekdays 10–12:30, Sat. 9:30–12.*

7 **Panorama Guth.** Artist Henk Guth found canvases too restrictive for his vision of central Australia, so he painted his panoramic, unstintingly realistic work in the round. Panorama Guth, inside an unusual crenellated building, has a circumference of 200 feet and stands 20 feet high. There is also a collection of Aboriginal artifacts downstairs. ⊠ *65 Hartley St.* ☎ *08/8952–2013* ▦ *A$5.50* ⊙ *Feb.–mid-Dec. Mon.–Sat. 9–5, Sun. noon–5.*

4 **The Residency.** The high white picket fence on the corner of Parsons and Hartley marks the Residency. Built in 1927 for John Cawood, the first government resident to be appointed to central Australia, it is now a museum with displays depicting the social and economic history of the area. ⊠ *Cnr. Parsons and Hartley Sts.* ☎ *08/8951–5688* ▦ *Donations accepted* ⊙ *Daily 10–5.*

8 **Royal Flying Doctor Service (RFDS).** Directed from the RFDS radio base, doctors use aircraft to make house calls on settlements and homes hundreds of miles apart. Like the School of the Air (⇨ Around Alice), the RFDS is still a vital part of life in the Outback. The visitor center here exhibits historical displays and has an audiovisual show. Tours take place every half hour April through November. ✉ *8–10 Stuart Terr.* ☎ *08/8952–1129* ⊕ *www.rfds.org.au* ✄ *A$5.50* ☾ *Mon.–Sat. 9–4, Sun. 1–4.*

Todd Mall. Cafés, galleries, banks, and tourist shops line this pedestrian area, the heart of Alice Springs. ✉ *Todd St. between Wills and Gregory Terrs.*

Around Alice

★ ⑪ **Alice Springs Cultural Precinct.** Part of this distinctive, multiroof building with a huge, curved, rammed-earth wall commemorates the work of Theodor Strehlow (1908–78). The anthropologist grew up with and later spent many years studying the Arrernte (Aranda) people, central Australia Aborigines who traditionally lived on the land extending north to central Mt. Stuart and south beyond the border with South Australia. The precinct also houses the Aviation Museum, the Museum of Central Australia, and the Araluen Centre for Arts and Entertainment. It's located 2 km (1 mi) southwest of town. ✉ *Larapinta Dr.* ☎ *08/8951–1120* ⊕ *www.nt.gov.au/dam* ✄ *A$8* ☾ *Daily 10–5.*

★ ⑮ **Alice Springs Desert Park.** This combined zoo, botanic gardens, and museum makes a convenient stop on the way to the western ranges. The focus is on the desert, which makes up 70% of the Australian landmass. The 75-acre area presents 320 types of plants and 120 animal species in a range of Australian ecosystems—including the largest nocturnal house in the Southern Hemisphere. The park is 6½ km (4 mi) west of Alice Springs. ✉ *Larapinta Dr.* ☎ *08/8951–8788* ⊕ *www. alicespringsdesertpark.com.au* ✄ *A$18* ☾ *Daily 7:30–6.*

> **off the beaten path**

MACDONNELL SIDING – This station 10 km (6 mi) south of Alice Springs is the resting place of the now-restored *Old Ghan,* a train named for the Afghans who led camel trains on the route from Adelaide. The train began passenger service on August 6, 1929, and over the next 51 years it provided a vital, if erratic, link with the south. In times of flood it could take up to three months to complete the journey. Today the *Ghan* still runs between Adelaide and Alice Springs using a modern train.

Between April and October you can ride the *Old Ghan* 10 km (6 mi) along the original track to Mt. Ertiva. There are morning trips Wednesday and Sunday at 11 for A$19.90, which includes entrance to the museum. Breakfast and dinner rides cost A$39.95 and A$55, respectively. There is a special Saturday Night Dinner on the Ghan trip, as well as Breakfast like a King every Thursday from May to August. ✉ *Stuart Hwy.* ☎ *08/8955–5047 or 1300/880042* ⊕ *www. maintraxnt.com.au* ✄ *A$5.50* ☾ *Daily 9–5.*

❾ **Alice Springs Telegraph Station Historical Reserve.** This reserve 3 km (2 mi) north of Alice Springs was the first white settlement in the area, at the original Alice Springs and the spring itself. The restored telegraph-station buildings are evocative reminders of the Red Centre as it existed at the turn of the 20th century. Within the buildings, exhibits of life at the station and a display of early photographs chronicle its history from 1872. ✉ *Stuart Hwy.* ☎ *08/8952–3993* ✄ *A$7* ☾ *Daily 8–5.*

⑭ **National Road Transport Hall of Fame.** Wander through exhibits of the huge roadtrains, which replaced the former camel trains hauling supplies and equipment through Central Australia. Look for the first roadtrain, which arrived from England in 1934. A 1942 former U.S. Army Diamond T, the first commercially operated cattle train, is also on display.

The museum is 8 km (5 mi) south of Alice Springs. ⊠ *Stuart Hwy.* ☎ *08/ 8952–7161* ⊕ *www.roadtransporthall.com* ☒ *A$8.80* ⊙ *Daily 9–5.*

⑩ **School of the Air.** Operating in many remote areas of Australia, the School of the Air has an ingenious way of teaching its faraway students: children take their classes by correspondence course, supplemented by lessons over the Royal Flying Doctor radio network. Observing the teacher–student relationship by way of radio is fascinating. ⊠ *Head St.* ☎ *08/8951–6834* ⊕ *www.assoa.nt.edu.au* ☒ *A$3.50* ⊙ *Mon.–Sat. 8:30–4:30, Sun. 1:30–4:30.*

> **off the beaten path**
>
> **RAINBOW VALLEY CONSERVATION RESERVE** – View amazing rock formations, which take on rainbow colors in the early morning and late afternoon light, in the sandstone cliffs of the James Range. The colors were caused by water dissolving the red iron in the sandstone, and further erosion created dramatic rock faces and squared towers. To reach the reserve, head is 75 km (45 mi) south of town, then turn left at Stuart's Well. The next 22 km (13 mi) are on a dirt track, requiring a four-wheel-drive vehicle. ⊠ *Stuart Hwy.* ☎ *08/ 8999–5511* ☒ *Free* ⊙ *Daily 8–8.*

Where to Eat

Bush tucker and Mod Oz cuisines have taken off in the Northern Territory over the past 15 years. There's an emphasis on such native game as kangaroo, emu, and barramundi, as well as camel, buffalo, and even crocodile. These are often prepared with native bush fruits, herbs, and spices, and served with Aussie damper (bread) flavored with bush herbs like lemon myrtle.

Pioneer cowboy-theme restaurants specializing in big, hearty steaks and other grilled meats are also popular. These restaurants are found right in the heart of town, as are simple cafés, budget restaurants, and pubs— the latter serve cheap, no-frills meals. Well-known chef Jimmy Shu, who has run restaurants in Melbourne and Malaysia, recently opened a Hanuman Thai, which is proving to be as big a draw as its sister property in Darwin.

$–$$ ✕ **Bojangles Saloon and Restaurant.** The Outback theme of this lively restau-
★ rant includes cowhide seats, tables made from Ghan railway benches, and a life-size replica of bushranger Ned Kelly. Food is classic Northern Territory Tucker: barramundi, kangaroo, camel, emu, thick slabs of ribs, and huge steaks. Nightly entertainment includes the Australian bush band Bloodwood, and all-day blues music concerts on Sundays draw crowds. Beware of Jangles, an 8-foot python who lives behind the bar. ⊠ *80 Todd St.* ☎ *08/8952–2873* ☒ *AE, DC, MC, V.*

$–$$ ✕ **Hanuman Thai.** Purple velvet cushions on timber chairs, parked around
Fodor'sChoice solid timber tables, match the plum-color walls at this comfortable, re-
★ laxing Thai restaurant in the Rydges Plaza Resort. Everyone comes at least once for the grilled Hanuman oysters, seasoned with lemongrass and tangy lime juice, which have converted even avowed seafood-haters. The *Pla Sam Rod* (three-flavored—sweet, sour, spicy—fish) is also popular. Desserts include black rice brûlée and banana spring rolls with dates and malted ice cream. If you like the flavors here and you're traveling north, there's a sister property in Darwin. ⊠ *Barrett Dr.,* ☎ *08/ 8953–7188* ☒ *AE, DC, MC, V* ✍ *Reservations essential.*

$–$$ ✕ **Oriental Gourmet.** Come here for the best Chinese food in the Red Centre. There are no surprises on the menu—honey prawns, beef with black bean sauce, duck with lemon sauce, and the like—but all the dishes are fresh, simple, and soundly prepared. ✉ *80 Hartley St.* ☎ *08/8953–0888* 🖃 *AE, DC, MC, V* ☾ *No lunch.*

\$–\$\$ ✕ **The Outback Bar and Grill.** Yellow walls behind chairs painted in a scramble of bold colors add decorative cheer to this airy Todd Mall restaurant. The menu includes such regional specialties as barramundi, kangaroo, steak, and Outback Burgers. ✉ *75 Todd Mall* ☎ *08/8952–7131* 🖃 *AE, DC, MC, V.*

\$–\$\$ ✕ **Overlander Steakhouse.** When locals take out-of-town guests to a restaurant, this is the one they choose. The atmosphere is all Outback, with old saddles, lamps, and equipment from local cattle stations, plus a live nightly Australian floor show. Overall, this folkloric experience maintains a hearty standard of cooking, presenting Northern Territory specialties. Dip into an appetizer of vol-au-vent filled with crocodile, or the mixed grill of kangaroo, camel, and barramundi. ✉ *72 Hartley St.* ☎ *08/8952–2159* 🖃 *AE, DC, MC, V* ☾ *No lunch.*

★ \$–\$\$ ✕ **Red Ochre.** At this funky, café-style restaurant you can explore the Outback with your knife and fork by tasting innovative dishes made with local ingredients. Earth-yellow walls are the backdrop to attractive art, and eating here is a sunny pleasure. The theme is native Oz foods; look for smoked kangaroo, bush-tomato salsa, aged prime beef, and emu carpaccio. The Taste of the Territory combines kebabs of camel, crocodile, and kangaroo. Make sure to sample from the cosmopolitan wine list. ✉ *Todd Mall* ☎ *08/8952–9614* 🖃 *AE, DC, MC, V.*

¢–\$ ✕ **Bar Doppio.** Take a seat at this al fresco café and sip one of Alice's top-notch espressos as you watch the Todd Mall shoppers stroll by. A casual crowd comes for filling, inexpensive offerings, which include vegetarian dishes, fish, and Turkish bread with a variety of dips. ✉ *Fan Arcade* ☎ *08/8952–6525* 🖃 *No credit cards* ☾ *No dinner Sun.–Thurs.*

¢–\$ ✕ **Todd Tavern.** The only traditional pub in Alice Springs serves cheap, hearty meals all day. Theme-dinner nights, which cost A\$6.95, include steak and endless salad on Wednesday, schnitzel on Thursday, and a traditional roast and vegetables dinner on Sunday. Pick your wine from the on-site bottle shop. ✉ *1 Todd Mall* ☎ *08/8952–1255* 🖃 *AE, DC, MC, V.*

Where to Stay

Alice Springs has a handful of elite hotels and many medium-priced accommodations, as well as numerous backpacker spots, a youth hostel, three caravan parks, and small bed-and-breakfasts in private homes. Most accommodations are in the heart of town or within 5 km (3 mi). Most hotels have air-conditioning, swimming pools, barbecue facilities, guest laundries, and free off-street parking, and many also have spacious grounds with children's playgrounds and picnic areas. Shuttle buses run between in-town hotels and the airport.

Although rates don't change much between low and high travel seasons, you can find bargains during the very hot months of December through February. The best way to find good deals is to surf the Internet, or to contact the Central Australian Tourism Visitors Centre before booking.

Hotels & Motels

\$\$\$ 🏨 **Alice Springs Resort.** High ceilings and potted palms grace the spacious, airy reception and restaurant areas of this hotel on the east bank of the Todd River. Many of the earth-tone rooms open directly onto a large lawn, which at dusk is covered in hungry pink-and-gray galahs, one of Australia's native bird species. It's just a few minutes' stroll to the heart of town. ✉ *34 Stott Terr., 0870* ☎ *08/8951–4545* 🖷 *08/ 8953–0995* ⊕ *www.voyages.com.au* ⇗ *144 rooms* ♿ *Restaurant, in-*

room data ports, pool, 2 bars, laundry service, Internet, meeting rooms, travel services, free parking; no smoking ☰ *AE, DC, MC, V.*

★ **$$-$$$** 🏨 **Crowne Plaza Resort Alice Springs.** Pastel hues and landscaped lawns are the hallmarks of the best hotel in Alice Springs, even if it's a mile from town. The rooms, appointed with bleached wood furniture, all have balconies with views over the pool and the low, barren mountains. The highly regarded Hanuman Thai restaurant is a local favorite. You can catch a cab into town for A$6–A$9. ⊠ *Barrett Dr. 0870* ☎ *08/8950–8000* 🖷 *08/8952–3822* ⊕ *www.crowneplaza.com.au* ⇆ *235 rooms, 7 suites* ♻ *2 restaurants, some microwaves, room TVs with movies, 2 tennis courts, pool, health club, sauna, 2 bars, laundry facilities, Internet, meeting rooms, travel services, free parking* ☰ *AE, DC, MC, V.*

$-$$ 🏨 **Novotel Outback Alice Springs Resort.** Shadowed by the mountain range along the town's southern periphery, the modern resort has rooms with exposed-brick walls, comfortable furnishings, and molded fiberglass bathrooms. A pool and barbecue area invite families to gather. It's 1½ km (1 mi) to Alice Springs, but there's a courtesy shuttle. ⊠ *Stephens Rd., 0870* ☎ *08/8952–6100 or 1800/810664* 🖷 *08/8952–1988* ⊕ *www.accorhotels.com.au* ⇆ *140 rooms* ♻ *Restaurant, room TVs with movies, tennis court, pool, spa, bar, laundry service, Internet, meeting room, free parking* ☰ *AE, DC, MC, V.*

★ **$** 🏨 **Desert Rose Inn.** This motel provides the best value for families staying in Alice Springs. Budget rooms are cramped and standards are unexceptional, but the family studios are more spacious. Exposed brick walls set the tone for these rooms, which contain a double bed, two single beds, a balcony, and a kitchenette with a sink, a microwave, and a breakfast table. Most rooms have a bath or shower. ⊠ *15–17 Railway Terr., 0870* ☎ *08/8952–1411 or 1800/896116* 🖷 *08/8952–3232* ⊕ *www.desertroseinn.com.au* ⇆ *48 rooms, 25 studios* ♻ *Some kitchenettes, pool, laundry service, free parking* ☰ *MC, V.*

★ **$** 🏨 **Mercure Inn Diplomat Hotel Alice Springs.** The location of the Diplomat—300 feet from the town center—is ideal if you don't have a car. Comfortable, carpeted rooms are decorated with dark bedspreads and drapes, and the hotel is just remote enough to guarantee peaceful evenings. Avoid ground-floor rooms if you want privacy; the glass doors open onto the central pool and parking lot. ⊠ *Gregory Terr. and Hartley St., 0870* ☎ *08/8952–8977 or 1800/804885* 🖷 *08/8953–0225* ⊕ *www.accorhotels.com.au* ⇆ *82 rooms* ♻ *Restaurant, room TVs with movies, pool, bar, laundry service, free parking; no-smoking rooms* ☰ *AE, DC, MC, V.*

¢-$ 🏨 **Alice on Todd Apartments.** On the banks of the Todd River about a mile from town, these self-contained apartments are priced at a steal. Studios sleep two, and one-bedrooms sleep four. Each apartment has a patio or balcony. Make friends at the barbecue area, then hop across the dry riverbed to try your luck at Lasseters Hotel Casino. ⊠ *Cnr. South Terr. and Strehlow St.,* ☎ *08/8953–8033* 🖷 *08/8952–9902* ⊕ *www.aliceontodd.com* ⇆ *15 studios, 4 one-bedroom, and 15 two-bedroom apartments* ♻ *Picnic area, kitchens, pool, recreation room, laundry facilities, Internet, free parking* ☰ *MC, V.*

¢ 🏨 **Heavitree Gap Outback Lodge.** See wild, black-footed rock wallabies fed nightly at this resort settled into the base of the MacDonnell Ranges. There's a huge camping area—plus four-bed bunkhouses and lodge rooms, all with air-conditioning and kitchenettes. Nightly entertainment includes a bush balladeer. A free shuttle runs to Alice Springs. ⊠ *Palm Circuit* ☎ *08/8950–4444* 🖷 *08/8952–9394* ⊕ *www.aurora-resorts.com.au* ⇆ *60 rooms, 16 bunkhouses, 90 powered sites* ♻ *Restaurant, grocery, picnic area, kitchenettes, room TVs with movies, pool, bicycles, playground, laundry facilities* ☰ *AE, DC, MC, V.*

¢ ⊡ **Melanka Lodge.** Budget accommodations include 30 three- or four-bed dorm rooms, 40 doubles with shared bath, 5 rooms with private bath, and 18 family rooms with private bath. An Internet café and a games room are on-site. The property is just south of the main shopping area. ⊠ *94 Todd St., 0870* ☎ *08/8952–2233 or 1800/896110* 🖷 *08/8952–2890* ⊕ *www.southernlodges.com.au* ⊅ *93 rooms* ⟁ *Restaurant, 2 pools, bar, recreation room, laundry service, meeting room, travel services, free parking; no-smoking rooms* ⊟ *AE, DC, MC, V.*

¢ ⊡ **Outback Motor Lodge.** Simple, clean accommodations have kitchen facilities and bathrooms with showers. The only public areas are the lawn around a small pool and the office. ⊠ *South Terr. 0870* ☎ *08/8952–3888 or 1800/896133* 🖷 *08/8953–2166* ⊕ *www.outbackmotorlodge.com.au* ⊅ *42 rooms* ⟁ *Kitchenettes, some microwaves, room TVs with movies, pool, laundry facilities, Internet, car rental, free parking, some pets allowed; no-smoking rooms* ⊟ *AE, DC, MC, V.*

¢ ⊡ **Todd Tavern.** After a rollicking night at the only real pub in town, you can crash in one of the clean, comfortable rooms. Some have private bathrooms; all have tea- and coffee-making equipment. The tavern has a bar, restaurant, gaming, and gambling facilities (such as the Australian TAB, where you can bet on horse races across the country), slot machines, and a bottle shop. ⊠ *1 Todd Mall 0870* ☎ *08/8952–1255* 🖷 *08/8952–3830* ⊕ *www.toddtavern.com.au* ⊅ *23 rooms* ⟁ *Restaurant, fans, refrigerators, pub, sports bar; no room phones, no room TVs* ⊟ *AE, DC, MC, V.*

¢ ⊡ **YHA Hostel.** This facility in the center of town has several dorm rooms and two family rooms, all with shared bath. ⊠ *Leichhardt Terr. and Parsons St., 0870* ☎ *08/8952–8855* 🖷 *08/8952–4144* ⊕ *www.yha. com.au* ⊅ *22 rooms* ⟁ *Pool, recreation room, laundry facilities, Internet, travel services; no room phones, no room TVs, no kids under 7, no smoking* ⊟ *MC, V.*

Caravan, Trailer, RV Park

★ ¢–$ ⚠ **MacDonnell Ranges Holiday Park.** Tucked behind the ranges 5 km (3 mi) south of town, this extensive, well-planned park has many trees, good children's facilities, Internet access, nightly entertainment—and a free pancake breakfast on Sundays. Most of the sites have electrical hookups, and 48 have a private shower and toilet. Facilities for people with disabilities are also provided. A free shuttle bus runs from the airport. ⊠ *Palm Pl., off Palm Circuit 0871* ⊙ *Box 9025* ☎ *08/8952–6111 or 1800/ 808373* 🖷 *08/8952–5236* ⊕ *www.macrange.com.au* ⊅ *360 sites* ⟁ *Flush toilets, full hook-ups, drinking water, showers, grills, picnic tables, restaurant, electricity, public telephone, general store, service station, playground, 2 pools* ⊟ *AE, MC, V.*

Nightlife & the Arts

Lasseters Hotel Casino (⊠ Barrett Dr. ☎ 08/8950–7777 or 1800/808975) has the full range of games: blackjack, roulette, slot machines, keno, and the lively Australian game of two-up. It's free to get into this late-night local haunt, which is open from midday until about 3 AM. The Irish pub has entertainment Wednesday through Sunday.

Sounds of Starlight (⊠ 40 Todd Mall ☎ 08/8953–0826), affiliated with the Aboriginal Dreamtime Art Gallery, is the place to enjoy Outback theater performances and didgeridoo music. Concerts are held at 8 PM Tuesday through Saturday (A$19).

Sports & the Outdoors

Camel Riding

Take a camel to dinner or breakfast, or just ramble along the dry Todd River bed, astride a "ship of the desert." **Frontier Camel Farm** (✉ Ross Hwy. ☎ 08/8953–0444) has short rides, river rambles, and breakfast rides beginning at 6:30 AM, as well as 4 PM dinner rides which include a three-course meal, wine, and beer. Prices range from A$10 for a short ride to A$100 for a dinner date. Transfers from Alice Springs hotels are included with the breakfast and dinner tours.

Hot-Air Ballooning

At dawn on most mornings, you can glimpse hot-air balloons floating in the sky around Alice Springs. **Outback Ballooning** (✉ 35 Kennett Ct. ☎ 1800/809790) makes hotel pickups about an hour before dawn and returns between 9 AM and 10 AM. The A$190 fee covers 30 minutes of flying time and a champagne breakfast. A 60-minute flight costs A$290.

Quad-Bike Riding

Hop aboard a motorbike with huge wheels and explore the Red Centre's oldest working cattle station with **Outback Quad Adventures** (✉ Undoolya Station ☎ 08/8953–0697). The company collects you from Alice Springs and takes you to the station 17 km (10 mi) out of town on the edge of the MacDonnell Ranges. No special license is needed, and all tours are escorted by guides with two-way radios. Half-day (A$170) and full-day tours (A$290) run year-round and include meals or light refreshments.

Shopping

Apart from the ubiquitous souvenir shops, the main focus of shopping in Alice Springs is Aboriginal art and artifacts. Central Australian Aboriginal art is characterized by intricate patterns of dots, commonly called sand paintings because they were originally drawn on sand as ceremonial devices. The **Aboriginal Desert Art Gallery** (✉ 87 Todd St. ☎ 08/8953–1005) is one of the best local galleries. The **Aboriginal Dreamtime Art Gallery** (✉ 63 Todd Mall ☎ 08/8952–8861) represents an impressive number of important Aboriginal artists. The **Todd Mall Markets** (✉ Todd St. ☎ 08/8952–9299) are held every second Sunday morning from February to December. Local arts, crafts, and food are displayed in the stalls to a background of live entertainment.

Alice Springs A to Z

To research prices, get advice from other travelers, and book travel arrangements, visit www.fodors.com.

AIR TRAVEL

Qantas serves the local airport. The flights from Sydney, Melbourne, and Brisbane take 3 hours; from Adelaide, it's 2 hours.
🛪 Qantas ☎ 13-1313 ⊕ www.qantas.com.

AIRPORT

Alice Springs Airport, with its bright, cool passenger terminal, is 15 km (9 mi) southeast of town.
🛪 Alice Springs Airport ☎ 08/8951-1211 ⊕ www.ntapl.com.au.

AIRPORT TRANSFERS Alice Springs Airport Shuttle Service meets every flight. The ride to your hotel costs A$10 each way. On request, the bus will also pick you up at your hotel and take you to the airport. Alice Springs Taxis maintains a stand at the airport. The fare to most parts of town is A$20–A$25.

🚹 **Alice Springs Airport Shuttle Service** ✉ Shop 6, Capricornia Centre, Gregory Terr. ☎ 08/8953-0310 or 1800/621188. **Alice Springs Taxis** ☎ 08/8952-1877.

BUS TRAVEL

Greyhound-operated interstate buses and McCafferty's buses arrive and depart from the Coles Complex. AAT Kings coaches, which run day and extended tours, have a separate terminal.

🚹 **Bus Lines AAT Kings** ✉ 74 Todd St. ☎ 08/8952-1700 or 1800/896111 ⊕ www. aatkings.com. **Greyhound/McCafferty's** ✉ Coles Complex, Gregory Terr. ☎ 08/ 8952-3952 or 13-2030 ⊕ www.greyhound.com.au ⊕ www.mccaffertys.com.au.

CAR RENTAL

Avis, Budget, Hertz, Thrifty, and the local agency, Territory Rent-a-Car, all have offices in Alice Springs.

🚹 **Agencies Avis** ✉ 52 Hartley St. ☎ 08/8953-5533 ⊕ www.avis.com.au. **Budget** ✉ Gregory Terr. ☎ 08/8952-8899 ⊕ www.budget.com.au. **Hertz** ✉ 76 Hartley St. ☎ 08/ 8952-2644 ⊕ www.hertznt.com.au. **Thrifty/Territory Rent-a-Car** ✉ 71 Hartley St. ☎ 08/8952-9999 or 08/8952-2400 ⊕ www.thrifty.com.au.

CAR TRAVEL

There is only one road into Alice Springs, and it runs north to south: the Stuart Highway, commonly called the Track. The town center lies east of the highway. The 1,610-km (1,000-mi) drive from Adelaide takes about 24 hours. From Darwin the 1,515-km (940-mi) drive is about 100 km (62 mi) shorter than from the south.

If you plan on going into the desert, renting a car is a smart idea. It's 440 km (273 mi) from Alice Springs to Ayers Rock Resort. The trip takes about five hours. The paved, scenic road is in very good condition.

The N.T. Road Report provides the latest information about conditions on the many unpaved roads in the area. In the event of a breakdown, contact the Automobile Association of N.T. in Alice Springs.

🚹 **Automobile Association of N.T.** ✉ 58 Sargent St. ☎ 08/8952-1087 ⊕ www.aant. com.au. **N.T. Road Report** ☎ 08/8955-5577 or 1800/246199 ⊕ www.ntholidays.com. au.

EMERGENCIES

In case of an emergency, dial 000 to reach an ambulance, the fire department, or the police.

🚹 **Doctors & Dentists Central Clinic** ✉ 76 Todd St. ☎ 08/8952-1088. **Department of Health Dental Clinic** ✉ Flynn Dr. ☎ 08/8951-6713.

🚹 **Hospital Alice Springs Hospital** ✉ Gap Rd. ☎ 08/8951-7777.

🚹 **Pharmacies Alice Springs Pharmacy** ✉ Shop 19, Hartley St. ☎ 08/8952-1554. **Plaza Amcal Chemist** ✉ Alice Plaza, Todd Mall ☎ 1800/068119.

TOURS

The narrated *Alice Wanderer* bus completes a 70-minute circuit of most tourist attractions in and around Alice Springs 9 to 5 daily. You can leave and rejoin the bus whenever you like for a flat rate of A$30.

Several companies conduct half-day tours of Alice Springs. All include visits to the Royal Flying Doctor Service Base, School of the Air, Telegraph Station, and Anzac Hill scenic lookout. AAT Kings and Tailormade Tours & Airport Limousines run three-hour tours.

🚹 **Tour Operators AAT Kings** ✉ 74 Todd St. ☎ 08/8952-1700 or 1800/334009 ⊕ www. aatkings.com. *Alice Wanderer* ✉ Box 2110, Alice Springs, NT 0871 ☎ 08/8952-2111 ⊕ www.alicewanderer.com.au. **Tailormade Tours & Airport Limousines** ✉ 23 Gosse St. ☎ 08/8952-1731 or 1800/806641.

TRAIN TRAVEL
The *Ghan,* named after the Afghan camel-train drivers who traveled the route before the railway, provides one of the world's classic rail journeys. The train leaves Adelaide at 5:15 PM Sunday and Friday, arriving in Alice Springs at 11:55 AM Monday and Saturday. On Mondays at 4 PM it continues to Darwin via Katherine, arriving at 4 PM Tuesday. Trains from Darwin depart Wednesday at 10 AM. Return trains leave Alice Springs at 2 PM Thursday and Saturday, arriving in Adelaide at 9 AM Tuesday and Sunday. Alice Springs's railway station is 2½ km (1½ mi) west of Todd Mall.

🚂 **Ghan** Great Southern Railway ☎ Bookings 13-2147, holiday packages 1300/132147 ⊕ www.trainways.com.au.

VISITOR INFORMATION
The Central Australian Tourism Industry Association dispenses information, advice, and maps and will book tours and cars. For additional information on buildings of historical significance in and around Alice Springs, contact the National Trust, open weekdays 10:30–2:30.

🚩 Tourist Information **Central Australian Tourism Industry Association** ✉ Gregory Terr., 0870 ☎ 08/8952-5800 ⊕ www.centralaustraliantourism.com or www.ntholidays. com.au. **National Trust** ✉ Old Hartley Street School, Hartley St. ☎ 08/8952-4516.

SIDE TRIPS FROM ALICE SPRINGS

East MacDonnell Ranges

Spectacular scenery and Aboriginal rock art found in the MacDonnell Ranges east of the Alice are well worth a day or more of exploring. Emily Gap (a sacred site), Jessie Gap, and Corroboree Rock are all within the first 44 km (27 mi) east of Alice Springs. Beyond these are Trephina Gorge, John Hayes Rockhole, and N'Dhala Gorge Nature Park (with numerous hide-and-seek Aboriginal rock carvings). Arltunga Historical Reserve, 110 km (69 mi) northeast of Alice, contains the ruins of a former 19th-century gold-rush site. There's no gold today, but there is a pub, a store, and a visitors' center. If you fancy fossicking for your own semiprecious stones, you can take your pick—and shovel—at Gemtree in the Harts Ranges, 140 km (87 mi) northeast of Alice. Here you can join a tag-along tour in your car (conventional vehicles are suitable), with guides showing you where to look for gems. The desert is a rich source of garnets and zircons.

Caravan, Trailer, RV Park
¢ 🏕 **Gemtree.** Fossick for gems by day and sleep under the stars at night at this bush-style caravan park. Powered sites are A\$22, campsites are A\$9 for two adults, and two-person cabins run A\$65 per night. It's A\$60 to join a tag-along gem-fossicking tour, including equipment. Although it's rustic, located 140 km (87 mi) northeast of Alice Springs, the park has its own golf course. ✉ *Plenty Hwy.* ☎ *08/8956–9855* 🖷 *08/8956 9860* ⊕ *www.gemtree.com.au* ⇆ *50 powered sites, 20 campsites, 2 cabins* ♨ *Laundry facilities, fire pits, general store* 🖃 *MC, V.*

West MacDonnell Ranges

The MacDonnell Ranges west of Alice Springs are, like the eastern ranges, broken by a series of chasms and gorges, many of which can be visited in a single day. To reach them, drive out of town on Larapinta Drive, the western continuation of Stott Terrace.

CloseUp

THE HEARTLAND

FOR MOST AUSTRALIANS, the Red Centre is the mystical and legendary core of the continent, and Uluru is its beautiful focal point. Whether they have been there or not, to locals its image symbolizes a steady pulse that radiates deep through the red earth, through the heartland, and all the way to the coasts.

Little more than a thumbprint within the vast Australian continent, the Red Centre is barren and isolated. Its hard, relentless topography and lack of the conveniences found in most areas of civilization make this one of the most difficult areas of the country in which to explore, much less survive. But the early pioneers—some foolish, some hardy—managed to set up bases that thrived. They created cattle stations, introduced electricity, and implemented telegraph services, enabling them to maintain a lifestyle that, if not luxurious, was at least reasonably comfortable.

The people who now sparsely populate the Red Centre are a breed of their own. Many were born and grew up here, but many others were "blow-ins," immigrants from far-flung countries and folk from other Australian states who took up the challenge to make a life in the desert and stayed on as they succeeded. Either way, folks out here have at least a few common characteristics. They're laconic and down-to-earth, canny and astute, and very likely to try to pull your leg when you least expect it.

And no one could survive the isolation without a good sense of humor: Where else in the world would you hold a bottomless boat race in a dry riverbed? The Henley-on-Todd, as it is known, is a sight to behold, with dozens of would-be skippers bumbling along within the bottomless boat frames. A traditional German Octoberfest also takes place every year, another unlikely event in this dry, desolate place. Like the Henley-on-Todd, the event is marked by hilarity, and includes such competitions as tug-of-war, spitting the dummy, and stein-lifting championships—plus a requisite amount of beer drinking.

As the small towns grew and businesses quietly prospered in the mid-1800s, a rail link between Alice Springs and Adelaide was planned. However, the undercurrent of challenge and humor that touches all life here ran through this project as well. Construction began in 1877, but things went wrong from the start. No one had seen rain for ages, and no one expected it; hence, the track was laid right across a floodplain. It wasn't long before locals realized their mistake, when intermittent, heavy floods regularly washed the tracks away. The railway is still in operation today and all works well, but its history is one of many local jokes here.

For some, the Red Centre is the real Australia, a special place where you will meet people whose generous and sincere hospitality may move you. The land and all its riches offer some of the most spectacular and unique sights on the planet, along with a sense of timelessness that will slow you down and fill your spirit. Take a moment to shade your eyes from the sun and pick up on the subtleties that nature has carefully protected and camouflaged here, and you will soon discover that the Red Centre is not the dead center.

—Bev Malzard

John Flynn's Grave is on a rise with the stark ranges behind, providing a memorable setting 6 km (4 mi) west of Alice Springs. ☒ *Larapinta Dr.* ☎ *no phone* ☒ *Free* ☉ *Daily 24 hrs.*

Simpsons Gap National Park isn't dramatic, but it is the closest gorge to town. Stark-white ghost gums, red rocks, and the purple-hazed mountains will give you a taste of the scenery to be seen farther into the ranges. The gap itself can be crowded, but it's only 200 yards from the parking lot. ☒ *Larapinta Dr., 17 km (10½ mi) west of Alice Springs, then 5½ km (3½ mi) on side road* ☎ *no phone* ☒ *Free* ☉ *Daily 8–8.*

Standley Chasm is one of the most impressive canyons in the MacDonnell Ranges. At midday, when the sun is directly overhead, the 10-yard-wide canyon glows red from the reflected light. The walk from the parking lot takes about 20 minutes and is rocky toward the end. There is a kiosk at the park entrance. ☒ *Larapinta Dr., 40 km (25 mi) west of Alice Springs, then 9 km (5½ mi) on Standley Chasm Rd.* ☎ *08/8956–7440* ☒ *A$6* ☉ *Daily 8:30–5.*

Namatjira Drive

A ride along Namatjira Drive takes you past the striking and diverse landscape of this remote desert region to scenic, accessible national parks and gorges. Beyond Standley Chasm, the mileage starts adding up, and you should be prepared for rough road conditions.

Ellery Creek Big Hole Scenic Reserve (☒ Namatjira Dr.), 88 km (55 mi) west of Alice Springs, is believed to have the coolest swimming hole in the Red Centre. It's also the deepest and most permanent water hole in the area; thus, you may catch glimpses of wild creatures quenching their thirst. Take the 3-km (2-mi) Dolomite Walk for a close-up look at this fascinating geological site.

Serpentine Gorge (☒ Namatjira Dr.), 99 km (61 mi) west of Alice Springs, requires a refreshing swim through the gorge for the best perspective. A lookout above the cliffs provides a sweeping view. Aboriginal myth has it that the pool is the home of a fierce serpent; hence the name. If you don't fancy the swim, you can rock-hop upstream to reach a flooded chasm. Note that the last 4 km (2½ mi) to the gorge is on rough track.

Ormiston Gorge and Pound National Park (☒ Namatjira Dr.), 128 km (79 mi) west of Alice Springs, is one of the few truly breathtaking sights of the western ranges. A short climb takes you to Gum Tree Lookout, from where you can see the spectacular 820-foot-high gorge walls rising from the pools below. Unfortunately, it can be crowded at times. Trails include the 7-km (4-mi) Pound Walk.

Glen Helen Gorge National Park (☒ Namatjira Dr.), 140 km (87 mi) west of Alice Springs, has the largest gorge, a water hole, and the rather sporadic coursing of the Finke River.

Where to Stay & Eat

★ $ ✕☒ **Glen Helen Resort.** This homestead resort in the West MacDonnell Ranges doesn't have a pool, but there's a natural swimming hole at the front door. You can camp, stay in one of the 10 four-person Stockman's Quarters with shared facilities, or splurge on an air-conditioned motel room. There's a restaurant, and entertainment three times a week. ☒ *Namatjira Dr., Alice Springs, 0871* ☝ *Box 2629,* ✛ *135 km (84 mi) west of Alice Springs* ☎ *08/8956–7489* ☒ *08/8956–7495* ☝ *www. southernlodges.com.au* ☝ *25 rooms, 105 unpowered sites, 22 powered sites* ☝ *Restaurant, grocery, picnic area, refrigerators, bar, beer garden, laundry facilities, travel services* ☒ *AE, MC, V.*

Hermannsburg & Beyond

One alternative after passing Standley Chasm is to continue on Larapinta Drive in the direction of Hermannsburg to see a restored mission, and beyond that to a national park. Hermannsburg itself has tea rooms, a supermarket, and a service station. The buildings of the early **Lutheran Mission**, dating to the late 19th century, have been restored, and visitors are welcome. Aboriginal artist Albert Namatjira was born into the Arrernte community at the mission in 1902. ⊠ *Larapinta Dr., 132 km (82 mi) from Alice Springs* ☎ *no phone* 🖃 *A$4* ☉ *Daily 9–4.*

Palm Valley in **Finke Gorge National Park** is a remnant of a time when Australia had a wetter climate and supported palm trees over large areas. The foliage here includes *Livistonia mariae,* an ancient, endemic variety of cabbage palm. The area is like a slice of the tropical north dropped into the middle of the Red Centre. You need a four-wheel-drive vehicle to continue past Hermannsburg to get here.

ULURU & KATA TJUTA

It isn't difficult to see why the Aborigines attach spiritual significance to Uluru (Ayers Rock). It's an awe-inspiring sight, rising above the plain and dramatically changing color throughout the day. The Anangu people are the traditional owners of the land around Uluru and Kata Tjuta. They believe they are direct descendants of the beings—some of whom include a python, an emu, a blue-tongue lizard, and a poisonous snake—who formed the land and its physical features during the Tjukurpa (creation period). Tjukurpa also refers to the Anangu religion, law, and moral system, a knowledge of past and present handed down from memory through stories and other oral traditions.

Rising more than 1,100 feet from the flat surrounding plain, Uluru is one of the world's largest monoliths, and because it's a sacred site, visitors should not climb the rock. Kata Tjuta (the Olgas), 53 km (33 mi) west, is a series of 36 gigantic rock domes hiding a maze of fascinating gorges and crevasses. The names Ayers Rock and the Olgas are used out of familiarity alone; at the sites themselves, the Aboriginal Uluru and Kata Tjuta are the respective names of preference.

Uluru and Kata Tjuta have very different compositions. The great monolith of Uluru is a type of sandstone called arkose, while the rock domes at Kata Tjuta are composed of conglomerate. It was once thought that they rest upon the sandy terrain like pebbles; however, both formations are in fact the tips of tilted rock strata that extend into the earth for thousands of meters. Perhaps two-thirds of each formation extends below the surface, tilted during a period of intense geological activity more than 300 million years ago—the arkose by nearly 90 degrees and the conglomerate only about 15 degrees. The rock surrounding the formations fractured and quickly eroded away about 40 million years ago, leaving the present structures standing as separate entities. But this is just one interpretation—ask your Aboriginal guide to relate the ancient stories of the Rock.

Both of these intriguing sights lie within Uluru–Kata Tjuta National Park, which is protected as a World Heritage Site. As such, it is one of just a few parks in the world recognized in this way for both its landscape and cultural values. The whole experience is a bit like seeing the Grand Canyon turned inside out, and you'll likely remember a visit here for a lifetime.

On the Way to Uluṟu

The 440-km (273-mi) drive to Uluṟu from Alice Springs along the Stuart and Lasseter highways takes about five hours, but you can see some interesting sights along the way if you're prepared to make a few detours.

Neil and Jayne Waters, owners of **Camels Australia,** offer everything from quick jaunts to five-day safaris. Day trips include a light lunch. Book all rides at least a day in advance. It's A\$35 for a one-hour ride; A\$150 daily for safaris, including camping gear and meals; and A\$110 for day treks with lunch. ⊠ *Stuart Hwy., 93 km (58 mi) south of Alice Springs* ☎ *08/8956–0925* 🖷 *08/8956–0909* ⊕ *www.camels-australia.com.au.*

The **Henbury Meteorite Craters,** a group of 12 depressions between 6 feet and 600 feet across, are believed to have been formed by a meteorite shower about 5,000 years ago. One is 60 feet deep. To get here, you must travel off the highway on an unpaved road. ⊠ *Ernest Giles Rd., 134 km (83 mi) south of Alice Springs and 13 km (8 mi) west of Stuart Hwy.*

A ride through **Watarrka National Park** takes you past desert foliage and wildflowers and to ⇨ **King's Canyon.** The park is accessible by car on the Mereenie Track from Glen Helen. To make this loop around the West MacDonnell Ranges, you'll need an Aboriginal Land Entry Permit, which is A\$2.20 from the **Central Australian Visitor Information Centre** (☎ 08/8952–5800 or 1800/645199) in Alice Springs. ⊠ *Luritja Rd., 167 km (104 mi) from the turnoff on Lasseter Hwy.*

FodorśChoice **Kings Canyon,** in ⇨ **Watarrka National Park,** is one of the finest sights
★ in Central Australia. Sheltered within the sheer cliff walls of the canyon is a world of ferns and rock pools, permanent springs, and woodlands. The main path is the 6-km (4-mi) Canyon Walk, which starts with a fairly steep climb to the top of the escarpment and leads to a delightful water hole in the so-called Garden of Eden halfway through the four-hour walk. ⊠ *Luritja Rd., 167 km (104 mi) from the turnoff on Lasseter Hwy.*

South of Kings Canyon, on the Lasseter Highway heading toward Uluṟu, you can see **Mt. Conner** from the side of the road. Located on Curtain Springs Cattle Station, and often mistaken for Uluṟu from a distance, it's actually a huge mesa. Nearby Curtain Springs Roadhouse is a good stopover for refreshments; you can also arrange guided tours of Mt Conner, the cattle station, and Lake Amadeus. The roadhouse has caravan sites and cabins with private facilities. ⊠ *Lasseter Hwy., 41 km (25 mi) from the turnoff on Luritja Rd.* ☎ *08/8956–2906.*

Where to Stay & Eat

\$–\$\$\$\$ ✕🛏 **Kings Canyon Resort.** This resort, 6 km (4 mi) from the canyon, is
FodorśChoice the only place to stay within Watarrka National Park. Check into one
★ of the deluxe spa rooms, then take the four-hour Canyon Walk, so you can return to the whirlpool bath. There's only a glass wall separating the whirlpool from views of the canyon, but each room is totally private. Accommodations include two- and four-bed lodge rooms, as well as a campground. Book the Sounds of Firelight Dinner to nosh in style around a campfire under the stars. ⊠ *PMB 136, Alice Springs, NT 0871* ☎ *08/8956–7442 or 1800/817622* 🖷 *08/8956–7410* ⊕ *www.voyages. com.au* 🛏 *164 rooms, 52 powered caravan sites, 200 tent sites* ⚙ *Restaurant, café, grocery, picnic, refrigerators, some room TVs with movies, tennis court, 2 pools, bicycles, hiking, 2 bars, shop, laundry facilities, travel services, free parking* ▭ *AE, DC, MC, V.*

Uluru & Kata Tjuta

The Ayers Rock Resort area serves as the base for exploration of Uluru and Kata Tjuta. Allow about 20 minutes to drive to Uluru from the resort area; Kata Tjuta will take another 30 minutes. The park entrance fee of A$17 is valid for a week. The sunset-viewing area lies 13 km (8 mi) from the resort on the way to Uluru.

Uluru

Fodor'sChoice ★ An inevitable sensation of excitement builds as you approach the great rock—Uluru just keeps looming larger and larger. After entering the park through a toll gate, you'll come upon the serpentine shape of the **Uluru–Kata Tjuta Cultural Centre** (☎ 08/8956–2299), two buildings that reflect the Kuniya and Liru stories of two ancestral snakes who fought a battle on the southern side of Uluru. The center, on the right side of the road just before you reach the rock, highlights Aboriginal history, along with information on the return of the park to Aboriginal ownership in 1985. The center contains the park's ranger station, an art shop, and a pottery store with lovely collectibles.

As you work your way around Uluru, your perspective of the great rock changes significantly. Four hours will allow you to walk the 10 km (6 mi) around the rock with time to explore the several deep crevices along the way; or you can drive around it on the paved road. Be aware that some places are Aboriginal sacred sites and cannot be entered. These are clearly signposted. Aboriginal art can be found in caves at the base of the rock.

Only one trail leads to the top of the rock, and the Aboriginal owners of Uluru don't encourage people to climb it. They don't prohibit it either, but the ranger station displays a well-reasoned argument why you should reconsider your intentions to ascend. A local Aborigine was once heard to say, "Why would anyone want to climb it? There's no food or water up there!"

If you decide to climb, it's about 1½ km (1 mi) from the base; the round-trip walk takes about two hours. Be careful: the ascent is very steep. Don't attempt the climb if you aren't in good condition. You'll also need to wear sturdy hiking boots, a hat, sunscreen, and bring drinking water. Once you are on top of the rock, the trail is much easier. The climb is prohibited when temperatures rise above 36°C (97°F).

The other popular way of experiencing Uluru is far less taxing but no less intense: watching the sun sink against it from one of the two sunset-viewing areas. As the last rays of daylight strike, the rock seems lit from within and it positively glows. Just as quickly, the light is extinguished and the color changes to a somber mauve and finally to black.

SHOPPING The **Cultural Centre** (☎ 08/8956–3139) houses the **Ininti Store** (☎ 08/8956–2437), which carries souvenirs, and the adjoining **Maruku Arts and Crafts Centre** (☎ 08/8956–2558), which is owned by Aborigines and sells Aboriginal painting and handicrafts. There is also a display of traditional huts and shelters. The Cultural Centre is open daily 7:30 to 5:30; Maruku is open daily 8:30 to 5.

Kata Tjuta

Fodor'sChoice ★ In many ways, Kata Tjuta is more satisfying to explore than Uluru. The latter rock is one immense block, so you feel as if you're always on the outside looking in—but you can really come to grips with Kata Tjuta. As the Aboriginal name, Kata Tjuta (many heads), suggests, this is a jumble of huge rocks containing numerous hidden gorges and chasms.

There are three main walks, the first from the parking lot into **Olga Gorge,** the deepest valley between the rocks. This is a mile walk, and the round-trip journey takes about one hour. The **Kata Tjuṯa Viewing Area,** 26 km (16 mi) along the Kata Tjuṯa Road, offers a magnificent vista and is a relaxing place for a break. Interpretive panels give you an under-standing of the natural life around you. More rewarding but also more difficult is a walk that continues through the major cleft between the Olgas known as the Valley of the Winds. Experienced walkers can com-plete this 6-km (4-mi) walk in about four hours. The Valley of the Winds walk is closed when temperatures rise above 36°C (97°F).

Ayers Rock Resort

The properties at Ayers Rock Resort, which serves as the base for ex-ploration of Uluṟu and Kata Tjuṯa, are all run by the same company—Voyages Hotels and Resorts—and share many of the same facilities.

Where to Stay & Eat

Indoor dining is limited to hotel restaurants and the less-expensive Gecko's Cafe. If you eat away from your hotel, you can have the meals billed to your room. All hotel reservations can be made through Voy-ages Hotel and Resorts on-site, or the resort's central reservations ser-vice in Sydney. **Central reservations service** (☎ 1300/134044 or 02/ 9339–1030 ⊕ www.voyages.com.au).

Fodor'sChoice ★ The most memorable dining experience of the region the A$120 **Sounds of Silence Dinner in the Desert,** an elegant outdoor meal served away from civilization. Champagne and Northern Territory specialty dishes—in-cluding bush salads—are served upon tables covered with crisp white linens, right in the desert. An astronomer takes you on a stargazing tour of the Southern sky while you dine. In winter, hot mulled wine is served around a campfire. Dinners can be reserved through the resort's cen-tral service.

DINING $$–$$$ **Fodor'sChoice** ★ ✕ **Kuniya Restaurant.** Named after the python that battled the Liru snake in Aboriginal creation stories, this restaurant in the Sails of the Desert hotel is the best in town. Its decor reflects local legends, with two mag-nificent wooden panels at the entrance marked by images of Kuniya and Liru burnt into the wood. A "Kuniya Dreaming" mural is on the rear wall. Entrées and main courses are named after the Australian states. Specialties include kangaroo, Emperor fish, lamb, and tiger prawns. ⊠ *Yulara Dr.* ☎ 08/8957–7714 ➡ *AE, DC, MC, V.*

$–$$ ✕ **Gecko's Cafe.** All-day dining options here include inexpensive appe-tizers and a range of pastas and wood-fired pizzas. You can also stop in for a quick coffee or slice of cake. ⊠ *Town Sq., Yulara Centre* ☎ 08/ 8957–7722 ➡ *AE, DC, MC, V.*

HOTELS & MOTELS $$$$ ▦ **Desert Gardens.** A lawn, pool, and extensive gardens with native flora make up the grounds at the Desert Garden, a small, two-story hotel with impeccable style and service. The modern rooms are small but com-fortable and well kept. Some of the deluxe rooms have whirlpool baths. The Whitegums, open for breakfast and dinner, serves light salads of local fruits, nuts, and berries. The relaxed Bunya Bar prepares light snacks for lunch, with an emphasis on fresh, healthful, affordable meals. The Palya Bar serves poolside snacks and drinks. ⊠ *Yulara Dr., Ayers Rock Resort, Yulara, 0872* ☎ 08/8957–7714 ➡ 08/8957–7716 ⊕ *www. voyages.com.au* ➥ *218 rooms* △ *2 restaurants, pool, 2 bars, laundry facilities, baby-sitting, travel services, free parking; no smoking* ➡ *AE, DC, MC, V.*

$$$$ ⊞ **Emu Walk Apartments.** These one- and two-bedroom apartments have fully equipped kitchens (complete with champagne glasses), living rooms, and daily maid service. Each unit contains a sofa bed, so one-bedrooms can sleep four, and the balconied two-bedrooms can accommodate six or eight. There's no restaurant on-site, but you're welcome to dine in any of the Ayers Rock Resort's eateries. ⊠ *Yulara Dr., Ayers Rock Resort, Yulara, 0872* ☎ *08/8957–7888* 🖷 *08/8957–7742* ⊕ *www.voyages. com.au* ➥ *40 one-bedroom and 20 two-bedroom apartments* ♙ *Kitchens, laundry facilities* ▤ *AE, DC, MC, V.*

$$$$ ⊞ **Longitude 131°.** Popping out of the desert like a row of white cones,
Fodor'sChoice   a gathering of luxury "tents" make up this unique resort. Each unit—
★   actually a fully enclosed, prefabricated unit on stilts—has a balcony with floor-to-ceiling sliding-glass doors for a panoramic view of the Rock from the king-size bed. Set just 2 km (1 mi) from the boundary of the Uluru–Kata Tjuta National Park, this is the closest accommodations to the main sites. There's a two-night minimum stay, but the price includes meals, drinks, and tours. You can park free at Sails in the Desert and hop a free transfer bus here. ⊠ *Ayers Rock Resort, Yulara* ☎ *08/8957–7131* ⊕ *www. voyages.com.au* ➥ *15 tents* ♙ *Restaurant, in-room safes, refrigerators, pool, bar, lounge, dry-cleaning, laundry service, business services, travel services; no room TVs* ▤ *AE, DC, MC, V* ⑩ FAP.

$$$$ ⊞ **Sails in the Desert.** With architectural shade sails for sun protection, manicured lawns, Aboriginal art, and numerous facilities, this is the resort's best traditional option. Ocher-tone rooms have balconies overlooking lawns and gardens; a viewing tower looks out toward Uluru in the distance. Six deluxe rooms have whirlpool baths. ⊠ *Yulara Dr., Ayers Rock Resort, Yulara, 0872* ☎ *08/8957–7417* 🖷 *08/8957–7474* ⊕ *www. voyages.com.au* ➥ *230 rooms, 2 suites* ♙ *3 restaurants, putting green, 2 tennis courts, pool, bar, shops, dry cleaning, laundry service, Internet, business services, meeting rooms, travel services, free parking; no smoking* ▤ *AE, DC, MC, V.*

$$$$ ⊞ **The Lost Camel.** This funky new hotel, formerly staff quarters, has brightly painted rooms of lime, purple, and orange that are furnished with traditional Aboriginal artifacts. Grouped around central courtyards, the rooms have irons, ironing boards, and tea- and coffee-making equipment. The lobby lounge has a café, wine bar, and plasma screen with cable channels. ⊠ *Yulara Dr., Ayers Rock Resort, Yulara, 0872* ☎ *08/ 8957–5650* 🖷 *08/8957–7755* ⊕ *www.voyages.com.au* ➥ *99 rooms* ♙ *Café, minibars, refrigerators, pool, lobby lounge, wine bar, free parking; no room TVs* ▤ *AE, DC, MC, V.*

★ $$–$$$$ ⊞ **Outback Pioneer Hotel and Lodge.** Although the theme is the 1860s Outback, complete with rustic decor and evening bush games, you won't be roughing it here—not with a restaurant, pool, and laundry facilities. Guests at the adjoining Outback Pioneer Lodge, an air-conditioned budget accommodation, have access to the hotel's facilities. The Bough House serves hearty central Australian dishes as well as lighter food, and the fully equipped kitchen at the Pioneer Self-Cook Barbecue opens at 6:30 PM. A shuttle bus connects the lodge to the other properties every 15 minutes. ⊠ *Yulara Dr., Ayers Rock Resort, Yulara, 0872* ☎ *08/ 8957–7605* 🖷 *08/8957–7615* ⊕ *www.voyages.com.au* ➥ *167 hotels rooms, 125 with private facilities, 168 lodge bunk beds* ♙ *Restaurant, grill, pool, laundry facilities, Internet, travel services, free parking; no room phones, no TV in some rooms, no smoking* ▤ *AE, DC, MC, V.*

CARAVAN,   ⚠ **Ayers Rock Campground.** This large campground amid rolling green
TRAILER, RV   lawns has 220 tent sites (A$12.60 for two), 198 powered sites (A$15
PARK   for two), and 14 air-conditioned cabins (A$148 per night). Cabins come
¢–$ with linens, full kitchens, and TVs—but no bathrooms. There's also a

well-equipped camper's kitchen for public use, as well as a grocery and
an Outback-style shelter with free gas barbecues. ☒ *Yulara Dr., Ayers
Rock Resort, Yulara, 0872* ☎ *08/8956–2055* 🖷 *08/8956–2260* ☞ *418
sites, 14 cabins* ☼ *Flush toilets, full hook-ups, drinking water, laundry
facilities, showers, grills, picnic tables, public telephone, general store,
pool* ☰ *MC, V.*

Child Care
The **Child Care Centre** (☒ Next to Community Hall ☎ 08/8956–2097)
will look after children between the ages of 6 months and 8 years on
weekdays from 8:30 to 5. Baby-sitting is available outside these times
by arrangement with the center. General costs are A$20 an hour, A$45
for a half day (5 hours), and A$65 a day. After-hours baby-sitting costs
A$15 per hour.

Shopping
Ayers Rock Resort has a news agency, a very reasonably priced supermarket (open daily 8 AM–9 PM), a take-away food outlet, and a couple
of souvenir shops. Each of the hotels houses an Ayers Rock Logo Shop
selling Australian-made garments and leather goods. The **Mulgara Gallery
and Craft Works Gallery** (☒ Yulara Dr. ☎ 08/8956–2460), in the foyer
of the Sails in the Desert Hotel, specializes in high-quality Australian
arts and crafts, including Aboriginal works and opal jewelry.

Uluṟu & Kata Tjuṯa A to Z

*To research prices, get advice from other travelers, and book travel ar-
rangements, visit www.fodors.com.*

AIR TRAVEL
Qantas serves Connellan Airport, which is 5 km (3 mi) north of the re-
sort complex. AAT Kings runs a complimentary shuttle bus between the
airport and Yulara that meets every flight.
🛈 **Qantas** ☎ 13–1313 ⊕ www.qantas.com.
🛈 **Connellan Airport** ☎ 08/8956–2388.
🛈 **AAT Kings** ☎ 08/8952–1700.

BUS TRAVEL
Bus companies traveling to Ayers Rock Resort from Alice Springs include AAT Kings and Greyhound Pioneer. AAT Kings also conducts daily
tours of the area.
🛈 **Bus Lines AAT Kings** ☎ 08/8952–1700 or 1800/334009 ⊕ www.aatkings.com.
Greyhound Pioneer ☒ Todd St. ☎ 08/8952–7888 or 08/8956–2171 ⊕ www.greyhound.
com.au.

CAR RENTAL
Avis, Hertz, and Thrifty/Territory Rent-a-Car all rent cars at the resort.
🛈 **Agencies Avis** ☎ 08/8956–2266 ⊕ www.avis.com.au. **Hertz** ☎ 08/8956–2244
⊕ www.hertznt.com. **Thrifty/Territory Rent-a-Car** ☎ 08/8956–2030 ⊕ www.thrifty.
com.au.

CAR TRAVEL
The 440-km (273-mi) trip from Alice Springs to Ayers Rock Resort takes
about five hours. The paved Lasseter Highway is in fine condition.

From the resort it's 19 km (12 mi) to Uluṟu or 53 km (33 mi) to Kata
Tjuṯa. The road to Kata Tjuṯa is paved. Routes between hotels and sights
are clearly marked, and because prices are competitive with those for
the bus tours—especially for larger parties—renting a car may be best.

EMERGENCIES

In case of an emergency, dial 000 to reach an ambulance, the fire department, or the police. The medical clinic at the Flying Doctor Base is open weekdays 9–noon and 2–5 and weekends 10–11.

🛈 **Ambulance** ☎ 08/8952-5733. **Medical Clinic** ✉ Flying Doctor Base, near police station ☎ 08/8956-2286 ⊕ www.rfds.org.au/central/yulara. **Police** ☎ 08/8956-2166.

TAXIS

For a chauffeur-driven limousine, contact V.I.P. Chauffeur Cars. Sunworth Transport Service can whisk you from the resorts to the sights for much less than the cost of a guided bus tour—plus, you can go at your own convenience.

🛈 Taxi Companies **Sunworth Transport Service** ☎ 08/8956-2152. **V.I.P. Chauffeur Cars** ☎ 08/8956-2283.

TOURS

Anangu Tours, owned and operated by local Aboriginal people, offers the Aboriginal Uluru Tour (A$108 with breakfast), led by an Aboriginal guide; the Kuniya Sunset Tour (A$84); the Anangu Culture Pass—which combines the first two tours over one or two days (A$172); the self-drive Liru Tour (A$52); and the self-drive Kuniya Tour (A$52). Guides are Aborigines who work with interpreters.

Several free slide shows about local wildlife and flora are given at the auditorium near the resort's visitor center next to the Desert Gardens Hotel on Yulara Drive.

Central Australia has some of the clearest and cleanest air in the world—just look up into the night sky. A small observatory with a telescope is set up on the resort grounds for just this purpose. Viewing times vary with the seasons; sessions last for about an hour, and can be booked through Discovery Ecotours for A$30.

🛈 Tour Operators **Anangu Tours** ☎ 08/8956-2123. **Discovery Ecotours** ☎ 08/8956-2563 or 1800/803174 ⊕ www.discoveryecotours.com.au.

AIRPLANE & HELICOPTER TOURS

The best views of Uluru and Kata Tjuta are from the air. Light-plane tours, with courtesy hotel pickup, include 40-minute flights over Ayers Rock and the Olgas, and day tours to Kings Canyon. Prices range from A$129 to A$499 per person; for options, contact Ayers Rock Scenic Flights. Helicopter flights are A$85 per person for 15 minutes over Ayers Rock, or A$160 for 30 minutes over the Olgas and the Rock. A flight over both sights and Lake Amadeus costs A$290 for 55 minutes. Book the helicopter (3 seats) for a Kings Canyon tour for A$1,530.

🛈 Tour Operators **Ayers Rock Helicopters** ☎ 08/8956-2077 ⊕ www.helicoptergroup.com.au. **Ayers Rock Scenic Flights** ☎ 08/8956-2345 🖷 08/8956-2472 ⊕ www.generalflyingservices.com.au.

MOTORCYCLE TOURS

The balmy desert climate makes Uluru Motorcycle Tours enjoyable (and popular), and provides the chance for unique vacation photographs. Guides communicate with their passengers by helmet intercoms. Prices range from A$80 for a half hour, 30-km "Pat's Special" ride to A$125 for the Uluru Cruise. A 4½-hour sunrise or sunset tour of Ayers Rock and the Olgas is A$345, including a light breakfast at sunrise or champagne at sunset.

🛈 **Uluru Motorcycle Tours** ☎ 08/8956-2019 🖷 08/8956-2196.

WALKING TOURS

The Mala Walk is free and led by Aboriginal rangers who show you the land from their perspective. The walk starts from the base of the climbing trail at Uluru at 10 AM. Discovery Ecotours specializes in small-group tours of Uluru with guides who have extensive local knowledge. The Uluru Walk, a 10-km (6-mi) hike around the base of Uluru, gives fascinating insight into the significance of the area to the Aboriginal people. It departs daily, includes breakfast, and costs A$92. Book at least a day in advance.

Discovery Ecotours ☎ 08/8956-2563 or 1800/803174. **Mala Walk** ☎ 08/8956-2299.

VISITOR INFORMATION

The Uluru–Kata Tjuṯa Cultural Centre is on the park road just before you reach the rock. It also contains the park's ranger station. The cultural center is open daily 7–6 from November to March, and 7–5:30 April to October. A visitor center next to the Desert Gardens Hotel on Yulara Drive is open daily 8:30–5.

Tourist Information **Uluru-Kata Tjuṯa Cultural Centre** ☎ 08/8956-3138. **Visitor Center** ☎ 08/8957-7377.

DARWIN, THE TOP END & THE KIMBERLEY

11

FODOR'S CHOICE

The Bush Camp Faraway Bay, near Kununurra

Cockatoo Island Resort, in the Buccaneer Archipelago

El Questro Wilderness Park, near Kununurra

Hanuman Thai and Nonya Restaurant, in Darwin

Kakadu National Park, near Darwin

Purnululu (Bungle Bungle) National Park, near Kununurra

Seven Spirit Bay, lodge on the Cobourg Peninsula

HIGHLY RECOMMENDED

RESTAURANTS Matso's Café, in Broome

Pee Wee's at the Point, in Darwin

HOTELS Cable Beach Club Resort, in Broome

El Questro, near Kununurra

Jan's Bed & Breakfast, in Katherine

Kimberley Hotel, in Halls Creek

McAlpine House, in Broome

Moonlight Bay Quality Suites, in Broome

Novotel Atrium, in Darwin

Saville Park Suites, in Darwin

SIGHTS Indo Pacific Marine aquarium, in Darwin

Museum and Art Gallery of the Northern Territory, in Darwin

Pearl Luggers museum, in Broome

By David
McGonigal
and Chips
Mackinolty
Updated by
Jad Davenport

THE TOP END IS A GEOGRAPHIC DESCRIPTION—but it's also a state of mind. Isolated from the rest of Australia by thousands of miles of desert and lonely scrubland, Top Enders are different and proud of it. From the remote wetlands and stone country of Arnhem Land—home to thousands of Aboriginal people—to the lush tropical city of Darwin, the Top End is a gateway to a region where people from 50 different national and cultural backgrounds live in what they regard as the real Australia. It's an isolation that contributes to strong feelings of independence from the rest of the country—Southerners are regarded with a mixture of pity and ridicule.

For thousands of years, this area of Northern Australia has been home to Aboriginal people. Stunning examples of ancient Aboriginal rock art remain—on cliffs, in hidden valleys, and in Darwin art galleries. Today, however, the region is a melting pot of cultures and traditions. Darwin and Broome—closer to the cities of Asia than to any Australian counterparts—host the nation's most racially diverse populations: Aborigines, Anglos, and Asians sharing a tropical lifestyle. Here, the year is divided into two seasons: the Wet (December–April) and the Dry (May–November). The Dry is a period of idyllic weather with warm days and cool nights. So to make up for those seven months of the year when there is barely a cloud in the sky, the Wet season brings monsoonal storms that dump an average 65 inches of rain in a few short months—and even the rain is warm! Heralded by the notorious heat and humidity of the buildup, the Wet is a time of year when roads wash out, rivers become impassable, and cyclones threaten the region. However, you shouldn't put off visiting larger towns like Darwin and Broome entirely during the Wet. For a start, the sights are much less crowded than during the Dry, plus the rain paints the landscape vivid green. You can also catch spectacular electrical storms, particularly over the ocean, and the region between Darwin and Kakadu National Park has the world's highest recorded rate of lightning strikes—up to 1,000 during a single storm.

During the Wet of 1974–75, Cyclone Tracy ripped through Darwin with winds of 136 mph, killing 66 people and destroying or damaging more than 80% of its buildings. Thankfully, though, having learned a lesson from that disastrous Christmas, Darwin is now much better prepared for cyclones.

The starkness of the isolation of the Top End and Western Australia's Kimberley is reflected in its tiny population. Although the Northern Territory occupies one-sixth of Australia's landmass, its population of 192,000 makes up just over 1% of the continent's citizenry—an average density of around one person per 8 square km (3 square mi). In many areas kangaroos and cattle vastly outnumber the locals. The Kimberley, an area of land larger than the state of Kansas, is home to only 30,000 people. Traveling by road from Darwin to Broome is the best way to see the Kimberley, but you pass through only nine communities in 2,016 km (1,250 mi), from such tiny settlements as Timber Creek to bigger towns like Katherine.

The Kimberley possesses some of the most dramatic landscapes in Australia. A land of rugged ranges, tropical wetlands, and desert, of vast cattle stations and wonderful national parks, including the bizarre, beautiful, red-and-black-striped sandstone domes and towers of Purnululu National Park, the Kimberley is still the frontier. Like Top Enders, the people of the Kimberley region see themselves as living in a land apart from the rest of the nation, and it's easy to see why—landscape and distance combine to make the Kimberley one of the world's few uniquely open spaces.

See Chapter 13 for more information on four-wheel-driving in the Top End and the Kimberley's great outdoors.

Exploring Darwin, the Top End & the Kimberley

The telltale recurring phrase "tyranny of distance" was first used to describe Australia's relationship to the rest of the world. In many ways it still describes the Top End and the Kimberley, with vast distances setting this region apart from the rest of the nation. This is not an area that you can justly contemplate—nor travel, for that matter—in a few days. And especially if you plan to get out to the Kimberley, you should consider seeing it over a couple of weeks and combining it with another week visiting the Red Centre for full effect.

About the Restaurants

WHAT IT COSTS In Australian Dollars				
$$$$	$$$	$$	$	¢
AT DINNER over $50	$36–$50	$21–$35	$10–$20	under $10

Prices are for a main course at dinner.

About the Hotels

Apart from Darwin hotels and Top End resorts, accommodations fall into the more basic category. With the local scenery as spectacular as it is, however, these shouldn't be discouraging words.

WHAT IT COSTS In Australian Dollars				
$$$$	$$$	$$	$	¢
FOR 2 PEOPLE over $300	$201–$300	$151–$200	$100–$150	under $100

Prices are for two people in a standard double room in high season, including tax and service, based on the European Plan (with no meals) unless otherwise noted.

Timing

Unless you're used to heat and humidity, the best time to tour is in the Dry, roughly May through August, keeping in mind that inland nights in July can be chilly. Note that May and June are when the waterfalls of Kakadu and the Kimberley are at their most dramatic, still full to overflowing following the Wet. When you're on the road, early starts beat the heat and get you to swimming holes in the middle of the day—the crucial time for cooling off. Most boat tours in the region run throughout the day, but morning and evening cruises are best for several reasons: to avoid the heat, to see animals when they are out feeding, to catch sunrises and sunsets, and to take advantage of the ideal light for photography (by noon the light is often harsh and flat).

DARWIN

There is no other city in Australia that dates its history by a single cataclysmic event. For the people of Darwin—including the vast majority who weren't here at the time—everything is dated as before or after 1974's Cyclone Tracy. It wasn't just the death toll. Officially 66 people died on that terrible Christmas Eve, compared to the 292 who died on 1942's first day of Japanese bombing raids. It was the immensity of the destruction wrought by Tracy that has marked Australia's northern capital. Casualties of war are one terrible thing, but the helplessness of an entire population faced with natural disaster is something else again. Within a week of Tracy, Australia's biggest peacetime airlift reduced the population from

If you have 3 days

Start from ⊞ **Darwin** just after dawn and head east on the Arnhem Highway to Fogg Dam to view the bird life. Continue into ⊞ **Kakadu National Park,** and picnic at the rock-art site at Ubirr. Take a scenic flight in the afternoon, then a trip to the Bowali Visitors Centre, and you can overnight in ⊞ **Jabiru.** On the second day, head to Nourlangie Rock; then continue to the Yellow Water cruise at ⊞ **Cooinda** and stay there for the night. A visit to the Warradjan Aboriginal Cultural Centre is a must on the third day, followed by a drive to ⊞ **Litchfield National Park** via Batchelor. Depending on your time, visit Florence, Tjaynera, or Wangi falls for a picnic lunch followed by a stop at Tolmer Falls before returning to Darwin.

If you have 5 days

From ⊞ **Darwin,** drive to ⊞ **Litchfield National Park,** entering through Batchelor. A swim at the Florence Falls plunge pool and a picnic in the rain forest will help you sleep well here. An early start on the second day will allow you to reach ⊞ **Kakadu National Park** and the rock-art site at Ubirr just after dawn. After Ubirr, stop at Bowali Visitors Centre before continuing to Nourlangie Rock for lunch. In the early afternoon visit the Aboriginal Cultural Centre, then take the evening Yellow Water cruise at ⊞ **Cooinda** and overnight near there. On the third day head down to the southern half of Kakadu National Park. After lunch continue to Edith Falls to camp in ⊞ **Nitmiluk (Katherine Gorge) National Park** or head into ⊞ **Katherine** for the night. Next morning cruise up Katherine Gorge in Nitmiluk National Park. After lunch head south to **Cutta Cutta Caves** and the thermal pools at **Mataranka.** Return to Katherine for the night, then on day five meander back toward Darwin, exploring some of the small roads down "the Track" (the Stuart Highway) along the way.

If you have 10 days

Take the five-day tour above, then from Mataranka head back through ⊞ **Katherine** and take the Victoria Highway, passing through mesa formations and Timber Creek to ⊞ **Kununurra** for the night. On the sixth day, take in the spectacular landscapes of **Purnululu National Park** by four wheel drive or with a guided tour, and spend the night in ⊞ **Halls Creek.** It'll be a long haul west the seventh day on the Great Northern Highway, but you can make it to **Geikie Gorge National Park** for an afternoon boat tour, a welcome and interesting respite before heading off to camp the night at ⊞ **Windjana Gorge National Park.** Another early start on day eight will get you to ⊞ **Broome,** the fascinating old pearling town. Spend the night, then take a fishing charter the ninth day or just amble around this attractive and historic town for a while. Spend a second night and then fly back to Darwin.

47,000 people to 12,000, with many refusing to return to a city that, for them, had died.

It's a tribute to those who stayed and those who have come to live here after Tracy that the rebuilt city now thrives as an administrative and commercial center for northern Australia. Old Darwin has been replaced by something of an edifice complex—such buildings as Parliament House and the Supreme Court seem all a bit too grand for such a small city, especially one that prides itself on its being relaxed. Here Aborigines, Asians, and Anglos live together in an alluring combination of Outback openness and cosmopolitan multiculturalism.

The seductiveness of contemporary Darwin lifestyles belies a Top End history of failed attempts by Europeans dating back to 1824 to establish an enclave in a climate that was harsh and unyielding to new arrivals. The original 1869 settlement, called Palmerston, was built on a parcel of mangrove wetlands and scrub forest that had changed little in 15 million years. It was not until 1911, after it had already weathered the disastrous cyclones of 1878, 1882, and 1897, that the town was named after the scientist who had visited these shores aboard the *Beagle* in 1839.

Today Darwin is the best place from which to explore the beauty and diversity of Australia's Top End, as well as the wonders of Kakadu, Nitmiluk (Katherine Gorge), and the mighty Kimberley region.

Exploring Darwin

The orientation point for visitors is the Mall at Smith Street. The downtown grid of streets around the Mall is at the very tip of a peninsula. Most of the suburbs and outlying attractions lie out beyond the airport.

Numbers in the text correspond to numbers in the margin and on the Darwin map.

a good walk

From the Smith Street Mall head southwest down Knuckey Street across Mitchell Street. On the right, at the intersection with the Esplanade, is the 1925 **Lyons Cottage** ❶ ▶ museum, which focuses on local history, including early settlement, pearling, and relations with Indonesian and Chinese groups. On the other side of Knuckey Street, the **Old Admiralty House** ❷ is elevated on columns, once a common architectural feature of Darwin. Farther southeast, behind the Esplanade, stands the modern **Northern Territory Parliament House** ❸.

On a corner in front of the Parliament building, on the Esplanade, is the **Overland Telegraph Memorial** ❹, the site of Australia's first telegraph connection with the rest of the world in 1871. Facing the memorial is **Government House** ❺, which has remarkably withstood the ravages of cyclones and Japanese bombing in World War II.

On the opposite side of the Esplanade, between Mitchell and Smith streets, are the **Old Police Station and Court House** ❻, which date to 1884, with their long veranda and old stone facades. They currently function as governmental offices. **Survivor's Lookout** ❼, a memorial to the victims of Japan's first bombing of Australia in 1942, is across the road.

To get to the wharf area, take the stairs down the cliff face. Directly at the bottom of the stairs is the entrance to Darwin's **World War II Storage Tunnels** ❽, which secured fuel stores in World War II. Inside there are photographs of Darwin during wartime.

A walk of 435 feet to the east leads to **Stokes Hill Wharf** ❾. The wharf now has a dual function: serving ships and serving locals with restaurants, weekend markets, and a good fishing spot. The wharf is a great place to wind up at sunset for a drink and a bite to eat. The view of the harbor is fantastic, and chances are good you might see some local dolphins waiting for fish scraps. For a different perspective on fish, stop in at the wharf's **Indo Pacific Marine** ❿, where a large indoor tank with a coral-reef ecosystem and its astonishing collection of fish reside. In the same building, the **Australian Pearling Exhibition** ⓫ has a lively presentation of northern Australia's history of hunting and cultivating pearls.

Bushwalking

The national parks of the Top End and the Kimberley are ideal for hiking—Australians call it bushwalking—and suit a variety of fitness levels. Major rock-art sites in Kakadu, for example, incorporate bushwalks from an hour or so to a half day in length. Park rangers supply maps and route information for walks that last overnight and longer. The rugged adventures require care and planning, but you'll be rewarded with unforgettable memories of trekking through some of the most remote places on earth. Bring a net to wrap around your face and head to combat the Outback flies, which have the annoying habit of swarming around your eyes, ears, and mouth.

11

Gourmet Game

The menus in Darwin seem to indicate that there is little the average Territorian won't eat—buffalo, crocodile, camel, and kangaroo are all frequently featured. Another local favorite, barramundi, is one of the tastiest fish in the world. Buffalo can be tough, but a tender piece is like a gamey piece of beef. Opinion is divided about crocodile; it, too, can be tough, but (like every other reptile, it seems) a good piece tastes like chicken. The newest eating precinct of Cullen Bay, only five minutes from the city and overlooking the marina near where Darwin Harbour cruises embark, has chic indoor and outdoor eating venues with great views of the harbor.

Stargazing

From Darwin to Broome, camping out under the stars is one of the real pleasures of traveling through the Outback. It can be a bit of a trial in the Wet—if you don't get rained on, you still have to contend with the mosquitoes—but camping in the Dry is perfect. Depending on personal taste, you may not even need a tent. Most locals just take a swag—a heavy canvas wrapped around a rolled mattress. The region abounds in out-of-the-way spots to pull up and sleep in the open. Wherever you go, ask a local to tell you the best place to throw down your swag, brew a billy (pot) of tea, and contemplate the glories of the southern night sky.

Returning up the cliff to Smith Street, look to your right for **Christ Church Cathedral ⑫. Browns Mart Community Arts Theatre ⑬**, a theater, is on the same side of Smith Street farther down.

Stop in at the Victoria Hotel, across Bennett Street on the left-hand side of Smith Street, and proceed to the balcony for a drink—a fine way to conclude a walking tour of Darwin.

TIMING   This scenic stroll takes just a couple of hours unless you pause to take in the exhibits. Start the walk just after breakfast, with a detour through a bit of Bicentennial Park, and you'll reach the cafés of Stokes Hill Wharf in time for mid-morning coffee. Head inside Indo Pacific Marine and the Australian Pearling Exhibition to beat the noon heat, and top off the afternoon with a bite at the Victoria Hotel. Summer temperatures can be exhausting, so if you're traveling during warmer months dress lightly and carry an umbrella for extra shade. Keep in mind that museum hours can be shortened during the Wet.

City Center

⑪ **Australian Pearling Exhibition.** Since the early 19th century, fortune seekers have hunted for pearls in Australia's northern waters. Exhibits at

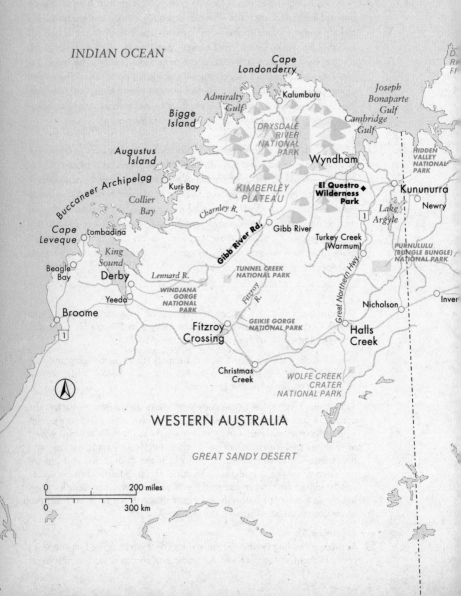

Timor Sea

INDIAN OCEAN

Cape
Londonderry

*Admiralty
Gulf*

Bigge
Island

Kalumburu

*DRYSDALE
RIVER
NATIONAL
PARK*

*Joseph
Bonaparte
Gulf*

*Cambridge
Gulf*

*Augustus
Island*

Wyndham

*HIDDEN
VALLEY
NATIONAL
PARK*

Buccaneer Archipelag

Kuri Bay

*KIMBERLEY
PLATEAU*

**El Questro
Wilderness
Park**

Kununurra

Newry

*Collier
Bay*

Charnley R.

Gibb River Rd.

Gibb River

Turkey Creek
(Warmum)

*Lake
Argyle*

Cape
Leveque

Lombadina

Turkey Creek
(Warmum)

*PURNULULU
(BUNGLE BUNGLE)
NATIONAL PARK*

*King
Sound*

Beagle
Bay

Derby

Lennard R.

*TUNNEL CREEK
NATIONAL PARK*

Great Northern Hwy.

Yeeda

*WINDJANA
GORGE
NATIONAL
PARK*

*Fitzroy
R.*

Nicholson

Inver

Broome

Fitzroy
Crossing

*GEIKIE GORGE
NATIONAL PARK*

Halls
Creek

Christmas
Creek

*WOLFE CREEK
CRATER
NATIONAL PARK*

WESTERN AUSTRALIA

GREAT SANDY DESERT

0		200 miles
0		300 km

AUSTRALIA

Bat
Is

D.
R
F

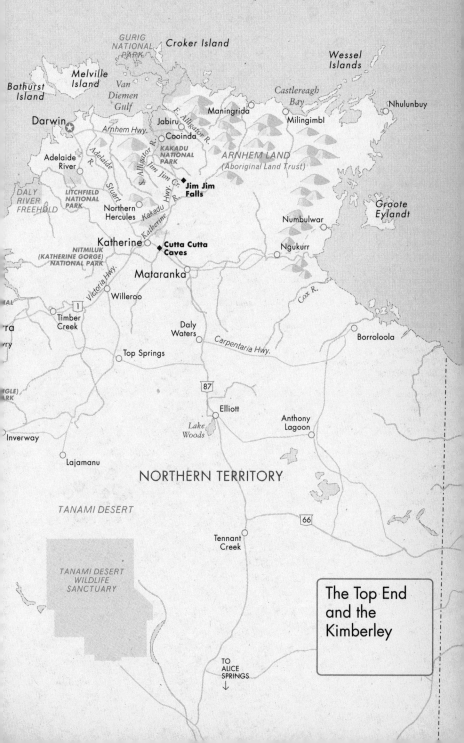

Arafura Sea

GURIG NATIONAL PARK

Croker Island

Wessel Islands

Melville Island

Van Diemen Gulf

Bathurst Island

Castlereagh Bay

Nhulunbuy

Darwin

Arnhem Hwy.

Jabiru

Maningrida

Milingimbl

Cooinda

KAKADU NATIONAL PARK

ARNHEM LAND
(Aboriginal Land Trust)

Adelaide River

Adelaide R.

S. Alligator R.

E. Alligator R.

Jim Jim Cr.

Jim Jim Falls

Groote Eylandt

DALY RIVER FREEHOLD

LITCHFIELD NATIONAL PARK

Northern Hercules

Stuart

Kakadu Hwy.

Numbulwar

Katherine

Katherine R.

Cutta Cutta Caves

Ngukurr

NITMILUK (KATHERINE GORGE) NATIONAL PARK

Mataranka

Victoria Hwy.

Willeroo

Cox R.

1

Timber Creek

Daly Waters

Carpentaria Hwy.

Borroloola

Top Springs

87

INVERWAY

Elliott

Lake Woods

Anthony Lagoon

Lajamanu

NORTHERN TERRITORY

TANAMI DESERT

66

TANAMI DESERT WILDLIFE SANCTUARY

Tennant Creek

The Top End
and the
Kimberley

TO ALICE SPRINGS
↓

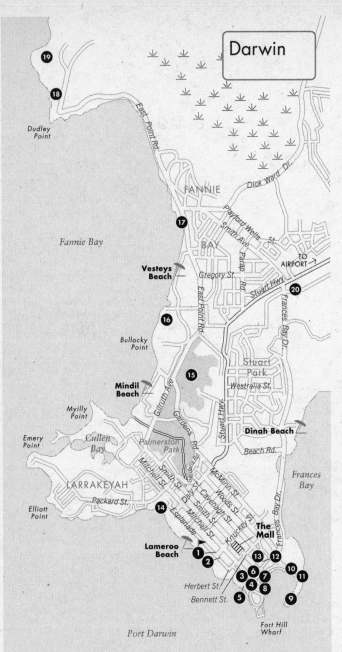

Darwin

this museum cover everything from pearl farming to pearl jewelry settings. ⊠ *Stokes Hill Wharf, Wharf Precinct* ☎ *08/8999–6573* 🖃 *A$6.60* 🕓 *Daily 10–5.*

⓭ Browns Mart Community Arts Theatre. Erected in 1885, this building has seen duty as an emporium, a mining exchange, and currently as a theater. ⊠ *Smith St. and Harry Chan Ave., City Center* ☎ *08/8981–5522* 🖃 *Free* 🕓 *During performances.*

need a break?

The balcony of the **Victoria Hotel** is a good place for a little refreshment. A Darwin institution since its construction in 1894, the Vic has been hit by every cyclone and rebuilt afterward. ⊠ *27 Smith St. Mall, City Center* ☎ *08/8981–4011.*

⓬ Christ Church Cathedral. Darwin's Anglican church was largely destroyed by Cyclone Tracy, and the remains of the original 1902 structure have been incorporated into the renovated building. ⊠ *Smith St. and Esplanade S, Wharf Precinct* 🖃 *Free* 🕓 *During worship hours.*

❺ Government House. The oldest building in Darwin, Government House has been the home of the administrator for the area since 1870. Despite being bombed by Japanese aircraft in 1942 and damaged by the cyclones of 1897, 1937, and 1974, the building looks much as it did in 1879 when it was first completed. The house, which is not open to the public, faces the Overland Telegraph Memorial. ⊠ *Esplanade S, Wharf Precinct.*

★ ❿ Indo Pacific Marine. If you'd rather ogle fish than eat them, visit this marine interpretative center at Stokes Hill Wharf. Housed in a large, open tank is one of the few self-contained coral-reef ecosystems in the Southern Hemisphere. Other exhibits include a static display of rare, deepwater coral skeletons and an exhibit explaining the effects of global warming on the planet. Night tours, which begin at 7:30 and take you by flashlight to view fluorescent reef plants and animals, include a lecture, a seafood buffet dinner, and wine. The pearling exhibition has videos and museum-style displays that track the history of this important local industry. ⊠ *Stokes Hill Wharf, Wharf Precinct* ☎ *08/8981–1294 Indo Pacific* 🖃 *A$16.40, night tours A$68* 🕓 *Apr.–Oct. daily 10–5; Nov.–Mar., daily 9–1.*

❶ Lyons Cottage. One of several buildings dating to the early settlement of northern Australia in downtown Darwin, Lyons Cottage was built in 1925 for executives of the British-Australian Telegraph Company (B.A.T.). The stone building is now a historical museum with exhibits on the town's history, Chinese immigrants, pearl diving, early explorers, and the Macassans, who came by boat from Indonesia, touched down in Australia, and had contact with the Aborigines centuries ago. ⊠ *Knuckey St. and Esplanade, Bicentennial Park* ☎ *08/8981–1750* 🖃 *Free* 🕓 *Daily 10–4:30.*

❸ Northern Territory Parliament House. Australia's northernmost Parliament resides in a gleaming state-of-the-art home set on cliffs at the edge of the sea. Ninety-minute tours of the building are conducted on Saturday at 10 and noon (reservations are essential). Spend your spare time in the extensive library brushing up on local history, or relax with a drink at the Speaker's Corner Cafe. ⊠ *Esplanade and Smith Sts., East Esplanade* ☎ *08/8946–1509* 🖃 *Free* 🕓 *Weekdays 8–6, weekends 9–6.*

❷ Old Admiralty House. In Darwin's steamy climate the most suitable design for a house is to elevate it on columns. This style of building was once common in Darwin, but the Old Admiralty House is one of only a few of its kind to survive Cyclone Tracy in 1974. The house was built in 1937 to provide lodging for the naval officer commanding northern Australia. ⊠ *Knuckey St. and Esplanade, Bicentennial Park.*

⑥ Old Police Station and Court House. These side-by-side 1884 buildings were reconstructed after Cyclone Tracy to serve as offices for the Northern Territory administrator. Their long verandas and stone facades are typical of buildings from the period. ⊠ *Esplanade S between Mitchell and Smith Sts., East Esplanade* ☎ *08/8999–7103.*

④ Overland Telegraph Memorial. On the harbor side of the Esplanade—near the front of Parliament House—is a cairn that marks the place where the first international telegraph cable came ashore from Java in 1871. A monumental event in Australia's history, this provided the first direct link with the mother country, England. Before that, information and orders from "home" took months to arrive by ship.

⑨ Stokes Hill Wharf. This working pier receives cargo ships, trawlers, defense vessels, and, occasionally, huge cruise liners. With the best views of Darwin Harbor, it's also a favorite spot for Darwinites to fish. When the mackerel are running, you can join scores of locals over a few beers in late-night fishing parties. The cluster of cafés and restaurants gets busy on weekends and when cruise ships arrive. ⊠ *McMinn St., Darwin Harbour* ☎ *08/8981–4268.*

⑦ Survivor's Lookout. On the site of World War II's first Japanese bombing raid on Australia, this memorial commemorates those who died, including sailors of the USS *Peary.* The shaded viewing platform holds a panoramic illustrated map describing the events of that fateful day. The lookout is also the gateway, via stairs down the cliff face, to the wharf precinct. ⊠ *Esplanade S, East Esplanade.*

⑧ World War II Storage Tunnels. Darwin's storage tunnels were built during World War II to protect fuel from Japanese bombing raids on the city. Carved into solid rock, the main tunnel is 22 feet high and 210 feet deep. There is a self-guided tour of the atmospheric tunnels, which now house photographic records of the war period. The entrance to the tunnels is at the bottom of the stairs below Survivor's Lookout. ⊠ *Esplanade S., Darwin Harbour* ☎ *08/8985–6333* 💰 *A\$4.50* ⊙ *May–Sept. daily 9–5; Oct.–Nov., Jan. and Mar.–Apr., Tues.–Fri. 10–2, weekends 10–4.*

Around Darwin

⑭ Aquascene. You can hand-feed hundreds of fish at this beach on the northwestern end of the Esplanade. At high tide, people wade into the water with buckets of bread to feed the schools of batfish, bream, catfish, milkfish, and mullet that come inshore in a feeding frenzy. ⊠ *Daly St. and Esplanade, Doctor's Gully* ☎ *08/8981–7837* 💰 *A\$6* ⊙ *Daily at high tide (times vary).*

⑳ Australian Aviation Heritage Centre. Due to its isolation and sparse population, the Northern Territory played an important role in the expansion of aviation in Australia, and this impressive museum traces the history of flight Down Under. Planes on exhibition include a massive B-52 bomber on permanent loan from the United States—one of very few not on U.S. soil—as well as a Japanese Zero shot down on the first day of bombing raids in 1942. ⊠ *557 Stuart Hwy., 8 km (5 mi) northeast of the city center, Winnellie* ☎ *08/8947–2145* 💰 *A\$11* ⊙ *Daily 9–5.*

☙ Darwin Crocodile Farm. With more than 8,000 fresh- and saltwater crocodiles, this farm supplies much of the meat on menus around the Territory. The best time to visit is during the daily feeding and tour (weekdays at 2 PM and weekends at noon), when the generally immobile reptiles become very active. ⊠ *Stuart Hwy., past the Arnhem Hwy. turnoff*

40 km (25 mi) south of Darwin, Berry Springs ☎ *08/8988–1450* ⊠ *A$10* ⊘ *Daily 9–4.*

⑮ Darwin's Botanic Gardens. Darwin's gardens make an ideal spot in which to escape the tropical heat. First planted in 1879, they were, like so much else, largely destroyed by Cyclone Tracy. The gardens have since been replanted with 400 species of figs and palms, wetland flora, and a rain forest. A popular walk takes visitors on a self-guided tour of plants Aborigines used for medicinal purposes. There's also a waterfall and a children's playground with an evolutionary theme. The greenhouse displays ferns and orchids. ⊠ *Gardens Rd. and Geranium St., Mindil Beach* ☎ *08/8981–1958* ⊠ *Free* ⊘ *Weekdays 7:30–5, weekends 8:30–5.*

⑲ East Point Military Museum. This hub of local military history is attractively set in tropical gardens at the edge of Fannie Bay. Exhibits detail the city's role as a major naval base in World War II and include some of the actual weapons and vehicles, observation towers, and bunkers used to defend the city against frequent Japanese attacks. ⊠ *E. Point Rd., Fannie Bay* ☎ *08/8981–9702* ⊠ *A$9* ⊘ *Daily 9:30–5.*

⑱ East Point Reserve and Lake Alexander. East Point Road leads past the beaches of Fannie Bay onto the headland occupied by the East Point Reserve. This is a pleasant expanse of small beaches, cliffs, lawns, and forest, where wallabies can be seen grazing at dawn and dusk. There is also a saltwater lake safe for swimming. ⊠ *E. Point Rd., Fannie Bay* ⊠ *Free* ⊘ *Daily 6 AM–9 PM.*

⑰ Fannie Bay Gaol. If the sordid stuff of prison life stirs your blood, take a trip out to the gaol (pronounced "jail"), which served as a prison from 1883 to 1979. It's now a museum where you can look into the former living conditions and even the gallows where the last execution in the Northern Territory took place in 1952. ⊠ *E. Point Rd., Fannie Bay* ☎ *08/8999–8290* ⊠ *Free* ⊘ *Daily 10–4:30.*

Fogg Dam. Built as a water supply for the ill-fated rice-growing project of Humpty Doo in the late 1950s, Fogg Dam has remained untouched by commercialism in its remote location 68 km (42 mi) east of Darwin. The project failed largely because the birds of the region regarded the rice crop as a rather tasty smorgasbord. The birds have remained, and they provide an unforgettable sight at sunrise and sunset during the Dry. Exercise care not to get stuck driving through this swampland, however, and wear clothes that you don't mind getting dirty. ⊕ *From Darwin, take the Stuart Highway to the Arnhem Highway. After 24 km (15 mi) turn left and continue for another 6 km (4 mi); then turn right and drive the last ¾ km (½ mi) to the dam.*

★ ⑯ Museum and Art Gallery of the Northern Territory. Natural history, Pacific Island cultures, and visual arts exhibits fill this regional museum. One room is devoted to Cyclone Tracy, and the Gallery of Aboriginal Man has displays of Aboriginal art and culture that provide solid insight into the lives of the most ancient inhabitants of the Top End. You can also see "Sweetheart," a five-meter stuffed saltwater crocodile that attacked 15 local boats in the 1970s. ⊠ *Conacher St., Bullocky Point, Fannie Bay* ☎ *08/8999–8201* ⊕ *www.nt.gov.au* ⊠ *Donation suggested* ⊘ *Weekdays 9–5, weekends 10–5.*

Territory Wildlife Park. Set in 1,000 acres of natural bushland, this impressive park is dedicated to the Northern Territory's native fauna and flora. In addition to saltwater crocodiles, water buffalo, dingoes, and waterbirds, it also has an underwater viewing area from which to observe freshwater fish and a nocturnal house kept dark for viewing animals. ⊠ *Cox Peninsula Rd., 47 km (29 mi) south of Darwin, Berry Springs* ☎ *08/8988–7200* 🎫 *A$18* ⊘ *Daily 8:30–4, exit open until 6.*

Where to Eat

$–$$ ✕ **The Buzz Café.** This is just one of many thriving waterfront eateries on the finger peninsula northwest of downtown, where Darwinites come to socialize. The accent is on fresh seafood presented in a contemporary Australian style. ⊠ *The Slipway, Cullen Bay* ☎ *08/8941–1141* ▭ *AE, DC, MC, V.*

$–$$ ✕ **Crustaceans on the Wharf.** In a renovated corrugated-iron storage shed at the end of a commercial pier, this large restaurant is dominated by a traditional Makassar fishing prau. Open to sea breezes, it's an ideal place to escape the city's summer heat. Seafood takes the foreground, and Greek dips can be followed by chili bugs (small lobsters), lightly cooked calamari, or chili mud crabs, a specialty of the house. ⊠ *Stokes Hill Wharf, Wharf Precinct* ☎ *08/8981–8658* ▭ *AE, DC, MC, V* ⊘ *Closed Sun. Oct.–Apr. No lunch.*

$–$$ ✕ **Twilight On Lindsay.** Tropical gardens surround this air-conditioned restaurant in an old-style, elevated house. The menu is regularly updated, but the theme remains modern Australian with Mediterranean and French influences. Popular choices include kangaroo, crocodile, and barramundi. ⊠ *2 Lindsay St., City Center* ☎ *08/8981–8631* ▭ *AE, DC, MC, V* ⊘ *No lunch weekends.*

¢–$$ ✕ **E'voo In The Boardroom.** This intimate restaurant, atop the MGM Grand Hotel Casino, serves modern Australian cuisine. The somewhat nondescript interior belies a varied menu with Asian and Mediterranean undertones (E'voo stands for Extra Virgin Olive Oil). It also has a very good Australian wine list. ⊠ *Gilruth Ave., Mindil Beach,* ☎ *08/8943–8888* ⬧ *Reservations essential* ▭ *AE, DC, MC, V* ⊘ *Closed Sun.–Mon. No lunch Tues.–Thurs. and Sat.*

★ **¢–$$** ✕ **Pee Wee's at the Point.** Uninterrupted views of Darwin Harbour at East Point Reserve make this restaurant a favorite with locals and visitors. The cooking is modern Australian with a touch of creole spice, and the carefully considered wine list has good values. ⊠ *Alec Fong Ling Dr., East Point Reserve, Fannie Bay* ☎ *08/8981–6868* ⬧ *Reservations essential* ▭ *AE, DC, MC, V* ⊘ *No lunch.*

$ ✕ **Roma Bar.** The decorative theme here seems only accidentally Italian, and the clientele is similarly eclectic: office workers, lawyers, and magistrates from the business district mingle with artists, entertainers, and students. You might enjoy the good coffee and somewhat rowdy hubbub of business-suited and barefoot Darwinites in their natural habitat. The menu is full of straightforward fare—fresh green salads, pasta, and focaccia. ⊠ *30 Cavenagh St., City Center* ☎ *08/8981–6729* ▭ *No credit cards* ⊘ *No dinner.*

¢–$ ✕ **Asian Pot.** This casual eatery, in a food court beneath the All Seasons Hotel, has cheap, tasty meals that reflect Darwin's proximity to Southeast Asia. Note that the restaurant is open until 9 PM for dinner during the Dry. ⊠ *Smith and Knuckey Sts., City Center* ☎ *08/8941–9833* ▭ *No credit cards* ⊘ *Closed Sun. No dinner in the Wet.*

¢–$ ✕ **Hanuman Thai and Nonya Restaurant.** Dark furniture and warm colors make the perfect backdrop for fine food and a wine list that includes the best from every grape-growing region in Australia. By drawing on Thai, Nonya (Malaysian), and Indian tandoori culinary traditions, Hanuman's chefs turn local herbs, vegetables, and seafood into sumptuous and innovative dishes. Of special note are Hanuman oysters, lightly cooked in a spicy coriander-and-lemongrass sauce; barramundi baked with ginger flower; and any of the curries. ⊠ *28 Mitchell St., City Center* ☎ *08/8941–3500* ▭ *AE, DC, MC, V* ⊘ *No lunch weekends.*

FodorśChoice
★

Where to Stay

City Center

$$$ ⊞ **Carlton.** With its colorful, round exterior, this five-story hotel is one of the most striking and unusual in Darwin. The rooms, arranged around a central foyer, are decorated in subtle greens and pinks and accented by natural wood. Most have city or harbor views. ⊠ *Esplanade, Bicentennial Park, 0800* ☎ *08/8980–0800 or 1800/891119* 🖷 *08/8980–0888* ⊕ *www.carlton-darwin.com.au* ↻ *164 rooms, 33 suites* ♣ *Restaurant, minibars, cable TV, pool, exercise equipment, gym, hair salon, 2 saunas, 3 bars, shops, laundry service, Internet, business services, travel services, free parking* ▭ *AE, DC, MC, V.*

$$$ ⊞ **Darwin Central Hotel.** The city's architectural obsession with corrugated iron is vividly illustrated in this unusual-looking modern hotel. As the name implies, it's the city's most central accommodation, overlooking the Smith Street Mall. All rooms have city views and cool color schemes, and they surround a delightful eight-story atrium. ⊠ *Smith and Knuckey Sts., City Center, 0800* ☎ *08/8944–9000 or 1300/364263* 🖷 *08/8944–9100* ↻ *102 rooms, 30 suites* ♣ *2 restaurants, minibars, pool, bar, laundry service, free parking* ▭ *AE, DC, MC, V.*

★ **$$$** ⊞ **Novotel Atrium.** Vying for the title of Darwin's prettiest hotel, the Atrium has seven floors served by glass elevators opening onto a central, vine-hung atrium. The hotel's bar and restaurant are set around a tiny artificial stream amid palm trees and ferns. The pastel-blue guest rooms are attractive and airy. ⊠ *Peel St. and Esplanade, Lameroo Beach, 0800* ☎ *08/8941–0755* 🖷 *08/8981–9025* ⊕ *www.noveteldarwin.com.au* ↻ *138 rooms, 17 suites* ♣ *Restaurant, in-room data ports, minibars, pool, wading pool, bar, laundry service, Internet, meeting rooms, travel services, free parking* ▭ *AE, DC, MC, V.*

$$$ ⊞ **Rydges Plaza Hotel.** This 12-story hotel in the business district is the tallest in Darwin. Rooms have pleasant, cool pastel furnishings, and some have harbor views. With its piano bar and elegant armchairs, the high-ceiling lobby can seem a bit formal if you're coming straight from a fishing trip, but it's a popular spot for an evening drink. ⊠ *32 Mitchell St., City Center, 0800* ☎ *08/8982–0000 or 1800/891107* 🖷 *08/8981–1765* ⊕ *www.rydges.com/darwin* ↻ *233 rooms, 12 suites* ♣ *Restaurant, in-room data ports, minibars, room TVs with movies, pool, gym, hair salon, spa, 2 bars, piano bar, shops, laundry service, business services, meeting rooms, travel services, free parking* ▭ *AE, DC, MC, V.*

★ **$$$** ⊞ **Saville Park Suites.** Spectacular views of the harbor and city are highlights of this eight-story hotel. Rooms are light, open, and equipped with kitchen facilities. Washers, dryers, and flexible room configurations make the apartment-style suites ideal for larger groups. ⊠ *88 Esplanade, Bicentennial Park, 0800* ☎ *08/8943–4333 or 1800/681686* 🖷 *08/8943–4388* ⊕ *www.savillesuites.com.au/darwin.html* ↻ *64 rooms, 140 suites* ♣ *Restaurant, in-room data ports, kitchenettes, minibars, room TVs with movies and video games, pool, hair salon, spa, bicycles, bar, baby-sitting, laundry facilities, laundry service, business services, car rental, travel services, free parking* ▭ *AE, DC, MC, V.*

$$–$$$ ⊞ **MGM Grand Hotel Casino.** Shaped like pyramids with square tops, this casino and the smaller adjoining hotel are two of the most distinctive structures in the city. The three-story hotel has beachfront accommodations set amid lush lawns and gardens. Dark marble, cherry-wood furniture, and Italian-designer lighting fixtures fill the rooms. ⊠ *Gilruth Ave., Mindil Beach, 0800* ☎ *08/8943–8888 or 1800/891118* 🖷 *08/8943–8999* ⊕ *www.mgmgrand.com.au* ↻ *96 rooms, 16 suites* ♣ *2* restaurants, coffee shop, in-room data ports, in-room safes, some in-room hot tubs, minibars, refrigerators, room TVs with movies, tennis court, 2 pools, wading pool, gym, health club, massage, sauna, spa, beach, 8 bars, casino, nightclub, shops, baby-sitting, laundry service, concierge, business services, convention center, meeting rooms, car rental, travel services, free parking ☐ AE, DC, MC, V.

¢ ⊡ **Value Inn.** A step up from the Youth Hostel, this is a one-of-a-kind, self-service hotel where you check in using a credit card that doubles as your room key. This large hotel bills itself as having the best rates for double rooms in town, and doesn't disappoint. While front-desk service is nonexistent (follow directions on the automated check-in outside), the small double rooms are comfortable and clean. Best of all, you are right in the heart of downtown. ✉ 50 Mitchell St., City Center ☎ 08/8981–4733 🖨 08/8981–4730 ⊕ www.valueinn.com.au ⇆ 93 rooms ♨ Pool, dry cleaning ☐ AE, DC, MC, V.

¢ ⊡ **YHA Hostel.** This hostel provides the cheapest accommodations in town. Sleeping areas are basic but clean, bright, and airy. You need to supply or rent sheets, but there is a fully equipped kitchen on-site. Two rooms sleep eight, 68 rooms sleep three to four and are suitable for families, and there are 11 twin and 12 double rooms (two of the latter have private bathrooms). There's a common area for watching television, and a quiet room for reading or writing letters. Nonmembers pay a A$3.50 nightly charge. ✉ 69A Mitchell St., City Center, 0800 ☎ 08/8981–3995 🖨 08/8981–6674 ⊕ www.yha.com.au ⇆ 93 rooms, 2 with bath ♨ Pool, recreation room, laundry facilities, travel services, free parking; no room phones, no room TVs ☐ MC, V.

Gurig National Park

$$$$ ⊡ **Seven Spirit Bay Wilderness Lodge.** This wilderness lodge on the pristine Cobourg Peninsula is accessible only by a one-hour flight. Hexagonal huts with private outdoor bathrooms are linked by winding paths to the main complex, lagoon-style pool, and ocean beyond. A resident naturalist heads photographic tours and bushwalks to see dingoes, wallabies, crocodiles, buffalo, and Timorese ponies. Meals, which are included, emphasize light, modern Australian cooking using seafood from the surrounding waters and herbs from the resort gardens. ✎ Box 4721, Darwin, 0801 ☎ 03/9826–2471 🖨 03/9824–1113 ⊕ www. sevenspiritbay.com ⇆ 24 bungalows ♨ Restaurant, minibars, pool, bar, lounge, library, laundry service, meeting room, airstrip, travel services; no a/c, no room TVs, no kids under 6 ☐ AE, MC, V ⑩ FAP.

Fodor's Choice ★

Nightlife & the Arts

Bars & Lounges

The atmospheric **Blue Heelers** (✉ Cnr. Mitchell and Herbert Sts., City Center ☎ 08/8941–7945) is a typically laid-back watering hole with good dancing and Australian Outback decor. Irish flavor and pub food is available at **Kitty O'Shea's** (✉ Mitchell and Herbert Sts., City Center ☎ 08/8941–7947). **Rorke's Drift** (✉ 46 Mitchell St., City Center ☎ 08/8941–7171), up Mitchell Street, resembles an English pub. There's a varied menu available until 10 PM. **Shenannigans Hotel** (✉ 69 Mitchell St., City Center ☎ 08/8981–2100) has Guinness on tap, along with those other two famous Irish beers, Kilkenny and Harp. Traditional pub food is also available.

The young and hip frequent **Time Nightclub** (✉ 3 Edmunds St., City Center ☎ 08/8981–9761), next door to Squire's tavern, where you can dance the night away to techno and funk. For a beer and live music, visit the

Top End Hotel (⊠ Daly and Mitchell Sts., Bicentennial Park ☎ 08/8981–6511), where the pleasant outdoor Lizard Bar serves meaty Australian fare.

Casino

MGM Grand Hotel Casino (⊠ Gilruth Ave., Mindil Beach ☎ 08/8943–8888) is one of Darwin's most popular sources of evening entertainment. Slot machines are open 24 hours, while gaming tables are open from noon until 3 AM weekdays and until 4 AM weekends.

Theaters & Concerts

The **Darwin Entertainment Centre** (⊠ 93 Mitchell St., City Center ☎ 08/8980–3333), behind the Carlton Hotel, has a large theater that regularly stages concerts, dance, and drama. It also doubles as booking office for other touring concerts in town—especially those at the Amphitheatre, Australia's best outdoor concert venue (entrance next to Botanic Gardens on Gardens Road). Check the *Northern Territory News* or the *Sunday Territorian* for current shows.

Sports & the Outdoors

Bicycling

Darwin is fairly flat and has a good network of bike paths, so cycling is a good way to get around—although you might need something waterproof during the Wet. **Darwin Tennis Centre** (⊠ Gilruth Ave., The Gardens ☎ 08/8985–2844) has bike rentals available at a number of hotels and motels including the YHA, next door to Shenannigans Hotel on Mitchell Street. Prices range from A$4 per hour to A$16 per day with discounts for weekly hire.

Fishing

Barramundi, the best-known fish of the Top End, can weigh up to 110 pounds and are excellent fighting fish that taste great on the barbie afterward. Contact the **Northern Territory Department of Primary Industry and Fisheries** (☎ 08/8999–5511) for more information on licenses and catch limits.

Cullen Bay Dive (⊠ 66 Marina Blvd., Cullen Bay ☎ 08/8981–3049) charters fishing vessels that go for snapper, trevelly, and mackerel. Trips cost about A$185 per person for a full day, or A$110 per person for a half day.

Golf

You can rent clubs at all three courses in the Darwin area.

The city's only 18-hole, par-72 course is the **Darwin Golf Club** (⊠ Links Rd., Marrara ☎ 08/8927–1322, 08/8927–1015 for reservations). Greens fees are A$22 for 9 holes and A$32 for 18, with motorized carts for A$21 to A$32. The 9-hole, par-34 **Gardens Park Golf Links** (⊠ Gardens Rd., The Gardens ☎ 08/8981–6365) costs A$13 weekdays and A$14.50 weekends. The 9-hole **Palmerston Golf and Country Club** (⊠ Dwyer Circuit, Palmerston ☎ 08/8932–1324) can also be played as an 18-hole, par-70 course. Fees are A$15 and A$20, respectively.

Health & Fitness Clubs

A popular gym is **Carlton Hotel Gymnasium** (⊠ Esplanade, Bicentennial Park ☎ 08/8980–0888). The fee is A$7 per visit, or A$84 monthly. The most central commercial gym is **Time Out Fitness Centre** (⊠ 5–2798 Dashwood Pl., City Center ☎ 08/8941–8711).

Running

The waterfront Bicentennial Park, which runs parallel to the Esplanade, has a popular jogging trail. For a longer run, the beachfront parks along the shores of Fannie Bay to East Point provide generally flat terrain and a great view.

Tennis

The **Darwin Tennis Centre** (✉ Gilruth Ave., The Gardens ☎ 08/8985–2844), near the Botanic Gardens, has four lighted courts. Prices range from A$11 per hour off-peak to A$16 per hour peak. All equipment is available for hire.

Water Sports

Marine stingers (jellyfish) and saltwater crocodiles restrict water activities around Darwin. The beaches of Fannie Bay, such as Mindil and Vesteys, and those of Nightcliff are nonetheless popular—though not for swimming—especially on weekends.

For diving, contact **Cullen Bay Dive** (✉ 66 Marina Blvd., Cullen Bay ☎ 08/8981–3049), which runs reef trips and dives on wrecks from World War II and Cyclone Tracy. Training and classes are available, including PADI and Technical Diving certification courses. Prices range from A$70 for two dives with your own gear, up to A$150 for two dives with all gear.

Shopping

Aboriginal Art

The best buys in Darwin are Aboriginal paintings and artifacts. Among the top Aboriginal-art sellers is the **Raintree Aboriginal Art Gallery** (✉ Shop 3, 20 Knuckey St., City Center ☎ 08/8981–2732). At **Framed** (✉ 55 Stuart Hwy., The Gardens ☎ 08/8981–2994 ⊕ www.framed.com.au), a gallery near the Botanic Gardens, you can find expensive but exquisite art pieces. It's open Mon.–Fri. 9–5:30, weekends and holidays 11–4.

Markets

The **Mindil Beach Sunset Market** (✉ Beach Rd., Mindil Beach ☎ 08/8981–3454) is an extravaganza that takes place Thursdays 5–10 PM April–October as well as Sundays June to September. Come in the late afternoon to snack at hundreds of food stalls, shop at artisans' booths, and watch singers, dancers, and musicians. Or join the other Darwinites with a bottle of wine to watch the sun plunge into the harbor.

The **Darwin Night Markets** (✉ 52 Mitchell St., City Center ☎ 0418/60–0830) are open daily 5 PM–11 PM and include arts, crafts, souvenirs, and Aboriginal artifacts. North of downtown, the **Parap Markets** (✉ Parap Sq., Parap) are open Saturday 8 AM–2 PM and have a great selection of ethnic Asian food. The **Rapid Creek Markets** (✉ Rapid Creek Shopping Centre, Trower Rd., Rapid Creek), open Sunday 8–2, specialize in Asian produce and cuisine.

Darwin A to Z

To research prices, get advice from other travelers, and book travel arrangements, visit www.fodors.com.

AIR TRAVEL

Darwin's International Airport is serviced from overseas by Qantas, Garuda, Malaysia Airlines, and Royal Brunei. Qantas and Garuda fly from Darwin to Bali several times a week. Malaysia Airlines flies twice weekly nonstop to Kuala Lumpur. Royal Brunei connects Darwin with Bandar Seri Begawan.

Qantas and its subsidiary Air North, along with Virgin Blue Airlines, fly into Darwin regularly from other parts of Australia and also operate a number of regional flights within the Top End. Air North flies west to Kununurra and Broome, south to Katherine and Alice Springs, and east to Cairns and Brisbane. Check the Qantas Web site for last-minute regional air specials.

Carriers Air North ☎ 08/8945-2866 or 1800/627474. **Garuda Indonesia** ☎ 1300/365330 ⊕ www.garudaindonesia.com. **Malaysia Airlines** ☎ 13-2627. **Qantas** ☎ 13-1313 ⊕ www.qantas.com. **Royal Brunei** ☎ 08/8941-0966. **Virgin Blue Airlines** ☎ 13-6789 ⊕ www.virginblue.com.au.

AIRPORTS

The airport is 15 km (9 mi) northeast of the city by car. After leaving the terminal, turn left onto McMillans Road and left again onto Bagot Road. Continue until you cross the overpass that merges onto the Stuart Highway, which later becomes Daly Street. Turn left onto Smith Street to reach the Smith Street Mall in the heart of the city.

The Darwin Airport Shuttle has regular service between the airport and the city's hotels. The cost is A$5.50 per person one-way or A$10 round-trip; book a day in advance. Taxis are available from the taxi rank at the airport. The journey downtown costs about A$15.

Darwin International Airport ☎ 08/8945-5944.
Darwin Airport Shuttle ☎ 1800/358945.

BUS TRAVEL

Greyhound Pioneer terminates at the Mitchell Street Shopping Precinct, which is the old Darwin Transit Centre. There is daily service to and from Alice Springs, Katherine, Broome, and Perth. McCafferty's terminates at 71 Smith Street in the middle of town. It also operates daily services to and from Darwin.

Bus Station Darwin Transit Centre ✉ 69 Mitchell St., City Center.
Bus Lines Greyhound Pioneer ☎ 08/8981-8700, 13-2030 central reservations ⊕ www.greyhound.com.au. **McCafferty's** ☎ 08/8941-0911, 13-1499 central reservations ⊕ www.mccaffertys.com.au.

BUS TRAVEL WITHIN DARWIN

The bus network in Darwin links the city with its far-flung suburbs. The main bus terminal (Darwin Bus) is on Harry Chan Avenue, near the Bennett Street end of Smith Street Mall. The 24-hour Darwin City Shuttle runs anywhere within a 4-km (6-mi) radius of downtown for A$2.

Darwin Bus ☎ 08/8924-7666. **Darwin City Shuttle** ☎ 08/8985-3666.

CAR RENTAL

Avis, Budget, and Hertz are the major international agencies; locally, you can depend on Britz-Rentals and Advance Car Rental. Four-wheel-drive vehicles are available.

Agencies Advance Car Rental ✉ 86 Mitchell St., City Center ☎ 1800/002227. **Avis** ✉ Airport ✉ 91 Smith St., City Center ☎ 08/8981-9922. **Britz-Rentals** ✉ 44-46 Stuart Hwy., Stuart Park ☎ 08/8981-2081. **Budget** ✉ Airport ✉ 108 Mitchell St., City Center ☎ 08/8981-9800. **Europcar** ✉ Airport ✉ 77 Cavenagh St., City Center ☎ 08/8941-0300 **Hertz** ✉ Airport ✉ Smith and Daly Sts., City Center ☎ 08/8941-0944.

CAR TRAVEL

The best way to get around Darwin is by car. The Stuart Highway is Darwin's land connection with the rest of Australia, and anyone arriving by car will enter the city on this road. By road Darwin is 20 hours from Alice Springs, 27 hours from Broome, 47 hours from Brisbane, and 58 hours from Perth.

For drivers headed outside the Northern Territory, one-way drop-off fees can be prohibitive, often twice as much as twice a weekly rental. Also, very few travelers, even Australians, drive the highways after dark.

EMERGENCIES

In an emergency, dial **000** to reach an ambulance, the police, or the fire department.

🔲 Doctors & Dentists **Night & Day Medical & Dental Surgery** ⊠ Casuarina Shopping Centre, Trower Rd., Casuarina ☎ 08/8927-1899. **Trower Road A/H Medical Centre** ⊠ Trower Rd., Casuarina ☎ 08/8927-6905.

🔲 Hospital **Royal Darwin Hospital** ⊠ Rocklands Dr., Tiwi ☎ 08/8922-8888.

MONEY MATTERS

Banking hours are Monday through Thursday from 9:30 to 4 and Friday from 9:30 to 5. Currency exchange facilities are available on Smith Street Mall and Mitchell Street.

TAXIS

In town, look for Yellow Cab Co., Darwin Radio Taxis, and Unique Minibus, among others, for local transport.

🔲 Taxi Companies **Darwin Radio Taxis** ☎ 08/8981-3777. **Metro Minibus** ☎ 08/8932-5577. **Unique Minibus** ☎ 08/8928-1100. **Yellow Cab Co.** ☎ 08/131924.

TOURS

Top End Tourism has information on adventure tours in the area.

Every day but Sunday, Darwin Day Tours conduct afternoon trips for A$48, and for A$10 more (May to September) you can take in a sunset harbor cruise with a glass of champagne. Tours include historic buildings, the main harbor, the Botanic Gardens, the Museum and Art Gallery of the Northern Territory, East Point Military Reserve, and Stokes Hill Wharf. Alternatively, for A$25 you can hop on and off the Tour Tub "City Sights" bus, which takes in most of Darwin's attractions. It picks up at Knuckey Street, at the end of Smith Street Mall, and runs daily 9–4.

Daytime and sunset cruises allow you to cool off and explore a beautiful harbor five times the size of Sydney's. Cruises are available on the *Spirit of Darwin*. Trips depart from Cullen Bay Marina at 1:45 and 5:45 daily (except Sunday) between April and October. The tours last two hours, cost A$34, and serve alcohol.

🔲 Boat Tour **Spirit of Darwin** ☎ 08/8981-3711.
🔲 Bus Tours **Darwin Day Tours** ☎ 1800/811633. **Tour Tub** ☎ 1800/632225.

TRAIN TRAVEL

The Ghan train connects Darwin with Adelaide via Alice Springs. The two-night journey, which departs twice weekly, is $A1,740 for a sleeper car (with all meals), $A440 for a reclining seat. Book two sleeper seats and you can take your car on the Motorail vehicle carrier for just $A99.

🔲 Ghan ☎ 13-2147, ⊕ www.trainways.com.

VISITOR INFORMATION

🔲 Top End Tourism ⊠ Beagle House, Mitchell and Knuckey Sts., City Center ☎ 08/8936-2499 ⊕ www.tourismtopend.com.au.

KAKADU NATIONAL PARK

FodorśChoice ★ Kakadu National Park is a jewel among the many Top End parks, and many come to the region just to experience this tropical wilderness. Beginning 256 km (159 mi) east of Darwin, the park covers 19,800 square km (7,645 square mi) and protects a large system of unspoiled rivers and creeks, as well as a rich Aboriginal heritage that extends back to the earliest days of humankind. The superb gathering of Aboriginal rock art may be Kakadu's highlight.

Two major types of Aboriginal artwork can be seen here. The Mimi style, which is the oldest, is believed to be up to 20,000 years old. Aborigines believe that Mimi spirits created the red-ocher stick figures to depict hunting scenes and other pictures of life at the time. The more recent artwork, known as X-ray painting, dates back less than 9,000 years and depicts freshwater animals—especially fish, turtles, and geese—living in floodplains created after the last ice age.

Most of the region is virtually inaccessible during the Wet, so it is strongly advisable to visit the park between May and September. As the dry season progresses, billabongs (water holes) become increasingly important to the more than 280 species of birds that inhabit the park. Huge flocks often gather at Yellow Water, South Alligator River, and Margella Creek. If you do visit during the Wet, scenic flights over the wetlands and Arnhem Land escarpment provide unforgettable moments.

Orientation

Bowali Visitors Centre has state-of-the-art audiovisual displays and traditional exhibits that give an introduction to the park's ecosystems and its bird population, the world's most diverse. ⊠ *Arnhem and Kakadu Hwys.* ☎ *08/8938–1120* ☑ *Free* ☉ *Daily 8–5.*

Warradjan Aboriginal Cultural Centre is at Yellow Water near Cooinda. The cultural center—named after the pig-nose turtle unique to the Top End—provides an excellent experience of local Bininj culture. Displays take you through the Aboriginal Creation period, following the path of the creation ancestor Rainbow Serpent through the ancient landscape of Kakadu. ⊠ *Kakadu Hwy., Cooinda* ☎ *08/8979–0051* ☑ *Free* ☉ *Daily 9–5.*

Exploring Kakadu National Park

Like the main Kakadu escarpment, **Nourlangie Rock** is a remnant of an ancient plateau that is slowly eroding, leaving sheer cliffs rising high above the floodplains. The main attraction at Nourlangie Rock is the **Anbangbang Gallery**, an excellent frieze of Aboriginal rock paintings. To reach the paintings, drive 19 km (12 mi) from the park headquarters down the Kakadu Highway to the left-hand turnoff to Nourlangie Rock, then follow this paved road (accessible year-round) about 11 km (7 mi) to the parking area and paintings.

Ubirr has an impressive array of Aboriginal paintings scattered through six shelters in the rock. The main gallery contains a 49-foot frieze of X-ray paintings depicting animals, birds, and fish. A 1-km (½-mi) path around the rock leads to all the galleries. It's just a short clamber to the top for wonderful views over the surrounding wetlands, particularly at sunset. ⊕ *43 km (27 mi) north of the park headquarters along a paved road.* ☑ *Free* ☉ *Apr.–Nov. 8–sunset, Dec.–Mar. 2–sunset.*

The best way to gain a true appreciation of the natural beauty of Kakadu is to visit the waterfalls running off the escarpment. Some 39 km (24 mi) south of the park headquarters along the Kakadu Highway, a track leads off to the left toward **Jim Jim Falls**. From the parking lot you have to walk 1 km (½ mi) over boulders to reach the falls and the plunge pools it has created at the base of the escarpment. After May, the water flow over the falls may cease, but the pools remain well worth visiting. This unpaved road is suitable only for four-wheel-drive vehicles and is closed in the Wet. Even in good conditions, the 60-km (37-mi) ride to Jim Jim takes about two hours.

As you approach the **Twin Falls,** the ravine opens up dramatically to reveal a beautiful sandy beach scattered with palm trees, as well as the crystal waters of the falls spilling onto the end of the beach. This spot is a bit difficult to reach, but the trip is rewarding. After a short walk from the parking lot, you must swim along a small creek for a few hundred yards to reach the falls—many people use inflatable air beds as rafts to transport their lunch and towels. The parking lot is 10 km (6 mi) farther on the dirt road from Jim Jim Falls.

Where to Stay
There are several lodges in the park, and campgrounds at Merl, Muirella Park, Mardugal, and Gumlom have toilets, showers, and water. Sites are A$5 per night.

$$ ⊞ **Aurora Kakadu Resort.** This comfortable hotel has doubles, dorms that sleep four, and family rooms. Rates are significantly lower during the Wet. Fuel is available. *⌖ Box 221, Winnellie 0822 ⊹ 2½ km (1½ mi) before Arnhem Hwy. crosses South Alligator River ☎ 08/8979–0166 or 1800/818845 ⊟ 08/8979–0147 ⊕ www.aurora-resorts.com.au ⤴ 138 rooms ⌂ Restaurant, tennis court, pool, spa, shops, laundry service, free parking ⊟ AE, DC, MC, V.*

$$ ⊞ **Gagudju Crocodile Holiday Inn.** Shaped like a crocodile, this unusual hotel with spacious rooms is the best of the area's accommodation options. The reception, a de facto art gallery, is through the mouth, and the swimming pool is in the open courtyard in the belly. *⊠ Flinders St., Jabiru, 0886 ☎ 08/8979–2800 or 1300/666747 ⊟ 08/8979–2707 ⤴ 110 rooms ⌂ Restaurant, pool, bar, shop, travel services, free parking ⊟ AE, DC, MC, V.*

$ ⊞ **Gagudju Lodge Cooinda.** Conveniently located near Yellow Water, this facility has light, airy lodge rooms looking out to tropical gardens. Forty-eight budget rooms are also available. *⊠ Kakadu Hwy., Cooinda 0886 ☎ 08/8979–0145 or 1800/500401 ⊟ 08/8979–0148 ⊕ www. gagudjulodgecooinda.com.au ⤴ 82 rooms ⌂ Restaurant, pool, bar, free parking ⊟ AE, MC, V.*

¢ ⚠ **Aurora Kakadu Lodge and Caravan Park.** A privately operated campground is available at Aurora. Power-equipped sites for motorhomes and basic tent sites set in lush grounds are both available, and within walking distance of trailheads, waterfalls, shops, and the lagoon-style pool. *⊠ Jabiru Dr., Jabiru, 0886 ☎ 08/8979–2422 or 1800/811154 ⊕ www. aurora-resorts.com.au ⤴ 138 rooms ⌂ Flush toilets, pit toilets, full hookups, drinking water, showers, fire pits, general store, pool.*

¢ ⚠ **Gagudju Lodge Cooinda Campground.** Campsites are set in the tropical forest near the resort. Some are supplied with power for motorhomes, but basic, bare-bones tent sites with shared bath facilities are also available. *⊠ Flinders St., Jabiru, 0886 ☎ 08/8979–2800 or 1800/ 808123 ⊟ 08/8979–2707 ⤴ 80 powered sites, 300 unpowered sites ⌂ Pit toilets, full hook-ups, showers, fire pits.*

Kakadu National Park A to Z

To research prices, get advice from other travelers, and book travel arrangements, visit www.fodors.com.

CAR TRAVEL
From Darwin take the Arnhem Highway east to Jabiru. Although four-wheel-drive vehicles are not necessary to travel to the park, they are re-

quired for many of the unpaved roads within, including the track to Jim Jim Falls. The entrance fee is A$16.25 per person.

TOURS

During the Dry, park rangers conduct free walks and tours at several popular locations. You can pick up a program at the entry station or at either of the visitor centers.

Kakadu Air makes scenic flights out of Jabiru, one hour for A$125 or a half hour for A$75. In the Dry, the flight encompasses the Northern Region, including floodplains, East Alligator River, and Jabiru Township. During the Wet, Jim Jim and Twin Falls are included. Gunbalanya Air also provides tours of the region.

The Gagudju Lodge Cooinda arranges boat tours of Yellow Water, the major water hole where innumerable birds and crocodiles gather. There are six tours throughout the day; the first (6:45 AM) is the coolest. Tours, which run most of the year, cost A$33 for 90 minutes and A$38.50 for two hours.

Billy Can Tours provides a range of two-, three-, and four-day camping and accommodation tours in Kakadu. Far Out Adventures runs customized tours of Kakadu, as well as other regions of the Top End, for small groups. Odyssey Safaris has deluxe four-wheel-drive tours into Kakadu as well as other areas of northern Australia including the Kimberley, and Litchfield and Nitmiluk national parks.

Air Tours Kakadu Air ☎ 1800/089113. **Gunbalanya Air** ☎ 08/8979-3384.
Boat Tours Gagudju Lodge Cooinda ☎ 08/8979-0111.
Vehicle Tours Billy Can Tours Box 4407, Darwin, 0801 ☎ 08/8981-9813 or 1800/813484 ☎ 08/8941-0803 ⊕ www.billycan.com.au. **Far Out Adventures** ⊠ 5 Rutt Ct., Katherine ☎ 08/8972-2552 ☎ 08/8972-2228 ⊕ www.farout.com.au. **Odyssey Safaris** Box 3012, Darwin, 0801 ☎ 08/8948-0091 or 1800/891190 ☎ 08/8948-0646 ⊕ www.odysaf.com.au.

VISITOR INFORMATION

You can contact the Kakadu National Park directly for information, or Top End Tourism.

Tourist Information Kakadu National Park Box 71, Jabiru, 0886 ☎ 08/8938-1120. **Top End Tourism** ⊠ Beagle House, Mitchell and Knuckey Sts., Darwin, 0800 ☎ 08/8981-4300.

LITCHFIELD NATIONAL PARK

Litchfield, one of the Northern Territory's newest and smallest parks, is also one of the most accessible from Darwin. Convenience hasn't spoiled the park's beauty, however. Almost all of the park's 1,340 square km (515 square mi) are covered by an untouched wilderness of monsoonal rain forests, rivers, and escarpment—cliffs formed by erosion. The highlights of this dramatic landscape are four separate spectacular waterfalls supplied by natural springs year-round from aquifers deep under the plateau. The park is not considered to be crocodile-free, hence swimming holes are regularly monitored and posted by park service staff. Even then, however, swim at your own risk.

Exploring Litchfield National Park

Lovely trails lead to Florence, Tjaynera, and Wangi falls, all of which have secluded plunge pools. **Tolmer Falls** looks out over a natural rock arch and is within a short walk of the parking lot. Near Tolmer Falls—accessible only by four-wheel-drive vehicles—is a series of large, free-standing sandstone pillars known as the **Lost City.**

Along the way look for groves of extremely slow-growing cycad palms, an ancient plant species that is unique to the area, the larger specimens of which are thought to be hundreds of years old. **Magnetic Termite Mounds,** which have an eerie resemblance to eroded grave markers, dot the black-soil plains of the park's northern area. To regulate the internal temperature of the mounds, termites orient them to take advantage of the early-morning sun.

Where to Stay

You have to camp if you want to stay in Litchfield National Park. In Batchelor, there are a couple of restaurants and a number of caravan parks, as well as a moderately priced motel.

⚠ **Campgrounds** are available at Florence Falls, Wangi Falls, Buley Rockhole, and Sandy Creek. These are basic—Buley has no shower facilities and Sandy Creek is accessible only by four-wheel-drive vehicles—but the price can't be beat. You never pay more than A$6.60 per person per night. ☎ *08/8976–0282 Parks and Wildlife Commission.*

$–$$ 🏨 **Rum Jungle Motor Inn.** This modern motel is a good base for exploring Litchfield National Park. ✉ *49 Rum Jungle Rd., Batchelor, 0845* ☎ *08/8976–0123* 🖷 *08/8976–0230* 🛏 *22 rooms* ♨ *Restaurant, pool, free parking* 🖃 *MC, V.*

Litchfield National Park A to Z

To research prices, get advice from other travelers, and book travel arrangements, visit www.fodors.com.

CAR TRAVEL

Litchfield is an easy 122 km (76 mi) from Darwin. Take the Stuart Highway 85 km (53 mi) south to the turnoff for the town of Batchelor, and continue on the Batchelor Road to the park's northern border. As you enter the park you will see a sign telling you to tune your radio to 88 on the FM dial. This station provides up-to-date information on the park, such as current road and campsite conditions, and how to get to the park's main areas of interest. Most of the park is accessible by conventional vehicles; four-wheel-drive vehicles are advised after the rains and are necessary to enter the park from Berry Springs or Adelaide River. You can make a loop through the park by connecting the Batchelor and Berry Springs entrances.

TOURS

Billy Can Tours provides a number of excursions to Litchfield, along with some that combine Litchfield with Kakadu and Nitmiluk (Katherine Gorge) national parks.

🎫 **Billy Can Tours** 📫 Box 4407, Darwin, 0801 ☎ 08/8981–9813 or 1800/813484 🖷 08/8941–0803.

VISITOR INFORMATION

🎫 **Parks and Wildlife Commission of the Northern Territory** 📫 Box 45, Batchelor, 0845 ☎ 08/8976–0282 🖷 08/8976–0292 ⊕ www.nt.gov.au/paw.

KATHERINE

317 km (196 mi) southeast of Darwin.

If you're heading west to the Kimberley or south to the Red Centre, Katherine River is the last permanently flowing water you'll see until you get to Adelaide—2,741 km (1,700 mi) to the south! A veritable oasis, Katherine is the crossroads of the region, making it the second-largest town in the Top End with a booming population of more than 11,000. The town was first established to service the Overland Telegraph that linked the south with Asia and Europe and it had the first cattle and sheep runs in the Top End. The Springvale Homestead 8 km (5 mi) west of town is the oldest still standing in the Northern Territory.

Katherine is now a regional administrative and supply center for the cattle industry, as well as being the site for the largest military air base in northern Australia. The focus of the town is on the Katherine River, popular for fishing, swimming, and canoeing. In a region best known for the spectacular 13 gorges of Nitmiluk National Park, Katherine makes a good base for exploring Cutta Cutta Caves and Mataranka.

Among other things, Katherine is home to the world's largest school classroom, the **Katherine School of the Air** (⊠ Giles St. ☎ 08/8972–1833 🖃 A$5), which broadcasts to about 250 students over 800,000 square km (308,880 square mi) of isolated cattle country. Tours are available on weekdays from mid-March through April.

off the beaten path

MANYALLALUK – The region is a focus for Aboriginal cultures quite different from those of the rest of the Top End and the Red Centre— and tours are available by Aboriginal people themselves. The community of Manyallaluk is on Aboriginal-owned land 100 km (62 mi) southeast of Katherine by road.

Where to Stay & Eat

★ ¢–$ ✕🖼 **Jan's Bed & Breakfast.** This cozy lodging is a real Top End find: a cool, comfortable retreat set in tropical gardens. Antiques and artifacts fill the interior, and a small outdoor hot tub is the perfect place to recuperate from a long walk at nearby Katherine Gorge. Northern Territory hospitality here includes delicious home-cooked food. ⊠ *13 Pearce St., Katherine, 0850* ☎ *08/8971–1005* 🖶 *08/8971–1309* ✍ *jcomleybbaccom@yahoo.com.au* 🛏 *3 rooms* ♨ *Dining room, outdoor hot tub, laundry facilities, free parking; no room phones, no room TVs* 🖃 *MC, V* ⦿*BP.*

¢–$ ✕🖼 **Knotts Crossing Resort.** Nestled on the banks of the Katherine River, well-designed motel rooms and low-slung cabins make up this resort. Two pools and an outside bar are favorite hangouts after a hot day. Katie's bistro serves local fish. Self-catering rooms and caravan and camping sites are also available. ⊠ *Cameron and Giles Sts., Katherine, 0850* ☎ *08/ 8972–2511 or 1800/222511* 🖶 *08/8972–2628* ⊕ *www.knottscrossing. com.au* 🛏 *123 rooms* ♨ *Restaurant, some kitchens, 2 pools, bar, laundry facilities, free parking* 🖃 *AE, DC, MC, V.*

Nitmiluk (Katherine Gorge) National Park

31 km (19 mi) north of Katherine.

One of the Territory's most famous parks, Nitmiluk—named after a site at the mouth of the first gorge—is owned by the local Jawoyn Aboriginal tribe and leased back to the Parks and Wildlife Commission. Katherine Gorge, the park's European name, is derived from the area's most striking feature. The power of the Katherine River in flood during the Wet has created an enormous system of gorges—13 in all—connected by the river. Rapids separate the gorges, much to the delight of canoeists, and there really is no better way to see the gorges than by boat. Regularly scheduled flat-bottom tour boats take people on (two-hour to full-day) safaris to the fifth gorge, a trip that requires hiking to circumnavigate each rapid. During the Wet, jet boats provide access into the flooded gorges. In general the best time to visit is during the Dry, from May through early November.

For more adventurous travelers, the park has over 100 km of the best bushwalking trails in the Top End. Ten well-marked walking tracks, ranging from one hour to five days, lead hikers on trails parallel to the Katherine River and north toward Edith Falls at the edge of the park. Some of the longer, overnight walks lead past Aboriginal paintings and through swamps, heath, cascades, waterfalls, and rain forest. The best is the four-day, 66-km (41-mi) **Jatbula Trail,** which passes a number of Edenesque pools and spectacular waterfall on its route from **Katherine Gorge** to **Edith Falls.** Walkers should register with the Nitmiluk Visitor Centre before departure.

The park's **Nitmiluk Visitor Centre** (☎ 08/8972–1253 🖷 08/8971–0715) is a beautiful ocher-color building crouching in the bush near the mouth of the gorge. It houses an interpretive center, an open-air children's playground, and souvenir and restaurant facilities.

Where to Stay

Campgrounds located near the Katherine River and opposite the Nitmiluk Visitor Centre, cost A$8 per person per night. Bush camping along the river past the second set of rapids is allowed with the ranger's permission. The cost is A$13 per person per night.

Sports & the Outdoors

Canoes can be rented from Nitmiluk Visitor Centre or at the gorge boat ramp for A$41 (double) and A$27 (single) per half day and for a whole day at A$56 for a two-person canoe and A$38 for a single. A A$20 deposit is required; that becomes A$60 if you are going on a longer overnight trip up the gorge.

Exciting multiday trips down less-frequented parts of the Katherine and other river systems in this area are run by an excellent local tour company, **Gecko Canoeing** (☎ 08/8972–2224 or 1800/634319 ⊕ www.geckocanoeing.com.au).

Cutta Cutta Caves

29 km (18 mi) south of Katherine.

The Cutta Cutta Caves, a series of limestone caverns, shelter the rare Ghost and Orange Horseshoe bats. Ranger-led tours take place daily throughout the day for A$11. ☎ 08/8972–1940.

Mataranka

106 km (66 mi) southeast of Katherine.

The tiny township of Mataranka is the original center of Australia's literary expression for the Outback, the "never never"—as in Jeannie Gunn's novel, *We of the Never Never,* about turn-of-the-20th-century life in the area. West of the upper reaches of the Roper River, Mataranka was a major army base during World War II, and its most famous attraction, the palm-shrouded **Mataranka Thermal Pool,** was first developed as a recreation site by American troops during that period.

Katherine A to Z

To research prices, get advice from other travelers, and book travel arrangements, visit www.fodors.com.

AIR TRAVEL

Air North serves Katherine to and from Darwin at least once daily. The flight time is one hour, and the airport is 10 minutes south of town.
🔝 **Air North** ☎ 08/8945-2866 or 1800/627474.

BUS TRAVEL

Greyhound Pioneer runs between Darwin and Alice Springs with a stop at Katherine. It's about 16 hours from Alice Springs to Katherine and 4 hours from Katherine to Darwin.
🔝 **Greyhound Pioneer** ☎ 08/8981-8700 or 13-2030 ⊕ www.greyhound.com.au.

CAR RENTAL

🔝 Agencies **Hertz** ✉ Katherine Airport ☎ 08/8971-1111. **Europcar** ✉ Katherine Airport ☎ 131-390.

CAR TRAVEL

Katherine is 317 km (196 mi) southeast of Darwin via the Stuart Highway. Driving to Katherine will allow you to stop along the way at Litchfield National Park and get around easily to Nitmiluk National Park and other sights nearby. And you may want to continue on to Kununurra, 564 km (350 mi) west, or to Alice Springs, 1,145 km (710 mi) to the south.

EMERGENCIES

In case of an emergency, call the police or the Katherine Hospital.
🔝 **Katherine Hospital** ☎ 08/8973-9211. **Police** ☎ 08/8972-0111.

TOURS

Manyallaluk Tours hosts a series of one- to three-day tours with Aboriginal guides that focus on bush tucker (food), art and artifact manufacture, interaction with Aboriginal people, and extensive rock-art sites.

Billy Can Tours combines excursions to Nitmiluk with Litchfield and Kakadu national parks. Based in Katherine, Far Out Adventures runs fully catered four-wheel-drive tours of Nitmiluk, Kakadu, and other less-explored parts of the region.

Gecko Canoeing, also based in Katherine, provides the chance to explore the Katherine River and some of the other tropical savannah river systems on an escorted canoe safari. Trips range from one to several days (with fully catered overnight camping). Nitmiluk Tours has two- (A$33), four- (A$47), and eight-hour (A$88) trips up the Katherine Gorge aboard a flat-bottom boat.
🔝 Aboriginal Tours **Manyallaluk Tours** ☎08/8975-4727 or 1800/644727 🖨08/8975-4724.
🔝 Boat Tours **Gecko Canoeing** ☎ 08/8972-2224 or 1800/634319 🖨 08/8972-2294 ⊕ www.geckocanoeing.com.au. **Nitmiluk Tours** ☎ 08/8972-2044.
🔝 Park Tours **Billy Can Tours** ☎ 08/8981-9813 or 1800/813484 🖨 08/8941-0803 ⊕ www.billycan.com.au. **Far Out Adventures** ☎ 08/8972-2552 🖨 08/8972-2228 ⊕ www.farout.com.au.

VISITOR INFORMATION

Katherine Visitors Information Centre is open weekdays 8:30–5, weekends and holidays 10–3. Parks and Wildlife Commission of the Northern Territory can provide information on Nitmiluk National Park.
🔝 Tourist Information **Katherine Visitors Information Centre** ✉ Lindsay St. and Stuart Hwy. ☎ 1800/653142 ⊕ www.krol.com.au. **Parks and Wildlife Commission of the Northern Territory** ✏ Box 344, 0851 ☎ 08/8973-8888 🖨 08/8973-8899 ⊕ www.nt.gov.au/paw.

THE KIMBERLEY

Perched on the northwestern hump of the loneliest Australian state, only half as far from Indonesia as it is from Sydney, the Kimberley remains a frontier of sorts. The first European explorers, dubbed by one of their descendants as "cattle kings in grass castles," ventured into the heart of the region in 1879 to establish cattle runs. They subsequently became embroiled in one of the country's longest-lasting conflicts between white settlers and Aboriginal people, who were led by Jandamarra of the Bunuba people.

The Kimberley remains sparsely populated, with only 30,000 people living in an area of 351,200 square km (135,600 square mi). That's 12 square km (4½ square mi) per person. The region is dotted with cattle stations and raked with desert ranges, rivers, tropical forests, and towering cliffs. Several of the country's most spectacular national parks are here, including Purnululu (Bungle Bungle) National Park, a vast area of bizarrely shaped and colored rock formations that became widely known to white Australians only in 1983. Facilities in this remote region are few, but if you're looking for a genuine bush experience, the Kimberley represents the opportunity of a lifetime.

This section begins in Kununurra, just over the northwestern border of the Northern Territory, in Western Australia.

Kununurra

315 km (195 mi) west of Katherine, 827 km (513 mi) southwest of Darwin.

Population 6,000, Kununurra is the eastern gateway to the Kimberley. It's a modern planned town with little of historical interest, developed in the 1960s for the nearby Lake Argyle and Ord River irrigation scheme. However, it does provide a convenient base from which to explore local attractions such as Mirima National Park (a mini Bungle Bungle on the edge of town), Lake Argyle, and the River Ord. The town is also the starting point for adventure tours of the Kimberley.

Where to Stay & Eat

$–$$ ✕ **Chopsticks Chinese Restaurant.** As its name suggests, this restaurant in the Country Club Hotel serves Aussie-style Chinese cuisine. Included on the menu are local dishes such as barramundi and Szechuan specialties like honey chili king prawns. ⊠ *47 Coolibah Dr.* ☎ *08/9168–1024* ⊟ *AE, DC, MC, V.*

¢–$ ✕ **George Room in Gulliver's Tavern.** Lots of dark jarrah timber gives the restaurant an Old English atmosphere. Although the tavern alongside it has simple counter meals, the George aims for greater things with steaks and seafood. ⊠ *196 Cottontree Ave.* ☎ *08/9168–1435* ♧ *Reservations essential* ⊟ *AE, DC, MC, V* ☉ *Closed Sun. No lunch.*

$$ ▦ **Kununurra Lakeside Resort.** On the shores of Lake Kununurra, at the edge of town, sits an understated, tranquil resort. Views of the sun setting over the lake—especially toward the end of the Dry—are worth the stay. The resort also has a small campground. ☝ *Box 1129, Casuarina Way, 6743* ☎ *08/9169–1092 or 1800/786692* ⨋ *08/9168–2741* ✍ *lakeside@agn.net.au* ⟿ *50 rooms* ♧ *2 restaurants, pool, 2 bars, laundry facilities* ⊟ *AE, DC, MC, V.*

$$ ▦ **Mercure Inn Kununurra.** Set amid tropical gardens, the inn provides a comfortable base from which to explore the Eastern Kimberley. Rooms

are brightly furnished. ⊠ *Victoria Hwy., 6743* ☎*08/9168–1455 or 1800/ 656565* 🖷 *08/9168–2622* ⊕ *www.accorhotel.com* ↩ *60 rooms* ♿ *Restaurant, pool, bar, laundry facilities* ⊟ *AE, DC, MC, V.*

$–$$ 🏨 **Country Club Hotel.** Kununurra's newest accommodation sits in the center of town, encircled by tropical gardens around its own little rain forest. Standard, ground-floor rooms are basic but clean; there are also two-story units, as well as a budget section. The hotel has several spots to dine, including one beside the pool. ⊠ *47 Coolibah Dr., 6743* ☎*08/ 9168–1024* 🖷 *08/9168–1189* ⊕ *www.countryclubhotel.com.au* ↩ *90 rooms* ♿ *Restaurant, grill, pool, 2 bars, laundry facilities, free parking* ⊟ *AE, DC, MC, V.*

¢–$ 🏨 **Duncan House.** This quiet bed-and-breakfast is close to the center of Kununurra. Rooms have TVs, refrigerators, and tea- and coffee-making facilities. ⊠ *167 Coolibah Dr., 6743* ☎☎ *08/9168–2436* ✉ *john-sonk@bigpond.com* ↩ *9 rooms* ♿ *Dining room, refrigerators, free parking* ⊟ *AE, DC, MC, V* ⦿ *BP.*

Shopping

The **Diversion Gallery** (⊠ 99 Riverfig Ave. ☎08/9168–1781) has examples of art from the Kimberley region. **Waringarri Arts** (⊠ 16 Speargrass Rd. ☎ 08/9168–2212) sells a large selection of local Aboriginal art.

Gibb River Road, El Questro, & Beyond

Gibb River Road is the cattle-carrying route through the heart of the Kimberley. It also provides an alternative—albeit a rough one—to the Great Northern Highway between Kununurra–Wyndham and Derby.

Fodor'sChoice
★
Should you decide to take the Gibb River Road, consider stopping for a break at the 1-million acre **El Questro Wilderness Park,** a working ranch in some of the most rugged country in Australia. Besides providing an opportunity to see Outback station life, El Questro has a full complement of such recreational activities as fishing and swimming, and horse, camel, and helicopter rides. On individually tailored walking and four-wheel-drive tours through the bush, you can bird-watch or examine ancient spirit figures depicted in the unique *wandjina* style of Kimberley Aboriginal rock painting—one of the world's most striking forms of spiritual art. ✛ *Turnoff for El Questro 27 km (17 mi) west of Kununurra on Gibb River Rd.* ☎*08/9169–1777* 🎟 *Wilderness permits are required, A\$12.50 for 7 days.*

Branching off toward the coast from Gibb River Road, 241 km (149 mi) from where it begins in the east, is the turnoff for the extraordinary **Mitchell Plateau and Falls:** The natural attraction is 162 slow-going km (100 mi) north on Kalumburu Road.

Adcock Gorge, 380 km (236 mi) from Kununurra on Gibb River Road, conjures up images of Eden with its large swimming hole, lush vegetation, and flocks of tropical parrots. **Bell Gorge,** 433 km (268 mi) from Kununurra, is a series of small falls that are framed by ancient rock and drop into a deep pool. The Gorge is reached by a 29-km (18-mi) four-wheel-drive track from the Gibb River Road. There are campsites at nearby Silent Grove and Bell Creek.

Lennard Gorge, 456 km (283 mi) from Kununurra and 191 km (118 mi) from Derby, is a half-hour drive down a rough four-wheel-drive track. But the discomfort is worth it—Lennard is one of the Kimberley's most spectacular gorges. Here, a thin section of the Lennard River is surrounded by high cliffs that bubble with several breathtaking waterfalls.

Where to Stay

Camping is permitted at a number of gorges and on some cattle stations along Kalumburu Road and the Gibb River. Just off Kalumburu Road, there are campsites at Mitchell Plateau (at King Edward River on the early part of the Mitchell Plateau Track) and at Mitchell Falls Car Park; the latter grounds have toilets. No other facilities are available, however. Off the Gibb River Road is the atmospheric Silent Grove campsite (close to Bell Gorge), which has showers, toilets, firewood, and secluded sites (with no facilities) beside Bell Creek. Access is restricted from December to April.

Information on camping can be obtained from the **Department of Conservation and Land Management** (⌂ Box 942, Kununurra, WA 6743 ☎ 08/9168–4200 ⊕ www.calm.wa.gov.au).

$$$$
Fodor'sChoice
★
🏨 **The Bush Camp Faraway Bay.** Faraway by both name and nature, this idyllic holiday hideaway is perched upon a cliff along the remote Kimberley coast 280 km (173 mi) northwest of Kununurra. Catering to a maximum of 12 guests, the camp oozes tranquillity. You can explore the nearby untouched coastline by boat and on foot, or simply sit back and enjoy the scenery. Accommodations are simple, bush-style cabins overlooking the bay, with sea breezes running through them even on the hottest days. The rate includes all meals, beverages, transfers, and activities. ⌂ Box 901, Kununurra, 6743 ☎ 08/9169–1214 🖷 08/9168–2224 ⊕ www.holiday-wa.net/bushcamp.htm ➥ 8 cabins ⚘ Restaurant, pool, boating, bar, laundry service ▭ AE, DC, MC, V ⦿ FAP.

★ **$–$$**
🏨 **El Questro.** The location at the top of a cliff face above the Chamberlain River rates as one of the most spectacular in Australia. Three independent accommodation facilities are on-site, each different in style and budget: the luxury Homestead, the tent cabins at Emma Gorge Resort, and the Station Township bungalows and riverside campgrounds. All areas have a restaurant, and rates at the Homestead include drinks and food, laundry, activities, and round-trip transport from Kununurra. ⌂ Box 909, Kununurra, 6743 ☎ 08/9169–1777, 08/9161–4388 Emma Gorge Resort 🖷 08/9169–1383 ⊕ www.elquestro.com.au ➥ 6 suites, 18 tent cabins, 12 bungalows, 28 campsites ⚘ 3 restaurants, tennis court, 2 pools, massage, spa, 2 bars, shops, laundry facilities, 2 airstrips, helipad, travel services, free parking ▭ AE, DC, MC, V ⊘ Closed Nov.–Apr.

Wyndham

105 km (65 mi) northwest of Kununurra.

The small, historic port on the Cambridge Gulf was established in 1886 to service the Halls Creek goldfields, and it looks as if nothing much has happened in Wyndham in the century since. The wharf is the best location in the Kimberley for spotting saltwater crocodiles as they bask on the mud flats below. There are also excellent bird-watching possibilities at the nearby Parry Lagoons Reserve, a short drive from the town.

Purnululu (Bungle Bungle) National Park

Fodor'sChoice
★
252 km (156 mi) south and southwest of Wyndham and Kununurra.

Purnululu (Bungle Bungle) National Park covers nearly 3,120 square km (1,200 square mi) in the southeast corner of the Kimberley. Australians of European descent first "discovered" its great beehive-shape domes—their English name is the Bungle Bungle—in 1983, proving how much about this vast continent remains outside of "white" experience. The local Kidja Aboriginal tribe knew about these scenic wonders long ago, of course, and called the area Purnululu.

The park's orange silica—and black lichen—striped mounds bubble up on the landscape. Climbing is not permitted because the sandstone layer beneath the thin crust of lichen and silica is fragile and would quickly erode without protection. Walking tracks follow rocky, dry creek beds. One popular walk leads hikers along the **Piccaninny Creek to Piccaninny Gorge,** passing through gorges with towering 328-foot cliffs to which slender fan palms cling.

The mounds are best seen from April through October and are closed from January through March. Anyone who has the time and a sense of adventure should spend a few days at Purnululu National Park. Facilities are primitive, but the views and experience are incomparable.

The ideal way to see the park is to arrive by air. There is an airstrip at Purnululu National Park suitable for light aircraft, where tour operators fly clients in from Kununurra, Broome, and Halls Creek to be collected by guides with four-wheel-drive vehicles. April through December, the most popular of these fly-drive tours includes one night of camping.

Where to Stay
Camping is permitted only at two designated campgrounds in Purnululu National Park. None of the campsites has facilities—both the Bellburn Creek and Walardi campgrounds have simple pit toilets—and fresh drinking water is available only at Bellburn Creek. The nearest accommodations are in Kununurra, and most visitors fly in from there.

Halls Creek

352 km (218 mi) southwest of Kununurra.

Old Halls Creek is the site of the short-lived Kimberley gold rush of 1885. Set on the edge of the Great Sandy Desert, the town has been a crumbling shell since its citizens decided in 1948 to move 15 km (9 mi) away to the site of the present Halls Creek, which has a better water supply. The old town is a fascinating place to explore, however, and small gold nuggets are still found in the surrounding gullies.

Halls Creek is the closest town to the **Wolfe Creek Meteorite Crater,** the world's second largest after the Coon Butte Crater in Arizona. The crater is 1-km (½-mi) wide and was formed as a result of a meteor that weighed tens of thousands of tons colliding with the earth about 300,000 years ago. Its shape has been well preserved in the dry desert climate, and it's best viewed from the air. **Oasis Air** (☎ 1800/501462) operates scenic flights over Wolfe Creek Meteorite Crater. **Northern Air Charter** (☎ 08/9168–5100) also has trips which take you to view Wolfe Creek Meteorite Crater from above.

Where to Stay & Eat
★ **$$** ✕🏠 **Kimberley Hotel.** Originally a simple Outback pub with a few rooms, this hotel at the end of the airstrip now has green lawns, airy quarters with pine furnishings and tile floors, and a swimming pool, making it an oasis in this dusty desert town. The high-ceiling restaurant, which overlooks the lawns and pool, has an excellent wine list and serves mostly meat and seafood dishes. ✉ *Box 244, Roberta Ave., Halls Creek, 6770* ☎ *08/9168–6101 or 1800/355228* 🖷 *08/9168–6071* 🛏 *60 rooms* ⟁ *Restaurant, pool, bar, free parking* ➡ *AE, DC, MC, V.*

Fitzroy Crossing

290 km (180 mi) west of Halls Creek, 391 km (242 mi) east of Broome.

The main attraction of Fitzroy Crossing is as a departure point for **Geikie Gorge National Park,** which cuts through one of the best-preserved fossilized coral reefs in the world. The town has a couple of basic motels and restaurants.

The **Crossing Inn** (⊠ Skulthorpe Rd. ☎ 08/9191–5080) is the place to meet some of the Kimberley's more colorful characters, especially on weekend afternoons. The **Fitzroy River Lodge** (⊠ Great Northern Rd. ☎ 08/9191–5080 or 1800/355226) is a comfortable lodging, with a restaurant, bar, pool, and a shady campground on the banks of the Fitzroy. Prices run from A\$11 per person for an unpowered camping site to A\$130 per night for one of the safari-style lodges and A\$167 per night for one of the 40 motel rooms.

Geikie Gorge National Park

16 km (10 mi) northeast of Fitzroy Crossing.

Geikie Gorge is part of a 350-million-year-old reef system formed from fossilized layers of algae—evolutionary precursors of coral reefs—when this area was still part of the Indian Ocean. The limestone walls you see now were cut and shaped by the mighty Fitzroy River; during the Wet, the normally placid waters roar through the region. The walls of the gorge are stained red from iron oxide, except where they have been leached of the mineral and turned white by the floods, which have washed as high as 52 feet from the bottom of the gorge.

When the Indian Ocean receded, it stranded a number of sea creatures, which managed to adapt to their altered conditions. Geikie is one of the few places in the world where freshwater barramundi, mussels, stingrays, and prawns swim. The park is also home to the freshwater archerfish, which can spit water as far as a yard to knock insects out of the air. Aborigines call this place Kangu, meaning "big fishing hole."

Although there is a 5-km (3-mi) walking trail along the west side of the gorge, the opposite side is off-limits because it is a wildlife sanctuary.

The best way to see the gorge is aboard one of the several daily one-hour boat tours led by **National Park Ranger** (⌂ Box 37, Fitzroy Crossing, WA 6765 ☎ 08/9191–5121 or 08/9191–5112 ⊕ www.calm.wa.gov. au). The rangers are extremely knowledgeable and helpful in pointing out the vegetation, strange limestone formations, and the many freshwater crocodiles along the way. You may also see part of the noisy fruit bat colony that inhabits the region.

Tunnel Creek & Windjana Gorge National Parks

Tunnel Creek is 111 km (69 mi) north of Fitzroy Crossing; Windjana Gorge is 145 km (90 mi) northwest of Fitzroy Crossing.

On the back road between Fitzroy Crossing and the coastal town of Derby are two geological oddities. **Tunnel Creek** was created when a stream cut an underground course through a fault line in a formation of limestone. You can follow the tunnel's path on foot for 1 km (½ mi), with the only natural light coming from those areas where the tunnel roof has collapsed. Flying foxes and other types of bats inhabit the tunnel. About 100 years ago, a band of outlaws and their Aboriginal leader Jandamarra—nicknamed "Pigeon"—used the caves as a hideout.

Windjana Gorge has cliffs nearly 325 feet high, which were carved out by the flooding of the Lennard River. During the Wet, the Lennard is a roaring torrent, but it dwindles to just a few still pools in the Dry.

Derby

256 km (158 mi) west of Fitzroy Crossing, 226 km (140 mi) northeast of Broome, 897 km (556 mi) west of Kununurra via Halls Creek, 758 km (470 mi) west of Kununurra via the Gibb River Road.

With its port, Derby has long been the main administrative and economic center of the western Kimberley, as well as a convenient base from which to explore Geikie Gorge, Windjana Gorge, and Tunnel Creek. It's a friendly town, and there's a lot to recommend Derby—beyond its collection of attractive giant boab trees (kin to Africa's baobab trees), which have enormously fat trunks. The hollow trunk of one of these trees was reputedly used as a prison at one time. Known as the Prison Tree, this boab has a circumference of 45 feet and is 6 km (4 mi) south of town. Derby's other claim to fame is that the King Sound, on which it sits, experiences the world's second-highest tides.

Where to Stay & Eat

$$$
Fodor'sChoice
★
Cockatoo Island Resort. This exclusive resort in the Buccaneer Archipelago is a 25-minute flight over the King Sound from Derby. Spacious rooms are in the elegant main lodge, while villas are fitted with polished jarrah-wood flooring, pottery and antiques, and private balconies overlooking the sea. The highlight is the cliff-top swimming pool with a sweeping view out over the sparkling ocean. Meals are included, and bushwalking, fishing, visits to isolated islands and beaches, and whale-watching can be arranged. *⌂ Box 444, Darwin, 0801 ☎ 08/8946–4455 🖷 08/8941–7246 ⊕ www.holiday-wa.net/cockatoo.htm ✆ 34 rooms, 16 villas ♧ Restaurant, tennis court, pool, hot tub, boating, fishing, billiards, hiking, bar, laundry service, meeting rooms, travel services ⊟ AE, DC, MC, V ⊙ FAP.*

$
✕☒ King Sound Resort Hotel. With its cool pool and en-suite accommodations, the King Sound is a bit of an oasis in the hot, dusty surrounds of Derby. The bistro serves solid if uninspired food, and the people are as friendly as can be. *⌂ Box 75, Loch St., Derby, 6728 ☎ 08/9193–1044 🖷 08/9191–1649 ✆ 58 rooms ♧ Restaurant, pool, bar, laundry service, free parking ⊟ AE, DC, MC, V.*

Broome

221 km (137 mi) southwest of Derby, 1,032 km (640 mi) southwest of Kununurra via Halls Creek, 1,544 km (957 mi) southwest of Katherine, 1,859 km (1,152 mi) southwest of Darwin.

Broome is the holiday capital of the Kimberley. It's the only town in the region with sandy beaches, so it has seen the growth of several resorts and has become the base from which most strike out to see more of the region. Long ago, Broome depended on pearling for its livelihood. Early in the 20th century, 300 to 400 sailing boats employing 3,000 men provided most of the world's mother-of-pearl shell. Many of the pearlers were Japanese, Malay, and Filipino, and the town is still a wonderful multicultural center today. Each August during the famous Shinju Matsuri (Pearl Festival), Broome looks back to the good old days. All but a few of the traditional old wooden luggers (boats used in the pearling industry) have disappeared, and Broome cultivates most of its pearls at nearby Kuri Bay. It retains the air of its boisterous shantytown days with wooden sidewalks and a charming Chinatown. However, with the arrival of relatively large numbers of tourists, it is becoming more upscale all the time.

Attractions in and around the town are growing, and there are several operators that have multiday cruises out of Broome along the magnificent Kimberley coast. The myriad deserted islands and beaches, with 35-foot tides that create horizontal waterfalls and whirlpools, make it an adventurer's delight. Broome marks the end of the Kimberley.

From here it's another 2,250 km (1,395 mi) south to Perth, or 1,859 km (1,152 mi) back to Darwin.

City Center

At **Broome Crocodile Park** there are more than 1,500 saltwater (estuarine) crocodiles, as well as many of the less fearsome freshwater variety. The park is also home to a collection of South American caimans and some grinning alligators from the United States. Feeding time is 3 PM during the Dry and 3:45 PM during the Wet. ⊠ *Cable Beach Rd.* ☎ *08/9193-7824* ⊠ *A$15* ⊗ *Apr.–Oct., weekdays 10–5, weekends 3:30–5; Nov.–Mar., daily 3:30–5.*

The life-size bronze statues of **The Cultured Pearling Monument** are near Chinatown. The monument depicts three pioneers of the cultured pearling industry that is so intertwined with the city's development and history. ⊠ *Carnarvon St.*

More than 900 pearl divers are buried in the **Japanese Cemetery,** on the road out to Broome's deep-water port. The graves are a testimony to the contribution of the Japanese to the development of the industry in Broome, as well as to the perils of gathering the pearls in the early days. ⊠ *Port Dr.*

★ The **Pearl Luggers** historical display sheds light on the difficulties and immense skill involved in pearl harvesting. It has two restored luggers, along with other such pearling equipment as diving suits. Informative videos run all day. This is a must-see for those interested in Broome's history. ⊠ *44 Dampier Terr.* ☎ *08/9192-2059* ⊠ *A$15* ⊗ *May–Dec., daily 9:30–5; Jan.–Apr., weekdays 10–4, weekends 10–1.*

Opened in 1916, **Sun Pictures** is the world's oldest operating picture garden. Here, silent movies—accompanied by a pianist—were once shown to the public. These days current releases are shown in the undeniably pleasant outdoors. ⊠ *Carnarvon St.* ☎ *08/9192-3738* ⊕ *www. sunpictures.com.au* ⊠ *A$12* ⊗ *Daily 6:30 PM–11 PM.*

Around Broome

The **Broome Bird Observatory,** a nonprofit research and education facility, provides the perfect opportunity to see many of the Kimberley's 310 bird species, some of which migrate annually from Siberia. On the shores of Roebuck Bay, just 18 km (11 mi) from Broome, the observatory has a prolific number of migratory waders. ⊠ *Crab Creek Rd.* ☎ *08/9193-5600* ⊠ *Donations suggested* ⊗ *By appointment.*

You can watch demonstrations of the cultured pearling process, including the seeding of a live oyster at **Willie Creek Pearl Farm,** 38 km (23½ mi) north of Broome. Drive out to the farm yourself, or catch a tour bus leaving from town. ⊠ *Cape Leveque Rd.* ☎ *08/9193-6000* ⊕ *www. williecreekpearls.com.au* ⊠ *A$25, coach tour A$55* ⊗ *Guided tours at 9 AM and 2 PM.*

Where to Stay & Eat

★ **$–$$** ✕ **Matso's Café, Art Gallery, and Broome Brewery.** An unusual eatery, this place has something for everyone: good food, its own brewed beer, and

Kimberley artwork adorning the walls. This old-world establishment is popular with locals. The café and brewery are both open for breakfast and until late at night. ⊠ *60 Hammersley St.* ☎ *08/9193–5811* 🖃 *AE, DC, MC, V.*

$$ ✕⊡ **Blue Seas Resort.** This apartment-style resort surrounds two central pools, but it's also close to Cable Beach. Stylish rooms have top-class furnishings and include a microwave, dishwasher, CD player, and the all-important air-conditioning. There's also a sofa bed in addition to the queen-size bed, so each apartment can accommodate up to four people. ⊠ *10 Sanctuary Rd., Cable Beach, 6725* ☎ *1800/637415 or 08/9192–0999* 🖨 *08/9192–1900* ⊕ *www.blueseasresort.com.au* 📡 *44 apartments* ⚬ *Kitchens, microwaves, room TVs with movies, 2 pools, lounge, laundry facilities, free parking* 🖃 *AE, MC, V.*

★ $$$–$$$$ ⊡ **Cable Beach Club Resort Broome.** Just a few minutes out of town opposite the broad, beautiful Cable Beach—the only sandy beach near any Kimberley town—this resort is the area's most luxurious accommodation. Single and double bungalows are spread through tropical gardens; studio rooms and suites are also available. The decor is colonial with a hint of Asian influence. ⊡ *Cable Beach Rd., 6725* ☎ *08/9192–0400 or 1800/199099* 🖨 *08/9192–2249* ⊕ *www.cablebeachclub.com* 📡 *260 rooms, 3 suites (dry season); 100 rooms (wet season)* ⚬ *4 restaurants (1 seasonal), coffee shop, grill, minibars, room TVs with movies, 12 tennis courts, 2 pools, gym, health club, massage, beach, 4 bars, shops, laundry service, concierge, Internet, business services, meeting rooms, travel services, free parking* 🖃 *AE, DC, MC, V.*

★ $$$–$$$$ ⊡ **McAlpine House.** Originally built for a pearling master, this atmospheric luxury guest house is set amid tropical gardens and full of exquisite Javanese teak furniture. With an inviting pool, an airy library, and a personalized approach to service, this is a good place to recover from the rigors of a regional tour, as well as a great place to simply hang out for a day or two. Breakfast can be either light and tropical in style (with fruits and pastries) or a substantial affair. Dinner is also available on request. ⊠ *84 Herbert St., Broome, 6725* ☎ *08/9192–3886* 🖨 *08/9192–3887* ⊕ *www.mcalpinehouse.com* 📡 *6 rooms* ⚬ *Dining room, pool, bar, library, laundry facilities, free parking* 🖃 *AE, DC, MC, V.*

$$$ ⊡ **Mangrove Hotel.** Overlooking Roebuck Bay, this highly regarded hotel has the best location of any accommodation in Broome. All the spacious rooms have private balconies or patios, many with bay views. ⊡ *47 Carnarvon St., 6725* ☎ *08/9192–1303 or 1800/094818* 🖨 *08/9193–5169* ⊕ *www.mangrovehotel.com.au* 📡 *68 rooms with shower* ⚬ *Restaurant, refrigerators, 2 pools, outdoor hot tub, 2 bars, laundry facilities, business services, meeting rooms, travel services, free parking* 🖃 *AE, DC, MC, V.*

★ $$$ ⊡ **Moonlight Bay Quality Suites.** Beside the Mangrove Hotel and with most of its rooms sharing equally good views, this complex of 57 luxurious, self-contained apartments has the twin benefits of location and convenience. This is a great place to recuperate by the pool after a rugged Kimberley tour. ⊡ *Box 198, Carnarvon St., 6725* ☎ *08/9193–7888 or 1800/818878* 🖨 *08/9193–7999* ✉ *moonlite@tpg.com.au* 📡 *57 apartments* ⚬ *Kitchens, pool, spa, gym, restaurant, laundry facilities, free parking* 🖃 *AE, DC, MC, V.*

Shopping

ABORIGINAL ART Prices for Aboriginal art in the Kimberley are generally well below those in Darwin or Alice Springs. **Matso's Café, Art Gallery, and Broome Brewery** (⊠ *60 Hammersley St.* ☎ *08/9193–5811*) specializes in Kimberley arts and crafts, displaying works by the region's most talented Aboriginal artists.

JEWELRY   The number of jewelry stores in Broome is completely out of proportion to the size of the town. **Broome Pearls** (⊠ 27 Dampier Terr. ☎ 08/9192–2061) specializes in high-quality, expensive pearls and jewelry.

Linneys (⊠ Dampier Terr. ☎ 08/9192–2430) sells high-end jewelry. Family-owned **Paspaley Pearling** (⊠ 2 Short St. ☎ 08/9192–2203), in Chinatown, sells pearls and stylish local jewelry.

The Kimberley A to Z

To research prices, get advice from other travelers, and book travel arrangements, visit www.fodors.com.

AIR TRAVEL

Distances in this part of the continent are colossal. Flying is the fastest and easiest way to get to Kimberley.

Qantas and its subsidiaries fly to Broome from Brisbane, Sydney, Melbourne, and Adelaide via Perth. On Saturdays there are faster flights from Sydney and Melbourne via Alice Springs (with connections from Brisbane and Adelaide). Air North has an extensive air network throughout the Top End, linking Broome and Kununurra with Darwin, Alice Springs, and Perth.

🛪 Carriers **Air North** ☎ 08/8945–2866 or 1800/627474. **Qantas** ☎ 13–1313.

BUS TRAVEL

Greyhound Pioneer runs the 1,859 km (1,152 mi) between Darwin and Broome in just under 24 hours. Greyhound also operates the 32-hour regular route and a 27-hour express daily between Perth and Broome.

🛪 **Greyhound Pioneer** ☎ 13–2030 ⊕ www.greyhound.com.au.

CAR TRAVEL

The unpaved, 700 km (434 mi) Gibb River Road runs through a remote area, and the trip should be done only with a great deal of caution. The road is passable by conventional vehicles only after it has been recently graded. At other times you need a four-wheel-drive vehicle, and in the Wet it's mostly impassable.

The Bungle Bungle are 252 km (156 mi) south of Kununurra along the Great Northern Highway. A rough, 55-km (34-mi) unpaved road, negotiable only in a four-wheel-drive vehicle, is the last stretch of road leading to the park from the turnoff near the Turkey Creek–Warmum Community. That part of the drive takes about 2½ hours.

From Broome to Geikie Gorge National Park, follow the Great Northern Highway east 391 km (242 mi) to Fitzroy Crossing, then 16 km (10 mi) north on a paved side road to the park. Camping is not permitted at the gorge, so you must stay in Fitzroy Crossing.

From Darwin to Kununurra and the eastern extent of the Kimberley it's 827 km (513 mi). From Darwin to Broome on the far side of the Kimberley it's 1,859 km (1,152 mi), a long, two-day drive. The route runs from Darwin to Katherine along the Stuart Highway, and then along the Victoria Highway to Kununurra. The entire road is paved but quite narrow in parts—especially so, it may seem, when a road train (an extremely long truck) is coming the other way. Drive with care. Fuel and supplies can be bought at small settlements along the way, but you should always keep supplies in abundance.

EMERGENCIES

In an emergency dial **000** to reach an ambulance, the fire department, or the police.

Doctors Royal Flying Doctor Service ⊠ Derby ☎ 08/9191-1211.

Hospitals Broome District Hospital ⊠ Robinson St. ☎ 08/9192-9222. **Derby Regional Hospital** ⊠ Loch St. ☎ 08/9193-3333. **Kununurra District Hospital** ⊠ Coolibah Dr. ☎ 08/9168-1522.

TOURS

Kimberley Wilderness Adventures conducts several tours from Broome and Kununurra, which include excursions along Gibb River Road and into Purnululu National Park. East Kimberley Tours also runs multi-day adventures along Gibb River Road, and fly-drive packages into Purnululu.

Broome Day Tours conducts several tours via air-conditioned coach with informative commentary, in the Western Kimberley region—including a three-hour Broome Explorer tour of the town's major sights, and day trips farther afield to Windjana Gorge, Tunnel Creek, and Geikie Gorge. Another company that can show the Kimberley is Flak Track Tours.

Alligator Airways operates both fixed-wing floatplanes from Lake Kununurra and land-based flights from Kununurra airport. A two-hour scenic flight costs A$190. Belray Diamond Tours has a daily air tour (subject to numbers) from Kununurra to the Argyle Diamond Mine, the world's largest, which produces about 8 tons of diamonds a year. Slingair Tours conducts two-hour flights over the Bungle Bungle for A$185.

Take a helicopter flight with Slingair Heliwork. A 30-minute excursion from their helipad in the Purnululu National Park costs A$180, while an alternative two-hour tour of the Bungle Bungle and Lake Argyle is A$190.

Lake Argyle Cruises operates excellent trips on Australia's largest expanse of fresh water, the man-made Lake Argyle. Tours run daily March to October, and it's A$35 for the two-hour morning cruise, A$105 for the six-hour cruise, and A$44 for the sunset cruise.

Pearl Sea Coastal Cruises has multiday Kimberley adventures along the region's magnificent coastline in their luxury *Kimberley Quest* cruiser. All meals and excursions (including fishing trips) are included in the cost. Cruising season runs from March to October.

Astro Tours organizes entertaining, informative night sky tours of the Broome area, as well as four-wheel-drive Outback stargazing adventures farther afield. Amesz Tours runs 9- or 14-day, four-wheel-drive safaris from Broome to Darwin, traveling right across the Kimberley and the Top End to Kakadu. A 13-day tour in a four-wheel-drive vehicle covers the region in more detail with a smaller group. Discover the Kimberley Tours operates four-wheel-drive adventures into the Bungle Bungle massif.

Adventure Tours Broome Day Tours ⌖ Box 2470, Broome, WA 6725 ☎ 1800/801068 🖷 08/9193-5575 ⊕ www.broomedaytours.com. **East Kimberley Tours** ⌖ Box 537, Kununurra, 6743 ☎ 08/9168-2213 ⊕ www.eastkimberleytours.com.au. **Flak Track Tours** ⌖ Box 1202, Broome, 6725 ☎ 08/8894-2228 🖷 08/9192-1275. **Kimberley Wilderness Adventures** ⌖ Box 564, Kununurra, 6743 ☎ 08/9168-1711 or 1800/804005.

Air Tours Alligator Airways ☎ 08/9168-1333 or 1800/632533 ⊕ www.alligatorairways.com.au. **Belray Diamond Tours** ⌖ Box 10, Kununurra, 6743 ☎ 08/9168-1014 or 1800/632533 🖷 08/9168-2704 ⊕ www.kimberlycoast.com/2302.htm. **Slingair Heliwork** ☎ 1800/095500 ⊕ www.slingair.com.au.

🚩 Boat Tours **Lake Argyle Cruises** ✆ Box 710, Kununurra, 6743 ☎ 08/9168-7361 🖷 08/9168-7461. **Pearl Sea Coastal Cruises** ✆ Box 2838, Broome, 6725 ☎ 08/9192-3829 or 08/9193-6131 🖷 08/9193-6303 ⊕ www.pearlseacruises.com.

🚩 Four-Wheel-Drive Tours **Astro Tours** ✆ Box 2537, Broome, WA 6725 ☎ 0500/831111 🖷 08/9193-5362. **Discover the Kimberley Tours** ✆ Box 2615, Broome, 6725 ☎ 08/9193-7267 or 1800/636802 ⊕ www.bunglebungle.com.au.

VISITOR INFORMATION

West Australian Main Roads Information Service provides information on road conditions, including the Gibb River Road.

🚩 Tourist Information **Broome Tourist Bureau** ✉ Great Northern Hwy., Broome ☎ 08/9192-2222 🖷 08/9192-2063 ⊕ www.ebroome.com/tourism. **Derby Tourist Bureau** ✉ 2 Clarendon St., Derby ☎ 08/9191-1426 🖷 08/9191-1609 ⊕ www.nttc.com.au. **Kununurra Tourist Bureau** ✉ Coolibah Dr., Kununurra ☎ 08/9168-1177 🖷 08/9168-2598. **West Australian Main Roads Information Service** ☎ 1800/013314 ⊕ www.mrwa.wa.gov.au/realtime/kimberley.htm. **Western Australian Tourism Commission** ✉ 16 St. Georges Terr., Perth ☎ 08/9220-1700 or 1300/361351 🖷 08/9481-1702 or 08/9481-0190 ⊕ www.westernaustralia.net.

PERTH & WESTERN AUSTRALIA

12

FODOR'S CHOICE

Basil's on Hannan, restaurant in Kalgoorlie

Burswood International Resort Casino, in Burswood

Busselton Jetty, in Busselton

Cape Leeuwin–Naturaliste National Park, near Dunsborough

Cape Lodge, in Yallingup

Clifton Best Western, in Bunbury

The Loose Box, restaurant in Mundaring

Mead's of Mosman Bay, restaurant in Mosman Park

Monkey Mia, dolphin sanctuary near Denham

Ningaloo Reef Marine Park, near Exmouth

Wentworth Plaza Flag Inn, in Perth

Western Australian Maritime Museum, in Fremantle

HIGHLY RECOMMENDED

RESTAURANTS Flutes Café, in Willyabrup

Perugino, in West Perth

Valley Café, in Margaret River

HOTELS Balneaire Seaside Resort, in Middleton Beach

Esplanade Hotel, in Albany

Hyatt Regency, in Perth

Joondalup Resort Hotel, in Connolly

Rendezvous Observation City Hotel, in Scarborough

SIGHTS Margaret River

By Helen Ayers
and Lorraine
Ironside

Updated by
Graham
Hodgson and
Shamara
Williams

THOSE WHO MAKE IT to the "undiscovered state" are stunned by the diversity of places to go and things to do. Far-flung beaches invite you to relax, while at Monkey Mia, Ningaloo Reef, and Bunbury you can swim with dolphins, manta rays, and whale sharks. Eerie limestone formations at Nambung National Park and the caves of Cape Leeuwin–Naturaliste National Park are just two of the geological wonders of this state. Add exquisite food, charming wineries, seaside parks, rare hardwood forests, and historic towns to the mix, and you have an eclectic and compelling list of reasons to visit Western Australia.

Although the existence of the south land—*terra australis*—was known long before Dutch seafarer Dirk Hartog first landed on the coast of "New Holland" in 1616 in today's Shark Bay, the panorama was so bleak he didn't even bother to plant his flag and claim it for the Dutch crown. It took an intrepid English seaman, William Dampier, to see past the daunting prospect of endless sands, rugged cliffs, heat, flies, and sparse scrubby plains to claim the land for Britain, 20,000 km (12,400 mi) away.

Still, nothing can quite prepare you for what lies beyond the capital city of Perth. The scenery is magnificent, from the awesome, rugged north to the green pastures, orchards, vineyards, and hardwood forests of the south. Along the coastlines, sparkling green waves break upon vast, deserted beaches. The sheer emptiness—the utter silence broken only by the mournful cry of the crow circling high overhead wherever you wander throughout this enormous state—often begs description.

Western Australia is a state blessed by wealth and cursed by distance. In every direction Perth is 3,200 km (2,000 mi) from any other major city in the world—hence its fond title as "the most isolated city on earth." The state itself is *huge*, about 1 million square mi (twice the size of Texas), but though it makes up one-third of Australia's landmass it's home to just 1.9 million people, with around 1.4 million in the Perth metropolitan area itself. Sheep stations here can be the size of Kentucky.

Perched as it is on the edge of the continent, Perth is much closer to Indonesia than to its overland Australian cousins. Indeed, many West Australians take their vacations in Bali rather than in eastern Australia. Such social isolation would ordinarily doom a community to life as a backwater, and for much of its history Perth (and Western Australia) has been the "Cinderella state." A gold rush around Kalgoorlie and Coolgardie in the 1890s saw wealth flow back to the capital, but it did little to change Perth's insularity. In the 1970s, however, the discovery of massive mineral deposits throughout the state attracted international interest and began an economic upswing that still continues. What currently drives the economy are finds at the Pilbara, the richest source of iron ore in the world; huge natural gas reserves on the Northwest Shelf; gold in the Goldfields; and bauxite (transformed into alumina) and mineral sands in the South West.

For some, highly paid work on one of Western Australia's many strip mines or natural gas wells is a necessary hardship to endure before returning to easy living in Perth. It's this attitude that defines Western Australia's unique character, an ambitious, yet relaxed frame of mind that combines with a fresh, outdoor lifestyle amid one of the world's most livable climates. Little wonder Western Australia is attractive to travelers worldwide—and even inspires some to move here.

The Kimberley region in Western Australia's tropical north is closer geographically and in character to the Northern Territory city of Darwin than it is to Perth. For this reason, information about Broome and the Kimberley is included in Chapter 11.

Planning your time out west requires you to focus on a couple of areas. It's unlikely you'll cover the whole state, even if you decide to permanently relocate. To narrow down your choices, consider whether you have a few days to spend in and around Perth and Fremantle. Does the thought of cooler air and the coastal scenery of the South West appeal to you, or would you rather get in a car and drive to far reaches east or north? Or, do you want to trek north along the coast to Monkey Mia or Ningaloo Reef Marine Park to frolic in and under the waves with amazing sea creatures?

12

If you have 3 days

Spend most of the first day knocking around 🚆 **Perth**'s city center, or take the train to pleasantly restored 🚆 **Fremantle** and stroll through the streets and stop for breaks at sidewalk cafés. In the evening in either city, have dinner overlooking the water. Over the next two days, take a ferry to 🚆 **Rottnest Island** and cycle around, walk on the beach, fish, or try to spot the small local marsupials called quokkas. Then either stay the night or head back to town. If you're feeling ambitious, you could drive a couple of hours north to the **Nambung National Park** Pinnacles, captivating coastal rock formations that look like anything from tombstones to trance-state druids moving en masse to the sea. The historic towns of **York** and **New Norcia** also make good day trips from Perth.

If you have 5 days

This in-between-length trip allows you to take on some of the larger distances in Western Australia, provided that you have the right mode of transportation. Fly north to 🚆 **Monkey Mia** to learn about and interact with dolphins, or to **Ningaloo Reef Marine Park** to dive with whale sharks and watch the annual coral spawning. Or, drive a couple of hours to the **South West** coastal area to see spring wildflowers, wineries, orchards, forests, grazing dairy and beef herds, and national parks, and to generally enjoy the good life. You'll have enough time for a day or two around 🚆 **Perth** before flying to the old goldfields towns of 🚆 **Kalgoorlie** and **Coolgardie.** They may remind you of America's Wild West—except that camel teams rather than stagecoaches used to pull into town—but this is pure Oz all the way.

If you have 7 days or more

With seven days you can consider all options, mixing parts of the three- and five-day itineraries. Of course, you could opt to spend the entire week leisurely making your way along the coast of the 🚆 **South West,** tasting the top-quality regional wines and locally grown foods. Or, you could head for the caves and rough shorelines that define **Cape Leeuwin–Naturaliste National Park,** then head inland through the charming villages and hamlets of the **Blackwood River Valley. Stirling Range National Park** is a place for hiking, especially in spring amid the vast wildflowers. If you plan to go north to view 🚆 **Karijini National Park** and its stunning gorges and rockscapes, taking a plane will give you more time to explore. Alternately, you could drive north to 🚆 **New Norcia,** cut across to 🚆 **Nambung National Park,** then take the coastal road north to the historic city of **Geraldton.** From here, you may want to continue to the Western Australian city of Broome and the Kimberley region, or even beyond them to Darwin.

Exploring Perth & Western Australia

Most trips to Western Australia begin in Perth. Apart from its own points of interest, there are a few great day trips to take from the city: to Rottnest Island, to the historic towns of New Norcia or York, and north to the coastal Nambung National Park. The port city of Fremantle is a good place to unwind, and, if you have the time, a tour of the South West—with its seashore, parks, hardwood forests, wildflowers, and first-rate wineries and restaurants—is highly recommended. The old goldfield towns east of Perth are a slice of the dust-blown Australia of yore. There are also a few long-distance forays worth your while: to the meetings of land and sea creatures at Monkey Mia and Ningaloo Reef Marine Park, and to the ancient rock formations inland at Karijini National Park. You'll have to take a tour or drive to these sights.

About the Restaurants

WHAT IT COSTS In Australian Dollars				
$$$$	$$$	$$	$	¢
RESTAURANTS over $50	$36–$50	$21–$35	$10–$20	under $10

Restaurant prices are per person for a main course at dinner.

About the Hotels

Perth has experienced a hotel-trade boom at all levels, from the luxurious to the frill-free. In the countryside, bed-and-breakfasts are a great option. In farther-flung parts of the state—and there are plenty of these—much of the lodging is motel style.

WHAT IT COSTS In Australian Dollars				
$$$$	$$$	$$	$	¢
HOTELS over $300	$201–$300	$151–$200	$100–$150	under $100

Hotel prices are for two people in a standard double room in high season, including tax and service, based on the European Plan (with no meals) unless otherwise noted.

When to Visit

Generally speaking, there is no wrong time to visit Western Australia. For Perth and south, you'll see a gorgeous abundance of wildflowers in spring (September through November), while you can watch pods of whales swim along the coast during fall (February through May). Although winter (May through August) is the wettest season, it's also when the orchards and forests are lush and green. North of Perth, winter is the dry season, and it can get chilly inland throughout the state. Summer (December through February) is *hot*, when temperatures can rise to 40°C (100°F). This is when most locals take holidays and head to the beaches.

PERTH

In its early days Perth was a poor country cousin to older Western Australian towns, including Albany and Fremantle. However, gold rushes around Kalgoorlie and Coolgardie in the late 19th century caused wealth to flow back to the capital, and 20th-century mineral finds transformed it into a modern city. Buoyed by mineral wealth and foreign investment,

12

Beaches

You'll find some of Australia's finest beaches in Western Australia, stretching from the snow-white salt beaches of Frenchman's Bay in the south to beyond Port Hedland in the north. In a day's drive from Perth, you can enjoy a sojourn just about anywhere along the coast in the South West, or explore the emerald waters of the Batavia Coast, north of where the Pinnacles keep watch over the turbulent Indian Ocean.

Food

Although Perth's cuisine has been shaped by such external influences as the postwar European immigration and an influx of Asian cultures, an indigenous West Coast cuisine is emerging. Like much of the innovative cooking in Australia, this style fuses Asian, European, and native Australian herbs and spices with French, Mediterranean, and Asian techniques to bring out the best in what is grown locally. In Western Australia's case, this means some of the country's finest seafood, as well as beef, lamb, kangaroo, venison, and emu.

The Outdoors

Western Australia's national parks are full of natural wonders, including fascinating rock formations, exotic bird life, jarrah and karri hardwood forests, and, in spring, great expanses of wildflowers. The parks rank among the best in Australia, in many cases because they are remote and uncrowded. Plan for long journeys to reach some, but others are easily accessible, being close to Perth and in the South West.

Water Sports

Wind-in-your-hair types can get their fill of jet skiing and parasailing in Perth. Divers should seriously consider going all the way north to Exmouth to take the scuba trip of a lifetime with whale sharks at Ningaloo Reef Marine Park. And in the South West, particularly near Margaret River, surfing is a way of life, with major international surf festivals each year.

Perth continues to grow. High-rise buildings dot the skyline, and an influx of immigrants gives the city a healthy diversity.

But, despite the expansion, the city has maintained its relaxed pace of living. Residents live for the water—half of Perth is always heading for its boats, the old joke goes, while the other half is already on them. And who can blame them? Some of the finest sands, sailing, and fishing in the world are on the city's doorstep. Seaside villages and great beaches, including Trigg and Cottesloe, lie just north of the harbor city of Fremantle, which now forms part of a Perth–Fremantle urban strip.

Although Perth's suburbs sprawl north and south of the city center, the city center is best managed on foot. The main business thoroughfare is St. George's Terrace, an elegant street along which many of the most intriguing sights are located. Shopping is best along Hay and Murray streets. Northbridge, on the opposite side of the central railway station, is a funky restaurant and nightlife precinct. Perth's literal highlight is King's Park, 1,000-acres of greenery atop Mt. Eliza, which affords panoramic views of the city.

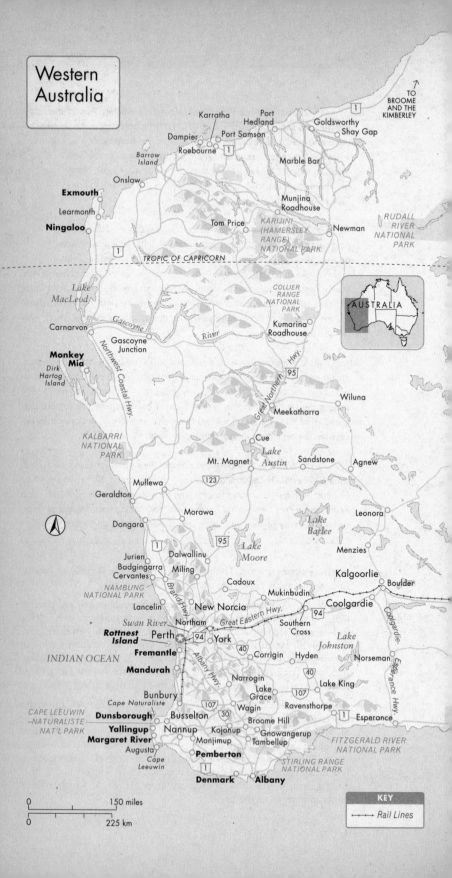

Western Australia

TO
BROOME AND THE
KIMBERLEY

Karratha
Port Hedland
Dampier
Port Samson
Roebourne
Goldsworthy
Shay Gap
Marble Bar
Barrow Island
Onslow
Exmouth
Learmonth
Munjina Roadhouse
Ningaloo
Tom Price
KARIJINI (HAMERSLEY RANGE) NATIONAL PARK
Newman
RUDALL RIVER NATIONAL PARK

TROPIC OF CAPRICORN

Lake MacLeod
COLLIER RANGE NATIONAL PARK
Gascoyne
Carnarvon
Gascoyne Junction
River
Kumarina Roadhouse
Monkey Mia
Dirk Hartog Island
Northwest Coastal Hwy.
Great Northern Hwy.
95
Wiluna
Meekatharra
KALBARRI NATIONAL PARK
Cue
Lake Austin
Sandstone
Agnew
Mt. Magnet
Mullewa
123
Geraldton
Morawa
Lake Barlee
Leonora
Dongara
95
Lake Moore
Menzies
Jurien
Badgingarra
Cervantes
Dalwallinu
Miling
Cadoux
Kalgoorlie
Boulder
NAMBUNG NATIONAL PARK
Mukinbudin
Coolgardie
Lancelin
New Norcia
94
Swan River
Northam
Great Eastern Hwy.
Southern Cross
Lake Johnston
Rottnest Island
Perth
94
York
Coolgardie-Esperance Hwy.
Brand Hwy.
INDIAN OCEAN
Fremantle
40
Corrigin
Hyden
Mandurah
Norseman
Narrogin
Lake Grace
Lake King
Bunbury
Albany Hwy.
Wagin
107
Ravensthorpe
Cape Naturaliste
Dunsborough
Busselton
30
Broome Hill
1
Esperance
CAPE LEEUWIN–NATURALISTE NAT'L PARK
Yallingup
Nannup
Kojonup
Gnowangerup
FITZGERALD RIVER NATIONAL PARK
Margaret River
Manjimup
Tambellup
Augusta
Pemberton
STIRLING RANGE NATIONAL PARK
Cape Leeuwin
1
Denmark
Albany

AUSTRALIA

0   150 miles
0   225 km

KEY
——•—— Rail Lines

Exploring Perth

Because of its relative colonial youth, Perth has an advantage over most other capital cities in that it was laid out with elegance and foresight. Streets were planned so that pedestrian traffic could flow smoothly from one avenue to the next, and this compact city remains easy to negotiate on foot. Most of the points of interest are in the downtown area close to the banks of the Swan River. Although the East End of the city has long been the fashionable part of town, the West End is fast becoming the chic shopping precinct.

Central Business District

The city center, a pleasant blend of old and new, runs along Perth's major business thoroughfare, St. George's Terrace, as well as on parallel Hay and Murray streets.

Numbers in the text correspond to numbers in the margin and on the Perth map.

a good walk

Start at the **General Post Office** ❶ ▐, a solid sandstone edifice facing **Forrest Place** ❷, one of the city's bustling pedestrian malls and a venue for regular free concerts and street theater. Head east along Murray Street, passing the **Forrest Chase Shopping Plaza** ❸. Beyond this, near the corner at Irwin Street, three blocks away, is the **Perth Fire Station Museum** ❹, which displays historic fire-fighting artifacts.

Continue east on Murray Street to Victoria Square, one of Perth's finest plazas, which is dominated by **St. Mary's Cathedral** ❺. Turn right onto Victoria Avenue for a block, then right again on Hay Street, passing two of Perth's newer buildings—the Central Fire Station on your right and the **Law Courts** ❻ on your left. Turn left onto Pier Street and head toward St. George's Terrace. On the corner, adjacent to the simple, gothic-style **St. George's Cathedral** ❼ is the Deanery, one of Perth's oldest houses.

Look across St. George's Terrace for the Gothic Revival turrets and English-style gardens of **Government House** ❽, then stroll south to **Supreme Court Gardens** ❾, where you'll see stately Moreton Bay fig trees, some of the finest in Perth. At the western end of the gardens is the charming Georgian **Francis Burt Law Museum** ❿. Turn left down Barrack Street toward the Swan River to view the **Swan Bells Tower** ⓫.

Return to St. George's Terrace and walk west for a look at many of Perth's newest and most impressive office buildings, including the notable **Bankwest Tower** ⓬. Continuing on St. George's Terrace, you'll pass **the Cloisters** ⓭ on your right, built as a boys' high school in 1858. At the top of the terrace is the lone remnant of the first military barracks, the **Barracks Arch** ⓮, which stands in front of **Parliament House** ⓯.

For a detour into the greener reaches of Perth, head down Harvest Terrace to Malcolm Street, then circle the roundabout to get to **King's Park** ⓰. The huge botanic garden within its bounds is a great place for an introduction to Western Australia's flora and natural bushland. In spring, the native wildflowers alone are worth the trip. You can return to the city on the Number 33 bus if you'd like to end the tour here.

From Barracks Arch, turn around and walk back along St. George's Terrace to Milligan Street and turn left. When you reach Hay Street, turn right and walk toward the opulent Edwardian exterior of **His Majesty's Theatre** ⓱ at the corner of King and Hay streets. Continue to the Hay Street Mall, one of many city streets closed to traffic, where you'll find **London Court** ⓲, a shopping arcade running north to south between Hay

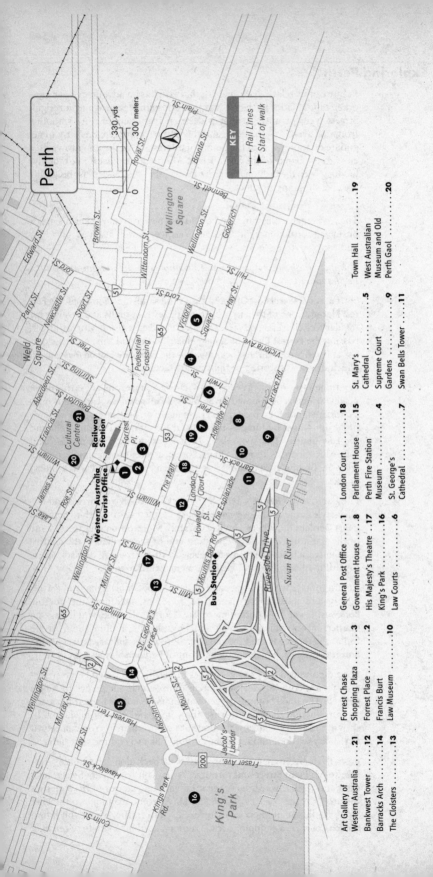

Perth

330 yds
300 meters

KEY

Rail Lines
Start of walk

Western Australia Tourist Office

Railway Station

Cultural Centre

Bus Station

King's Park

Swan River

Art Gallery of Western Australia **21**	
Bankwest Tower **12**	
Barracks Arch **14**	
The Cloisters **13**	
Forest Chase Shopping Plaza **3**	Forrest Place **2**
Francis Burt Law Museum **10**	
General Post Office **1**	Government House **8**
His Majesty's Theatre **17**	King's Park **16**
Law Courts **6**	
London Court **18**	Parliament House **15**
Perth Fire Station Museum **4**	St. George's Cathedral **7**
St. Mary's Cathedral **5**	Supreme Court Gardens **9**
Swan Bells Tower **11**	
Town Hall **19**	West Australian Museum and Old Perth Gaol **20**

Street and St. George's Terrace. The mechanical clock with three-dimensional animated figures chimes every quarter hour. Pause at the intersection of Hay and Barrack streets, at **Town Hall** ⑲, one of Perth's handsome, convict-built structures. From here you can take a break, or continue four blocks northeast on Barrack Street toward the James Street Mall, where you can wander through the **Western Australian Museum and Old Perth Gaol** ⑳, or the **Art Gallery of Western Australia** ㉑.

TIMING It will take about two hours just to pace off the above route, without the Western Australian Museum or the Art Gallery of Western Australia, and you can lengthen this by stopping in shops and gardens. The heat from December through February can make all but early morning or evening strolls uncomfortable.

What to See

㉑ **Art Gallery of Western Australia.** More than 1,000 treasures from the state's art collection are on display, including one of the best exhibits of Aboriginal art in Australia. Other works include Australian and international paintings, sculpture, prints, crafts, and decorative arts. Free guided tours run at 1 PM Tuesdays, Wednesdays, and Sundays, and 12:30 on Fridays. There's also a shop and café. ⊠ *47 James St. Mall, CBD* ☎ *08/ 9492–6600* ⊕ *www.artgallery.wa.gov.au* ⊠ *Free* ☉ *Daily 10–5.*

⑫ **Bankwest Tower.** This 1988 tower wraps around the historic 1895 **Palace Hotel,** now used for bank offices. The hotel typifies the ornate architecture that dominated the city during the late 19th century. ⊠ *108 St. George's Terr., at William St., CBD.*

⑭ **Barracks Arch.** Perth's oddest architectural curiosity, this freestanding brick arch in the middle of the city center stands more or less in front of the seat of government—the highway actually comes between them. All that remains of the former headquarters (demolished in 1966) of the Pensioner Forces is this Tudor-style edifice, built in the 1860s with Flemish bond brickwork, a memorial to the earliest settlers. ⊠ *St. George's Terr. and Malcolm St., CBD* ☎ *08/9321–6088.*

⑬ **The Cloisters.** Originally built as a school for boys, this 1858 brick building now houses mining company offices. ⊠ *200 St. George's Terr., at Mill St., CBD* ☎ *no phone.*

③ **Forrest Chase Shopping Plaza.** This major shopping complex, with its myriad merchants, is anchored by the Myer department store. ⊠ *Murray St., between Forrest Pl. and Barrack St., CBD* ☎ *08/9322–9111.*

② **Forrest Place.** In addition to having shops, this bustling pedestrian mall hosts street theater and free outdoor concerts. ⊠ *Forrest Pl., at Murray St., CBD.*

⑩ **Francis Burt Law Museum.** A former courthouse and Perth's oldest public building, this charming 1836 Georgian structure sits amid the ⇨ **Supreme Court Gardens.** Visits to trial reenactments and the adjacent Supreme Court are possible. ⊠ *5/33 Barrack St., CBD* ☎ *08/ 9325–4787* ⊕ *www.francisburt.lawsocietywa.asn.au* ⊠ *Donation* ☉ *Feb.–Dec., weekdays 10–2:30.*

▶ ① **General Post Office.** A handsome, colonnaded sandstone building, the post office forms an impressive backdrop to the city's major public square, Forrest Place. ⊠ *Forrest Pl., between Murray and Wellington Sts., CBD.*

⑧ **Government House.** This is the official residence of the governor and home to members of the royal family during visits to Perth. It was constructed between 1859 and 1864 in Gothic Revival style, with arches and turrets reminiscent of the Tower of London. You can't tour the house, but the gardens are open to the public on Tuesdays noon to 2. ✉ *Supreme Court Gardens, CBD.*

⓱ His Majesty's Theatre. Restoration has transformed this Edwardian 1904 building, one of Perth's most gracious, into a handsome home for the Western Australian opera and ballet companies. The busiest month for performances is February, during the Perth International Arts Festival. Free general tours take place weekdays between 10 and 4; free backstage tours are by arrangement only. Tours can usually be booked in advance. ✉ *825 Hay St., CBD* ☎ *08/9265–0900* ⊕ *www.hismajestystheatre.com.au* ✎ *Tours: Free* ☉ *Box office weekdays 9–5:30.*

⓰ King's Park. Once a gathering place for Aboriginal people and established as a public park in 1890, this 1,000-acre park now overlooks downtown Perth. It was named to mark the accession of Edward VII in 1901, and in springtime the gardens blaze with orchids, kangaroo paw, banksias, and other wildflowers. A highlight is the 17-acre botanic garden, displaying flora from all over Australia. Free walks depart daily; ask at the information kiosk near Fraser's Restaurant about themed and seasonal tours. ✉ *Fraser Ave. and King's Park Rd., West Perth* ☎ *08/9480–3600* ✎ *Free* ☉ *Daily, 24 hours.*

❻ Law Courts. The 1903 building is surrounded by lively gardens, and inside the atmosphere can be almost as colorful. Many cases tried here are high profile—and guests can be part of the viewing gallery. ✉ *30 St. George's Terr., CBD* ☎ *08/9425–2222* ✎ *Free* ☉ *During trials.*

⓲ London Court. Gold-mining entrepreneur Claude de Bernales built this outdoor shopping arcade in 1937. Today it's a magnet for buskers and anyone with a camera. Along its length you'll find statues of Sir Walter Raleigh and Dick Whittington, the legendary lord mayor of London. Costumed mechanical knights joust with one another when the clock strikes the quarter hour. ✉ *Between St. George's Terr. and Hay St., CBD.*

⓯ Parliament House. From its position on the hill at the top of St. George's Terrace, this building dominates Perth's skyline and serves as a respectable backdrop for the Barracks Arch. Shady old Moreton Bay fig trees and landscaped gardens make the lodge of Western Australian government one of the most pleasant spots in the city. Drop in for a free one-hour tour Monday or Thursday at 10:30; groups are accommodated by appointment. You can visit the Public Galleries whenever Parliament is sitting. ✉ *Harvest Terr., West Perth* ☎ *08/9222–7429* ✎ *Free* ☉ *Tours: Mon. and Thurs. 10:30.*

Perth Concert Hall. When it was built, this small rectangular 1960s concert hall was considered both elegant and architecturally impressive. Although its architectural merit may now seem questionable to some, its acoustics are still clean and clear. The hall serves as the city's main music performance venue. ✉ *5 St. George's Terr., CBD* ☎ *08/9321–9900* ⊕ *www.perthconcerthall.com.au* ✎ *Ticket prices vary* ☉ *During performances.*

❹ Perth Fire Station Museum. Also known as the Old Fire Station, the building is now a museum housing an exhibit on the history of the fire brigade. Photos trace its beginnings, when horses and carts were used, to the present day. There's also a splendid display of old vehicles and equipment. The old limestone building is a fine example of colonial architecture. ✉ *Murray and Irwin Sts., CBD* ☎ *08/9323–9468* ✎ *Free* ☉ *Weekdays 10–3.*

❼ St. George's Cathedral. The church and its **Deanery** form one of the city's most distinctive European-style complexes. Built during the late 1850s as a home for the first dean of Perth, the Deanery is one of the few remaining houses in Western Australia from this period. It is now used as offices for the Anglican Church and is not open to the public. ⊠ *Pier St. and St. George's Terr., CBD* ☎ *08/9325–5766* ⊠ *Free* ☉ *Weekdays 7:30–5, Sunday services at 8, 10, and 5.*

❺ **St. Mary's Cathedral.** One of Perth's most appealing plazas, **Victoria Square,** is the happy home of the Gothic Revival St. Mary's. Its environs house the headquarters for the Roman Catholic Church. ⊠ *Victoria Sq., CBD* ☎ *08/9221–7238* ⊠ *Free* ☉ *Mass weekdays 7 AM and 12:10 PM, Saturday 7 AM and 6:30 PM, Sunday 7:30, 9, 10, 11:30, and 5.*

🦢 **Scitech Discovery Centre.** The center's interactive displays of science and technology educate and entertain children of all ages. There are more than 100 hands-on exhibits, including a stand where you can freeze your own shadow, and another where you can play the Mystical Laser Harp. Scitech was inducted into the Western Australian Tourist Commission's Hall of Fame as an outstanding Major Tourist Attraction. ⊠ *City West Railway Parade, at Sutherland St., West Perth* ☎ *08/9481–5789* ⊕ *www.scitech.org.au* ⊠ *A$12* ☉ *Daily 10–5.*

❾ **Supreme Court Gardens.** This favorite lunch spot for hundreds of office workers is also home to some of the finest Moreton Bay fig trees in the state. A band shell in the rear of the gardens hosts summer concerts, which take place in the evenings from December through February and twice weekly as part of the Perth International Arts Festival. ⊠ *Barrack St. and Adelaide Terr., CBD* ☎ *08/9461–3333* ⊠ *Free* ☉ *Daily 9–5.*

⓫ **Swan Bells Tower.** Comprising one of the largest musical instruments on Earth, the 12 ancient bells installed in the tower are originally from St. Martin-in-the-Fields Church of London, England. The same bells rang to celebrate the destruction of the Spanish Armada in 1588, the homecoming of Captain James Cook in 1771, and the coronation of every British monarch. The tower contains fascinating displays on the history of the bells and bell ringing, and provides stunning views of the Perth skyline. ⊠ *Barrack Sq., cnr. Barrack St. and Riverside Dr.* ☎ *08/9218–8183* ⊕ *www.swanbells.com.au* ⊠ *A$6* ☉ *Daily 10–6.*

⓳ **Town Hall.** During the 1860s, convicts built this hall in the style of a Jacobean English market. Today the building is used for public events. ⊠ *Hay and Barrack Sts., CBD* ☎ *08/9229–2960.*

⓴ **West Australian Museum and Old Perth Gaol.** The state's largest and most comprehensive museum includes some of Perth's oldest structures, such as the Old Perth Gaol. Built of stone in 1856, this was Perth's first prison until 1888. Today, it has been reconstructed in the museum courtyard, and you can go inside the cells for a taste of life in Perth's criminal past. Exhibitions include Diamonds to Dinosaurs, which uses fossils, rocks, and gemstones to take you back 3½ billion years into Western Australia's past; and Katta Djinoong: First Peoples of Western Australia, which has a fascinating collection of primitive tools and lifestyle items used thousands of years ago by Australia's Aborigines. In the Marine Gallery there's an 80-foot-long blue whale skeleton that washed ashore in the South West. ⊠ *James St., CBD* ☎ *08/9427–2700* ⊕ *www.museum.wa.gov.au* ⊠ *Free* ☉ *Daily 9:30–5.*

Around Perth

🦢 **Cohunu Koala Park.** The 40-acre Cohunu (pronounced co-*hu*-na) lets you cuddle with a koala. But take time to view other native animals, such as emus and wombats, in their natural surroundings, too. Cohunu has a walk-through aviary that's the largest in the Southern Hemisphere.

Kids love the park's miniature railway. A revolving restaurant overlooks the city. Gosnells is the nearest railway station. ⊠ *Mill Rd. E., Gosnells* ☎ *08/9390–6090* 🖷 *08/9495–1341* ⊕ *www.cohunu.com.au* 🖂 *A$18* ⊘ *Daily 10–5; koala cuddle daily 10–4.*

☾ **Museum of Childhood.** A pioneer in the conservation of childhood heritage in Australia, this museum is an enchanting hands-on journey for both children and parents. Its 18,000 items constitute the largest and most diverse children's collection the country. Among the most prized exhibits are an original alphabet manuscript written, illustrated, and bound by William Makepeace Thackeray in 1833 and dolls from around the world. ⊠ *Thomas Sten Bldg., Edith Cowan University Campus, Bay Rd., Claremont* ☎ *08/9442–1373* 🖷 *08/9442–1314* ⊕ *www.cowan.edu.au/ses/museum* 🖂 *A$4* ⊘ *Weekdays 10–4; Sun. 2–4.*

☾ **Perth Zoo.** Some 2,000 creatures—from 280 different species—are housed in this gathering of spacious natural habitats. Popular attractions include the Australian Walkabout, the Penguin Plunge, and the Australian Bushwalk. Wander down the dry river bed, which meanders through the African Savannah, or delve through the thick foliage in the Asian Rainforest. To reach the zoo, it's a five-minute walk across the Narrows Bridge, or a ferry ride across the Swan River from the bottom of Barrack Street and then a 10-minute walk following the signs. ⊠ *20 Labouchere Rd., South Perth* ☎ *08/9367–7988* ☎ *08/9474–3551* 🖷 *08/9367–3921* ⊕ *www.perthzoo.wa.gov.au* 🖂 *A$14* ⊘ *Daily 9–5.*

☾ **Whiteman Park.** Barbecue facilities, picnic spots, bike trails, vintage trains and electric trams, and historic wagons and tractors fill this enormous recreation area linked by more than 30 km (19 mi) of bushwalking trails and bike paths. Watch potters, blacksmiths, leather workers, toy makers, printers, and stained-glass artists at work in their shops. Naturally, the wildlife includes kangaroos. ⊠ *Lord St., Swan Valley, West Swan* ☎ *08/9249–2446* 🖂 *A$5 per car (up to 6 people)* ⊘ *Daily 10–4.*

Where to Eat

Northbridge, northwest of the railway station, is *the* dining and nightclubbing center of Perth, and reasonably priced restaurants proliferate. Elsewhere around Perth are seafood and international restaurants, many with stunning views over the Swan River or city. A trend that perfectly suits the mild Western Australian climate is the introduction of cantilevered windows in many restaurants, making for a seamless transition between indoor and alfresco dining.

Chinese

$$$–$$$$ ✕ **Genting Palace.** This elegant restaurant at Burswood International Resort Casino serves some of the best Chinese food in the city. Cantonese flavors predominate, but several Szechuan, Shanghai, and Chiu Chow dishes stand out as well. Start with King prawn salad or hot-and-sour soup, then sample the fresh seafood: eel, jellyfish, fresh green-lip abalone, and lobster, among other choices. Dim sum lunch is served weekends 10:30–2:30. ⊠ *Burswood International Resort Casino, Great Eastern Hwy., Burswood* ☎ *08/9362–7551* ⊕ *www.burswood.com.au* ⊟ AE, DC, MC, V.

$$–$$$ ✕ **Shun Fung on the River.** Right on the waterfront next to the Swan Bells, this Chinese restaurant has rapidly gained accolades as one of Perth's classiest. The huge selection of fresh seafood shines, including the abalone in oyster sauce, and the steamed Sydney rock oysters with chili and black-bean sauce. Banquet menus (8–10 courses) are a specialty, and an extensive collection of rare vintage wines complements the menu.

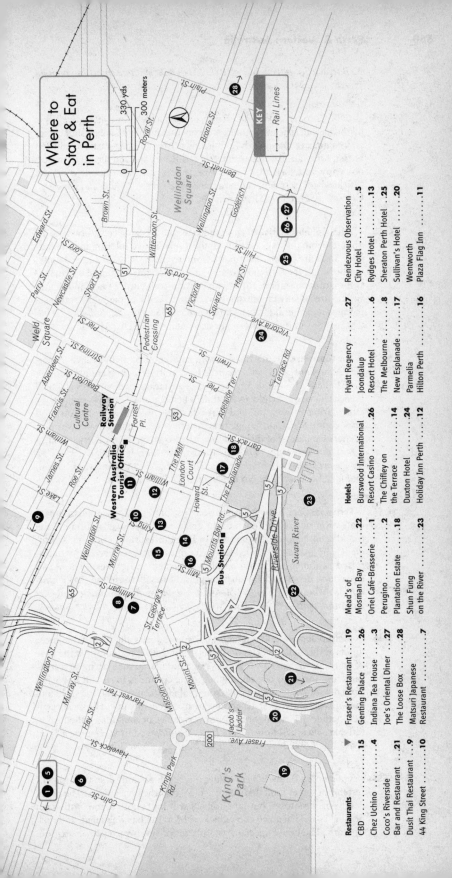

Where to Stay & Eat in Perth

0 — 330 yds
0 — 300 meters

KEY

⊢⊢⊢ Rail Lines

Restaurants

CBD	**15**
Chez Uchino	**4**
Coco's Riverside Bar and Restaurant	**21**
Dusit Thai Restaurant	**9**
44 King Street	**10**
Fraser's Restaurant	**19**
Genting Palace	**26**
Indiana Tea House	**3**
Joe's Oriental Diner	**27**
The Loose Box	**28**
Matsuri Japanese Restaurant	**7**
Mead's of Mosman Bay	**22**
Oriel Café-Brasserie	**1**
Perugino	**2**
Plantation Estate	**18**
Shun Fung on the River	**23**

Hotels

Burswood International Resort Casino	**26**
The Chifley on the Terrace	**14**
Duxton Hotel	**24**
Holiday Inn Perth	**12**
Hyatt Regency	**27**
Joondalup Resort Hotel	**6**
The Melbourne	**8**
New Esplanade	**17**
Parmelia	
Hilton Perth	**16**
Rendezvous Observation City Hotel	**5**
Rydges Hotel	**13**
Sheraton Perth Hotel	**25**
Sullivan's Hotel	**20**
Wentworth Plaza Flag Inn	**11**

Western Australia Tourist Office **11**
Railway Station
Cultural Centre
Bus Station
King's Park
Swan River
Wellington Square
Weld Square

☒ *Barrack Sq. Jetty, CBD* ☎ *08/9221–1868* ⊕ *www.shunfung.com.au*
⊟ *AE, DC, MC, V.*

Contemporary

$$–$$$ ✕ **CBD.** Chrome and jarrah furniture, linen napery, and attractive silver fill this casual, spacious restaurant. From the confident kitchen staff comes an imaginative menu with tantalizing twists. The bag-steamed chicken breast, for example, is marinated in red-bean curd and served with rice, bok choy, and coriander pesto. Twenty-four varieties of table wine and "stickies" (dessert wine) are available by the glass. ☒ *Hay and King Sts., CBD* ☎ *08/9263–1859* ⊟ *AE, DC, MC, V.*

Eclectic

¢–$$ ✕ **Oriel Café-Brasserie.** At this quintessential 24-hour Perth brasserie 10 minutes from the city center, both the dimly lighted interior and the outdoor areas are crowded with tables and overflow with people and noise. For breakfast try *rösti* (potato-and-bacon) with poached eggs, or banana-and-macadamia-nut muffins with passion-fruit curd. Lunch and dinner entrées are equally tantalizing—visualize baked snapper with sesame asparagus and shiitake-mushroom glaze. ☒ *483 Hay St., Subiaco* ☎ *08/ 9382–1886* ⌲ *Reservations not accepted* ⊟ *AE, DC, MC, V.*

French

$$$$ ✕ **The Loose Box.** Perth's finest French restaurant is run by French owner-
Fodor'sChoice chef Alain Fabregues, who received his country's highest culinary honor,
★ the Meilleur Ouvrier de France. His degustation menu applies classical French culinary principles to Australia's best seasonal bounty—fresh yabby tails marinated with dill and pernod, snails braised with shallots, and duck confit. Separate dining areas each have cozy intimacy and warmth. All herbs and most of the vegetables are grown on the property. ☒ *6825 Great Eastern Hwy., Darling Range, Mundaring* ☎ *08/9295–1787* ⌲ *Reservations essential* ⊟ *AE, DC, MC, V* ☾ *Closed Mon., Tues., and last 2 wks of July. No lunch Sat., Wed., and Thurs.*

Italian

★ **$$** ✕ **Perugino.** Chef Giuseppe Pagliaricci's use of fresh produce and his imaginative yet simple approach to the cuisine of his native Umbria are the foundation beneath this impressive Perth institution. Look for *scottadito* (baby goat chops grilled with olive oil and herbs) and *coniglio* (farm-raised rabbit in a tomato sauce with garlic and chilies). The A$60 five-course degustation menu highlights the best of the house. ☒ *77 Outram St., West Perth* ☎ *08/9321–5420* ⊕ *www.perugino.com.au* ⌲ *Reservations essential* ⊟ *AE, DC, MC, V* ☾ *Closed Sun. No lunch Sat.*

Japanese

$–$$ ✕ **Matsuri Japanese Restaurant.** Discerning diners fill every table most nights at this palatial glass-and-steel ground-floor restaurant at the base of an office tower. This is Perth's most popular casual Japanese restaurant, and for good reason: the authentic cuisine is fresh and flavorful. Served with steamed rice, miso soup, salad, and green tea, the sushi and sashimi sets start at A$12 and make an excellent value. House specialties include delicate light tempura vegetables or *una don* (grilled eel in teriyaki sauce). ☒ *Lower level 1, QV1 building, 250 St. George's Terr., CBD* ☎ *08/9322–7737* ⊟ *AE, DC, MC, V* ☾ *No lunch Sat.*

Modern Australian

$$–$$$$ ✕ **Indiana Tea House.** Overlooking the beach at Cottesloe, this opulent restaurant serves food that's as spectacular as the ocean views. The menu emphasizes seafood, but landlubbers will find choices, too, with such highlights as Thai green curry chicken, Moreton Bay bug salad, and rack of lamb. The house specialty is a platter of seven varieties of seafood, served with salad and sauces. Despite the revamped colonial exterior, you're more likely to find Indiana Jones than Somerset Maugham among the wicker chairs and cool Indian decor. ⊠ *99 Marine Parade, Cottesloe* ☎ *08/9385–5005* ⊕ *www.indiana.com.au* ⌖ *Reservations essential* ⊟ *AE, DC, MC, V.*

$$$ ✕ **Chez Uchino.** One of Perth's most innovative chefs, Osamu Uchino consistently earns praise for his spacious, airy restaurant. He skillfully fuses Japanese cuisine and French techniques, with interesting results: panfried sea scallops in bouillabaisse, served with vegetable julienne; beef teriyaki topped with freshwater lobsters; and duck confit. The minimalist, no-smoking dining room is elegant and just a 15-minute cab ride from downtown. ⊠ *622 Stirling Hwy., Mosman Park* ☎ *08/9385–2202* ⌖ *Reservations essential* ⊟ *AE, DC, MC, V* ⊘ *Closed Sun.–Tues. No lunch.*

$$$ ✕ **Plantation Estate.** Reminiscent of a colonial planter's mansion, this restaurant, with its scrubbed wooden paneling emulating the decay of the tropics, attracts crowds of dining cognoscenti. The kitchen flourishes under the guidance of master chef Craig Young, with breakfasts that include *nasi goreng* (Indonesian fried rice) and vanilla flapjacks with berry compote, double cream, and maple syrup. Among the dinner choices are local freshwater lobsters and seafood stir-fry with organic noodles, snow peas, lemongrass, and coconut cream. ⊠ *29 Esplanade, at Mends St., South Perth* ☎ *08/9474–5566* ⊟ *AE, DC, MC, V.*

$$–$$$ ✕ **44 King Street.** Noted for its cutting-edge interpretations of modern Australian cuisine, this no-smoking restaurant redefines the criteria for fast and furious feeding. The seasonal menu changes weekly: try Caesar salad with candied bacon, or pizza with tomato, chèvre, roasted pepper, and black olives. Winter brings savory soups and slow-cooked dishes, while the summer menu highlights outstanding seafood salads. The coffee, cakes, and wines are excellent, and the service is superefficient. ⊠ *44 King St., CBD* ☎ *08/9321–4476* ⊟ *AE, DC, MC, V.*

$$–$$$ ✕ **Fraser's Restaurant.** When the weather is fair—most of the time in Perth—the large outdoor area at this elegant bi-level restaurant in King's Park fills with happy diners, here to enjoy the food and the vistas of the city and Swan River. Local seafood is a specialty. The menu changes each day according to what the markets offer. The special might be rabbit loin and peach salad with Thai dressing, wok-fried baby octopus with chili jam and bean sprouts, or freshly shucked Ceduna oysters with tomato and red-onion salsa. The restaurant serves an excellent breakfast daily from 7. ⊠ *Fraser Ave., King's Park, West Perth* ☎ *08/9481–7100* ⊕ *www.frasersrestaurant.com.au* ⌖ *Reservations essential* ⊟ *AE, DC, MC, V.*

$–$$ ✕ **Coco's Riverside Bar and Restaurant.** Overlooking the Swan River in South Perth, this fine restaurant also offers fine views of the Perth skyline. The menu changes daily, depending on availability of fresh produce, with most items available in either appetizer or main-course portions. The beef, aged in the restaurant's own cool room, has a formidable reputation. Try the wok-seared, spicy-crust king prawns; or the fresh Albany King George whiting fillets, shallow-fried in a light tempura batter. There is an extensive vintage wine cellar. ⊠ *Southshore Centre, 85 The Esplanade, South Perth* ☎ *08/9474–3030* ⊕ *www.cocosperth.com* ⌖ *Reservations essential* ⊟ *AE, DC, MC, V.*

Pan-Asian

$$ ✕ **Joe's Oriental Diner.** Wood, natural brick, terra-cotta, and teak antiques reinforce the Southeast Asian theme at this restaurant serving Thai, Indonesian, Malaysian, and Singaporean dishes. Start with one of the hearty soups before moving on to such delicious noodle dishes as *kway teow*

(noodles with bean sprouts, prawns, and chicken) and *laksa* (rice noodles in a rich and spicy coconut-milk soup with chicken, bean curd, and prawns). "Joe's favorite selections" include stir-fried seafood with ginger and oyster sauce, and yabbies with chili-bean sauce. ⊠ *Hyatt Regency, 99 Adelaide Terr., CBD* ☏ *08/9225–1268* ⊟ *AE, DC, MC, V* ⊘ *Closed Sun. No lunch Sat.*

Seafood

$$$–$$$$
FodorsChoice
★

✕ **Mead's of Mosman Bay.** Visitors are divided about whether the seafood or the setting—on the Swan River surrounded by yachts and the mansions of Western Australia's elite—is more spectacular. A hip bar area and an oyster bar add to the experience, but culinary excellence is the main draw. While gazing at a squadron of pelicans lazily gliding over the river, you can feast on Thai parcel of king prawns and snapper served with fresh mango, or char-grilled baby squid in chili. The restaurant is a 15-minute cab ride from town. ⊠ *15 Johnson Parade, Mosman Park* ☏ *08/9383–3388* ⊕ *www.meads.com.au* ⊟ *AE, DC, MC, V.*

Thai

$$–$$$

✕ **Dusit Thai Restaurant.** Celebrate the taste of Thailand at this upscale Northbridge restaurant, where fresh, authentic Thai food is lovingly prepared and presented amid a setting of traditional sculptures, ornaments, and images. Start with *gai hor bai-toey* (marinated chicken breast wrapped in pandang leaves); spicy, sour *tom yum* soup; or coconut-milk-sweetened *tom kha* (chicken soup). Main-course specialties include *gang keo-wan jai* (green curry chicken) and *pard ki-mow moo* (stir-fried spicy pork with runner beans and basil). Complete the experience with sticky rice and ice cream for dessert. ⊠ *249 James St., Northbridge* ☏ *08/9328–7647* ⊟ *AE, DC, MC, V* ⊘ *No lunch Sat.–Wed. No dinner Mon.*

Where to Stay

$$$$

🛏 **Duxton Hotel.** Soothing autumn colors, CD players, paintings by local artists, and furniture crafted from Australian timber fill the comfortable rooms of this hotel within easy walking distance of the central business district and right next to the Perth Concert Hall. Be sure to request a room with a view of the Swan River. The Brasserie provides casual dining. ⊠ *1 St. George's Terr., CBD, 6000* ☏ *08/9261–8000 or 1800/681118* 🖷 *08/9261–8020* ⊕ *www.duxton.com* ⇨ *291 rooms, 15 suites* ♣ *Restaurant, room service, pool, gym, sauna, spa, steam room, bar, laundry service, business services, free parking* ⊟ *AE, DC, MC, V.*

$$$$

🛏 **Parmelia Hilton Perth.** Enter this opulent hotel, one of Perth's finest, through a foyer of rich wood paneling and an elliptical parquet floor. Marvel at the many antiques, including Chinese silk tapestries and Mussolini's mirror (near the elevator). Many of the 55 alcove rooms overlook the hotel pool and city; 81 rooms have private balconies. All suites enjoy river views, and 10 have crystal chandeliers, gilt mirrors, deep-pile carpeting, and luxurious marble bathrooms. There's personal service around-the-clock, with a valet and seamstress on call and a business center open 24 hours. ⊠ *Mill St., CBD, 6000* ☏ *08/9215–2000* 🖷 *08/9215–2001* ⊕ *www.hilton.com* ⇨ *273 rooms, 55 suites* ♣ *2 restaurants, room service, in-room data ports, pool, health club, sauna, bicycles, 4 bars, nightclub, dry cleaning, laundry service, concierge, business services, car rental, free parking, parking (fee)* ⊟ *AE, DC, MC, V.*

$$$
FodorsChoice
★

🛏 **Burswood International Resort Casino.** From the 10-story glass atrium atop its pyramid-shape exterior to its 18-hole golf course, Burswood is a distinctive luxury resort. Spacious rooms each have a Japanese shoji screen between the bedroom and bathroom and a view of either the river or the city. Suites have spa baths. The adjoining casino is one of the largest in the Southern Hemisphere, open around-the-clock for roulette, blackjack, baccarat, keno, and video games. ☺ *P.O. Box 500 Victoria Park, 6979* ✉ *Great Eastern Hwy., Burswood 6100* ☎ *08/9362–7777* 🖶 *08/9470–2553* 🌐 *www.burswood.com.au* 🛏 *413 rooms, 16 suites* ᓚ *9 restaurants, room service, in-room data ports, 18-hole golf course, 4 tennis courts, 2 pools, 1 indoor pool, health club, sauna, spa, 6 bars, casino, dance club, video-game room, shops, baby-sitting, playground, laundry service, business services, concierge, free parking; no-smoking rooms* ▭ *AE, DC, MC, V.*

★ **$$$** ▦ **Hyatt Regency.** A setting on the banks of the Swan River, within walking distance of Perth's central business district, makes this hotel an enchanting and convenient place to stay. Standard rooms are subdued and spacious, and the two floors of the Regency Club rooms and suites, reached by a private elevator, have stunning city or river views and include a complimentary Continental breakfast and evening drinks and canapés. The Conservatory, a sitting area with tasteful cane furniture and a fountain under a large domed atrium, is a great place to relax. ✉ *99 Adelaide Terr., CBD, 6000* ☎ *08/9225–1234* 🖶 *08/9325–8899 or 08/9325–8785* 🌐 *www.hyatt.com* 🛏 *367 rooms, 32 suites* ᓚ *3 restaurants, room service, in-room safes, tennis court, pool, health club, 2 bars, shops, baby-sitting, dry cleaning, laundry service, Internet, business services, concierge, meeting room, free parking* ▭ *AE, DC, MC, V* ❑ *CP.*

$$$ ▦ **Rydges Hotel.** Soothing earth tones and ultramodern furnishings of chrome, glass, black leather, and velveteen fill the rooms at this 16-story hotel. Rooms above the 12th floor afford commanding views of the river and city. King executive suites have floor-to-ceiling windows and goldfish tanks, and Executive Club floors include security-key access and oversize desks with printer, scanner, and fax capabilities. Complimentary membership passes are provided for a private fitness center nearby. ✉ *Hay and King Sts., Northbridge, 6000* ☎ *08/9263–1800* 🖶 *08/9263–1801* 🌐 *www.rydges.com/perth* 🛏 *245 rooms, 6 suites* ᓚ *Restaurant, cable TV, pool, gym, bar, laundry service, business services, parking (fee)* ▭ *AE, DC, MC, V.*

$$$ ▦ **Sheraton Perth Hotel.** Towering above the Swan River, this hotel has a pretty setting and a convenient location not far from the Perth Concert Hall. Rooms, done in Tasmanian oak, all have sweeping river views. The Brasserie provides laid-back, California-style dining. ✉ *207 Adelaide Terr., CBD, 6000* ☎ *08/9224–7777* 🖶 *08/9224–7788* 🌐 *www.sheraton.com/perth* 🛏 *388 rooms, 18 suites* ᓚ *2 restaurants, in-room data ports, in-room safes, cable TV, pool, health club, steam room, bicycles, 2 bars, dry cleaning, laundry service, concierge, business services, parking (fee)* ▭ *AE, DC, MC, V.*

★ **$$–$$$** ▦ **Joondalup Resort Hotel.** Golf is the main attraction at this resort with three 9-hole championship courses, though there are plenty of other facilities, such as a free-form pool, a jogging track, an airy bistro-bar, and meeting rooms. The two-story, palm-shaded building resembles a southern plantation owner's mansion. The hotel's only drawback is that it's 30 km (19 mi) from the city center. ✉ *Country Club Blvd., Connolly, 6027* ☎ *08/9400–8888* 🖶 *08/9400–8889* 🌐 *www.joondalupresort.com.au* 🛏 *69 rooms, 4 suites, 6 villas* ᓚ *2 restaurants, in-room data ports, in-room safes, in-room VCRs, 3 9-hole golf courses, 3 tennis courts, pool, gym, sauna, spa, 2 bars, laundry service, business services, meeting rooms, free parking* ▭ *AE, DC, MC, V.*

$$ ▦ **The Chifley on the Terrace.** This bright, breezy business hotel offers a wealth of innovations you might expect to find only in much pricier establishments, such as roomy baths with aromatherapy oils, and convenient Internet connections in every room. Rooms are kitted out in earth tones, and executive suites have open-plan bathrooms with a spa tub. A casual, alfresco bistro is attached to the foyer. ⊠ *185 St. George's Terr., CBD, 6000* ☎ *08/9226–3355* 🖷 *08/9226–1055* ⊕ *www. chifleyhotels.com* 🔊 *58 rooms, 27 suites* ↳ *Restaurant, in-room data ports, cable TV, bar, laundry service, business services, free parking* 🖃 *AE, DC, MC, V.*

★ **\$\$**   🏨 **Rendezvous Observation City Hotel.** Watching the sun sink into the Indian Ocean from this beachside resort is a memorable experience. Elegant blues, golds, and mauves decorate the stylish rooms, all with superb ocean views, and marble bathrooms and mirrored wardrobes add just the right touch of luxury. Dine at the epicurean Savannahs Restaurant, or enjoy alfresco beachside fare at Café Estrada. Just 10 minutes by freeway from the city center, this hotel makes a great alternative to downtown properties. ⊠ *The Esplanade, Scarborough, 6019* ☎ *08/9245–1000* 🖷 *08/9245–1345* ⊕ *www.rendezvoushotels.com* 🔊 *333 rooms, 6 suites* ↳ *4 restaurants, cable TV, 2 tennis courts, pool, gym, sauna, spa, 4 bars, playground, concierge, free parking* 🖃 *AE, DC, MC, V.*

\$ 🏨 **Holiday Inn Perth.** This hotel lies just a minute's walk from the central business district, major shopping areas, cinemas, and restaurants. The bar and brasserie, with warm terra-cotta tiles and wrought-iron furniture, each have a Mediterranean feel. Rooms are of typical Holiday Inn minimalist design. ⊠ *778 Hay St., CBD, 6000* ☎ *08/9261–7200* 🖷 *08/9261–7277* ⊕ *www.perth-cityctr.holiday-inn.com* 🔊 *180 rooms, 1 suite* ↳ *Restaurant, cable TV, indoor pool, health club, sauna, spa, bar, laundry service, free parking* 🖃 *AE, DC, MC, V.*

\$ 🏨 **The Melbourne.** A restored 1890s building listed on the National Heritage Register houses this stylish boutique hotel. The Perth landmark retains all the original design elements of the era, including a grand staircase and elevator. The elegant Louisiana's Restaurant serves excellent Australian cuisine. Have a drink in the Mississippi Bar, with its atmospheric period photographs of river paddle steamers, or the Orleans Bar. ⊠ *Hay St. at Milligan St., CBD, 6000* ☎ *08/9320–3333* 🖷 *08/9320–3344* ⊕ *www.melbournehotel.com.au* 🔊 *32 rooms, 3 suites* ↳ *Restaurant, room service, cable TV, 2 bars, dry cleaning, laundry service, convention center, meeting rooms, free parking* 🖃 *AE, DC, MC, V.*

\$ 🏨 **Sullivan's Hotel.** "The guest reigns supreme" should be the motto for this innovative, family-run hotel opposite waterfront parkland. Poolside barbecues, free movies, and drinks service (at bar prices) to your room are all part of the fun, while the free shuttle and guest showers for those arriving early or departing late are part of the excellent service. The spacious, open foyer complements the design of the light, airy rooms. ⊠ *166 Mounts Bay Rd., CBD, 6000* ☎ *08/9321–8022* 🖷 *08/ 9481–6762* ⊕ *www.sullivans.com.au* 🔊 *70 rooms* ↳ *Restaurant, picnic area, pool, bicycles, bar, laundry service, free parking* 🖃 *AE, DC, MC, V.*

¢–\$ 🏨 **New Esplanade.** Ideally situated on the Esplanade, this hotel enjoys the same million-dollar view of the Swan River for which flamboyant mining tycoons have forked over fortunes. And it's just a chopstick's toss from the Grand Palace, one of the more popular Chinese restaurants in town. Shades of green and cream contrast nicely with the teak woodwork in the comfortable, spacious rooms. ⊠ *18 Esplanade, CBD, 6000* ☎ *08/9325–2000* 🖷 *08/9221–2190* ⊕ *www.newesplanade.com. au* 🔊 *65 rooms* ↳ *Restaurant, bar, free parking* 🖃 *AE, DC, MC, V.*

¢–\$ 🏨 **Wentworth Plaza Flag Inn.** A Federation-era inn, the Wentworth
FodorśChoice   merged with the equally old Royal on Wellington Street to form one large,
★   grand hotel. The rooms recapture period ambience, with accommodations ranging from two-room apartments and single rooms with a private bath to inexpensive, traditional rooms that share facilities on the

Royal Hotel side. Downstairs, the Garage Bar, Horsefeathers, Bobby Dazzler, and Moon and Sixpence are popular watering holes where you can rub shoulders with locals. ☒ *300 Murray St., CBD, 6000* ☎ *08/9481–1000* 🖷 *08/9321–2443* 🌐 *www.holidaycity.com/flag-perth* 🛏 *96 rooms* ⚴ *Restaurant, room service, 4 bars, laundry facilities, free parking* ▭ *AE, DC, MC, V.*

Nightlife & the Arts

Details on cultural events in Perth are published in the comprehensive Saturday edition of the *West Australian*. A free weekly, *X-Press Magazine*, lists music, concerts, movies, entertainment reviews, and who's playing at pubs, clubs, and hotels. *Scoop* magazine (🌐 www.scoop.com.au), published quarterly, is an excellent guide to the essential Western Australian lifestyle.

The Arts

Local talent dominates the arts scene in Perth, although the acclaimed **Perth International Arts Festival (PIAF)** (☒ University of Western Australia, Mounts Bay Rd., Crawley, 6009 ☎ 08/9380–2000 🌐 www.perthfestival.com.au), held during January and February in venues throughout the city, attracts world-class names in music, dance, and theater. This is Australia's oldest and biggest annual arts festival, and it's been running for more than 50 years. As part of the festival, the PIAF Sunset Cinema Season, adjacent to Winthrop Hall on Mounts Bay Road at the University of Western Australia, screens films outdoors December–March.

BALLET The **West Australian Ballet Company** (☒ 825 Hay St., CBD ☎ 08/9481–0707), one of just three ballet companies in Australia, focuses on classical ballet but also has contemporary ballet and dance in its diverse repertoire. Performances are at His Majesty's Theatre, although you can also see the 17-person troupe at such outdoor venues as the Quarry Amphitheatre (at City Beach) and on country tours.

CONCERTS The **Perth Concert Hall** (☒ 5 St. George's Terr., CBD ☎ 08/9231–9900 🌐 www.perthconcerthall.com.au), a modern building overlooking the Swan River, stages regular recitals by the excellent West Australian Symphony Orchestra, as well as Australian and international artists. Adding to the appeal of the fine auditorium is the 3,000-pipe organ surrounded by a 160-person choir gallery.

OPERA The **West Australian Opera Company** (☒ 825 Hay St., CBD ☎ 08/9321–5869) presents three seasons annually—in April, August, and November—at His Majesty's Theatre. The company's repertoire includes classic opera, Gilbert and Sullivan operettas, and occasional musicals.

THEATER The casual **Effie Crump Theatre** (☒ 81 Brisbane St. at William St., Northbridge ☎ 08/9227–7226), upstairs in the Brisbane Hotel, showcases light comedies (often bordering on the bizarre or surreal) and musicals. The opulent Edwardian **His Majesty's Theatre** (☒ 825 Hay St., CBD ☎ 08/9265–0900 🌐 www.hismajestystheatre.com.au), opened in 1904, is loved by all who step inside. Home to the WA Opera Company and the West Australian Ballet Company, it hosts most theatrical productions in Perth. The **Playhouse Theatre** (☒ 3 Pier St., CBD ☎ 08/9231–2377) stages local productions. For outdoor performances, the **Quarry Amphitheatre** (☒ Ocean Dr., City Beach ☎ 08/9385–7144) is popular, particularly during the Perth International Arts Festival. The **Regal Theatre** (☒ 474 Hay St. at Rokeby Rd., Subiaco ☎ 08/9484–1133) hosts local performances.

Nightlife

BARS   Architect Michael Patroni transformed a number of Perth's dilapidated pubs and bars into stylish, popular spots. The **Bog** (✉ 361 Newcastle St., Northbridge ☎ 08/9228–0900) is a favorite on the Irish music scene, with live music every night from 6 PM to 6 AM. You'll find fast and furious Celtic music playing on both floors, plus good drinks and plenty of chill-out spaces. Admission is free. The **Brass Monkey** (✉ 209 William St., Northbridge ☎ 08/9227–9596) is in a huge, old, crimson-painted building with potted plants flowing over the antique verandas. An instrumental trio plays on Friday nights, and a cover band plays popular tunes on Thursday and Saturday. There's no cover charge. **Carnegie's** (✉ 356 Murray St. at King St., CBD ☎ 08/9481–3222), a relaxed, up-scale café by day, turns into an attractive pub during the afternoon and then a disco late at night. With rock-and-roll decor, a raised dance floor, and DJs playing music from the 1960s to today's Top 40, the bar attracts an older clientele from the business and tourist sectors. The **Grosvenor Hotel** (✉ 339 Hay St., CBD ☎ 08/9325–3799) has alternative-style music and is popular with the younger crowd. The **Oriel Café-Brasserie** (✉ 483 Hay St., Subiaco ☎ 08/9382–1886) is a fun place for snacks and drinks. **Queen's Tavern** (✉ 520 Beaufort St., Highgate ☎ 08/9328–7267) has an excellent outdoor beer garden. The bar at the **Subiaco Hotel** (✉ 465 Hay St., Subiaco ☎ 08/9381–3069) attracts a lively after-work crowd during the week.

JAZZ & BLUES   For blues Tuesday night, try the **Charles Hotel** (✉ 509 Charles St., North Perth ☎ 08/9444–1051). The **Hyde Park Hotel** (✉ 331 Bulwer St., North Perth ☎ 08/9328–6166), a no-nonsense Aussie pub, hosts contemporary jazz Monday night and Dixieland Tuesday night.

NIGHTCLUBS   Most luxury hotels in Perth have upscale nightclubs that appeal to the over-30 crowd. The **Burswood International Resort Casino** (✉ Great Eastern Hwy., Burswood ☎ 08/9362–7777) showcases lyric-style cabaret, with national and international performers and shows. There's also a retro nightclub, The Ruby Room. **Club A** (✉ The Esplanade, next to the lookout, Scarborough ☎ 08/9340–5735) is one of the city's top dance spots, attracting 18–35 year olds. **The Hip-e Club** (✉ 663 Newcastle St., Leederville ☎ 08/9227–8899), a Perth legend, capitalizes on its hippy-era image with a neon kaleidoscope, three-dimensional color explosions, murals, and '60s paraphernalia decorating the walls.

Margeaux's (✉ Parmelia Hilton Perth, Mill St., CBD ☎ 08/9322–3622) is an exclusive late-night drinking and dancing venue. **Varga Lounge** (✉ 161 James St., Northbridge ☎ 08/9328–7200) mixes it up with techno, rap, hip-hop, and other dance styles.

Midway between Perth and Fremantle is **BayView** (✉ 20 St. Quentin's Ave., Claremont ☎ 08/9385–1331), an upscale cocktail bar–cum–nightclub that attracts 18–40 year olds. Many people arrive after the nearby Red Rock Hotel closes at midnight.

Sports & the Outdoors

Participant Sports

BEACHES   Perth's beaches and waterways are among its greatest attractions. If possible, plan to make an excursion to the seaside during your stay.

Traveling north from Fremantle, the first beach you come to is **Leighton.** Here you'll find Windsurfers and the astonishing wave-jumpers who ride boards against the surf and hurl themselves airborne. **Cottesloe** and **North Cottesloe** attract family groups. **Trigg,** a top surf site and arguably

Perth's best beach, overlooks an emerald-green bay. **Scarborough** is favored by teenagers and young adults. **Swanbourne** (between North Cottesloe and City Beach) is a "clothing-optional" beach.

BICYCLING Perth and Fremantle have an extensive and expanding network of cycleways, which means you can ride along the rivers and coast without having to worry about traffic. Most freeways also have a separated cycle path. Bicycle helmets are compulsory. Details on trails and free brochures are available from the **Western Australia Visitor Centre** (⊠ Forrest Pl. and Wellington St., CBD ☎ 08/9483–1111).

GOLF Perth has numerous public golf courses, all of which rent out clubs. The **Western Australia Golf Association** (☎ 08/9367–2490) can provide details on golf courses in Western Australia.

The 18-hole, par-70 course at **Burswood International Resort Casino** (⊠ Great Eastern Hwy., Burswood ☎ 08/9362–7576) is closest to the city. The finest golfing venue is the **Joondalup Country Club** (⊠ Country Club Blvd., Joondalup ☎ 08/9400–8888 ⊕ www.joondalupresort.com. au), 25 minutes north of Perth, which offers three challenging 9-hole, par-36 courses.

HEALTH CLUB Health clubs with spas, saunas, and exercise equipment are available to guests of most luxury hotels.

Lords Health Club and Sports Centre (⊠ 588 Hay St., Subiaco ☎ 08/ 9381–4777 health club, 08/9381–6666 sports center ⊕ www.lords. com.au) has fitness equipment, aerobics, a heated indoor pool, indoor tennis and squash courts, a sauna, and a spa. The club is open weekdays 6 AM–9 PM, weekends 8–6; a A$16.50 day pass covers the pool, aerobics, and gym equipment.

MOTORCYCLING **Deluxe Trike Tours** (☎ 08/9405–4949) runs one- to eight-hour excursions on a trike (three-wheeled motorcycle that seats three people) or aboard the more familiar Harley-Davidson motorcycles.

RUNNING Jogging tracks lead along the Swan River and through King's Park.

SKYDIVING The **Western Australian Skydiving Academy** (⊠ Shop 9–10, 143 William St., Northbridge ☎ 08/9227–6066) conducts everything from tandem jumps to accelerated free-fall courses. A tandem jump starts from A$220 for 6,000 feet up to A$380 for the maximum jump—14,000 ft. Tandem jumps don't require training, just 20 minutes of instruction. The accelerated free-fall course, which takes nine hours, costs A$650.

SWIMMING Aside from Perth's glorious beaches, there are three Olympic-size pools at **Challenge Stadium** (⊠ Stephenson Ave., Mt. Claremont ☎ 08/ 9441–8222). Admission costs A$4.40, and the pools are open weekdays 5:30 AM–9:30 PM, Saturday 5:30 AM–6 PM, and Sunday 8–6.

TENNIS **Tennis West** (☎ 08/9361–1112 ⊕ www.tenniswest.com.au) provides details on tennis courts in the metropolitan area.

WATER SPORTS Parasailing is available on the South Perth foreshore every weekend, weather and winds permitting. It's A$75 for a single for 15 minutes and A$120 tandem. Contact **South Perth Parasailing** (⊠ Narrows Bridge, South Perth ☎ 08/9447–7450).

If you want to enjoy the Swan River at a leisurely pace, hire a catamaran or a sailboard from **Funcats Surfcat Hire** (⊠ Coode St., South Perth ☎ 0408/926–003) at the Coode Street jetty. It costs A$24 per hour, and advance reservations are essential on weekends.

Spectator Sports

AUSTRALIAN- RULES FOOTBALL
This unique blend of an Aboriginal game and Gaelic football first came to life in Melbourne and is now a national sport with teams competing from every state. The Australian Football League (AFL) plays every weekend throughout the winter (March–September) at Subiaco Oval and at the Western Australia Cricket Association (WACA) grounds. Top Western Australian teams are the Eagles and the Fremantle Dockers. The local league, Westar, plays every Saturday around the metropolitan area. For details contact the **West Australian Football Commission** (☎ 08/9381–5599 ⊕ www.wafl.com.au).

CRICKET
The national summer game is played professionally at the **Western Australia Cricket Association** (WACA; ☎ 08/9265–7222 ⊕ www.waca.com. au) grounds in Nelson Crescent, East Perth.

Shopping

Shopping in Perth is a delight, with pedestrian malls the latest European-style craze. Hay Street Mall and Murray Street Mall are the main city shopping areas, linked by numerous arcades with small shops. In the suburbs, top retail strips include Napoleon Street in the suburb of Cottesloe (for clothing and cooking items), Hampden Road in Nedlands (for crafts), and Beaufort Street in Mount Lawley (for antiques).

Australiana

Australian souvenirs and knickknacks are on sale at small shops throughout the city and suburbs. **Looking East** (⊠ Unit 3, 160 Hampden Rd., Nedlands ☎ 08/9389–5569) sells contemporary, minimalist Aussie clothing, furnishings, and pottery. **Maalia Mia** (⊠ 8991 West Swan Rd., Henley Brook ☎ 08/9296–0704 ⊕ www.maalimia.com.au), an Aboriginal-owned and -operated cultural center, art gallery, and gift shop, sells art and artifacts purchased only from Aboriginal artists. Boomerangs, didgeridoos, and clapping sticks are made on site. **Purely Australian Clothing Company** (☎ 08/9325–4328 ⊕ www.purelyaustralian.com) carries the most comprehensive selection of Oz-abilia in Perth, with stores in London Court, Hay Street Mall, and City Arcade. **R. M. Williams** (⊠ Carillon Arcade, Hay Street Mall, CBD ☎ 08/9321–7786) sells everything for the Australian bushman, including moleskin pants, hand-tooled leather boots, and Akubra hats.

Crafts

Craftwest (⊠ 357–365 Murray St., CBD ☎ 08/9226–2799) carries a large selection of Western Australian crafts and giftware, including some Aboriginal art, jewelry, cards, and accessories. You can find authentic Aboriginal artifacts at **Creative Native** (⊠ 32 King St., CBD ☎ 08/ 9322–3398 ⊕ www.creativenative.com.au); the Dreamtime Gallery, upstairs, is one of Australia's finest. A former car dealer's workshop has been transformed into the Outback for **Indigenart** (⊠ 115 Hay St., Subiaco ☎ 08/9388–2899 ⊕ www.indigenart.com.au), an art gallery–cum–Aboriginal culture center where you can view works and talk with the Aboriginal creators.

Gems

Cartier (⊠ 41 King St., CBD ☎ 08/9321–8877 ⊕ www.cartier.com) crafts stunning pieces using the prized pink diamonds from the Argyle diamond mines. Opals from South Australia's Coober Pedy are available at **Costello's** (⊠ 5–6 London Ct., CBD ☎ 08/9325–8588 ⊕ www. costellos.com.au). **Linneys** (⊠ 37 Rokeby Rd., Subiaco ☎ 08/9382–4077 ⊕ www.linneys.com.au), whose designers and craftspeople have won national awards, carries an excellent selection of Broome pearls, Argyle diamonds, and Kalgoorlie gold, and will set the gems and pearls in the design of your choice. **Rosendorf's** (✉ Hay St. Mall, CBD ☎ 08/9321–4015), regarded as Perth's premier diamond jeweler, specializes in white and colored diamonds. They also have outlets in Karrinyup and Graden City shopping centers in the suburbs.

Malls

Forrest Place, flanked by the post office and the Forrest Chase Shopping Plaza, is the largest mall area in the city. **David Jones** (☎ 08/9210–4000) department store opens onto the Murray Street pedestrian mall. **Myer** (☎ 08/9221–3444) is a popular department store that carries various goods and sundries. Hay Street Mall, running parallel to Murray Street and linked by numerous arcades, also has extensive shopping facilities.

Perth A to Z

To research prices, get advice from other travelers, and book travel arrangements, visit www.fodors.com.

AIR TRAVEL

International airlines serving Perth International Airport include: Air New Zealand, British Airways, Qantas, Singapore Airlines, and South African Airlines, among others. Qantas and Virgin Blue connect Perth to other Australian capital cities.

Airlink (the regional subsidiary of Qantas) and Skywest connect Perth with other towns in the state.

🛪 Carriers **Airlink** ☎ 13–1313. **Air New Zealand** ☎ 13–2476. **British Airways** ☎ 08/9425–7711. **Qantas** ☎ 13–1313. **Singapore Airlines** ☎ 13–1011. **Skywest** ☎ 13–6789. **South African Airlines** ☎ 08/9321–2435. **Virgin Blue** ☎ 13–6789.

AIRPORTS & TRANSFERS

Perth International Airport has two separate terminals. The domestic terminal is about 11 km (7 mi) from Perth, and the international terminal is about 16 km (10 mi) from the city.

🛪 Airport Information **Perth International Airport** ☎ 08/9478–8888 🌐 www.perthairport.com.

AIRPORT
TRANSFERS
Taxis are available 24 hours a day. Trips to the city cost about A$30 and take around a half-hour. Shuttle buses run between terminals (A$6), as well as to hotels in Perth and Fremantle. Transperth bus services are cheaper, but may not drop you off near your hotel.

BIKE TRAVEL

Perth's climate and its network of excellent trails make cycling a safe and enjoyable way to discover the city. But beware: the summer temperature can exceed 40°C (100°F) in the shade. Wearing a bicycle helmet is required by law, and carrying water is always prudent. You can rent a bicycle for A$25 a day or A$55 a week, including obligatory helmet, from About Bike Hire. The office is located behind Causeway Car Park at the southeastern end of Riverside Drive, and it's open Monday–Saturday 10–6 and Sunday 9–6. Free brochures detailing trails, including stops at historical spots, are available from the Perth Visitor Centre.

🚲 **About Bike Hire** ☎ 08/9221-2665 🌐 www.aboutbikehire.com.au.

BOAT & FERRY TRAVEL

Perth Water Transport ferries make daily runs from 6:50 AM to 7:15 PM between Barrack Street Jetty in Perth to Mends Street, across the Swan River in South Perth. Reduced service runs on weekends and holidays.

🛥 **Perth Water Transport** ☎ 08/9221-2722.

BUSINESS SERVICES

All major hotels provide fax, photocopy, and computer services for guests, although there may be a fee. Serviced Office Specialists has round-the-clock services, including, data entry, word processing, e-mailing, and faxing.

🖪 **Serviced Office Specialists** ✉ Level 21, 197 St. George's Terr., CBD ☎ 08/9214-3838.

BUS TRAVEL

Greyhound Pioneer Australia buses are routed through the Western Australian Government Railways terminal in East Perth. It's 60 hours to Darwin, 36 hours to Adelaide, 48 hours to Melbourne, and 60 hours to Sydney.

🖪 **Western Australian Government Railways** ✉ West Parade, East Perth ☎ 13-1053.
🖪 **Greyhound Pioneer Australia** ☎ 13-2030 ⊕ www.greyhound.com.au.

BUS TRAVEL WITHIN PERTH

The Perth central business district and suburban areas are well connected by the Transperth line. The main terminals are at Perth Central Bus Station on Mounts Bay Road and at Wellington Street Bus Station.

FARES & SCHEDULES
Transperth tickets are valid for two hours and can be used on Transperth trains and ferries. Buses run daily between 6 AM and 11:30 PM, with reduced service on weekends and holidays.

Rides within the city center are free. CAT (Central Area Transit) buses circle the city center, running approximately every 10 minutes on weekdays from 7 to 6, Saturday 9 to 5. Routes and timetables are available from Transperth.

🖪 **Transperth** ☎ 13-2213 ⊕ www.transperth.wa.gov.au.

CAR RENTALS

All major car-rental companies, including Hertz and Avis, have depots at both the international and domestic airports. A good budget alternative is Network Car Rental, which can arrange airport pickup and drop-off.

🖪 **Agencies Avis** ☎ 08/9325-7677 or 1800/225533. **Hertz** ☎ 08/9321-7777 or 1800/550067. **Budget Car Rental** ☎ 13-2727.

CAR TRAVEL

The Eyre Highway crosses the continent from Port Augusta in South Australia to Western Australia's transportation gateway, Norseman. From there, take the Coolgardie–Esperance Highway north to Coolgardie, and the Great Eastern Highway on to Perth. Driving to Perth—2,580 km (1,600 mi) and 30 hours from Adelaide, and 4,032 km (2,500 mi) and 56 hours from Sydney—is an arduous journey, which should be undertaken only with a car (and mental faculties) in top condition. Spare tires and drinking water are essential. Service stations and motels are spaced at regular intervals along the route.

Driving in Perth is relatively easy; just remember to stay on the left-hand side of the road. Peak traffic hours are 7:30 to 9 AM heading into Perth and 4:30 to 6 PM heading away from the city center. Country roads are generally well-maintained and have little traffic. There are no freeways and few two-lane highways outside of the Perth metropolitan area. "Self-Drive Tours within WA," a free 72-page booklet that suggests itineraries around Perth, Fremantle, and the state, is available from the Western Australia Visitor Centre and major car-rental companies.

EMERGENCIES

In case of an emergency, dial 000 to reach an ambulance, the police, or the fire department.

Perth Dental Hospital recommends private practitioners for emergency service. Royal Perth Hospital has a 24-hour emergency room.

⚠ Perth Dental Hospital ⊠ 196 Goderich St., East Perth ☎ 08/9220-5777, 08/9325-3452 after hours. **Police** ☎ 08/9222-1111. **Royal Perth Hospital** ⊠ Victoria Sq., East Perth ☎ 08/9224-2244.

MAIL, INTERNET & SHIPPING

You will find lots of places where you can access the Internet cheaply in Perth and Fremantle. Coin-operated terminals can be found around both cities and at the airport. In Perth and Northbridge these are often found along Williams and Wellington streets.

The main post office, on Forest Place, is open weekdays 9–5:30 and Saturday 9–noon. Federal Express and DHL can provide overnight mail services.

⚠ Main Post Office ☎ 08/9237-5000.

⚠ DHL ☎ 13-1406. **Federal Express** ☎ 13-2610.

⚠ Malibu City Dive and Travel ⊠ 126 Barrack St., Northbridge ☎ 08/9225-7555.

MONEY MATTERS

Banks with dependable check-cashing and money-changing services include ANZ, Challenge Bank, Commonwealth, and National Australia Bank. ATMs—which accept Cirrus, Plus, Visa, and MasterCard—are ubiquitous and nearly always reliable.

⚠ Banks ANZ ☎ 13-1314. **Challenge Bank** ☎ 13-1862. **Commonwealth** ☎ 13-221. **National Australia Bank** ☎ 13-2265.

TAXIS

Cab fare between 6 AM and 6 PM weekdays is an initial A$2.90 plus A$1.17 every 1 km (½ mi). From 6 PM to 6 AM and on weekends the rate rises to A$4.20 plus A$1.17 per km (½ mi).

⚠ Black and White ☎ 08/9333-3322. **Swan Taxis** ☎ 13-1330.

TOURS

BOAT TOURS Boat Torque runs excursions to Rottnest Island twice daily from Perth and four times daily from Fremantle; they also have whale-watching September–late November and wine cruises.

For a trip upriver to the famous Swan River wineries, the ferry *Mystique,* another craft in the fleet of Boat Torque, makes daily trips from the Barrack Street Jetty, serving wine coming and going and lunch at one of the wineries.

Captain Cook Cruises has trips on the Swan River, traveling from Perth to the Indian Ocean at Fremantle. Cruises cost A$12–A$60 and may include meals. Oceanic Cruises runs several boat cruises, including tours of the Swan River with stops at wineries. Golden Sun Cruises also has tours upriver to the vineyards, as well as trips to Fremantle.

⚠ Boat Torque ⊠ Barrack St. Ferry Terminal, CBD ☎ 08/9221-5844 or 1300/368686. **Captain Cook Cruises** ☎ 08/9325-3341. **Golden Sun Cruises** ⊠ No. 4, Barrack Sq. Jetty ☎ 08/9325-9916. **Oceanic Cruises** ⊠ Pier 2A, Barrack Sq. Jetty, CBD ☎ 08/9325-1911.

EXCURSIONS West Coach Rail and Coach uses trains and buses in conjunction with local operators to provide tours to popular destinations such as Margaret River, Kalbarri, Albany, and Kalgoorlie.

⚠ West Coach Rail and Coach ☎ 08/9221-9522.

ORIENTATION TOURS Australian Pacific Touring and Feature Tours conduct day tours of Perth and its major attractions.

⚠ Australian Pacific Touring ☎ 1800/675222. **Feature Tours** ☎ 08/9475-2900.

WILDFLOWER
TOUR

Springtime in Western Australia (August–November) is synonymous with wildflowers, as 8,000 species blanket an area that stretches 645 km (400 mi) north and 403 km (250 mi) south of Perth. Tours of these areas, by companies such as Feature Tours, are popular, and early reservations are essential.
🛈 Feature Tours ☎ 08/9475-2900.

TRAINS

Crossing the Nullarbor Plain from the eastern states is one of the great rail journeys of the world. The *Indian Pacific* makes three-day runs from Sydney on Monday and Thursday and two-day runs from Adelaide on Tuesday and Friday.

Fastrack trains run from Perth to Fremantle, Midland, Armadale, Joondalup, and en route stations weekdays 5:30 AM–11:30 PM, with reduced service on weekends and public holidays. Suburban and Bunbury trains depart from the city station on Wellington Street.

The Transperth train systems provide a quick, easy way to get around Perth. The east–west line runs to Midland and Fremantle, while the north line runs to Joondalup, and the southeast line runs to Armadale. Perth to Fremantle takes about 30 minutes. Tickets must be purchased at vending machines before boarding.
🛈 **Western Australian Government Railways** ✉ East Perth Terminal, West Parade, East Perth ☎ 08/9326-2000 or 13-1053 ⊕ www.wagr.wa.gov.au.

VISITOR INFORMATION

🛈 **Western Australia Visitor Centre** ✉ Forrest Pl. and Wellington St., CBD, 6000 ☎1300/ 361351, 61/89483-1111 from outside Australia ⊕ www.westernaustralia.net.

FREMANTLE

Located about 19 km (12 mi) southwest of Perth, Fremantle is the jewel in Western Australia's crown. The major state port since Europeans first settled here in the early 1800s, the town basks in its maritime heritage. This is a city where locals know each other, and everyone smiles and says "hello" as they pass in the street.

Modern Fremantle is a far cry from the barren, sandy plain that greeted the first wave of English settlers back in 1829, at the newly constituted Swan River Colony. Most were city dwellers, and after five months at sea in sailing ships, they landed on salt-marsh flats that sorely tested their fortitude. Living in tents, with packing cases for chairs, they found no edible crops, and the nearest fresh water was a distant 51 km (32 mi)— and a tortuous trip up the salty waters of the Swan. As a result they soon moved the settlement upriver to the vicinity of present-day Perth.

Fremantle remained the location of the seaport, however, and it is to this day Western Australia's premier port. Local architects have brought about a stunning transformation of the town without defacing the colonial streetscape or its fine limestone buildings. In the leafy suburbs, every other house is a restored 19th-century gem.

Like all great port cities, Freo (as the locals call it) is cosmopolitan, with mariners from all parts of the world strolling the streets—including 20,000 U.S. Navy personnel on rest and recreation throughout the year. You'll also find plenty of interesting local (and sometimes eccentric) residents, who find the atmosphere of Freo much more interesting than the coastal suburbs north and south of the city.

Exploring Fremantle

An ideal place to start a leisurely stroll around town is South Terrace, known as the Fremantle cappuccino strip. Soak up the ambience as you wander alongside locals through sidewalk cafés or browse in bookstores, art galleries, and souvenir shops. No matter how aimlessly you meander, you'll invariably end up where you began, along the broad sidewalk of the cappuccino strip.

Between Phillimore Street and Marine Terrace in the West End, you'll find a collection of some of the best-preserved heritage buildings in the state. The Fremantle Railway Station on Elder Place is a good place to start a walk.

What to See

Outside the port gates on the western end of town is **Arthur's Head**, a limestone cliff with cottages built to house employees of the Customs Department. Nearby **J-Shed** contains the workshop of perhaps the nation's foremost exponent of public art, the sculptor Greg James. His extraordinarily lifelike figures grace a number of Perth and metropolitan sites, including King's Square.

Seagulls squawk overhead, boat horns blare in the distance, and the tangy scent of the sea permeates the air along **Marine Terrace,** which skirts the water's edge. At the end of Marine Terrace, you can visit the **Kidogo Arthouse,** a gallery and arts center that specializes in the works of local artists. Or pause for fresh fish-and-chips (a legacy of British immigration) or the ubiquitous hamburger as you watch the tide roll in from the old sea wall. Try dangling your feet from the wooden jetty that was rebuilt on the spot where it stood in the days of tall ships.

Like most of Fremantle, the fine, Gothic Revival **Fremantle Museum and Arts Centre** was built by convicts in the 19th century. First used as a lunatic asylum (the ghosts of one or two demented souls are said to haunt the halls), by 1900 it was overcrowded and nearly shut down. It eventually became a home for elderly women until 1942, when the U.S. Navy made it into their local headquarters. Artifacts trace the early days of Fremantle's settlement in one wing, while another wing houses the **Arts Centre**. The complex contains a restaurant and gift shop, and Sunday afternoon courtyard concerts are a regular feature. ⊠ *Ord and Finnerty Sts.* ☎ *08/9430–7966* 🖾 *Free* ☉ *Sun.–Fri. 10:30–4:30, Sat. 1–5.*

The 1855 former **Fremantle Prison** is one of Western Australia's premier sites where, between 1888 and 1964, 44 inmates met their fate on the prison gallows. Tours include the prison's famous classic-art cell, a superb collection of drawings made by convict James Walsh to decorate his quarters. Reservations are essential for candlelight tours. ⊠ *1 The Terr.* ☎ *08/9336–9200* 🖾 *A$14.30, including tour every 30 min.* ☉ *Daily 10–6; last tour at 5. Candlelight tours Wed. and Fri. at 7:30.*

The **Fremantle Market,** housed in a classic Victorian building, sells everything from potatoes to paintings, incense to antiques, and sausages to Chinese take-out from around 150 stalls. On weekends and public holidays the Market can get super-crowded, but a small café and bar make it a wonderful place to refresh yourself while buskers and street musicians entertain. ⊠ *South Terr. and Henderson St.* ☎ *08/9335–2515* ☉ *Fri. 9–9, Sat. 9–5, Sun. 10–5.*

For a glimpse of local color, wander through **High Street Mall,** in the center of the business district. This pedestrian mall is the haunt of people from all walks of Fremantle life, including retired Italian fishermen whiling away their days in conversation. ⊠ *High, Market, William, and Adelaide Sts.*

One of the oldest commercial heritage-listed structures in Western Australia is **Moores' Building,** an exhibition and performance space run by the Artists' Performance Centre. ⊠ *46 Henry St.* ☎ *08/9335–8366* ⊙ *Exhibitions daily 10–5.*

A landmark of early Fremantle atop the limestone cliff known as Arthur's Head, the **Round House** was built in 1831 by convicts to house other convicts. This curious, 12-sided building is the state's oldest surviving structure. From its ramparts, there are great vistas of High Street out to the Indian Ocean. Underneath, a tunnel was carved through the cliffs in the mid-1800s to give ships lying at anchor offshore easy access from town. ⊠ *West end of High St.* ☎ *08/9336–6897* ⊠ *Free* ⊙ *Daily 10:30–3:30.*

Bounded by High, Queen, and William streets, **King's Square** is at the heart of the central business district. Shaded as it is by the spreading branches of 100-year-old Moreton Bay fig trees, it makes a perfect place for a rest. Medieval-style benches complete the picture of old-world elegance. Bordering the square are **St. John's Anglican Church** and the **town hall.**

� The **Spare Parts Puppet Theatre** stages imaginative productions for children several times a year. Spare Parts has built up an international reputation and regularly tours abroad. The foyer is a showplace for its puppetry. ⊠ *1 Short St., opposite the railway station* ☎ *08/9335–5044* ⊠ *Free* ⊙ *Daily 10–5.*

FodorśChoice   Fremantle's major attraction, the **Western Australian Maritime Museum,**
★   covers three distinct areas: the Maritime Museum, the Submarine Ovens, and the Shipwreck Gallery. Resembling an upside-down boat, the Maritime Museum sits on the edge of Fremantle Harbour, where is houses *Australia 11*—winner of the 1983 America's Cup. Adjacent is the *Submarine Ovens,* a former Royal Australian Navy World War II submarine. The Shipwreck Gallery houses the recovered remains of the *Dutch East Indiaman,* the *Batavia* (wrecked offshore in 1629), and the 1872 *SS Xantho* steamer. Tours of the Ovens take one hour. ⊠ *Victoria Quay* ☎ *08/9335–8921* ⊕ *www.mm.wa.gov.au* ⊠ *Maritime Museum only: A\$10 day pass; Maritime Museum and Ovens: A\$15; Shipwreck Gallery: Free* ⊙ *Daily except Christmas and Good Friday 9:30–5; Submarine Ovens Fri.–Sun. and school holidays.*

Where to Eat

Italian

\$\$ ✕ **Gino's Café** Located at the start of the cappuccino strip and graced with an alfresco dining terrace, Gino's is the hottest property on the block. Lunch and dinner selections include excellent pasta dishes and local seafood specialties. It's always crowded, so reservations are recommended. ⊠ *South Terr. at Collie St.* ☎ *08/9336–1464* ▤ *MC, V.*

\$–\$\$ ✕ **Capri.** You may need to queue, but the traditional complimentary minestrone soup and crusty bread alone are worth the wait at this Fremantle favorite, where the warm welcome makes you feel like part of the family. Enjoy fried calamari with a squeeze of fresh lemon, panfried scallopini in white wine, rich spaghetti Bolognese, and fresh salads. Simple white-linen tablecloths, carafes of chilled water, and the sounds of laughter and clinking glasses round out the experience. ⊠ *21 South Terr.* ☎ *08/9335–1399* ▤ *MC, V.*

Japanese

$–$$ ╳ **Dai's Japanese Restaurant.** Dai, who was master-trained in one of Kyoto's best hotels, hand-catches his own fish every morning, then returns to his restaurant to prepare them. The result is the freshest sushi you are likely to find in the region. It's a rustic place, nothing flashy, but the sushi and sashimi are sheer magic. ✉ *310 South Terr.* ☎ *08/9335–1303* ▭ *AE, DC, MC, V* ☾ *Closed Sun.–Mon. No lunch.*

Seafood

$$$$ ╳ **The Essex.** This 1886 cottage is one of the top places for fine dining in Western Australia. Candles, plush carpets, and antiques convey a sense of tranquillity. Fresh local seafood is the house specialty—try the Cajun-grilled calamari, or the Balmain bugs (mini lobsters) served with seafood ravioli. The extensive wine list includes some of Australia's best vintages. ✉ *20 Essex St.* ☎ *08/9335–5725* ▭ *AE, DC, MC, V.*

$–$$ ╳ **Joe's Fish Shack.** Fremantle's quirkiest restaurant looks like everyone's vision of a run-down, weather-beaten Maine diner. With uninterrupted harbor views, authentic nautical bric-a-brac, and great food, you can't go wrong. Recommendations include the salt-and-pepper squid, stuffed tiger prawns, and the chili mussels. An outdoor dining area provides restaurant food at take-away prices. ✉ *42 Mews Rd.* ☎ *08/9336–7161* ▭ *AE, DC, MC, V.*

¢–$ **Cicerello's.** More than a century of Fremantle history and fishing lies behind the family name, and the Fremantle experience isn't complete without a visit to one of the country's best-known and beloved fish-and-chip shops. Now housed in a boatshed-style building fronting the famous Fishing Boat Harbour, the restaurant serves up the real thing: freshly caught oysters, mussels, crabs, fish, lobsters, and chips. And it's all wrapped up in real butcher's paper—no cardboard boxes or plastic plates here. ✉ *Fishing Boat Harbour* ☎ *08/9335–1911* ▭ *No credit cards.*

Turkish

$ ╳ **Istanbul Cuisine.** This bright, breezy street-front venue serves specialties from the Turkish cities of Samsun, Adana, and Iskendar. A secret of this restaurant's success is the fresh-baked Turkish flat bread that accompanies every meal. Start with one of the traditional dips—hummus, eggplant, or potato—then move on to delicacies like grilled lamb and *burek* (meat- or vegetable-stuffed pastries). Kavuma chicken, a house specialty, is grilled with capsicum and served with tabbouleh and steamed rice. Save room for sweet, sticky baklava. Traditional music and belly dancing take place Friday and Saturday nights. ✉ *19B Essex St.* ☎ *08/9335–6068* ▭ *MC, V* ⏣ *BYOB* ☾ *Closed Mon.*

Where to Stay

★ $$$ ⌂ **Esplanade Hotel.** Part of an original colonial hotel, this establishment has provided seafront accommodation and spectacular ocean views to West Australians for more than a century. The property is geared toward business travelers, and the stylish bright-pastel rooms have work desks and in-room data ports. Studio rooms and complimentary valet parking are also available. Café Panache, right on the Esplanade, draws crowds all day. ⌖ *Marine Terr. and Essex St., Box 1102, 6160* ☎ *08/9432–4000* or *1800/998201* ☏ *08/9430–4539* ⊕ *www.esplanadehotelfremantle.com.au* ⇆ *259 rooms; 7 suites* ⌂ *2 restaurants, café, in-room data ports, 2 pools, dry cleaning, laundry service, business services, meeting rooms, free parking* ▭ *AE, DC, MC, V.*

$ ⌂ **Fothergills of Fremantle.** Antiques and Italian pottery furnish this 1892 two-story limestone terrace house opposite the old Fremantle prison, just a few minutes' walk from the heart of town. Service and food are excellent at this B&B, and although the house is some distance from the waterfront, the balconies afford sweeping views of the harbor. Breakfast in the elegant Provençal-style dining room is included. ⊠ 20–22 Ord St., 6160 ☎ 08/9335–6784 🖶 08/9430–7789 ⊕ www.iinet.net. au/~fotherg ➪ 2 rooms ⚒ Dining room, refrigerators, laundry service, free parking ▤ AE, DC, MC, V ¶O¶ BP.

¢–$ 🏠 **Fremantle Colonial Cottages.** These cottages next to the old Fremantle prison have been restored in colonial style. Each has a kitchen and laundry facilities. ⊠ 215 High St., 6160 ☎ 08/9430–6568 🖶 08/9430–6405 ➪ 3 cottages ⚒ Kitchenettes, laundry facilities, laundry service, free parking ▤ AE, DC, MC, V.

Nightlife

After a hot day there's nothing more pleasant than relaxing at one of the sidewalk tables on the cappuccino strip for a drink and a meal. This area, along South Terrace, opens at 6 AM and closes around 3 AM. **The Dôme** (☎ 08/9336–3040) is a big, airy space, a little frantic at busy periods. **Marconi** (☎ 08/9335–3215) may be small, but it has an attractive alfresco atmosphere. If you're in the mood for fun, try the totally over-the-top **Miss Maud's** (☎ 08/9336–1599). **Old Papas** (☎ 08/9335–4655) is a popular coffee spot right on the street. If you're hungry, try their fine pasta.

Bars

Many great pubs and nightlife venues have sprung up along the boardwalk of Fremantle's Fishing Boat Harbour.

Describing itself as "Friends of the Guinness," **National Hotel** (⊠ 98 High St. ☎ 08/9335–1786) hosts live Irish music on Friday and Sunday.

Rosie O'Grady's (⊠ William St. opposite town hall ☎ 08/9335–1645), once a fine old Australian hotel, is now an Irish pub.

Thanks to its selection of home-brewed beers, the **Sail and Anchor Pub–Brewery** (⊠ 64 South Terr. ☎ 08/9335–8433) is a popular watering hole. A shady courtyard beer garden makes a nice fair-weather gathering place.

Music

The Bog (⊠ 189 High St. ☎ 08/9336–7751) has the atmosphere and entertainment of a traditional Irish pub. The friendly staff are mostly Irish backpackers who entertain patrons with their lively personalities.

The Clink (⊠ 14–16 South Terr. ☎ 08/9336–1919), Fremantle's classiest nightclub, caters to a well-dressed, sophisticated clientele. The Electro Lounge provides some rest from nonstop dancing.

Many local bands and soloists owe their big breaks to **Fly By Night Musicians Club** (⊠ Parry St. ☎ 08/9430–5976), a smoke-free venue.

In the heart of Fremantle's cappuccino strip, **Metropolis Concert Club Fremantle** (⊠ 58 South Terr. ☎ 08/9336–1609), a nonstop techno and funk dance venue, is a great place to be on Saturday night.

Shopping

At **Bannister Street Craftworks** (⊠ 8–12 Bannister St. ☎ 08/9336–2035), a restored 19th-century warehouse, craftspeople have gathered in their own workshops to turn out everything from screen printing to woodwork, handblown glass, leather goods, and souvenirs. The artists, working as a cooperative, invite you to come in and watch as they demonstrate their skills, or just to browse among the exhibits.

Into Camelot (✉ Shop 9, South Terr. Piazza ☏ 08/9335–4698), a medieval-style dress shop, sells romantic wedding gowns and cloaks, street and evening wear, and peasant smocks for all occasions. Period boots, classic Saxon and Celtic jewelry, and masks (feathered and plain) are all available at affordable prices.

Kakulas Sisters (✉ 29–31 Market St. ☏ 08/9430–4445), a unique produce shop, overflows with fragrances and sacks of goodies from across the globe, including Costa Rican coffee beans, Colorado black-eyed beans, Brazilian quince and guava pastries, and Japanese teas.

🍂 A fairy theme pervades **The Pickled Fairy & Other Myths** (✉ Shop 7B, South Terrace Piazza ☏ 08/9430–5827), making it a paradise for children (and the child within). Celtic jewelry is sold along with books on magic and mythology.

Fremantle A to Z

To research prices, get advice from other travelers, and book travel arrangements, visit www.fodors.com.

BUS TRAVEL

Bus information for service from Perth is available from Transperth.
🚌 **Transperth** ☏ 13-6213.

EMERGENCIES

In case of an emergency, dial 000 to reach an ambulance, the police, or the fire department.
🚑 **Fremantle Hospital** ✉ Alma St. ☏ 08/9431-3333.

TOURS

Trams West has five trams and runs several tours, including sightseeing trips along the harbor, a fish-and-chips tour, and a history trail. A tour around Fremantle is a great way to orient yourself and get to know each area of the port city. A tour leaves every hour on the hour from the Fremantle Town Hall 10–4 daily.
🚃 **Trams West** ✉ 39a Malsbury St., Bicton 6157 ☏ 08/9339-8719 ⊕ www.tramswest.com.au.

TRAIN TRAVEL

Trains bound for Fremantle depart from Perth approximately every 20–30 minutes from the Perth Central Station on Wellington Street. All services originate at Perth Railway Station, and you can travel from Perth to Fremantle (or vice versa) in about 30 minutes. Tickets must be purchased prior to travel at the Ticket Vending Machines.
🚆 **Western Australian Government Railways** ☏ 08/9326-2813 or 08/9326-2000 or 13-1053

VISITOR INFORMATION

🛈 Tourist Information **Fremantle Tourist Bureau** ✉ Kings Sq. off William St. ☏ 08/9431-7878 ☏ 08/9431-7755 ⊗ Daily 9–5. **Tourist Information Centre** ✉ Esplanade Park, opposite Esplanade Hotel ☏ 08/9339-8719 ⊗ Daily 7:30–4.

SIDE TRIPS FROM PERTH

Rottnest Island

23 km (14 mi) west of Perth.

A pleasant cruise down the Swan River or across from Fremantle, sunny Rottnest Island makes an ideal day trip from Perth. It's easy to fall in love with the island's bleached beaches, rocky coves, blue-green waters, and particularly its unique wallaby-like inhabitants called quokkas.

The most convenient way to get around Rottnest is by bicycle, as cars are not allowed on the island and bus service is infrequent. A bicycle tour of the island covers 26 km (16 mi) and can take as little as three hours, although you really need an entire day to enjoy the beautiful surroundings. It's impossible to get lost, since the one main road circles the island and will always bring you back to your starting point.

Heading south from Thomson Bay, between Government House and Herschell lakes, you'll encounter a **quokka colony.** Quokkas are marsupials, small wallabies that were mistaken for rats by the first discoverers. In fact, the island's name means "rats' nest" in Dutch. Another colony lies down the road to the east, near the amphitheater at the civic center in sparkling **Geordie Bay.** Here, tame quokkas will come and eat right out of your hand.

Past the quokka colony you'll find **gun emplacements** from World War II. As you continue south to **Bickley Bay,** you can spot the wreckage of ships that came to rest on Rottnest's rocky coastline.

Follow the main road past Porpoise, Salmon, Strickland, and Wilson bays to **West End,** the westernmost point on the island and another graveyard for unfortunate vessels. If you've brought a fishing rod, now is the time to unpack it. As you head back to Thomson Bay, you'll pass a dozen rocky inlets and bays. **Parakeet Bay,** the prettiest, is at the northernmost tip of the island.

At the Thomson Bay settlement, visit the **Rottnest Museum** (⊠ Digby Ave. ☎ 08/9372–9752), which includes memorabilia recalling the island's long and turbulent past. Displays show local geology, natural history, and maritime lore; there's also a convict building and an Aboriginal prison. It's open daily 11–4.

Rent bikes at **Rottnest Bike Hire** (☎ 08/9292–5105), open daily 8:30–5 in the main settlement at Thomson Bay. It's A$20 a day for a double-seater 10-speed mountain bike, A$15 a day for a single-seater. A returnable deposit of A$25 for two people applies.

Where to Stay & Eat

$$ ✕🏠 **The Rottnest Hotel.** The Rottnest Hotel—affectionately known as the Quokka Arms, after the island's small marsupials—affords extraordinary bay views. Once a stately colonial mansion, the hotel was the official summer residence for the governors of Western Australia. Comfortable rooms have TVs, coffeemakers, and private baths. Although there's a popular beer garden, there are also two restaurants: one for fine dining, the other casual. The former, which requires reservations, has a more typical à la carte menu, whereas at the latter, you can barbecue your own steaks or seafood before helping yourself to the salad bar. ⊠ *Main Rd., Thomson Bay* ☎ *08/9292–5011* ✐ *rottnesthotel@axismgt.com.au* 🛏 *18 rooms* ♨ *2 restaurants, pool, bar* 🚭 *AE, MC, V.*

$$ ✕🏠 **Rottnest Island Resort.** The resort has 80 rooms with cable TV and coffeemakers from A$175 per night. When you're not walking around the island, you can take a dip in the pool or reflect on the day in the bar. Seafood is the highlight of the lunches and dinners at the **Marlin Restaurant;** try Thai seafood salad, seafood chowder, and bruschetta with prawns and mango. A buffet lunch is served from 11 to 2, with à la carte offerings 12:30–3 and at night. Reservations are essential. ⊠ *Main Rd.,*

Thomson Bay ☎ *08/9292–5161* ⤳ *80 rooms* ♨ *Restaurant, pool, bar* ⊟ *AE, DC, MC, V.*

York

90 km (56 mi) east of Perth.

Founded in the 1830s, this town stands as an excellent example of historic restoration. It sits in the lovely Avon Valley east of Perth, and its restored main street, Avon Terrace, evokes the days of the 1890s gold rush. The tiny town is easy to explore on foot and contains attractive edifices made of local sandstone. If you plan to spend the night, consider the romantic, colonial-style **Settler's House** (✉ 125 Avon Terr. ☎ 08/9641–1096), where the pleasant, unhurried atmosphere of the 19th century is re-created with antique-furnished sitting rooms and four-poster beds. The rate (A$110) includes a continental breakfast.

The **York Motor Museum** houses more than 100 classic and vintage cars, motorcycles, and even some horse-drawn vehicles. There is an ongoing program to get some of the vehicles back into working order, and motor-coach rides are available. ✉ *Avon Terr.* ☎ *08/9641–1288* 🖅 *A$7.50* 🕑 *Daily 9:30–4.*

New Norcia

129 km (80 mi) north of Perth.

In 1846 a small band of Benedictine monks arrived in Australia to establish a mission for Aborigines. They settled in New Norcia and built boarding schools and orphanages. Eventually, New Norcia became what is still Australia's only monastic town. Today the monks in the community continue to live a life of prayer and work. Their devotion and labor produce the best olive oil in the state, pressed from the fruit of century-old trees. Daily two-hour **guided walking tours** of the town, museum, and art gallery (A$12) start at 11 and 1:30. You can book tours at the museum or art gallery (☎ 08/9654–8056) The **New Norcia Heritage Trail** is a short, self-guided walk highlighting New Norcia's historical and cultural significance and its unique blend of architectural styles. It features the role of Benedictine monks in agriculture, in industry, and in the colony's early development. Suitable for all walkers, the 2 km (1.2 mi) trail, with an optional 1.7 km (1 mi) loop, has an accompanying pamphlet available from the New Norcia Museum and Art Gallery at A$3.

Where to Stay

¢ 🏨 **Monastery Guest House.** Hidden behind the walls of the southern cloister, this small guesthouse offers visitors the opportunity to experience true Benedictine hospitality. The guesthouse can accommodate 22 guests in 7 single rooms with shared facilities for male guests and 8 twin-share rooms with en-suites for females and couples. Quarters are very basic, but comfortable. Although the payment is set by donations, there's a suggested rate of A$45 per person per night for full board. Spiritual direction is available on request. ✉ *New Norcia, 6509* ☎ *08/ 9654–8002* ⤳ *15 rooms* ♨ *Free parking* ⊟ *No credit cards.*

¢ 🏨 **New Norcia Hotel.** Opened in 1927 as a hostel to accommodate parents of the children who were boarding at the town's colleges, the New Norcia Hotel still captures its heritage with high, molded, pressed-metal ceilings and a massive divided central staircase. Rooms have coffeemakers. ✉ *New Norcia, 6509* ☎ *08/9654–8034* 🖷 *08/9654–8011* ⤳ *16 rooms with shared bath; 1 suite* ♨ *Dining room, refrigerators, room TVs, lounge, pub, laundry facilities, free parking* ⊟ *MC, V.*

en route From New Norcia, a scenic back road leads via Mogumber to the Brand Highway, providing access to Nambung National Park.

Nambung National Park

245 km (152 mi) north of Perth.

Nambung National Park, on the Swan coastal plain, is best known for the Pinnacles Desert, in the center of the park. Over the years, wind and drifting sand have sculpted forms that loom as high as 15 ft. These eerie limestone forms, which resemble African anthills, are the fossilized roots of ancient coastal plants fused with sand.

You can walk among the Pinnacles on a 1,650-foot-long trail from the parking area or drive the scenic, one-way, 3-km (2-mi) Pinnacles Desert Loop (not suitable for large RVs or buses). The best time to visit the park is August–October, when the heath blazes with wildflowers. Entrance fees are A$8 per car or A$3 per bus passenger.

Where to Stay

¢ ⊞ **Best Western Cervantes Pinnacles Motel.** This modern, air-conditioned establishment is one of the better choices in this area. The Europa Anchor Restaurant serves seafood dishes, including an extraordinary seafood platter. You can book park tours here through Cervantes Pinnacles Adventure Tours. ⊠ *7 Aragon St., Cervantes, 6511* ☎ *08/ 9652-7145* 📠 *08/9652-7214* ⊕ *www.bestwestern.com.au* 🛏 *40 rooms* ⚭ *Restaurant, pool, laundry facilities, free parking* ▭ *AE, DC, MC, V.*

Batavia Coast

A drive along the Batavia Coast, which starts at Greenhead and runs up to Kalbarri, takes you past white sand and an emerald sea. The drive from Perth can take more than six hours, so if you make the trip, plan to stay overnight.

The little seaside town of **Dongara**, on the coastal road from Jurien to Geraldton, makes for a pleasant stopover. A superb grove of Moreton Bay fig trees shades its main street. If you want to overnight here you can stay at **Priory Lodge** (⊠ 6 St. Dominic's Rd., 6525 ☎📠 08/ 9927–1090), which has inexpensive rooms in a tastefully restored Dominican priory.

At the National Trust–listed **Greenough Historical Hamlet,** you'll find a dozen restored colonial buildings dating from 1858—including a jail with original leg irons and a historic courthouse. The village lies between Dongara and Geraldton. Greenough Trail Guides and self-tour guide booklets are available at the Greenough Hamlet, on entry. ⊠ *Brand Hwy., Greenough* ☎ *08/9926–1660* ⊕ *www.greenough.wa.gov.au* 🎫 *A$4.50* ⊙ *Daily 9–4.*

Grand old architecture and a scenic marine drive make **Geraldton**, 12 km (7 mi) north of Greenough and the fourth-largest city in Western Australia, one of the state's hidden gems. Dominating the skyline is the Byzantine **St. Francis Xavier Cathedral,** open daily, which—along with numerous other sacred and secular buildings in the district—was designed by the gifted priest and architect Monsignor John Hawes. The huge Batavia Coast Marina has a pedestrian plaza, shopping arcades, and the Western Australian Museum.

Side Trips From Perth A to Z

To research prices, get advice from other travelers, and book travel arrangements, visit www.fodors.com.

AIR TRAVEL

Speedy air service to Rottnest Island is available with Rottnest Air Taxi. Round-trip fare is from A$60 per person, and the service operates on demand. Skywest has flights to Geraldton on Tuesdays, Wednesdays, and Thursdays.

Rottnest Air Taxi ☎ 0411/264547. **Skywest** ☎ 08/9478-9999

BOAT & FERRY TRAVEL

Daily ferry services operate from Perth, Fremantle, and Hillary's Boat Harbour with Rottnest Express (Fremantle), Oceanic Cruises (Fremantle and Perth), and Boat Torque Cruises (Fremantle, Perth, and Hillarys). The ferries take approximately 25 minutes from Fremantle, 45 minutes from Hillary's, or an hour-plus from Perth—though the latter trip also includes a scenic cruise on the Swan River. Round-trip prices, including entry to Rottnest, are A$40 per person from Fremantle and A$55 per person from Perth. Timetables and detailed prices are available from the ferry companies.

Boat & Ferry Information **Boat Torque Cruises** ☎ 08/9430-5844 in Fremantle; 08/9246-1039 in Hillary's; 08/9421-5888 in Perth. **Oceanic Cruises** ☎ 08/9430-5127 in Fremantle; 08/9325-1191 in Perth. **Rottnest Express** ☎ 08/9335-6406.

BUS TRAVEL

Western Australian Government Railways provides a daily bus service to Geraldton from Perth. There are also regular services to York, Cervantes, Dongara, and Greenough.

Western Australian Government Railways ✉ East Perth Railway Terminal, West Parade Perth ☎ 131-053 ⊕ www.wagr.wa.gov.au.

CAR TRAVEL

To reach Nambung National Park from Perth, travel north about 193 km (120 mi) on the Brand Highway toward Badgingarra, then turn west toward Cervantes and south into the park.

EMERGENCIES

In case of an emergency, dial 000 to reach an ambulance, the police, or the fire department. The Nursing Post, operated by qualified nurses, is open daily 8:30 to 5.

Rottnest Nursing Post ☎ 08/9292-5030.

TOURS

The Rottnest Island Authority runs a daily two-hour coach tour of the island's highlights, including convict-built cottages, World War II gun emplacements, and salt lakes. The Oliver Hill Railway made its debut in the mid-nineties, utilizing 6 km (4 mi) of reconstructed railway line to reach the island's gun batteries. Information is available from the Rottnest Island Visitor Centre.

The Western Australia Visitor Centre and Cervantes Pinnacles Adventure Tours can arrange tours of Nambung National Park.

Cervantes Pinnacles Adventure Tours ✉ Best Western Cervantes Pinnacles Motel, 7 Aragon St., Cervantes, 6511 ☎ 08/9652-7145. **Rottnest Island Authority** ✉ Thomson Bay ☎ 08/9372-9752. **Western Australia Visitor Centre** ✉ Forrest Pl. and Wellington St., Perth, 6000 ☎ 08/9483-1111.

VISITOR INFORMATION

Cervantes Tourist Information Centre ⊠ Cnr. Aragon and Seville Sts. ☎ 08/9652-7041. **Dongara Denison Tourist Information Centre** ⊠ 9 Waldeck St. Dongara ☎ 08/9927-1404 ⊕ www.lobstercapital.com.au. **Geraldton Visitor Centre** ⊠ Cnr. Chapman Rd. and Bayley St., Geraldton ☎ 08/9921-3999 ⊕ www.geraldtontourist. com.au. **Greenough Hamlet Tourist Information Centre** ⊠ 4 Hull St., Greenough ☎ 08/9926-1084. **Kalbarri Visitor Centre** ⊠ Grey St., Kalbarri ☎ 08/9937-1104 ⊕ www.kalbarriwa.info. **Nambung National Park** ⊠ Ranger's HQ, Bradley Loop, Cervantes ☎ 08/9652-7043. **New Norcia Tourist Information Centre** ⊠ New Norcia Museum and Art Gallery, Great Northern Hwy. ☎ 08/9654-8056. **Rottnest Visitor Information Centre** ⊠ Adjacent to Dome Café, Thompson Bay beachfront ☎ 08/9372-9752. **York Tourist Bureau** ⊠ 81 Avon Terr., York ☎ 08/9641-1301 ⊕ www. yorktouristbureau.com.au.

THE SOUTH WEST

With a balmy Mediterranean climate, world-class wines, and pristine white, sandy beaches, it's easy to see why the South West is Western Australia's most popular visitor destination. But it's not all coastal beauty— inland, rare hardwood forest make excellent hiking terrain. Add in easy access by road or passenger train from Perth and plenty of affordable, comfortable accommodations, and you have an ideal break from the city.

Mandurah

75 km (47 mi) south of Perth.

On the shores of the perfect horseshoe-shape Peel Inlet, this attractive city lends itself to strolls along a scenic boardwalk fronted by fine civic buildings and shaded by mangrove trees. Opposite the boardwalk are several stylish cafés, including Santorini's Fish Café, Cicerello's, and the Choice Café. You can cruise more than 150 square km (60 square mi) of inland waterways, or take in the views along the **Estuary Scenic Drive.** The nearby San Marco and Mandurah Quays (Keys) are prototypes for the laid-back Western Australia lifestyle. See ⊕ www.peeltour.net.au for information about Mandurah and surrounds.

Where to Stay

$ 🏨 **Atrium Hotel.** Overlooking the ornamental lake that adjoins Peel Inlet, this hotel is a restful retreat built around a palm tree-lined indoor swimming pool. Bland rooms in neutral colors have basic but comfortable modern furnishings. ⊠ *65 Ormsby Terr., 6210* ☎ *08/9535-6633* 🖷 *08/9581-4151* ⊕ *www.the-atrium.com.au* 🛏 *116 rooms* 🍴 *Restaurant, kitchenettes (some), tennis court, 2 pools, wading pool, sauna, spa, bar, lobby lounge, laundry facilities, convention center, free parking* ▭ *AE, DC, MC, V.*

Bunbury

184 km (114 mi) south of Perth, 109 km (68 mi) south of Mandurah.

Bunbury is the major seaport of the South West, with a spectacular mangrove boardwalk along the Leschenault Inlet. With its own cappuccino strip and entertainment precinct, the town is surprisingly sophisticated. Around 90 bottle-nosed dolphins regularly visit the excellent **Dolphin Discovery Centre** on Koombana Bay. Their favorite time is 8 to noon (mainly October–April), and you're encouraged to enter the water with them. Admission includes the Interpretive Centre and Interaction Beach. Swim tours are available December through April for A$99 per person. ⊠ *Koombana Dr.* ☎ *08/9791-3088* ⊕ *www.dolphindiscovery.com.au* 🎫 *A$2* ☉ *June–Aug., daily 9–3; Sept.–May, daily 8–5.*

Where to Stay & Eat

¢–$ ╳▥ **Clifton Best Western.** With 42 tourism and restaurant awards since
FodorsChoice 1990, this small hotel is the most awarded lodging in the region. In ad-
★ dition to the typical motel-style rooms, you can upgrade to one of four
tastefully appointed suites furnished with antiques in the adjacent 1885
Grittleton Lodge. Louisa's, regarded as one of the best country restaurants in Western Australia, serves casual, brasserie-style fare paired
with a strong local wine list. Excellent entrées include Thai snapper and
lobster curry with coconut rice. ⊠ *15 Clifton St., 6230* ☎ *08/9721–4300
hotel, 08/9721–9959 Louisa's Restaurant* ⊕ *www.theclifton.com.au*
↪ *48 rooms, 4 suites* ♨ *Restaurant, pool, hot tub, sauna, laundry facilities, free parking* ▭ *AE, DC, MC, V.*

$ ▥ **Lord Forrest Hotel.** Conveniently located in the center of town, the hotel
is within walking distance of the cappuccino strip, cinemas, shops, and
restaurants. Greenery dangles down from garden beds lining the walkway around the eight-story atrium, where sunlight streams through
clerestory windows. Rooms are pleasantly furnished and decorated in
pastels; upper floors have city views. ⊠ *20 Symmons St., 6230* ☎ *1800/
097811* ⊕ *www.lordforresthotel.com.au* ↪ *102 rooms, 13 suites* ♨ *2
restaurants, indoor pool, sauna, spa, 2 bars, nightclub, free parking* ▭ *AE,
DC, MC, V.*

Nightlife

Fitzgerald's (⊠ 22 Victoria St. ☎ 08/9791–2371) is Bunbury's authentic Irish Bar, located in the historic Customs House Bond Store.

For late-night action, check out the extraordinary purple-painted **Reef
Hotel** (⊠ 12 Victoria St. ☎ 08/9791–6677), marked by a giant ele-
phant's head.

off the
beaten
path

Inland 20 km (12 mi) from Bunbury is the village of **Dardanup,** a
gathering of one general store, one pub, and one gas station.
However, you can take a heritage walk to see its interesting 19th-
century buildings. The town is the entry point to the **Ferguson
Valley,** which you'll find by taking the winding Ferguson Valley Road
that heads up into the Darling Scarp. Here you'll discover tiny
wineries, art and craft galleries, and farm-stay lodgings. Come April
to November, when the pastures are green from seasonal rains.
Wineries open for tasting include **Willow Bridge** (⊠ Gardincourt Dr.
☎ 08/9728–0055), open daily 11 to 5. Another winery is **Ferguson
Falls** (⊠ Pile Rd. ☎ 08/9728–1083), open weekends 10 to 5. You'll
find more information at ⊕ www.dardanup.wa.gov.au.

en route

From Bunbury to Busselton, take the scenic route through the only
natural **tuart forest** in the world. These magnificent tuart trees, a
type of eucalypt or gum tree that thrives in arid conditions, have been
standing on this land for 400 years.

Busselton

53 km (33 mi) south of Bunbury.

Seaside Busselton, a popular weekend getaway spot with good dining
and lodging, was settled by the Bussell family in 1834, and it is among
the state's oldest towns. The small **Old Butter Factory** museum records
Busselton's history and that of the South West dairy industry's early years.
⊠ *Peel Terr.* ☎ 08/9754–2166 ▱ A$4 ⊙ *Wed.–Mon. 2–5.*

FodorsChoice At the 1.9-km (1.2-mi) **Busselton Jetty,** the longest timber jetty in the South-
★ ern Hemisphere, an hourly train takes you almost to the end. Close to

the end of the jetty is the **Busselton Underwater Observatory,** which takes you beneath the waves to see more than 300 coral species growing here. Train departures are on the hour, weather permitting. The site is closed on Christmas. ⊠ *Main Beachfront, Busselton* ☎ *08/9754–3689* ⊕ *www. downsouth.com.au* ⊠ *Jetty: A$2.50; train A$7.50; interpretive center: free; underwater observatory: call for prices* ⊗ *Jetty: Daily 24 hours; train: Dec.–April, daily 9–5, May–Nov. daily 10–4; interpretive center Dec.–April daily 8–6, May–Nov. daily 9–5.*

Where to Stay

$ ▦ **Abbey Beach Resort.** The biggest resort outside Perth is on the beachfront 8 km (5 mi) west of Busselton. Its U-shape houses an impressive lobby, restaurant, and bar, as well as two sizeable outdoor pools and a heated indoor pool. ⊠ *595 Bussell Hwy., 6280* ☎ *08/9755–4600* ☎ *08/ 9755–4610* ⊕ *www.abbeybeach.com.au* ⤳ *213 apartments, studios and rooms. Apartments have kitchen facilities and sleep up to 8.* ⚭ *Restaurant, café, tennis courts, 2 pools, indoor pool, gym, sauna, hot tub, squash, bicycles, 2 bars, free parking* ⊟ *AE, DC, MC, V.*

$ ▦ **Geographe Bayview Resort.** The bright, cheerful rooms at this stylish resort 6 km (4 mi) west of Busselton are set in 28 acres of beautiful gardens just a two-minute walk from the beach. Self-contained villas that sleep eight are also available. On-site dining includes Spinnakers Café and the more elegant Tuart Restaurant. ⊠ *Bussell Hwy., 6280* ☎ *08/ 9755–4166 or 08/9755–4075* ⊕ *www.geographebayview.com.au* ⤳ *27 rooms, 70 villas* ⚭ *Restaurant, café, picnic area, refrigerators, putting green, tennis court, 2 pools, beach, windsurfing, free parking* ⊟ *AE, DC, MC, V.*

¢ ▦ **Prospect Villa.** Laura Ashley fabrics decorate the rooms, and Victorian bric-a-brac provides an atmospheric backdrop for this comfortable 1850s B&B. The two-story house stands 100 yards or so from town but a half-mile from the Geographe Bay beaches. ⊠ *1 Pries Ave., 6280* ☎ *08/ 9752–1509, 08/9752–2273 after 7 PM* ⤳ *4 rooms* ⚭ *Dining room, laundry service, free parking* ⊟ *AE, MC, V* ⦿ *CP.*

Dunsborough

21 km (13 mi) west of Busselton.

An attractive seaside town, Dunsborough is perfect for a few days of swimming, sunning, and fishing, and it's close to the wineries of Margaret River. Along with Eagle Bay and Yallingup, this booming holiday resort is popular with families from Perth. Offshore, you can dive on the wreck of the **HMAS Swan,** the former Royal Australian Navy ship deliberately sunk in Geographe Bay at the end of its useful life. Meelup Beach is a pretty cove with protected waters ideal for safe swimming. September through December you can take a cruise to see migrating humpback and southern right whales.

Where to Stay & Eat

$–$$$ ✕ **Wise Vineyard Restaurant.** Verdant bushland and a carefully manicured vineyard surround Heath Townsend's restaurant at the Wise winery. Simple ingredients are transformed into culinary delights, such as a risotto of green peas, mint, and chorizo, or smoked salmon with an herb pancake and avocado salad. Views of Eagle Bay complete the dining experience. Six homey cottages are available for accommodation. ⊠ *Meelup Rd., Dunsborough* ☎ *08/9755–3331* ⊟ *AE, DC, MC, V* ⊗ *No dinner Mon.–Thurs.*

$–$$ ▦ **Broadwater Sanctuary Resort.** Sunny public areas and extensive sports facilities make this the accommodation of choice on the Southwest beach strip. Romantic king rooms, done in pastel colors, have deluxe facilities, while the two- and three-bedroom apartments have a lounge, dining room, and kitchen. Many rooms have superb ocean views. The casual, airy restaurant serves fusion cuisine using fresh local produce, cheeses, and olive oils. A selection of Margaret River wines is on hand to complement the meal. ⊠ *Caves Rd., Marybrook, 6281* ☎ *08/9756–9777* 🖷 *08/9756–8788* ⊕ *www.broadwaters.com.au* ⌔ *50 rooms, 50 apartments* ⚖ *Restaurant, café, picnic area, room service, putting green, 2 tennis courts, pool, gym, spa, beach, volleyball, bar, playground, concierge, business services, meeting rooms, travel services, free parking* ⊟ *AE, DC, MC, V.*

Cape Leeuwin–Naturaliste National Park

Fodor'sChoice *The northernmost part of the park is 266 km (165 mi) south of Perth,*
★ *25 km (16 mi) northwest of Dunsborough.*

This 150-km (93-mi) stretch of coastline on the southwest tip of the continent is one of Australia's most fascinating areas. The limestone Leeuwin–Naturaliste Ridge directly below the park contains more than 360 known caves. Evidence dates both human and animal habitation here to more than 40,000 years ago.

At the northern end of the park stands **Cape Naturaliste Lighthouse,** open daily 9:30–5. A 1½-km- (1-mi-) long trail leads from Cape Naturaliste to Canal Rocks, passing rugged cliffs, quiet bays, and curving beaches. This is also the start of the 120-km (75-mi) Cape to Cape Walk.

The coastal scenery changes drastically from north to south: rocks at some points, calm sandy beaches at others, all interspersed with heathlands, eucalyptus forests, and swamps. It would take days to explore all the intricacies of this park.

Four major cave systems are easily accessible: **Jewel** (☎ 08/9757–7411), open daily 9:30–3:30; **Lake** (☎ 08/9757–7411), open daily 9–5; **Mammoth** (☎ 08/9757–7411), open daily 8:30–4:30; and **Ngilgi** (☎ 08/9755–2152), near Yallingup, open daily 9:30–3:30. Admission is A$9–A$12 per cave and includes a guided tour. The **CaveWorks** (☎ 08/9757–7411) display center at Lake Cave presents a good introduction to the whole cave system.

The view from the top of the lighthouse at **Cape Leeuwin** allows you to witness the meeting of the Southern and the Indian oceans. In some places, this alliance results in giant swells that crash against the rocks. In others, small coves are blessed with calm waters ideal for swimming.

Where to Stay

If you don't plan to camp, consider staying at Dunsborough or Margaret River. Campgrounds with toilets, showers, and an information center are located north in Injidup. Campsites (including firewood) cost A$9 per adult per night, A$2 per child. Facilities include toilets and barbecue facilities. For more information on camping in WA, visit ⊕ www.calm.wa.gov.au/tourism/camping.html.

Margaret River

★ *181 km (112 mi) south of Perth, 38 km (24 mi) south of Cape Naturaliste.*

The town of Margaret River is thought of as the center of the South West's wine region, though vineyards and wineries stretch from well north of

Bunbury to the south coast. Nevertheless, close to Margaret River are some 80 wineries offering tastings and sales of some of the best wines in the world, as the area produces about 25% of Australia's fine wines. The **Margaret River Visitor Center** (⊠ Bussell Hwy. ☎ 08/9757–2911), open daily 9–5, can provide a brochure with details on individual cellars. Also, each November, the World Masters Surf Circuit championships take place at Surfers Point, just 8 km (5 mi) outside of Margaret River.

Cape Mentelle (⊠ Wallcliffe Rd. ☎ 08/9757–3266) was one of the first and is still one of the most notable wineries in the area. The rammed-earth winery and tasting rooms, so typical of the buildings in the Margaret River district, are as handsome and memorable as the wine. Wine maker Vanya Cullen produces one of Australia's best chardonnays and an outstanding cabernet merlot at **Cullen Wines** (⊠ Caves Rd., Willyabrup ☎ 08/9755–5277), a family-run business. **Leeuwin Estate** (⊠ Stevens Rd. ☎ 08/9757–6253), one of the area's leading wineries, has tastings, guided tours (A$6.60), and a restaurant with daily lunch and Saturday dinner. Tours run three times daily, at 11, 12, and 3. Thousands flock to the estate's concerts in February to hear international superstars— Michael Crawford, Dame Kiri Te Kanawa, George Benson, Tom Jones, Diana Ross—perform under the stars against a backdrop of flood-lit karri trees. **Vasse Felix** (⊠ Harmans Rd. S, Cowaramup ☎ 08/9755–5242) has an excellent upstairs restaurant and a basement cellar within picturesque grounds.

Eagle's Heritage, set in a natural bush environment, has the largest collection of birds of prey in Australia. It is also a rehabilitation center for sick and injured birds of prey. The ancient art of falconry is shown in the free-flight display, with tours at 11 and 1:30. ⊠ *Boodjidup Rd.* ☎ *08/ 9757–2960* ⊡ *A$7* ☉ *Daily 10–5.*

Where to Stay & Eat

★ **$$–$$$** ✕ **Flutes Café.** The pastoral setting here—over the dammed waters of the Willyabrup Brook and encircled by olive groves in the midst of the Brookland Valley Vineyard—is almost as compelling as the food. The modern Australian cooking makes use of prime local produce. Margaret River venison, Capel marron (freshwater crayfish), and water buffalo are all excellent, prepared simply yet with flair. ⊠ *Caves Rd., Willyabrup* ☎ *08/9755–6250* ⚬ *Reservations essential* ☰ *AE, DC, MC, V.*

$$–$$$ ✕ **Vat 107.** The setting is open and airy, the service friendly, and the food highly pleasing at Vat 107. "Bio-dynamic" and organic products star in offerings that include Malaysian-style *laksa lemak* (spicy, coconut-based curry with tiger prawns, tofu, hokkien noodles, and coriander), and seared sea scallops with asparagus, Cloverdene pecorino, and Parmesan oil. There are also plenty of vegetarian choices. Luxury studio apartments are upstairs if you want to stay. ⊠ *107 Bussell Hwy.* ☎ *08/9758–8877* ☰ *AE, DC, MC, V* ☉ *Closed Mon.*

$$ ✕ **Lamont's.** A lovely lake-side setting fronts this fine, well-known restaurant. The seasonal menu, which reflects fresh local produce, highlights the signature dish of local marron (a freshwater crustacean of exceptional flavor)—served grilled with fresh tomato and basil, or poached with a lime and chive buerre blanc. ⊠ *Gunyulgup Valley Dr., Yallingup* ☎ *08/9755–2434* ⊕ *www.lamonts.com.au* ☰ *AE, DC, MC, V* ☉ *No dinner Sun.–Thurs.*

★ **$–$$** ✕ **Valley Café.** Relax and take in the superb valley views at this out-of-the-way, colorful café. Try the lime chicken with Kashmiri spices, or the crispy squid. *Laksa* (Malaysian coconut-milk curry) is also popular.

✉ *Carters Rd. at Caves Rd.* ☎ *08/9757–3225* ▭ *AE, DC, MC, V*
🕙 *No dinner Mon.–Tues.*

$$$ 🏨 **Cape Lodge.** The Cape Dutch architecture perfectly suits this elegant
Fodor'sChoice lodge set in the midst of Margaret River wine country. Accommodations,
★ set in four different buildings, are in opulent, comfortable suites, some
with their own balcony or terrace overlooking a private lake. The Con-
servatory Restaurant uses fresh local produce to create an ever-chang-
ing menu that is complemented by an impressive selection of local
wines. The sumptuous, free gourmet breakfast can be served in your suite
or in the sunny conservatory. ✉ *Caves Rd., Yallingup, 6282* ☎ *08/
9755–6311* 🖷 *08/9755–6322* ⊕ *www.capelodge.com.au* 🛏 *18 suites*
⚓ *Restaurant, room service, tennis court, pool, free parking; no kids
under 15* ▭ *AE, DC, MC, V* ⦿ *CP.*

$$–$$$ 🏨 **Gilgara Homestead.** This stunning property, a replica of an 1870 sta-
tion homestead, sits amid 23 gently rolling, bucolic acres. Antiques and
lace furnish the romantic rooms, so it's no surprise that honeymooners
frequently choose to stay here. A rose-covered veranda, open fireplaces,
and a cozy lounge add to the charm. You might breakfast surrounded
by spectacular blue wrens and sacred ibises, or catch a few kangaroos
lounging near the front door. Rates include a Mediterranean-style break-
fast. ✉ *Caves Rd., 6285* ☎ *08/9757–2705* 🖷 *08/9757–3259* ⊕ *www.
gilgara.com.au* 🛏 *6 rooms* ⚓ *Horseback riding; no kids under 15*
▭ *AE, DC, MC, V* ⦿ *BP.*

$$–$$$ 🏨 **Heritage Trail Lodge.** Nestled among the trees, this luxury retreat is
located only about ½-km (¼-mi) from Margaret River township. Spa-
cious suites have a spa bath, a king-size bed, and a private balcony over-
looking the forest. Walk the trails early, then enjoy a complimentary
gourmet continental breakfast of local produce in the conservatory.
✉ *31 Bussell Hwy., 6285* ☎ *08/9757–9595* 🖷 *08/9757–9596* ⊕ *www.
heritage-trail-lodge.com.au* 🛏 *10 suites* ⚓ *Dining room, hiking, free
parking* ▭ *AE, DC, MC, V* ⦿ *CP.*

$$ 🏨 **Basildene Manor.** Each of the guest rooms and the breakfast room have
been lovingly refurbished in this circa 1912 house built by a former light-
house keeper. Rich lilac, gold, and red colors decorate the rooms. This
grand, two-story house, on the outskirts of Margaret River, has long
been regarded as one of the region's finest inns. ✉ *Wallcliffe Rd., 6285*
☎ *08/9757–3140* 🖷 *08/9757–3383* 🛏 *17 rooms* ⚓ *Dining room, library, free parking* ▭ *AE, DC, MC, V* ⦿ *BP.*

Nannup

*100 km (62 mi) east of Margaret River, 71 km (44 mi) southeast of Bus-
selton.*

Quaint timber cottages and several historic buildings characterize this
small, lovely town. Several scenic drives wind through the area, including the Blackwood River Tourist Drive, a 10-km (6-mi) ride along
the river, surrounded by hills with karri and jarrah forests. You can also
canoe on the Blackwood River and wander through the Blythe Gardens.

Where to Stay

$ 🏨 **Holberry House.** A charming colonial building with exposed beams,
stone fireplaces, and an elegant lounge sits amid timbered acres overlooking the Blackwood Valley. Tennis, golf, canoeing, and hiking are
all nearby. Rates include a continental buffet breakfast, and light evening
meals are available. ✉ *Grange Rd., 6275* ☎ *08/9756–1276* 🖷 *08/
9756–1394* ⊕ *www.holberryhouse.com* 🛏 *7 rooms* ⚓ *Restaurant,
pool, free parking; no kids under 10, no smoking* ▭ *MC, V* ⦿ *BP.*

An alternative route from Nannup to Albany is along the Brockman Highway and then the South Western Highway. The road follows the picturesque Blackwood River valley through tall karri forests and rolling hillscapes to **Bridgetown,** where the international Bridgetown Blues Festival takes place in mid-November. The **Bridgetown Information Centre** (☎ 1800/777140 ⊕ www.blackwood.com.au) can provide details on local accommodations and events.

Pemberton

280 km (150 mi) southeast of Perth.

Pemberton is the heartland of the magnificent karri forest of Western Australia. These timber giants—said to be the third tallest tree in the world behind mountain ash and Californian redwood—grow in their natural state only in this southern region of Western Australia.

Pemberton was settled in 1913, and has relied on harvesting the karri trees since. Take a walk through pristine forest in national parks, such as **Warren National Park** where you can climb the **Dave Evans Bicentennial Tree.** Just outside Pemberton is **Gloucester Tree,** which also allows you to climb to the top 200 feet (60 meters) above the ground. These tall trees are still used during the summer as platforms to watch for and report bushfires.

Pemberton also has numerous artisans working in woods from the region. A must-see experience, **Fine Woodcraft Gallery** offers some outstanding examples of wood as art, as well as more practical pieces such as fine furniture. ⊠ *Dickinson St.* ☎ *08/9776–1399* ⊙ *Daily 9–5.*

Where to Stay

There's plenty of lodging in Pemberton and surrounding forest and farmland areas. Much is self-contained chalets and cottages; however, there are also motels, bed and breakfasts, and farm-stays.

$$ 🏨 **Karri Valley Resort.** Built on the edge of a huge man-made lake, the resort has 32 rooms in a two-story timber building, as well as 10 two- and three-bedroom villas scattered through the forest upslope from the lake. The resort is about 20 minutes drive from Pemberton close to **Beedelup National Park,** with 400-year-old karri trees. ⊠ *Vasse Hwy., 6260* ☎ *1800/245757 or 08/9776–2020* ⊕ *www.karrivalleyresort.com. au* ⇨ *32 rooms, 10 chalets* ⚭ *Restaurant, miniature golf, boating, shop, laundry, free parking* ☐ *AE, DC, MC, V.*

Denmark

197 km (122 mi) southeast of Pemberton, 219 km (136 mi) southeast of Nannup.

Denmark is a quaint old town nestling on a river—"where forest meets the sea" as the town motto goes. It's an ideal place to pause for a day or two to enjoy such sights as the historic butter factory or the artists' studios tucked away on hillside farms.

Have a picnic alongside the river, or follow its course to the sparkling white beaches and clear waters of Wilson's Inlet, where the swimming is superb. The **Old Butter Factory** sells the work of local craftspeople and artists as well as antiques and collectibles from the Languedoc region of southern France. Adjoining is the popular Mary Rose Restaurant. ⊠ *11 North St.* ☎ *08/9848–2525* ⊙ *Mon.–Sat. 10–4:30, Sun. 11–4:30.*

Where to Stay

$$ ⊞ **Chimes at Karri Mia.** This secluded 60-acre property is the only luxury guesthouse in the region. Deep sage and cream décor, cedar blinds, and a mix of modern furniture and intricately carved Indonesian antiques garnish the suites. King-size beds, whirlpool tubs, and views of the ocean add to the comfort and beauty. The Observatory restaurant serves local venison and vegetarian entrées and has a walk-in wine cellar with outstanding regional wines. ⊠ *Mt. Shadforth Rd., 6333* ☎ *08/9848–2255* 🖷 *08/9848–2277* ⊕ *www.chimes-at-karrimia.com.au* ➡ *10 suites* ♿ *Restaurant, minibars, in-room VCRs, massage, hiking, laundry service, free parking; no kids under 14* ⊟ *AE, DC, MC, V* ⧖ *BP.*

¢ ⊞ **Rannoch West Holiday Farm.** A classic 1945 farm-stay owned and operated by George and Dorothy Brenton, Rannoch West tends livestock close to the famed Valley of the Giants forest. Natural attractions abound in the area, as do wineries. You can lodge in the homestead on a B&B basis (with dinner available on request), or stay in one of two self-catering pioneer cottages. One has three bedrooms and one has five bedrooms, but each sleeps up to 10. ⊠ *South Coast Hwy., 6333* ☎ *08/9840–8032* ➡ *3 rooms, 2 with bath; 2 cottages* ♿ *Kitchenettes (some), refrigerators, horseback riding, free parking* ⊟ *No credit cards.*

Albany

410 km (254 mi) southeast of Perth via Rte. 30, 55 km (34 mi) east of Denmark, 377 km (234 mi) east of Margaret River.

Lying on the southernmost tip of Western Australia's rugged coastline, this sophisticated port city is a surprising find. The earliest settlement in Western Australia, it was founded in 1826 as a penal outpost—three years earlier than northern Swan River, which later became Perth. Originally named Frederickstown after Frederick, Duke of York and Albany, the town was in 1831 renamed Albany by Governor James Stirling. Its 1840s whaling fleet turned it into a boomtown, and though the whaling heyday ended in 1978, the town's heritage is still very much evident. Solid stone buildings, clustered around the beautiful waterways of Princess Royal Harbour, spread out around King George Sound.

To Albany's fine harbor, whalers brought in huge numbers of sperm whales every season—the greatest number being 1,174, in 1975—until the practice was stopped in 1978. Today, whales are found in King George Sound between May and October. The old whaling station has been converted to the **Whaleworld** museum, which has memorable displays of cetaceans (whales and dolphins) and pinnipeds (seals and sea lions), as well as the restored whaling brig *Cheyne IV*. The museum lies 20 km (12½ mi) from Albany along the shores of Frenchman's Bay. ⊠ *Cheynes Beach* ☎ *08/9844–4021* ⊕ *www.whaleworld.org* 🎟 *A$13* ◷ *Daily 9–4:30, ½-hr tours on the hr 10–4.*

Built in 1851, **The Old Gaol** on Stirling Terrace served as the district jail from 1872 until it was closed in the 1930s. Restored by the Albany Historical Society in 1968, it now contains a collection of social and historical artifacts. A ticket also grants you access to **Patrick Taylor Cottage,** a wattle-and-daub (twig-and-mud) dwelling built on Duke Street in 1832 and believed to be the oldest in the district. It contains more than 2,000 items, including period costumes, old clocks, silverware, and kitchenware. ⊠ *Stirling Terr.* ☎ *08/9841–1401* 🎟 *A$4* ◷ *Daily 10–4.*

The 1850 Residency building once accommodated government officials and later became offices. Since 1985 it has housed the **Western Australian Museum Albany,** one of the finest small museums in Australia and a focal point for both the social and natural history of the Albany region. Exhibits explore the local Noongar Aboriginal peoples, as well as local geology, flora, and fauna. Also worth visiting are the adjoining saddlery and artisans' gallery. The lovely sandstone building affords sweeping views of the harbor. ⊠ *Residency Rd.* ☎ *08/9841–4844* 🖃 *Donations accepted* ☉ *Daily 10–5.*

⟳ Adjacent to the Residency Museum is a faithful replica of the brig **Amity,** on which Albany's original settlers arrived. Local artisans used timber from the surrounding forest to build the replica. If you board the ship, climb below deck and try to imagine how 45 men, plus livestock, could fit into such a small craft. ⊠ *Port Rd.* ☎ *08/9841–6885* 🖃 *Free* ☉ *Daily 9–5.*

Created for snorkelers and divers, the **Albany Artificial Reef** is set on the former Royal Australian Navy ship *HMAS Perth.* Most of the original ship is intact, including the mast, forward gun, both funnels, and the main radar dishes. It was scuttled in 100 feet of water in King George Sound, close to Whale World Museum. ⊠ *Frenchman's Bay Rd.* ☎ *08/9841–9333* 🖃 *A$7.50* ☉ *Daily, daylight hours.*

The 963-km (597-mi) **Bibbulmun Walking Trail** (☎ 08/9481–0551) meanders through scenic forest country all the way from Perth to Albany, the southern trailhead. The motif of the rainbow serpent *Waugal* marks the trail.

The **coastline** around Albany is spectacular. Be sure to spend some time in the peninsular **Torndirrup National Park. Porongurup National Park,** about 39 km (24 mi) north of Albany, has ancient granite formations.

Where to Stay & Eat

$$–$$$ ✕ **Genevieve's.** The restaurant takes its name from a veteran English motorcar made famous by a witty British movie of 1953. Delicious bistro-style breakfasts and à la carte dining are created from local produce—the seafood is caught daily in King George Sound. Among other entrées, the Thai chili squid and the crispy Mount Barker duck are superb. ⊠ *Esplanade Hotel, the Esplanade, Middleton Beach* ☎ *08/9842–1711* 🖃 *AE, DC, MC, V* ☉ *No lunch.*

$$–$$$ ✕ **Kooka's.** Kookaburras of every description frequent this timeless colonial cottage—on lamp shades, trays, saltshakers, teapots, and ornaments. The Australian menu changes every two to three months. Highlights might include fillet of steak stuffed with blue Castello cheese or Moroccan-spiced quail. ⊠ *204 Stirling Terr.* ☎ *08/9841–5889* 🖃 *AE, DC, MC, V* 🍽 *BYOB* ☉ *Closed Sun.–Mon. No lunch Sat.*

$$ ✕ **Gosyu-Ya.** When Perth restaurateur Jun Fujiki, proprietor of no fewer than five popular Japanese restaurants, wanted a change of pace, Albany seemed a logical choice. The town's first Japanese restaurant has quickly become one of its most popular eating venues. Specialties include grilled fish, Japanese steaks, and *amimoto-no-sara* (seafood platter). ⊠ *1 Mermaid Ave., Emu Point* ☎ *08/9844–1111* 🖃 *AE, DC, MC, V* ☉ *Closed Sun.–Mon. No lunch.*

$–$$ ✕ **Shamrock Café.** This Irish-theme café has become one of the most popular such establishments in the state. The walls positively groan with Irish memorabilia. Specialties include soda bread, potato bread, and huge Irish breakfasts for just A$7. ⊠ *184 York St.* ☎ *08/9841–4201* 🖃 *Reservations not accepted* 🖃 *MC, V.*

★ $$–$$$ 🏨 **Esplanade Hotel.** The elegant, colonial-style hotel is renowned for its high-quality accommodations and views over Middleton Beach. The rooms are decorated in subdued tones, with timber and cane furniture in keeping with the colonial-style public areas. In winter there are open wood fires blazing in the bars and restaurant. ⊠ *Cnr. Adelaide and*

Flinders, 6330 ☎ *1800/678757 or 08/9842–1711* 🖷 *08/9841–7527*
🌐 *www.albanyesplanade.com.au* 🖵 *40 rooms, 8 suites* ⚭ *Restaurant,
tennis court, pool, health club, sauna, 2 bars, library, laundry facilities,
free parking* ⊟ *AE, DC, MC, V.*

★ $$ 🏨 **Balneaire Seaside Resort.** This luxury accommodation brings a bit of
the south of France to the south of the state, just a short stroll from a
prime stretch of Middleton Beach. Two- and three-bedroom, villa-style
apartments overlook lush gardens and a central courtyard designed to
resemble a Provençal village square. Soft aquas, blues, and yellows dec-
orate each fully equipped villa. ✉ *27 Adelaide Crescent, Middleton Beach,
6330* ☎ *08/9842–2877* 🖷 *08/9842–2899* 🌐 *www.balneaire.com.au*
🖵 *28 apartments* ⚭ *Café, kitchens, beach, playground, laundry facil-
ities, free parking* ⊟ *AE, DC, MC, V.*

The Arts

Once the seat of local government, the **Albany Town Hall Theatre** now
administers to the town's artistic needs as a performing-arts venue. The
box office is open weekdays 10–4:30. ✉ *York St.* ☎ *08/9841–1661.*

Sports & the Outdoors

GOLF The 18-hole, par-79 **Grove Park Golf Course** (☎ 08/9844–4277) is about
10 km (6 mi) outside of Albany. Clubs, bags, and caddies can be hired.
The cost is A$8 for 9 holes, A$13 for 18 holes.

PLAYGROUND **Middleton Beach Park** has a playground at either end, one for 8- to 12-
year-olds and one for toddlers to 7-year-olds. The park sits just across
the road from the popular Beachside Café restaurant.

Stirling Range National Park

403 km (250 mi) south of Perth, 71 km (44 mi) north of Albany.

During the height of the wildflower season (September and October),
the Stirling Ranges, north of Albany, rival any botanical park in the world.
Rising from the flat countryside, the ranges fill the horizon with a kalei-
doscope of color. More than 1,000 wildflower species have been iden-
tified, including 69 species of orchid. This profusion of flowers attracts
equal numbers of insects, reptiles, and birds, as well as a host of noc-
turnal honey possums. Emus and kangaroos are frequent visitors as well.

The Stirlings, together with the ranges of the adjacent Porongurup Na-
tional Park, are considered the only true mountain range in southwest
Australia. They were formed by the uplifting and buckling of sediments
laid down by a now-dry ancient sea. An extensive road system, includ-
ing the super-scenic Stirling Range Drive, makes travel from peak to peak
easy. Treks begin at designated parking areas. Don't be fooled by ap-
parently short distances—a 3-km (2-mi) walk up 3,541-foot Bluff Knoll
takes about three hours round-trip. Take plenty of water and wet-
weather gear—the park's location near the south coast makes Stirling
subject to sudden storms. Before attempting longer hikes, register your
intended routes in the ranger's log book, and log out upon return.
✉ *Stirling Range Dr., Amelup via Borden* ☎ *08/9827–9230.*

Where to Stay & Eat

Albany is close enough to serve as a good base for exploring the park.

The **Bluff Knoll Café** (✉ Chester Pass Rd., Borden ☎ 08/9827–9293), op-
posite the Stirling Range Retreat, has a liquor license and is open every
day except Christmas. **The Lily** (✉ Chester Pass Rd., Amelup ☎ 08/
9827–9205), north of the Stirling Range Retreat, is a café-vineyard
serving lunch and candlelight dinners in a full-scale replica of a wind-
mill in Puttershoek, Holland.

The only camping within the park is at △ **Moingup Springs** (☎ 08/9827–9230) which has toilets, water, and barbecues. Campfires are prohibited. Fees are A$8 per night for two adults, A$4 for additional adults. The △ **Stirling Range Retreat** (✉ Chester Pass Rd., Borden, 6333 ☎ 08/9827–9229) lies just north of the park's boundary opposite Bluff Knoll. Hot and cold showers, laundry facilities, swimming pool, powered and unpowered sites, chalets, and cabins are available. Campfires are permitted. Camping fees are A$20 for two adults; other accommodations start at A$25 per night.

South West A to Z

To research prices, get advice from other travelers, and book travel arrangements, visit www.fodors.com.

AIR TRAVEL

CARRIERS   Skywest provides daily service to the southern coastal town of Albany.
🛈 **Skywest** ☎ 13-2300 ⊕ www.skywest.com.au.

CAR TRAVEL

A comprehensive network of highways makes exploring the South West practical and easy. Take Highway 1 down the coast from Perth to Bunbury, switch to Route 10 through Busselton and Margaret River, Karridale, and finally Bridgetown, where you rejoin Highway 1 south to Albany via Manjimup.

From Perth, you can reach Stirling Range National Park by traveling along the Albany Highway to Kojonup, proceeding east via Broome Hill and Gnowangerup, and then veering south through Borden onto the Albany Road. For a more scenic route, head south from Kojonup and then proceed east along the Stirling Range Drive.

EMERGENCIES

In case of an emergency, dial 000 to reach an ambulance, the police, or the fire department.
🛈 **Albany Regional Hospital** ✉ Warden Ave., Albany ☎ 08/9841-2955. **South West Health Campus** ✉ Bussel Hwy., Bunbury ☎ 08/9722-1000 **Mandurah-Peel Regional Hospital** ✉ Lakes Rd., Mandurah ☎ 08/9531-8000

MAIL, INTERNET & SHIPPING

Internet and e-mail access is available in most public libraries. Some towns have an Internet café. Cyber Corner Café in Margaret River is open daily 10–8. Log on in Busselton at Novatech 2000. The Margaret River post office has express mail services.
🛈 **Cyber Corner Café** ✉ Shop 2/70, Wilmot St., Margaret River ☎ 08/9757-9388. **Novatech 2000** ✉ Prince St. Busselton ☎ 08/9754-2838
🛈 **Australia Post** ✉ Townview Terr., Margaret River ☎ 08/9757-2250.

TOUR OPERATORS

Skywest provides three- to five-day packages throughout the South West that incorporate coaches and hotels or four-wheel-driving and camping. Westcoast Rail and Coach runs regular tours of the South West, with departures from Perth railway stations.
🛈 **Skywest** ☎ 13-1300. **Westcoast Rail and Coach** ☎ 08/9221-9522

VISITOR INFORMATION

The Western Australia Visitor Centre maintains an excellent library of free information for visitors, including B&B and farm-stay accommodations throughout the region.

Farm and Country Holidays Association of Western Australia has extensive details of farm-stay accommodations throughout the state, from small holdings with rustic cottages to sheep stations of more than 654,000 acres where guests stay in sheep shearers' quarters and participate in station activities.

All major centers in the South West have visitor information centers that can arrange tours, book accommodations, and provide free information service for your travels. ▪ **Albany Visitor Centre** ✉ ☎ 1800/644088. **Bridgetown Information Centre** ✉ 154 Hampton St., Bridgetown ☎ 08/9761-1740. **Bunbury Visitor Information Centre** ✉ Old Railway Station, Carmody Pl., Bunbury ☎ 1800/287286. **Busselton Tourist Bureau** ✉ 38 Peel Terr., Busselton ☎ 08/9752-1288. **Farm & Country Holidays Association of Western Australia** ⊕ www.farmstaywa.com. **Mandurah Visitor Centre** ✉ 75 Mandurah Terr., Mandurah ☎ 08/9550-3999. **Margaret River Visitor Centre** ✉ Bussell Hwy., Margaret River ☎ 08/9757-2911. **Pemberton Visitor Centre** ✉ Brockman St., Pemberton ☎ 08/9776-1133. **Western Australia Visitor Centre** ✉ 469 Wellington St., Perth ☎ 1300/361351.

THE GOLDFIELDS

Since the day in 1893 when Paddy Hannan stumbled over a sizable gold nugget on the site of what is now Kalgoorlie, Western Australia's goldfields have ranked among the richest in the world. In fact, this "Golden Mile" is said to have had the world's highest concentration of gold. In the area's heyday, more than 100,000 men and women scattered throughout the area, all hoping to make their fortunes. It's still an astonishingly productive area, and the population of Kalgoorlie-Boulder is now increasing rapidly after falling to below 25,000 in the 1980s. Many nearby communities, however, are now nothing more than ghost towns.

Kalgoorlie-Boulder

602 km (373 mi) east of Perth.

Comprising the twin cities of Kalgoorlie and Boulder—locals call the conurbation Kal—Kalgoorlie-Boulder retains the rough-and-ready air of a frontier town, with streets wide enough to accommodate the camel teams that were once a common sight here. Open-cut mines gouge the earth everywhere, with the Super Pit—951 feet deep, 4 km (2½ mi) long, and 1½ km (1 mi) wide—expected to reach a depth of 1,969 feet by 2010.

The center of Kalgoorlie is compact enough to explore on foot. Hannan Street, named after the man who discovered gold here, is the main thoroughfare and contains the bulk of the hotels and places of interest.

The miners in Kalgoorlie favored slaking their thirst at the **Exchange Hotel** before filling their bellies, but now you can do both at once. A superb example of a goldfields pub, the redecorated Exchange is replete with exquisite stained glass and pressed-tin ceilings. ✉ *Hannan and Maritana Sts.* ☎ *08/9021-2833.*

Hannan's North Tourist Mine provides a comprehensive look at the century-old goldfields, with audiovisual displays, a reconstructed prospector's camp, historic buildings, and opportunities to go underground or to witness a real gold-pour. The **Australian Prospectors' and Mining Hall of Fame** (✉ Broadarrow Rd. ☎ 08/9091-2122) explores the history of mining in the region with exhibits and films. ✉ *Eastern Bypass Rd.* ☎ *08/9091-4074* ⊕ *www.mininghall.com* 💲 *Tour A$16.50, tour and Miners' Hall of Fame A$20* ⊙ *Daily 9:30-4:30; call for tour times.*

Built in 1908, **Kalgoorlie Town Hall** serves as an excellent example of a common style used around the goldfields. Be sure to look up at the stamped-tin ceiling. The cast-iron Edwardian seats in the balcony were imported from England at the turn of the 20th century. An art collection also graces the walls. The building, which is on Hannan Street a block south of the post office, is open weekdays 9–4:30.

The **Museum of the Goldfields** is housed partly within the historic British Arms—once the narrowest pub in the Southern Hemisphere. This outstanding small museum paints a colorful portrait of life in this boisterous town. The hands-on exhibits are a hit with children. Outside are a re-creation of a sandalwood cutter's camp and a replica of the first bank in Western Australia. ✉ *17 Hannan St.* ☎ *08/9021–8533* ✉ *Donation suggested* ⊙ *Daily 10–4:30.*

Outside Kalgoorlie Town Hall stands **Paddy Hannan,** arguably the most photographed statue in the nation. This life-size bronze replica of the town's founder replaces the weathered original, which now stands inside the Town Hall.

Built from local pink stone, Kalgoorlie's **Post Office** has dominated Hannan Street since it was constructed in 1899.

The **York Hotel,** opposite the post office, is one of the few hotels in Kalgoorlie to remain untouched by time. Take a look at its fine staircase and intricate cupola.

Not to be missed is the rustic **Bush Two-up Ring,** about 5 km (3 mi) out of Kalgoorlie, one of the few places in Australia where this popular gambling game may legally be played. Contact the Kalgoorlie-Boulder Visitor Centre for information. ☎ *08/9021–1966* ⊙ *5 AM–dark.*

The history of Kalgoorlie would not be complete without the infamous **Hay Street** and its "red light" district. Today only three brothels remain. The million-dollar complex at **Langtrees 181** (✉ Hay St. ☎ 08/9026–2181) even offers tours.

Where to Stay & Eat

$$–$$$ ✕ **Amalfi Motel.** This al fresco, à la carte dining experience includes Asian dishes, pasta, Cajun chicken, filet of beef, char-grilled squid, and other Australian brasserie foods. Snapper Crévette, lamb cutlets with sweet date couscous, and steaks that hang off the plate are house specialties. Don't miss the Indian herb bread. ✉ *Midas Motel, 409 Hannan St.* ☎ *08/9021–3088* ⚭ *Reservations essential* ▭ *AE, DC, MC, V.*

$ ✕ **Basil's on Hannan.** This pretty café in the heart of town owes its
Fodor's Choice   Mediterranean air to terra-cotta, wrought iron, and indoor-garden
★   decor. In addition to terrific coffee, the restaurant serves casual fare such as pastas and veal dishes. The popular Sunday brunch includes something different for Kalgoorlie—namely focaccia, seafood fettuccine, and a renowned Caesar salad. ✉ *168 Hannan St.* ☎ *08/9021–7832* ▭ *AE, MC, V* ⛀ *BYOB* ⊙ *No dinner Sun.*

$ ▥ **Mercure Hotel Plaza.** Though just a stone's throw from busy Hannan Street, this modern hotel complex has a quiet location, on a tree-lined street. In the morning you can open your windows to the sound of kookaburras and the heady smell of eucalyptus. Rooms in the refurbished four-story building have balconies. The higher floors enjoy views over the low-rise town. ✉ *45 Egan St., 6430* ☎ *08/9021–4544* ⎙ *08/9091–2195* ⊕ *www.mercure.com/mercure* ⇗ *100 rooms*

    & *Restaurant, room service, refrigerators, pool, spa, bar, free parking*
    ☱ *AE, DC, MC, V.*

$ ⊡ **Yelverton Apartment Hotel.** This comfortable Kalgoorlie hotel is named for Charles Yelverton O'Connor, the engineer who masterminded the 350-mi pipeline that brought a regular water supply from Mundaring Weir (near Perth) to Kalgoorlie in 1903. Roomy one- and two-bedroom apartments have full kitchens. Spa suites have king-size beds, and two-bedroom apartments can accommodate six. Furnishings and fittings are contemporary and high-quality. ✉ *210 Egan St., 6430* ☎ *08/9022–8181* 🖷 *08/9022–8191* ⊕ *www.yelvertonmotel.com.au* 🛏 *50 apartments* & *Room service, in-room safes, pool, laundry, dry cleaning, laundry facilities, Internet, meeting rooms, free parking* ☱ *AE, DC, MC, V* ⊺◎| *BP.*

¢ ⊡ **York Hotel.** The historic York, dating from 1901, has retained its lovely stained-glass windows and pressed-tin ceilings. Its staircase and dining room are a historian's dream. Rooms are small but functional, and rates include breakfast. ✉ *259 Hannan St., 6430* ☎ *08/9021–2337* ⊕ *www.yorkhotelkalgoorlie.com* 🛏 *16 rooms without bath* & *Restaurant* ☱ *AE, MC, V* ⊺◎| *BP.*

Coolgardie

561 km (348 mi) east of Perth, 39 km (24 mi) west of Kalgoorlie.

Tiny Coolgardie is probably the best-maintained ghost town in Australia. A great deal of effort has gone into preserving this historic community, where some 150 markers placed around town indicate important historical sights.

The Coolgardie Railway Station operated until 1971 and now houses the **Railway Station Museum**'s display on the history of rail transport. The museum also exhibits photographs, books, and artifacts that together paint a gripping portrayal of a famous mining rescue that was once carried out in these goldfields. ✉ *Woodward St.* ☎ *08/9026–6388* ⊠ *Donation suggested* ⊘ *Sat.–Thurs. 9–4.*

One of the most unusual museums in Australia, **Ben Prior's Open Air Museum** displays the machinery, boilers, and other equipment used to mine the region at the turn of the 20th century. If you didn't know it was a museum, you would think this was a private junkyard. Relics from Coolgardie's boom years include covered wagons, old cars, and statues of explorers. ✉ *Bayley St.* ☎ *08/9021–1966* ⊠ *Free* ⊘ *Daily 24 hrs.*

The stark, weathered headstones in the **Coolgardie Cemetery,** on the Great Eastern Highway about 1 km (½ mi) east of town, recall stories of tragedy and the grim struggle for survival in a harsh, unrelenting environment. Many of the graves remain unmarked because the identities of their occupants were lost during the wild rush to the eastern goldfields. Look for the graves of several Afghan camel drivers at the rear of the cemetery.

Coolgardie Camel Farm lets you take a look at the animals that played a vital role in opening inland Australia. Camel rides are available, including trips around the yard and one-hour, daylong, or overnight treks. Longer trips allow the chance to hunt for gems and gold. Reservations are essential for multiday excursions. ✉ *Great Eastern Hwy., 4 km (2½ mi) west of Coolgardie* ☎ *08/9026–6159* ⊠ *A$3.50* ⊘ *Public holidays and school holidays.*

Goldfields A to Z

To research prices, get advice from other travelers, and book travel arrangements, visit www.fodors.com.

AIR TRAVEL

QANTASLINK operates daily services from Perth to Kalgoorlie and twice weekly from Adelaide to Kalgoorlie. Skywest operates services between Perth and Kalgoorlie daily except Saturday.

🛈 **QANTASLINK** ☎ 13-1313. **Skywest** ☎ 1300/660088

BUS TRAVEL

Greyhound Pioneer Australia operates daily services from Perth to Adelaide, with stops at Coolgardie, Kalgoorlie, and Norseman. Perth–Goldfields Express operates a regular luxury coach service linking Perth to Kalgoorlie, Menzies, Leonora, Laverton, Wiluna, and Warburton. Western Australia Government Railways operates a return service linking Kalgoorlie with Esperance three days a week.

🛈 Bus Information **Greyhound Pioneer Australia** ☎ 08/9481-7066 or 13-2030 ⊕ www.greyhound.com.au. **Perth–Goldfields Express** ✉ 16 Lane St. Kalgoorlie ☎ 08/9021-2954. **Western Australia Government Railways** ☎ 131-053.

EMERGENCIES

In case of an emergency, dial 000 to reach an ambulance, the police, or the fire department.

🛈 **Kalgoorlie Regional Hospital** ✉ Piccadilly St., Kalgoorlie ☎ 08/9080-5888.

MAIL, INTERNET & SHIPPING

The Netzone Internet Lounge in Kalgoorlie is open weekdays 10–7 and weekends 10–5. Kalgoorlie's main post office is on Hannan Street.

🛈 **Netzone Internet Lounge** ✉ St. Barbara's Sq. ☎ 08/9022-8342.
🛈 **Australia Post Kalgoorlie** ✉ 204 Hannon St. ☎ 08/9024-1093.

TAXIS

Kalgoorlie taxis are available around-the-clock.

🛈 **Twin City Cabs** ☎ 131-008.

TOURS

Goldfields Air Services has an air tour that gives you a bird's-eye view of the open-cut mining technique now used instead of more traditional shaft mining. Goldrush Tours runs excellent tours on the goldfields' history and ghost towns, the profusion of wildflowers in the area, and the ghost town of Coolgardie. Boulder is home to the Loop Line Railroad, whose train the *Rattler* offers tours of the Golden Mile by rail. The train leaves from the Boulder Railway Station. Yamatji Bitja offers individually tailored experiences with an Aboriginal guide.

🛈 Tour Operators **Goldfields Air Services** ☎ 08/9093-2116. **Goldrush Tours** ✉ 16 Lane St. ☎ 08/9021-2954 ⊕ www.goldrushtours.info. **Loop Line Railroad** ✉ Burt St. ☎ 08/9093-3055. **Yamatji Bitja** ✉ 16 Richardson St., Boulder ☎ 08/9093-3745.

TRAIN TRAVEL

The clean and efficient *Prospector* is an appropriate name for the train that runs a daily seven-hour service between Perth and Kalgoorlie. It departs from the East Perth Railway Terminal. The Indian Pacific stops at Kalgoorlie four times a week as its journeys across the continent from Perth to Sydney via Adelaide.

🛈 Train Information *Prospector* ☎ 131-053. **Indian Pacific** ☎ 132-147.

VISITOR INFORMATION

The Coolgardie Tourist Bureau is open weekdays 9 to 5. Staff members at the Kalgoorlie/Boulder Tourist Centre are as enthusiastic and welcoming as they are knowledgeable. The office is open weekdays 8:30 to 5, weekends and holidays 9 to 3.

🛈 Tourist Information **Coolgardie Tourist Bureau** ✉ 62 Bayley St., Coolgardie ☎ 08/9026-6090 **Kalgoorlie/Boulder Tourist Centre** ✉ 250 Hannan St. ☎ 08/9021-1966 🖷 08/9021-2180 ⊕ www.kalgoorlieanwagoldfields.com.au.

KARIJINI NATIONAL PARK

Fodor'sChoice
★

1,411 km (875 mi) northeast of Perth, 285 km (177 mi) south of Port Hedland.

The huge rocks, crags, and gorges that make up the Hamersley Range, in the Pilbara region of the northwestern corner of the state, are among the most ancient land surfaces in the world. Sediments deposited by an inland sea more than 2½ billion years ago were forced up by movements in the Earth's crust and slowly weathered by natural elements through succeeding centuries. Much of the 320-km (200-mi) range is being mined for its rich iron deposits, but a small section is incorporated into the national park. Towering cliffs, lush fern-filled gullies, and richly colored stone make this one of the most beautiful parks in Australia.

Karijini has trails for hikers of every level. The one-hour Dales Gorge trail is the most popular and easily accessible, with the Fortescue Falls and Ferns pool (a leisurely 20 minutes from the car park) as a highlight. Other trails are far more challenging and should be undertaken only by experienced hikers, who must brave freezing water, cling to rock ledges, and scramble over boulders through the Joffre, Knox, and Hancock gorges. Notify a ranger before hiking into any of these gorges.

Because summer temperatures often top 43°C (110°F), it's best to visit during the cooler months, from April through early November.

Where to Stay

There are a couple of basic motels in the fast-growing mining town of Tom Price, about 50 km (31 mi) west of the Park.

Food and supplies can be purchased in nearby Tom Price or Wittenoom, where hotel and motel accommodations can be arranged. Drinking water is available at Yampire and Joffre roads and at Mujina Roadhouse.

Camping is permitted only in designated sites at Circular Pool, Joffre Turnoff, and Weano. Campsites have no facilities except toilets, but gas barbecues are free. The burning of wood is prohibited. Nightly fees are A$8 per car, plus A$8 park entry.

Lodging is available at **Auski Tourist Village Munjina** (✉ Cnr. Great Northern Hwy. and Wittenoom turnoff, Port Hedland ☎ 08/9716-6988), also known as the Munjina Roadhouse, about 70 km (43 mi) northeast of the major park attractions. It's A$100–A$120 (seasonal) for a motel room, A$12 for a camping site.

Karijini National Park A to Z

CAR TRAVEL

You can best reach this remote park by flying from Perth to Port Hedland and renting a car from there, or by flying to Broome (⇨ The Kimberley *in* Chapter 11) and driving 551 km (342 mi) on the Great Northern Highway to Port Hedland. Turn south from Port Hedland to the park. Tom Price is 80 km (50 mi) from the Hamersley Gorge turnoff. All roads within the park are unsealed.

TOURS

Design a Tour has tours departing from Port Hedland, Exmouth, Perth, Broome, Tom Price, or Auski Munjina. The season runs from April to October. (✉ Box 627 Albany ☎ 08/9841–7788 ⊕ www.dat.com.au).

Lestok Tours has full-day trips to Karijini National Park Gorges, departing from Tom Price, with swimming and guided walks through the gorges. (✉ Tom Price, 6751 ☎ 08/9189–2032).

Red Rock Abseiling Adventures has experienced and qualified instructors who will guide you on a half-day rapelling experience in the park. No previous experience is required. (✆ P. O. Box 559, Tom Price, 6751 ☎ 08/ 9189–2206).

VISITOR INFORMATION

The Tom Price Visitor Centre is open weekdays April to September 8:30 to 5:30 and weekends and holidays 9 to noon. October to March it's open weekdays 8:30 to 2:30, Saturday 9 to noon, and closed Sundays and holidays. The Pilbara Tourism and Convention Bureau is open weekdays April to November 8:30 to 5, and weekends and public holidays 9 to 4. Hours from December to March are 9 to 5 weekdays, 9 to noon Saturday, and closed Sunday and holidays.

🛈 Tourist Information **Pilbara Tourism and Convention Bureau** ✉ Shop 12, Karratha Village Shopping Centre, Sharpe Ave., Karratha, 6714 ☎ 08/9185–5455. **Tom Price Visitor Centre** ✉ Central Rd., Tom Price, 6751 ☎ 08/9188–1112. **Western Australia Visitor Centre** ✉ Forrest Pl. and Wellington St., Perth, 6000 ☎ 1300/361351.

MONKEY MIA & NINGALOO REEF

Two marine wonders await in the northwestern corner of the state. At Monkey Mia, a World Heritage Site, dolphins interact freely with human beings. Ningaloo Reef Marine Park is a great spot to see coral and observe whales, manta rays, and other marine life.

Monkey Mia

Fodor'sChoice *985 km (611 mi) north of Perth, 450 km (280 mi) from Karijini Na-*
★ *tional Park.*

Monkey Mia is a World Heritage Site and the setting for one of the world's most extraordinary natural wonders; nowhere else do wild dolphins interact so freely with human beings. In 1964 a woman from one of the makeshift fishing camps in the area hand-fed one of the dolphins that regularly followed the fishing boats home. Other dolphins followed that lead, and an extensive family of wild dolphins now comes of its own accord to be fed. For many, standing in the shallow waters of Shark Bay to hand-feed a dolphin is the experience of a lifetime. There are no set feeding times. Dolphins show up at any hour of the day at the public beach, where park rangers feed them. Rangers share their food with people who want to get close to the sea creatures. There is also a Dolphin Information Centre, which has videos and information. ✉ *Follow Hwy. 1 north from Perth for 806 km (500 mi) to Denham/Hamelin Rd., then follow signs* ☎ *08/9948–1366* ☉ *Information center daily 7–4:30.*

Where to Stay

$$ 🏨 **Monkey Mia Dolphin Resort.** This resort has everything from backpacker accommodations to canvas condos to motel-style units. Eight cedar units open straight onto Dolphin Beach, while the others are set in a tropical garden. Dolphin-watch cruises leave the resort's jetty daily at 10:30 AM. ✆ *Box 119, Denham, 6537* ☎ *08/9948–1320* 🖷 *08/ 9948–1034* ⊕ *www.monkeymia.com.au* ⇝ *60 rooms* ⌂ *Restaurant,*

tennis, pool, hot tub, volleyball, bar, shop, laundry facilities, free parking ⊟ AE, DC, MC, V.

en route Between Monkey Mia and Ningaloo Reef Marine Park, and 904 km (560 mi) north of Perth, the town of **Carnarvon** is a popular stopover. Stroll the *Fascine,* a palm-lined harborside boardwalk, where the Gascoyne River flows into the Indian Ocean.

Ningaloo Reef Marine Park

Fodor'sChoice
★
1,512 km (937 mi) north of Perth, 550 km (341 mi) from Monkey Mia.

Some of Australia's most pristine coral reef runs 251 km (156 mi) along the coast of the Exmouth Peninsula, very far north of Perth. A happy conjunction of migratory routes and accessibility makes it one of the best places on Earth to see huge manta rays, giant whale sharks, humpback whales, nesting turtles, and the annual coral spawning. Exmouth makes a good overnight base for exploring the marine park.

Also worth seeing near Exmouth is the **Cape Range National Park,** including the Yardie Creek Gorge. ⊠ *Follow North West Coastal Hwy. north 1,170 km (725 mi) to Minilya turnoff; Exmouth is 374 km (232 mi) farther north.*

Where to Stay

¢–$$$ 🏨 **Bayview Coral Bay.** On the beachfront overlooking Coral Bay, this venue offers a wide range of lodging types. The Holiday units sleep up to 6, while cabins sleep 4. Most of the camper spots have electricity. This is an ideal spot for families and those seeking a relaxing environment near the water. ⊠ *Robinson St., 6701* 🕾 *08/9942–5932* 🖷 *08/9385–7413* ◿ *8 Holiday units, 12 cabins, 250 camper spots* ⚲ *Café, 2 tennis courts, pool, beach volleyball, playground, free parking* ⊟ MC, V.

$ 🏨 **Ningaloo Reef Resort.** Rooms at this beachfront Coral Bay resort have views over the bay. ⊠ *Robinson St., 6701* 🕾 *08/9942–5934* 🖷 *08/ 9942–5953* ◿ *34 rooms* ⚲ *Restaurant, kitchens (some), pool, dive shop, bar, recreation room, free parking; no a/c in some rooms* ⊟ AE, MC, V.

Monkey Mia & Ningaloo Reef A to Z

AIR TRAVEL
Skywest operates four return flights a week from Perth to Shark Bay airport, which serves Monkey Mia, on Monday, Wednesday, Friday, and Saturday.
🛈 **Skywest** 🕾 13-1300.

BUS TRAVEL
Greyhound Pioneer Australia buses drive from Perth to Shark Bay, Carnarvon, Coral Bay, and Exmouth. Services to Monkey Mia are on Monday, Thursday, Friday, and Saturday, returning on Monday, Wednesday, Thursday, and Saturday.
🛈 **Greyhound Pioneer Australia** 🕾 13-2030 ⊕ www.greyhound.com.au.

TOURS
Ningaloo Reef Marine National Park, accessible from both Exmouth and Coral Bay, has opportunities to mix with the local wildlife. Coral Bay Adventures takes small groups out to the reef to swim with the whale sharks from March to June. Their glass-bottom boat allows you to view the coral and tropical fish life without getting wet

▣ Tour Operators **Aristocat 2 Wildlife Cruises** ⊠ Monkey Mia jetty ☎ 08/9948-1446
⊕ www.monkey-mia.net. **Coral Bay Adventures** ☎ 08/9942-5955. **Coral Bay
Ocean Game Fishing** ☎ 08/9942-5874. **Exmouth Diving Centre** ⊠ Payne St.
☎ 08/9949-1201. **Ningaloo Reef Dive** ☎ 08/9942-5824. **Sportfishing Safaris**
☎ 08/9948-1846 ⊕ www.sportfish.com.au.

VISITOR INFORMATION

▣ Tourist Information **Carnarvon Tourist Bureau** ⊠ Robinson St., Carnarvon, 6701
☎ 08/9941-1146 ⊟ 08/9941-1149 ⊕ www.outbackcoast.com. **Exmouth Tourist Bureau** ⊠ Murat Rd. Exmouth ☎ 08/9949-1176. **Shark Bay Tourist Bureau** ⊠ 71 Knight
St., Denham ☎ 08/9948-1253.

UNDERSTANDING AUSTRALIA

THE LAND OF OZ

THOSE WHO LIVE IN AUSTRALIA call it "Oz." The name fits. This is a land so different from any other that it can sometimes seem as though it were conjured rather than created. Australia casts its spell through paradoxes: it is a developed nation, poised for the Century of the Pacific Rim, yet it is largely unpopulated, a land of vast frontiers—and with a frontier spirit in its people that was lost in other nations long ago, when life became crowded or comfortable or both.

Yet for all their cherished "bushman" heritage, 90% of the 19½ million residents of Australia cluster in the cities and townships along the eastern seaboard, which stretches from Brisbane to Adelaide in an arc of about 3,300 km (2,050 mi). Few Australians have visited much of their huge, empty land, yet their souls dwell in the dusty, Technicolor Outback.

To realize the sparseness of the sixth-largest country in the world, imagine a land the size of the continental United States with virtually no human population for the first 3,200 km (2,000 mi) inland from the West Coast—as if nothing but sand and spinifex lay between Los Angeles and Chicago. In Australia, sheep —and kangaroos—outnumber people.

Despite the immensity of the land, local cultural variations, and a sectionalism that often has the six states snarling at one another, Australia is a nation of one texture. From the Kimberley, in the far northwest, to Melbourne, some 3,700 km (2,312 mi) southeast, the same Australian accent flattens the vowels and puts on cozy suffixes ("Brissy" for Brisbane, "Fre-o" for Fremantle).

You don't need to head into the Outback to sense the land's enormous power. Whereas in Europe and America cities intrude upon the countryside, in Australia the country tends to invade the cities. When the British first arrived in Australia in 1770, Captain James Cook called the area just south of Sydney Botany Bay because of the profusion of flowers and trees. Even today, with a population of 4 million, Sydney seems to be, above all, a slice of nature. On hills around a sparkling blue harbor, plants and flowering shrubs soften red-tile roofs.

In the large, stately city of Melbourne you find a high, vast sky whose light overwhelms, and a silence that allows you to hear the rustle of a gum (eucalyptus) tree as you exit from the airport terminal. With its gray-green acacias and purple-flowering jacarandas, much of Brisbane looks like a horticultural exhibit, and it's possible to become lost in dreams while strolling through King's Park in Perth, where a riot of boronia, orchid, and kangaroo paw spreads beneath magnificent gums.

For tens of thousands of years the Aborigines and nature shared this continent together. The Aborigines arrived during the Ice Age, before sea levels rose and isolated Australia from the rest of Asia. Some 300,000 Aborigines inhabited the land when Captain Arthur Phillip arrived with the first convict settlers in 1788, and as Europeans built their penal colony on the shores of Sydney Harbour, the Aborigines were pushed out further. Some may have welcomed European accoutrements, but they could not cope with alcohol, and thousands died from smallpox, venereal disease, and, tragically, at the hands of the new white settlers.

The days when Australia was a penal colony are not so distant. The country's unique origin as a place of crime and punishment haunted Australians for a century and a half. It was only after World War II that most people could bring themselves to talk about their criminal ancestry. Today, it is fashionable to boast of it. Tracing one's ancestry back to the First Fleet—the 11 ships which arrived from England in 1788 with convicts and soldiers—is a badge of honor.

A legacy of the convict era remains in some Australian attitudes. This is a society that looks to the government for solutions to its problems. In part, geographic necessity dictates the posture, but it also stems from the nation's origins as a government camp.

At the same time, an anti-authoritarian streak seems to echo the contempt of convicts for their keepers and "betters." This attitude, too, has been perpetuated by geographic realities. The farmer in the tough Outback was not inclined—and still isn't—to respect the city bureaucrat who does not know how to mend a fence or cook a meal in the desert. Thus, in one and the same Australian, you find both the government-dependent mind-set and the anti-authoritarian rhetoric. It is no coincidence, then, that the historical figure who stands out most clearly as an Australian hero is Ned Kelly, a bushranger (highwayman) who killed policemen.

Out of this past, distance from European norms, and nature's influence have fostered a casual and easygoing lifestyle. A businessperson can sound as folksy as a worker, and an academic can look like a worker while boozing and cheering at a football game. It is still an oddity to Australian cab drivers for anyone traveling alone to ride in the backseat, although you are perfectly free to do so.

The nation's spirit dwells somewhere within a triangle, the points of which are diffidence, innocence, and skepticism. Aussies can neither be easily fooled nor easily enthused. They like to believe others will be reasonable, but at arm's length many a proposed scheme will seem flawed or not worth the bother. In spite of that skepticism, there is a seductive softness to Aussie life. People still say "sorry" if they bump into you on the street, and the word for thank you, "ta," is uttered even after you yourself have said thank you in a shop or restaurant. And whether the topic is the weather, the absurdity of politicians, or the way the world is going to pot, Australians tend to want your agreement.

This desire for affirmation may be due, in part, to the fact that Australians lived in the shadow of Great Britain for so long, during which time they developed something of an inferiority complex. The emergence of distinctly Australian traditions—such as Mod Oz cuisine—is part of a growing nationalism helping the country forge its own unique identity. A few decades ago, a basic meal of meat pies and beer or fish-and-chips were, in an unspoken way, defiantly asserted to be adequate "tucker" for any real Australian. Today, dressed in T-shirts and sandals, diners in Melbourne and Sydney peer lengthily at wine lists and discuss the right dressing to drizzle over goat's cheese and arugula. Along with the new dining trends, Australia has established an internationally acclaimed film industry, a leading Aboriginal artist community, vibrant theater and performing arts programs, and a host of respected wineries.

* * *

T TAKES TIME to establish an identity rooted in one's own geographic and climatic experience, however, and Australia can seem quite British at times and somewhat American at others. Political, legal, and educational institutions derive from Britain. Each state capital is named after a colonial politician (Perth, Brisbane, Sydney, Hobart, Melbourne) or a British royal figure (Adelaide). Dry, sun-scorched towns bear names from England's green, temperate land. Each day in the leading newspapers a "Vice Regal" column lists the activities and visitors at the state and national government houses, where the representative of the British queen is the formal head of state. Only since 1984 has it been required that a civil servant in Australia be an Australian—previously it was sufficient to be British.

American culture influences entertainment, technology, defense arrangements, and business. Television channels are well stocked with American programs, and American popular music and clothing styles attract youth in Sydney and Melbourne, as they do in much of the world. Books from the United States have made a major advance in Australian intellectual circles since the 1960s. American ideas of management and problem-solving are sweeping away cobwebs as the presence of multilateral corporations grows.

Immigration has also influenced cultural trends in Australia, and the overseas arrivals have come in waves over the decades. A flood of Europeans headed for Australia after WWII, including immigrants from Italy, Yugoslavia, Malta, Eastern Europe, and Greece. Students from Asia arrived in the 1960s and '70s, including many Vietnamese escaping from their war-torn lands. Australians' own love of travel has also introduced them to the nearby countries of Southeast Asia, and now Indonesia, Japan, and other regional members are priorities in Australia's political and economic agendas.

Currently about half of Australia's inhabitants were either born outside Australia or have at least one parent who was. So far, less than 10% of the population is of Asian descent, but Asians comprise more than half the immigrants who have arrived since 1984. Just over 2% of Australians are Aborigines.

Thus, Australian urban life has become more cosmopolitan, with Chinese restaurants, Italian cafés, and Vietnamese and Lebanese grocery stores in virtually every suburb. Former residents of Greece and Italy teach school classes that are half Vietnamese and Chinese—yesterday's students teaching today's—with gum trees outside the window and cricket played during the sports hour.

* * *

AUSTRALIA HAS REMAINED pleasant and peaceable by taking a practical (if sometimes hit-or-miss) approach to issues. Some Australians wonder if this approach will adequately address tomorrow's challenges. Government ministers have suggested that Australia should forget about being the "lucky country" and strive to be a "clever country"—competing in Asia through high-tech development, ingenuity, and flexibility.

For now, Australia is a young nation with an identity that is still crystallizing. Its last half century has brought it to an exciting stage of development. Greater ethnic diversity, creative excellence, and the pleasures of a comfortable, safe, and healthy life have instilled in its people pride and sophistication.

—Ross Terrill

Updated by Josie Gibson

AUSTRALIA'S ANIMALS

USTRALIA'S ANIMALS ARE among nature's oddest creations. So weird are the creatures that hop, burrow, slither, and amble across the Australian landmass that, until the 20th century, it was believed that the continent's fauna had a different evolutionary starting point from the rest of the Earth's species.

Nowhere is this more evident than in Australia's parched interior. About four-fifths of Australia's entire landmass receives less than 16 inches of rainfall per year, and here, on the earth's driest inhabited continent, life-forms have evolved with unique characteristics that enable them to survive, often acquiring a stark and surreal beauty in the process.

In times of drought, the water-holding frog locks itself away in an underground chamber, where it remains in a state of suspended animation waiting for rain for up to seven years. Despite its ferocious appearance, the heavy armor of another desert dweller, the thorny devil, also serves as a water-conservation measure. Its exaggerated spikes and spines give the creature an enormous surface area on which dew condenses and is then channeled into its mouth.

One of the most fascinating groups of all Australian animals is the monotremes. Classified as mammals, they also exhibit some of the characteristics of reptiles, who preceded them on the evolutionary scale. Monotremes lay eggs, as reptiles do. However, they are warm-blooded and suckle their young with milk, mammalian adaptations that considerably increase their chances of survival. Only three species of monotremes survive: the platypus, a reclusive crustacean-eater found in freshwater streams in eastern Australia, and two species of echidna, a small, spiny termite-eater.

Australia's animal life was shaped by its plants, and they, in turn, were determined by the climate, which dramatically changed around 15 million years ago. Moist, rain-bearing winds that once irrigated the heart of the continent died, the great inland sea dried up, and the inland rain forests vanished—flamingos and freshwater dolphins along with them. As forests gave way to grassland, the marsupials thrived.

The kangaroo is a superb example of adaptation. In the parched, semidesert that covers most of central Australia, kangaroos must forage for food over a wide area. Their powerful hind legs act as springs that absorb the energy of each leap, enabling them to travel long distances while using relatively little energy.

Young kangaroos are born underdeveloped, when they are barely an inch long. The mother then enters estrus again within days of giving birth. The second embryo develops for just a week and stays dormant until its older sibling leaves the pouch, at which time it enters a 30-day gestation period before being born.

Kangaroos, wallabies, and their midsize relations range enormously in size, habitat, and location. In Australia, you'll find everything from rat-size specimens to the 6-ft, 200-pound red kangaroos, and you'll find them everywhere from the cool, misty forests of Tasmania to the northern tip of Cape York.

Best loved of all Australia's animals is the koala. A tree-dwelling herbivore, the koala eats a diet entirely of eucalyptus leaves, which are low in nutrients and high in toxins. As a result, koalas must restrict their energy level. Typically, a koala will spend about 20 hours of each day dozing in a tree fork. Even the koala's brain has adapted to its harsh regimen. A human brain uses about 17% of the body's energy, but the koala saves on the wasteful expenditure by starting out with a brain the size of a small walnut.

However deficient in the cerebellum it may be, though, one thing that the koala will not tolerate is being called a bear. Cute and cuddly as it is—and despite its resemblance to every child's favorite bed mate—the koala is a marsupial, not a bear.

—Michael Gebicki

BOOKS & MOVIES

Books

Most of the following books are available in bookstores in the United States and Australia.

Aboriginal Culture. In the acclaimed *Australian Dreaming: 40,000 Years of Aboriginal History,* author Jennifer Isaacs has paired stunning color photographs with the story of the original Australians. Geoffrey Blainey's *Triumph of the Nomads* is a highly readable appraisal of the knowledge and technology that allowed the Aborigines to live in their harsh environment.

One of the most celebrated contemporary works by an Aboriginal writer is *My Place,* by Sally Morgan. Bruce Chatwin's *The Songlines* is a fictional rendering of the Aboriginal relationship with the earth.

Fiction. Peter Carey's inventive novels have won many awards, including the 1988 Booker Prize, the British Commonwealth's highest literary award. His work includes the novels *Jack Maggs, Illywhacker, Bliss,* and *Oscar and Lucinda.* Elizabeth Jolley is another leading contemporary author whose often humorous novels and stories, such as *The Sugar Mother* and *Woman in a Lampshade,* are set in her home state of Western Australia. Also recommended are *The Chant of Jimmie Blacksmith* and *The Playmaker,* Australian-subject books by Thomas Keneally, the author of *Schindler's Ark,* which became the film *Schindler's List.* Patrick White is Australia's most celebrated novelist, winner of the Nobel Prize in 1973. Among his works are *Voss* and *Flaws in the Glass.* Murray Bail's *Eucalyptus* is an allegorical romantic fantasy in which the Australian landscape is examined through the eyes of a naturalist and interwoven with the question, "How do you win a woman's heart?" *Remembering Babylon,* by David Malouf, tells the story of a 13-year-old British cabin boy who is cast ashore in northern Australia and adopted by Aborigines in the mid-19th century, and the traumatic collision of cultures that results when he is thrust back into white society.

History & Society. Barry Hill's generously illustrated *The Rock: Travelling to Uluru weaves together oral and natural history in its account of The Handback, when white Australians gave ownership of Uluru back to the Aborigines in 1985.*

Robert Hughes spins Australia's convict origins into a fascinating narrative web in *The Fatal Shore.* The book traces the birth of the nation from the arrival of the First Fleet in 1788 through the end of convict transportation in 1868. Marcus Clarke's classic, *For the Term of His Natural Life,* was written in 1870 and brings to life the grim conditions endured by convicts.

Frontier Country: Australia's Outback Heritage is acclaimed as a definitive work of the history of the Outback. It encompasses the continent's 40,000 years of evolution. Aeneus Gunn's 1908 *We of the Never Never* describes her life as the wife of a pioneering homesteader in the Northern Territory. Henry Lawson also captured the spirit of Australian life at the turn of the 20th century in books such as *While the Billy Boils* and *The Country I Come From.* Dame Mary Durack grew up in the Kimberley, daughter of a pioneering pastoralist family. Her many books include *Kings in Grass Castles* and *Sons in the Saddle.* As a young American journalist, Tony Horowitz spent many months rambling through the Australian Outback, and the result is *One for the Road,* an exuberant, wildly hilarious, and illuminating look at the "real Australia." The writing is crisp and the observations from this Pulitzer prize–winning author are finely crafted. For another American take on traveling in Australia, read Bill Bryson's funny and insightful *In a Sunburned Country. Tracks,* by Robyn Davidson, tells of the author's solitary journey from Alice Springs to the west coast—a six-month, 2,720-km (1,686-mi) odyssey across the trackless deserts of central Australia. The book is finely written and sharply personal, juggling courage, desperation, reflection, and moments of quiet heroism. *The Road from Coorain,* by Jill Ker Conway, tells of her life until the age of 23, when she left Australia for graduate school at Harvard. It's a fragrant, lyrical account of Australian rural society and the author's blooming consciousness.

Ross Terrill's *The Australians* takes a penetrating look at the social fabric of today's Australia. Although it was published in the late 1980s, *Sydney,* by Jan Morris, is a brilliant portrait of the contemporary mood, manners, and morals of the city.

For a wry look at the seedier side of Australia, read crime writers Peter Corris (Sydney) and Shane Maloney (Melbourne). Try Corris's novel *The Greenwich Apartments* and Maloney's *The Brush Off.*

Movies

From its early appearance on the world film scene with Charles Tait's 1906 *The Story of the Kelly Gang,* widely held to be the first feature-length moving picture, Australia didn't always hold its own against Hollywood. In the past several decades, however, it has come to reclaim its international stature, with popular and critical successes alike. Looking past the megahit comedy *Crocodile Dundee* (1986), there are a number of great Aussie films to choose from at your local video rental store. *Muriel's Wedding* (1995), *Strictly Ballroom* (1991), *The Man from Snowy River* (1981), and *My Brilliant Career* (1977) are spirited dramas that stand out for their bigheartedness. Peter Weir's tragic *Gallipoli* (1980)—starring a young Mel Gibson—and his eerie *Picnic at Hanging Rock* (1975) are in a class of their own. *Oscar and Lucinda* (1997) is a lush adaptation of the Peter Carey novel by the same name. *Shine* (1996) features an Oscar-winning performance by native son Geoffrey Rush. The computer-animated *Babe* (1995) and sequel *Babe: Pig in the City* (1998) delight and astonish adults and children alike. Based loosely on the life of Australian artist Norman Lindsay, who scandalized Australian society with his voluptuous nudes, *Sirens* (1994) stars Hugh Grant as a sexually repressed clergyman, as well as a scantily clad Elle Macpherson. Following the often hilarious and sometimes poignant footsteps of a troupe of cross-dressing males on tour across Outback Australia, *The Adventures of Priscilla, Queen of the Desert* (1994) has become a cult classic. A crime thriller centering on love and the lives that intersect with one character, *Lantana* (2001) stormed the box offices in Australia with an all-star cast including Geoffrey Rush, Barbara Hershey, Anthony LaPaglia, and Kerry Armstrong. *Rabbit Proof Fence* (2002) was the first film to tackle the subject of the Stolen Generation: the name given to the thousands of Aboriginal children who were forcibly taken from their families by the government during the first two-thirds of the 20th century. Directed by Phillip Noyce, the movie scooped all the Australian Film Institute Awards that year.

The 1999 opening of the giant Fox Studios production facility close to the heart of Sydney has meant a boom for Australia's movie industry. The list of hit movies that have been filmed at least partly in Australia include *The Matrix* (1999), *Mission Impossible II* (1999), and *The Thin Red Line* (1998).

CHRONOLOGY

45 million years ago	Australian continent separates from Asia and Antarctica.
120,000– 50,000 years ago	First humans are thought to have arrived from Southeast Asia, although Australian Aborigines believe life was created here in the Dreamtime.
25,000 years ago	Aborigines arrive in Australia's southern island, Tasmania.
1558–1603	Portuguese ships arrive in Australian waters.
1606	Aborigines believed to have sighted Dutchman William Jansz as he sails past the northern coast of Australia.
1642	Aborigines in southern Australia meet Dutch explorer Abel Tasman; 46 years later they encounter Englishman William Dampier on Australia's northwest coast.
1770	British Captain James Cook explores Botany Bay.
1788	The British First Fleet under Captain Arthur Phillip arrives in Port Jackson (Sydney) and Botany Bay.
1797	First organized commerce in Australia as Spanish merino sheep are imported to New South Wales, marking the birth of Australia's wool industry.
1804	White settlement begun in Van Dieman's Land (Tasmania), the prelude to the island becoming a major British penal colony.
1813	Explorers Gregory Blaxland and William Wentworth cross the Blue Mountains east of Sydney, opening up exploration of the vast inland.
1814	The colony, known to this point as New Holland, becomes Australia (from *terra australis,* "the great south land") at the suggestion of Governor Matthew Flinders.
1823	Explorer John Oxley discovers Brisbane River.
1824	Explorers Hume and Hovell reach Port Phillip (later to become Melbourne) from Sydney.
1828	Brisbane founded.
1836	South Australia founded.
1840	Explorer Edward John Eyre survives attack by Aborigines to reach West Australian coast from Adelaide.
1850	Port Phillip (Victoria), Van Dieman's Land (Tasmania), Western Australia, and South Australia become separate colonies.
1851	Gold discovered at Bathurst, New South Wales, in May and Ballarat, Victoria, in August. Gold rushes begin.
1854	First steam train runs in Australia. Miners, angry at what they see as excessive regulation, rebel at Ballarat; dozens killed at the Eureka Stockade.
1855	New South Wales, Victoria, South Australia, and Van Dieman's Land (now called Tasmania) elect parliaments. Women not allowed to vote.

1856   Queensland becomes separate colony. Workers in building industry win the right to an eight-hour day.

1858   First recorded Australian Rules football match.

1859   Thomas Austin of Geelong imports 24 English rabbits. Rabbit plague begins, and continues to this day.

1861   First "Selection Acts" in New South Wales's attempt to put small farmers on the land. Explorers Burke and Wills die at the remote central Australian water hole, Cooper's Creek. Chinese attacked at the gold mining settlement of Lambing Flat, New South Wales.

1863   First South Pacific islanders brought to Queensland to work in sugarcane fields. The practice, resembling slavery, becomes known as "blackbirding."

1869   Opening of Suez Canal dramatically reduces sailing time from Europe to Australia.

1872   First telegraph cable linking Britain and Australia. W. C. Gosse becomes first white man to see Uluru (Ayers Rock). New South Wales Marriage Act allows women to maintain control of their own money after they marry.

1876   Explorer Ernest Giles's final expedition confirms that central Australia is virtually a desert. Stump-Jump plough invented in South Australia, enabling the cultivation of thousands of acres of scrubland and helping small-holders to make some sort of living from marginal farmland.

1879   First consignments of Australian frozen beef sold in London.

1880   Melbourne stages World Exhibition. Notorious bushranger Ned Kelly hanged in Melbourne.

1883   Sydney–Melbourne rail line opens. Two thousand Melbourne tailoresses strike for better conditions.

1884   Formation of Women's Suffrage Movement, demanding women's right to vote.

1886   Amalgamated Shearers' Union formed, with membership growing to some 20,000 over the next four years. Gold and silver discovered at Mt. Lyell in Tasmania. Gold discovered at Mt. Morgan in Queensland and the Kimberleys in Western Australia.

1890   Economic depression hits. Many thousands become unemployed amid widespread strikes at Broken Hill, New South Wales, and in the pastoral and shipping industries. Western Australia elects its first parliament.

1891   American Jessie Ackerman begins the first public lecture tour by a woman in Australia, on issues affecting women's lives.

1892   Gold discovered at Coolgardie in Western Australia.

1893   Gold discovered at Kalgoorlie in Western Australia. Quickly established as Australia's richest-ever goldfield, it sparks a new rush.

1894   National shearers' strike. South Australian women win the right to vote.

1895   Start of a devastating seven-year drought in eastern Australia.

1899   Federation of the states agreed to by a majority of Australians. Troops land in South Africa to fight on the side of Britain in the Boer War. West Australian women win the right to vote.

1900   The Commonwealth of Australia formed.

1901   Opening of the first Australian federal parliament with Edward Barton as prime minister. Australian population is 3,773,248 (excluding Aborigines, estimated to number 150,000).

1902   Drought breaks in eastern Australia. Drought and rabbit plague have halved the nation's sheep and cattle population over the preceding 10 years. Australia linked to America by telegraph cable from Southport in Queensland. Australia begins administration of Southwest New Guinea. Women in New South Wales win the right to vote in state parliament.

1903   Women win the right to vote for federal parliament. Three women stand for election. Women in Tasmania win the right to vote in state parliament.

1905   Queen Victoria of Britain's birthday made a national public holiday, to be called Empire Day. Women in Queensland win the right to vote in state parliament.

1908   Women in Victoria win the right to vote in state parliament.

1910   Australia's own money replaces British gold, silver, and copper coins.

1911   Explorer and scientist Douglas Mawson departs Hobart for Antarctica on the first of several expeditions.

1913   Site of Canberra declared open.

1914   Australia enters World War I in support of Britain and its allies.

1915   Australian troops land at Gallipoli, Turkey, on April 25, later to be commemorated as Anzac Day.

1917   First train crosses the Nullabor Plain from the eastern states to Perth, Western Australia.

1918   At end of World War I, Australian dead total 60,000. First wireless messages exchanged between England and Australia.

1919   Thousands of Australians die in the Spanish influenza epidemic that claims at least 10 million people worldwide. Pioneering airman Ross Smith flies from England to Australia. Country Party formed to represent Australia's farmers (later renamed the National Party).

1920   Communist Party of Australia formed.

1921   West Australian Edith Cowan becomes the first woman elected to an Australian parliament.

1923   Vegemite invented in Melbourne by Fred Walker. Australia's first radio stations begin broadcasting in Sydney. Australian Council of Trade Unions formed. Making of Australia's first "talkie" movies. Massacre of Aborigines at Coniston, Western Australia. Beginning of the Great Depression. Legendary cricketer Don Bradman makes world record score of 452.

1930   Sharp falls in prices of Australian wool, wheat, and minerals. Industry slows markedly as unemployment soars. Australia linked to London by telephone.

1931   More than 30% of Australian workers unemployed. Sydney Harbour Bridge opens.

1933   Australia outraged at English cricket team's "bodyline" bowling tactics in test matches. Australian *Women's Weekly* begins publication. Australia gains control of a sector of Antarctica.

1937   Tasmanian Les Vaughan invents Defender snail and slug killer.

1939   "Black Friday" in Victoria and New South Wales as bushfires devastate vast areas of bush and countryside, killing more than 100 people. Britain declares war on Germany, and Australia enters the conflict in support of Britain.

1941   Fifteen thousand Australian soldiers defend Tobruk in the Libyan desert and become famous as the "Rats of Tobruk."

1942   Japanese warplanes bomb Darwin, Broome, and Townsville. Japanese midget submarines enter Sydney Harbour but do little damage.

1944   Australia's Liberal Party formed, led by Robert Menzies.

1945   War ends in Europe and the Pacific. Prime Minister John Curtin dies.

1946   Missile testing site established with British Government at Woomera, South Australia.

1947   Introduction of 40-hour week for Australian workers. Scheme launched to boost immigration from Europe.

1948   First Holden car produced in Australia.

1950   War in Korea. Australia sends troops.

1953   Uranium mined at Rum Jungle, Northern Territory. Oil discovered in the Exmouth Gulf, Western Australia.

1956   Olympic Games in Melbourne. Australia wins 13 gold medals. First television broadcasts. First atomic bomb testing at Maralinga, South Australia.

1959   Australian population reaches 10 million.

1961   Discovery of huge iron ore deposits at Pilbara in Western Australia.

1963   United States establishes naval base at North-West Cape in Western Australia.

1964   The Beatles visit Australia, creating wild scenes in the streets of several capital cities.

1965   Battalion of Australian soldiers sent to South Vietnam.

1966   Oil and gas discovered in Bass Strait, off the Victorian coast. Robert Menzies resigns as prime minister and is replaced by Harold Holt. Conscripted Australian soldiers sent to South Vietnam. Northern Territory Aborigines appeal to the United Nations for help in obtaining equal rights. Decimal currency introduced, with pounds, shillings, and pence replaced by dollars and cents. Beginning of change to metric weights and measures.

1967   American president Lyndon Johnson visits Australia. Prime Minister Harold Holt disappears in the surf at Portsea, Victoria. John Gorton becomes prime minister. Excavation at Lake Mungo in western New South Wales produces strong evidence of human occupation of Australia 40,000 years ago.

1971   Neville Bonner becomes the first Aboriginal elected to the Australian parliament.

1972   Labor's Gough Whitlam becomes prime minister. Australian troops brought home from Vietnam. Conscription ends.

1973   Sydney Opera House opens. Traditional lands given back to Gurindji people at Wave Hill.

1974   Cyclone Tracy destroys much of Darwin.

1975   Papua New Guinea granted independence from Australia.

1977   Refugee boats from Vietnam begin arriving in Darwin.

1981   South Australian government returns the northeastern part of the state to the Pitjantjantjara Aboriginal people. Australia's population reaches 14,922,300. Unlike the 1901 census, Aboriginal people were included in the count, their population put at 159,600.

1983   Australia wins the America's Cup yacht race. Uluru (Ayers Rock) returned to Aboriginal people by the Commonwealth government.

1985   A Royal Commission into Britain's atomic bomb tests recommends London pay compensation to Australians who became ill as a result of their involvement. Bantamweight boxer Jeff Fenech defeats Japan's Satoshi Shingaki to win the world title.

1986   Queen Elizabeth II signs away the last British legal powers over Australia.

1987   The Federal Labor government of Bob Hawke wins a historic third term in office. Michael and Lindy Chamberlain are pardoned over the famous disappearance of their baby, Azaria, at Uluru (Ayers Rock) in 1980. American 39-ft yacht, *Stars and Stripes,* wins back the America's Cup from Australia. Media magnate Rupert Murdoch buys the *Herald* and *Weekly Times,* Australia's biggest publishing and broadcasting group.

1988   The biggest crowd ever seen in Australia crushes around Sydney Harbour to celebrate the 200th anniversary of the arrival of the First Fleet. Queen Elizabeth II opens Australia's new Parliament House in Canberra.

1989   An earthquake rocks the New South Wales city of Newcastle, killing 12 people. Christopher Skase and Alan Bond, two of Australia's most colorful corporate high-flyers, are investigated over massive corporate debts.

1992   Australia's national carrier, Qantas, is put up for sale. A full High Court judgment abolishes the concept of *terra nullius*—that Australia was no one's land when European settlers arrived.

1993   After a long legislative process, Australia establishes the Native Title Act to deal with the land rights of indigenous Australians. Sydney secures the right to host the 2000 Olympic Games.

1995   Canberra joins the international community in condemning French nuclear tests at Mururoa Atoll, near Tahiti.

1996   In one of the greatest comebacks in Australian political history, John Howard becomes prime minister, thereby leading the Liberal–National Party coalition back to power after 13 years in opposition. Gunman Martin Bryant kills 35 people in a massacre at Port Arthur, Tasmania.

1998   John Howard's conservative government is reelected, paving the way for major tax changes.

1999   Australian peacekeeping troops are deployed in East Timor to help quell bloodshed between pro- and anti-Indonesian groups. Australians vote "No" in a referendum on whether the country should become a republic. Elaborate celebrations mark the new millennium—although many people are convinced the fireworks are a year early.

2000   Sydney stages the Olympics Games, which the IOC president hails as "The Best Games Ever." Melbourne hosts international political and business heavyweights at the World Economic Forum. Australians come to terms with the imposition of a Goods and Services Tax and other tax reforms.

2001   John Howard defies the polls to lead his conservative coalition government to a third term in office. Australian troops head to Afghanistan as part of the international fight against terrorism.

2002   Australia's iconic second airline, Ansett, folds, leaving thousands of workers without jobs.

AUSTRALIAN VOCABULARY

Copping an earful of 'strine—to use the local vernacular—is one of the distinct pleasures of a trip here. However, it's becoming increasingly scarce. In the era of the global village, many of the words that once formed a colorful adjunct to the English language have fallen from popular usage, especially in urban areas, which is where more than 90% of the population lives. Letters to the editor frequently lament the Americanization of the language and that, for example, such trusty and traditional expressions as "blokes" have been largely replaced by "guys." Australians now say, "Get a life," where a decade ago they would have said, "Cop it sweet!" The store assistant who hands you your change is more likely to say, "Have a nice day" than "Farewell," and expressions such as "sheilas" (women) and "fair dinkum" (true) are rarely heard these days except in country pubs.

Australians tend to shorten many common words, and most are easy enough to decipher—"Chrissie" (Christmas), "footie" (football), and "bikie" (biker), for example. Others, though—such as "postie" (mailman), "cozzie" (bathing suit), and "garbo" (garbage collector)—require some lateral thinking. Note, however, that it is not essential to have a grasp of 'strine to travel, eat, and find a bed in Australia. English will serve you perfectly well. Still, here are a few translations to help you:

Abo: Aborigine (derogatory)

Ankle biter: Infant

Back of Bourke: Very far away

Banana bender: Native of Queensland

Battler: One who works very hard and barely scrapes by

Beyond the black stump: Extremely rare

Billabong: Ox-bow lake

Blowie: Blowfly, Australia's native bird

Bludger: Idler

Blue: Disagreement

Bodgy: Inferior quality

Boofhead: Nerd

Bull bar: Device fitted to the front of a vehicle to minimize collision damage

Cockie: Farmer

Crook: Sick or dysfunctional

Crow eater: Native of South Australia

Dag: Fashion victim

Damper: Camp bread

Derro: Hobo

Digger: Australian army personnel, also used as an affectionate greeting between males ("G'day, digger!")

Doona: Eiderdown

Drongo: Nerd

Dummy: Pacifier

Dunny: Outside toilet

Earbash: Chatter egregiously

Esky: A cooler

Fag: A cigarette; less commonly used in the derogatory American sense to denote a homosexual male

Furphy: Rumor

Galah: Nerd; literally, a noisy species of parrot

Greenie: A conservationist

Gutless: Cowardly

Have a crack: Try hard

Hoon: Hoodlum

Jackaroo: A male station hand

Jillaroo: A female station hand

Larrikin: Prankster

Lollies: Candy

Middy: 10-fluid-ounce glass of beer

Mug: Gullible person

Offsider: Assistant

Pom, Pommie: Native of England

Ripper: Great, outstanding

Rubber: Eraser

Rubbish: To criticize

Sandgroper: Native of Western Australia

Septic or seppo: An American (from rhyming slang; septic tank equals Yank)

Shout: To send a round of drinks

Smoko: Coffee break

Spit the dummy: To become enraged

'Strine: Aussie slang

Stubbie: Small, short-necked bottle of beer

Swag: Bedroll

Tall poppy: One who excels

Togs: Bathing suit

Tucker: Food

Ute: Pickup truck

Walkabout: To excuse oneself, usually without explanation

Whinger: Whiner

Whiteant: To undermine (named after a common termite)

Wog: Anyone not of Anglo-Saxon background (usually derogatory)

Yobbo, Yob: Uncouth male

INDEX

NOTES

NOTES

NOTES

FODOR'S KEY TO THE GUIDES

America's guidebook leader publishes guides for every kind of traveler.
Check out our many series and find your perfect match.

FODOR'S GOLD GUIDES

America's favorite travel-guide series offers the most detailed insider reviews of hotels, restaurants, and attractions in all price ranges, plus great background information, smart tips, and useful maps.

COMPASS AMERICAN GUIDES

Stunning guides from top local writers and photographers, with gorgeous photos, literary excerpts, and colorful anecdotes. A must-have for culture mavens, history buffs, and new residents.

FODOR'S CITYPACKS

Concise city coverage in a guide plus a foldout map. The right choice for urban travelers who want everything under one cover.

FODOR'S EXPLORING GUIDES

Hundreds of color photos bring your destination to life. Lively stories lend insight into the culture, history, and people.

FODOR'S TRAVEL HISTORIC AMERICA

For travelers who want to experience history firsthand, this series gives in-depth coverage of historic sights, plus nearby restaurants and hotels. Themes include the Thirteen Colonies, the Old West, and the Lewis and Clark Trail.

FODOR'S POCKET GUIDES

For travelers who need only the essentials. The best of Fodor's in pocket-size packages for just $9.95.

FODOR'S FLASHMAPS

Every resident's map guide, with 60 easy-to-follow maps of public transit, parks, museums, zip codes, and more.

FODOR'S CITYGUIDES

Sourcebooks for living in the city: thousands of in-the-know listings for restaurants, shops, sports, nightlife, and other city resources.

FODOR'S AROUND THE CITY WITH KIDS

Up to 68 great ideas for family days, recommended by resident parents. Perfect for exploring in your own backyard or on the road.

FODOR'S HOW TO GUIDES

Get tips from the pros on planning the perfect trip. Learn how to pack, fly hassle-free, plan a honeymoon or cruise, stay healthy on the road, and travel with your baby.

FODOR'S LANGUAGES FOR TRAVELERS

Practice the local language before you hit the road. Available in phrase books, cassette sets, and CD sets.

KAREN BROWN'S GUIDES

Engaging guides—many with easy-to-follow inn-to-inn itineraries—to the most charming inns and B&Bs in the U.S.A. and Europe.

BAEDEKER'S GUIDES

Comprehensive guides, trusted since 1829, packed with A–Z reviews and star ratings.

OTHER GREAT TITLES FROM FODOR'S

Baseball Vacations, The Complete Guide to the National Parks, Family Vacations, Golf Digest's Places to Play, Great American Drives of the East, Great American Drives of the West, Great American Vacations, Healthy Escapes, National Parks of the West, Skiing USA.